IRB WORLD RUGBY YEARBOOK 2011

EDITED BY PAUL MORGAN AND JOHN GRIFFITHS

Vision Sports Publishing
19-23 High Street
Kingston upon Thames
Surrey, KT1 1LL

www.visionsp.co.uk

Published by
Vision Sports Publishing in 2010

ISBN 13: 978-1905326-87-7

All pictures by Getty Images unless otherwise stated
Illustrations by Ann Cakebread

Typeset by Palimpsest Book Production Ltd, Falkirk, Stirlingshire

Printed and bound in the UK by
Ashford Colour Press Ltd

The IRB World Rugby Yearbook is an independent publication supported by the International Rugby Board but the views throughout, expressed by the different authors, do not necessarily reflect the policies and opinions of the IRB.

International Rugby Board
Huguenot House
35-38 St Stephen's Green
Dublin 2, Ireland

t +353-1-240-9200
f +353-1-240-9201
e irb@irb.com

www.irb.com

Contents

THE COUNTRIES

THE COMBINED TEAMS

CROSS-BORDER TOURNAMENTS

THE BACK ROW

Emirates

Introduction

By HH Sheikh Ahmed Bin Saeed Al Maktoum

Chairman and Chief Executive, Emirates Airline & Group

As we enter this special Rugby World Cup year, it gives me great pride that Emirates is supporting the IRB with the sport's showpiece event.

As a Rugby World Cup 2011 Worldwide Partner, Emirates is hugely excited about the tournament's September kick-off. We are looking forward to flying thousands of rugby fans to New Zealand to watch their teams battle it out to lift the prestigious Webb Ellis Cup.

It has been almost a quarter of a century since New Zealand hosted and won the inaugural Rugby World Cup in 1987. The whole country has a keen sense of anticipation as it counts down to welcoming the world to their culturally diverse, fascinating and rugby-mad country.

From the kick-off of the opening match in Auckland on September 9 through to the final on October 23, I am confident New Zealand will be an outstanding host. No doubt the All Blacks will be desperate to get their hands on the trophy on home soil and not many would doubt their chances.

Looking back to 2010, it was another fantastic year of rugby for Emirates. As title sponsor of four of the IRB Sevens World Series tournaments, Emirates was delighted to see such a closely fought competition – won for the first time by Samoa. New Zealand pushed them all the way to the final event of the season at the Emirates Airline Edinburgh Sevens, but the Samoans finished worthy Series winners.

Dennis Muhanji of Kenya in action during day two of the Emirates Airline London Sevens at Twickenham in May.

These are exciting times for Sevens rugby. With the announcement that the sport will feature at the 2016 Olympic Games, the next few years promise to see it thrive around the world. The tournaments continue to grow and are proving to be a successful way of introducing more and more supporters to the game.

Emirates has a long-term commitment to rugby – ensuring its involvement in the game reaches far and wide. The airline is not only a Worldwide Partner of Rugby World Cup 2011, it is also title sponsor of the Dubai, George, London and Edinburgh Sevens events; shirt sponsor of the Samoa, USA and England sevens teams; sponsor of the USA Eagles and Western Force teams as well as the Warrington Wolves and the Rugby Football League; and official sponsor of the IRB Referees and the IRB Awards.

I hope you enjoy this latest edition of the IRB Yearbook and, together with Emirates, are looking forward to what will be a thrilling year of international rugby.

Rugby Breaking New Frontiers

A message from Bernard Lapasset, Chairman of the International Rugby Board

A year ago we were celebrating Rugby Sevens' inclusion onto the Olympic Games programme, starting with the 2016 Games in Rio de Janeiro.

Over the next ten years rugby will break new frontiers on and off the field of play as we look forward to Rugby World Cups in England in 2015 and Japan in 2019 and Olympic Games in 2016 and 2020. Each event will provide the IRB with an opportunity to further promote the game and spearhead growth in key international markets.

Importantly, it is the certainty, the opportunity to map out the next decade, that will provide the game with the biggest benefits as we work in collaboration with our unions to develop a framework that will ensure rugby continues to flourish around the world.

Planning for Rugby World Cup 2015 and 2019 is already underway. We are working with both host unions to ensure that the appropriate processes, platforms and knowledge transfer elements are in place to deliver not only outstanding sporting spectacles, but tournaments that will advance the growth and competitiveness of rugby around the world.

Rugby Sevens' participation in the Olympic Games has already seen major benefits for our member unions. Many have already forged strong relationships with their National Olympic Committees and we are working in collaboration with our unions and the International Olympic Committee to ensure that our debut in Rio is a major success.

With the huge success of the IRB Sevens and its inclusion in the 2016 Olympics, Sevens is helping take rugby to a whole new audience.

Inclusion will also provide the impetus for growth within existing rugby countries and also new rugby nations and in 2011 the IRB will announce its Strategic Plan for Rugby Sevens, a blueprint that will benefit both Sevens and fifteens rugby, while also delivering a new structure for the HSBC Sevens World Series and Olympic Qualification. These are exciting times.

Further building blocks were delivered in 2010 when the IRB Council approved a funding structure and regulatory amendments to allow Argentina to compete in the new Four Nations competition from 2012. This major development will mean that for the first time the Rugby World Cup 2007 bronze medallists will have a platform for an expanded programme of Test rugby and an opportunity to consolidate their position as a major player on the world stage.

The decision is the culmination of a process that began with the historic Woking Forum in November 2007 where all stakeholders agreed that integration into a major competition structure was a priority for the Pumas. In making the dream a reality I would like to thank SANZAR and the Australia, New Zealand and South Africa Unions for their full support in the process.

In May 2010 we announced that traditional tours will return to the international rugby calendar after the IRB Council approved a new global ten-year playing schedule that will shape the Test landscape in the run-up to Rugby World Cup 2019 in Japan.

The schedule, which commences in 2012, will lead to more meaningful Tests between SANZAR and Six Nations Unions during the June window, providing an attractive and equitable commercial model that will see northern hemisphere unions tour southern hemisphere unions on a rotational basis.

Most years within the schedule will involve a three-Test series against only one visiting nation in June, with midweek matches also set to be incorporated into the touring side's itinerary at the agreement of the respective unions.

The new schedule meets the IRB's strategic goal of providing the platform to grow and increase the profile of the game around the world while also recognising the commercial requirements of the Tier 1 and Tier 2 Unions.

A core component of the new schedule is an integrated Test schedule for targeted Strategic Investment Unions, providing the platform for increased competition and growth through the delivery of more ranking tests between Tier 2 nations and matches against touring Tier 1 sides for the first time in several years, with Tests in North America, Japan and the Pacific Islands. Such commitment was underlined with the top 25 Ranked Unions all in action for the first time during November 2010.

Increased competition pathways will increase global competitiveness and as we look towards Rugby World Cup 2011 the IRB is confident that we will see improvements in performance from many of the so-called smaller nations.

Despite the challenging global economic climate the IRB maintained its commitment to investment in the game and between 2009 and 2012 £48 million will be invested in the Game in the form of High Performance investment aimed at increasing global playing standards. The total investment in global rugby during the period will be upwards of £153 million and is made possible by the commercial success of Rugby World Cup.

As we count down to Rugby World Cup 2011 in New Zealand I am delighted to say that the tournament will write another memorable chapter in the Rugby World Cup success story.

The tournament, the seventh edition of rugby's showcase event, will be the biggest sporting event of the year and the biggest event ever to be hosted in New Zealand and will be watched by a record number of people around the world.

Rugby World Cup 2011 will attract over 60,000 overseas fans from upwards of 100 countries and deliver a global television audience of four billion, while the impact on the New Zealand economy is likely to around NZD$500 million. It will also lay the foundation for rugby's growth through a strong commercial programme.

As we look to an exciting decade ahead, it is important as we reach out to new markets, new audiences and new players and fans that we do not lose sight of the core values of our game and the spirit and ethos of teamwork, fair play, respect and integrity. Over the next 12 months the IRB will be working with its Member Unions to deliver an education programme that will ensure that all that we hold dear about the sport is protected as we welcome new men, women and children to the global rugby family.

The Front Row

THE KICK OFF

How To Win a World Cup!

By Victor Matfield

Victory in a Rugby World Cup Final is the pinnacle of any player's career and looking back at South Africa's journey to lifting the trophy in 2007, I would say it all really began in 2004 when Jake White was appointed coach and he brought together the players who formed the nucleus of the squad that was ultimately successful in France.

We had a terrible World Cup in 2003 but when Jake came in, we talked about the style of play we wanted to adopt and how we could move forward. It was a decision taken between the players and the coaching staff and that democratic process ensured everyone was on board. Jake made it clear he believed in us as a group of players and we respected his trust. It meant that by the time the World Cup arrived, we were an experienced, tight-knit group.

Of course, it wasn't all plain sailing. We struggled in 2006 in particular, losing five Tests on the bounce at one stage, but with hindsight it was a blessing. You often find out more about yourself as a team in adversity than you do when things are going well and that poor run of results collectively forced us to sit down and identify what we were doing wrong.

We came to the conclusion it was a case of minor alterations rather than major surgery. We realised more accuracy and patience were required and as the World Cup got closer we put the lessons into practice.

Even though a World Cup is a long tournament, you do all the hard work before the competition begins or a ball is kicked. We were in training camps

The celebrations begin: with fellow lock Bakkies Botha and the Webb Ellis Cup.

during 2006 doing plenty of conditioning work simply because there was no time in 2007. For South African players, it was Super Rugby, then the Tri-Nations and then the World Cup was upon us, so by the time we touched down in France, all the serious physical conditioning was behind us and training sessions were all about fine tuning and refining our structures.

Reaching the final meant we were away from home for seven weeks but boredom and homesickness were not a factor. We had our families with us for long periods during the tournament and we had a lot of freedom in terms of going out and sightseeing in Paris. I think that was hugely important because it kept spirits high in the squad.

It is always important to be able to switch off from rugby, to get away from it all, but it's even more important in the pressurised environment of a World Cup and in that respect France were the perfect hosts. The country has a long, proud rugby tradition but we were still able to walk the streets with our families or rent a car for a day and not get mobbed by people asking for autographs.

Behind the scenes, the role of the coach and the captain were crucial. Jake was under huge pressure going into the tournament and he did get stressed at times but he kept a lid on it. He also got a lot of support from the rest of the coaching team and the likes of Eddie Jones, who had been there and done that before in 2003, and I think that was another big factor in our success.

As was John Smit. Supporters only see the captain on the pitch for the 80 minutes but I'd have to say what happens on the pitch is only 10 per cent of the job a good captain does, especially when a group of players are away together at a tournament for a long period.

The captain sets the tone for everything, from the team meetings to training sessions. He's ultimately responsible for the atmosphere in the camp and John was superb in France. He struck the perfect balance between keeping everyone focused and making sure we stayed relaxed. Of course, he's world class out on the pitch but what he contributed off it in 2007 was absolutely crucial.

There were more than one or two rows and disagreements within the squad in 2007 though. Some might see that as a sign of disunity or low morale but I thought it was a positive because it's always better to get something off your chest and move on rather than let it fester and ultimately affect team spirit.

It's inevitable when you've got 30 players and a coaching staff of 20 together for seven weeks that tempers will flare when there's a clash of heads in training or if a big tackle comes in unexpectedly. People won't always see eye to eye but it doesn't need to be a problem. Players had their say when they weren't happy and we moved on as a squad.

Looking back at the final in Paris, it was as close and tough as we expected and I think what got us through against England was our experience and sense of togetherness. We had been building up to that game for three years, so all the trials and tribulations we experienced on the way ultimately pulled us through.

Happy days: posing with the trophy after the match...

We had hammered England in the group stages but there was definitely no sense of complacency ahead of the final. England were poor in the first game but when they beat Australia in the quarter-finals and then France in the semi-final, we were under no illusions that they had turned things around. English teams are always physically challenging and that side was no different but we stayed patient, stuck to our game plan and got over the line.

New Zealand host the 2011 World Cup and we know it will be incredibly difficult to defend our title. No country has yet won back-to-back World Cups, so we could make history but, as champions, we are also there to be shot at.

I've no doubt New Zealand will do a fantastic job of staging the tournament but I think it will be a different dynamic. It's a smaller country than France and rugby is the number one sport, so it will be harder to escape during the competition. As I said, we were able to wander the streets of Paris in relative anonymity in 2007 but I can't see that being the case in New Zealand because people are absolutely crazy about their rugby over there.

... and back home in South Africa when we paraded it through the streets of Johannesburg.

I think we will have to make a conscious effort to arrange more activities and get out of the cities so the squad can unwind, forget about rugby for a day or two and refresh minds and bodies.

Our form going into the tournament has not been great and our performances in the 2010 Tri-Nations were disappointing but I'm still confident we are capable of lifting the trophy. Our recent results have not been part of the grand plan but the way we struggled in 2010 reminds me of the team's problems in 2006 and we showed then that it is possible to turn the ship around.

We have to be brutally honest about what has gone wrong and not be afraid to change things. It worked for us four years ago and I don't believe there is currently any shortage of talent in South African rugby.

The fact the Bulls and the Sharks contested an all-South African final in Super Rugby in 2010 tells its own story and there are young players on the domestic scene who are keeping the older, more experienced players on their toes.

We know we have no divine right to lift the World Cup again but we definitely won't come up short in terms of preparation or commitment. We will probably be one of the most experienced squads in New Zealand and when it comes down to tournament rugby, that's a huge asset. At this stage, I really don't think there is a favourite for the trophy. Previous tournaments have proved that form and reputation can often count for little and I'm sure it will be the same in New Zealand.

The Stadium of Four Million

By Paul Morgan

There is only one country in the world where the live televising of the Rugby World Cup final would appear simultaneously on five channels! That's right, five different TV channels, not one or two but five and that country is, of course, New Zealand.

So considering this level of obsession with the great sport of rugby union, it is in many ways apt that the seventh staging of the Rugby World Cup should appear in the land of the long white cloud, and that they become the first nation to host it twice.

Those of us who have been lucky enough to visit New Zealand on rugby tours will testify to this obsession and it is true that when you meet someone in the street (any street) they can dissect the Wallaby lineout as well as Graham Henry.

We've heard all the doom-mongers talk about the lack of beds and infrastructure but one thing I can guarantee anyone lucky enough to go to New Zealand in September or October 2011 is a party they'll never forget.

Touring in many 'rugby' countries can be beset by indifference. I have turned up in many towns on Lions tours to be greeted by a population that barely knows what rugby is. That will definitely not be the case in New Zealand. The matches in all 12 venues will be welcomed with a frenzy and will be the biggest show in town by a long way.

My enthusiasm for a New Zealand World Cup can be explained by those many and enjoyable trips to the country. For a rugby fan there is no better place to watch the game, because the sport is knitted into the fabric of every part of life in New Zealand. They have a Rugby Channel for goodness sake. Not a sports channel that shows lots of rugby as many countries have. They have a Rugby Channel that shows nothing but rugby – that alone should make you appreciate how

A huge rugby ball celebrates the imminent Rugby World Cup in New Zealand at Circular Quay, Sydney, Australia.

enthusiastic the Kiwis will be to put on a great show. It guarantees that every restaurant, hotel, pub and fan zone will go rugby crazy in those two months.

As a journalist I want to be at the centre of the action, following the event that the country is talking about. That is guaranteed in New Zealand.

What other country would move their school terms to accommodate a Rugby World Cup? Only New Zealand. Their commitment was probably reflected best at the announcement of New Zealand's successful bid, by the IRB in 2005. Every country's delegation contained government dignitaries but New Zealand Prime Minister Helen Clark had taken the trouble to break from her busy schedule to make the trip to Ireland. In that gesture you will appreciate what rugby, and holding the Rugby World Cup in 2011, means to New Zealand.

As part of now former Prime Minister Clark's commitment in a country where the confirmation of a new All Blacks captain would lead the evening news, the guarantee given to the IRB is underpinned by a partnership with the New Zealand Government and a joint funding commitment from both partners, not something that most countries could guarantee.

This is an incredibly proud moment for New Zealand, thanks to the successful Government-rugby union partnership that underlined the New Zealand Rugby Union's bid for the hosting rights.

"The contest to host the competition was particularly competitive, and we are honoured that the International Rugby Board chose New Zealand to showcase this tournament," Prime Minister Clark said.

"It is an enormous vote of confidence in our country's ability to host major events, and also shows the important role that small countries like New Zealand can play in international sporting events.

"We believe this event will be a spectacle to remember – for everyone who loves rugby – the players, and fans and spectators from around the world."

The New Zealand Government have even appointed a Rugby World Cup minister. Think the Olympics for Great Britain and you get the idea. Rugby World Cup Minister Murray McCully can't wait for September 2011 to come around.

"RWC 2011 is an unprecedented opportunity for New Zealand. It will be the biggest event ever held in this country, and we plan to make the most of it," Mr McCully said. "The Cup will inject over $500 million (£250 million) into the economy, with around half of that going into Auckland.

"It will also attract over 60,000 international visitors and a global television audience of over four billion. New Zealand will be in the international spotlight like never before, and we will be ready.

"I think 2011 will be a golden year for us in New Zealand. Rugby World Cup is not just an opportunity to invite people down to a place with a rich rugby heritage but also an opportunity to meet our business people – particularly in the food and beverage area but in other sectors as well.

"Whilst we cannot offer the glitz and glamour of bigger venues, we can offer a rugby heritage that is different and which will be appreciated by real rugby followers, as well as all of the opportunities to see some of the economic activities that we are involved in and meet our business people."

And if you are lucky enough to make the trip to New Zealand it won't be just about the rugby as McCully explains. "We are encouraging New Zealanders to be a 'nation of four million hosts' to make the tournament an unforgettable experience for players and supporters," he adds. "We'll also have a festival programme – offering a calendar of events that will allow visitors and New Zealanders to experience the best of our sporting and cultural life, and a showcase programme – to show the world the very best of everything that New Zealand, as a small trading nation, has to offer.

"RWC 2011 is an unprecedented opportunity to raise our international profile, boost our economy and make lasting gains in trade and tourism."

In terms of stadiums no one should worry about New Zealand's ability to get the tournament staged. The new 60,000-seater Eden Park that will host both semis and the final opened ahead of schedule, in October 2010. In 2011, the ground will become the first stadium in the world to host two Rugby World Cup finals.

Two new stands – the South and East – are at the forefront of a quarter of a billion New Zealand dollar redevelopment and the new ground will continue to host Auckland during the ITM Cup, ahead of its first international contest with the Rugby League Four Nations playing a double-header there.The South Stand is a six level structure that alone holds 21,500 spectators and features retractable seating in front of it.

Radio New Zealand reported that the opening would begin with a dawn blessing of four tekoteko (carved poles) which will be blessed by Ngati Whatua o Orakei. Representing the four Maori gods Tanemahuta, Rongo, Tumatauenga and Tawhirimatea, they stand guard at the four corners of the park.

The ground will host the 2011 tournament opener between the All Blacks and Tonga, as well as other pool matches, the semi finals, bronze final and the final itself.

Also featured will be a new internal concourse connecting the stands from within, access for vehicles into the ground has been improved; while new changing rooms, big enough to hold lineout drills, will be connected directly to the coaches box.

And it isn't all talk from the Government in New Zealand as they went further, confirming that any profits from the tournament will be shared on a 50/50 basis between the NZRU and the New Zealand Government. While any shortfall/ losses on the tournament will be met by a one-third/two-thirds split between the NZRU and the New Zealand Government respectively. This will truly be a country-backed World Cup, rather than one just supported by a rugby union.

Back in 2005 New Zealand's bid was built around the theme that the tournament would be hosted in New Zealand's 'Stadium of Four Million' and that it would be an 'All Black' experience for all involved.

A view of the 'new' Eden Park under construction. The stadium now has a capacity of 60,000.

It is worth looking back and considering what New Zealand's bid promised to deliver:

1. A tournament for players
2. An environment where players can perform at their very best
3. Rugby facilities that are excellent and close at hand
4. A tournament based on traditional rugby values

When you talk to New Zealanders about the event there is measurable excitement in their voices, and none are more excited than Rugby New Zealand 2011 Chief Executive Martin Snedden. The former Kiwi Test cricketer is heading up the countdown to September 2011 with the gusto of a salesman that believes 100 per cent in the product he is selling.

"Every time I get the opportunity to watch live sport, it reminds me there is really nothing quite like being a part of the crowd," he says. "When the promise that the New Zealand Rugby Union made in its 2005 bid, that RWC 2011 would be staged within our 'Stadium of Four Million', it was a great bid concept and our 'stadium' is truly coming to life.

"I'm not a big football fan, although I'll admit that I am sometimes fascinated by how the powerhouse clubs like Manchester United and Chelsea have turned a game of sport, for better or worse, into a huge commercial enterprise.

"And yet, despite feeling fairly ambivalent about the game, I can unequivocally state that the best spectator experience of my life (and I've been lucky enough to have been to a lot of great events over the last 30 or so years) was being part of

North Harbour Stadium in Albany, Auckland, which will host three Rugby World Cup matches.

the crowd at Wellington Regional Stadium in November 2009 when the New Zealand 'All Whites' beat Bahrain to qualify for the FIFA World Cup 2010 finals in South Africa.

"New Zealand is a rugby-mad country and has been like this for more than a century, but if an alien from outer space had happened to drop into the stadium that night it would have thought that Wellington was the centre of the football, and not the rugby, universe.

"The whole day was perfect. In the hours before the match the city centre was full of fans, many of them out-of-towners, enjoying the restaurants, the bars, the beautiful harbour and each other's company. There was a tangible air of excitement, a real buzz. As football is still a growing sport in this country there was no sign of any obsessive 'win at all costs' fan mentality. It seemed to me that the vast majority just wanted to be part of the fun and to be there in case history was made.

"I've talked to lots of people since about the experience that night. Everyone loved it, including those around New Zealand watching on TV. But I've noticed that the smile and the gleam in the eye is invariably strongest on the faces of those who were actually there that night, inside the stadium.

"Our Rugby World Cup will capture New Zealand. It's already well on the way to doing so. For us, this is a genuine once-in-a-lifetime opportunity, something really unique.

"Yes, as Kiwis we will back the All Blacks to the hilt, but right across the nation our people will warmly embrace and care for all the participating teams and their supporters.

"Just as happened in Wellington for the All Whites, together with our thousands of international visitors we will fill the stadia for all the 48 RWC 2011 matches and, with the players, create an incredibly special in-stadia experience.

"We will be there for the action, there for the fun but we will also be there just to make sure that, in case history is made, we can say we were part of it.

I can't wait!"

The Kiwi enthusiasm isn't in question, but never doubt that the IRB has been closely monitoring the progress made Down Under. Senior International Rugby Board (IRB) and Rugby World Cup Limited (RWCL) officials visited New Zealand to celebrate the 365-day countdown to RWC 2011 and expressed their confidence in New Zealand's preparations for the tournament.

The delegation, which included IRB and RWCL Chairman Bernard Lapasset, IRB Vice Chairman and RWCL Director Bill Beaumont and IRB CEO and RWCL Managing Director Mike Miller, were impressed with the progress made since their last visit and enjoyed the positive feeling about the tournament as they travelled around the country.

Mr Lapasset stressed the confidence and excitement that supporters around the world had conveyed to him. "Planning and preparations are at an advanced stage. As the countdown enters its final year, the global rugby community awaits a tournament that will provide the seventh chapter of the RWC story in a country that is totally immersed in rugby's tradition and culture," he said.

RWCL and its commercial partners marked one year to go with a number of events in New Zealand. These included bringing the RWC commercial family together for a two-day RWC 2011 Sponsors Workshop, reviewing spectacular plans for the commercial hospitality pavilion at Eden Park and host broadcasters SKY NZ hosting those showcasing New Zealand to the world with a World Broadcasters Meeting.

Drawing on his experience as the Chairman of the RWC 2007 Organising Committee in France, Mr Lapasset highlighted the critical nature of the partnerships around the tournament. He praised the role of the Prime Minister, John Key, and the RWC Minister Murray McCully, and the strong relationship that had been built with them.

RWCL has seen how this partnership is being reflected at all levels between tournament partners around the country to provide lasting legacies beyond next year's tournament.

Having driven RWC's growth at recent tournaments beyond being just 48 matches of rugby, the RWCL Directors were also impressed with the launch of the REAL Festival. They left confident that the excitement that continues to build in supporters around the world will be matched by the 'Stadium of Four Million'.

In terms of the players they clearly can't wait, with one of Australia's finest, Quade Cooper, turning down a lucrative contract with rugby league to allow him to get a crack at lifting the Webb Ellis Cup.

"It was obviously a big decision," said the 22-year-old, who turned down a three-year offer from the Parramatta Eels to stay in rugby union.

"I had huge things weighing on my mind. There was a World Cup to be won, some of my best mates were in the team, and there was something I felt we were building towards with the way we were improving.

"I feel I made the right decision. To go on this tour with these guys and prepare for a World Cup next year is pretty massive."

Like Cooper I can't wait for the World Cup to start. I'm sure it is the same for rugby fans all over the world.

Rugby World Cup Fixtures

Date	Time (NZ)	Pool	Match Details	Location	Stadium
Fri Sept 9	20.30	A	New Zealand v Tonga	Auckland	Eden Park
Sat Sept 10	13.00	B	Scotland v Play off winner	Invercargill	Rugby Park Stadium
Sat Sept 10	15.30	D	Fiji v Namibia	Rotorua	Rotorua International Stadium
Sat Sept 10	18.00	A	France v Japan	North Shore	North Harbour Stadium
Sat Sept 10	20.30	B	Argentina v England	Christchurch	Stadium Christchurch
Sun Sept 11	15.30	C	Australia v Italy	Christchurch	Stadium Christchurch
Sun Sept 11	18.00	C	Ireland v USA	New Plymouth	Stadium Taranaki
Sun Sept 11	20.30	D	South Africa v Wales	Wellington	Wellington Regional Stadium
Wed Sept 14	14.30	D	Samoa v Namibia	Rotorua	Rotorua International Stadium
Wed Sept 14	17.00	A	Tonga v Canada	Whangarei	Northland Events Centre
Wed Sept 14	19.30	B	Scotland v Georgia	Dunedin	Dunedin (TBA)
Thurs Sept 15	19.30	C	Russia v USA	New Plymouth	Stadium Taranaki
Fri Sept 16	20.00	A	New Zealand v Japan	Hamilton	Waikato Stadium
Sat Sept 17	15.30	B	Argentina v Play off winner	Invercargill	Rugby Park Stadium
Sat Sept 17	18.00	D	South Africa v Fiji	Wellington	Wellington Regional Stadium
Sat Sept 17	20.30	C	Australia v Ireland	Auckland	Eden Park
Sun Sept 18	15.30	D	Wales v Samoa	Hamilton	Waikato Stadium
Sun Sept 18	18.00	B	England v Georgia	Christchurch	Stadium Christchurch
Sun Sept 18	20.30	A	France v Canada	Napier	McLean Park
Tues Sept 20	19.30	C	Italy v Russia	Nelson	Trafalgar Park
Wed Sept 21	19.30	A	Tonga v Japan	Whangarei	Northland Events Centre
Thurs Sept 22	20.00	D	South Africa v Namibia	North Shore	North Harbour Stadium
Fri Sept 23	20.30	C	Australia v USA	Wellington	Wellington Regional Stadium
Sat Sept 24	18.00	B	England v Play off winner	Dunedin	Dunedin (TBA)
Sat Sept 24	20.30	A	New Zealand v France	Auckland	Eden Park
Sun Sept 25	15.30	D	Fiji v Samoa	Auckland	Eden Park
Sun Sept 25	18.00	C	Ireland v Russia	Rotorua	Rotorua International Stadium
Sun Sept 25	20.30	B	Argentina v Scotland	Christchurch	Stadium Christchurch
Mon Sept 26	19.30	D	Wales v Namibia	New Plymouth	Stadium Taranaki
Tues Sept 27	17.00	A	Canada v Japan	Napier	McLean Park
Tues Sept 27	19.30	C	Italy v USA	Nelson	Trafalgar Park
Wed Sept 28	19.30	B	Georgia v Play off winner	Palmerston North	Arena Manawatu
Fri Sept 30	20.30	D	South Africa v Samoa	North Shore	North Harbour Stadium
Sat Oct 1	15.30	C	Australia v Russia	Christchurch	Stadium Christchurch
Sat Oct 1	18.00	A	France v Tonga	Wellington	Wellington Regional Stadium
Sat Oct 1	20.30	B	England v Scotland	Auckland	Eden Park
Sun Oct 2	13.00	B	Argentina v Georgia	Palmerston North	Arena Manawatu
Sun Oct 2	15.30	A	New Zealand v Canada	Wellington	Wellington Regional Stadium
Sun Oct 2	18.00	D	Wales v Fiji	Hamilton	Waikato Stadium
Sun Oct 2	20.30	C	Ireland v Italy	Dunedin	Dunedin (TBA)
Sat Oct 8	18.00		QF1: W Pool C v RU Pool D	Wellington	Wellington Regional Stadium
Sat Oct 8	20.30		QF2: W Pool B v RU Pool A	Christchurch	Stadium Christchurch
Sun Oct 9	18.00		QF3: W Pool D v RU Pool C	Wellington	Wellington Regional Stadium
Sun Oct 9	20.30		QF4: W Pool A v RU Pool B	Christchurch	Stadium Christchurch
Sat Oct 15	21.00		SF1: W QF1 v W QF2	Auckland	Eden Park
Sun Oct 16	21.00		SF2: W QF3 v W QF4	Auckland	Eden Park
Fri Oct 21	20.30		Bronze Final	Auckland	Eden Park
Sun Oct 23	21.00		Final	Auckland	Eden Park

iRB
RUGBY
WORLD CUP
2011
2011
World Cup
Stadiums
North Island
❶ Whangarei
Northland Events
Centre
Capacity: 20,000
❷ Auckland
North Harbour
Stadium, Capacity: 30,000
Eden Park
Capacity: 60,000
❸ Hamilton
Waikato Stadium
Capacity: 30,800
❹ Rotorua
Rotorua
International Stadium
Capacity: 34,000
❺ New Plymouth
Stadium Taranaki
Capacity: 25,500
❻ Napier
McLean Park
Capacity: 16,000
❼ Palmerston North
Arena Manawatu
Capacity: 18,300
❽ Wellington
Wellington
Regional Stadium
Capacity: 40,000
South Island
❾ Nelson
Trafalgar Park
Capacity: 20,080
❿ Christchurch
Stadium Christchurch
Capacity: 45,000
⓫ Dunedin
TBC
Capacity: 29,000
⓬ Invercargill
Rugby Park
Capacity: 16,500
1
2
3
4
5
6
7
8
9
10
11
12

The Road to Eden Park

By Iain Spragg

There will be a new nation competing alongside the game's traditional heavyweights for the Webb Ellis Cup in New Zealand after Russia successfully qualified for a Rugby World Cup for the first time in their short history as a distinct union.

The Rugby Union of Russia was only established in 1992 following the break-up of the old Soviet Union and just 18 years later, the Bears were celebrating booking a place at RWC 2011 after an historic 21-21 draw with the Romanians in Sochi on 27 February 2010. The draw meant Russia were guaranteed a top-two finish in the European Nations Cup and one of the region's two qualification places at RWC 2011. However, it would be another three weeks before they knew they would enter Pool C with Australia, Ireland, Italy and USA, their first opponents in New Plymouth's Stadium Taranaki on 15 September 2011.

"To qualify for the Rugby World Cup is absolutely enormous for us," said Howard Thomas, the RUR's Chief Executive. "To get across the line in the European Nations Cup I would say is the hardest route to qualify for tier two countries. We have a very competitive league with the likes of Georgia, Romania and Portugal and I'm proud of the players and everyone involved.

"Having said that we know we have to step up enormously. We look at the last World Cup and see how well Georgia did, and obviously Portugal and Romania had their moments and also Namibia. In all the games you play you want to make it a competitive game of rugby. We want to make sure that our defence is up for it, physically we're up for it and fitness-wise we're up for it."

Wing Alexander Gvozdovskiy was the hero for Russia with two tries against Romania. Yury Kushnarev converted one of them and also landed three penalties in the 21-21 stalemate that ensured the qualification.

"For me this is probably the top of my dreams, to play for my country, my national team and to qualify for the World Cup," admitted wing Vasily Artemyev after the team had earned qualification.

From Europe, the Russians were joined by Georgia in qualifying for the finals on the same weekend after they beat Spain 17-9 at the National Stadium in Tbilisi. It was the Lelos' seventh victory in their previous eight European Nations Cup matches and guaranteed them a third consecutive World Cup appearance.

"Though I am not Georgian, I understand perfectly well how the Georgians must feel now and share with them the excitement any local rugby supporter must experience now that the national team has won its third World Cup ticket in a row and that the word 'Georgia' will resound on the international stage once again," said coach and former Wallaby centre Tim Lane.

The final day meeting between Georgia and Russia would not only decide the ENC champion, but also who qualified as Europe 1 and 2 for RWC 2011. Georgia claimed the title after triumphing 36-8 and, in the process, booked their place in Pool B at RWC 2011 with Argentina, England, Scotland and the Play-off Winner.

Georgia will be back at the Rugby World Cup 2011 after winning the European Nations Cup.

The title decider was played in the Akçabaat Fatih Stadium in Trabzon, Turkey, but some 6,000 Georgian fans were still in attendance to see their side run in five tries to one. The match, despite political tensions between the two countries following the brief war of 2008, was played in an excellent spirit.

"For Georgian rugby, another World Cup appearance means a big surge in popularity," said lock Ilia Zedginidze, who captained Georgia at RWC 2007 in France. "It will bring a fresh wave of children and teenagers into youth rugby teams, another boost for development, another chance to go forward. And as regards myself, I am happy to be a part of this process and grateful to everyone who supports us on our way."

Away from Europe, Canada became the first of the eight teams who did not pre-qualify to confirm their place at RWC 2011 after beating old rivals USA in a home and away play-off in July 2009. Canada, who have appeared at every Rugby World Cup, lost the first leg 12-6 in Charleston but made the most of home advantage in Edmonton seven days later with a 41-18 victory that gave them a 47-30 aggregate triumph.

James Pritchard, Adam Kleeberger and Justin Mensah-Coker all scored tries in the first half at Ellerslie Rugby Park to establish Canadian supremacy and, despite a revival from the Eagles after the break, further scores from Ed Fairhurst and DTH van der Merwe secured the all-important win.

"There was a lot on this game and we let ourselves down last week," said Canada coach Kieran Crowley. "We didn't turn up in the first match and we wanted to put things right so it's been a long week waiting for this game, so we're pretty happy."

Victory confirmed Canada's place in Pool A alongside hosts New Zealand, France, Tonga and the Asian qualifier, which nearly a year later was confirmed as Japan. The Samoans joined the party a week later. In truth, there was little doubt about their involvement after they had overwhelmed Papua New Guinea 115-7 in Apia in the first leg of their Oceania qualifier, and they rubber stamped their progress to RWC 2011 in the return game in Port Moresby with a 72-13 win, including a hat-trick from wing Mikaele Pesamino.

Japan again emerged as Asia's top nation, heading to the Rugby World Cup.

"They were a lot harder in front of their home crowd," admitted Samoa captain Gavin Williams after the final whistle. "If they can improve that much in the space of a week, then PNG rugby is heading the right way forward."

Samoa were rewarded for their efforts with a place in Pool D alongside South Africa, Wales, Fiji and Namibia, who were duly confirmed as the Africa 1 qualifier in November 2009. The same month, the USA were presented with a chance to redeem themselves after losing to Canada and they did not disappoint at the second time of asking as Eddie O'Sullivan's side overcame Uruguay over two games to become the Americas 2 qualifier.

The Eagles had narrowly beaten Los Teros 27-22 – surviving a late Uruguayan rally – in the first leg, but were far more convincing in the second match at Broward County Regional Park in Lauderhill, Florida. Louis Stanfill and Kevin Swiryn scored first-half tries for the home side to ease any early nerves and when captain Todd Clever crashed over for his two scores after the break, the USA were home and dry with the 27-6 win giving the Eagles a 54-28 aggregate success.

"I was very happy with our defence," O'Sullivan said. "It went very well today.

We scrummaged better and stopped their rolling maul, which were the two parts of the game that we needed to improve from last week. I feel happy with the way we finished, although Uruguay made us work for it.

"It's tough to hit the ground running after not being together since July, and although we qualified, which was our ultimate goal – they were a little rusty early on. I can't be too hard on them, though, they got the job done and you can't forget that we scored eight tries in the last two games."

Namibia then became the fourth team to confirm their place at New Zealand 2011. Tunisia stood between them and a World Cup place but over two legs the Welwitschias proved the stronger of the two sides and emerged 40-23 aggregate winners. A tight 18-13 triumph for Namibia in Tunis in the first leg left the outcome hanging in the balance, but a fortnight later they proved too strong for their visitors as they battled their way to a crucial 22-10 victory in Windhoek.

Tunisia began the encounter the more confident looking side and scored the first try through wing Abbes Kherfani, while Namibia had to rely on the boot of fly-half Emile Wessels to keep them in contention. The critical score for the home side however came on the hour mark when No 8 Tinus du Plessis crashed over in the Hage Geingob Rugby Stadium and when the final whistle sounded, the Welwitschias were through.

In May 2010, Japan were confirmed as the 19th of the 20 nations who will converge on New Zealand for RWC 2011 after winning a third successive HSBC Asian 5 Nations title, overcoming the challenge of Kazakhstan, Hong Kong, Arabian Gulf and Korea. Coached by former All Black wing John Kirwan, the Brave Blossoms were in dominant form throughout the competition and began their season with a 71-13 win over Korea. The Japanese never looked back and signed off with a 94-5 victory over Hong Kong in the Prince Chichibu Memorial Stadium in Tokyo. The result maintained Japan's proud record of appearing in every World Cup and sent them through to Pool A to face the All Blacks, France, Tonga and Canada.

"Every Rugby World Cup is special for the athletes," said Kirwan after a qualifying campaign which saw his side score an incredible 326 points in four games. "If we perform well in New Zealand and give it our best effort we will have a great time. I think for Japan it is also an opportunity for us to measure our improvement. We drew with Canada in 2007 and will be looking for a win this time around. I want to show the world how much we have improved and I hope we have the courage to play our style of rugby.

"Our goal is to be first, a top ten team at the World Cup in 2011, then top eight by 2015. Canada and Tonga will be important matches and if we can win these two games, then we automatically qualify for 2015. We are hoping to get great support from the Japanese fans travelling to New Zealand. It is a popular destination for Japanese tourists and I am sure they will be encouraged by the added motivation of cheering on their team."

The final place will be taken by either Romania or Uruguay, who meet home and away in the cross-continental play-off in November 2010. In the first phase of this play-off in July, Romania overcame Tunisia 56-13, while Uruguay beat Kazakhstan 44-7.

Happy Birthday!

By Chris Thau

The International Rugby Board, the Game's governing body, will mark its 125th year in 2011. The idea of an International Board was conceived in 1886, at a time when international rugby exchanges had begun 15 years earlier with the match between England and Scotland. Matches were then confined to the four Home Unions, with the Rugby Football Union and Scottish Football Union as they were named at the time very much the dominant forces.

However, from an administration point of view this formative period was very informal, with the players themselves acting as both administrators and players of the newly formed unions. The Irish, with two governing bodies – one in Belfast and the other in Dublin – were making efforts to unify the Game in Ireland into one union. The Welsh, very much the new boys on the international stage, were trying hard to catch up with the established powers in England and Scotland in particular.

The Scots, who originally were members of the RFU until the formation of SFU in 1873, became increasingly frustrated with the process of Law change and alteration as the Rules of the Game, as they were called at the time, were guarded by the Rugby Football Union, their authors and owners.

The first half of the 1880s proved a fruitful period when the Game evolved at pace, having improved tremendously since the move to 15-a-side in 1877. During the early and mid 1880s the new running game, pioneered by Oxford University under the captaincy of Harry Vassall and practised by the Scottish schools Loretto and Fettes in particular, was making great inroads. In Wales, the Cardiff club started using four backs, a format pioneered by Frank Hancock and then adopted by Wales under his captaincy in 1886.

The advent of umpires and then of the referee as well as the introduction of the whistle and flags in 1885 did a lot to help the increasingly complicated management of the Game. However, as a result of the way the Laws were administered in domestic matches by the three new unions, variations of the Rules became widespread, leading to endless disputes between clubs and, occasionally, between unions. This is how the process that led to the formation of the Board had commenced in 1884, based on the different interpretations of the definition of a "knock-on" in Scotland and England.

A disputed try in the match between England and Scotland on 1 March at Blackheath was the trigger point. According to various records, one of the Scottish players CW Berry knocked a ball back during play which was gathered by England's RS Kindersley, who scored a try.

The Scottish players argued that it was illegal to knock the ball back, which was accurate according to the Law as it applied in Scotland. The English replied that irrespective of whether it was illegal or not – and in their opinion knocking a ball back was not illegal – a team may not be allowed to take advantage of their own mistake.

It is worth mentioning that the match referee George Scriven, the captain of Ireland and President of the Irish Union, did not have a whistle yet and the umpires, JHS Graham of Scotland and J McLaren of England, did not have flags.

After long deliberations – "for the best part of half an hour, the players stood about the field not knowing what to do" – referee Scriven eventually awarded the try to England despite the protestations of the Scots. WN Bolton converted and England won by one goal to an unconverted try, scored by J Jamieson. After the match, Scotland suggested adjudication but England rejected the proposal, arguing that the decision of the referee – the sole judge of fact – should be allowed to stand. After the match the Scottish Union asked the matter to be dealt with by a neutral body, a call rejected by the RFU.

The IRB was formed in 1886 following a disagreement between England and Scotland over a disputed try that led to the Scots refusing to play the English for four years.

The Scots felt so strongly about the entire episode that the fixture with England was cancelled the following season, despite the correspondence between the two unions. At the IRFU meeting in December 1885, William J Moore and Robert G Warren put forward an historic motion in which the term "international board" is used for the first time. "The Honorary Secretary be directed to write to the Honorary Secretaries of the English and Scotch Unions stating that an international board would be very useful for the settlement of international disputes." The Irish Union Secretary HG Cook wrote to the two unions and a conference was held in Dublin on 6 February 1886, and the IRFB came into existence after that.

The first meeting of the Board with former Scotland full-back James Stewart Carrick in the chair and his countryman James A Gardner as secretary was held in Manchester in 1887. The three founding unions were represented by Edward McAlister and Thomas Lyle from Ireland, Carrick and Gardner from Scotland and

Horace S Lyne and Richard Mullock from Wales. The minutes of the first meeting were signed by Lyne, who had played for Wales only two years earlier and served on the Board for a record 51 years until his retirement in 1938.

Following the Dublin conference, Scotland awarded the disputed 1884 match to England, on the understanding that the RFU would join an International Board composed of an equal number of representatives of each of the four unions. That was not the case, however, as England felt, rightly or wrongly, that given the size of their union and number of clubs their representation should be bigger.

However, the main issue remained the Laws, with the Game's lawmakers unwilling to relinquish control. Significantly, the second Board meeting, chaired by McAlister, was attended by the RFU's Rowland Hill, though not in a "representative capacity".

The IRB administrates all levels and forms of the international game, including Sevens.

The three founding unions decided to suspend their fixtures against England at the third meeting of the Board on 5 December 1887, until such time as England agreed to join the International Rugby Board. The decision was reinforced by a resolution on 29 September 1888 that "no International match with England can take place until the English Rugby Union agrees to join the International Board."

As a result there were no matches between England and the three unions for two seasons – 1887-88 and 1888-89. The trio resumed their matches with England in 1890 when the four unions had agreed to refer the matter to arbitration and that until the results of the arbitration were made public, further international matches should be played under the Laws of the country in which each match took place.

Significantly, the adjudicators – the Lord Justice Clerk, Lord Kingsburgh and the President of the Football Association, Major FA Marindin – ruled that "all international matches shall be played by the laws approved by the Board," which was the original source of the dispute.

On the matter of representation, the arbitrators ruled in favour of England, who were given six seats on the Board, matching the six of the other three unions which meant that England could never be out-voted by the others. The level of English representation on the Board remained unchanged for 22 years until 1911 when the RFU, reacting to a proposal by Scotland, agreed to reduce its representation from six to four.

One of the earliest and arguably most significant decisions of the 12-strong

Board, under the Chairmanship of former England captain Edward Temple Gurdon – another Board stalwart who attended 51 meetings of the organisation in the 38 years he represented England – was to allocate points to its various forms of scoring at the February 1892 meeting.

It is worth pointing out that, until after the Second World War, the leading overseas unions – the New South Wales Union (formed in 1874), the Queensland Rugby Union (formed in 1878), the South African Rugby Board (formed in 1889) and the New Zealand Rugby Union (formed in 1892) – had no representation on the IRFB, being represented by the English Union.

After the War, the RFU representation was reduced to two to enable the admission of the three Dominions and once the Australian Rugby Union was formed in 1949, the three southern hemisphere unions – the NZRU, SARB and ARU – joined the IRFB, having been allocated one seat each. This lasted until 1958, when it was agreed that all seven member unions would have two representatives each. France joined the Board in 1978, when the By-Laws were altered to enable the Fédération Française de Rugby to become a member.

In 1982, a proposal to hold a Rugby World Cup tournament was discussed at the IRFB Annual Meeting and a year later the Australian Rugby Union suggested that the plans for a RWC tournament were further investigated. Three proposals were received by the Board from three member unions in 1983, and in 1984 the Board agreed that New Zealand and Australia should prepare a feasibility study for consideration in 1985. On 21 March 1985 at the IRFB General Meeting in Paris, it was "resolved to hold a RWC tournament on a trial basis." The Rugby World Cup held in New Zealand and Australia in 1987 was a great success and paved the way for the tournament to continue on a four-year basis.

In 1986, marking the centenary of the formation of the IRFB, the Board agreed to expand and invited the rest of the playing world to join as associate members. The associate membership was a short-lived administrative option, as very soon afterwards full membership was granted to all playing nations.

After the first Rugby World Cup, in 1988 a permanent full-time secretariat, with former Wales and British Lion Keith Rowlands as chief executive, was temporarily installed in London. The IRFB office was then moved to Bristol and from there to Dublin in 1996, as the Rugby World Cup became a permanent feature of the international sporting calendar.

The success of RWC 1987 – the first tournament to make a profit – was followed by the 1991 tournament held in the UK, Ireland and France. RWC 1991 gave a glimpse of the huge commercial potential of the Game, but more significantly, and unlike the previous 'by invitation only', it was open to all unions in IRFB membership.

The meritocratic nature of the event fired up the imagination of the smaller nations, who flocked in to join the IRB – as it became known in 1998-99. The numbers grew steadily from 1991 when 38 unions took part in the RWC qualifying rounds to 96 unions for RWC 2007.

In 1995 the Board declared the Game open, while in 2009 Rugby Sevens joined the Olympic family when the International Olympic Committee voted to include the sport in the 2016 Olympic Games in Rio de Janeiro.

IRB Awards

Another thrilling Year

By Iain Spragg

Thrilling young New Zealand winger, Julian Savea, the IRB Junior Player of the Year.

Two of the three IRB Awards 2010 in association with Emirates Airline to have already been presented this year have gone to flying New Zealand wings in Julian Savea and Carla Hohepa. The other recipient was Mikaele Pesamino, who was named IRB Sevens Player of the Year in May after helping Samoa claim a first ever IRB Sevens World Series crown.

Exciting wing Savea was named IRB Junior Player of the Year 2010 in June, becoming the eighth New Zealander to claim the coveted award since its inception back in 2001. Hohepa, meanwhile, was presented with the IRB Women's Personality of the Year in September after helping the Black Ferns win a fourth successive Women's Rugby World Cup title.

Savea received his award from IRB Vice Chairman Bill Beaumont after helping New Zealand Under-20s win a third successive IRB Junior World Championship title with a scintillating 62-17 defeat of Australia at the

IRB Women's Personality of the Year, Carla Hohepa, in World Cup Final action v England.

Estadio El Coloso del Parque in Rosario, Argentina, on 21 June.

The Wellington-born wing beat off stiff competition from his compatriot and captain Tyler Bleyendaal, Australia centre Robbie Coleman and Argentina No 10 Ignacio Rodriguez Muedra to collect the honour. Savea was the tournament's top try-scorer with eight – although none of them in the final – and by winning the award he follows in the footsteps of previous New Zealand recipients such as Luke McAlister, Isaia Toeava, Jerome Kaino and 2009 winner Aaron Cruden.

"The IRB Junior World Championship has shown us the future stars of the world game, which looks to be in very good hands," said Beaumont after presenting Savea with his award. "The IRB Junior Player of the Year award is essential in recognising achievement at this level and Julian should feel extremely proud that he has won this award given the very talented players on show here over the past three weeks."

A product of Rongotai College in eastern Wellington, the wing was selected for the New Zealand secondary schools side in 2008 and the following year he debuted for the Sevens national team in Adelaide. The reward for his outstanding performances in the IRB Junior World Championship was a place in the Wellington Lions squad to play in the 2010 ITM Cup.

"I feel pretty stoked," Savea said after collecting his award. "Once again, credit to the boys as without them I wouldn't be here."

Hohepa would also pay tribute to her team-mates after being named the IRB Women's Personality of the Year 2010 within minutes of playing a pivotal role in New Zealand's victory in the Women's Rugby World Cup final on 5 September.

The 25-year-old wing ended the tournament as joint top try-scorer with seven, including a crucial score in the 13-10 win over hosts England in the final at the Twickenham Stoop to secure New Zealand's fourth consecutive title to extend their reign as women's world champions dating back to 1998.

"I can't take all the credit for it but it's an awesome honour to win this award," Hohepa said. "The whole team performance in the final was fantastic, everyone has put 100 per cent in and it showed out there today."

Hohepa edged out England duo Maggie Alphonsi and Danielle Waterman, as well as Australia wing Nicole Beck to become the first New Zealander to claim the coveted award since former Black Ferns' captain Farah Palmer in 2005.

Samoa's dazzling Mikaele Pesamino, the IRB Sevens Player of the Year, who scored an astonishing 56 tries during the 2009-10 IRB Sevens season.

The IRB Sevens Player of the Year 2010 accolade was presented to Pesamino in Edinburgh after a series of scintillating displays which helped inspire Samoa to their historic Sevens World Series title.

The 26-year-old speedster scored a phenomenal 56 tries – 23 more than New Zealand's Kurt Baker in second place – as Samoa beat Gordon Tietjens' eight-time Series champions to the 2010 crown, courtesy of their 44-14 victory over Australia in the final of the Emirates Airline Edinburgh Sevens at Murrayfield.

"I wanted to be the top try scorer this year and I wanted to be the Player of the Year and I feel great," Pesamino said after collecting his award and becoming only the second Samoan, after Uale Mai in 2006, to receive it. "I feel happy, not only for me but also for my team-mates, my family all the way from Samoa.

"They pray for us, they cheer for us, and also our fans, our younger players, this is our best gift for them for our Independence Day next week. It is Sunday today in Samoa and the people will go to church and the pastors will talk and I think they will talk about rugby on this day.

"Our Prime Minister said that we would have a national holiday if we won the Series and we'll celebrate, we'll enjoy tonight and this is our best gift to our people."

IRB World Rankings
All Blacks on Top
By Karen Bond

The last 12 months have seen no fewer than nine nations achieve their highest-ever positions in the IRB World Rankings, including the year's biggest climbers in Colombia with a 12-place elevation to 53rd on the back of victories over Peru and Venezuela at the South American 'B' Championship in December.

Japan, Namibia, Kenya, Senegal, Malaysia, India, Israel and Andorra also rose to new heights over the course of the year, while Sri Lanka closed to within one place of their best ever position of 42nd and Scotland matched their highest standing of seventh by beating Argentina in their own backyard in June.

Some stays at these new highs were brief, Japan's elevation to 12th on the back of beating Samoa in the ANZ Pacific Nations Cup lasting only a week in June, others showed the strides being made by developing countries such as Malaysia who now occupy 57th spot, having repeated their 11-place gain of the previous year.

Malaysia's gain largely came on the back of beating Chinese Taipei 35-8 in the HSBC Asian 5 Nations Division I. Sri Lanka also overwhelmed the same nation, who had elected to send a young side to the tournament, en route to securing promotion to the elite level of Asian rugby. Chinese Taipei have slumped 10 to their lowest ever position of 61st, but it is China who experienced the biggest drop over the last 12 months, falling 18 places to a worst ever 67th after crashing 94-5 to India and 56-3 to Thailand in Division II of the A5N. These heavy losses helped India and Thailand to climb 10 places to 73rd and 60th respectively.

Another nation to suffer a fall, albeit nowhere near the magnitude of China, was South Africa who had begun last October as the number one ranked side only to lose it to New Zealand the following month after losing 20-13 to France. Things got worse for the Springboks with defeat by Australia in Bloemfontein – the fifth loss in a disappointing 2010 Tri-Nations campaign – seeing them drop to third.

New Zealand's impressive run of 14 consecutive Test victories over the last 12 months has seen Richie McCaw's men surge clear at the top, their clean sweep of the Tri-Nations stretching their advantage over Australia to 9.21 rating points, just two tenths shy of the biggest ever cushion they enjoyed over France back on 25 June 2007.

While New Zealand pulled clear at the top, there was plenty of movement amid the world's leading 20 nations with only Georgia (17) and Romania (19) entering October in the same position they had done so 12 months earlier. Namibia, though, are the biggest movers with a five place elevation on the back of their IRB Nations Cup success in June to enter the top 20 for the first time.

Morocco and Senegal were two other African nations on the rise, climbing eight and seven places respectively after victories over Ivory Coast in the Africa Cup pool stages. Morocco also beat Tunisia, who are the continent's biggest fallers in the IRB World Rankings, dropping eight places to 35th, although Uganda, Ivory Coast, Zimbabwe and Botswana also fell.

The biggest movers in the North America and Caribbean region over the last 12 months were Bermuda, who rose four places to 54th on the back of other results and a 26-15 away win over the Cayman Islands in May. The Cayman Islands fell eight places in the same period, while USA came close to matching Bermuda's climb with a three-place rise to 15th.

With victory over Argentina in June 2010 Scotland lifted themselves to 7th in the IRB World Rankings.

In South America, there were few climbers besides Colombia with Brazil rising one to 28th. On the flip side, there were plenty of nations slipping with Peru dropping seven to 78th. Two other nations to fall seven places were Poland and Korea, the latter after losing all four matches in the A5N Top 5, including a first ever loss to the Arabian Gulf.

There was better news in Europe for Andorra, the region's biggest climber with a 10-place elevation to 62nd, while Malta, Belgium, Austria and Israel all rose six or seven places. Finally, in Oceania, the only other nation besides New Zealand and Australia to register an improved ranking was Niue, who climbed one place to 68th. Fiji, Samoa and Tonga all fell one place, while Papua New Guinea and the Cook Islands remain 50th and 55th respectively.

The IRB World Rankings were introduced in October 2003 and are published every Monday on www.irb.com. They are calculated using a points exchange system in which teams take points off each other based on the match result. Whatever one team gains, the other team loses. The exchanges are determined by the match result, the relative strength of the team and the margin of victory. There is also an allowance for home advantage.

Ninety-five of the IRB's Member Unions have a rating, typically between 0 and 100 with the top side in the world usually having a rating above 90 – New Zealand's was 94.77 at the time of writing. Any match that is not a full international between two countries or a Test against the Lions or Pacific Islanders does not count towards the rankings. Likewise neither does a match against a country that is not a Full Member Union of the IRB. For more details, visit www.irb.com.

IRB WORLD RANKINGS 01/10/09 – 30/09/10

POSITION	MEMBER UNION	RATING POINTS	MOVERS
1	New Zealand	94.77	Up 1
2	Australia	85.56	Up 1
3	South Africa	85.22	Down 2
4	France	82.75	Up 1
5	Ireland	82.03	Down 1
6	England	81.82	Up 1
7	Scotland	79.81	Up 3
8	Argentina	79.70	Down 2
9	Wales	78.58	Down 1
10	Fiji	72.97	Down 1
11	Italy	72.97	Up 1
12	Samoa	72.74	Down 1
13	Japan	72.49	Up 1
14	Canada	69.43	Down 1
15	USA	67.86	Up 3
16	Tonga	67.06	Down 1
17	Georgia	66.38	
18	Russia	65.80	Down 2
19	Romania	65.10	
20	Namibia	62.69	Up 5
21	Uruguay	61.38	
22	Portugal	61.27	Down 2
23	Spain	57.70	Down 1
24	Chile	56.97	Down 1
25	Morocco	56.11	Up 8
26	Belgium	55.36	Up 6
27	Kazakhstan	55.28	Up 1
28	Brazil	54.56	Up 1
29	Ukraine	54.35	Up 1
30	Germany	53.22	Down 4
31	Korea	53.03	Down 7
32	Kenya	52.85	Up 10
33	Czech Republic	52.52	Up 2
34	Hong Kong	52.49	
35	Tunisia	52.24	Down 8
36	Netherlands	51.67	
37	Moldova	51.61	Up 3
38	Poland	51.50	Down 7
39	Lithuania	50.41	Down 1
40	Arabian Gulf	50.41	Up 5
41	Paraguay	50.23	Down 4
42	Croatia	49.72	Up 1
43	Sri Lanka	48.62	Up 10
44	Uganda	48.13	Down 3
45	Ivory Coast	47.52	Down 6
46	Trinidad & Tobago	47.19	
47	Madagascar	46.45	Up 1
48	Malta	46.44	Up 6

IRB WORLD RANKINGS 01/10/09 – 30/09/10

POSITION	MEMBER UNION	RATING POINTS	MOVERS
49	Sweden	46.36	Down 5
50	Papua New Guinea	46.19	
51	Zimbabwe	46.15	Down 4
52	Singapore	45.03	
53	Colombia	44.99	Up 12
54	Bermuda	44.74	Up 4
55	Cook Islands	44.61	
56	Senegal	43.83	Up 7
57	Malaysia	43.05	Up 11
58	Latvia	43.03	Up 1
59	Venezuela	42.79	Down 3
60	Thailand	42.70	Up 10
61	Chinese Taipei	42.58	Down 10
62	Andorra	42.29	Up 10
63	Switzerland	42.19	Down 6
64	Serbia	42.06	Down 4
65	Slovenia	41.52	Down 4
66	Guyana	41.52	Up 1
67	China	41.39	Down 18
68	Niue Islands	41.11	Up 1
69	Hungary	41.01	Down 5
70	Cayman	40.97	Down 8
71	Denmark	40.52	Down 5
72	Zambia	39.97	Up 1
73	India	39.61	Up 10
74	Israel	39.57	Up 6
75	St Vincent & The Grenadines	39.30	Down 1
76	Barbados	39.21	
77	Solomon Islands	39.06	
78	Peru	38.81	Down 7
79	Cameroon	38.21	Down 1
80	Botswana	38.17	Down 5
81	St Lucia	37.57	Down 2
82	Norway	37.13	Up 3
83	Guam	36.80	Down 2
84	Swaziland	36.68	Down 2
85	Jamaica	36.61	Down 1
86	Bahamas	36.33	
87	Austria	36.29	Up 6
88	Tahiti	36.25	Down 1
89	Bosnia & Herzegovina	36.18	Up 1
90	Bulgaria	36.08	Down 1
91	Nigeria	35.29	
92	Monaco	35.17	Down 4
93	Vanuatu	34.77	Down 1
94	Luxembourg	32.65	
95	Finland	28.59	

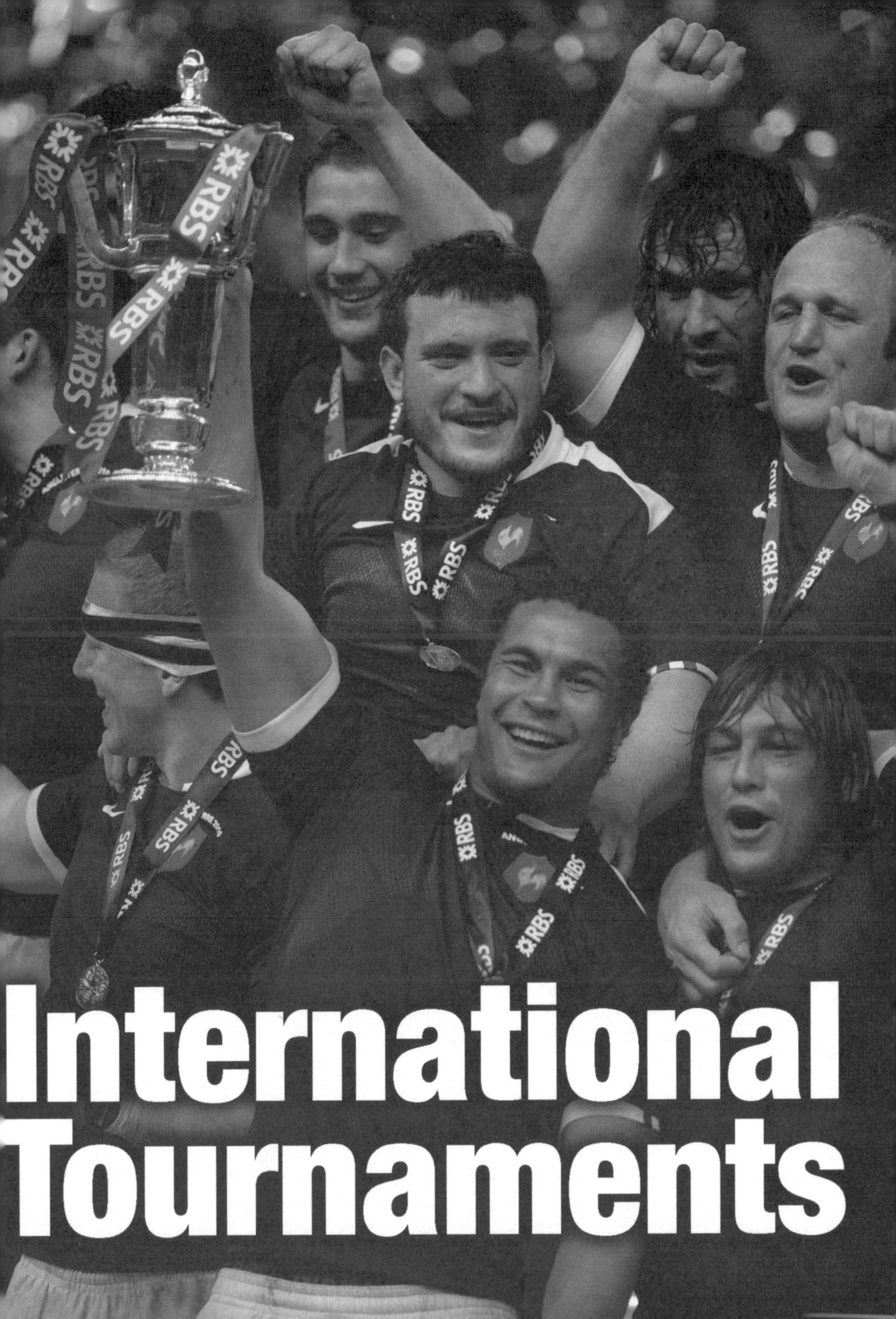

International Tournaments

RUGBY WORLD CUP TOURNAMENTS 1987–2007

(FINAL STAGES ONLY)

OVERALL RECORDS

MOST MATCHES WON IN FINAL STAGES

30	New Zealand
28	Australia
26	France
25	England

MOST OVERALL POINTS IN FINAL STAGES

249	J P Wilkinson	England	1999–2007
227	A G Hastings	Scotland	1987–1995
195	M P Lynagh	Australia	1987–1995
170	G J Fox	New Zealand	1987–1991
163	A P Mehrtens	New Zealand	1995–1999

MOST OVERALL TRIES IN FINAL STAGES

15	J T Lomu	New Zealand	1995–1999
13	D C Howlett	New Zealand	2003–2007
11	R Underwood	England	1987–1995
11	J T Rokocoko	New Zealand	2003–2007
11	C E Latham	Australia	1999–2007

MOST OVERALL CONVERSIONS IN FINAL STAGES

39	A G Hastings	Scotland	1987–1995
37	G J Fox	New Zealand	1987–1991
36	M P Lynagh	Australia	1987–1995
29	D W Carter	New Zealand	2003–2007
27	P J Grayson	England	1999–2003

MOST OVERALL PENALTY GOALS IN FINAL STAGES

53	J P Wilkinson	England	1999–2007
36	A G Hastings	Scotland	1987–1995
35	G Quesada	Argentina	1999–2003
33	M P Lynagh	Australia	1987–1995
33	A P Mehrtens	New Zealand	1995–1999

MOST OVERALL DROPPED GOALS IN FINAL STAGES

13	J P Wilkinson	England	1999–2007
6	J H de Beer	South Africa	1999
5	C R Andrew	England	1987–1995
5	G L Rees	Canada	1987–1999
4	J M Hernández	Argentina	2003–2007

MOST MATCH APPEARANCES IN FINAL STAGES

22	J Leonard	England	1991–2003
20	G M Gregan	Australia	1995–2007
19	M J Catt	England	1995–2007
18	M O Johnson	England	1995–2003
18	B P Lima	Samoa	1991–2007
18	R Ibañez	France	1999–2007

LEADING SCORERS

MOST POINTS IN ONE COMPETITION

126	G J Fox	New Zealand	1987
113	J P Wilkinson	England	2003
112	T Lacroix	France	1995
105	P C Montgomery	South Africa	2007
104	A G Hastings	Scotland	1995
103	F Michalak	France	2003
102	G Quesada	Argentina	1999
101	M Burke	Australia	1999

MOST PENALTY GOALS IN ONE COMPETITION

31	G Quesada	Argentina	1999
26	T Lacroix	France	1995
23	J P Wilkinson	England	2003
21	G J Fox	New Zealand	1987
21	E J Flatley	Australia	2003
20	C R Andrew	England	1995

MOST TRIES IN ONE COMPETITION

8	J T Lomu	New Zealand	1999
8	B G Habana	South Africa	2007
7	M C G Ellis	New Zealand	1995
7	J T Lomu	New Zealand	1995
7	D C Howlett	New Zealand	2003
7	J M Muliaina	New Zealand	2003
7	D A Mitchell	Australia	2007

MOST DROPPED GOALS IN ONE COMPETITION

8	J P Wilkinson	England	2003
6	J H de Beer	South Africa	1999
5	J P Wilkinson	England	2007
4	J M Hernández	Argentina	2007

MOST CONVERSIONS IN ONE COMPETITION

30	G J Fox	New Zealand	1987
22	P C Montgomery	South Africa	2007
20	S D Culhane	New Zealand	1995
20	M P Lynagh	Australia	1987
20	L R MacDonald	New Zealand	2003
20	N J Evans	New Zealand	2007

MOST POINTS IN A MATCH

BY THE TEAM

145	New Zealand v Japan	1995
142	Australia v Namibia	2003
111	England v Uruguay	2003
108	New Zealand v Portugal	2007
101	New Zealand v Italy	1999
101	England v Tonga	1999

BY A PLAYER

45	S D Culhane	New Zealand v Japan	1995
44	A G Hastings	Scotland v Ivory Coast	1995
42	M S Rogers	Australia v Namibia	2003
36	T E Brown	New Zealand v Italy	1999
36	P J Grayson	England v Tonga	1999
34	J H de Beer	South Africa v England	1999
33	N J Evans	New Zealand v Portugal	2007
32	J P Wilkinson	England v Italy	1999

MOST TRIES IN A MATCH

BY THE TEAM

22	Australia v Namibia	2003
21	New Zealand v Japan	1995
17	England v Uruguay	2003
16	New Zealand v Portugal	2007
14	New Zealand v Italy	1999

BY A PLAYER

6	M C G Ellis	New Zealand v Japan	1995
5	C E Latham	Australia v Namibia	2003
5	O J Lewsey	England v Uruguay	2003
4	I C Evans	Wales v Canada	1987
4	C I Green	New Zealand v Fiji	1987
4	J A Gallagher	New Zealand v Fiji	1987
4	B F Robinson	Ireland v Zimbabwe	1991
4	A G Hastings	Scotland v Ivory Coast	1995
4	C M Williams	South Africa v Western Samoa	1995
4	J T Lomu	New Zealand v England	1995
4	K G M Wood	Ireland v United States	1999
4	J M Muliaina	New Zealand v Canada	2003
4	B G Habana	South Africa v Samoa	2007

MOST CONVERSIONS IN A MATCH

BY THE TEAM

20	New Zealand v Japan	1995
16	Australia v Namibia	2003
14	New Zealand v Portugal	2007
13	New Zealand v Tonga	2003
13	England v Uruguay	2003

BY A PLAYER

20	S D Culhane	New Zealand v Japan	1995
16	M S Rogers	Australia v Namibia	2003
14	N J Evans	New Zealand v Portugal	2007
12	P J Grayson	England v Tonga	1999
12	L R MacDonald	New Zealand v Tonga	2003

MOST PENALTY GOALS IN A MATCH

BY THE TEAM

8	Australia v South Africa	1999
8	Argentina v Samoa	1999
8	Scotland v Tonga	1995
8	France v Ireland	1995

BY A PLAYER

8	M Burke	Australia v South Africa	1999
8	G Quesada	Argentina v Samoa	1999
8	A G Hastings	Scotland v Tonga	1995
8	T Lacroix	France v Ireland	1995

MOST DROPPED GOALS IN A MATCH

BY THE TEAM

5	South Africa v England	1999
3	Fiji v Romania	1991
3	England v France	2003
3	Argentina v Ireland	2007

BY A PLAYER

5	J H de Beer	South Africa v England	1999
3	J P Wilkinson	England v France	2003
3	J M Hernández	Argentina v Ireland	2007

Ross Setford/Getty Images

Simon Culhane's 23-year-old record for most points in a match still stands.

RUGBY WORLD CUP TOURNAMENTS 1987–2007

FIRST TOURNAMENT: 1987 IN AUSTRALIA & NEW ZEALAND

POOL 1

Australia	19	**England**	6
USA	21	**Japan**	18
England	60	**Japan**	7
Australia	47	**USA**	12
England	34	**USA**	6
Australia	42	**Japan**	23

	P	W	D	L	F	A	Pts
Australia	3	3	0	0	108	41	6
England	3	2	0	1	100	32	4
USA	3	1	0	2	39	99	2
Japan	3	0	0	3	48	123	0

POOL 2

Canada	37	**Tonga**	4
Wales	13	**Ireland**	6
Wales	29	**Tonga**	16
Ireland	46	**Canada**	19
Wales	40	**Canada**	9
Ireland	32	**Tonga**	9

	P	W	D	L	F	A	Pts
Wales	3	3	0	0	82	31	6
Ireland	3	2	0	1	84	41	4
Canada	3	1	0	2	65	90	2
Tonga	3	0	0	3	29	98	0

POOL 3

New Zealand	70	**Italy**	6
Fiji	28	**Argentina**	9
New Zealand	74	**Fiji**	13
Argentina	25	**Italy**	16
Italy	18	**Fiji**	15
New Zealand	46	**Argentina**	15

	P	W	D	L	F	A	Pts
New Zealand	3	3	0	0	190	34	6
Fiji	3	1	0	2	56	101	2
Argentina	3	1	0	2	49	90	2
Italy	3	1	0	2	40	110	2

POOL 4

Romania	21	**Zimbabwe**	20
France	20	**Scotland**	20
France	55	**Romania**	12
Scotland	60	**Zimbabwe**	21
France	70	**Zimbabwe**	12
Scotland	55	**Romania**	28

	P	W	D	L	F	A	Pts
France	3	2	1	0	145	44	5
Scotland	3	2	1	0	135	69	5
Romania	3	1	0	2	61	130	2
Zimbabwe	3	0	0	3	53	151	0

QUARTER-FINALS

New Zealand	30	**Scotland**	3
France	31	**Fiji**	16
Australia	33	**Ireland**	15
Wales	16	**England**	3

SEMI-FINALS

France	30	**Australia**	24
New Zealand	49	**Wales**	6

THIRD PLACE MATCH

Wales	22	**Australia**	21

First World Cup Final, Eden Park, Auckland, 20 June 1987

NEW ZEALAND 29 (1G 4PG 1DG 2T)
FRANCE 9 (1G 1PG)

NEW ZEALAND: J A Gallagher; J J Kirwan, J T Stanley, W T Taylor, C I Green; G J Fox, D E Kirk (captain); S C McDowell, S B T Fitzpatrick, J A Drake, M J Pierce, G W Whetton, A J Whetton, W T Shelford, M N Jones

SCORERS *Tries*: Jones, Kirk, Kirwan *Conversion*: Fox *Penalty Goals*: Fox (4) *Drop Goal*: Fox

FRANCE: S Blanco; D Camberabero, P Sella, D Charvet, P Lagisquet; F Mesnel, P Berbizier; P Ondarts, D Dubroca (captain), J–P Garuet, A Lorieux, J Condom, E Champ, L Rodriguez, D Erbani

SCORERS *Try*: Berbizier *Conversion*: Camberabero *Penalty Goal*: Camberabero

REFEREE K V J Fitzgerald (Australia)

Ross Land/Getty Images

David Kirk delights a nation by lifting the first Rugby World Cup.

SECOND TOURNAMENT: 1991 IN BRITAIN, IRELAND & FRANCE

POOL 1

New Zealand	18	**England**	12
Italy	30	**USA**	9
New Zealand	46	**USA**	6
England	36	**Italy**	6
England	37	**USA**	9
New Zealand	31	**Italy**	21

	P	W	D	L	F	A	Pts
New Zealand	3	3	0	0	95	39	9
England	3	2	0	1	85	33	7
Italy	3	1	0	2	57	76	5
USA	3	0	0	3	24	113	3

POOL 2

Scotland	47	**Japan**	9
Ireland	55	**Zimbabwe**	11
Ireland	32	**Japan**	16
Scotland	51	**Zimbabwe**	12
Scotland	24	**Ireland**	15
Japan	52	**Zimbabwe**	8

	P	W	D	L	F	A	Pts
Scotland	3	3	0	0	122	36	9
Ireland	3	2	0	1	102	51	7
Japan	3	1	0	2	77	87	5
Zimbabwe	3	0	0	3	31	158	3

POOL 3

Australia	32	**Argentina**	19
Western Samoa	16	**Wales**	13
Australia	9	**Western Samoa**	3
Wales	16	**Argentina**	7
Australia	38	**Wales**	3
Western Samoa	35	**Argentina**	12

	P	W	D	L	F	A	Pts
Australia	3	3	0	0	79	25	9
Western Samoa	3	2	0	1	54	34	7
Wales	3	1	0	2	32	61	5
Argentina	3	0	0	3	38	83	3

POOL 4

France	30	**Romania**	3
Canada	13	**Fiji**	3
France	33	**Fiji**	9
Canada	19	**Romania**	11
Romania	17	**Fiji**	15
France	19	**Canada**	13

	P	W	D	L	F	A	Pts
France	3	3	0	0	82	25	9
Canada	3	2	0	1	45	33	7
Romania	3	1	0	2	31	64	5
Fiji	3	0	0	3	27	63	3

QUARTER-FINALS

England	19	**France**	10
Scotland	28	**Western Samoa**	6
Australia	19	**Ireland**	18
New Zealand	29	**Canada**	13

SEMI-FINALS

England	9	**Scotland**	6
Australia	16	**New Zealand**	6

THIRD PLACE MATCH

New Zealand	13	**Scotland**	6

Second World Cup Final, Twickenham, 2 November 1991

AUSTRALIA 12 (1G 2PG)
ENGLAND 6 (2PG)

AUSTRALIA: M C Roebuck; D I Campese, J S Little, T J Horan, R H Egerton; M P Lynagh, N C Farr-Jones (captain); A J Daly, P N Kearns, E J A McKenzie, R J McCall, J A Eales, S P Poidevin, T Coker, V Ofahengaue

SCORERS *Try***:** Daly *Conversion*: Lynagh *Penalty Goals*: Lynagh (2)

ENGLAND: J M Webb; S J Halliday, W D C Carling (captain), J C Guscott, R Underwood; C R Andrew, R J Hill; J Leonard, B C Moore, J A Probyn, P J Ackford, W A Dooley, M G Skinner, M C Teague, P J Winterbottom

SCORER *Penalty Goals***:** Webb (2)

REFEREE W D Bevan (Wales)

Getty Images

Michael Lynagh (bottom right) leads the Aussie celebrations in 1991.

THIRD TOURNAMENT: 1995 IN SOUTH AFRICA

POOL A

South Africa	27	Australia	18
Canada	34	Romania	3
South Africa	21	Romania	8
Australia	27	Canada	11
Australia	42	Romania	3
South Africa	20	Canada	0

	P	W	D	L	F	A	Pts
South Africa	3	3	0	0	68	26	9
Australia	3	2	0	1	87	41	7
Canada	3	1	0	2	45	50	5
Romania	3	0	0	3	14	97	3

POOL B

Western Samoa	42	Italy	18
England	24	Argentina	18
Western Samoa	32	Argentina	26
England	27	Italy	20
Italy	31	Argentina	25
England	44	Western Samoa	22

	P	W	D	L	F	A	Pts
England	3	3	0	0	95	60	9
Western Samoa	3	2	0	1	96	88	7
Italy	3	1	0	2	69	94	5
Argentina	3	0	0	3	69	87	3

POOL C

Wales	57	Japan	10
New Zealand	43	Ireland	19
Ireland	50	Japan	28
New Zealand	34	Wales	9
New Zealand	145	Japan	17
Ireland	24	Wales	23

	P	W	D	L	F	A	Pts
New Zealand	3	3	0	0	222	45	9
Ireland	3	2	0	1	93	94	7
Wales	3	1	0	2	89	68	5
Japan	3	0	0	3	55	252	3

POOL D

Scotland	89	Ivory Coast	0
France	38	Tonga	10
France	54	Ivory Coast	18
Scotland	41	Tonga	5
Tonga	29	Ivory Coast	11
France	22	Scotland	19

	P	W	D	L	F	A	Pts
France	3	3	0	0	114	47	9
Scotland	3	2	0	1	149	27	7
Tonga	3	1	0	2	44	90	5
Ivory Coast	3	0	0	3	29	172	3

QUARTER-FINALS

France	36	Ireland	12
South Africa	42	Western Samoa	14
England	25	Australia	22
New Zealand	48	Scotland	30

SEMI-FINALS

South Africa	19	France	15
New Zealand	45	England	29

THIRD PLACE MATCH

France	19	England	9

Third World Cup Final, Ellis Park, Johannesburg, 24 June 1995

SOUTH AFRICA 15 (3PG 2DG)
NEW ZEALAND 12 (3PG 1DG) *

SOUTH AFRICA: A J Joubert; J T Small, J C Mulder, H P Le Roux, C M Williams; J T Stransky, J H van der Westhuizen; J P du Randt, C L C Rossouw, I S Swart, J J Wiese, J J Strydom, J F Pienaar (captain), M G Andrews, R J Kruger Substitutions: G L Pagel for Swart (68 mins); R A W Straeuli for Andrews (90 mins); B Venter for Small (97 mins)

SCORER *Penalty Goals*: Stransky (3) *Drop Goals*: Stransky (2)

NEW ZEALAND: G M Osborne; J W Wilson, F E Bunce, W K Little, J T Lomu; A P Mehrtens, G T M Bachop; C W Dowd, S B T Fitzpatrick (captain), O M Brown, I D Jones, R M Brooke, M R Brewer, Z V Brooke, J A Kronfeld Substitutions: J W Joseph for Brewer (40 mins); M C G Ellis for Wilson (55 mins); R W Loe for Dowd (83 mins); A D Strachan for Bachop (temp 66 to 71 mins)

SCORER *Penalty Goals*: Mehrtens (3) *Drop Goal*: Mehrtens

REFEREE E F Morrison (England)

* after extra time: 9–9 after normal time

Getty Images

The Springboks celebrate an incredible win at Ellis Park in 1995.

FOURTH TOURNAMENT: 1999 IN BRITAIN, IRELAND & FRANCE

POOL A

Spain	15	Uruguay	27
South Africa	46	Scotland	29
Scotland	43	Uruguay	12
South Africa	47	Spain	3
South Africa	39	Uruguay	3
Scotland	48	Spain	0

	P	W	D	L	F	A	Pts
South Africa	3	3	0	0	132	35	9
Scotland	3	2	0	1	120	58	7
Uruguay	3	1	0	2	42	97	5
Spain	3	0	0	3	18	122	3

POOL B

England	67	**Italy**	7
New Zealand	45	**Tonga**	9
England	16	**New Zealand**	30
Italy	25	**Tonga**	28
New Zealand	101	**Italy**	3
England	101	**Tonga**	10

	P	W	D	L	F	A	Pts
New Zealand	3	3	0	0	176	28	9
England	3	2	0	1	184	47	7
Tonga	3	1	0	2	47	171	5
Italy	3	0	0	3	35	196	3

POOL C

Fiji	67	**Namibia**	18
France	33	**Canada**	20
France	47	**Namibia**	13
Fiji	38	**Canada**	22
Canada	72	**Namibia**	11
France	28	**Fiji**	19

	P	W	D	L	F	A	Pts
France	3	3	0	0	108	52	9
Fiji	3	2	0	1	124	68	7
Canada	3	1	0	2	114	82	5
Namibia	3	0	0	3	42	186	3

POOL D

Wales	23	**Argentina**	18
Samoa	43	**Japan**	9
Wales	64	**Japan**	15
Argentina	32	**Samoa**	16
Wales	31	**Samoa**	38
Argentina	33	**Japan**	12

	P	W	D	L	F	A	Pts
Wales	3	2	0	1	118	71	7
Samoa	3	2	0	1	97	72	7
Argentina	3	2	0	1	83	51	7
Japan	3	0	0	3	36	140	3

POOL E

Ireland	53	**United States**	8
Australia	57	**Romania**	9
United States	25	**Romania**	27
Ireland	3	**Australia**	23
Australia	55	**United States**	19
Ireland	44	**Romania**	14

	P	W	D	L	F	A	Pts
Australia	3	3	0	0	135	31	9
Ireland	3	2	0	1	100	45	7
Romania	3	1	0	2	50	126	5
United States	3	0	0	3	52	135	3

PLAY-OFFS FOR QUARTER-FINAL PLACES

England	45	**Fiji**	24
Scotland	35	**Samoa**	20
Ireland	24	**Argentina**	28

QUARTER-FINALS

Wales	9	**Australia**	24
South Africa	44	**England**	21
France	47	**Argentina**	26
Scotland	18	**New Zealand**	30

Fourth World Cup Final, Millennium Stadium, Cardiff, 6 November 1999

AUSTRALIA 35 (2G 7PG) FRANCE 12 (4PG)

AUSTRALIA: M Burke; B N Tune, D J Herbert, T J Horan, J W Roff; S J Larkham, G M Gregan; R L L Harry, M A Foley, A T Blades, D T Giffin, J A Eales (captain), M J Cockbain, R S T Kefu, D J Wilson Substitutions J S Little for Herbert (46 mins); O D A Finegan for Cockbain (52 mins); M R Connors for Wilson (73 mins); D J Crowley for Harry (75 mins); J A Paul for Foley (85 mins); C J Whitaker for Gregan (86 mins); N P Grey for Horan (86 mins)

SCORERS *Tries*: Tune, Finegan *Conversions*: Burke (2) *Penalty Goals*: Burke (7)

FRANCE: X Garbajosa; P Bernat Salles, R Dourthe, E Ntamack, C Dominici; C Lamaison, F Galthié; C Soulette, R Ibañez (captain), F Tournaire, A Benazzi, F Pelous, M Lièvremont, C Juillet, O Magne Substitutions O Brouzet for Juillet (HT); P de Villiers for Soulette (47 mins); A Costes for Magne (temp 19 to 22 mins) and for Lièvremont (67 mins); U Mola for Garbajosa (67 mins); S Glas for Dourthe (temp 49 to 55 mins and from 74 mins); S Castaignède for Galthié (76 mins); M Dal Maso for Ibañez (79 mins)

SCORER *Penalty Goals*: Lamaison (4)

REFEREE A J Watson (South Africa)

Dave Rogers/Getty Images

The Wallabies start the party after their victory against France in 1999.

FIFTH TOURNAMENT: 2003 IN AUSTRALIA

POOL A

Australia	24	**Argentina**	8
Ireland	45	**Romania**	17
Argentina	67	**Namibia**	14
Australia	90	**Romania**	8
Ireland	64	**Namibia**	7
Argentina	50	**Romania**	3
Australia	142	**Namibia**	0
Ireland	16	**Argentina**	15
Romania	37	**Namibia**	7
Australia	17	**Ireland**	16

	P	W	D	L	F	A	Pts
Australia	4	4	0	0	273	32	18
Ireland	4	3	0	1	141	56	14
Argentina	4	2	0	2	140	57	11
Romania	4	1	0	3	65	192	5
Namibia	4	0	0	4	28	310	0

POOL C

South Africa	72	**Uruguay**	6
England	84	**Georgia**	6
Samoa	60	**Uruguay**	13
England	25	**South Africa**	6
Samoa	46	**Georgia**	9
South Africa	46	**Georgia**	19
England	35	**Samoa**	22
Uruguay	24	**Georgia**	12
South Africa	60	**Samoa**	10
England	111	**Uruguay**	13

	P	W	D	L	F	A	Pts
England	4	4	0	0	255	47	19
South Africa	4	3	0	1	184	60	15
Samoa	4	2	0	2	138	117	10
Uruguay	4	1	0	3	56	255	4
Georgia	4	0	0	4	46	200	0

POOL B

France	61	**Fiji**	18
Scotland	32	**Japan**	11
Fiji	19	**United States**	18
France	51	**Japan**	29
Scotland	39	**United States**	15
Fiji	41	**Japan**	13
France	51	**Scotland**	9
United States	39	**Japan**	26
France	41	**United States**	14
Scotland	22	**Fiji**	20

	P	W	D	L	F	A	Pts
France	4	4	0	0	204	70	20
Scotland	4	3	0	1	102	97	14
Fiji	4	2	0	2	98	114	9
United States	4	1	0	3	86	125	6
Japan	4	0	0	4	79	163	0

POOL D

New Zealand	70	**Italy**	7
Wales	41	**Canada**	10
Italy	36	**Tonga**	12
New Zealand	68	**Canada**	6
Wales	27	**Tonga**	20
Italy	19	**Canada**	14
New Zealand	91	**Tonga**	7
Wales	27	**Italy**	15
Canada	24	**Tonga**	7
New Zealand	53	**Wales**	37

	P	W	D	L	F	A	Pts
New Zealand	4	4	0	0	282	57	20
Wales	4	3	0	1	132	98	14
Italy	4	2	0	2	77	123	8
Canada	4	1	0	3	54	135	5
Tonga	4	0	0	4	46	178	1

QUARTER-FINALS

New Zealand	29	**South Africa**	9
Australia	33	**Scotland**	16
France	43	**Ireland**	21
England	28	**Wales**	17

SEMI-FINALS

Australia	22	**New Zealand**	10
England	24	**France**	7

THIRD PLACE MATCH

New Zealand	40	**France**	13

Fifth World Cup Final, Telstra Stadium, Sydney, 22 November 2003

ENGLAND 20 (4PG 1DG 1T) AUSTRALIA 17 (4PG 1T) *

ENGLAND: J Robinson; O J Lewsey, W J H Greenwood, M J Tindall, B C Cohen; J P Wilkinson, M J S Dawson; T J Woodman, S Thompson, P J Vickery, M O Johnson (captain), B J Kay, R A Hill, L B N Dallaglio, N A Back Substitutions: M J Catt for Tindall (78 mins); J Leonard for Vickery (80 mins); I R Balshaw for Lewsey (85 mins); L W Moody for Hill (93 mins)

SCORERS *Try*: Robinson *Penalty Goals*: Wilkinson (4) *Dropped Goal*: Wilkinson

AUSTRALIA: M S Rogers; W J Sailor, S A Mortlock, E J Flatley, L Tuqiri; S J Larkham, G M Gregan (captain); W K Young, B J Cannon, A K E Baxter, J B Harrison, N C Sharpe, G B Smith, D J Lyons, P R Waugh Substitutions: D T Giffin for Sharpe (48 mins); J A Paul for Cannon (56 mins); M J Cockbain for Lyons (56 mins); J W Roff for Sailor (70 mins); M J Dunning for Young (92 mins); M J Giteau for Larkham (temp 18 to 30 mins; 55 to 63 mins; 85 to 93 mins)

SCORERS *Try*: Tuqiri *Penalty Goals*: Flatley (4)

REFEREE A J Watson (South Africa)

* after extra time: 14–14 after normal time

Mark Dadswell/Getty Images

The moment Jonny Wilkinson realises he has kicked the most famous drop-goal in the history of English rugby.

SIXTH TOURNAMENT: 2007 IN FRANCE, WALES & SCOTLAND

POOL A

England	28	United States	10
South Africa	59	Samoa	7
United States	15	Tonga	25
England	0	South Africa	36
Samoa	15	Tonga	19
South Africa	30	Tonga	25
England	44	Samoa	22
Samoa	25	United States	21
England	36	Tonga	20
South Africa	64	United States	15

	P	W	D	L	F	A	Pts
South Africa	4	4	0	0	189	47	19
England	4	3	0	1	108	88	14
Tonga	4	2	0	2	89	96	9
Samoa	4	1	0	3	69	143	5
United States	4	0	0	4	61	142	1

POOL B

Australia	91	Japan	3
Wales	42	Canada	17
Japan	31	Fiji	35
Wales	20	Australia	32
Fiji	29	Canada	16
Wales	72	Japan	18
Australia	55	Fiji	12
Canada	12	Japan	12
Australia	37	Canada	6
Wales	34	Fiji	38

	P	W	D	L	F	A	Pts
Australia	4	4	0	0	215	41	20
Fiji	4	3	0	1	114	136	15
Wales	4	2	0	2	168	105	12
Japan	4	0	1	3	64	210	3
Canada	4	0	1	3	51	120	2

POOL C

New Zealand	76	Italy	14
Scotland	56	Portugal	10
Italy	24	Romania	18
New Zealand	108	Portugal	13
Scotland	42	Romania	0
Italy	31	Portugal	5
Scotland	0	New Zealand	40
Romania	14	Portugal	10
New Zealand	85	Romania	8
Scotland	18	Italy	16

	P	W	D	L	F	A	Pts
New Zealand	4	4	0	0	309	35	20
Scotland	4	3	0	1	116	66	14
Italy	4	2	0	2	85	117	9
Romania	4	1	0	3	40	161	5
Portugal	4	0	0	4	38	209	1

POOL D

France	12	Argentina	17
Ireland	32	Namibia	17
Argentina	33	Georgia	3
Ireland	14	Georgia	10
France	87	Namibia	10
France	25	Ireland	3
Argentina	63	Namibia	3
Georgia	30	Namibia	0
France	64	Georgia	7
Ireland	15	Argentina	30

	P	W	D	L	F	A	Pts
Argentina	4	4	0	0	143	33	18
France	4	3	0	1	188	37	15
Ireland	4	2	0	2	64	82	9
Georgia	4	1	0	3	50	111	5
Namibia	4	0	0	4	30	212	0

QUARTER-FINALS

Australia	10	England	12
New Zealand	18	France	20
South Africa	37	Fiji	20
Argentina	19	Scotland	13

SEMI-FINALS

France	9	England	14
South Africa	37	Argentina	13

BRONZE MEDAL MATCH

France	10	Argentina	34

Sixth World Cup Final, Stade de France, Paris, 20 October 2007

SOUTH AFRICA 15 (5PG) ENGLAND 6 (2PG)

SOUTH AFRICA: P C Montgomery; J–P R Pietersen, J Fourie, F P L Steyn, B G Habana; A D James, P F du Preez; J P du Randt, J W Smit (*captain*), C J van der Linde, J P Botha, V Matfield, J H Smith, D J Rossouw, S W P Burger *Substitutions:* J L van Heerden for Rossouw (72 mins); B W du Plessis for Smit (temp 71 to 76 mins)

SCORERS *Penalty Goals*: Montgomery (4), Steyn

ENGLAND: J T Robinson; P H Sackey, M Tait, M J Catt, M J Cueto; J P Wilkinson, A C T Gomarsall; A J Sheridan, M P Regan, P J Vickery (*captain*), S D Shaw, B J Kay, M E Corry, N Easter, L W Moody *Substitutions:* M J H Stevens for Vickery (40 mins); D Hipkiss for Robinson (46 mins); T Flood for Catt (50 mins); G S Chuter for Regan (62 mins); J P R Worsley for Moody (62 mins); L B N Dallaglio for Easter (64 mins); P C Richards for Worsley (70 mins)

SCORER *Penalty Goals*: Wilkinson (2)

REFEREE A C Rolland (Ireland)

Julian Finney/Getty Images

Coach Jake White (centre) with skipper John Smit and star man Bryan Habana (left).

Ethan Miller/Getty Images

The IRB Sevens World Series found a new home in 2010, Las Vegas.

DELIGHT FOR SAMOA

By Nigel Starmer-Smith

Getty Images

It's ours! Samoa lift the IRB Sevens World Series trophy in Edinburgh.

The 11th season of the IRB Sevens World Series dawned with the announcement in Copenhagen by the IOC of the inclusion of Rugby Sevens, for men and women, in the Olympic Games in Rio, in 2016.

I'm sure that it was not by chance that the thrill, which followed this news of Olympic status, coincided with a truly exciting series and increasing competitiveness at all levels across the Rugby Sevens world.

Seven nations contested one or more of the tournament finals, with four different winners, and once again the overall champion of the IRB Sevens World Series was not decided until the Cup semi-finals on the final day of the final tournament, at Murrayfield.

Samoa, who had competed in every IRB Sevens World Series event since the first one in Dubai 1999, finally in their 92nd appearance realised their dream of becoming the IRB Sevens World Series champions.

No wonder that the celebrations back home in the South Pacific island of population 180,000 lasted for many more days than the officially granted national holiday! The season began as though New Zealand were set to brush aside every challenge and swiftly make amends for their previous title-less season.

Make amends they certainly did, in the traditional opening event in the Emirates Dubai Sevens, though briefly out of sorts whilst winning their Cup quarter-final against Kenya, the experienced core of Gordon Tietjen's squad steadied the ship and swept past Fiji and Samoa to take the title.

There was little to suggest that the 24–12 win over Samoa would be their only win over the eventual champions, but by the end of the season New Zealand had only lost seven games – and six of those defeats were at the hands of Samoa!

But in George, at the Emirates South Africa Sevens, there were no such problems to impede New Zealand's continued advance on their way to a second winning final. Albeit they needed all their resilience and discipline to edge past England by just three points and then Kenya – again as in Dubai by just 17–14. More comfortable was the final, 21–12 over Fiji, and more heartening still was the performance of a brilliant 23-year-old Sherwin Stowers from Counties Manakau. Now a new star in the firmament, scoring 15 tries in the opening two events.

It was from this point on that New Zealand ran into the buffers, in the shape of the Samoans, who blocked their path as they came home to their own spectacular Wellington event. Not that Samoa were to recapture the glory days of their first-ever Sevens title in 2007. It was to be the turn of their closest Pacific rivals, Fiji, to thrill the crowd in their one truly supreme tournament performance in a season marred not just by cyclone worries back home, but in rugby terms the loss of brilliant talents through a move to fifteens like Vucago, Roko and Kolonisau, through injury as befell Cakau and Lutumailagi and personal matters that beset Naba and Ryder.

All-in-all a difficult season for coach Iliesa Tanivula. It saddens me that we are unlikely to witness again especially the sparkle and instinctive Sevens genius that William Ryder brought to the game. He helped Fiji on this occasion to their Cup Final win in Wellington 2010, with victory over Samoa 19–14, but he never recaptured the supreme heights his rare talent attained when scoring a hat-trick in the Wellington Cup Final four years earlier.

From Wellington to the bright lights of Las Vegas, staging the USA Sevens for the first time. It was fun, it was different and the crowd rolled in.

And it was here that Samoa's three-title sequence began, adapting to the conditions with their tight game-avoiding kicks, using short contestable restarts, moving away from physical contact, and relying on the outstanding duo of the season Alafoti Fa'osiliva, a mobile powerhouse, and the ultimate 'finisher' Mikaele Pesamino, later to be named as the IRB Player of the Season, scoring 56 tries, getting on for twice as many as anyone else. Not forgetting the outstanding influence of captain Lolo Lui and the fortuitous return to the Sevens' fold of Uale Mai.

Samoa's win over New Zealand in Wellington's semi-final was to be followed up by a 33–12 romp when they next met, this time in the Vegas Final itself.

But new challenges were emerging from all parts of the globe.

First it was Australia, who had never made a Cup Final since 2002. But under the guiding hand of Michael O'Connor his troupe of young Wallabies – average age 21, and six still in their teens – were creating waves.

In Bradman's Adelaide Oval the scene gives way for a couple of days a year to the family friendly rock and pop and dancing entertainment that has become an integral and fun part of all IRB World Sevens Series events. And it was here that Samoa, unchanged in personnel unsurprisingly stuck to their Vegas winning formula.

Yet again there were surprises in store – not Australia this time, but the USA, making their first Cup Final.

At Hong Kong was Samoa's chance to take the overall lead for the first time in the race for the champion's title. And what a contest unfolded as the four previous HK winners, Fiji, New Zealand, Samoa and England battled through to the Cup semi-finals. The Cup Final itself was equally enthralling as those semis, but for the fifth time in a row Samoa had the last word.

The fabulous win, 24–21, for the first time in Sevens history put Samoa ahead of the pack in the race for the overall Sevens World Series title, with a lead of just three tournament points over New Zealand. So, as last year, all rested on the London and Edinburgh events.

For South Africa, the reigning IRB Sevens World Series champions, it had thus far been a frustrating experience. Renfred Dazel, and former captains Kyle Brown, Mzwandile Stick and Neil Powell had all been sidelined, and even at the final events new young stars Sampie Mastriet and Branco du Preez were whisked away to the Springboks Junior World Cup training squad.

All of this was familiar territory for New Zealand and Australia (and England, too, to an extent) who have to cope virtually without any access to their leading 15-a-side exponents. But on this occasion at Twickenham Stick, Dazel and Powell were all back in the Springbok squad, and so too Fabian Juries after his two-year absence. And 'Fab' he proved still to be, alongside the superb Frankie Horne and new star Cecil Afrika. A first Cup Final of the season, but this time it was against Australia.

A ruthless, newly-confident Australia ran rings round England in the opening pool round, with James Stannard running the show, before making their first final for eight years, to face South Africa.

Michael O'Connor's young Wallabies kept their composure, and flair, enough to celebrate the receipt of a silver Cup for the first time since February 2002 at Ballymore in Brisbane.

One week later, and the season's champions title still remained to be decided between Samoa and New Zealand. Samoa, seven points ahead, knew their target for guaranteed success was a place in the Cup Final at Murrayfield.

They certainly wavered in the Pool round as Argentina, maybe inspired by the farewell appearance of the Pumas' Sevens legend Santiago Gomez–Cora, beat them with ease.

Finals day and what a climax! Samoa, comfortable and clinical in victory over South Africa; New Zealand, an easy win over Argentina. But then a game to cap the season, as England, having lost to Canada the previous day, produced a performance against Samoa, which showed their true potential and capabilities. A riveting spectacle was locked all square at 12-all at the end of normal time.

In fact it was Samoa's coolness under immense pressure that created the winning drop-goal chance in extra-time, scored appropriately by captain Lolo Lui. The Overall IRB Sevens World Series title was theirs!

Samoa crowned it gloriously turning the Final into a virtual exhibition of their outstanding talents – and amazing fitness levels!

There was the tearful farewell in Edinburgh of Argentina's Santiago Gomez–Cora, the top try-scorer of all time, with 270 to his eternal credit. An end of an era, too, with the retirement of Springbok Marius Schoeman who did so much to bring Springbok Sevens to new heights. And, on a happier note, there was the broad grin as Scotland coach Steve Gemmell saluted his boys at the final whistle when winning the Plate at Murrayfield, on his final IRB sevens event. Or, live on TV by chance, the (successful, fortunately!) invitation by USA's Kevin Swiryn asking his girlfriend if she would be his bride! Well, where better to pop the question than Las Vegas! What a year. What memories – here's to the next!

IRB SEVENS WORLD SERIES 2009–10 RESULTS

DUBAI: 4–5 DECEMBER

New Zealand (24), **Samoa** (20), **Fiji** (16), **England** (16), **Australia** (12), **South Africa** (8), **Argentina** (6), **Kenya** (6), **Wales** (4)

SOUTH AFRICA: 11–12 DECEMBER

New Zealand (24), **Fiji** (20), **Argentina** (16), **Kenya** (16), **England** (12), **South Africa** (8), **Australia** (6), **Samoa** (6), **Wales** (4)

NEW ZEALAND: 5–6 FEBRUARY

Fiji (24), **Samoa** (20), **England** (16), **New Zealand** (16), **Australia** (12), **South Africa** (8), **Kenya** (6), **Canada** (6), **Wales** (4)

USA: 13–14 FEBRUARY

Samoa (24), **New Zealand** (20), **Australia** (16), **Kenya** (16), **South Africa** (12), **Fiji** (8), **Wales** (6), **England** (6), **United States** (4)

AUSTRALIA: 19–21 MARCH

Samoa (24), **United States** (20), **Australia** (16), **Argentina** (16), **New Zealand** (12), **South Africa** (8), **Fiji** (6), **Wales** (6), **England** (4)

HONG KONG: 26–28 MARCH

Samoa (30), **New Zealand** (25), **Fiji** (20), **England** (20), **Australia** (16), **South Africa** (10), **Kenya** (8), **United States** (8), **Canada** (5)

ENGLAND: 22–23 MAY

Australia (24), **South Africa** (20), **Samoa** (16), **Argentina** (16), **New Zealand** (12), **Fiji** (8), **England** (6), **Wales** (6), **Kenya** (6), **Canada** (4)

SCOTLAND: 29–30 MAY

Samoa (24), **Australia** (20), **England** (16), **New Zealand** (16), **Scotland** (12), **Argentina** (8), **South Africa** (6), **Fiji** (6), **Wales** (4)

FINAL STANDINGS

Samoa - 164	**Argentina** - 62
New Zealand - 149	**Kenya** - 52
Australia - 122	**Wales** - 34
Fiji - 108	**United States** - 32
England - 96	**Canada** - 15
South Africa - 80	**Scotland** - 12

PREVIOUS WINNERS

1999–2000: New Zealand
2000–01: New Zealand
2001–02: New Zealand
2002–03: New Zealand
2003–04: New Zealand
2004–05: New Zealand
2005–06: Fiji
2006–07: New Zealand
2007–08: New Zealand
2008–09: South Africa
2009–10: Samoa

Ryan Pierse/Getty Images

The consumate Sevens player, Mikaele Pesamino.

FRANCE GRAB NINTH SLAM

By Ireland's David Wallace

Franck Fife/AFP/Getty Images

The France team can hardly contain their delight at their Slam.

There is no getting away from the fact that everyone in the Ireland set-up was bitterly disappointed to surrender our hard-earned RBS Six Nations crown to France.

I would have to say that Marc Lièvremont's side were ultimately the best side in the tournament both in terms of consistency and in their level of performance but that does not really soften the blow from a partisan, Irish perspective.

The euphoria of winning the Grand Slam in 2009 was unbelievable and I'm sure it will stay with every player involved but if that was a massive high, the way we performed and the results we achieved in 2010 was definitely a low in my Test career. Expectations were high and we did not meet those expectations.

Professional sport is all about setting yourself new targets, even if you have enjoyed significant success and won silverware, and at the start of the campaign Declan Kidney made it clear to the squad that 2009 was over and done with and retaining the Championship was our one and only target. We did not hit that target and by that measure, our Six Nations season was a failure.

We were acutely aware ahead of the tournament that, as champions, we had become a target for the other sides. We knew we were a scalp that everyone wanted to take. Winning a Grand Slam is a huge challenge but I now know from first-hand experience that achieving it back-to-back is even harder.

For Ireland, it was a season of contrast, which is probably best summed up in our performances against England at Twickenham and Scotland at Croke Park.

Our 20–16 win over the English was definitely our best 80 minutes of rugby in the Championship. The scoreline suggests it was a close match but I felt we were the dominant team and the fact we outscored them three tries to one is testament to the attacking rugby we played.

Going away from home and relying on your kicking game can get you results but to travel to London and score the tries we did through Tommy Bowe and Keith Earls was fantastic.

We've had a couple of good results at Twickenham in recent years but victories there remain a rare commodity and we were delighted with the performance.

And then there was the Scotland game in Dublin. It was our last match of the Six Nations and although we already knew the title had probably gone, the Triple Crown was up for grabs and we were focused on signing off on a positive note. The fact we were beaten 23–20 to Dan Parks' late penalty was hard to swallow.

Scotland certainly played well. True, they needed the late penalty to clinch it but we have to look honestly at ourselves and admit we did not deserve to win the match. We didn't do enough and even if Parks had not landed what was a superb kick under immense pressure, the game would have probably finished all square.

I mentioned Tommy Bowe earlier and I thought his Player of the Championship award was thoroughly deserved. He was relatively young when he first came into the Ireland squad but he has matured quickly and for me, he is now second to none in world rugby on the wing. Tommy is incredibly powerful and he's got great endurance but he also brings an amazing vision to the side and it's those attributes that make him such a complete player.

For France, it was obviously a great season. It was Lièvremont's third season as coach and after repeatedly chopping and changing his players in the first two matches he settled on a more consistent starting XV and reaped the rewards.

I think he admitted himself that it had taken time to find his best side but there's no argument he found it in 2010. I can speak from experience that familiarity with your team-mates at any level of the game is priceless.

It is always the same story with France. Their talent is never in question and when they get their selection right and find some consistency in terms of the way they play, they are dangerous.

We played the French in Paris and made the fatal mistake of letting them get away from us in the first half. We came back strongly at them after the break but it was a case of leaving ourselves too much to do with too little time and they emerged 33–10 winners. We were not happy with the display but I have to admit some of their rugby in the first 40 minutes was very impressive.

France's two standout performers throughout the tournament I thought were Imanol Harinordoquy at No 8 and Morgan Parra at scrum-half.

Parra pulled the strings beautifully and Harinordoquy was immense in the back row. I also came up against him in the Heineken Cup semi-final between Munster and Biarritz and despite his broken nose I would say he was the difference between the two sides.

England finished the Six Nations in third but had a mixed campaign. They carry a huge weight of expectation on their shoulders ahead of every Six Nations but looked like a side still in a rebuilding phase and I would expect they will emerge stronger contenders next season.

They kicked off well enough with a big win over Wales at Twickenham but struggled to recapture their best form against Italy and Scotland.

They gave France a real test in Paris in the last game of the tournament, which underlined why England can never be

TRIVIA

Scotland's best RBS Six Nations campaign for a number of years had a big impact on Rugby World's Team of the Tournament as selected by the world's best-selling rugby magazine. The line-up was: Clément Poitrenaud; Sean Lamont, James Hook, Yannick Jauzion, Shane Williams; Stephen Jones, Tomas O'Leary; Tim Payne, Ross Ford, Allan Jacobsen, Quintin Geldenhuys, Paul O'Connell, Thierry Dusautoir, John Barclay, Johnnie Beattie. Dusautoir and O'Connell are the only survivors from the 2009 team.

underestimated, but I don't think Martin Johnson would claim his side is the finished article just yet.

It was also a tough season for Wales, who finished fourth and I'm sure Warren Gatland would have wanted more. Wales won the Grand Slam in 2008 and like Ireland, once you achieve that, you're not going to be happy with a mid-table finish.

Our game with Wales, which we won 27–12 at Croke Park, was certainly an emotional one because it was Brian O'Driscoll's 100th cap for the country. I say emotional but the truth was Brian treated it just like any other match because he knows the minute you start believing the hype, you will come a cropper. He's always been that kind of guy and I think it's his level-headedness as much as his talent that has been the foundation of his career.

Like everyone else, I was pleased to see Scotland's unquestionable improvement in the Championship, even if they did beat us in Dublin.

They had struggled in previous seasons but I felt they emerged as a genuine force again in 2010 and that can only be good news for the tournament. Every country wants to win the title but the bigger picture is the overall strength of the competition and Andy Robinson's side certainly brought a welcome extra dimension to proceedings.

I thought the Scottish pack was impressive. Their lineout worked really well and the back row trio of Johnnie Beattie, Kelly Brown and

Mike Hewitt/Getty Images

Ireland had to settle for second, even after beating England at Twickenham.

John Barclay were outstanding. You really can't play Test rugby without a forward platform and Scotland appear to have settled on a strong one.

The turning point was probably the 15–15 draw with England at Murrayfield. I think it gave them a lot of confidence and when we played them at Croke Park a week later, you could sense they were a side that felt they were making real progress. It was a season in which the green shoots of recovery were clearly there to see and they underlined the fact in the summer when they won their two Tests in Argentina, which is no mean feat for any side.

Italy finished with the wooden spoon and once again the Six Nations was a real struggle for them. Given their relatively modest player base, it is always going to be a challenge for them to compete for the title but I strongly believe the tournament is better for their inclusion and after being admitted in 2000, they have made small but solid improvement.

Having a smaller pool of players to select from leaves Italy vulnerable to injuries to key players and there's no doubt they badly missed Sergio Parisse. He is a world-class player and there probably isn't a single Test side that wouldn't find a place for him. All of Italy's play goes through Parisse and without him they lacked inspirational leadership and a tireless ball carrier.

The good news for Italian rugby is the introduction of Benetton Treviso and Aironi to the Magners League for the 2010–11 season.

The only way to move forward at Test level is having your players exposed to a higher level of rugby for their clubs on a regular basis and the expansion of the Magners League will definitely provide that. We will all have to wait and see how long it takes to bear fruit for the national team but there's no doubt it will eventually help strengthen the Test side.

FIXTURES 2011

WALES and England will make history in the 2011 RBS Six Nations by starting the Championship on a Friday night.

Wales are hosts and England make the short journey over the Severn Bridge for what promises to be a tantilising encounter.

Ireland's first match back at Aviva Stadium after four years at Croke Park is at home to Les Bleus the following weekend.

The tournament takes on extra significance with the Rugby World Cup 2011 just months away and David Pickering, Chairman of the Six Nations Council, said: "The RBS Six Nations Championship remains the envy of the rugby world, a tournament played with pride and passion and drenched in history and tradition."

Fri 4 February
Wales v England
(Millennium Stadium, Cardiff, 7.45pm)

Sat 5 February
Italy v Ireland
(Stadio Flaminio, Rome, 2.30pm)
France v Scotland
(Stade de France, Paris, 5pm)

Sat 12 February
England v Italy
(Twickenham, London, 2.30pm)
Scotland v Wales
(Murrayfield, Edinburgh, 5pm)

Sun 13 February
Ireland v France
(Aviva Stadium, Dublin, 3pm)

Sat 26 February
Italy v Wales
(Stadio Flaminio, Rome, 2.30pm)
England v France
(Twickenham, London, 5pm)

Sun 27 February
Scotland v Ireland
(Murrayfield, Edinburgh, 3pm)

Sat 12 March
Italy v France
(Stadio Flaminio, Rome, 2.30pm)
Wales v Ireland
(Millennium Stadium, Cardiff, 5pm)

Sun 13 March
England v Scotland
(Twickenham, London, 2pm)

Sat 19 March
Scotland v Italy
(Murrayfield, Edinburgh, 2.30pm)
Ireland v England
(Aviva Stadium, Dublin, 5pm)
France v Wales
(Stade de France, Paris, 7.45pm)

All times listed are GMT

SIX NATIONS 2010 FINAL TABLE

	P	W	D	L	For	Against	Pts
France	5	5	0	0	135	69	**10**
Ireland	5	3	0	2	106	95	**6**
England	5	2	1	2	88	76	**5**
Wales	5	2	0	3	113	117	**4**
Scotland	5	1	1	3	83	100	**3**
Italy	5	1	0	4	69	137	**2**

Points: Win 2; Draw 1; Defeat 0.

There were 594 points scored at an average of 39.6 a match. The Championship record (803 points at an average of 53.5 a match) was set in 2000. Stephen Jones was the leading individual points scorer with 63, 26 points shy of the Championship record Jonny Wilkinson set in 2001. Four players, Tommy Bowe, James Hook, Shane Williams and Keith Earls, were the Championship's leading try-scorers with three each, five short of the all-time record shared between England's Cyril Lowe (1914) and Scotland's Ian Smith (1925).

Dave Rogers/Getty Images

France celebrate their ninth Grand Slam, in Paris.

2010 MATCH STATS

6 February, Croke Park, Dublin

IRELAND 29 (2G 5PG) ITALY 11 (2PG 1T)

IRELAND: R D J Kearney; T J Bowe, B G O'Driscoll (*captain*), G W D'Arcy, A D Trimble; R J R O'Gara, T G O'Leary; C E Healy, J P Flannery, J J Hayes, L F M Cullen, P J O'Connell, K McLaughlin, J P R Heaslip, D P Wallace *Substitutions:* R Best for Flannery (55 mins); K G Earls for Trimble (55 mins); D Ryan for O'Connell (60 mins); P W Wallace for O'Gara (65 mins); T G Court for Hayes (72 mins); S O'Brien for D P Wallace (72 mins); E G Reddan for O'Leary (73 mins)

SCORERS *Tries:* Heaslip, O'Leary *Conversions:* O'Gara (2) *Penalty Goals:* O'Gara (4), P Wallace

ITALY: L McLean; P K Robertson, G-J Canale, G Garcia, Mirco Bergamasco; C Gower, T Tebaldi; S Perugini, L Ghiraldini (*captain*), M-L Castrogiovanni, C-A Del Fava, Q Geldenhuys, J Sole, A Zanni, Mauro Bergamasco *Substitutions:* M Bortolami for Del Fava (49 mins); M Aguero for Castrogiovanni (55 mins); A Masi for Robertson (57 mins); S Picone for Tebaldi (65 mins); F Ongaro for Ghiraldini (72 mins); Castrogiovanni back for Perugini (73 mins); R Bocchino for Gower (temp 65 to 73 mins)

SCORERS *Try:* Robertson *Penalty Goals:* Gower, Mirco Bergamasco

REFEREE R Poite (France)

YELLOW CARD G Garcia (32 mins)

6 February, Twickenham

ENGLAND 30 (3G 3PG) WALES 17 (2G 1PG)

ENGLAND: D A Armitage; M J Cueto, M J M Tait, T G A L Flood, Y C C Monye; J P Wilkinson, D S Care; T A N Payne, D M Hartley, D G Wilson, S D Shaw, S W Borthwick (*captain*), J A W Haskell, N J Easter, L W Moody *Substitutions:* S G Thompson for Hartley (59 mins); D R Cole for Wilson (59 mins); L P Deacon for Shaw (69 mins); P K Hodgson for Care (75 mins); S E Armitage for Moody (76 mins); D J Hipkiss for Flood (76 mins)

SCORERS *Tries:* Haskell (2), Care *Conversions:* Wilkinson (3) *Penalty Goals:* Wilkinson (3)

WALES: L M Byrne; T James, J W Hook, J H Roberts, S M Williams; S M Jones, G J Cooper; P James, G J Williams, A R Jones, L C Charteris, A-W Jones, A Powell, R P Jones (*captain*), M E Williams *Substitutions:* H Bennett for G J Williams (53 mins); B S Davies for Charteris (temp 13 to 16 mins and 53 mins); S L Halfpenny for T James (64 mins); R S Rees for Cooper (67 mins); J Thomas for Powell (67 mins)

SCORERS *Tries:* A R Jones, Hook *Conversions:* S M Jones (2) *Penalty Goal:* S M Jones

REFEREE A C Rolland (Ireland)

YELLOW CARD A-W Jones (33 mins)

7 February, Murrayfield

SCOTLAND 9 (3PG) FRANCE 18 (1G 2PG 1T)

SCOTLAND: C D Paterson; T H Evans, M B Evans, G A Morrison, S F Lamont; P J Godman, C P Cusiter (*captain*); A G Dickinson, R W Ford, M J Low, N J Hines, A D Kellock, K D R Brown, J W Beattie, J A Barclay *Substitutions:* H F G Southwell for Godman (51 mins); A F Jacobsen for Low (51 mins); S Lawson for Ford (65 mins); R J Gray for Hines (67 mins); Low back for Dickinson (69 mins)

SCORER *Penalty Goals:* Paterson (3)

FRANCE: C Poitrenaud; B Fall, M Bastareaud, Y Jauzion, A Rougerie; F Trinh-Duc, M Parra; T Domingo, W Servat, N Mas, L Nallet, P Papé, T Dusautoir (*captain*), I Harinordoquy, F Ouedraogo *Substitutions:* V Clerc for Rougerie (4 mins); L Ducalcon for Mas (45 mins); D Szarzewski for Servat (50 mins); J Pierre for Papé (65 mins); J Bonnaire for Dusautoir (66 mins); F Michalak for Parra (71 mins); D Marty for Bastareaud (71 mins)

SCORERS *Tries:* Bastareaud (2) *Conversion:* Parra *Penalty Goals:* Parra (2)

REFEREE N Owens (Wales)

13 February, Millennium Stadium, Cardiff

WALES 31 (2G 4PG 1T)
SCOTLAND 24 (1G 2PG 2DG 1T)

WALES: L M Byrne; S L Halfpenny, J W Hook, J H Roberts, S M Williams; S M Jones, G J Cooper; P James, G J Williams, A R Jones, J Thomas, A-W Jones, A Powell, R P Jones (*captain*), M E Williams *Substitutions:* R S Rees for Cooper (40 mins); H Bennett for G J Williams (48 mins); G D Jenkins for James (48 mins); B S Davies for Powell (48 mins); James back for Jenkins (59 mins); S Warburton for M E Williams (67 mins)

SCORERS *Tries:* Byrne, Halfpenny, S M Williams *Conversions:* S M Jones (2) *Penalty Goals:* S M Jones (4)

SCOTLAND: C D Paterson; R P Lamont, S F Lamont, G A Morrison, T H Evans; D A Parks, C P Cusiter (*captain*); A G Dickinson, R W Ford, E A Murray, J L Hamilton, A D Kellock, K D R Brown, J W Beattie, J A Barclay *Substitutions:* M B Evans for T H Evans (temp 13 to 26 mins) and for Paterson (29 mins); M R L Blair for T H Evans (35 mins); A F Jacobsen for Dickinson (56 mins); S Lawson for Ford (56 mins); P J Godman for R P Lamont (67 mins); R J Gray for Hamilton (77 mins); A R MacDonald for Brown (temp 49 to 56 mins) and for Parks (77 mins)

SCORERS *Tries:* Barclay, M B Evans *Conversion:* Paterson *Penalty Goals:* Parks (2) *Dropped Goals:* Parks (2)

REFEREE G Clancy (Ireland)

YELLOW CARDS S Lawson (73 mins); P J Godman (79 mins)

13 February, Stade de France, Paris

FRANCE 33 (3G 2PG 2DG) IRELAND 10 (1G 1PG)

FRANCE: C Poitrenaud; V Clerc, M Bastareaud, Y Jauzion, A Palisson; F Trinh-Duc, M Parra; T Domingo, W Servat, N Mas, L Nallet, P Papé, T Dusautoir (*captain*), I Harinordoquy, F Ouedraogo *Substitutions:* J Malzieu for Palisson (23 mins); D Marty for Clerc (47 mins); D Szarzewski for Servat (48 mins); S Marconnet for Mas (48 mins); J Bonnaire for Harinordoquy (61 mins); F Michalak for Jauzion (66 mins); Mas back for Marconnet (72 mins); J Pierre for Papé (73 mins)

SCORERS *Tries:* Servat, Jauzion, Poitrenaud *Conversions:* Parra (3) *Penalty Goals:* Parra (2) *Dropped Goals:* Parra, Michalak

IRELAND: R D J Kearney; T J Bowe, B G O'Driscoll (*captain*), G W D'Arcy, K G Earls; R J R O'Gara, T G O'Leary; C E Healy, J P Flannery, J J Hayes, L F M Cullen, P J O'Connell, S P H Ferris, J P R Heaslip, D P Wallace *Substitutions:* P W Wallace for O'Driscoll (temp 18 to 19 mins) and for Kearney (34 mins); T G Court for Ferris (temp 19 to 28 mins) and for Hayes (48 mins); R Best for Flannery (60 mins); D Ryan for Cullen (60 mins); J Sexton for O'Gara (68 mins); E G Reddan for O'Leary (68 mins)

SCORERS *Try:* D P Wallace *Conversion:* O'Gara *Penalty Goal:* O'Gara

REFEREE W Barnes (England)

YELLOW CARD C E Healy (17 mins)

14 February, Stadio Flaminio, Rome

ITALY 12 (4PG) ENGLAND 17 (3PG 1DG 1T)

ITALY: L McLean; A Masi, G-J Canale, G Garcia, Mirco Bergamasco; C Gower, T Tebaldi; S Perugini, L Ghiraldini (*captain*), M-L Castrogiovanni, Q Geldenhuys, M Bortolami, J Sole, A Zanni, Mauro Bergamasco *Substitutions:* M Aguero for Perugini (52 mins); P Canavosio for Tebaldi (52 mins); P Derbyshire for Sole (69 mins); F Ongaro for Ghiraldini (75 mins); P K Robertson for Masi (temp 54 to 61 mins) and for Garcia (75 mins); Perugini back for Sole (temp 59 to 69 mins)

SCORER *Penalty Goals:* Mirco Bergamasco (4)

ENGLAND: D A Armitage; M J Cueto, M J M Tait, R J Flutey, Y C C Monye; J P Wilkinson, D S Care; T A N Payne, D M Hartley, D R Cole, S D Shaw, S W Borthwick (*captain*), J A W Haskell, N J Easter, L W Moody *Substitutions:* M Mullan for Payne (58 mins); D G Wilson for Cole (64 mins); L P Deacon for Shaw (64 mins); S G Thompson for Hartley (69 mins); S E Armitage for Moody (72 mins); P K Hodgson for Care (75 mins)

SCORERS *Try:* Tait *Penalty Goals:* Wilkinson (3) *Dropped Goal:* Wilkinson

REFEREE C Berdos (France)

YELLOW CARD M-L Castrogiovanni (57 mins)

26 February, Millennium Stadium, Cardiff

WALES 20 (2G 2PG) FRANCE 26 (2G 4PG)

WALES: L M Byrne; S L Halfpenny, J W Hook, J H Roberts, S M Williams; S M Jones, R S Rees; P James, H Bennett, A R Jones, B S Davies, D L Jones, J Thomas, R P Jones (*captain*), M E Williams *Substitution:* L C Charteris for D L Jones (24 mins)

SCORERS *Tries:* Halfpenny, S M Williams *Conversions:* S M Jones (2) *Penalty Goals:* S M Jones (2)

FRANCE: C Poitrenaud; J Malzieu, M Bastareaud, Y Jauzion, A Palisson; F Trinh-Duc, M Parra; T Domingo, W Servat, N Mas, L Nallet, J Pierre, T Dusautoir (*captain*), I Harinordoquy, J Bonnaire *Substitutions:* D Szarzewski for Servat (51 mins); J-B Poux for Domingo (54 mins); S Chabal for Pierre (63 mins); F Michalak for Trinh-Duc (63 mins); D Marty for Bastareaud (69 mins); A Lapandry for Harinordoquy (69 mins); M Andreu for Poitrenaud (77 mins); Servat back for Szarzewski (temp 69 to 71 mins)

SCORERS *Tries:* Palisson, Trinh-Duc *Conversions:* Parra (2) *Penalty Goals:* Parra (3), Michalak

REFEREE J I Kaplan (South Africa)

YELLOW CARD M Parra (63 mins)

27 February, Stadio Flaminio, Rome

ITALY 16 (1G 3PG) SCOTLAND 12 (3PG 1DG)

ITALY: L McLean; A Masi, G-J Canale, G Garcia, Mirco Bergamasco; C Gower, T Tebaldi; S Perugini, L Ghiraldini (*captain*), M-L Castrogiovanni, Q Geldenhuys, M Bortolami, J Sole, A Zanni, Mauro Bergamasco *Substitutions:* P Canavosio for Tebaldi (51 mins); C-A del Fava for Bortolami (68 mins); M Aguero for Perugini (68 mins); P K Robertson for Garcia (68 mins); F Ongaro for Ghiraldini (72 mins);

SCORERS *Try:* Canavosio *Conversion:* Mirco Bergamasco *Penalty Goals:* Mirco Bergamasco (3)

SCOTLAND: H F G Southwell; S F Lamont, M B Evans, G A Morrison, S C J Danielli; D A Parks, C P Cusiter (*captain*); A F Jacobsen, R W Ford, E A Murray, J L Hamilton, A D Kellock, K D R Brown, J W Beattie, J A Barclay *Substitutions:* A K Strokosch for Beattie (54 mins); M R L Blair for Cusiter (54 mins); N J de Luca for Danielli (63 mins); A G Dickinson for Murray (68 mins); N J Hines for Hamilton (68 mins); Murray back for Jacobsen (71 mins)

SCORER *Penalty Goals:* Parks (3) *Dropped Goal:* Parks

REFEREE D Pearson (England)

27 February, Twickenham

ENGLAND 16 (1G 2PG 1DG)
IRELAND 20 (1G 1PG 2T)

ENGLAND: D A Armitage; M J Cueto, M J M Tait, R J Flutey, Y C C Monye; J P Wilkinson, D S Care; T A N Payne, D M Hartley, D R Cole, S D Shaw, S W Borthwick (*captain*), J A W Haskell, N J Easter, L W Moody *Substitutions:* L P Deacon for Shaw (4 mins); B J Foden for Armitage (48 mins); J P R Worsley for Moody (53 mins); L A Mears for Hartley (63 mins); D G Wilson for Cole (72 mins); P K Hodgson for Care (72 mins)

SCORERS *Try:* Cole *Conversion:* Wilkinson *Penalty Goals:* Wilkinson (2) *Dropped Goal:* Wilkinson

IRELAND: G E A Murphy; T J Bowe, B G O'Driscoll (*captain*), G W D'Arcy, K G Earls; J Sexton, T G O'Leary; C E Healy, R Best, J J Hayes, D P O'Callaghan, P J O'Connell, S P H Ferris, J P R Heaslip, D P Wallace *Substitutions:* T D Buckley for Hayes (61 mins); A D Trimble for O'Driscoll (63 mins); L F M Cullen for O'Callaghan (68 mins); R J R O'Gara for Sexton (68 mins); S Jennings for Wallace (69 mins)

SCORERS *Tries:* Bowe (2), Earls *Conversion:* O'Gara *Penalty Goal:* Sexton

REFEREE S M Lawrence (South Africa)

13 March, Croke Park, Dublin

IRELAND 27 (3PG 1DG 3T) WALES 12 (4PG)

IRELAND: G E A Murphy; T J Bowe, B G O'Driscoll (*captain*), G W D'Arcy, K G Earls; J Sexton, T G O'Leary; C E Healy, R Best, J J Hayes, D P O'Callaghan, P J O'Connell, S P H Ferris, J P R Heaslip, D P Wallace *Substitutions:* R D J Kearney for D'Arcy (22 mins); T D Buckley for Hayes (73 mins); R J R O'Gara for Earls (77 mins); L F M Cullen for O'Connell (78 mins); S Jennings for Ferris (78 mins); E G Reddan for O'Leary (78 mins); S Cronin for Best (79 mins)

SCORERS *Tries:* Earls (2), O'Leary *Penalty Goals:* Sexton (3) *Dropped Goal:* Sexton

WALES: L M Byrne; S L Halfpenny, J W Hook, J H Roberts, S M Williams; S M Jones, R S Rees; P James, M Rees, A R Jones, B S Davies, L C Charteris, J Thomas, G L Delve, M E Williams (*captain*) *Substitutions:* H Bennett for M Rees (56 mins); I M Gough for Davies (58 mins); D J Peel for R S Rees (61 mins); A M Bishop for Byrne (63 mins); S Warburton for M E Williams (66 mins); A R Gill for James (77 mins)

SCORER *Penalty Goals:* S M Jones (4)

REFEREE C Joubert (South Africa)

YELLOW CARD L M Byrne (24 mins)

13 March, Murrayfield

SCOTLAND 15 (4PG 1DG) ENGLAND 15 (5PG)

SCOTLAND: H F G Southwell; S F Lamont, N J de Luca, G A Morrison, M B Evans; D A Parks, C P Cusiter (*captain*); A F Jacobsen, R W Ford, E A Murray, J L Hamilton, A D Kellock, K D R Brown, J W Beattie, J A Barclay *Substitutions:* N J Hines for Hamilton (51 mins); A R MacDonald for Brown (55 mins); R G M Lawson for Cusiter (60 mins); S Lawson for Ford (64 mins); S C J Danielli for Southwell (66 mins); G Cross for Jacobsen (71 mins); P J Godman for Parks (71 mins)

SCORER *Penalty Goals:* Parks (4) *Dropped Goal:* Parks

ENGLAND: D A Armitage; M J Cueto, M J M Tait, R J Flutey, Y C C Monye; J P Wilkinson, D S Care; T A N Payne, D M Hartley, D R Cole, L P Deacon, S W Borthwick (*captain*), J A W Haskell, N J Easter, J P R Worsley *Substitutions:* T G A L Flood for Wilkinson (44 mins); B J Foden for Armitage (49 mins); B R Youngs for Monye (55 mins); L W Moody for Haskell (61 mins); S G Thompson for Hartley (61 mins); C L Lawes for Deacon (73 mins); D G Wilson for Cole (76 mins)

SCORERS *Penalty Goals:* Wilkinson (3), Flood (2)

REFEREE M Jonker (South Africa)

14 March, Stade de France, Paris

FRANCE 46 (5G 2PG 1T) ITALY 20 (2G 2PG)

FRANCE: C Poitrenaud; M Andreu, D Marty, Y Jauzion, A Palisson; F Trinh-Duc, M Parra; T Domingo, W Servat, N Mas, L Nallet, J Pierre, T Dusautoir (*captain*), I Harinordoquy, J Bonnaire *Substitutions:* D Szarzewski for Servat (40 mins); J-B Poux for Mas (40 mins); S Chabal for Nallet (48 mins); A Lapandry for Dusautoir (57 mins); D Yachvili for Trinh-Duc (57 mins); J Malzieu for Poitrenaud (62 mins); M Bastareaud for Jauzion (69 mins); Mas back for Domingo (70 mins)

SCORERS *Tries:* Marty (2), Harinordoquy, Andreu, Jauzion, Lapandry *Conversions:* Parra (5) *Penalty Goals:* Parra (2)

ITALY: L McLean; A Masi, G-J Canale, G Garcia, Mirco Bergamasco; C Gower, T Tebaldi; S Perugini, L Ghiraldini (*captain*), M-L Castrogiovanni, Q Geldenhuys, M Bortolami, J Sole, A Zanni, Mauro Bergamasco *Substitutions:* P Canavosio for Tebaldi (30 mins); C-A del Fava for Bortolami (55 mins); P K Robertson for Garcia (temp 7 to 12 mins and 60 mins); P Derbyshire for Sole (63 mins); M Aguero for Castrogiovanni (66 mins); F Ongaro for Ghiraldini (66 mins); R Bocchino for Gower (71 mins)

SCORERS *Tries:* Canavosio, Del Fava *Conversions:* Mirco Bergamasco (2) *Penalty Goals:* Mirco Bergamasco (2)

REFEREE D A Lewis (Ireland)

YELLOW CARD G Garcia (14 mins)

20 March, Millennium Stadium, Cardiff

WALES 33 (3G 4PG) ITALY 10 (1G 1PG)

WALES: L M Byrne; T W J Prydie, J W Hook, J H Roberts, S M Williams; S M Jones, W M Phillips; G D Jenkins, M Rees, A R Jones, B S Davies, L C Charteris, J Thomas, R P Jones (*captain*), S Warburton *Substitutions:* I M Gough for Davies (14 mins); T G L Shanklin for Roberts (62 mins); H Bennett for Rees (62 mins); P James for A R Jones (temp 2 to 9 mins and 62 mins); G L Delve for R P Jones (66 mins); A M Bishop for S M Jones (69 mins); D J Peel for Phillips (69 mins)

SCORERS *Tries:* Hook (2), S M Williams *Conversions:* S M Jones (3) *Penalty Goals:* S M Jones (4)

ITALY: L McLean; P K Robertson, G-J Canale, G Garcia, Mirco Bergamasco; C Gower, P Canavosio; S Perugini, L Ghiraldini (*captain*), M-L Castrogiovanni, Q Geldenhuys, M Bortolami, J Sole, A Zanni, Mauro Bergamasco *Substitutions:* M Pratichetti for Canale (3 mins); T Tebaldi for Canavosio (24 mins); M Aguero for Perugini (54 mins); M Vosawai for Sole (54 mins); R Bocchino for Tebaldi (62 mins); F Ongaro for Ghiraldini (64 mins); V Bernabo for Bortolami (72 mins)

SCORERS *Try:* McLean *Conversion:* Mirco Bergamasco *Penalty Goal:* Mirco Bergamasco

REFEREE W Barnes (England)

YELLOW CARD Mauro Bergamasco (55 mins)

20 March, Croke Park, Dublin

IRELAND 20 (2G 2PG) SCOTLAND 23 (5PG 1DG 1T)

IRELAND: G E A Murphy; T J Bowe, B G O'Driscoll (*captain*), G W D'Arcy, K G Earls; J Sexton, T G O'Leary; C E Healy, R Best, J J Hayes, D P O'Callaghan, P J O'Connell, S P H Ferris, J P R Heaslip, D P Wallace *Substitutions:* R D J Kearney for Murphy (26 mins); R J R O'Gara for Sexton (51 mins); T D Buckley for Hayes (79 mins)

SCORERS *Tries:* O'Driscoll, Bowe *Conversions:* Sexton, O'Gara *Penalty Goals:* Sexton, O'Gara

SCOTLAND: H F G Southwell; M B Evans, N J de Luca, G A Morrison, S F Lamont; D A Parks, C P Cusiter (*captain*); A F Jacobsen, R W Ford, E A Murray, J L Hamilton, A D Kellock, K D R Brown, J W Beattie, J A Barclay *Substitutions:* M R L Blair for Cusiter (51 mins); R J Gray for Hamilton (51 mins); A G Dickinson for Jacobsen (65 mins); S Lawson for Ford (71 mins); S C J Danielli for Lamont (73 mins); A R MacDonald for Brown (temp 26 to 33 mins; 38 to 40 mins and 50 to 57 mins)

SCORERS *Try:* Beattie *Penalty Goals:* Parks (5) *Dropped Goal:* Parks

REFEREE J I Kaplan (South Africa)

20 March, Stade de France, Paris

FRANCE 12 (3PG 1DG)
ENGLAND 10 (1G 1PG)

FRANCE: C Poitrenaud; M Andreu, M Bastareaud, Y Jauzion, A Palisson; F Trinh-Duc, M Parra; T Domingo, W Servat, N Mas, L Nallet, J Pierre, T Dusautoir (*captain*), I Harinordoquy, J Bonnaire *Substitutions:* D Marty for Bastareaud (49 mins); D Szarzewski for Servat (52 mins); J-B Poux for Domingo (54 mins); S Chabal for Pierre (58 mins); A Lapandry for Harinordoquy (60 mins); J Malzieu for Andreu (72 mins)

SCORERS *Penalty Goals:* Parra (3) *Dropped Goal:* Trinh-Duc

ENGLAND: B J Foden; M J Cueto, M J Tindall, R J Flutey, C J Ashton; T G A L Flood, D S Care; T A N Payne, D M Hartley, D R Cole, S D Shaw, L P Deacon, J P R Worsley, N J Easter, L W Moody (*captain*) *Substitutions:* T P Palmer for Shaw (14 mins); D G Wilson for Cole (40 mins); S G Thompson for Hartley (40 mins); M J M Tait for Tindall (52 mins); J P Wilkinson for Flutey (60 mins); J A W Haskell for Worsley (63 mins); Cole back for Payne (64 mins)

SCORERS *Try:* Foden *Conversion:* Flood *Penalty Goal:* Wilkinson

REFEREE B J Lawrence (New Zealand)

Dave Rogers/Getty Images

The 12–10 win over England got the party started.

INTERNATIONAL CHAMPIONSHIP RECORDS 1883–2010

PREVIOUS WINNERS

1883 England	1884 England	1885 Not completed
1886 England & Scotland	1887 Scotland	1888 Not completed
1889 Not completed	1890 England & Scotland	1891 Scotland
1892 England	1893 Wales	1894 Ireland
1895 Scotland	1896 Ireland	1897 Not completed
1898 Not completed	1899 Ireland	1900 Wales
1901 Scotland	1902 Wales	1903 Scotland
1904 Scotland	1905 Wales	1906 Ireland & Wales
1907 Scotland	1908 Wales	1909 Wales
1910 England	1911 Wales	1912 England & Ireland
1913 England	1914 England	1920 England & Scotland & Wales
1921 England	1922 Wales	1923 England
1924 England	1925 Scotland	1926 Scotland & Ireland
1927 Scotland & Ireland	1928 England	1929 Scotland
1930 England	1931 Wales	1932 England & Ireland & Wales
1933 Scotland	1934 England	1935 Ireland
1936 Wales	1937 England	1938 Scotland
1939 England & Ireland & Wales	1947 England & Wales	1948 Ireland
1949 Ireland	1950 Wales	1951 Ireland
1952 Wales	1953 England	1954 England & Wales & France
1955 Wales & France	1956 Wales	1957 England
1958 England	1959 France	1960 England & France
1961 France	1962 France	1963 England
1964 Scotland & Wales	1965 Wales	1966 Wales
1967 France	1968 France	1969 Wales
1970 Wales & France	1971 Wales	1972 Not completed
1973 Five Nations tie	1974 Ireland	1975 Wales
1976 Wales	1977 France	1978 Wales
1979 Wales	1980 England	1981 France
1982 Ireland	1983 Ireland & France	1984 Scotland
1985 Ireland	1986 Scotland & France	1987 France
1988 Wales & France	1989 France	1990 Scotland
1991 England	1992 England	1993 France
1994 Wales	1995 England	1996 England
1997 France	1998 France	1999 Scotland
2000 England	2001 England	2002 France
2003 England	2004 France	2005 Wales
2006 France	2007 France	2008 Wales
2009 Ireland	2010 France	

England have won the title outright 25 times; Wales 24; France 17; Scotland 14; Ireland 11; Italy 0.

TRIPLE CROWN WINNERS

England (23 times) 1883, 1884, 1892, 1913, 1914, 1921, 1923, 1924, 1928, 1934, 1937, 1954, 1957, 1960, 1980, 1991, 1992, 1995, 1996, 1997, 1998, 2002, 2003.

Wales (19 times) 1893, 1900, 1902, 1905, 1908, 1909, 1911, 1950, 1952, 1965, 1969, 1971, 1976, 1977, 1978, 1979, 1988, 2005, 2008.

Scotland (10 times) 1891, 1895, 1901, 1903, 1907, 1925, 1933, 1938, 1984, 1990.

Ireland (10 times) 1894, 1899, 1948, 1949, 1982, 1985, 2004, 2006, 2007, 2009.

GRAND SLAM WINNERS

England (12 times) 1913, 1914, 1921, 1923, 1924, 1928, 1957, 1980, 1991, 1992, 1995, 2003.

Wales (Ten times) 1908, 1909, 1911, 1950, 1952, 1971, 1976, 1978, 2005, 2008.

France (Nine times) 1968, 1977, 1981, 1987, 1997, 1998, 2002, 2004, 2010.

Scotland (Three times) 1925, 1984, 1990.

Ireland (Twice) 1948, 2009

THE SIX NATIONS CHAMPIONSHIP 2000–2010:

COMPOSITE TABLE

	P	W	D	L	Pts
France	55	41	0	14	**82**
Ireland	55	39	0	16	**78**
England	55	35	1	19	**71**
Wales	55	25	2	28	**52**
Scotland	55	15	2	38	**32**
Italy	55	7	1	47	**15**

CHIEF RECORDS

RECORD	DETAIL		SET
Most team points in season	229 by England	in five matches	2001
Most team tries in season	29 by England	in five matches	2001
Highest team score	80 by England	80–23 v Italy	2001
Biggest team win	57 by England	80–23 v Italy	2001
Most team tries in match	12 by Scotland	v Wales	1887
Most appearances	56 for Ireland	C M H Gibson	1964 – 1979
Most points in matches	529 for England	J P Wilkinson	1998 – 2010
Most points in season	89 for England	J P Wilkinson	2001
Most points in match	35 for England	J P Wilkinson	v Italy, 2001
Most tries in matches	24 for Scotland	I S Smith	1924 – 1933
Most tries in season	8 for England	C N Lowe	1914
	8 for Scotland	I S Smith	1925
Most tries in match	5 for Scotland	G C Lindsay	v Wales, 1887
Most cons in matches	85 for England	J P Wilkinson	1998 – 2010
Most cons in season	24 for England	J P Wilkinson	2001
Most cons in match	9 for England	J P Wilkinson	v Italy, 2001
Most pens in matches	105 for Ireland	R J R O'Gara	2000 – 2010
Most pens in season	18 for England	S D Hodgkinson	1991
	18 for England	J P Wilkinson	2000
	18 for France	G Merceron	2002
Most pens in match	7 for England	S D Hodgkinson	v Wales, 1991
	7 for England	C R Andrew	v Scotland, 1995
	7 for England	J P Wilkinson	v France, 1999
	7 for Wales	N R Jenkins	v Italy, 2000
	7 for France	G Merceron	v Italy, 2002
	7 for Scotland	C D Paterson	v Wales, 2007
Most drops in matches	11 for England	J P Wilkinson	1998 – 2010
Most drops in season	5 for France	G Camberabero	1967
	5 for Italy	D Dominguez	2000
	5 for Wales	N R Jenkins	2001
	5 for England	J P Wilkinson	2003
	5 for Scotland	D A Parks	2010
Most drops in match	3 for France	P Albaladejo	v Ireland, 1960
	3 for France	J-P Lescarboura	v England, 1985
	3 for Italy	D Dominguez	v Scotland 2000
	3 for Wales	N R Jenkins	v Scotland 2001

WOMEN'S SIX NATIONS

ENGLAND CONTINUE TO DOMINATE

By Paul Morgan

When the Wales team of the 1970s won three Grand Slams and two Triple Crowns they were rightly lauded as one of the best sides the game has ever seen. But in 2010 England's women overtook this record in clinching their fifth successive RBS Six Nations title, and their fourth of that run with a Grand Slam.

The only defeat in what has been a remarkable run on their way to European domination was 10–9 to Wales in 2009, England rattling up scores of tries and hundreds of points in between.

Their latest Grand Slam, in 2010, was certainly one of contrasting fortunes for Catherine Spencer's side.

At times it was the easiest of their Slams as they stormed through the first four rounds but in the last game, against France, they only clinched their clean sweep by one point.

In the French game at a passionate and foreboding stadium in Rennes England had to dig deeper than in recent seasons to emerge 11–10 victors.

Amy Turner's try put England 5–3 ahead at half-time while France had Claire Canal sent off on the half-hour mark.

Celine Allainmat's try put France ahead before Katy McLean gave England the lead again with a 64th-minute penalty.

And it says much for the way England have developed under coach Gary Street that the coach was relaxed throughout what became a frantic second half.

"Even though this was a tight game, the victory was never in doubt in my mind," said Street.

"We knew France would throw everything they had at us and they made us work very hard for this win. But we showed great character and mental strength to turn this around."

France had looked anything but dangerous in large parts of the Championship losing to struggling Scotland but with their management experimenting with the side ahead of the Women's Rugby World Cup 2010 it was no surprise to insiders that they pushed England so close.

England's cause was helped by the dismissal of Canal, who brought an unacceptable side to the game in to the Women's Six Nations by admitting making contact with the eyes of Jo McGilchrist, an offence which later led to her being banned for 13 weeks. A one-off in the women's game, we all hope.

England headed to Rennes with an incredible record, conceding just five points in four games. Ireland scored the only try against the women in white, who went on to capitalise on that sensational defence in the World Cup (see pages 84–90).

In fact it took until round three for England to concede their first points as they beat Ireland 22–5 at Esher, their home ground for the Championship.

Kate O'Loughlin took the accolades as the first woman to cross England's line in 2010, although replies from Maggie Alphonsi, Emily Scarratt, Claire Allan and Turner rounded off the victory in the second half.

England were barely troubled in their games against Wales (31–0), Scotland (51–0) and Italy (41–0), the reality beginning to sink in that England could field an A team in the majority of their Six Nations games and still win.

Below England the other five sides produced one of the most inconsistent tournaments on record with Scotland beating France, Wales beating Scotland and Italy beating Wales and drawing with Scotland.

The subsequent Women's Rugby World Cup did hold the key to some of these scorelines as coaches tweaked their line-ups and gave players the chance to show they could play at the highest level.

The French finished second, their best win coming in round two when they beat Ireland 19–9 in Blois. The French policy of moving their games around the country is commendable and could be a consideration for England in future years, as they can only develop the game so much when all their matches are played in the London area.

The trip to Blois brought snowy conditions to the Championship and an unforgettable performance from France winger Fanny Horta, who scored two stunning tries.

Wales had high hopes after their shock victory over England in 2009, but slumped to a series of defeats, to take the wooden spoon.

Their only win came on Valentine's Day, wing Caryl James helping herself to two tries as Wales got their campaign up and running with victory over Scotland in Bridgend.

Wales lost to England in their opening fixture but bounced back in style with three tries in the first half against the Scots putting them in the driving seat before eventually going on to win 28–12.

Wales coach Jason Lewis believed the victory over Scotland had got his side "back on track" but they failed to build on the platform, unable to record any more wins in the Championship.

Wales were one of three sides marooned at the bottom of the table on one win, but they fell below both Scotland and Italy by virtue of their draw in round three.

All of the rugby world will delight at the continued success of Italy, who are also starting to excel at Sevens with the Olympics just around the corner.

The win over Wales and the draw against Scotland could be landmark results for the Italians who finished equal fourth with the Scots.

Ireland continued their progression to finish joint second with the French, three victories showing the potential in a country where there is still a small player base. Ireland continued to move forward at the World Cup and it is hoped this will lead to a compelling recruitment campaign for women's rugby in the Emerald Isle, where they have the ability to become one of Europe's superpowers.

RESULTS	
Ireland 22 **Italy** 5	**England** 22 **Ireland** 5
England 31 **Wales** 0	**Ireland** 18 **Wales** 3
Scotland 10 **France** 8	**Scotland** 0 **England** 51
France 19 **Ireland** 9	**France** 45 **Italy** 14
Italy 0 **England** 41	**Ireland** 15 **Scotland** 3
Wales 28 **Scotland** 12	**France** 10 **England** 11
Wales 3 **France** 15	**Wales** 15 **Italy** 19
Italy 6 **Scotland** 6	

FINAL TABLE

	P	W	D	L	DIFF	Pts
England	5	5	0	0	+141	**10**
France	5	3	0	2	+50	**6**
Ireland	5	3	0	2	+17	**6**
Scotland	5	1	1	3	–77	**3**
Italy	5	1	1	3	–85	**3**
Wales	5	1	0	4	–46	**2**

ALL BLACKS INTO DOUBLE FIGURES

By Iain Spragg

Since its inaugural season back in 1996 the Tri–Nations trophy has, at times, felt like the exclusive preserve of New Zealand and after surrendering their title to South Africa in 2009, the All Blacks were back to their irresistible best as they reclaimed their crown as the undisputed kings of southern hemisphere rugby.

In the 15th instalment of the competition, Graham Henry's Kiwis swept aside the challenge of both Australia and South Africa with devastating aplomb, becoming the first side to lift the trophy without suffering a single defeat since the number of matches was increased from four to six in 2006.

It was the New Zealanders' tenth Tri–Nations crown in total since they were first anointed champions and the 184 points they amassed in the 2010 campaign was a new record for the competition, eclipsing the 179 they had accumulated four years earlier.

The All Blacks wrapped up the title in late August with a game to spare when they overcame South Africa 29–22 in Soweto in front of a staggering 95,000-strong crowd, staging a second-half fightback against the Springboks to secure the trophy and condemn Springbok skipper John Smit to defeat on the occasion of his 100th Test cap.

"I'm proud of our boys," New Zealand skipper Richie McCaw said after the crucial victory, a result which meant the openside flanker had personally been involved in seven triumphant Tri–Nations campaigns. "We kept believing in what we were doing. We got some pressure on in that second half and perhaps their weary legs gave us a few opportunities that we managed to take. I'm happy we won but I feel sorry for John. For a guy like that, he probably deserved better, but that's the way rugby goes. It's a cruel game sometimes."

The penultimate Tri–Nations before the addition of the Argentineans to the schedule in 2012 began with the clash between Henry's team and South Africa in Auckland, but any hopes the defending champions harboured of laying down an early marker in the tournament were dashed by a compelling New Zealand performance.

It took the All Blacks 18 minutes to pierce the South African defence at Eden Park as Conrad Smith crossed the whitewash and further tries from Ma'a Nonu, Kieran Read and Tony Woodcock served to both crush the Springbok resistance and signal Kiwi intent as Henry's team emerged convincing 32–12 winners.

Seven days later the two old foes did battle again in Wellington and although Peter de Villiers' side reduced the margin of defeat, New Zealand still ran in four tries in a 31–17 victory that produced a winning bonus point for the second successive weekend.

"We were prepared to play rugby from a fair way out from the goal line and were prepared to attack from our own half and that resulted in a couple of tries," Henry said after the final whistle at the Westpac Stadium. "The new interpretation of the tackle law has changed the game a lot. It allows you to get continuity of possession and to build to score points and the guys did that exceptionally well."

Battered and bruised, South Africa now decamped to Australia for the final leg of their three games on the road but if any of the Springbok squad believed respite would be found against the Wallabies, last crowned champions in 2001, they were in for a rude awakening in Brisbane.

Tries from winger Drew Mitchell and scrum-half Will Genia proved decisive for the home side while the Springboks saw both Jaque Fourie and BJ Botha yellow carded as their indiscipline came back to haunt them once again. Matt Giteau contributed 15 points with the boot and the Wallabies claimed an encouraging 30–13 win.

"We wanted to build as much pressure as we could and to do that you've got to keep the ball," said Australia coach Robbie Deans. "It wasn't always successful but we asked enough to sap them and it made it more difficult when they did get the ball in terms of their attack.

"I'm clearly happy with the performance. There was a lot of stuff to be proud of, particularly the defence. We know next week we've got a New Zealand team coming who will do that plus a bit. They've got a lot of patience, they'll work us around and we'll have to finish the opportunities that we get."

Sadly for Wallaby fans, Deans' side did not heed his words of warning in Melbourne seven days later as the Kiwis came calling and although the home side did finish off three attacking moves for three tries through Adam Ashley–Cooper, Rocky Elsom and Drew Mitchell, they were completely blown away by the All Blacks' own attacking game and allowed the Kiwis to cross the whitewash eight times in a devastating 49–28 defeat.

Dan Carter began the try deluge for the New Zealanders in the ninth minute and replacement Corey Flynn completed the rout in the 79th. In between, Mils Muliaina helped himself to a brace.

It was now a simple question of whether the Wallabies or the Springboks could halt the All Blacks' regal procession to the trophy and the Kiwis provided a brusque answer in Christchurch in early August when they beat Australia 20–10 to take another step closer to the title.

In contrast to the encounter between the two sides in Melbourne, the game was a good, old-fashioned arm wrestle. Tries from Muliaina and Smith and 10 points from Carter gave the All Blacks the edge in the Bledisloe Cup clash and although a rejuvenated Wallaby side crossed through Kurtley Beale, the Kiwis were in resolute mood and recorded their 13th consecutive Test victory and ninth in a row against Australia.

"Some big hits went in but the boys played defensively for each other and the boys are pretty happy with that," said McCaw after the game. "Such hard defensive games take their toll and the players' tanks were fairly empty with 10 minutes to go, but we felt we started to get on top of them physically towards the end.

"Last week both teams wanted to use the ball a lot but the difference was we had to defend a lot in that second half. In tight Test matches, you've got to do that. I'm very happy. It's an important Cup and we wanted to put a performance in to put it away so happy with that."

A perfect four from four left New Zealand on the brink of glory and a fortnight later the fixture list conspired to present them with the chance to dethrone the Springboks in their own backyard. It was an opportunity which they seized in dramatic style.

Wounded and under the hopeful scrutiny of their own fans, South Africa were quickest out of the blocks in Johannesburg. Two Morne Steyn penalties cancelled out an earlier three-pointer from Carter and when Schalk Burger crashed over in the 19th minute, South Africa had established a 13–6 advantage. Woodcock went over four minutes before the break to reduce the deficit but as the half-time whistle sounded, the home side were 16–14 ahead.

Scoring opportunities were at a premium in the second period but two Steyn penalties edged the Springboks 22–14 clear and with just 18 minutes left on the clock, the All Blacks found themselves with their backs firmly against the wall for the first time in the tournament.

A 66th-minute Carter penalty gnawed away at the lead but it was not until the final three minutes of the match that New Zealand were able to complete their revival as McCaw and substitute Israel Dagg breached the desperate South African defence for tries that set up their 29–22 triumph.

"They don't get any bigger than that," said Henry. "It was a huge Test match, played in front of that crowd in that stadium. I just felt so proud of what they've achieved. The character, backed by their guts and togetherness was superb. So I think it was a very special win by the All Blacks today, an outstanding result and something we will never forget as far as we're concerned."

The champions now took a well-earned break as the Springboks and Australia prepared for a two-match, head-to-head which would go a long way to deciding who finished as runners-up and who would face the ignominy of third place.

The first clash in Pretoria was significant because it ended with South Africa's first victory. The Wallabies led at half-time at Loftus Versfeld but the Springboks came storming back, scoring five tries in total to finish 44–31 winners and end their four-game losing streak.

"I was worried when we gave them those tries, especially in the state we were in, the confidence being low," De Villiers admitted. "So to give them a start like that it took really a lot of heart and character to come back and win a game a like this."

The rematch in Bloemfontein a week later however did not follow the same script and an epic, high-scoring Tri–Nations encounter was finally settled with the final kick of the match – a 55-metre monster – when Beale landed the crucial penalty. The Wallabies emerged 41–39 winners and the Springboks were condemned to finish bottom of the table.

"I didn't know who was supposed to take the kick. I was busy looking for Matt Giteau, but he'd left the field," admitted Beale after the dramatic denouement. "When I stepped up to take that final kick, I knew I couldn't let the boys down. The guys wanted me to take the kick and I knew I had to stick to the process and not worry about the crowd. It's definitely a career highlight. To win a match for the Wallabies, it doesn't get better."

The tournament of course was not quite finished. Champions New Zealand still had to travel to Sydney to face the Wallabies to bring down the curtain on the 2010 Tri–Nations and the trans-Tasman rivals served up a suitably entertaining encounter.

Australia briefly threatened to spoil the party, leading 22–9 midway through the second half thanks to tries from James O'Connor and Ashley–Cooper but tries from McCaw and Kieran Read were just enough to secure a 23–22 win for the visitors and confirm the All Blacks as the first to complete a six-game Tri–Nations clean sweep.

It was also a 14th Test victory from 14 in 2009–10 for Henry's side and, perhaps more significantly, an ominous early shot across southern hemisphere bows ahead of Rugby World Cup 2011.

TRI-NATIONS 2010: FINAL TABLE

	P	W	D	L	F	A	Bonus Pts	Pts
New Zealand	6	6	0	0	184	111	**3**	**27**
Australia	6	2	0	4	162	188	**3**	**11**
South Africa	6	1	0	5	147	194	**3**	**7**

Points: win 4; draw 2; four or more tries, or defeat by seven or fewer points 1

10 July, Eden Park, Auckland

NEW ZEALAND 32 (3G 2PG 1T)
SOUTH AFRICA 12 (4PG)

NEW ZEALAND: J M Muliaina; C S Jane, C G Smith, M A Nonu, J T Rokocoko; D W Carter, Q J Cowan; T D Woodcock, K F Mealamu, O T Franks, B C Thorn, T J S Donnelly, J Kaino, K J Read, R H McCaw (captain)

SUBSTITUTIONS: P A T Weepu for Cowan (54 mins); R D Kahui for Rokocoko (58 mins); B J Franks for O T Franks (64 mins); S L Whitelock for Donnelly (71 mins); L J Messam for Kaino (72 mins); C R Flynn for Mealamu (78 mins)

SCORERS *Tries*: Smith, Nonu, Read, Woodcock *Conversions*: Carter (3) *Penalty Goals*: Carter (2)

SOUTH AFRICA: Z Kirchner; J de Villiers, J Fourie, W Olivier, B G Habana; M Steyn, E R Januarie; G G Steenkamp, J W Smit (captain), J N du Plessis, J P Botha, V Matfield, L–F P Louw, P J Spies, S W P Burger

SUBSTITUTIONS: D J Rossouw for Louw (51 mins); A Bekker for J P Botha (51 mins); B J Botha for Du Plessis (57 mins); A D James for Steyn (70 mins); G G Aplon for Olivier (71 mins); M C Ralepelle for Smit (71 mins); R Pienaar for Januarie (75 mins)

SCORER *Penalty Goals*: Steyn (4)

REFEREE D A Lewis (Ireland)

YELLOW CARD J P Botha (12 mins)

17 July, Westpac Stadium, Wellington

NEW ZEALAND 31 (1G 3PG 3T)
SOUTH AFRICA 17 (2G 1PG)

NEW ZEALAND: J M Muliaina; C S Jane, C G Smith, M A Nonu, R M N Ranger; D W Carter, P A T Weepu; T D Woodcock, K F Mealamu, O T Franks, B C Thorn, T J S Donnelly, J Kaino, K J Read, R H McCaw (captain)

SUBSTITUTIONS: S L Whitelock for Donnelly (62 mins); Q J Cowan for Weepu (62 mins); I J A Dagg for Ranger (62 mins); B J Franks for O T Franks (68 mins); A W Cruden for Nonu (73 mins); L J Messam for McCaw (75 mins); C R Flynn for Mealamu (75 mins)

SCORERS *Tries*: Nonu, Muliaina, Ranger, Dagg *Conversion*: Carter *Penalty Goals*: Carter (2), Weepu

SOUTH AFRICA: Z Kirchner; J de Villiers, J Fourie, W Olivier, B G Habana; M Steyn, E R Januarie; G G Steenkamp, J W Smit (captain), C J van der Linde, D J Rossouw, V Matfield, L–F P Louw, P J Spies, S W P Burger

SUBSTITUTIONS: G G Aplon for De Villiers (40 mins); B J Botha for Van der Linde (40 mins); A Bekker for Rossouw (53 mins); R Pienaar for Januarie (53 mins); R Kankowski for Spies (69 mins); M C Ralepelle for Smit (75 mins);

SCORERS *Tries*: Rossouw, Burger *Conversions*: Steyn (2) *Penalty Goal*: Steyn

REFEREE A C Rolland (Ireland)

YELLOW CARD D J Rossouw (3 mins)

24 July, Suncorp Stadium, Brisbane

AUSTRALIA 30 (1G 6PG 1T)
SOUTH AFRICA 13 (1PG 2T)

AUSTRALIA: A P Ashley–Cooper; J D O'Connor, R G Horne, M J Giteau, D A Mitchell; Q S Cooper, S W Genia; B A Robinson, S M Fainga'a, R S L Ma'afu, D W Mumm, N C Sharpe, R D Elsom (captain), R N Brown, D W Pocock

SUBSTITUTIONS: S T Moore for Fainga'a (53 mins); J A Slipper for Robinson (58 mins); R A Simmons for Mumm (67 mins); B McCalman for Brown (69 mins); B S Barnes for Giteau (72 mins)

SCORERS *Tries*: Mitchell, Genia *Conversion*: O'Connor *Penalty Goals*: Giteau (5), O'Connor

SOUTH AFRICA: Z Kirchner; G G Aplon, J Fourie, W Olivier, B G Habana; M Steyn, R Pienaar; G G Steenkamp, J W Smit (captain), B J Botha, D J Rossouw, V Matfield, R Kankowski, P J Spies, S W P Burger

SUBSTITUTIONS: A D James for Steyn (54 mins); J L de Jongh for Olivier (54 mins); D J Potgieter for Kankowski (55 mins); P R van der Merwe for Rossouw (67 mins); C J Van der Linde for Spies (temp 48 to 55 mins) and for Botha (67 mins); F Hougaard for Pienaar (72 mins); M C Ralepelle for Smit (72 mins);

SCORERS *Tries*: Fourie, Steenkamp *Penalty Goal*: Steyn

REFEREE G Clancy (Ireland)

YELLOW CARDS J Fourie (2 mins); B J Botha (45 mins); Q S Cooper (53 mins)

31 July, Etihad Stadium, Melbourne

AUSTRALIA 28 (2G 3PG 1T)
NEW ZEALAND 49 (4G 2PG 3T)

AUSTRALIA: A P Ashley–Cooper; J D O'Connor, R G Horne, B S Barnes, D A Mitchell; M J Giteau, S W Genia; B A Robinson, S T Moore, R S L Ma'afu, D W Mumm, N C Sharpe, R D Elsom (captain), R N Brown, D W Pocock

SUBSTITUTIONS: R A Simmons for Sharpe (47 mins); S M Fainga'a for Moore (47 mins); K J Beale for Horne (56 mins); J A Slipper for Ma'afu (59 mins); L Burgess for Genia (75 mins); A S Fainga'a for Giteau (76 mins)

SCORERS *Tries*: Mitchell, Ashley–Cooper, Elsom *Conversions*: Giteau (2) *Penalty Goals*: Giteau (3)

NEW ZEALAND: J M Muliaina; C S Jane, C G Smith, M A Nonu, J T Rokocoko; D W Carter, Q J Cowan; T D Woodcock, K F Mealamu, O T Franks, B C Thorn, T J S Donnelly, J Kaino, K J Read, R H McCaw (captain)

SUBSTITUTIONS: P A T Weepu for Cowan (33 mins); B J Franks for O T Franks (43 mins); S L Whitelock for Thorn (57 mins); A W Cruden for Nonu (71 mins); C R Flynn for Mealamu (71 mins); V V J Vito for Donnelly (73 mins); I J A Dagg for Jane (75 mins)

SCORERS *Tries*: Muliaina (2), Carter, McCaw, Jane, Rokocoko, Flynn *Conversions*: Carter (4) *Penalty Goals*: Carter (2)

REFEREE C Joubert (South Africa)

YELLOW CARDS O T Franks (21 mins); D A Mitchell (28 mins and 43 mins)

RED CARD D A Mitchell (43 mins)

7 August, AMI Stadium, Lancaster Park, Christchurch

NEW ZEALAND 20 (2G 2PG)
AUSTRALIA 10 (1G 1PG)

NEW ZEALAND: J M Muliaina; C S Jane, C G Smith, M A Nonu, J T Rokocoko; D W Carter, P A T Weepu; T D Woodcock, K F Mealamu, O T Franks, B C Thorn, T J S Donnelly, J Kaino, K J Read, R H McCaw (captain)

SUBSTITUTIONS: B J Franks for O T Franks (42 mins); S L Whitelock for Donnelly (49 mins); V V J Vito for Kaino (69 mins); A S Mathewson for Weepu (76 mins); C R Flynn for Mealamu (76 mins)

SCORERS *Tries*: Muliaina, Smith *Conversions*: Carter (2) *Penalty Goals*: Carter (2)

AUSTRALIA: K J Beale; J D O'Connor, A P Ashley–Cooper, A S Fainga'a, D A Mitchell; M J Giteau, S W Genia; B A Robinson, S M Fainga'a, R S L Ma'afu, D W Mumm, N C Sharpe, R D Elsom (captain), R N Brown, D W Pocock

SUBSTITUTIONS: M J Hodgson for Brown (55 mins); R A Simmons for Sharpe (64 mins); J A Slipper for Ma'afu (64 mins)

SCORERS *Try*: Beale *Conversion*: Giteau *Penalty Goal*: Giteau

REFEREE J I Kaplan (South Africa)

21 August, FNB Stadium, Soweto

SOUTH AFRICA 22 (1G 5PG)
NEW ZEALAND 29 (1G 4PG 2T)

SOUTH AFRICA: G G Aplon; J–P R Pietersen, J L de Jongh, J de Villiers, B G Habana; M Steyn, F Hougaard; G G Steenkamp, J W Smit (captain), J N du Plessis, P R van der Merwe, V Matfield, J H Smith, P J Spies, S W P Burger

SUBSTITUTIONS: L–F P Louw for Smith (58 mins); C J van der Linde for Du Plessis (61 mins); D J Rossouw for Van der Merwe (temp 24 to 37 mins and 69 mins); E R Januarie for Hougaard (75 mins)

SCORERS *Try*: Burger *Conversion*: Steyn *Penalty Goals*: Steyn (5)

NEW ZEALAND: J M Muliaina; C S Jane, C G Smith, M A Nonu, J T Rokocoko; D W Carter, Q J Cowan; T D Woodcock, K F Mealamu, B J Franks, B C Thorn, T J S Donnelly, J Kaino, K J Read, R H McCaw (captain)

SUBSTITUTIONS: P A T Weepu for Cowan (41 mins); S L Whitelock for Donnelly (49 mins); I J A Dagg for Rokocoko (57 mins); I F Afoa for Franks (62 mins); V V J Vito for Kaino (69 mins)

SCORERS *Tries*: Woodcock, McCaw, Dagg *Conversion*: Carter *Penalty Goals*: Carter (4)

REFEREE N Owens (Wales)

28 August, Loftus Versfeld, Pretoria

SOUTH AFRICA 44 (5G 3PG)
AUSTRALIA 31 (4G 1PG)

SOUTH AFRICA: F P L Steyn; J–P R Pietersen, J Fourie, J de Villiers, B G Habana; M Steyn, F Hougaard; G G Steenkamp, J W Smit (captain), J N du Plessis, P R van der Merwe, V Matfield, J H Smith, P J Spies, S W P Burger

SUBSTITUTIONS: D J Rossouw for Van der Merwe (48 mins); C J van der Linde for Du Plessis (53 mins); M C Ralepelle for Smit (59 mins); A D James for M Steyn (64 mins); Smit back for Van der Linde (79 mins)

SCORERS *Tries*: Smith, Steenkamp, Spies, F P L Steyn, Pietersen *Conversions*: M Steyn (4), James *Penalty Goals*: M Steyn (2), F P L Steyn

AUSTRALIA: K J Beale; J D O'Connor, A P Ashley–Cooper, M J Giteau, D A Mitchell; Q S Cooper, S W Genia; B A Robinson, S M Fainga'a, R S L Ma'afu, D W Mumm, N C Sharpe, R D Elsom (captain), R N Brown, D W Pocock

SUBSTITUTIONS: J A Slipper for Ma'afu (54 mins); B J McCalman for Brown (57 mins); R A Simmons for Sharpe (64 mins); S T Moore for Fainga'a (temp 16 to 38 mins)

SCORERS *Tries*: O'Connor (2), Genia, Mumm *Conversions*: Giteau (4) *Penalty Goal*: Giteau

REFEREE A C Rolland (Ireland)

4 September, Vodacom Park, Bloemfontein

SOUTH AFRICA 39 (3G 6PG) AUSTRALIA 41 (5G 2PG)

SOUTH AFRICA: F P L Steyn; J–P R Pietersen, J Fourie, J de Villiers, B G Habana; M Steyn, F Hougaard; G G Steenkamp, J W Smit (captain), J N du Plessis, D J Rossouw, V Matfield, J H Smith, P J Spies, S W P Burger

SUBSTITUTIONS: G G Aplon for Habana (50 mins); C J van der Linde for Du Plessis (54 mins); P R Van der Merwe for Rossouw (60 mins); M C Ralepelle for Smit (64 mins); R Kankowski for Spies (64 mins)

SCORERS *Tries*: Fourie, Steenkamp, De Villiers *Conversions*: M Steyn (3) *Penalty Goals*: M Steyn (6)

AUSTRALIA: K J Beale; J D O'Connor, A P Ashley–Cooper, M J Giteau, D A Mitchell; Q S Cooper, S W Genia; B A Robinson, S T Moore, R S L Ma'afu, M D Chisholm, N C Sharpe, R D Elsom (captain), B J McCalman, D W Pocock

SUBSTITUTIONS: J A Slipper for Ma'afu (21 mins); D W Mumm for Chisholm (53 mins); L Burgess for Genia (54 mins); S M Fainga'a for Moore (64 mins); B S Barnes for Giteau (70 mins); R N Brown for McCalman (70 mins); A S Fainga'a for Mitchell (73 mins); Moore back for Brown (temp 78 to 79 mins) and for S M Fainga'a (79 mins)

SCORERS *Tries*: Beale, O'Connor, Moore, Elsom, Mitchell *Conversions*: Giteau (4), O'Connor *Penalty Goals*: Giteau, Beale

REFEREE W Barnes (England)

YELLOW CARD S M Fainga'a (69 mins)

11 September, ANZ Stadium, Sydney

AUSTRALIA 22 (4PG 2T) NEW ZEALAND 23 (2G 3PG)

AUSTRALIA: K J Beale; J D O'Connor, A P Ashley–Cooper, M J Giteau, L D Turner; Q S Cooper, S W Genia; B A Robinson, S T Moore, R S L Ma'afu, M D Chisholm; N C Sharpe, R D Elsom (captain), B J McCalman, D W Pocock

SUBSTITUTIONS: J A Slipper for Ma'afu (52 mins); D W Mumm for Chisholm (55 mins); L Burgess for Genia (71 mins); R N Brown for McCalman (72 mins); B S Barnes for Cooper (temp 68 to 73 mins and 78 mins); A S Fainga'a for Ashley–Cooper (78 mins)

SCORER *Tries*: O'Connor, Ashley–Cooper *Penalty Goals*: Giteau (3), Beale

NEW ZEALAND: J M Muliaina; C S Jane, C G Smith, M A Nonu, I J A Dagg; A W Cruden, P A T Weepu; T D Woodcock, K F Mealamu, O T Franks, B C Thorn, T J S Donnelly, V V J Vito, K J Read, R H McCaw (captain)

SUBSTITUTIONS: C R Flynn for Mealamu (11 mins); J Kaino for Vito (48 mins); C R Slade for Cruden (60 mins); A F Boric for Donnelly (60 mins); I F Afoa for Franks (60 mins); R M N Ranger for Jane (68 mins); Q J Cowan for Weepu (78 mins)

SCORERS *Tries*: McCaw, Read *Conversions*: Weepu (2) *Penalty Goals*: Weepu (3)

REFEREE S M Lawrence (South Africa)

TRI-NATIONS RECORDS 1996–2010

PREVIOUS WINNERS

1996 New Zealand	1997 New Zealand	1998 South Africa	1999 New Zealand
2000 Australia	2001 Australia	2002 New Zealand	2003 New Zealand
2004 South Africa	2005 New Zealand	2006 New Zealand	2007 New Zealand
2008 New Zealand	2009 South Africa	2010 New Zealand	

GRAND SLAM WINNERS

New Zealand (Four times) 1996, 1997, 2003 and 2010.

South Africa (Once) 1998

TEAM RECORD	DETAIL		SET
Most team points in season	184 by N Zealand	in six matches	2010
Most team tries in season	22 by N Zealand	in six matches	2010
Highest team score	61 by S Africa	61–22 v Australia (h)	1997
Biggest team win	49 by Australia	49–0 v S Africa (h)	2006
Most team tries in match	8 by S Africa	v Australia	1997
	8 by S Africa	v Australia	2008

INDIVIDUAL RECORD	DETAIL		SET
Most appearances	48 for Australia	G M Gregan	1996 to 2007
Most points in matches	426 for N Zealand	D W Carter	2003 to 2010
Most points in season	99 for N Zealand	D W Carter	2006
Most points in match	31 for S Africa	M Steyn	v N Zealand (h) 2009
Most tries in matches	16 for N Zealand	C M Cullen	1996 to 2002
Most tries in season	7 for N Zealand	C M Cullen	2000
Most tries in match	4 for S Africa	J L Nokwe	v Australia (h) 2008
Most cons in matches	54 for N Zealand	D W Carter	2003 to 2010
Most cons in season	14 for N Zealand	D W Carter	2006
Most cons in match	6 for S Africa	J H de Beer	v Australia (h),1997
Most pens in matches	94 for N Zealand	D W Carter	2003 to 2010
Most pens in season	23 for S Africa	M Steyn	2009
Most pens in match	9 for N Zealand	A P Mehrtens	v Australia (h) 1999
Most drops in matches	4 for S Africa	A S Pretorius	2002 to 2006
Most drops in season	3 for S Africa	M Steyn	2009
Most drops in match	2 for S Africa	J H de Beer	v N Zealand (h) 1997
	2 for S Africa	F P L Steyn	v Australia (h) 2007

From 1996 to 2005 inclusive, each nation played four matches in a season. The nations have each played six matches since, except in 2007 (World Cup year) when they reverted to four.

BLACK FERNS STAY ON TOP OF THE WORLD

By Paul Morgan

In the rugby world we are often stopped in our tracks by a great try, great match or great tournament. You think back over the last 20 years and there's Jonah Lomu smashing through the England team in 1995, Sir Clive Woodward lifting the World Cup in 2003 or Dan Carter destroying the Lions in 2005, before masterminding a European Grand Slam for New Zealand.

Joining these world-tilting events in 2010 was the Women's Rugby World Cup, a tournament that left an indelible mark on anyone who saw a game, whether on TV or at one of the two venues.

Never before has a tournament outside of a Rugby World Cup captured the imagination of the rugby public as this Women's Rugby World Cup did and it could be the most significant event in the history of the women's game.

An incredible crowd of more than 13,000 saw the final between hosts England and defending champions New Zealand, which was without question the best game of women's rugby ever staged. And those 13,000 didn't pay a token £5. There was no 'buy one ticket get two free' offers. These 13,000 paid upwards of £20 a seat or used their £60 tournament pass and created one of the best atmospheres experienced at the Twickenham Stoop in recent years.

When England wing Charlotte Barras scored her side's only try in the second half the ear-splitting noise was louder than anything I had experienced at the ground in 20 years of covering matches there.

Ultimately the Black Ferns were too streetwise, particularly at the breakdown to give up their crown, lifting their fourth successive Women's

Rugby World Cup. A remarkable achievement by one of sport's (not just rugby's) great teams.

Even in the final frantic minutes, with England trailing by three points, the women in white were prevented from having even the opportunity to strike a fatal blow.

The Black Ferns survived having three yellow cards in the final as they fell foul of referee Sarah Corrigan at the breakdown.

The scores were tied at 10–10 until the 66th minute when Kelly Brazier landed the winning penalty.

"I was pretty nervous [with the penalty]. The crowd were making a lot of noise," admitted Brazier.

"I just thought of it as another kick and thankfully it went straight through the posts. Relief, but obviously there was still a bit of time on the clock so I knew it wasn't over yet."

There were many great stories in the New Zealand team, but perhaps none greater than Anna Richards'. The 45-year-old fly-half was playing in her fourth World Cup final, having not even made the initial squad, only being called up for her fifth tournament because of injury.

"It feels awesome, it feels kind of surreal. It was an awesome atmosphere and kind of a strange game with all the sin-binnings. It was a weird game actually, but nice to come out on top," Richards said.

"It definitely ebbed and flowed. I thought we had the better first 15 or 20 and then England came back when we had a couple of sin-binnings. It was a real ebb and flow game; a real typical final."

Richards knew the key to the victory was the way they coped with the yellow cards, adding: "Our composure was crucial, especially when we were down to 14 and 13 at some stages, and we believed in ourselves.

"It feels really good to win my fourth World Cup. I will believe it later but I am really happy. It doesn't get any better – it's the best."

The Black Ferns achieved what most people expected them to, but that should take nothing away from Melissa Ruscoe's side. The pressure on them to win was huge, as they knew anything less would be seen as a failure back home.

"The girls just put their whole heart into it and got us through the game," said Ruscoe. "It's a patience game and rugby is a game of 80 minutes and it certainly went the full distance. We knew if we could just get back down their end, no one has scored on us from their own 22."

Heroines were created in the tournament, particularly in the ranks of the hosts and to hear Will Greenwood, the former England World Cup winner declare that Maggie Alphonsi could play for a side in the RFU Championship shows the huge strides that were made in terms of perception and visibility for the women's game.

England's players sank to their knees at the final whistle but even defeat didn't dim the performance of Alphonsi, who confirmed her status as one of the best players in the world and still appreciated the effect the tournament had on women's rugby.

"It is heartbreaking. We have worked for four years to achieve this and to come out with a loss is hard work," Alphonsi said.

"But I have to look at the game, it was a great game of rugby and advert for women's rugby. At the end of this tournament if you look at it we have got so many spectators who have seen some great women's rugby and hopefully we will get more girls taking up the sport.

"New Zealand were great, they played really well. Our English girls played awesome as well but unfortunately the best team won on the day, but in four years time we will be back.

"Our defence was amazing, it was solid, the breakdown was really good, and just a few penalties that killed us a little bit. But I take my hat off to our English girls, we were fantastic, dug in from the start and we chased every person down. Gutted but at the same time I am proud of my girls and the tournament itself."

New Zealand also had the IRB Women's Personality of the Year 2010, awarded in association with Emirates Airline, in their ranks as flying wing Carla Hohepa was crowned at the end of the tournament.

The 25-year-old fought off stiff competition to take the coveted award from England duo Alphonsi and Nolli Waterman and Australia wing Nicole Beck. "I can't take all the credit for it but it's an awesome honour to win this award. The whole team performance was fantastic, everyone has put 100% in and it showed out there today," said Hohepa.

England's assault on the title was based on their incredible defence, and they ended the tournament conceding the fewest points with 23 across the five matches, 10 fewer than champions New Zealand. Kazakhstan conceded the most at 203, with Scotland, South Africa, Sweden and Wales all leaking more than a century of points.

Behind the top two there were big breakthroughs elsewhere, most notably for Australia, who finished third after perennially ending up outside the top four, beating France 22–8 in the play-off.

"We came here, we made history," said Australia captain Cheryl Soon. "First would have been nice, or top two, but after our loss against England our goal was to finish third and we achieved that so we are very pleased with the result."

The third place has massive repercussions for the Wallaroos as they will now avoid the Black Ferns in the pool stages next time around, and make a real tilt on making their first final.

The USA, meanwhile, edged the North American tussle for fifth place, beating Canada 23–20.

"Whenever we play Canada we know it's going to be tough for us and we like to think this is the one that counted but I'm just glad we had them there," said USA coach Kathy Flores.

"I'm glad we didn't drop but we would like to be higher than fifth. We came in fifth, we stayed fifth, but we've still got a lot of work to do."

Ireland are another side moving forward, and they can be rightly delighted with their campaign which ended with them finishing seventh, following a 32–8 win over Scotland.

"This is huge for the girls. Seventh in the world is a great achievement for us. I know it's only one place further on for us than four years ago but the standard of this World Cup has been hugely impressive so this is a huge achievement for us," said Ireland coach Philip Doyle.

Kazakhstan ensured they ended Women's Rugby World Cup 2010 on a high by recording their first win of the tournament with a 12–8 victory over Sweden to claim 11th, while Wales recovered from defeats to New Zealand, South Africa and Australia to beat South Africa 29–17 to finish ninth.

"We wanted to finish the tournament on a high and with a good performance to show people that we can play good rugby," said Wales co-captain Mellissa Berry. "It was a fantastic performance by our girls. You don't come here looking at ninth-12th ranking, but the situation we had after the pool stages you want to get to the best you can, so all credit to our girls for digging in and showing people we can come away with the result."

But it wasn't just the rugby that made this the best Women's Rugby World Cup to date – the structure was spot on with the venue for the pool matches and some of the play-offs, Surrey Sports Park, being one of the stars of the show. Housing all the teams there was inspirational and created an Olympic Village-type atmosphere, which must be preserved for future tournaments to come.

Roll on 2014!

Facts and stats from the tournament

- The Black Ferns have now won 19 consecutive World Cup matches since their only defeat, a 7–0 loss to USA in the 1991 semi-finals.
- The three-point winning margin in the 2010 final is the closest any team has come to beating New Zealand in their four World Cup winning campaigns since.
- Thirty thousand fans attended the 30 matches at Women's Rugby World Cup 2010, be it at Surrey Sports Park or the Twickenham Stoop.
- The honour as the leading try scorer of the tournament is shared between Black Ferns flyer Carla Hohepa and Canada wing Heather Moyse with seven. Moyse matched her tally of seven four years ago, which made her the top try-scorer then.

- Nine players scored four tries at WRWC 2010 with Ireland No 8 Joy Neville the only forward among them.
- Kelly Brazier's title-winning penalty means she ends Women's Rugby World Cup 2010 as the leading point scorer with 48, taking her above Canada fly half Anna Schnell by two points with USA No.10 Christy Ringgenberg third best on 44 points.
- Kazakhstan and Sweden were the only sides to average less than a try a match.
- A total of 65 yellow cards were handed out across the 36 matches with Kazakhstan receiving the most at 10, one more than South Africa. By contrast England and Scotland had only one player sin-binned in the duration of the tournament.
- Kazakhstan received the tournament's only two red cards with scrum-half Amina Baratova's against South Africa and then second row Svetlana Karatygina in their victory over Sweden.

WOMEN'S RUGBY WORLD CUP 2010 STATISTICS

POOL A

Wales	12	**Australia**	26
New Zealand	55	**South Africa**	3
Wales	10	**South Africa**	15
New Zealand	32	**Australia**	5
New Zealand	41	**Wales**	8
Australia	62	**South Africa**	0

	P	W	D	L	PF	PA	BP	P
New Zealand	3	3	0	0	128	16	3	15
Australia	3	2	0	1	93	44	2	10
South Africa	3	1	0	2	18	127	0	4
Wales	3	0	0	3	30	82	1	1

POOL B

USA	51	**Kazakhstan**	0
England	27	**Ireland**	0
USA	12	**Ireland**	22
England	82	**Kazakhstan**	0
Ireland	37	**Kazakhstan**	3
England	37	**USA**	10

	P	W	D	L	PF	PA	BP	P
England	3	3	0	0	146	10	3	15
Ireland	3	2	0	1	59	42	2	10
USA	3	1	0	2	73	59	1	5
Kazakhstan	3	0	0	3	170	0	0	0

POOL C

Canada	37	**Scotland**	10
France	15	**Sweden**	9
France	17	**Scotland**	7
Canada	40	**Sweden**	10
Scotland	32	**Sweden**	5
France	23	**Canada**	8

	P	W	D	L	PF	PA	BP	P
France	3	3	0	0	55	24	1	13
Canada	3	2	0	1	85	43	2	10
Scotland	3	1	0	2	49	59	1	5
Sweden	3	0	0	3	24	87	1	1

PLAY-OFFS

9TH – 12TH SEMI FINALS	**South Africa** 25–10 **Kazakhstan**
	Wales 32–10 **Sweden**
5TH – 8TH SEMI FINALS	**Canada** 41–0 **Scotland**
	Ireland 3–40 **USA**
SEMI FINALS	**New Zealand** 45–7 **France**
	England 15–0 **Australia**
11TH PLACE PLAY-OFF	**Sweden** 8–12 **Kazakhstan**
9TH PLACE PLAY-OFF	**Wales** 29–17 **South Africa**
7TH PLACE PLAY-OFF	**Ireland** 32–8 **Scotland**
5TH PLACE PLAY-OFF	**USA** 23–20 **Canada**
3RD PLACE PLAY-OFF	**France** 8–22 **Australia**

WOMEN'S RUGBY WORLD CUP FINAL

5 September, Twickenham Stoop

NEW ZEALAND 13 (1G, 2PG)
ENGLAND 10 (1G, 1PG)

NEW ZEALAND: V Grant; C Hohepa, H Manuel, K Brazier, R Wickliffe; A Richards, E Jensen; R McKay, F Fa'amausili, M Bosman, V Robinson, V Heighway, M Ruscoe (captain), J Lavea, C Robertson.

SUBSTITUTIONS: S Te Ohaere–Fox for Bosman (64 mins), L Itunu for C Robertson (69 mins), J Sione for J Lavea (69 mins), T Hina for R Wickliffe (70 mins).

SCORERS: *Try*: Hohepa, *Conversion*: Brazier, *Penalties*: Brazier (2).

ENGLAND: D Waterman; C Barras, E Scarratt, R Burford, K Merchant; K McLean, A Turner; R Clark, A Garnett, S Hemming, T Taylor, J McGilchrist, S Hunter, M Alphonsi, C Spencer (captain).

SUBSTITUTIONS: A Richardson for R Burford (50 mins), C Purdy for R Clark (64 mins), B Essex for T Taylor (64 mins), LT Mason for A Turner (69), E Croker for A Garnett (69 mins), A Penrith for K Merchant (69 mins), S Beale for C Spencer (70 mins).

SCORERS: *Try*: Barras, *Conversion*: McLean. *Penalty*: McLean

REFEREE: S Corrigan (Australia)

YELLOW CARDS: A Richards (22 mins), M Bosman (29 mins), M Ruscoe (57 mins).

The final standings of Women's Rugby World Cup 2010 are:

Champions. New Zealand	Runners-up. England
3. Australia	4. France
5. USA	6. Canada
7. Ireland	8. Scotland
9. Wales	10. South Africa
11. Kazakhstan	12. Sweden

Winners of the IRB Women's Personality of the Year Award:

2010 – Carla Hohepa (New Zealand)
2009 – Debby Hodgkinson (Australia)
2008 – Carol Isherwood (England)
2007 – Sarah Corrigan (Australia)
2006 – Maggie Alphonsi (England)
2005 – Farah Palmer (New Zealand)
2004 – Donna Kennedy (Scotland)
2003 – Kathy Flores (USA)
2002 – Monique Hirovanaa (New Zealand)
2001 – Shelley Rae (England)

A NEW BLACK ERA IS ON THE WAY

By Karen Bond

IRB

New Zealand celebrate a hat-trick of world titles.

That the silverware remained in New Zealand's hands for a third year in a row was perhaps not all that surprising given their recent dominance of age grade rugby, but the manner of their title-clinching victory over Australia at the Estadio El Coloso del Parque in the Argentine city of Rosario in late June was totally unexpected.

The Baby Blacks produced an exceptional display of rugby to destroy an Australian Under-20 side with no shortage of talent, crossing for seven tries in a dominant 62–17 victory which left renowned commentator Nigel Starmer–Smith to describe them as "up in the stratosphere somewhere" in comparison to New Zealand's two previous IRB Junior World Championship winning squads.

They possessed all the qualities traditionally associated with New Zealand squads at any age, but it was their strength and skill levels across the park that stood out, alongside the mobility and handling of their forward pack, their consistent performances and the confidence they had in each other to realise their goal of winning the prestigious tournament.

This confidence stemmed from a 'Wolf Pack' philosophy adopted by the whole squad and the saying that 'the strength of the pack is the wolf and the strength of the wolf is his pack'. Put simply every player knew that there was always someone who had his back, always someone to pick him up after a mistake with the 'Join the Pack' call, all of which helped to create their own family on tour.

Few people, though, would have been brave enough to predict such a runaway victory, even after Pool A winners New Zealand had brushed aside the challenge of South Africa 36–7 in the semi finals. Not least because Australia had been equally impressive in denying England a third successive final appearance only days after beating the Baby Boks 42–35 in a truly enthralling Pool C decider in Santa Fe.

Both finalists had played some great free-flowing rugby along the way and a youthful Australian side under the guidance of David Nucifora, and featuring a number of players with IRB Sevens World Series experience, were expected to truly test the Baby Blacks. In reality, New Zealand never looked like ending a 14-match winning run in the Championship after hooker Liam Coltman touched down just 33 seconds into the final with Australia unable to get out of their own half for long periods.

Captain Tyler Bleyendaal, just like his predecessor Aaron Cruden 12 months previously, pulled the strings with another impressive display at fly half, creating two tries for teammates and scoring one of his own in a 28-point haul before limping off just past the hour mark having become the tournament's leading point scorer in the process.

Tries from Tom Marshall, Sean Polwart and a hat-trick from Telusa Veainu gave New Zealand a victory margin that in no way flattered them, but Australia deserve credit for the way they refused to just throw in the towel and admit defeat as the scoreboard ticked over, instead continuing to play the brand of rugby that had served them so well to that point.

It was also a fitting send-off for New Zealand coach Dave Rennie, who has overseen all three successes and admitted afterwards it was "pretty close" to a perfect performance. There was another reason for the Baby Blacks to celebrate with wing Julian Savea named IRB Junior Player of the Year 2010 following an impressive tournament where at times he was unstoppable on the way to equalling Zac Guildford's record of eight tries in a single Championship.

Guildford and Cruden have already graduated to the All Blacks ranks in the last year as the Championship continues to provide an important stepping stone, reaching a significant milestone when Rhys Ruddock's debut for Ireland – having been called up from the Under 20 squad in Argentina

– against Australia in June meant that all 17 nations to have played in the tournament had given at least one JWC graduate their senior test debut.

The tournament, though, is about more than just unearthing the next generation of world stars and will certainly have left its mark on the rugby communities in the Litoral region of Argentina with fans attending matches in their tens of thousands across the three venues in Rosario, Santa Fe and Paraná and creating an atmosphere to savour with their enthusiasm.

None more so than in Rosario during the pool stages when 16,000 people turned up to see Argentina take on England in their opening Pool B match, creating a cacophony of noise to try and inspire Los Pumitas to victory. The results may not have gone their way with defeats against England and France, but they finally had something to celebrate after beating Ireland 24–21.

This victory guaranteed Argentina's place in the 2011 Championship and left them fighting for fifth to eighth place, an improvement on 11th last year. It also earned them a meeting with Pool A runners-up Wales, one that would go down in the history books as the first to be decided by a kicking competition after sudden-death extra-time could not break the 19–19 deadlock.

It came down to a battle of nerves with Fernando Luna proving Argentina's hero when he slotted the winning kick moments after Rhys Downes had missed for Wales with the shootout tied at 8–8. Los Pumitas, though, had to settle for sixth place after losing to France for the second time in a tournament, while Wales again proved too strong for Fiji in the seventh place play-off in Santa Fe.

South Africa, meanwhile, bounced back from the disappointing loss to New Zealand to match their previous finishes of third with a 27–22 defeat of England in Rosario thanks to tries from Nico Scheepers, his early replacement Sibusiso Sithole (2) and their impressive full back Patrick Lambie.

Ireland and Scotland went into the final day without any pressure after overcoming Samoa and Tonga respectively on day four to leave the islanders to battle over relegation to the IRB Junior World Rugby Trophy in 2011. Ireland, as Six Nations champions, had arrived with higher expectations than ninth, but after a disappointing pool phase they did finish strongly with a 53–23 defeat of Scotland.

There was to be no happy ending for Samoa, though, after they ended the tournament as the only side without a win, losing the must-win encounter with Tonga 23–3 in Paraná to finish 12th and be relegated to the Trophy next year. Their place will be taken by the 2010 Trophy winner and Junior World Championship 2011 hosts Italy, who will join the other 10 nations in trying to find a way to stop New Zealand claiming a fourth title in a row.

IRB JUNIOR WORLD CHAMPIONSHIP 2010 RESULTS

POOL A

Round One: **New Zealand** 44–11 **Fiji**, **Wales** 22–13 **Samoa**. Round Two: **Wales** 31–3 **Fiji**, **New Zealand** 77–7 **Samoa**. Round Three: **New Zealand** 43–10 **Wales**, **Samoa** 12–15 **Fiji**.

POOL B

Round One: **France** 25–22 **Ireland**, **Argentina** 22–48 **England**. Round Two: **England** 36–21 **Ireland**, **Argentina** 23–31 **France**. Round Three: **England** 17–9 **France**, **Argentina** 24–21 **Ireland**.

POOL C

Round One: **South Africa** 40–14 **Tonga**, **Australia** 58–13 **Scotland**. Round Two: **Australia** 67–5 **Tonga**, **South Africa** 73–0 **Scotland**. Round Three: **Scotland** 27–3 **Tonga**, **South Africa** 35–42 **Australia**.

POOL TABLES

POOL A

	P	W	D	L	F	A	BP	PTS
New Zealand	3	3	0	0	164	28	3	**15**
Wales	3	2	0	1	63	59	0	**8**
Fiji	3	1	0	2	29	87	0	**4**
Samoa	3	0	0	3	32	114	1	**1**

POOL B

	P	W	D	L	F	A	BP	PTS
England	3	3	0	0	101	52	1	**13**
France	3	2	0	1	65	62	1	**9**
Argentina	3	1	0	2	69	100	0	**4**
Ireland	3	0	0	3	64	85	2	**2**

POOL C

	P	W	D	L	F	A	BP	PTS
Australia	3	3	0	0	167	53	3	**15**
South Africa	3	2	0	1	148	56	4	**12**
Scotland	3	1	0	2	40	134	0	**4**
Tonga	3	0	0	3	22	134	0	**0**

PLAY-OFFS – FIRST PHASE

Ninth Place Semi-Finals	**Ireland** 37–10 **Samoa**
	Scotland 28–8 **Tonga**
Fifth Place Semi-Finals	**Wales** 19–19 **Argentina** – Argentina win 9–8 after kicking competition
	France 44–9 **Fiji**
Semi-Finals	**Australia** 28–16 **England**
	New Zealand 36–7 **South Africa**

PLAY-OFFS – SECOND PHASE

11th Place Play-off	**Samoa** 3–23 **Tonga**
Ninth Place Play-off	**Ireland** 53–23 **Scotland**
Seventh Place Play-off	**Wales** 39–15 **Fiji**
Fifth Place Play-off	**Argentina** 23–37 **France**

THIRD PLACE PLAY-OFF

ENGLAND 22 (2G 1T 1PG) SOUTH AFRICA 27 (2G 2T 1PG)

FINAL

21 June 2010, Estadio El Coloso del Parque, Rosario

AUSTRALIA 17 (2G 1PG)
NEW ZEALAND 62 (6G 1T 5PG)

AUSTRALIA: L Morahan; D Shipperley, K Sitauti, R Coleman, A Toua; M Toomua, N White; S Manu, S Siliva, P Alo–Emile, P Battye, G Peterson, C Faingaa, L Gill, J Schatz (captain).

SUBSTITUTIONS: E Quirk for Faingaa (45 mins); C Ah–Nau for Manu (55 mins); I Prior for White (55 mins); J Lance for Shipperley (59 mins), L Jones for Peterson (68 mins); G Jeloudev for Sitauti (72 mins); S Robertson for Siliva (73 mins).

SCORERS: *Tries*: Morahan, Sitauti *Conversions*: Toomua (2) *Penalty*: Toomua

NEW ZEALAND: T Marshall; J Savea, S Timu, C Ngatai, T Veainu; T Bleyendaal (captain), T Kerr–Barlow; A Taavao–Matau, L Coltman, J Allen, L Moli, B Thomson, L Whitelock, S Polwart, R Grice.

SUBSTITUTIONS: T Franklin for Thomson (52 mins); P Ngauamo for Grice (63 mins); H Parker for Bleyendaal (64 mins); W Ioane for Taavao–Matau (68 mins); K Hammington for Kerr–Barlow (68 mins); J Woodward for Marshall (68 mins); Richard Haddon for Grice (73 mins); R Grice for Ngauamo (73 mins); Ngauamo for Coltman.

SCORERS: *Tries*: Veainu (3), Bleyendaal, Coltman, Marshall, Polwart *Conversions*: Bleyendaal (4), Parker (2) *Penalties*: Bleyendaal (5).

YELLOW CARD: L Coltman (62)

REFEREE: P Gauzere (France)

FINAL STANDINGS

1. New Zealand	**2. Australia**
3. South Africa	**4. England**
5. France	**6. Argentina**
7. Wales	**8. Fiji**
9. Ireland	**10. Scotland**
11. Tonga	**12. Samoa**

ITALY REALISE TARGET IN MOSCOW

By Chris Tau

Italy may have already been guaranteed a return to the IRB Junior World Championship in 2011 as hosts of the IRB's premier age grade tournament, but they were determined to take their place among the world's elite nations at Under 20 level in their own right as IRB Junior World Rugby Trophy 2010 winners.

Their intentions to claim the title were evident on day one in the Russian capital of Moscow when Papua New Guinea were cast aside 74–0 with defending champions Romania beaten 30–7 in Pool A of what was a hugely competitive tournament with Japan, Canada and Uruguay also having played in last year's Junior World Championship.

Uruguay, the inaugural Trophy winners in 2008, proved a sterner test and it was only a penalty try awarded at the death that enabled Italy to snatch a 16–12 victory and take their place in the final against Japan, the Pool B winners who also had to battle hard to reach the title decider.

Japan had kicked off their own campaign with a 31–17 defeat of Russia, before being held to an exciting 20–20 draw by a lively and talented Zimbabwe team. Canada stood in their way on the last round of pool matches, but a try-blitz either side of half-time saw the Asian champions to a 38–17 win.

The final of the first IRB 15-a-side tournament to be played in Russia took place at the Slava Stadium on 30 May with Tommaso Benvenuti, the dashing outside centre who plays for Benetton Treviso and was one of 14 veterans of the JWC 2009 squad present in Moscow, opening the scoring with a second minute try to calm any Italian nerves.

Antonio Denti touched down a second before the clock had reached 10 minutes with an Alberto Chillon penalty giving Italy a 15–0 half-time lead. A similar start to the second half, with tries from Michele Mortali and

Gabriele Cicchinelli, put the title beyond reach of the gallant Japanese despite a late consolation try from Mao Enoki making the final score 36–7.

Japan may have missed out on the title, but manager Takashi Hasunuma knows the importance of the tournament for the next generation of Brave Blossoms. "Many of these boys will form the core of the Japan team who compete in Rugby World Cup 2019 in Japan. This is why the tournament is very important for us in so many ways." One of those players could well be Takaaki Nakazuru, the top try-scorer.

In the third place play-off, Russia confirmed their status as the surprise package of the tournament by defeating Romania 23–20 in a match which made history as the first 15-a-side international match to be decided via nail-biting sudden-death extra-time.

Russia played their dynamic game, based on a well-drilled pack with back row twins Veniamin and Yuri Vengerov proving adept at being in the right place at the right time. The scores were locked at 20–20 when fly-half Denis Kukishev kept his cool, landing the penalty which secured third place.

Romania's Gabriel Conache was left to rue missed opportunities, which included six penalty attempts and a conversion in normal time, not to mention a drop-goal in extra-time, to allow Kukishev to be the match-winner and secure a third place which coach Andrey Cherevichny labelled "a good springboard for the future".

IRB JUNIOR WORLD RUGBY TROPHY 2010 RESULTS

POOL A

Round One; **Italy** 74–0 **Papua New Guinea**, **Uruguay** 12–15 **Romania**. Round Two: **Uruguay** 42–14 **Papua New Guinea**, **Italy** 30–7 **Romania**. Round Three: **Romania** 48–12 **Papua New Guinea**, **Italy** 16–12 **Uruguay**

POOL B

Round One: **Canada** 22–6 **Zimbabwe**, **Russia** 17–31 **Japan**. Round Two: **Japan** 20–20 **Zimbabwe**, **Russia** 17–15 **Canada**. Round Three: **Russia** 21–19 **Zimbabwe**, **Canada** 17–38 **Japan**

PLAY-OFFS

Seventh Place Play-off: **Papua New Guinea** 22–46 **Zimbabwe**. Fifth Place Play-off: **Uruguay** 13–11 **Canada**. Third Place Play-off: **Romania** 20–23 **Russia**. Final: **Italy** 36–7 **Japan**

International Records and Statistics

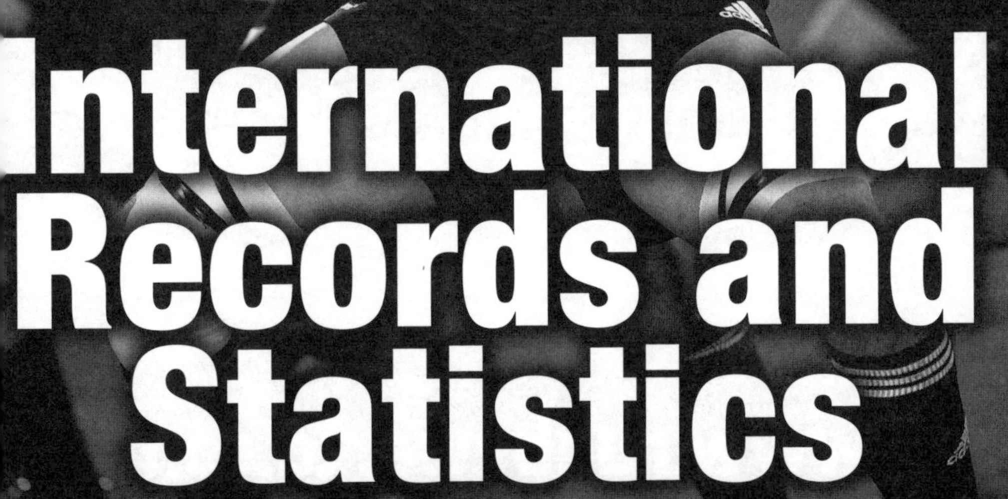

INTERNATIONAL RECORDS

RESULTS OF INTERNATIONAL MATCHES

MATCH RECORDS UP TO 29TH OCTOBER 2010

Cap matches involving senior executive council member unions only. Years for International Championship matches are for the second half of the season: eg 1972 means season 1971-72. Years for matches against touring teams from the Southern Hemisphere refer to the actual year of the match.
Points-scoring was first introduced in 1886, when an International Board was formed by Scotland, Ireland and Wales. Points values varied among the countries until 1890, when England agreed to join the Board, and uniform values were adopted.

Northern Hemisphere seasons	Try	Conversion	Penalty Goal	Dropped goal	Goal from mark
1890–91	1	2	2	3	3
1891–92 to 1892–93	2	3	3	4	4
1893–94 to 1904–05	3	2	3	4	4
1905–06 to 1947–48	3	2	3	4	3
1948–49 to 1970–71	3	2	3	3	3
1971–72 to 1991–92	4	2	3	3	3*
1992–93 onwards	5	2	3	3	–

**The goal from mark ceased to exist when the free-kick clause was introduced, 1977-78.*

WC indicates a fixture played during the Rugby World Cup finals. LC indicates a fixture played in the Latin Cup. TN indicates a fixture played in the Tri Nations.

ENGLAND V SCOTLAND

Played 127 England won 67, Scotland won 42, Drawn 18
Highest scores England 43-3 in 2001 and 43-22 in 2005, Scotland 33-6 in 1986
Biggest wins England 43-3 in 2001, Scotland 33-6 in 1986

1871 Raeburn Place (Edinburgh) **Scotland** 1G 1T to 1T
1872 The Oval (London) **England** 1G 1DG 2T to 1DG
1873 Glasgow **Drawn** no score
1874 The Oval **England** 1DG to 1T
1875 Raeburn Place **Drawn** no score
1876 The Oval **England** 1G 1T to 0
1877 Raeburn Place **Scotland** 1 DG to 0
1878 The Oval **Drawn** no score
1879 Raeburn Place **Drawn** Scotland 1DG England 1G
1880 Manchester **England** 2G 3T to 1G
1881 Raeburn Place **Drawn** Scotland 1G 1T England 1DG 1T
1882 Manchester **Scotland** 2T to 0
1883 Raeburn Place **England** 2T to 1T
1884 Blackheath (London) **England** 1G to 1T
1885 No Match
1886 Raeburn Place **Drawn** no score
1887 Manchester **Drawn** 1T each
1888 No Match
1889 No Match
1890 Raeburn Place **England** 1G 1T to 0
1891 Richmond (London) **Scotland** 9-3
1892 Raeburn Place **England** 5-0
1893 Leeds **Scotland** 8-0
1894 Raeburn Place **Scotland** 6-0
1895 Richmond **Scotland** 6-3
1896 Glasgow **Scotland** 11-0
1897 Manchester **England** 12-3
1898 Powderhall (Edinburgh) **Drawn** 3-3
1899 Blackheath **Scotland** 5-0
1900 Inverleith (Edinburgh) **Drawn** 0-0
1901 Blackheath **Scotland** 18-3
1902 Inverleith **England** 6-3
1903 Richmond **Scotland** 10-6
1904 Inverleith **Scotland** 6-3
1905 Richmond **Scotland** 8-0
1906 Inverleith **England** 9-3
1907 Blackheath **Scotland** 8-3
1908 Inverleith **Scotland** 16-10
1909 Richmond **Scotland** 18-8
1910 Inverleith **England** 14-5
1911 Twickenham **England** 13-8
1912 Inverleith **Scotland** 8-3
1913 Twickenham **England** 3-0
1914 Inverleith **England** 16-15
1920 Twickenham **England** 13-4
1921 Inverleith **England** 18-0
1922 Twickenham **England** 11-5
1923 Inverleith **England** 8-6
1924 Twickenham **England** 19-0
1925 Murrayfield **Scotland** 14-11
1926 Twickenham **Scotland** 17-9
1927 Murrayfield **Scotland** 21-13
1928 Twickenham **England** 6-0
1929 Murrayfield **Scotland** 12-6
1930 Twickenham **Drawn** 0-0
1931 Murrayfield **Scotland** 28-19
1932 Twickenham **England** 16-3
1933 Murrayfield **Scotland** 3-0
1934 Twickenham **England** 6-3
1935 Murrayfield **Scotland** 10-7
1936 Twickenham **England** 9-8
1937 Murrayfield **England** 6-3
1938 Twickenham **Scotland** 21-16
1939 Murrayfield **England** 9-6
1947 Twickenham **England** 24-5
1948 Murrayfield **Scotland** 6-3
1949 Twickenham **England** 19-3
1950 Murrayfield **Scotland** 13-11
1951 Twickenham **England** 5-3
1952 Murrayfield **England** 19-3
1953 Twickenham **England** 26-8
1954 Murrayfield **England** 13-3
1955 Twickenham **England** 9-6
1956 Murrayfield **England** 11-6
1957 Twickenham **England** 16-3
1958 Murrayfield **Drawn** 3-3
1959 Twickenham **Drawn** 3-3
1960 Murrayfield **England** 21-12
1961 Twickenham **England** 6-0
1962 Murrayfield **Drawn** 3-3
1963 Twickenham **England** 10-8

1964 Murrayfield **Scotland** 15-6
1965 Twickenham **Drawn** 3-3
1966 Murrayfield **Scotland** 6-3
1967 Twickenham **England** 27-14
1968 Murrayfield **England** 8-6
1969 Twickenham **England** 8-3
1970 Murrayfield **Scotland** 14-5
1971 Twickenham **Scotland** 16-15
1971 Murrayfield **Scotland** 26-6
Special centenary match – non-championship
1972 Murrayfield **Scotland** 23-9
1973 Twickenham **England** 20-13
1974 Murrayfield **Scotland** 16-14
1975 Twickenham **England** 7-6
1976 Murrayfield **Scotland** 22-12
1977 Twickenham **England** 26-6
1978 Murrayfield **England** 15-0
1979 Twickenham **Drawn** 7-7
1980 Murrayfield **England** 30-18
1981 Twickenham **England** 23-17
1982 Murrayfield **Drawn** 9-9
1983 Twickenham **Scotland** 22-12
1984 Murrayfield **Scotland** 18-6
1985 Twickenham **England** 10-7
1986 Murrayfield **Scotland** 33-6
1987 Twickenham **England** 21-12
1988 Murrayfield **England** 9-6
1989 Twickenham **Drawn** 12-12
1990 Murrayfield **Scotland** 13-7
1991 Twickenham **England** 21-12
1991 Murrayfield WC **England** 9-6
1992 Murrayfield **England** 25-7
1993 Twickenham **England** 26-12
1994 Murrayfield **England** 15-14
1995 Twickenham **England** 24-12
1996 Murrayfield **England** 18-9
1997 Twickenham **England** 41-13
1998 Murrayfield **England** 34-20
1999 Twickenham **England** 24-21
2000 Murrayfield **Scotland** 19-13
2001 Twickenham **England** 43-3
2002 Murrayfield **England** 29-3
2003 Twickenham **England** 40-9
2004 Murrayfield **England** 35-13
2005 Twickenham **England** 43-22
2006 Murrayfield **Scotland** 18-12
2007 Twickenham **England** 42-20
2008 Murrayfield **Scotland** 15-9
2009 Twickenham **England** 26-12
2010 Murrayfield **Drawn** 15-15

ENGLAND v IRELAND

Played 123 England won 70, Ireland won 45, Drawn 8
Highest scores England 50-18 in 2000, Ireland 43-13 in 2007
Biggest wins England 46-6 in 1997, Ireland 43-13 in 2007

1875 The Oval (London) **England** 1G 1DG 1T to 0
1876 Dublin **England** 1G 1T to 0
1877 The Oval **England** 2G 2T to 0
1878 Dublin **England** 2G 1T to 0
1879 The Oval **England** 2G 1DG 2T to 0
1880 Dublin **England** 1G 1T to 1T
1881 Manchester **England** 2G 2T to 0
1882 Dublin **Drawn** 2T each
1883 Manchester **England** 1G 3T to 1T
1884 Dublin **England** 1G to 0
1885 Manchester **England** 2T to 1T
1886 Dublin **England** 1T to 0
1887 Dublin **Ireland** 2G to 0
1888 No Match
1889 No Match
1890 Blackheath (London) **England** 3T to 0
1891 Dublin **England** 9-0
1892 Manchester **England** 7-0
1893 Dublin **England** 4-0
1894 Blackheath **Ireland** 7-5
1895 Dublin **England** 6-3
1896 Leeds **Ireland** 10-4
1897 Dublin **Ireland** 13-9
1898 Richmond (London) **Ireland** 9-6
1899 Dublin **Ireland** 6-0
1900 Richmond **England** 15-4
1901 Dublin **Ireland** 10-6
1902 Leicester **England** 6-3
1903 Dublin **Ireland** 6-0

1904 Blackheath **England** 19-0
1905 Cork **Ireland** 17-3
1906 Leicester **Ireland** 16-6
1907 Dublin **Ireland** 17-9
1908 Richmond **England** 13-3
1909 Dublin **England** 11-5
1910 Twickenham **Drawn** 0-0
1911 Dublin **Ireland** 3-0
1912 Twickenham **England** 15-0
1913 Dublin **England** 15-4
1914 Twickenham **England** 17-12
1920 Dublin **England** 14-11
1921 Twickenham **England** 15-0
1922 Dublin **England** 12-3
1923 Leicester **England** 23-5
1924 Belfast **England** 14-3
1925 Twickenham **Drawn** 6-6
1926 Dublin **Ireland** 19-15
1927 Twickenham **England** 8-6
1928 Dublin **England** 7-6
1929 Twickenham **Ireland** 6-5
1930 Dublin **Ireland** 4-3
1931 Twickenham **Ireland** 6-5
1932 Dublin **England** 11-8
1933 Twickenham **England** 17-6
1934 Dublin **England** 13-3
1935 Twickenham **England** 14-3
1936 Dublin **Ireland** 6-3
1937 Twickenham **England** 9-8
1938 Dublin **England** 36-14
1939 Twickenham **Ireland** 5-0
1947 Dublin **Ireland** 22-0
1948 Twickenham **Ireland** 11-10
1949 Dublin **Ireland** 14-5
1950 Twickenham **England** 3-0
1951 Dublin **Ireland** 3-0
1952 Twickenham **England** 3-0
1953 Dublin **Drawn** 9-9
1954 Twickenham **England** 14-3
1955 Dublin **Drawn** 6-6
1956 Twickenham **England** 20-0
1957 Dublin **England** 6-0
1958 Twickenham **England** 6-0
1959 Dublin **England** 3-0
1960 Twickenham **England** 8-5
1961 Dublin **Ireland** 11-8
1962 Twickenham **England** 16-0
1963 Dublin **Drawn** 0-0
1964 Twickenham **Ireland** 18-5
1965 Dublin **Ireland** 5-0
1966 Twickenham **Drawn** 6-6
1967 Dublin **England** 8-3
1968 Twickenham **Drawn** 9-9
1969 Dublin **Ireland** 17-15
1970 Twickenham **England** 9-3
1971 Dublin **England** 9-6
1972 Twickenham **Ireland** 16-12
1973 Dublin **Ireland** 18-9
1974 Twickenham **Ireland** 26-21
1975 Dublin **Ireland** 12-9
1976 Twickenham **Ireland** 13-12
1977 Dublin **England** 4-0
1978 Twickenham **England** 15-9
1979 Dublin **Ireland** 12-7
1980 Twickenham **England** 24-9
1981 Dublin **England** 10-6
1982 Twickenham **Ireland** 16-15
1983 Dublin **Ireland** 25-15
1984 Twickenham **England** 12-9
1985 Dublin **Ireland** 13-10
1986 Twickenham **England** 25-20
1987 Dublin **Ireland** 17-0
1988 Twickenham **England** 35-3
1988 Dublin **England** 21-10
Non-championship match
1989 Dublin **England** 16-3
1990 Twickenham **England** 23-0
1991 Dublin **England** 16-7
1992 Twickenham **England** 38-9
1993 Dublin **Ireland** 17-3
1994 Twickenham **Ireland** 13-12
1995 Dublin **England** 20-8
1996 Twickenham **England** 28-15
1997 Dublin **England** 46-6
1998 Twickenham **England** 35-17
1999 Dublin **England** 27-15
2000 Twickenham **England** 50-18
2001 Dublin **Ireland** 20-14
2002 Twickenham **England** 45-11
2003 Dublin **England** 42-6
2004 Twickenham **Ireland** 19-13
2005 Dublin **Ireland** 19-13
2006 Twickenham **Ireland** 28-24
2007 Dublin **Ireland** 43-13
2008 Twickenham **England** 33-10
2009 Dublin **Ireland** 14-13
2010 Twickenham **Ireland** 20-16

ENGLAND v WALES

Played 119 England won 54 Wales won 53, Drawn 12
Highest scores England 62-5 in 2007, Wales 34-21 in 1967
Biggest wins England 62-5 in 2007, Wales 25-0 in 1905

1881 Blackheath (London) **England** 7G 1DG 6T to 0
1882 No Match
1883 Swansea **England** 2G 4T to 0
1884 Leeds **England** 1G 2T to 1G
1885 Swansea **England** 1G 4T to 1G 1T
1886 Blackheath **England** 1GM 2T to 1G
1887 Llanelli **Drawn** no score
1888 No Match
1889 No Match
1890 Dewsbury **Wales** 1T to 0
1891 Newport **England** 7-3
1892 Blackheath **England** 17-0
1893 Cardiff **Wales** 12-11
1894 Birkenhead **England** 24-3
1895 Swansea **England** 14-6
1896 Blackheath **England** 25-0
1897 Newport **Wales** 11-0
1898 Blackheath **England** 14-7
1899 Swansea **Wales** 26-3
1900 Gloucester **Wales** 13-3
1901 Cardiff **Wales** 13-0
1902 Blackheath **Wales** 9-8
1903 Swansea **Wales** 21-5
1904 Leicester **Drawn** 14-14
1905 Cardiff **Wales** 25-0
1906 Richmond (London) **Wales** 16-3
1907 Swansea **Wales** 22-0
1908 Bristol **Wales** 28-18
1909 Cardiff **Wales** 8-0
1910 Twickenham **England** 11-6
1911 Swansea **Wales** 15-11
1912 Twickenham **England** 8-0
1913 Cardiff **England** 12-0
1914 Twickenham **England** 10-9
1920 Swansea **Wales** 19-5
1921 Twickenham **England** 18-3
1922 Cardiff **Wales** 28-6
1923 Twickenham **England** 7-3
1924 Swansea **England** 17-9
1925 Twickenham **England** 12-6
1926 Cardiff **Drawn** 3-3
1927 Twickenham **England** 11-9
1928 Swansea **England** 10-8
1929 Twickenham **England** 8-3
1930 Cardiff **England** 11-3
1931 Twickenham **Drawn** 11-11
1932 Swansea **Wales** 12-5
1933 Twickenham **Wales** 7-3
1934 Cardiff **England** 9-0
1935 Twickenham **Drawn** 3-3
1936 Swansea **Drawn** 0-0
1937 Twickenham **England** 4-3
1938 Cardiff **Wales** 14-8
1939 Twickenham **England** 3-0
1947 Cardiff **England** 9-6
1948 Twickenham **Drawn** 3-3
1949 Cardiff **Wales** 9-3
1950 Twickenham **Wales** 11-5
1951 Swansea **Wales** 23-5
1952 Twickenham **Wales** 8-6
1953 Cardiff **England** 8-3
1954 Twickenham **England** 9-6
1955 Cardiff **Wales** 3-0
1956 Twickenham **Wales** 8-3
1957 Cardiff **England** 3-0
1958 Twickenham **Drawn** 3-3
1959 Cardiff **Wales** 5-0
1960 Twickenham **England** 14-6
1961 Cardiff **Wales** 6-3
1962 Twickenham **Drawn** 0-0
1963 Cardiff **England** 13-6
1964 Twickenham **Drawn** 6-6
1965 Cardiff **Wales** 14-3
1966 Twickenham **Wales** 11-6
1967 Cardiff **Wales** 34-21
1968 Twickenham **Drawn** 11-11
1969 Cardiff **Wales** 30-9
1970 Twickenham **Wales** 17-13
1971 Cardiff **Wales** 22-6
1972 Twickenham **Wales** 12-3
1973 Cardiff **Wales** 25-9
1974 Twickenham **England** 16-12
1975 Cardiff **Wales** 20-4
1976 Twickenham **Wales** 21-9
1977 Cardiff **Wales** 14-9

1978 Twickenham **Wales** 9-6
1979 Cardiff **Wales** 27-3
1980 Twickenham **England** 9-8
1981 Cardiff **Wales** 21-19
1982 Twickenham **England** 17-7
1983 Cardiff **Drawn** 13-13
1984 Twickenham **Wales** 24-15
1985 Cardiff **Wales** 24-15
1986 Twickenham **England** 21-18
1987 Cardiff **Wales** 19-12
1987 Brisbane WC **Wales** 16-3
1988 Twickenham **Wales** 11-3
1989 Cardiff **Wales** 12-9
1990 Twickenham **England** 34-6
1991 Cardiff **England** 25-6
1992 Twickenham **England** 24-0
1993 Cardiff **Wales** 10-9
1994 Twickenham **England** 15-8
1995 Cardiff **England** 23-9
1996 Twickenham **England** 21-15
1997 Cardiff **England** 34-13
1998 Twickenham **England** 60-26
1999 Wembley **Wales** 32-31
2000 Twickenham **England** 46-12
2001 Cardiff **England** 44-15
2002 Twickenham **England** 50-10
2003 Cardiff **England** 26-9
2003 Cardiff **England** 43-9
Non-championship match
2003 Brisbane WC **England** 28-17
2004 Twickenham **England** 31-21
2005 Cardiff **Wales** 11-9
2006 Twickenham **England** 47-13
2007 Cardiff **Wales** 27-18
2007 Twickenham **England** 62-5
Non-championship match
2008 Twickenham **Wales** 26-19
2009 Cardiff **Wales** 23-15
2010 Twickenham **England** 30-17

ENGLAND v FRANCE

Played 93 England won 50, France won 36, Drawn 7
Highest scores England 48-19 in 2001, France 37-12 in 1972
Biggest wins England 37-0 in 1911, France 37-12 in 1972 and 31-6 in 2006

1906 Paris **England** 35-8
1907 Richmond (London) **England** 41-13
1908 Paris **England** 19-0
1909 Leicester **England** 22-0
1910 Paris **England** 11-3
1911 Twickenham **England** 37-0
1912 Paris **England** 18-8
1913 Twickenham **England** 20-0
1914 Paris **England** 39-13
1920 Twickenham **England** 8-3
1921 Paris **England** 10-6
1922 Twickenham **Drawn** 11-11
1923 Paris **England** 12-3
1924 Twickenham **England** 19-7
1925 Paris **England** 13-11
1926 Twickenham **England** 11-0
1927 Paris **France** 3-0
1928 Twickenham **England** 18-8
1929 Paris **England** 16-6
1930 Twickenham **England** 11-5
1931 Paris **France** 14-13
1947 Twickenham **England** 6-3
1948 Paris **France** 15-0
1949 Twickenham **England** 8-3
1950 Paris **France** 6-3
1951 Twickenham **France** 11-3
1952 Paris **England** 6-3
1953 Twickenham **England** 11-0
1954 Paris **France** 11-3
1955 Twickenham **France** 16-9
1956 Paris **France** 14-9
1957 Twickenham **England** 9-5
1958 Paris **England** 14-0
1959 Twickenham **Drawn** 3-3
1960 Paris **Drawn** 3-3
1961 Twickenham **Drawn** 5-5
1962 Paris **France** 13-0
1963 Twickenham **England** 6-5
1964 Paris **England** 6-3
1965 Twickenham **England** 9-6
1966 Paris **France** 13-0
1967 Twickenham **France** 16-12
1968 Paris **France** 14-9
1969 Twickenham **England** 22-8
1970 Paris **France** 35-13
1971 Twickenham **Drawn** 14-14
1972 Paris **France** 37-12
1973 Twickenham **England** 14-6

1974 Paris **Drawn** 12-12
1975 Twickenham **France** 27-20
1976 Paris **France** 30-9
1977 Twickenham **France** 4-3
1978 Paris **France** 15-6
1979 Twickenham **England** 7-6
1980 Paris **England** 17-13
1981 Twickenham **France** 16-12
1982 Paris **England** 27-15
1983 Twickenham **France** 19-15
1984 Paris **France** 32-18
1985 Twickenham **Drawn** 9-9
1986 Paris **France** 29-10
1987 Twickenham **France** 19-15
1988 Paris **France** 10-9
1989 Twickenham **England** 11-0
1990 Paris **England** 26-7
1991 Twickenham **England** 21-19
1991 Paris WC **England** 19-10
1992 Paris **England** 31-13
1993 Twickenham **England** 16-15
1994 Paris **England** 18-14
1995 Twickenham **England** 31-10
1995 Pretoria WC **France 19-9**
1996 Paris **France** 15-12
1997 Twickenham **France** 23-20
1998 Paris **France** 24-17
1999 Twickenham **England** 21-10
2000 Paris **England** 15-9
2001 Twickenham **England** 48-19
2002 Paris **France** 20-15
2003 Twickenham **England** 25-17
2003 Marseilles **France** 17-16
Non-championship match
2003 Twickenham **England** 45-14
Non-championship match
2003 Sydney WC **England** 24-7
2004 Paris **France** 24-21
2005 Twickenham **France** 18-17
2006 Paris **France** 31-6
2007 Twickenham **England** 26-18
2007 Twickenham **France** 21-15
Non-championship match
2007 Marseilles **France** 22-9
Non-championship match
2007 Paris WC **England** 14-9
2008 Paris **England** 24-13
2009 Twickenham **England** 34-10
2010 Paris **France** 12-10

ENGLAND v SOUTH AFRICA

Played 31 England won 12, South Africa won 18, Drawn 1
Highest scores England 53-3 in 2002, South Africa 58-10 in 2007
Biggest wins England 53-3 in 2002, South Africa 58-10 in 2007

1906 Crystal Palace (London) **Drawn** 3-3
1913 Twickenham **South Africa** 9-3
1932 Twickenham **South Africa** 7-0
1952 Twickenham **South Africa** 8-3
1961 Twickenham **South Africa** 5-0
1969 Twickenham **England** 11-8
1972 Johannesburg **England** 18-9
1984 *1* Port Elizabeth **South Africa** 33-15
2 Johannesburg **South Africa** 35-9
South Africa won series 2-0
1992 Twickenham **England** 33-16
1994 *1* Pretoria **England** 32-15
2 Cape Town **South Africa** 27-9
Series drawn 1-1
1995 Twickenham **South Africa** 24-14
1997 Twickenham **South Africa** 29-11
1998 Cape Town **South Africa** 18-0
1998 Twickenham **England** 13-7
1999 Paris WC **South Africa** 44-21
2000 *1* Pretoria **South Africa** 18-13
2 Bloemfontein **England** 27-22
Series drawn 1-1
2000 Twickenham **England** 25-17
2001 Twickenham **England** 29-9
2002 Twickenham **England** 53-3
2003 Perth WC **England** 25-6
2004 Twickenham **England** 32-16
2006 1 Twickenham **England** 23-21
2 Twickenham **South Africa** 25-14
Series drawn 1-1
2007 1 Bloemfontein **South Africa** 58-10
2 Pretoria **South Africa** 55-22
South Africa won series 2-0
2007 Paris WC **South Africa** 36-0
2007 Paris WC **South Africa** 15-6
2008 Twickenham **South Africa** 42-6

ENGLAND v NEW ZEALAND

Played 33 England won 6, New Zealand won 26, Drawn 1
Highest scores England 31-28 in 2002, New Zealand 64-22 in 1998
Biggest wins England 13-0 in 1936, New Zealand 64-22 in 1998

1905	Crystal Palace (London) **New Zealand** 15-0
1925	Twickenham **New Zealand** 17-11
1936	Twickenham **England** 13-0
1954	Twickenham **New Zealand** 5-0
1963	*1* Auckland **New Zealand** 21-11
	2 Christchurch **New Zealand** 9-6
	New Zealand won series 2-0
1964	Twickenham **New Zealand** 14-0
1967	Twickenham **New Zealand** 23-11
1973	Twickenham **New Zealand** 9-0
1973	Auckland **England** 16-10
1978	Twickenham **New Zealand** 16-6
1979	Twickenham **New Zealand** 10-9
1983	Twickenham **England** 15-9
1985	*1* Christchurch **New Zealand** 18-13
	2 Wellington **New Zealand** 42-15
	New Zealand won series 2-0
1991	Twickenham WC **New Zealand** 18-12
1993	Twickenham **England** 15-9
1995	Cape Town WC **New Zealand 45-29**
1997	*1* Manchester **New Zealand** 25-8
	2 Twickenham **Drawn** 26-26
	New Zealand won series 1-0, with 1 draw
1998	*1* Dunedin **New Zealand** 64-22
	2 Auckland **New Zealand** 40-10
	New Zealand won series 2-0
1999	Twickenham WC **New Zealand** 30-16
2002	Twickenham **England** 31-28
2003	Wellington **England** 15-13
2004	*1* Dunedin **New Zealand** 36-3
	2 Auckland **New Zealand** 36-12
	New Zealand won series 2-0
2005	Twickenham **New Zealand** 23-19
2006	Twickenham **New Zealand** 41-20
2008	*1* Auckland **New Zealand** 37-20
	2 Christchurch **New Zealand** 44-12
	New Zealand won series 2-0
2008	Twickenham **New Zealand** 32-6
2009	Twickenham **New Zealand** 19-6

ENGLAND v AUSTRALIA

Played 39 England won 15, Australia won 23, Drawn 1
Highest scores England 32-31 in 2002, Australia 76-0 in 1998
Biggest wins England 20-3 in 1973 & 23-6 in 1976, Australia 76-0 in 1998

1909	Blackheath (London) **Australia** 9-3
1928	Twickenham **England** 18-11
1948	Twickenham **Australia** 11-0
1958	Twickenham **England** 9-6
1963	Sydney **Australia** 18-9
1967	Twickenham **Australia** 23-11
1973	Twickenham **England** 20-3
1975	*1* Sydney **Australia** 16-9
	2 Brisbane **Australia** 30-21
	Australia won series 2-0
1976	Twickenham **England** 23-6
1982	Twickenham **England** 15-11
1984	Twickenham **Australia** 19-3
1987	Sydney WC **Australia** 19-6
1988	*1* Brisbane **Australia** 22-16
	2 Sydney **Australia** 28-8
	Australia won series 2-0
1988	Twickenham **England** 28-19
1991	Sydney **Australia** 40-15
1991	Twickenham WC **Australia** 12-6
1995	Cape Town WC **England** 25-22
1997	Sydney **Australia** 25-6
1997	Twickenham **Drawn** 15-15
1998	Brisbane **Australia** 76-0
1998	Twickenham **Australia** 12-11
1999	Sydney **Australia** 22-15
2000	Twickenham **England** 22-19
2001	Twickenham **England** 21-15
2002	Twickenham **England** 32-31
2003	Melbourne **England** 25-14
2003	Sydney WC **England** 20-17 (aet)
2004	Brisbane **Australia** 51-15

2004 Twickenham **Australia** 21-19	2008 Twickenham **Australia** 28-14
2005 Twickenham **England** 26-16	2009 Twickenham **Australia** 18-9
2006 1 Sydney **Australia** 34-3	2010 1 Perth **Australia** 27-17
2 Melbourne **Australia** 43-18	2 Sydney **England** 21-20
Australia won series 2-0	Series drawn 1-1
2007 Marseilles WC **England** 12-10	

ENGLAND v NEW ZEALAND NATIVES

Played 1 England won 1
Highest score England 7-0 in 1889, NZ Natives 0-7 in 1889
Biggest win England 7-0 in 1889, NZ Natives no win

1889 Blackheath **England** 1G 4T to 0

ENGLAND v RFU PRESIDENT'S XV

Played 1 President's XV won 1
Highest score England 11-28 in 1971, RFU President's XV 28-11 in 1971
Biggest win RFU President's XV 28-11 in 1971

1971 Twickenham **President's XV** 28-11

ENGLAND v ARGENTINA

Played 15 England won 10, Argentina won 4, Drawn 1
Highest scores England 51-0 in 1990, Argentina 33-13 in 1997
Biggest wins England 51-0 in 1990, Argentina 33-13 in 1997

1981 *1* Buenos Aires **Drawn** 19-19
2 Buenos Aires **England** 12-6
England won series 1-0 with 1 draw
1990 *1* Buenos Aires **England** 25-12
2 Buenos Aires **Argentina** 15-13
Series drawn 1-1
1990 Twickenham **England** 51-0
1995 Durban WC **England** 24-18
1996 Twickenham **England** 20-18
1997 *1* Buenos Aires **England** 46-20
2 Buenos Aires **Argentina** 33-13
Series drawn 1-1
2000 Twickenham **England** 19-0
2002 Buenos Aires **England** 26-18
2006 Twickenham **Argentina** 25-18
2009 1 Manchester **England** 37-15
2 Salta **Argentina** 24-22
Series drawn 1-1
2009 Twickenham **England** 16-9

ENGLAND v ROMANIA

Played 4 England won 4
Highest scores England 134-0 in 2001, Romania 15-22 in 1985
Biggest win England 134-0 in 2001, Romania no win

1985	Twickenham **England** 22-15	1994	Twickenham **England** 54-3
1989	Bucharest **England** 58-3	2001	Twickenham **England** 134-0

ENGLAND v JAPAN

Played 1 England won 1
Highest score England 60-7 in 1987, Japan 7-60 in 1987
Biggest win England 60-7 in 1987, Japan no win

1987	Sydney WC **England** 60-7

ENGLAND v UNITED STATES

Played 5 England won 5
Highest scores England 106-8 in 1999, United States 19-48 in 2001
Biggest win England 106-8 in 1999, United States no win

1987	Sydney WC **England** 34-6	2001	San Francisco **England** 48-19
1991	Twickenham WC **England** 37-9	2007	Lens WC **England** 28-10
1999	Twickenham **England** 106-8		

ENGLAND v FIJI

Played 4 England won 4
Highest scores England 58-23 in 1989, Fiji 24-45 in 1999
Biggest win England 58-23 in 1989, Fiji no win

1988	Suva **England** 25-12	1991	Suva **England** 28-12
1989	Twickenham **England** 58-23	1999	Twickenham WC **England** 45-24

ENGLAND v ITALY

Played 16 England won 16
Highest scores England 80-23 in 2001, Italy 23-80 in 2001
Biggest win England 67-7 in 1999, Italy no win

1991 Twickenham WC **England** 36-6
1995 Durban WC **England 27-20**
1996 Twickenham **England** 54-21
1998 Huddersfield **England** 23-15
1999 Twickenham WC **England** 67-7
2000 Rome **England** 59-12
2001 Twickenham **England** 80-23
2002 Rome **England** 45-9
2003 Twickenham **England** 40-5
2004 Rome **England** 50-9
2005 Twickenham **England** 39-7
2006 Rome **England** 31-16
2007 Twickenham **England** 20-7
2008 Rome **England** 23-19
2009 Twickenham **England** 36-11
2010 Rome **England** 17-12

ENGLAND v CANADA

Played 6 England won 6
Highest scores England 70-0 in 2004, Canada 20-59 in 2001
Biggest win England 70-0 in 2004, Canada no win

1992 Wembley **England** 26-13
1994 Twickenham **England** 60-19
1999 Twickenham **England** 36-11
2001 *1* Markham **England** 22-10
2 Burnaby **England** 59-20
England won series 2-0
2004 Twickenham **England** 70-0

ENGLAND v SAMOA

Played 5 England won 5
Highest scores England 44-22 in 1995 and 44-22 in 2007, Samoa 22-44 in 1995, 22-35 in 2003 and 22-44 in 2007
Biggest win England 40-3 in 2005, Samoa no win

1995 Durban WC **England** 44-22
1995 Twickenham **England** 27-9
2003 Melbourne WC **England** 35-22
2005 Twickenham **England** 40-3
2007 Nantes WC **England** 44-22

ENGLAND v THE NETHERLANDS

Played 1 England won 1
Highest scores England 110-0 in 1998, The Netherlands 0-110 in 1998
Biggest win England 110-0 in 1998, The Netherlands no win

1998 Huddersfield **England** 110-0

ENGLAND v TONGA

Played 2 England won 2
Highest scores England 101-10 in 1999, Tonga 20-36 in 2007
Biggest win England 101-10 in 1999, Tonga no win

1999 Twickenham WC **England** 101-10
2007 Paris WC **England** 36-20

ENGLAND v GEORGIA

Played 1 England won 1
Highest scores England 84-6 in 2003, Georgia 6-84 in 2003
Biggest win England 84-6 in 2003, Georgia no win

2003 Perth WC **England** 84-6

ENGLAND v URUGUAY

Played 1 England won 1
Highest scores England 111-13 in 2003, Uruguay 13-111 in 2003
Biggest win England 111-13 in 2003, Uruguay no win

2003 Brisbane WC **England** 111-13

ENGLAND v PACIFIC ISLANDS

Played 1 England won 1
Highest scores England 39-13 in 2008, Pacific Islands 13-39 in 2008
Biggest win England 39-13 in 2008, Pacific Islands no win

2008 Twickenham **England** 39-13

SCOTLAND v IRELAND

Played 124 Scotland won 63, Ireland won 55, Drawn 5, Abandoned 1
Highest scores Scotland 38-10 in 1997, Ireland 44-22 in 2000
Biggest wins Scotland 38-10 in 1997, Ireland 36-6 in 2003

1877 Belfast **Scotland** 4G 2DG 2T to 0
1878 No Match
1879 Belfast **Scotland** 1G 1DG 1T to 0
1880 Glasgow **Scotland** 1G 2DG 2T to 0
1881 Belfast **Ireland** 1DG to 1T
1882 Glasgow **Scotland** 2T to 0
1883 Belfast **Scotland** 1G 1T to 0
1884 Raeburn Place (Edinburgh) **Scotland** 2G 2T to 1T
1885 Belfast **Abandoned** Ireland 0 Scotland 1T
1885 Raeburn Place **Scotland** 1G 2T to 0
1886 Raeburn Place **Scotland** 3G 1DG 2T to 0
1887 Belfast **Scotland** 1G 1GM 2T to 0
1888 Raeburn Place **Scotland** 1G to 0
1889 Belfast **Scotland** 1DG to 0
1890 Raeburn Place **Scotland** 1DG 1T to 0
1891 Belfast **Scotland** 14-0
1892 Raeburn Place **Scotland** 2-0
1893 Belfast **Drawn** 0-0
1894 Dublin **Ireland** 5-0

1895 Raeburn Place **Scotland** 6-0
1896 Dublin **Drawn** 0-0
1897 Powderhall (Edinburgh) **Scotland** 8-3
1898 Belfast **Scotland** 8-0
1899 Inverleith (Edinburgh) **Ireland** 9-3
1900 Dublin **Drawn** 0-0
1901 Inverleith **Scotland** 9-5
1902 Belfast **Ireland** 5-0
1903 Inverleith **Scotland** 3-0
1904 Dublin **Scotland** 19-3
1905 Inverleith **Ireland** 11-5
1906 Dublin **Scotland** 13-6
1907 Inverleith **Scotland** 15-3
1908 Dublin **Ireland** 16-11
1909 Inverleith **Scotland** 9-3
1910 Belfast **Scotland** 14-0
1911 Inverleith **Ireland** 16-10
1912 Dublin **Ireland** 10-8
1913 Inverleith **Scotland** 29-14
1914 Dublin **Ireland** 6-0
1920 Inverleith **Scotland** 19-0
1921 Dublin **Ireland** 9-8
1922 Inverleith **Scotland** 6-3
1923 Dublin **Scotland** 13-3
1924 Inverleith **Scotland** 13-8
1925 Dublin **Scotland** 14-8
1926 Murrayfield **Ireland** 3-0
1927 Dublin **Ireland** 6-0
1928 Murrayfield **Ireland** 13-5
1929 Dublin **Scotland** 16-7
1930 Murrayfield **Ireland** 14-11
1931 Dublin **Ireland** 8-5
1932 Murrayfield **Ireland** 20-8
1933 Dublin **Scotland** 8-6
1934 Murrayfield **Scotland** 16-9
1935 Dublin **Ireland** 12-5
1936 Murrayfield **Ireland** 10-4
1937 Dublin **Ireland** 11-4
1938 Murrayfield **Scotland** 23-14
1939 Dublin **Ireland** 12-3
1947 Murrayfield **Ireland** 3-0
1948 Dublin **Ireland** 6-0
1949 Murrayfield **Ireland** 13-3
1950 Dublin **Ireland** 21-0
1951 Murrayfield **Ireland** 6-5
1952 Dublin **Ireland** 12-8
1953 Murrayfield **Ireland** 26-8
1954 Belfast **Ireland** 6-0
1955 Murrayfield **Scotland** 12-3
1956 Dublin **Ireland** 14-10
1957 Murrayfield **Ireland** 5-3
1958 Dublin **Ireland** 12-6
1959 Murrayfield **Ireland** 8-3
1960 Dublin **Scotland** 6-5
1961 Murrayfield **Scotland** 16-8
1962 Dublin **Scotland** 20-6
1963 Murrayfield **Scotland** 3-0
1964 Dublin **Scotland** 6-3
1965 Murrayfield **Ireland** 16-6
1966 Dublin **Scotland** 11-3
1967 Murrayfield **Ireland** 5-3
1968 Dublin **Ireland** 14-6
1969 Murrayfield **Ireland** 16-0
1970 Dublin **Ireland** 16-11
1971 Murrayfield **Ireland** 17-5
1972 No Match
1973 Murrayfield **Scotland** 19-14
1974 Dublin **Ireland** 9-6
1975 Murrayfield **Scotland** 20-13
1976 Dublin **Scotland** 15-6
1977 Murrayfield **Scotland** 21-18
1978 Dublin **Ireland** 12-9
1979 Murrayfield **Drawn** 11-11
1980 Dublin **Ireland** 22-15
1981 Murrayfield **Scotland** 10-9
1982 Dublin **Ireland** 21-12
1983 Murrayfield **Ireland** 15-13
1984 Dublin **Scotland** 32-9
1985 Murrayfield **Ireland** 18-15
1986 Dublin **Scotland** 10-9
1987 Murrayfield **Scotland** 16-12
1988 Dublin **Ireland** 22-18
1989 Murrayfield **Scotland** 37-21
1990 Dublin **Scotland** 13-10
1991 Murrayfield **Scotland** 28-25
1991 Murrayfield WC **Scotland** 24-15
1992 Dublin **Scotland** 18-10
1993 Murrayfield **Scotland** 15-3
1994 Dublin **Drawn** 6-6
1995 Murrayfield **Scotland** 26-13
1996 Dublin **Scotland** 16-10
1997 Murrayfield **Scotland** 38-10
1998 Dublin **Scotland** 17-16
1999 Murrayfield **Scotland** 30-13
2000 Dublin **Ireland** 44-22
2001 Murrayfield **Scotland** 32-10
2002 Dublin **Ireland** 43-22
2003 Murrayfield **Ireland** 36-6
2003 Murrayfield **Ireland** 29-10
Non-championship match
2004 Dublin **Ireland** 37-16
2005 Murrayfield **Ireland** 40-13
2006 Dublin **Ireland** 15-9
2007 Murrayfield **Ireland** 19-18
2007 Murrayfield **Scotland** 31-21
Non-championship match
2008 Dublin **Ireland** 34-13
2009 Murrayfield **Ireland** 22-15
2010 Dublin **Scotland** 23-20

SCOTLAND v WALES

Played 115 Scotland won 48, Wales won 64, Drawn 3
Highest scores Scotland 35-10 in 1924, Wales 46-22 in 2005
Biggest wins Scotland 35-10 in 1924, Wales 46-22 in 2005

1883 Raeburn Place (Edinburgh) **Scotland** 3G to 1G
1884 Newport **Scotland** 1DG 1T to 0
1885 Glasgow **Drawn** no score
1886 Cardiff **Scotland** 2G 1T to 0
1887 Raeburn Place **Scotland** 4G 8T to 0
1888 Newport **Wales** 1T to 0
1889 Raeburn Place **Scotland** 2T to 0
1890 Cardiff **Scotland** 1G 2T to 1T
1891 Raeburn Place **Scotland** 15-0
1892 Swansea **Scotland** 7-2
1893 Raeburn Place **Wales** 9-0
1894 Newport **Wales** 7-0
1895 Raeburn Place **Scotland** 5-4
1896 Cardiff **Wales** 6-0
1897 No Match
1898 No Match
1899 Inverleith (Edinburgh) **Scotland** 21-10
1900 Swansea **Wales** 12-3
1901 Inverleith **Scotland** 18-8
1902 Cardiff **Wales** 14-5
1903 Inverleith **Scotland** 6-0
1904 Swansea **Wales** 21-3
1905 Inverleith **Wales** 6-3
1906 Cardiff **Wales** 9-3
1907 Inverleith **Scotland** 6-3
1908 Swansea **Wales** 6-5
1909 Inverleith **Wales** 5-3
1910 Cardiff **Wales** 14-0
1911 Inverleith **Wales** 32-10
1912 Swansea **Wales** 21-6
1913 Inverleith **Wales** 8-0
1914 Cardiff **Wales** 24-5
1920 Inverleith **Scotland** 9-5
1921 Swansea **Scotland** 14-8
1922 Inverleith **Drawn** 9-9
1923 Cardiff **Scotland** 11-8
1924 Inverleith **Scotland** 35-10
1925 Swansea **Scotland** 24-14
1926 Murrayfield **Scotland** 8-5
1927 Cardiff **Scotland** 5-0
1928 Murrayfield **Wales** 13-0
1929 Swansea **Wales** 14-7
1930 Murrayfield **Scotland** 12-9
1931 Cardiff **Wales** 13-8
1932 Murrayfield **Wales** 6-0
1933 Swansea **Scotland** 11-3
1934 Murrayfield **Wales** 13-6
1935 Cardiff **Wales** 10-6
1936 Murrayfield **Wales** 13-3
1937 Swansea **Scotland** 13-6
1938 Murrayfield **Scotland** 8-6
1939 Cardiff **Wales** 11-3
1947 Murrayfield **Wales** 22-8
1948 Cardiff **Wales** 14-0
1949 Murrayfield **Scotland** 6-5
1950 Swansea **Wales** 12-0
1951 Murrayfield **Scotland** 19-0
1952 Cardiff **Wales** 11-0
1953 Murrayfield **Wales** 12-0
1954 Swansea **Wales** 15-3
1955 Murrayfield **Scotland** 14-8
1956 Cardiff **Wales** 9-3
1957 Murrayfield **Scotland** 9-6
1958 Cardiff **Wales** 8-3
1959 Murrayfield **Scotland** 6-5
1960 Cardiff **Wales** 8-0
1961 Murrayfield **Scotland** 3-0
1962 Cardiff **Scotland** 8-3
1963 Murrayfield **Wales** 6-0
1964 Cardiff **Wales** 11-3
1965 Murrayfield **Wales** 14-12
1966 Cardiff **Wales** 8-3
1967 Murrayfield **Scotland** 11-5
1968 Cardiff **Wales** 5-0
1969 Murrayfield **Wales** 17-3
1970 Cardiff **Wales** 18-9
1971 Murrayfield **Wales** 19-18
1972 Cardiff **Wales** 35-12
1973 Murrayfield **Scotland** 10-9
1974 Cardiff **Wales** 6-0
1975 Murrayfield **Scotland** 12-10
1976 Cardiff **Wales** 28-6
1977 Murrayfield **Wales** 18-9
1978 Cardiff **Wales** 22-14
1979 Murrayfield **Wales** 19-13

1980 Cardiff **Wales** 17-6
1981 Murrayfield **Scotland** 15-6
1982 Cardiff **Scotland** 34-18
1983 Murrayfield **Wales** 19-15
1984 Cardiff **Scotland** 15-9
1985 Murrayfield **Wales** 25-21
1986 Cardiff **Wales** 22-15
1987 Murrayfield **Scotland** 21-15
1988 Cardiff **Wales** 25-20
1989 Murrayfield **Scotland** 23-7
1990 Cardiff **Scotland** 13-9
1991 Murrayfield **Scotland** 32-12
1992 Cardiff **Wales** 15-12
1993 Murrayfield **Scotland** 20-0
1994 Cardiff **Wales** 29-6
1995 Murrayfield **Scotland** 26-13
1996 Cardiff **Scotland** 16-14
1997 Murrayfield **Wales** 34-19
1998 Wembley **Wales** 19-13
1999 Murrayfield **Scotland** 33-20
2000 Cardiff **Wales** 26-18
2001 Murrayfield **Drawn** 28-28
2002 Cardiff **Scotland** 27-22
2003 Murrayfield **Scotland** 30-22
2003 Cardiff **Wales** 23-9
Non-championship match
2004 Cardiff **Wales** 23-10
2005 Murrayfield **Wales** 46-22
2006 Cardiff **Wales** 28-18
2007 Murrayfield **Scotland** 21-9
2008 Cardiff **Wales** 30-15
2009 Murrayfield **Wales** 26-13
2010 Cardiff **Wales** 31-24

SCOTLAND v FRANCE

Played 83 Scotland won 34, France won 46, Drawn 3
Highest scores Scotland 36-22 in 1999, France 51-16 in 1998 and 51-9 in 2003
Biggest wins Scotland 31-3 in 1912, France 51-9 in 2003

1910 Inverleith (Edinburgh) **Scotland** 27-0
1911 Paris **France** 16-15
1912 Inverleith **Scotland** 31-3
1913 Paris **Scotland** 21-3
1914 No Match
1920 Paris **Scotland** 5-0
1921 Inverleith **France** 3-0
1922 Paris **Drawn** 3-3
1923 Inverleith **Scotland** 16-3
1924 Paris **France** 12-10
1925 Inverleith **Scotland** 25-4
1926 Paris **Scotland** 20-6
1927 Murrayfield **Scotland** 23-6
1928 Paris **Scotland** 15-6
1929 Murrayfield **Scotland** 6-3
1930 Paris **France** 7-3
1931 Murrayfield **Scotland** 6-4
1947 Paris **France** 8-3
1948 Murrayfield **Scotland** 9-8
1949 Paris **Scotland** 8-0
1950 Murrayfield **Scotland** 8-5
1951 Paris **France** 14-12
1952 Murrayfield **France** 13-11
1953 Paris **France** 11-5
1954 Murrayfield **France** 3-0
1955 Paris **France** 15-0
1956 Murrayfield **Scotland** 12-0
1957 Paris **Scotland** 6-0
1958 Murrayfield **Scotland** 11-9
1959 Paris **France** 9-0
1960 Murrayfield **France** 13-11
1961 Paris **France** 11-0
1962 Murrayfield **France** 11-3
1963 Paris **Scotland** 11-6
1964 Murrayfield **Scotland** 10-0
1965 Paris **France** 16-8
1966 Murrayfield **Drawn** 3-3
1967 Paris **Scotland** 9-8
1968 Murrayfield **France** 8-6
1969 Paris **Scotland** 6-3
1970 Murrayfield **France** 11-9
1971 Paris **France** 13-8
1972 Murrayfield **Scotland** 20-9
1973 Paris **France** 16-13
1974 Murrayfield **Scotland** 19-6
1975 Paris **France** 10-9
1976 Murrayfield **France** 13-6
1977 Paris **France** 23-3
1978 Murrayfield **France** 19-16
1979 Paris **France** 21-17

1980 Murrayfield **Scotland** 22-14
1981 Paris **France** 16-9
1982 Murrayfield **Scotland** 16-7
1983 Paris **France** 19-15
1984 Murrayfield **Scotland** 21-12
1985 Paris **France** 11-3
1986 Murrayfield **Scotland** 18-17
1987 Paris **France** 28-22
1987 Christchurch WC **Drawn** 20-20
1988 Murrayfield **Scotland** 23-12
1989 Paris **France** 19-3
1990 Murrayfield **Scotland** 21-0
1991 Paris **France** 15-9
1992 Murrayfield **Scotland** 10-6
1993 Paris **France** 11-3
1994 Murrayfield **France** 20-12
1995 Paris **Scotland** 23-21
1995 Pretoria WC **France** 22-19
1996 Murrayfield **Scotland** 19-14
1997 Paris **France** 47-20
1998 Murrayfield **France** 51-16
1999 Paris **Scotland** 36-22
2000 Murrayfield **France** 28-16
2001 Paris **France** 16-6
2002 Murrayfield **France** 22-10
2003 Paris **France** 38-3
2003 Sydney WC **France** 51-9
2004 Murrayfield **France** 31-0
2005 Paris **France** 16-9
2006 Murrayfield **Scotland** 20-16
2007 Paris **France** 46-19
2008 Murrayfield **France** 27-6
2009 Paris **France** 22-13
2010 Murrayfield **France** 18-9

SCOTLAND v SOUTH AFRICA

Played 20 Scotland won 4, South Africa won 16, Drawn 0
Highest scores Scotland 29-46 in 1999, South Africa 68-10 in 1997
Biggest wins Scotland 21-6 in 2002, South Africa 68-10 in 1997

1906 Glasgow **Scotland** 6-0
1912 Inverleith **South Africa** 16-0
1932 Murrayfield **South Africa** 6-3
1951 Murrayfield **South Africa** 44-0
1960 Port Elizabeth **South Africa** 18-10
1961 Murrayfield **South Africa** 12-5
1965 Murrayfield **Scotland** 8-5
1969 Murrayfield **Scotland** 6-3
1994 Murrayfield **South Africa** 34-10
1997 Murrayfield **South Africa** 68-10
1998 Murrayfield **South Africa** 35-10
1999 Murrayfield WC **South Africa** 46-29
2002 Murrayfield **Scotland** 21-6
2003 *1* Durban **South Africa** 29-25
2 Johannesburg **South Africa** 28-19
South Africa won series 2-0
2004 Murrayfield **South Africa** 45-10
2006 1 Durban **South Africa** 36-16
2 Port Elizabeth **South Africa** 29-15
South Africa won series 2-0
2007 Murrayfield **South Africa** 27-3
2008 Murrayfield **South Africa** 14-10

SCOTLAND v NEW ZEALAND

Played 27 Scotland won 0, New Zealand won 25, Drawn 2
Highest scores Scotland 31-62 in 1996, New Zealand 69-20 in 2000
Biggest wins Scotland no win, New Zealand 69-20 in 2000

1905 Inverleith (Edinburgh) **New Zealand** 12-7
1935 Murrayfield **New Zealand** 18-8
1954 Murrayfield **New Zealand** 3-0
1964 Murrayfield **Drawn** 0-0
1967 Murrayfield **New Zealand** 14-3

1972 Murrayfield **New Zealand** 14-9
1975 Auckland **New Zealand** 24-0
1978 Murrayfield **New Zealand** 18-9
1979 Murrayfield **New Zealand** 20-6
1981 *1* Dunedin **New Zealand** 11-4
2 Auckland **New Zealand** 40-15
New Zealand won series 2-0
1983 Murrayfield **Drawn** 25-25
1987 Christchurch WC **New Zealand** 30-3
1990 *1* Dunedin **New Zealand** 31-16
2 Auckland **New Zealand** 21-18
New Zealand won series 2-0
1991 Cardiff WC **New Zealand** 13-6
1993 Murrayfield **New Zealand** 51-15
1995 Pretoria WC **New Zealand** 48-30
1996 *1* Dunedin **New Zealand** 62-31
2 Auckland **New Zealand** 36-12
New Zealand won series 2-0
1999 Murrayfield WC **New Zealand** 30-18
2000 *1* Dunedin **New Zealand** 69-20
2 Auckland **New Zealand** 48-14
New Zealand won series 2-0
2001 Murrayfield **New Zealand** 37-6
2005 Murrayfield **New Zealand** 29-10
2007 Murrayfield WC **New Zealand** 40-0
2008 Murrayfield **New Zealand** 32-6

SCOTLAND v AUSTRALIA

Played 26 Scotland won 8, Australia won 18, Drawn 0
Highest scores Scotland 24-15 in 1981, Australia 45-3 in 1998
Biggest wins Scotland 24-15 in 1981, Australia 45-3 in 1998

1927 Murrayfield **Scotland** 10-8
1947 Murrayfield **Australia** 16-7
1958 Murrayfield **Scotland** 12-8
1966 Murrayfield **Scotland** 11-5
1968 Murrayfield **Scotland** 9-3
1970 Sydney **Australia** 23-3
1975 Murrayfield **Scotland** 10-3
1981 Murrayfield **Scotland** 24-15
1982 *1* Brisbane **Scotland** 12-7
2 Sydney **Australia** 33-9
Series drawn 1-1
1984 Murrayfield **Australia** 37-12
1988 Murrayfield **Australia** 32-13
1992 *1* Sydney **Australia** 27-12
2 Brisbane **Australia** 37-13
Australia won series 2-0
1996 Murrayfield **Australia** 29-19
1997 Murrayfield **Australia** 37-8
1998 *1* Sydney **Australia** 45-3
2 Brisbane **Australia** 33-11
Australia won series 2-0
2000 Murrayfield **Australia** 30-9
2003 Brisbane WC **Australia** 33-16
2004 1 Melbourne **Australia** 35-15
2 Sydney **Australia** 34-13
Australia won series 2-0
2004 1 Murrayfield **Australia** 31-14
2 Glasgow **Australia** 31-17
Australia won series 2-0
2006 Murrayfield **Australia** 44-15
2009 Murrayfield **Scotland** 9-8

SCOTLAND v SRU PRESIDENT'S XV

Played 1 Scotland won 1
Highest scores Scotland 27-16 in 1972, SRU President's XV 16-27 in 1973
Biggest win Scotland 27-16 in 1973, SRU President's XV no win

1973 Murrayfield **Scotland** 27-16

SCOTLAND v ROMANIA

Played 12 Scotland won 10 Romania won 2, Drawn 0
Highest scores Scotland 60-19 in 1999, Romania 28-55 in 1987 & 28-22 in 1984
Biggest wins Scotland 48-6 in 2006 and 42-0 in 2007, Romania 28-22 in 1984 & 18-12 in 1991

1981	Murrayfield **Scotland** 12-6	1995	Murrayfield **Scotland** 49-16
1984	Bucharest **Romania** 28-22	1999	Glasgow **Scotland** 60-19
1986	Bucharest **Scotland** 33-18	2002	Murrayfield **Scotland** 37-10
1987	Dunedin WC **Scotland** 55-28	2005	Bucharest **Scotland** 39-19
1989	Murrayfield **Scotland** 32-0	2006	Murrayfield **Scotland** 48-6
1991	Bucharest **Romania** 18-12	2007	Murrayfield WC **Scotland** 42-0

SCOTLAND v ZIMBABWE

Played 2 Scotland won 2
Highest scores Scotland 60-21 in 1987, Zimbabwe 21-60 in 1987
Biggest win Scotland 60-21 in 1987 & 51-12 in 1991, Zimbabwe no win

1987	Wellington WC **Scotland** 60-21	1991	Murrayfield WC **Scotland** 51-12

SCOTLAND v FIJI

Played 5 Scotland won 4, Fiji won 1
Highest scores Scotland 38-17 in 1989, Fiji 51-26 in 1998
Biggest win Scotland 38-17 in 1989, Fiji 51-26 in 1998

1989	Murrayfield **Scotland** 38-17	2003	Sydney WC **Scotland** 22-20
1998	Suva **Fiji** 51-26	2009	Murrayfield **Scotland** 23-10
2002	Murrayfield **Scotland** 36-22		

SCOTLAND v ARGENTINA

Played 12 Scotland won 4, Argentina won 8, Drawn 0
Highest scores Scotland 49-3 in 1990, Argentina 31-22 in 1999
Biggest wins Scotland 49-3 in 1990, Argentina 31-22 in 1999 and 25-16 in 2001

1990	Murrayfield **Scotland** 49-3		Argentina won series 2-0
1994	*1* Buenos Aires **Argentina** 16-15	1999	Murrayfield **Argentina** 31-22
	2 Buenos Aires **Argentina** 19-17	2001	Murrayfield **Argentina** 25-16

2005	Murrayfield **Argentina** 23-19	2009	Murrayfield **Argentina** 9-6
2007	Paris WC **Argentina** 19-13	2010	1 Tucumán **Scotland** 24-16
2008	*1* Rosario **Argentina** 21-15		2 Mar del Plata **Scotland** 13-9
	2 Buenos Aires **Scotland** 26-14		Scotland won series 2-0
	Series drawn 1-1		

SCOTLAND v JAPAN

Played 3 Scotland won 3
Highest scores Scotland 100-8 in 2004, Japan 11-32 in 2003
Biggest win Scotland 100-8 in 2004, Japan no win

1991	Murrayfield WC **Scotland** 47-9	2004	Perth **Scotland** 100-8
2003	Townsville WC **Scotland** 32-11		

SCOTLAND v SAMOA

Played 6 Scotland won 5, Drawn 1
Highest scores Scotland 38-3 in 2004, Samoa 20-35 in 1999
Biggest win Scotland 38-3 in 2004, Samoa no win

1991	Murrayfield WC **Scotland** 28-6	2000	Murrayfield **Scotland** 31-8
1995	Murrayfield **Drawn** 15-15	2004	Wellington (NZ) **Scotland** 38-3
1999	Murrayfield WC **Scotland** 35-20	2005	Murrayfield **Scotland** 18-11

SCOTLAND v CANADA

Played 3 Scotland won 2, Canada won 1
Highest scores Scotland 41-0 in 2008, Canada 26-23 in 2002
Biggest win Scotland 41-0 in 2008, Canada 26-23 in 2002

1995	Murrayfield **Scotland** 22-6	2008	Aberdeen **Scotland** 41-0
2002	Vancouver **Canada** 26-23		

SCOTLAND v IVORY COAST

Played 1 Scotland won 1
Highest scores Scotland 89-0 in 1995, Ivory Coast 0-89 in 1995
Biggest win Scotland 89-0 in 1995, Ivory Coast no win

1995	Rustenburg WC **Scotland** 89-0

SCOTLAND v TONGA

Played 2 Scotland won 2
Highest scores Scotland 43-20 in 2001, Tonga 20-43 in 2001
Biggest win Scotland 41-5 in 1995, Tonga no win

1995 Pretoria WC **Scotland** 41-5	2001 Murrayfield **Scotland** 43-20

SCOTLAND v ITALY

Played 16 Scotland won 10, Italy won 6
Highest scores Scotland 47-15 in 2003, Italy 37-17 in 2007
Biggest wins Scotland 47-15 in 2003, Italy 37-17 in 2007

1996 Murrayfield **Scotland** 29-22	2004 Rome **Italy** 20-14
1998 Treviso **Italy** 25-21	2005 Murrayfield **Scotland** 18-10
1999 Murrayfield **Scotland** 30-12	2006 Rome **Scotland** 13-10
2000 Rome **Italy** 34-20	2007 Murrayfield **Italy** 37-17
2001 Murrayfield **Scotland** 23-19	2007 Saint Etienne WC **Scotland** 18-16
2002 Rome **Scotland** 29-12	2008 Rome **Italy** 23-20
2003 Murrayfield **Scotland** 33-25	2009 Murrayfield **Scotland** 26-6
2003 Murrayfield **Scotland** 47-15 Non-championship match	2010 Rome **Italy** 16-12

SCOTLAND v URUGUAY

Played 1 Scotland won 1
Highest scores Scotland 43-12 in 1999, Uruguay 12-43 in 1999
Biggest win Scotland 43-12 in 1999, Uruguay no win

1999 Murrayfield WC **Scotland** 43-12

SCOTLAND v SPAIN

Played 1 Scotland won 1
Highest scores Scotland 48-0 in 1999, Spain 0-48 in 1999
Biggest win Scotland 48-0 in 1999, Spain no win

1999 Murrayfield WC **Scotland** 48-0

SCOTLAND v UNITED STATES

Played 3 Scotland won 3
Highest scores Scotland 65-23 in 2002, United States 23-65 in 2002
Biggest win Scotland 53-6 in 2000, United States no win

2000 Murrayfield **Scotland** 53-6
2002 San Francisco **Scotland** 65-23
2003 Brisbane WC **Scotland** 39-15

SCOTLAND v PACIFIC ISLANDS

Played 1 Scotland won 1
Highest scores Scotland 34-22 in 2006, Pacific Islands 22-34 in 2006
Biggest win Scotland 34-22 in 2006, Pacific Islands no win

2006 Murrayfield **Scotland** 34-22

SCOTLAND v PORTUGAL

Played 1 Scotland won 1
Highest scores Scotland 56-10 in 2007, Portugal 10-56 in 2007
Biggest win Scotland 56-10 in 2007, Portugal no win

2007 Saint Etienne WC **Scotland** 56-10

IRELAND v WALES

Played 115 Ireland won 47, Wales won 62, Drawn 6
Highest scores Ireland 54-10 in 2002, Wales 34-9 in 1976
Biggest wins Ireland 54-10 in 2002, Wales 29-0 in 1907

1882 Dublin **Wales** 2G 2T to 0
1883 No Match
1884 Cardiff **Wales** 1DG 2T to 0
1885 No Match
1886 No Match
1887 Birkenhead **Wales** 1DG 1T to 3T
1888 Dublin **Ireland** 1G 1DG 1T to 0
1889 Swansea **Ireland** 2T to 0
1890 Dublin **Drawn** 1G each
1891 Llanelli **Wales** 6-4
1892 Dublin **Ireland** 9-0
1893 Llanelli **Wales** 2-0
1894 Belfast **Ireland** 3-0
1895 Cardiff **Wales** 5-3
1896 Dublin **Ireland** 8-4
1897 No Match
1898 Limerick **Wales** 11-3
1899 Cardiff **Ireland** 3-0

1900 Belfast **Wales** 3-0
1901 Swansea **Wales** 10-9
1902 Dublin **Wales** 15-0
1903 Cardiff **Wales** 18-0
1904 Belfast **Ireland** 14-12
1905 Swansea **Wales** 10-3
1906 Belfast **Ireland** 11-6
1907 Cardiff **Wales** 29-0
1908 Belfast **Wales** 11-5
1909 Swansea **Wales** 18-5
1910 Dublin **Wales** 19-3
1911 Cardiff **Wales** 16-0
1912 Belfast **Ireland** 12-5
1913 Swansea **Wales** 16-13
1914 Belfast **Wales** 11-3
1920 Cardiff **Wales** 28-4
1921 Belfast **Wales** 6-0
1922 Swansea **Wales** 11-5
1923 Dublin **Ireland** 5-4
1924 Cardiff **Ireland** 13-10
1925 Belfast **Ireland** 19-3
1926 Swansea **Wales** 11-8
1927 Dublin **Ireland** 19-9
1928 Cardiff **Ireland** 13-10
1929 Belfast **Drawn** 5-5
1930 Swansea **Wales** 12-7
1931 Belfast **Wales** 15-3
1932 Cardiff **Ireland** 12-10
1933 Belfast **Ireland** 10-5
1934 Swansea **Wales** 13-0
1935 Belfast **Ireland** 9-3
1936 Cardiff **Wales** 3-0
1937 Belfast **Ireland** 5-3
1938 Swansea **Wales** 11-5
1939 Belfast **Wales** 7-0
1947 Swansea **Wales** 6-0
1948 Belfast **Ireland** 6-3
1949 Swansea **Ireland** 5-0
1950 Belfast **Wales** 6-3
1951 Cardiff **Drawn** 3-3
1952 Dublin **Wales** 14-3
1953 Swansea **Wales** 5-3
1954 Dublin **Wales** 12-9
1955 Cardiff **Wales** 21-3
1956 Dublin **Ireland** 11-3
1957 Cardiff **Wales** 6-5
1958 Dublin **Wales** 9-6
1959 Cardiff **Wales** 8-6
1960 Dublin **Wales** 10-9
1961 Cardiff **Wales** 9-0
1962 Dublin **Drawn** 3-3
1963 Cardiff **Ireland** 14-6
1964 Dublin **Wales** 15-6
1965 Cardiff **Wales** 14-8
1966 Dublin **Ireland** 9-6
1967 Cardiff **Ireland** 3-0
1968 Dublin **Ireland** 9-6
1969 Cardiff **Wales** 24-11
1970 Dublin **Ireland** 14-0
1971 Cardiff **Wales** 23-9
1972 No Match
1973 Cardiff **Wales** 16-12
1974 Dublin **Drawn** 9-9
1975 Cardiff **Wales** 32-4
1976 Dublin **Wales** 34-9
1977 Cardiff **Wales** 25-9
1978 Dublin **Wales** 20-16
1979 Cardiff **Wales** 24-21
1980 Dublin **Ireland** 21-7
1981 Cardiff **Wales** 9-8
1982 Dublin **Ireland** 20-12
1983 Cardiff **Wales** 23-9
1984 Dublin **Wales** 18-9
1985 Cardiff **Ireland** 21-9
1986 Dublin **Wales** 19-12
1987 Cardiff **Ireland** 15-11
1987 Wellington WC **Wales** 13-6
1988 Dublin **Wales** 12-9
1989 Cardiff **Ireland** 19-13
1990 Dublin **Ireland** 14-8
1991 Cardiff **Drawn** 21-21
1992 Dublin **Wales** 16-15
1993 Cardiff **Ireland** 19-14
1994 Dublin **Wales** 17-15
1995 Cardiff **Ireland** 16-12
1995 Johannesburg WC **Ireland** 24-23
1996 Dublin **Ireland** 30-17
1997 Cardiff **Ireland** 26-25
1998 Dublin **Wales** 30-21
1999 Wembley **Ireland** 29-23
2000 Dublin **Wales** 23-19
2001 Cardiff **Ireland** 36-6
2002 Dublin **Ireland** 54-10
2003 Cardiff **Ireland** 25-24
2003 Dublin **Ireland** 35-12
2004 Dublin **Ireland** 36-15
2005 Cardiff **Wales** 32-20
2006 Dublin **Ireland** 31-5
2007 Cardiff **Ireland** 19-9
2008 Dublin **Wales** 16-12
2009 Cardiff **Ireland** 17-15
2010 Dublin **Ireland** 27-12

IRELAND v FRANCE

Played 86 Ireland won 29, France won 52, Drawn 5
Highest scores Ireland 31-43 in 2006, France 45-10 in 1996
Biggest wins Ireland 24-0 in 1913, France 44-5 in 2002

1909 Dublin **Ireland** 19-8
1910 Paris **Ireland** 8-3
1911 Cork **Ireland** 25-5
1912 Paris **Ireland** 11-6
1913 Cork **Ireland** 24-0
1914 Paris **Ireland** 8-6
1920 Dublin **France** 15-7
1921 Paris **France** 20-10
1922 Dublin **Ireland** 8-3
1923 Paris **France** 14-8
1924 Dublin **Ireland** 6-0
1925 Paris **Ireland** 9-3
1926 Belfast **Ireland** 11-0
1927 Paris **Ireland** 8-3
1928 Belfast **Ireland** 12-8
1929 Paris **Ireland** 6-0
1930 Belfast **France** 5-0
1931 Paris **France** 3-0
1947 Dublin **France** 12-8
1948 Paris **Ireland** 13-6
1949 Dublin **France** 16-9
1950 Paris **Drawn** 3-3
1951 Dublin **Ireland** 9-8
1952 Paris **Ireland** 11-8
1953 Belfast **Ireland** 16-3
1954 Paris **France** 8-0
1955 Dublin **France** 5-3
1956 Paris **France** 14-8
1957 Dublin **Ireland** 11-6
1958 Paris **France** 11-6
1959 Dublin **Ireland** 9-5
1960 Paris **France** 23-6
1961 Dublin **France** 15-3
1962 Paris **France** 11-0
1963 Dublin **France** 24-5
1964 Paris **France** 27-6
1965 Dublin **Drawn** 3-3
1966 Paris **France** 11-6
1967 Dublin **France** 11-6
1968 Paris **France** 16-6
1969 Dublin **Ireland** 17-9
1970 Paris **France** 8-0
1971 Dublin **Drawn** 9-9
1972 Paris **Ireland** 14-9
1972 Dublin **Ireland** 24-14
Non-championship match
1973 Dublin **Ireland** 6-4
1974 Paris **France** 9-6
1975 Dublin **Ireland** 25-6
1976 Paris **France** 26-3
1977 Dublin **France** 15-6
1978 Paris **France** 10-9
1979 Dublin **Drawn** 9-9
1980 Paris **France** 19-18
1981 Dublin **France** 19-13
1982 Paris **France** 22-9
1983 Dublin **Ireland** 22-16
1984 Paris **France** 25-12
1985 Dublin **Drawn** 15-15
1986 Paris **France** 29-9
1987 Dublin **France** 19-13
1988 Paris **France** 25-6
1989 Dublin **France** 26-21
1990 Paris **France** 31-12
1991 Dublin **France** 21-13
1992 Paris **France** 44-12
1993 Dublin **France** 21-6
1994 Paris **France** 35-15
1995 Dublin **France** 25-7
1995 Durban WC **France** 36-12
1996 Paris **France** 45-10
1997 Dublin **France** 32-15
1998 Paris **France** 18-16
1999 Dublin **France** 10-9
2000 Paris **Ireland** 27-25
2001 Dublin **Ireland** 22-15
2002 Paris **France** 44-5
2003 Dublin **Ireland** 15-12
2003 Melbourne WC **France** 43-21
2004 Paris **France** 35-17
2005 Dublin **France** 26-19
2006 Paris **France** 43-31
2007 Dublin **France** 20-17
2007 Paris WC **France** 25-3
2008 Paris **France** 26-21
2009 Dublin **Ireland** 30-21
2010 Paris **France** 33-10

IRELAND v SOUTH AFRICA

Played 19 Ireland won 4, South Africa won 14, Drawn 1
Highest scores Ireland 32-15 in 2006, South Africa 38-0 in 1912
Biggest wins Ireland 32-15 in 2006, South Africa 38-0 in 1912

1906	Belfast **South Africa** 15-12
1912	Dublin **South Africa** 38-0
1931	Dublin **South Africa** 8-3
1951	Dublin **South Africa** 17-5
1960	Dublin **South Africa** 8-3
1961	Cape Town **South Africa** 24-8
1965	Dublin **Ireland** 9-6
1970	Dublin **Drawn** 8-8
1981	*1* Cape Town **South Africa** 23-15
	2 Durban **South Africa** 12-10
	South Africa won series 2-0
1998	*1* Bloemfontein **South Africa** 37-13
	2 Pretoria **South Africa** 33-0
	South Africa won series 2-0
1998	Dublin **South Africa** 27-13
2000	Dublin **South Africa** 28-18
2004	1 Bloemfontein **South Africa** 31-17
	2 Cape Town **South Africa** 26-17
	South Africa won series 2-0
2004	Dublin **Ireland** 17-12
2006	Dublin **Ireland** 32-15
2009	Dublin **Ireland** 15-10

IRELAND v NEW ZEALAND

Played 23 Ireland won 0, New Zealand won 22, Drawn 1
Highest scores Ireland 29-40 in 2001, New Zealand 66-28 in 2010
Biggest win Ireland no win, New Zealand 59-6 in 1992

1905	Dublin **New Zealand** 15-0
1924	Dublin **New Zealand** 6-0
1935	Dublin **New Zealand** 17-9
1954	Dublin **New Zealand** 14-3
1963	Dublin **New Zealand** 6-5
1973	Dublin **Drawn** 10-10
1974	Dublin **New Zealand** 15-6
1976	Wellington **New Zealand** 11-3
1978	Dublin **New Zealand** 10-6
1989	Dublin **New Zealand** 23-6
1992	*1* Dunedin **New Zealand** 24-21
	2 Wellington **New Zealand** 59-6
	New Zealand won series 2-0
1995	Johannesburg WC **New Zealand 43-19**
1997	Dublin **New Zealand** 63-15
2001	Dublin **New Zealand** 40-29
2002	*1* Dunedin **New Zealand** 15-6
	2 Auckland **New Zealand** 40-8
	New Zealand won series 2-0
2005	Dublin **New Zealand** 45-7
2006	1 Hamilton **New Zealand** 34-23
	2 Auckland **New Zealand** 27-17
	New Zealand won series 2-0
2008	Wellington **New Zealand** 21-11
2008	Dublin **New Zealand** 22-3
2010	New Plymouth **New Zealand** 66-28

IRELAND v AUSTRALIA

Played 29 Ireland won 8, Australia won 20, Drawn 1
Highest scores Ireland 27-12 in 1979, Australia 46-10 in 1999
Biggest wins Ireland 27-12 in 1979 & 21-6 in 2006, Australia 46-10 in 1999

1927	Dublin **Australia** 5-3
1947	Dublin **Australia** 16-3
1958	Dublin **Ireland** 9-6
1967	Dublin **Ireland** 15-8
1967	Sydney **Ireland** 11-5
1968	Dublin **Ireland** 10-3
1976	Dublin **Australia** 20-10
1979	*1* Brisbane **Ireland** 27-12
	2 Sydney **Ireland** 9-3
	Ireland won series 2-0
1981	Dublin **Australia** 16-12
1984	Dublin **Australia** 16-9
1987	Sydney WC **Australia** 33-15
1991	Dublin WC **Australia** 19-18
1992	Dublin **Australia** 42-17
1994	*1* Brisbane **Australia** 33-13
	2 Sydney **Australia** 32-18
	Australia won series 2-0
1996	Dublin **Australia** 22-12
1999	*1* Brisbane **Australia** 46-10
	2 Perth **Australia** 32-26
	Australia won series 2-0
1999	Dublin WC **Australia** 23-3
2002	Dublin **Ireland** 18-9
2003	Perth **Australia** 45-16
2003	Melbourne WC **Australia** 17-16
2005	Dublin **Australia** 30-14
2006	Perth **Australia** 37-15
2006	Dublin **Ireland** 21-6
2008	Melbourne **Australia** 18-12
2009	Dublin **Drawn** 20-20
2010	Brisbane **Australia** 22-15

IRELAND v NEW ZEALAND NATIVES

Played 1 New Zealand Natives won 1
Highest scores Ireland 4-13 in 1888, Zew Zealand Natives 13-4 in 1888
Biggest win Ireland no win, New Zealand Natives 13-4 in 1888

1888	Dublin **New Zealand Natives** 4G 1T to 1G 1T

IRELAND v IRU PRESIDENT'S XV

Played 1 Drawn 1
Highest scores Ireland 18-18 in 1974, IRFU President's XV 18-18 in 1974

1974	Dublin **Drawn** 18-18

IRELAND v ROMANIA

Played 8 Ireland won 8
Highest scores Ireland 60-0 in 1986, Romania 35-53 in 1998
Biggest win Ireland 60-0 in 1986, Romania no win

1986	Dublin **Ireland** 60-0	2001	Bucharest **Ireland** 37-3
1993	Dublin **Ireland** 25-3	2002	Limerick **Ireland** 39-8
1998	Dublin **Ireland** 53-35	2003	Gosford WC **Ireland** 45-17
1999	Dublin WC **Ireland** 44-14	2005	Dublin **Ireland** 43-12

IRELAND v CANADA

Played 5 Ireland won 4 Drawn 1
Highest scores Ireland 55-0 in 2008, Canada 27-27 in 2000
Biggest win Ireland 55-0 in 2008, Canada no win

1987	Dunedin WC **Ireland** 46-19	2008	Limerick **Ireland** 55-0
1997	Dublin **Ireland** 33-11	2009	Vancouver **Ireland** 25-6
2000	Markham **Drawn** 27-27		

IRELAND v TONGA

Played 2 Ireland won 2
Highest scores Ireland 40-19 in 2003, Tonga 19-40 in 2003
Biggest win Ireland 32-9 in 1987, Tonga no win

1987	Brisbane WC **Ireland** 32-9	2003	Nuku'alofa **Ireland** 40-19

IRELAND v SAMOA

Played 4 Ireland won 3, Samoa won 1, Drawn 0
Highest scores Ireland 49-22 in 1988, Samoa 40-25 in 1996
Biggest wins Ireland 49-22 in 1988 and 35-8 in 2001, Samoa 40-25 in 1996

1988	Dublin **Ireland** 49-22	2001	Dublin **Ireland** 35-8
1996	Dublin **Samoa** 40-25	2003	Apia **Ireland** 40-14

IRELAND v ITALY

Played 18 Ireland won 15, Italy won 3, Drawn 0
Highest scores Ireland 61-6 in 2003, Italy 37-29 in 1997 & 37-22 in 1997
Biggest wins Ireland 61-6 in 2003, Italy 37-22 in 1997

1988	Dublin **Ireland** 31-15
1995	Treviso **Italy** 22-12
1997	Dublin **Italy** 37-29
1997	Bologna **Italy** 37-22
1999	Dublin **Ireland** 39-30
2000	Dublin **Ireland** 60-13
2001	Rome **Ireland** 41-22
2002	Dublin **Ireland** 32-17
2003	Rome **Ireland** 37-13
2003	Limerick **Ireland** 61-6
	Non-championship match
2004	Dublin **Ireland** 19-3
2005	Rome **Ireland** 28-17
2006	Dublin **Ireland** 26-16
2007	Rome **Ireland** 51-24
2007	Belfast **Ireland** 23-20
	Non-championship match
2008	Dublin **Ireland** 16-11
2009	Rome **Ireland** 38-9
2010	Dublin **Ireland** 29-11

IRELAND v ARGENTINA

Played 11 Ireland won 6 Argentina won 5
Highest scores Ireland 32-24 in 1999, Argentina 34-23 in 2000
Biggest win Ireland 17-3 in 2008, Argentina 16-0 in 2007

1990	Dublin **Ireland** 20-18
1999	Dublin **Ireland** 32-24
1999	Lens WC **Argentina** 28-24
2000	Buenos Aires **Argentina** 34-23
2002	Dublin **Ireland** 16-7
2003	Adelaide WC **Ireland** 16-15
2004	Dublin **Ireland** 21-19
2007	1 Santa Fé **Argentina** 22-20
	2 Buenos Aires **Argentina** 16-0
	Argentina won series 2-0
2007	Paris WC **Argentina** 30-15
2008	Dublin **Ireland** 17-3

IRELAND v NAMIBIA

Played 4 Ireland won 2, Namibia won 2
Highest scores Ireland 64-7 in 2003, Namibia 26-15 in 1991
Biggest win Ireland 64-7 in 2003, Namibia 26-15 in 1991

1991	*1* Windhoek **Namibia** 15-6
	2 Windhoek **Namibia** 26-15
	Namibia won series 2-0
2003	Sydney WC **Ireland** 64-7
2007	Bordeaux WC **Ireland** 32-17

IRELAND v ZIMBABWE

Played 1 Ireland won 1
Highest scores Ireland 55-11 in 1991, Zimbabwe 11-55 in 1991
Biggest win Ireland 55-11 in 1991, Zimbabwe no win

1991	Dublin WC **Ireland** 55-11

IRELAND v JAPAN

Played 5 Ireland won 5
Highest scores Ireland 78-9 in 2000, Japan 28-50 in 1995
Biggest win Ireland 78-9 in 2000, Japan no win

1991	Dublin WC **Ireland** 32-16	2005	1 Osaka **Ireland** 44-12
1995	Bloemfontein WC **Ireland 50-28**		2 Tokyo **Ireland** 47-18
2000	Dublin **Ireland** 78-9		Ireland won series 2-0

IRELAND v UNITED STATES

Played 6 Ireland won 6
Highest scores Ireland 83-3 in 2000, United States 18-25 in 1996
Biggest win Ireland 83-3 in 2000, United States no win

1994	Dublin **Ireland** 26-15	2000	Manchester (NH) **Ireland** 83-3
1996	Atlanta **Ireland** 25-18	2004	Dublin **Ireland** 55-6
1999	Dublin WC **Ireland** 53-8	2009	Santa Clara **Ireland** 27-10

IRELAND v FIJI

Played 3 Ireland won 3
Highest scores Ireland 64-17 in 2002, Fiji 17-64 in 2002
Biggest win Ireland 64-17 in 2002, Fiji no win

1995	Dublin **Ireland** 44-8	2009	Dublin **Ireland** 41-6
2002	Dublin **Ireland** 64-17		

IRELAND v GEORGIA

Played 3 Ireland won 3
Highest scores Ireland 70-0 in 1998, Georgia 14-63 in 2002
Biggest win Ireland 70-0 in 1998, Georgia no win

1998 Dublin **Ireland** 70-0
2002 Dublin **Ireland** 63-14
2007 Bordeaux WC **Ireland** 14-10

IRELAND v RUSSIA

Played 1 Ireland won 1
Highest scores Ireland 35-3 in 2002, Russia 3-35 in 2002
Biggest win Ireland 35-3 in 2002, Russia no win

2002 Krasnoyarsk **Ireland** 35-3

IRELAND v PACIFIC ISLANDS

Played 1 Ireland won 1
Highest scores Ireland 61-17 in 2006, Pacific Islands 17-61 in 2006
Biggest win Ireland 61-17 in 2006, Pacific Islands no win

2006 Dublin **Ireland** 61-17

WALES v FRANCE

Played 87 Wales won 43, France won 41, Drawn 3
Highest scores Wales 49-14 in 1910, France 51-0 in 1998
Biggest wins Wales 47-5 in 1909, France 51-0 in 1998

1908 Cardiff **Wales** 36-4
1909 Paris **Wales** 47-5
1910 Swansea **Wales** 49-14
1911 Paris **Wales** 15-0
1912 Newport **Wales** 14-8
1913 Paris **Wales** 11-8
1914 Swansea **Wales** 31-0
1920 Paris **Wales** 6-5
1921 Cardiff **Wales** 12-4
1922 Paris **Wales** 11-3
1923 Swansea **Wales** 16-8
1924 Paris **Wales** 10-6
1925 Cardiff **Wales** 11-5
1926 Paris **Wales** 7-5
1927 Swansea **Wales** 25-7
1928 Paris **France** 8-3

1929 Cardiff **Wales** 8-3
1930 Paris **Wales** 11-0
1931 Swansea **Wales** 35-3
1947 Paris **Wales** 3-0
1948 Swansea **France** 11-3
1949 Paris **France** 5-3
1950 Cardiff **Wales** 21-0
1951 Paris **France** 8-3
1952 Swansea **Wales** 9-5
1953 Paris **Wales** 6-3
1954 Cardiff **Wales** 19-13
1955 Paris **Wales** 16-11
1956 Cardiff **Wales** 5-3
1957 Paris **Wales** 19-13
1958 Cardiff **France** 16-6
1959 Paris **France** 11-3
1960 Cardiff **France** 16-8
1961 Paris **France** 8-6
1962 Cardiff **Wales** 3-0
1963 Paris **France** 5-3
1964 Cardiff **Drawn** 11-11
1965 Paris **France** 22-13
1966 Cardiff **Wales** 9-8
1967 Paris **France** 20-14
1968 Cardiff **France** 14-9
1969 Paris **Drawn** 8-8
1970 Cardiff **Wales** 11-6
1971 Paris **Wales** 9-5
1972 Cardiff **Wales** 20-6
1973 Paris **France** 12-3
1974 Cardiff **Drawn** 16-16
1975 Paris **Wales** 25-10
1976 Cardiff **Wales** 19-13
1977 Paris **France** 16-9
1978 Cardiff **Wales** 16-7
1979 Paris **France** 14-13
1980 Cardiff **Wales** 18-9
1981 Paris **France** 19-15
1982 Cardiff **Wales** 22-12
1983 Paris **France** 16-9
1984 Cardiff **France** 21-16
1985 Paris **France** 14-3
1986 Cardiff **France** 23-15
1987 Paris **France** 16-9
1988 Cardiff **France** 10-9
1989 Paris **France** 31-12
1990 Cardiff **France** 29-19
1991 Paris **France** 36-3
1991 Cardiff **France** 22-9
Non-championship match
1992 Cardiff **France** 12-9
1993 Paris **France** 26-10
1994 Cardiff **Wales** 24-15
1995 Paris **France** 21-9
1996 Cardiff **Wales** 16-15
1996 Cardiff **France** 40-33
Non-championship match
1997 Paris **France 27-22**
1998 Wembley **France** 51-0
1999 Paris **Wales** 34-33
1999 Cardiff **Wales** 34-23
Non-championship match
2000 Cardiff **France** 36-3
2001 Paris **Wales** 43-35
2002 Cardiff **France** 37-33
2003 Paris **France** 33-5
2004 Cardiff **France** 29-22
2005 Paris **Wales** 24-18
2006 Cardiff **France** 21-16
2007 Paris **France** 32-21
2007 Cardiff **France** 34-7
Non-championship match
2008 Cardiff **Wales** 29-12
2009 Paris **France** 21-16
2010 Cardiff **France** 26-20

WALES v SOUTH AFRICA

Played 24 Wales won 1, South Africa won 22, Drawn 1
Highest scores Wales 36-38 in 2004, South Africa 96-13 in 1998
Biggest win Wales 29-19 in 1999, South Africa 96-13 in 1998

1906 Swansea **South Africa** 11-0
1912 Cardiff **South Africa** 3-0
1931 Swansea **South Africa** 8-3
1951 Cardiff **South Africa** 6-3
1960 Cardiff **South Africa** 3-0
1964 Durban **South Africa** 24-3

1970 Cardiff **Drawn** 6-6
1994 Cardiff **South Africa** 20-12
1995 Johannesburg **South Africa** 40-11
1996 Cardiff **South Africa** 37-20
1998 Pretoria **South Africa** 96-13
1998 Wembley **South Africa** 28-20
1999 Cardiff **Wales** 29-19
2000 Cardiff **South Africa** 23-13
2002 *1* Bloemfontein **South Africa** 34-19
2 Cape Town **South Africa** 19-8
SA won series 2-0
2004 Pretoria **South Africa** 53-18
2004 Cardiff **South Africa** 38-36
2005 Cardiff **South Africa** 33-16
2007 Cardiff **South Africa** 34-12
2008 *1* Bloemfontein **South Africa** 43-17
2 Pretoria **South Africa** 37-21
SA won series 2-0
2008 Cardiff **South Africa** 20-15
2010 Cardiff **South Africa** 34-31

WALES v NEW ZEALAND

Played 27 Wales won 3, New Zealand won 24, Drawn 0
Highest scores Wales 37-53 in 2003, New Zealand 55-3 in 2003
Biggest wins Wales 13-8 in 1953, New Zealand 55-3 in 2003

1905 Cardiff **Wales** 3-0
1924 Swansea **New Zealand** 19-0
1935 Cardiff **Wales** 13-12
1953 Cardiff **Wales** 13-8
1963 Cardiff **New Zealand** 6-0
1967 Cardiff **New Zealand** 13-6
1969 *1* Christchurch **New Zealand** 19-0
2 Auckland **New Zealand** 33-12
New Zealand won series 2-0
1972 Cardiff **New Zealand** 19-16
1978 Cardiff **New Zealand** 13-12
1980 Cardiff **New Zealand** 23-3
1987 Brisbane WC **New Zealand** 49-6
1988 *1* Christchurch **New Zealand** 52-3
2 Auckland **New Zealand** 54-9
New Zealand won series 2-0
1989 Cardiff **New Zealand** 34-9
1995 Johannesburg WC **New Zealand 34-9**
1997 Wembley **New Zealand** 42-7
2002 Cardiff **New Zealand** 43-17
2003 Hamilton **New Zealand** 55-3
2003 Sydney WC **New Zealand** 53-37
2004 Cardiff **New Zealand** 26-25
2005 Cardiff **New Zealand** 41-3
2006 Cardiff **New Zealand** 45-10
2008 Cardiff **New Zealand** 29-9
2009 Cardiff **New Zealand** 19-12
2010 1 Dunedin **New Zealand** 42-9
2 Hamilton **New Zealand** 29-10
New Zealand won series 2-0

WALES v AUSTRALIA

Played 29 Wales won 10, Australia won 18, Drawn 1
Highest scores Wales 29-29 in 2006, Australia 63-6 in 1991
Biggest wins Wales 28-3 in 1975, Australia 63-6 in 1991

1908 Cardiff **Wales** 9-6
1927 Cardiff **Australia** 18-8
1947 Cardiff **Wales** 6-0
1958 Cardiff **Wales** 9-3
1966 Cardiff **Australia** 14-11
1969 Sydney **Wales** 19-16
1973 Cardiff **Wales** 24-0
1975 Cardiff **Wales** 28-3
1978 *1* Brisbane **Australia** 18-8
2 Sydney **Australia** 19-17
Australia won series 2-0
1981 Cardiff **Wales** 18-13
1984 Cardiff **Australia** 28-9
1987 Rotorua WC **Wales** 22-21
1991 Brisbane **Australia** 63-6
1991 Cardiff WC **Australia** 38-3
1992 Cardiff **Australia** 23-6
1996 *1* Brisbane **Australia** 56-25

	2 Sydney **Australia** 42-3
	Australia won series 2-0
1996	Cardiff **Australia** 28-19
1999	Cardiff WC **Australia** 24-9
2001	Cardiff **Australia** 21-13
2003	Sydney **Australia** 30-10
2005	Cardiff **Wales** 24-22
2006	Cardiff **Drawn** 29-29
2007	1 Sydney **Australia** 29-23
	2 Brisbane **Australia** 31-0
	Australia won series 2-0
2007	Cardiff WC **Australia** 32-20
2008	Cardiff **Wales** 21-18
2009	Cardiff **Australia** 33-12

WALES v NEW ZEALAND NATIVES

Played 1 Wales won 1
Highest scores Wales 5-0 in 1888, New Zealand Natives 0-5 in 1888
Biggest win Wales 5-0 in 1888, New Zealand Natives no win

1888	Swansea **Wales** 1G 2T to 0

WALES v NEW ZEALAND ARMY

Played 1 New Zealand Army won 1
Highest scores Wales 3-6 in 1919, New Zealand Army 6-3 in 1919
Biggest win Wales no win, New Zealand Army 6-3 in 1919

1919	Swansea **New Zealand Army** 6-3

WALES v ROMANIA

Played 8 Wales won 6, Romania won 2
Highest scores Wales 81-9 in 2001, Romania 24-6 in 1983
Biggest wins Wales 81-9 in 2001, Romania 24-6 in 1983

1983	Bucharest **Romania** 24-6
1988	Cardiff **Romania** 15-9
1994	Bucharest **Wales** 16-9
1997	Wrexham **Wales** 70-21
2001	Cardiff **Wales** 81-9
2002	Wrexham **Wales** 40-3
2003	Wrexham **Wales** 54-8
2004	Cardiff **Wales** 66-7

WALES v FIJI

Played 7 Wales won 6, Fiji won 1
Highest scores Wales 58-14 in 2002, Fiji 38-34 in 2007
Biggest win Wales 58-14 in 2002, Fiji 38-34 in 2007

1985	Cardiff **Wales** 40-3	2002	Cardiff **Wales** 58-14
1986	Suva **Wales** 22-15	2005	Cardiff **Wales** 11-10
1994	Suva **Wales** 23-8	2007	Nantes WC **Fiji** 38-34
1995	Cardiff **Wales** 19-15		

WALES v TONGA

Played 6 Wales won 6
Highest scores Wales 51-7 in 2001, Tonga 20-27 in 2003
Biggest win Wales 51-7 in 2001, Tonga no win

1986	Nuku'Alofa **Wales** 15-7	1997	Swansea **Wales** 46-12
1987	Palmerston North WC **Wales** 29-16	2001	Cardiff **Wales** 51-7
1994	Nuku'Alofa **Wales** 18-9	2003	Canberra WC **Wales** 27-20

WALES v SAMOA

Played 7 Wales won 4, Samoa won 3, Drawn 0
Highest scores Wales 50-6 in 2000, Samoa 38-31 in 1999
Biggest wins Wales 50-6 in 2000, Samoa 34-9 in 1994

1986	Apia **Wales** 32-14	1999	Cardiff WC **Samoa** 38-31
1988	Cardiff **Wales** 28-6	2000	Cardiff **Wales** 50-6
1991	Cardiff WC **Samoa** 16-13	2009	Cardiff **Wales** 17-13
1994	Moamoa **Samoa** 34-9		

WALES v CANADA

Played 12 Wales won 11, Canada won 1, Drawn 0
Highest scores Wales 61-26 in 2006, Canada 26-24 in 1993 & 26-61 in 2006
Biggest wins Wales 60-3 in 2005, Canada 26-24 in 1993

1987	Invercargill WC **Wales** 40-9	1994	Toronto **Wales** 33-15
1993	Cardiff **Canada** 26-24	1997	Toronto **Wales** 28-25

1999	Cardiff **Wales** 33-19	2006	Cardiff **Wales** 61-26
2002	Cardiff **Wales** 32-21	2007	Nantes WC **Wales** 42-17
2003	Melbourne WC **Wales** 41-10	2008	Cardiff **Wales** 34-13
2005	Toronto **Wales** 60-3	2009	Toronto **Wales** 32-23

WALES v UNITED STATES

Played 7 Wales won 7
Highest scores Wales 77-3 in 2005, United States 23-28 in 1997
Biggest win Wales 77-3 in 2005, United States no win

1987	Cardiff **Wales** 46-0		Wales won series 2-0
1997	Cardiff **Wales** 34-14	2000	Cardiff **Wales** 42-11
1997	*1* Wilmington **Wales** 30-20	2005	Hartford **Wales** 77-3
	2 San Francisco **Wales** 28-23	2009	Chicago **Wales** 48-15

WALES v NAMIBIA

Played 3 Wales won 3
Highest scores Wales 38-23 in 1993, Namibia 30-34 in 1990
Biggest win Wales 38-23 in 1993, Namibia no win

1990	*1* Windhoek **Wales** 18-9		Wales won series 2-0
	2 Windhoek **Wales** 34-30	1993	Windhoek **Wales** 38-23

WALES v BARBARIANS

Played 2 Wales won 1, Barbarians won 1
Highest scores Wales 31-10 in 1996, Barbarians 31-24 in 1990
Biggest wins Wales 31-10 in 1996, Barbarians 31-24 in 1990

1990	Cardiff **Barbarians** 31-24	1996	Cardiff **Wales** 31-10

WALES v ARGENTINA

Played 12 Wales won 8, Argentina won 4
Highest scores Wales 44-50 in 2004, Argentina 50-44 in 2004
Biggest win Wales 33-16 in 2009, Argentina 45-27 in 2006

1991	Cardiff WC **Wales** 16-7
1998	Llanelli **Wales** 43-30
1999	*1* Buenos Aires **Wales** 36-26
	2 Buenos Aires **Wales** 23-16
	Wales won series 2-0
1999	Cardiff WC **Wales** 23-18
2001	Cardiff **Argentina** 30-16
2004	1 Tucumán **Argentina** 50-44
	2 Buenos Aires **Wales** 35-20
	Series drawn 1-1
2006	1 Puerto Madryn **Argentina** 27-25
	2 Buenos Aires **Argentina** 45-27
	Argentina won series 2-0
2007	Cardiff **Wales** 27-20
2009	Cardiff **Wales** 33-16

WALES v ZIMBABWE

Played 3 Wales won 3
Highest scores Wales 49-11 in 1998, Zimbabwe 14-35 in 1993
Biggest win Wales 49-11 in 1998, Zimbabwe no win

1993	*1* Bulawayo **Wales** 35-14
	2 Harare **Wales** 42-13
	Wales won series 2-0
1998	Harare **Wales** 49-11

WALES v JAPAN

Played 7 Wales won 7
Highest scores Wales 98-0 in 2004, Japan 30-53 in 2001
Biggest win Wales 98-0 in 2004, Japan no win

1993	Cardiff **Wales** 55-5
1995	Bloemfontein WC **Wales 57-10**
1999	Cardiff WC **Wales** 64-15
2001	*1* Osaka **Wales** 64-10
	2 Tokyo **Wales** 53-30
	Wales won series 2-0
2004	Cardiff **Wales** 98-0
2007	Cardiff WC **Wales** 72-18

WALES v PORTUGAL

Played 1 Wales won 1
Highest scores Wales 102-11 in 1994, Portugal 11-102 in 1994
Biggest win Wales 102-11 in 1994, Portugal no win

1994	Lisbon **Wales** 102-11

WALES v SPAIN

Played 1 Wales won 1
Highest scores Wales 54-0 in 1994, Spain 0-54 in 1994
Bigegst win Wales 54-0 in 1994, Spain no win

1994 Madrid **Wales** 54-0

WALES v ITALY

Played 17 Wales won 14, Italy won 2, Drawn 1
Highest scores Wales 60-21 in 1999, Italy 30-22 in 2003
Biggest win Wales 60-21 in 1999 and 47-8 in 2008, Italy 30-22 in 2003

1994 Cardiff **Wales** 29-19
1996 Cardiff **Wales** 31-26
1996 Rome **Wales** 31-22
1998 Llanelli **Wales** 23-20
1999 Treviso **Wales** 60-21
2000 Cardiff **Wales** 47-16
2001 Rome **Wales** 33-23
2002 Cardiff **Wales** 44-20
2003 Rome **Italy** 30-22
2003 Canberra WC **Wales** 27-15
2004 Cardiff **Wales** 44-10
2005 Rome **Wales** 38-8
2006 Cardiff **Drawn** 18-18
2007 Rome **Italy** 23-20
2008 Cardiff **Wales** 47-8
2009 Rome **Wales** 20-15
2010 Cardiff **Wales** 33-10

WALES v PACIFIC ISLANDS

Played 1 Wales won 1
Highest scores Wales 38-20 in 2006, Pacific Islands 20-38 in 2006
Biggest win Wales 38-20 in 2006, Pacific Islands no win

2006 Cardiff **Wales** 38-20

BRITISH/IRISH ISLES v SOUTH AFRICA

Played 46 British/Irish won 17, South Africa won 23, Drawn 6
Highest scores: British/Irish 28–9 in 1974 & 2009, South Africa 35–16 in 1997
Biggest wins: British/Irish 28–9 in 1974 & 2009, South Africa 34–14 in 1962

1891 *1* Port Elizabeth **British/Irish** 4-0
2 Kimberley **British/Irish** 3-0
3 Cape Town **British/Irish** 4-0
British/Irish won series 3-0
1896 *1* Port Elizabeth **British/Irish** 8-0
2 Johannesburg **British/Irish** 17-8
3 Kimberley **British/Irish** 9-3
4 Cape Town **South Africa** 5-0
British/Irish won series 3-1
1903 *1* Johannesburg **Drawn** 10-10
2 Kimberley **Drawn** 0-0
3 Cape Town **South Africa** 8-0
South Africa won series 1-0 with two drawn

1910 *1* Johannesburg **South Africa** 14–10
2 Port Elizabeth **British/Irish** 8–3
3 Cape Town **South Africa** 21–5
South Africa won series 2-1

1924 *1* Durban **South Africa** 7–3
2 Johannesburg **South Africa** 17–0
3 Port Elizabeth **Drawn** 3–3
4 Cape Town **South Africa** 16–9
South Africa won series 3-0, with 1 draw

1938 *1* Johannesburg **South Africa** 26–12
2 Port Elizabeth **South Africa** 19–3
3 Cape Town **British/Irish** 21–16
South Africa won series 2-1

1955 *1* Johannesburg **British/Irish** 23–22
2 Cape Town **South Africa** 25–9
3 Pretoria **British/Irish** 9–6
4 Port Elizabeth **South Africa** 22–8
Series drawn 2-2

1962 *1* Johannesburg **Drawn** 3–3
2 Durban **South Africa** 3–0
3 Cape Town **South Africa** 8–3
4 Bloemfontein **South Africa** 34–14
South Africa won series 3-0, with 1 draw

1968 *1* Pretoria **South Africa** 25–20
2 Port Elizabeth **Drawn** 6–6
3 Cape Town **South Africa** 11–6
4 Johannesburg **South Africa** 19–6
South Africa won series 3-0, with 1 draw

1974 *1* Cape Town **British/Irish** 12–3
2 Pretoria **British/Irish** 28–9
3 Port Elizabeth **British/Irish** 26–9
4 Johannesburg **Drawn** 13–13
British/Irish won series 3-0, with 1 draw

1980 *1* Cape Town **South Africa** 26–22
2 Bloemfontein **South Africa** 26–19
3 Port Elizabeth **South Africa** 12–10
4 Pretoria **British/Irish** 17–13
South Africa won series 3-1

1997 *1* Cape Town **British/Irish** 25-16
2 Durban **British/Irish** 18-15
3 Johannesburg **South Africa** 35-16
British/Irish won series 2-1

2009 1 Durban **South Africa** 26–21
2 Pretoria **South Africa** 28–25
3 Johannesburg **British/Irish** 28–9
South Africa won series 2-1

BRITISH/IRISH ISLES v NEW ZEALAND

Played 35 British/Irish won 6, New Zealand won 27, Drawn 2
Highest scores: British/Irish 20–7 in 1993, New Zealand 48–18 in 2005
Biggest wins: British/Irish 20–7 in 1993, New Zealand 38–6 in 1983

1904 Wellington **New Zealand** 9-3

1930 *1* Dunedin **British/Irish** 6–3
2 Christchurch **New Zealand** 13–10
3 Auckland **New Zealand** 15–10
4 Wellington **New Zealand** 22–8
New Zealand won series 3-1

1950 *1* Dunedin **Drawn** 9–9
2 Christchurch **New Zealand** 8–0
3 Wellington **New Zealand** 6–3
4 Auckland **New Zealand** 11–8
New Zealand won series 3-0, with 1 draw

1959 *1* Dunedin **New Zealand** 18–17
2 Wellington **New Zealand** 11–8
3 Christchurch **New Zealand** 22–8
4 Auckland **British/Irish** 9–6
New Zealand won series 3-1

1966 *1* Dunedin **New Zealand** 20–3
2 Wellington **New Zealand** 16–12
3 Christchurch **New Zealand** 19–6
4 Auckland **New Zealand** 24–11
New Zealand won series 4-0

1971 *1* Dunedin **British/Irish** 9–3
2 Christchurch **New Zealand** 22–12
3 Wellington **British/Irish** 13–3
4 Auckland **Drawn** 14–14
British/Irish won series 2-1, with 1 draw

1977 *1* Wellington **New Zealand** 16–12
2 Christchurch **British/Irish** 13–9
3 Dunedin **New Zealand** 19–7
4 Auckland **New Zealand** 10–9
New Zealand won series 3-1

1983 *1* Christchurch **New Zealand** 16–12
2 Wellington **New Zealand** 9–0
3 Dunedin **New Zealand** 15–8
4 Auckland **New Zealand** 38–6

New Zealand won series 4-0

1993 *1* Christchurch **New Zealand** 20–18
2 Wellington **British/Irish** 20–7
3 Auckland **New Zealand** 30–13
New Zealand won series 2-1

2005 1 Christchurch **New Zealand** 21–3
2 Wellington **New Zealand** 48–18
3 Auckland **New Zealand** 38–19
New Zealand won series 3-0

ANGLO-WELSH v NEW ZEALAND

Played 3 New Zealand won 2, Drawn 1
Highest scores Anglo Welsh 5-32 in 1908, New Zealand 32-5 in 1908
Biggest win Anglo Welsh no win, New Zealand 29-0 in 1908

1908 *1* Dunedin **New Zealand** 32-5
2 Wellington **Drawn** 3-3
3 Auckland **New Zealand** 29-0
New Zealand won series 2-0 with one drawn

BRITISH/IRISH ISLES v AUSTRALIA

Played 20 British/Irish won 15, Australia won 5, Drawn 0
Highest scores: British/Irish 31–0 in 1966, Australia 35–14 in 2001
Biggest wins: British/Irish 31–0 in 1966, Australia 35–14 in 2001

1899 *1* Sydney **Australia** 13-3
2 Brisbane **British/Irish** 11-0
3 Sydney **British/Irish** 11-10
4 Sydney **British/Irish** 13-0
British/Irish won series 3-1

1904 *1* Sydney **British/Irish** 17-0
2 Brisbane **British/Irish** 17-3
3 Sydney **British/Irish** 16-0
British/Irish won series 3-0

1930 Sydney **Australia** 6–5

1950 *1* Brisbane **British/Irish** 19–6
2 Sydney **British/Irish** 24–3
British/Irish won series 2-0

1959 *1* Brisbane **British/Irish** 17–6
2 Sydney **British/Irish** 24–3
British/Irish won series 2-0

1966 *1* Sydney **British/Irish** 11–8
2 Brisbane **British/Irish** 31–0
British/Irish won series 2-0

1989 *1* Sydney **Australia** 30–12
2 Brisbane **British/Irish** 19–12
3 Sydney **British/Irish** 19–18
British/Irish won series 2-1

2001 *1* Brisbane **British/Irish** 29-13
2 Melbourne **Australia** 35-14
3 Sydney **Australia** 29-23
Australia won series 2-1

BRITISH/IRISH ISLES v ARGENTINA

Played 1 British/Irish won 0, Argentina won 0, Drawn 1
Highest scores: British/Irish 25-25 in 2005, Argentina 25–25 in 2005
Biggest wins: British/Irish no win to date, Argentina no win to date

2005 Cardiff **Drawn** 25-25

FRANCE v SOUTH AFRICA

Played 38 France won 11, South Africa won 21, Drawn 6
Highest scores France 36-26 in 2006, South Africa 52-10 in 1997
Biggest wins France 30-10 in 2002, South Africa 52-10 in 1997

1913 Bordeaux **South Africa** 38-5
1952 Paris **South Africa** 25-3
1958 *1* Cape Town **Drawn** 3-3
2 Johannesburg **France** 9-5
France won series 1-0, with 1 draw
1961 Paris **Drawn** 0-0
1964 Springs (SA) **France** 8-6
1967 *1* Durban **South Africa** 26-3
2 Bloemfontein **South Africa** 16-3
3 Johannesburg **France** 19-14
4 Cape Town **Drawn** 6-6
South Africa won series 2-1, with 1 draw
1968 *1* Bordeaux **South Africa** 12-9
2 Paris **South Africa** 16-11
South Africa won series 2-0
1971 *1* Bloemfontein **South Africa** 22-9
2 Durban **Drawn** 8-8
South Africa won series 1-0, with 1 draw
1974 *1* Toulouse **South Africa** 13-4
2 Paris **South Africa** 10-8
South Africa won series 2-0
1975 *1* Bloemfontein **South Africa** 38-25
2 Pretoria **South Africa** 33-18
South Africa won series 2-0
1980 Pretoria **South Africa** 37-15
1992 *1* Lyons **South Africa** 20-15
2 Paris **France** 29-16
Series drawn 1-1
1993 *1* Durban **Drawn** 20-20
2 Johannesburg **France** 18-17
France won series 1-0, with 1 draw
1995 Durban WC **South Africa 19-15**
1996 *1* Bordeaux **South Africa** 22-12
2 Paris **South Africa** 13-12
South Africa won series 2-0
1997 *1* Lyons **South Africa** 36-32
2 Paris **South Africa** 52-10
South Africa won series 2-0
2001 *1* Johannesburg **France** 32-23
2 Durban **South Africa** 20-15
Series drawn 1-1
2001 Paris **France** 20-10
2002 Marseilles **France** 30-10
2005 1 Durban **Drawn** 30-30
2 Port Elizabeth **South Africa** 27-13
South Africa won series 1-0, with 1 draw
2005 Paris **France** 26-20
2006 Cape Town **France** 36-26
2009 Toulouse **France** 20-13
2010 Cape Town **South Africa** 42-17

FRANCE v NEW ZEALAND

Played 49 France won 12, New Zealand won 36, Drawn 1
Highest scores France 43-31 in 1999, New Zealand 61-10 in 2007
Biggest wins France 22-8 in 1994, New Zealand 61-10 in 2007

1906 Paris **New Zealand** 38-8
1925 Toulouse **New Zealand** 30-6
1954 Paris **France** 3-0
1961 1 Auckland **New Zealand** 13-6
2 Wellington **New Zealand** 5-3
3 Christchurch **New Zealand** 32-3
New Zealand won series 3-0
1964 Paris **New Zealand** 12-3
1967 Paris **New Zealand** 21-15
1968 1 Christchurch **New Zealand** 12-9
2 Wellington **New Zealand** 9-3
3 Auckland **New Zealand** 19-12
New Zealand won series 3-0
1973 Paris **France** 13-6
1977 1 Toulouse **France** 18-13
2 Paris **New Zealand** 15-3

	Series drawn 1-1
1979	1 Christchurch **New Zealand** 23-9
	2 Auckland **France** 24-19
	Series drawn 1-1
1981	1 Toulouse **New Zealand** 13-9
	2 Paris **New Zealand** 18-6
	New Zealand won series 2-0
1984	1 Christchurch **New Zealand** 10-9
	2 Auckland **New Zealand** 31-18
	New Zealand won series 2-0
1986	Christchurch **New Zealand** 18-9
1986	1 Toulouse **New Zealand** 19-7
	2 Nantes **France** 16-3
	Series drawn 1-1
1987	Auckland WC **New Zealand** 29-9
1989	1 Christchurch **New Zealand** 25-17
	2 Auckland **New Zealand** 34-20
	New Zealand won series 2-0
1990	1 Nantes **New Zealand** 24-3
	2 Paris **New Zealand** 30-12
	New Zealand won series 2-0
1994	1 Christchurch **France** 22-8
	2 Auckland **France** 23-20
	France won series 2-0
1995	1 Toulouse **France** 22-15
	2 Paris **New Zealand** 37-12
	Series drawn 1-1
1999	Wellington **New Zealand** 54-7
1999	Twickenham WC **France** 43-31
2000	1 Paris **New Zealand** 39-26
	2 Marseilles **France** 42-33
	Series drawn 1-1
2001	Wellington **New Zealand** 37-12
2002	Paris **Drawn** 20-20
2003	Christchurch **New Zealand** 31-23
2003	Sydney WC **New Zealand** 40-13
2004	Paris **New Zealand** 45-6
2006	1 Lyons **New Zealand** 47-3
	2 Paris **New Zealand** 23-11
	New Zealand won series 2-0
2007	1 Auckland **New Zealand** 42-11
	2 Wellington **New Zealand** 61-10
	New Zealand won series 2-0
2007	Cardiff WC **France** 20-18
2009	1 Dunedin **France** 27-22
	2 Wellington **New Zealand** 14-10
	Series drawn 1-1
2009	Marseilles **New Zealand** 39-12

FRANCE v AUSTRALIA

Played 40 France won 16, Australia won 22, Drawn 2
Highest scores France 34-6 in 1976, Australia 48-31 in 1990
Biggest wins France 34-6 in 1976, Australia 40-10 in 2008

1928	Paris **Australia** 11-8
1948	Paris **France** 13-6
1958	Paris **France** 19-0
1961	Sydney **France** 15-8
1967	Paris **France** 20-14
1968	Sydney **Australia** 11-10
1971	*1* Toulouse **Australia** 13-11
	2 Paris **France** 18-9
	Series drawn 1-1
1972	*1* Sydney **Drawn** 14-14
	2 Brisbane **France** 16-15
	France won series 1-0, with 1 draw
1976	*1* Bordeaux **France** 18-15
	2 Paris **France** 34-6
	France won series 2-0
1981	*1* Brisbane **Australia** 17-15
	2 Sydney **Australia** 24-14
	Australia won series 2-0
1983	*1* Clermont-Ferrand **Drawn** 15-15
	2 Paris **France** 15-6
	France won series 1-0, with 1 draw
1986	Sydney **Australia** 27-14
1987	Sydney WC **France** 30-24
1989	*1* Strasbourg **Australia** 32-15
	2 Lille **France** 25-19
	Series drawn 1-1
1990	*1* Sydney **Australia** 21-9
	2 Brisbane **Australia** 48-31
	3 Sydney **France** 28-19
	Australia won series 2-1
1993	*1* Bordeaux **France** 16-13
	2 Paris **Australia** 24-3
	Series drawn 1-1
1997	*1* Sydney **Australia** 29-15

	2 Brisbane **Australia** 26-19
	Australia won series 2-0
1998	Paris **Australia** 32-21
1999	Cardiff WC **Australia** 35-12
2000	Paris **Australia** 18-13
2001	Marseilles **France** 14-13
2002	*1* Melbourne **Australia** 29-17
	2 Sydney **Australia** 31-25
	Australia won series 2-0
2004	Paris **France** 27-14
2005	Brisbane **Australia** 37-31
2005	Marseilles **France** 26-16
2008	*1* Sydney **Australia** 34-13
	2 Brisbane **Australia** 40-10
	Australia won series 2-0
2008	Paris **Australia** 18-13
2009	Sydney **Australia** 22-6

FRANCE v UNITED STATES

Played 7 France won 6, United States won 1, Drawn 0
Highest scores France 41-9 in 1991 and 41-14 in 2003, United States 31-39 in 2004
Biggest wins France 41-9 in 1991, United States 17-3 in 1924

1920	Paris **France** 14-5
1924	Paris **United States** 17-3
1976	Chicago **France** 33-14
1991	*1* Denver **France** 41-9
	2 Colorado Springs **France** 10-3*
	*Abandoned after 43 mins
	France won series 2-0
2003	Wollongong WC **France** 41-14
2004	Hartford **France** 39-31

FRANCE v ROMANIA

Played 49 France won 39, Romania won 8, Drawn 2
Highest scores France 67-20 in 2000, Romania 21-33 in 1991
Biggest wins France 59-3 in 1924, Romania 15-0 in 1980

1924	Paris **France** 59-3
1938	Bucharest **France** 11-8
1957	Bucharest **France** 18-15
1957	Bordeaux **France** 39-0
1960	Bucharest **Romania** 11-5
1961	Bayonne **Drawn** 5-5
1962	Bucharest **Romania** 3-0
1963	Toulouse **Drawn** 6-6
1964	Bucharest **France** 9-6
1965	Lyons **France** 8-3
1966	Bucharest **France** 9-3
1967	Nantes **France** 11-3
1968	Bucharest **Romania** 15-14
1969	Tarbes **France** 14-9
1970	Bucharest **France** 14-3
1971	Béziers **France** 31-12
1972	Constanza **France** 15-6
1973	Valence **France** 7-6
1974	Bucharest **Romania** 15-10
1975	Bordeaux **France** 36-12
1976	Bucharest **Romania** 15-12
1977	Clermont-Ferrand **France** 9-6
1978	Bucharest **France** 9-6
1979	Montauban **France** 30-12
1980	Bucharest **Romania** 15-0
1981	Narbonne **France** 17-9
1982	Bucharest **Romania** 13-9
1983	Toulouse **France** 26-15
1984	Bucharest **France** 18-3
1986	Lille **France** 25-13
1986	Bucharest **France** 20-3
1987	Wellington WC **France** 55-12
1987	Agen **France** 49-3
1988	Bucharest **France** 16-12
1990	Auch **Romania** 12-6
1991	Bucharest **France** 33-21

1991	Béziers WC **France** 30-3	1997	Bucharest **France** 51-20
1992	Le Havre **France** 25-6	1997	Lourdes LC **France 39-3**
1993	Bucharest **France** 37-20	1999	Castres **France** 62-8
1993	Brive **France** 51-0	2000	Bucharest **France** 67-20
1995	Bucharest **France** 24-15	2003	Lens **France** 56-8
1995	Tucumán LC **France 52-8**	2006	Bucharest **France** 62-14
1996	Aurillac **France** 64-12		

FRANCE v NEW ZEALAND MAORI

Played 1 New Zealand Maori won 1
Highest scores France 3-12 in 1926, New Zealand Maori 12-3 in 1926
Biggest win France no win, New Zealand Maori 12-3 in 1926

1926	Paris **New Zealand Maori** 12-3

FRANCE v GERMANY

Played 15 France won 13, Germany won 2, Drawn 0
Highest scores France 38-17 in 1933, Germany 17-16 in 1927 & 17-38 in 1933
Biggest wins France 34-0 in 1931, Germany 3-0 in 1938

1927	Paris **France** 30-5	1934	Hanover **France** 13-9
1927	Frankfurt **Germany** 17-16	1935	Paris **France** 18-3
1928	Hanover **France** 14-3	1936	*1* Berlin **France** 19-14
1929	Paris **France** 24-0		*2* Hanover **France** 6-3
1930	Berlin **France** 31-0		France won series 2-0
1931	Paris **France** 34-0	1937	Paris **France** 27-6
1932	Frankfurt **France** 20-4	1938	Frankfurt **Germany** 3-0
1933	Paris **France** 38-17	1938	Bucharest **France** 8-5

FRANCE v ITALY

Played 31 France won 30, Italy won 1, Drawn 0
Highest scores France 60-13 in 1967, Italy 40-32 in 1997
Biggest wins France 60-13 in 1967, Italy 40-32 in 1997

1937	Paris **France** 43-5	1953	Lyons **France** 22-8
1952	Milan **France** 17-8	1954	Rome **France** 39-12

1955	Grenoble **France** 24-0	1997	Grenoble **Italy** 40-32
1956	Padua **France** 16-3	1997	Auch LC **France 30-19**
1957	Agen **France** 38-6	2000	Paris **France** 42-31
1958	Naples **France** 11-3	2001	Rome **France** 30-19
1959	Nantes **France** 22-0	2002	Paris **France** 33-12
1960	Treviso **France** 26-0	2003	Rome **France** 53-27
1961	Chambéry **France** 17-0	2004	Paris **France** 25-0
1962	Brescia **France** 6-3	2005	Rome **France** 56-13
1963	Grenoble **France** 14-12	2006	Paris **France** 37-12
1964	Parma **France** 12-3	2007	Rome **France** 39-3
1965	Pau **France** 21-0	2008	Paris **France** 25-13
1966	Naples **France** 21-0	2009	Rome **France** 50-8
1967	Toulon **France** 60-13	2010	Paris **France** 46-20
1995	Buenos Aires LC **France 34-22**		

FRANCE v BRITISH XVs

Played 5 France won 2, British XVs won 3, Drawn 0
Highest scores France 27-29 in 1989, British XV 36-3 in 1940
Biggest wins France 21-9 in 1945, British XV 36-3 in 1940

1940	Paris **British XV** 36-3	1946	Paris **France** 10-0
1945	Paris **France** 21-9	1989	Paris **British XV** 29-27
1945	Richmond **British XV** 27-6		

FRANCE v WALES XVs

Played 2 France won 1, Wales XV won 1
Highest scores France 12-0 in 1946, Wales XV 8-0 in 1945
Biggest win France 12-0 in 1946, Wales XV 8-0 in 1945

1945	Swansea **Wales XV** 8-0	1946	Paris **France** 12-0

FRANCE v IRELAND XVs

Played 1 France won 1
Highest scores France 4-3 in 1946, Ireland XV 3-4 in 1946
Biggest win France 4-3 in 1946, Ireland XV no win

1946	Dublin **France** 4-3

FRANCE v NEW ZEALAND ARMY

Played 1 New Zealand Army won 1
Highest scores France 9-14 in 1946, New Zealand Army 14-9 in 1946
Biggest win France no win, New Zealand Army 14-9 in 1946

1946 Paris **New Zealand Army** 14-9

FRANCE v ARGENTINA

Played 43 France won 31, Argentina won 11, Drawn 1
Highest scores France 47-12 in 1995 & 47-26 in 1999, Argentina 41-13 in 2010
Biggest wins France 47-12 in 1995, Argentina 41-13 in 2010

1949	*1* Buenos Aires **France** 5-0
	2 Buenos Aires **France** 12-3
	France won series 2-0
1954	*1* Buenos Aires **France** 22-8
	2 Buenos Aires **France** 30-3
	France won series 2-0
1960	*1* Buenos Aires **France** 37-3
	2 Buenos Aires **France** 12-3
	3 Buenos Aires **France** 29-6
	France won series 3-0
1974	*1* Buenos Aires **France** 20-15
	2 Buenos Aires **France** 31-27
	France won series 2-0
1975	*1* Lyons **France** 29-6
	2 Paris **France** 36-21
	France won series 2-0
1977	*1* Buenos Aires **France** 26-3
	2 Buenos Aires **Drawn** 18-18
	France won series 1-0, with 1 draw
1982	*1* Toulouse **France** 25-12
	2 Paris **France** 13-6
	France won series 2-0
1985	*1* Buenos Aires **Argentina** 24-16
	2 Buenos Aires **France** 23-15
	Series drawn 1-1
1986	*1* Buenos Aires **Argentina** 15-13
	2 Buenos Aires **France** 22-9
	Series drawn 1-1
1988	*1* Buenos Aires **France** 18-15
	2 Buenos Aires **Argentina** 18-6
	Series drawn 1-1
1988	*1* Nantes **France** 29-9
	2 Lille **France** 28-18
	France won series 2-0
1992	*1* Buenos Aires **France** 27-12
	2 Buenos Aires **France** 33-9
	France won series 2-0
1992	Nantes **Argentina** 24-20
1995	Buenos Aires LC **France** 47-12
1996	*1* Buenos Aires **France** 34-27
	2 Buenos Aires **France** 34-15
	France won series 2-0
1997	Tarbes LC **France** 32-27
1998	*1* Buenos Aires **France** 35-18
	2 Buenos Aires **France** 37-12
	France won series 2-0
1998	Nantes **France** 34-14
1999	Dublin WC **France** 47-26
2002	Buenos Aires **Argentina** 28-27
2003	*1* Buenos Aires **Argentina** 10-6
	2 Buenos Aires **Argentina** 33-32
	Argentina won series 2-0
2004	Marseilles **Argentina** 24-14
2006	Paris **France** 27-26
2007	Paris WC **Argentina** 17-12
2007	Paris WC **Argentina** 34-10
2008	Marseilles **France** 12-6
2010	Buenos Aires **Argentina** 41-13

FRANCE v CZECHOSLOVAKIA

Played 2 France won 2
Highest scores France 28-3 in 1956, Czechoslovakia 6-19 in 1968
Biggest win France 28-3 in 1956, Czechoslovakia no win

1956 Toulouse **France** 28-3	1968 Prague **France** 19-6

FRANCE v FIJI

Played 7 France won 7
Highest scores France 77-10 in 2001, Fiji 19-28 in 1999
Biggest win France 77-10 in 2001, Fiji no win

1964 Paris **France** 21-3	1999 Toulouse WC **France** 28-19
1987 Auckland WC **France** 31-16	2001 Saint Etienne **France** 77-10
1991 Grenoble WC **France** 33-9	2003 Brisbane WC **France** 61-18
1998 Suva **France** 34-9	

FRANCE v JAPAN

Played 2 France won 2
Highest scores France 51-29 in 2003, Japan 29-51 in 2003
Biggest win France 51-29 in 2003, Japan no win

1973 Bordeaux **France** 30-18	2003 Townsville WC **France** 51-29

FRANCE v ZIMBABWE

Played 1 France won 1
Highest scores France 70-12 in 1987, Zimbabwe 12-70 in 1987
Biggest win France 70-12 in 1987, Zimbabwe no win

1987 Auckland WC **France** 70-12

FRANCE v CANADA

Played 7 France won 6, Canada won 1, Drawn 0
Highest scores France 50-6 in 2005, Canada 20-33 in 1999
Biggest wins France 50-6 in 2005, Canada 18-16 in 1994

1991	Agen WC **France** 19-13	2002	Paris **France** 35-3
1994	Nepean **Canada** 18-16	2004	Toronto **France** 47-13
1994	Besançon **France** 28-9	2005	Nantes **France** 50-6
1999	Béziers WC **France** 33-20		

FRANCE v TONGA

Played 3 France won 2, Tonga won 1
Highest scores France 43-8 in 2005, Tonga 20-16 in 1999
Biggest win France 43-8 in 2005, Tonga 20-16 in 1999

1995	Pretoria WC **France** 38-10	2005	Toulouse **France** 43-8
1999	Nuku'alofa **Tonga** 20-16		

FRANCE v IVORY COAST

Played 1 France won 1
Highest scores France 54-18 in 1995, Ivory Coast 18-54 in 1995
Biggest win France 54-18 in 1995, Ivory Coast no win

1995	Rustenburg WC **France** 54-18

FRANCE v SAMOA

Played 2 France won 2
Highest scores France 43-5 in 2009, Samoa 22-39 in 1999
Biggest win France 43-5 in 2009, Samoa no win

1999	Apia **France** 39-22	2009	Paris **France** 43-5

FRANCE v NAMIBIA

Played 2 France won 2
Highest scores France 87-10 in 2007, Namibia 13-47 in 1999
Biggest win France 87-10 in 2007, Namibia no win

1999 Bordeaux WC **France** 47-13
2007 Toulouse WC **France** 87-10

FRANCE v GEORGIA

Played 1 France won 1
Highest scores France 64-7 in 2007, Georgia 7-64 in 2007
Biggest win France 64-7 in 2007, Georgia no win

2007 Marseilles WC **France** 64-7

FRANCE v PACIFIC ISLANDS

Played 1 Wales won 1
Highest scores France 42-17 in 2008, Pacific Islands 17-42 in 2008
Biggest win France 42-17 in 2008, Pacific Islands no win

2008 Sochaux **France** 42-17

SOUTH AFRICA v NEW ZEALAND

Played 81 New Zealand won 45, South Africa won 33, Drawn 3
Highest scores New Zealand 55-35 in 1997, South Africa 46-40 in 2000
Biggest wins New Zealand 52-16 in 2003, South Africa 17-0 in 1928

1921 *1* Dunedin **New Zealand** 13-5
2 Auckland **South Africa** 9-5
3 Wellington **Drawn** 0-0
Series drawn 1-1, with 1 draw
1928 *1* Durban **South Africa** 17-0
2 Johannesburg **New Zealand** 7-6
3 Port Elizabeth **South Africa** 11-6
4 Cape Town **New Zealand** 13-5
Series drawn 2-2
1937 *1* Wellington **New Zealand** 13-7
2 Christchurch **South Africa** 13-6
3 Auckland **South Africa** 17-6
South Africa won series 2-1
1949 *1* Cape Town **South Africa** 15-11
2 Johannesburg **South Africa** 12-6
3 Durban **South Africa** 9-3
4 Port Elizabeth **South Africa** 11-8
South Africa won series 4-0
1956 *1* Dunedin **New Zealand** 10-6
2 Wellington **South Africa** 8-3
3 Christchurch **New Zealand** 17-10
4 Auckland **New Zealand** 11-5
New Zealand won series 3-1
1960 *1* Johannesburg **South Africa** 13-0
2 Cape Town **New Zealand** 11-3
3 Bloemfontein **Drawn** 11-11
4 Port Elizabeth **South Africa** 8-3
South Africa won series 2-1, with 1 draw
1965 *1* Wellington **New Zealand** 6-3
2 Dunedin **New Zealand** 13-0
3 Christchurch **South Africa** 19-16
4 Auckland **New Zealand** 20-3
New Zealand won series 3-1
1970 *1* Pretoria **South Africa** 17-6
2 Cape Town **New Zealand** 9-8
3 Port Elizabeth **South Africa** 14-3
4 Johannesburg **South Africa** 20-17
South Africa won series 3-1
1976 *1* Durban **South Africa** 16-7
2 Bloemfontein **New Zealand** 15-9

3 Cape Town **South Africa** 15-10
4 Johannesburg **South Africa** 15-14
South Africa won series 3-1
1981 *1* Christchurch **New Zealand** 14-9
2 Wellington **South Africa** 24-12
3 Auckland **New Zealand** 25-22
New Zealand won series 2-1
1992 Johannesburg **New Zealand** 27-24
1994 *1* Dunedin **New Zealand** 22-14
2 Wellington **New Zealand** 13-9
3 Auckland **Drawn** 18-18
New Zealand won series 2-0, with 1 draw
1995 Johannesburg WC **South Africa** 15-12 (*aet*)
1996 Christchurch TN **New Zealand** 15-11
1996 Cape Town TN **New Zealand** 29-18
1996 *1* Durban **New Zealand** 23-19
2 Pretoria **New Zealand** 33-26
3 Johannesburg **South Africa** 32-22
New Zealand won series 2-1
1997 Johannesburg TN **New Zealand** 35-32
1997 Auckland TN **New Zealand** 55-35
1998 Wellington TN **South Africa** 13-3
1998 Durban TN **South Africa** 24-23
1999 Dunedin TN **New Zealand** 28-0
1999 Pretoria TN **New Zealand** 34-18
1999 Cardiff WC **South Africa** 22-18
2000 Christchurch TN **New Zealand** 25-12
2000 Johannesburg TN **South Africa** 46-40
2001 Cape Town TN **New Zealand** 12-3
2001 Auckland TN **New Zealand** 26-15
2002 Wellington TN **New Zealand** 41-20
2002 Durban TN **New Zealand** 30-23
2003 Pretoria TN **New Zealand** 52-16
2003 Dunedin TN **New Zealand** 19-11
2003 Melbourne WC **New Zealand** 29-9
2004 Christchurch TN **New Zealand** 23-21
2004 Johannesburg TN **South Africa** 40-26
2005 Cape Town TN **South Africa** 22-16
2005 Dunedin TN **New Zealand** 31-27
2006 Wellington TN **New Zealand** 35-17
2006 Pretoria TN **New Zealand** 45-26
2006 Rustenburg TN **South Africa** 21-20
2007 Durban TN **New Zealand** 26-21
2007 Christchurch TN **New Zealand** 33-6
2008 Wellington TN **New Zealand** 19-8
2008 Dunedin TN **South Africa** 30-28
2008 Cape Town TN **New Zealand** 19-0
2009 Bloemfontein TN **South Africa** 28-19
2009 Durban TN **South Africa** 31-19
2009 Hamilton TN **South Africa** 32-29
2010 Auckland TN **New Zealand** 32-12
2010 Wellington TN **New Zealand** 31-17
2010 Soweto TN **New Zealand** 29-22

SOUTH AFRICA v AUSTRALIA

Played 71 South Africa won 41, Australia won 29, Drawn 1
Highest scores South Africa 61-22 in 1997, Australia 49-0 in 2006
Biggest wins South Africa 53-8 in 2008, Australia 49-0 in 2006

1933 *1* Cape Town **South Africa** 17-3
2 Durban **Australia** 21-6
3 Johannesburg **South Africa** 12-3
4 Port Elizabeth **South Africa** 11-0
5 Bloemfontein **Australia** 15-4
South Africa won series 3-2
1937 *1* Sydney **South Africa** 9-5
2 Sydney **South Africa** 26-17
South Africa won series 2-0
1953 *1* Johannesburg **South Africa** 25-3
2 Cape Town **Australia** 18-14
3 Durban **South Africa** 18-8
4 Port Elizabeth **South Africa** 22-9
South Africa won series 3-1
1956 *1* Sydney **South Africa** 9-0
2 Brisbane **South Africa** 9-0
South Africa won series 2-0
1961 *1* Johannesburg **South Africa** 28-3
2 Port Elizabeth **South Africa** 23-11
South Africa won series 2-0
1963 *1* Pretoria **South Africa** 14-3
2 Cape Town **Australia** 9-5
3 Johannesburg **Australia** 11-9
4 Port Elizabeth **South Africa** 22-6
Series drawn 2-2
1965 *1* Sydney **Australia** 18-11
2 Brisbane **Australia** 12-8
Australia won series 2-0
1969 *1* Johannesburg **South Africa** 30-11
2 Durban **South Africa** 16-9
3 Cape Town **South Africa** 11-3
4 Bloemfontein **South Africa** 19-8
South Africa won series 4-0
1971 *1* Sydney **South Africa** 19-11
2 Brisbane **South Africa** 14-6
3 Sydney **South Africa** 18-6
South Africa won series 3-0
1992 Cape Town **Australia** 26-3

1993 *1* Sydney **South Africa** 19-12
2 Brisbane **Australia** 28-20
3 Sydney **Australia** 19-12
Australia won series 2-1
1995 Cape Town WC **South Africa** 27-18
1996 Sydney TN **Australia** 21-16
1996 Bloemfontein TN **South Africa** 25-19
1997 Brisbane TN **Australia** 32-20
1997 Pretoria TN **South Africa** 61-22
1998 Perth TN **South Africa** 14-13
1998 Johannesburg TN **South Africa** 29-15
1999 Brisbane TN **Australia** 32-6
1999 Cape Town TN **South Africa** 10-9
1999 Twickenham WC **Australia** 27-21
2000 Melbourne **Australia** 44-23
2000 Sydney TN **Australia** 26-6
2000 Durban TN **Australia** 19-18
2001 Pretoria TN **South Africa** 20-15
2001 Perth TN **Drawn** 14-14
2002 Brisbane TN **Australia** 38-27
2002 Johannesburg TN **South Africa** 33-31
2003 Cape Town TN **South Africa** 26-22
2003 Brisbane TN **Australia** 29-9
2004 Perth TN **Australia** 30-26
2004 Durban TN **South Africa** 23-19
2005 Sydney **Australia** 30-12
2005 Johannesburg **South Africa** 33-20
2005 Pretoria TN **South Africa** 22-16
2005 Perth TN **South Africa** 22-19
2006 Brisbane TN **Australia** 49-0
2006 Sydney TN **Australia** 20-18
2006 Johannesburg TN **South Africa** 24-16
2007 Cape Town TN **South Africa** 22-19
2007 Sydney TN **Australia** 25-17
2008 Perth TN **Australia** 16-9
2008 Durban TN **Australia** 27-15
2008 Johannesburg TN **South Africa** 53-8
2009 Cape Town TN **South Africa** 29-17
2009 Perth TN **South Africa** 32-25
2009 Brisbane TN **Australia** 21-6
2010 Brisbane TN **Australia** 30-13
2010 Pretoria TN **South Africa** 44-31
2010 Bloemfontein TN **Australia** 41-39

SOUTH AFRICA v WORLD XVs

Played 3 South Africa won 3
Highest scores South Africa 45-24 in 1977, World XV 24-45 in 1977
Biggest win South Africa 45-24 in 1977, World XV no win

1977 Pretoria **South Africa** 45-24
1989 *1* Cape Town **South Africa** 20-19
2 Johannesburg **South Africa** 22-16
South Africa won series 2-0

SOUTH AFRICA v SOUTH AMERICA

Played 8 South Africa won 7, South America won 1, Drawn 0
Highest scores South Africa 50-18 in 1982, South America 21-12 in 1982
Biggest wins South Africa 50-18 in 1982, South America 21-12 in 1982

1980 *1* Johannesburg **South Africa** 24-9
2 Durban **South Africa** 18-9
South Africa won series 2-0
1980 *1* Montevideo **South Africa** 22-13
2 Santiago **South Africa** 30-16
South Africa won series 2-0
1982 *1* Pretoria **South Africa** 50-18
2 Bloemfontein **South America** 21-12
Series drawn 1-1
1984 *1* Pretoria **South Africa** 32-15
2 Cape Town **South Africa** 22-13
South Africa won series 2-0

SOUTH AFRICA v UNITED STATES

Played 3 South Africa won 3
Highest scores South Africa 64-10 in 2007, United States 20-43 in 2001
Biggest win South Africa 64-10 in 2007, United States no win

1981	Glenville **South Africa** 38-7
2001	Houston **South Africa** 43-20
2007	Montpellier WC **South Africa** 64-10

SOUTH AFRICA v NEW ZEALAND CAVALIERS

Played 4 South Africa won 3, New Zealand Cavaliers won 1, Drawn 0
Highest scores South Africa 33-18 in 1986, New Zealand Cavaliers 19-18 in 1986
Biggest wins South Africa 33-18 in 1986, New Zealand Cavaliers 19-18 in 1986

1986	*1* Cape Town **South Africa** 21-15
	2 Durban **New Zealand Cavaliers** 19-18
	3 Pretoria **South Africa** 33-18
	4 Johannesburg **South Africa** 24-10
	South Africa won series 3-1

SOUTH AFRICA v ARGENTINA

Played 13 South Africa won 13
Highest scores South Africa 63-9 in 2008, Argentina 33-37 in 2000
Biggest wins South Africa 63-9 in 2008, Argentina no win

1993	*1* Buenos Aires **South Africa** 29-26
	2 Buenos Aires **South Africa** 52-23
	South Africa won series 2-0
1994	*1* Port Elizabeth **South Africa** 42-22
	2 Johannesburg **South Africa** 46-26
	South Africa won series 2-0
1996	*1* Buenos Aires **South Africa** 46-15
	2 Buenos Aires **South Africa** 44-21
	South Africa win series 2-0
2000	Buenos Aires **South Africa** 37-33
2002	Springs **South Africa** 49-29
2003	Port Elizabeth **South Africa** 26-25
2004	Buenos Aires **South Africa** 39-7
2005	Buenos Aires **South Africa** 34-23
2007	Paris WC **South Africa** 37-13
2008	Johannesburg **South Africa** 63-9

SOUTH AFRICA v SAMOA

Played 6 South Africa won 6
Highest scores South Africa 60-8 in 1995, 60-18 in 2002 and 60-10 in 2003, Samoa 18-60 in 2002
Biggest win South Africa 60-8 in 1995 and 59-7 in 2007, Samoa no win

1995	Johannesburg **South Africa** 60-8	2003	Brisbane WC **South Africa** 60-10
1995	Johannesburg WC **South Africa** 42-14	2007	Johannesburg **South Africa** 35-8
2002	Pretoria **South Africa** 60-18	2007	Paris WC **South Africa** 59-7

SOUTH AFRICA v ROMANIA

Played 1 South Africa won 1
Highest score South Africa 21-8 in 1995, Romania 8-21 in 1995
Biggest win South Africa 21-8 in 1995, Romania no win

1995	Cape Town WC **South Africa** 21-8

SOUTH AFRICA v CANADA

Played 2 South Africa won 2
Highest scores South Africa 51-18 in 2000, Canada 18-51 in 2000
Biggest win South Africa 51-18 in 2000, Canada no win

1995	Port Elizabeth WC **South Africa** 20-0	2000	East London **South Africa** 51-18

SOUTH AFRICA v ITALY

Played 10 South Africa won 10
Highest scores South Africa 101-0 in 1999, Italy 31-62 in 1997
Biggest win South Africa 101-0 in 1999, Italy no win

1995	Rome **South Africa** 40-21	2001	Genoa **South Africa** 54-26
1997	Bologna **South Africa** 62-31	2008	Cape Town **South Africa** 26-0
1999	*1* Port Elizabeth **South Africa** 74-3	2009	Udine **South Africa** 32-10
	2 Durban **South Africa** 101-0	2010	*1* Witbank **South Africa** 29-13
	South Africa won series 2-0		*2* East London **South Africa** 55-11
2001	Port Elizabeth **South Africa** 60-14		South Africa won series 2-0

SOUTH AFRICA v FIJI

Played 2 South Africa won 2
Highest scores South Africa 43-18 in 1996, Fiji 20-37 in 2007
Biggest win South Africa 43-18 in 1996, Fiji no win

1996 Pretoria **South Africa** 43-18	2007 Marseilles WC **South Africa** 37-20

SOUTH AFRICA v TONGA

Played 2 South Africa won 2
Higest scores South Africa 74-10 in 1997, Tonga 25-30 in 2007
Biggest win South Africa 74-10 in 1997, Tonga no win

1997 Cape Town **South Africa** 74-10	2007 Lens WC **South Africa** 30-25

SOUTH AFRICA v SPAIN

Played 1 South Africa won 1
Highest scores South Africa 47-3 in 1999, Spain 3-47 in 1999
Biggest win South Africa 47-3 in 1999, Spain no win

1999 Murrayfield WC **South Africa** 47-3

SOUTH AFRICA v URUGUAY

Played 3 South Africa won 3
Highest scores South Africa 134-3 in 2005, Uruguay 6-72 in 2003
Biggest win South Africa 134-3 in 2005, Uruguay no win

1999 Glasgow WC **South Africa** 39-3	Perth WC **South Africa** 72-6
2003 Glasgow *WC* **South Africa** 39-3	2005 East London **South Africa** 134-3

SOUTH AFRICA v GEORGIA

Played 1 South Africa won 1
Highest scores South Africa 46-19 in 2003, Georgia 19-46 in 2003
Biggest win South Africa 46-19 in 2003, Georgia no win

2003 Sydney WC **South Africa** 46-19

SOUTH AFRICA v PACIFIC ISLANDS

Played 1 South Africa won 1
Highest scores South Africa 38-24 in 2004, Pacific Islands 24-38 in 2004
Biggest win South Africa 38-24 in 2004, Pacific Islands no win

2004 Gosford (Aus) **South Africa** 38-24

SOUTH AFRICA v NAMIBIA

Played 1 South Africa won 1
Highest scores South Africa 105-13 in 2007, Namibia 13-105 in 2007
Biggest win South Africa 105-13 in 2007, Namibia no win

2007 Cape Town **South Africa** 105-13

NEW ZEALAND v AUSTRALIA

Played 139 New Zealand won 95, Australia won 39, Drawn 5
Highest scores New Zealand 50-21 in 2003, Australia 35-39 in 2000
Biggest wins New Zealand 43-6 in 1996, Australia 28-7 in 1999

1903 Sydney **New Zealand** 22-3
1905 Dunedin **New Zealand** 14-3
1907 *1* Sydney **New Zealand** 26-6
2 Brisbane **New Zealand** 14-5
3 Sydney **Drawn** 5-5
New Zealand won series 2-0, with 1 draw
1910 *1* Sydney **New Zealand** 6-0
2 Sydney **Australia** 11-0
3 Sydney **New Zealand** 28-13
New Zealand won series 2-1
1913 *1* Wellington **New Zealand** 30-5
2 Dunedin **New Zealand** 25-13
3 Christchurch **Australia** 16-5
New Zealand won series 2-1
1914 *1* Sydney **New Zealand** 5-0
2 Brisbane **New Zealand** 17-0
3 Sydney **New Zealand** 22-7

New Zealand won series 3-0
1929 *1* Sydney **Australia** 9-8
2 Brisbane **Australia** 17-9
3 Sydney **Australia** 15-13
Australia won series 3-0
1931 Auckland **New Zealand** 20-13
1932 *1* Sydney **Australia** 22-17
2 Brisbane **New Zealand** 21-3
3 Sydney **New Zealand** 21-13
New Zealand won series 2-1
1934 *1* Sydney **Australia** 25-11
2 Sydney **Drawn** 3-3
Australia won series 1-0, with 1 draw
1936 *1* Wellington **New Zealand** 11-6
2 Dunedin **New Zealand** 38-13
New Zealand won series 2-0
1938 *1* Sydney **New Zealand** 24-9
2 Brisbane **New Zealand** 20-14
3 Sydney **New Zealand** 14-6
New Zealand won series 3-0
1946 *1* Dunedin **New Zealand** 31-8
2 Auckland **New Zealand** 14-10
New Zealand won series 2-0
1947 *1* Brisbane **New Zealand** 13-5
2 Sydney **New Zealand** 27-14
New Zealand won series 2-0
1949 *1* Wellington **Australia** 11-6
2 Auckland **Australia** 16-9
Australia won series 2-0
1951 *1* Sydney **New Zealand** 8-0
2 Sydney **New Zealand** 17-11
3 Brisbane **New Zealand** 16-6
New Zealand won series 3-0
1952 *1* Christchurch **Australia** 14-9
2 Wellington **New Zealand** 15-8
Series drawn 1-1
1955 *1* Wellington **New Zealand** 16-8
2 Dunedin **New Zealand** 8-0
3 Auckland **Australia** 8-3
New Zealand won series 2-1
1957 *1* Sydney **New Zealand** 25-11
2 Brisbane **New Zealand** 22-9
New Zealand won series 2-0
1958 *1* Wellington **New Zealand** 25-3
2 Christchurch **Australia** 6-3
3 Auckland **New Zealand** 17-8
New Zealand won series 2-1
1962 *1* Brisbane **New Zealand** 20-6
2 Sydney **New Zealand** 14-5
New Zealand won series 2-0
1962 *1* Wellington **Drawn** 9-9
2 Dunedin **New Zealand** 3-0
3 Auckland **New Zealand** 16-8
New Zealand won series 2-0, with1 draw
1964 *1* Dunedin **New Zealand** 14-9
2 Christchurch **New Zealand** 18-3
3 Wellington **Australia** 20-5
New Zealand won series 2-1
1967 Wellington **New Zealand** 29-9
1968 *1* Sydney **New Zealand** 27-11
2 Brisbane **New Zealand** 19-18
New Zealand won series 2-0
1972 *1* Wellington **New Zealand** 29-6
2 Christchurch **New Zealand** 30-17
3 Auckland **New Zealand** 38-3
New Zealand won series 3-0
1974 *1* Sydney **New Zealand** 11-6
2 Brisbane **Drawn** 16-16
3 Sydney **New Zealand** 16-6
New Zealand won series 2-0, with 1 draw
1978 *1* Wellington **New Zealand** 13-12
2 Christchurch **New Zealand** 22-6
3 Auckland **Australia** 30-16
New Zealand won series 2-1
1979 Sydney **Australia** 12-6
1980 *1* Sydney **Australia** 13-9
2 Brisbane **New Zealand** 12-9
3 Sydney **Australia** 26-10
Australia won series 2-1
1982 *1* Christchurch **New Zealand** 23-16
2 Wellington **Australia** 19-16
3 Auckland **New Zealand** 33-18
New Zealand won series 2-1
1983 Sydney **New Zealand** 18-8
1984 *1* Sydney **Australia** 16-9
2 Brisbane **New Zealand** 19-15
3 Sydney **New Zealand** 25-24
New Zealand won series 2-1
1985 Auckland **New Zealand** 10-9
1986 *1* Wellington **Australia** 13-12
2 Dunedin **New Zealand** 13-12
3 Auckland **Australia** 22-9
Australia won series 2-1
1987 Sydney **New Zealand** 30-16
1988 *1* Sydney **New Zealand** 32-7
2 Brisbane **Drawn** 19-19

	3 Sydney **New Zealand** 30-9
	New Zealand won series 2-0, with 1 draw
1989	Auckland **New Zealand** 24-12
1990	*1* Christchurch **New Zealand** 21-6
	2 Auckland **New Zealand** 27-17
	3 Wellington **Australia** 21-9
	New Zealand won series 2-1
1991	*1* Sydney **Australia** 21-12
	2 Auckland **New Zealand** 6-3
1991	Dublin WC **Australia** 16-6
1992	*1* Sydney **Australia** 16-15
	2 Brisbane **Australia** 19-17
	3 Sydney **New Zealand** 26-23
	Australia won series 2-1
1993	Dunedin **New Zealand** 25-10
1994	Sydney **Australia** 20-16
1995	Auckland **New Zealand** 28-16
1995	Sydney **New Zealand** 34-23
1996	Wellington TN **New Zealand** 43-6
1996	Brisbane TN **New Zealand** 32-25
	New Zealand won series 2-0
1997	Christchurch **New Zealand** 30-13
1997	Melbourne TN **New Zealand** 33-18
1997	Dunedin TN **New Zealand** 36-24
	New Zealand won series 3-0
1998	Melbourne TN **Australia** 24-16
1998	Christchurch TN **Australia** 27-23
1998	Sydney Australia 19-14
	Australia won series 3-0
1999	Auckland TN **New Zealand** 34-15
1999	Sydney TN **Australia** 28-7
	Series drawn 1-1
2000	Sydney TN **New Zealand** 39-35
2000	Wellington TN **Australia** 24-23
	Series drawn 1-1
2001	Dunedin TN **Australia** 23-15
2001	Sydney TN **Australia** 29-26
	Australia won series 2-0
2002	Christchurch TN **New Zealand** 12-6
2002	Sydney TN **Australia** 16-14
	Series drawn 1-1
2003	Sydney TN **New Zealand** 50-21
2003	Auckland TN **New Zealand** 21-17
	New Zealand won series 2-0
2003	Sydney WC **Australia** 22-10
2004	Wellington TN **New Zealand** 16-7
2004	Sydney TN **Australia** 23-18
	Series drawn 1-1
2005	Sydney TN **New Zealand** 30-13
2005	Auckland TN **New Zealand** 34-24
	New Zealand won series 2-0
2006	Christchurch TN **New Zealand** 32-12
2006	Brisbane TN **New Zealand** 13-9
2006	Auckland TN **New Zealand** 34-27
	New Zealand won series 3-0
2007	Melbourne TN **Australia** 20-15
2007	Auckland TN **New Zealand** 26-12
	Series drawn 1-1
2008	Sydney TN **Australia** 34-19
2008	Auckland TN **New Zealand** 39-10
2008	Brisbane TN **New Zealand** 28-24
2008	Hong Kong **New Zealand** 19-14
	New Zealand won series 3-1
2009	Auckland TN **New Zealand** 22-16
2009	Sydney TN **New Zealand** 19-18
2009	Wellington TN **New Zealand** 33-6
2009	Tokyo **New Zealand** 32-19
	New Zealand won series 4-0
2010	Melbourne TN **New Zealand** 49-28
2010	Christchurch TN **New Zealand** 20-10
2010	Sydney TN **New Zealand** 23-22

NEW ZEALAND v UNITED STATES

Played 2 New Zealand won 2
Highest scores New Zealand 51-3 in 1913, United States 6-46 in 1991
Biggest win New Zealand 51-3 in 1913, United States no win

1913	Berkeley **New Zealand** 51-3
1991	Gloucester WC **New Zealand** 46-6

NEW ZEALAND v ROMANIA

Played 2 New Zealand won 2
Highest score New Zealand 85-8 in 2007, Romania 8-85 in 2007
Biggest win New Zealand 85-8 in 2007, Romania no win

1981 Bucharest **New Zealand** 14-6
2007 Toulouse WC **New Zealand** 85-8

NEW ZEALAND v ARGENTINA

Played 13 New Zealand won 12, Drawn 1
Highest scores New Zealand 93-8 in 1997, Argentina 21-21 in 1985
Biggest win New Zealand 93-8 in 1997, Argentina no win

1985 *1* Buenos Aires **New Zealand** 33-20
2 Buenos Aires **Drawn** 21-21
New Zealand won series 1-0, with 1 draw
1987 Wellington *WC* **New Zealand** 46-15
1989 *1* Dunedin **New Zealand** 60-9
2 Wellington **New Zealand** 49-12
New Zealand won series 2-0
1991 *1* Buenos Aires **New Zealand** 28-14
2 Buenos Aires **New Zealand** 36-6
New Zealand won series 2-0
1997 *1* Wellington **New Zealand** 93-8
2 Hamilton **New Zealand** 62-10
New Zealand won series 2-0
2001 Christchurch **New Zealand** 67-19
2001 Buenos Aires **New Zealand** 24-20
2004 Hamilton **New Zealand** 41-7
2006 Buenos Aires **New Zealand** 25-19

NEW ZEALAND v ITALY

Played 11 New Zealand won 11
Highest scores New Zealand 101-3 in 1999, Italy 21-31 in 1991
Biggest win New Zealand 101-3 in 1999, Italy no win

1987 Auckland WC **New Zealand** 70-6
1991 Leicester WC **New Zealand** 31-21
1995 Bologna **New Zealand** 70-6
1999 Huddersfield WC **New Zealand** 101-3
2000 Genoa **New Zealand** 56-19
2002 Hamilton **New Zealand** 64-10
2003 Melbourne WC **New Zealand** 70-7
2004 Rome **New Zealand** 59-10
2007 Marseilles WC **New Zealand** 76-14
2009 Christchurch **New Zealand** 27-6
2009 Milan **New Zealand** 20-6

NEW ZEALAND v FIJI

Played 4 New Zealand won 4
Highest scores New Zealand 91-0 in 2005, Fiji 18-68 in 2002
Biggest win New Zealand 91-0 in 2005, Fiji no win

1987	Christchurch WC **New Zealand** 74-13	2002	Wellington **New Zealand** 68-18
1997	Albany **New Zealand** 71-5	2005	Albany **New Zealand** 91-0

NEW ZEALAND v CANADA

Played 4 New Zealand won 4
Highest scores New Zealand 73-7 in 1995, Canada 13-29 in 1991 & 13-64 in 2007
Biggest win New Zealand 73-7 in 1995, Canada no win

1991	Lille WC **New Zealand** 29-13	2003	Melbourne WC **New Zealand** 68-6
1995	Auckland **New Zealand** 73-7	2007	Hamilton **New Zealand** 64-13

NEW ZEALAND v WORLD XVs

Played 3 New Zealand won 2, World XV won 1, Drawn 0
Highest scores New Zealand 54-26 in 1992, World XV 28-14 in 1992
Biggest wins New Zealand 54-26 in 1992, World XV 28-14 in 1992

1992	*1* Christchurch **World XV** 28-14	*3* Auckland **New Zealand** 26-15
	2 Wellington **New Zealand** 54-26	New Zealand won series 2-1

NEW ZEALAND v SAMOA

Played 5 New Zealand won 5
Highest scores New Zealand 101-14 in 2008, Samoa 14-101 in 2008
Biggest win New Zealand 101-14 in 2008, Samoa no win

1993	Auckland **New Zealand** 35-13	2001	Albany **New Zealand** 50-6
1996	Napier **New Zealand** 51-10	2008	New Plymouth **New Zealand** 101-14
1999	Albany **New Zealand** 71-13		

NEW ZEALAND v JAPAN

Played 1 New Zealand won 1
Highest scores New Zealand 145-17 in 1995, Japan 17-145 in 1995
Biggest win New Zealand 145-17 in 1995, Japan no win

1995 Bloemfontein WC **New Zealand** 145-17

NEW ZEALAND v TONGA

Played 3 New Zealand won 3
Highest scores New Zealand 102-0 in 2000, Tonga 9-45 in 1999
Biggest win New Zealand 102-0 in 2000, Tonga no win

1999 Bristol WC **New Zealand** 45-9
2000 Albany **New Zealand** 102-0
2003 Brisbane WC **New Zealand** 91-7

NEW ZEALAND v PACIFIC ISLANDS

Played 1 New Zealand won 1
Highest scores New Zealand 41-26 in 2004, Pacific Islands 26-41 in 2004
Biggest win New Zealand 41-26 in 2004, Pacific Islands no win

2004 Albany **New Zealand 41-26**

NEW ZEALAND v PORTUGAL

Played 1 New Zealand won 1
Highest scores New Zealand 108-13 in 2007, Portugal 13-108 in 2007
Biggest win New Zealand 108-13 in 2007, Portugal no win

2007 Lyons WC **New Zealand** 108-13

AUSTRALIA v UNITED STATES

Played 6 Australia won 6
Highest scores Australia 67-9 in 1990, United States 19-55 in 1999
Biggest win Australia 67-9 in 1990, United States no win

1912 Berkeley **Australia** 12-8
1976 Los Angeles **Australia** 24-12
1983 Sydney **Australia** 49-3
1987 Brisbane WC **Australia** 47-12
1990 Brisbane **Australia** 67-9
1999 Limerick WC **Australia** 55-19

AUSTRALIA v NEW ZEALAND XVs

Played 24 Australia won 6, New Zealand XVs won 18, Drawn 0
Highest scores Australia 26-20 in 1926, New Zealand XV 38-11 in 1923 and 38-8 in 1924
Biggest win Australia 17-0 in 1921, New Zealand XV 38-8 in 1924

1920 *1* Sydney **New Zealand XV** 26-15
2 Sydney **New Zealand XV** 14-6
3 Sydney **New Zealand XV** 24-13
New Zealand XV won series 3-0
1921 Christchurch **Australia** 17-0
1922 *1* Sydney **New Zealand XV** 26-19
2 Sydney **Australia** 14-8
3 Sydney **Australia** 8-6
Australia won series 2-1
1923 *1* Dunedin **New Zealand XV** 19-9
2 Christchurch **New Zealand XV** 34-6
3 Wellington **New Zealand XV** 38-11
New Zealand XV won series 3-0
1924 *1* Sydney **Australia** 20-16
2 Sydney **New Zealand XV** 21-5
3 Sydney **New Zealand XV** 38-8
New Zealand XV won series 2-1
1925 *1* Sydney **New Zealand XV** 26-3
2 Sydney **New Zealand XV** 4-0
3 Sydney **New Zealand XV** 11-3
New Zealand XV won series 3-0
1925 Auckland **New Zealand XV** 36-10
1926 *1* Sydney **Australia** 26-20
2 Sydney **New Zealand XV** 11-6
3 Sydney **New Zealand XV** 14-0
4 Sydney **New Zealand XV** 28-21
New Zealand XV won series 3-1
1928 *1* Wellington **New Zealand XV** 15-12
2 Dunedin **New Zealand XV** 16-14
3 Christchurch **Australia** 11-8
New Zealand XV won series 2-1

AUSTRALIA v SOUTH AFRICA XVs

Played 3 South Africa XVs won 3
Highest scores Australia 11-16 in 1921, South Africa XV 28-9 in 1921
Biggest win Australia no win, South Africa XV 28-9 in 1921

1921 *1* Sydney **South Africa XV** 25-10
2 Sydney **South Africa XV** 16-11
3 Sydney **South Africa XV** 28-9
South Africa XV won series 3-0

AUSTRALIA v NEW ZEALAND MAORIS

Played 16 Australia won 8, New Zealand Maoris won 6, Drawn 2
Highest scores Australia 31-6 in 1936, New Zealand Maoris 25-22 in 1922
Biggest wins Australia 31-6 in 1936, New Zealand Maoris 20-0 in 1946

1922 *1* Sydney **New Zealand Maoris** 25-22
2 Sydney **Australia** 28-13
3 Sydney **New Zealand Maoris** 23-22
New Zealand Maoris won series 2-1
1923 *1* Sydney **Australia** 27-23
2 Sydney **Australia** 21-16
3 Sydney **Australia** 14-12
Australia won series 3-0
1928 Wellington **New Zealand Maoris** 9-8
1931 Palmerston North **Australia** 14-3
1936 Palmerston North **Australia** 31-6
1946 Hamilton **New Zealand Maoris** 20-0
1949 *1* Sydney **New Zealand Maoris** 12-3
2 Brisbane **Drawn** 8-8
3 Sydney **Australia** 18-3
Series drawn 1-1, with 1 draw
1958 *1* Brisbane **Australia** 15-14
2 Sydney **Drawn** 3-3
3 Melbourne **New Zealand Maoris** 13-6
Series drawn 1-1, with 1 draw

AUSTRALIA v FIJI

Played 19 Australia won 16, Fiji won 2, Drawn 1
Highest scores Australia 66-20 in 1998, Fiji 28-52 in 1985
Biggest wins Australia 49-0 in 2007, Fiji 17-15 in 1952 & 18-16 in 1954

1952 *1* Sydney **Australia** 15-9
2 Sydney **Fiji** 17-15
Series drawn 1-1
1954 *1* Brisbane **Australia** 22-19
2 Sydney **Fiji** 18-16
Series drawn 1-1
1961 *1* Brisbane **Australia** 24-6
2 Sydney **Australia** 20-14
3 Melbourne **Drawn** 3-3
Australia won series 2-0, with 1 draw
1972 Suva **Australia** 21-19
1976 *1* Sydney **Australia** 22-6
2 Brisbane **Australia** 21-9
3 Sydney **Australia** 27-17
Australia won series 3-0
1980 Suva **Australia** 22-9
1984 Suva **Australia** 16-3
1985 *1* Brisbane **Australia** 52-28
2 Sydney **Australia** 31-9
Australia won series 2-0
1998 Sydney **Australia** 66-20
2007 Perth **Australia** 49-0
2007 Montpellier WC **Australia** 55-12
2010 Canberra **Australia** 49-3

AUSTRALIA v TONGA

Played 4 Australia won 3, Tonga won 1, Drawn 0
Highest scores Australia 74-0 in 1998, Tonga 16-11 in 1973
Biggest wins Australia 74-0 in 1998, Tonga 16-11 in 1973

1973 *1* Sydney **Australia** 30-12	1993 Brisbane **Australia** 52-14
2 Brisbane **Tonga** 16-11	1998 Canberra **Australia** 74-0
Series drawn 1-1	

AUSTRALIA v JAPAN

Played 4 Australia won 4
Highest scores Australia 91-3 in 2007, Japan 25-50 in 1973
Biggest win Australia 91-3 in 2007, Japan no win

1975 *1* Sydney **Australia** 37-7	1987 Sydney WC **Australia** 42-23
2 Brisbane **Australia** 50-25	2007 Lyons WC **Australia** 91-3
Australia won series 2-0	

AUSTRALIA v ARGENTINA

Played 17 Australia won 12, Argentina won 4, Drawn 1
Highest scores Australia 53-7 in 1995 & 53-6 in 2000, Argentina 27-19 in 1987
Biggest wins Australia 53-6 in 2000, Argentina 18-3 in 1983

1979 *1* Buenos Aires **Argentina** 24-13	1991 Llanelli WC **Australia** 32-19
2 Buenos Aires **Australia** 17-12	1995 *1* Brisbane **Australia** 53-7
Series drawn 1-1	*2* Sydney **Australia** 30-13
1983 *1* Brisbane **Argentina** 18-3	Australia won series 2-0
2 Sydney **Australia** 29-13	1997 *1* Buenos Aires **Australia** 23-15
Series drawn 1-1	*2* Buenos Aires **Argentina** 18-16
1986 *1* Brisbane **Australia** 39-19	Series drawn 1-1
2 Sydney **Australia** 26-0	2000 *1* Brisbane **Australia** 53-6
Australia won series 2-0	*2* Canberra **Australia** 32-25
1987 *1* Buenos Aires **Drawn** 19-19	Australia won series 2-0
2 Buenos Aires **Argentina** 27-19	2002 Buenos Aires **Australia** 17-6
Argentina won series 1-0, with 1 draw	2003 Sydney WC **Australia** 24-8

AUSTRALIA v SAMOA

Played 4 Australia won 4
Highest scores Australia 74-7 in 2005, Samoa 13-25 in 1998
Biggest win Australia 73-3 in 1994, Samoa no win

1991 Pontypool WC **Australia** 9-3
1994 Sydney **Australia** 73-3
1998 Brisbane **Australia** 25-13
2005 Sydney **Australia** 74-7

AUSTRALIA v ITALY

Played 12 Australia won 12
Highest scores Australia 69-21 in 2005, Italy 21-69 in 2005
Biggest win Australia 55-6 in 1988, Italy no win

1983 Rovigo **Australia** 29-7
1986 Brisbane **Australia** 39-18
1988 Rome **Australia** 55-6
1994 1 Brisbane **Australia** 23-20
2 Melbourne **Australia** 20-7
Australia won series 2-0
1996 Padua **Australia** 40-18
2002 Genoa **Australia** 34-3
2005 Melbourne **Australia** 69-21
2006 Rome **Australia** 25-18
2008 Padua **Australia** 30-20
2009 1 Canberra **Australia** 31-8
2 Melbourne **Australia** 34-12
Australia won series 2-0

AUSTRALIA v CANADA

Played 6 Australia won 6
Highest scores Australia 74-9 in 1996, Canada 16-43 in 1993
Biggest win Australia 74-9 in 1996, Canada no win

1985 *1* Sydney **Australia** 59-3
2 Brisbane **Australia** 43-15
Australia won series 2-0
1993 Calgary **Australia** 43-16
1995 Port Elizabeth WC **Australia** 27-11
1996 Brisbane **Australia** 74-9
2007 Bordeaux WC **Australia** 37-6

AUSTRALIA v KOREA

Played 1 Australia won 1
Highest scores Australia 65-18 in 1987, Korea 18-65 in 1987
Biggest win Australia 65-18 in 1987, Korea no win

1987 Brisbane **Australia** 65-18

AUSTRALIA v ROMANIA

Played 3 Australia won 3
Highest scores Australia 90-8 in 2003, Romania 9-57 in 1999
Biggest win Australia 90-8 in 2003, Romania no win

1995 Stellenbosch WC **Australia** 42-3
1999 Belfast WC **Australia** 57-9
2003 Brisbane WC **Australia** 90-8

AUSTRALIA v SPAIN

Played 1 Australia won 1
Highest scores Australia 92-10 in 2001, Spain 10-92 in 2001
Biggest win Australia 92-10 in 2001, Spain no win

2001 Madrid **Australia** 92-10

AUSTRALIA v NAMIBIA

Played 1 Australia won 1
Highest scores Australia 142-0 in 2003, Namibia 0-142 in 2003
Biggest win Australia 142-0 in 2003, Namibia no win

2003 Adelaide WC **Australia** 142-0

AUSTRALIA v PACIFIC ISLANDS

Played 1 Australia won 1
Highest scores Australia 29-14 in 2004, Pacific Islands 14-29 in 2004
Biggest win Australia 29-14 in 2004, Pacific Islands no win

2004 Adelaide **Australia** 29-14

MN Chan/Getty Images

Japan's Daisuke Ohata (left), with 69, is still the world record holder for most tries in Tests.

WORLD INTERNATIONAL RECORDS

The match and career records cover **official Test matches** *played by the dozen Executive Council Member Unions of the International Board (England, Scotland, Ireland, Wales, France, Italy, South Africa, New Zealand, Australia, Argentina, Canada and Japan) from 1871 up to 29 October 2010. Figures include Test performances for the (British/Irish Isles) Lions and (South American) Jaguars (shown in brackets). Where a world record has been set in a Test match played by another nation in membership of the IRB, this is shown as a footnote to the relevant table.*

MATCH RECORDS

MOST CONSECUTIVE TEST WINS

17 by N Zealand	1965 *SA* 4, 1966 *BI* 1,2,3,4, 1967 *A, E, W, F, S,* 1968 *A* 1, 2, *F* 1,2,3, 1969 *W* 1,2
17 by S Africa	1997 *A* 2, *It, F* 1,2, *E, S,* 1998 *I* 1,2, *W* 1, *E* 1, *A* 1, *NZ* 1,2, *A* 2, *W* 2, *S, I* 3

MOST CONSECUTIVE TESTS WITHOUT DEFEAT

Matches	Wins	Draws	Period
23 by N Zealand	22	1	1987 to 1990
17 by N Zealand	15	2	1961 to 1964
17 by N Zealand	17	0	1965 to 1969
17 by S Africa	17	0	1997 to 1998

* Between 2006 and 2010 Lithuania won 18 consecutive Test matches

MOST POINTS IN A MATCH

BY THE TEAM

Pts.	Opponents	Venue	Year
155 by Japan	Chinese Taipei	Tokyo	2002
152 by Argentina	Paraguay	Mendoza	2002
147 by Argentina	Venezuela	Santiago	2004
145 by N Zealand	Japan	Bloemfontein	1995
144 by Argentina	Paraguay	Montevideo	2003
142 by Australia	Namibia	Adelaide	2003
134 by Japan	Chinese Taipei	Singapore	1998
134 by England	Romania	Twickenham	2001
134 by S Africa	Uruguay	East London	2005
120 by Japan	Chinese Taipei	Tainan	2002

Hong Kong scored 164 points against Singapore at Kuala Lumpur in 1994

BY A PLAYER

Pts.	Player	Opponents	Venue	Year
60 for Japan	T Kurihara	Chinese Taipei	Tainan	2002
50 for Argentina	E Morgan	Paraguay	San Pablo	1973
45 for N Zealand	S D Culhane	Japan	Bloemfontein	1995
45 for Argentina	J-M Nuñez-Piossek	Paraguay	Montevideo	2003
44 for Scotland	A G Hastings	Ivory Coast	Rustenburg	1995
44 for England	C C Hodgson	Romania	Twickenham	2001
42 for Australia	M S Rogers	Namibia	Adelaide	2003
40 for Argentina	G M Jorge	Brazil	Sao Paulo	1993
40 for Japan	D Ohata	Chinese Taipei	Tokyo	2002
40 for Scotland	C D Paterson	Japan	Perth	2004
39 for Australia	M C Burke	Canada	Brisbane	1996

MOST TRIES IN A MATCH

BY THE TEAM

Tries	Opponents	Venue	Year
24 by Argentina	Paraguay	Mendoza	2002
24 by Argentina	Paraguay	Montevideo	2003
23 by Japan	Chinese Taipei	Tokyo	2002
23 by Argentina	Venezuela	Santiago	2004
22 by Australia	Namibia	Adelaide	2003
21 by N Zealand	Japan	Bloemfontein	1995
21 by S Africa	Uruguay	East London	2005
20 by Argentina	Brazil	Montevideo	1989
20 by Japan	Chinese Taipei	Singapore	1998
20 by England	Romania	Twickenham	2001
19 by Argentina	Brazil	Santiago	1979
19 by Argentina	Paraguay	Asuncion	1985

Hong Kong scored 26 tries against Singapore at Kuala Lumpur in 1994

BY A PLAYER

Tries	Player	Opponents	Venue	Year
11 for Argentina	U O'Farrell	Brazil	Buenos Aires	1951
9 for Argentina	J-M Nuñez-Piossek	Paraguay	Montevideo	2003
8 for Argentina	G M Jorge	Brazil	Sao Paulo	1993
8 for Japan	D Ohata	Chinese Taipei	Tokyo	2002
6 for Argentina	E Morgan	Paraguay	San Pablo	1973
6 for Argentina	G M Jorge	Brazil	Montevideo	1989
6 for N Zealand	M C G Ellis	Japan	Bloemfontein	1995
6 for Japan	T Kurihara	Chinese Taipei	Tainan	2002
6 for S Africa	T Chavhanga	Uruguay	East London	2005
6 for Japan	D Ohata	Hong Kong	Tokyo	2005
5 for Scotland	G C Lindsay	Wales	Raeburn Place	1887
5 for England	D Lambert	France	Richmond	1907
5 for Argentina	H Goti	Brazil	Montevideo	1961
5 for Argentina	M R Jurado	Brazil	Montevideo	1971
5 for England	R Underwood	Fiji	Twickenham	1989
5 for N Zealand	J W Wilson	Fiji	Albany	1997
5 for Japan	T Masuho	Chinese Taipei	Singapore	1998
5 for Argentina	P Grande	Paraguay	Asuncion	1998
5 for S Africa	C S Terblanche	Italy	Durban	1999
5 for England	O J Lewsey	Uruguay	Brisbane	2003
5 for Australia	C E Latham	Namibia	Adelaide	2003
5 for Argentina	F Higgs	Venezuela	Santiago	2004

MOST CONVERSIONS IN A MATCH

BY THE TEAM

Cons	Opponents	Venue	Year
20 by N Zealand	Japan	Bloemfontein	1995
20 by Japan	Chinese Taipei	Tokyo	2002
17 by Japan	Chinese Taipei	Singapore	1998
16 by Argentina	Paraguay	Mendoza	2002
16 by Australia	Namibia	Adelaide	2003
16 by Argentina	Venezuela	Santiago	2004
15 by Argentina	Brazil	Santiago	1979
15 by England	Netherlands	Huddersfield	1998
15 by Japan	Chinese Taipei	Tainan	2002

BY A PLAYER

Cons	Player	Opponents	Venue	Year
20 for N Zealand	S D Culhane	Japan	Bloemfontein	1995
16 for Argentina	J-L Cilley	Paraguay	Mendoza	2002
16 for Australia	M S Rogers	Namibia	Adelaide	2003
15 for England	P J Grayson	Netherlands	Huddersfield	1998
15 for Japan	T Kurihara	Chinese Taipei	Tainan	2002

MOST PENALTIES IN A MATCH

BY THE TEAM

Penalties	Opponents	Venue	Year
9 by Japan	Tonga	Tokyo	1999
9 by N Zealand	Australia	Auckland	1999
9 by Wales	France	Cardiff	1999
9 by N Zealand	France	Paris	2000

Portugal scored nine penalties against Georgia at Lisbon in 2000

BY A PLAYER

Penalties	Player	Opponents	Venue	Year
9 for Japan	K Hirose	Tonga	Tokyo	1999
9 for N Zealand	A P Mehrtens	Australia	Auckland	1999
9 for Wales	N R Jenkins	France	Cardiff	1999
9 for N Zealand	A P Mehrtens	France	Paris	2000

Nine penalties were scored for Portugal by T Teixeira against Georgia at Lisbon in 2000

MOST DROPPED GOALS IN A MATCH

BY THE TEAM

Drops	Opponents	Venue	Year
5 by South Africa	England	Paris	1999
4 by South Africa	England	Twickenham	2006
3 by several nations			

BY A PLAYER

Drops	Player	Opponents	Venue	Year
5 by South Africa	J H de Beer	England	Paris	1999
4 by South Africa	A S Pretorius	England	Twickenham	2006
3 by several nations				

CAREER RECORDS

MOST TEST APPEARANCES

Caps	Player	Career Span
139	G M Gregan (Australia)	1994 to 2007
119 (5)	J Leonard (England/Lions)	1990 to 2004
118	F Pelous (France)	1995 to 2007
111	P Sella (France)	1982 to 1995
110	G B Smith (Australia)	2000 to 2009
109 (6)	B G O'Driscoll (Ireland/Lions)	1999 to 2010
104 (2)	J J Hayes (Ireland/Lions)	2000 to 2010
103 (3)	Gareth Thomas (Wales/Lions)	1995 to 2007
102	S J Larkham (Australia)	1996 to 2007
102	P C Montgomery (S Africa)	1997 to 2008
102	J W Smit (S Africa)	2000 to 2010
101	D I Campese (Australia)	1982 to 1996
101	A Troncon (Italy)	1994 to 2007
101 (2)	R J R O'Gara (Ireland/Lions)	2000 to 2010
101	V Matfield (S Africa)	2001 to 2010
100	C D Paterson (Scotland)	1999 to 2010
99 (4)	M E Williams (Wales/Lions)	1996 to 2010
98	R Ibañez (France)	1996 to 2007
97 (6)	S M Jones (Wales/Lions)	1998 to 2010
96 (2)	C L Charvis (Wales/Lions)	1996 to 2007
93	S Blanco (France)	1980 to 1991
92	S B T Fitzpatrick (N Zealand)	1986 to 1997
92 (8)	M O Johnson (England/Lions)	1993 to 2003
92	G O Llewellyn (Wales)	1989 to 2004
92	M E O'Kelly (Ireland)	1997 to 2009

MOST CONSECUTIVE TESTS

Tests	Player	Career span
63	S B T Fitzpatrick (N Zealand)	1986 to 1995
62	J W C Roff (Australia)	1996 to 2001
53	G O Edwards (Wales)	1967 to 1978
52	W J McBride (Ireland)	1964 to 1975
51	C M Cullen (N Zealand)	1996 to 2000

MOST TESTS AS CAPTAIN

Tests	Captain	Career span
76	J W Smit (S Africa)	2003 to 2010
67 (1)	B G O'Driscoll (Ireland/Lions)	2002 to 2010
59	W D C Carling (England)	1988 to 1996
59	G M Gregan (Australia)	2001 to 2007
55	J A Eales (Australia)	1996 to 2001
52	R H McCaw (N Zealand)	2004 to 2010
51	S B T Fitzpatrick (N Zealand)	1992 to 1997
46 (8)	H Porta (Argentina/Jaguars)	1971 to 1990
45 (6)	M O Johnson (England/Lions)	1997 to 2003
42	F Pelous (France)	1997 to 2006
41	L Arbizu (Argentina)	1992 to 2002
41	R Ibañez (France)	1996 to 2007
37	M Giovanelli (Italy)	1992 to 1999
36	N C Farr-Jones (Australia)	1988 to 1992
36	G H Teichmann (S Africa)	1996 to 1999
36	K G M Wood (Ireland)	1996 to 2003

MOST POINTS IN TESTS

Points	Player	Tests	Career Span
1178 (67)	J P Wilkinson (England/Lions)	86 (6)	1998 to 2010
1118	D W Carter (N Zealand)	74	2003 to 2010
1090 (41)	N R Jenkins Wales/Lions))	91 (4)	1991 to 2002
1010 (27)	D Dominguez (Italy/Argentina)	76 (2)	1989 to 2003
967	A P Mehrtens (N Zealand)	70	1995 to 2004
963 (0)	R J R O'Gara (Ireland/Lions)	101(2)	2000 to 2010
911	M P Lynagh (Australia)	72	1984 to 1995
893	P C Montgomery (S Africa)	102	1997 to 2008
878	M C Burke (Australia)	81	1993 to 2004
868 (53)	S M Jones (Wales/Lions)	97 (6)	1998 to 2010
752	C D Paterson (Scotland)	100	1999 to 2010
733 (66)	A G Hastings (Scotland/Lions)	67 (6)	1986 to 1995

MOST TRIES IN TESTS

Tries	Player	Tests	Career Span
69	D Ohata (Japan)	58	1996 to 2006
64	D I Campese (Australia)	101	1982 to 1996
53 (2)	S M Williams (Wales/Lions)	77 (4)	2000 to 2010
50 (1)	R Underwood (England/Lions)	91 (6)	1984 to 1996
49	D C Howlett (N Zealand)	62	2000 to 2007
46	C M Cullen (N Zealand)	58	1996 to 2002
46	J T Rokocoko (N Zealand)	66	2003 to 2010
44	J W Wilson (N Zealand)	60	1993 to 2001
41 (1)	Gareth Thomas (Wales/Lions)	103 (3)	1995 to 2007
41 (1)	B G O'Driscoll (Ireland/Lions)	109 (6)	1999 to 2010
40	C E Latham (Australia)	78	1998 to 2007
40	H Onozawa (Japan)	56	2001 to 2010
38	S Blanco (France)	93	1980 to 1991
38	J H van der Westhuizen (S Africa)	89	1993 to 2003
38	B G Habana (S Africa)	66	2004 to 2010
37	J T Lomu (N Zealand)	63	1994 to 2002
37*	J F Umaga (N Zealand)	74	1997 to 2005

* includes a penalty try

MOST CONVERSIONS IN TESTS

Cons	Player	Tests	Career Span
192	D W Carter (N Zealand)	74	2003 to 2010
169	A P Mehrtens (N Zealand)	70	1995 to 2004
156 (7)	J P Wilkinson (England/Lions)	86 (6)	1998 to 2010
154 (0)	R J R O'Gara (Ireland/Lions)	101 (2)	2000 to 2010
153	P C Montgomery (S Africa)	102	1997 to 2008
140	M P Lynagh (Australia)	72	1984 to 1995
139 (7)	S M Jones (Wales/Lions)	97 (6)	1998 to 2010
133 (6)	D Dominguez (Italy/Argentina)	76 (2)	1989 to 2003
131 (1)	N R Jenkins (Wales/Lions)	91 (4)	1991 to 2002
118	G J Fox (N Zealand)	46	1985 to 1993

MOST PENALTY GOALS IN TESTS

Pens	Player	Tests	Career Span
248 (13)	N R Jenkins (Wales/Lions)	91 (4)	1991 to 2002
244 (16)	J P Wilkinson (England/Lions)	86 (6)	1998 to 2010
214 (5)	D Dominguez (Italy/Argentina)	76 (2)	1989 to 2003
196	D W Carter (N Zealand)	74	2003 to 2010
188	A P Mehrtens (N Zealand)	70	1995 to 2004
181 (0)	R J R O'Gara (Ireland/Lions)	101 (2)	2000 to 2010
178 (12)	S M Jones (Wales/Lions)	97 (6)	1998 to 2010
177	M P Lynagh (Australia)	72	1984 to 1995
174	M C Burke (Australia)	81	1993 to 2004
160 (20)	A G Hastings (Scotland/Lions)	67 (6)	1986 to 1995
153	C D Paterson (Scotland)	100	1999 to 2010

MOST DROPPED GOALS IN TESTS

Drops	Player	Tests	Career Span
33 (0)	J P Wilkinson (England/Lions)	86 (6)	1998 to 2010
28 (2)	H Porta (Argentina/Jaguars)	68 (8)	1971 to 1999
23 (2)	C R Andrew (England/Lions)	76 (5)	1985 to 1997
19 (0)	D Dominguez (Italy/Argentina)	76 (2)	1989 to 2003
18	H E Botha (S Africa)	28	1980 to 1992
17	S Bettarello (Italy)	55	1979 to 1988
15	J-P Lescarboura (France)	28	1982 to 1990

Official Ticket Sales Channels

A number of entities are offering Rugby World Cup 2011 tickets and ticket-inclusive packages for sale without authorisation to do so. Rugby World Cup Limited would like to emphasise to all Rugby supporters that they should only purchase tickets or ticket-inclusive packages from the following official ticket sales channels to ensure they receive genuine and valid tickets:

1. Individual tickets can be purchased from Rugby New Zealand 2011 Limited (the Tournament Organisers) from late 2010. See **www.rugbyworldcup.com/tickets** for details.

2. Official travel packages (including match tickets) can be purchased from one of the appointed Official Travel Agents, details of which are available at **www.rth2011.com.**

3. Official hospitality packages (including match tickets) can be purchased from one of the appointed Official Corporate Hospitality Agents, details of which are available at **www.rth2011.com**.

Supporters purchasing tickets or ticket-inclusive packages from unofficial sources run the risk of tickets not arriving, receiving counterfeit tickets or having their tickets cancelled (and being refused entry to or evicted from match venues).

Match tickets are non-transferable except as set out in the Rugby World Cup 2011 Ticket General Terms and Conditions. Specific legislation has also been passed in New Zealand to prohibit ticket-scalping and offering, giving away, or selling a match ticket in connection with the promotion of goods or services without the authorisation of Rugby World Cup Limited.

Don't be let down – ensure you only purchase Rugby World Cup 2011 tickets and ticket-inclusive packages from official ticket sales channels.

New Zealand 2011

The Countries

ARGENTINA

ARGENTINA'S 2009–10 TEST RECORD

OPPONENTS	DATE	VENUE	RESULT
England	14 Nov	A	**Lost** 9–16
Wales	21 Nov	A	**Lost** 16–33
Scotland	28 Nov	A	**Won** 9–6
Uruguay	21 May	A	**Won** 38–0
Chile	23 May	A	**Won** 48–9
Scotland	12 Jun	H	**Lost** 16–24
Scotland	19 Jun	H	**Lost** 9–13
France	26 Jun	H	**Won** 41–13

HISTORY IN THE MAKING

By Frankie Deges

The year of 2010 will be looked back on as an historic time for rugby in Argentina, even if the benefits may not be felt immediately. It was a year of highs and lows, but one of steady progress. The undoubted highlight was the decision by the IRB Council to pave the way for Argentina to join an expanded Four Nations competition from 2012.

The overwhelming support for the amendment to Regulation 9 – which created a new Four Nations Player Release Period – and the IRB's commitment to fund £7 million over five years, continued a journey which had begun in England back in 2007 when the Woking Forum witnessed a commitment by the global rugby community to ensure Argentina gained integration into an annual tournament.

This calendar year will also be remembered for the record-breaking IRB Junior World Championship, which was staged across three venues in the Litoral region of the country – Rosario, Santa Fe and Paraná – in June. Despite being played in a soccer-mad nation in the middle of a FIFA World Cup, more than 100,000 fans attended matches as the region truly embraced the tournament, highlighting the strength and love of the game in Argentina. To cap it all, Los Pumitas secured their best-ever finish in the premier Under-20 tournament, with sixth place on home soil.

Their senior counterparts, Los Pumas, ran hot and cold on the pitch, winning only one of their matches in the November window – against Scotland.

They blew cold in suffering a series loss to the same opponents at home in June, but then hot to beat France by a record score that same month. The promotion of home-based players was one positive aspect, particularly with Rugby World Cup year looming.

The date 12 May 2010, though, will go down as the day when, collectively, the top rugby nations stood up for Argentina rugby and honoured their pledge for the Pumas to have an unprecedented competition calendar from 2012.

With an invitation to play in an enlarged SANZAR Four Nations from 2012, the main stumbling block was linked to player release and the ability of Los Pumas to field their best players. With most Pumas based overseas – in France, UK and Ireland – it was still an issue on how players would turn out for their national side. That was, until the IRB Council voted to adjust Regulation 9.

IRB Chairman Bernard Lapasset put the decision into context in saying: "It represents an historic milestone in the process of Argentina's integration into an expanded Tri Nations tournament and is an extremely exciting development for the Unión Argentina de Rugby and rugby around the world.

"This regulatory amendment, coupled with the significant financial assistance of the IRB and SANZAR, represents the global rugby community's support of this important programme and I would like to thank all parties and in particular SANZAR for their dedication to making Argentina's Four Nations dream a reality. We will continue to work in close collaboration with all stakeholders to make Argentina's transition as smooth as possible."

Former Puma captain Agustín Pichot, a member of the UAR High Performance Committee and an ambassador for the Argentine cause, was in London that day and commented that: "This is the work of many people. A lot of history written on the field of play and the success of 2007 were instrumental in generating opportunities. We've worked hard for this and I personally believe that we are now part of the oval world."

This announcement came around the same time as Argentina's first professional team, Los Pampas XV, were completing their involvement in SARU's Vodacom Cup. Based in South Africa for three months, this team comprising young up and coming players proved an important investment in the game.

"As a first experience, we are more than happy," admitted coach Daniel Hourcade, a former assistant coach of Portugal from 2006–2008. "We had to find our feet in a difficult environment, adjust to a stronger game and adapt to new rule interpretations. Despite not qualifying for the quarters, it was a success. Players grew during the tournament."

Los Pampas XV kicked off with a 27–27 draw against Eastern Province. Then, it was three wins and three losses in seven games. Victories came against SWD Eagles 36–17, Border 73–14 and Free State 36–24, with defeats suffered against Boland Kavaliers 26–13, Western Province 19–16 – albeit with the last kick of the match – and the Sharks XV 24–19. They came painstakingly close to a spot in the last eight.

The Jaguars, Argentina's second string, enjoyed a solid 2009–10 with more games than Los Pumas. They played in the inaugural Americas Rugby Championship and beat the USA Selects 57–10 and the BC Bears, the top Canadian provincial side, 35–11 to claim the title, before ending the trip to North America with a 42–16 win over Canada A in a friendly match.

Following the Americas Rugby Championship success, the Jaguars joined Los Pumas on tour in November, beating Portugal 24–13 in Lisbon and losing to both Georgia 24–22 in Tbilisi and Ireland A 31–0. Before heading for Europe, an Argentina XV, featuring many of the Jaguars, beat Uruguay in a two-match series, 55–13 at home and 54–22 away. Many of these players also turned out for Los Pampas XV.

At the conclusion of that tour, and featuring some overseas-based players, Argentina beat Uruguay 38–0 and Chile 48–9 to, again, win the South American Championship.

The Jaguars team, though, that headed to the IRB Nations Cup in June would have a different look to it, coach Hourcade admitting "with France wanting to play a second game on tour, the top 47 players were unavailable for Jaguar selection, so we travelled to Romania for the Nations Cup with a young side." Losses duly followed against Italy A (20–22) and Romania (24–8), but defending champions Scotland A were beaten 33–13.

Los Pumas had also been without a number of incumbent Test players for their European tour in November, although this was not entirely a bad thing for coach Santiago Phelan. He said: "This opened opportunities for new players, mostly those who had come through the High Performance Units. With this in mind, we performed pretty well against England after a four-month hiatus."

A week later at the Millennium Stadium, crucial mistakes and lapses of concentration cost Argentina dearly as a Shane Williams' brace saw Los Pumas lose 33–16 to Wales. "The character of the team was seen during the following week. With two losses on their backs, they continued to work hard and the reward came against Scotland," Phelan added.

This reward was a much celebrated 9–6 win, courtesy of drop-goal two minutes from full-time by Martín Rodríguez, who had started the year as a star performer for Argentina Sevens and ended it as the sole point-scorer on a tour in which he played his first three Tests. He scored the only try in those three games, a trend Phelan described as "very worrying". Six months after the Murrayfield win Los Pumas failed to ignite against Scotland, who found ways to trouble their hosts, who they will face in Pool B at RWC 2011. A 24–16 loss in Tucumán and 13–9 defeat in Mar del Plata gave cause for concern in Argentina.

Fortunately, a week later in Buenos Aires, Argentina restored their dented pride with a solid, auspicious win against France. Fly-half Contepomi was "on fire", scoring 31 of the Pumas' points in a record

41–13 win. “We showed how well we can play. We want an attacking team and we hadn’t attacked very well in the previous five Tests. We corrected that and we can now look forward to the final stretch in our Rugby World Cup 2011 preparations,” concluded Phelan.

Rugby World Cup 2011 may come too early for some of the Jaguars or those who performed so well in the IRB Junior World Championship on home soil. The success of the tournament was not built on Los Pumitas’ performance – despite their highest ever finish and providing some thrilling entertainment along the way – but on the confirmation of Argentina as a host for major international tournaments.

The crowds amassed despite the cold weather and the strength of FIFA’s World Cup, to join in a tournament that, as the slogan said, had “the future stars of world rugby” playing in the Litoral region. Tomas de la Vega and Ignacio Rodriguez Muedra were two of the better performers for the host team, led with charm and determination by captain Alan Kessen in a tournament which was ultimately won by a dominant New Zealand side for the third year in succession. Muedra did earn a nomination for the IRB Junior Player of the Year award, the first Argentinean to ever make the shortlist.

Argentine rugby is now working hard to ensure all the platforms are in place for continued growth and maximising the opportunities that will ultimately come their way in the years ahead. Sevens has regained its programme and the team will slowly return to chasing top IRB Sevens World Series honours. Iconic captain Santiago Gomez Cora has retired after scoring 230 tries – a Series record. His mantle will now pass to the younger generation coming through. The Under-20s are now the end of the line that starts at Under-17s and player identification is working well.

Playing numbers from Under-15 to senior rugby have grown almost 40% since 2000, to 47,000 – before Rugby World Cup 2003 the figure was around 39,000. Numbers below that age-group multiply from year to year and inclusion in the Four Nations could see that grow further.

With no professional set-up it is the clubs that take on the challenge. The UAR and its provincial affiliates are working hard. The challenge is not being taken lightly with plans in place to ensure the growth is managed and the game developed with strength and ensuring the right message is sent out.

Argentina may have only won two of its last six Test matches and dropped to eighth in the IRB World Rankings, but it is the long-term benefit that is crucial here. Being competitive at the highest level will need a huge support base – and that is the challenge.

ARGENTINA INTERNATIONAL STATISTICS

MATCH RECORDS UP TO 29TH OCTOBER 2010

WINNING MARGIN

Date	Opponent	Result	Winning Margin
01/05/2002	Paraguay	152–0	**152**
27/04/2003	Paraguay	144–0	**144**
01/05/2004	Venezuela	147–7	**140**
02/10/1993	Brazil	114–3	**111**
09/10/1979	Brazil	109–3	**106**

MOST POINTS IN A MATCH
BY THE TEAM

Date	Opponent	Result	Points
01/05/2002	Paraguay	152–0	**152**
01/05/2004	Venezuela	147–7	**147**
27/04/2003	Paraguay	144–0	**144**
02/10/1993	Brazil	114–3	**114**
09/10/1979	Brazil	109–3	**109**

MOST TRIES IN A MATCH
BY THE TEAM

Date	Opponent	Result	Tries
01/05/2002	Paraguay	152–0	**24**
27/04/2003	Paraguay	144–0	**24**
01/05/2004	Venezuela	147–7	**23**
08/10/1989	Brazil	103–0	**20**

MOST CONVERSIONS IN A MATCH
BY THE TEAM

Date	Opponent	Result	Cons
01/05/2002	Paraguay	152–0	**16**
01/05/2004	Venezuela	147–7	**16**
09/10/1979	Brazil	109–3	**15**
21/09/1985	Paraguay	102–3	**13**
14/10/1973	Paraguay	98–3	**13**

MOST PENALTIES IN A MATCH
BY THE TEAM

Date	Opponent	Result	Pens
10/10/1999	Samoa	32–16	**8**
10/03/1995	Canada	29–26	**8**
17/06/2006	Wales	45–27	**8**

MOST DROP GOALS IN A MATCH
BY THE TEAM

Date	Opponent	Result	DGs
27/10/1979	Australia	24–13	**3**
02/11/1985	New Zealand	21–21	**3**
26/05/2001	Canada	20–6	**3**
21/09/1975	Uruguay	30–15	**3**
07/08/1971	SA Gazelles	12–0	**3**
30/09/2007	Ireland	30–15	**3**

MOST POINTS IN A MATCH
BY A PLAYER

Date	Player	Opponent	Points
14/10/1973	Eduardo Morgan	Paraguay	**50**
27/04/2003	José María Nuñez Piossek	Paraguay	**45**
02/10/1993	Gustavo Jorge	Brazil	**40**
24/10/1977	Martin Sansot	Brazil	**36**
13/09/1951	Uriel O'Farrell	Brazil	**33**

MOST TRIES IN A MATCH BY A PLAYER

Date	Player	Opponent	Tries
13/09/1951	Uriel O'Farrell	Brazil	11
27/04/2003	José María Nuñez Piossek	Paraguay	9
02/10/1993	Gustavo Jorge	Brazil	8
08/10/1989	Gustavo Jorge	Brazil	6
14/10/1973	Eduardo Morgan	Paraguay	6

MOST CONVERSIONS IN A MATCH BY A PLAYER

Date	Player	Opponent	Cons
01/05/2002	Jose Cilley	Paraguay	16
21/09/1985	Hugo Porta	Paraguay	13
14/10/1973	Eduardo Morgan	Paraguay	13
25/09/1975	Eduardo de Forteza	Paraguay	11

MOST PENALTIES IN A MATCH BY A PLAYER

Date	Player	Opponent	Pens
10/10/1999	Gonzalo Quesada	Samoa	8
10/03/1995	Santiago Meson	Canada	8
17/06/2006	Federico Todeschini	Wales	8

MOST DROP GOALS IN A MATCH BY A PLAYER

Date	Player	Opponent	DGs
27/10/1979	Hugo Porta	Australia	3
02/11/1985	Hugo Porta	New Zealand	3
07/08/1971	Tomas Harris-Smith	SA Gazelles	3
26/05/2001	Juan Fernández Miranda	Canada	3
30/09/2007	Juan Martín Hernández	Ireland	3

MOST CAPPED PLAYERS

Name	Caps
Lisandro Arbizu	86
Rolando Martin	86
Pedro Sporleder	78
Mario Ledesma	75
Federico Méndez	73

LEADING TRY SCORERS

Name	Tries
José María Nuñez Piossek	29
Diego Cuesta Silva	28
Gustavo Jorge	24
Facundo Soler	18
Rolando Martin	18

LEADING CONVERSIONS SCORERS

Name	Cons
Hugo Porta	84
Gonzalo Quesada	68
Santiago Meson	68
Felipe Contepomi	59
Juan Fernández Miranda	41

LEADING PENALTY SCORERS

Name	Pens
Felipe Contepomi	110
Gonzalo Quesada	103
Hugo Porta	102
Santiago Meson	63
Federico Todeschini	54

LEADING DROP GOAL SCORERS

Name	DGs
Hugo Porta	26
Lisandro Arbizu	11
Tomas Harris-Smith	6
Gonzalo Quesada	6
Juan Martín Hernández	6

LEADING POINTS SCORERS

Name	Pts.
Hugo Porta	593
Felipe Contepomi	522
Gonzalo Quesada	483
Santiago Meson	370
Federico Todeschini	256

ARGENTINA INTERNATIONAL PLAYERS
UP TO 29TH OCTOBER 2010

Note: Years given for International Championship matches are for second half of season; eg 1972 means season 1971–72. Years for all other matches refer to the actual year of the match.

A Abadie 2007 *CHL*, 2009 *E*, *W*, *S*
A Abella 1969 *Ur*, *CHL*
C Abud 1975 *Par*, *Bra*, *CHL*
H Achaval 1948 *OCC*
J Aguilar 1983 *CHL*, *Ur*
A Aguirre 1997 *Par*, *CHL*
ME Aguirre 1990 *E*, *S*, 1991 *Sa*
B Agulla 2010 *Ur*, *CHL*
H Agulla 2005 *Sa*, 2006 *Ur*, *E*, *It*, 2007 *It*, *F*, *Nm*, *I*, *S*, *SA*, *F*, 2008 *S*, *It*, *SA*, *F*, *It*, *I*, 2009 *E*, *E*, *E*, *W*, *S*, 2010 *Ur*, *CHL*, *S*, *S*, *F*
P Albacete 2003 *Par*, *Ur*, *F*, *SA*, *Ur*, *C*, *A*, *R*, 2004 *W*, *W*, *NZ*, *F*, *I*, 2005 *It*, *It*, 2006 *E*, *It*, *F*, 2007 *W*, *F*, *Geo*, *Nm*, *I*, *S*, *SA*, *F*, 2008 *SA*, *F*, *It*, *I*, 2009 *E*, *E*, *E*, *W*, *S*, 2010 *S*, *S*, *F*
DL Albanese 1995 *Ur*, *C*, *E*, *F*, 1996 *Ur*, *F*, *SA*, *E*, 1997 *NZ*, *Ur*, *R*, *It*, *F*, *A*, *A*, 1998 *Ur*, *F*, *F*, *R*, *US*, *C*, *It*, *F*, *W*, 1999 *WXV*, *W*, *W*, *S*, *I*, *W*, *Sa*, *J*, *I*, *F*, 2000 *I*, *A*, *A*, *SA*, 2001 *NZ*, *It*, *W*, *S*, *NZ*, 2002 *F*, *E*, *SA*, *A*, *It*, *I*, 2003 *F*, *F*, *SA*, *US*, *C*, *A*, *Nm*, *I*
F Albarracin 2007 *CHL*
M Albina 2001 *Ur*, *US*, 2003 *Par*, *Ur*, *Fj*, 2004 *CHL*, *Ven*, *W*, *W*, 2005 *J*
C Aldao 1961 *CHL*, *Bra*, *Ur*
P Alexenicer 1997 *Par*, *CHL*
C Alfonso 1936 *BI*
H Alfonso 1936 *BI*, *BI*, *CHL*
G Allen 1977 *Par*
JG Allen 1981 *C*, 1985 *F*, *F*, *Ur*, *NZ*, *NZ*, 1986 *F*, *F*, *A*, *A*, 1987 *Ur*, *Fj*, *It*, *NZ*, *Sp*, *A*, *A*, 1988 *F*, *F*, *F*, *F*, 1989 *Bra*, *CHL*, *Par*, *Ur*, *US*
L Allen 1951 *Ur*, *Bra*, *CHL*
M Allen 1990 *C*, *E*, *S*, 1991 *NZ*, *CHL*
A Allub 1997 *Par*, *Ur*, *It*, *F*, *A*, *A*, 1998 *Ur*, *F*, *F*, *US*, *C*, *J*, *It*, *F*, *W*, 1999 *WXV*, *W*, *W*, *S*, *I*, *W*, *Sa*, *J*, *I*, *F*, 2000 *I*, *A*, *A*, *SA*, *E*, 2001 *NZ*
M Alonso 1973 *R*, *R*, *S*, 1977 *F*, *F*
A Altberg 1972 *SAG*, *SAG*, 1973 *R*, *R*, *Par*
J Altube 1998 *Par*, *CHL*, *Ur*
C Alvarez 1958 *Ur*, *Per*, *CHL*, 1959 *JSB*, *JSB*, 1960 *F*
GM Alvarez 1975 *Ur*, *Par*, *Bra*, *CHL*, 1976 *Ur*, *NZ*, 1977 *Bra*, *Ur*, *Par*, *CHL*
R Álvarez Kairelis 1998 *Par*, *CHL*, *Ur*, 2001 *Ur*, *US*, *C*, *W*, *S*, *NZ*, 2002 *F*, *E*, *SA*, *A*, *It*, *I*, 2003 *F*, *SA*, *Fj*, *Ur*, *C*, *Nm*, *I*, 2004 *F*, *I*, 2006 *W*, *W*, *NZ*, *CHL*, *Ur*, 2007 *I*, *It*, *W*, *F*, *Geo*, *Nm*, *I*, *S*, *SA*, *F*, 2008 *SA*, *F*, *It*, *I*, 2009 *E*
F Amelong 2007 *CHL*
A Amuchastegui 2001 *Ur*, 2002 *Ur*, *Par*, *CHL*
GP Angaut 1987 *NZ*, *Ur*, *CHL*, 1990 *S*, 1991 *NZ*, *Sa*
J-J Angelillo 1987 *Ur*, *CHL*, *A*, 1988 *F*, *F*, *F*, 1989 *It*, *Bra*, *CHL*, *Par*, *Ur*, *US*, 1990 *C*, *US*, *E*, *E*, 1994 *US*, *S*, *S*, *US*, 1995 *Par*, *CHL*, *R*, *F*
W Aniz 1960 *F*
R Annichini 1983 *CHL*, *Ur*, 1985 *F*, *CHL*, *Par*
A Anthony 1965 *OCC*, *CHL*, 1967 *Ur*, *CHL*, 1968 *W*, *W*, 1969 *S*, *S*, *Ur*, *CHL*, 1970 *I*, *I*, 1971 *SAG*, *SAG*, *OCC*, 1972 *SAG*, *SAG*, 1974 *F*, *F*
F Aranguren 2007 *CHL*
L Arbizu 1990 *I*, *S*, 1991 *NZ*, *NZ*, *CHL*, *A*, *W*, *Sa*, 1992 *F*, *F*, *Sp*, *Sp*, *R*, *F*, 1993 *J*, *J*, *Bra*, *CHL*, *Par*, *Ur*, *SA*, *SA*, 1995 *Ur*, *A*, *A*, *E*, *Sa*, *It*, *Par*, *CHL*, *Ur*, *R*, *It*, *F*, 1996 *Ur*, *US*, *Ur*, *C*, *SA*, *SA*, *E*, 1997 *E*, *E*, *NZ*, *NZ*, *R*, *It*, *F*, *A*, *A*, 1998 *Ur*, *F*, *F*, *R*, *US*, *C*, *It*, *F*, *W*, 1999 *W*, *W*, *S*, *I*, *W*, *Sa*, *J*, *I*, *F*, 2000 *A*, *A*, *SA*, *E*, 2001 *NZ*, *It*, *W*, *S*, *NZ*, 2002 *F*, *A*, *It*, *I*, 2003 *F*, *F*, *US*, *C*, 2005 *BI*, *It*, *It*
F Argerich 1979 *Ur*
G Aristide 1997 *E*
J Arocena Messones 2005 *C*, *Sa*
E Arriaga 1936 *CHL*, *CHL*
S Artese 2004 *SA*, 2005 *C*
G Ascarate 2010 *CHL*
M Avellaneda 1948 *OCC*, *OCC*, 1951 *Bra*, *CHL*
M Avramovic 2005 *J*, *C*, *Sa*, 2006 *CHL*, *Ur*, *E*, *It*, 2007 *I*, 2008 *It*, *SA*, *I*, 2009 *E*
M Ayerra 1927 *GBR*
MI Ayerza 2004 *SA*, 2005 *J*, *It*, *Sa*, 2006 *W*, *W*, *CHL*, *Ur*, *E*, *It*, *F*, 2007 *I*, *I*, *Geo*, *F*, 2008 *S*, *S*, *SA*, *F*, *It*, *I*, 2009 *E*, *E*, *E*, *W*, *S*, 2010 *S*, *S*, *F*
G Azcarate 2007 *CHL*
M Azpiroz 1956 *OCC*, 1958 *Ur*, *Per*, *CHL*, 1959 *JSB*, *JSB*
J Bach 1975 *Par*, *Bra*, *CHL*
A Badano 1977 *Bra*, *Ur*, *Par*, *CHL*
J Baeck 1983 *Par*
M Baeck 1985 *Ur*, *CHL*, *Par*, 1990 *US*, *E*, *E*
DR Baetti Sabah 1980 *WXV*, *Fj*, *Fj*, 1981 *E*, *E*, *C*, 1983 *WXV*, 1987 *Ur*, *Par*, *CHL*, 1988 *F*, *F*, 1989 *It*, *NZ*, *NZ*
R Baez 2010 *CHL*
L Balfour 1977 *Bra*, *Ur*, *Par*, *CHL*
C Barrea 1996 *Ur*, *C*, *SA*
O Bartolucci 1996 *US*, *C*, *SA*, 1998 *Ur*, *CHL*, *Ur*, 1999 *WXV*, *W*, *W*, *S*, *I*, *W*, *Sa*, 2000 *I*, *A*, *A*, *SA*, *E*, 2001 *US*, *C*, 2003 *Par*, *Ur*
E Basile 1983 *CHL*, *Ur*
L Bavio 1954 *F*
R Bazan 1951 *Ur*, *Bra*, *CHL*, 1956 *OCC*
D Beccar Varela 1975 *CHL*, *F*, *F*, 1976 *Ur*, *W*, *NZ*, 1977 *F*, *F*
G Beccar Varela 1976 *W*, *NZ*, *NZ*, 1977 *F*, *F*
M Beccar Varela 1965 *Rho*, *OCC*, *OCC*
G Begino 2007 *CHL*
JW Beith 1936 *BI*
J Benzi 1965 *Rho*, 1969 *S*, *Ur*, *CHL*
E Bergamaschi 2001 *US*
O Bernacchi 1954 *F*, 1956 *OCC*, *OCC*, 1958 *Ur*, *Per*, *CHL*
G Bernardi 1997 *CHL*
O Bernat 1932 *JSB*
MM Berro 1964 *Ur*, *Bra*, *CHL*
MJS Bertranou 1989 *It*, *NZ*, *NZ*, *CHL*, *Par*, 1990 *C*, *US*, *C*, *E*, *E*, *I*, *E*, *S*, 1993 *SA*
E Bianchetti 1959 *JSB*, *JSB*
G Blacksley 1971 *SAG*
T Blades 1938 *CHL*
G Bocca 1998 *J*, *Par*
C Bofelli 1997 *Ur*, 1998 *Par*, 2004 *CHL*, *Ur*, *Ven*
S Boffelli 2005 *C*
L Borges 2001 *Ur*, 2003 *Par*, *CHL*, *Ur*, 2004 *CHL*, *Ur*, *Ven*, *W*, *W*, *NZ*, *F*, *I*, *SA*, 2005 *SA*, *S*, 2006 *W*, *W*, *CHL*, *Ur*, 2007 *W*, *F*, *Geo*, *I*, *S*, *SA*, 2008 *S*, *It*, 2009 *E*, *W*, *S*, 2010 *Ur*, *S*
C Bori 1975 *CHL*, *F*
F Bosch 2004 *CHL*, *SA*, 2005 *J*, *Sa*

MA Bosch 1991 *A, Sa*, 1992 *F, F*
MT Bosch 2007 *It*, 2008 *It*
N Bossicovich 1995 *Ur, C*
CA Bottarini 1973 *Par, Ur, Bra, I*, 1974 *F*, 1975 *F, F*, 1979 *Ur, CHL, Bra*, 1983 *CHL, Par, Ur*
R Botting 1927 *GBR, GBR, GBR*
L Bouza 1992 *Sp*
M Bouza 1966 *SAG, SAG*, 1967 *Ur, CHL*
P Bouza 1996 *Ur, F, F, E*, 1997 *E, NZ, NZ, Ur, R*, 1998 *Ur*, 2002 *Ur, Par, CHL*, 2003 *Par, CHL, Ur, US, Ur, Nm, R*, 2004 *CHL, Ur, Ven, W, NZ, SA*, 2005 *J, BI, It, It, C, SA, S, It*, 2006 *CHL, Ur*, 2007 *I, I*
A Bovet 1910 *GBR*
N Bozzo 1975 *Bra*
JG Braceras 1971 *Bra, Par*, 1976 *W, NZ*, 1977 *F*
W Braddon 1927 *GBR*
EN Branca 1976 *Ur, W, NZ, NZ*, 1977 *F, F*, 1980 *Fj*, 1981 *E, E, C*, 1983 *WXV, A, A*, 1985 *F, F, Ur, CHL, Par, NZ, NZ*, 1986 *F, F, A, A*, 1987 *Ur, Fj, It, NZ, Sp, A, A*, 1988 *F, F, F, F*, 1989 *Bra, Par, Ur*, 1990 *E, E*
M Brandi 1997 *Par, CHL*, 1998 *Par, CHL, Ur*
J Bridger 1932 *JSB*
J Brolese 1998 *CHL, Ur*
E Brouchou 1975 *CHL, Ur, Par, Bra, CHL*
R Bruno 2010 *Ur, CHL*
F Buabse 1991 *Ur, Par, Bra*, 1992 *Sp*
PM Buabse 1989 *NZ, US*, 1991 *Sa*, 1993 *Bra*, 1995 *Ur, C, A*
E Buckley 1938 *CHL*
R Bullrich 1991 *Ur, Bra*, 1992 *R*, 1993 *Bra, CHL, SA*, 1994 *SA, SA*
S Bunader 1989 *US*, 1990 *C*
K Bush 1938 *CHL*
E Bustamante 1927 *GBR, GBR, GBR, GBR*
F Bustillo 1977 *F, F, Bra, Ur, Par, CHL*
G Bustos 2001 *Ur*, 2003 *Par, Ur*, 2004 *CHL, Ven*
CJ Cáceres 2010 *Ur, CHL*
E Caffarone 1949 *F, F*, 1951 *Bra, CHL*, 1952 *I, I*, 1954 *F, F*
M Caldwell 1956 *OCC*
G Camacho 2009 *E, E*
GF Camardon 1990 *E*, 1991 *NZ, CHL, A, W, Sa*, 1992 *F, F, Sp, R, F*, 1993 *J, Par, Ur, SA, SA*, 1995 *A*, 1996 *Ur, US, Ur, C, SA, E*, 1999 *W, W, Sa, J, I, F*, 2001 *US, C, NZ, It, W, S, NZ*, 2002 *F, E, SA, It, I*
PJ Camerlinckx 1989 *Bra, Par, Ur*, 1990 *C, US*, 1994 *S*, 1995 *CHL*, 1996 *Ur, F, F, US, Ur, C, SA, SA, E*, 1997 *E, E, NZ, NZ, Ur, R, It, F, A, A*, 1998 *R, US, C, F, W*, 1999 *WXV, W*
A Cameron 1936 *BI, BI, CHL, CHL*, 1938 *CHL*
R Cameron 1927 *GBR, GBR*
J Caminotti 1987 *Ur, Par, CHL*
M Campo 1975 *CHL*, 1978 *E, It*, 1979 *NZ, NZ, A, A*, 1980 *WXV, Fj*, 1981 *E, E, C*, 1982 *F, F, Sp*, 1983 *WXV, A, A*, 1987 *Ur, Fj, NZ*
A Campos 2007 *CHL*, 2008 *S, It, F, It*, 2009 *E, W, S*, 2010 *Ur, S, F*
A Canalda 1999 *S, I, F*, 2000 *A*, 2001 *Ur, US, C, Ur*
R Cano 1997 *Par*
J Capalbo 1975 *Bra*, 1977 *Bra, Ur, CHL*
AE Capelletti 1977 *F, F*, 1978 *E, It*, 1979 *NZ, NZ, A, A*, 1980 *WXV, Fj, Fj*, 1981 *E, E*
R Carballo 2005 *C*, 2006 *W, CHL, Ur*, 2008 *SA, It, I*, 2010 *S, F*
N Carbone 1969 *Ur, CHL*, 1971 *SAG*, 1973 *I, S*
PF Cardinali 2001 *US, Ur*, 2002 *Ur, Par*, 2004 *W*, 2007 *I*
M Carizza 2004 *SA*, 2005 *J, BI, SA, S, It*, 2006 *W, CHL, Ur*, 2007 *It*, 2008 *It*, 2009 *E, E, E, W, S*, 2010 *S, S, F*
J Carlos Galvalisi 1983 *Par, Ur*
MA Carluccio 1973 *R, R, Ur, Bra, I*, 1975 *F, F*, 1976 *NZ*, 1977 *F, F*
M Carmona 1997 *Par, CHL*
S Carossio 1985 *NZ*, 1987 *It, NZ*
J Carracedo 1971 *CHL, Bra, Par*, 1972 *SAG, SAG*, 1973 *R, R, Par, Ur, Bra, CHL, I, S*, 1975 *F*, 1976 *W, NZ, NZ*, 1977 *F*
J Carrasco 2001 *Ur*
M Carreras 1991 *NZ, NZ, CHL, A, W, Sa*, 1992 *F*
M Carreras 1987 *Par*
M Carrique 1983 *Par, Ur*
J Casanegra 1959 *JSB, JSB*, 1960 *F, F*
GF Casas 1971 *OCC*, 1973 *Par, CHL, I*, 1975 *F, F*
DM Cash 1985 *F, F, Ur, CHL, NZ, NZ*, 1986 *F, F, A, A*, 1987 *Ur, Fj, It, NZ, Sp, A, A*, 1988 *F, F, F, F*, 1989 *It, NZ, NZ, US*, 1990 *C, US, C, E, I, E, S*, 1991 *NZ, NZ, CHL, A, Sa*, 1992 *F, F*
R Castagna 1977 *F*
A Castellina 2004 *CHL, Ur, Ven*
R Castro 1971 *CHL, Bra, Par*
J Cato 1975 *Ur, Par*
R Cazenave 1965 *Rho, JSB, OCC, CHL*, 1966 *SAG, SAG*
A Cerioni 1975 *F*, 1978 *E, It*, 1979 *CHL, Bra*
G Cernegoy 1938 *CHL*
H Cespedes 1997 *Ur, CHL*
M Chesta 1966 *SAG, SAG*, 1967 *Ur, CHL*, 1968 *W, W*
W Chiswell 1949 *F*
V Christianson 1954 *F, F*, 1956 *OCC*
E Cilley 1932 *JSB, JSB*
J Cilley 1936 *BI, CHL, CHL*, 1938 *CHL*
JL Cilley 1994 *SA*, 1995 *Sa, It, Par, CHL*, 1996 *Ur, F, F, SA, SA*, 1999 *WXV, W*, 2000 *A*, 2001 *Ur*, 2002 *Par*
J Clement 1987 *Par*, 1989 *Bra*
R Cobelo 1987 *Ur, Par, CHL*
I Comas 1951 *Bra, CHL*, 1958 *Per, CHL*, 1960 *F*
MA Comuzzi 2009 *E, W*
A Conen 1951 *CHL*, 1952 *I, I*
J Conrard 1927 *GBR, GBR*
CA Contepomi 1964 *Bra, CHL*
F Contepomi 1998 *CHL, Ur, F, W*, 1999 *W, S, I, J, I, F*, 2000 *I, A, A, SA, E*, 2001 *Ur, US, C, NZ, It, W, S, NZ*, 2002 *F, E, SA, A, It, I*, 2003 *F, F, SA, US, C, A, Nm, I*, 2004 *W, W, F, I*, 2005 *BI, It, It, SA, S, It*, 2006 *W, NZ, E, F*, 2007 *I, W, F, Geo, Nm, I, S, SA, F*, 2008 *S, S, SA, F, It*, 2010 *S, S, F*
M Contepomi 1998 *US, C, It, F, W*, 1999 *S, I, W, Sa, F*, 2003 *Ur, F, Fj, Ur, A, R*, 2004 *CHL, Ur, Ven, W, W, NZ, F, I, SA*, 2005 *SA, S*, 2006 *It, F*, 2007 *I, It, W, F, Nm, I, S, SA, F*
F Conti 1988 *F*
GEF Cooke 1927 *GBR*
KAM Cookson 1932 *JSB*
N Cooper 1936 *BI, CHL, CHL*
R Cooper 1927 *GBR, GBR, GBR, GBR*
J Copello 1975 *CHL, Ur, Bra*
C Cordeiro 1983 *Par*
J Coria 1987 *Ur, Par, CHL*, 1989 *Bra*
I Corleto 1998 *J, F, W*, 1999 *WXV, I, J, I, F*, 2000 *I, A, SA, E*, 2001 *W, S, NZ*, 2002 *F, E, SA, A, It, I*, 2003 *F, Fj, US, Ur, C, A, I*, 2006 *It, F*, 2007 *W, F, Geo, Nm, I, S, SA, F*
L Cornella 2001 *Ur*
ME Corral 1993 *J, Bra, Par, Ur, SA, SA*, 1994 *US, S, SA, SA*, 1995 *Ur, C, A, A, E, Sa, It*
M Cortese 2005 *Sa*, 2010 *Ur, CHL*
F Cortopasso 2003 *CHL, Ur*
A Costa Repetto 2005 *C, Sa*
JD Costante 1971 *OCC, OCC, CHL, Bra, Par, Ur*, 1976 *Ur, W, NZ*, 1977 *F*
AF Courreges 1979 *Ur, Par, Bra*, 1982 *F, F, Sp*, 1983 *WXV, A, A*, 1987 *Sp, A, A*, 1988 *F*
PH Cox 1938 *CHL*
A Creevy 2005 *J, Sa*, 2006 *Ur*, 2009 *S*, 2010 *S, S, F*
P Cremaschi 1993 *J, J*, 1995 *Par, CHL, Ur, It*
RH Crexell 1990 *I, S*, 1991 *Par*, 1992 *Sp*, 1993 *J*, 1995 *Ur, C, A, E, Sa, It, Par, CHL, Ur*
L Criscuolo 1992 *F, F*, 1993 *Bra, SA*, 1996 *Ur, F, F*
J Cruz Legora 2001 *Ur*, 2002 *Par, CHL*
J Cruz Meabe 1997 *Par*
AG Cubelli 1977 *Bra, Ur, CHL*, 1978 *E, It*, 1979 *A, A*, 1980 *WXV, Fj*, 1983 *Par*, 1985 *F, F, Ur, Par, NZ, NZ*, 1990 *S*
T Cubelli 2010 *Ur, CHL*
D Cuesta Silva 1983 *CHL, Ur*, 1985 *F, F, Ur, CHL, NZ, NZ*, 1986 *F, F, A, A*, 1987 *Ur, Fj, It, Sp, A, A*, 1988 *F, F, F, F*, 1989 *It, NZ, NZ*, 1990 *C, E, E, I, E, S*, 1991 *NZ, NZ, CHL, A, W, Sa*, 1992 *F, F, Sp, R, F*, 1993 *J, J, Bra, Par, Ur, SA, SA*, 1994 *US, S, S, US, SA*, 1995 *Ur, C, E, Sa, It, Par, R, It, F*
J Cuesta Silva 1927 *GBR, GBR, GBR, GBR*
B Cuezzo 2007 *CHL*
M Cutler 1969 *Ur*, 1971 *CHL, Bra, Par, Ur*
A Da Milano 1964 *Bra, CHL*

F D'Agnillo 1975 *Ur, Bra*, 1977 *Bra, Ur, Par, CHL*
JL Damioli 1991 *Ur, Par, Bra*
H Dande 2001 *Ur, C*, 2004 *CHL, Ven*
J Dartiguelongue 1964 *Bra, CHL*, 1968 *W, W*
S Dassen 1983 *CHL, Par, Ur*
H Davel 1936 *BI*
R de Abelleyra 1932 *JSB, JSB*
L de Chazal 2001 *Ur, C*, 2004 *SA*, 2005 *C*
E de Forteza 1975 *Ur, Par, Bra, CHL*
R de la Arena 1992 *F, Sp*
JC De Pablo 1948 *OCC*
G de Robertis 2005 *Sa*, 2006 *CHL, Ur*
R de Vedia 1982 *F, Sp*
T de Vedia 2007 *I, I*, 2008 *S*
R del Busto 2007 *CHL*
F del Castillo 1994 *US, SA*, 1995 *Ur, C, A*, 1996 *Ur, F*, 1997 *Par, Ur*, 1998 *Ur*
GJ del Castillo 1991 *NZ, NZ, CHL, A, W*, 1993 *J*, 1994 *S, S, US, SA*, 1995 *C, A*
L del Chazal 1983 *CHL, Par, Ur*
R Dell'Acqua 1956 *OCC*
S Dengra 1982 *F, Sp*, 1983 *WXV, A, A*, 1986 *A*, 1987 *It, NZ, Sp, A, A*, 1988 *F, F, F, F*, 1989 *It, NZ, NZ*
C Derkheim 1927 *GBR*
M Devoto 1975 *Par, Bra*, 1977 *Par*
PM Devoto 1982 *F, F, Sp*, 1983 *WXV*
R Devoto 1960 *F*
M Diaz 1997 *Par, CHL*, 1998 *J, Par, CHL*
F Diaz Alberdi 1997 *Ur*, 1999 *WXV, S, I*, 2000 *A, A*
J Diez 1956 *OCC*
R Dillon 1956 *OCC*
P Dinisio 1989 *NZ*, 1990 *C, US*
M Dip 1979 *Par, Bra*
D Dominguez 1989 *CHL, Par*
E Dominguez 1949 *F, F*, 1952 *I, I*, 1954 *F, F*
A Donnelly 1910 *GBR*
L Dorado 1949 *F*
J Dumas 1973 *R, R, Ur, Bra, S*
M Dumas 1966 *SAG, SAG*
MA Durand 1997 *CHL*, 1998 *Par, CHL, Ur, It, F, W*, 2000 *SA*, 2001 *Ur, US, C, It, NZ*, 2002 *F, SA, A, It, I*, 2003 *CHL, Ur, Fj, US, Ur, C, A, Nm, R*, 2004 *CHL, Ur, Ven, W, W, NZ, F, I, SA*, 2005 *SA, S, It*, 2006 *W, NZ, CHL, Ur, It, F*, 2007 *I, I, It, W, F, Geo, I, F*, 2008 *S, S, It, SA, F, It, I*
C Echeverria 1932 *JSB*
G Ehrman 1948 *OCC*, 1949 *F, F*, 1951 *Ur, Bra, CHL*, 1952 *I, I*, 1954 *F, F*
O Elia 1954 *F*
R Elliot 1936 *BI, BI*, 1938 *CHL*
J Escalante 1975 *Ur, Par, CHL*, 1978 *It*, 1979 *Ur, CHL, Par, Bra*
N Escary 1927 *GBR, GBR*, 1932 *JSB, JSB*
R Espagnol 1971 *SAG*
AM Etchegaray 1964 *Ur, Bra, CHL*, 1965 *Rho, JSB, CHL*, 1967 *Ur, CHL*, 1968 *W, W*, 1969 *S, S*, 1971 *SAG, OCC, OCC*, 1972 *SAG, SAG*, 1973 *Par, Bra, I*, 1974 *F, F*, 1976 *Ur, W, NZ, NZ*
R Etchegoyen 1991 *Ur, Par, Bra*
C Ezcurra 1958 *Ur, Per, CHL*
E Ezcurra 1990 *I, E, S*
R Fariello 1973 *Par, Ur, CHL, S*
M Farina 1968 *W, W*, 1969 *S, S*
D Farrell 1951 *Ur*
P Felisari 1956 *OCC*
JJ Fernandez 1971 *SAG, CHL, Bra, Par, Ur*, 1972 *SAG, SAG*, 1973 *R, R, Par, Ur, CHL, I, S*, 1974 *F, F*, 1975 *F*, 1976 *Ur, W, NZ, NZ*, 1977 *F, F*
S Fernández 2008 *It, I*, 2009 *E, E, E, W, S*, 2010 *S, S, F*
Pablo Fernandez Bravo 1993 *SA, SA*
E Fernandez del Casal 1951 *Ur, Bra, CHL*, 1952 *I, I*, 1956 *OCC, OCC*
CI Fernandez Lobbe 1996 *US*, 1997 *E, E*, 1998 *Ur, F, F, R, US, Ur, C, J, It, F*, 1999 *WXV, W, W, S, I, W, Sa, J, I, F*, 2000 *I, A, A, SA, E*, 2001 *NZ, It, W, S, NZ*, 2002 *F, E, SA, A, It, I*, 2003 *F, F, SA, US, C, A, Nm, I*, 2004 *W, W, NZ*, 2005 *SA, S, It*, 2006 *W, W, NZ, E, F*, 2007 *It, W, F, Nm, I, S, SA*, 2008 *S, S*
JM Fernandez Lobbe 2004 *Ur, Ven*, 2005 *S, It, Sa*, 2006 *W, W, NZ, E, It, F*, 2007 *I, I, It, W, F, Geo, Nm, I, S, SA, F*, 2008 *S, S, SA, F, It, I*, 2009 *E, E, E, W, S*, 2010 *S, S, F*
JC Fernández Miranda 1997 *Ur, R, It*, 1998 *Ur, Ur, It*, 1999 *WXV*, 2000 *I*, 2001 *US, C*, 2002 *Ur, Par, CHL, It, I*, 2003 *Par, CHL, Ur, Fj, US, Nm, R*, 2004 *W, NZ, SA*, 2005 *J, C, Sa*, 2006 *CHL, Ur*, 2007 *It*
N Fernandez Miranda 1994 *US, S, S, US*, 1995 *CHL, Ur*, 1996 *F, SA, SA, E*, 1997 *E, E, NZ, NZ, Ur, R*, 1998 *Ur, R, US, C, It*, 1999 *WXV, I, F*, 2002 *Ur, CHL, It*, 2003 *CHL, Ur, F, F, SA, US, Ur, Nm, R*, 2004 *W, NZ*, 2005 *J, BI, It, It*, 2006 *W, It*, 2007 *It, Geo, Nm*
N Ferrari 1992 *Sp, Sp*
G Fessia 2005 *C*, 2007 *I*, 2009 *E*, 2010 *S, S, F*
JG Figallo 2010 *F*
A Figuerola 2008 *It, I*, 2009 *E, W, S*, 2010 *S, S*
R Follett 1948 *OCC, OCC*, 1952 *I, I*, 1954 *F*
G Foster 1971 *CHL, Bra, Par, Ur*
R Foster 1965 *Rho, JSB, OCC, OCC, CHL*, 1966 *SAG, SAG*, 1970 *I, I*, 1971 *SAG, SAG, OCC*, 1972 *SAG, SAG*
P Franchi 1987 *Ur, Par, CHL*
JL Francombe 1932 *JSB, JSB*, 1936 *BI, BI*
J Freixas 2003 *CHL, Ur*
R Frigerio 1948 *OCC, OCC*, 1954 *F*
J Frigoli 1936 *BI, BI, CHL, CHL*
P Fuselli 1998 *J, Par*
E Gahan 1954 *F, F*
M Gaitán 1998 *Ur*, 2002 *Par, CHL*, 2003 *Fj, US, Nm, R*, 2004 *W*, 2007 *It, W*
AM Galindo 2004 *Ur, Ven*, 2008 *S, It, SA, F, It*, 2009 *E*, 2010 *Ur*
R Gallo 1964 *Bra*
P Gambarini 2006 *W, CHL, Ur*, 2007 *I, It, CHL*, 2008 *S*
E Garbarino 1992 *Sp, Sp*
FL Garcia 1994 *SA*, 1995 *A, A, Par, CHL*, 1996 *Ur, F, F*, 1997 *NZ*, 1998 *Ur, R, Ur, J*
J Garcia 1998 *Par, Ur*, 2000 *A*
PT Garcia 1948 *OCC*
E Garcia Hamilton 1993 *Bra*
P Garcia Hamilton 1998 *CHL*
HM Garcia Simon 1990 *I*, 1992 *F*
G Garcia-Orsetti 1992 *R, F*
PA Garreton 1987 *Sp, Ur, CHL, A, A*, 1988 *F, F, F, F*, 1989 *It, NZ, Bra, CHL, Ur, US*, 1990 *C, E, E, I, E, S*, 1991 *NZ, NZ, CHL, A, W, Sa*, 1992 *F, F*, 1993 *J, J*
P Garzon 1990 *C*, 1991 *Par, Bra*
G Gasso 1983 *CHL, Par*
JM Gauweloose 1975 *F, F*, 1976 *W, NZ, NZ*, 1977 *F, F*, 1981 *C*
E Gavina 1956 *OCC, OCC*, 1958 *Ur, Per, CHL*, 1959 *JSB, JSB*, 1960 *F, F*, 1961 *CHL, Bra, Ur*
OST Gebbie 1910 *GBR*
FA Genoud 2004 *CHL, Ur, Ven*, 2005 *J, BI, It*
J Genoud 1952 *I, I*, 1956 *OCC, OCC*
M Gerosa 1987 *Ur, CHL*
D Giambroni 2001 *Ur*
D Giannantonio 1996 *Ur*, 1997 *Par, Ur, It, A, A*, 1998 *Ur, F, F*, 2000 *A*, 2002 *E*
MC Giargia 1973 *Par, Ur, Bra*, 1975 *Par, CHL*
R Giles 1948 *OCC*, 1949 *F, F*, 1951 *Ur*, 1952 *I, I*
C Giuliano 1959 *JSB, JSB*, 1960 *F*
L Glastra 1948 *OCC, OCC*, 1952 *I, I*
M Glastra 1979 *Ur, CHL*, 1981 *C*
FE Gomez 1985 *Ur*, 1987 *Ur, Fj, It, NZ*, 1989 *NZ*, 1990 *C, E, E*
JF Gomez 2006 *It*, 2008 *S, S, It*
N Gomez 1997 *Par, CHL*
PM Gomez Cora 2001 *Ur*, 2004 *NZ, SA*, 2005 *Sa*, 2006 *E*
D Gonzalez 1988 *F, F*
D Gonzalez 1987 *Par*
T Gonzalez 1975 *Ur, CHL*
L González Amorosino 2007 *CHL*, 2009 *E, E*, 2010 *S, S, F*
S Gonzalez Bonorino 2001 *Ur, US, C*, 2002 *Par, CHL*, 2003 *F, SA*, 2007 *I, I, It, W, F, Geo*, 2008 *S, S*
E Gonzalez del Solar 1960 *F*, 1961 *CHL, Bra, Ur*
N Gonzalez del Solar 1964 *Ur, Bra, CHL*, 1965 *Rho, JSB, OCC, OCC, CHL*

H Goti 1961 *CHL, Bra, Ur,* 1964 *Ur, Bra, CHL,* 1965 *Rho,* 1966 *SAG*
LM Gradin 1965 *OCC, OCC, CHL,* 1966 *SAG, SAG,* 1969 *CHL,* 1970 *I, I,* 1973 *R, R, Par, Ur, CHL, S*
P Grande 1998 *Par, CHL, Ur*
RD Grau 1993 *J, Bra, CHL,* 1995 *Par, CHL,* 1996 *F, F, US, Ur, C, SA, SA, E,* 1997 *E, E, NZ, NZ, A, A,* 1998 *Ur, F, It, F,* 1999 *W, W, S, I, W, F,* 2000 *A, SA, E,* 2001 *NZ, W, S, NZ,* 2002 *F, E, SA, A, It,* 2003 *F, SA, US, Ur, C, A, I*
L Gravano 1997 *CHL,* 1998 *CHL, Ur*
LH Gribell 1910 *GBR*
B Grigolon 1948 *OCC,* 1954 *F, F*
V Grimoldi 1927 *GBR, GBR*
J Grondona 1990 *C*
R Grosse 1952 *I, I,* 1954 *F, F*
P Guarrochena 1977 *Par*
A Guastella 1956 *OCC,* 1959 *JSB, JSB,* 1960 *F*
J Guidi 1958 *Ur, Per, CHL,* 1959 *JSB,* 1960 *F,* 1961 *CHL, Bra, Ur*
E Guiñazu 2003 *Par, CHL, Ur,* 2004 *CHL, Ur, Ven, W, W, SA,* 2005 *J, It,* 2007 *I, It, F,* 2009 *E*
JA Guzman 2007 *CHL,* 2010 *Ur, CHL*
SN Guzmán 2010 *S*
D Halle 1989 *Bra, CHL, Ur, US,* 1990 *US*
A Hamilton 1936 *BI*
R Handley 1966 *SAG, SAG,* 1968 *W, W,* 1969 *S, S, Ur, CHL,* 1970 *I, I,* 1971 *SAG, SAG,* 1972 *SAG, SAG*
G Hardie 1948 *OCC*
TA Harris-Smith 1969 *S, S,* 1971 *SAG, OCC, OCC,* 1973 *Par, Ur*
V Harris-smith 1936 *BI*
O Hasan Jalil 1995 *Ur,* 1996 *Ur, C, SA, SA,* 1997 *E, E, NZ, R, It, F, A,* 1998 *Ur, F, F, R, US, C, It, F, W,* 1999 *W, W, S, W, Sa, J, I,* 2000 *SA, E,* 2001 *NZ, It, W, S, NZ,* 2002 *F, E, SA, A, It, I,* 2003 *US, C, A, R,* 2004 *W, W, NZ, F, I,* 2005 *It, It, SA, S, It,* 2006 *NZ, E, F,* 2007 *It, Geo, Nm, I, S, SA, F*
WM Hayman 1910 *GBR*
BH Heatlie 1910 *GBR*
P Henn 2004 *CHL, Ur, Ven,* 2005 *J, It, C,* 2007 *It*
F Henrys 1910 *GBR*
F Heriot 1910 *GBR*
JM Hernández 2003 *Par, Ur, F, F, SA, C, A, Nm, R,* 2004 *F, I, SA,* 2005 *SA, S, It,* 2006 *W, W, NZ, E, It, F,* 2007 *F, Geo, I, S, SA, F,* 2008 *It, F, It,* 2009 *E, E*
M Hernandez 1927 *GBR, GBR, GBR*
L Herrera 1991 *Ur, Par*
FA Higgs 2004 *Ur, Ven,* 2005 *J*
D Hine 1938 *CHL*
C Hirsch 1960 *F*
C Hirsch 1960 *F*
E Hirsch 1954 *F,* 1956 *OCC*
R Hogg 1958 *Ur, Per, CHL,* 1959 *JSB, JSB,* 1961 *CHL, Bra, Ur*
S Hogg 1956 *OCC, OCC,* 1958 *Ur, Per, CHL,* 1959 *JSB, JSB*
E Holmberg 1948 *OCC*
B Holmes 1949 *F, F*
E Holmgren 1958 *Ur, Per, CHL,* 1959 *JSB, JSB,* 1960 *F, F*
G Holmgren 1985 *NZ, NZ*
E Horan 1956 *OCC*
L Hughes 1936 *CHL*
M Hughes 1954 *F, F*
M Hughes 1949 *F, F*
CA Huntley Robertson 1932 *JSB, JSB*
A Iachetti 1975 *Ur, Par,* 1977 *Ur, Par, CHL,* 1978 *E, It,* 1979 *NZ, NZ, A, A,* 1980 *WXV, Fj, Fj,* 1981 *E, E,* 1982 *F, F, Sp,* 1987 *Ur, Par, A, A,* 1988 *F, F, F, F,* 1989 *It, NZ,* 1990 *C, E, E*
A Iachetti 1977 *Bra,* 1987 *CHL*
ME Iachetti 1979 *NZ, NZ, A, A*
M Iglesias 1973 *R,* 1974 *F, F*
G Illia 1965 *Rho*
J Imhoff 2010 *CHL*
JL Imhoff 1967 *Ur, CHL*
V Inchausti 1936 *BI, CHL, CHL*
F Insua 1971 *CHL, Bra, Par, Ur,* 1972 *SAG, SAG,* 1973 *R, R, Bra, CHL, I, S,* 1974 *F, F,* 1976 *Ur, W, NZ, NZ,* 1977 *F, F*
R Iraneta 1974 *F,* 1976 *Ur, W, NZ*
FJ Irarrazabal 1991 *Sa,* 1992 *Sp, Sp*
S Irazoqui 1993 *J, CHL, Par, Ur,* 1995 *E, Sa, Par*
A Irigoyen 1997 *Par*
C Jacobi 1979 *CHL, Par*
AG Jacobs 1927 *GBR, GBR*
Jaugust 1975 *CHL*
AGW Jones 1948 *OCC*
GM Jorge 1989 *Bra, CHL, Par, Ur,* 1990 *I, E,* 1992 *F, F, Sp, Sp, R, F,* 1993 *J, J, Bra, CHL, Ur, SA, SA,* 1994 *US, S, S, US*
E Jurado 1995 *A, A, E, Sa, It, Par, CHL, Ur, R, It, F,* 1996 *SA, E,* 1997 *E, E, NZ, NZ, Ur, R, It, F, A, A,* 1998 *Ur, F, Ur, C, It,* 1999 *W*
E Karplus 1959 *JSB, JSB,* 1960 *F, F, F*
A Ker 1936 *CHL,* 1938 *CHL*
E Kossler 1960 *F, F, F*
EH Laborde 1991 *A, W, Sa*
G Laborde 1979 *CHL, Bra*
J Lacarra 1989 *Par, Ur*
R Lagarde 1956 *OCC*
A Lalanne 2008 *SA,* 2009 *E, E, W, S,* 2010 *S*
M Lamas 1998 *Par, CHL*
M Landajo 2010 *Ur, CHL*
TR Landajo 1977 *F, Bra, Ur, CHL,* 1978 *E,* 1979 *A, A,* 1980 *WXV, Fj, Fj,* 1981 *E, E*
M Lanfranco 1991 *Ur, Par, Bra*
AR Lanusse 1932 *JSB*
M Lanusse 1951 *Ur, Bra, CHL*
J Lanza 1985 *F, Ur, Par, NZ, NZ,* 1986 *F, F, A, A,* 1987 *Ur, Fj, It, NZ*
P Lanza 1983 *CHL, Par, Ur,* 1985 *F, F, Ur, CHL, Par, NZ, NZ,* 1986 *F, F, A, A,* 1987 *It, NZ*
J Lasalle 1964 *Ur*
J Lavayen 1961 *CHL, Bra, Ur*
CG Lazcano Miranda 1998 *CHL,* 2004 *CHL, Ur, Ven,* 2005 *J*
RA le Fort 1990 *I, E,* 1991 *NZ, NZ, CHL, A, W,* 1992 *R, F,* 1993 *J, SA, SA,* 1995 *Ur, It*
F Lecot 2003 *Par, Ur,* 2005 *J,* 2007 *CHL*
ME Ledesma 1996 *Ur, C,* 1997 *NZ, NZ, Ur, R, It, F, A, A,* 1998 *Ur, F, F, Ur, C, J, Ur, F, W,* 1999 *WXV, W, W, Sa, J, I, F,* 2000 *SA,* 2001 *It, W, NZ,* 2002 *F, E, SA, A, It, I,* 2003 *F, SA, Fj, US, C, A, Nm, R,* 2004 *W, NZ, F, I,* 2005 *BI, It, It, SA, S, It,* 2006 *W, W, NZ, CHL, Ur, E, It, F,* 2007 *W, F, Geo, I, S, SA,* 2008 *SA, F, It, I,* 2009 *E, E, W,* 2010 *S, S, F*
P Ledesma 2008 *It, SA*
J Legora 1996 *F, F, US, Ur,* 1997 *CHL,* 1998 *Par*
JM Leguizamón 2005 *J, BI, It, It, SA, S, It,* 2006 *W, NZ, CHL, Ur, E, It, F,* 2007 *I, I, It, W, F, Geo, Nm, S, SA, F,* 2008 *S, S, It, SA, I,* 2009 *E, E,* 2010 *S, S, F*
GP Leiros 1973 *Bra, I*
C Lennon 1958 *Ur, Per*
TC Leonardi 2009 *E, W, S*
FJ Leonelli Morey 2001 *Ur,* 2004 *Ur, Ven,* 2005 *J, BI, It, C, SA, S, It,* 2006 *W, W,* 2007 *I, I, It,* 2008 *F, I,* 2009 *E*
M Lerga 1995 *Par, CHL, Ur*
Lesianado 1948 *OCC*
I Lewis 1932 *JSB*
GA Llanes 1990 *I, E, S,* 1991 *NZ, NZ, CHL, A, W,* 1992 *F, F, Sp, R, F,* 1993 *Bra, CHL, SA, SA,* 1994 *US, S, S, SA, SA,* 1995 *A, A, E, Sa, It, R, It, F,* 1996 *SA, SA, E,* 1997 *E, E, NZ, NZ, R, It, F,* 1998 *Ur, F,* 2000 *A*
G Llanos 2005 *C*
MA Lobato 2010 *Ur, CHL*
L Lobrauco 1996 *US,* 1997 *CHL,* 1998 *J, CHL, Ur*
MH Loffreda 1978 *E,* 1979 *NZ, NZ, A, A,* 1980 *WXV, Fj, Fj,* 1981 *E, E, C,* 1982 *F, F, Sp,* 1983 *WXV, A, A,* 1985 *Ur, CHL, Par,* 1987 *Ur, Par, CHL, A, A,* 1988 *F, F, F, F,* 1989 *It, NZ, Bra, CHL, Par, Ur, US,* 1990 *C, US, E, E,* 1994 *US, S, S, US, SA, SA*
G Logan 1936 *BI, BI*
GM Longo Elía 1999 *W, W, S, I, W, Sa, I, F,* 2000 *I, A, A, SA, E,* 2001 *US, NZ, It, W, S, NZ,* 2002 *F, E, SA, A, It, I,* 2003 *F, F, SA, Fj, C, A, I,* 2004 *W, W, NZ, F, I,* 2005 *It, It, SA,* 2006 *W, W, NZ, E, It, F,* 2007 *W, Nm, I, S, SA, F*
L Lopez Fleming 2004 *Ur, Ven, W,* 2005 *BI, C, Sa*
A Lopresti 1997 *Par, CHL*
J Loures 1954 *F*

R Loyola 1964 *Ur, CHL*, 1965 *Rho, JSB, OCC, OCC, CHL*, 1966 *SAG, SAG*, 1968 *W, W*, 1969 *S, S*, 1970 *I, I*, 1971 *CHL, Bra, Par, Ur*
E Lozada 2006 *E, It*, 2007 *I, I, Geo, F*, 2008 *S, S, It, SA, F, It, I*, 2009 *E, E*
F Lucioni 1927 *GBR*
R Lucke 1975 *Ur, Par, Bra, CHL*, 1976 *Ur*, 1981 *C*
M Lugano 2001 *Ur*
J Luna 1995 *Par, CHL, Ur, R, It, F*, 1997 *Par, CHL*
P Macadam 1949 *F, F*
AM Macome 1990 *I, E*, 1995 *Ur, C*
RM Madero 1978 *E, It*, 1979 *NZ, NZ, A, A*, 1980 *WXV, Fj, Fj*, 1981 *E, E, C*, 1982 *F, F, Sp*, 1983 *WXV, A, A*, 1985 *F, NZ*, 1986 *A, A*, 1987 *Ur, It, NZ, Sp, Ur, Par, CHL, A, A*, 1988 *F, F, F*, 1989 *It, NZ, NZ*, 1990 *E, E*
L Makin 1927 *GBR*
A Mamanna 1991 *Par*, 1997 *Par*
Manguiamell 1975 *CHL*
J Manuel Belgrano 1956 *OCC*
A Marguery 1991 *Ur, Bra*, 1993 *CHL, Par*
R Martin 1938 *CHL*
RA Martin 1994 *US, S, S, US, SA, SA*, 1995 *Ur, C, A, A, E, Sa, It, CHL, Ur, R, It, F*, 1996 *Ur, F, F, Ur, C, SA, SA, E*, 1997 *E, E, NZ, NZ, It, F, A, A*, 1998 *Ur, F, F, R, US, Ur, J, Par, CHL, Ur, It, W*, 1999 *WXV, W, W, S, I, W, Sa, J, I, F*, 2000 *I, A, A, SA, E*, 2001 *Ur, US, C, NZ, It, W, S, NZ*, 2002 *Ur, Par, CHL, F, E, SA, A, It, I*, 2003 *Par, CHL, Ur, F, SA, Ur, C, A, R, I*
F Martin Aramburu 2004 *CHL, Ven, W, NZ, F, I*, 2005 *It, SA, S, It*, 2006 *NZ*, 2007 *Geo, F*, 2008 *S, SA, F, It, I*, 2009 *E, S*
J Martin Copella 1989 *CHL, Par*
C Martinez 1969 *Ur, CHL*, 1970 *I, I*
E Martinez 1971 *CHL, Bra, Ur*
O Martinez Basante 1954 *F*
M Martinez Mosquera 1971 *CHL*
RC Mastai 1975 *CHL, F*, 1976 *Ur, W, NZ, NZ*, 1977 *F, F, Bra, Ur, Par, CHL*, 1980 *WXV*
R Matarazzo 1971 *SAG, SAG, Par, Ur*, 1972 *SAG, SAG*, 1973 *R, R, Par, Ur, CHL, I, S*, 1974 *F, F*
H Maurer 1932 *JSB, JSB*
L Maurette 1948 *OCC, OCC*
C Mazzini 1977 *F, F*
CJ McCarthy 1910 *GBR*
G McCormick 1964 *Bra, CHL*, 1965 *Rho, OCC, OCC, CHL*, 1966 *SAG, SAG*
M McCormick 1927 *GBR*
A Memoli 1979 *Ur, Par, Bra*
FE Méndez 1990 *I, E*, 1991 *NZ, NZ, CHL, A, W*, 1992 *F, F, Sp, Sp, R, F*, 1994 *S, US, SA, SA*, 1995 *Ur, C, A, A, E, Sa, It, Par, CHL, Ur, R, It, F*, 1996 *SA, SA*, 1997 *E*, 1998 *Ur, F, F, R, US, Ur, C, It, F, W*, 1999 *W, W*, 2000 *I, A, A, SA, E*, 2001 *NZ, It, W, S, NZ*, 2002 *Ur, CHL, F, E, SA, A*, 2003 *F, F, SA, Fj, Ur, Nm, I*, 2004 *CHL, Ur, W, W, NZ, SA*, 2005 *BI*
FJ Mendez 1991 *Ur, Par, Bra*, 1992 *Sp, Sp*
H Mendez 1967 *Ur, CHL*
L Mendez 1958 *Ur, Per, CHL*, 1959 *JSB*
CI Mendy 1987 *Ur, Par, CHL, A, A*, 1988 *F, F, F, F*, 1989 *It, NZ, NZ, US*, 1990 *C*, 1991 *Ur, Bra*
D Mercol 2001 *Ur*
FJ Merello 2007 *CHL*, 2010 *Ur, CHL*
I Merlo 1993 *Bra, CHL*
P Merlo 1985 *CHL, Par*
SE Meson 1987 *Par*, 1989 *Bra, Par, Ur, US*, 1990 *US, C, S*, 1991 *NZ, NZ, CHL, Sa*, 1992 *F, F, Sp, R, F*, 1993 *J, Bra, Par, Ur, SA, SA*, 1994 *US, S, S, US*, 1995 *Ur, C, A, A*, 1996 *US, C*, 1997 *CHL*
I Mieres 2007 *CHL*, 2010 *Ur, CHL*
BH Miguens 1983 *WXV, A, A*, 1985 *F, F, NZ, NZ*, 1986 *F, F, A, A*, 1987 *Sp*
E Miguens 1975 *CHL, Ur, Par, CHL*
H Miguens 1969 *S, S, Ur, CHL*, 1970 *I, I*, 1971 *OCC*, 1972 *SAG, SAG*, 1973 *R, R, Par, Ur, Bra, CHL, I, S*, 1975 *F*
J Miguens 1982 *F*, 1985 *F, F*, 1986 *F, F, A, A*
GE Milano 1982 *F, F, Sp*, 1983 *WXV, A, A*, 1985 *F, F, Ur, CHL, Par, NZ, NZ*, 1986 *F, F, A, A*, 1987 *Ur, Fj, Sp, Ur, CHL, A, A*, 1988 *F, F, F*, 1989 *It, NZ, NZ*
A Mimesi 1998 *J, Par, CHL*
B Minguez 1975 *Par, Bra, CHL*, 1979 *Ur, CHL, Par*, 1983 *WXV, A, A*, 1985 *Ur, CHL*
B Mitchelstein 1936 *BI*
E Mitchelstein 1956 *OCC*, 1960 *F, F*
C Mold 1910 *GBR*
LE Molina 1985 *CHL*, 1987 *Ur, Fj, It, NZ*, 1989 *NZ, NZ, Bra, CHL, Par*, 1990 *C, E*, 1991 *W*
M Molina 1998 *Par, CHL, Ur*
G Montes de Oca 1961 *CHL, Bra, Ur*
E Montpelat 1948 *OCC, OCC*
G Morales Oliver 2001 *Ur, US, C*
C Morea 1951 *Ur, Bra, CHL*
FR Morel 1979 *A, A*, 1980 *WXV, Fj, Fj*, 1981 *E, E, C*, 1982 *F*, 1985 *F, F, Ur, Par, NZ, NZ*, 1986 *F, F, A*, 1987 *Ur, Fj*
A Moreno 1998 *Par, CHL, Ur*
D Morgan 1967 *CHL*, 1970 *I, I*, 1971 *SAG, SAG, OCC, OCC*, 1972 *SAG, SAG*
E Morgan 1969 *S, S*, 1972 *SAG, SAG*, 1973 *R, R, Par, Ur, Bra, CHL, I, S*, 1975 *CHL, F, F*
G Morgan 1977 *Bra, Ur, Par, CHL*, 1979 *Ur, Par, Bra*
M Morgan 1971 *SAG, OCC, OCC*
JS Morganti 1951 *Ur, Bra, CHL*
J Mostany 1987 *Ur, Fj, NZ*
E Muliero 1997 *CHL*
S Muller 1927 *GBR*
R Muniz 1975 *Par, Bra, CHL*
M Nannini 2001 *Ur*, 2002 *Ur, Par, CHL*, 2003 *Par, CHL*
A Navajas 1932 *JSB, JSB*
E Naveyra 1998 *CHL*
G Nazassi 1997 *CHL*
ML Negri 1979 *CHL, Bra*
E Neri 1960 *F, F*, 1961 *CHL, Bra, Ur*, 1964 *Ur, Bra, CHL*, 1965 *Rho, JSB, OCC*, 1966 *SAG, SAG*
CM Neyra 1975 *CHL, F, F*, 1976 *W, NZ, NZ*, 1983 *WXV*
A Nicholson 1979 *Ur, Par, Bra*
HM Nicola 1971 *SAG, OCC, OCC, CHL, Bra, Par, Ur*, 1975 *CHL, F, F*, 1978 *E, It*, 1979 *NZ, NZ*
EP Noriega 1991 *Par*, 1992 *Sp, Sp, R, F*, 1993 *J, J, CHL, Par, Ur, SA, SA*, 1994 *US, S, S, US, SA, SA*, 1995 *Ur, C, A, A, E, Sa, It*
JM Nuñez Piossek 2001 *Ur, NZ*, 2002 *Ur, Par, CHL, A*, 2003 *Par, Ur, F, SA, Ur, C, A, R, I*, 2004 *CHL, Ur, W, W*, 2005 *BI, It, It*, 2006 *W, W, NZ, E, F*, 2008 *S, SA*
R Ochoa 1956 *OCC*
M Odriozola 1961 *CHL, Ur*
J O'Farrell 1948 *OCC*, 1951 *Ur, Bra*, 1956 *OCC*
U O'Farrell 1951 *Ur, Bra, CHL*
C Ohanian 1998 *Ur, Par, Ur*
C Olivera 1958 *Ur, Per, CHL*, 1959 *JSB, JSB*
R Olivieri 1960 *F, F, F*, 1961 *CHL, Bra, Ur*
J Orengo 1996 *Ur*, 1997 *Ur, R, It*, 1998 *Ur, F, F, R, US, C, F, W*, 1999 *WXV, W*, 2000 *A, SA, E*, 2001 *Ur, US, C, NZ, W, S, NZ*, 2002 *F, E, SA, A, It, I*, 2003 *F, SA, Ur, C, A, I*, 2004 *W, W*
JP Orlandi 2008 *F, It, I*, 2009 *E, E*
C Orti 1949 *F, F*
L Ortiz 2003 *Par, CHL, Ur*
A Orzabal 1974 *F, F*
L Ostiglia 1999 *W, W, S, I, W, J, F*, 2001 *NZ, It, W, S*, 2002 *E, SA*, 2003 *Par, CHL, Ur, F, F, SA, Nm, I*, 2004 *W, W, NZ, F, I, SA*, 2007 *F, Nm, I, S, SA*
B Otaño 1960 *F, F, F*, 1961 *CHL, Bra, Ur*, 1964 *Ur, Bra, CHL*, 1965 *Rho, JSB, OCC, OCC, CHL*, 1966 *SAG, SAG*, 1968 *W, W*, 1969 *S, S, Ur, CHL*, 1970 *I, I*, 1971 *SAG, OCC, OCC*
J Otaola 1970 *I*, 1971 *CHL, Bra, Par, Ur*, 1974 *F, F*
M Pacheco 1938 *CHL*
RL Pacheco 2010 *Ur, CHL*
A Palma 1949 *F, F*, 1952 *I, I*, 1954 *F, F*
JMC Palma 1982 *F, Sp*, 1983 *WXV, A, A*
R Palma 1985 *CHL, Par*
M Palou 1996 *US, Ur*
M Parra 1975 *Ur, Bra, CHL*
A Pasalagua 1927 *GBR, GBR*
M Pascual 1965 *Rho, JSB, OCC, OCC, CHL*, 1966 *SAG, SAG*, 1967 *Ur, CHL*, 1968 *W, W*, 1969 *S, S, Ur, CHL*, 1970 *I, I*, 1971 *SAG, SAG, OCC, OCC*

HR Pascuali 1936 *BI*
H Pasman 1936 *CHL*
R Passaglia 1977 *Bra, Ur, CHL*, 1978 *E, It*
G Paz 1979 *Ur, CHL, Par, Bra*, 1983 *CHL, Par, Ur*
JJ Paz 1991 *Ur, Bra*
F Peralta 2001 *Ur*
S Peretti 1993 *Bra, Par, SA*
L Pereyra 2010 *Ur, CHL*
N Perez 1968 *W*
RN Perez 1992 *F, F, Sp, R, F*, 1993 *Bra, Par, Ur, SA*, 1995 *Ur, R, It, F*, 1996 *US, Ur, C, SA, SA*, 1998 *Ur*, 1999 *WXV, I*
J Perez Cobo 1979 *NZ, NZ*, 1980 *Fj*, 1981 *E, E, C*
M Peri Brusa 1998 *CHL*
R Pesce 1958 *Ur, Per, CHL*
TA Petersen 1978 *E, It*, 1979 *NZ, NZ, A, A*, 1980 *Fj, Fj*, 1981 *E, E, C*, 1982 *F*, 1983 *WXV, A, A*, 1985 *F, F, Ur, CHL, Par, NZ, NZ*, 1986 *F, F, A*
AD Petrilli 2004 *SA*, 2005 *J, C*
J Petrone 1949 *F, F*
R Petti 1995 *Par, CHL*
M Pfister 1994 *SA, SA*, 1996 *F*, 1998 *R, Ur, J*
S Phelan 1997 *Ur, CHL, R, It*, 1998 *Ur, F, F, R, US, C, It*, 1999 *S, I, W, Sa, J, I, F*, 2000 *I, A, A, SA, E*, 2001 *NZ, It, W, S, NZ*, 2002 *Ur, Par, CHL, F, E, SA, A, It, I*, 2003 *CHL, Ur, F, SA, Fj, C, A, R*
A Phillips 1948 *OCC*, 1949 *F, F*
JP Piccardo 1981 *E*, 1983 *CHL, Par, Ur*
A Pichot 1995 *A, R, It, F*, 1996 *Ur, F, F*, 1997 *It, F, A, A*, 1998 *Ur, F, F, R, It, F, W*, 1999 *WXV, W, W, S, I, W, Sa, J, I, F*, 2000 *I, A, A, SA, E*, 2001 *Ur, US, C, NZ, It, W, S, NZ*, 2002 *F, E, SA, A, It, I*, 2003 *Ur, C, A, R, I*, 2004 *F, I, SA*, 2005 *It, C, SA, S, It*, 2006 *W, W, NZ, CHL, Ur, E, F*, 2007 *W, F, Nm, I, S, SA, F*
G Pimentel 1971 *Bra*
R Pineo 1954 *F*
E Pittinari 1991 *Ur, Par, Bra*
E Poggi 1965 *JSB, OCC, OCC, CHL*, 1966 *SAG*, 1967 *Ur*, 1969 *Ur*
C Pollano 1927 *GBR*
S Ponce 2007 *CHL*
R Pont Lezica 1951 *Ur, Bra, CHL*
H Porta 1971 *CHL, Bra, Par, Ur*, 1972 *SAG, SAG*, 1973 *R, R, Ur, Bra, CHL, I, S*, 1974 *F, F*, 1975 *F, F*, 1976 *Ur, W, NZ, NZ*, 1977 *F, F*, 1978 *E, It*, 1979 *NZ, NZ, A, A*, 1980 *WXV, Fj, Fj*, 1981 *E, E, C*, 1982 *F, F, Sp*, 1983 *A, A*, 1985 *F, F, Ur, CHL, Par, NZ, NZ*, 1986 *F, F, A*, 1987 *Fj, It, NZ, Sp, A, A*, 1990 *I, E, S*, 1999 *WXV*
O Portillo 1995 *Par, CHL*, 1997 *Par, CHL*
J Posse 1977 *Par*
S Posse 1991 *Par*, 1993 *Bra, CHL, Ur*
C Promanzio 1995 *C*, 1996 *Ur, F, F, E*, 1997 *E, E, NZ, Ur*, 1998 *R, J*
U Propato 1956 *OCC*
L Proto 2010 *Ur, CHL*
A Puccio 1979 *CHL, Par, Bra*
M Puigdeval 1964 *Ur, Bra*
J Pulido 1960 *F*
JC Queirolo 1964 *Ur, Bra, CHL*
G Quesada 1996 *US, Ur, C, SA, E*, 1997 *E, E, NZ, NZ*, 1998 *Ur, F, R, US, C, It*, 1999 *WXV, W, S, I, W, Sa, J, I, F*, 2000 *I, SA, E*, 2001 *NZ, It, NZ*, 2002 *F, E, SA*, 2003 *F, SA, Ur, C, Nm, R, I*
E Quetglas 1965 *CHL*
G Quinones 2001 *Ur*, 2004 *Ur, Ven*
R Raimundez 1959 *JSB, JSB*
C Ramallo 1979 *Ur, CHL, Par*
S Ratcliff 1936 *CHL*
F Rave 1997 *Par*
M Reggiardo 1996 *Ur, F, F, E*, 1997 *E, E, NZ, NZ, R, F, A, A*, 1998 *Ur, F, F, R, US, Ur, C, It, W*, 1999 *W, W, S, I, W, Sa, J, I, F*, 2000 *I, SA*, 2001 *NZ, It, W, S, NZ*, 2002 *F, E, SA, A, It, I*, 2003 *F, SA, Fj, US, Ur, A, Nm, I*, 2005 *BI*
A Reid 1910 *GBR*
C Reyes 1927 *GBR, GBR, GBR*
M Ricci 1987 *Sp*
A Riganti 1927 *GBR, GBR, GBR*
MA Righentini 1989 *NZ*
Rinaldi 1975 *CHL*
J Rios 1960 *F, F*
G Rivero 1996 *Ur, US, Ur*
G Roan 2010 *Ur, CHL*
T Roan 2007 *CHL*
F Robson 1927 *GBR*
M Roby 1992 *Sp*, 1993 *J*
A Rocca 1989 *US*, 1990 *C, US, C, E*, 1991 *Ur, Bra*
O Rocha 1974 *F, F*
D Rodriguez 1998 *J, Par, CHL, Ur*
D Rodriguez 2001 *Ur*, 2002 *Ur, Par, CHL*
EE Rodriguez 1979 *NZ, NZ, A, A*, 1980 *WXV, Fj, Fj*, 1981 *E, E, C*, 1983 *WXV, A, A*
F Rodriguez 2007 *CHL*
M Rodríguez 2009 *E, W, S*, 2010 *S, S, F*
A Rodriguez Jurado 1927 *GBR, GBR, GBR, GBR*, 1932 *JSB, JSB*, 1936 *CHL, CHL*
M Rodriguez Jurado 1971 *SAG, OCC, CHL, Bra, Par, Ur*
A Rodriguez-Jurado 1965 *JSB, OCC, OCC, CHL*, 1966 *SAG, SAG*, 1968 *W, W*, 1969 *S, CHL*, 1970 *I*, 1971 *SAG*, 1973 *R, Par, Bra, CHL, I, S*, 1974 *F, F*, 1975 *F, F*, 1976 *Ur*
L Roldan 2001 *Ur, C*
AS Romagnoli 2004 *CHL, Ur, Ven*
R Roncero 1998 *J*, 2002 *Ur, Par, CHL*, 2003 *Fj, US, Nm, R*, 2004 *W, W, NZ, F, I*, 2005 *It, SA, S, It*, 2006 *W, W, NZ*, 2007 *W, F, Nm, I, S, SA, F*, 2008 *It, SA, F, It, I*, 2009 *E, E, E, W, S*, 2010 *S, S, F*
S Rondinelli 2005 *C, Sa*
S Rosatti 1977 *Par, CHL*
M Rospide 2003 *Par, CHL, Ur*, 2005 *C*
F Rossi 1991 *Ur, Par, Bra*, 1998 *Ur, F*
D Rotondo 1997 *Par, CHL*
MA Ruiz 1997 *NZ, CHL, R, It, F, A, A*, 1998 *Ur, F, F, R, US, Ur, C, J, It, F, W*, 1999 *WXV, W, Sa, J, F*, 2001 *Ur*, 2002 *Ur, Par, CHL*
JE Saffery 1910 *GBR*
CMS Sainz Trapaga 1979 *Ur, Par, Bra*
A Salinas 1954 *F*, 1956 *OCC*, 1958 *Ur, CHL*, 1960 *F, F*
S Salvat 1987 *Ur, Fj, It*, 1988 *F*, 1989 *It, NZ*, 1990 *C, US, C, E, E*, 1991 *Ur, Par, Bra*, 1992 *Sp, F*, 1993 *Bra, CHL, Par, Ur, SA, SA*, 1994 *SA, SA*, 1995 *Ur, C, A, A, E, Sa, It, Par, CHL, Ur, R, It, F*
T Salzman 1936 *BI, CHL, CHL*
M Sambucetti 2001 *Ur, US, C, Ur*, 2002 *Ur, CHL*, 2003 *Par, CHL, Fj*, 2005 *BI, It, Sa*, 2009 *W*
H San Martin 2009 *W, S*
FT Sanchez 2010 *Ur, CHL*
T Sanderson 1932 *JSB*
D Sanes 1985 *CHL, Par*, 1986 *F, F*, 1987 *Ur, Par, CHL*, 1989 *Bra, CHL, Ur*
EJ Sanguinetti 1975 *Ur, Par, CHL*, 1978 *It*, 1979 *A*, 1982 *F, F, Sp*
G Sanguinetti 1979 *Ur, CHL, Par, Bra*
J Sansot 1948 *OCC*
M Sansot 1975 *CHL, F, F*, 1976 *Ur, W, NZ, NZ*, 1977 *Bra, CHL*, 1978 *E, It*, 1979 *NZ, NZ, A, A*, 1980 *WXV, Fj*, 1983 *WXV*
Jm Santamarina 1991 *NZ, NZ, CHL, A, W, Sa*, 1992 *F, Sp, R, F*, 1993 *J, J*, 1994 *US, S, US*, 1995 *A, A, E, Sa, It, Ur, R, It, F*, 1999 *WXV*
J Santiago 1948 *OCC*, 1952 *I, I*
JR Sanz 1973 *Par, Ur, Bra, CHL*, 1974 *F, F*, 1976 *Ur*, 1977 *F, F*
S Sanz 2003 *US*, 2004 *CHL, Ven*, 2005 *BI, It, Sa*, 2007 *CHL*
M Sarandon 1948 *OCC, OCC*, 1949 *F, F*, 1951 *Ur, Bra, CHL*, 1952 *I, I*, 1954 *F*
J Sartori 1979 *CHL, Par, Bra*
R Sauze 1983 *Par*
FW Saywer 1910 *GBR*
JM Scarpatti 2001 *Ur*
JM Scelzo 1996 *US, SA*, 1997 *R, It, F, A*, 1998 *Ur, F, US, Ur, C, CHL, F*, 1999 *WXV, I, Sa, I, F*, 2000 *I, A, A*, 2003 *F, F, Fj, Ur, C, Nm, R, I*, 2005 *SA, S, It*, 2006 *W, W, NZ, CHL, Ur, E, It, F*, 2007 *W, F, Nm, I, S, SA*, 2009 *E, W, S*, 2010 *S, S, F*
F Schacht 1989 *Bra, CHL, Par, Ur, US*, 1990 *C*
E Scharemberg 1961 *CHL, Bra, Ur*, 1964 *Ur, Bra*, 1965 *Rho, JSB, OCC, OCC*, 1967 *Ur, CHL*

AM Schiavio 1983 *CHL*, *Ur*, 1986 *A*, 1987 *Fj*, *It*, *NZ*
E Schiavio 1936 *BI*, *BI*, *CHL*, *CHL*
R Schmidt 1960 *F*, *F*, *F*, 1961 *Bra*, 1964 *Ur*, 1965 *JSB*
G Schmitt 1964 *Ur*, *CHL*
M Schusterman 2001 *Ur*, 2003 *Par*, *Fj*, 2004 *W*, *W*, *NZ*, *F*, 2005 *BI*, *It*, *It*, *SA*, *S*, 2006 *W*, *CHL*, *Ur*, *E*, 2007 *I*, *It*, *Geo*
AA Scolni 1983 *CHL*, *Par*, *Ur*, 1985 *F*, 1987 *Sp*, *A*, 1988 *F*, *F*, *F*, *F*, 1989 *NZ*, *US*, 1990 *C*, *US*, *E*, *E*, *I*, *E*, *S*
J Seaton 1968 *W*, *W*, 1969 *Ur*, *CHL*
R Seaton 1967 *Ur*, *CHL*
H Senillosa 2002 *Ur*, *Par*, *CHL*, 2003 *Par*, *CHL*, *Ur*, *F*, *SA*, *Fj*, *US*, *Nm*, *R*, 2004 *CHL*, *Ur*, *Ven*, *W*, *W*, *NZ*, *F*, *I*, 2005 *It*, *It*, 2006 *CHL*, *It*, *F*, 2007 *I*, *I*, *F*, *Geo*, *Nm*, *I*, *S*, *F*, 2008 *It*
R Serra 1927 *GBR*, *GBR*, *GBR*
F Serra Miras 2003 *CHL*, 2005 *J*, 2006 *W*, *CHL*, *Ur*, 2007 *I*, *It*, *W*, *Nm*, 2008 *S*
C Serrano 1978 *It*, 1980 *Fj*, 1983 *CHL*, *Par*, *Ur*
R Sharpe 1948 *OCC*
HL Silva 1965 *JSB*, *OCC*, 1967 *Ur*, *CHL*, 1968 *W*, *W*, 1969 *S*, *S*, *Ur*, *CHL*, 1970 *I*, *I*, 1971 *SAG*, *SAG*, *OCC*, *OCC*, *Ur*, 1978 *E*, 1979 *NZ*, *NZ*, *A*, *A*, 1980 *WXV*
R Silva 1998 *J*
F Silvestre 1988 *F*, 1989 *Bra*, *Par*, *Ur*, *US*, 1990 *C*, *US*
D Silvetti 1993 *J*
J Simes 1989 *Bra*, *CHL*, 1990 *C*, *US*, 1993 *J*, *J*, 1996 *Ur*, *F*, *F*, *US*, *C*
HG Simon 1991 *NZ*, *NZ*, *A*, *W*, *Sa*
E Simone 1996 *US*, *SA*, *SA*, *E*, 1997 *E*, *E*, *NZ*, *NZ*, *R*, *F*, *A*, *A*, 1998 *Ur*, *F*, *F*, *US*, *Ur*, *C*, *J*, *It*, *F*, *W*, 1999 *WXV*, *W*, *S*, *I*, *W*, *Sa*, *J*, *I*, *F*, 2000 *I*, *SA*, 2001 *Ur*, *US*, *It*, *Ur*, 2002 *Ur*, *CHL*
A Smidt 2010 *Ur*, *CHL*
A Soares-Gache 1978 *It*, 1979 *NZ*, *NZ*, 1981 *C*, 1982 *F*, *Sp*, 1983 *WXV*, *A*, *A*, 1987 *Sp*, *A*, *A*, 1988 *F*
T Solari 1996 *Ur*, *C*, *SA*, 1997 *E*, *E*, *NZ*, *NZ*, 1998 *Ur*
F Soler 1996 *Ur*, *F*, *F*, *SA*, *SA*, 1997 *E*, *E*, *NZ*, *NZ*, *Ur*, *R*, *It*, *F*, 1998 *Ur*, *F*, *F*, *R*, *US*, *C*, *It*, *W*, 2001 *Ur*, *US*, 2002 *Ur*, *Par*, *CHL*
JS Soler Valls 1989 *It*, *Bra*, *Par*, *Ur*
H Solveira 1951 *Ur*
J Sommer 1927 *GBR*
E Sorhaburu 1958 *Ur*, *Per*, 1960 *F*, 1961 *CHL*, *Ur*
E Spain 1965 *JSB*, *OCC*, *OCC*, *CHL*, 1967 *Ur*, *CHL*
PL Sporleder 1990 *I*, *E*, *S*, 1991 *NZ*, *NZ*, *CHL*, *A*, *W*, *Sa*, 1992 *F*, *F*, *Sp*, *Sp*, *R*, *F*, 1993 *J*, *J*, *Bra*, *CHL*, *Par*, *Ur*, *SA*, *SA*, 1994 *US*, *S*, *S*, *US*, *SA*, *SA*, 1995 *A*, *A*, *E*, *Sa*, *It*, 1996 *Ur*, *F*, *F*, *Ur*, *C*, *SA*, *SA*, *E*, 1997 *E*, *E*, *NZ*, *NZ*, *Par*, *Ur*, *R*, *It*, *F*, *A*, *A*, 1998 *Ur*, *F*, *R*, *US*, *Ur*, *C*, *Ur*, *It*, *F*, *W*, 1999 *WXV*, *W*, *W*, *J*, 2002 *Ur*, *Par*, *CHL*, *It*, *I*, 2003 *Par*, *CHL*, *Ur*, *F*, *Fj*, *US*, *Nm*, *R*
J Stanfield 1932 *JSB*
A Stewart 1936 *BI*
J Stewart 1932 *JSB*, *JSB*
BM Stortoni 1998 *J*, *Par*, 2001 *Ur*, *US*, *C*, *NZ*, *It*, *NZ*, 2002 *Ur*, *Par*, *CHL*, 2003 *F*, *Fj*, *US*, 2005 *BI*, *It*, *It*, *S*, *It*, 2007 *I*, 2008 *S*, *S*, *It*, *SA*, *F*, *It*, *I*
J Stuart 2007 *CHL*, 2008 *S*, *It*
M Sugasti 1995 *Par*, *CHL*
W Sutton 1936 *CHL*
C Swain 1948 *OCC*, 1949 *F*, *F*, 1951 *Ur*, *Bra*, *CHL*, 1952 *I*, *I*
J Tagliabue 1936 *CHL*, *CHL*
L Tahier 1964 *Ur*, *CHL*
F Talbot 1936 *BI*, *BI*, 1938 *CHL*
H Talbot 1936 *BI*, *BI*, *CHL*, *CHL*, 1938 *CHL*
HF Talbot 1910 *GBR*
A Tejeda 2008 *S*, *S*, *It*
EG Teran 1975 *CHL*, 1977 *Bra*, *Ur*, *Par*, *CHL*, 1979 *CHL*, *Par*, *Bra*
G Teran 1988 *F*
MJ Teran 1991 *NZ*, *NZ*, *CHL*, *A*, *W*, *Sa*, 1992 *F*, *Sp*, *R*, *F*, 1993 *J*, *J*, *Ur*, *SA*, *SA*, 1994 *US*, *S*, *S*, *US*, *SA*, *SA*, 1995 *A*, *A*, *E*, *Sa*, *It*, *Ur*, *R*, *It*, *F*
FN Tetaz Chaparro 2010 *CHL*
GP Tiesi 2004 *SA*, 2005 *J*, *C*, *It*, *Sa*, 2006 *W*, *W*, *NZ*, *CHL*, *Ur*, *E*, 2007 *Geo*, *Nm*, *SA*, 2008 *S*, *S*, *F*, *It*, 2009 *E*, *E*, *E*, *W*, *S*, 2010 *S*, *S*, *F*
FJ Todeschini 1998 *R*, *Ur*, 2005 *J*, *BI*, *It*, *It*, *S*, 2006 *W*, *W*, *NZ*, *CHL*, *Ur*, *E*, *It*, *F*, 2007 *I*, *W*, *Geo*, *Nm*, 2008 *S*, *S*
A Tolomei 1991 *Par*, *Bra*, 1993 *Bra*, *CHL*, *Par*
N Tompkins 1948 *OCC*, 1949 *F*, *F*, 1952 *I*, *I*
JA Topping 1938 *CHL*
E Torello 1983 *Par*, 1989 *CHL*
F Torino 1927 *GBR*, *GBR*
NC Tozer 1932 *JSB*, *JSB*
AA Travaglini 1967 *Ur*, *CHL*, 1968 *W*, 1969 *S*, *S*, 1970 *I*, *I*, 1971 *SAG*, *SAG*, *OCC*, *OCC*, 1972 *SAG*, *SAG*, 1973 *R*, *Par*, *Ur*, *Bra*, *CHL*, *I*, *S*, 1974 *F*, *F*, 1975 *F*, *F*, 1976 *Ur*, *W*, *NZ*, *NZ*
G Travaglini 1978 *E*, *It*, 1979 *NZ*, *NZ*, *A*, *A*, 1980 *WXV*, *Fj*, *Fj*, 1981 *E*, *E*, 1982 *F*, *F*, *Sp*, 1983 *WXV*, *A*, 1987 *Ur*, *Fj*, *It*, *NZ*
R Travaglini 1996 *US*, *Ur*, *C*, 1997 *NZ*, *R*, *F*, 1998 *Ur*, *C*, 1999 *WXV*
J Trucco 1977 *Bra*, *Ur*, *Par*, *CHL*
A Turner 1932 *JSB*, *JSB*
FA Turnes 1985 *F*, *F*, *Ur*, *NZ*, *NZ*, 1986 *F*, *F*, *A*, *A*, 1987 *Ur*, *Fj*, *NZ*, *Sp*, *A*, *A*, 1988 *F*, *F*, *F*, *F*, 1989 *It*, *NZ*, *NZ*, 1997 *Ur*, *F*, *A*, *A*
G Ugartemendia 1991 *Ur*, 1993 *J*, *CHL*, *Par*, *Ur*, *SA*, *SA*, 1994 *US*, *SA*, *SA*, 1997 *Ur*, 1998 *Par*, 2000 *E*
M Urbano 1991 *Ur*, *Bra*, 1995 *Par*, *CHL*, *R*, *It*, *F*
B Urdapilleta 2007 *CHL*, 2008 *SA*, 2009 *W*, 2010 *Ur*
EM Ure 1980 *WXV*, *Fj*, *Fj*, 1981 *E*, *E*, 1982 *F*, *F*, *Sp*, 1983 *A*, 1985 *F*, *F*, *NZ*, *NZ*, 1986 *F*, *F*, *A*
J Uriarte 1986 *A*, 1987 *Par*
E Valesani 1986 *A*, *A*
MR Valesani 1989 *It*, *NZ*, *NZ*, *CHL*, *Par*, *Ur*, *US*, 1990 *C*, *US*, *C*
GB Varela 1979 *Ur*, *CHL*
L Varela 1961 *CHL*, *Bra*, *Ur*
F Varella 1960 *F*
GM Varone 1982 *F*
C Vazquez 1927 *GBR*, *GBR*, *GBR*
A Velazquez 1971 *CHL*, *Par*
R Ventura 1975 *CHL*, *Ur*, *Bra*, *CHL*, 1977 *Bra*, *Ur*, 1978 *It*, 1979 *Ur*, *CHL*, *Par*, 1983 *CHL*, *Par*, *Ur*
E Verardo 1958 *CHL*, 1959 *JSB*, *JSB*, 1964 *Ur*, *Bra*, *CHL*, 1967 *Ur*, *CHL*
N Vergallo 2005 *Sa*, 2006 *CHL*, *Ur*, 2007 *I*, *I*, *CHL*, 2008 *S*, *S*, *It*, *SA*, *F*, *It*, *I*, 2009 *E*, 2010 *F*
AV Vernet Basualdo 2004 *SA*, 2005 *J*, 2006 *It*, 2007 *I*, *Geo*, *Nm*, *I*, *F*, 2008 *SA*, *It*, 2009 *E*, *E*, *S*
G Veron 1997 *Par*
M Viazzo 2010 *Ur*, *CHL*
J Vibart 1960 *F*
H Vidou 1987 *Par*, 1990 *C*, *US*, *E*, *E*, 1991 *NZ*
H Vidou 1960 *F*, 1961 *Bra*
C Viel Temperley 1993 *Bra*, *CHL*, *Par*, *Ur*, 1994 *US*, *S*, *S*, *US*, *SA*, *SA*, 1995 *Ur*, *C*, *A*, *A*, *E*, *Sa*, *It*, *Par*, *Ur*, *R*, *It*, *F*, 1996 *SA*, 1997 *E*, *NZ*
E Vila 1975 *CHL*, *Ur*, *Par*, *CHL*
JJ Villar 2001 *Ur*, *US*, *C*, 2002 *Par*, *CHL*
D Villen 1998 *J*, *Par*
M Viola 1993 *Bra*
J Virasoro 1973 *R*, *R*, *Ur*, *Bra*, *CHL*, *S*
JL Visca 1985 *Par*
J Walther 1971 *OCC*
M Walther 1967 *Ur*, *CHL*, 1968 *W*, *W*, 1969 *S*, *S*, *Ur*, *CHL*, 1970 *I*, *I*, 1971 *SAG*, *OCC*, *OCC*, 1973 *Bra*, *CHL*, 1974 *F*, *F*
WA Watson 1910 *GBR*
F Werner 1996 *US*, 1997 *Ur*
Wessek 1960 *F*
R Wilkins 1936 *CHL*, *CHL*
J Wittman 1971 *SAG*, *SAG*, *OCC*, *OCC*, *Ur*, 1972 *SAG*, *SAG*, 1973 *R*
L Yanez 1965 *Rho*, *JSB*, *OCC*, *OCC*, *CHL*, 1966 *SAG*, *SAG*, 1968 *W*, *W*, 1969 *S*, *S*, *Ur*, *CHL*, 1970 *I*, *I*, 1971 *SAG*, *OCC*, *OCC*, *Ur*
EP Yanguela 1956 *OCC*
M Yanguela 1987 *It*
B Yustini 1954 *F*, 1956 *OCC*
R Zanero 1990 *C*
E Zapiola 1998 *Par*
A Zappa 1927 *GBR*

AUSTRALIA

AUSTRALIA'S 2009–10 TEST RECORD

OPPONENTS	DATE	VENUE	RESULT
New Zealand	31 Oct	N	**Lost** 19–32
England	7 Nov	A	**Won** 18–9
Ireland	15 Nov	A	**Drew** 20–20
Scotland	21 Nov	A	**Lost** 8–9
Wales	28 Nov	A	**Won** 33–12
Fiji	5 June	H	**Won** 49–3
England	12 June	H	**Won** 27–17
England	19 June	H	**Lost** 21–20
Ireland	26 June	H	**Won** 22–15
South Africa	24 July	H	**Won** 30–13
New Zealand	31 July	H	**Lost** 28–49
New Zealand	7 Aug	A	**Lost** 10–20
South Africa	28 Aug	A	**Lost** 31–44
South Africa	4 Sep	A	**Won** 41–39
New Zealand	11 Sep	H	**Lost** 22–23

WALLABIES ON THE FRONT FOOT

By Matt Burke

With only seven wins in 15 Tests, I couldn't say it was a vintage season for the Wallabies but I thought there was genuine hope for the future in some of their performances and overall I'd give Robbie Deans and his players a pass mark for their efforts.

I think there's a debate in every country about the balance between results and the brand of rugby the side plays. Australia arguably came up short in terms of results but they produced some really entertaining stuff over the season and if what is essentially a young squad can learn some of the harsh lessons that Test rugby regularly dishes out, they can move forward with some confidence.

It is certainly true their inexperience was exposed on a number of occasions. The 9–8 defeat to Scotland at Murrayfield in November in particular was hard to swallow because they had their chances to put the Scots away but failed to get themselves out of jail. It was the end of a long season and conditions were cold and wet in Edinburgh but the Wallabies should not use those factors as excuses at this level.

Good teams can play in all conditions, at any stage of the season, and Australia couldn't do it. The good news is, collectively, they are still young enough to learn and improve.

The conclusion of the Tri–Nations saw some sections of the Australian press questioning Deans' future as coach but personally I think he has done a decent job and I see no reason why he shouldn't be given the opportunity to at least fulfil his original contract and take the side through to the 2011 World Cup.

The 2009–10 season was only his second full campaign since his appointment and it was always going to take time for him to shape the squad and move some of the players he inherited on. He got rid of some of the elder statesmen like Phil Waugh and Al Baxter and his squad for the Tri–Nations was brimming with youngsters, which can only be good for the future.

To my eye, the Wallabies were still coming to terms with the new skill sets, defensive patterns and structures Deans is trying to introduce. There were definitely signs the message was getting through but there's no overnight fix when you're trying to build a new team.

Hannah Johnston/Getty Images

Rocky Elsom led Australia with pride and passion in 2010.

What I admire about Deans is he sticks to his guns and even when it seems he's making odd decisions, there's method to his madness. I'm thinking in particular about the two Tests against England and his selections in the Wallaby front row.

He picked Ben Daley, Saia Faingaa and Salesi Ma'afu for the first Test in Perth and although Australia won the match, the front three were bashed up by the English. Deans could have panicked but he stuck with the guys for the second Test in Sydney and I think that proves he's a good operator.

The Wallabies' problems up front in recent years are well documented. Deans knows it and so do the opposition. But he hasn't got a lot of time before the World Cup, so he took the decision to throw the guys in at the deep end but, more importantly, he stuck with them even though they had a rough ride.

Of course, there are still worries about the front row. You can have the best backline in the world but if you can't get at least parity up front, you are going to struggle. When I played in the UK for Newcastle, we had some great players out wide but not the greatest pack and we didn't get enough of the ball.

Considering the physical nature of the two Tests against the English, the Wallabies bounced back impressively in the Tri–Nations and although two wins from six was hardly world-beating form, I thought some of their rugby over the course of the tournament was the best they produced all year.

The standout performance was their 30–13 win over South Africa in Brisbane in their first game of the tournament. True, it was not a great Springbok side but it was a comprehensive win against the reigning world champions and one of which the guys should have been proud.

I was also impressed by their displays in the two Tests in South Africa. The 44–31 defeat in Pretoria was obviously disappointing in terms of the final result but Australia scored four tries at Loftus Versfeld and I thought they showed promise.

The 41–39 win in Bloemfontein a week later was even better. Yes, it needed a magnificent long-range kick from Kurtley Beale to wrap things up but they would have felt choked not to have won a match in which they outscored the Springboks five tries to three. It was a display full of aggression and enthusiasm.

The Wallabies' clashes with New Zealand were a different story. They were blown away by the All Blacks in Melbourne, pushed them close in Christchurch and then came the big disappointment, the 23–22 reverse in Sydney in the final game of the Tri–Nations.

The problem with that game was it was there for the taking. Australia were 22–9 up with 15 minutes left but they allowed the All Blacks back into it and they scored two late tries for the win. It was a sad way to end the season for the Wallabies and led to criticism of the side not being able to play for the full 80 minutes.

I think it's true the team did show glimpses of indecision in Sydney and although I'm generally optimistic about the future, I'd have to agree they need to wise up quickly when it comes to closing games out. Test matches are not usually won in the first 20 minutes but Australia repeatedly produced their best rugby in the opening quarter of games only to go into their shell and pay a heavy price.

In contrast, the All Blacks in Sydney gave an abject lesson in how to finish. They had been outscored two tries to nil after the hour mark, they trailed and the clock was ticking. But they refused to panic, they patiently went through their phases and finally found a way through the Wallaby defence.

The Kiwis are the masters at doing exactly what they need to do in the final 20 minutes of a match and I hope some of Australia's younger players learned from what happened at ANZ Stadium. It was Test rugby at its harshest.

In terms of individual performances for the Wallabies, I was very impressed by the half back pairing of Will Genia and Quade Cooper. They still don't have many caps between them but they brought a dynamism and control to some of the Wallaby play that belied their relative inexperience.

Nine and ten at international level is pretty unforgiving because if you make mistakes, they are magnified but Genia and Cooper stepped up to the plate and gave the side a cutting edge that was really encouraging. If form and fitness allows Deans to keep them as a unit, they can only get better.

I also liked the Wallaby back three. As modern rugby dictates, the personnel in that back three changed on a reasonably regular basis but I'm talking about Drew Mitchell, Kurtley Beale, Adam–Ashley Cooper and James O'Connor.

All of them did well on an individual basis but as a unit I thought Australia's back three was superb on the counter attack and made some scorching runs, which is why the Wallabies always looked dangerous out wide even if the forwards were not dominating.

In the pack, Rocky Elsom led by example again even though there had been some doubts whether Deans would retain him as captain. His back row colleague David Pocock also caught the eye and prop Benn Robinson was solid enough in the scrum but really impressed with his mobility about the park.

The Wallabies are still a work in progress but for me they are definitely heading in the right direction.

AUSTRALIA INTERNATIONAL STATISTICS

MATCH RECORDS UP TO 29TH OCTOBER 2010

MOST CONSECUTIVE TEST WINS

10 1991 Arg, WS, W, I, NZ, E, 1992 S 1,2, NZ 1,2
10 1998 NZ 3, Fj, Tg, Sm, F, E 2, 1999 I 1,2, E, SA 1
10 1999 NZ 2, R, I 3, US, W, SA 3, F, 2000 Arg 1,2,SA 1

MOST CONSECUTIVE TESTS WITHOUT DEFEAT

Matches	Wins	Draws	Period
10	10	0	1991 to 1992
10	10	0	1998 to 1999
10	10	0	1999 to 2000

MOST POINTS IN A MATCH

BY THE TEAM

Pts	Opponents	Venue	Year
142	Namibia	Adelaide	2003
92	Spain	Madrid	2001
91	Japan	Lyons	2007
90	Romania	Brisbane	2003
76	England	Brisbane	1998
74	Canada	Brisbane	1996
74	Tonga	Canberra	1998
74	W Samoa	Sydney	2005
73	W Samoa	Sydney	1994
69	Italy	Melbourne	2005
67	United States	Brisbane	1990

BY A PLAYER

Pts	Player	Opponents	Venue	Year
42	M S Rogers	Namibia	Adelaide	2003
39	M C Burke	Canada	Brisbane	1996
30	E J Flatley	Romania	Brisbane	2003
29	S A Mortlock	South Africa	Melbourne	2000
28	M P Lynagh	Argentina	Brisbane	1995
27	M J Giteau	Fiji	Montpellier	2007
25	M C Burke	Scotland	Sydney	1998
25	M C Burke	France	Cardiff	1999
25	M C Burke	British/Irish Lions	Melbourne	2001
25	E J Flatley*	Ireland	Perth	2003
25	C E Latham	Namibia	Adelaide	2003
24	M P Lynagh	United States	Brisbane	1990
24	M P Lynagh	France	Brisbane	1990
24	M C Burke	New Zealand	Melbourne	1998
24	M C Burke	South Africa	Twickenham	1999

* includes a penalty try

MOST TRIES IN A MATCH

BY THE TEAM

Tries	Opponents	Venue	Year
22	Namibia	Adelaide	2003
13	South Korea	Brisbane	1987
13	Spain	Madrid	2001
13	Romania	Brisbane	2003
13	Japan	Lyons	2007
12	United States	Brisbane	1990
12	Wales	Brisbane	1991
12	Tonga	Canberra	1998
12	Samoa	Sydney	2005
11	Western Samoa	Sydney	1994
11	England	Brisbane	1998
11	Italy	Melbourne	2005

BY A PLAYER

Tries	Player	Opponents	Venue	Year
5	C E Latham	Namibia	Adelaide	2003
4	G Cornelsen	New Zealand	Auckland	1978
4	D I Campese	United States	Sydney	1983
4	J S Little	Tonga	Canberra	1998
4	C E Latham	Argentina	Brisbane	2000
4	L D Tuqiri	Italy	Melbourne	2005

MOST CONVERSIONS IN A MATCH

BY THE TEAM

Cons	Opponents	Venue	Year
16	Namibia	Adelaide	2003
12	Spain	Madrid	2001
11	Romania	Brisbane	2003
10	Japan	Lyons	2007
9	Canada	Brisbane	1996
9	Fiji	Parramatta	1998
8	Italy	Rome	1988
8	United States	Brisbane	1990
7	Canada	Sydney	1985
7	Tonga	Canberra	1998
7	Samoa	Sydney	2005
7	Italy	Melbourne	2005
7	Fiji	Canberra	2010

BY A PLAYER

Cons	Player	Opponents	Venue	Year
16	M S Rogers	Namibia	Adelaide	2003
11	E J Flatley	Romania	Brisbane	2003
10	M C Burke	Spain	Madrid	2001
9	M C Burke	Canada	Brisbane	1996
9	J A Eales	Fiji	Parramatta	1998
8	M P Lynagh	Italy	Rome	1988
8	M P Lynagh	United States	Brisbane	1990
7	M P Lynagh	Canada	Sydney	1985
7	S A Mortlock	Japan	Lyons	2007

MOST PENALTIES IN A MATCH

BY THE TEAM

Pens	Opponents	Venue	Year
8	South Africa	Twickenham	1999
7	New Zealand	Sydney	1999
7	France	Cardiff	1999
7	Wales	Cardiff	2001
7	England	Twickenham	2008
6	New Zealand	Sydney	1984
6	France	Sydney	1986
6	England	Brisbane	1988
6	Argentina	Buenos Aires	1997
6	Ireland	Perth	1999
6	France	Paris	2000
6	British/Irish Lions	Melbourne	2001
6	New Zealand	Sydney	2004
6	Italy	Padua	2008
6	New Zealand	Sydney	2009
6	South Africa	Brisbane	2010

BY A PLAYER

Pens	Player	Opponents	Venue	Year
8	M C Burke	South Africa	Twickenham	1999
7	M C Burke	New Zealand	Sydney	1999
7	M C Burke	France	Cardiff	1999
7	M C Burke	Wales	Cardiff	2001
6	M P Lynagh	France	Sydney	1986
6	M P Lynagh	England	Brisbane	1988
6	D J Knox	Argentina	Buenos Aires	1997
6	M C Burke	France	Paris	2000
6	M C Burke	British/Irish Lions	Melbourne	2001
6	M J Giteau	England	Twickenham	2008
6	M J Giteau	New Zealand	Sydney	2009

MOST DROPPED GOALS IN A MATCH

BY THE TEAM

Drops	Opponents	Venue	Year
3	England	Twickenham	1967
3	Ireland	Dublin	1984
3	Fiji	Brisbane	1985

BY A PLAYER

Drops	Player	Opponent	Venue	Year
3	P F Hawthorne	England	Twickenham	1967
2	M G Ella	Ireland	Dublin	1984
2	D J Knox	Fiji	Brisbane	1985

CAREER RECORDS

MOST CAPPED PLAYERS

Caps	Player	Career Span
139	G M Gregan	1994 to 2007
110	G B Smith	2000 to 2009
102	S J Larkham	1996 to 2007
101	D I Campese	1982 to 1996
88	N C Sharpe	2002 to 2010
87	M J Giteau	2002 to 2010
86	J A Eales	1991 to 2001
86	J W C Roff	1995 to 2004
81	M C Burke	1993 to 2004
80	T J Horan	1989 to 2000
80	S A Mortlock	2000 to 2009
79	D J Wilson	1992 to 2000
79	P R Waugh	2000 to 2009
78	C E Latham	1998 to 2007
75	J S Little	1989 to 2000
72	M P Lynagh	1984 to 1995
72	J A Paul	1998 to 2006
69	A K E Baxter	2003 to 2009
67	P N Kearns	1989 to 1999
67	D J Herbert	1994 to 2002
67	L D Tuqiri	2003 to 2008
63	N C Farr Jones	1984 to 1993
63	M J Cockbain	1997 to 2003
60	R S T Kefu	1997 to 2003
59	S P Poidevin	1980 to 1991
59	R D Elsom	2005 to 2010

MOST CONSECUTIVE TESTS

Tests	Player	Career Span
62	J W C Roff	1996 to 2001
46	P N Kearns	1989 to 1995
44	G B Smith	2003 to 2006
42	D I Campese	1990 to 1995
37	P G Johnson	1959 to 1968

MOST TESTS AS CAPTAIN

Tests	Captain	Career Span
59	G M Gregan	2001 to 2007
55	J A Eales	1996 to 2001
36	N C Farr Jones	1988 to 1992
29	S A Mortlock	2006 to 2009
19	A G Slack	1984 to 1987
16	J E Thornett	1962 to 1967
16	G V Davis	1969 to 1972

MOST POINTS IN TESTS

Pts	Player	Tests	Career Span
911	M P Lynagh	72	1984 to 1995
878	M C Burke	81	1993 to 2004
664	M J Giteau	87	2002 to 2010
489	S A Mortlock	80	2000 to 2009
315	D I Campese	101	1982 to 1996
260	P E McLean	30	1974 to 1982
249*	J W Roff	86	1995 to 2004
200	C E Latham	78	1998 to 2007
187*	E J Flatley	38	1997 to 2005
173	J A Eales	86	1991 to 2001

* Roff and Flatley's totals include a penalty try

MOST TRIES IN TESTS

Tries	Player	Tests	Career Span
64	D I Campese	101	1982 to 1996
40	C E Latham	78	1998 to 2007
31*	J W Roff	86	1995 to 2004
30	T J Horan	80	1989 to 2000
30	L D Tuqiri	67	2003 to 2008
29	M C Burke	81	1993 to 2004
29	S A Mortlock	80	2000 to 2009
28	M J Giteau	87	2002 to 2010
25	S J Larkham	102	1996 to 2007
24	B N Tune	47	1996 to 2006
22	D A Mitchell	50	2005 to 2010
21	J S Little	75	1989 to 2000

* Roff's total includes a penalty try

MOST CONVERSIONS IN TESTS

Cons	Player	Tests	Career Span
140	M P Lynagh	72	1984 to 1995
104	M C Burke	81	1993 to 2004
100	M J Giteau	87	2002 to 2010
61	S A Mortlock	80	2000 to 2009
31	J A Eales	86	1991 to 2001
30	E J Flatley	38	1997 to 2005
27	P E McLean	30	1974 to 1982
27	M S Rogers	45	2002 to 2006
20	J W Roff	86	1995 to 2004
19	D J Knox	13	1985 to 1997

MOST PENALTY GOALS IN TESTS

Pens	Player	Tests	Career Span
177	M P Lynagh	72	1984 to 1995
174	M C Burke	81	1993 to 2004
104	M J Giteau	87	2002 to 2010
74	S A Mortlock	80	2000 to 2009
62	P E McLean	30	1974 to 1982
34	J A Eales	86	1991 to 2001
34	E J Flatley	38	1997 to 2005
23	M C Roebuck	23	1991 to 1993

MOST DROPPED GOALS IN TESTS

Drops	Player	Tests	Career Span
9	P F Hawthorne	21	1962 to 1967
9	M P Lynagh	72	1984 to 1995
8	M G Ella	25	1980 to 1984
5	B S Barnes	26	2007 to 2010
4	P E McLean	30	1974 to 1982
4	M J Giteau	87	2002 to 2010

TRI-NATIONS RECORDS

RECORD	DETAIL	HOLDER	SET
Most points in season	162	in six matches	2010
Most tries in season	17	in six matches	2010
Highest Score	49	49–0 v S Africa (h)	2006
Biggest win	49	49–0 v S Africa (h)	2006
Highest score conceded	61	22–61 v S Africa (a)	1997
Biggest defeat	45	8–53 v S Africa (a)	2008
Most appearances	48	G M Gregan	1996 to 2007
Most points in matches	271	M C Burke	1996 to 2004
Most points in season	72	M J Giteau	2009
Most points in match	24	M C Burke	v N Zealand (h) 1998
Most tries in matches	9	J W C Roff	1996 to 2003
	9	S A Mortlock	2000 to 2009
	9	L D Tuqiri	2003 to 2008
Most tries in season	4	S A Mortlock	2000
	4	J D O'Connor	2010
Most tries in match	2	B N Tune	v S Africa (h) 1997
	2	S J Larkham	v N Zealand (a) 1997
	2	M C Burke	v N Zealand (h) 1998
	2	J W C Roff	v S Africa (h) 1999
	2	S A Mortlock	v N Zealand (h) 2000
	2	C E Latham	v S Africa (h) 2002
	2	M J Giteau	v S Africa (h) 2006
	2	L D Tuqiri	v N Zealand (a) 2006
	2	M J Giteau	v S Africa (h) 2009
	2	J D O'Connor	v S Africa (a) 2010
Most cons in matches	36	M J Giteau	2003 to 2010
Most cons in season	12	S A Mortlock	2006
Most cons in match	5	S A Mortlock	v S Africa (h) 2006
Most pens in matches	65	M C Burke	1996 to 2004
Most pens in season	14	M C Burke	2001
	14	M J Giteau	2009
	14	M J Giteau	2010
Most pens in match	7	M C Burke	v N Zealand (h) 1999

MISCELLANEOUS RECORDS

RECORD	HOLDER	DETAIL
Longest Test Career	G M Cooke	1932–1948
Youngest Test Cap	B W Ford	18 yrs 90 days in 1957
Oldest Test Cap	A R Miller	38 yrs 113 days in 1967

CAREER RECORDS OF AUSTRALIA INTERNATIONAL PLAYERS (UP TO 29TH OCTOBER 2010)

PLAYER	DEBUT	CAPS	T	C	P	D	PTS
BACKS							
A P Ashley-Cooper	2005 v SA	46	14	0	0	0	70
B S Barnes	2007 v J	26	4	1	0	5	37
K J Beale	2009 v W	9	4	0	2	0	26
L Burgess	2008 v I	27	1	0	0	0	5
Q S Cooper	2008 v It	19	5	1	3	0	36
R P Cross	2008 v F	18	6	0	0	0	30
A S Fainga'a	2010 v NZ	4	0	0	0	0	0
S W Genia	2009 v NZ	18	3	0	0	0	15
M J Giteau	2002 v E	87	28	100	104	4	664
R G Horne	2010 v Fj	6	0	0	0	0	0
P J Hynes	2008 v I	22	4	0	0	0	20
D N Ioane	2007 v W	11	5	0	0	0	25
D A Mitchell	2005 v SA	50	22	0	0	0	110
S A Mortlock	2000 v Arg	80	29	61	74	0	489
S H Norton-Knight	2007 v W	2	1	0	0	0	5
J D O'Connor	2008 v It	23	8	7	3	0	63
P J A Tahu	2008 v NZ	4	0	0	0	0	0
L D Tuqiri	2003 v I	67	30	0	0	0	150
L D Turner	2008 v F	12	3	0	0	0	15
J J Valentine	2006 v E	6	0	0	0	0	0
FORWARDS:							
B E Alexander	2008 v F	19	0	0	0	0	0
A K E Baxter	2003 v NZ	69	1	0	0	0	5
R N Brown	2008 v NZ	22	1	0	0	0	5
M D Chisholm	2004 v S	53	6	0	0	0	30
P J M Cowan	2009 v It	4	0	0	0	0	0
B P Daley	2010 v E	3	0	0	0	0	0
M J Dunning	2003 v Nm	45	0	0	0	0	0
H Edmonds	2010 v Fj	3	0	0	0	0	0
R D Elsom	2005 v Sm	59	11	0	0	0	55
S M Fainga'a	2010 v Fj	9	0	0	0	0	0
A L Freier	2002 v Arg	25	2	0	0	0	10
M J Hodgson	2010 v Fj	3	0	0	0	0	0
S A Hoiles	2004 v S	16	3	0	0	0	15

J E Horwill	2007 v Fj	24	5	0	0	0	25
S M Kepu	2008 v It	3	0	0	0	0	0
P J Kimlin	2009 v It	2	0	0	0	0	0
R S L Ma'afu	2010 v Fj	10	0	0	0	0	0
B J McCalman	2010 v SA	4	0	0	0	0	0
H J McMeniman	2005 v Sm	21	0	0	0	0	0
S T Moore	2005 v Sm	51	3	0	0	0	15
D W Mumm	2008 v I	30	1	0	0	0	5
W L Palu	2006 v E	36	1	0	0	0	5
D W Pocock	2008 v NZ	25	1	0	0	0	5
T Polota-Nau	2005 v E	23	2	0	0	0	10
B A Robinson	2006 v SA	37	1	0	0	0	5
N C Sharpe	2002 v F	88	7	0	0	0	35
G T Shepherdson	2006 v I	18	1	0	0	0	5
R A Simmons	2010 v SA	4	0	0	0	0	0
J A Slipper	2010 v E	9	0	0	0	0	0
G B Smith	2000 v F	110	9	0	0	0	45
D J Vickerman	2002 v F	55	0	0	0	0	0

Mark Nolan/Getty Images

George Smith has become only the fifth player in history to reach 110 caps.

AUSTRALIA INTERNATIONAL PLAYERS

UP TO 29TH OCTOBER 2010

Note: Years given for International Championship matches are for second half of season; eg 1972 means season 1971–72. Years for all other matches refer to the actual year of the match. Entries in square brackets denote matches played in RWC Finals.

Abrahams, A M F (NSW) 1967 NZ, 1968 NZ 1, 1969 W
Adams, N J (NSW) 1955 NZ 1
Adamson, R W (NSW) 1912 US
Alexander, B E (ACT) 2008 F1(R),2(R),It,F3, 2009 It1(R),2,F(R), NZ1(R),SA1(R), NZ2(t&R),SA2,3,NZ3,4,E,I,S,W, 2010 Fj
Allan, T (NSW) 1946 NZ 1, M, NZ 2, 1947 NZ 2, S, I, W, 1948 E, F, 1949 M 1,2,3, NZ 1,2
Anderson, R P (NSW) 1925 NZ 1
Anlezark, E A (NSW) 1905 NZ
Armstrong, A R (NSW) 1923 NZ 1,2
Ashley-Cooper, A P (ACT) 2005 SA4(R), 2007 W1,2,Fj,SA1(R), NZ1,SA2,NZ2, [J,Fj, C,E], 2008 F1(R),2,SA1,NZ1,2,SA3,NZ3,4, It,E,F3, 2009 It1(R),2(t&R),F,NZ1,SA1, NZ2,SA2,3,NZ3,4,E,I,S,W, 2010 Fj,E2(R),I,SA1,NZ1,2,SA2,3,NZ3
Austin, L R (NSW) 1963 E
Baker, R L (NSW) 1904 BI 1,2
Baker, W H (NSW) 1914 NZ 1,2,3
Ballesty, J P (NSW) 1968 NZ 1,2, F, I, S, 1969 W, SA 2,3,4,
Bannon, D P (NSW) 1946 M
Bardsley, E J (NSW) 1928 NZ 1,3, M (R)
Barker, H S (NSW) 1952 Fj 1,2, NZ 1,2, 1953 SA 4, 1954 Fj 1,2
Barnes, B S (Q, NSW) 2007 [J(R),W,Fj,E], 2008 I,F1,2,SA1,NZ1,2, SA2,NZ4(R),It, 2009 It1,2,F,NZ1,SA1,NZ2,SA3,NZ3, 2010 E1, SA1(R),NZ1,SA3(R),NZ3(t&R)
Barnett, J T (NSW) 1907 NZ 1,2,3, 1908 W, 1909 E
Barry, M J (Q) 1971 SA 3
Bartholomeusz, M A (ACT) 2002 It (R)
Barton, R F D (NSW) 1899 BI 3
Batch, P G (Q) 1975 S, W, 1976 E, Fj 1,2,3, F 1,2, 1978 W 1,2, NZ 1,2,3, 1979 Arg 2
Batterham, R P (NSW) 1967 NZ, 1970 S
Battishall, B R (NSW) 1973 E
Baxter, A J (NSW) 1949 M 1,2,3, NZ 1,2, 1951 NZ 1,2, 1952 NZ 1,2
Baxter, A K E (NSW) 2003 NZ 2(R), [Arg,R,I(R),S(R),NZ(R),E], 2004 S1,2,E1,PI,NZ1, SA1,NZ2,SA2,S3,F,S4,E2, 2005 It,F1, SA1,2,3(R),NZ1,SA4,NZ2,F2,E,I(R),W(R), 2006 E1(R),2(R),I1(R), NZ1(R),SA1(R),NZ3(R),SA3(R),W,It,I2,S(R), 2007 Fj,SA1(R), NZ1(R),SA2(R),NZ2(R), [J,W(R),C,E(R)], 2008 I(R),F1,2,SA1, NZ1,2,SA2(R),3(R), NZ3,4,E,F3,W, 2009 It1,F,NZ1,SA1,NZ2
Baxter, T J (Q) 1958 NZ 3
Beale, K J (NSW) 2009 W(R), 2010 Fj,E1(R),I(R),NZ1(R),2,SA2,3, NZ3
Beith, B McN (NSW) 1914 NZ 3, 1920 NZ 1,2,3
Bell, K R (Q) 1968 S
Bell, M D NSW) 1996 C
Bennett, W G (Q) 1931 M, 1933 SA 1,2,3,
Bermingham, J V (Q) 1934 NZ 1,2, 1937 SA 1
Berne, J E (NSW) 1975 S
Besomo, K S (NSW) 1979 I 2
Betts, T N (Q) 1951 NZ 2,3, 1954 Fj 2
Biilmann, R R (NSW) 1933 SA 1,2,3,4
Birt, R S W (Q) 1914 NZ 2
Black, J W (NSW) 1985 C 1,2, NZ, Fj 1
Blackwood, J G (NSW) 1922 M 1, NZ 1,2,3, 1923 M 1, NZ 1,2,3, 1924 NZ 1,2,3, 1925 NZ 1,4, 1926 NZ 1,2,3, 1927 I, W, S, 1928 E, F
Blades, A T (NSW) 1996 S, I, W 3, 1997 NZ 1(R), E 1(R), SA 1(R), NZ 3, SA 2, Arg 1,2, E 2, S, 1998 E 1, S 1,2, NZ 1, SA 1, NZ 2, SA 2, NZ 3, Fj, WS, F, E 2, 1999 I 1(R), SA 2, NZ 2, [R, I 3, W, SA 3, F]
Blades, C D (NSW) 1997 E 1
Blake, R C (Q) 2006 E1,2, NZ2,SA2,NZ3,SA3,W
Blair, M R (NSW) 1928 F, 1931 M, NZ
Bland, G V (NSW) 1928 NZ 3, M, 1932 NZ 1,2,3, 1933 SA 1,2,4,5
Blomley, J (NSW) 1949 M 1,2,3, NZ 1,2, 1950 BI 1,2
Boland, S B (Q) 1899 BI 3,4, 1903 NZ
Bond, G S G (ACT) 2001 SA 2(R), Sp (R), E (R), F, W
Bond, J H (NSW) 1920 NZ 1,2,3, 1921 NZ
Bondfield, C (NSW) 1925 NZ 2
Bonis, E T (Q) 1929 NZ 1,2,3, 1930 BI, 1931 M, NZ, 1932 NZ 1,2,3, 1933 SA 1,2,3,4,5, 1934 NZ 1,2, 1936 NZ 1,2, M, 1937 SA 1, 1938 NZ 1
Bonner, J E (NSW) 1922 NZ 1,2,3, 1923 M 1,2,3, 1924 NZ 1,2
Bosler, J M (NSW) 1953 SA 1
Bouffler, R G (NSW) 1899 BI 3
Bourke, T K (Q) 1947 NZ 2
Bowden, R (NSW) 1926 NZ 4
Bowen, S (NSW) 1993 SA 1,2,3, 1995 [R], NZ 1,2, 1996 C, NZ 1, SA 2
Bowers, A J A (NSW) 1923 M 2(R),3, NZ, 3, 1925 NZ 1,4, 1926 NZ 1, 1927 I
Bowman, T M (NSW) 1998 E 1, S 1,2, NZ 1, SA 1, NZ 2, SA 2, NZ 3, Fj, WS, F, E 2, 1999 I 1,2, SA 2, [US]
Boyce, E S (NSW) 1962 NZ 1,2, 1964 NZ 1,2,3, 1965 SA 1,2, 1966 W, S, 1967 E, I 1, F, I 2
Boyce, J S (NSW) 1962 NZ 3,4,5, 1963 E, SA 1,2,3,4, 1964 NZ 1,3, 1965 SA 1,2
Boyd, A (NSW) 1899 BI 3
Boyd, A F McC (Q) 1958 M 1
Brass, J E (NSW) 1966 BI 2, W, S, 1967 E, I 1, F, I 2, NZ, 1968 NZ 1, F, I, S
Breckenridge, J W (NSW) 1925 NZ 2(R),3, 1927 I, W, S, 1928 E, F, 1929 NZ 1,2,3, 1930 BI
Brial, M C (NSW) 1993 F 1(R), 2, 1996 W 1(R), 2, C, NZ 1, SA 1, NZ 2, SA 2, It, I, W 3, 1997 NZ 2
Bridle, O L (V) 1931 M, 1932 NZ 1,2,3, 1933 SA 3,4,5, 1934 NZ 1,2, 1936 NZ 1,2, M
Broad, E G (Q) 1949 M 1
Brockhoff, J D (NSW) 1949 M 2,3, NZ 1,2, 1950 BI 1,2, 1951 NZ 2,3
Brown, B R (Q) 1972 NZ 1,3
Brown, J V (NSW) 1956 SA 1,2, 1957 NZ 1,2, 1958 W, I, E, S, F
Brown, R C (NSW) 1975 E 1,2
Brown, R N (WF) 2008 NZ3(R),4,It,E,W, 2009 It1,F,NZ1,SA1, NZ2,SA2,S(R), 2010 Fj, E1,2,I,SA1,NZ1,2,SA2,3(R),NZ3(R)
Brown, S W (NSW) 1953 SA 2,3,4
Bryant, H (NSW) 1925 NZ 1,3,4
Buchan, A J (NSW) 1946 NZ 1,2, 1947 NZ 1,2, S, I, W, 1948 E, F, 1949 M 3
Buchanan, P N (NSW) 1923 M 2(R),3
Bull, D (NSW) 1928 M
Buntine, H (NSW) 1923 NZ 1(R), 1924 NZ 2
Burdon, A (NSW) 1903 NZ, 1904 BI 1,2, 1905 NZ
Burge, A B (NSW) 1907 NZ 3, 1908 W
Burge, P H (NSW) 1907 NZ 1,2,3
Burge, R (NSW) 1928 NZ 1,2,3(R), M (R)
Burgess, L (NSW) 2008 I,F1,2,SA1,NZ1,2,4,It,E,F3,W, 2009 It1,2, F,NZ1,SA1,NZ2, SA2,NZ3(R),S(R),W(R), 2010 Fj,E1,I,NZ1(R), SA3(R),NZ3(R)
Burke, B T (NSW) 1988 S (R)
Burke, C T (NSW) 1946 NZ 2, 1947 NZ 1,2, S, I, W, 1948 E, F, 1949 M 2,3, NZ 1,2, 1950 BI 1,2, 1951 NZ 1,2,3, 1953 SA 2,3,4, 1954 Fj 1, 1955 NZ 1,2,3, 1956 SA 1,2,
Burke, M C (NSW) 1993 SA 3(R), F 1, 1994 I 1,2, It 1,2, 1995 [C, R, E], NZ 1,2, 1996 W 1,2, C, NZ 1, SA 1, NZ 2, SA 2, It, S, I, W 3, 1997 E 1, NZ 2 , 1998 E 1, S 1,2, NZ 1, SA 1, NZ 2, SA 2, NZ 3, 1999 I 2(R), E (R), SA 1, NZ 1, SA 2, NZ 2, [R, I 3, US, W, SA 3, F], 2000 F, S, E, 2001 BI 1(R),2,3, SA 1, NZ 1, SA 2, NZ 2, Sp, E, F, W, 2002 F 1,2, NZ 1, SA 1, NZ 2, SA 2, Arg, I, E, It, 2003 SA 1, NZ 1, SA 2(R), NZ 2(R),[Arg,R, Nm(R),I], 2004 S1(R),PI(R),SA1(R),NZ2(t&R),SA2(R)
Burke, M P (NSW) 1984 E (R), I, 1985 C 1,2, NZ, Fj 1,2, 1986 It (R), F, Arg 1,2, NZ 1,2,3, 1987 SK, [US, J, I, F, W], NZ, Arg 1,2

Burnet, D R (NSW) 1972 F 1,2, NZ 1,2,3, Fj
Butler, O F (NSW) 1969 SA 1,2, 1970 S, 1971 SA 2,3, F 1,2
Calcraft, W J (NSW) 1985 C 1, 1986 It, Arg 2
Caldwell, B C (NSW) 1928 NZ 3
Cameron, A S (NSW) 1951 NZ 1,2,3, 1952 Fj 1,2, NZ 1,2, 1953 SA 1,2,3,4, 1954 Fj 1,2, 1955 NZ 1,2,3, 1956 SA 1,2, 1957 NZ 1, 1958 I
Campbell, A M (ACT) 2005 F1(R), 2006 It(R),I2(R),S
Campbell, J D (NSW) 1910 NZ 1,2,3
Campbell, W A (Q) 1984 Fj, 1986 It, F, Arg 1,2, NZ 1,2,3, 1987 SK, [E, US, J (R), I, F], NZ, 1988 E, 1989 BI 1,2,3, NZ, 1990 NZ 2,3
Campese, D I (ACT, NSW) 1982 NZ 1,2,3, 1983 US, Arg 1,2, NZ, It, F 1,2, 1984 Fj, NZ 1,2,3, E, I, W, S, 1985 Fj 1,2, 1986 It, F, Arg 1,2, NZ 1,2,3, 1987 [E, US, J, I, F, W], NZ, 1988 E 1,2, NZ 1,2,3, E, S, It, 1989 BI 1,2,3, NZ, F 1,2, 1990 F 2,3, US, NZ 1,2,3, 1991 W, E, NZ 1,2, [Arg, WS, W, I, NZ, E], 1992 S 1,2, NZ 1,2,3, SA, I, W, 1993 Tg, NZ, SA 1,2,3, C, F 1,2, 1994 I 1,2, It 1,2, WS, NZ, 1995 Arg 1,2, [SA, C, E], NZ 2(R), 1996 W 1,2, C, NZ 1, SA 1, NZ 2, SA 2, It, W3
Canniffe, W D (Q) 1907 NZ 2
Cannon, B J (NSW, WF) 2001 BI 2(R), NZ 1(R), Sp (R), F (R), W (R), 2002 F 1(R),2, SA 1(t),2(R), I (t), It (R), 2003 I (R), W (R), E (R), SA 1, NZ 1, SA 2, NZ 2, [Arg,R,I,S,NZ,E], 2004 S1,2,E1, PI,NZ1,2,SA2,S3(R),4(R), 2005 NZ1(R),SA4,NZ2,F2,E,I,W, 2006 W(R),It
Caputo, M E (ACT) 1996 W 1,2, 1997 F 1,2, NZ 1
Carberry, C M (NSW, Q) 1973 Tg 2, E, 1976 I, US, Fj 1,2,3, 1981 F 1,2, I, W, S, 1982 E
Cardy, A M (NSW) 1966 BI 1,2, W, S, 1967 E, I 1, F, 1968 NZ 1,2
Carew, P J (Q) 1899 BI 1,2,3,4
Carmichael, P (Q) 1904 BI 2, 1907 NZ 1, 1908 W, 1909 E
Carozza, P V (Q) 1990 F 1,2,3, NZ 2,3, 1992 S 1,2, NZ 1,2,3, SA, I, W, 1993 Tg, NZ
Carpenter, M G (V) 1938 NZ 1,2,
Carr, E T A (NSW) 1913 NZ 1,2,3, 1914 NZ 1,2,3
Carr, E W (NSW) 1921 SA 1,2,3, NZ (R)
Carroll, D B (NSW) 1908 W, 1912 US
Carroll, J C (NSW) 1953 SA 1
Carroll, J H (NSW) 1958 M 2,3, NZ 1,2,3, 1959 BI 1,2
Carson, J (NSW) 1899 BI 1
Carson, P J (NSW) 1979 NZ, 1980 NZ 3
Carter, D G (NSW) 1988 E 1,2, NZ 1, 1989 F 1,2
Casey, T V (NSW) 1963 SA 2,3,4, 1964 NZ 1,2,3
Catchpole, K W (NSW) 1961 Fj 1,2,3, SA 1,2, F, 1962 NZ 1,2,4, 1963 SA 2,3,4, 1964 NZ 1,2,3, 1965 SA 1,2, 1966 BI 1,2, W, S, 1967 E, I 1, F, I 2, NZ, 1968 NZ 1
Cawsey, R M (NSW) 1949 M 1, NZ 1,2
Cerutti, W H (NSW) 1928 NZ 1,2,3, M, 1929 NZ 1,2,3, 1930 BI, 1931 M, NZ, 1932 NZ 1,2,3, 1933 SA 1,2,3,4,5, 1936 M, 1937 SA 1,2
Challoner, R L (NSW) 1899 BI 2
Chambers, R (NSW) 1920 NZ 1,3
Chapman, G A (NSW) 1962 NZ 3,4,5
Chisholm, M D (ACT) 2004 S3(R), 2005 Sm,It,F1,SA1,2,3(R), NZ1(R),2,F2,E(t&R), I(R),W(R), 2006 E1(R),2,I1,NZ1,SA1(R), NZ2(R),SA2(R),NZ3(t&R),SA3(R),W(R), It,I2,S(t&R), 2007 W1, 2(R),Fj,SA1(R),NZ1(R),2(R), [W(R),Fj,C], 2008 NZ4,It,E, F3(R),W, 2009 SA2,3,NZ3,4,E,I,S,W(R), 2010 E1(R),2(R),I,SA3,NZ3
Clark, J G (Q) 1931 M, NZ, 1932 NZ 1,2, 1933 SA 1
Clarken, J C (NSW) 1905 NZ, 1910 NZ 1,2,3
Cleary, M A (NSW) 1961 Fj 1,2,3, SA 1,2, F
Clements, P (NSW) 1982 NZ 3
Clifford, M (NSW) 1938 NZ 3
Cobb, W G (NSW) 1899 BI 3,4
Cockbain, M J (Q) 1997 F 2(R), NZ 1, SA 1,2, 1998 E 1, S 1,2, NZ 1, SA 1, NZ 2, SA 2, NZ 3, Fj, Tg (R), WS, F, E 2, 1999 I 1,2, E, SA 1, NZ 1, SA 2, NZ 2, [US (t&R), W, SA 3, F], 2000 Arg 1,2, SA 2(t&R),3(t&R), F, S, E (R), 2001 BI 1(R),2(R),3(R), SA 1(R), NZ 1(R), SA 2(R), NZ 2(R), Sp (R), E (R), F (t+R), W, 2002 F 1(R),2(R), NZ 1(R), SA 1(R), NZ 2(R), SA 2(R), Arg, I, E, It, 2003 [Arg(R),R(R),Nm(R),I(R),S(R),NZ(R),E(R)]
Cocks, M R (NSW, Q) 1972 F 1,2, NZ 2,3, Fj, 1973 Tg 1,2, W, E, 1975 J 1
Codey, D (NSW Country, Q) 1983 Arg 1, 1984 E, W, S, 1985 C 2, NZ, 1986 F, Arg 1, 1987 [US, J, F (R), W], NZ
Cody, E W (NSW) 1913 NZ 1,2,3
Coker, T (Q, ACT) 1987 [E, US, F, W], 1991 NZ 2, [Arg, WS, NZ, E], 1992 NZ 1,2,3, W (R), 1993 Tg, NZ, 1995 Arg 2, NZ 1(R), 1997 F 1(R), 2, NZ 1, E 1, NZ 2(R), SA 1(R), NZ 3, SA 2, Arg 1,2
Colbert, R (NSW) 1952 Fj 2, NZ 1,2, 1953 SA 2,3,4
Cole, J W (NSW) 1968 NZ 1,2, F, I, S, 1969 W, SA 1,2,3,4, 1970 S, 1971 SA 1,2,3, F 1,2, 1972 NZ 1,2,3, 1973 Tg 1,2, 1974 NZ 1,2,3
Collins, P K (NSW) 1937 SA 2, 1938 NZ 2,3
Colton, A J (Q) 1899 BI 1,3
Colton, T (Q) 1904 BI 1,2
Comrie-Thomson, I R (NSW) 1926 NZ 4, 1928 NZ 1,2,3 M
Connor, D M (Q) 1958 W, I, E, S, F, M 2,3, NZ 1,2,3, 1959 BI 1,2
Connors, M R (Q) 1999 SA 1(R), NZ 1(R), SA 2(R), NZ 2, [R (R), I 3, US, W (R), SA 3(R), F(R)], 2000 Arg 1(R),2(R), SA 1, NZ 1, SA 2, NZ 2(t&R), SA 3, F (R), S (R), E (R)
Constable, R (Q) 1994 I 2(t & R)
Cook, M T (Q) 1986 F, 1987 SK, [J], 1988 E 1,2, NZ 1,2,3, E, S, It
Cooke, B P (Q) 1979 I 1
Cooke, G M (Q) 1932 NZ 1,2,3, 1933 SA 1,2,3, 1946 NZ 2, 1947 NZ 2, S, I, W, 1948 E, F
Coolican, J E (NSW) 1982 NZ 1, 1983 It, F 1,2
Cooney, R C (NSW) 1922 M 2
Cooper, Q S (Q) 2008 It(R),F3(R),W(R), 2009 It1(R),2,SA2(R),3(R), E,I,S,W, 2010 Fj, E1,2,I,SA1,2,3,NZ3
Cordingley, S J (Q, Grenoble) 2000 Arg 1(R), SA 1(R), F, S, E, 2006 E2,I1(R),NZ1(R), SA1(R),NZ2(R),SA2(R), 2007 Fj(R), [Fj(R),C], 2008 I(R),F1(R),2(t&R),SA1(R),2,3, NZ3,F3(R)
Corfe, A C (Q) 1899 BI 2
Cornelsen, G (NSW) 1974 NZ 2,3, 1975 J 2, S, W, 1976 E, F 1,2, 1978 W 1,2, NZ 1,2,3, 1979 I 1,2, NZ, Arg 1,2, 1980 NZ 1,2,3, 1981 I, W, S, 1982 E
Cornes, J R (Q) 1972 Fj
Cornforth, R G W (NSW) 1947 NZ 1, 1950 BI 2
Cornish, P (ACT) 1990 F 2,3, NZ 1
Costello, P P S (Q) 1950 BI 2
Cottrell, N V (Q) 1949 M 1,2,3, NZ 1,2, 1950 BI 1,2, 1951 NZ 1,2,3, 1952 Fj 1,2, NZ 1,2
Cowan, P J M (WF) 2009 It2,SA3(R),NZ3(R), 2010 Fj(R)
Cowper, D L (V) 1931 NZ, 1932 NZ 1,2,3, 1933 SA 1,2,3,4,5
Cox, B P (NSW) 1952 Fj 1,2, NZ 1,2, 1954 Fj 2, 1955 NZ 1, 1956 SA 2, 1957 NZ 1,2
Cox, M H (NSW) 1981 W, S
Cox, P A (NSW) 1979 Arg 1,2, 1980 Fj, NZ 1,2, 1981 W (R), S, 1982 S 1,2, NZ 1,2,3, 1984 Fj, NZ 1,2,3
Craig, R R (NSW) 1908 W
Crakanthorp, J S (NSW) 1923 NZ 3
Cremin, J F (NSW) 1946 NZ 1,2, 1947 NZ 1
Crittle, C P (NSW) 1962 NZ 4,5, 1963 SA 2,3,4, 1964 NZ 1,2,3, 1965 SA 1,2, 1966 BI 1,2, S, 1967 E, I
Croft, B H D (NSW) 1928 M
Croft, D N (Q) 2002 Arg (t&R), I (R), E (t&R), It (R), 2003 [Nm]
Cross, J R (NSW) 1955 NZ 1,2,3
Cross, K A (NSW) 1949 M 1, NZ 1,2, 1950 BI 1,2, 1951 NZ 2,3, 1952 NZ 1, 1953 SA 1,2,3,4, 1954 Fj 1,2, 1955 NZ 3, 1956 SA 1,2, 1957 NZ 1,2
Cross, R P (WF) 2008 F1(R),2(R),SA1(R),NZ1,2(R),SA2(R),3(R), NZ3,4,E,W, 2009 It2,F(R),NZ2(R),SA2,NZ4,E(R),S
Crossman, O C (NSW) 1923 M 1(R),2,3, 1924, NZ 1,2,3, 1925 NZ 1,3,4, 1926 NZ 1,2,3,4, 1929 NZ 2, 1930 BI
Crowe, P J (NSW) 1976 F 2, 1978 W 1,2, 1979 I 2, NZ, Arg 1
Crowley, D J (Q) 1989 BI 1,2,3, 1991 [WS], 1992 I, W, 1993 C (R), 1995 Arg 1,2, [SA, E], NZ 1, 1996 W 2(R), C, NZ 1, SA 1,2, I, W 3, 1998 E 1(R), S 1(R),2(R), NZ 1(R), SA 1, NZ 2, SA 2, NZ 3, Tg, WS, 1999 I 1,2(R), E (R), SA 1, NZ 1(R), [R (R), I 3(t&R), US, F(R)]
Curley, T G P (NSW) 1957 NZ 1,2, 1958 W, I, E, S, F, M 1, NZ 1,2,3
Curran, D J (NSW) 1980 NZ 3, 1981 F 1,2, W, 1983 Arg 1
Currie, E W (Q) 1899 BI 2
Cutler, S A G (NSW) 1982 NZ 2(R), 1984 NZ 1,2,3, E, I, W, S, 1985 C 1,2, NZ, Fj 1,2, 1986 It, F, NZ 1,2,3, 1987 SK, [E, J, I, F, W], NZ, Arg 1,2, 1988 E 1,2, NZ 1,2,3, E, S, It, 1989 BI 1,2,3, NZ, 1991 [WS]
Daley, B P (Q) 2010 E1,2,I
Daly, A J (NSW) 1989 NZ, F 1,2, 1990 F 1,2,3, US, NZ 1,2,3, 1991 W, E, NZ 1,2, [Arg, W, I, NZ, E], 1992 S 1,2, NZ 1,2,3, SA, 1993 Tg, NZ, SA 1,2,3, C, F 1,2, 1994 I 1,2, It 1,2, WS, NZ, 1995 [C, R]
D'Arcy, A M (Q) 1980 Fj, NZ 3, 1981 F 1,2, I, W, S, 1982 E, S 1,2
Darveniza, P (NSW) 1969 W, SA 2,3,4
Darwin, B J (ACT) 2001 BI 1(R), SA 1(R), NZ 1(R), SA 2(R), NZ 2(t&R), Sp, E, F, W, 2002 NZ 1(R), SA 1(R), NZ 2(R), SA 2, Arg (R), I (R), E (R), It (R), 2003 I (R), W (t&R), E (R), SA 1(R), NZ 1(R), [Arg(R),R(R),Nm,I,S,NZ]
Davidson, R A L (NSW) 1952 Fj 1,2, NZ 1,2, 1953 SA 1, 1957 NZ 1,2, 1958 W, I, E, S, F, M 1
Davis, C C (NSW) 1949 NZ 1, 1951 NZ 1,2,3

Davis, E H (V) 1947 S, W, 1949 M 1,2
Davis, G V (NSW) 1963 E, SA 1,2,3,4, 1964 NZ 1,2,3, 1965 SA 1, 1966 BI 1,2, W, S, 1967 E, I 1, F, I 2, NZ, 1968 NZ 1,2, F, I, S, 1969 W, SA 1,2,3,4, 1970 S, 1971 SA 1,2,3, F 1,2, 1972 F 1,2, NZ 1,2,3
Davis, G W G (NSW) 1955 NZ 2,3
Davis, R A (NSW) 1974 NZ 1,2,3
Davis, T S R (NSW) 1920 NZ 1,2,3, 1921 SA 1,2,3, NZ, 1922 M 1,2,3, NZ 1,2,3, 1923 M 3, NZ 1,2,3, 1924 NZ 1,2, 1925 NZ 1
Davis, W (NSW) 1899 BI 1,3,4
Dawson, W L (NSW) 1946 NZ 1,2
Diett, L J (NSW) 1959 BI 1,2
Dix, W (NSW) 1907 NZ 1,2,3, 1909 E
Dixon, E J (Q) 1904 BI 3
Donald, K J (Q) 1957 NZ 1, 1958 W, I, E, S, M 2,3, 1959 BI 1,2
Dore, E (Q) 1904 BI 1
Dore, M J (Q) 1905 NZ
Dorr, R W (V) 1936 M, 1937 SA 1
Douglas, J A (V) 1962 NZ 3,4,5
Douglas, W A (NSW) 1922 NZ 3(R)
Dowse, J H (NSW) 1961 Fj 1,2, SA 1,2
Dunbar, A R (NSW) 1910 NZ 1,2,3, 1912 US
Duncan, J L (NSW) 1926 NZ 4
Dunlop, E E (V) 1932 NZ 3, 1934 NZ 1
Dunn, P K (NSW) 1958 NZ 1,2,3, 1959 BI 1,2
Dunn, V A (NSW) 1920 NZ 1,2,3, 1921 SA 1,2,3, NZ
Dunning, M J (NSW, WF) 2003 [Nm,E(R)], 2004 S1(R),2(R), E1(R),NZ1(R),SA1(R), NZ2(t&R),SA2(R),S3(R),F(R),S4(R), E2(R),2005 Sm,It(R),F1(t&R),SA1(R),2(R),3, NZ1(t&R),SA4(t&R), NZ2(R),F2,E,W, 2007 W1,2(R),Fj,SA1,NZ1,SA2,NZ2, [J,W,Fj,E], 2008 I,SA1(R),NZ1(R),SA2,3,NZ4(R),It, 2009 E(R),W(R)
Dunworth, D A (Q) 1971 F 1,2, 1972 F 1,2, 1976 Fj 2
Dwyer, L J (NSW) 1910 NZ 1,2,3, 1912 US, 1913 NZ 3, 1914 NZ 1,2,3
Dyson, F J (Q) 2000 Arg 1,2, SA 1, NZ 1, SA 2, NZ 2, SA 3, F, S, E
Eales, J A (Q) 1991 W, E, NZ 1,2, [Arg, WS, W, I, NZ, E], 1992 S 1,2, NZ 1,2,3, SA, I, 1994 I 1,2, It 1,2, WS, NZ, 1995 Arg 1,2, [SA, C, R, E], NZ 1,2, 1996 W 1,2, C, NZ 1, SA 1, NZ 2, SA 2, It, S, I, 1997 F 1,2, NZ 1, E 1, NZ 2, SA 1, Arg 1,2, E 2, S, 1998 E 1, S 1,2, NZ 1, SA 1, NZ 2, SA 2, NZ 3, Fj, Tg, WS, F, E 2, 1999 [R, I 3, W, SA 3, F], 2000 Arg 1,2, SA 1, NZ 1, SA 2, NZ 2, SA 3, F, S, E, 2001 BI 1,2,3, SA 1, NZ 1, SA 2, NZ 2
Eastes, C C (NSW) 1946 NZ 1,2, 1947 NZ 1,2, 1949 M 1,2
Edmonds, H (ACT) 2010 Fj,E1(R),2(R)
Edmonds, M H M (NSW) 1998 Tg, 2001 SA 1(R)
Egerton, R H (NSW) 1991 W, E, NZ 1,2, [Arg, W, I, NZ, E]
Ella, G A (NSW) 1982 NZ 1,2, 1983 F 1,2, 1988 E 2, NZ 1
Ella, G J (NSW) 1982 S 1, 1983 It, 1985 C 2(R), Fj 2
Ella, M G (NSW) 1980 NZ 1,2,3, 1981 F 2, S, 1982 E, S 1, NZ 1,2,3, 1983 US, Arg 1,2, NZ, It, F 1,2, 1984 Fj, NZ 1,2,3, E, I, W, S
Ellem, M A (NSW) 1976 Fj 3(R)
Elliott, F M (NSW) 1957 NZ 1
Elliott, R E (NSW) 1920 NZ 1, 1921 NZ, 1922 M 1,2, NZ 1(R),2,3, 1923 M 1,2,3, NZ 1,2,3
Ellis, C S (NSW) 1899 BI 1,2,3,4
Ellis, K J (NSW) 1958 NZ 1,2,3, 1959 BI 1,2
Ellwood, B J (NSW) 1958 NZ 1,2,3, 1961 Fj 2,3, SA 1, F, 1962 NZ 1,2,3,4,5, 1963 SA 1,2,3,4, 1964 NZ 3, 1965 SA 1,2, 1966 BI 1
Elsom, R D (NSW, ACT) 2005 Sm,It,F1,SA1,2,3(R),4,NZ2,F2, 2006 E1,2,I1,NZ1,SA1, NZ2,SA2,NZ3,SA3,W,It,I2,S, 2007 W1,2,SA1,NZ1,SA2,NZ2, [J,W,Fj,E], 2008 I,F1,2,SA1,NZ1, SA2,3,NZ3, 2009 NZ2,SA2,3,NZ3,4,E,I,S,W, 2010 Fj,E1,2,I,SA1, NZ1,2,SA2, 3,NZ3
Emanuel, D M (NSW) 1957 NZ 2, 1958 W, I, E, S, F, M 1,2,3
Emery, N A (NSW) 1947 NZ 2, S, I, W, 1948 E, F, 1949 M 2,3, NZ 1,2
Erasmus, D J (NSW) 1923 NZ 1,2
Erby, A B (NSW) 1923 M 1,2, NZ 2,3, 1925 NZ 2
Evans, L J (Q) 1903 NZ, 1904 BI 1,3
Evans, W T (Q) 1899 BI 1,2
Fahey, E J (NSW) 1912 US, 1913 NZ 1,2, 1914 NZ 3
Fainga'a, A S (Q) 2010 NZ1(R),2,SA3(R),NZ3(R)
Fainga'a, S M (Q) 2010 Fj(R),E1,2,I,SA1,NZ1(R),2,SA2,3(R)
Fairfax, R L (NSW) 1971 F 1,2, 1972 F 1,2, NZ 1, Fj, 1973 W, E
Farmer, E H (Q) 1910 NZ 1
Farquhar, C R (NSW) 1920 NZ 2
Farr-Jones, N C (NSW) 1984 E, I, W, S, 1985 C 1,2, NZ, Fj 1,2, 1986 It, F, Arg 1,2, NZ 1,2,3, 1987 SK, [E, I, F, W (R)], NZ, Arg 2, 1988 E 1,2, NZ 1,2,3, E, S, It, 1989 BI 1,2,3, NZ, F 1,2, 1990 F 1,2,3, US, NZ 1,2,3, 1991 W, E, NZ 1,2, [Arg, WS, I, NZ, E], 1992 S 1,2, NZ 1,2,3, SA, 1993 NZ, SA 1,2,3
Fava, S G (ACT, WF) 2005 E(R),I(R), 2006 NZ1(R),SA1,NZ2
Fay, G (NSW) 1971 SA 2, 1972 NZ 1,2,3, 1973 Tg 1,2, W, E, 1974 NZ 1,2,3, 1975 E 1,2, J 1, S, W, 1976 I, US, 1978 W 1,2, NZ 1,2,3, 1979 I 1
Fenwicke, P T (NSW) 1957 NZ 1, 1958 W, I, E, 1959 BI 1,2
Ferguson, R T (NSW) 1922 M 3, NZ 1, 1923 M 3, NZ 3
Fihelly, J A (Q) 1907 NZ 2
Finau, S F (NSW) 1997 NZ 3
Finegan, O D A (ACT) 1996 W 1,2, C, NZ 1, SA 1(t), S, W 3, 1997 SA 1, NZ 3, SA 2, Arg 1,2, E 2, S, 1998 E 1(R), S 1(t + R),2(t + R), NZ 1(R), SA 1(t),2(R), NZ 3(R), Fj (R), Tg, WS (t + R), F (R), E 2(R), 1999 NZ 2(R), [R, I 3(R), US, W (R), SA 3(R), F (R)], 2001 BI 1,2,3, SA 1, NZ 1, SA 2, NZ 2, Sp, E, F, W, 2002 F 1,2, NZ 1, SA 1, NZ 2, SA 2, I, 2003 SA 1(t&R), NZ 1(R), SA 2(R), NZ 2(R)
Finlay, A N (NSW) 1926 NZ 1,2,3, 1927 I, W, S, 1928 E, F, 1929 NZ 1,2,3, 1930 BI
Finley, F G (NSW) 1904 BI 3
Finnane, S C (NSW) 1975 E 1, J 1,2, 1976 E, 1978 W 1,2
Fitter, D E S (ACT) 2005 I,W
FitzSimons, P (NSW) 1989 F 1,2, 1990 F 1,2,3, US, NZ 1
Flanagan, P (Q) 1907 NZ 1,2
Flatley, E J (Q) 1997 E 2, S, 2000 S (R), 2001 BI 1(R),2(R),3, SA 1, NZ 1(R),2(R), Sp (R), F (R), W, 2002 F 1(R),2(R), NZ 1(t+R), SA 1(R), NZ 2(t), Arg (R), I (R), E, It, 2003 I, W, SA 1, NZ 1, SA 2, NZ 2, [Arg,R,I,S,NZ,E], 2004 S3(R),F(R),S4(R),E2, 2005 NZ1(R)
Flett, J A (NSW) 1990 US, NZ 2,3, 1991 [WS]
Flynn, J P (Q) 1914 NZ 1,2
Fogarty, J R (Q) 1949 M 2,3
Foley, M A (Q) 1995 [C (R), R], 1996 W 2(R), NZ 1, SA 1, NZ 2, SA 2, It, S, I, W 3, 1997 NZ 1(R), E 1, NZ 2, SA 1, NZ 3, SA 2, Arg 1,2, E 2, S, 1998 Tg (R), F (R), E 2(R), 1999 NZ 2(R), [US, W, SA 3, F], 2000 Arg 1,2, SA 1, NZ 1, SA 2, NZ 2, SA 3, F, S, E, 2001 BI 1(R),2,3, SA 1, NZ 1, SA 2, NZ 2, Sp, E, F, W
Foote, R H (NSW) 1924 NZ 2,3, 1926 NZ 2
Forbes, C F (Q) 1953 SA 2,3,4, 1954 Fj 1, 1956 SA 1,2
Ford, B (Q) 1957 NZ 2
Ford, E E (NSW) 1927 I, W, S, 1928 E, F, 1929 NZ 1,3
Ford, J A (NSW) 1925 NZ 4, 1926 NZ 1,2, 1927 I, W, S, 1928 E, 1929 NZ 1,2,3, 1930 BI
Forman, T R (NSW) 1968 I, S, 1969 W, SA 1,2,3,4
Fowles, D G (NSW) 1921 SA 1,2,3, 1922 M 2,3, 1923 M 2,3
Fox, C L (NSW) 1920 NZ 1,2,3, 1921 SA 1, NZ, 1922 M 1,2, NZ 1, 1924 NZ 1,2,3, 1925 NZ 1,2,3, 1926 NZ 1,3, 1928 F
Fox, O G (NSW) 1958 F
Francis, E (Q) 1914 NZ 1,2
Frawley, D (Q, NSW) 1986 Arg 2(R), 1987 Arg 1,2, 1988 E 1,2, NZ 1,2,3, S, It
Freedman, J E (NSW) 1962 NZ 3,4,5, 1963 SA 1
Freeman, E (NSW) 1946 NZ 1(R), M
Freier, A L (NSW) 2002 Arg (R), I, E (R), It, 2003 SA 1(R), NZ 1(t), 2005 NZ2(R), 2006 E2, 2007 W1(R),2(R),Fj,SA1(R),NZ1(R),SA2, NZ2(R), [J(R),W(R),Fj(R),C,E(R)], 2008 I(R),F1(R),2(R),NZ3(R), W(t&R)
Freney, M E (Q) 1972 NZ 1,2,3, 1973 Tg 1, W, E (R)
Friend, W S (NSW) 1920 NZ 3, 1921 SA 1,2,3, 1922 NZ 1,2,3, 1923 M 1,2,3
Furness, D C (NSW) 1946 M
Futter, F C (NSW) 1904 BI 3
Gardner, J M (Q) 1987 Arg 2, 1988 E 1, NZ 1, E
Gardner, W C (NSW) 1950 BI 1
Garner, R L (NSW) 1949 NZ 1,2
Gavin, K A (NSW) 1909 E
Gavin, T B (NSW) 1988 NZ 2,3, S, It (R), 1989 NZ (R), F 1,2, 1990 F 1,2,3, US, NZ 1,2,3, 1991 W, E, NZ 1, 1992 S 1,2, SA, I, W, 1993 Tg, NZ, SA 1,2,3, C, F 1,2, 1994 I 1,2, It 1,2, WS, NZ, 1995 Arg 1,2, [SA, C, R, E], NZ 1,2, 1996 NZ 2(R), SA 2, W 3
Gelling, A M (NSW) 1972 NZ 1, Fj
Genia, S W (Q) 2009 NZ1(R),SA1(R),NZ2(R),SA2(R),3,NZ3,4,E,I,S, W, 2010 E2,SA1, NZ1,2,SA2,3,NZ3
George, H W (NSW) 1910 NZ 1,2,3, 1912 US, 1913 NZ 1,3, 1914 NZ 1,3
George, W G (NSW) 1923 M 1,3, NZ 1,2, 1924 NZ 3, 1925 NZ 2,3, 1926 NZ 4, 1928 NZ 1,2,3, M
Gerrard, M A (ACT) 2005 It(R),SA1(R),NZ1,2,E,I,W, 2006 E1,2,I1,NZ1,SA1,NZ2, SA2,NZ3(t),SA3(R),I2,S, 2007 W1,2(R),SA2,NZ2, [J(R)]
Gibbons, E de C (NSW) 1936 NZ 1,2, M
Gibbs, P R (V) 1966 S

Giffin, D T (ACT) 1996 W 3, 1997 F 1,2, 1999 I 1,2, E, SA 1, NZ 1, SA 2, NZ 2, [R, I 3, US (R), W, SA 3, F], 2000 Arg 1,2, SA 1, NZ 1, SA 2, NZ 2, SA 3, F, S, E, 2001 BI 1,2, SA 1, NZ 2, Sp, E, F, W, 2002 Arg (R), I, E (R), It (R), 2003 I, W, E, SA 1, NZ 1, SA 2, NZ 2, [Arg,Nm(R),I,NZ(t&R),E(R)]
Gilbert, H (NSW) 1910 NZ 1,2,3
Girvan, B (ACT) 1988 E
Giteau, M J (ACT, WF) 2002 E (R), It (R), 2003 SA 2(R), NZ 2(R), [Arg(R),R(R),Nm, I(R),S(R),E(t)], 2004 S1,E1,PI,NZ1,SA1,NZ2, SA2,S3,F,S4,E2, 2005 Sm,It,F1,SA1,2,3, NZ1,SA4,F2,E(t&R), 2006 NZ1(R),SA1,NZ2,SA2,NZ3,SA3,W,It,I2,S, 2007 W1,2,SA1, NZ1,SA2,NZ2, [J,W,Fj,E], 2008 I,F1,2,SA1,NZ1,2,SA2,3, NZ3,4,It(R),E,F3,W, 2009 It1, F,NZ1,SA1,NZ2,SA2,3,NZ3,4,E,I,S, W, 2010 Fj,E2,I,SA1,NZ1,2,SA2,3,NZ3
Gordon, G C (NSW) 1929 NZ 1
Gordon, K M (NSW) 1950 BI 1,2
Gould, R G (Q) 1980 NZ 1,2,3, 1981 I, W, S, 1982 S 2, NZ 1,2,3, 1983 US, Arg 1, F 1,2, 1984 NZ 1,2,3, E, I, W, S, 1985 NZ, 1986 It, 1987 SK, [E]
Gourley, S R (NSW) 1988 S, It, 1989 BI 1,2,3
Graham, C S (Q) 1899 BI 2
Graham, R (NSW) 1973 Tg 1,2, W, E, 1974 NZ 2,3, 1975 E 2, J 1,2, S, W, 1976 I, US, Fj 1,2,3, F 1,2
Gralton, A S I (Q) 1899 BI 1,4, 1903 NZ
Grant, J C (NSW) 1988 E 1, NZ 2,3, E
Graves, R H (NSW) 1907 NZ 1(R)
Greatorex, E N (NSW) 1923 M 3, NZ 3, 1924 NZ 1,2,3, 1925 NZ 1, 1928 E, F
Gregan, G M (ACT) 1994 It 1,2, WS, NZ, 1995 Arg 1,2, [SA, C (R), R, E], 1996 W 1, C (t), SA 1, NZ 2, SA 2, It, I, W 3, 1997 F 1,2, NZ 1, E 1, NZ 2, SA 1, NZ 3, SA 2, Arg 1,2, E 2, S, 1998 E 1, S 1,2, NZ 1, SA 1, NZ 2, SA 2, NZ 3, Fj, WS, F, E 2, 1999 I 1,2, E, SA 1, NZ 1, SA 2, NZ 2, [R, I 3, W, SA 3, F], 2000 Arg 1,2, SA 1, NZ 1, SA 2, NZ 2, SA 3, 2001 BI 1,2,3, SA 1, NZ 1, SA 2, NZ 2, Sp, E, F, W, 2002 F 1,2, NZ 1, SA 1, NZ 2, SA 2, Arg, I, E, It, 2003 I, W, E, SA 1, NZ 1, SA 2, NZ 2, [Arg,R,I,S,NZ,E], 2004 S1,2,E1, PI,SA1,NZ2,SA2,S3,F,S4,E2, 2005 It,F1,SA1,2,3,NZ1,SA4,NZ2,F2,E,I,W, 2006 E1, 2(R),I1,NZ1,SA1,NZ2,SA2,NZ3,SA3, 2007 W1(R),2(R),Fj,SA1,NZ1,SA2,NZ2, [J,W,Fj,C(R),E]
Gregory, S C (Q) 1968 NZ 3, F, I, S, 1969 SA 1,3, 1971 SA 1,3, F 1,2, 1972 F 1,2, 1973 Tg 1,2, W, E
Grey, G O (NSW) 1972 F 2(R), NZ 1,2,3, Fj (R)
Grey, N P (NSW) 1998 S 2(R), SA 2(R), Fj (R), Tg (R), F, E 2, 1999 I 1(R),2(R), E, SA 1, NZ 1, SA 2, NZ 2(t&R), [R (R), I 3(R), US, SA 3(R), F (R)], 2000 S (R), E (R), 2001 BI 1,2,3, SA 1, NZ 1, SA 2, NZ 2, Sp, E, F, 2003 I (R), W (R), E, [Nm,NZ(t)]
Griffin, T S (NSW) 1907 NZ 1,3, 1908 W, 1910 NZ 1,2, 1912 US
Grigg, P C (Q) 1980 NZ 3, 1982 S 2, NZ 1,2,3, 1983 Arg 2, NZ, 1984 Fj, W, S, 1985 C 1,2, NZ, Fj 1,2, 1986 Arg 1,2, NZ 1,2, 1987 SK, [E, J, I, F, W]
Grimmond, D N (NSW) 1964 NZ 2
Gudsell, K E (NSW) 1951 NZ 1,2,3
Guerassimoff, J (Q) 1963 SA 2,3,4, 1964 NZ 1,2,3, 1965 SA 2, 1966 BI 1,2, 1967 E, I, F
Gunther, W J (NSW) 1957 NZ 2
Hall, D (Q) 1980 Fj, NZ 1,2,3, 1981 F 1,2, 1982 S 1,2, NZ 1,2, 1983 US, Arg 1,2, NZ, It
Hamalainen, H A (Q) 1929 NZ 1,2,3
Hamilton, B G (NSW) 1946 M
Hammand, C A (NSW) 1908 W, 1909 E
Hammon, J D C (V) 1937 SA 2
Handy, C B (Q) 1978 NZ 3, 1979 NZ, Arg 1,2, 1980 NZ 1,2
Hanley, R G (Q) 1983 US (R), It (R), 1985 Fj 2(R)
Hardcastle, P A (NSW) 1946 NZ 1, M, NZ 2, 1947 NZ 1, 1949 M 3
Hardcastle, W R (NSW) 1899 BI 4, 1903 NZ
Harding, M A (NSW) 1983 It
Hardman, S P (Q) 2002 F 2(R), 2006 SA1(R), 2007 SA2(t&R), [C(R)]
Hardy, M D (ACT) 1997 F 1(t), 2(R), NZ 1(R), 3(R), Arg 1(R), 2(R), 1998 Tg, WS
Harrison, J B (ACT, NSW) 2001 BI 3, NZ 1, SA 2, Sp, E, F, W (R), 2002 F 1,2, NZ 1, SA 1, NZ 2, SA 2, Arg, I (R), E, It, 2003 [R(R),Nm,S,NZ,E], 2004 S1,2,E1,PI,NZ1,SA1, NZ2,SA2,S3,F,S4,E2
Harry, R L L (NSW) 1996 W 1,2, NZ 1, SA 1(t), NZ 2, It, S, 1997 F 1,2, NZ 1,2, SA 1, NZ 3, SA 2, Arg 1,2, E 2, S, 1998 E 1, S 1,2, NZ 1, Fj, 1999 SA 2, NZ 2, [R, I 3, W, SA 3, F], 2000 Arg 1,2, SA 1, NZ 1, SA 2, NZ 2, SA 3
Hartill, M N (NSW) 1986 NZ 1,2,3, 1987 SK, [J], Arg 1, 1988 NZ 1,2, E, It, 1989 BI 1(R), 2,3, F 1,2, 1995 Arg 1(R), 2(R), [C], NZ 1,2
Harvey, P B (Q) 1949 M 1,2
Harvey, R M (NSW) 1958 F, M 3
Hatherell, W I (Q) 1952 Fj 1,2
Hauser, R G (Q) 1975 J 1(R), 2, W (R), 1976 E, I, US, Fj 1,2,3, F 1,2, 1978 W 1,2, 1979 I 1,2
Hawker, M J (NSW) 1980 Fj, NZ 1,2,3, 1981 F 1,2, I, W, 1982 E, S 1,2, NZ 1,2,3, 1983 US, Arg 1,2, NZ, It, F 1,2, 1984 NZ 1,2,3, 1987 NZ
Hawthorne, P F (NSW) 1962 NZ 3,4,5, 1963 E, SA 1,2,3,4, 1964 NZ 1,2,3, 1965 SA 1,2, 1966 BI 1,2, W, 1967 E, I 1, F, I 2, NZ
Hayes, E S (Q) 1934 NZ 1,2, 1938 NZ 1,2,3
Heath, A (NSW) 1996 C, SA 1, NZ 2, SA 2, It, 1997 NZ 2, SA 1, E 2(R)
Heenan, D P (Q, ACT) 2003 W, 2006 E1
Heinrich, E L (NSW) 1961 Fj 1,2,3, SA 2, F, 1962 NZ 1,2,3, 1963 E, SA 1
Heinrich, V W (NSW) 1954 Fj 1,2
Heming, R J (NSW) 1961 Fj 2,3, SA 1,2, F, 1962 NZ 2,3,4,5, 1963 SA 2,3,4, 1964 NZ 1,2,3, 1965 SA 1,2, 1966 BI 1,2, W, 1967 F
Hemingway, W H (NSW) 1928 NZ 2,3, 1931 M, NZ, 1932 NZ 3
Henderson, N J (ACT) 2004 PI(R), 2005 Sm(R), 2006 It(R)
Henjak, M T (ACT) 2004 E1(R),NZ1(R), 2005 Sm(R),I(R)
Henry, A R (Q) 1899 BI 2
Herbert, A G (Q) 1987 SK (R), [F (R)], 1990 F 1(R), US, NZ 2,3, 1991 [WS], 1992 NZ 3(R), 1993 NZ (R), SA 2(R)
Herbert, D J (Q) 1994 I 2, It 1,2, WS (R), 1995 Arg 1,2, [SA, R], 1996 C, SA 2, It, S, I, 1997 NZ 1, 1998 E 1, S 1,2, NZ 1, SA 1, NZ 2, SA 2, Fj, Tg, WS, F, E 2, 1999 I 1,2, E, SA 1, NZ 1, SA 2, NZ 2, [R, I 3, W, SA 3, F], 2000 Arg 1,2, SA 1, NZ 1, SA 2, NZ 2, SA 3, F, S, E, 2001 BI 1,2,3, SA 1, NZ 1, SA 2, NZ 2, Sp, E, 2002 F 1,2, NZ 1, SA 1, NZ 2, SA 2, Arg, I, E, It
Herd, H V (NSW) 1931 M
Hickey, J (NSW) 1908 W, 1909 E
Hill, J (NSW) 1925 NZ 1
Hillhouse, D W (Q) 1975 S, 1976 E, Fj 1,2,3, F 1,2, 1978 W 1,2, 1983 US, Arg 1,2, NZ, It, F 1,2
Hills, E F (V) 1950 BI 1,2
Hindmarsh, J A (Q) 1904 BI 1
Hindmarsh, J C (NSW) 1975 J 2, S, W, 1976 US, Fj 1,2,3, F 1,2
Hipwell, J N B (NSW) 1968 NZ 1(R), 2, F, I, S, 1969 W, SA 1,2,3,4, 1970 S, 1971 SA 1,2, F 1,2, 1972 F 1,2, 1973 Tg 1, W, E, 1974 NZ 1,2,3, 1975 E 1,2, J 1, S, W, 1978 NZ 1,2,3, 1981 F 1,2, I, W, 1982 E
Hirschberg, W A (NSW) 1905 NZ
Hodgins, C H (NSW) 1910 NZ 1,2,3
Hodgson, A J (NSW) 1933 SA 2,3,4, 1934 NZ 1, 1936 NZ 1,2, M, 1937 SA 2, 1938 NZ 1,2,3
Hodgson, M J (WF) 2010 Fj(R),E1(R),NZ2(R)
Hoiles, S A (NSW, ACT) 2004 S4(R),E2(R), 2006 W(R), 2007 W1(R),2(R),Fj(R), SA1(R),NZ1(R),SA2,NZ2, [J(R),W(R),Fj(R),C(R), E(R)] 2006 W(R), 2007 W1(R),2(R), Fj(R),SA1(R),NZ1(R),SA2, NZ2, [J(R),W(R),Fj(R),C(R),E(R)], 2008 F2
Holbeck, J C (ACT) 1997 NZ 1(R), E 1, NZ 2, SA 1, NZ 3, SA 2, 2001 BI 3(R)
Holdsworth, J W (NSW) 1921 SA 1,2,3, 1922 M 2,3, NZ 1(R)
Holmes, G S (Q) 2005 F2(R),E(t&R),I, 2006 E1,2,I1,NZ1,SA1,NZ2,SA2,NZ3, 2007 [Fj(R),C]
Holt, N C (Q) 1984 Fj
Honan, B D (Q) 1968 NZ 1(R), 2, F, I, S, 1969 SA 1,2,3,4
Honan, R E (Q) 1964 NZ 1,2
Horan, T J (Q) 1989 NZ, F 1,2, 1990 F 1, NZ 1,2,3, 1991 W, E, NZ 1,2, [Arg, WS, W, I, NZ, E], 1992 S 1,2, NZ 1,2,3, SA, I, W, 1993 Tg, NZ, SA 1,2,3, C, F 1,2, 1995 [C, R, E], NZ 1,2, 1996 W 1,2, C, NZ 1, SA 1, It, S, I, W 3, 1997 F 1,2, NZ 1, E 1, NZ 2, Arg 1,2, E 2, S, 1998 E 1, S 1,2, NZ 1, SA 1, NZ 2, SA 2, NZ 3, Fj, Tg, WS, 1999 I 1,2, E, SA 1, NZ 1, SA 2, NZ 2, [R, I 3, W, SA 3, F], 2000 Arg 1
Horne, R G (NSW) 2010 Fj,E1,2,I,SA1,NZ1
Horodam, D J (Q) 1913 NZ 2
Horsley, G R (Q) 1954 Fj 2
Horton, P A (NSW) 1974 NZ 1,2,3, 1975 E 1,2, J 1,2, S, W, 1976 E, F 1,2, 1978 W 1,2, NZ 1,2,3, 1979 NZ, Arg 1
Horwill, J E (Q) 2007 Fj, 2008 I,F1,2,SA1,NZ1,2,SA2,3,NZ3, 2009 It1,2,F,NZ1,SA1,NZ2,SA2,3,NZ3,4,E,I,S,W
Hoskins, J E (NSW) 1924 NZ 1,2,3
How, R A (NSW) 1967 I 2
Howard, J (Q) 1938 NZ 1,2
Howard, J L (NSW) 1970 S, 1971 SA 1, 1972 F 1(R), NZ 2, 1973 Tg 1,2, W
Howard, P W (Q, ACT) 1993 NZ, 1994 WS, NZ, 1995 NZ 1(R), 2(t), 1996 W 1,2, SA 1, NZ 2, SA 2, It, S, W 3, 1997 F 1,2, NZ 1, Arg 1,2, E 2, S
Howell, M L (NSW) 1946 NZ 1(R), 1947 NZ 1, S, I, W

Hughes, B D (NSW) 1913 NZ 2,3
Hughes, J C (NSW) 1907 NZ 1,3
Hughes, N McL (NSW) 1953 SA 1,2,3,4, 1955 NZ 1,2,3, 1956 SA 1,2, 1958 W, I, E, S, F
Humphreys, O W (NSW) 1920 NZ 3, 1921 NZ, 1922 M 1,2,3, 1925 NZ 1
Hutchinson, E E (NSW) 1937 SA 1,2
Hutchinson, F E (NSW) 1936 NZ 1,2, 1938 NZ 1,3
Huxley, J L (ACT) 2007 W1,2,Fj,SA1,NZ1,SA2, [W(R),Fj(R),C]
Hynes, P J (Q) 2008 I,F1,2,SA1,NZ1,2,SA2,3,NZ3,4,E,F3,W, 2009 It2,NZ2(R),SA2, 3(R),NZ4,E,I,S,W
Ide, W P J (Q) 1938 NZ 2,3
Ioane, D N (WF, Q) 2007 W2, 2008 It,F3,W, 2009 NZ4,E,I,W, 2010 Fj,E1,2
Ives, W N (NSW) 1926 NZ 1,2,3,4, 1929 NZ 3
James, P M (Q) 1958 M 2,3
James, S L (NSW) 1987 SK (R), [E (R)], NZ, Arg 1,2, 1988 NZ 2(R)
Jamieson, A E (NSW) 1925 NZ 3(R)
Jaques, T (ACT) 2000 SA 1(R), NZ 1(R)
Jessep, E M (V) 1934 NZ 1,2
Johansson, L D T (Q) 2005 NZ2(R),F2(R),E(R)
Johnson, A P (NSW) 1946 NZ 1, M
Johnson, B B (NSW) 1952 Fj 1,2, NZ 1,2, 1953 SA 2,3,4, 1955 NZ 1,2
Johnson, P G (NSW) 1959 BI 1,2, 1961 Fj 1,2,3, SA 1,2, F, 1962 NZ 1,2,3,4,5, 1963 E, SA 1,2,3,4, 1964 NZ 1,2,3, 1965 SA 1,2, 1966 BI 1,2, W, S, 1967 E, I 1, F, I 2, NZ, 1968 NZ 1,2, F, I, S, 1970 S, 1971 SA 1,2, F 1,2
Johnstone, B (Q) 1993 Tg (R)
Jones, G G (Q) 1952 Fj 1,2, 1953 SA 1,2,3,4, 1954 Fj 1,2, 1955 NZ 1,2,3, 1956 SA 1
Jones, H (NSW) 1913 NZ 1,2,3
Jones, P A (NSW) 1963 E, SA 1
Jorgensen, P (NSW) 1992 S 1(R), 2(R)
Joyce, J E (NSW) 1903 NZ
Judd, H A (NSW) 1903 NZ, 1904 BI 1,2,3, 1905 NZ
Judd, P B (NSW) 1925 NZ 4, 1926 NZ 1,2,3,4, 1927 I, W, S, 1928 E, 1931 M, NZ
Junee, D K (NSW) 1989 F 1(R), 2(R), 1994 WS (R), NZ (R)
Kafer, R B (ACT) 1999 NZ 2, [R, US (R)], 2000 Arg 1(R),2, SA 1, NZ 1(t&R), SA 2(R),3(R), F, S, E
Kahl, P R (Q) 1992 W
Kanaar, A (NSW) 2005 NZ2(R)
Kassulke, N (Q) 1985 C 1,2
Kay, A R (V) 1958 NZ 2, 1959 BI 2
Kay, P (NSW) 1988 E 2
Kearney, K H (NSW) 1947 NZ 1,2, S, I, W, 1948 E, F
Kearns, P N (NSW) 1989 NZ, F 1,2, 1990 F 1,2,3, US, NZ 1,2,3, 1991 W, E, NZ 1,2, [Arg, WS, W, I, NZ, E], 1992 S 1,2, NZ 1,2,3, SA, I, W, 1993 Tg, NZ, SA 1,2,3, C, F 1,2, 1994 I 1,2, It 1,2, WS, NZ, 1995 Arg 1,2, [SA, C, E], NZ 1,2, 1998 E 1, S 1,2, NZ 1, SA 1, NZ 2, SA 2, NZ 3, Fj, WS, F, E 2, 1999 I 2(R), SA 1(R),2, NZ 2, [R, I 3]
Kefu, R S T (Q) 1997 SA 2(R), 1998 E 1, S 1,2, NZ 1, SA 1, NZ 2, SA 2, NZ 3, Fj (R), Tg, WS (R), F, E 2, 1999 I 1,2, E, SA 1, NZ 1(R), SA 2, NZ 2, [R, I 3, SA 3, F], 2000 SA 1(t&R), NZ 1(R), SA 2(R), NZ 2, SA 3(R), F, S, E, 2001 BI 1,2,3, SA 1, NZ 1, SA 2, NZ 2, Sp, E, F, W, 2002 F 1, NZ 1, SA 1, NZ 2, SA 2, Arg, I, E, It, 2003 I, W, E, SA 1, NZ 1, SA 2, NZ 2
Kefu, S (Q) 2001 W (R), 2003 I, W, E, SA 1, NZ 1(R)
Kelaher, J D (NSW) 1933 SA 1,2,3,4,5, 1934 NZ 1,2, 1936 NZ 1,2, M, 1937 SA 1,2, 1938 NZ 3
Kelaher, T P (NSW) 1992 NZ 1, I (R), 1993 NZ
Kelleher, R J (Q) 1969 SA 2,3
Keller, D H (NSW) 1947 NZ 1, S, I, W, 1948 E, F
Kelly, A J (NSW) 1899 BI 1
Kelly, R L F (NSW) 1936 NZ 1,2, M, 1937 SA 1,2, 1938 NZ 1,2
Kent, A (Q) 1912 US
Kepu, S M (NSW) 2008 It(R),F3(R), 2009 S(R)
Kerr, F R (V) 1938 NZ 1
Kimlin, P J (ACT) 2009 It1(R),2
King, S C (NSW) 1926 NZ 1,2,3,4(R), 1927 W, S, 1928 E, F, 1929 NZ 1,2,3, 1930 BI, 1932 NZ 1,2
Knight, M (NSW) 1978 W 1,2, NZ 1
Knight, S O (NSW) 1969 SA 2,4, 1970 S, 1971 SA 1,2,3
Knox, D J (NSW, ACT) 1985 Fj 1,2, 1990 US (R), 1994 WS, NZ, 1996 It, S, I, 1997 SA 1, NZ 3, SA 2, Arg 1,2
Kraefft, D F (NSW) 1947 NZ 2, S, I, W, 1948 E, F
Kreutzer, S D (Q) 1914 NZ 2
Lamb, J S (NSW) 1928 NZ 1,2, M
Lambie, J K (NSW) 1974 NZ 1,2,3, 1975 W
Lane, R E (NSW) 1921 SA 1
Lane, T A (Q) 1985 C 1,2, NZ
Lang, C W P (V) 1938 NZ 2,3
Langford, J F (ACT) 1997 NZ 3, SA 2, E 2, S
Larkham, S J (ACT) 1996 W 2(R), 1997 F 1,2, NZ 1,2(R), SA 1, NZ 3, SA 2, Arg 1,2, E 2, S, 1998 E 1, S 1,2, NZ 1, SA 1, NZ 2, SA 2, NZ 3, Fj, Tg (t), WS, F, E 2, 1999 [I 3, US, W, SA 3, F], 2000 Arg 1,2, SA 1, NZ 1, SA 2, NZ 2, SA 3, 2001 BI 1,2, NZ 1, SA 2, NZ 2, Sp, E, F, W, 2002 F 1,2, NZ 1, SA 1, NZ 2, SA 2, Arg, I, E, 2003 SA 1(R), NZ 1, SA 2, NZ 2,[Arg,R,I,S, NZ,E], 2004S1,2,E1,PI,NZ1,SA1,NZ2,SA2,S3,F,S4, 2005 Sm(R), It,F1,SA1,2,3, 2006 E1,2,I1,NZ1,SA1,NZ2,SA2,NZ3,SA3,W,It,I2, S, 2007 W2,Fj,SA1, NZ1,SA2,NZ2, [J]
Larkin, E R (NSW) 1903 NZ
Larkin, K K (Q) 1958 M 2,3
Latham, C E (Q) 1998 F, E 2, 1999 I 1,2, E, [US], 2000 Arg 1,2, SA 1, NZ 1, SA 2, NZ 2, SA 3, F, S, E, 2001 BI 1,2(R), SA 1(R), NZ 1(R), SA 2, NZ 2, Sp, E, F, W (R), 2002 F 1,2, NZ 1, SA 1, NZ 2, SA 2, 2003 I, W, E, NZ 1(R), SA 2, NZ 2,[Nm], 2004 S1(R), 2(R),E1(R),PI(t&R),NZ1,SA1,NZ2,SA2,S3,F,S4,E2, 2005 Sm,F1,SA2,3,F2,E,I,W, 2006 E1,2,I1,NZ1,SA1,NZ2, SA2,NZ3,SA3,W,It,I2,S, 2007 NZ2(R), [J,W,Fj,C,E]
Latimer, N B (NSW) 1957 NZ 2
Lawton, R (Q) 1988 E 1, NZ 2(R), 3, S
Lawton, T (NSW, Q) 1920 NZ 1,2, 1925 NZ 4, 1927 I, W, S, 1928 E, F, 1929 NZ 1,2,3, 1930 BI, 1932 NZ 1,2
Lawton, T A (Q) 1983 F 1(R), 2, 1984 Fj, NZ 1,2,3, E, I, W, S, 1985 C 1,2, NZ, Fj 1, 1986 It, F, Arg 1,2, NZ 1,2,3, 1987 SK, [E, US, I, F, W], NZ, Arg 1,2, 1988 E 1,2, NZ 1,2,3, E, S, It, 1989 BI 1,2,3
Laycock, W M B (NSW) 1925 NZ 2,3,4, 1926 NZ 2
Leeds, A J (NSW) 1986 NZ 3, 1987 [US, W], NZ, Arg 1,2, 1988 E 1,2, NZ 1,2,3, E, S, It
Lenehan, J K (NSW) 1958 W, E, S, F, M 1,2,3, 1959 BI 1,2, 1961 SA 1,2, F, 1962 NZ 2,3,4,5, 1965 SA 1,2, 1966 W, S, 1967 E, I 1, F, I 2
L'Estrange, R D (Q) 1971 F 1,2, 1972 NZ 1,2,3, 1973 Tg 1,2, W, E, 1974 NZ 1,2,3, 1975 S, W, 1976 I, US
Lewis, L S (Q) 1934 NZ 1,2, 1936 NZ 2, 1938 NZ 1
Lidbury, S (NSW) 1987 Arg 1, 1988 E 2
Lillicrap, C P (Q) 1985 Fj 2, 1987 [US, I, F, W], 1989 BI 1, 1991 [WS]
Lindsay, R T G (Q) 1932 NZ 3
Lisle, R J (NSW) 1961 Fj 1,2,3, SA 1
Little, J S (Q, NSW) 1989 F 1,2, 1990 F 1,2,3, US, 1991 W, E, NZ 1,2, [Arg, W, I, NZ, E], 1992 NZ 1,2,3, SA, I, W, 1993 Tg, NZ, SA 1,2,3, C, F 1,2, 1994 WS, NZ, 1995 Arg 1,2, [SA, C, E], NZ 1,2, 1996 It (R), I, W 3, 1997 F 1,2, E 1, NZ 2, SA 1, NZ 3, SA 2, 1998 E 1(R), S 2(R), NZ 2, SA 2(R), NZ 3, Fj, Tg, WS, F, E 2, 1999 I 1(R),2, SA 2(R), NZ 2, [R, I 3(t&R), US, W (R), SA 3(t&R), F (R)], 2000 Arg 1(R),2(R), SA 1(R), NZ 1, SA 2, NZ 2, SA 3
Livermore, A E (Q) 1946 NZ 1, M
Loane, M E (Q) 1973 Tg 1,2, 1974 NZ 1, 1975 E 1,2, J 1, 1976 E, I, Fj 1,2,3, F 1,2, 1978 W 1,2, 1979 I 1,2, NZ, Arg 1,2, 1981 F 1,2, I, W, S, 1982 E, S 1,2
Logan, D L (NSW) 1958 M 1
Loudon, D B (NSW) 1921 NZ, 1922 M 1,2,3
Loudon, R B (NSW) 1923 NZ 1(R), 2,3, 1928 NZ 1,2,3, M, 1929 NZ 2, 1933 SA 2,3,4,5, 1934 NZ 2
Love, E W (NSW) 1932 NZ 1,2,3
Lowth, D R (NSW) 1958 NZ 1
Lucas, B C (Q) 1905 NZ
Lucas, P W (NSW) 1982 NZ 1,2,3
Lutge, D (NSW) 1903 NZ, 1904 BI 1,2,3
Lynagh, M P (Q) 1984 Fj, E, I, W, S, 1985 C 1,2, NZ, 1986 It, F, Arg 1,2, NZ 1,2,3, 1987 [E, US, J, I, F, W], Arg 1,2, 1988 E 1,2, NZ 1,3(R), E, S, It, 1989 BI 1,2,3, NZ, F 1,2, 1990 F 1,2,3, US, NZ 1,2,3, 1991 W, E, NZ 1,2, [Arg, WS, W, I, NZ, E], 1992 S 1,2, NZ 1,2,3, SA, I, 1993 Tg, C, F 1,2, 1994 I 1,2, It 1, 1995 Arg 1,2, [SA, C, E]
Lyons, D J (NSW) 2000 Arg 1(t&R),2(R), 2001 BI 1(R), SA 1(R), 2002 F 1(R),2, NZ 1(R), SA 1(R), NZ 2(R), SA 2(t+R), 2003 I, W, E, SA 1, [Arg,R,Nm,I,S,NZ,E], 2004 S1,2,E1,PI,NZ1,SA1,NZ2, SA2,S3(R),F(R),S4,E2, 2005 Sm,It,F1,SA1,2,NZ1,SA4, 2006 S, 2007 Fj,SA2(R), [C]
McArthur, M (NSW) 1909 E
McBain, M I (Q) 1983 It, F 1, 1985 Fj 2, 1986 It (R), 1987 [J], 1988 E 2(R), 1989 BI 1(R)
MacBride, J W T (NSW) 1946 NZ 1, M, NZ 2, 1947 NZ 1,2, S, I, W, 1948 E, F
McCabe, A J M (NSW) 1909 E
McCall, R J (Q) 1989 F 1,2, 1990 F 1,2,3, US, NZ 1,2,3, 1991 W, E, NZ 1,2, [Arg, W, I, NZ, E], 1992 S 1,2, NZ 1,2,3, SA, I, W, 1993 Tg, NZ, SA 1,2,3, C, F 1,2, 1994 It 2, 1995 Arg 1,2, [SA, R, E]

McCalman, B J (WF) 2010 SA1(R),2(R),3,NZ3
McCarthy, F J C (Q) 1950 BI 1
McCowan, R H (Q) 1899 BI 1,2,4
McCue, P A (NSW) 1907 NZ 1,3, 1908 W, 1909 E
McDermott, L C (Q) 1962 NZ 1,2
McDonald, B S (NSW) 1969 SA 4, 1970 S
McDonald, J C (Q) 1938 NZ 2,3
Macdougall, D G (NSW) 1961 Fj 1, SA 1
Macdougall, S G (NSW, ACT) 1971 SA 3, 1973 E, 1974 NZ 1,2,3, 1975 E 1,2, 1976 E
McGhie, G H (Q) 1929 NZ 2,3, 1930 BI
McGill, A N (NSW) 1968 NZ 1,2, F, 1969 W, SA 1,2,3,4, 1970 S, 1971 SA 1,2,3, F 1,2, 1972 F 1,2, NZ 1,2,3, 1973 Tg 1,2
McIntyre, A J (Q) 1982 NZ 1,2,3, 1983 F 1,2, 1984 Fj, NZ 1,2,3, E, I, W, S, 1985 C 1,2, NZ, Fj 1,2, 1986 It, F, Arg 1,2, 1987 [E, US, I, F, W], NZ, Arg 2, 1988 E 1,2, NZ 1,2,3, E, S, It, 1989 NZ
McIsaac, T P (WF) 2006 E1,I1,NZ1,2(R),SA2,3(R),W,I2
McKay, G R (NSW) 1920 NZ 2, 1921 SA 2,3, 1922 M 1,2,3
MacKay, L J (NSW) 2005 NZ2(R)
McKenzie, E J A (NSW, ACT) 1990 F 1,2,3, US, NZ 1,2,3, 1991 W, E, NZ 1,2, [Arg, W, I, NZ, E], 1992 S 1,2, NZ 1,2,3, SA, I, W, 1993 Tg, NZ, SA 1,2,3, C, F 1,2, 1994 I 1,2, It 1,2, WS, NZ, 1995 Arg 1,2, [SA, C (R), R, E], NZ 2, 1996 W 1,2, 1997 F 1,2, NZ 1, E 1
McKid, W A (NSW) 1976 E, Fj 1, 1978 NZ 2,3, 1979 I 1,2
McKinnon, A (Q) 1904 BI 2
McKivat, C H (NSW) 1907 NZ 1,3, 1908 W, 1909 E
McLaren, S D (NSW) 1926 NZ 4
McLaughlin, R E M (NSW) 1936 NZ 1,2
McLean, A D (Q) 1933 SA 1,2,3,4,5, 1934 NZ 1,2, 1936 NZ 1,2, M
McLean, J D (Q) 1904 BI 2,3, 1905 NZ
McLean, J J (Q) 1971 SA 2,3, F 1,2, 1972 F 1,2, NZ 1,2,3, Fj, 1973 W, E, 1974 NZ 1
McLean, P E (Q) 1974 NZ 1,2,3, 1975 J 1,2, S, W, 1976 E, I, Fj 1,2,3, F 1,2, 1978 W 1,2, NZ 2, 1979 I 1,2, NZ, Arg 1,2, 1980 Fj, 1981 F 1,2, I, W, S, 1982 E, S 2
McLean, P W (Q) 1978 NZ 1,2,3, 1979 I 1,2, NZ, Arg 1,2, 1980 Fj (R), NZ 3, 1981 I, W, S, 1982 E, S 1,2
McLean, R A (NSW) 1971 SA 1,2,3, F 1,2
McLean, W M (Q) 1946 NZ 1, M, NZ 2, 1947 NZ 1,2
McMahon, M J (Q) 1913 NZ 1
McMaster, R E (Q) 1946 NZ 1, M, NZ 2, 1947 NZ 1,2, I, W
McMeniman, H J (Q) 2005 Sm(R),It(R),F2(R),E,I,W, 2007 SA2(R), NZ2(R), [J(R), Fj(R),C,E(t&R)], 2008 F2(R),SA1(t&R),NZ2(R),SA3, NZ3(R),It,E,F3,W
MacMillan, D I (Q) 1950 BI 1,2
McMullen, K V (NSW) 1962 NZ 3,5, 1963 E, SA 1
McShane, J M S (NSW) 1937 SA 1,2
Ma'afu, R S L (ACT) 2010 Fj,E1,2,I,SA1,NZ1,2,SA2,3,NZ3
Mackay, G (NSW) 1926 NZ 4
Mackney, W A R (NSW) 1933 SA 1,5, 1934 NZ 1,2
Magrath, E (NSW) 1961 Fj 1, SA 2, F
Maguire, D J (Q) 1989 BI 1,2,3
Malcolm, S J (NSW) 1927 S, 1928 E, F, NZ 1,2, M, 1929 NZ 1,2,3, 1930 BI, 1931 NZ, 1932 NZ 1,2,3, 1933 SA 4,5, 1934 NZ 1,2
Malone, J H (NSW) 1936 NZ 1,2, M, 1937 SA 2
Malouf, B P (NSW) 1982 NZ 1
Mandible, E F (NSW) 1907 NZ 2,3, 1908 W
Manning, J (NSW) 1904 BI 2
Manning, R C S (Q) 1967 NZ
Mansfield, B W (NSW) 1975 J 2
Manu, D T (NSW) 1995 [R (t)], NZ 1,2, 1996 W 1,2(R), SA 1, NZ 2, It, S, I, 1997 F 1, NZ 1(t), E 1, NZ 2, SA 1
Marks, H (NSW) 1899 BI 1,2
Marks, R J P (Q) 1962 NZ 4,5, 1963 E, SA 2,3,4, 1964 NZ 1,2,3, 1965 SA 1,2, 1966 W, S, 1967 E, I 1, F, I 2
Marrott, R (NSW) 1920 NZ 1,3
Marrott, W J (NSW) 1922 NZ 2,3, 1923 M 1,2,3, NZ 1,2
Marshall, J S (NSW) 1949 M 1
Martin, G J (Q) 1989 BI 1,2,3, NZ, F 1,2, 1990 F 1,3(R), NZ 1
Martin, M C (NSW) 1980 Fj, NZ 1,2, 1981 F 1,2, W (R)
Massey-Westropp, M (NSW) 1914 NZ 3
Mathers, M J (NSW) 1980 Fj, NZ 2(R)
Maund, J W (NSW) 1903 NZ
Mayne, A V (NSW) 1920 NZ 1,2,3, 1922 M 1
Meadows, J E C (V, Q) 1974 NZ 1, 1975 S, W, 1976 I, US, Fj 1,3, F 1,2, 1978 NZ 1,2,3, 1979 I 1,2, 1981 I, S, 1982 E, NZ 2,3, 1983 US, Arg 2, NZ
Meadows, R W (NSW) 1958 M 1,2,3, NZ 1,2,3
Meagher, F W (NSW) 1923 NZ 3, 1924 NZ 3, 1925 NZ 4, 1926 NZ 1,2,3, 1927 I, W
Meibusch, J H (Q) 1904 BI 3
Meibusch, L S (Q) 1912 US
Melrose, T C (NSW) 1978 NZ 3, 1979 I 1,2, NZ, Arg 1,2
Merrick, S (NSW) 1995 NZ 1,2
Messenger, H H (NSW) 1907 NZ 2,3
Middleton, S A (NSW) 1909 E, 1910 NZ 1,2,3
Miller, A R (NSW) 1952 Fj 1,2, NZ 1,2, 1953 SA 1,2,3,4, 1954 Fj 1,2, 1955 NZ 1,2,3, 1956 SA 1,2, 1957 NZ 1,2, 1958 W, E, S, F, M 1,2,3, 1959 BI 1,2, 1961 Fj 1,2,3, SA 2, F, 1962 NZ 1,2, 1966 BI 1,2, W, S, 1967 I 1, F, I 2, NZ
Miller, J M (NSW) 1962 NZ 1, 1963 E, SA 1, 1966 W, S, 1967 E
Miller, J S (Q) 1986 NZ 2,3, 1987 SK, [US, I, F], NZ, Arg 1,2, 1988 E 1,2, NZ 2,3, E, S, It, 1989 BI 1,2,3, NZ, 1990 F 1,3, 1991 W, [WS, W, I]
Miller, S W J (NSW) 1899 BI 3
Mingey, N (NSW) 1920 NZ 3, 1921 SA 1,2,3, 1923 M 1, NZ 1,2
Mitchell, D A (Q, WF, NSW) 2005 SA1(R),2(R),3(R),NZ1,SA4, NZ2,F2(R),E,I,W, 2007 W1,2,Fj,SA1,2(R),NZ2, [J(R),W,Fj,C,E(R)], 2008 SA1(R),NZ2(R),SA2,3(R),NZ4,E,F3, W, 2009 It1,F,NZ1,SA1, NZ2,SA2(R),3,NZ3,E,I,S,W, 2010 Fj(t&R),E1,2,I,SA1,NZ1,2, SA2,3
Monaghan, L E (NSW) 1973 E, 1974 NZ 1,2,3, 1975 E 1,2, S, W, 1976 E, I, US, F 1, 1978 W 1,2, NZ 1, 1979 I 1,2
Monti, C I A (Q) 1938 NZ 2
Moon, B J (Q) 1978 NZ 2,3, 1979 I 1,2, NZ, Arg 1,2, 1980 Fj, NZ 1,2,3, 1981 F 1,2, I, W, S, 1982 E, S 1,2, 1983 US, Arg 1,2, NZ, It, F 1,2, 1984 Fj, NZ 1,2,3, E, 1986 It, F, Arg 1,2
Mooney, T P (Q) 1954 Fj 1,2
Moore, R C (ACT, NSW) 1999 [US], 2001 BI 2,3, SA 1, NZ 1, SA 2, NZ 2, Sp (R), E (R), F (R), W (R), 2002 F 1(R),2(R), SA 2(R)
Moore, S T (Q, ACT) 2005 Sm(R),It(R),F1(R),SA2(R),3(R),F2(t&R), 2006 It(t),I2(R),S, 2007 W1,2,Fj(R),SA1,NZ1,2, [J,W,Fj,E], 2008 I,F1,2,SA1,NZ1,2,SA2,3(R),NZ3,4,It,E, F3,W, 2009 It1,F,NZ1, SA1,NZ2,SA2,3(R),NZ3(R),4,E,I,S,W, 2010 SA1(R),NZ1,SA2(t), 3,NZ3
Moran, H M (NSW) 1908 W
Morgan, G (Q) 1992 NZ 1(R), 3(R), W, 1993 Tg, NZ, SA 1,2,3, C, F 1,2, 1994 I 1,2, It 1, WS, NZ, 1996 W 1,2, C, NZ 1, SA 1, NZ 2, 1997 E 1, NZ 2
Morrissey, C V (NSW) 1925 NZ 2,3,4, 1926 NZ 2,3
Morrissey, W (Q) 1914 NZ 2
Mortlock, S A (ACT) 2000 Arg 1,2, SA 1, NZ 1, SA 2, NZ 2, SA 3, F, S, E, 2002 F 1,2, NZ 1, SA 1, NZ 2, SA 2, Arg, I, E, It, 2003 [R(R),Nm,S,NZ,E], 2004 S2,E1,PI,NZ1,SA1, NZ2,SA2,S3, F,S4, 2005 Sm,It,F1,SA2,3(R),NZ1, 2006 E1,2,I1,NZ1,SA1, NZ2,SA2,NZ3, SA3,It,I2,S, 2007 W1,2,Fj(R),SA1,NZ1,SA2,NZ2, [J,W,E], 2008 I,F1,2,SA1,NZ2,SA2, 3,NZ3,4,It,E,F3,W, 2009 It1,F,NZ1,SA1
Morton, A R (NSW) 1957 NZ 1,2, 1958 F, M 1,2,3, NZ 1,2,3, 1959 BI 1,2
Mossop, R P (NSW) 1949 NZ 1,2, 1950 BI 1,2, 1951 NZ 1
Moutray, I E (NSW) 1963 SA 2
Mulligan, P J (NSW) 1925 NZ 1(R)
Mumm, D W (NSW) 2008 I(t&R),F1(R),2,SA2(R),3(R),NZ4,It,E(R), F3,W(R), 2009 It1, 2,F,NZ1(t),SA1(R),NZ2(R),4(R),E(R),S(R),W, 2010 Fj,E1,2,I,SA1,NZ1,2,SA2,3(R), NZ3(R)
Munsie, A (NSW) 1928 NZ 2
Murdoch, A R (NSW) 1993 F 1, 1996 W 1
Murphy, P J (Q) 1910 NZ 1,2,3, 1913 NZ 1,2,3, 1914 NZ 1,2,3
Murphy, W (Q) 1912 US
Nasser, B P (Q) 1989 F 1,2, 1990 F 1,2,3, US, NZ 2, 1991 [WS]
Newman, E W (NSW) 1922 NZ 1
Nicholson, F C (Q) 1904 BI 3
Nicholson, F V (Q) 1903 NZ, 1904 BI 1
Niuqila, A S (NSW) 1988 S, It, 1989 BI 1
Noriega, E P (ACT, NSW) 1998 F, E 2, 1999 I 1,2, E, SA 1, NZ 1, SA 2(R), NZ 2(R), 2002 F 1,2, NZ 1, SA 1, NZ 2, Arg, I, E, It, 2003 I, W, E, SA 1, NZ 1, SA 2
Norton-Knight, S H (NSW) 2007 W1,Fj(R)
Nothling, O E (NSW) 1921 SA 1,2,3, NZ, 1922 M 1,2,3, NZ 1,2,3, 1923 M 1,2,3, NZ 1,2,3, 1924 NZ 1,2,3
Nucifora, D V (Q) 1991 [Arg (R)], 1993 C (R)
O'Brien, F W H (NSW) 1937 SA 2, 1938 NZ 3
O'Connor, J A (NSW) 1928 NZ 1,2,3, M
O'Connor, J D (WF) 2008 It(R), 2009 It1,2,F(R),NZ1(R),SA1(R), NZ2,SA2,3,NZ3,4, I(R),S(R),W(R), 2010 E1,2,I,SA1,NZ1,2,SA2,3, NZ3
O'Connor, M (ACT) 1994 I 1
O'Connor, M D (ACT, Q) 1979 Arg 1,2, 1980 Fj, NZ 1,2,3, 1981 F 1,2, I, 1982 E, S 1,2
O'Donnell, C (NSW) 1913 NZ 1,2
O'Donnell, I C (NSW) 1899 BI 3,4
O'Donnell, J B (NSW) 1928 NZ 1,3, M
O'Donnell, J M (NSW) 1899 BI 4
O'Gorman, J F (NSW) 1961 Fj 1, SA 1,2, F, 1962 NZ 2, 1963 E, SA 1,2,3,4, 1965 SA 1,2, 1966 W, S, 1967 E, I 1, F, I 2

O'Neill, D J (Q) 1964 NZ 1,2
O'Neill, J M (Q) 1952 NZ 1,2, 1956 SA 1,2
Ofahengaue, V (NSW) 1990 NZ 1,2,3, 1991 W, E, NZ 1,2, [Arg, W, I, NZ, E], 1992 S 1,2, SA, I, W, 1994 WS, NZ, 1995 Arg 1,2(R), [SA, C, E], NZ 1,2, 1997 Arg 1(t + R), 2(R), E 2, S, 1998 E 1(R), S 1(R),2(R), NZ 1(R), SA 1(R), NZ 2(R), SA 2(R), NZ 3(R), Fj, WS, F (R)
Ormiston, I W L (NSW) 1920 NZ 1,2,3
Osborne, D H (V) 1975 E 1,2, J 1
Outterside, R (NSW) 1959 BI 1,2
Oxenham, A McE (Q) 1904 BI 2, 1907 NZ 2
Oxlade, A M (Q) 1904 BI 2,3, 1905 NZ, 1907 NZ 2
Oxlade, B D (Q) 1938 NZ 1,2,3
Palfreyman, J R L (NSW) 1929 NZ 1, 1930 BI, 1931 NZ, 1932 NZ 3
Palu, W L (NSW) 2006 E2(t&R),I1(R),SA2,NZ3,SA3,W,It,I2,S(R), 2007 W1,2,SA1, NZ1, [J,W,Fj,E], 2008 I,F1,SA1,NZ1,2,SA2,3, NZ3,It(R),E(R),F3, 2009 NZ1,SA1, NZ3(t&R),4,E,I,S,W
Panoho, G M (Q) 1998 SA 2(R), NZ 3(R), Fj (R), Tg, WS (R), 1999 I 2, E, SA 1(R), NZ 1, 2000 Arg 1(R),2(R), SA 1(R), NZ 1(R), SA 2(R),3(R), F (R), S (R), E (R), 2001 BI 1, 2003 SA 2(R), NZ 2
Papworth, B (NSW) 1985 Fj 1,2, 1986 It, Arg 1,2, NZ 1,2,3, 1987 [E, US, J (R), I, F], NZ, Arg 1,2
Parker, A J (Q) 1983 Arg 1(R), 2, NZ
Parkinson, C E (Q) 1907 NZ 2
Pashley, J J (NSW) 1954 Fj 1,2, 1958 M 1,2,3
Paul, J A (ACT) 1998 S 1(R), NZ 1(R), SA 1(t), Fj (R), Tg, 1999 I 1,2, E, SA 1, NZ 1, [R (R), I 3(R), W (t), F (R)], 2000 Arg 1(R),2(R), SA 1(R), NZ 1(R), SA 2(R), NZ 2(R), SA 3(R), F (R), S (R), E (R), 2001 BI 1, 2002 F 1, NZ 1, SA 1, NZ 2, SA 2, Arg, E, 2003 I, W, E, SA 2(t&R), NZ2(R),[Arg(R),R(R),Nm,I(R),S(R), NZ(R),E(R)], 2004 S1(R),2(R), E1(R),PI(R),NZ1(t&R),SA1, NZ2(R),SA2(R),S3,F,S4,E2, 2005 Sm,It,F1,SA1,2,3,NZ1, 2006 E1(R),2(R),I1(R),NZ1(R),SA1,NZ2,SA2(R),NZ3,SA3
Pauling, T P (NSW) 1936 NZ 1, 1937 SA 1
Payne, S J (NSW) 1996 W 2, C, NZ 1, S, 1997 F 1(t), NZ 2(R), Arg 2(t)
Pearse, G K (NSW) 1975 W (R), 1976 I, US, Fj 1,2,3, 1978 NZ 1,2,3
Penman, A P (NSW) 1905 NZ
Perrin, P D (Q) 1962 NZ 1
Perrin, T D (NSW) 1931 M, NZ
Phelps, R (NSW) 1955 NZ 2,3, 1956 SA 1,2, 1957 NZ 1,2, 1958 W, I, E, S, F, M 1, NZ 1,2,3, 1961 Fj 1,2,3, SA 1,2, F, 1962 NZ 1,2
Phipps, J A (NSW) 1953 SA 1,2,3,4, 1954 Fj 1,2, 1955 NZ 1,2,3, 1956 SA 1,2
Phipps, W J (NSW) 1928 NZ 2
Piggott, H R (NSW) 1922 M 3(R)
Pilecki, S J (Q) 1978 W 1,2, NZ 1,2, 1979 I 1,2, NZ, Arg 1,2, 1980 Fj, NZ 1,2, 1982 S 1,2, 1983 US, Arg 1,2, NZ
Pini, M (Q) 1994 I 1, It 2, WS, NZ, 1995 Arg 1,2, [SA, R (t)]
Piper, B J C (NSW) 1946 NZ 1, M, NZ 2, 1947 NZ 1, S, I, W, 1948 E, F, 1949 M, 1,2,3
Pocock, D W (WF) 2008 NZ4(R),It(R), 2009 It1(R),2,F(R),NZ1(R), SA1(R),NZ2(R), SA2(R),3,NZ3,4,E(R),I,W, 2010 Fj,E1,2,I,SA1, NZ1,2,SA2,3,NZ3
Poidevin, S P (NSW) 1980 Fj, NZ 1,2,3, 1981 F 1,2, I, W, S, 1982 E, NZ 1,2,3, 1983 US, Arg 1,2, NZ, It, F 1,2, 1984 Fj, NZ 1,2,3, E, I, W, S, 1985 C 1,2, NZ, Fj 1,2, 1986 It, F, Arg 1,2, NZ 1,2,3, 1987 SK, [E, J, I, F, W], Arg 1, 1988 NZ 1,2,3, 1989 NZ, 1991 E, NZ 1,2, [Arg, W, I, NZ, E]
Polota-Nau, T (NSW) 2005 E(R),I(R), 2006 S(R), 2008 SA1(R), NZ1(R),2(R),SA2(R),3, It(R),E(R), 2009 It1(R),2,F(R),SA1(R), NZ2(t&R),SA2(R),3,NZ3,4(R),E(R),I(R),S(R), W(R)
Pope, A M (Q) 1968 NZ 2(R)
Potter, R T (Q) 1961 Fj 2
Potts, J M (NSW) 1957 NZ 1,2, 1958 W, I, 1959 BI 1
Prentice, C W (NSW) 1914 NZ 3
Prentice, W S (NSW) 1908 W, 1909 E, 1910 NZ 1,2,3, 1912 US
Price, R A (NSW) 1974 NZ 1,2,3, 1975 E 1,2, J 1,2, 1976 US
Primmer, C J (Q) 1951 NZ 1,3
Proctor, I J (NSW)) 1967 NZ
Prosser, R B (NSW) 1967 E, I 1,2, NZ, 1968 NZ 1,2, F, I, S, 1969 W, SA 1,2,3,4, 1971 SA 1,2,3, F 1,2, 1972 F 1,2, NZ 1,2,3, Fj
Pugh, G H (NSW) 1912 US
Purcell, M P (Q) 1966 W, S, 1967 I 2
Purkis, E M (NSW) 1958 S, M 1
Pym, J E (NSW) 1923 M 1
Rainbow, A E (NSW) 1925 NZ 1
Ramalli, C (NSW) 1938 NZ 2,3
Ramsay, K M (NSW) 1936 M, 1937 SA 1, 1938 NZ 1,3
Rankin, R (NSW) 1936 NZ 1,2, M, 1937 SA 1,2, 1938 NZ 1,2
Rathbone, C (ACT) 2004 S1,2(R),E1,PI,NZ1,SA1,NZ2,SA2,S3, F,S4, 2005 Sm,NZ1(R), SA4,NZ2, 2006E1(R),2(R),I1(R),SA1(R), NZ2(R),SA2(R),NZ3,SA3,W,It,I2
Rathie, D S (Q) 1972 F 1,2
Raymond, R L (NSW) 1920 NZ 1,2, 1921 SA 2,3, NZ, 1922 M 1,2,3, NZ 1,2,3, 1923 M 1,2
Redwood, C (Q) 1903 NZ, 1904 BI 1,2,3
Reid, E J (NSW) 1925 NZ 2,3,4
Reid, T W (NSW) 1961 Fj 1,2,3, SA 1, 1962 NZ 1
Reilly, N P (Q) 1968 NZ 1,2, F, I, S, 1969 W, SA 1,2,3,4
Reynolds, L J (NSW) 1910 NZ 2(R), 3
Reynolds, R J (NSW) 1984 Fj, NZ 1,2,3, 1985 Fj 1,2, 1986 Arg 1,2, NZ 1, 1987 [J]
Richards, E W (Q) 1904 BI 1,3, 1905 NZ, 1907 NZ 1(R), 2
Richards, G (NSW) 1978 NZ 2(R), 3, 1981 F 1
Richards, T J (Q) 1908 W, 1909 E, 1912 US
Richards, V S (NSW) 1936 NZ 1,2(R), M, 1937 SA 1, 1938 NZ 1
Richardson, G C (Q) 1971 SA 1,2,3, 1972 NZ 2,3, Fj, 1973 Tg 1,2, W
Rigney, W A (NSW) 1925 NZ 2,4, 1926 NZ 4
Riley, S A (NSW) 1903 NZ
Ritchie, E V (NSW) 1924 NZ 1,3, 1925 NZ 2,3
Roberts, B T (NSW) 1956 SA 2
Roberts, H F (Q) 1961 Fj 1,3, SA 2, F
Robertson, I J (NSW) 1975 J 1,2
Robinson, B A (NSW) 2006 SA3,I2(R),S, 2007 W1(R),2,Fj(R), 2008 I,F1,2,SA1, NZ1,2,SA2,3,NZ3,4,E,W, 2009 It1,F,NZ1,SA1, NZ2,SA2,3,NZ3,4,E,I,S,W, 2010 SA1,NZ1,2,SA2,3,NZ3
Robinson, B J (ACT) 1996 It (R), S (R), I (R), 1997 F 1,2, NZ 1, E 1, NZ 2, SA 1(R), NZ 3(R), SA 2(R), Arg 1,2, E 2, S, 1998 Tg
Roche, C (Q) 1982 S 1,2, NZ 1,2,3, 1983 US, Arg 1,2, NZ, It, F 1,2, 1984 Fj, NZ 1,2,3, I
Rodriguez, E E (NSW) 1984 Fj, NZ 1,2,3, E, I, W, S, 1985 C 1,2, NZ, Fj 1, 1986 It, F, Arg 1,2, NZ 1,2,3, 1987 SK, [E, J, W (R)], NZ, Arg 1,2
Roe, J A (Q) 2003 [Nm(R)], 2004 E1(R),SA1(R),NZ2(R),SA2(t&R), S3,F, 2005 Sm(R), It(R),F1(R),SA1(R),3,NZ1,SA4(t&R),NZ2(R), F2(R),E,I,W
Roebuck, M C (NSW) 1991 W, E, NZ 1,2, [Arg, WS, W, I, NZ, E], 1992 S 1,2, NZ 2,3, SA, I, W, 1993 Tg, SA 1,2,3, C, F 2
Roff, J W (ACT) 1995 [C, R], NZ 1,2, 1996 W 1,2, NZ 1, SA 1, NZ 2, SA 2(R), S, I, W 3, 1997 F 1,2, NZ 1, E 1, NZ 2, SA 1, NZ 3, SA 2, Arg 1,2, E 2, S, 1998 E 1, S 1,2, NZ 1, SA 1, NZ 2, SA 2, NZ 3, Fj, Tg, WS, F, E 2, 1999 I 1,2, E, SA 1, NZ 1, SA 2, NZ 2(R), [R (R), I 3, US (R), W, SA 3, F], 2000 Arg 1,2, SA 1, NZ 1, SA 2, NZ 2, SA 3, F, S, E, 2001 BI 1,2,3, SA 1, NZ 1, SA 2, NZ 2, Sp, E, F, W, 2003 I, W, E, SA 1, [Arg,R,I,S(R), NZ(t&R),E(R)], 2004 S1,2,E1,PI
Rogers, M S (NSW) 2002 F 1(R),2(R), NZ 1(R), SA 1(R), NZ 2(R), SA 2(t&R), Arg, 2003 E (R), SA 1, NZ 1, SA 2, NZ 2, [Arg,R, Nm,I,S,NZ,E],2004S3(R),F(R),S4(R), E2(R), 2005 Sm(R),It, F1(R),SA1,4,NZ2,F2,E,I,W, 2006 E1,2,I1,NZ1,SA1(R),NZ2(R), SA2(R),NZ3(R),W,It,I2(R),S(R)
Rose, H A (NSW), 1967 I 2, NZ, 1968 NZ 1,2, F, I, S, 1969 W, SA 1,2,3,4, 1970 S
Rosenblum, M E (NSW) 1928 NZ 1,2,3, M
Rosenblum, R G (NSW) 1969 SA 1,3, 1970 S
Rosewell, J S H (NSW) 1907 NZ 1,3
Ross, A W (NSW) 1925 NZ 1,2,3, 1926 NZ 1,2,3, 1927 I, W, S, 1928 E, F, 1929 NZ 1, 1930 BI, 1931 M, NZ, 1932 NZ 2,3, 1933 SA 5, 1934 NZ 1,2
Ross, W S (Q) 1979 I 1,2, Arg 2, 1980 Fj, NZ 1,2,3, 1982 S 1,2, 1983 US, Arg 1,2, NZ
Rothwell, P R (NSW) 1951 NZ 1,2,3, 1952 Fj 1
Row, F L (NSW) 1899 BI 1,3,4
Row, N E (NSW) 1907 NZ 1,3, 1909 E, 1910 NZ 1,2,3
Rowles, P G (NSW) 1972 Fj, 1973 E
Roxburgh, J R (NSW) 1968 NZ 1,2, F, 1969 W, SA 1,2,3,4, 1970 S
Ruebner, G (NSW) 1966 BI 1,2
Russell, C J (NSW) 1907 NZ 1,2,3, 1908 W, 1909 E
Ryan, J R (NSW) 1975 J 2, 1976 I, US, Fj 1,2,3
Ryan, K J (Q) 1958 E, M 1, NZ 1,2,3
Ryan, P F (NSW) 1963 E, SA 1, 1966 BI 1,2
Rylance, M H (NSW) 1926 NZ 4(R)
Sailor, W J (Q) 2002 F 1,2, Arg (R), I, E, It, 2003 I, W, E, SA 1, NZ 1, SA 2, NZ 2, [Arg,R,I,S,NZ,E], 2004 S1,2,NZ1(R),2(R), SA2(R),S3(R),F(R),S4(R),E2, 2005 Sm,It,F1,SA1,2,3,F2,I(R),W(R)
Samo, R U (ACT) 2004 S1,2,E1,PI,NZ1,S4(R)
Sampson, J H (NSW) 1899 BI 4
Sayle, J L (NSW) 1967 NZ
Schulte, B G (Q) 1946 NZ 1, M
Scott, P R I (NSW) 1962 NZ 1,2
Scott-Young, S J (Q) 1990 F 2,3(R), US, NZ 3, 1992 NZ 1,2,3
Shambrook, G G (Q) 1976 Fj 2,3

Sharpe, N C (Q, WF) 2002 F 1,2, NZ 1, SA 1, NZ 2, SA 2, 2003 I, W, E, SA 1(R), NZ 1(R), SA 2(R), NZ 2(R),[Arg,R,Nm,I,S,NZ,E], 2004 S1,2,E1,PI,NZ1,SA1,NZ2,SA2, 2005 Sm,It,F1,SA1,2,3, NZ1,SA4,NZ2,F2,E,I,W, 2006 E1,2,I1,NZ1,SA1,NZ2,SA2,NZ3, SA3,W,It,I2,S, 2007 W1,2,SA1,NZ1,SA2,NZ2, [J,W,C,E], 2008 I,F1,SA1,NZ1,2,3,4,E, F3,W, 2009 It1,F,NZ1,SA1,NZ2, 2010 Fj,E1,2,SA1,NZ1,2,SA2,3,NZ3
Shaw, A A (Q) 1973 W, E, 1975 E 1,2, J 2, S, W, 1976 E, I, US, Fj 1,2,3, F 1,2, 1978 W 1,2, NZ 1,2,3, 1979 I 1,2, NZ, Arg 1,2, 1980 Fj, NZ 1,2,3, 1981 F 1,2, I, W, S, 1982 S 1,2
Shaw, C (NSW) 1925 NZ 2,3,4(R)
Shaw, G A (NSW) 1969 W, SA 1(R), 1970 S, 1971 SA 1,2,3, F 1,2, 1973 W, E, 1974 NZ 1,2,3, 1975 E 1,2, J 1,2, W, 1976 E, I, US, Fj 1,2,3, F 1,2, 1979 NZ
Sheehan, B R (ACT) 2006 SA3(R), 2008 SA2(R),3(R)
Sheehan, W B J (NSW) 1921 SA 1,2,3, 1922 NZ 1,2,3, 1923 M 1,2, NZ 1,2,3, 1924 NZ 1,2, 1926 NZ 1,2,3, 1927 W, S
Shehadie, N M (NSW) 1947 NZ 2, 1948 E, F, 1949 M 1,2,3, NZ 1,2, 1950 BI 1,2, 1951 NZ 1,2,3, 1952 Fj 1,2, NZ 2, 1953 SA 1,2,3,4, 1954 Fj 1,2, 1955 NZ 1,2,3, 1956 SA 1,2, 1957 NZ 2, 1958 W, I
Sheil, A G R (Q) 1956 SA 1
Shepherd, C B (WF) 2006 E1(R),2(R),I1(R),SA3,W, 2007 [C], 2008 I,F1,2(R)
Shepherd, D J (V) 1964 NZ 3, 1965 SA 1,2, 1966 BI 1,2
Shepherdson, G T (ACT) 2006 I1,NZ1,SA1,NZ2(R),SA2(R),It,I2,S, 2007 W1,2,SA1, NZ1,SA2,NZ2, [J(R),W,Fj,E]
Shute, J L (NSW) 1920 NZ 3, 1922 M 2,3
Simmons, R A (Q) 2010 SA1(R),NZ1(R),2(R),SA2(R)
Simpson, R J (NSW) 1913 NZ 2
Skinner, A J (NSW) 1969 W, SA 4, 1970 S
Slack, A G (Q) 1978 W 1,2, NZ 1,2, 1979 NZ, Arg 1,2, 1980 Fj, 1981 I, W, S, 1982 E, S 1, NZ 3, 1983 US, Arg 1,2 NZ, It, 1984 Fj, NZ 1,2,3, E, I, W, S, 1986 It, F, NZ 1,2,3, 1987 SK, [E, US, J, I, F, W]
Slater, S H (NSW) 1910 NZ 3
Slattery, P J (Q) 1990 US (R), 1991 W (R), E (R), [WS (R), W, I (R)], 1992 I, W, 1993 Tg, C, F 1,2, 1994 I 1,2, It 1(R), 1995 [C, R (R)]
Slipper, J A (Q) 2010 E1(R),2(R),I(R),SA1(R),NZ1(R),2(R),SA2(R), 3(R),NZ3(R)
Smairl, A M (NSW) 1928 NZ 1,2,3
Smith, B A (Q) 1987 SK, [US, J, I (R), W], Arg 1
Smith, D P (Q) 1993 SA 1,2,3, C, F 2, 1994 I 1,2, It 1,2, WS, NZ, 1995 Arg 1,2, [SA, R, E], NZ 1,2, 1998 SA 1(R), NZ 3(R), Fj
Smith, F B (NSW) 1905 NZ, 1907 NZ 1,2,3
Smith, G B (ACT) 2000 F, S, E, 2001 BI 1,2,3, SA 1, NZ 1, SA 2, NZ 2, Sp, E, F (R), W (R), 2002 F 1,2, NZ 1, SA 1, NZ 2, SA 2, Arg, I, E, It, 2003 I, NZ 1, SA 2, NZ 2, [Arg,R, Nm,I,S,NZ,E], 2004 S1,2(R),E1(t&R),PI(R),NZ1(R),SA1,NZ2,SA2,S3,F,S4,E2, 2005 Sm,It,F1,SA1,2,3,NZ1,SA4(R),NZ2,F2,E,I,W, 2006 E1,2, I1,NZ1,SA1,NZ2,SA2,NZ3(t), SA3(R),It,I2(R),S, 2007 W1(R),2, Fj(R),SA1,NZ1,SA2,NZ2, [J,W,C,E], 2008 I,F1,2(R), SA1,NZ1,2, SA2,3(R),NZ3,4,E,F3,W(R), 2009 It1,2,F,NZ1,SA1,NZ2,SA2,3, NZ3,4(R),E, I(t),S,W(R)
Smith, L M (NSW) 1905 NZ
Smith, N C (NSW) 1922 NZ 2,3, 1923 NZ 1, 1924 NZ 1,3(R), 1925 NZ 2,3
Smith, P V (NSW) 1967 NZ, 1968 NZ 1,2, F, I, S, 1969 W, SA 1
Smith, R A (NSW) 1971 SA 1,2, 1972 F 1,2, NZ 1,2(R), 3, Fj, 1975 E 1,2, J 1,2, S, W, 1976 E, I, US, Fj 1,2,3, F 1,2
Smith, T S (NSW) 1921 SA 1,2,3, NZ, 1922 M 2,3, NZ 1,2,3, 1925 NZ 1,3,4
Snell, H W (NSW) 1925 NZ 2,3, 1928 NZ 3
Solomon, H J (NSW) 1949 M 3, NZ 2, 1950 BI 1,2, 1951 NZ 1,2, 1952 Fj 1,2, NZ 1,2, 1953 SA 1,2,3, 1955 NZ 1
Spooner, N R (Q) 1999 I 1,2
Spragg, S A (NSW) 1899 BI 1,2,3,4
Staniforth, S N G (NSW,WF) 1999 [US], 2002 I, It, 2006 SA3(R), I2(R),S, 2007 Fj, NZ1(R),SA2(R),NZ2(R), [W(R),Fj(R)]
Stanley, R G (NSW) 1921 NZ, 1922 M 1,2,3, NZ 1,2,3, 1923 M 2,3, NZ 1,2,3, 1924 NZ 1,3
Stapleton, E T (NSW) 1951 NZ 1,2,3, 1952 Fj 1,2, NZ 1,2, 1953 SA 1,2,3,4, 1954 Fj 1, 1955 NZ 1,2,3, 1958 NZ 1
Steggall, J C (Q) 1931 M, NZ, 1932 NZ 1,2,3, 1933 SA 1,2,3,4,5
Stegman, T R (NSW) 1973 Tg 1,2
Stephens, O G (NSW) 1973 Tg 1,2, W, 1974 NZ 2,3
Stewart, A A (NSW) 1979 NZ, Arg 1,2
Stiles, N B (Q) 2001 BI 1,2,3, SA 1, NZ 1, SA 2, NZ 2, Sp, E, F, W, 2002 I
Stone, A H (NSW) 1937 SA 2, 1938 NZ 2,3
Stone, C G (NSW) 1938 NZ 1
Stone, J M (NSW) 1946 M, NZ 2
Storey, G P (NSW) 1926 NZ 4, 1927 I, W, S, 1928 E, F, 1929 NZ 3(R), 1930 BI
Storey, K P (NSW) 1936 NZ 2
Storey, N J D (NSW) 1962 NZ 1
Strachan, D J (NSW) 1955 NZ 2,3
Strauss, C P (NSW) 1999 I 1(R),2(R), E (R), SA 1(R), NZ 1, SA 2(R), NZ 2(R), [R (R), I 3(R), US, W]
Street, N O (NSW) 1899 BI 2
Streeter, S F (NSW) 1978 NZ 1
Stuart, R (NSW) 1910 NZ 2,3
Stumbles, B D (NSW) 1972 NZ 1(R), 2,3, Fj
Sturtridge, G S (V) 1929 NZ 2, 1932 NZ 1,2,3, 1933 SA 1,2,3, 4,5
Sullivan, P D (NSW) 1971 SA 1,2,3, F 1,2, 1972 F 1,2, NZ 1,2, Fj, 1973 Tg 1,2, W
Summons, A J (NSW) 1958 W, I, E, S, M 2, NZ 1,2,3, 1959 BI 1,2
Suttor, D C (NSW) 1913 NZ 1,2,3
Swannell, B I (NSW) 1905 NZ
Sweeney, T L (Q) 1953 SA 1
Taafe, B S (NSW) 1969 SA 1, 1972 F 1,2
Tabua, I (Q) 1993 SA 2,3, C, F 1, 1994 I 1,2, It 1,2, 1995 [C, R]
Tahu, P J A (NSW) 2008 NZ1(R),SA2(R),3,It
Tancred, A J (NSW) 1927 I, W, S
Tancred, H E (NSW) 1923 M 1,2
Tancred, J L (NSW) 1926 NZ 3,4, 1928 F
Tanner, W H (Q) 1899 BI 1,2
Tarleton, K (NSW) 1925 NZ 2,3
Tasker, W G (NSW) 1913 NZ 1,2,3, 1914 NZ 1,2,3
Tate, M J (NSW) 1951 NZ 3, 1952 Fj 1,2, NZ 1,2, 1953 SA 1, 1954 Fj 1,2
Taylor, D A (Q) 1968 NZ 1,2, F, I, S
Taylor, H C (NSW) 1923 NZ 1,2,3, 1924 NZ 4
Taylor, J I (NSW) 1971 SA 1, 1972 F 1,2, Fj
Taylor, J M (NSW) 1922 M 1,2
Teitzel, R G (Q) 1966 W, S, 1967 E, I 1, F, I 2, NZ
Telford, D G (NSW) 1926 NZ 3(R)
Thompson, C E (NSW) 1922 M 1, 1923 M 1,2, NZ 1, 1924 NZ 2,3
Thompson, E G (Q) 1929 NZ 1,2,3, 1930 BI
Thompson, F (NSW) 1913 NZ 1,2,3, 1914 NZ 1,3
Thompson, J (Q) 1914 NZ 1, 2
Thompson, P D (Q) 1950 BI 1
Thompson, R J (WA) 1971 SA 3, F 2(R), 1972 Fj
Thorn, A M (NSW) 1921 SA 1,2,3, NZ, 1922 M 1,3
Thorn, E J (NSW) 1922 NZ 1,2,3, 1923 NZ 1,2,3, 1924 NZ 1,2,3, 1925 NZ 1,2, 1926 NZ 1,2,3,4
Thornett, J E (NSW) 1955 NZ 1,2,3, 1956 SA 1,2, 1958 W, I, S, F, M 2,3, NZ 2,3, 1959 BI 1,2, 1961 Fj 2,3, SA 1,2, F, 1962 NZ 2,3,4,5, 1963 E, SA 1,2,3,4, 1964 NZ 1,2,3, 1965 SA 1,2, 1966 BI 1,2, 1967 F
Thornett, R N (NSW) 1961 Fj 1,2,3, SA 1,2, F, 1962 NZ 1,2,3,4,5
Thorpe, A C (NSW) 1929 NZ 1(R)
Timbury, F R V (Q) 1910 NZ 1,2,
Tindall, E N (NSW) 1973 Tg 2
Toby, A E (NSW) 1925 NZ 1,4
Tolhurst, H A (NSW) 1931 M, NZ
Tombs, R C (NSW) 1992 S 1,2, 1994 I 2, It 1, 1996 NZ 2
Tonkin, A E J (NSW) 1947 S, I, W, 1948 E, F, 1950 BI 2
Tooth, R M (NSW) 1951 NZ 1,2,3, 1954 Fj 1,2, 1955 NZ 1,2,3, 1957 NZ 1,2
Towers, C H T (NSW) 1926 NZ 1,3(R),4, 1927 I, 1928 E, F, NZ 1,2,3, M, 1929 NZ 1,3, 1930 BI, 1931 M, NZ, 1934 NZ 1,2, 1937 SA 1,2
Trivett, R K (Q) 1966 BI 1,2
Tune, B N (Q) 1996 W 2, C, NZ 1, SA 1, NZ 2, SA 2, 1997 F 1,2, NZ 1, E 1, NZ 2, SA 1, NZ 3, SA 2, Arg, 1,2, E 2, S, 1998 E 1, S 1,2, NZ 1, SA 1,2, NZ 3, 1999 I 1, E, SA 1, NZ 1, SA 2, NZ 2, [R, I 3, W, SA 3, F], 2000 SA 2(R), NZ 2(t&R), SA 3(R), 2001 F (R), W, 2002 NZ 1, SA 1, NZ 2, SA 2, Arg, 2006 NZ1(R)
Tuqiri, L D (NSW) 2003 I (R), W (R), E (R), SA 1(R), NZ 1, SA 2, NZ 2, [Arg(R),R(R), Nm,I(R),S,NZ,E], 2004 S1,2,E1,PI,NZ1,SA1, NZ2,SA2,S3,F,S4,E2, 2005 It,F1,SA1,2,3, NZ1,SA4,NZ2,F2, E,I,W, 2006 E1,2,I1,NZ1,SA1,NZ2,SA2,NZ3,W,It,I2,S, 2007 Fj,SA1, NZ1, [J,W,Fj,C,E], 2008 I,F1,SA1,NZ1,2,SA2,3,NZ3,W(R)
Turinui, M P (NSW) 2003 I, W, E, 2003 [Nm(R)], 2004 S1(R),2,E2, 2005 Sm,It(R), F1(R),SA1,2(t&R),3,NZ1,SA4,NZ2,F2,E,I,W
Turnbull, A (V) 1961 Fj 3
Turnbull, R V (NSW) 1968 I
Turner, L D (NSW) 2008 F2,It, 2009 It1,2,F,NZ1,SA1,NZ2,SA2,3, NZ3, 2010 NZ3
Tuynman, S N (NSW) 1983 F 1,2, 1984 E, I, W, S, 1985 C 1,2, NZ, Fj 1,2, 1986 It, F, Arg 1,2, NZ 1,2,3, 1987 SK, [E, US, J, I, W], NZ, Arg 1(R), 2, 1988 E, It, 1989 BI 1,2,3, NZ, 1990 NZ 1
Tweedale, E (NSW) 1946 NZ 1,2, 1947 NZ 2, S, I, 1948 E, F, 1949 M 1,2,3
Valentine, J J (Q, WF) 2006 E1(R),W(R),I2(R),S(R), 2009 It2(R),F(R)

Vaughan, D (NSW) 1983 US, Arg 1, It, F 1,2
Vaughan, G N (V) 1958 E, S, F, M 1,2,3
Verge, A (NSW) 1904 BI 1,2
Vickerman, D J (ACT, NSW) 2002 F 2(R), Arg, E, It, 2003 I (R), W (R), E (R), SA 1, NZ 1, SA 2, NZ 2, [Arg(R),R,I(R),S(R)], 2004 S1(t&R),2(R),E1(R),PI(R),NZ1(R), SA1(R),NZ2(R),SA2(R),S3,F,S4, E2, 2005 SA2(R),3,NZ1,SA4, 2006 E1,2,I1,NZ1,SA1, NZ2,SA2, NZ3,SA3,W, 2007 W1(R),2,Fj,SA1,NZ1,SA2,NZ2, [J,W,Fj,E], 2008 NZ1(R), 2(t&R),SA2
Walden, R J (NSW) 1934 NZ 2, 1936 NZ 1,2, M
Walker, A K (NSW) 1947 NZ 1, 1948 E, F, 1950 BI 1,2
Walker, A M (ACT) 2000 NZ 1(R), 2001 BI 1,2,3, SA 1, NZ 1,2(R)
Walker, A S B (NSW) 1912 US, 1920 NZ 1,2, 1921 SA 1,2,3, NZ, 1922 M 1,3, NZ 1,2,3, 1923 M 2,3, 1924 NZ 1,2
Walker, L F (NSW) 1988 NZ 2,3, S, It, 1989 BI 1,2,3, NZ
Walker, L R (NSW) 1982 NZ 2,3
Wallace, A C (NSW) 1921 NZ, 1926 NZ 3,4, 1927 I, W, S, 1928 E, F
Wallace, T M (NSW) 1994 It 1(R), 2
Wallach, C (NSW) 1913 NZ 1,3, 1914 NZ 1,2,3
Walsh, J J (NSW) 1953 SA 1,2,3,4
Walsh, P B (NSW) 1904 BI 1,2,3
Walsham, K P (NSW) 1962 NZ 3, 1963 E
Ward, P G (NSW) 1899 BI 1,2,3,4
Ward, T (Q) 1899 BI 2
Watson, G W (Q) 1907 NZ 1
Watson, W T (NSW) 1912 US, 1913 NZ 1,2,3, 1914 NZ 1, 1920 NZ 1,2,3
Waugh, P R (NSW) 2000 E (R), 2001 NZ 1(R), SA 2(R), NZ 2(R), Sp (R), E (R), F, W, 2003 I (R), W, E, SA 1, NZ 1, SA 2, NZ2, [Arg,R,I,S,NZ,E], 2004 S1(R),2,E1,PI,NZ1, SA1,NZ2,SA2, S3,F,S4,E2,2005 SA1(R),2(R),3,NZ1(R),SA4,NZ2,F2,E,I,W, 2006 E1(R),2(R),I1(R),NZ1(R),SA1(R),NZ2(R),SA2(R),NZ3,SA3,W,I2,S(R, 2007 W1,2(R), Fj,SA1(R),NZ1(R),SA2(R),NZ2(R) , [W(R),Fj,C(R), E(R)], 2008 I(R),F1(R),2,SA1(R), NZ1(R),2,SA2(t&R),3,NZ4(R),It,W, 2009 It2(R),F(R)
Waugh, W W (NSW, ACT) 1993 SA 1, 1995 [C], NZ 1,2, 1996 S, I, 1997 Arg 1,2
Weatherstone, L J (ACT) 1975 E 1,2, J 1,2, S (R), 1976 E, I
Webb, W (NSW) 1899 BI 3,4
Welborn J P (NSW) 1996 SA 2, It, 1998 Tg, 1999 E, SA 1, NZ 1
Wells, B G (NSW) 1958 M 1
Westfield, R E (NSW) 1928 NZ 1,2,3, M, 1929 NZ 2,3
Whitaker, C J (NSW) 1998 SA 2(R), Fj (R), Tg, 1999 NZ 2(R), [R (R), US, F (R)], 2000 S (R), 2001 Sp (R), W (R), 2002 Arg (R), It (R), 2003 I (R), W (R), SA 2(R),[Arg(R),Nm,S(R)], 2004 PI(R),NZ1, 2005 Sm,It(R),F1(R),SA1(R),2(R),NZ1(t&R),SA4(R),NZ2(R),F2(R), E(R),W(R)
White, C J B (NSW) 1899 BI 1, 1903 NZ, 1904 BI 1
White, J M (NSW) 1904 BI 3
White, J P L (NSW) 1958 NZ 1,2,3, 1961 Fj 1,2,3, SA 1,2, F, 1962 NZ 1,2,3,4,5, 1963 E, SA 1,2,3,4, 1964 NZ 1,2,3, 1965 SA 1,2
White, M C (Q) 1931 M, NZ 1932 NZ 1,2, 1933 SA 1,2,3,4,5
White, S W (NSW) 1956 SA 1,2, 1958 I, E, S, M 2,3
White, W G S (Q) 1933 SA 1,2,3,4,5, 1934 NZ 1,2, 1936 NZ 1,2, M
White, W J (NSW) 1928 NZ 1, M, 1932 NZ 1
Wickham, S M (NSW) 1903 NZ, 1904 BI 1,2,3, 1905 NZ
Williams, D (Q) 1913 NZ 3, 1914 NZ 1,2,3
Williams, I M (NSW) 1987 Arg 1,2, 1988 E 1,2, NZ 1,2,3, 1989 BI 2,3, NZ, F 1,2, 1990 F 1,2,3, US, NZ 1
Williams, J L (NSW) 1963 SA 1,3,4
Williams, R W (ACT) 1999 I 1(t&R),2(t&R), E (R), [US], 2000 Arg 1,2, SA 1, NZ 1, SA 2, NZ 2, SA 3, F (R), S (R), E
Williams, S A (NSW) 1980 Fj, NZ 1,2, 1981 F 1,2, 1982 E, NZ 1,2,3, 1983 US, Arg 1(R), 2, NZ, It, F 1,2, 1984 NZ 1,2,3, E, I, W, S, 1985 C 1,2, NZ, Fj 1,2
Wilson, B J (NSW) 1949 NZ 1,2
Wilson, C R (Q) 1957 NZ 1, 1958 NZ 1,2,3
Wilson, D J (Q) 1992 S 1,2, NZ 1,2,3, SA, I, W, 1993 Tg, NZ, SA 1,2,3, C, F 1,2, 1994 I 1,2, It 1,2, WS, NZ, 1995 Arg 1,2, [SA, R, E], 1996 W 1,2, C, NZ 1, SA 1, NZ 2, SA 2, It, S, I, W 3, 1997 F 1,2, NZ 1, E 1(t + R), NZ 2(R), SA 1, NZ 3, SA 2, E 2(R), S (R), 1998 E 1, S 1,2, NZ 1, SA 1, NZ 2, SA 2, NZ 3, Fj, WS, F, E 2, 1999 I 1,2, E, SA 1, NZ 1, SA 2, NZ 2, [R, I 3, W, SA 3, F], 2000 Arg 1,2, SA 1, NZ 1, SA 2, NZ 2, SA 3
Wilson, V W (Q) 1937 SA 1,2, 1938 NZ 1,2,3
Windon, C J (NSW) 1946 NZ 1,2, 1947 NZ 1, S, I, W, 1948 E, F, 1949 M 1,2,3, NZ 1,2, 1951 NZ 1,2,3, 1952 Fj 1,2, NZ 1,2
Windon, K S (NSW) 1937 SA 1,2, 1946 M
Windsor, J C (Q) 1947 NZ 2
Winning, K C (Q) 1951 NZ 1
Wogan, L W (NSW) 1913 NZ 1,2,3, 1914 NZ 1,2,3, 1920 NZ 1,2,3, 1921 SA 1,2,3, NZ, 1922 M 3, NZ 1,2,3, 1923 M 1,2, 1924 NZ 1,2,3
Wood, F (NSW) 1907 NZ 1,2,3, 1910 NZ 1,2,3, 1913 NZ 1,2,3, 1914 NZ 1,2,3
Wood, R N (Q) 1972 Fj
Woods, H F (NSW) 1925 NZ 4, 1926 NZ 1,2,3, 1927 I, W, S, 1928 E
Wright, K J (NSW) 1975 E 1,2, J 1, 1976 US, F 1,2, 1978 NZ 1,2,3
Wyld, G (NSW) 1920 NZ 2
Yanz, K (NSW) 1958 F
Young, W K (ACT, NSW) 2000 F, S, E, 2002 F 1,2, NZ 1, SA 1, NZ 2, SA 2, Arg, E, It, 2003 I, W, E, SA 1, NZ 1, SA 2, NZ 2, [Arg,R,I,S,NZ,E], 2004 S1,2,E1,PI,NZ1,SA1, NZ2,SA2,S3,F,S4, E2, 2005 Sm,It,F1,SA1,2,3,NZ1,SA4,NZ2

CANADA

CANADA'S 2009–10 TEST RECORD

OPPONENTS	DATE	VENUE	RESULT
Japan	15 Nov	A	**Lost** 8–46
Japan	21 Nov	A	**Lost** 6–27
Russia	28 Nov	H	**Won** 22–6
Uruguay	5 Jun	N	**Won** 48–6
France A	13 Jun	N	**Won** 33–27
England Saxons	19 Jun	N	**Lost** 18–38

CHURCHILL BRINGS MUCH CHEER

By Doug Crosse

Mike Stobe/Getty Images

Canada had an impressive Churchill Cup campaign before falling to England in the final.

While Canada ended 2009 with a disappointing tour to Japan and first-ever win over Russia, the rebound from that tough Asian jaunt was significant in 2010 with an impressive run at the Churchill Cup in Denver and the New York City area.

Opening the tournament against Uruguay, Kieran Crowley's charges had a good day, running in six tries in a 48–6 victory. DTH van der Merwe showed his ever-improving style with a pair of superb tries, cementing his mantle as the offensive hub of the team.

A week later against a tough France A squad, it was a thrilling come from behind 33–27 victory that propelled Canada into its first ever Churchill Cup championship game against the England Saxons. Lock Brian Erichsen was the hero of the game, recovering from a knock to the head that required eight stitches to score a scorching 40-metre try.

In the Cup final in Harrison, New Jersey, the Saxons jumped out to a quick lead before Canada fought back to 20–13 with tries from Matt Evans and Chauncey O'Toole. Agonisingly, Canada left 11 points on the field in missed penalty and conversion kicks as the Saxons pulled clear in the second half.

"I am very pleased with the progress we have made," said Crowley. "Today, against England, we had a few problems against a fully professional team, but it was four tries to three, and defensively we did pretty well."

"We have added to our depth with some players, and the more time we can give them at this level the better they will get.

"If you look at the calibre of [the Saxons'] players they are all Premiership players. They made us pay for mistakes and when we had a breakdown in the system. We have got to take the positives out of it."

The tour to Japan seven months earlier had not yielded so many positives for Crowley, Canada having slumped to a heavy seven-try, 46–8 loss in the opening match in Sendai. Six days later in Tokyo the margin of defeat was smaller (27–6), but Canada still had no answer to a side they will face again at RWC 2011.

The Canadian women enjoyed a more profitable tour in November, travelling to France for a two-Test series to officially begin their countdown to Women's Rugby World Cup 2010 in England.

The first Test in Dijon, at a time when the rivals had just been drawn in the same WRWC 2010 pool, saw Canada record a first win over France for 11 years with tries from Araba Chintoh and Cheryl Phillips sealing a 14–5 win.

A week later, in the curtain raiser for the French men's match with Samoa at the Stade de France, the series was levelled after the French women triumphed 22–0.

The win, though, was significant for confidence in the Canadian ranks going into January and the first of four matches against their USA counterparts in the run-in to the World Cup.

Canada won three of the matches, taking the first in Florida 18–8 only to see the USA snatch an 11–10 victory in the dying seconds four days later. Four months on and Canada this time won the series with 14–8 and 34–22 victories.

These wins suggested the Canadians travelled to the World Cup in good form, hoping to better their fourth place finishes at the last three tournaments. Certainly the support shown by the Canadian rugby community to help underwrite the cost was an important aspect for the women given the 'pay to play' model in Canada.

Canada kicked off their campaign with a satisfying 37–10 win over Scotland and 40–10 defeat of Sweden. However, when it came to the Pool C decider against France, Canada had no answer to the French flair and fell 23–8. Worse was to follow when Australia's 62–0 defeat of South Africa meant they beat Canada to the remaining semi-final spot.

The title dream had ended, but Canada bounced back to beat Scotland

41–0 before losing a close encounter with USA 23–20 to finish sixth, a disappointing final chapter for a number of players, including Maria Gallo, captain Leslie Cripps, Anna Schnell and Gillian Florence, a veteran of five World Cups.

The next generation of Canadian men had travelled to Russia in May for the IRB Junior World Rugby Trophy, hoping to secure an immediate return to the Junior World Championship for 2011.

Canada's Under-20s began with a 22–6 win over Zimbabwe, only to then fall 17–15 to the hosts and 38–17 to Japan in their final pool match.

This pitted Tim Murdy's team into the fifth place play-off against Uruguay, the 2008 Trophy winners coming out on top 13–11 to leave Canada sixth overall.

Canada may not have been a core member of the IRB Sevens World Series in 2009–10, but they were determined to make the most of their opportunities on the circuit to develop players for the future with the 2016 Olympic Games in mind.

In their first event in Wellington, Canada reached the NZI Sevens Cup quarter-finals after Nathan Hirayama's last-gasp conversion saw them past France.

Canada went on to claim two Bowl titles in the remainder of the season, beating world champions Wales 35–19 in Hong Kong and Russia 21–12 at the London Sevens.

On the domestic scene, the Canadian Rugby Championship – the new senior men's competition – saw the two favourites bow out early after Ontario Blues and the BC Bears fell to the Rock and Prairie Wolf Pack respectively.

The final pool match saw the Wolf Pack and the Rock meet in St John's to determine home advantage for the championship decider. The lead changed twice in the final two minutes as first the Wolf Pack and then the Rock scored tries, the last one from No 8 Ken Goodland giving the Rock a 27–23 win. The two sides met a fortnight later in a nationally televised final with the Rock prevailing 19–8 in extremely wet conditions to win a fourth national title in 15 seasons.

British Columbia, meanwhile, played Ontario in the National Women's League final in a sizzling hot Toronto in July. With World Cup selectors looking on, British Columbia, featuring many Canadian national team players, were too strong and ran out 34–22 winners.

In the National Under-20 men's tournament, the Vancouver Wave made the difficult 11-hour cross-country flight to St. John's Newfoundland to play the Rock. It was a close contest, but the hometown heroes ruled the day 13–10.

CANADA INTERNATIONAL STATISTICS

MATCH RECORDS UP TO 29TH OCTOBER 2010

WINNING MARGIN

Date	Opponent	Result	Winning Margin
24/06/2006	Barbados	69–3	**66**
14/10/1999	Namibia	72–11	**61**
12/08/2006	USA	56–7	**49**
06/07/1996	Hong Kong	57–9	**48**

MOST POINTS IN A MATCH

BY THE TEAM

Date	Opponent	Result	Pts.
14/10/1999	Namibia	72–11	**72**
24/06/2006	Barbados	69–3	**69**
15/07/2000	Japan	62–18	**62**
06/07/1996	Hong Kong	57–9	**57**
12/08/2006	USA	56–7	**56**

MOST TRIES IN A MATCH

BY THE TEAM

Date	Opponent	Result	Tries
24/06/2006	Barbados	69–3	**11**
14/10/1999	Namibia	72–11	**9**
11/05/1991	Japan	49–26	**8**
15/07/2000	Japan	62–18	**8**

MOST CONVERSIONS IN A MATCH

BY THE TEAM

Date	Opponent	Result	Cons
14/10/1999	Namibia	72–11	**9**
15/07/2000	Japan	62–18	**8**
24/06/2006	Barbados	69–3	**7**
02/06/2007	USA	52–10	**7**
11/05/1991	Japan	49–26	**7**

MOST PENALTIES IN A MATCH

BY THE TEAM

Date	Opponent	Result	Pens
25/05/1991	Scotland	24–19	**8**
22/08/1998	Argentina	28–54	**7**

MOST DROP GOALS IN A MATCH

BY THE TEAM

Date	Opponent	Result	DGs
08/11/1986	USA	27–16	**2**
04/07/2001	Fiji	23–52	**2**
08/06/1980	USA	16–0	**2**
24/05/1997	Hong Kong	35–27	**2**

MOST POINTS IN A MATCH

BY A PLAYER

Date	Player	Opponent	Pts.
12/08/2006	James Pritchard	USA	**36**
24/06/2006	James Pritchard	Barbados	**29**
14/10/1999	Gareth Rees	Namibia	**27**
13/07/1996	Bobby Ross	Japan	**26**
25/05/1991	Mark Wyatt	Scotland	**24**

MOST TRIES IN A MATCH

BY A PLAYER

Date	Player	Opponent	Tries
15/07/2000	Kyle Nichols	Japan	**4**
24/06/2006	James Pritchard	Barbados	**3**
12/08/2006	James Pritchard	USA	**3**
10/05/1987	Steve Gray	USA	**3**

MOST CONVERSIONS IN A MATCH

BY A PLAYER

Date	Player	Opponent	Cons
14/10/1999	Gareth Rees	Namibia	9
15/07/2000	Jared Barker	Japan	8
24/06/2006	James Pritchard	Barbados	7
02/06/2007	James Pritchard	USA	7
11/05/1991	Mark Wyatt	Japan	7

MOST PENALTIES IN A MATCH

BY A PLAYER

Date	Player	Opponent	Pens
25/05/1991	Mark Wyatt	Scotland	8
22/08/1998	Gareth Rees	Argentina	7

MOST DROP GOALS IN A MATCH

BY A PLAYER

Date	Player	Opponent	DGs
04/07/2001	Bobby Ross	Fiji	2
24/05/1997	Bobby Ross	Hong Kong	2

MOST CAPPED PLAYERS

Name	Caps
Al Charron	76
Winston Stanley	66
Scott Stewart	64
Rod Snow	62
Bobby Ross	58

LEADING TRY SCORERS

Name	Tries
Winston Stanley	24
Morgan Williams	13
Pat Palmer	10
Kyle Nichols	10
James Pritchard	10

LEADING CONVERSIONS SCORERS

Name	Cons
James Pritchard	53
Bobby Ross	52
Gareth Rees	51
Jared Barker	24
Mark Wyatt	24

LEADING PENALTY SCORERS

Name	Pens
Gareth Rees	110
Bobby Ross	84
Mark Wyatt	64
Jared Barker	55
James Pritchard	49

LEADING DROP GOAL SCORERS

Name	DGs
Bobby Ross	10
Gareth Rees	9
Mark Wyatt	5

LEADING POINTS SCORERS

Name	Pts.
Gareth Rees	491
Bobby Ross	421
James Pritchard	303
Mark Wyatt	263
Jared Barker	226

CANADA INTERNATIONAL PLAYERS
UP TO 29TH OCTOBER 2010

Note: Years given for International Championship matches are for second half of season; eg 1972 means season 1971–72. Years for all other matches refer to the actual year of the match.

AD Abrams 2003 *US, NZ, Tg*, 2004 *US, J, EngA, US, F, It, E*, 2005 *US, J, W, EngA, US, Ar, F, R*, 2006 *S, E, US, It*
MJ Alder 1976 *Bb*
P Aldous 1971 *W*
AS Arthurs 1988 *US*
M Ashton 1971 *W*
F Asselin 1999 *Fj*, 2000 *Tg, US, SA*, 2001 *Ur, Ar, Fj*, 2002 *S, US, US, Ur, Ur, CHL, W, F*
O Atkinson 2005 *J, Ar*, 2006 *E, US, It*
S Ault 2006 *W, It*, 2008 *US, Pt*, 2009 *Geo, US, US*
JC Bain 1932 *J*
RG Banks 1999 *J, Fj, Sa, US, Tg, W, E, F, Nm*, 2000 *US, SA, I, J, It*, 2001 *US, Ur, Ar, E, Fj, J*, 2002 *S, US, US, Ur, CHL, Ur, CHL, W, F*, 2003 *E, US, M, M, Ur, NZ, It*
S Barber 1973 *W*, 1976 *Bb*
M Barbieri 2006 *E, US*
B Barker 1966 *BI*, 1971 *W*
J Barker 2000 *Tg, J, It*, 2002 *S, US, US, Ur, CHL, Ur, CHL, W*, 2003 *US, NZ, It*, 2004 *US, J, F, It*
T Bauer 1977 *US, E*, 1978 *US, F*, 1979 *US*
D Baugh 1998 *J, HK, US, HK, J, Ur, Ar*, 1999 *J, Fj, Sa, US, Tg, W, E, F, Fj, Nm*, 2000 *US, SA, I, It*, 2001 *E, E*, 2002 *S, US, Ur, CHL*
A Bianco 1966 *BI*
AJ Bibby 1979 *US, F*, 1980 *W, US, NZ*, 1981 *US, Ar*
R Bice 1996 *US, A*, 1997 *US, J, HK, US, W, I*, 1998 *US, US, HK, J, Ur, US, Ar*, 1999 *J, Fj, Sa, US, Tg, W, F*
P Bickerton 2004 *US, J*
D Biddle 2006 *S, E, Bar*, 2007 *M, W, Fj, A*
JM Billingsley 1974 *Tg*, 1977 *US*, 1978 *F*, 1979 *US*, 1980 *W*, 1983 *US, It, It*, 1984 *US*
WG Bjarneson 1962 *Bb*
TJH Blackwell 1973 *W*
N Blevins 2009 *J, J*
B Bonenberg 1983 *US, It, It*
J Boone 1932 *J, J*
T Bourne 1967 *E*
R Breen 1986 *US*, 1987 *W*, 1990 *US*, 1991 *J, S, US, R*, 1993 *E, US*
R Breen 1983 *E*, 1987 *US*
R Brewer 1967 *E*
STT Brown 1989 *I, US*
N Browne 1973 *W*, 1974 *Tg*
T Browne 1964 *Fj*
S Bryan 1996 *Ur, US, Ar*, 1997 *HK, J, US, W*, 1998 *HK, J, US, Ar*, 1999 *Fj, Sa, US, Tg, W, E, F, Fj, Nm*
T Bunyan 1964 *Fj*
M Burak 2004 *US, J, EngA, US, F, It, E*, 2005 *EngA, US, Ar, F, R*, 2006 *US, Bar, W*, 2007 *IrA, M, NZ, Pt, W, Fj, J, A*, 2008 *I, W, S*, 2009 *I, W, Geo, IrA, US, US*
C Burford 1970 *Fj*
D Burgess 1962 *Bb, W23*, 1964 *Fj*
D Burleigh 2001 *Ur, Ar, E, E*
JB Burnham 1966 *BI*, 1967 *E*, 1970 *Fj*, 1971 *W*
H Buydens 2006 *E*, 2008 *US*
H Calder 1964 *Fj*
GE Cameron 1932 *J*
JWD Cannon 2001 *US, Ar, E, E, Fj, J*, 2002 *S, US, Ur, CHL, Ur, CHL, W, F*, 2003 *E, M, M, Ur, US, Ar, NZ, It*, 2004 *US, F, It, E*, 2005 *W, EngA, US, F*
R Card 1996 *US, A, Ur, US, Ar*, 1997 *US, J, HK*
ME Cardinal 1986 *US*, 1987 *US, Tg, I, US*, 1991 *S*, 1993 *A*, 1994 *US, F, E, F*, 1995 *S, Fj, NZ, R, SA*, 1996 *US, US, HK, J, A, HK, J*, 1997 *US, US, W, I*, 1998 *US, HK*, 1999 *Fj, US, W, E, Fj, Nm*
LAG Carlson 2002 *Ur, W*, 2003 *E*
A Carpenter 2005 *US, J, EngA, US, Ar, F, R*, 2006 *S, E, US, W, It*, 2007 *IrA, M, US, NZ, Pt, W, Fj, J, A*, 2008 *US, Pt, I, W, S*, 2009 *I, W, Geo, IrA, ArJ, US, J, J, Rus*, 2010 *Ur, F, E*
NS Carr 1985 *A, A*
DJ Carson 1980 *W, US, NZ*, 1981 *US, Ar*, 1982 *J, E, US*, 1983 *It, It*
SFB Carson 1977 *E*
MP Chambers 1962 *Bb, W23*, 1964 *Fj*, 1966 *BI*
AJ Charron 1990 *Ar, US, Ar*, 1991 *J, S, Fj, F, NZ*, 1992 *US*, 1993 *E, E, US, A, W*, 1994 *US, F, W*, 1995 *Fj, NZ, R, A, SA, US*, 1996 *US, US, A, HK, J, Ur, US, Ar*, 1997 *US, J, HK, HK, J, US, W, I*, 1998 *US, HK, J, Ur, US, Ar*, 1999 *Fj, Sa, US, Tg, W, E, F, Fj, Nm*, 2000 *Tg, US, SA, Sa, Fj, J, It*, 2001 *Ur, Ar, E, E*, 2002 *S, US, US, Ur, CHL, Ur, CHL, F*, 2003 *W, It, Tg*
L Chung 1978 *F*
N Clapinson 1995 *US*, 1996 *US*
RM Clark 1962 *Bb*
D Clarke 1996 *A*
ME Clarkin 1985 *A, A*
B Collins 2004 *US, J*
W Collins 1977 *US, E*
GG Cooke 2000 *Tg, US*, 2001 *Fj, J*, 2003 *E, US, M, M, Ur, US, Ar, W, NZ, Tg*, 2004 *EngA, US, It, E*, 2005 *US, J, W, Ar, F, R*, 2006 *US*
I Cooper 1993 *W*
JA Cordle 1998 *HK, J*, 1999 *J, Fj, Sa*, 2001 *J*
GER Cox 1932 *J*
S Creagh 1988 *US*
J Cudmore 2002 *US, CHL, W, F*, 2003 *E, US, W, NZ, It, Tg*, 2004 *US, F, It, E*, 2005 *W, F*, 2006 *US*, 2007 *Pt, W, Fj*
L Cudmore 2008 *US*
C Culpan 2006 *E*, 2007 *IrA, M, US, NZ, Pt, W, Fj, J*
TJ Cummings 1964 *Fj*, 1966 *BI*, 1973 *W*
Z Cvitak 1983 *E*
N Dala 2007 *IrA, US*, 2008 *US*, 2009 *I, W, Geo, IrA, ArJ, US, US, J, J*, 2010 *Ur, E*
MJW Dandy 1977 *E, E*
M Danskin 2001 *J*, 2004 *EngA, F*
D Daypuck 2004 *EngA, F, It, E*, 2005 *US, J, W, EngA, Ar, F, R*, 2006 *S, US, US, W, It*, 2007 *IrA, M, A*
H de Goede 1976 *Bb*, 1977 *US, E, E*, 1978 *US*, 1979 *US, F*, 1980 *W, US, NZ*, 1981 *US*, 1982 *J, J, E, US*, 1984 *US*, 1985 *US*, 1986 *J, US*, 1987 *US, Tg, I, W*
HW de Goede 1974 *Tg*
F Deacy 1973 *W*
J Delaney 1983 *E*
P Densmore 2005 *EngA*
JD Devlin 1985 *US*, 1986 *US*
M di Girolamo 2001 *Ur, Ar*, 2002 *US, Ur, CHL, Ur, W, F*, 2003 *US, M, M, Ur, W, NZ, It, Tg*, 2004 *EngA, US, F, It, E*
GA Dixon 2000 *US, SA, I, Sa, Fj, J, It*, 2001 *US, Ar, E, E*
D Docherty 1973 *W*
T Dolezel 2009 *Rus*, 2010 *Ur*
WJ Donaldson 1978 *F*, 1979 *US, F*, 1980 *W, US, NZ*, 1981 *US*, 1982 *E, US*, 1983 *US, It, It*, 1984 *US*

A Douglas 1974 *Tg*
JT Douglas 2003 *M, M, Ur, US, Ar, NZ, It*, 2004 *US, F*
A du Temple 1932 *J, J*
S Duke 2008 *S*, 2009 *W, Geo, IrA, ArJ, J, J, Rus*
G Dukelow 1980 *W, US, NZ*, 1981 *US*, 1982 *J, J, E, US*, 1983 *US, It, It, E*, 1984 *US*, 1990 *US*
PJ Dunkley 1998 *J, HK, US, HK, J, US, Ar*, 1999 *J, Fj, Sa, US, Tg, E, F, Fj, Nm*, 2000 *Tg, SA, I, Sa, Fj*, 2001 *US, Ar, E, Fj, J*, 2002 *S, US, US, Ur, CHL, W, F*, 2003 *M, M, Ur, Ar*, 2005 *W*
C Dunning 2005 *EngA, US, Ar, F, R*
B Ebl 1995 *NZ*, 1998 *J, HK*
DC Eburne 1977 *US, E, E*
MA Eckardt 1974 *Tg*, 1977 *US, E, E*, 1978 *US*
IJ Edwards 1967 *E*
B Ellison 1964 *Fj*
G Ellwand 1973 *W*
GD Ennis 1986 *J, US*, 1987 *US, Tg, I, W*, 1988 *US*, 1989 *I, US*, 1990 *Ar, US, Ar*, 1991 *J, S, US, Fj, R, F, NZ*, 1993 *E, E*, 1994 *US, W*, 1995 *Fj, NZ, R, A, SA*, 1998 *J, HK, US, US*
B Erichsen 2009 *Rus*, 2010 *Ur, F, E*
EA Evans 1986 *US*, 1987 *US, Tg, I, US*, 1989 *I, US*, 1990 *Ar, Ar*, 1991 *J, S, US, Fj, R, F, NZ*, 1992 *US, E*, 1993 *E, E*, 1994 *US, F, W, E, F*, 1995 *S, Ur, Ar, Fj, NZ, R, A, SA*, 1996 *J, HK, J*, 1997 *US, J, HK, J, US, W, I*, 1998 *J, HK, US, US, US, Ar*
M Evans 2008 *I, W, S*, 2009 *W, Geo, IrA, ArJ, US, US, J, Rus*, 2010 *Ur, F, E*
I Exner 2005 *EngA, US*
A Fagan 2008 *Pt*
EG Fairhurst 2001 *US, Ar*, 2002 *US, Ur, CHL, Ur, CHL, W, F*, 2003 *E, M, M, US, NZ, Tg*, 2004 *US, J, EngA, US, F, It, E*, 2005 *US, W, EngA, US, F*, 2006 *S, E, US, Bar, US, W, It*, 2007 *IrA, M, US, NZ, Pt, W, A*, 2008 *US, I, W, S*, 2009 *I, W, Geo, IrA, ArJ, US, US*, 2010 *Ur*
SC Fauth 2000 *Tg, US, SA, I, Sa, Fj, J, It*, 2001 *US, Ar, E, E, Fj, J*, 2002 *S, US, US, Ur, CHL, CHL, W, F*, 2003 *US, M, Ur, US, Ar, NZ, Tg*
M Felix 1985 *A, A*, 1996 *Ur, US*
P Fleck 2004 *US, J, It, E*, 2005 *US, W*
I Fleming 1976 *Bb*
AC Forbes 1932 *J, J*
F Forster 1983 *US, It, It*
AE Foster 1970 *Fj*, 1976 *Bb*, 1977 *US, E, E*
C Fowler 1988 *US*, 1990 *US*
TE Fraine 1967 *E*
RP Frame 1986 *J*, 1987 *US, Tg, I, W, US*
S Franklin 2007 *IrA, M, US, NZ, J*, 2008 *US, S*, 2009 *I*
G Fraser 1983 *E*
P Frize 1962 *Bb, W23*
GW Fumano 1967 *E*, 1970 *Fj*
QA Fyffe 2003 *E, US, NZ, It, Tg*, 2004 *US, J, EngA, US, F, It*, 2005 *US, J, W, Ar*
F Gainer 2004 *US, J, EngA, US, F, It, E*, 2005 *J, W, EngA, US, F, R*, 2006 *W, It*
A Godziek 1982 *J, E, US*, 1983 *US, It, It, E*, 1984 *US*
G Gonis 1978 *US*
GG Gonis 1977 *US, E, E*
I Gordon 1991 *S*, 1992 *US, E*, 1993 *US, A, W*, 1994 *F, W, E, F*, 1995 *S, R, SA, US*, 1996 *US, HK, J, A, HK*, 1997 *US, J, HK*, 1998 *J, HK, US, J, US, Ar*
JD Graf 1989 *I, US*, 1990 *Ar*, 1991 *S, R*, 1992 *US, E*, 1993 *E, E, US, A*, 1994 *US, F, W, E, F*, 1995 *S, Ur, Ar, Fj, NZ, R, A, SA, US*, 1996 *US, HK, J, A, HK, J*, 1997 *US, J, HK, HK, US, W, I*, 1998 *J, HK, US, US, HK, J, Ur, US, Ar*, 1999 *J, Fj, Sa, US, Tg, F, Nm*
W Granleese 1962 *W23*
G Grant 1977 *E, E*, 1978 *US*, 1979 *US, F*, 1980 *W*
I Grant 1983 *US, It, It, E*
PR Grantham 1962 *Bb, W23*, 1966 *BI*
SD Gray 1984 *US*, 1987 *US, W, US*, 1989 *I*, 1990 *Ar, US, Ar*, 1991 *J, S, Fj, F, NZ*, 1992 *US, E*, 1993 *E, E, US, A, W*, 1994 *US, F, W, E, F*, 1995 *S, Ar, Fj, NZ, R, A, SA, US*, 1996 *US, US, HK, J, A, HK, J, US, Ar*, 1997 *US, J, HK, J, US*
GR Greig 1973 *W*
J Greig 1977 *US, E*
JR Grieg 1978 *US*, 1979 *US, F*, 1980 *W, US, NZ*, 1981 *Ar*
J Grout 1995 *Ur*
G Gudmundseth 1973 *W*
N Hadley 1987 *US*, 1989 *I, US*, 1990 *Ar*, 1991 *S, US, Fj, R, F, NZ*, 1992 *US, E*, 1993 *E*, 1994 *E, F*
J Haley 1996 *Ur*
J Hall 1996 *US*, 1997 *HK*, 1998 *J, HK, J, US, Ar*
R Hamilton 2010 *Ur, E*
WT Handson 1985 *A, A, US*, 1986 *J, US*, 1987 *US, Tg, I, W*
JP Hawthorn 1982 *J, J, E*, 1983 *US, It, It*
A Healy 1996 *HK, J, HK, J, Ur, US, Ar*, 1997 *US, HK, HK, I*, 1998 *HK, J, Ur*, 1999 *J*
AR Heaman 1988 *US*
C Hearn 2008 *I, W, S*, 2009 *I, W, Geo, IrA, US, US, J, J*, 2010 *Ur, F, E*
B Henderson 2005 *J, F, R*
S Hendry 1996 *Ur, US, Ar*
G Henrikson 1971 *W*
L Hillier 1973 *W*
RE Hindson 1973 *W*, 1976 *Bb*, 1977 *US, E, E*, 1978 *US, F*, 1979 *US, F*, 1980 *W, US, NZ*, 1981 *US, Ar*, 1982 *J, J, E, US*, 1983 *US, It, It*, 1984 *US*, 1985 *A, A, US*, 1986 *J*, 1987 *US, I, W*, 1990 *Ar*
RE Hindson 1974 *Tg*
G Hirayama 1977 *E, E*, 1978 *US*, 1979 *US, F*, 1980 *W, US, NZ*, 1981 *US*, 1982 *J, E, US*
N Hirayama 2007 *M*, 2008 *Pt, S*, 2009 *J, J, Rus*
M Holmes 1987 *US*
T Hotson 2008 *US, Pt, I, W, S*, 2009 *I, W, Geo, IrA, ArJ, US, US, J, J, Rus*, 2010 *Ur, E*
P Howlett 1974 *Tg*
BM Hunnings 1932 *J, J*
E Hunt 1966 *BI*, 1967 *E*
S Hunter 2005 *R*
J Hutchinson 1993 *E, A, W*, 1995 *S, Ar, Fj, A, SA, US*, 1996 *US, US, HK, J, A, HK, J, Ur, US, Ar*, 1997 *US, J, HK, HK, J, US, W, I*, 1998 *J, HK, US, US, HK, J, Ur, US, Ar*, 1999 *J, Fj, Sa, US, Tg, W, E, F, Fj, Nm*, 2000 *US, Sa, Fj, J*
I Hyde-Lay 1986 *J*, 1987 *US*, 1988 *US*
M Irvine 2000 *Tg, SA, I, Sa, Fj, J*, 2001 *US, Ar*
DC Jackart 1991 *J, S, US, Fj, R, F*, 1992 *US, E*, 1993 *E, E, US, A, W*, 1994 *US, F, W, E, F*, 1995 *S, Ar, Fj*
J Jackson 2003 *Ur, US, Ar, W, It, Tg*, 2004 *EngA, US, It, E*, 2005 *W, US, Ar, R*, 2006 *S*, 2007 *IrA, M, US, NZ, J*, 2008 *I, W, S*, 2009 *J*
RO Jackson 1970 *Fj*, 1971 *W*
MB James 1994 *US, F, W, E, F*, 1995 *S, Ur, Ar, Fj, NZ, R, A, US*, 1996 *US, US, HK, J, A, HK, J*, 1997 *J, US, W, I*, 1998 *US, US, Ur, US, Ar*, 1999 *Sa, W, E, F, Fj, Nm*, 2000 *It*, 2002 *S, US, US, Ur, CHL, W, F*, 2003 *M, M, Ur, US, Ar, W, Tg*, 2005 *F*, 2006 *US*, 2007 *Pt, W, Fj, J, A*
G Jennings 1981 *Ar*, 1983 *US, It, It, E*
O Johnson 1970 *Fj*
G Johnston 1978 *F*
RR Johnstone 2001 *Ur, Fj, J*, 2002 *CHL, Ur, CHL*, 2003 *E*
C Jones 1983 *E*, 1987 *US*
EL Jones 1982 *J*, 1983 *US*
TK Kariya 1967 *E*, 1970 *Fj*, 1971 *W*
A Kennedy 1985 *A, A*
I Kennedy 1993 *A, W*
ED Kettleson 1985 *US*
B Keys 2008 *US, Pt, I, W, S*, 2009 *Geo, ArJ, US, J*
MMG King 2002 *US, Ur*, 2003 *M, US, Ar, NZ*, 2005 *US, J, W, EngA, US, Ar*
A Kingham 1974 *Tg*
A Kleeberger 2005 *F, R*, 2006 *S, E, US, Bar, It*, 2007 *IrA, M, US, NZ, Pt, J*, 2008 *US, Pt, I, W, S*, 2009 *I, W, Geo, IrA, ArJ, US, US, J, J, Rus*, 2010 *Ur, F, E*
ERP Knaggs 2000 *Tg, US, SA, I, Sa, Fj, J*, 2001 *US, Ur, Ar, E, E, Fj, J*, 2002 *S*, 2003 *E, Ur, Ar, NZ*
JD Knauer 1992 *E*, 1993 *E, E, US, W*
MJ Kokan 1984 *US*, 1985 *US*
P Kyle 1984 *US*
A La Carte 2004 *US, J*
M Langley 2004 *EngA*, 2005 *Ar*
MJ Lawson 2002 *US, Ur, CHL, Ur, CHL, F*, 2003 *E, US, M, M, Ur, US, Ar, W, It, Tg*, 2004 *F, It, E*, 2005 *US, J, F, R*, 2006 *US, W*
P le Blanc 1994 *F*, 1995 *Ur, Fj, NZ*
CE le Fevre 1976 *Bb*
J Lecky 1962 *Bb, W23*
JL Lecky 1982 *J, US*, 1983 *US, It, It*, 1984 *US*, 1985 *A, US*, 1986 *J, US*, 1987 *I, W, US*, 1991 *J, S, Fj, R*
GB Legh 1973 *W*, 1974 *Tg*, 1976 *Bb*
LSF Leroy 1932 *J*
D Lillywhite 1964 *Fj*

J Lorenz 1964 *Fj*, 1966 *BI*, 1970 *Fj*, 1971 *W*
DC Lougheed 1990 *Ar*, 1991 *J*, *US*, 1992 *US*, *E*, 1993 *E*, *E*, *US*, 1994 *F*, *W*, *E*, *F*, 1995 *Fj*, *NZ*, *R*, *A*, *SA*, 1996 *A*, *HK*, 1997 *J*, *W*, *I*, 1998 *US*, *Ar*, 1999 *US*, *Tg*, *W*, *E*, *F*, *Fj*, *Nm*, 2003 *W*, *It*
J Loveday 1993 *E*, *E*, *US*, *A*, 1996 *HK*, *J*, 1998 *J*, *Ur*, 1999 *Sa*, *US*
B Luke 2004 *US*, *J*
M Luke 1974 *Tg*, 1976 *Bb*, 1977 *US*, *E*, *E*, 1978 *US*, *F*, 1979 *US*, *F*, 1980 *W*, *US*, *NZ*, 1981 *US*, 1982 *J*, *US*
S Lytton 1995 *Ur*, *Ar*, *US*, 1996 *US*, *HK*, *J*, *J*, *US*, *Ar*
G MacDonald 1970 *Fj*
GDT MacDonald 1998 *HK*
P Mack 2009 *I*, *W*, *Geo*, *IrA*, *US*, *US*, *J*, *J*, *Rus*
I MacKay 1993 *A*, *W*
MacKenzie 2008 *Pt*, *I*, 2010 *Ur*, *F*, *E*
GI MacKinnon 1985 *US*, 1986 *J*, 1988 *US*, 1989 *I*, *US*, 1990 *Ar*, *Ar*, 1991 *J*, *S*, *Fj*, *R*, *F*, *NZ*, 1992 *US*, *E*, 1993 *E*, 1994 *US*, *F*, *W*, *E*, *F*, 1995 *S*, *Ur*, *Ar*, *Fj*, *NZ*, *A*, *SA*
S MacKinnon 1992 *US*, 1995 *Ur*, *Ar*, *Fj*
C MacLachlan 1981 *Ar*, 1982 *J*, *E*
P Maclean 1983 *US*, *It*, *It*, *E*
I Macmillan 1981 *Ar*, 1982 *J*, *J*, *E*, *US*
M MacSween 2009 *Rus*
B Major 2001 *Fj*, *J*
D Major 1999 *E*, *Fj*, *Nm*, 2000 *Tg*, *US*, *SA*, *I*, *Fj*, 2001 *Ur*, *E*, *E*
A Marshall 1997 *J*, 1998 *Ur*
J Marshall 2008 *S*, 2010 *Ur*, *E*
P Mason 1974 *Tg*
B McCarthy 1996 *US*, *Ar*, 1998 *J*, *HK*, *J*
J McDonald 1974 *Tg*
RN McDonald 1966 *BI*, 1967 *E*, 1970 *Fj*
AG McGann 1985 *A*, *A*
R McGeein 1973 *W*
RI McInnes 1979 *F*, 1980 *NZ*, 1981 *US*, *Ar*, 1982 *J*, *J*, *E*, *US*, 1983 *US*, *It*, *It*, 1984 *US*, 1985 *US*
B McKee 1962 *Bb*, *W23*
B Mckee 1966 *BI*, 1970 *Fj*
S McKeen 2004 *US*, *J*, *EngA*, *US*, *F*, *It*, *E*, 2005 *US*, *J*, *W*, *EngA*, *F*, *R*, 2006 *S*, *US*, *US*, *W*, *It*, 2007 *IrA*, *US*, *NZ*, 2009 *ArJ*
JR McKellar 1985 *A*, *A*, 1986 *J*, 1987 *W*
JH McKenna 1967 *E*
C McKenzie 1992 *US*, *E*, 1993 *E*, *US*, *A*, *W*, 1994 *US*, *F*, *W*, *E*, *F*, 1995 *S*, *Ur*, *Ar*, *Fj*, *NZ*, *R*, *SA*, 1996 *US*, *HK*, *J*, *J*, 1997 *J*, *HK*, *I*
SG McTavish 1970 *Fj*, 1971 *W*, 1976 *Bb*, 1977 *US*, *E*, *E*, 1978 *US*, *F*, 1979 *US*, *F*, 1980 *W*, *US*, 1981 *US*, *Ar*, 1982 *J*, *J*, *E*, *US*, 1985 *US*, 1987 *US*, *Tg*, *I*
R McWhinney 2005 *F*, *R*
J Mensah-Coker 2006 *S*, *E*, *US*, *Bar*, *US*, *W*, *It*, 2007 *US*, *NZ*, *Pt*, *J*, *A*, 2008 *US*, *I*, *W*, *S*, 2009 *IrA*, *US*, *US*, *J*, *J*, *Rus*, 2010 *Ur*, *F*, *E*
C Michaluk 1995 *SA*, 1996 *US*, *J*, 1997 *US*, *HK*
N Milau 2000 *US*, *J*
DRW Milne 1966 *BI*, 1967 *E*
AB Mitchell 1932 *J*, *J*
P Monaghan 1982 *J*
A Monro 2006 *E*, *US*, *Bar*, *US*, *W*, *It*, 2007 *M*, *W*, *A*, 2008 *US*, *Pt*, *I*, *W*, 2009 *I*, *W*, *Geo*, *IrA*, *ArJ*, *US*, *US*, *J*, *J*, *Rus*, 2010 *Ur*, *F*
D Moonlight 2003 *E*, 2004 *EngA*, *E*, 2005 *US*
J Moonlight 2009 *Geo*, *IrA*
DL Moore 1962 *Bb*, *W23*
K Morgan 1997 *HK*, *HK*, *J*, *W*
VJP Moroney 1962 *Bb*
B Mosychuk 1996 *Ur*, 1997 *J*
J Moyes 1981 *Ar*, 1982 *J*, *J*, *E*, *US*
PT Murphy 2000 *Tg*, *US*, *SA*, *I*, *Sa*, *Fj*, *J*, 2001 *Fj*, *J*, 2002 *S*, *US*, *US*, *Ur*, *CHL*, *W*, *F*, 2003 *US*, *M*, *M*, 2004 *F*
WA Murray 1932 *J*
K Myhre 1970 *Fj*
J Newton 1962 *W23*
GN Niblo 1932 *J*, *J*
K Nichols 1996 *Ur*, 1998 *J*, *HK*, *US*, *US*, *Ur*, 1999 *J*, *Fj*, *Sa*, *US*, *Tg*, *Fj*, *Nm*, 2000 *Tg*, *US*, *SA*, *I*, *Sa*, *Fj*, *J*, *It*, 2001 *Ur*, *E*, *Fj*, *J*, 2002 *S*
D Nikas 1995 *Ur*
S O'Leary 2004 *US*, *J*, *EngA*, *E*, 2005 *J*
C O'Toole 2009 *I*, *ArJ*, *US*, *J*, *J*, *Rus*, 2010 *Ur*, *F*, *E*
S Pacey 2005 *W*
C Pack 2006 *S*, *US*
J Pagano 1997 *I*, 1998 *J*, *HK*, *US*, *HK*, *J*, *US*, 1999 *J*, *Fj*, *Nm*
DV Pahl 1971 *W*
P Palmer 1983 *E*, 1984 *US*, 1985 *A*, 1986 *J*, *US*, 1987 *Tg*, *I*, *W*, 1988 *US*, 1990 *Ar*, *US*, 1991 *J*, *US*, *Fj*, *R*, *F*, 1992 *US*
K Parfrey 2005 *J*
A Pasutto 2004 *US*, *J*
L Patterson 1964 *Fj*
J Pavey 1964 *Fj*
K Peace 1978 *F*, 1979 *US*, *F*, 1980 *W*, *US*
J Penaluna 1996 *Ur*
DN Penney 1995 *US*, 1996 *US*, *A*, *US*, *Ar*, 1997 *HK*, 1999 *E*
JM Phelan 1980 *NZ*, 1981 *Ar*, 1982 *J*, *J*, 1985 *A*, *A*
M Phinney 2006 *S*, *E*
EC Pinkham 1932 *J*
C Plater 2003 *E*
D Pletch 2004 *US*, *J*, *EngA*, *It*, *E*, 2005 *US*, *J*, *W*, *EngA*, 2006 *S*, *E*, *US*, *Bar*, *US*, *W*, *It*, 2007 *IrA*, *M*, *US*, *NZ*, *Pt*, *W*, *Fj*, *J*, *A*, 2009 *IrA*, *ArJ*, *US*, *US*, *J*, *J*, *Rus*
M Pletch 2005 *Ar*, 2006 *S*, *E*, *US*, *Bar*, *W*, *It*, 2007 *IrA*, *M*, *US*, *NZ*, *Pt*, *W*, *J*, *A*, 2008 *US*, *Pt*, *I*, *W*, *S*, 2009 *W*, *Geo*, *IrA*, *ArJ*, *US*, *US*, *J*, *Rus*
C Pollard 1964 *Fj*
JF Porter 1964 *Fj*
J Pritchard 2003 *M*, *M*, *Ur*, *US*, *Ar*, *W*, *Tg*, 2006 *S*, *US*, *Bar*, *US*, *W*, 2007 *IrA*, *M*, *US*, *NZ*, *Pt*, *W*, *Fj*, *J*, *A*, 2008 *US*, *Pt*, *I*, *W*, *S*, 2009 *I*, *W*, *Geo*, *IrA*, *ArJ*, *US*, *US*, *J*, *J*, *Rus*, 2010 *Ur*, *E*
G Puil 1962 *Bb*, *W23*
M Pyke 2004 *US*, *J*, *US*, *It*, 2005 *US*, *F*, *R*, 2006 *S*, *E*, *US*, *Bar*, *US*, *W*, *It*, 2007 *IrA*, *M*, *US*, *NZ*, *Pt*, *W*, *Fj*, *J*, *A*, 2008 *US*
DLJ Quigley 1976 *Bb*, 1979 *F*
RE Radu 1985 *A*, 1986 *US*, 1987 *US*, *Tg*, *I*, *US*, 1988 *US*, 1989 *I*, *US*, 1990 *Ar*, *Ar*, 1991 *US*
D Ramsey 2005 *US*
GL Rees 1986 *US*, 1987 *US*, *Tg*, *I*, *W*, *US*, 1989 *I*, *US*, 1990 *Ar*, *Ar*, 1991 *J*, *S*, *US*, *Fj*, *R*, *F*, *NZ*, 1992 *US*, *E*, 1993 *E*, *E*, *US*, *W*, 1994 *US*, *F*, *W*, *E*, *F*, 1995 *S*, *Fj*, *NZ*, *R*, *A*, *SA*, 1996 *HK*, *J*, 1997 *US*, *J*, *HK*, *J*, *US*, *W*, *I*, 1998 *US*, *US*, *Ur*, *US*, *Ar*, 1999 *Sa*, *Tg*, *W*, *E*, *F*, *Fj*, *Nm*
J Reid 2003 *M*, *US*, *Ar*, *NZ*, *Tg*
G Relph 1974 *Tg*
S Richmond 2004 *EngA*, *US*, *F*, *It*, *E*, 2005 *US*, *W*, *EngA*, *US*
PD Riordan 2003 *E*, 2004 *US*, *J*, *EngA*, *US*, 2006 *S*, *E*, *US*, *Bar*, *US*, *W*, *It*, 2007 *IrA*, *M*, *US*, *NZ*, *Pt*, *W*, *Fj*, *J*, *A*, 2008 *US*, *Pt*, *I*, *W*, 2009 *I*, *W*, *Geo*, *IrA*, *ArJ*, *US*, *US*, *J*, *J*, *Rus*, 2010 *Ur*, *F*, *E*
JR Robertsen 1985 *A*, *A*, *US*, 1986 *US*, 1987 *Tg*, *US*, 1989 *I*, *US*, 1990 *Ar*, *US*, *Ar*, 1991 *Fj*, *F*
C Robertson 1997 *HK*, 1998 *US*, *US*, *HK*, *J*, *Ur*, 2001 *Ur*
AK Robinson 1998 *HK*
G Robinson 1966 *BI*
R Robson 1998 *HK*, *US*, 1999 *J*, *Tg*
S Rodgers 2005 *US*
RP Ross 1989 *I*, *US*, 1990 *US*, 1995 *Ar*, *NZ*, 1996 *US*, *US*, *HK*, *J*, *A*, *HK*, *J*, *Ur*, *US*, *Ar*, 1997 *US*, *J*, *HK*, *HK*, *J*, *US*, *W*, 1998 *J*, *HK*, *US*, *US*, *HK*, *J*, *Ur*, *US*, 1999 *J*, *Fj*, *Sa*, *US*, *W*, *E*, *F*, *Nm*, 2001 *Ur*, *E*, *E*, *Fj*, *J*, 2002 *S*, *US*, *US*, *Ur*, *CHL*, *Ur*, *CHL*, *F*, 2003 *E*, *US*, *M*, *Ur*, *Ar*, *W*, *Tg*
JG Rowland 1932 *J*, *J*
G Rowlands 1995 *Ar*, *NZ*, *A*, *US*, 1996 *US*, *US*
GC Rowles 1964 *Fj*
RJ Russell 1979 *US*, 1983 *E*, 1985 *A*, *A*
JB Ryan 1966 *BI*, 1967 *E*
IH Saundry 1932 *J*, *J*
MD Schiefler 1981 *US*, *Ar*, 1982 *J*, *E*, *US*, 1983 *US*, 1984 *US*
MD Schielfer 1980 *US*, *NZ*
M Schmid 1996 *Ur*, *US*, *Ar*, 1997 *US*, *J*, *US*, *W*, *I*, 1998 *US*, *HK*, *J*, *Ur*, *Ar*, 1999 *Sa*, *US*, *W*, *E*, *F*, *Fj*, *Nm*, 2001 *US*, *Ur*, *E*, *E*
M Scholz 2009 *Rus*
T Scott 1976 *Bb*
R Scurfield 1964 *Fj*
S Selkirk 1932 *J*
JD Shaw 1978 *F*
CJ Shergold 1980 *US*, *NZ*, 1981 *US*
DM Shick 1970 *Fj*, 1971 *W*
J Sinclair 2008 *Pt*, *I*, *W*, *S*, 2009 *I*, *IrA*, *ArJ*, *US*, *US*, *J*, *J*, *Rus*
DC Sinnott 1979 *F*, 1981 *US*, *Ar*
FG Skillings 1932 *J*, *J*
DM Slater 1971 *W*

C Smith 1995 *Ur, US*, 1996 *HK, J, Ur, US, Ar*, 1997 *US*, 1998 *J, HK, US, HK, Ur*, 1999 *J, Fj, Sa, US, Tg, W, E, F*
RJ Smith 2003 *E, M, M, Ur, US, Ar, W, NZ, Tg*, 2004 *US, J, EngA, US, F, It, E*, 2005 *US, J, W, EngA, US, Ar, F, R*, 2006 *S, Bar, US, W, It*, 2007 *IrA, M, US, NZ, Pt, W, Fj, J*, 2008 *US, Pt, I, W, S*, 2009 *I, W, US, US*, 2010 *E*
C Smythe 1997 *J, HK*
RGA Snow 1995 *Ar, NZ, R, A, SA, US*, 1996 *HK, J, A, HK, J*, 1997 *US, HK, J, W, I*, 1998 *US, US, US, Ar*, 1999 *J, Fj, Sa, US, W, E, F, Fj, Nm*, 2000 *I, J, It*, 2001 *US, Ar, E, E, Fj, J*, 2002 *S, US, US, Ur, CHL, Ur, CHL, W, F*, 2003 *Ur, US, Ar, W, NZ, It, Tg*, 2006 *US, Bar, US*, 2007 *Pt, W, Fj, J, A*
DA Speirs 1988 *US*, 1989 *I, US*, 1991 *Fj, NZ*
D Spicer 2004 *E*, 2005 *R*, 2006 *S, E, US, Bar, US, W*, 2007 *IrA, US, NZ, Pt, W, Fj, J*, 2008 *US*, 2009 *I, W*
WE Spofford 1981 *Ar*
W Stanley 1994 *US, F*, 1995 *S, Ur, Ar, R, A, SA, US*, 1996 *US, US, A, HK, J*, 1997 *US, J, HK, HK, US, W, I*, 1998 *US, US, HK, Ur, US, Ar*, 1999 *J, Fj, Sa, US, Tg, W, E, F, Fj, Nm*, 2000 *Tg, US, SA, I, Sa, Fj, J, It*, 2001 *E, E*, 2002 *S, US, US, Ur, CHL, Ur, CHL, W, F*, 2003 *E, US, M, M, Ur, US, Ar, W, It, Tg*
AI Stanton 1971 *W*, 1973 *W*, 1974 *Tg*
E Stapleton 1978 *US, F*
D Steen 1966 *BI*
SM Stephen 2005 *EngA, US*, 2006 *S, E, US, Bar, US, W*, 2007 *US, NZ, Pt, W, Fj, A*, 2008 *I, W, S*, 2009 *I, W*
C Stewart 1991 *S, US, Fj, R, F, NZ*, 1994 *E, F*, 1995 *S, Fj, NZ, R, A, SA*
DS Stewart 1989 *US*, 1990 *Ar*, 1991 *US, Fj, R, F, NZ*, 1992 *E*, 1993 *E, E, US, A, W*, 1994 *US, F, W, E, F*, 1995 *S, Fj, NZ, R, A, SA, US*, 1996 *US, US, A, HK, J, Ur, US, Ar*, 1997 *US, J, HK, HK, J, US, W, I*, 1998 *US, J, Ur, Ar*, 1999 *Sa, US, Tg, W, E, F, Fj, Nm*, 2000 *US, SA, I, Sa, Fj, It*, 2001 *US, Ur, Ar, E, E*
R Stewart 2005 *R*
B Stoikos 2001 *Ur*
G Stover 1962 *Bb*
R Strang 1983 *E*
C Strubin 2004 *EngA*
IC Stuart 1984 *US*, 1985 *A, A*, 1986 *J*, 1987 *US, Tg, I, W, US*, 1988 *US*, 1989 *US*, 1990 *Ar, US, Ar*, 1992 *E*, 1993 *A, W*, 1994 *US, F, W, E*
JD Stubbs 1962 *Bb, W23*
FJ Sturrock 1971 *W*
CW Suter 1932 *J*
KF Svoboda 1985 *A, A, US*, 1986 *J, US*, 1987 *W*, 1990 *Ar, US, Ar*, 1991 *J, US, R, F*, 1992 *US, E*, 1993 *E, E, US*, 1994 *F, W, F*, 1995 *Fj, A, US*
P Szabo 1989 *I, US*, 1990 *Ar, US, Ar*, 1991 *NZ*, 1993 *US, A, W*
JN Tait 1997 *US, J, HK, HK, J, US, W, I*, 1998 *US, Ur, Ar*, 1999 *J, Fj, Sa, US, Tg, W, E, F, Fj, Nm*, 2000 *Tg, US, SA, I, Sa, Fj, J, It*, 2001 *US, Ur, Ar, E, E*, 2002 *US, W, F*
L Tait 2005 *US, J, W, EngA*, 2006 *S, E, US, Bar, US, W, It*, 2007 *M, US, NZ, Pt, W, Fj, A*, 2009 *I, W*, 2010 *Ur, F, E*
WG Taylor 1978 *F*, 1979 *US, F*, 1980 *W, US, NZ*, 1981 *US, Ar*, 1983 *US, It*
J Thiel 1998 *HK, J, Ur*, 1999 *J, Fj, Sa, US, Tg, W, E, F, Fj, Nm*, 2000 *SA, I, Sa, Fj, J*, 2001 *US, Ar, E, E*, 2002 *S, US, US, Ur, CHL, Ur, W, F*, 2003 *Ur, US, Ar, W, It*, 2004 *F*, 2007 *Pt, W, Fj, J, A*, 2008 *I, W*
S Thompson 2001 *Fj, J*
W Thomson 1970 *Fj*
A Tiedemann 2009 *W, Geo, IrA, US*, 2010 *Ur, F, E*
K Tkachuk 2000 *Tg, US, SA, Sa, Fj, It*, 2001 *Fj, J*, 2002 *CHL, Ur, CHL, W, F*, 2003 *E, US, M, M, Ur, US, Ar, W, NZ, It, Tg*, 2004 *EngA, US, F, It, E*, 2005 *US, J, W, Ar, F, R*, 2006 *US, W, It*, 2007 *IrA, M, US, NZ*, 2008 *US, Pt, I, W, S*, 2009 *I, W, Geo, US, US, J, J, Rus*
H Toews 1997 *HK*, 1998 *J, HK, HK, Ur*, 1999 *Tg*, 2000 *US, Sa, J, It*, 2001 *Fj, J*
R Toews 1993 *W*, 1994 *US, F, W, E*, 1995 *S, Ur, Ar, Fj*, 1996 *US, HK, J, A*, 1997 *US, I*
J Tomlinson 1996 *A*, 2001 *Ur*
N Trenkel 2007 *A*
DM Tucker 1985 *A, A, US*, 1986 *US*, 1987 *US, W*
A Tyler 2005 *Ar*
A Tynan 1995 *Ur, Ar, US*, 1997 *J*
CJ Tynan 1987 *US*, 1988 *US*, 1990 *Ar, US, Ar*, 1991 *J, US, Fj, F, NZ*, 1992 *US*, 1993 *E, E, US, W*, 1995 *NZ*, 1996 *US, J*, 1997 *HK, J*, 1998 *US*
DN Ure 1962 *Bb, W23*
PC Vaesen 1985 *US*, 1986 *J*, 1987 *US, Tg, US*
D van Camp 2005 *J, R*, 2006 *It*, 2007 *IrA, M, US, NZ*, 2008 *Pt, W*, 2009 *I, Geo, ArJ*
R van den Brink 1986 *US*, 1987 *Tg*, 1988 *US*, 1991 *J, US, R, F, NZ*
D van der Merwe 2006 *Bar, It*, 2007 *Pt, W, Fj, J, A*, 2009 *I, W, Geo, IrA, ArJ, US, US*, 2010 *Ur, F, E*
D Van Eeuwen 1978 *F*, 1979 *US*
A van Staveren 2000 *Tg, Sa, Fj*, 2002 *US, US, Ur, CHL, Ur, CHL, W, F*, 2003 *E, US, M, M, Ur, US, W, NZ, Tg*
J Verstraten 2000 *US, SA, Fj, J*
J Vivian 1983 *E*, 1984 *US*
F Walsh 2008 *I, W, S*, 2009 *IrA, ArJ, US*
KC Walt 1976 *Bb*, 1977 *US, E, E*, 1978 *US, F*
JM Ward 1962 *W23*
M Webb 2004 *US, J, US, F, It*, 2005 *US, J, W, EngA, US, Ar, F*, 2006 *US, W, It*, 2007 *M, J, A*, 2008 *US*
M Weingart 2004 *J*, 2005 *J, EngA, US, F, R*, 2007 *Pt*
GJM Wessels 1962 *W23*
WR Wharton 1932 *J, J*
S White 2009 *J, J, Rus*, 2010 *Ur, F, E*
K Whitley 1995 *S*
C Whittaker 1993 *US, A*, 1995 *Ur*, 1996 *A*, 1997 *J*, 1998 *J, HK, US, US, HK, J, US, Ar*, 1999 *J, Fj, US*
LW Whitty 1967 *E*
DW Whyte 1974 *Tg*, 1977 *US, E, E*
RR Wickland 1966 *BI*, 1967 *E*
JP Wiley 1977 *US, E, E*, 1978 *US, F*, 1979 *US*, 1980 *W, US, NZ*, 1981 *US*
K Wilke 1971 *W*, 1973 *W*, 1976 *Bb*, 1978 *US*
K Wilkinson 1976 *Bb*, 1978 *F*, 1979 *F*
BN Williams 1962 *W23*
J Williams 2001 *US, Ur, Ar, Fj, J*
M Williams 1999 *Tg, W, E, F, Fj, Nm*, 2000 *Tg, SA, I, Sa, Fj, J, It*, 2001 *E, E, Fj, J*, 2002 *S, US, US, Ur, CHL, W, F*, 2003 *E, US, M, M, Ur, US, Ar, W, It, Tg*, 2004 *EngA, US, F*, 2005 *W, Ar, F, R*, 2006 *E, US, Bar, US, W, It*, 2007 *IrA, M, US, NZ, W, Fj, J, A*, 2008 *Pt, W, S*
M Williams 1992 *E*, 1993 *A, W*
MH Williams 1978 *US, F*, 1980 *US*
MH Williams 1982 *J*
A Wilson 2008 *US*
E Wilson 2010 *E*
PG Wilson 1932 *J, J*
RS Wilson 1962 *Bb*
K Wirachowski 1992 *E*, 1993 *US*, 1996 *US, HK, Ur, US, Ar*, 1997 *US, HK*, 2000 *It*, 2001 *Ur, E, Fj, J*, 2002 *S, CHL*, 2003 *E, US, M*
T Wish 2004 *US, J*
K Witkowski 2005 *EngA, Ar*, 2006 *E*
N Witkowski 1998 *US, J*, 2000 *Tg, US, SA, I, Sa, Fj, J, It*, 2001 *US, E, E*, 2002 *S, US, US, Ur, CHL, Ur, CHL, W, F*, 2003 *E, US, M, M, Ur, Ar, W, NZ, Tg*, 2005 *EngA, US*, 2006 *E*
AH Woller 1967 *E*
S Wood 1977 *E*
TA Woods 1984 *US*, 1986 *J, US*, 1987 *US, Tg, I, W*, 1988 *US*, 1989 *I, US*, 1990 *Ar, US*, 1991 *S, F, NZ*, 1996 *US, US*, 1997 *US, J*
D Wooldridge 2009 *I, Geo, IrA, ArJ, J, J, Rus*, 2010 *Ur, F, E*
MA Wyatt 1982 *J, J, E, US*, 1983 *US, It, It, E*, 1985 *A, A, US*, 1986 *J, US*, 1987 *Tg, I, W, US*, 1988 *US*, 1989 *I, US*, 1990 *Ar, US, Ar*, 1991 *J, S, US, R, F, NZ*
H Wyndham 1973 *W*
JJ Yeganegi 1996 *US*, 1998 *J*
C Yukes 2001 *Ur, Fj, J*, 2002 *S, US, Ur, Ur*, 2003 *E, US, M, M, US, Ar, W, NZ, It, Tg*, 2004 *US, J, EngA, US, F, It, E*, 2005 *W, EngA, US*, 2006 *Bar, US*, 2007 *IrA, US, NZ, Pt, W, Fj, J, A*

ENGLAND

ENGLAND'S 2009–10 TEST RECORD

OPPONENTS	DATE	VENUE	RESULT
Australia	7 November	H	**Lost** 9–18
Argentina	14 November	H	**Won** 16–9
New Zealand	21 November	H	**Lost** 6–19
Wales	6 February	H	**Won** 30–17
Italy	14 February	A	**Won** 17–12
Ireland	27 February	H	**Lost** 16–20
Scotland	13 March	A	**Drew** 15–15
France	20 March	A	**Lost** 10–12
Australia	12 June	A	**Lost** 17–27
Australia	19 June	A	**Won** 21–20

ENGLAND SHOW SIGNS OF RECOVERY

By Paul Morgan

AFP

England manager Martin Johnson (right) had plenty to smile about at the end of the season.

If a single, solitary result can symbolise the beginning of a new era for a struggling team, not to mention its beleaguered manager, then England and Martin Johnson may just have had their Road to Damascus moment at the very end of what was a punishing and largely underwhelming season.

It came against the Wallabies in Sydney, in June. Beaten in the first Test in Perth seven days earlier, England were on the ropes after a disjointed and disappointing campaign but shocked the Australians, and perhaps even themselves, with a vibrant, free-flowing performance and 21–20 win at the Olympic Stadium.

That such a desperately-needed victory came in the same city where they had lifted the World Cup back in 2003 was doubtless not lost on Johnson, who led England to glory that day, and after another campaign dominated by trials and tribulations rather than tries and triumphs. It was a result that history may yet reflect on as the turning point in Johnson's coaching career.

However it was not merely that England had triumphed on Australian soil for only the third time in their history but the fact his side finally played an adventurous, attacking brand of rugby that had been conspicuous by its absence throughout the autumn internationals and a workmanlike but ultimately uninspiring Six Nations challenge.

England had thrown off the shackles, delighted their travelling supporters and beaten the Wallabies in their own backyard.

It was England's first victory over a Tri–Nations side since the 2007 World Cup and the first one down south since 2003. For Johnson, the high profile win that, if only privately, he knew he desperately needed.

"It is really good for the players and coaches," he said after the match. "It doesn't happen that often, so to win one here is pretty special. I have said all week I don't worry about my record or my job, I worry about this team getting better. Today we showed we can play.

"We knew we could, we just had to go and do it. We have still got to be better and more consistent but we have won the Test match. We still made mistakes and had to weather a few storms but that is Test rugby. We kept fighting back."

England's new season began with an injury crisis as Johnson lost 11 of his 32-man squad, including seven probable starters, in the build-up to the autumn internationals in 2009 but whether a completely clean bill of health would have affected their fortunes through November at Twickenham is a moot point.

The team started those November Tests against Australia, with Jonny Wilkinson in the starting XV for the first time in nearly two years, but the iconic fly-half was powerless to prevent the Wallabies emerging 18–9 winners.

A week later Argentina were the visitors at HQ but supporters yearning for their side to produce a dominant display were disappointed as England laboured to a turgid 16–9 victory that was eventually secured by the only try of the game from wing Matt Banahan late in the second half.

In fairness, the side's display in the third Test of the autumn against New Zealand the following weekend was much improved but it was not good enough to deny the All Blacks a 19–6 victory and Johnson was forced to contemplate an unconvincing three-match series in which his team scraped a single win against the Pumas and, more ominously, scored just one try.

The manager's squad for the Six Nations included rugby league converts Chris Ashton and Shontayne Hape but neither made the starting line-up for the tournament opener against Wales at Twickenham, a game that marked the centenary of international rugby at the famous old stadium. Hape would have played but for injury.

England were to emerge 30–17 winners and although the Twickenham faithful witnessed tries from James Haskell (2) and Danny Care, had it not been for the yellow card shown to Wales lock Alun Wyn Jones in the 34th minute for a cynical trip on Dylan Hartley, the home side scoring 17 unanswered points during his ten minutes in the sin-bin, the match would likely have been far closer.

Leicester prop Dan Cole and Brive centre Riki Flutey were drafted into the starting XV to face Italy in the second game but England's old failings were once again very much in evidence as they struggled to break down a stubborn Azzurri defence in Rome and it was Matthew Tait's try early in the second-half that proved decisive as the visitors ran out nervous 17–12 victors.

The dreams of a first Grand Slam since 2003 briefly lived on but were dashed at Twickenham in late February when a pair of Tommy Bowe tries gave Ireland a 20–16 triumph and England's campaign began to disintegrate, drawing 15–15 with Scotland at Murrayfield before a brave 12–10 defeat to France at the Stade de France.

England limped home third in the final table but three successive games without a victory meant Johnson could boast a mere eight wins in his 19 Tests in charge as he began his preparations for the summer tour.

"It's so frustrating, we were so near," admitted flanker Lewis Moody, who had replaced the injured Steve Borthwick as England captain for the loss in Paris. "It was a good performance by France but we should have finished them off. France have been the most consistent team of the tournament, they are deserved winners.

"But I'm very proud of the boys, they worked their socks off. The penalty count probably cost us and I'm bitterly disappointed. To come off the field with a loss is painful. The guys played some good rugby in defeat but knowing this team still has another 30 per cent to give fills me with confidence for the future. This team knows where it has to go now and I think that showed on the pitch."

With the pressure on him growing, Johnson named his squad for the tour of Australia and New Zealand by including nine uncapped players in a 44-strong tour party and once a pay dispute between the players and the RFU had been resolved and the Barbarians beaten 35–26 at Twickenham, England headed Down Under.

The tour began with a 28–28 midweek draw with the Australian Barbarians in Perth but the first Test was a familiar story as the tourists' scrum completely dominated yet England were unable to shackle the Wallabies out wide. Australia fly-half Quade Cooper scored two tries and captain Rocky Elsom added a third and although the men in white were awarded two penalty tries after annihilating the home scrum, the Wallabies held on for a 27–17 victory.

The midweek side recorded the first win of the tour with a 15–9 success against the Australian Barbarians three days later and their victory seemed to inspire the squad as England came out for the second Test in Sydney rejuvenated and brimming with attacking intent.

During the first-half in particular, England were a revelation and superbly taken tries from scrum-half Ben Youngs and wing Ashton were no less than Johnson's team deserved. Australia rallied after the break but the tourists held their nerve for a morale-boosting win and rare triumph for the northern hemisphere over their southern counterparts.

England had one final assignment before disbanding for their summer holidays in the shape of the New Zealand Maori in Napier but there was to be no final victory as what was effectively a second string team were overwhelmed by the home side.

The tourists surged into a 13–0 lead courtesy of two Charlie Hodgson penalties and a Steffon Armitage try but the Maori were not to be denied a famous scalp and a Hosea Gear hat-trick laid the foundation for a 35–28 win.

"It rankles losing that game because there was a definite chance to win it," said Johnson as he reflected on a tour, which had ultimately strengthened his position as England manager. "I am a bit grumpy. There are so many good things to come out of this tour but it was a bit annoying not to finish it off. But ultimately the Maori probably deserved it.

"There were some harsh lessons for some players but that is why we are here. If you look at the results, we have done OK but the effect of the tour on the team and the wider squad has been absolutely fantastic.

"A few people doubted whether it was a good idea to take these midweek games and this extra one against the Maori after a two-Test series and a long season. But the midweek guys have kept their end up and done a fantastic job. Some guys have really put themselves in contention for the bigger squad."

ENGLAND INTERNATIONAL STATISTICS

MATCH RECORDS UP TO 29TH OCTOBER 2010

MOST CONSECUTIVE TEST WINS

14 2002 W, It, Arg, NZ, A, SA, 2003 F1, W1, It, S, I, NZ, A, W2

11 2000 SA 2, A, Arg, SA3, 2001 W, It, S, F, C1, 2, US

10 1882 W, 1883 I,S, 1884 W,I,S, 1885 W,I, 1886 W,I

10 1994 R,C, 1995 I,F,W,S, Arg, It, WS, A

10 2003 F,Gg,SA,Sm,U,W,F,A, 2004 It,S

MOST CONSECUTIVE TESTS WITHOUT DEFEAT

Matches	Wins	Draws	Periods
14	14	0	2002 to 2003
12	10	2	1882 to 1887
11	10	1	1922 to 1924
11	11	0	2000 to 2001

MOST POINTS IN A MATCH

BY THE TEAM

Pts	Opponents	Venue	Year
134	Romania	Twickenham	2001
111	Uruguay	Brisbane	2003
110	Netherlands	Huddersfield	1998
106	U S A	Twickenham	1999
101	Tonga	Twickenham	1999
84	Georgia	Perth	2003
80	Italy	Twickenham	2001

BY A PLAYER

Pts	Player	Opponents	Venue	Year
44	C Hodgson	Romania	Twickenham	2001
36	P J Grayson	Tonga	Twickenham	1999
35	J P Wilkinson	Italy	Twickenham	2001
32	J P Wilkinson	Italy	Twickenham	1999
30	C R Andrew	Canada	Twickenham	1994
30	P J Grayson	Netherlands	Huddersfield	1998
30	J P Wilkinson	Wales	Twickenham	2002
29	D J H Walder	Canada	Burnaby	2001
27	C R Andrew	South Africa	Pretoria	1994
27	J P Wilkinson	South Africa	Bloemfontein	2000
27	C C Hodgson	South Africa	Twickenham	2004
27	J P Wilkinson	Scotland	Twickenham	2007
26	J P Wilkinson	United States	Twickenham	1999

MOST TRIES IN A MATCH

BY THE TEAM

Tries	Opponents	Venue	Year
20	Romania	Twickenham	2001
17	Uruguay	Brisbane	2003
16	Netherlands	Huddersfield	1998
16	United States	Twickenham	1999
13	Wales	Blackheath	1881
13	Tonga	Twickenham	1999
12	Georgia	Perth	2003
12	Canada	Twickenham	2004
10	Japan	Sydney	1987
10	Fiji	Twickenham	1989
10	Italy	Twickenham	2001

BY A PLAYER

Tries	Player	Opponents	Venue	Year
5	D Lambert	France	Richmond	1907
5	R Underwood	Fiji	Twickenham	1989
5	O J Lewsey	Uruguay	Brisbane	2003
4	G W Burton	Wales	Blackheath	1881
4	A Hudson	France	Paris	1906
4	R W Poulton	France	Paris	1914
4	C Oti	Romania	Bucharest	1989
4	J C Guscott	Netherlands	Huddersfield	1998
4	N A Back	Netherlands	Huddersfield	1998
4	J C Guscott	United States	Twickenham	1999
4	J Robinson	Romania	Twickenham	2001
4	N Easter	Wales	Twickenham	2007

MOST CONVERSIONS IN A MATCH

BY THE TEAM

Cons	Opponents	Venue	Year
15	Netherlands	Huddersfield	1998
14	Romania	Twickenham	2001
13	United States	Twickenham	1999
13	Uruguay	Brisbane	2003
12	Tonga	Twickenham	1999
9	Italy	Twickenham	2001
9	Georgia	Perth	2003
8	Romania	Bucharest	1989
7	Wales	Blackheath	1881
7	Japan	Sydney	1987
7	Argentina	Twickenham	1990
7	Wales	Twickenham	1998
7	Wales	Twickenham	2007

BY A PLAYER

Cons	Player	Opponents	Venue	Year
15	P J Grayson	Netherlands	Huddersfield	1998
14	C Hodgson	Romania	Twickenham	2001
13	J P Wilkinson	United States	Twickenham	1999
12	P J Grayson	Tonga	Twickenham	1999
11	P J Grayson	Uruguay	Brisbane	2003
9	J P Wilkinson	Italy	Twickenham	2001
8	S D Hodgkinson	Romania	Bucharest	1989
7	J M Webb	Japan	Sydney	1987
7	S D Hodgkinson	Argentina	Twickenham	1990
7	P J Grayson	Wales	Twickenham	1998
7	J P Wilkinson	Wales	Twickenham	2007

MOST PENALTIES IN A MATCH

BY THE TEAM

Pens	Opponents	Venue	Year
8	South Africa	Bloemfontein	2000
7	Wales	Cardiff	1991
7	Scotland	Twickenham	1995
7	France	Twickenham	1999
7	Fiji	Twickenham	1999
7	South Africa	Paris	1999
7	South Africa	Twickenham	2001
6	Wales	Twickenham	1986
6	Canada	Twickenham	1994
6	Argentina	Durban	1995
6	Scotland	Murrayfield	1996
6	Ireland	Twickenham	1996
6	South Africa	Twickenham	2000
6	Australia	Twickenham	2002
6	Wales	Brisbane	2003

BY A PLAYER

Pens	Player	Opponents	Venue	Year
8	J P Wilkinson	South Africa	Bloemfontein	2000
7	S D Hodgkinson	Wales	Cardiff	1991
7	C R Andrew	Scotland	Twickenham	1995
7	J P Wilkinson	France	Twickenham	1999
7	J P Wilkinson	Fiji	Twickenham	1999
7	J P Wilkinson	South Africa	Twickenham	2001
6	C R Andrew	Wales	Twickenham	1986
6	C R Andrew	Canada	Twickenham	1994
6	C R Andrew	Argentina	Durban	1995
6	P J Grayson	Scotland	Murrayfield	1996
6	P J Grayson	Ireland	Twickenham	1996
6	P J Grayson	South Africa	Paris	1999
6	J P Wilkinson	South Africa	Twickenham	2000
6	J P Wilkinson	Australia	Twickenham	2002
6	J P Wilkinson	Wales	Brisbane	2003

MOST DROPPED GOALS IN A MATCH

BY THE TEAM

Drops	Opponents	Venue	Year
3	France	Sydney	2003
2	Ireland	Twickenham	1970
2	France	Paris	1978
2	France	Paris	1980
2	Romania	Twickenham	1985
2	Fiji	Suva	1991
2	Argentina	Durban	1995
2	France	Paris	1996
2	Australia	Twickenham	2001
2	Wales	Cardiff	2003
2	Ireland	Dublin	2003
2	South Africa	Perth	2003
2	Samoa	Nantes	2007
2	Tonga	Paris	2007
2	Argentina	Manchester	2009

BY A PLAYER

Drops	Player	Opponents	Venue	Year
3	J P Wilkinson	France	Sydney	2003
2	R Hiller	Ireland	Twickenham	1970
2	A G B Old	France	Paris	1978
2	J P Horton	France	Paris	1980
2	C R Andrew	Romania	Twickenham	1985
2	C R Andrew	Fiji	Suva	1991
2	C R Andrew	Argentina	Durban	1995
2	P J Grayson	France	Paris	1996
2	J P Wilkinson	Australia	Twickenham	2001
2	J P Wilkinson	Wales	Cardiff	2003
2	J P Wilkinson	Ireland	Dublin	2003
2	J P Wilkinson	South Africa	Perth	2003
2	J P Wilkinson	Samoa	Nantes	2007
2	J P Wilkinson	Tonga	Paris	2007
2	A J Goode	Argentina	Manchester	2009

CAREER RECORDS

MOST CAPPED PLAYERS

Caps	Player	Career Span
114	J Leonard	1990 to 2004
85	R Underwood	1984 to 1996
85	L B N Dallaglio	1995 to 2007
84	M O Johnson	1993 to 2003
80	J P Wilkinson	1998 to 2010
77	M J S Dawson	1995 to 2006
77	J P R Worsley	1999 to 2010
75	M J Catt	1994 to 2007
73	P J Vickery	1998 to 2009
72	W D C Carling	1988 to 1997
71	C R Andrew	1985 to 1997
71	R A Hill	1997 to 2004
69	D J Grewcock	1997 to 2007
66	N A Back	1994 to 2003
65	J C Guscott	1989 to 1999
64	B C Moore	1987 to 1995
64	M E Corry	1997 to 2007
63	M J Tindall	2000 to 2010
63	L W Moody	2001 to 2010
62	B J Kay	2001 to 2009
59	S D Shaw	1996 to 2010
58	P J Winterbottom	1982 to 1993
57	B C Cohen	2000 to 2006
57	S W Borthwick	2001 to 2010
57	S G Thompson	2002 to 2010
55	W A Dooley	1985 to 1993
55	W J H Greenwood	1997 to 2004
55	O J Lewsey	1998 to 2007
54	G C Rowntree	1995 to 2006
51	A S Healey	1997 to 2003
51	K P P Bracken	1993 to 2003
51	J T Robinson	2001 to 2007
51	J M White	2000 to 2009

MOST CONSECUTIVE TESTS

Tests	Player	Span
44	W D C Carling	1989 to 1995
40	J Leonard	1990 to 1995
36	J V Pullin	1968 to 1975
33	W B Beaumont	1975 to 1982
30	R Underwood	1992 to 1996

MOST TESTS AS CAPTAIN

Tests	Captain	Span
59	W D C Carling	1988 to 1996
39	M O Johnson	1998 to 2003
22	L B N Dallaglio	1997 to 2004
21	W B Beaumont	1978 to 1982
21	S W Borthwick	2008 to 2010
17	M E Corry	2005 to 2007
15	P J Vickery	2002 to 2008
13	W W Wakefield	1924 to 1926
13	N M Hall	1949 to 1955
13	E Evans	1956 to 1958
13	R E G Jeeps	1960 to 1962
13	J V Pullin	1972 to 1975

MOST POINTS IN TESTS

Points	Player	Tests	Career
1111	J P Wilkinson	80	1998 to 2010
400	P J Grayson	32	1995 to 2004
396	C R Andrew	71	1985 to 1997
296	J M Webb	33	1987 to 1993
259	C C Hodgson	31	2001 to 2008
240	W H Hare	25	1974 to 1984
210	R Underwood	85	1984 to 1996

MOST TRIES IN TESTS

Tries	Player	Tests	Career
49	R Underwood	85	1984 to 1996
31	W J H Greenwood	55	1997 to 2004
31	B C Cohen	57	2000 to 2006
30	J C Guscott	65	1989 to 1999
28	J T Robinson	51	2001 to 2007
24	D D Luger	38	1998 to 2003
22	O J Lewsey	55	1998 to 2007
18	C N Lowe	25	1913 to 1923
17	L B N Dallaglio	85	1995 to 2007
16	N A Back	66	1994 to 2003
16	M J S Dawson	77	1995 to 2006
15	A S Healey	51	1997 to 2003
15	M J Cueto	41	2004 to 2010
13	T Underwood	27	1992 to 1998
13	M J Tindall	63	2000 to 2010
13	I R Balshaw	35	2000 to 2008

MOST CONVERSIONS IN TESTS

Cons	Player	Tests	Career
149	J P Wilkinson	80	1998 to 2010
78	P J Grayson	32	1995 to 2004
44	C C Hodgson	31	2001 to 2008
41	J M Webb	33	1987 to 1993
35	S D Hodgkinson	14	1989 to 1991
33	C R Andrew	71	1985 to 1997
17	L Stokes	12	1875 to 1881

MOST PENALTY GOALS IN TESTS

Pens	Player	Tests	Career
228	J P Wilkinson	80	1998 to 2010
86	C R Andrew	71	1985 to 1997
72	P J Grayson	32	1995 to 2004
67	W H Hare	25	1974 to 1984
66	J M Webb	33	1987 to 1993
44	C C Hodgson	31	2001 to 2008
43	S D Hodgkinson	14	1989 to 1991

MOST DROPPED GOALS IN TESTS

Drops	Player	Tests	Career
33	J P Wilkinson	80	1998 to 2010
21	C R Andrew	71	1985 to 1997
6	P J Grayson	32	1995 to 2004
4	J P Horton	13	1978 to 1984
4	L Cusworth	12	1979 to 1988
4	A J Goode	17	2005 to 2009

INTERNATIONAL CHAMPIONSHIP RECORDS

RECORD	DETAIL		SET
Most points in season	229	in five matches	2001
Most tries in season	29	in five matches	2001
Highest Score	80	80–23 v Italy	2001
Biggest win	57	80–23 v Italy	2001
Highest score conceded	43	13–43 v Ireland	2007
Biggest defeat	30	13–43 v Ireland	2007
Most appearances	54	J Leonard	1991–2004
Most points in matches	529	J P Wilkinson	1998–2010
Most points in season	89	J P Wilkinson	2001
Most points in match	35	J P Wilkinson	v Italy, 2001
Most tries in matches	18	C N Lowe	1913–1923
	18	R Underwood	1984–1996
Most tries in season	8	C N Lowe	1914
Most tries in match	4	R W Poulton	v France, 1914
Most cons in matches	85	J P Wilkinson	1998–2010
Most cons in season	24	J P Wilkinson	2001
Most cons in match	9	J P Wilkinson	v Italy, 2001
Most pens in matches	102	J P Wilkinson	1998–2010
Most pens in season	18	S D Hodgkinson	1991
	18	J P Wilkinson	2000
Most pens in match	7	S D Hodgkinson	v Wales, 1991
	7	C R Andrew	v Scotland, 1995
	7	J P Wilkinson	v France, 1999
Most drops in matches	11	J P Wilkinson	1998–2010
Most drops in season	5	J P Wilkinson	2003
Most drops in match	2	R Hiller	v Ireland, 1970
	2	A G B Old	v France, 1978
	2	J P Horton	v France, 1980
	2	P J Grayson	v France, 1996
	2	J P Wilkinson	v Wales, 2003
	2	J P Wilkinson	v Ireland, 2003

MISCELLANEOUS RECORDS

RECORD	HOLDER	DETAIL
Longest Test Career	J Leonard	1990 to 2004
Youngest Test Cap	H C C Laird	18 yrs 134 days in 1927
Oldest Test Cap	F Gilbert	38 yrs 362 days in 1923

CAREER RECORDS OF ENGLAND INTERNATIONAL PLAYERS (UP TO 29TH OCTOBER 2010)

PLAYER BACKS	DEBUT	CAPS	T	C	P	D	PTS
A O Allen	2006 v NZ	2	0	0	0	0	0
D A Armitage	2008 v PI	16	5	0	2	1	34
C J Ashton	2010 v F	3	1	0	0	0	5
M A Banahan	2009 v Arg	5	3	0	0	0	15
O J Barkley	2001 v US	23	2	9	18	0	82
M N Brown	2007 v SA	3	0	0	0	0	0
D S Care	2008 v NZ	21	2	0	0	1	13
D J Cipriani	2008 v W	7	1	7	10	0	49
M J Cueto	2004 v C	41	15	0	0	0	75
H A Ellis	2004 v SA	27	5	0	0	0	25
A Erinle	2009 v A	2	0	0	0	0	0
T G A L Flood	2006 v Arg	31	3	11	15	1	85
R J Flutey	2008 v PI	13	4	0	0	0	20
B J Foden	2009 v It	6	1	0	0	0	5
S J J Geraghty	2007 v F	6	0	1	1	0	5
A J Goode	2005 v It	17	1	15	20	4	107
S E Hape	2010 v A	2	0	0	0	0	0
D J Hipkiss	2007 v W	13	0	0	0	0	0
C C Hodgson	2001 v R	31	6	44	44	3	259
P K Hodgson	2008 v I	9	0	0	0	0	0
T A May	2009 v Arg	2	0	0	0	0	0
Y C C Monye	2008 v PI	13	1	0	0	0	5
O C Morgan	2007 v S	2	0	0	0	0	0
J D Noon	2001 v C	38	7	0	0	0	35
T O Ojo	2008 v NZ	2	2	0	0	0	10
P H Sackey	2006 v NZ	22	11	0	0	0	55
J D Simpson-Daniel	2002 v NZ	10	3	0	0	0	15
D Strettle	2007 v I	6	1	0	0	0	5
M J M Tait	2005 v W	38	5	0	0	0	25
M J Tindall	2000 v I	63	13	2	0	0	69
T W Varndell	2005 v Sm	4	3	0	0	0	15
S B Vesty	2009 v Arg	2	0	0	0	0	0
R E P Wigglesworth	2008 v It	5	1	0	0	0	5

J P Wilkinson	1998 v I	80	6	149	228	33	1111
B R Youngs	2010 v S	3	1	0	0	0	5

FORWARDS

S E Armitage	2009 v It	5	0	0	0	0	0
D S C Bell	2005 v It	5	0	0	0	0	0
S W Borthwick	2001 v F	57	2	0	0	0	10
A T Brown	2006 v A	3	0	0	0	0	0
M I Cairns	2007 v SA	1	0	0	0	0	0
G S Chuter	2006 v A	24	1	0	0	0	5
D R Cole	2010 v W	7	1	0	0	0	5
J S Crane	2008 v SA	3	0	0	0	0	0
T R Croft	2008 v F	18	0	0	0	0	0
L P Deacon	2005 v Sm	18	0	0	0	0	0
P P L Doran-Jones	2009 v Arg	1	0	0	0	0	0
N J Easter	2007 v It	34	5	0	0	0	25
P T Freshwater	2005 v Sm	10	0	0	0	0	0
D M Hartley	2008 v PI	19	0	0	0	0	0
J A W Haskell	2007 v W	28	2	0	0	0	10
J D Hobson	2008 v NZ	1	0	0	0	0	0
B J Kay	2001 v C	62	2	0	0	0	10
N J Kennedy	2008 v PI	7	1	0	0	0	5
C L Lawes	2009 v A	4	0	0	0	0	0
M R Lipman	2004 v NZ	10	0	0	0	0	0
L A Mears	2005 v Sm	35	1	0	0	0	5
L W Moody	2001 v C	63	9	0	0	0	45
M Mullan	2010 v It	1	0	0	0	0	0
L J W Narraway	2008 v W	7	0	0	0	0	0
D J Paice	2008 v NZ	2	0	0	0	0	0
T P Palmer	2001 v US	16	0	0	0	0	0
T A N Payne	2004 v A	22	0	0	0	0	0
T Rees	2007 v S	15	1	0	0	0	5
C D C Robshaw	2009 v Arg	1	0	0	0	0	0
S D Shaw	1996 v It	59	2	0	0	0	10
A J Sheridan	2004 v C	32	0	0	0	0	0
B D Skirving	2007 v SA	1	0	0	0	0	0
M J H Stevens	2004 v NZ	32	0	0	0	0	0
S G Thompson	2002 v S	57	3	0	0	0	15
S C Turner	2007 v W	3	0	0	0	0	0
P J Vickery	1998 v W	73	2	0	0	0	10
J M White	2000 v SA	51	0	0	0	0	0
D G Wilson	2009 v Arg	11	0	0	0	0	0
J P R Worsley	1999 v Tg	77	10	0	0	0	50

ENGLAND INTERNATIONAL PLAYERS

UP TO 29TH OCTOBER 2010

Note: Years given for International Championship matches are for second half of season; eg 1972 means season 1971–72. Years for all other matches refer to the actual year of the match. Entries in square brackets denote matches played in RWC Finals.

Aarvold, C D (Cambridge U, W Hartlepool, Headingley, Blackheath) 1928 A, W, I, F, S, 1929 W, I, F, 1931 W, S, F, 1932 SA, W, I, S, 1933 W

Abbott, S R (Wasps, Harlequins) 2003 W2, F3, [Sm, U, W(R)], 2004 NZ1(t&R), 2, 2006 I, A2(R)

Abendanon, N A (Bath) 2007 SA2(R), F2

Ackford, P J (Harlequins) 1988 A, 1989 S, I, F, W, R, Fj, 1990 I, F, W, S, Arg 3, 1991 W, S, I, F, A, [NZ, It, F, S, A]

Adams, A A (London Hospital) 1910 F

Adams, F R (Richmond) 1875 I, S, 1876 S, 1877 I, 1878 S, 1879 S, I

Adebayo, A A (Bath) 1996, It, 1997 Arg 1, 2, A 2, NZ 1, 1998 S

Adey, G J (Leicester) 1976 I, F

Adkins, S J (Coventry) 1950 I, F, S, 1953 W, I, F, S

Agar, A E (Harlequins) 1952 SA, W, S, I, F, 1953 W, I

Alcock, A (Guy's Hospital) 1906 SA

Alderson, F H R (Hartlepool R) 1891 W, I, S, 1892 W, S, 1893 W

Alexander, H (Richmond) 1900 I, S, 1901 W, I, S, 1902 W, I

Alexander, W (Northern) 1927 F

Allen, A O (Gloucester) 2006 NZ, Arg

Allison, D F (Coventry) 1956 W, I, S, F, 1957 W, 1958 W, S

Allport, A (Blackheath) 1892 W, 1893 I, 1894 W, I, S

Anderson, S (Rockcliff) 1899 I

Anderson, W F (Orrell) 1973 NZ 1

Anderton, C (Manchester FW) 1889 M

Andrew, C R (Cambridge U, Nottingham, Wasps, Toulouse, Newcastle) 1985 R, F, S, I, W, 1986 W, S, I, F, 1987 I, F, W, [J (R), US], 1988 S, I 1, 2, A 1, 2, Fj, A, 1989 S, I, F, W, R, Fj, 1990 I, F, W, S, Arg 3, 1991 W, S, I, F, Fj, A, [NZ, It, US, F, S, A], 1992 S, I, F, W, C, SA, 1993 F, W, NZ, 1994 S, I, F, W, SA 1, 2, R, C, 1995 I, F, W, S, [Arg, It, A, NZ, F], 1997 W (R)

Appleford, G N (London Irish) 2002 Arg

Archer, G S (Bristol, Army, Newcastle) 1996 S, I, 1997 A 2, NZ 1, SA, NZ 2, 1998 F, W, S, I, A 1, NZ 1, H, It, 1999 Tg, Fj, 2000 I, F, W, It, S

Archer, H (Bridgwater A) 1909 W, F, I

Armitage, D A (London Irish) 2008 PI, A, SA, NZ3, 2009 It, W, I, F, S, Arg 1, 2, 2010 W, It, I, S, A2(R)

Armitage, S E (London Irish) 2009 It, Arg 1, 2, 2010 W(R), It(R)

Armstrong, R (Northern) 1925 W

Arthur, T G (Wasps) 1966 W, I

Ashby, R C (Wasps) 1966 I, F, 1967 A

Ashcroft, A (Waterloo) 1956 W, I, S, F, 1957 W, I, F, S, 1958 W, A, I, F, S, 1959 I, F, S

Ashcroft, A H (Birkenhead Park) 1909 A

Ashford, W (Richmond) 1897 W, I, 1898 S, W

Ashton, C J (Northampton) 2010 F, A1, 2

Ashworth, A (Oldham) 1892 I

Askew, J G (Cambridge U) 1930 W, I, F

Aslett, A R (Richmond) 1926 W, I, F, S, 1929 S, F

Assinder, E W (O Edwardians) 1909 A, W

Aston, R L (Blackheath) 1890 S, I

Auty, J R (Headingley) 1935 S

Back, N A (Leicester) 1994 S, I, 1995 [Arg (t), It, WS], 1997 NZ 1(R), SA, NZ 2, 1998 F, W, S, I, H, It, A 2, SA 2, 1999 S, I, F, W, A, US, C, [It, NZ, Fj, SA], 2000 I, F, W, It, S, SA 1, 2, A, Arg, SA 3, 2001 W, It, S, F, I, A, R, SA, 2002 S, I, F, W, It, NZ (t + R), A, SA, 2003 F 1, W 1, S, I, NZ, A, F 3, [Gg, SA, Sm, W, F, A]

Bailey, M D (Cambridge U, Wasps) 1984 SA 1, 2, 1987 [US], 1989 Fj, 1990 I, F, S (R)

Bainbridge, S (Gosforth, Fylde) 1982 F, W, 1983 F, W, S, I, NZ, 1984 S, I, F, W, 1985 NZ 1, 2, 1987 F, W, S, [J, US]

Baker, D G S (OMTs) 1955 W, I, F, S

Baker, E M (Moseley) 1895 W, I, S, 1896 W, I, S, 1897 W

Baker, H C (Clifton) 1887 W

Balshaw, I R (Bath, Leeds, Gloucester) 2000 I (R), F (R), It (R), S (R), A (R), Arg, SA 3(R), 2001 W, It, S, F, I, 2002 S (R), I (R), 2003 F2, 3, [Sm, U, A(R)], 2004 It, S, I, 2005 It, S, 2006 A1, 2, NZ, Arg, 2007 It, SA1, 2008 W, It, F, S, I

Banahan, M A (Bath) 2009 Arg 1, 2, A, Arg 3, NZ

Bance, J F (Bedford) 1954 S

Barkley, O J (Bath) 2001 US (R), 2004 It(R), I(t), W, F, NZ2(R), A1(R), 2005 W(R), F, I, It, S, A(R), Sm(R), 2006 A1, 2(R), 2007 F2, 3(R), [US, Sm, Tg], 2008 NZ1, 2(R)

Barley, B (Wakefield) 1984 I, F, W, A, 1988 A 1, 2, Fj

Barnes, S (Bristol, Bath) 1984 A, 1985 R (R), NZ 1, 2, 1986 S (R), F (R), 1987 I (R), 1988 Fj, 1993 S, I

Barr, R J (Leicester) 1932 SA, W, I

Barrett, E I M (Lennox) 1903 S

Barrington, T J M (Bristol) 1931 W, I

Barrington-Ward, L E (Edinburgh U) 1910 W, I, F, S

Barron, J H (Bingley) 1896 S, 1897 W, I

Bartlett, J T (Waterloo) 1951 W

Bartlett, R M (Harlequins) 1957 W, I, F, S, 1958 I, F, S

Barton, J (Coventry) 1967 I, F, W, 1972 F

Batchelor, T B (Oxford U) 1907 F

Bates, S M (Wasps) 1989 R

Bateson, A H (Otley) 1930 W, I, F, S

Bateson, H D (Liverpool) 1879 I

Batson, T (Blackheath) 1872 S, 1874 S, 1875 I

Batten, J M (Cambridge U) 1874 S

Baume, J L (Northern) 1950 S

Baxendell, J J N (Sale) 1998 NZ 2, SA 1

Baxter, J (Birkenhead Park) 1900 W, I, S

Bayfield, M C (Northampton) 1991 Fj, A, 1992 S, I, F, W, C, SA, 1993 F, W, S, I, 1994 S, I, SA 1, 2, R, C, 1995 I, F, W, S, [Arg, It, A, NZ, F], SA, WS, 1996 F, W

Bazley, R C (Waterloo) 1952 I, F, 1953 W, I, F, S, 1955 W, I, F, S

Beal, N D (Northampton) 1996 Arg, 1997 A 1, 1998 NZ 1, 2, SA 1, H (R), SA 2, 1999 S, F (R), A (t), C (R), [It (R), Tg (R), Fj, SA]

Beaumont, W B (Fylde) 1975 I, A 1(R), 2, 1976 A, W, S, I, F, 1977 S, I, F, W, 1978 F, W, S, I, NZ, 1979 S, I, F, W, NZ, 1980 I, F, W, S, 1981 W, S, I, F, Arg 1, 2, 1982 A, S

Bedford, H (Morley) 1889 M, 1890 S, I

Bedford, L L (Headingley) 1931 W, I

Beer, I D S (Harlequins) 1955 F, S

Beese, M C (Liverpool) 1972 W, I, F

Beim, T D (Sale) 1998 NZ 1(R), 2

Bell, D S C (Bath) 2005 It(R), S, 2009 A(R), Arg 3, NZ

Bell, F J (Northern) 1900 W

Bell, H (New Brighton) 1884 I

Bell, J L (Darlington) 1878 I

Bell, P J (Blackheath) 1968 W, I, F, S

Bell, R W (Northern) 1900 W, I, S

Bendon, G J (Wasps) 1959 W, I, F, S

Bennett, N O (St Mary's Hospital, Waterloo) 1947 W, S, F, 1948 A, W, I, S

Bennett, W N (Bedford, London Welsh) 1975 S, A1, 1976 S (R), 1979 S, I, F, W
Bennetts, B B (Penzance) 1909 A, W
Bentley, J (Sale, Newcastle) 1988 I 2, A 1, 1997 A 1, SA
Bentley, J E (Gipsies) 1871 S, 1872 S
Benton, S (Gloucester) 1998 A 1
Berridge, M J (Northampton) 1949 W, I
Berry, H (Gloucester) 1910 W, I, F, S
Berry, J (Tyldesley) 1891 W, I, S
Berry, J T W (Leicester) 1939 W, I, S
Beswick, E (Swinton) 1882 I, S
Biggs, J M (UCH) 1878 S, 1879 I
Birkett, J G G (Harlequins) 1906 S, F, SA, 1907 F, W, S, 1908 F, W, I , S, 1910 W, I, S, 1911 W, F, I , S, 1912 W, I , S, F
Birkett L (Clapham R) 1875 S, 1877 I, S
Birkett, R H (Clapham R) 1871 S, 1875 S, 1876 S, 1877 I
Bishop, C C (Blackheath) 1927 F
Black, B H (Blackheath) 1930 W, I, F, S, 1931 W, I, S, F, 1932 S, 1933 W
Blacklock, J H (Aspatria) 1898 I, 1899 I
Blakeway, P J (Gloucester) 1980 I, F, W, S, 1981 W, S, I, F, 1982 I, F, W, 1984 I, F, W, SA 1, 1985 R, F, S, I
Blakiston, A F (Northampton) 1920 S, 1921 W, I, S, F, 1922 W, 1923 S, F, 1924 W, I, F, S, 1925 NZ, W, I, S, F
Blatherwick, T (Manchester) 1878 I
Body, J A (Gipsies) 1872 S, 1873 S
Bolton, C A (United Services) 1909 F
Bolton, R (Harlequins) 1933 W, 1936 S, 1937 S, 1938 W, I
Bolton, W N (Blackheath) 1882 I, S, 1883 W, I, S, 1884 W, I, S, 1885 I, 1887 I, S
Bonaventura, M S (Blackheath) 1931 W
Bond, A M (Sale) 1978 NZ, 1979 S, I, NZ, 1980 I, 1982 I
Bonham-Carter, E (Oxford U) 1891 S
Bonsor, F (Bradford) 1886 W, I, S, 1887 W, S, 1889 M
Boobbyer, B (Rosslyn Park) 1950 W, I, F, S, 1951 W, F, 1952 S, I, F
Booth, L A (Headingley) 1933 W, I, S, 1934 S, 1935 W, I, S
Borthwick, S W (Bath, Saracens) 2001 F, C 1, 2(R), US, R, 2003 A(t), W 2(t), F 2, 2004 I, F(R), NZ1(R), 2, A1, C, SA, A2, 2005 W(R), It(R), S(R), A, NZ, Sm, 2006 W, It, S, F, I, 2007 W2, F3, [SA1(t&R), Sm(R), Tg], 2008 W, It, F, S, I, NZ1, 2, PI, A, SA, NZ3, 2009 It, W, I, F, S, Arg 1, 2, A, Arg 3, NZ, 2010 W, It, I, S
Botting, I J (Oxford U) 1950 W, I
Boughton, H J (Gloucester) 1935 W, I, S
Boyle, C W (Oxford U) 1873 S
Boyle, S B (Gloucester) 1983 W, S, I
Boylen, F (Hartlepool R) 1908 F, W, I, S
Bracken, K P P (Bristol, Saracens) 1993 NZ, 1994 S, I, C, 1995 I, F, W, S, [It, WS (t)], SA, 1996 It (R), 1997 Arg 1, 2, A 2, NZ 1, 2, 1998 F, W, 1999 S(R), I, F, A, 2000 SA 1, 2, A, 2001 It (R), S (R), F (R), C 1, 2, US, I (R), A, R (R), SA, 2002 S, I, F, W, It, 2003 W 1, It(R), I(t), NZ, A, F3, [SA, U(R), W(R), F(t&R)]
Bradby, M S (United Services) 1922 I, F
Bradley, R (W Hartlepool) 1903 W
Bradshaw, H (Bramley) 1892 S, 1893 W, I, S, 1894 W, I, S
Brain, S E (Coventry) 1984 SA 2, A (R), 1985 R, F, S, I, W, NZ 1, 2, 1986 W, S, I, F
Braithwaite, J (Leicester) 1905 NZ
Braithwaite-Exley, B (Headingley) 1949 W
Brettargh, A T (Liverpool OB) 1900 W, 1903 I, S, 1904 W, I, S, 1905 I, S
Brewer, J (Gipsies) 1876 I
Briggs, A (Bradford) 1892 W, I, S
Brinn, A (Gloucester) 1972 W, I, S
Broadley, T (Bingley) 1893 W, S, 1894 W, I, S, 1896 S
Bromet, W E (Richmond) 1891 W, I, 1892 W, I, S, 1893 W, I, S, 1895 W, I, S, 1896 I
Brook, P W P (Harlequins) 1930 S, 1931 F, 1936 S
Brooke, T J (Richmond) 1968 F, S
Brooks, F G (Bedford) 1906 SA
Brooks, M J (Oxford U) 1874 S
Brophy, T J (Liverpool) 1964 I, F, S, 1965 W, I, 1966 W, I, F
Brough, J W (Silloth) 1925 NZ, W
Brougham, H (Harlequins) 1912 W, I, S, F
Brown, A A (Exeter) 1938 S
Brown A T (Gloucester) 2006 A1, 2007 SA1, 2
Brown, L G (Oxford U, Blackheath) 1911 W, F, I, S, 1913 SA, W, F, I, S, 1914 W, I, S, F, 1921 W, I, S, F, 1922 W
Brown, M N (Harlequins) 2007 SA1, 2, 2008 NZ1
Brown S P (Richmond) 1998 A 1, SA 1
Brown, T W (Bristol) 1928 S, 1929 W, I, S, F, 1932 S, 1933 W, I, S
Brunton, J (N Durham) 1914 W, I, S
Brutton, E B (Cambridge U) 1886 S
Bryden, C C (Clapham R) 1876 I, 1877 S
Bryden, H A (Clapham R) 1874 S
Buckingham, R A (Leicester) 1927 F
Bucknall, A L (Richmond) 1969 SA, 1970 I, W, S, F, 1971 W, I, F, S (2[1C])
Buckton, J R D (Saracens) 1988 A (R), 1990 Arg 1, 2
Budd, A J (Blackheath) 1878 I, 1879 S, I, 1881 W, S
Budworth, R T D (Blackheath) 1890 W, 1891 W, S
Bull, A G (Northampton) 1914 W
Bullough, E (Wigan) 1892 W, I, S
Bulpitt, M P (Blackheath) 1970 S
Bulteel, A J (Manchester) 1876 I
Bunting, W L (Moseley) 1897 I, S, 1898 I, S, W, 1899 S, 1900 S, 1901 I, S
Burland, D W (Bristol) 1931 W, I, F, 1932 I, S, 1933 W, I, S
Burns, B H (Blackheath) 1871 S
Burton, G W (Blackheath) 1879 S, I, 1880 S, 1881 I, W, S
Burton, H C (Richmond) 1926 W
Burton, M A (Gloucester) 1972 W, I, F, S, SA, 1974 F, W, 1975 S, A 1, 2, 1976 A, W, S, I, F, 1978 F, W
Bush, J A (Clifton) 1872 S, 1873 S, 1875 S, 1876 I, S
Butcher, C J S (Harlequins) 1984 SA 1, 2, A
Butcher, W V (Streatham) 1903 S, 1904 W, I, S, 1905 W, I, S
Butler, A G (Harlequins) 1937 W, I
Butler, P E (Gloucester) 1975 A 1, 1976 F
Butterfield, J (Northampton) 1953 F, S, 1954 W, NZ, I, S, F, 1955 W, I, F, S, 1956 W, I, S, F, 1957 W, I, F, S, 1958 W, A, I, F, S, 1959 W, I, F, S
Byrne, F A (Moseley) 1897 W
Byrne, J F (Moseley) 1894 W, I, S, 1895 I, S, 1896 I, 1897 W, I, S, 1898 I, S, W, 1899 I
Cain, J J (Waterloo) 1950 W
Cairns, M I (Saracens) 2007 SA1(R)
Callard, J E B (Bath) 1993 NZ, 1994 S, I, 1995 [WS], SA
Campbell, D A (Cambridge U) 1937 W, I
Candler, P L (St Bart's Hospital) 1935 W, 1936 NZ, W, I, S, 1937 W, I, S, 1938 W, S
Cannell, L B (Oxford U, St Mary's Hospital) 1948 F, 1949 W, I, F, S, 1950 W, I, F, S, 1952 SA, W, 1953 W, I, F, 1956 I, S, F, 1957 W, I
Caplan, D W N (Headingley) 1978 S, I
Cardus, R M (Roundhay) 1979 F, W
Care, D S (Harlequins) 2008 NZ1(R), 2, PI, A, SA, NZ3, 2009 I(R), F(R), S(R), Arg 1, 2, A, Arg 3(R), NZ(R), 2010 W, It, I, S, F, A1, 2(R)
Carey, G M (Blackheath) 1895 W, I, S, 1896 W, I
Carleton, J (Orrell) 1979 NZ, 1980 I, F, W, S, 1981 W, S, I, F, Arg 1, 2, 1982 A, S, I, F, W, 1983 F, W, S, I, NZ, 1984 S, I, F, W, A
Carling, W D C (Durham U, Harlequins) 1988 F, W, S, I 1, 2, A2, Fj, A, 1989 S, I, F, W, Fj, 1990 I, F, W, S, Arg 1, 2, 3, 1991 W, S, I, F, Fj, A, [NZ, It, US, F, S, A], 1992 S, I, F, W, C, SA, 1993 F, W, S, I, NZ, 1994 S, I, F, W, SA 1, 2, R, C, 1995 I, F, W, S, [Arg, WS, A, NZ, F], SA, WS, 1996 F, W, S, I, It, Arg, 1997 S, I, F, W
Carpenter, A D (Gloucester) 1932 SA
Carr, R S L (Manchester) 1939 W, I, S
Cartwright, V H (Nottingham) 1903 W, I, S, 1904 W, S, 1905 W, I, S, NZ, 1906 W, I, S, F, SA
Catcheside, H C (Percy Park) 1924 W, I, F, S, 1926 W, I, 1927 I, S
Catt, M J (Bath, London Irish) 1994 W (R), C (R), 1995 I, F, W, S, [Arg, It, WS, A, NZ, F], SA, WS, 1996 F, W, S, I, It, Arg, 1997 W, Arg 1, A 1, 2, NZ 1, SA, 1998 F, W (R), I, A 2(R), SA 2, 1999 S, F, W, A, C (R), [Tg (R), Fj, SA (R)], 2000 I, F, W, It, S, SA 1, 2, A, Arg, 2001 W, It, S, F, I, A, R (R), SA, 2003 [Sm(R), U, W(R), F, A(R)], 2004 W(R), F(R), NZ1, A1, 2006 A1, 2, 2007 F1, W1, F2, [US, SA1, A, F, SA2]
Cattell, R H B (Blackheath) 1895 W, I, S, 1896 W, I, S, 1900 W
Cave, J W (Richmond) 1889 M
Cave, W T C (Blackheath) 1905 W
Challis, R (Bristol) 1957 I, F, S
Chambers, E L (Bedford) 1908 F, 1910 W, I
Chantrill, B S (Bristol) 1924 W, I, F, S

Chapman, C E (Cambridge U) 1884 W
Chapman D E (Richmond) 1998 A 1(R)
Chapman, F E (Hartlepool) 1910 W, I, F, S, 1912 W, 1914 W, I
Cheesman, W I (OMTs) 1913 SA, W, F, I
Cheston, E C (Richmond) 1873 S, 1874 S, 1875 I, S, 1876 S
Chilcott, G J (Bath) 1984 A, 1986 I, F, 1987 F (R), W, [J, US, W (R)], 1988 I 2(R), Fj, 1989 I (R), F, W, R
Christophers, P D (Bristol) 2002 Arg, SA, 2003 W 1 (R)
Christopherson, P (Blackheath) 1891 W, S
Chuter, G S (Leicester) 2006 A1(R), 2, NZ, Arg, SA1, 2(R), 2007 S, It, I, F1, W1, 2(R), [US(R), SA1(R), Sm, Tg, A(R), F(R), SA2(R)], 2008 S(R), I(R), 2009 Arg 2(R), 2010 A1(R), 2(R)
Cipriani, D J (Wasps) 2008 W(R), It(R), I, PI, A, SA, NZ3(R)
Clark, C W H (Liverpool) 1876 I
Clarke, A J (Coventry) 1935 W, I, S, 1936 NZ, W, I
Clarke, B B (Bath, Richmond) 1992 SA, 1993 F, W, S, I, NZ, 1994 S, F, W, SA 1, 2, R, C, 1995 I, F, W, S, [Arg, It, A, NZ, F], SA, WS, 1996 F, W, S, I, Arg (R), 1997 W, Arg 1, 2, A 1(R), 1998 A 1(t), NZ 1, 2, SA 1, H, It, 1999 A (R)
Clarke, S J S (Cambridge U, Blackheath) 1963 W, I, F, S, NZ 1, 2, A, 1964 NZ, W, I, 1965 I, F, S
Clayton, J H (Liverpool) 1871 S
Clements, J W (O Cranleighans) 1959 I, F, S
Cleveland, C R (Blackheath) 1887 W, S
Clibborn, W G (Richmond) 1886 W, I, S, 1887 W, I, S
Clough, F J (Cambridge U, Orrell) 1986 I, F, 1987 [J (R), US]
Coates, C H (Yorkshire W) 1880 S, 1881 S, 1882 S
Coates, V H M (Bath) 1913 SA, W, F, I, S
Cobby, W (Hull) 1900 W
Cockerham, A (Bradford Olicana) 1900 W
Cockerill, R (Leicester) 1997 Arg 1(R), 2, A 2(t+R), NZ 1, SA, NZ 2, 1998 W, S, I, A 1, NZ 1, 2, SA 1, H, It, A 2, SA 2, 1999 S, I, F, W, A, C (R), [It, NZ, Tg (R), Fj (R)]
Codling, A J (Harlequins) 2002 Arg
Cohen, B C (Northampton) 2000 I, F, W, It, S, SA 2, Arg, SA 3, 2001 W, It, S, F, R, 2002 S, I, F, W, It, NZ, A, SA, 2003 F 1, W 1, S, I, NZ, A, F2, 3, [Gg, SA, Sm, W, F, A], 2004 It, S, I, W, F, NZ1, 2, A1, C(R), A2(R), 2005 F(R), A, NZ, 2006 W, It, S, F, I, NZ, Arg, SA1, 2
Colclough, M J (Angoul'me, Wasps, Swansea) 1978 S, I, 1979 NZ, 1980 F, W, S, 1981 W, S, I, F, 1982 A, S, I, F, W, 1983 F, NZ, 1984 S, I, F, W, 1986 W, S, I, F
Cole, D R (Leicester) 2010 W(R), It, I, S, F, A1, 2
Coley, E (Northampton) 1929 F, 1932 W
Collins, P J (Camborne) 1952 S, I, F
Collins, W E (O Cheltonians) 1874 S, 1875 I, S, 1876 I, S
Considine, S G U (Bath) 1925 F
Conway, G S (Cambridge U, Rugby, Manchester) 1920 F, I, S, 1921 F, 1922 W, I, F, S, 1923 W, I, S, F, 1924 W, I, F, S, 1925 NZ, 1927 W
Cook, J G (Bedford) 1937 S
Cook, P W (Richmond) 1965 I, F
Cooke, D A (Harlequins) 1976 W, S, I, F
Cooke, D H (Harlequins) 1981 W, S, I, F, 1984 I, 1985 R, F, S, I, W, NZ 1, 2
Cooke, P (Richmond) 1939 W, I
Coop, T (Leigh) 1892 S
Cooper, J G (Moseley) 1909 A, W
Cooper, M J (Moseley) 1973 F, S, NZ 2(R), 1975 F, W, 1976 A, W, 1977 S, I, F, W
Coopper, S F (Blackheath) 1900 W, 1902 W, I, 1905 W, I, S, 1907 W
Corbett, L J (Bristol) 1921 F, 1923 W, I, 1924 W, I, F, S, 1925 NZ, W, I, S, F, 1927 W, I, S, F
Corless, B J (Coventry, Moseley) 1976 A, I (R), 1977 S, I, F, W, 1978 F, W, S, I
Corry, M E (Bristol, Leicester) 1997 Arg 1, 2, 1998 H, It, SA 2(t), 1999 F(R), A, C (t), [It (R), NZ (t+R), SA (R)], 2000 I (R), F (R), W (R), It (R), S (R), Arg (R), SA 3(t), 2001 W (R), It (R), F (t), C 1, I, 2002 F (t+R), W (t), 2003 W 2, F 2, 3, [U], 2004 A1(R), C, SA, A2, 2005 F, I, It, S, A, NZ, Sm, 2006 W, It, S, F, I, NZ, Arg, SA1, 2, 2007 S, It, I, F1, W1, 2, F2(R), 3, [US(R), SA1, Sm, Tg, A, F, SA2]
Cotton, F E (Loughborough Colls, Coventry, Sale) 1971 S (2[1C]), P, 1973 W, I, F, S, NZ 2, A, 1974 S, I, 1975 I, F, W, 1976 A, W, S, I, F, 1977 S, I, F, W, 1978 S, I, 1979 NZ, 1980 I, F, W, S, 1981 W
Coulman, M J (Moseley) 1967 A, I, F, S, W, 1968 W, I, F, S
Coulson, T J (Coventry) 1927 W, 1928 A, W
Court, E D (Blackheath) 1885 W
Coverdale, H (Blackheath) 1910 F, 1912 I, F, 1920 W
Cove-Smith, R (OMTs) 1921 S, F, 1922 I, F, S, 1923 W, I, S, F, 1924 W, I, S, F, 1925 NZ, W, I, S, F, 1927 W, I, S, F, 1928 A, W, I, F, S, 1929 W, I
Cowling, R J (Leicester) 1977 S, I, F, W, 1978 F, NZ, 1979 S, I
Cowman, A R (Loughborough Colls, Coventry) 1971 S (2[1C]), P, 1973 W, I
Cox, N S (Sunderland) 1901 S
Crane, J S (Leicester) 2008 SA(R), 2009 Arg 1(R), A
Cranmer, P (Richmond, Moseley) 1934 W, I, S, 1935 W, I, S, 1936 NZ, W, I, S, 1937 W, I, S, 1938 W, I, S
Creed, R N (Coventry) 1971 P
Cridlan, A G (Blackheath) 1935 W, I, S
Croft, T R (Leicester) 2008 F(R), S, I, NZ2(R), PI, A, SA(R), NZ3(R), 2009 It(R), W(R), I(R), F, S, A, Arg 3, NZ(R), 2010 A1, 2
Crompton, C A (Blackheath) 1871 S
Crompton, D E (Bristol) 2007 SA1(R)
Crosse, C W (Oxford U) 1874 S, 1875 I
Cueto, M J (Sale) 2004 C, SA, A2, 2005 W, F, I, It, S, A, NZ, Sm, 2006 W, It, S, F, I, SA1, 2, 2007 W1, F3, [US, Sm, Tg, SA2], 2009 It, W, I, F, S, Arg 1, 2, A, Arg 3, NZ, 2010 W, It, I, S, F, A1, 2
Cumberlege, B S (Blackheath) 1920 W, I, S, 1921 W, I, S, F, 1922 W
Cumming, D C (Blackheath) 1925 S, F
Cunliffe, F L (RMA) 1874 S
Currey, F I (Marlborough N) 1872 S
Currie, J D (Oxford U, Harlequins, Bristol) 1956 W, I, S, F, 1957 W, I, F, S, 1958 W, A, I, F, S, 1959 W, I, F, S, 1960 W, I, F, S, 1961 SA, 1962 W, I, F
Cusani, D A (Orrell) 1987 I
Cusworth, L (Leicester) 1979 NZ, 1982 F, W, 1983 F, W, NZ, 1984 S, I, F, W, 1988 F, W
D'Agnilar, F B G (Royal Engineers) 1872 S
Dallaglio, L B N (Wasps) 1995 SA (R), WS, 1996 F, W, S, I, It, Arg, 1997 S, I, F, A 1, 2, NZ 1, SA, NZ 2, 1998 F, W, S, I, A 2, SA 2, 1999 S, I, F, W, US, C, [It, NZ, Tg, Fj, SA], 2000 I, F, W, It, S, SA 1, 2, A, Arg, SA 3, 2001 W, It, S, F, 2002 It (R), NZ, A (t), SA(R), 2003 F 1 (R), W 1, It, S, I, NZ, A, [Gg, SA, Sm, U, W, F, A], 2004 It, S, I, W, F, NZ1, 2, A1, 2006 W(t&R), It(R), S(R), F(R), 2007 W2(R), F2, 3(R), [US, Tg(R), A(R), F(R), SA2(R)]
Dalton, T J (Coventry) 1969 S(R)
Danby, T (Harlequins) 1949 W
Daniell, J (Richmond) 1899 W, 1900 I, S, 1902 I, S, 1904 I, S
Darby, A J L (Birkenhead Park) 1899 I
Davenport, A (Ravenscourt Park) 1871 S
Davey, J (Redruth) 1908 S, 1909 W
Davey, R F (Teignmouth) 1931 W
Davidson, Jas (Aspatria) 1897 S, 1898 S, W, 1899 I, S
Davidson, Jos (Aspatria) 1899 W, S
Davies, G H (Cambridge U, Coventry, Wasps) 1981 S, I, F, Arg 1, 2, 1982 A, S, I, 1983 F, W, S, 1984 S, SA 1, 2, 1985 R (R), NZ 1, 2, 1986 W, S, I, F
Davies, P H (Sale) 1927 I
Davies, V G (Harlequins) 1922 W, 1925 NZ
Davies, W J A (United Services, RN) 1913 SA, W, F, I, S, 1914 I, S, F, 1920 F, I, S, 1921 W, I, S, F, 1922 I, F, S, 1923 W, I, S, F
Davies, W P C (Harlequins) 1953 S, 1954 NZ, I, 1955 W, I, F, S, 1956 W, 1957 F, S, 1958 W
Davis, A M (Torquay Ath, Harlequins) 1963 W, I, S, NZ 1, 2, 1964 NZ, W, I, F, S, 1966 W, 1967 A, 1969 SA, 1970 I, W, S
Dawe, R G R (Bath) 1987 I, F, W, [US], 1995 [WS]
Dawson, E F (RIEC) 1878 I
Dawson, M J S (Northampton, Wasps) 1995 WS, 1996 F, W, S, I, 1997 A 1, SA, NZ 2(R), 1998 W (R), S, I, NZ 1, 2, SA 1, H, It, A 2, SA 2, 1999 S, F(R), W, A(R), US, C, [It, NZ, Tg, Fj (R), SA], 2000 I, F, W, It, S, A (R), Arg, SA 3, 2001 W, It, S, F, I, 2002 W (R), It (R), NZ, A, SA, 2003 It, S, I, A(R), F3(R), [Gg, Sm, W, F, A], 2004It(R), S(R), I, W, F, NZ1, 2(R), A1(R), 2005 W, F(R), I(R), It(R), S(R), A, NZ, 2006 W(R), It(R), S(t&R), F, I(R)
Day, H L V (Leicester) 1920 W, 1922 W, F, 1926 S
Deacon, L P (Leicester) 2005 Sm, 2006 A1, 2(R), 2007 S, It,

I, F1(R), W1(R), 2009 Arg 1, 2, A, Arg 3, NZ(R), 2010 W(R), It(R), I(R), S, F
Dean, G J (Harlequins) 1931 I
Dee, J M (Hartlepool R) 1962 S, 1963 NZ 1
Devitt, Sir T G (Blackheath) 1926 I, F, 1928 A, W
Dewhurst, J H (Richmond) 1887 W, I, S, 1890 W
De Glanville, P R (Bath) 1992 SA (R), 1993 W (R), NZ, 1994 S, I, F, W, SA 1, 2, C (R), 1995 [Arg (R), It, WS], SA (R), 1996 W (R), I (R), It, 1997 S, I, F, W, Arg 1, 2, A 1, 2, NZ 1, 2, 1998 W (R), S (R), I (R), A 2, SA 2, 1999 A (R), US, [It, NZ, Fj (R), SA]
De Winton, R F C (Marlborough N) 1893 W
Dibble, R (Bridgwater A) 1906 S, F, SA, 1908 F, W, I, S, 1909 A, W, F, I, S, 1910 S, 1911 W, F, S, 1912 W, I, S
Dicks, J (Northampton) 1934 W, I, S, 1935 W, I, S, 1936 S, 1937 I
Dillon, E W (Blackheath) 1904 W, I, S, 1905 W
Dingle, A J (Hartlepool R) 1913 I, 1914 S, F
Diprose, A J (Saracens) 1997 Arg 1, 2, A 2, NZ 1, 1998 W (R), S (R), I, A 1, NZ 2, SA 1
Dixon, P J (Harlequins, Gosforth) 1971 P, 1972 W, I, F, S, 1973 I, F, S, 1974 S, I, F, W, 1975 I, 1976 F, 1977 S, I, F, W, 1978 F, S, I, NZ
Dobbs, G E B (Devonport A) 1906 W, I
Doble, S A (Moseley) 1972 SA, 1973 NZ 1, W
Dobson, D D (Newton Abbot) 1902 W, I, S, 1903 W, I, S
Dobson, T H (Bradford) 1895 S
Dodge, P W (Leicester) 1978 W, S, I, NZ, 1979 S, I, F, W, 1980 W, S, 1981 W, S, I, F, Arg 1, 2, 1982 A, S, F, W, 1983 F, W, S, I, NZ, 1985 R, F, S, I, W, NZ 1, 2
Donnelly, M P (Oxford U) 1947 I
Dooley, W A (Preston Grasshoppers, Fylde) 1985 R, F, S, I, W, NZ 2(R), 1986 W, S, I, F, 1987 F, W, [A, US, W], 1988 F, W, S, I 1, 2, A 1, 2, Fj, A, 1989 S, I, F, W, R, Fj, 1990 I, F, W, S, Arg 1, 2, 3, 1991 W, S, I, F, [NZ, US, F, S, A], 1992 S, I, F, W, C, SA, 1993 W, S, I
Doran-Jones, P P L (Gloucester) 2009 Arg 3(R)
Dovey, B A (Rosslyn Park) 1963 W, I
Down, P J (Bristol) 1909 A
Dowson, A O (Moseley) 1899 S
Drake-Lee, N J (Cambridge U, Leicester) 1963 W, I, F, S, 1964 NZ, W, I, 1965 W
Duckett, H (Bradford) 1893 I, S
Duckham, D J (Coventry) 1969 I, F, S, W, SA, 1970 I, W, S, F, 1971 W, I, F, S (2[1C]), P, 1972 W, I, F, S, 1973 NZ 1, W, I, F, S, NZ 2, A, 1974 S, I, F, W, 1975 I, F, W, 1976 A, W, S
Dudgeon, H W (Richmond) 1897 S, 1898 I, S, W, 1899 W, I, S
Dugdale, J M (Ravenscourt Park) 1871 S
Dun, A F (Wasps) 1984 W
Duncan, R F H (Guy's Hospital) 1922 I, F, S
Duncombe, N S (Harlequins) 2002 S (R), I (R)
Dunkley, P E (Harlequins) 1931 I, S, 1936 NZ, W, I, S
Duthie, J (W Hartlepool) 1903 W
Dyson, J W (Huddersfield) 1890 S, 1892 S, 1893 I, S
Easter, N J (Harlequins) 2007 It, F1, SA1, 2, W2, F3, [SA1, Sm, Tg, A, F, SA2], 2008 It, F, S, I, PI, A, SA, NZ3, 2009 It, W, I, F, S, Arg 1, 2, 2010 W, It, I, S, F, A1, 2
Ebdon, P J (Wellington) 1897 W, I
Eddison, J H (Headingley) 1912 W, I, S, F
Edgar, C S (Birkenhead Park) 1901 S
Edwards, R (Newport) 1921 W, I, S, F, 1922 W, F, 1923 W, 1924 W, F, S, 1925 NZ
Egerton, D W (Bath) 1988 I 2, A 1, Fj (R), A, 1989 Fj, 1990 I, Arg 2(R)
Elliot, C H (Sunderland) 1886 W
Elliot, E W (Sunderland) 1901 W, I, S, 1904 W
Elliot, W (United Services, RN) 1932 I, S, 1933 W, I, S, 1934 W, I
Elliott, A E (St Thomas's Hospital) 1894 S
Ellis, H A (Leicester) 2004 SA(R), A2(R), 2005 W(R), F, I, It, S, Sm, 2006 W, It, S, F(R), I, 2007 S, It, I, F1, W1, 2008 PI(R), A(R), SA(R), NZ3(R), 2009 It, W, I, F, S
Ellis, J (Wakefield) 1939 S
Ellis, S S (Queen's House) 1880 I
Emmott, C (Bradford) 1892 W
Enthoven, H J (Richmond) 1878 I
Erinle, A O (Biarritz) 2009 A(R), NZ
Estcourt, N S D (Blackheath) 1955 S
Evans, B J (Leicester) 1988 A 2, Fj
Evans, E (Sale) 1948 A, 1950 W, 1951 I, F, S, 1952 SA, W, S, I, F, 1953 I, F, S, 1954 W, NZ, I, F, 1956 W, I, S, F, 1957 W, I, F, S, 1958 W, A, I, F, S
Evans, G W (Coventry) 1972 S, 1973 W (R), F, S, NZ 2, 1974 S, I, F, W
Evans, N L (RNEC) 1932 W, I, S, 1933 W, I
Evanson, A M (Richmond) 1883 W, I, S, 1884 S
Evanson, W A D (Richmond) 1875 S, 1877 S, 1878 S, 1879 S, I
Evershed, F (Blackheath) 1889 M, 1890 W, S, I, 1892 W, I, S, 1893 W, I, S
Eyres, W C T (Richmond) 1927 I
Fagan, A R St L (Richmond) 1887 I
Fairbrother, K E (Coventry) 1969 I, F, S, W, SA, 1970 I, W, S, F, 1971 W, I, F
Faithfull, C K T (Harlequins) 1924 I, 1926 F, S
Fallas, H (Wakefield T) 1884 I
Farrell, A D (Saracens) 2007 S, It, I, W2, F3, [US(R), SA1, Tg(R)]
Fegan, J H C (Blackheath) 1895 W, I, S
Fernandes, C W L (Leeds) 1881 I, W, S
Fidler, J H (Gloucester) 1981 Arg 1, 2, 1984 SA 1, 2
Fidler, R J (Gloucester) 1998 NZ 2, SA 1
Field, E (Middlesex W) 1893 W, I
Fielding, K J (Moseley, Loughborough Colls) 1969 I, F, S, SA, 1970 I, F, 1972 W, I, F, S
Finch, R T (Cambridge U) 1880 S
Finlan, J F (Moseley) 1967 I, F, S, W, NZ, 1968 W, I, 1969 I, F, S, W, 1970 F, 1973 NZ 1
Finlinson, H W (Blackheath) 1895 W, I, S
Finney, S (RIE Coll) 1872 S, 1873 S
Firth, F (Halifax) 1894 W, I, S
Flatman, D L (Saracens) 2000 SA 1(t), 2(t+R), A (t), Arg (t+R), 2001 F (t), C 2(t+R), US (t+R), 2002 Arg
Fletcher, N C (OMTs) 1901 W, I, S, 1903 S
Fletcher, T (Seaton) 1897 W
Fletcher, W R B (Marlborough N) 1873 S, 1875 S
Flood, T G A L (Newcastle, Leicester) 2006 Arg(R), SA2(R), 2007 S(R), It(R), F1, W1, SA1, 2, W2(t), [A(R), F(R), SA2(R)], 2008 W, It, F, S, I, NZ2, PI(R), A(R), SA(R), NZ3, 2009 W(R), I, F, S, 2010 W, S(R), F, A1, 2
Flutey, R J (Wasps, Brive) 2008 PI, A, SA, NZ3, 2009 It, W, I, F, S, 2010 It, I, S, F
Foden, B J (Northampton) 2009 It(R), 2010 I(R), S(R), F, A1, 2
Fookes, E F (Sowerby Bridge) 1896 W, I, S, 1897 W, I, S, 1898 I, W, 1899 I, S
Ford, P J (Gloucester) 1964 W, I, F, S
Forrest, J W (United Services, RN) 1930 W, I, F, S, 1931 W, I, S, F, 1934 I, S
Forrest, R (Wellington) 1899 W, 1900 S, 1902 I, S, 1903 I, S
Forrester, J (Gloucester) 2005 W(t), Sm(t&R)
Foulds, R T (Waterloo) 1929 W, I
Fowler, F D (Manchester) 1878 S, 1879 S
Fowler, H (Oxford U) 1878 S, 1881 W, S
Fowler, R H (Leeds) 1877 I
Fox, F H (Wellington) 1890 W, S
Francis, T E S (Cambridge U) 1926 W, I, F, S
Frankcom, G P (Cambridge U, Bedford) 1965 W, I, F, S
Fraser, E C (Blackheath) 1875 I
Fraser, G (Richmond) 1902 W, I, S, 1903 W, I
Freakes, H D (Oxford U) 1938 W, 1939 W, I
Freeman, H (Marlborough N) 1872 S, 1873 S, 1874 S
French, R J (St Helens) 1961 W, I, F, S
Freshwater, P T (Perpignan) 2005 v Sm(R), 2006 S(t&R), I(R), Arg, 2007 S, It, I, F3, [SA1(R), Sm(R)]
Fry, H A (Liverpool) 1934 W, I, S
Fry, T W (Queen's House) 1880 I, S, 1881 W
Fuller, H G (Cambridge U) 1882 I, S, 1883 W, I, S, 1884 W
Gadney, B C (Leicester, Headingley) 1932 I, S, 1933 I, S, 1934 W, I, S, 1935 S, 1936 NZ, W, I, S, 1937 S, 1938 W
Gamlin, H T (Blackheath) 1899 W, S, 1900 W, I, S, 1901 S, 1902 W, I, S, 1903 W, I, S, 1904 W, I, S
Gardner, E R (Devonport Services) 1921 W, I, S, 1922 W, I, F, 1923 W, I, S, F
Gardner, H P (Richmond) 1878 I
Garforth, D J (Leicester) 1997 W (R), Arg 1, 2, A 1, NZ 1, SA, NZ 2, 1998 F, W (R), S, I, H, It, A 2, SA 2, 1999 S, I, F, W, A, C (R), [It (R), NZ (R), Fj], 2000 It
Garnett, H W T (Bradford) 1877 S
Gavins, M N (Leicester) 1961 W

Gay, D J (Bath) 1968 W, I, F, S
Gent, D R (Gloucester) 1905 NZ, 1906 W, I, 1910 W, I
Genth, J S M (Manchester) 1874 S, 1875 S
George, J T (Falmouth) 1947 S, F, 1949 I
Geraghty, S J J (London Irish, Northampton) 2007 F1(R), W1(R), 2009 It(R), A, Arg 3, NZ(R)
Gerrard, R A (Bath) 1932 SA, W, I, S, 1933 W, I, S, 1934 W, I, S, 1936 NZ, W, I, S
Gibbs, G A (Bristol) 1947 F, 1948 I
Gibbs, J C (Harlequins) 1925 NZ, W, 1926 F, 1927 W, I, S, F
Gibbs, N (Harlequins) 1954 S, F
Giblin, L F (Blackheath) 1896 W, I, 1897 S
Gibson, A S (Manchester) 1871 S
Gibson, C O P (Northern) 1901 W
Gibson, G R (Northern) 1899 W, 1901 S
Gibson, T A (Northern) 1905 W, S
Gilbert, F G (Devonport Services) 1923 W, I
Gilbert, R (Devonport A) 1908 W, I, S
Giles, J L (Coventry) 1935 W, I, 1937 W, I, 1938 I, S
Gittings, W J (Coventry) 1967 NZ
Glover, P B (Bath) 1967 A, 1971 F, P
Godfray, R E (Richmond) 1905 NZ
Godwin, H O (Coventry) 1959 F, S, 1963 S, NZ 1, 2, A, 1964 NZ, I, F, S, 1967 NZ
Gomarsall, A C T (Wasps, Bedford, Gloucester, Harlequins) 1996 It, Arg, 1997 S, I, F, Arg 2(R) 2000 It (R), 2002 Arg, SA(R), 2003 F 1, W 1(R), 2, F2(R), [Gg(R), U], 2004 It, S, NZ1(R), 2, A1, C, SA, A2, 2007 SA1, 2, F2(R), 3(R), [SA1(R), Sm, Tg, A, F, SA2], 2008 W, It
Goode, A J (Leicester, Brive) 2005 It(R), S(R), 2006 W(R), F(R), I, A1(R), 2, SA1(R), 2, 2009 It, W, I(R), F(R), S(R), Arg1, 2, 3(R)
Gordon-Smith, G W (Blackheath) 1900 W, I, S
Gotley, A L H (Oxford U) 1910 F, S, 1911 W, F, I, S
Graham, D (Aspatria) 1901 W
Graham, H J (Wimbledon H) 1875 I, S, 1876 I, S
Graham, J D G (Wimbledon H) 1876 I
Gray, A (Otley) 1947 W, I, S
Grayson, P J (Northampton) 1995 WS, 1996 F, W, S, I, 1997 S, I, F, A 2(t), SA (R), NZ 2, 1998 F, W, S, I, H, It, A 2, 1999 I, [NZ (R), Tg, Fj (R), SA], 2003 S(R), I(t), F2, 3(R), [Gg(R), U], 2004 It, S, I
Green, J (Skipton) 1905 I, 1906 S, F, SA, 1907 F, W, I, S
Green, J F (West Kent) 1871 S
Green, W R (Wasps) 1997 A 2, 1998 NZ 1(t+R), 1999 US (R), 2003 W 2(R)
Greening, P B T (Gloucester, Wasps) 1996 It (R), 1997 W (R), Arg 1 1998 NZ 1(R), 2(R), 1999 A (R), US, C, [It (R), NZ (R), Tg, Fj, SA], 2000 I, F, W, It, S, SA 1, 2, A, SA 3, 2001 F, I
Greenstock, N J J (Wasps) 1997 Arg 1, 2, A 1, SA
Greenwell, J H (Rockcliff) 1893 W, I
Greenwood, J E (Cambridge U, Leicester) 1912 F, 1913 SA, W, F, I, S, 1914 W, S, F, 1920 W, F, I, S
Greenwood, J R H (Waterloo) 1966 I, F, S, 1967 A, 1969 I
Greenwood, W J H (Leicester, Harlequins) 1997 A 2, NZ 1, SA, NZ 2, 1998 F, W, S, I, H, It, 1999 C, [It, Tg, Fj, SA], 2000 Arg (R), SA 3, 2001 W, It, S, F, I, A, R, SA, 2002 S, I, F, W, It, NZ, A, SA, 2003 F 1, W 1, It, S, I, NZ, A, F3, [Gg, SA, U(R), W, F, A], 2004 It, S, I, W, F, C(R), SA(R), A2(R)
Greg, W (Manchester) 1876 I, S
Gregory, G G (Bristol) 1931 I, S, F, 1932 SA, W, I, S, 1933 W, I, S, 1934 W, I, S
Gregory, J A (Blackheath) 1949 W
Grewcock, D J (Coventry, Saracens, Bath) 1997 Arg 2, SA, 1998 W (R), S (R), I (R), A 1, NZ 1, SA 2(R), 1999 S (R), A (R), US, C, [It, NZ, Tg (R), SA], 2000 SA 1, 2, A, Arg, SA 3, 2001 W, It, S, I, A, R (R), SA, 2002 S (R), I (R), F (R), W, It, NZ, SA (R), 2003 F 1 (R), W 1 (R), It, S (R), I (t), W 2, F 2, [U], 2004 It, S, W, F, NZ1, 2(R), C, SA, A2, 2005 W, F, I, It, S, A, NZ, 2006 W, It, S, F, I(R), NZ, Arg, 2007 S, It, I
Grylls, W M (Redruth) 1905 I
Guest, R H (Waterloo) 1939 W, I, S, 1947 W, I, S, F, 1948 A, W, I, S, 1949 F, S
Guillemard, A G (West Kent) 1871 S, 1872 S
Gummer, C H A (Plymouth A) 1929 F
Gunner, C R (Marlborough N) 1876 I
Gurdon, C (Richmond) 1880 I, S, 1881 I, W, S, 1882 I, S, 1883 S, 1884 W, S, 1885 I, 1886 W, I, S
Gurdon, E T (Richmond) 1878 S, 1879 I, 1880 S, 1881 I, W, S, 1882 S, 1883 W, I, S, 1884 W, I, S, 1885 W, I, 1886 S
Guscott, J C (Bath) 1989 R, Fj, 1990 I, F, W, S, Arg 3, 1991 W, S, I, F, Fj, A, [NZ, It, F, S, A], 1992 S, I, F, W, C, SA, 1993 F, W, S, I, 1994 R, C, 1995 I, F, W, S, [Arg, It, A, NZ, F], SA, WS, 1996 F, W, S, I, Arg, 1997 I (R), W (R), 1998 F, W, S, I, H, It, A 2, SA 2, 1999 S, I, F, A, US, C, [It (R), NZ, Tg]
Haag, M (Bath) 1997 Arg 1, 2
Haigh, L (Manchester) 1910 W, I, S, 1911 W, F, I, S
Hale, P M (Moseley) 1969 SA, 1970 I, W
Hall, C (Gloucester) 1901 I, S
Hall, J (N Durham) 1894 W, I, S
Hall, J P (Bath) 1984 S (R), I, F, SA 1, 2, A, 1985 R, F, S, I, W, NZ 1, 2, 1986 W, S, 1987 I, F, W, S, 1990 Arg 3, 1994 S
Hall, N M (Richmond) 1947 W, I, S, F, 1949 W, I, 1952 SA, W, S, I, F, 1953 W, I, F, S, 1955 W, I
Halliday, S J (Bath, Harlequins) 1986 W, S, 1987 S, 1988 S, I 1, 2, A 1, A, 1989 S, I, F, W, R, Fj (R), 1990 W, S, 1991 [US, S, A], 1992 S, I, F, W
Hamersley, A St G (Marlborough N) 1871 S, 1872 S, 1873 S, 1874 S
Hamilton-Hill, E A (Harlequins) 1936 NZ, W, I
Hamilton-Wickes, R H (Cambridge U) 1924 I, 1925 NZ, W, I, S, F, 1926 W, I, S, 1927 W
Hammett, E D G (Newport) 1920 W, F, S, 1921 W, I, S, F, 1922 W
Hammond, C E L (Harlequins) 1905 S, NZ, 1906 W, I, S, F, 1908 W, I
Hancock, A W (Northampton) 1965 F, S, 1966 F
Hancock, G E (Birkenhead Park) 1939 W, I, S
Hancock, J H (Newport) 1955 W, I
Hancock, P F (Blackheath) 1886 W, I, 1890 W
Hancock, P S (Richmond) 1904 W, I, S
Handford, F G (Manchester) 1909 W, F, I, S
Hands, R H M (Blackheath) 1910 F, S
Hanley, J (Plymouth A) 1927 W, S, F, 1928 W, I, F, S
Hanley, S M (Sale) 1999 W
Hannaford, R C (Bristol) 1971 W, I, F
Hanvey, R J (Aspatria) 1926 W, I, F, S
Hape, S E (Bath) 2010 A1, 2
Harding, E H (Devonport Services) 1931 I
Harding, R M (Bristol) 1985 R, F, S, 1987 S, [A, J, W], 1988 I 1(R), 2, A 1, 2, Fj
Harding, V S J (Saracens) 1961 F, S, 1962 W, I, F, S
Hardwick, P F (Percy Park) 1902 I, S, 1903 W, I, S, 1904 W, I, S
Hardwick, R J K (Coventry) 1996 It (R)
Hardy, E M P (Blackheath) 1951 I, F, S
Hare, W H (Nottingham, Leicester) 1974 W, 1978 F, NZ, 1979 NZ, 1980 I, F, W, S, 1981 W, S, Arg 1, 2, 1982 F, W, 1983 F, W, S, I, NZ, 1984 S, I, F, W, SA 1, 2
Harper, C H (Exeter) 1899 W
Harriman, A T (Harlequins) 1988 A
Harris, S W (Blackheath) 1920 I, S
Harris, T W (Northampton) 1929 S, 1932 I
Harrison, A C (Hartlepool R) 1931 I, S
Harrison, A L (United Services, RN) 1914 I, F
Harrison, G (Hull) 1877 I, S, 1879 S, I, 1880 S, 1885 W, I
Harrison, H C (United Services, RN) 1909 S, 1914 I, S, F
Harrison, M E (Wakefield) 1985 NZ 1, 2, 1986 S, I, F, 1987 I, F, W, S, [A, J, US, W], 1988 F, W
Hartley, B C (Blackheath) 1901 S, 1902 S
Hartley, D M (Northampton) 2008 PI(R), A(R), SA(R), NZ3(R), 2009 It(R), W(R), I(R), F(R), S(R), Arg 1, 2, A(R), Arg 3, NZ, 2010 W, It, I, S, F
Haskell, J A W (Wasps, Stade Français) 2007 W1, F2, 2008 W, It, F, I(R), NZ1, 2, PI(t&R), A(R), SA, NZ3, 2009 It, W, I, F(R), S(R), Arg 1, 2(R), A(R), Arg 3, NZ, 2010 W, It, I, S, F(R), A1(R)
Haslett, L W (Birkenhead Park) 1926 I, F
Hastings, G W D (Gloucester) 1955 W, I, F, S, 1957 W, I, F, S, 1958 W, A, I, F, S
Havelock, H (Hartlepool R) 1908 F, W, I
Hawcridge, J J (Bradford) 1885 W, I
Hayward, L W (Cheltenham) 1910 I
Hazell, A R (Gloucester) 2004 C, SA(t&R), 2005 W, F(t), It(R), S(R), 2007 SA1
Hazell, D St G (Leicester) 1955 W, I, F, S
Healey, A S (Leicester) 1997 I (R), W, A 1(R), 2(R), NZ 1(R), SA (R), NZ 2, 1998 F, W, S, I, A 1, NZ 1, 2, H, It, A 2, SA 2(R), 1999 US, C, [It, NZ, Tg, Fj, SA (R)], 2000 I, F, W, It, S, SA 1, 2, A, SA 3(R), 2001 W (R), It, S, F, I (R), A, R, SA, 2002 S, I, F, W, It (R), NZ (R), A (R), SA(R), 2003 F2

Hearn, R D (Bedford) 1966 F, S, 1967 I, F, S, W
Heath, A H (Oxford U) 1876 S
Heaton, J (Waterloo) 1935 W, I, S, 1939 W, I, S, 1947 I, S, F
Henderson, A P (Edinburgh Wands) 1947 W, I, S, F, 1948 I, S, F, 1949 W, I
Henderson, R S F (Blackheath) 1883 W, S, 1884 W, S, 1885 W
Heppell, W G (Devonport A) 1903 I
Herbert, A J (Wasps) 1958 F, S, 1959 W, I, F, S
Hesford, R (Bristol) 1981 S (R), 1982 A, S, F (R), 1983 F (R), 1985 R, F, S, I, W
Heslop, N J (Orrell) 1990 Arg 1, 2, 3, 1991 W, S, I, F, [US, F], 1992 W (R)
Hetherington, J G G (Northampton) 1958 A, I, 1959 W, I, F, S
Hewitt, E N (Coventry) 1951 W, I, F
Hewitt, W W (Queen's House) 1881 I, W, S, 1882 I
Hickson, J L (Bradford) 1887 W, I, S, 1890 W, S, I
Higgins, R (Liverpool) 1954 W, NZ, I, S, 1955 W, I, F, S, 1957 W, I, F, S, 1959 W
Hignell, A J (Cambridge U, Bristol) 1975 A 2, 1976 A, W, S, I, 1977 S, I, F, W, 1978 W, 1979 S, I, F, W
Hill, B A (Blackheath) 1903 I, S, 1904 W, I, 1905 W, NZ, 1906 SA, 1907 F, W
Hill, R A (Saracens) 1997 S, I, F, W, A 1, 2, NZ 1, SA, NZ 2, 1998 F, W, H (R), It (R), A 2, SA 2, 1999 S, I, F, W, A, US, C, [It, NZ, Tg, Fj (R), SA], 2000 I, F, W, It, S, SA 1, 2, A, Arg, SA 3, 2001 W, It, S, F, I, A, SA, 2002 S, I, F, W, It, NZ, A, SA, 2003 F 1, W 1, It, S, I, NZ, A, F 3, [Gg, F, A], 2004 It, S, I, W, F, NZ1, 2, A1
Hill, R J (Bath) 1984 SA 1, 2, 1985 I (R), NZ 2(R), 1986 F (R), 1987 I, F, W, [US], 1989 Fj, 1990 I, F, W, S, Arg 1, 2, 3, 1991 W, S, I, F, Fj, A, [NZ, It, US, F, S, A]
Hillard, R J (Oxford U) 1925 NZ
Hiller, R (Harlequins) 1968 W, I, F, S, 1969 I, F, S, W, SA, 1970 I, W, S, 1971 I, F, S (2[1C]), P, 1972 W, I
Hind, A E (Leicester) 1905 NZ, 1906 W
Hind, G R (Blackheath) 1910 S, 1911 I
Hipkiss, D J (Leicester) 2007 W2, F3, [Sm(R), Tg(R), F(R), SA2(R)], 2008 NZ3(R), 2009 Arg 1, 2, A, Arg 3, NZ, 2010 W(R)
Hobbs, R F A (Blackheath) 1899 S, 1903 W
Hobbs, R G S (Richmond) 1932 SA, W, I, S
Hobson, J D (Bristol) 2008 NZ2(R)
Hodges, H A (Nottingham) 1906 W, I
Hodgkinson, S D (Nottingham) 1989 R, Fj, 1990 I, F, W, S, Arg 1, 2, 3, 1991 W, S, I, F, [US]
Hodgson, C C (Sale) 2001 R, 2002 S (R), I (R), It (R), Arg, 2003 F 1, W 1, It (R), 2004 NZ1, 2, A1, C, SA, A2, 2005 W, F, I, It, S, A, NZ, Sm, 2006 W, It, S, F, NZ, Arg, SA1, 2008 S(R), NZ1
Hodgson, J McD (Northern) 1932 SA, W, I, S, 1934 W, I, 1936 I
Hodgson, P K (London Irish) 2008 I(R), 2009 Arg 1(R), 2(R), A(R), Arg 3, NZ, 2010 W(R), It(R), I(R)
Hodgson, S A M (Durham City) 1960 W, I, F, S, 1961 SA, W, 1962 W, I, F, S, 1964 W
Hofmeyr, M B (Oxford U) 1950 W, F, S
Hogarth, T B (Hartlepool R) 1906 F
Holford, G (Gloucester) 1920 W, F
Holland, D (Devonport A) 1912 W, I, S
Holliday, T E (Aspatria) 1923 S, F, 1925 I, S, F, 1926 F, S
Holmes, C B (Manchester) 1947 S, 1948 I, F
Holmes, E (Manningham) 1890 S, I
Holmes, W A (Nuneaton) 1950 W, I, F, S, 1951 W, I, F, S, 1952 SA, S, I, F, 1953 W, I, F, S
Holmes, W B (Cambridge U) 1949 W, I, F, S
Hook, W G (Gloucester) 1951 S, 1952 SA, W
Hooper, C A (Middlesex W) 1894 W, I, S
Hopley, D P (Wasps) 1995 [WS (R)], SA, WS
Hopley, F J V (Blackheath) 1907 F, W, 1908 I
Horak, M J (London Irish) 2002 Arg
Hordern, P C (Gloucester) 1931 I, S, F, 1934 W
Horley, C H (Swinton) 1885 I
Hornby, A N (Manchester) 1877 I, S, 1878 S, I, 1880 I, 1881 I, S, 1882 I, S
Horrocks-Taylor, J P (Cambridge U, Leicester, Middlesbrough) 1958 W, A, 1961 S, 1962 S, 1963 NZ 1, 2, A, 1964 NZ, W
Horsfall, E L (Harlequins) 1949 W
Horton, A L (Blackheath) 1965 W, I, F, S, 1966 F, S, 1967 NZ
Horton, J P (Bath) 1978 W, S, I, NZ, 1980 I, F, W, S, 1981 W, 1983 S, I, 1984 SA 1, 2
Horton, N E (Moseley, Toulouse) 1969 I, F, S, W, 1971 I, F, S, 1974 S, 1975 W, 1977 S, I, F, W, 1978 F, W, 1979 S, I, F, W, 1980 I
Hosen, R W (Bristol, Northampton) 1963 NZ 1, 2, A, 1964 F, S, 1967 A, I, F, S, W
Hosking, G R d'A (Devonport Services) 1949 W, I, F, S, 1950 W
Houghton, S (Runcorn) 1892 I, 1896 W
Howard, P D (O Millhillians) 1930 W, I, F, S, 1931 W, I, S, F
Hubbard, G C (Blackheath) 1892 W, I
Hubbard, J C (Harlequins) 1930 S
Hudson, A (Gloucester) 1906 W, I, F, 1908 F, W, I, S, 1910 F
Hughes, G E (Barrow) 1896 S
Hull, P A (Bristol, RAF) 1994 SA 1, 2, R, C
Hulme, F C (Birkenhead Park) 1903 W, I, 1905 W, I
Hunt, J T (Manchester) 1882 I, S, 1884 W
Hunt, R (Manchester) 1880 I, 1881 W, S, 1882 I
Hunt, W H (Manchester) 1876 S, 1877 I, S, 1878 I
Hunter, I (Northampton) 1992 C, 1993 F, W, 1994 F, W, 1995 [WS, F]
Huntsman, R P (Headingley) 1985 NZ 1, 2
Hurst, A C B (Wasps) 1962 S
Huskisson, T F (OMTs) 1937 W, I, S, 1938 W, I, 1939 W, I, S
Hutchinson, F (Headingley) 1909 F, I, S
Hutchinson, J E (Durham City) 1906 I
Hutchinson, W C (RIE Coll) 1876 S, 1877 I
Hutchinson, W H H (Hull) 1875 I, 1876 I
Huth, H (Huddersfield) 1879 S
Hyde, J P (Northampton) 1950 F, S
Hynes, W B (United Services, RN) 1912 F
Ibbitson, E D (Headingley) 1909 W, F, I, S
Imrie, H M (Durham City) 1906 NZ, 1907 I
Inglis, R E (Blackheath) 1886 W, I, S
Irvin, S H (Devonport A) 1905 W
Isherwood, F W (Ravenscourt Park) 1872 S
Jackett, E J (Leicester, Falmouth) 1905 NZ, 1906 W, I, S, F, SA, 1907 W, I, S, 1909 W, F, I, S
Jackson, A H (Blackheath) 1878 I, 1880 I
Jackson, B S (Broughton Park) 1970 S (R), F
Jackson, P B (Coventry) 1956 W, I, F, 1957 W, I, F, S, 1958 W, A, F, S, 1959 W, I, F, S, 1961 S, 1963 W, I, F, S
Jackson, W J (Halifax) 1894 S
Jacob, F (Cambridge U) 1897 W, I, S, 1898 I, S, W, 1899 W, I
Jacob, H P (Blackheath) 1924 W, I, F, S, 1930 F
Jacob, P G (Blackheath) 1898 I
Jacobs, C R (Northampton) 1956 W, I, S, F, 1957 W, I, F, S, 1958 W, A, I, F, S, 1960 W, I, F, S, 1961 SA, W, I, F, S, 1963 NZ 1, 2, A, 1964 W, I, F, S
Jago, R A (Devonport A) 1906 W, I, SA, 1907 W, I
Janion, J P A G (Bedford) 1971 W, I, F, S (2[1C]), P, 1972 W, S, SA, 1973 A, 1975 A 1, 2
Jarman, J W (Bristol) 1900 W
Jeavons, N C (Moseley) 1981 S, I, F, Arg 1, 2, 1982 A, S, I, F, W, 1983 F, W, S, I
Jeeps, R E G (Northampton) 1956 W, 1957 W, I, F, S, 1958 W, A, I, F, S, 1959 I, 1960 W, I, F, S, 1961 SA, W, I, F, S, 1962 W, I, F, S
Jeffery, G L (Blackheath) 1886 W, I, S, 1887 W, I, S
Jennins, C R (Waterloo) 1967 A, I, F
Jewitt, J (Hartlepool R) 1902 W
Johns, W A (Gloucester) 1909 W, F, I, S, 1910 W, I, F
Johnson, M O (Leicester) 1993 F, NZ, 1994 S, I, F, W, R, C, 1995 I, F, W, S, [Arg, It, WS, A, NZ, F], SA, WS, 1996 F, W, S, I, It, Arg, 1997 S, I, F, W, A 2, NZ 1, 2, 1998 F, W, S, I, H, It, A 2, SA 2, 1999 S, I, F, W, A, US, C, [It, NZ, Tg, Fj, SA], 2000 SA 1, 2, A, Arg, SA 3, 2001 W, It, S, F, SA, 2002 S, I, F, It (t+R), NZ, A, SA, 2003 F 1, W 1, S, I, NZ, A, F 3, [Gg, SA, Sm, U(R), W, F, A]
Johnston, J B (Saracens) 2002 Arg, NZ (R)
Johnston, W R (Bristol) 1910 W, I, S, 1912 W, I, S, F, 1913 SA, W, F, I, S, 1914 W, I, S, F
Jones, C M (Sale) 2004 It(R), S, I(R), W, NZ1, 2005 W, 2006 A1(R), 2, SA1(R), 2, 2007 SA1, 2(R)
Jones, F P (New Brighton) 1893 S
Jones, H A (Barnstaple) 1950 W, I, F
Jorden, A M (Cambridge U, Blackheath, Bedford) 1970 F, 1973 I, F, S, 1974 F, 1975 W, S
Jowett, D (Heckmondwike) 1889 M, 1890 S, I, 1891 W, I, S

Judd, P E (Coventry) 1962 W, I, F, S, 1963 S, NZ 1, 2, A, 1964 NZ, 1965 I, F, S, 1966 W, I, F, S, 1967 A, I, F, S, W, NZ
Kay, B J (Leicester) 2001 C 1, 2, A, R, SA (t+R), 2002 S, I, F, W, It, Arg, NZ (R), A, SA, 2003 F 1, W 1, It, S, I, NZ, A, F 3, [Gg, SA, Sm, W, F, A], 2004 It, S, I, W, F, C(R), SA(R), 2005 W, F, I, It, S, 2006 A2, NZ, Arg, SA1, 2(R), 2007 F2, [US, SA1, Sm, Tg, A, F, SA2], 2008 W(R), It(R), F(R), S(R), I(R), NZ1(R), 2(R), 2009 Arg 1(R), 2(t&R)
Kayll, H E (Sunderland) 1878 S
Keeling, J H (Guy's Hospital) 1948 A, W
Keen, B W (Newcastle U) 1968 W, I, F, S
Keeton, G H (Leicester) 1904 W, I, S
Kelly, G A (Bedford) 1947 W, I, S, 1948 W
Kelly, T S (London Devonians) 1906 W, I, S, F, SA, 1907 F, W, I, S, 1908 F, I, S
Kemble, A T (Liverpool) 1885 W, I, 1887 I
Kemp, D T (Blackheath) 1935 W
Kemp, T A (Richmond) 1937 W, I, 1939 S, 1948 A, W
Kendall, P D (Birkenhead Park) 1901 S, 1902 W, 1903 S
Kendall-Carpenter, J MacG K (Oxford U, Bath) 1949 I, F, S, 1950 W, I, F, S, 1951 I, F, S, 1952 SA, W, S, I, F, 1953 W, I, F, S, 1954 W, NZ, I, F
Kendrew, D A (Leicester) 1930 W, I, 1933 I, S, 1934 S, 1935 W, I, 1936 NZ, W, I
Kennedy, N J (London Irish) 2008 PI, NZ3, 2009 It, W, I, F(R), S(R)
Kennedy, R D (Camborne S of M) 1949 I, F, S
Kent, C P (Rosslyn Park) 1977 S, I, F, W, 1978 F (R)
Kent, T (Salford) 1891 W, I, S, 1892 W, I, S
Kershaw, C A (United Services, RN) 1920 W, F, I, S, 1921 W, I, S, F, 1922 W, I, F, S, 1923 W, I, S, F
Kewley, E (Liverpool) 1874 S, 1875 S, 1876 I, S, 1877 I, S, 1878 S
Kewney, A L (Leicester) 1906 W, I, S, F, 1909 A, W, F, I, S, 1911 W, F, I, S, 1912 I, S, 1913 SA
Key, A (O Cranleighans) 1930 I, 1933 W
Keyworth, M (Swansea) 1976 A, W, S, I
Kilner, B (Wakefield T) 1880 I
Kindersley, R S (Exeter) 1883 W, 1884 S, 1885 W
King, A D (Wasps) 1997 Arg 2(R), 1998 SA 2(R), 2000 It (R), 2001 C 2(R), 2003 W2
King, I (Harrogate) 1954 W, NZ, I
King, J A (Headingley) 1911 W, F, I, S, 1912 W, I, S, 1913 SA, W, F, I, S
King, Q E M A (Army) 1921 S
Kingston, P (Gloucester) 1975 A 1, 2, 1979 I, F, W
Kitching, A E (Blackheath) 1913 I
Kittermaster, H J (Harlequins) 1925 NZ, W, I, 1926 W, I, F, S
Knight, F (Plymouth) 1909 A
Knight, P M (Bristol) 1972 F, S, SA
Knowles, E (Millom) 1896 S, 1897 S
Knowles, T C (Birkenhead Park) 1931 S
Krige, J A (Guy's Hospital) 1920 W
Labuschagne, N A (Harlequins, Guy's Hospital) 1953 W, 1955 W, I, F, S
Lagden, R O (Richmond) 1911 S
Laird, H C C (Harlequins) 1927 W, I, S, 1928 A, W, I, F, S, 1929 W, I
Lambert, D (Harlequins) 1907 F, 1908 F, W, S, 1911 W, F, I
Lampkowski, M S (Headingley) 1976 A, W, S, I
Lapage, W N (United Services, RN) 1908 F, W, I, S
Larter, P J (Northampton, RAF) 1967 A, NZ, 1968 W, I, F, S, 1969 I, F, S, W, SA, 1970 I, W, F, S, 1971 W, I, F, S (2[1C]), P, 1972 SA, 1973 NZ 1, W
Law, A F (Richmond) 1877 S
Law, D E (Birkenhead Park) 1927 I
Lawes, C L (Northampton) 2009 A(R), 2010 S(R), A1(R), 2
Lawrence, Hon H A (Richmond) 1873 S, 1874 S, 1875 I, S
Lawrie, P W (Leicester) 1910 S, 1911 S
Lawson, R G (Workington) 1925 I
Lawson, T M (Workington) 1928 A, W
Leadbetter, M M (Broughton Park) 1970 F
Leadbetter, V H (Edinburgh Wands) 1954 S, F
Leake, W R M (Harlequins) 1891 W, I, S
Leather, G (Liverpool) 1907 I
Lee, F H (Marlborough N) 1876 S, 1877 I
Lee, H (Blackheath) 1907 F
Le Fleming, J (Blackheath) 1887 W
Leonard, J (Saracens, Harlequins) 1990 Arg 1, 2, 3, 1991 W, S, I, F, Fj, A, [NZ, It, US, F, S, A], 1992 S, I, F, W, C, SA, 1993 F, W, S, I, NZ, 1994 S, I, F, W, SA 1, 2, R, C, 1995 I, F, W, S, [Arg, It, A, NZ, F], SA, WS, 1996 F, W, S, I, It, Arg, 1997 S, I, F, W, A 2, NZ 1, SA, NZ 2, 1998 F, W, S, I, H, It, A 2 SA 2, 1999 S, I, F, W, A, C (R), [It, NZ, Fj, SA], 2000 I, F, W, It, S, SA 1, 2, A, Arg, SA 3, 2001 W, It, S, F, I, R, 2002 S (R), I (R), F (R), It (R), A, SA, 2003 F 1, S, I, NZ, W 2, F 2(t+R), 3(R), [Gg(t&R), SA(R), Sm, U, W, F(t&R), A(R)], 2004 It(R)
Leslie-Jones, F A (Richmond) 1895 W, I
Lewis, A O (Bath) 1952 SA, W, S, I, F, 1953 W, I, F, S, 1954 F
Lewsey, O J (Wasps) 1998 NZ 1, 2, SA 1, 2001 C 1, 2, US, 2003 It, S, I, NZ, A, F2, 3(t+R), [Gg, SA, U, F, A], 2004 It, S, I, W, F, NZ1, 2, A1, C, SA, A2, 2005 W, F, I, It, S, A, NZ, Sm, 2006 W, S, F, Arg(R), SA1, 2, 2007 S, It, I, F1, 2, 3, [US, SA1, Sm, Tg, A, F]
Leyland, R (Waterloo) 1935 W, I, S
Linnett, M S (Moseley) 1989 Fj
Lipman, M R (Bath) 2004 NZ2(R), A1(R), 2006 A2, 2008 It, F, S, I, PI(R), A(R), NZ3
Livesay, R O'H (Blackheath) 1898 W, 1899 W
Lloyd, L D (Leicester) 2000 SA 1(R), 2(R), 2001 C 1, 2, US
Lloyd, R H (Harlequins) 1967 NZ, 1968 W, I, F, S
Locke, H M (Birkenhead Park) 1923 S, F, 1924 W, F, S, 1925 W, I, S, F, 1927 W, I, S
Lockwood, R E (Heckmondwike) 1887 W, I, S, 1889 M, 1891 W, I, S, 1892 W, I, S, 1893 W, I, 1894 W, I
Login, S H M (RN Coll) 1876 I
Lohden, F C (Blackheath) 1893 W
Long, A E (Bath) 1997 A 2, 2001 US (R)
Longland, R J (Northampton) 1932 S, 1933 W, S, 1934 W, I, S, 1935 W, I, S, 1936 NZ, W, I, S, 1937 W, I, S, 1938 W, I, S
Lowe, C N (Cambridge U, Blackheath) 1913 SA, W, F, I, S, 1914 W, I, S, F, 1920 W, F, I, S, 1921 W, I, S, F, 1922 W, I, F, S, 1923 W, I, S, F
Lowrie, F W (Wakefield T) 1889 M, 1890 W
Lowry, W M (Birkenhead Park) 1920 F
Lozowski, R A P (Wasps) 1984 A
Luddington, W G E (Devonport Services) 1923 W, I, S, F, 1924 W, I, F, S, 1925 W, I, S, F, 1926 W
Luger, D D (Harlequins, Saracens) 1998 H, It, SA 2, 1999 S, I, F, W, A, US, C, [It, NZ, Tg, Fj, SA], 2000 SA 1, A, Arg, SA 3, 2001 W, I, A, R, SA, 2002 F (R), W, It, 2003 F 1, W 1, It, S (R), I (R), NZ(R), W 2, [Gg(R), SA(R), U, W]
Lund, M B (Sale) 2006 A1, 2(R), NZ(R), Arg(t&R), 2007 S, It, I, F1(R), W1(R), SA2
Luscombe, F (Gipsies) 1872 S, 1873 S, 1875 I, S, 1876 I, S
Luscombe, J H (Gipsies) 1871 S
Luxmoore, A F C C (Richmond) 1900 S, 1901 W
Luya, H F (Waterloo, Headingley) 1948 W, I, S, F, 1949 W
Lyon, A (Liverpool) 1871 S
Lyon, G H d'O (United Services, RN) 1908 S, 1909 A
McCanlis, M A (Gloucester) 1931 W, I
McCarthy, N (Gloucester) 1999 I (t), US (R), 2000 It (R)
McFadyean, C W (Moseley) 1966 I, F, S, 1967 A, I, F, S, W, NZ, 1968 W, I
MacIlwaine, A H (United Services, Hull & E Riding) 1912 W, I, S, F, 1920 I
Mackie, O G (Wakefield T, Cambridge U) 1897 S, 1898 I
Mackinlay, J E H (St George's Hospital) 1872 S, 1873 S, 1875 I
MacLaren, W (Manchester) 1871 S
MacLennan, R R F (OMTs) 1925 I, S, F
McLeod, N F (RIE Coll) 1879 S, I
Madge, R J P (Exeter) 1948 A, W, I, S
Malir, F W S (Otley) 1930 W, I, S
Mallett, J A (Bath) 1995 [WS (R)]
Mallinder, J (Sale) 1997 Arg 1, 2
Mangles, R H (Richmond) 1897 W, I
Manley, D C (Exeter) 1963 W, I, F, S
Mann, W E (United Services, Army) 1911 W, F, I
Mantell, N D (Rosslyn Park) 1975 A 1
Mapletoft, M S (Gloucester) 1997 Arg 2
Markendale, E T (Manchester R) 1880 I
Marques, R W D (Cambridge U, Harlequins) 1956 W, I, S, F, 1957 W, I, F, S, 1958 W, A, I, F, S, 1959 W, I, F, S, 1960 W, I, F, S, 1961 SA, W
Marquis, J C (Birkenhead Park) 1900 I, S

Marriott, C J B (Blackheath) 1884 W, I, S, 1886 W, I, S, 1887 I
Marriott, E E (Manchester) 1876 I
Marriott, V R (Harlequins) 1963 NZ 1, 2, A, 1964 NZ
Marsden, G H (Morley) 1900 W, I, S
Marsh, H (RIE Coll) 1873 S
Marsh, J (Swinton) 1892 I
Marshall, H (Blackheath) 1893 W
Marshall, M W (Blackheath) 1873 S, 1874 S, 1875 I, S, 1876 I, S, 1877 I, S, 1878 S, I
Marshall, R M (Oxford U) 1938 I, S, 1939 W, I, S
Martin, C R (Bath) 1985 F, S, I, W
Martin, N O (Harlequins) 1972 F (R)
Martindale, S A (Kendal) 1929 F
Massey, E J (Leicester) 1925 W, I, S
Mather, B-J (Sale) 1999 W
Mathias, J L (Bristol) 1905 W, I, S, NZ
Matters, J C (RNE Coll) 1899 S
Matthews, J R C (Harlequins) 1949 F, S, 1950 I, F, S, 1952 SA, W, S, I, F
Maud, P (Blackheath) 1893 W, I
Maxwell, A W (New Brighton, Headingley) 1975 A 1, 1976 A, W, S, I, F, 1978 F
Maxwell-Hyslop, J E (Oxford U) 1922 I, F, S
May, T A (Newcastle) 2009 Arg 1, 2
Maynard, A F (Cambridge U) 1914 W, I, S
Mears, L A (Bath) 2005 Sm(R), 2006 W(R), It(R), F(R), I, A1, 2(R), NZ(R), Arg(R), SA1(R), 2, 2007 S(R), It(R), I(R), W1(R), F2(R), 3(R), [Tg(R)], 2008 W(R), It(R), F(R), S, I, NZ1, 2, PI, A, SA, NZ3, 2009 It, W, I, F, S, 2010 I(R)
Meikle, G W C (Waterloo) 1934 W, I, S
Meikle, S S C (Waterloo) 1929 S
Mellish, F W (Blackheath) 1920 W, F, I, S, 1921 W, I
Melville, N D (Wasps) 1984 A, 1985 I, W, NZ 1, 2, 1986 W, S, I, F, 1988 F, W, S, I 1
Merriam, L P B (Blackheath) 1920 W, F
Michell, A T (Oxford U) 1875 I, S, 1876 I
Middleton, B B (Birkenhead Park) 1882 I, 1883 I
Middleton, J A (Richmond) 1922 S
Miles, J H (Leicester) 1903 W
Millett, H (Richmond) 1920 F
Mills, F W (Marlborough N) 1872 S, 1873 S
Mills, S G F (Gloucester) 1981 Arg 1, 2, 1983 W, 1984 SA 1, A
Mills, W A (Devonport A) 1906 W, I, S, F, SA, 1907 F, W, I, S, 1908 F, W
Milman, D L K (Bedford) 1937 W, 1938 W, I, S
Milton, C H (Camborne S of M) 1906 I
Milton, J G (Camborne S of M) 1904 W, I, S, 1905 S, 1907 I
Milton, W H (Marlborough N) 1874 S, 1875 I
Mitchell, F (Blackheath) 1895 W, I, S, 1896 W, I, S
Mitchell, W G (Richmond) 1890 W, S, I, 1891 W, I, S, 1893 S
Mobbs, E R (Northampton) 1909 A, W, F, I, S, 1910 I, F
Moberley, W O (Ravenscourt Park) 1872 S
Monye, Y C C (Harlequins) 2008 PI, A, SA, NZ3, 2009 F, S, A, Arg 3, NZ, 2010 W, It, I, S
Moody, L W (Leicester) 2001 C 1, 2, US, I (R), R, SA (R), 2002 I (R), W, It, Arg, NZ, A, SA, 2003 F 1, W 2, F 2, 3(R), [Gg(R), SA, Sm(R), U, W, F(R), A(R)], 2004 C, SA, A2, 2005 F, I, It, S, A, NZ, Sm, 2006 W, It, S, F, I, A1, NZ, Arg, SA1(R), 2(R), W2(R), 2007 [US(R), SA1(R), Sm(R), Tg, A, F, SA2], 2008 W, 2009 A, Arg 3, NZ, 2010 W, It, I, S(R), F, A1, 2
Moore, B C (Nottingham, Harlequins) 1987 S, [A, J, W], 1988 F, W, S, I 1, 2, A 1, 2, Fj, A, 1989 S, I, F, W, R, Fj, 1990 I, F, W, S, Arg 1, 2, 1991 W, S, I, F, Fj, A, [NZ, It, F, S, A], 1992 S, I, F, W, SA, 1993 F, W, S, I, NZ, 1994 S, I, F, W, SA 1, 2, R, C, 1995 I, F, W, S, [Arg, It, WS (R), A, NZ, F]
Moore, E J (Blackheath) 1883 I, S
Moore, N J N H (Bristol) 1904 W, I, S
Moore, P B C (Blackheath) 1951 W
Moore, W K T (Leicester) 1947 W, I, 1949 F, S, 1950 I, F, S
Mordell, R J (Rosslyn Park) 1978 W
Morfitt, S (W Hartlepool) 1894 W, I, S, 1896 W, I, S
Morgan, J R (Hawick) 1920 W
Morgan, O C (Gloucester) 2007 S, I
Morgan, W G D (Medicals, Newcastle) 1960 W, I, F, S, 1961 SA, W, I, F, S
Morley, A J (Bristol) 1972 SA, 1973 NZ 1, W, I, 1975 S, A 1, 2
Morris, A D W (United Services, RN) 1909 A, W, F
Morris, C D (Liverpool St Helens, Orrell) 1988 A, 1989 S, I, F, W, 1992 S, I, F, W, C, SA, 1993 F, W, S, I, 1994 F, W, SA 1, 2, R, 1995 S (t), [Arg, WS, A, NZ, F]
Morris, R (Northampton) 2003 W 1, It
Morrison, P H (Cambridge U) 1890 W, S, I, 1891 I
Morse, S (Marlborough N) 1873 S, 1874 S, 1875 S
Mortimer, W (Marlborough N) 1899 W
Morton, H J S (Blackheath) 1909 I, S, 1910 W, I
Moss, F (Broughton) 1885 W, I, 1886 W
Mullan, M J (Worcester) 2010 It(R)
Mullins, A R (Harlequins) 1989 Fj
Mycock, J (Sale) 1947 W, I, S, F, 1948 A
Myers, E (Bradford) 1920 I, S, 1921 W, I, 1922 W, I, F, S, 1923 W, I, S, F, 1924 W, I, F, S, 1925 S, F
Myers, H (Keighley) 1898 I
Nanson, W M B (Carlisle) 1907 F, W
Narraway, L J W (Gloucester) 2008 W, It(R), S(R), NZ1, 2, 2009 W(R), I(R)
Nash, E H (Richmond) 1875 I
Neale, B A (Rosslyn Park) 1951 I, F, S
Neale, M E (Blackheath) 1912 F
Neame, S (O Cheltonians) 1879 S, I, 1880 I, S
Neary, A (Broughton Park) 1971 W, I, F, S (2[1C]), P, 1972 W, I, F, S, SA, 1973 NZ 1, W, I, F, S, NZ 2, A, 1974 S, I, F, W, 1975 I, F, W, S, A 1, 1976 A, W, S, I, F, 1977 I, 1978 F (R), 1979 S, I, F, W, NZ, 1980 I, F, W, S
Nelmes, B G (Cardiff) 1975 A 1, 2, 1978 W, S, I, NZ
Newbold, C J (Blackheath) 1904 W, I, S, 1905 W, I, S
Newman, S C (Oxford U) 1947 F, 1948 A, W
Newton, A W (Blackheath) 1907 S
Newton, P A (Blackheath) 1882 S
Newton-Thompson, J O (Oxford U) 1947 S, F
Nichol, W (Brighouse R) 1892 W, S
Nicholas, P L (Exeter) 1902 W
Nicholson, B E (Harlequins) 1938 W, I
Nicholson, E S (Leicester) 1935 W, I, S, 1936 NZ, W
Nicholson, E T (Birkenhead Park) 1900 W, I
Nicholson, T (Rockcliff) 1893 I
Ninnes, B F (Coventry) 1971 W
Noon, J D (Newcastle) 2001 C 1, 2, US, 2003 W 2, F 2(t+R), 2005 W, F, I, It, S, A, NZ, 2006 W, It, S, F, I, 2006 A1(R), 2, NZ, Arg, SA1, 2, 2007 SA2, F2, [US, SA1], 2008 It, F, S, I, NZ1(R), 2, PI, A, SA, NZ3, 2009 It
Norman, D J (Leicester) 1932 SA, W
North, E H G (Blackheath) 1891 W, I, S
Northmore, S (Millom) 1897 I
Novak, M J (Harlequins) 1970 W, S, F
Novis, A L (Blackheath) 1929 S, F, 1930 W, I, F, 1933 I, S
Oakeley, F E (United Services, RN) 1913 S, 1914 I, S, F
Oakes, R F (Hartlepool R) 1897 W, I, S, 1898 I, S, W, 1899 W, S
Oakley, L F L (Bedford) 1951 W
Obolensky, A (Oxford U) 1936 NZ, W, I, S
Ojo, T O (London Irish) 2008 NZ1, 2
Ojomoh, S O (Bath, Gloucester) 1994 I, F, SA 1(R), 2, R, 1995 S (R), [Arg, WS, A (t), F], 1996 F, 1998 NZ 1
Old, A G B (Middlesbrough, Leicester, Sheffield) 1972 W, I, F, S, SA, 1973 NZ 2, A, 1974 S, I, F, W, 1975 I, A 2, 1976 S, I, 1978 F
Oldham, W L (Coventry) 1908 S, 1909 A
Olver, C J (Northampton) 1990 Arg 3, 1991 [US], 1992 C
O'Neill, A (Teignmouth, Torquay A) 1901 W, I, S
Openshaw, W E (Manchester) 1879 I
Orwin, J (Gloucester, RAF, Bedford) 1985 R, F, S, I, W, NZ 1, 2, 1988 F, W, S, I 1, 2, A 1, 2
Osborne, R R (Manchester) 1871 S
Osborne, S H (Oxford U) 1905 S
Oti, C (Cambridge U, Nottingham, Wasps) 1988 S, I 1, 1989 S, I, F, W, R, 1990 Arg 1, 2, 1991 Fj, A, [NZ, It]
Oughtred, B (Hartlepool R) 1901 S, 1902 W, I, S, 1903 W, I
Owen, J E (Coventry) 1963 W, I, F, S, A, 1964 NZ, 1965 W, I, F, S, 1966 I, F, S, 1967 NZ
Owen-Smith, H G O (St Mary's Hospital) 1934 W, I, S, 1936 NZ, W, I, S, 1937 W, I, S
Page, J J (Bedford, Northampton) 1971 W, I, F, S, 1975 S
Paice, D J (London Irish) 2008 NZ1(R), 2(R)
Pallant, J N (Notts) 1967 I, F, S
Palmer, A C (London Hospital) 1909 I, S
Palmer, F H (Richmond) 1905 W
Palmer, G V (Richmond) 1928 I, F, S
Palmer, J A (Bath) 1984 SA 1, 2, 1986 I (R)

Palmer, T P (Leeds, Wasps, Stade Français) 2001 US (R), 2006 Arg(R), SA1, 2, 2007 It(R), I(R), F1, W1, 2008 NZ1, 2, PI(R), A, SA, 2010 F(R), A1, 2
Pargetter, T A (Coventry) 1962 S, 1963 F, NZ 1
Parker, G W (Gloucester) 1938 I, S
Parker, Hon S (Liverpool) 1874 S, 1875 S
Parsons, E I (RAF) 1939 S
Parsons, M J (Northampton) 1968 W, I, F, S
Patterson, W M (Sale) 1961 SA, S
Pattisson, R M (Blackheath) 1883 I, S
Paul, H R (Gloucester) 2002 F(R), 2004 It(t&R), S(R), C, SA, A2
Paul, J E (RIE Coll) 1875 S
Payne, A T (Bristol) 1935 I, S
Payne, C M (Harlequins) 1964 I, F, S, 1965 I, F, S, 1966 W, I, F, S
Payne, J H (Broughton) 1882 S, 1883 W, I, S, 1884 I, 1885 W, I
Payne, T A N (Wasps) 2004 A1, 2006 A1(R), 2(R), 2007 F1, W1, 2008 It, NZ1(R), 2, SA, NZ3, 2009 Arg 1, 2, A, Arg 3, NZ, 2010 W, It, I, S, F, A1, 2
Pearce, G S (Northampton) 1979 S, I, F, W, 1981 Arg 1, 2, 1982 A, S, 1983 F, W, S, I, NZ, 1984 S, SA 2, A, 1985 R, F, S, I, W, NZ 1, 2, 1986 W, S, I, F, 1987 I, F, W, S, [A, US, W], 1988 Fj, 1991 [US]
Pears, D (Harlequins) 1990 Arg 1, 2, 1992 F (R), 1994 F
Pearson, A W (Blackheath) 1875 I, S, 1876 I, S, 1877 S, 1878 S, I
Peart, T G A H (Hartlepool R) 1964 F, S
Pease, F E (Hartlepool R) 1887 I
Penny, S H (Leicester) 1909 A
Penny, W J (United Hospitals) 1878 I, 1879 S, I
Percival, L J (Rugby) 1891 I, 1892 I, 1893 S
Periton, H G (Waterloo) 1925 W, 1926 W, I, F, S, 1927 W, I, S, F, 1928 A, I, F, S, 1929 W, I, S, F, 1930 W, I, F, S
Perrott, E S (O Cheltonians) 1875 I
Perry, D G (Bedford) 1963 F, S, NZ 1, 2, A 1964 NZ, W, I, 1965 W, I, F, S, 1966 W, I, F
Perry, M B (Bath) 1997 A 2, NZ 1, SA, NZ 2, 1998 W, S, I, A 1, NZ 1, 2, SA 1, H, It, A 2, 1999 I, F, W, A US, C, [It, NZ, Tg, Fj, SA], 2000 I, F, W, It, S, SA 1, 2, A, SA 3, 2001 W (R), F (R)
Perry, S A (Bristol) 2006 NZ, Arg, SA1(R), 2(R), 2007 I(R), F1(R), W1(R), SA1(R), 2(R), W2, F2, 3, [US, SA1]
Perry, S V (Cambridge U, Waterloo) 1947 W, I, 1948 A, W, I, S, F
Peters, J (Plymouth) 1906 S, F, 1907 I, S, 1908 W
Phillips, C (Birkenhead Park) 1880 S, 1881 I, S
Phillips, M S (Fylde) 1958 A, I, F, S, 1959 W, I, F, S, 1960 W, I, F, S, 1961 W, 1963 W, I, F, S, NZ 1, 2, A, 1964 NZ, W, I, F, S
Pickering, A S (Harrogate) 1907 I
Pickering, R D A (Bradford) 1967 I, F, S, W, 1968 F, S
Pickles, R C W (Bristol) 1922 I, F
Pierce, R (Liverpool) 1898 I, 1903 S
Pilkington, W N (Cambridge U) 1898 S
Pillman, C H (Blackheath) 1910 W, I, F, S, 1911 W, F, I, S, 1912 W, F, 1913 SA, W, F, I, S, 1914 W, I, S
Pillman, R L (Blackheath) 1914 F
Pinch, J (Lancaster) 1896 W, I, 1897 S
Pinching, W W (Guy's Hospital) 1872 S
Pitman, I J (Oxford U) 1922 S
Plummer, K C (Bristol) 1969 W, 1976 S, I, F
Pool-Jones, R J (Stade Francais) 1998 A 1
Poole, F O (Oxford U) 1895 W, I, S
Poole, R W (Hartlepool R) 1896 S
Pope, E B (Blackheath) 1931 W, S, F
Portus, G V (Blackheath) 1908 F, I
Potter, S (Leicester) 1998 A 1(t)
Poulton, R W (later Poulton Palmer) (Oxford U, Harlequins, Liverpool) 1909 F, I, S, 1910 W, 1911 S, 1912 W, I, S, 1913 SA, W, F, I, S, 1914 W, I, S, F
Powell, D L (Northampton) 1966 W, I, 1969 I, F, S, W, 1971 W, I, F, S (2[1C])
Pratten, W E (Blackheath) 1927 S, F
Preece, I (Coventry) 1948 I, S, F, 1949 F, S, 1950 W, I, F, S, 1951 W, I, F
Preece, P S (Coventry) 1972 SA, 1973 NZ 1, W, I, F, S, NZ 2, 1975 I, F, W, A 2, 1976 W (R)
Preedy, M (Gloucester) 1984 SA 1
Prentice, F D (Leicester) 1928 I, F, S
Prescott, R E (Harlequins) 1937 W, I, 1938 I, 1939 W, I, S
Preston, N J (Richmond) 1979 NZ, 1980 I, F
Price, H L (Harlequins) 1922 I, S, 1923 W, I
Price, J (Coventry) 1961 I
Price, P L A (RIE Coll) 1877 I, S, 1878 S
Price, T W (Cheltenham) 1948 S, F, 1949 W, I, F, S
Probyn, J A (Wasps, Askeans) 1988 F, W, S, I 1, 2, A 1, 2, A, 1989 S, I, R (R), 1990 I, F, W, S, Arg 1, 2, 3, 1991 W, S, I, F, Fj, A, [NZ, It, F, S, A], 1992 S, I, F, W, 1993 F, W, S, I
Prout, D H (Northampton) 1968 W, I
Pullin, J V (Bristol) 1966 W, 1968 W, I, F, S, 1969 I, F, S, W, SA, 1970 I, W, S, F, 1971 W, I, F, S (2[1C]), P, 1972 W, I, F, S, SA, 1973 NZ 1, W, I, F, S, NZ 2, A, 1974 S, I, F, W, 1975 I, W (R), S, A 1, 2, 1976 F
Purdy, S J (Rugby) 1962 S
Pyke, J (St Helens Recreation) 1892 W
Pym, J A (Blackheath) 1912 W, I, S, F
Quinn, J P (New Brighton) 1954 W, NZ, I, S, F
Rafter, M (Bristol) 1977 S, F, W, 1978 F, W, S, I, NZ, 1979 S, I, F, W, NZ, 1980 W(R), 1981 W, Arg 1, 2
Ralston, C W (Richmond) 1971 S (C), P, 1972 W, I, F, S, SA, 1973 NZ 1, W, I, F, S, NZ 2, A, 1974 S, I, F, W, 1975 I, F, W, S
Ramsden, H E (Bingley) 1898 S, W
Ranson, J M (Rosslyn Park) 1963 NZ 1, 2, A, 1964 W, I, F, S
Raphael, J E (OMTs) 1902 W, I, S, 1905 W, S, NZ, 1906 W, S, F
Ravenscroft, J (Birkenhead Park) 1881 I
Ravenscroft, S C W (Saracens) 1998 A 1, NZ 2(R)
Rawlinson, W C W (Blackheath) 1876 S
Redfern, S P (Leicester) 1984 I (R)
Redman, N C (Bath) 1984 A, 1986 S (R), 1987 I, S, [A, J, W], 1988 Fj, 1990 Arg 1, 2, 1991 Fj, [It, US], 1993 NZ, 1994 F, W, SA 1, 2, 1997 Arg 1, A 1
Redmond, G F (Cambridge U) 1970 F
Redwood, B W (Bristol) 1968 W, I
Rees, D L (Sale) 1997 A 2, NZ 1, SA, NZ 2, 1998 F, W, SA 2(R), 1999 S, I, F, A
Rees, G W (Nottingham) 1984 SA 2(R), A, 1986 I, F, 1987 F, W, S, [A, J, US, W], 1988 S (R), I 1, 2, A 1, 2, Fj, 1989 W (R), R (R), Fj (R), 1990 Arg 3(R), 1991 Fj, [US]
Rees, T (Wasps) 2007 S(R), It(R), I(R), F1, W1, F3, [US, SA1], 2008 W(R), NZ1, 2, PI, A, SA, NZ3(R)
Reeve, J S R (Harlequins) 1929 F, 1930 W, I, F, S, 1931 W, I, S
Regan, M (Liverpool) 1953 W, I, F, S, 1954 W, NZ, I, S, F, 1956 I, S, F
Regan, M P (Bristol, Bath, Leeds) 1995 SA, WS, 1996 F, W, S, I, It, Arg, 1997 S, I, F, W, A 1, NZ 2(R), 1998 F, 2000 SA 1(t), A(R), Arg, SA 3(t), 2001 It(R), S(R), C 2(R), R, 2003 F 1(t), It(R), W 2, [Gg(R), Sm], 2004 It(R), I(R), NZ1(R), 2, A1, 2007 SA1, 2, W2, F2, 3, [US, SA1, A, F, SA2], 2008 W, It, F
Rendall, P A G (Wasps, Askeans) 1984 W, SA 2, 1986 W, S, 1987 I, F, S, [A, J, W], 1988 F, W, S, I 1, 2, A 1, 2, A, 1989 S, I, F, W, R, 1990 I, F, W, S, 1991 [It (R)]
Rew, H (Blackheath) 1929 S, F, 1930 F, S, 1931 W, S, F, 1934 W, I, S
Reynolds, F J (O Cranleighans) 1937 S, 1938 I, S
Reynolds, S (Richmond) 1900 W, I, S, 1901 I
Rhodes, J (Castleford) 1896 W, I, S
Richards, D (Leicester) 1986 I, F, 1987 S, [A, J, US, W], 1988 F, W, S, I 1, A 1, 2, Fj, A, 1989 S, I, F, W, R, 1990 Arg 3, 1991 W, S, I, F, Fj, A, [NZ, It, US], 1992 S (R), F, W, C, 1993 NZ, 1994 W, SA 1, C, 1995 I, F, W, S, [WS, A, NZ], 1996 F (t), S, I
Richards, E E (Plymouth A) 1929 S, F
Richards, J (Bradford) 1891 W, I, S
Richards, P C (Gloucester, London Irish) 2006 A1, 2, NZ(R), Arg(R), SA1, 2, 2007 [US(R), SA1(R), Tg(R), A(t), F(R), SA2(R)], 2008 NZ2(R)
Richards, S B (Richmond) 1965 W, I, F, S, 1967 A, I, F, S, W
Richardson, J V (Birkenhead Park) 1928 A, W, I, F, S
Richardson, W R (Manchester) 1881 I
Rickards, C H (Gipsies) 1873 S
Rimmer, G (Waterloo) 1949 W, I, 1950 W, 1951 W, I, F, 1952 SA, W, 1954 W, NZ, I, S
Rimmer, L I (Bath) 1961 SA, W, I, F, S
Ripley, A G (Rosslyn Park) 1972 W, I, F, S, SA, 1973 NZ 1,

W, I, F, S, NZ 2, A, 1974 S, I, F, W, 1975 I, F, S, A 1, 2, 1976 A, W, S
Risman, A B W (Loughborough Coll) 1959 W, I, F, S, 1961 SA, W, I, F
Ritson, J A S (Northern) 1910 F, S, 1912 F, 1913 SA, W, F, I, S
Rittson-Thomas, G C (Oxford U) 1951 W, I, F
Robbins, G L (Coventry) 1986 W, S
Robbins, P G D (Oxford U, Moseley, Coventry) 1956 W, I, S, F, 1957 W, I, F, S, 1958 W, A, I, S, 1960 W, I, F, S, 1961 SA, W, 1962 S
Roberts, A D (Northern) 1911 W, F, I, S, 1912 I, S, F, 1914 I
Roberts, E W (RNE Coll) 1901 W, I, 1905 NZ, 1906 W, I, 1907 S
Roberts, G D (Harlequins) 1907 S, 1908 F, W
Roberts, J (Sale) 1960 W, I, F, S, 1961 SA, W, I, F, S, 1962 W, I, F, S, 1963 W, I, F, S, 1964 NZ
Roberts, R S (Coventry) 1932 I
Roberts, S (Swinton) 1887 W, I
Roberts, V G (Penryn, Harlequins) 1947 F, 1949 W, I, F, S, 1950 I, F, S, 1951 W, I, F, S, 1956 W, I, S, F
Robertshaw, A R (Bradford) 1886 W, I, S, 1887 W, S
Robinson, A (Blackheath) 1889 M, 1890 W, S, I
Robinson, E T (Coventry) 1954 S, 1961 I, F, S
Robinson, G C (Percy Park) 1897 I, S, 1898 I, 1899 W, 1900 I, S, 1901 I, S
Robinson, J T (Sale) 2001 It (R), S (R), F (R), I, A, R, SA, 2002 S, I, F, It, NZ, A, SA, 2003 F 1, W 1, S, I, NZ, A, F 3, [Gg, SA, Sm, U(R), W, F, A], 2004 It, S, I, W, F, C, SA, A2, 2005 W, F, I, 2007 S, It, F1, W1, SA1, W2, F3, [US, SA1, A, F, SA2]
Robinson, J J (Headingley) 1893 S, 1902 W, I, S
Robinson, R A (Bath) 1988 A 2, Fj, A, 1989 S, I, F, W, 1995 SA
Robshaw, C D C (Harlequins) 2009 Arg 2
Robson, A (Northern) 1924 W, I, F, S, 1926 W
Robson, M (Oxford U) 1930 W, I, F, S
Rodber, T A K (Army, Northampton) 1992 S, I, 1993 NZ, 1994 I, F, W, SA 1, 2, R, C, 1995 I, F, W, S, [Arg, It, WS (R), A, NZ, F], SA, WS, 1996 W, S (R), I (t), It, Arg, 1997 S, I, F, W, A 1, 1998 H (R), It (R), A 2, SA 2, 1999 S, I, F, W, A, US (R), [NZ (R), Fj (R)]
Rogers, D P (Bedford) 1961 I, F, S, 1962 W, I, F, 1963 W, I, F, S, NZ 1, 2, A, 1964 NZ, W, I, F, S, 1965 W, I, F, S, 1966 W, I, F, S, 1967 A, S, W, NZ, 1969 I, F, S, W
Rogers, J H (Moseley) 1890 W, S, I, 1891 S
Rogers, W L Y (Blackheath) 1905 W, I
Rollitt, D M (Bristol) 1967 I, F, S, W, 1969 I, F, S, W, 1975 S, A 1, 2
Roncoroni, A D S (West Herts, Richmond) 1933 W, I, S
Rose, W M H (Cambridge U, Coventry, Harlequins) 1981 I, F, 1982 A, S, I, 1987 I, F, W, S, [A]
Rossborough, P A (Coventry) 1971 W, 1973 NZ 2, A, 1974 S, I, 1975 I, F
Rosser, D W A (Wasps) 1965 W, I, F, S, 1966 W
Rotherham, Alan (Richmond) 1883 W, S, 1884 W, S, 1885 W, I, 1886 W, I, S, 1887 W, I, S
Rotherham, Arthur (Richmond) 1898 S, W, 1899 W, I, S
Roughley, D (Liverpool) 1973 A, 1974 S, I
Rowell, R E (Leicester) 1964 W, 1965 W
Rowley, A J (Coventry) 1932 SA
Rowley, H C (Manchester) 1879 S, I, 1880 I, S, 1881 I, W, S, 1882 I, S
Rowntree, G C (Leicester) 1995 S (t), [It, WS], WS, 1996 F, W, S, I, It, Arg, 1997 S, I, F, W, A 1, 1998 A 1, NZ 1, 2, SA 1, H (R), It (R), 1999 US, C, [It (R), Tg, Fj (R)], 2001 C 1, 2, US, I(R), A, R, SA, 2002 S, I, F, W, It, 2003 F 1(R), W 1, It, S, I, NZ, F 2, 2004 C, SA, A2, 2005 W, F, I, It, 2006 A1, 2
Royds, P M R (Blackheath) 1898 S, W, 1899 W
Royle, A V (Broughton R) 1889 M
Rudd, E L (Liverpool) 1965 W, I, S, 1966 W, I, S
Russell, R F (Leicester) 1905 NZ
Rutherford, D (Percy Park, Gloucester) 1960 W, I, F, S, 1961 SA, 1965 W, I, F, S, 1966 W, I, F, S, 1967 NZ
Ryalls, H J (New Brighton) 1885 W, I
Ryan, D (Wasps, Newcastle) 1990 Arg 1, 2, 1992 C, 1998 S
Ryan, P H (Richmond) 1955 W, I
Sackey, P H (Wasps) 2006 NZ, Arg, 2007 F2, 3(R), [SA1, Sm, Tg, A, F, SA2], 2008 W, It, F, S, I, PI, A, SA, NZ3, 2009 It, W, I
Sadler, E H (Army) 1933 I, S
Sagar, J W (Cambridge U) 1901 W, I
Salmon, J L B (Harlequins) 1985 NZ 1, 2, 1986 W, S, 1987 I, F, W, S, [A, J, US, W]
Sample, C H (Cambridge U) 1884 I, 1885 I, 1886 S
Sampson, P C (Wasps) 1998 SA 1, 2001 C 1, 2
Sanders, D L (Harlequins) 1954 W, NZ, I, S, F, 1956 W, I, S, F
Sanders, F W (Plymouth A) 1923 I, S, F
Sanderson, A (Sale) 2001 R (R), 2002 Arg, 2003 It(t + R), W 2(R), F 2
Sanderson, P H (Sale, Harlequins, Worcester) 1998 NZ 1, 2, SA 1, 2001 C 1(R), 2(R), US(t+R), 2005 A, NZ, Sm, 2006 A1, 2, NZ, Arg, SA1, 2, 2007 SA1(R)
Sandford, J R P (Marlborough N) 1906 I
Sangwin, R D (Hull and E Riding) 1964 NZ, W
Sargent, G A F (Gloucester) 1981 I (R)
Savage, K F (Northampton) 1966 W, I, F, S, 1967 A, I, F, S, W, NZ, 1968 W, F, S
Sawyer, C M (Broughton) 1880 S, 1881 I
Saxby, L E (Gloucester) 1932 SA, W
Scarbrough, D G R (Leeds, Saracens) 2003 W 2, 2007 SA2
Schofield, D F (Sale) 2007 SA1, 2(R)
Schofield, J W (Manchester) 1880 I
Scholfield, J A (Preston Grasshoppers) 1911 W
Schwarz, R O (Richmond) 1899 S, 1901 W, I
Scorfield, E S (Percy Park) 1910 F
Scott, C T (Blackheath) 1900 W, I, 1901 W, I
Scott, E K (St Mary's Hospital, Redruth) 1947 W, 1948 A, W, I, S
Scott, F S (Bristol) 1907 W
Scott, H (Manchester) 1955 F
Scott, J P (Rosslyn Park, Cardiff) 1978 F, W, S, I, NZ, 1979 S (R), I, F, W, NZ, 1980 I, F, W, S, 1981 W, S, I, F, Arg 1, 2, 1982 I, F, W, 1983 F, W, S, I, NZ, 1984 S, I, F, W, SA 1, 2
Scott, J S M (Oxford U) 1958 F
Scott, M T (Cambridge U) 1887 I, 1890 S, I
Scott, W M (Cambridge U) 1889 M
Seddon, R L (Broughton R) 1887 W, I, S
Sellar, K A (United Services, RN) 1927 W, I, S, 1928 A, W, I, F
Sever, H S (Sale) 1936 NZ, W, I, S, 1937 W, I, S, 1938 W, I, S
Shackleton, I R (Cambridge U) 1969 SA, 1970 I, W, S
Sharp, R A W (Oxford U, Wasps, Redruth) 1960 W, I, F, S, 1961 I, F, 1962 W, I, F, 1963 W, I, F, S, 1967 A
Shaw, C H (Moseley) 1906 S, SA, 1907 F, W, I, S
Shaw, F (Cleckheaton) 1898 I
Shaw, J F (RNE Coll) 1898 S, W
Shaw, S D (Bristol, Wasps) 1996 It, Arg, 1997 S, I, F, W, A 1, SA (R), 2000 I, F, W, It, S, SA 1(R), 2(R), 2001 C 1(R), 2, US, I, 2003 It (R), W 2, F 2(R), 3(R), 2004 It(t&R), S(R), NZ1, 2, A1, 2005 Sm(R), 2006 W(R), It(R), S(R), F(R), I, 2007 W2, F2, 3, [US, SA1, Sm, A, F, SA2], 2008 W, It, F, S, I, A(R), SA(R), 2009 F, S, NZ, 2010 W, It, I, F, A1, 2(R)
Sheasby, C M A (Wasps) 1996 It, Arg, 1997 W (R), Arg 1(R), 2(R), SA (R), NZ 2(t)
Sheppard, A (Bristol) 1981 W (R), 1985 W
Sheridan, A J (Sale) 2004 C(R), 2005 A, NZ, Sm, 2006 W, It, S, F(R), I, NZ, SA1, 2007 W2, F2, [US, SA1, Sm, Tg, A, F, SA2], 2008 W, F, S, I, NZ1, PI, A, 2009 It, W, I, F, S
Sherrard, C W (Blackheath) 1871 S, 1872 S
Sherriff, G A (Saracens) 1966 S, 1967 A, NZ
Shewring, H E (Bristol) 1905 I, NZ, 1906 W, S, F, SA, 1907 F, W, I, S
Shooter, J H (Morley) 1899 I, S, 1900 I, S
Shuttleworth, D W (Headingley) 1951 S, 1953 S
Sibree, H J H (Harlequins) 1908 F, 1909 I, S
Silk, N (Harlequins) 1965 W, I, F, S
Simms, K G (Cambridge U, Liverpool, Wasps) 1985 R, F, S, I, W, 1986 I, F, 1987 I, F, W, [A, J, W], 1988 F, W
Simpson, C P (Harlequins) 1965 W
Simpson, P D (Bath) 1983 NZ, 1984 S, 1987 I
Simpson, T (Rockcliff) 1902 S, 1903 W, I, S, 1904 I, S, 1905 I, S, 1906 S, SA, 1909 F
Simpson-Daniel, J D (Gloucester) 2002 NZ, A, 2003 W 1(t + R), It, W 2, 2004 I(R), NZ1, 2005 Sm, 2006 It(R), 2007 SA1(R)
Sims, D (Gloucester) 1998 NZ 1(R), 2, SA 1
Skinner, M G (Harlequins) 1988 F, W, S, I 1, 2, 1989 Fj, 1990 I, F, W, S, Arg 1, 2, 1991 Fj (R), [US, F, S, A], 1992 S, I, F, W
Skirving, B D (Saracens) 2007 SA2
Sladen, G M (United Services, RN) 1929 W, I, S
Sleightholme, J M (Bath) 1996 F, W, S, I, It, Arg, 1997 S, I, F, W, Arg 1, 2

Slemen, M A C (Liverpool) 1976 I, F, 1977 S, I, F, W, 1978 F, W, S, I, NZ, 1979 S, I, F, W, NZ, 1980 I, F, W, S, 1981 W, S, I, F, 1982 A, S, I, F, W, 1983 NZ, 1984 S
Slocock, L A N (Liverpool) 1907 F, W, I, S, 1908 F, W, I, S
Slow, C F (Leicester) 1934 S
Small, H D (Oxford U) 1950 W, I, F, S
Smallwood, A M (Leicester) 1920 F, I, 1921 W, I, S, F, 1922 I, S, 1923 W, I, S, F, 1925 I, S
Smart, C E (Newport) 1979 F, W, NZ, 1981 S, I, F, Arg 1, 2, 1982 A, S, I, F, W, 1983 F, W, S, I
Smart, S E J (Gloucester) 1913 SA, W, F, I, S, 1914 W, I, S, F, 1920 W, I, S
Smeddle, R W (Cambridge U) 1929 W, I, S, 1931 F
Smith, C C (Gloucester) 1901 W
Smith, D F (Richmond) 1910 W, I
Smith, J V (Cambridge U, Rosslyn Park) 1950 W, I, F, S
Smith, K (Roundhay) 1974 F, W, 1975 W, S
Smith, M J K (Oxford U) 1956 W
Smith, O J (Leicester) 2003 It (R), W 2(R), F 2, 2005 It(R), S(R)
Smith, S J (Sale) 1973 I, F, S, A, 1974 I, F, 1975 W (R), 1976 F, 1977 F (R), 1979 NZ, 1980 I, F, W, S, 1981 W, S, I, F, Arg 1, 2, 1982 A, S, I, F, W, 1983 F, W, S
Smith, S R (Richmond) 1959 W, F, S, 1964 F, S
Smith, S T (Wasps) 1985 R, F, S, I, W, NZ 1, 2, 1986 W, S
Smith, T H (Northampton) 1951 W
Soane, F (Bath) 1893 S, 1894 W, I, S
Sobey, W H (O Millhillians) 1930 W, F, S, 1932 SA, W
Solomon, B (Redruth) 1910 W
Sparks, R H W (Plymouth A) 1928 I, F, S, 1929 W, I, S, 1931 I, S, F
Speed, H (Castleford) 1894 W, I, S, 1896 S
Spence, F W (Birkenhead Park) 1890 I
Spencer, J (Harlequins) 1966 W
Spencer, J S (Cambridge U, Headingley) 1969 I, F, S, W, SA, 1970 I, W, S, F, 1971 W, I, S (2[1C]), P
Spong, R S (O Millhillians) 1929 F, 1930 W, I, F, S, 1931 F, 1932 SA, W
Spooner, R H (Liverpool) 1903 W
Springman, H H (Liverpool) 1879 S, 1887 S
Spurling, A (Blackheath) 1882 I
Spurling, N (Blackheath) 1886 I, S, 1887 W
Squires, P J (Harrogate) 1973 F, S, NZ 2, A, 1974 S, I, F, W, 1975 I, F, W, S, A 1, 2, 1976 A, W, 1977 S, I, F, W, 1978 F, W, S, I, NZ, 1979 S, I, F, W
Stafford R C (Bedford) 1912 W, I, S, F
Stafford, W F H (RE) 1874 S
Stanbury, E (Plymouth A) 1926 W, I, S, 1927 W, I, S, F, 1928 A, W, I, F, S, 1929 W, I, S, F
Standing, G (Blackheath) 1883 W, I
Stanger-Leathes, C F (Northern) 1905 I
Stark, K J (O Alleynians) 1927 W, I, S, F, 1928 A, W, I, F, S
Starks, A (Castleford) 1896 W, I
Starmer-Smith, N C (Harlequins) 1969 SA, 1970 I, W, S, F, 1971 S (C), P
Start, S P (United Services, RN) 1907 S
Steeds, J H (Saracens) 1949 F, S, 1950 I, F, S
Steele-Bodger, M R (Cambridge U) 1947 W, I, S, F, 1948 A, W, I, S, F
Steinthal, F E (Ilkley) 1913 W, F
Stephenson, M (Newcastle) 2001 C 1, 2, US
Stevens, C B (Penzance-Newlyn, Harlequins) 1969 SA, 1970 I, W, S, 1971 P, 1972 W, I, F, S, SA, 1973 NZ 1, W, I, F, S, NZ 2, A, 1974 S, I, F, W, 1975 I, F, W, S
Stevens, M J H (Bath) 2004 NZ1(R), 2(t), 2005 I, It, S, NZ(R), Sm, 2006 W, It, F, 2007 SA2, W2(R), F2, 3(R), [US(R), SA1, Sm, Tg, A(R), F(R), SA2(R)], 2008 W(R), It, F(R), S(R), I(R), NZ1, 2, PI, A(t&R), SA(R), NZ3(R)
Still, E R (Oxford U, Ravenscourt P) 1873 S
Stimpson, T R G (Newcastle, Leicester) 1996 It, 1997 S, I, F, W, A 1, NZ 2(t+R), 1998 A 1, NZ 1, 2(R), SA 1(R), 1999 US (R), C (R), 2000 SA 1, 2001 C 1(t), 2(R), 2002 W (R), Arg, SA (R)
Stirling, R V (Leicester, RAF, Wasps) 1951 W, I, F, S, 1952 SA, W, S, I, F, 1953 W, I, F, S, 1954 W, NZ, I, S, F
Stoddart, A E (Blackheath) 1885 W, I, 1886 W, I, S, 1889 M, 1890 W, I, 1893 W, S
Stoddart, W B (Liverpool) 1897 W, I, S
Stokes, F (Blackheath) 1871 S, 1872 S, 1873 S
Stokes, L (Blackheath) 1875 I, 1876 S, 1877 I, S, 1878 S, 1879 S, I, 1880 I, S, 1881 I, W, S
Stone, F le S (Blackheath) 1914 F
Stoop, A D (Harlequins) 1905 S, 1906 S, F, SA, 1907 F, W, 1910 W, I, S, 1911 W, F, I, S, 1912 W, S
Stoop, F M (Harlequins) 1910 S, 1911 F, I, 1913 SA
Stout, F M (Richmond) 1897 W, I, 1898 I, S, W, 1899 I, S, 1903 S, 1904 W, I, S, 1905 W, I, S
Stout, P W (Richmond) 1898 S, W, 1899 W, I, S
Strettle, D (Harlequins) 2007 I, F1, W1, 2, 2008 W, NZ1
Stringer, N C (Wasps) 1982 A (R), 1983 NZ (R), 1984 SA 1(R), A, 1985 R
Strong, E L (Oxford U) 1884 W, I, S
Sturnham B (Saracens) 1998 A 1, NZ 1(t), 2(t)
Summerscales, G E (Durham City) 1905 NZ
Sutcliffe, J W (Heckmondwike) 1889 M
Swarbrick, D W (Oxford U) 1947 W, I, F, 1948 A, W, 1949 I
Swayne, D H (Oxford U) 1931 W
Swayne, J W R (Bridgwater) 1929 W
Swift, A H (Swansea) 1981 Arg 1, 2, 1983 F, W, S, 1984 SA 2
Syddall, J P (Waterloo) 1982 I, 1984 A
Sykes, A R V (Blackheath) 1914 F
Sykes, F D (Northampton) 1955 F, S, 1963 NZ 2, A
Sykes, P W (Wasps) 1948 F, 1952 S, I, F, 1953 W, I, F
Syrett, R E (Wasps) 1958 W, A, I, F, 1960 W, I, F, S, 1962 W, I, F
Tait, M J M (Newcastle, Sale) 2005 W, 2006 A1, 2, SA1, 2, 2007 It(R), I(R), F1(R), W1, SA1, 2, W2, [US(R), SA1(R), Sm, Tg, A, F, SA2], 2008 It(t), F(R), S(R), I(t&R), NZ2, 2009 It(R), W(R), I(R), F(R), S(R), Arg 1(R), 2(R), NZ(R), 2010 W, It, I, S, F(R), A1(R)
Tallent, J A (Cambridge U, Blackheath) 1931 S, F, 1932 SA, W, 1935 I
Tanner, C C (Cambridge U, Gloucester) 1930 S, 1932 SA, W, I, S
Tarr, F N (Leicester) 1909 A, W, F, 1913 S
Tatham, W M (Oxford U) 1882 S, 1883 W, I, S, 1884 W, I, S
Taylor, A S (Blackheath) 1883 W, I, 1886 W, I
Taylor, E W (Rockcliff) 1892 I, 1893 I, 1894 W, I, S, 1895 W, I, S, 1896 W, I, 1897 W, I, S, 1899 I
Taylor, F (Leicester) 1920 F, I
Taylor, F M (Leicester) 1914 W
Taylor, H H (Blackheath) 1879 S, 1880 S, 1881 I, W, 1882 S
Taylor, J T (W Hartlepool) 1897 I, 1899 I, 1900 I, 1901 W, I, 1902 W, I, S, 1903 W, I, 1905 S
Taylor, P J (Northampton) 1955 W, I, 1962 W, I, F, S
Taylor, R B (Northampton) 1966 W, 1967 I, F, S, W, NZ, 1969 F, S, W, SA, 1970 I, W, S, F, 1971 S (2[1C])
Taylor, W J (Blackheath) 1928 A, W, I, F, S
Teague, M C (Gloucester, Moseley) 1985 F (R), NZ 1, 2, 1989 S, I, F, W, R, 1990 F, W, S, 1991 W, S, I, F, Fj, A, [NZ, It, F, S, A], 1992 SA, 1993 F, W, S, I
Teden, D E (Richmond) 1939 W, I, S
Teggin, A (Broughton R) 1884 I, 1885 W, 1886 I, S, 1887 I, S
Tetley, T S (Bradford) 1876 S
Thomas, C (Barnstaple) 1895 W, I, S, 1899 I
Thompson, P H (Headingley, Waterloo) 1956 W, I, S, F, 1957 W, I, F, S, 1958 W, A, I, F, S, 1959 W, I, F, S
Thompson, S G (Northampton, Brive) 2002 S, I, F, W, It, Arg, NZ, A, SA, 2003 F 1, W 1, It, S, I, NZ, A, F 2(R), 3, [Gg, SA, Sm(R), W, F, A], 2004 It, S, I, W, F, NZ1, A1(R), C, SA, A2, 2005 W, F, I, It, S, A, NZ, Sm, 2006 W, It, S, F, I(R), 2009 Arg 1(R), A, Arg 3(R), NZ(R), 2010 W(R), It(R), S(R), F(R), A1, 2
Thomson, G T (Halifax) 1878 S, 1882 I, S, 1883 W, I, S, 1884 I, S, 1885 I
Thomson, W B (Blackheath) 1892 W, 1895 W, I, S
Thorne, J D (Bristol) 1963 W, I, F
Tindall, M J (Bath, Gloucester) 2000 I, F, W, It, S, SA 1, 2, A Arg, SA 3, 2001 W (R), R, SA (R), 2002 S, I, F, W, It, NZ, A, SA, 2003 It, S, I, NZ, A, F 2, [Gg, SA, Sm, W, F(R), A], 2004 W, F, NZ1, 2, A1, C, SA, A2, 2005 A, NZ, Sm, 2006 W, It, S, F, I(t&R), 2007 S, It, I, F1, 2008 W, NZ1, 2, 2009 W, I, F, S, 2010 F, A1, 2
Tindall, V R (Liverpool U) 1951 W, I, F, S
Titterrell, A J (Sale) 2004 NZ2(R), C(R), 2005 It(R), S(R), 2007 SA2(R)
Tobin, F (Liverpool) 1871 S
Todd, A F (Blackheath) 1900 I, S

Todd, R (Manchester) 1877 S
Toft, H B (Waterloo) 1936 S, 1937 W, I, S, 1938 W, I, S, 1939 W, I, S
Toothill, J T (Bradford) 1890 S, I, 1891 W, I, 1892 W, I, S, 1893 W, I, S, 1894 W, I
Tosswill, L R (Exeter) 1902 W, I, S
Touzel, C J C (Liverpool) 1877 I, S
Towell, A C (Bedford) 1948 F, 1951 S
Travers, B H (Harlequins) 1947 W, I, 1948 A, W, 1949 F, S
Treadwell, W T (Wasps) 1966 I, F, S
Trick, D M (Bath) 1983 I, 1984 SA 1
Tristram, H B (Oxford U) 1883 S, 1884 W, S, 1885 W, 1887 S
Troop, C L (Aldershot S) 1933 I, S
Tucker, J S (Bristol) 1922 W, 1925 NZ, W, I, S, F, 1926 W, I, F, S, 1927 W, I, S, F, 1928 A, W, I, F, S, 1929 W, I, F, 1930 W, I, F, S, 1931 W
Tucker, W E (Blackheath) 1894 W, I, 1895 W, I, S
Tucker, W E (Blackheath) 1926 I, 1930 W, I
Turner, D P (Richmond) 1871 S, 1872 S, 1873 S, 1874 S, 1875 I, S
Turner, E B (St George's Hospital) 1876 I, 1877 I, 1878 I
Turner, G R (St George's Hospital) 1876 S
Turner, H J C (Manchester) 1871 S
Turner, M F (Blackheath) 1948 S, F
Turner, S C (Sale) 2007 W1(R), SA1, 2(R)
Turquand-Young, D (Richmond) 1928 A, W, 1929 I, S, F
Twynam, H T (Richmond) 1879 I, 1880 I, 1881 W, 1882<j> I, 1883 I, 1884 W, I, S
Ubogu, V E (Bath) 1992 C, SA, 1993 NZ, 1994 S, I, F, W, SA 1, 2, R, C, 1995 I, F, W, S, [Arg, WS, A, NZ, F], SA, 1999 F (R), W (R), A (R)
Underwood, A M (Exeter) 1962 W, I, F, S, 1964 I
Underwood, R (Leicester, RAF) 1984 I, F, W, A, 1985 R, F, S, I, W, 1986 W, I, F, 1987 I, F, W, S, [A, J, W], 1988 F, W, S, I 1, 2, A 1, 2, Fj, A, 1989 S, I, F, W, R, Fj, 1990 I, F, W, S, Arg 3, 1991 W, S, I, F, Fj, A, [NZ, It, US, F, S, A], 1992 S, I, F, W, SA, 1993 F, W, S, I, NZ, 1994 S, I, F, W, SA 1, 2, R, C, 1995 I, F, W, S, [Arg, It, WS, A, NZ, F], SA, WS, 1996 F, W, S, I
Underwood, T (Leicester, Newcastle) 1992 C, SA, 1993 S, I, NZ, 1994 S, I, W, SA 1, 2, R, C, 1995 I, F, W, S, [Arg, It, A, NZ], 1996 Arg, 1997 S, I, F, W, 1998 A 2, SA 2
Unwin, E J (Rosslyn Park, Army) 1937 S, 1938 W, I, S
Unwin, G T (Blackheath) 1898 S
Uren, R (Waterloo) 1948 I, S, F, 1950 I
Uttley, R M (Gosforth) 1973 I, F, S, NZ 2, A, 1974 I, F, W, 1975 F, W, S, A 1, 2, 1977 S, I, F, W, 1978 NZ 1979 S, 1980 I, F, W, S
Vainikolo, L P I (Gloucester) 2008 W(R), It, F, S, I
Valentine J (Swinton) 1890 W, 1896 W, I, S
Vanderspar, C H R (Richmond) 1873 S
Van Gisbergen, M C (Wasps) 2005 A(t)
Van Ryneveld, C B (Oxford U) 1949 W, I, F, S
Varley, H (Liversedge) 1892 S
Varndell, T W (Leicester) 2005 Sm(R), 2006 A1, 2, 2008 NZ2
Vassall, H (Blackheath) 1881 W, S, 1882 I, S, 1883 W
Vassall, H H (Blackheath) 1908 I
Vaughan, D B (Headingley) 1948 A, W, I, S, 1949 I, F, S, 1950 W
Vaughan-Jones, A (Army) 1932 I, S, 1933 W
Verelst, C L (Liverpool) 1876 I, 1878 I
Vernon, G F (Blackheath) 1878 S, I, 1880 I, S, 1881 I
Vesty, S B (Leicester) 2009 Arg 1(R), 2(R)
Vickery, G (Aberavon) 1905 I
Vickery, P J (Gloucester, Wasps) 1998 W, A 1, NZ 1, 2, SA 1, 1999 US, C, [It, NZ, Tg, SA], 2000 I, F, W, S, A, Arg (R), SA 3(R), 2001 W, It, S, A, SA, 2002 I, F, Arg, NZ, A, SA, 2003 NZ(R), A, [Gg, SA, Sm(R), U, W, F, A], 2004 It, S, I, W, F, 2005 W(R), F, A, NZ, 2006 SA1(R), 2, 2007 S, It, I, W2, F2(R), 3, [US, Tg(R), A, F, SA2], 2008 W, F, S, I, Pl(R), A, SA, NZ3, 2009 It, W, I, F, S
Vivyan, E J (Devonport A) 1901 W, 1904 W, I, S
Voyce, A T (Gloucester) 1920 I, S, 1921 W, I, S, F, 1922 W, I, F, S, 1923 W, I, S, F, 1924 W, I, F, S, 1925 NZ, W, I, S, F, 1926 W, I, F, S
Voyce, T M D (Bath, Wasps) 2001 US (R), 2004 NZ2, A1, 2005 Sm, 2006 W(R), It, F(R), I, A1
Vyvyan, H D (Saracens) 2004 C(R)
Wackett, J A S (Rosslyn Park) 1959 W, I
Wade, C G (Richmond) 1883 W, I, S, 1884 W, S, 1885 W, 1886 W, I
Wade, M R (Cambridge U) 1962 W, I, F
Wakefield, W W (Harlequins) 1920 W, F, I, S, 1921 W, I, S, F, 1922 W, I, F, S, 1923 W, I, S, F, 1924 W, I, F, S, 1925 NZ, W, I, S, F, 1926 W, I, F, S, 1927 S, F
Walder, D J H (Newcastle) 2001 C 1, 2, US, 2003 W 2(R)
Walker, G A (Blackheath) 1939 W, I
Walker, H W (Coventry) 1947 W, I, S, F, 1948 A, W, I, S, F
Walker, R (Manchester) 1874 S, 1875 I, 1876 S, 1879 S, 1880 S
Wallens, J N S (Waterloo) 1927 F
Walshe, N P J (Bath) 2006 A1(R), 2(R)
Walton, E J (Castleford) 1901 W, I, 1902 I, S
Walton, W (Castleford) 1894 S
Ward, G (Leicester) 1913 W, F, S, 1914 W, I, S
Ward, H (Bradford) 1895 W
Ward, J I (Richmond) 1881 I, 1882 I
Ward, J W (Castleford) 1896 W, I, S
Wardlow, C S (Northampton) 1969 SA (R), 1971 W, I, F, S (2[1C])
Warfield, P J (Rosslyn Park, Durham U) 1973 NZ 1, W, I, 1975 I, F, S
Warr, A L (Oxford U) 1934 W, I
Waters, F H H (Wasps) 2001 US, 2004 NZ2(R), A1(R)
Watkins, J A (Gloucester) 1972 SA, 1973 NZ 1, W, NZ 2, A, 1975 F, W
Watkins, J K (United Services, RN) 1939 W, I, S
Watson, F B (United Services, RN) 1908 S, 1909 S
Watson, J H D (Blackheath) 1914 W, S, F
Watt, D E J (Bristol) 1967 I, F, S, W
Webb, C S H (Devonport Services, RN) 1932 SA, W, I, S, 1933 W, I, S, 1935 S, 1936 NZ, W, I, S
Webb, J M (Bristol, Bath) 1987 [A (R), J, US, W], 1988 F, W, S, I 1, 2, A 1, 2, A, 1989 S, I, F, W, 1991 Fj, A, [NZ, It, F, S, A], 1992 S, I, F, W, C, SA, 1993 F, W, S, I
Webb, J W G (Northampton) 1926 F, S, 1929 S
Webb, R E (Coventry) 1967 S, W, NZ, 1968 I, F, S, 1969 I, F, S, W, 1972 I, F
Webb, St L H (Bedford) 1959 W, I, F, S
Webster, J G (Moseley) 1972 W, I, SA, 1973 NZ 1, W, NZ 2, 1974 S, W, 1975 I, F, W
Wedge, T G (St Ives) 1907 F, 1909 W
Weighill, R H G (RAF, Harlequins) 1947 S, F, 1948 S, F
Wells, C M (Cambridge U, Harlequins) 1893 S, 1894 W, S, 1896 S, 1897 W, S
West, B R (Loughborough Colls, Northampton) 1968 W, I, F, S, 1969 SA, 1970 I, W, S
West, D E (Leicester) 1998 F (R), S (R), 2000 Arg (R), 2001 W, It, S, F (t), C 1, 2, US, I (R), A, SA, 2002 F (R), W (R), It (R), 2003 W 2(R), F 2, 3(t+R), [U, F(R)]
West, R (Gloucester) 1995 [WS]
Weston, H T F (Northampton) 1901 S
Weston, L E (W of Scotland) 1972 F, S
Weston, M P (Richmond, Durham City) 1960 W, I, F, S, 1961 SA, W, I, F, S, 1962 W, I, F, 1963 W, I, F, S, NZ 1, 2, A, 1964 NZ, W, I, F, S, 1965 F, S, 1966 S, 1968 F, S
Weston, W H (Northampton) 1933 I, S, 1934 I, S, 1935 W, I, S, 1936 NZ, W, S, 1937 W, I, S, 1938 W, I, S
Wheatley, A A (Coventry) 1937 W, I, S, 1938 W, S
Wheatley, H F (Coventry) 1936 I, 1937 S, 1938 W, S, 1939 W, I, S
Wheeler, P J (Leicester) 1975 F, W, 1976 A, W, S, I, 1977 S, I, F, W, 1978 F, W, S, I, NZ, 1979 S, I, F, W, NZ, 1980 I, F, W, S, 1981 W, S, I, F, 1982 A, S, I, F, W, 1983 F, S, I, NZ, 1984 S, I, F, W
White, C (Gosforth) 1983 NZ, 1984 S, I, F
White, D F (Northampton) 1947 W, I, S, 1948 I, F, 1951 S, 1952 SA, W, S, I, F, 1953 W, I, S
White, J M (Saracens, Bristol, Leicester) 2000 SA 1, 2, Arg, SA 3, 2001 F, C 1, 2, US, I, R (R), 2002 S, W, It, 2003 F 1(R), W 2, F 2, 3, [Sm, U(R)], 2004 W(R), F(R), NZ1, 2, A1, C, SA, A2, 2005 W, 2006 W(R), It(R), S, F, I, A1, 2, NZ, Arg, SA1, 2, 2007 S(R), It(R), I(R), F1, W1, 2009 It(R), W(R), I(t&R), F(t&R), S(R), Arg 1(R), 2
White-Cooper, S (Harlequins) 2001 C 2, US
Whiteley, E C P (O Alleynians) 1931 S, F
Whiteley, W (Bramley) 1896 W
Whitely, H (Northern) 1929 W
Wightman, B J (Moseley, Coventry) 1959 W, 1963 W, I, NZ 2, A
Wigglesworth, H J (Thornes) 1884 I

Wigglesworth, R E P (Sale) 2008 It(R), F, S, I, NZ1
Wilkins, D T (United Services, RN, Roundhay) 1951 W, I, F, S, 1952 SA, W, S, I, F, 1953 W, I, F, S
Wilkinson, E (Bradford) 1886 W, I, S, 1887 W, S
Wilkinson, H (Halifax) 1929 W, I, S, 1930 F
Wilkinson, H J (Halifax) 1889 M
Wilkinson, J P (Newcastle, Toulon) 1998 I (R), A 1, NZ 1, 1999 S, I, F, W, A, US, C, [It, NZ, Fj, SA (R)], 2000 I, F, W, It, S, SA 2, A, Arg, SA 3, 2001 W, It, S, F, I, A, SA, 2002 S, I, F, W, It, NZ, A, SA, 2003 F 1, W 1, It, S, I, NZ, A, F 3, [Gg, SA, Sm, W, F, A], 2007 S, It, I, SA1, 2, W2, F2(R), F3, [Sm, Tg, A, F, SA2], 2008 W, It, F, S, I(R), 2009 A, Arg 3, NZ, 2010 W, It, I, S, F(R), A1(R), 2(R)
Wilkinson, P (Law Club) 1872 S
Wilkinson, R M (Bedford) 1975 A 2, 1976 A, W, S, I, F
Willcocks, T J (Plymouth) 1902 W
Willcox, J G (Oxford U, Harlequins) 1961 I, F, S, 1962 W, I, F, S, 1963 W, I, F, S, 1964 NZ, W, I, F, S
William-Powlett, P B R W (United Services, RN) 1922 S
Williams, C G (Gloucester, RAF) 1976 F
Williams, C S (Manchester) 1910 F
Williams, J E (O Millhillians, Sale) 1954 F, 1955 W, I, F, S, 1956 I, S, F, 1965 W
Williams, J M (Penzance-Newlyn) 1951 I, S
Williams, P N (Orrell) 1987 S, [A, J, W]
Williams, S G (Devonport A) 1902 W, I, S, 1903 I, S, 1907 I, S
Williams, S H (Newport) 1911 W, F, I, S
Williamson, R H (Oxford U) 1908 W, I, S, 1909 A, F
Wilson, A J (Camborne S of M) 1909 I
Wilson, C E (Blackheath) 1898 I
Wilson, C P (Cambridge U, Marlborough N) 1881 W
Wilson, D G (Newcastle, Bath) 2009 Arg 1, 2(R), A, NZ(R), 2010 W, It(R), I(R), S(R), F(R), A1(R), 2(t&R)
Wilson, D S (Met Police, Harlequins) 1953 F, 1954 W, NZ, I, S, F, 1955 F, S
Wilson, G S (Tyldesley) 1929 W, I
Wilson, K J (Gloucester) 1963 F
Wilson, R P (Liverpool OB) 1891 W, I, S
Wilson, W C (Richmond) 1907 I, S
Winn, C E (Rosslyn Park) 1952 SA, W, S, I, F, 1954 W, S, F
Winterbottom, P J (Headingley, Harlequins) 1982 A, S, I, F, W, 1983 F, W, S, I, NZ, 1984 S, F, W, SA 1, 2, 1986 W, S, I, F, 1987 I, F, W, [A, J, US, W], 1988 F, W, S, 1989 R, Fj, 1990 I, F, W, S, Arg 1, 2, 3, 1991 W, S, I, F, A, [NZ, It, F, S, A], 1992 S, I, F, W, C, SA, 1993 F, W, S, I
Winters, R A (Bristol) 2007 SA1(R), 2
Wintle, T C (Northampton) 1966 S, 1969 I, F, S, W
Wodehouse, N A (United Services, RN) 1910 F, 1911 W, F, I, S, 1912 W, I, S, F, 1913 SA, W, F, I, S
Wood, A (Halifax) 1884 I
Wood, A E (Gloucester, Cheltenham) 1908 F, W, I
Wood, G W (Leicester) 1914 W
Wood, M B (Wasps) 2001 C 2(R), US (R)
Wood, R (Liversedge) 1894 I
Wood, R D (Liverpool OB) 1901 I, 1903 W, I
Woodgate, E E (Paignton) 1952 W
Woodhead, E (Huddersfield) 1880 I
Woodman, T J (Gloucester) 1999 US (R), 2000 I (R), It (R), 2001 W (R), It (R), 2002 NZ, 2003 S (R), I(t + R), A, F 3, [Gg, SA, W(R), F, A], 2004 It, S, I, W, F, NZ1, 2
Woodruff, C G (Harlequins) 1951 W, I, F, S
Woods, S M J (Cambridge U, Wellington) 1890 W, S, I, 1891 W, I, S, 1892 I, S, 1893 W, I, 1895 W, I, S
Woods, T (Bridgwater) 1908 S
Woods, T (United Services, RN) 1920 S, 1921 W, I, S, F
Woodward, C R (Leicester) 1980 I (R), F, W, S, 1981 W, S, I, F, Arg 1, 2, 1982 A, S, I, F, W, 1983 I, NZ, 1984 S, I, F, W
Woodward, J E (Wasps) 1952 SA, W, S, 1953 W, I, F, S, 1954 W, NZ, I, S, F, 1955 W, I, 1956 S
Wooldridge, C S (Oxford U, Blackheath) 1883 W, I, S, 1884 W, I, S, 1885 I
Wordsworth, A J (Cambridge U) 1975 A 1(R)
Worsley, J P R (Wasps) 1999 [Tg, Fj], 2000 It (R), S (R), SA 1(R), 2(R), 2001 It (R), S (R), F (R), C 1, 2, US, A, R, SA, 2002 S, I, F, W (t+R), Arg, 2003 W 1(R), It, S(R), I(t), NZ(R), A(R), W 2, [SA(t), Sm, U], 2004 It, I, W(R), F, NZ1(R), 2, A1, SA, A2, 2005 W, F, I, It, S, 2006 W, It, S, F, I, A1(R), 2, SA1, 2, 2007 S, I, F1, W1, 2, F2, 3(R), [US, Sm, A(R), F(R), SA2(R)], 2008 NZ1(R), 2(R), 2009 It(R), W, I, F, S, Arg 3(R), NZ, 2010 I(R), S, F
Worsley, M A (London Irish, Harlequins) 2003 It(R), 2004 A1(R), 2005 S(R)
Worton, J R B (Harlequins, Army) 1926 W, 1927 W
Wrench, D F B (Harlequins) 1964 F, S
Wright, C C G (Cambridge U, Blackheath) 1909 I, S
Wright, F T (Edinburgh Acady, Manchester) 1881 S
Wright, I D (Northampton) 1971 W, I, F, S (R)
Wright. J C (Met Police) 1934 W
Wright, J F (Bradford) 1890 W
Wright, T P (Blackheath) 1960 W, I, F, S, 1961 SA, W, I, F, S, 1962 W, I, F, S
Wright, W H G (Plymouth) 1920 W, F
Wyatt, D M (Bedford) 1976 S (R)
Yarranton, P G (RAF, Wasps) 1954 W, NZ, I, 1955 F, S
Yates, K P (Bath, Saracens) 1997 Arg 1, 2, 2007 SA1, 2
Yiend, W (Hartlepool R, Gloucester) 1889 M, 1892 W, I, S, 1893 I, S
Young, A T (Cambridge U, Blackheath, Army) 1924 W, I, F, S, 1925 NZ, F, 1926 I, F, S, 1927 I, S, F, 1928 A, W, I, F, S, 1929 I
Young, J R C (Oxford U, Harlequins) 1958 I, 1960 W, I, F, S, 1961 SA, W, I, F
Young, M (Gosforth) 1977 S, I, F, W, 1978 F, W, S, I, NZ, 1979 S
Young, P D (Dublin Wands) 1954 W, NZ, I, S, F, 1955 W, I, F, S
Youngs, N G (Leicester) 1983 I, NZ, 1984 S, I, F, W
Youngs, B R (Leicester) 2010 S(R), A1(R), 2

TIGERS TRIUMPH IN BREATHTAKING FINALE

By Iain Spragg

Dave Rogers/Getty Images

Leicester stand at the top of the English game.

The Premiership play-off final may not have always served up the breathtaking showpiece encounter that the climax of the English domestic season demands but the 82,000 fans who packed Twickenham to witness Leicester's pulsating clash with Saracens were certainly treated to an epic spectacle in 2010.

The Tigers, appearing in an incredible sixth straight final, may have been the pre-match favourites but reputation and recent form counted for little at HQ as both sides played with real adventure and with time rapidly running out, Leicester held a slender 26–24 advantage.

Saracens then appeared to have one hand on the trophy when Glen Jackson's fifth penalty sailed through the posts with four minutes left on the clock to make it 27–26 in their favour but from the subsequent restart, Leicester regained possession through Scott Hamilton and surged forward. Hamilton offloaded to Dan Hipkiss who initially seemed to have been stopped in his tracks but was not held and the England centre burst through for the try which gave the Tigers a dramatic 33–27 triumph and their third title in four years.

"To win back-to-back titles is very hard," said Leicester coach Richard Cockerill after the dramatic denouement at Twickenham. "It's been a hard year with a lot of injuries at times but we battle on and do what we do and it's turned out to be quite good. Both teams had the right attitude – tries were scored, mistakes were made but it was played in the right spirit.

Cockerill added: "We're boring and we train every day. We work hard on the training field. You don't win kick-offs at the end and you don't steal line-outs at the end by luck. It is from hard work. I wondered how we would win the ball back. But Floody kicked it in the right spot, Scott Hamilton caught it, Danny Hipkiss finished off and we won the game."

The race for an all-important finish in the top four began in early September and although it was Leicester and Jim Mallinder's Northampton who finally occupied the top two places, it was Saracens who set the early pace with eight consecutive victories. The sequence was brought to an abrupt end with a 12–12 draw with Worcester in November, sparking a temporary slump for the London side, but Brendan Venter's team had already done enough and finished third. Bath held off the challenge of Wasps to claim the final play-off spot.

The first semi-final saw the Saints entertain Saracens at Franklin's Gardens and the away side scored the first of the game's five tries through Alex Goode, only for Soane Tonga'uiha to hit back for Northampton and establish an 8–7 lead at half-time.

Saracens crossed again through Chris Wyles after the break, the Saints replied with a Brian Mujati score and when Schalk Brits crashed over for the visitors in the closing minutes to leave the scores tied at 19–19, Jackson calmly slotted the subsequent penalty and Saracens were on their way to Twickenham.

"The margins between winning and losing are so small and there is no doubt we could have lost that game," Venter said afterwards. "We knew that we had to stop Northampton behind the gain-line and the guys tackled their hearts out. They have unbelievable character."

The second semi between Leicester and Bath was less dramatic or free-flowing. It was a war of attrition at Welford Road with try-scoring opportunities in short supply and after 80 minutes it was Toby Flood's five penalties for the Tigers to two successful kicks from Bath's Olly Barkley that proved the difference between the two sides.

"We had some opportunities in the first half but we carried the ball into contact when the pass was on," conceded Bath coach Steve Meehan after his team's 15–6 defeat. "In the second half, we found it difficult to get out of our half and get control of the football. And when we had it we showed a lack of patience. It's difficult to build pressure like that."

The final at HQ began at a breathless pace and it was Sarries who drew first blood with two Jackson penalties, only for Flood to land his first penalty to make it 6–3 to the Londoners. A superb converted try from Matt Smith for the Tigers began the try scoring but Saracens hit back with an equally stunning try of their own from captain Ernst Joubert. Flood and Jackson then exchanged penalties before Ben Youngs danced over for Leicester and at half-time, the Tigers had established a 20–14 lead.

The first 40 minutes had been compelling but the second period was sensational and when Joubert barged over for his second score, it was evident the match would be nail-bitingly close. Flood edged Leicester into a five-point lead as their pack took control in the scrum, but Jackson landed two penalties of his own to put Sarries into the lead inside the last five minutes. It was then left to Hipkiss to provide the coup de grace as the Tigers were crowned English club champions for a ninth time.

"Some clubs like to pay more money to our players because they think they're going to get some DNA from us," Cockerill said after the final whistle in anticipation of losing members of his squad in the summer. "Other teams wouldn't have coped with the injuries we had but we do. It's just the culture we have. If you're not very good or don't want to work hard, you're out of the door."

In the Championship, Exeter emerged from two tight play-off clashes 38–16 aggregate winners against Bristol to earn promotion to the Premiership. The Chiefs had finished the league season in second in the table, four points adrift of Bristol, but proved the stronger side at the crucial stage of the campaign.

"We have been working towards Premiership standards for a number of years and we can grow even more," head coach Rob Baxter said after his side's 28–10 win against Bristol at the Memorial Stadium which confirmed promotion. "We believe we will have the support, we also believe many of the players we have now can become better in the Premiership."

Further down the leagues, Esher were promoted from National League One with five league games to spare after a 31–12 victory over Blaydon in April while Macclesfield, Barking and Rosslyn Park were the three sides to emerge from the revamped National League Two.

In the Bill Beaumont Cup at Twickenham, Lancashire triumphed over Gloucestershire in a repeat of the 2009 final. The Lancastrians scored five unanswered tries at HQ in a 36–6 victory to earn a record 20th title.

GUINNESS PREMIERSHIP 2009–10 RESULTS

4 September: **Sale** 15 **Leicester** 12. 5 September: **Saracens** 18 **London Irish** 14, **Wasps** 26 **Harlequins** 15. 6 September: **Northampton** 20 **Worcester** 17, **Leeds** 9 **Newcastle** 9, **Gloucester** 24 **Bath** 5. 11 September: **Worcester** 27 **Leeds** 7. 12 September: **Bath** 15 **Wasps** 17, **Saracens** 19 **Northampton** 16, **Harlequins** 9 **Leicester** 15. 13 September: **London Irish** 40 **Gloucester** 10, **Newcastle** 16 **Sale** 16. 18 September: **Sale** 12 **Bath** 25. 19 September: **Gloucester** 14 **Northampton** 27, **Harlequins** 9 **Saracens** 22, **Leicester** 15 **Newcastle** 6. 20 September: **Leeds** 7 **London Irish** 56, **Wasps** 23 **Worcester** 3. 25 September: **Newcastle** 17 **Harlequins** 17. 26 September: **Northampton** 30 **Leeds** 10, **Worcester** 24 **Sale** 18, **Bath** 20 **Leicester** 20. 27 September: **London Irish** 28 **Wasps** 16, **Saracens** 19 **Gloucester** 16. 2 October: **Sale** 8 **London Irish** 11. 3 October: **Leicester** 19 **Worcester** 14, **Harlequins** 13 **Bath** 11. 4 October: **Leeds** 10 **Gloucester** 26, **Wasps** 20 **Northampton** 15. **Newcastle** 15 **Saracens** 22. 24 October: **Bath** 16 **Newcastle** 27, **Northampton** 21 **Sale** 16, **Worcester** 22 **Harlequins** 26, **London Irish** 18 **Leicester** 12, **Gloucester** 6 **Wasps** 35. 25 October: **Saracens** 21 **Leeds** 15. 30 October: **Sale** 28 **Gloucester** 23. 31 October: **Bath** 11 **Saracens** 12, **Harlequins** 9 **London Irish** 9, **Leicester** 29 **Northampton** 15. 1 November: **Wasps** 9 **Leeds** 15, **Newcastle** 14 **Worcester** 3. 20 November: **Gloucester** 12 **Leicester** 9, **Worcester** 12 **Bath** 12. 21 November: **Northampton** 26 **Harlequins** 17. 22 November: **Leeds** 17 **Sale** 24, **London Irish** 11 **Newcastle** 15, **Saracens** 22 **Wasps** 6. 27 November: **Newcastle** 8 **Northampton** 28, **Worcester** 12 **Saracens** 12. 28 November: **Harlequins** 35 **Gloucester** 29, **Leicester** 39 **Leeds** 6, **Bath** 0 **London Irish** 16. 4 December: **Leeds** 27 **Harlequins** 30. 5 December: **Gloucester** 25 **Newcastle** 13, **London Irish** 16 **Worcester** 16, **Northampton** 15 **Bath** 13, **Saracens** 15 **Sale** 13. 6 December: **Wasps** 24 **Leicester** 22. 26 December: **Worcester** 6 **Northampton** 26. 27 December: **Leicester** 32 **Sale** 6, **Bath** 24 **Gloucester** 8, **London Irish** 23 **Saracens** 19, **Newcastle** 15 **Leeds** 16, **Harlequins** 20 **Wasps** 21. 1 January: **Sale** 21 **Harlequins** 16. 2 January: **Gloucester** 13 **Worcester** 13, **Leeds** 15 **Bath** 20, **Northampton** 24 **London Irish** 22, **Saracens** 15 **Leicester** 22. 3 January: **Wasps** 6 **Newcastle** 12, 9 January: **Leicester** 34 **Wasps** 8. 13 February: **Gloucester** 46 **Harlequins** 6, **Northampton** 25 **Newcastle** 13, **Saracens** 25 **Worcester** 20. 14 February: **Leeds** 9 **Leicester** 14, **London Irish** 22 **Bath** 35, **Wasps** 22 **Sale** 16. 19 February: **Sale** 10 **Leeds** 19. 20 February: **Bath** 37 **Worcester** 13, **Harlequins** 13 **Northampton** 6, **Leicester** 33 **Gloucester** 11, **Newcastle** 12 **London Irish** 12. 21 February: **Wasps** 9 **Saracens** 0. 26 February: **Worcester** 13 **Newcastle** 0. 27 February: **Gloucester** 47 **Sale** 3, **Northampton** 19 **Leicester** 3. 28 February: **Leeds** 26 **Wasps** 10, **London Irish** 29 **Harlequins** 14, **Saracens** 14 **Bath** 16. 6 March: **Harlequins** 14 **Worcester** 11, **Leicester** 35 **London Irish** 19. 7 March: **Sale** 7 **Northampton** 15, **Leeds** 19 **Saracens** 12, **Wasps** 24 **Gloucester** 19, **Newcastle** 13 **Bath** 17. 19 March: **Sale** 19 **Wasps** 8. 27 March: **Bath** 24 **Harlequins** 13, **Gloucester** 19 **Leeds** 0, **Worcester** 18 **Leicester** 39, **Northampton** 14 **Wasps** 9. 28 March: **London Irish** 38 **Sale** 0, **Saracens** 58 **Newcastle** 15. 31 March: **Newcastle** 25 **Gloucester** 13. 2 April: **Sale** 17 **Worcester** 3. 3 April: **Harlequins** 23 **Newcastle** 14, **Leeds** 7 **Northampton** 14, **Leicester** 43 **Bath** 20, **Gloucester** 29 **Saracens** 28. 4 April: **Wasps** 33 **London Irish** 22. 9 April: **Sale** 19 **Saracens** 30. 10 April: **Harlequins** 46 **Leeds** 11, **Worcester** 13 **London Irish** 23. 17 April: **Bath** 34 **Sale** 15, **Northampton** 38 **Gloucester** 23, **Worcester** 20 **Wasps** 24, **Saracens** 37 **Harlequins** 18. 18 April: **London Irish** 13 **Leeds** 23, **Newcastle** 7 **Leicester** 31. 20 April: **Bath** 21 **Northampton** 20. 23 April: **Sale** 30 **Newcastle** 32. 24 April: **Gloucester** 34 **London Irish** 20, **Leicester** 40 **Harlequins** 22, **Northampton** 27 **Saracens** 28, **Wasps** 19 **Bath** 35. 25 April: **Leeds** 12 **Worcester** 10. 8 May: **Bath** 39 **Leeds** 3, **Harlequins** 35 **Sale** 20, **Leicester** 23 **Saracens** 32, **London Irish** 7, **Northampton** 31, **Newcastle** 21 **Wasps** 25, **Worcester** 22 **Gloucester** 23.

FINAL TABLE

	P	W	D	L	F	A	BP	PTS
Leicester	22	15	1	6	541	325	11	**73**
Northampton	22	16	0	6	472	322	7	**71**
Saracens	22	15	1	6	480	367	7	**69**
Bath	22	12	2	8	450	366	9	**61**
Wasps	22	13	0	9	394	399	5	**57**
London Irish	22	10	3	9	469	384	6	**52**
Gloucester	22	10	1	11	470	457	6	**48**
Harlequins	22	9	2	11	420	484	6	**46**
Newcastle	22	6	4	12	319	431	5	**37**
Leeds	22	7	1	14	283	493	6	**36**
Sale	22	6	1	15	333	495	6	**32**
Worcester	22	3	4	15	312	420	8	**28**

PREVIOUS ENGLISH CHAMPIONS

1987/1988: Leicester
1988/1989: Bath
1989/1990: Wasps
1990/1991: Bath
1991/1992: Bath
1992/1993: Bath
1993/1994: Bath
1994/1995: Leicester
1995/1996: Bath
1996/1997: Wasps
1997/1998: Newcastle
1998/1999: Leicester
1999/2000: Leicester
2000/2001: Leicester
2001/2002: Leicester
2002/2003: Wasps
2003/2004: Wasps
2004/2005: Wasps
2005/2006: Sale
2006/2007: Leicester
2007/2008: London Wasps
2008/2009: Leicester
2009/2010: Leicester

PLAY-OFF SEMI-FINALS

16 May, Franklin's Gardens, Northampton

NORTHAMPTON 19 (3PG, 2T) SARACENS 21 (3G)

NORTHAMPTON: B Foden; C Ashton, J Clarke, J Downey, B Reihana; S Myler, L Dickson; S Tonga'uiha, D Hartley (captain), B Mujati, I Fernandez Lobbe, J Kruger, P Dowson, N Best, R Wilson

SUBSTITUTIONS: J Ansbro for Reihana (42 mins); D Morris for Mujati (74 mins); C Lawes for Fernandez Lobbe (55 mins); B Sharman for Hartley (76 mins)

SCORERS *Tries*: Tonga'uiha, Mujati *Penalty Goals*: Myler (3)

SARACENS: A Goode; M Tagicakibau, A Powell, B Barritt, C Wyles; G Jackson, N De Kock; M Aguero, S Brits, P Du Plessis, H Vyvyan, M Botha, J Burger, A Saull, E Joubert (captain)

SUBSTITUTIONS: K Ratuvou for Powell (46 mins); R Gill for Aguero (63 mins); T Ryder for Botha (69 mins); J Melck for Saull (69 mins); D Hougaard for Goode (74 mins); J Marshall for De Kock (74 mins); R Skuse for Du Plessis (76 mins)

SCORERS *Tries*: Goode, Wyles, Brits *Conversions*: Jackson (3)

REFEREE W Barnes (London)

16 May, Welford Road, Leicester

LEICESTER 15 (5PG) BATH 6 (2PG)

LEICESTER: G Murphy (captain); S Hamilton, M Smith, A Allen, A Tuilagi; T Flood, B Youngs; M Ayerza, G Chuter, M Catstrogiovanni, L Deacon, G Parling, T Croft, L Moody, J Crane

SUBSTITUTIONS: D Cole for Catstrogiovanni (65 mins); C Newby for Moody (65 mins); B Woods for Croft (79 mins); J Murphy for Tuilagi (80 mins)

SCORERS *Penalty Goals*: Flood (5)

BATH: N Abendanon; J Maddock, M Carraro, O Barkley, M Banahan; B James, M Claasens (captain); D Flatman, L Mears, D Wilson, S Hooper, D Grewcock, A Beattie, J Salvi, L Watson

SUBSTITUTIONS: D Bell for Wilson (62 mins); P Dixon for Mears (66 mins); S Hape for Carraro (68 mins); D Barnes for Flatman (73 mins); P Short for Hooper (73 mins)

SCORERS *Penalty Goals*: Barkley (2)

REFEREE C White (Gloucestershire)

PLAY-OFF FINAL

29 May, Twickenham, London

LEICESTER 33 (3G, 4PT)
SARACENS 27 (1G, 5PG, 1T)

LEICESTER: G Murphy (captain); S Hamilton, M Smith, A Allen, A Tuilagi; T Flood, B Youngs; M Ayerza, G Chuter, M Castrogiovanni, L Deacon, G Parling, T Croft, L Moody, J Crane

SUBSTITUTIONS: D Hipkiss for Smith (68); D Cole for Castrogiovanni (67); C Newby for Moody (68);) J Staunton for Tuilagi (74)

SCORERS *Tries*: Smith, Youngs, Hipkiss *Conversions*: Flood (3) *Penalty Goals*: Flood (4)

SARACENS: A Goode; M Tagicakibau, A Powell, B Barritt, C Wyles; G Jackson, N de Kock; M Aguero, S Brits, P Du Plessis, S Borthwick, H Vyvyan, J Burger, A Saull, E Joubert (captain)

SUBSTITUTIONS: M Botha for Borthwick (45); R Gill for Aguero (49); K Ratuvou for Tagicakibau (57); J Marshall for de Kock (65); J Melck for Saull (65)

SCORERS *Tries*: Joubert (2) *Conversions*: Jackson *Penalty Goals*: Jackson (5)

REFEREE D Pearson (Northumberland)

Jamie McDonald/Getty Images

Dan Hipkiss bursts through the Saracens defence to win the final for the Leicester Tigers.

OTHER MAJOR DOMESTIC WINNERS

RFU CHAMPIONSHIP
Exeter Chiefs
NATIONAL ONE
Esher
NATIONAL TWO NORTH
Macclesfield
NATIONAL TWO SOUTH
Barking
NATIONAL THREE SOUTH-WEST
Taunton
NATIONAL THREE LONDON
Jersey
NATIONAL THREE MIDLANDS
Luctonians
NATIONAL THREE NORTH
Morley

FIJI

FIJI'S 2009–10 TEST RECORD

OPPONENTS	DATE	VENUE	RESULT
Scotland	14 Nov	A	**Lost** 10–23
Ireland	21 Nov	A	**Lost** 6–41
Romania	28 Nov	A	**Won** 29–18
Australia	5 Jun	A	**Lost** 3–49
Japan	12 Jun	H	**Won** 22–8
Tonga	19 Jun	N	**Won** 41–38
Samoa	26 Jun	A	**Lost** 9–31

RACING TO THE WORLD CUP

Fiji have struggled in the past 12 months to regain their reputation as the flamboyant 'Flying Fijians' who mesmerised the rugby world a few years ago in France.

Averaging 27 points per game with a free-flowing style of play, the Fijians were one of the star attractions of Rugby World Cup 2007, knocking out Wales and then coming so close to inflicting the same fate on eventual champions South Africa.

The three years since have not produced such highs for Fiji and in seven Tests from November 2009 to September 2010, their scoring average has plummeted to 17 points per game, against arguably weaker opposition.

The ebullience and enthusiasm that carried Fiji to such heights appears to be missing. Time to rediscover it is running out with RWC 2011 – when Fiji will face Wales and the Springboks again, as well as Samoa and Namibia in Pool D – now less than a year away.

Despite the fast-approaching World Cup, Fijian selectors still seem to be trying to find their best team with a raft of players making their debuts. In six Test matches in 2009, Fiji used 22 previously uncapped players, with another 12 utilised in their four Tests to October 2010.

Fiji ended 2009 with three Tests in Europe under the guidance of former Wallaby Glen Ella. Mike Brewer, the former All Black, became assistant coach with Fiji-born Australian Sam Domoni given the unusual title of coach-designate, meaning he was in effect Ella's understudy.

The tour wasn't without its controversy, the most publicised of which was Domoni's banning of the 'cibi' war dance on religious grounds. This move caused such a stir back home that at April's subsequent Annual General Meeting, Fiji Rugby Union (FRU) Council members wrote it into the Constitution that the 'cibi' must always be performed for Test matches.

In the opening game against Scotland, Fiji were caught somewhat flat-footed and disorganised, a reflection perhaps on the chaotic nature of their arrival in Edinburgh, having driven through the night in mini-vans after missing their connection at Heathrow.

The match was significant for the fact that Scarlets prop Deacon Manu and Clermont's hulking wing Napolioni Nalaga were making their long-awaited Fiji debuts. There was also a return to Test duty for Gloucester flanker Akapusi Qera after almost 18 months out with injury and Bath fly-half Nicky Little, who hadn't featured since that monumental RWC 2007 win over Wales.

New Zealand-born Manu qualifies through his mother and was brought in to help steady Fiji's front row. Though he only played the one game on that tour and missed the ANZ Pacific Nations Cup, he is expected to lead the Fiji pack at the World Cup. Indeed, he may even be captain.

Exeter utility back Josh Matavesi was picked at full-back and, at 19 years and 38 days, became Fiji's youngest Test player since Watisoni Nasolo in 1974.

So Fiji certainly had a mix of young and old, but they lost almost half of their lineouts and had two scrum put-ins turned over. Former Fiji Sevens captain Vereniki Goneva picked up the only try for the visitors at Murrayfield, and though the final score of 23–10 in Scotland's favour was hardly a disaster, Fiji hadn't shown much imagination.

In the 41–6 defeat by Ireland a week later, Fiji were competitive for about 50 minutes, trailing only 13–3 at the break. But when they took off 43-cap veteran full-back Norman Ligairi and moved the inexperienced Nasoni Roko to No 15, this signalled the start of the downfall.

Surprisingly, Fiji's best performance of the tour came when most of the top players had departed. Ligairi showed once again that the No 15 jersey remains his, while wing Jim Nagusa looked the complete player and teenager Matavesi offered a great variety of attack at fly-half. Indeed, the whole back-line played some delightful rugby as Fiji beat Romania 29–18 in Bucharest for their only win of the tour.

When the squad returned to Fiji, Ella went back to Australia and Brewer to the UK, allowing Domoni to take over the reins.

Having been a forwards coach at Sydney clubs Manly and Penrith, and later the skills coach at the Joondalup club in Perth, Domoni was taking a giant leap to become the main man as Fiji prepare for RWC 2011 in New Zealand.

His first assignment, in January, was to take Fiji A to play his old side, the NSW Waratahs, at Wade Park in Orange. The Waratahs' rampant form that day meant Fiji were soundly beaten 83–15.

Four months later, Domoni returned to Australia with the Test side to face the Wallabies in Canberra as part of their preparations for the annual Pacific Nations Cup challenge.

The match saw more players making their debut with Manu partnering newcomers West Harbour prop Campese Ma'afu and former age grade hooker Talemaitoga Tuapati in the front row.

Born and raised in Sydney to a Tongan father and Fijian mother, Ma'afu came face to face with his older brother Salesi, who was simultaneously making his Test debut for Australia.

"My first choice was Australia, but that didn't go my way," Campese said. "I wasn't really interested in Tonga, but now that I've been selected for Fiji there's a great opportunity ahead."

"It'll be tough for the family to decide who to cheer for," he joked before kick-off. "Though I bet mum will be cheering for me!"

The Canberra encounter also saw the Racing Métro duo of No 8 Jone Qovu and wing Sireli Bobo return for the first time since the last World Cup. Another returnee was Rupeni Caucaunibuca, stretching the white jersey over his 118kg frame for the first time since 2006.

Playing at centre, Caucau threw himself about, making a team high total of 18 tackles, but was not given any front-foot ball to start one of those famous blockbusting runs of his.

Caucau limped off midway through the second half as the Wallabies began to stamp their authority to secure a 49–3 victory. His shoulder injury kept him out of the PNC and delayed his return to French club Agen, who later announced they were releasing him.

Manu, Qovu, and Bobo all returned to their clubs in Europe and Waikato lock Dominiko Waqaniburotu, having only just made his debut, was given the captain's armband for the Pacific Nations Cup.

In the opening match against Japan in Lautoka, the Fijians took to the field with just 33 caps to their names – the lowest total in the professional era. Despite this inexperience and against John Kirwan's rapidly improving Japanese side, Fiji emerged 22–8 winners.

Fiji showed glimpses of their former selves with a running game that produced three excellent tries from deep in their own half to Nagusa, centre Iliesa Keresoni, and 20-year-old half-back Nikola Matawalu, who enjoyed a tremendous debut having been denied a visa to travel to Canberra the week before because he is in the Fiji Navy.

A week later the Fijians produced a remarkable comeback in Apia to defeat Tonga 41–38, having trailed 28–0 in the first half and 38–20 with 15 minutes to go. Though there were obvious positives to be taken from the win, Fiji's first-half defence will have given cause for concern as they fell off their tackles and had little in the way of a defensive pattern.

One player to catch the eye was Exeter centre Sireli Naqelevuki, who made no fewer than 10 line-breaks and seems certain to have a prominent role to play at the World Cup.

With the Pacific Nations Cup title up for grabs, Fiji then faced Samoa, needing to stop their hosts from taking a bonus point. A first title, though, was not to be as Samoa ran out 31–9 victors to become the first non New Zealand winner of the tournament.

On the Sevens scene, Fiji also had to play second fiddle to Samoa. The highlight of the 2009–10 season was undoubtedly the NZI Sevens success in Wellington, but that was as good as it got for Iliesa Tanivula's boys as Fiji finished fourth in the IRB Sevens World Series standings behind champions Samoa, New Zealand and Australia.

There was better news for Fiji in the IRB Pacific Rugby Cup on home soil as the Warriors became the first side to successfully defend the title after beating Fiji Barbarians 26–17 following a remarkable comeback in the final quarter.

This was followed by a best-ever finish of eighth at the IRB Junior World Championship 2010 in June from the next generation of 'Flying Fijians', the country's Under-20 players securing a final position better than both Ireland and Scotland in Argentina.

The Fiji Schoolboys also toured Australia in September, winning two of their four matches. Eleven months earlier history had been made when the Fiji Under-12s and Under-14s played a 'Test' series against Tonga, the first time primary school rugby had reached that level. Though the Fijians won all four matches, the series was hailed a great success and is planned again for November 2010.

On the domestic front, Naitasiri triumphed in the Digicel Cup, beating Nadroga 25–24 to win the provincial title for the first time since 2002.

FIJI INTERNATIONAL STATISTICS

MATCH RECORDS UP TO 29TH OCTOBER 2010

WINNING MARGIN

Date	Opponent	Result	Winning Margin
10/09/1983	Niue Island	120–4	**116**
21/08/1969	Solomon Islands	113–13	**100**
08/09/1983	Solomon Islands	86–0	**86**
30/08/1979	Papua New Guinea	86–0	**86**
23/08/1969	Papua New Guinea	88–3	**85**

MOST TRIES IN A MATCH
BY THE TEAM

Date	Opponent	Result	Tries
21/08/1969	Solomon Islands	113–13	**25**
10/09/1983	Niue Island	120–4	**21**
23/08/1969	Papua New Guinea	88–3	**20**
18/08/1969	Papua New Guinea	79–0	**19**
30/08/1979	Papua New Guinea	86–0	**18**

MOST POINTS IN A MATCH
BY THE TEAM

Date	Opponent	Result	Pts.
10/09/1983	Niue Island	120–4	**120**
21/08/1969	Solomon Islands	113–13	**113**
23/08/1969	Papua New Guinea	88–3	**88**
08/09/1983	Solomon Islands	86–0	**86**
30/08/1979	Papua New Guinea	86–0	**86**

MOST CONVERSIONS IN A MATCH
BY THE TEAM

Date	Opponent	Result	Cons
21/08/1969	Solomon Islands	113–13	**19**
10/09/1983	Niue Island	120–4	**18**

MOST PENALTIES IN A MATCH BY THE TEAM

Date	Opponent	Result	Pens
08/07/2001	Samoa	28–17	7

MOST DROP GOALS IN A MATCH BY THE TEAM

Date	Opponent	Result	DGs
02/07/1994	Samoa	20–13	3
12/10/1991	Romania	15–17	3

MOST POINTS IN A MATCH BY A PLAYER

Date	Player	Opponent	Pts.
10/09/1983	Severo Koroduadua	Niue Island	36
21/08/1969	Semesa Sikivou	Solomon Islands	27
28/08/1999	Nicky Little	Italy	25

MOST TRIES IN A MATCH BY A PLAYER

Date	Player	Opponent	Tries
30/08/1979	Tevita Makutu	Papua New Guinea	6
18/08/1969	George Sailosi	Papua New Guinea	5

MOST CONVERSIONS IN A MATCH BY A PLAYER

Date	Player	Opponent	Cons
10/09/1983	Severo Koroduadua	Niue Island	18
21/08/1969	Semesa Sikivou	Solomon Islands	12
07/10/1989	Severo Koroduadua	Belgium	10

MOST PENALTIES IN A MATCH BY A PLAYER

Date	Player	Opponent	Pens
08/07/2001	Nicky Little	Samoa	7
26/05/2000	Nicky Little	Tonga	6
25/05/2001	Nicky Little	Tonga	6
05/10/1996	Nicky Little	Hong Kong	6
08/07/1967	Inoke Tabualevu	Tonga	6

MOST DROP GOALS IN A MATCH BY A PLAYER

Date	Player	Opponent	Pens
02/07/1994	Opeti Turuva	Samoa	3
12/10/1991	Tomasi Rabaka	Romania	2

MOST CAPPED PLAYERS

Name	Caps
Nicky Little	65
Jacob Rauluni	50
Joeli Veitayaki	49
Emori Katalau	47

LEADING TRY SCORERS

Name	Tries
Senivalati Laulau	18
Norman Ligairi	16
Viliame Satala	16
Fero Lasagavibau	16

LEADING CONVERSIONS SCORERS

Name	Cons
Nicky Little	114
Severo Koroduadua	56
Waisale Serevi	40

LEADING PENALTY SCORERS

Name	Pens
Nicky Little	136
Severo Koroduadua	47
Waisale Serevi	27
Seremaia Bai	26

LEADING DROP GOAL SCORERS

Name	DGs
Opeti Turuva	5
Severo Koroduadua	5
Waisale Serevi	3

LEADING POINTS SCORERS

Name	
Nicky Little	652
Severo Koroduadua	268
Waisale Serevi	221
Seremaia Bai	151

FRANCE

FRANCE'S 2009–10 TEST RECORD

OPPONENTS	DATE	VENUE	RESULT
South Africa	13 November	H	**Won** 20–13
Samoa	21 November	H	**Won** 43–5
New Zealand	28 November	H	**Lost** 12–39
Scotland	7 February	A	**Won** 18–9
Ireland	13 February	H	**Won** 33–10
Wales	26 February	A	**Won** 26–20
Italy	14 March	H	**Won** 46–20
England	20 March	H	**Won** 12–10
South Africa	12 June	A	**Lost** 17–42
Argentina	26 June	A	**Lost** 13–41

LIÈVREMONT DELIVERS THE SLAM

By Iain Spragg

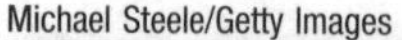
Michael Steele/Getty Images

France get their hands on the RBS Six Nations trophy.

They say patience is a virtue and for the FFR this was undoubtedly the case as Marc Lièvremont rewarded his employers' considerable faith in him and his coaching powers by steering France to the Six Nations Grand Slam, banishing the memories of his two previous and distinctly mediocre seasons at the helm.

Named as successor to Bernard Laporte in the wake of the 2007 World Cup, Lièvremont was widely perceived as an audacious rather assured appointment and after leading Les Bleus to third place in the Championship table for two years running, there was growing concern in French rugby that the FFR's gamble had backfired.

Despite registering victories over the All Blacks and the Springboks, Lièvremont had been criticised for his seemingly incoherent selection policy and on the eve of his third Championship campaign, his detractors lurked menacingly in the shadows.

At the end of the Six Nations however it was a hero's reception rather than his P45 that greeted the former French Under-21 and Dax coach after his side translated their potential into tangible results, completing the clean sweep in March at the Stade de France after a gritty, battling 12–10 victory over England.

The result gave France their first Grand Slam since 2004 and the ninth in their history. It was Lièvremont's first victory over the English at the third time of asking and also earned him his place in the record books as he became only the fourth man to win a Grand Slam as both player and coach, following in the footsteps of compatriots Jean–Claude Skrela and Jacques Fouroux, and England's Sir Clive Woodward.

"It is a very nice baby even if the birth was quite difficult," admitted Lièvremont as the party in Paris began.

"For the first time we have reached the end of a series or a tournament and I can be satisfied. We have a Grand Slam to celebrate.

"I am very proud of this team for the bravery they showed in the 80 minutes. It is five victories and a Grand Slam but we have to pay tribute to the England team. It was very difficult and they played their best against us. We owe a lot to our forwards tonight and I am happy for the forwards that Nicolas Mas was named man of the match. No scrum, no win."

Lièvremont named a 30-man squad ahead of the autumn Test series, recalling fly-half Frederic Michalak, but there was no place for him in the 22 for the opening, Friday night clash with world champions South Africa in Toulouse.

France had not lost to the Springboks at home for 12 years and although the visitors led by two points at half time, a try from Vincent Clerc and four penalties from the boot of Morgan Parra were enough to subdue the South African challenge and Les Bleus began their season with a hugely-encouraging 20–13 victory.

They returned to the Stade de France for the following weekend's clash with Samoa and the South Sea Islanders were unable to trouble France unduly as the home side ran in seven tries in a one-sided 43–5 win.

The autumn programme came to a conclusion with a mouth-watering showdown with New Zealand and Lièvremont made seven changes from the side that vanquished the Samoans as France looked to build on their victory over the Kiwis in Dunedin the previous summer.

The All Blacks however were hell bent on revenge in Marseille and an early try from Sitiveni Sivivatu established their supremacy. Les Bleus had to rely on penalties from Julien Dupuy to stay in contention but New Zealand crossed the whitewash three further times as they raced away to a convincing 39–12 victory.

"The All Blacks played very well," conceded Lièvremont. "They put a lot of pressure on us in defence and scored points when they needed to. We did manage to get back into the game after their first try but we struggled after that. We were not able to convert our opportunities into points."

"Sometimes, one has to accept defeat with dignity. When the All Blacks play like that, attacking the line with complete confidence, they are unstoppable. It's a big disappointment but don't forget all the work that has been done. I'm still very confident about this group and there is room for improvement ahead of the Six Nations tournament."

The coach named his squad for the Six Nations in January, drafting centre Mathieu Bastareaud back in but dropping experienced players Maxime Medard, Cedric Heymans, Florian Fritz and Lionel Beauxis from his back division as he fine tuned his preparations for the tournament opener against Scotland at Murrayfield.

Bastareaud had been sent home from France's tour of New Zealand in controversial circumstances the previous summer but the burly centre rewarded Lièvremont's show of faith with a two-try display against the Scots in Edinburgh, providing the platform for his side's 18–9 triumph and a winning start to the tournament.

The clash a week later with Six Nations champions Ireland, unbeaten in their previous 12 Tests, was arguably the sternest test of France's title credentials but Les Bleus made light work of Declan Kidney's side in Paris, scoring tries through Yannick Jauzion, Clement Poitrenaud and William Servat in a dominant 33–10 victory.

"It was a great performance," said wing Clerc. "We put up great defence against a great Irish team. We are surprised but we believe in ourselves and we played the perfect match today."

The Grand Slam was now firmly in France's sights and after going to Cardiff and beating Wales 26–20 in the Millennium Stadium in their third game of the campaign, surviving a spirited second-half comeback by the home side, the clean sweep was a real possibility.

The Italians offered little serious resistance in the penultimate match of the Championship season, crashing to a crushing 46–20 defeat in Paris, and the stage was set for Les Bleus' crunch clash with the old enemy England.

On recent form, France should have won with ease but, as ever, the visitors proved stubborn opponents in the Stade de France and stunned the crowd when Ben Foden scored the game's only try after five minutes. France however were not to be denied and three penalties from Parra and a drop-goal from fly-half Francois Trinh-Duc were just enough to secure an all-important 12–10 triumph.

"Despite the weather, we won this game and beat England with a lot at stake," said captain Thierry Dusautoir. "Honestly, I think we were better than England but we had to search for something else to win, more pragmatism. In the rain, and with all that pressure, we reacted well. For once the English did not beat us. We can be very proud with the end of the match."

Lièvremont now turned his attention to the summer tour of South Africa and Argentina and included uncapped duo Wenceslas Lauret and Jerome Porical in his 30-man squad.

There was perhaps always the danger of the side suffering from a Grand Slam hangover and so it proved against the Springboks in Cape Town in June as Les Bleus were brutally overpowered by the world champions, who exacted revenge for their defeat in Toulouse with a 42–17 win.

An exhausting flight to Argentina to face the Pumas a fortnight later was not ideal preparation for France's final game of the season and Les Bleus looked a shadow of themselves in the José Amalfitani Stadium as they slumped to a record 41–13 defeat.

France took an early lead with a Parra penalty but Argentina were in merciless mood in Buenos Aires and 31 points from fly-half Felipe Contepomi with two tries, three conversions and five penalties ensured Les Bleus' otherwise impressive season ended on a disappointing note.

"It is desolation," admitted Lièvremont after the game. "I don't know how we could sink so badly in these few weeks, to suffer two points records in South Africa and now here in Argentina."

The club season in France had reached a dramatic and emotional climax at the end of May as perennial bridesmaids Clermont Auvergne beat Perpignan in the Top 14 final in Paris, ending a century of waiting to lift the famous Bouclier de Brennus.

Les Jaunards were appearing in an 11th final in the club's history and after ten previous, heartbreaking falls at the final hurdle, they finally emerged victorious after beating their Catalan opponents 19–6 in the Stade de France.

Clermont had lost the finals of 2007, 2008 and 2009 to earn the side a reputation in French rugby as serial chokers on the big occasion but were crowned champions after dispatching Perpignan, the team who had beaten them 22–13 in the final 12 months earlier.

"This is the culmination of four years work and a dream for everyone," said emotional Clermont coach Vern Cotter after the final whistle. "It hasn't sunk in yet but the title is the result of the common love of my players.

"It has been three years of sheer frustration but every year we tried to come back stronger and full credit to the players. We are going to have a good night."

Clermont's route to the knockout stages of the Top 14 was relatively straight forward as Cotter's side comfortably finished third in the final table after 26 games, setting up a semi-final clash with second-place Toulon.

Perpignan came first on points difference and faced fourth-placed Toulouse in the last four at the Stade de la Mosson in Montpellier. Toulouse drew first blood with a seventh-minute score from 20-year-old scrum-half Nicolas Bezy but it was to prove the only try of the contest and seven immaculately struck penalties from the boot of Jerome Porical steered Perpignan to a 21–13 win and a second successive appearance in the final.

A day later, Les Jaunards faced Toulon in what was an infinitely more free-scoring encounter at Stade Geoffroy-Guichard in Saint-Etienne, a dramatic match which yielded four tries and a grand total of 64 points.

The clash could not be settled in 80 minutes but in extra-time it was Clermont who delivered the coup de grace with a try from centre Julien Malzieu and a sensational drop goal from fly-half Brock James to set up a repeat of the 2009 final.

The Stade de France was packed for the big rematch and proceedings were as tense as they had been 12 months earlier. Parra landed the first of his three successful penalties on ten minutes to give Clermont a platform and when Fijian wing Napolioni Nalaga powered his way over five minutes later, a score Parra converted, Cotter's team had suddenly established a 10-point lead.

Champions Perpignan responded with two penalties from Porical to reduce their arrears but at half-time they still trailed 13–6 courtesy of another three points from Parra.

The second period produced just six more points and the anticipated fightback from the Catalans failed to materialise. Parra's third penalty on 62 minutes extended his side's advantage and an outrageous drop goal from full-back Anthony Floch six minutes later hammered the final nail in Perpignan's coffin. Clermont were finally champions and the long-awaited celebrations could begin.

"We're happy for ourselves," said Clermont captain Aurelien Rougerie. "This squad really has a soul, a character. I'm very happy for us, this squad and obviously all the people who waited so long for this."

FRANCE INTERNATIONAL STATISTICS

MATCH RECORDS UP TO 29TH OCTOBER 2010

MOST CONSECUTIVE TEST WINS

10 1931 E,G, 1932 G, 1933 G, 1934 G, 1935 G, 1936 G1,2, 1937 G,It
8 1998 E, S, I, W, Arg 1,2, Fj, Arg 3
8 2001 SA3, A, Fj 2002 It, W, E, S,I
8 2004 I, It, W, S, E, US, C, A

MOST CONSECUTIVE TESTS WITHOUT DEFEAT

Matches	Wins	Draws	Period
10	10	0	1931 to 1938
10	8	2	1958 to 1959
10	9	1	1986 to 1987

MOST POINTS IN A MATCH

BY THE TEAM

Pts.	Opponents	Venue	Year
87	Namibia	Toulouse	2007
77	Fiji	Saint Etienne	2001
70	Zimbabwe	Auckland	1987
67	Romania	Bucharest	2000
64	Romania	Aurillac	1996
64	Georgia	Marseilles	2007
62	Romania	Castres	1999
62	Romania	Bucharest	2006
61	Fiji	Brisbane	2003
60	Italy	Toulon	1967
59	Romania	Paris	1924
56	Romania	Lens	2003
56	Italy	Rome	2005

BY A PLAYER

Pts.	Player	Opponents	Venue	Year
30	D Camberabero	Zimbabwe	Auckland	1987
28	C Lamaison	New Zealand	Twickenham	1999
28	F Michalak	Scotland	Sydney	2003
27	G Camberabero	Italy	Toulon	1967
27	C Lamaison	New Zealand	Marseilles	2000
27	G Merceron	South Africa	Johannesburg	2001
27	J-B Elissalde	Namibia	Toulouse	2007
26	T Lacroix	Ireland	Durban	1995
26	F Michalak	Fiji	Brisbane	2003
25	J-P Romeu	United States	Chicago	1976
25	P Berot	Romania	Agen	1987
25	T Lacroix	Tonga	Pretoria	1995

MOST TRIES IN A MATCH

BY THE TEAM

Tries	Opponents	Venue	Year
13	Romania	Paris	1924
13	Zimbabwe	Auckland	1987
13	Namibia	Toulouse	2007
12	Fiji	Saint Etienne	2001
11	Italy	Toulon	1967
10	Romania	Aurillac	1996
10	Romania	Bucharest	2000

BY A PLAYER

Tries	Player	Opponents	Venue	Year
4	A Jauréguy	Romania	Paris	1924
4	M Celhay	Italy	Paris	1937

MOST CONVERSIONS IN A MATCH

BY THE TEAM

Cons	Opponents	Venue	Year
11	Namibia	Toulouse	2007
9	Italy	Toulon	1967
9	Zimbabwe	Auckland	1987
8	Romania	Wellington	1987
8	Romania	Lens	2003

BY A PLAYER

Cons	Player	Opponents	Venue	Year
11	J-B Elissalde	Namibia	Toulouse	2007
9	G Camberabero	Italy	Toulon	1967
9	D Camberabero	Zimbabwe	Auckland	1987
8	G Laporte	Romania	Wellington	1987

MOST PENALTIES IN A MATCH

BY THE TEAM

Pens	Opponents	Venue	Year
8	Ireland	Durban	1995
7	Wales	Paris	2001
7	Italy	Paris	2002
6	Argentina	Buenos Aires	1977
6	Scotland	Paris	1997
6	Italy	Auch	1997
6	Ireland	Paris	2000
6	South Africa	Johannesburg	2001
6	Argentina	Buenos Aires	2003
6	Fiji	Brisbane	2003
6	England	Twickenham	2005
6	Wales	Paris	2007
6	England	Twickenham	2007

BY A PLAYER

Pens	Player	Opponents	Venue	Year
8	T Lacroix	Ireland	Durban	1995
7	G Merceron	Italy	Paris	2002
6	J-M Aguirre	Argentina	Buenos Aires	1977
6	C Lamaison	Scotland	Paris	1997
6	C Lamaison	Italy	Auch	1997
6	G Merceron	Ireland	Paris	2000
6	G Merceron	South Africa	Johannesburg	2001
6	F Michalak	Fiji	Brisbane	2003
6	D Yachvili	England	Twickenham	2005

MOST DROPPED GOALS IN A MATCH

BY THE TEAM

Drops	Opponents	Venue	Year
3	Ireland	Paris	1960
3	England	Twickenham	1985
3	New Zealand	Christchurch	1986
3	Australia	Sydney	1990
3	Scotland	Paris	1991
3	New Zealand	Christchurch	1994

BY A PLAYER

Drops	Player	Opponents	Venue	Year
3	P Albaladejo	Ireland	Paris	1960
3	J-P Lescarboura	England	Twickenham	1985
3	J-P Lescarboura	New Zealand	Christchurch	1986
3	D Camberabero	Australia	Sydney	1990

CAREER RECORDS

MOST CAPPED PLAYERS

Caps	Player	Career Span
118	F Pelous	1995 to 2007
111	P Sella	1982 to 1995
98	R Ibañez	1996 to 2007
93	S Blanco	1980 to 1991
89	O Magne	1997 to 2007
80	S Marconnet	1998 to 2010
78	A Benazzi	1990 to 2001
74	D Traille	2001 to 2009
71	J-L Sadourny	1991 to 2001
71	O Brouzet	1994 to 2003
71	C Califano	1994 to 2007
69	R Bertranne	1971 to 1981
69	P Saint-André	1990 to 1997
69	P de Villiers	1999 to 2007
68	Y Jauzion	2001 to 2010
67	C Dominici	1998 to 2007
64	F Galthié	1991 to 2003
63	M Crauste	1957 to 1966
63	B Dauga	1964 to 1972
63	S Betsen	1997 to 2007

MOST CONSECUTIVE TESTS

Tests	Player	Career Span
46	R Bertranne	1973 to 1979
45	P Sella	1982 to 1987
44	M Crauste	1960 to 1966
35	B Dauga	1964 to 1968

MOST TESTS AS CAPTAIN

Tests	Captain	Span
42	F Pelous	1997 to 2006
41	R Ibanez	1998 to 2007
34	J-P Rives	1978 to 1984
34	P Saint-André	1994 to 1997
25	D Dubroca	1986 to 1988
25	F Galthié	1999 to 2003
24	G Basquet	1948 to 1952
22	M Crauste	1961 to 1966

MOST POINTS IN TESTS

Pts	Player	Tests	Career
380	C Lamaison	37	1996 to 2001
367	T Lacroix	43	1989 to 1997
354	D Camberabero	36	1982 to 1993
267	G Merceron	32	1999 to 2003
265	J-P Romeu	34	1972 to 1977
264	D Yachvili	44	2002 to 2010
252	F Michalak	54	2001 to 2010
247	T Castaignède	54	1995 to 2007
233	S Blanco	93	1980 to 1991
214	J-B Elissalde	35	2000 to 2008
200	J-P Lescarboura	28	1982 to 1990

MOST TRIES IN TESTS

Tries	Player	Tests	Career
38	S Blanco	93	1980 to 1991
33*	P Saint-André	69	1990 to 1997
30	P Sella	111	1982 to 1995
26	E Ntamack	46	1994 to 2000
26	P Bernat Salles	41	1992 to 2001
25	C Dominici	67	1998 to 2007
23	C Darrouy	40	1957 to 1967

*Saint-André's total includes a penalty try against Romania in 1992

MOST CONVERSIONS IN TESTS

Cons	Player	Tests	Career
59	C Lamaison	37	1996 to 2001
48	D Camberabero	36	1982 to 1993
45	M Vannier	43	1953 to 1961
42	T Castaignède	54	1995 to 2007
40	J-B Elissalde	35	2000 to 2008
37	D Yachvili	44	2002 to 2010
36	R Dourthe	31	1995 to 2001
36	G Merceron	32	1999 to 2003
36	F Michalak	54	2001 to 2010
32	T Lacroix	43	1989 to 1997
29	P Villepreux	34	1967 to 1972

MOST PENALTY GOALS IN TESTS

Pens	Player	Tests	Career
89	T Lacroix	43	1989 to 1997
78	C Lamaison	37	1996 to 2001
59	D Camberabero	36	1982 to 1993
58	D Yachvili	44	2002 to 2010
57	G Merceron	32	1999 to 2003
56	J-P Romeu	34	1972 to 1977
39	F Michalak	54	2001 to 2010
38	J-B Elissalde	35	2000 to 2008
33	P Villepreux	34	1967 to 1972
33	P Bérot	19	1986 to 1989

MOST DROPPED GOALS IN TESTS

Drops	Player	Tests	Career
15	J-P Lescarboura	28	1982 to 1990
12	P Albaladejo	30	1954 to 1964
11	G Camberabero	14	1961 to 1968
11	D Camberabero	36	1982 to 1993
9	J-P Romeu	34	1972 to 1977

INTERNATIONAL CHAMPIONSHIP RECORDS

RECORD	DETAIL		SET
Most points in season	156	in five matches	2002
Most tries in season	18	in four matches	1998
	18	in five matches	2006
Highest Score	56	56-13 v Italy	2005
Biggest win	51	51–0 v Wales	1998
Highest score conceded	49	14-49 v Wales	1910
Biggest defeat	37	0-37 v England	1911
Most appearances	50	P Sella	1983–1995
Most points in matches	180	D Yachvili	2003–2010
Most points in season	80	G Merceron	2002
Most points in match	24	S Viars	v Ireland, 1992
	24	C Lamaison	v Scotland, 1997
	24	J-B Elissalde	v Wales, 2004
Most tries in matches	14	S Blanco	1981 – 1991
	14	P Sella	1983 – 1995
Most tries in season	5	P Estève	1983
	5	E Bonneval	1987
	5	E Ntamack	1999
	5	P Bernat Salles	2001
	5	V Clerc	2008
Most tries in match	3	M Crauste	v England, 1962
	3	C Darrouy	v Ireland, 1963
	3	E Bonneval	v Scotland, 1987
	3	D Venditti	v Ireland, 1997
	3	E Ntamack	v Wales, 1999
	3	V Clerc	v Ireland, 2008
Most cons in matches	25	D Yachvili	2003 – 2010
Most cons in season	11	M Parra	2010
Most cons in match	6	D Yachvili	v Italy, 2003
Most pens in matches	40	D Yachvili	2003 – 2010
Most pens in season	18	G Merceron	2002
Most pens in match	7	G Merceron	v Italy, 2002
Most drops in matches	9	J-P Lescarboura	1982 – 1988
Most drops in season	5	G Camberabero	1967
Most drops in match	3	P Albaladejo	v Ireland, 1960
	3	J-P Lescarboura	v England, 1985

MISCELLANEOUS RECORDS

RECORD	HOLDER	DETAIL
Longest Test Career	F Haget	1974 to 1987
	C Califano	1994 to 2007
Youngest Test Cap	C Dourthe	18 yrs 7 days in 1966
Oldest Test Cap	A Roques	37 yrs 329 days in 1963

CAREER RECORDS OF FRANCE INTERNATIONAL PLAYERS (UP TO 29TH OCTOBER 2010)

PLAYER BACKS	DEBUT	CAPS	T	C	P	D	PTS
M Andreu	2010 v W	4	2	0	0	0	10
J Arias	2009 v A	1	0	0	0	0	0
M Bastareaud	2009 v W	9	2	0	0	0	10
L Beauxis	2007 v It	15	1	18	21	2	110
V Clerc	2002 SA	43	22	0	0	0	110
Y David	2008 It	4	0	0	0	0	0
J Dupuy	2009 v NZ	6	0	4	9	0	35
J-B Elissalde	2000 v S	35	4	40	38	0	214
B Fall	2009 v Sm	2	1	0	0	0	5
A Floch	2008 v E	3	1	0	0	0	5
F Fritz	2005 v SA	19	3	0	0	2	21
C Heymans	2000 v It	54	15	0	0	0	75
Y Jauzion	2001 v SA	68	20	0	0	1	103
J Malzieu	2008 v S	16	4	0	0	0	20
D Marty	2005 v It	31	10	0	0	0	50
L Mazars	2007 v NZ	2	0	0	0	0	0
M Médard	2008 v Arg	14	5	0	0	1	28
M Mermoz	2008 v A	7	0	0	0	0	0
F Michalak	2001 v SA	54	9	36	39	6	252
A Palisson	2008 v A	9	2	0	0	0	10
M Parra	2008 v S	19	0	21	22	1	111
C Poitrenaud	2001 v SA	41	7	0	0	0	35
J Porical	2010 v Arg	1	0	0	1	0	3
A Rougerie	2001 v SA	57	22	0	0	0	110
D Skrela	2001 v NZ	19	0	14	27	1	112
B Thiéry	2007 v NZ	4	0	0	0	0	0
S Tillous-Borde	2008 v A	8	1	0	0	0	5
D Traille	2001 v SA	74	12	8	12	1	115
F Trinh-Duc	2008 v S	22	6	1	1	2	41
D Yachvili	2002 v C	44	2	37	58	2	264

FORWARDS	DEBUT	CAPS	T	C	P	D	PTS
F Barcella	2008 v It	12	0	0	0	0	0
J Bonnaire	2004 v S	54	6	0	0	0	30
R Boyoud	2008 v A	3	0	0	0	0	0
S Chabal	2000 v S	55	6	0	0	0	30
T Domingo	2009 v W	11	1	0	0	0	5
L Ducalcon	2010 v S	1	0	0	0	0	0
T Dusautoir	2006 v R	35	5	0	0	0	25
L Faure	2008 v S	8	0	0	0	0	0
G Guirado	2008 v It	5	0	0	0	0	0
I Harinordoquy	2002 v W	62	12	0	0	0	60
B Kayser	2008 v A	9	0	0	0	0	0
G Lamboley	2005 v S	14	1	0	0	0	5
A Lapandry	2009 v Sm	4	1	0	0	0	5
W Lauret	2010 v SA	1	0	0	0	0	0
B Lecouls	2008 v A	6	0	0	0	0	0
S Marconnet	1998 v Arg	80	3	0	0	0	15
N Mas	2003 v NZ	37	0	0	0	0	0
R Millo-Chluski	2005 v SA	14	0	0	0	0	0
L Nallet	2000 v R	56	6	0	0	0	30
F Ouedraogo	2007 v NZ	20	1	0	0	0	5
P Papé	2004 v I	26	2	0	0	0	10
L Picamoles	2008 v I	17	1	0	0	0	5
J Pierre	2007 v NZ	9	0	0	0	0	0
J-B Poux	2001 v Fj	28	3	0	0	0	15
J Puricelli	2009 v NZ	4	0	0	0	0	0
W Servat	2004 v I	30	2	0	0	0	10
D Szarzewski	2004 v C	48	6	0	0	0	30

FRANCE INTERNATIONAL PLAYERS
UP TO 29TH OCTOBER 2010

Note: Years given for International Championship matches are for second half of season; eg 1972 means season 1971–72. Years for all other matches refer to the actual year of the match. Entries in square brackets denote matches played in RWC Finals.

Abadie, A (Pau) 1964 I
Abadie, A (Graulhet) 1965 R, 1967 SA 1,3,4, NZ, 1968 S, I
Abadie, L (Tarbes) 1963 R
Accoceberry, G (Bègles) 1994 NZ 1,2, C 2, 1995 W, E, S, I, R 1, [Iv, S], It, 1996 I, W 1, R, Arg 1, W 2(R), SA 2, 1997 S, It 1
Aguerre, R (Biarritz O) 1979 S
Aguilar, D (Pau) 1937 G
Aguirre, J-M (Bagnères) 1971 A 2, 1972 S, 1973 W, I, J, R, 1974 I, W, Arg 2, R, SA 1, 1976 W (R), E, US, A 2, R, 1977 W, E, S, I, Arg 1,2, NZ 1,2, R, 1978 E, S, I, W, R, 1979 I, W, E, S, NZ 1,2, R, 1980 W, I
Ainciart, E (Bayonne) 1933 G, 1934 G, 1935 G, 1937 G, It, 1938 G 1
Albaladéjo, P (Dax) 1954 E, It, 1960 W, I, It, R, 1961 S, SA, E, W, I, NZ 1,2, A, 1962 S, E, W, I, 1963 S, I, E, W, It, 1964 S, NZ, W, It, I, SA, Fj
Albouy, A (Castres) 2002 It (R)
Alvarez, A-J (Tyrosse) 1945 B2, 1946 B, I, K, W, 1947 S, I, W, E, 1948 I, A, S, W, E, 1949 I, E, W, 1951 S, E, W
Amand, H (SF) 1906 NZ
Ambert, A (Toulouse) 1930 S, I, E, G, W
Amestoy, J-B (Mont-de-Marsan) 1964 NZ, E
André, G (RCF) 1913 SA, E, W, I, 1914 I, W, E
Andreu, M (Castres) 2010 W(R),It,E,SA(R)
Andrieu, M (Nîmes) 1986 Arg 2, NZ 1, R 2, NZ 2, 1987 [R, Z], R, 1988 E, S, I, W, Arg 1,2,3,4, R, 1989 I, W, E, S, NZ 2, B, A 2, 1990 W, E, I (R)
Anduran, J (SCUF) 1910 W
Aqua, J-L (Toulon) 1999 R, Tg, NZ 1(R)
Araou, R (Narbonne) 1924 R
Arcalis, R (Brive) 1950 S, I, 1951 I, E, W
Arias, J (SF) 2009 A(R)
Arino, M (Agen) 1962 R
Aristouy, P (Pau) 1948 S, 1949 Arg 2, 1950 S, I, E, W
Arlettaz, P (Perpignan) 1995 R 2
Armary, L (Lourdes) 1987 [R], R, 1988 S, I, W, Arg 3,4, R, 1989 W, S, A 1,2, 1990 W, E, S, I, A 1,2,3, NZ 1, 1991 W 2, 1992 S, I, R, Arg 1,2, SA 1,2, Arg, 1993 E, S, I, W, SA 1,2, R 2, A 1,2, 1994 I, W, NZ 1(t),2(t), 1995 I, R 1 [Tg, I, SA]
Arnal, J-M (RCF) 1914 I, W
Arnaudet, M (Lourdes) 1964 I, 1967 It, W
Arotca, R (Bayonne) 1938 R
Arrieta, J (SF) 1953 E, W
Arthapignet, P (see Harislur-Arthapignet)
Artiguste, E (Castres) 1999 WS
Astre, R (Béziers) 1971 R, 1972 I 1, 1973 E (R), 1975 E, S, I, SA 1,2, Arg 2, 1976 A 2, R
Attoub, D (Castres) 2006 R
Aucagne, D (Pau) 1997 W (R), S, It 1, R 1(R), A 1, R 2(R), SA 2(R), 1998 S (R), W (R), Arg 2(R), Fj (R), Arg 3, A, 1999 W 1(R), S (R)
Audebert, A (Montferrand) 2000 R, 2002 W (R)
Aué, J-M (Castres) 1998 W (R)
Augé, J (Dax) 1929 S, W
Augras-Fabre, L (Agen) 1931 I, S, W
August, B (Biarritz) 2007 W1(R)
Auradou, D (SF) 1999 E (R), S (R), WS (R), Tg, NZ 1, W 2(R), [Arg (R)], 2000 A (R), NZ 1,2, 2001 S, I, It, W, E (R), SA 1,2, NZ (R), SA 3, A, Fj, 2002 It, E, I (R), C (R), 2003 S (R), It (R), W (R), Arg, 1,2, NZ (R), R (R), E 2(R),3, [J(R),US,NZ] , 2004 I(R),It(R),S(R),E(R)
Averous, J-L (La Voulte) 1975 S, I, SA 1,2, 1976 I, W, E, US, A 1,2, R, 1977 W, E, S, I, Arg 1, R, 1978 E, S, I, 1979 NZ 1,2, 1980 E, S, 1981 A 2
Avril, D (Biarritz) 2005 A1
Azam, O (Montferrand, Gloucester) 1995 R 2, Arg (R), 2000 A (R), NZ 2(R), 2001 SA 2(R), NZ, 2002 E (R), I (R), Arg (R), A 1
Azarete, J-L (Dax, St Jean-de-Luz) 1969 W, R, 1970 S, I, W, R, 1971 S, I, E, SA 1,2, A 1, 1972 E, W, I 2, A 1, R, 1973 NZ, W, I, R, 1974 I, R, SA 1,2, 1975 W
Baby, B (Toulouse, Clermont-Auvergne) 2005 I,SA2(R),A1, 2008 Arg,PI,A3, 2009 I(R),S,W
Bacqué, N (Pau) 1997 R 2
Bader, E (Primevères) 1926 M, 1927 I, S
Badin, C (Chalon) 1973 W, I, 1975 Arg 1
Baillette, M (Perpignan) 1925 I, NZ, S, 1926 W, M, 1927 I, W, G 2, 1929 G, 1930 S, I, E, G, 1931 I, S, E, 1932 G
Baladie, G (Agen) 1945 B 1,2, W, 1946 B, I, K
Ballarin, J (Tarbes) 1924 E, 1925 NZ, S
Baquey, J (Toulouse) 1921 I
Barbazanges, A (Roanne) 1932 G, 1933 G
Barcella, F (Auch, Biarritz) 2008 It,W,Arg, 2009 S,W,It, NZ1,2,A,SA,NZ3, 2010 Arg1
Barrau, M (Beaumont, Toulouse) 1971 S, E, W, 1972 E, W, A 1,2, 1973 S, NZ, E, I, J, R, 1974 I, S
Barrau, M (Agen) 2004 US,C(R),NZ(R)
Barrère, P (Toulon) 1929 G, 1931 W
Barrière, R (Béziers) 1960 R
Barthe, F (SBUC) 1925 W, E
Barthe, J (Lourdes) 1954 Arg 1,2, 1955 S, 1956 I, W, It, E, Cz, 1957 S, I, E, W, R 1,2, 1958 S, E, A, W, It, I, SA 1,2, 1959 S, E, It, W
Basauri, R (Albi) 1954 Arg 1
Bascou, P (Bayonne) 1914 E
Basquet, G (Agen) 1945 W, 1946 B, I, K, W, 1947 S, I, W, E, 1948 I, A, S, W, E, 1949 S, I, E, W, Arg 1, 1950 S, I, E, W, 1951 S, I, E, W, 1952 S, I, SA, W, E, It
Bastareaud, M (SF) 2009 W,E,It(R),NZ1, 2010 S,I,W,It(R),E
Bastiat, J-P (Dax) 1969 R, 1970 S, I, W, 1971 S, I, SA 2, 1972 S, A 1, 1973 E, 1974 Arg 1,2, SA 2, 1975 W, Arg 1,2, R, 1976 S, I, W, E, A 1,2, R, 1977 W, E, S, I, 1978 E, S, I, W
Baudry, N (Montferrand) 1949 S, I, W, Arg 1,2
Baulon, R (Vienne, Bayonne) 1954 S, NZ, W, E, It, 1955 I, E, W, It, 1956 S, I, W, It, E, Cz, 1957 S, I, It
Baux, J-P (Lannemezan) 1968 NZ 1,2, SA 1,2
Bavozet, J (Lyon) 1911 S, E, W
Bayard, J (Toulouse) 1923 S, W, E, 1924 W, R, US
Bayardon, J (Chalon) 1964 S, NZ, E
Beaurin-Gressier, C (SF) 1907 E, 1908 E
Beauxis, L (SF) 2007 It(R),I(R),W1(R),E1(R),S,W2, [Nm(R),I(R) ,Gg,NZ,E,Arg 2(R)], 2009 I,S,A
Bégu, J (Dax) 1982 Arg 2(R), 1984 E, S
Béguerie, C (Agen) 1979 NZ 1
Béguet, L (RCF) 1922 I, 1923 S, W, E, I, 1924 S, I, E, R, US
Béhotéguy, A (Bayonne, Cognac) 1923 E, 1924 S, I, E, W, R, US, 1926 E, 1927 E, G 1,2, 1928 A, I, E, G, W, 1929 S, W, E
Béhotéguy, H (RCF, Cognac) 1923 W, 1928 A, I, E, G, W
Bélascain, C (Bayonne) 1977 R, 1978 E, S, I, W, R, 1979 I, W, E, S, 1982 W, E, S, I, 1983 E, S, I, W
Belletante, G (Nantes) 1951 I, E, W

Belot, F (Toulouse) 2000 I (R)

Benazzi, A (Agen) 1990 A 1,2,3, NZ 1,2, 1991 E, US 1(R),2, [R, Fj, C], 1992 SA 1(R),2, Arg, 1993 E, S, I, W, A 1,2, 1994 I, W, E, S, C 1, NZ 1,2, C 2, 1995 W, E, S, I, [Tg, Iv, S, I, SA, E], NZ 1,2, 1996 E, S, I, W 1, Arg 1,2, W 2, SA 1,2, 1997 I, W, E, S, R 1, A 1,2, It 2, R 2(R), Arg, SA 1,2, 1999 R, WS, W 2, [C, Nm (R), Fj, Arg, NZ 2, A], 2000 W, E, I, It (R), R, 2001 S (R), I (t&R), E

Bénésis, R (Narbonne) 1969 W, R, 1970 S, I, W, E, R, 1971 S, I, E, W, A 2, R, 1972 S, I 1, E, W, I 2, A 1, R, 1973 NZ, E, W, I, J, R, 1974 I, W, E, S

Benetière, J (Roanne) 1954 It, Arg 1

Benetton, P (Agen) 1989 B, 1990 NZ 2, 1991 US 2, 1992 Arg 1,2(R), SA 1(R),2, Arg, 1993 E, S, I, W, SA 1,2, R 2, A 1,2, 1994 I, W, E, S, C 1, NZ 1,2, C 2, 1995 W, E, S, I, [Tg, Iv (R), S], It, R 2(R), Arg, NZ 1,2, 1996 Arg 1,2, W 2, SA 1,2, 1997 I, It 1,2(R), R 2, Arg, SA 1,2 1998 E, S (R), I (R), W (R), Arg 1(R),2(R), Fj (R), 1999 I, W 1, S (R)

Benezech, L (RCF) 1994 E, S, C 1, NZ 1,2, C 2, 1995 W, E, [Iv, S, E], R 2, Arg, NZ 1,2

Berbizier, P (Lourdes, Agen) 1981 S, I, W, E, NZ 1,2, 1982 I, R, 1983 S, I, 1984 S (R), NZ 1,2, 1985 Arg 1,2, 1986 S, I, W, E, R 1, Arg 1, A, NZ 1, R 2, NZ 2,3, 1987 W, E, S, I, [S, R, Fj, A, NZ], R, 1988 E, S, I, W, Arg 1,2, 1989 I, W, E, S, NZ 1,2, B, A 1, 1990 W, E, 1991 S, I, W 1, E

Berejnoï, J-C (Tulle) 1963 R, 1964 S, W, It, I, SA, Fj, R, 1965 S, I, E, W, It, R, 1966 S, I, E, W, It, R, 1967 S, A, E, It, W, I, R

Bergès, B (Toulouse) 1926 I

Berges-Cau, R (Lourdes) 1976 E (R)

Bergese, F (Bayonne) 1936 G 2, 1937 G, It, 1938 G 1, R, G 2

Bergougnan, Y (Toulouse) 1945 B 1, W, 1946 B, I, K, W, 1947 S, I, W, E, 1948 S, W, E, 1949 S, E, Arg 1,2

Bernard, R (Bergerac) 1951 S, I, E, W

Bernat-Salles, P (Pau, Bègles-Bordeaux, Biarritz) 1992 Arg, 1993 R 1, SA 1,2, R 2, A 1,2, 1994 I, 1995 E, S, 1996 E (R), 1997 R 1, A 1,2, 1998 E, S, I, W, Arg 1,2, Fj, Arg 3(R), A 1999 I, W 1, R, Tg, [Nm, Fj, Arg, NZ 2, A], 2000 I, It, NZ 1(R),2, 2001 S, I, It, W, E

Bernon, J (Lourdes) 1922 I, 1923 S

Bérot, J-L (Toulouse) 1968 NZ 3, A, 1969 S, I, 1970 E, R, 1971 S, I, E, W, SA 1,2, A 1,2, R, 1972 S, I 1, E, W, A 1, 1974 I

Bérot, P (Agen) 1986 R 2, NZ 2,3, 1987 W, E, S, I, R, 1988 E, S, I, Arg 1,2,3,4, R, 1989 S, NZ 1,2

Bertrand, P (Bourg) 1951 I, E, W, 1953 S, I, E, W, It

Bertranne, R (Bagnères) 1971 E, W, SA 2, A 1,2, 1972 S, I 1, 1973 NZ, E, J, R, 1974 I, W, E, S, Arg 1,2, R, SA 1,2, 1975 W, E, S, I, SA 1,2, Arg 1,2, R, 1976 S, I, W, E, US, A 1,2, R, 1977 W, E, S, I, Arg 1,2, NZ 1,2, R, 1978 E, S, I, W, R, 1979 I, W, E, S, R, 1980 W, E, S, I, SA, R, 1981 S, I, W, E, R, NZ 1,2

Berty, D (Toulouse) 1990 NZ 2, 1992 R (R), 1993 R 2, 1995 NZ 1(R), 1996 W 2(R), SA 1

Besset, E (Grenoble) 1924 S

Besset, L (SCUF) 1914 W, E

Besson, M (CASG) 1924 I, 1925 I, E, 1926 S, W, 1927 I

Besson, P (Brive) 1963 S, I, E, 1965 R, 1968 SA 1

Betsen, S (Biarritz) 1997 It 1(R), 2000 W (R), E (R), A (R), NZ 1(R),2(R), 2001 S (R), I (R), It (R), W (R), SA 3(R), A, Fj, 2002 It, W, E, S, I, Arg, A 1,2, SA, NZ, C, 2003 E 1, S, I, It, W, R, E 2, [Fj,J,S,I,E], 2004 I,It,W,S,E,A,Arg,NZ, 2005 E,W,I,It, 2006 SA, NZ2(R),Arg(R), 2007 It,I,W1,E1,S,E2,W2, [Arg 1,I,Gg,NZ,E]

Bianchi, J (Toulon) 1986 Arg 1

Bichindaritz, J (Biarritz O) 1954 It, Arg 1,2

Bidabé, P (Biarritz) 2004 C, 2006 R

Bidart, L (La Rochelle) 1953 W

Biémouret, P (Agen) 1969 E, W, 1970 I, W, E, 1971 W, SA 1,2, A 1, 1972 E, W, I 2, A 2, R, 1973 S, NZ, E, W, I

Biénès, R (Cognac) 1950 S, I, E, W, 1951 S, I, E, W, 1952 S, I, SA, W, E, It, 1953 S, I, E, 1954 S, I, NZ, W, E, Arg 1,2, 1956 S, I, W, It, E

Bigot, C (Quillan) 1930 S, E, 1931 I, S

Bilbao, L (St Jean-de-Luz) 1978 I, 1979 I

Billac, E (Bayonne) 1920 S, E, W, I, US, 1921 S, W, 1922 W, 1923 E

Billière, M (Toulouse) 1968 NZ 3

Bioussa, A (Toulouse) 1924 W, US, 1925 I, NZ, S, E, 1926 S, I, E, 1928 E, G, W, 1929 I, S, W, E, 1930 S, I, E, G, W

Bioussa, C (Toulouse) 1913 W, I, 1914 I

Biraben, M (Dax) 1920 W, I, US, 1921 S, W, E, I, 1922 S, E, I

Blain, A (Carcassonne) 1934 G

Blanco, S (Biarritz O) 1980 SA, R, 1981 S, W, E, A 1,2, R, NZ 1,2, 1982 W, E, S, I, R, Arg 1,2, 1983 E, S, I, W, 1984 I, W, E, S, NZ 1,2, R, 1985 E, S, I, W, Arg 1,2, 1986 S, I, W, E, R 1, Arg 2, A, NZ 1, R 2, NZ 2,3, 1987 W, E, S, I, [S, R, Fj, A, NZ], R, 1988 E, S, I, W, Arg 1,2,3,4, R, 1989 I, W, E, S, NZ 1,2, B, A 1, 1990 E, S, I, R, A 1,2,3, NZ 1,2, 1991 S, I, W 1, E, R, US 1,2, W 2, [R, Fj, C, E]

Blond, J (SF) 1935 G, 1936 G 2, 1937 G, 1938 G 1, R, G 2

Blond, X (RCF) 1990 A 3, 1991 S, I, W 1, E, 1994 NZ 2(R)

Boffelli, V (Aurillac) 1971 A 2, R, 1972 S, I 1, 1973 J, R, 1974 I, W, E, S, Arg 1,2, R, SA 1,2, 1975 W, S, I

Bonal, J-M (Toulouse) 1968 E, W, Cz, NZ 2,3, SA 1,2, R, 1969 S, I, E, R, 1970 W, E

Bonamy, R (SB) 1928 A, I

Bondouy, P (Narbonne, Toulouse) 1997 S (R), It 1, A 2(R), R 2, 2000 R (R)

Bonetti, S (Biarritz) 2001 It, W, NZ (R)

Boniface, A (Mont-de-Marsan) 1954 I, NZ, W, E, It, Arg 1,2, 1955 S, I, 1956 S, I, W, It, Cz, 1957 S, I, W, R 2, 1958 S, E, 1959 E, 1961 NZ 1,3, A, R, 1962 E, W, I, It, R, 1963 S, I, E, W, It, R, 1964 S, NZ, E, W, It, 1965 W, It, R, 1966 S, I, E, W

Boniface, G (Mont-de-Marsan) 1960 W, I, It, R, Arg 1,2,3, 1961 S, SA, E, W, It, I, NZ 1,2,3, R, 1962 R, 1963 S, I, E, W, It, R, 1964 S, 1965 S, I, E, W, It, R, 1966 S, I, E, W

Bonnaire, J (Bourgoin, Clermont-Auvergne) 2004 S(t&R), A(R),NZ(R), 2005 S,E,W,I,It,SA1,2,A1,C,Tg,SA3, 2006 S,I,It(R), E(R),W,R,SA(R),NZ1,2,Arg, 2007 It,I(R),W1,E1,S,E2,3(R), [Arg1(R),Nm,I,Gg,NZ,E], 2008 S(R),I,E,It(R),W, 2009 E(R),It, SA(R),Sm,NZ3, 2010 S(R),I(R),W,It,E,SA,Arg1

Bonnes, E (Narbonne) 1924 W, R, US

Bonneval, E (Toulouse) 1984 NZ 2(R), 1985 W, Arg 1, 1986 W, E, R 1, Arg 1,2, A, R 2, NZ 2,3, 1987 W, E, S, I, [Z], 1988 E

Bonnus, F (Toulon) 1950 S, I, E, W

Bonnus, M (Toulon) 1937 It, 1938 G 1, R, G 2, 1940 B

Bontemps, D (La Rochelle) 1968 SA 2

Borchard, G (RCF) 1908 E, 1909 E, W, I, 1911 I

Borde, F (RCF) 1920 I, US, 1921 S, W, E, 1922 S, W, 1923 S, I, 1924 E, 1925 I, 1926 E

Bordenave, L (Toulon) 1948 A, S, W, E, 1949 S

Bory, D (Montferrand) 2000 I, It, A, NZ 1, 2001 S, I, SA 1,2,3, A, Fj, 2002 It, E, S, I, C, 2003 [US,NZ]

Boubée, J (Tarbes) 1921 S, E, I, 1922 E, W, 1923 E, I, 1925 NZ, S

Boudreaux, R (SCUF) 1910 W, S

Bouet, D (Dax) 1989 NZ 1,2, B, A 2, 1990 A 3

Bouguyon, G (Grenoble) 1961 SA, E, W, It, I, NZ 1,2,3, A

Bouic, G (Agen) 1996 SA 1

Bouilhou, J (Toulouse) 2001 NZ, 2003 Arg 1

Boujet, C (Grenoble) 1968 NZ 2, A (R), SA 1

Bouquet, J (Bourgoin, Vienne) 1954 S, 1955 E, 1956 S, I, W, It, E, Cz, 1957 S, E, W, R 2, 1958 S, E, 1959 S, It, W, I, 1960 S, E, W, I, R, 1961 S, SA, E, W, It, I, R, 1962 S, E, W, I

Bourdeu, J R (Lourdes) 1952 S, I, SA, W, E, It, 1953 S, I, E

Bourgarel, R (Toulouse) 1969 R, 1970 S, I, E, R, 1971 W, SA 1,2, 1973 S

Bourguignon, G (Narbonne) 1988 Arg 3, 1989 I, E, B, A 1, 1990 R

Bousquet, A (Béziers) 1921 E, I, 1924 R

Bousquet, R (Albi) 1926 M, 1927 I, S, W, E, G 1, 1929 W, E, 1930 W

Bousses, G (Bourgoin) 2006 S(R)

Boyau, M (SBUC) 1912 I, S, W, E, 1913 W, I

Boyer, P (Toulon) 1935 G

Boyet, B (Bourgoin) 2006 I(R), 2007 NZ1,2, 2008 A1,2(R)

Boyoud, R (Dax) 2008 A1(R),2, 2009 S(R)

Branca, G (SF) 1928 S, 1929 I, S

Branlat, A (RCF) 1906 NZ, E, 1908 W

Bréjassou, R (Tarbes) 1952 S, I, SA, W, E, 1953 W, E, 1954 S, I, NZ, 1955 S, I, E, W, It

Brèthes, R (St Séver) 1960 Arg 2

Bringeon, A (Biarritz O) 1925 W

Brouzet, O (Grenoble, Bègles, Northampton, Montferrand) 1994 S, NZ 2(R), 1995 E, S, I, R 1, [Tg, Iv, E (t)], It, Arg (R), 1996 W 1(R), 1997 R 1, A 1,2, It 2, Arg, SA 1,2, 1998 E, S, I, W,

Arg 1,2, Fj, Arg 3, A, 1999 I, W 1, E, S, R, [C (R), Nm, Fj (R), Arg, NZ 2(R), A (R)], 2000 W, E, S, I, It, A, NZ 1(R),2(R), 2001 SA 1,2, NZ, 2002 W, E, S, I, Arg, A 1(R),2, SA, NZ, C, 2003 E 1, S, I, It, W, E 3, [Fj(R),J,S(R),US,I(R)]

Bru, Y (Toulouse) 2001 A (R), Fj (R), 2002 It, 2003 Arg 2, NZ, R, E 2,3(R), [J,S(R),US,I(t&R),NZ], 2004 I(R),It(R),W(R),S(R),E(R)

Brugnaut, J (Dax) 2008 S,I(R)

Brun, G (Vienne) 1950 E, W, 1951 S, E, W, 1952 S, I, SA, W, E, It, 1953 E, W, It

Bruneau, M (SBUC) 1910 W, E, 1913 SA, E

Brunet, Y (Perpignan) 1975 SA 1, 1977 Arg 1

Bruno, S (Béziers, Sale) 2002 W (R), 2004 A(R),NZ(t&R), 2005 S(R),E,W,I,It,SA1,2(R),A1(R),2(R),C,SA3(R), 2006 S(R),I(R), 2007 I(R),E1(R),NZ1,2,E3(R),W2(R), [Gg,Arg 2(t&R)], 2008 A1,2

Brusque, N (Pau, Biarritz) 1997 R 2(R), 2002 W, E, S, I, Arg, A 2, SA, NZ, C, 2003 E 2, [Fj,S,I,E,NZ(R)], 2004 I,It,W,S,E,A,Arg, 2005 SA1(R),2,A1, 2006 S

Buchet, E (Nice) 1980 R, 1982 E, R (R), Arg 1,2

Buisson, H (see Empereur-Buisson)

Buonomo, Y (Béziers) 1971 A 2, R, 1972 I 1

Burgun, M (RCF) 1909 I, 1910 W, S, I, 1911 S, E, 1912 I, S, 1913 S, E, 1914 E

Bustaffa, D (Carcassonne) 1977 Arg 1,2, NZ 1,2, 1978 W, R, 1980 W, E, S, SA, R

Buzy, C-E (Lourdes) 1946 K, W, 1947 S, I, W, E, 1948 I, A, S, W, E, 1949 S, I, E, W, Arg 1,2

Caballero, Y (Montauban) 2008 A2(R)

Cabanier, J-M (Montauban) 1963 R, 1964 S, Fj, 1965 S, I, W, It, R, 1966 S, I, E, W, It, R, 1967 S, A, E, It, W, I, SA 1,3, NZ, R, 1968 S, I

Cabannes, L (RCF, Harlequins) 1990 NZ 2(R), 1991 S, I, W 1, E, US 2, W 2, [R, Fj, C, E], 1992 W, E, S, I, R, Arg 2, SA 1,2, 1993 E, S, I, W, R 1, SA 1,2, 1994 E, S, C 1, NZ 1,2, 1995 W, E, S, R 1, [Tg (R), Iv, S, I, SA, E], 1996 E, S, I, W 1, 1997 It 2, Arg, SA 1,2

Cabrol, H (Béziers) 1972 A 1(R),2, 1973 J, 1974 SA 2

Cadenat, J (SCUF) 1910 S, E, 1911 W, I, 1912 W, E, 1913 I

Cadieu, J-M (Toulouse) 1991 R, US 1, [R, Fj, C, E], 1992 W, I, R, Arg 1,2, SA 1

Cahuc, F (St Girons) 1922 S

Califano, C (Toulouse, Saracens, Gloucester) 1994 NZ 1,2, C 2, 1995 W, E, S, I, [Iv, S, I, SA, E], It, Arg, NZ 1,2, 1996 E, S, I, W 1, R, Arg 1,2, SA 1,2, 1997 I, W, E, A 1,2, It 2, R 2(R), Arg, SA 1,2, 1998 E, S, I, W, 1999 I, W 1, E (R), S, WS, Tg (R), NZ 1, W 2, [C, Nm, Fj], 2000 W, E, S, I, It, R, A, NZ 1,2(R), 2001 S (R), I (R), It, W, SA 1(R),2(R), NZ, 2003 E 1, S (R), I (R), 2007 NZ1,2

Cals, R (RCF) 1938 G 1

Calvo, G (Lourdes) 1961 NZ 1,3

Camberabero, D (La Voulte, Béziers) 1982 R, Arg 1,2, 1983 E, W, 1987 [R (R), Z, Fj (R), A, NZ], 1988 I, 1989 B, A 1, 1990 W, S, I, R, A 1,2,3, NZ 1,2, 1991 S, I, W 1, E, R, US 1,2, W 2, [R, Fj, C], 1993 E, S, I

Camberabero, G (La Voulte) 1961 NZ 3, 1962 R, 1964 R, 1967 A, E, It, W, I, SA 1,3,4, 1968 S, E, W

Camberabero, L (La Voulte) 1964 R, 1965 S, I, 1966 E, W, 1967 A, E, It, W, I, 1968 S, E, W

Cambré, T (Oloron) 1920 E, W, I, US

Camel, A (Toulouse) 1928 S, A, I, E, G, W, 1929 W, E, G, 1930 S, I, E, G, W, 1935 G

Camel, M (Toulouse) 1929 S, W, E

Camicas, F (Tarbes) 1927 G 2, 1928 S, I, E, G, W, 1929 I, S, W, E

Camo, E (Villeneuve) 1931 I, S, W, E, G, 1932 G

Campaès, A (Lourdes) 1965 W, 1967 NZ, 1968 S, I, E, W, Cz, NZ 1,2, A, 1969 S, W, 1972 R, 1973 NZ

Campan, O (Agen) 1993 SA 1(R),2(R), R 2(R), 1996 I, W 1, R

Candelon, J (Narbonne) 2005 SA1,A1(R)

Cantoni, J (Béziers) 1970 W, R, 1971 S, I, E, W, SA 1,2, R, 1972 S, I 1, 1973 S, NZ, W, I, 1975 W (R)

Capdouze, J (Pau) 1964 SA, Fj, R, 1965 S, I, E

Capendeguy, J-M (Bègles) 1967 NZ, R

Capitani, P (Toulon) 1954 Arg 1,2

Capmau, J-L (Toulouse) 1914 E

Carabignac, G (Agen) 1951 S, I, 1952 SA, W, E, 1953 S, I

Carbonne, J (Perpignan) 1927 W

Carbonneau, P (Toulouse, Brive, Pau) 1995 R 2, Arg, NZ 1,2, 1996 E, S, R (R), Arg 2, W 2, SA 1, 1997 I (R), W, E, S (R), R 1(R), A 1,2, 1998 E, S, I, W, Arg 1,2, Fj, Arg 3, A, 1999 I, W 1, E, S, 2000 NZ 2(R), 2001 I

Carminati, A (Béziers, Brive) 1986 R 2, NZ 2, 1987 [R, Z], 1988 I, W, Arg 1,2, 1989 I, W, S, NZ 1(R),2, A 2, 1990 S, 1995 It, R 2, Arg, NZ 1,2

Caron, L (Lyon O, Castres) 1947 E, 1948 I, A, W, E, 1949 S, I, E, W, Arg 1

Carpentier, M (Lourdes) 1980 E, SA, R, 1981 S, I, A 1, 1982 E, S

Carrère, C (Toulon) 1966 R, 1967 S, A, E, W, I, SA 1,3,4, NZ, R, 1968 S, I, E, W, Cz, NZ 3, A, R, 1969 S, I, 1970 S, I, W, E, 1971 E, W

Carrère, J (Vichy, Toulon) 1956 S, 1957 E, W, R 2, 1958 S, SA 1,2, 1959 I

Carrère, R (Mont-de-Marsan) 1953 E, It

Casadei, D (Brive) 1997 S, R 1, SA 2(R)

Casaux, L (Tarbes) 1959 I, It, 1962 S

Cassagne, P (Pau) 1957 It

Cassayet-Armagnac, A (Tarbes, Narbonne) 1920 S, E, W, US, 1921 W, E, I, 1922 S, E, W, 1923 S, W, E, I, 1924 S, E, W, R, US, 1925 I, NZ, S, W, 1926 S, I, E, W, M, 1927 I, S, W

Cassiède, M (Dax) 1961 NZ 3, A, R

Castaignède, S (Mont-de-Marsan) 1999 W 2, [C (R), Nm (R), Fj, Arg (R), NZ 2(R), A (R)]

Castaignède, T (Toulouse, Castres, Saracens) 1995 R 2, Arg, NZ 1,2, 1996 E, S, I, W 1, Arg 1,2, 1997 I, A 1,2, It 2, 1998 E, S, I, W, Arg 1,2, Fj, 1999 I, W 1, E, S, R, WS, Tg (R), NZ 1, W 2, [C], 2000 W, E, S, It, 2002 SA, NZ, C, 2003 E 1(R), S (R), It, W, Arg 1, 2005 A2(R),C,Tg,SA3, 2006 It,E,W,R,SA(R), 2007 NZ1,2

Castel, R (Toulouse, Béziers) 1996 I, W 1, W 2, SA 1(R),2, 1997 I (R), W, E (R), S (R), A 1(R), 1998 Arg 3(R), A (R), 1999 W 1(R), E, S

Castets, J (Toulon) 1923 W, E, I

Caujolle, J (Tarbes) 1909 E, 1913 SA, E, 1914 W, E

Caunègre, R (SB) 1938 R, G 2

Caussade, A (Lourdes) 1978 R, 1979 I, W, E, NZ 1,2, R, 1980 W, E, S, 1981 S (R), I

Caussarieu, G (Pau) 1929 I

Cayrefourcq, E (Tarbes) 1921 E

Cazalbou, J (Toulouse) 1997 It 2(R), R 2, Arg, SA 2(R)

Cazals, P (Mont-de-Marsan) 1961 NZ 1, A, R

Cazenave, A (Pau) 1927 E, G 1, 1928 S, A, G

Cazenave, F (RCF) 1950 E, 1952 S, 1954 I, NZ, W, E

Cécillon, M (Bourgoin) 1988 I, W, Arg 2,3,4, R, 1989 I, E, NZ 1,2, A 1, 1991 S, I, E (R), R, US 1, W 2, [E], 1992 W, E, S, I, R, Arg 1,2, SA 1,2, 1993 E, S, I, W, R 1, SA 1,2, R 2, A 1,2, 1994 I, W, NZ 1(R), 1995 I, R 1, [Tg, S (R), I, SA]

Celaya, M (Biarritz O, SBUC) 1953 E, W, It, 1954 I, E, It, Arg 1,2, 1955 S, I, E, W, It, 1956 S, I, W, It, E, Cz 1957 S, I, E, W, R 2, 1958 S, E, A, W, It, 1959 S, E, 1960 S, E, W, I, R, Arg 1,2,3, 1961 S, SA, E, W, It, I, NZ 1,2,3, A, R

Celhay, M (Bayonne) 1935 G, 1936 G 1, 1937 G, It, 1938 G 1, 1940 B

Cermeno, F (Perpignan) 2000 R

Cessieux, N (Lyon) 1906 NZ

Cester, E (TOEC, Valence) 1966 S, I, E, 1967 W, 1968 S, I, E, W, Cz, NZ 1,3, A, SA 1,2, R, 1969 S, I, E, W, 1970 S, I, W, E, 1971 A 1, 1972 R, 1973 S, NZ, W, I, J, R, 1974 I, W, E, S

Chabal, S (Bourgoin, Sale, Racing-Metro) 2000 S, 2001 SA 1,2, NZ (R), Fj (R), 2002 Arg (R), A 2, SA (R), NZ (t), C (R), 2003 E 1(R), S (R), I (R), Arg 2, NZ (R), E 2(R),3, [J(R),US,NZ], 2005 S,E,A2(R),Tg, 2007 It,I,E1,NZ1,2,E2(R),W2, [Arg1(R),Nm,I, NZ(R),E(R),Arg 2(R)], 2008 A1,2,Arg(R),PI(R),A3, 2009 I,S(R),W,E,It,NZ1(R),2,SA(R),Sm,NZ3, 2010 W(R),It(R),E(R)

Chaban-Delmas, J (CASG) 1945 B 2

Chabowski, H (Nice, Bourgoin) 1985 Arg 2, 1986 R 2, NZ 2, 1989 B (R)

Chadebech, P (Brive) 1982 R, Arg 1,2, 1986 S, I

Champ, E (Toulon) 1985 Arg 1,2, 1986 I, W, E, R 1, Arg 1,2, A, NZ 1, R 2, NZ 2,3, 1987 W, E, S, I, [S, R, Fj, A, NZ], R, 1988 E, S, Arg 1,3,4, R, 1989 W, S, A 1,2, 1990 W, E, NZ 1, 1991 R, US 1, [R, Fj, C, E]

Chapuy, L (SF) 1926 S

Charpentier, G (SF) 1911 E, 1912 W, E
Charton, P (Montferrand) 1940 B
Charvet, D (Toulouse) 1986 W, E, R 1, Arg 1, A, NZ 1,3, 1987 W, E, S, I, [S, R, Z, Fj, A, NZ], R, 1989 E (R), 1990 W, E, 1991 S, I
Chassagne, J (Montferrand) 1938 G 1
Chatau, A (Bayonne) 1913 SA
Chaud, E (Toulon) 1932 G, 1934 G, 1935 G
Chazalet, A (Bourgoin) 1999 Tg
Chenevay, C (Grenoble) 1968 SA 1
Chevallier, B (Montferrand) 1952 S, I, SA, W, E, It, 1953 E, W, It, 1954 S, I, NZ, W, Arg 1, 1955 S, I, E, W, It, 1956 S, I, W, It, E, Cz, 1957 S
Chiberry, J (Chambéry) 1955 It
Chilo, A (RCF) 1920 S, W, 1925 I, NZ
Cholley, G (Castres) 1975 E, S, I, SA 1,2, Arg 1,2, R, 1976 S, I, W, E, A 1,2, R, 1977 W, E, S, I, Arg 1,2, NZ 1,2, R, 1978 E, S, I, W, R, 1979 I, S
Chouly, D (Brive, Perpignan) 2007 NZ1(R),2, 2009 NZ2(R),A(R)
Choy J (Narbonne) 1930 S, I, E, G, W, 1931 I, 1933 G, 1934 G, 1935 G, 1936 G 2
Cigagna, A (Toulouse) 1995 [E]
Cimarosti, J (Castres) 1976 US (R)
Cistacq, J-C (Agen) 2000 R (R)
Clady, A (Lezignan) 1929 G, 1931 I, S, E, G
Clarac, H (St Girons) 1938 G 1
Claudel, R (Lyon) 1932 G, 1934 G
Clauzel, F (Béziers) 1924 E, W, 1925 W
Clavé, J (Agen) 1936 G 2, 1938 R, G 2
Claverie, H (Lourdes) 1954 NZ, W
Cléda, T (Pau) 1998 E (R), S (R), I (R), W (R), Arg 1(R), Fj (R), Arg 3(R), 1999 I (R), S
Clément, G (RCF) 1931 W
Clément, J (RCF) 1921 S, W, E, 1922 S, E, W, I, 1923 S, W, I
Clemente, M (Oloron) 1978 R, 1980 S, I
Clerc, V (Toulouse) 2002 SA, NZ, C, 2003 E 1, S, I, It (R), W (R), Arg 2, NZ, 2004 I,It,W, 2005 SA2,Tg, 2006 SA, 2007 I,W1,E1,S,E2,W2, [Nm,I,Gg(R),NZ,E,Arg 2(R)], 2008 S,I,E,It(t),W, 2009 NZ1,2,A(R),SA,Sm,NZ3, 2010 S(R),I,SA,Arg1
Cluchague, L (Biarritz O) 1924 S, 1925 E
Coderc, J (Chalon) 1932 G, 1933 G, 1934 G, 1935 G, 1936 G 1
Codorniou, D (Narbonne) 1979 NZ 1,2, R, 1980 W, E, S, I, 1981 S, W, E, A 2, 1983 E, S, I, W, A 1,2, R, 1984 I, W, E, S, NZ 1,2, R, 1985 E, S, I, W, Arg 1,2
Coeurveille, C (Agen) 1992 Arg 1(R),2
Cognet, L (Montferrand) 1932 G, 1936 G 1,2, 1937 G, It
Collazo, P (Bègles) 2000 R
Colombier, J (St Junien) 1952 SA, W, E
Colomine, G (Narbonne) 1979 NZ 1
Comba, F (SF) 1998 Arg 1,2, Fj, Arg 3, 1999 I, W 1, E, S, 2000 A, NZ 1,2, 2001 S, I
Combe, J (SF) 1910 S, E, I, 1911 S
Combes, G (Fumel) 1945 B 2
Communeau, M (SF) 1906 NZ, E, 1907 E, 1908 E, W, 1909 E, W, I, 1910 S, E, I, 1911 S, E, I, 1912 I, S, W, E, 1913 SA, E, W
Condom, J (Boucau, Biarritz O) 1982 R, 1983 E, S, I, W, A 1,2, R, 1984 I, W, E, S, NZ 1,2, R, 1985 E, S, I, W, Arg 1,2, 1986 S, I, W, E, R 1, Arg 1,2, NZ 1, R 2, NZ 2,3, 1987 W, E, S, I, [S, R, Z, A, NZ], R, 1988 E, S, W, Arg 1,2,3,4, R, 1989 I, W, E, S, NZ 1,2, A 1, 1990 I, R, A 2,3(R)
Conilh de Beyssac, J-J (SBUC) 1912 I, S, 1914 I, W, E
Constant, G (Perpignan) 1920 W
Correia, P (Albi) 2008 A2
Coscolla, G (Béziers) 1921 S, W
Costantino, J (Montferrand) 1973 R
Costes, A (Montferrand) 1994 C 2, 1995 R 1, [Iv], 1997 It 1, 1999 WS, Tg (R), NZ 1, [Nm (R), Fj (R), Arg (R), NZ 2(R), A (t&R)], 2000 S (R), I
Costes, F (Montferrand) 1979 E, S, NZ 1,2, R, 1980 W, I
Couffignal, H (Colomiers) 1993 R 1
Coulon, E (Grenoble) 1928 S
Courtiols, M (Bègles) 1991 R, US 1, W 2
Coux, J-F (Bourgoin) 2007 NZ1,2
Couzinet, D (Biarritz) 2004 US,C(R), 2008 A1(R)
Crabos, R (RCF) 1920 S, E, W, I, US, 1921 S, W, E, I, 1922 S, E, W, I, 1923 S, I, 1924 S, I
Crampagne, J (Bègles) 1967 SA 4
Crancée, R (Lourdes) 1960 Arg 3, 1961 S
Crauste, M (RCF, Lourdes) 1957 R 1,2, 1958 S, E, A, W, It, I, 1959 E, It, W, I, 1960 S, E, W, I, It, R, Arg 1,3, 1961 S, SA, E, W, It, I, NZ 1,2,3, A, R, 1962 S, E, W, I, It, R, 1963 S, I, E, W, It, R, 1964 S, NZ, E, W, It, I, SA, Fj, R, 1965 S, I, E, W, It, R, 1966 S, I, E, W, It
Cremaschi, M (Lourdes) 1980 R, 1981 R, NZ 1,2, 1982 W, S, 1983 A 1,2, R, 1984 I, W
Crenca, J-J (Agen) 1996 SA 2(R), 1999 R, Tg, WS (R), NZ 1(R), 2001 SA 1,2, NZ (R), SA 3, A, Fj, 2002 It, W, E, S, I, Arg, A 2, SA, NZ, C, 2003 E 1, S, I, It, W, R, E 2, [Fj,J(t&R),S,I,E,NZ(R)], 2004 I(R),It(R),W(R),S(R),E(R)
Crichton, W H (Le Havre) 1906 NZ, E
Cristina, J (Montferrand) 1979 R
Cussac, P (Biarritz O) 1934 G
Cutzach, A (Quillan) 1929 G
Daguerre, F (Biarritz O) 1936 G 1
Daguerre, J (CASG) 1933 G
Dal Maso, M (Mont-de-Marsan, Agen, Colomiers) 1988 R (R), 1990 NZ 2, 1996 SA 1(R),2, 1997 I, W, E, S, It 1, R 1(R), A 1,2, It 2, Arg, SA 1,2, 1998 W (R), Arg 1(t), Fj (R), 1999 R (R), WS (R), Tg, NZ 1(R), W 2(R), [Nm (R), Fj (R), Arg (R), A (R)], 2000 W, E, S, I, It
Danion, J (Toulon) 1924 I
Danos, P (Toulon, Béziers) 1954 Arg 1,2, 1957 R 2, 1958 S, E, W, It, I, SA 1,2, 1959 S, E, It, W, I, 1960 S, E
Dantiacq, D (Pau) 1997 R 1
Darbos, P (Dax) 1969 R
Darracq, R (Dax) 1957 It
Darrieussecq, A (Biarritz O) 1973 E
Darrieussecq, J (Mont-de-Marsan) 1953 It
Darrouy, C (Mont-de-Marsan) 1957 I, E, W, It, R 1, 1959 E, 1961 R, 1963 S, I, E, W, It, 1964 NZ, E, W, It, I, SA, Fj, R, 1965 S, I, E, It, R, 1966 S, I, E, W, It, R, 1967 S, A, E, It, W, I, SA 1,2,4
Daudé, J (Bourgoin) 2000 S
Daudignon, G (SF) 1928 S
Dauga, B (Mont-de-Marsan) 1964 S, NZ, E, W, It, I, SA, Fj, R, 1965 S, I, E, W, It, R, 1966 S, I, E, W, It, R, 1967 S, A, E, It, W, I, SA 1,2,3,4, NZ, R, 1968 S, I, NZ 1,2,3, A, SA 1,2, R, 1969 S, I, E, R, 1970 S, I, W, E, R, 1971 S, I, E, W, SA 1,2, A 1,2, R, 1972 S, I 1, W
Dauger, J (Bayonne) 1945 B 1,2, 1953 S
Daulouède, P (Tyrosse) 1937 G, It, 1938 G 1, 1940 B
David, Y (Bourgoin, Toulouse) 2008 It, 2009 SA,Sm(R),NZ3(R)
Debaty, V (Perpignan) 2006 R(R)
De Besombes, S (Perpignan) 1998 Arg 1(R), Fj (R)
Decamps, P (RCF) 1911 S
Dedet, J (SF) 1910 S, E, I, 1911 W, I, 1912 S, 1913 E, I
Dedeyn, P (RCF) 1906 NZ
Dedieu, P (Béziers) 1963 E, It, 1964 W, It, I, SA, Fj, R, 1965 S, I, E, W
De Gregorio, J (Grenoble) 1960 S, E, W, I, It, R, Arg 1,2, 1961 S, SA, E, W, It, I, 1962 S, E, W, 1963 S, W, It, 1964 NZ, E
Dehez, J-L (Agen) 1967 SA 2, 1969 R
De Jouvencel, E (SF) 1909 W, I
De Laborderie, M (RCF) 1921 I, 1922 I, 1925 W, E
Delage, C (Agen) 1983 S, I
De Malherbe, H (CASG) 1932 G, 1933 G
De Malmann, R (RCF) 1908 E, W, 1909 E, W, I, 1910 E, I
De Muizon, J J (SF) 1910 I
Delaigue, G (Toulon) 1973 J, R
Delaigue, Y (Toulon, Toulouse, Castres) 1994 S, NZ 2(R), C 2, 1995 I, R 1, [Tg, Iv], It, R 2(R), 1997 It 1, 2003 Arg 1,2, 2005 S,E,W,I,It,A2(R),Tg,SA3(R)
Delmotte, G (Toulon) 1999 R, Tg
Delque, A (Toulouse) 1937 It, 1938 G 1, R, G 2
De Rougemont, M (Toulon) 1995 E (t), R 1(t), [Iv], NZ 1,2, 1996 I (R), Arg 1,2, W 2, SA 1, 1997 E (R), S (R), It 1
Desbrosse, C (Toulouse) 1999 [Nm (R)], 2000 I
Descamps, P (SB) 1927 G 2
Desclaux, F (RCF) 1949 Arg 1,2, 1953 It
Desclaux, J (Perpignan) 1934 G, 1935 G, 1936 G 1,2, 1937 G, It, 1938 G 1, R, G 2, 1945 B 1
Deslandes, C (RCF) 1990 A 1, NZ 2, 1991 W 1, 1992 R, Arg 1,2
Desnoyer, L (Brive) 1974 R
Destarac, L (Tarbes) 1926 S, I, E, W, M, 1927 W, E, G 1,2

Desvouges, R (SF) 1914 W
Detrez, P-E (Nîmes) 1983 A 2(R), 1986 Arg 1(R),2, A (R), NZ1
Devergie, T (Nîmes) 1988 R, 1989 NZ 1,2, B, A 2, 1990 W, E, S, I, R, A 1,2,3, 1991 US 2, W 2, 1992 R (R), Arg 2(R)
De Villiers, P (SF) 1999 W 2, [Arg (R), NZ 2(R), A (R)], 2000 W (R), E (R), S (R), I (R), It (R), NZ 1(R),2, 2001 S, I, It, W, E, SA 1,2, NZ (R), SA 3, A, Fj, 2002 It, W, E, I, SA, NZ, C, 2003 Arg 1,2, NZ (R), 2004 I,It,W,S,E,US,C,NZ, 2005 S,I(R),It(R), SA1(R),2,A1(R),2,C,Tg(R),SA3, 2006 S,I,It,E,W,SA,NZ1,2,Arg, 2007 It,I,E1,S,W2, [Arg1,Nm,I,NZ,E]
Deygas, M (Vienne) 1937 It
Deylaud, C (Toulouse) 1992 R, Arg 1,2, SA 1, 1994 C 1, NZ 1,2, 1995 W, E, S, [Iv (R), S, I, SA], It, Arg
Diarra, I (Montauban) 2008 It
Dintrans, P (Tarbes) 1979 NZ 1,2, R, 1980 E, S, I, SA, R, 1981 S, I, W, E, A 1,2, R, NZ 1,2, 1982 W, E, S, I, R, Arg 1,2, 1983 E, W, A 1,2, R, 1984 I, W, E, S, NZ 1,2, R, 1985 E, S, I, W, Arg 1,2, 1987 [R], 1988 Arg 1,2,3, 1989 W, E, S, 1990 R
Dispagne, S (Toulouse) 1996 I (R), W 1
Dizabo, P (Tyrosse) 1948 A, S, E, 1949 S, I, E, W, Arg 2, 1950 S, I, 1960 Arg 1,2,3
Domec, A (Carcassonne) 1929 W
Domec, H (Lourdes) 1953 W, It, 1954 S, I, NZ, W, E, It, 1955 S, I, E, W, 1956 I, W, It, 1958 E, A, W, It, I
Domenech, A (Vichy, Brive) 1954 W, E, It, 1955 S, I, E, W, 1956 S, I, W, It, E, Cz, 1957 S, I, E, W, It, R 1,2, 1958 S, E, It, 1959 It, 1960 S, E, W, I, It, R, Arg 1,2,3, 1961 S, SA, E, W, It, I, NZ 1,2,3, A, R, 1962 S, E, W, I, It, R, 1963 W, It
Domercq, J (Bayonne) 1912 I, S
Domingo, T (Clermont-Auvergne) 2009 W(R),E(R),It(R),NZ2(R), Sm, 2010 S,I,W,It,E,SA
Dominici, C (SF) 1998 E, S, Arg 1,2, 1999 E, S, WS, NZ 1, W 2, [C, Fj, Arg, NZ 2, A], 2000 W, E, S, R, 2001 I (R), It, W, E, SA 1,2, NZ, Fj, 2003 Arg 1, R, E 2,3, [Fj,J,S,I,E], 2004 I,It,W,S,E,A(R),NZ(R), 2005 S,E,W,I,It, 2006 S,I,It,E,W,NZ1, 2(R),Arg, 2007 It,I,W1,E1,S(R),E3,W2(R), [Arg 1,Gg,NZ(R), (R),Arg 2]
Dorot, J (RCF) 1935 G
Dospital, P (Bayonne) 1977 R, 1980 I, 1981 S, I, W, E, 1982 I, R, Arg 1,2, 1983 E, S, I, W, 1984 E, S, NZ 1,2, R, 1985 E, S, I, W, Arg 1
Dourthe, C (Dax) 1966 R, 1967 S, A, E, W, I, SA 1,2,3, NZ, 1968 W, NZ 3, SA 1,2, 1969 W, 1971 SA 2(R), R, 1972 I 1,2, A 1,2, R, 1973 S, NZ, E, 1974 I, Arg 1,2, SA 1,2, 1975 W, E, S
Dourthe, M (Dax) 2000 NZ 2(t)
Dourthe, R (Dax, SF, Béziers) 1995 R 2, Arg, NZ 1,2, 1996 E, R, 1996 Arg 1,2, W 2, SA 1,2, 1997 W, A 1, 1999 I, W 1,2, [C, Nm, Fj, Arg, NZ 2, A], 2000 W, E, It, R, A, NZ 1,2, 2001 S, I
Doussau, E (Angoulême) 1938 R
Droitecourt, M (Montferrand) 1972 R, 1973 NZ (R), E, 1974 E, S, Arg 1, SA 2, 1975 SA 1,2, Arg 1,2, R, 1976 S, I, W, A 1, 1977 Arg 2
Dubertrand, A (Montferrand) 1971 A 1,2, R, 1972 I 2, 1974 I, W, E, SA 2, 1975 Arg 1,2, R, 1976 S, US
Dubois, D (Bègles) 1971 S
Dubroca, D (Agen) 1979 NZ 2, 1981 NZ 2(R), 1982 E, S, 1984 W, E, S, 1985 Arg 2, 1986 S, I, W, E, R 1, Arg 2, A, NZ 1, R 2, NZ 2,3, 1987 W, E, S, I, [S, Z, Fj, A, NZ], R, 1988 E, S, I, W
Ducalcon, L (Castres) 2010 S(R)
Duché, A (Limoges) 1929 G
Duclos, A (Lourdes) 1931 S
Ducousso, J (Tarbes) 1925 S, W, E
Dufau, G (RCF) 1948 I, A, 1949 I, W, 1950 S, E, W, 1951 S, I, E, W, 1952 SA, W, 1953 S, I, E, W, 1954 S, I, NZ, W, E, It, 1955 S, I, E, W, It, 1956 S, I, W, It, 1957 S, I, E, W, It, R 1
Dufau, J (Biarritz) 1912 I, S, W, E
Duffaut, Y (Agen) 1954 Arg 1,2
Duffour, R (Tarbes) 1911 W
Dufourcq, J (SBUC) 1906 NZ, E, 1907 E, 1908 W
Duhard, Y (Bagnères) 1980 E
Duhau, J (SF) 1928 I,1930 I, G, 1931 I, S, W, 1933 G
Dulaurens, C (Toulouse) 1926 I, 1928 S, 1929 W
Duluc, A (Béziers) 1934 G
Du Manoir, Y le P (RCF) 1925 I, NZ, S, W, E, 1926 S, 1927 I, S
Dupont, C (Lourdes) 1923 S, W, I, 1924 S, I, W, R, US, 1925 S, 1927 E, G 1,2, 1928 A, G, W, 1929 I
Dupont, J-L (Agen) 1983 S
Dupont, L (RCF) 1934 G, 1935 G, 1936 G 1,2, 1938 R, G 2
Dupouy, A (SB) 1924 W, R
Duprat, B (Bayonne) 1966 E, W, It, R, 1967 S, A, E, SA 2,3, 1968 S, I, 1972 E, W, I 2, A 1
Dupré, P (RCF) 1909 W
Dupuy, J (Leicester, SF) 2009 NZ1,2,A(R),SA,Sm(R),NZ3
Dupuy, J-V (Tarbes) 1956 S, I, W, It, E, Cz, 1957 S, I, E, W, It, R 2, 1958 S, E, SA 1,2, 1959 S, E, It, W, I, 1960 W, I, It, Arg 1,3, 1961 S, SA, E, NZ 2, R, 1962 S, E, W, I, It, 1963 W, It, R, 1964 S
Durand, N (Perpignan) 2007 NZ1,2
Dusautoir, T (Biarritz, Toulouse) 2006 R,SA,NZ1, 2007 E3,W2(R), [Nm,I,NZ,E,Arg 2], 2008 S,I,E,W,Arg,PI,A3, 2009 I,S,W,E,It,NZ1, 2,A,SA,Sm,NZ3, 2010 S,I,W,It,E,SA,Arg1
Du Souich, C J (see Judas du Souich)
Dutin, B (Mont-de-Marsan) 1968 NZ 2, A, SA 2, R
Dutour, F X (Toulouse) 1911 E, I, 1912 S, W, E, 1913 S
Dutrain, H (Toulouse) 1945 W, 1946 B, I, 1947 E, 1949 I, E, W, Arg 1
Dutrey, J (Lourdes) 1940 B
Duval, R (SF) 1908 E, W, 1909 E, 1911 E, W, I
Echavé, L (Agen) 1961 S
Elhorga, P (Agen) 2001 NZ, 2002 A 1,2, 2003 Arg 2, NZ (R), R, [Fj(R),US,I(R),NZ], 2004 I(R),It(R),S,E, 2005 S,E, 2006 NZ2,Arg, 2008 A1
Elissalde, E (Bayonne) 1936 G 2, 1940 B
Elissalde, J-B (La Rochelle, Toulouse) 2000 S (R), R (R), 2003 It (R), W (R), 2004 I,It,W,A,Arg, 2005 SA1,2(R),A1,2,SA3, 2006 S,I,It,W(R),NZ1(R),2, 2007 E2(R),3,W2(R), [Arg 1(R),Nm,I,Gg(R), NZ,E,Arg 2], 2008 S,I,W,Arg,PI
Elissalde, J-P (La Rochelle) 1980 SA, R, 1981 A 1,2, R
Empereur-Buisson, H (Béziers) 1931 E, G
Erbani, D (Agen) 1981 A 1,2, NZ 1,2, 1982 Arg 1,2, 1983 S (R), I, W, A 1,2, R, 1984 W, E, R, 1985 E, W (R), Arg 2, 1986 S, I, W, E, R 1, Arg 2, NZ 1,2(R),3, 1987 W, E, S, I, [S, R, Fj, A, NZ], 1988 E, S, 1989 I (R), W, E, S, NZ 1, A 2, 1990 W, E
Escaffre, P (Narbonne) 1933 G, 1934 G
Escommier, M (Montelimar) 1955 It
Esponda, J-M (RCF) 1967 SA 1,2, R, 1968 NZ 1,2, SA 2, R, 1969 S, I (R), E
Estève, A (Béziers) 1971 SA 1, 1972 I 1, E, W, I 2, A 2, R, 1973 S, NZ, E, I, 1974 I, W, E, S, R, SA 1,2, 1975 W, E
Estève, P (Narbonne, Lavelanet) 1982 R, Arg 1,2, 1983 E, S, I, W, A 1,2, R, 1984 I, W, E, S, NZ 1,2, R, 1985 E, S, I, W, 1986 S, I, 1987 [S, Z]
Etcheberry, J (Rochefort, Cognac) 1923 W, I, 1924 S, I, E, W, R, US, 1926 S, I, E, M, 1927 I, S, W, G 2
Etchenique, J-M (Biarritz O) 1974 R, SA 1, 1975 E, Arg 2
Etchepare, A (Bayonne) 1922 I
Etcheverry, M (Pau) 1971 S, I
Eutrope, A (SCUF) 1913 I
Fabre, E (Toulouse) 1937 It, 1938 G 1,2
Fabre, J (Toulouse) 1963 S, I, E, W, It, 1964 S, NZ, E
Fabre, L (Lezignan) 1930 G
Fabre, M (Béziers) 1981 A 1, R, NZ 1,2, 1982 I, R
Failliot, P (RCF) 1911 S, W, I, 1912 I, S, E, 1913 E, W
Fall, B (Bayonne) 2009 Sm, 2010 S
Fargues, G (Dax) 1923 I
Fauré, F (Tarbes) 1914 I, W, E
Faure, L (Sale) 2008 S,I,E,A1,PI,A3, 2009 I,E
Fauvel, J-P (Tulle) 1980 R
Favre, M (Lyon) 1913 E, W
Ferrand, L (Chalon) 1940 B
Ferrien, R (Tarbes) 1950 S, I, E, W
Finat, R (CASG) 1932 G, 1933 G
Fite, R (Brive) 1963 W, It
Floch, A (Clermont-Auvergne) 2008 E(R),It,W
Forest, M (Bourgoin) 2007 NZ1(R),2(R)
Forestier, J (SCUF) 1912 W
Forgues, F (Bayonne) 1911 S, E, W, 1912 I, W, E, 1913 S, SA, W, 1914 I, E
Fort, J (Agen) 1967 It, W, I, SA 1,2,3,4
Fourcade, G (BEC) 1909 E, W
Foures, H (Toulouse) 1951 S, I, E, W
Fournet, F (Montferrand) 1950 W

Fouroux, J (La Voulte) 1972 I 2, R, 1974 W, E, Arg 1,2, R, SA 1,2, 1975 W, Arg 1, R, 1976 S, I, W, E, US, A 1, 1977 W, E, S, I, Arg 1,2, NZ 1,2, R

Francquenelle, A (Vaugirard) 1911 S, 1913 W, I

Fritz, F (Toulouse) 2005 SA1,A2,SA3, 2006 S,I,It,E,W,SA,NZ1,2, Arg, 2007 It, 2009 I,E(R),It,NZ2(R),A, 2010 Arg1

Froment, R (Castres) 2004 US(R)

Furcade, R (Perpignan) 1952 S

Gabernet, S (Toulouse) 1980 E, S, 1981 S, I, W, E, A 1,2, R, NZ 1,2, 1982 I, 1983 A 2, R

Gachassin, J (Lourdes) 1961 S, I, 1963 R, 1964 S, NZ, E, W, It, I, SA, Fj, R, 1965 S, I, E, W, It, R, 1966 S, I, E, W, 1967 S, A, It, W, I, NZ, 1968 I, E, 1969 S, I

Galasso, A (Toulon, Montferrand) 2000 R (R), 2001 E (R)

Galau, H (Toulouse) 1924 S, I, E, W, US

Galia, J (Quillan) 1927 E, G 1,2, 1928 S, A, I, E, W, 1929 I, E, G, 1930 S, I, E, G, W, 1931 S, W, E, G

Gallart, P (Béziers) 1990 R, A 1,2(R),3, 1992 S, I, R, Arg 1,2, SA 1,2, Arg, 1994 I, W, E, 1995 I (t), R 1, [Tg]

Gallion, J (Toulon) 1978 E, S, I, W, 1979 I, W, E, S, NZ 2, R, 1980 W, E, S, I, 1983 A 1,2, R, 1984 I, W, E, S, R, 1985 E, S, I, W, 1986 Arg 2

Galthié, F (Colomiers, SF) 1991 R, US 1, [R, Fj, C, E], 1992 W, E, S, R, Arg, 1994 I, W, E, 1995 [SA, E], 1996 W 1(R), 1997 I, It 2, SA 1,2, 1998 W (R), Fj (R), 1999 R, WS (R), Tg, NZ 1(R), [Fj (R), Arg, NZ 2, A], 2000 W, E, A, NZ 1,2, 2001 S, It, W, E, SA 1,2, NZ, SA 3, A, Fj, 2002 E, S, I, SA, NZ, C, 2003 E 1, S, Arg 1,2, NZ, R, E 2, [Fj,J,S,I,E]

Galy, J (Perpignan) 1953 W

Garbajosa, X (Toulouse) 1998 I, W, Arg 2(R), Fj, 1999 W 1(R), E, S, WS, NZ 1, W 2, [C, Nm (R), Fj (R), Arg, NZ 2, A], 2000 A, NZ 1,2, 2001 S, I, E, 2002 It (R), W, SA (R), C (R), 2003 E 1, S, I, It, W, E 3

Garuet-Lempirou, J-P (Lourdes) 1983 A 1,2, R, 1984 I, NZ 1,2, R, 1985 E, S, I, W, Arg 1, 1986 S, I, W, E, R 1, Arg 1, NZ 1, R 2, NZ 2,3, 1987 W, E, S, I, [S, R, Fj, A, NZ], 1988 E, S, Arg 1,2, R, 1989 E (R), S, NZ 1,2, 1990 W, E

Gasc, J (Graulhet) 1977 NZ 2

Gasparotto, G (Montferrand) 1976 A 2, R

Gauby, G (Perpignan) 1956 Cz

Gaudermen, P (RCF) 1906 E

Gayraud, W (Toulouse) 1920 I

Gelez, F (Agen) 2001 SA 3, 2002 I (R), A 1, SA, NZ, C (R), 2003 S, I

Geneste, R (BEC) 1945 B 1, 1949 Arg 2

Genet, J-P (RCF) 1992 S, I, R

Gensane, R (Béziers) 1962 S, E, W, I, It, R, 1963 S

Gérald, G (RCF) 1927 E, G 2, 1928 S, 1929 I, S, W, E, G, 1930 S, I, E, G, W, 1931 I, S, E, G

Gérard, D (Bègles) 1999 Tg

Gérintes, G (CASG) 1924 R, 1925 I, 1926 W

Geschwind, P (RCF) 1936 G 1,2

Giacardy, M (SBUC) 1907 E

Gimbert, P (Bègles) 1991 R, US 1, 1992 W, E

Giordani, P (Dax) 1999 E, S

Glas, S (Bourgoin) 1996 S (t), I (R), W 1, R, Arg 2(R), W 2, SA 1,2, 1997 I, W, E, S, It 2(R), R 2, Arg, SA 1,2, 1998 E, S, I, W, Arg 1,2, Fj, Arg 3, A, 1999 W 2, [C,Nm, Arg (R), NZ 2(R), A (t&R)], 2000 I, 2001 E, SA 1,2, NZ

Gomès, A (SF) 1998 Arg 1,2, Fj, Arg 3, A, 1999 I (R)

Gommes, J (RCF) 1909 I

Gonnet, C-A (Albi) 1921 E, I, 1922 E, W, 1924 S, E, 1926 S, I, E, W, M, 1927 I, S, W, E, G 1

Gonzalez, J-M (Bayonne) 1992 Arg 1,2, SA 1,2, Arg, 1993 R 1, SA 1,2, R 2, A 1,2, 1994 I, W, E, S, C 1, NZ 1,2, C 2, 1995 W, E, S, I, R 1, [Tg, S, I, SA, E], It, Arg, 1996 E, S, I, W 1

Got, R (Perpignan) 1920 I, US, 1921 S, W, 1922 S, E, W, I, 1924 I, E, W, R, US

Gourdon, J-F (RCF, Bagnères) 1974 S, Arg 1,2, R, SA 1,2, 1975 W, E, S, I, R, 1976 S, I, W, E, 1978 E, S, 1979 W, E, S, R, 1980 I

Gourragne, J-F (Béziers) 1990 NZ 2, 1991 W 1

Goutta, B (Perpignan) 2004 C

Goyard, A (Lyon U) 1936 G 1,2, 1937 G, It, 1938 G 1, R, G 2

Graciet, R (SBUC) 1926 I, W, 1927 S, G 1, 1929 E, 1930 W

Grandclaude, J-P (Perpignan) 2005 E(R),W(R), 2007 NZ1

Graou, S (Auch, Colomiers) 1992 Arg (R), 1993 SA 1,2, R 2, A 2(R), 1995 R 2, Arg (t), NZ 2(R)

Gratton, J (Agen) 1984 NZ 2, R, 1985 E, S, I, W, Arg 1,2, 1986 S, NZ 1

Graule, V (Arl Perpignan) 1926 I, E, W, 1927 S, W, 1931 G

Greffe, M (Grenoble) 1968 W, Cz, NZ 1,2, SA 1

Griffard, J (Lyon U) 1932 G, 1933 G, 1934 G

Gruarin, A (Toulon) 1964 W, It, I, SA, Fj, R, 1965 S, I, E, W, It, 1966 S, I, E, W, It, R, 1967 S, A, E, It, W, I, NZ, 1968 S, I

Guélorget, P (RCF) 1931 E, G

Guichemerre, A (Dax) 1920 E, 1921 E, I, 1923 S

Guilbert, A (Toulon) 1975 E, S, I, SA 1,2, 1976 A 1, 1977 Arg 1,2, NZ 1,2, R, 1979 I, W, E

Guillemin, P (RCF) 1908 E, W, 1909 E, I, 1910 W, S, E, I, 1911 S, E, W

Guilleux, P (Agen) 1952 SA, It

Guirado, G (Perpignan) 2008 It(R), 2009 A(R),Sm(R), 2010 SA(R),Arg1(R)

Guiral, M (Agen) 1931 G, 1932 G, 1933 G

Guiraud, H (Nîmes) 1996 R

Haget, A (PUC) 1953 E, 1954 I, NZ, E, Arg 2, 1955 E, W, It, 1957 I, E, It, R 1, 1958 It, SA 2

Haget, F (Agen, Biarritz O) 1974 Arg 1,2, 1975 SA 2, Arg 1,2, R, 1976 S, 1978 S, I, W, R, 1979 I, W, E, S, NZ 1,2, R, 1980 W, S, I, 1984 S, NZ 1,2, R, 1985 E, S, I, 1986 S, I, W, E, R 1, Arg 1, A, NZ 1, 1987 S, I, [R, Fj]

Haget, H (CASG) 1928 S, 1930 G

Halet, R (Strasbourg) 1925 NZ, S, W

Hall, S (Béziers) 2002 It, W

Harinordoquy, I (Pau, Biarritz)) 2002 W, E, S, I, A 1,2, SA, NZ, C, 2003 E 1, S, I, It, W, Arg 1(R),2, NZ, R, E 2,3(R), [Fj,S,I,E], 2004 I,It,W,E,A,Arg,NZ, 2005 W(R),2006 R(R),SA, 2007 It(R),I,W1(R),E1(R),S,E3,W2, [Arg 1,Nm(R),NZ(R),E(R),Arg 2], 2008 A1,2,Arg,PI,A3, 2009 I,S,W,E,It,SA, 2010 S,I,W,It,E

Harislur-Arthapignet, P (Tarbes) 1988 Arg 4(R)

Harize, D (Cahors, Toulouse) 1975 SA 1,2, 1976 A 1,2, R, 1977 W, E, S, I

Hauc, J (Toulon) 1928 E, G, 1929 I, S, G

Hauser, M (Lourdes) 1969 E

Hedembaigt, M (Bayonne) 1913 S, SA, 1914 W

Hericé, D (Bègles) 1950 I

Herrero, A (Toulon) 1963 R, 1964 NZ, E, W, It, I, SA, Fj, R, 1965 S, I, E, W, 1966 W, It, R, 1967 S, A, E, It, I, R

Herrero, B (Nice) 1983 I, 1986 Arg 1

Heyer, F (Montferrand) 1990 A 2

Heymans, C (Agen, Toulouse) 2000 It (R) R, 2002 A 2(R), SA, NZ, 2004 W(R),US,C(R),A,Arg,NZ, 2005 I,It,SA1,2,A1,2,C,SA3, 2006 S,I,W(R),R,SA,NZ2,Arg, 2007 It,I(R),E1(R),S,E3,W2, [Arg 1,Nm,I,NZ,E], 2008 S,I,E,W(R),Arg,PI,A3, 2009 I(R),S,W,E,It, NZ1,2,A,SA,NZ3(R)

Hiquet, J-C (Agen) 1964 E

Hoche, M (PUC) 1957 I, E, W, It, R 1

Hondagné-Monge, M (Tarbes) 1988 Arg 2(R)

Hontas, P (Biarritz) 1990 S, I, R, 1991 R, 1992 Arg, 1993 E, S, I, W

Hortoland, J-P (Béziers) 1971 A 2

Houblain, H (SCUF) 1909 E, 1910 W

Houdet, R (SF) 1927 S, W, G 1, 1928 G, W, 1929 I, S, E, 1930 S, E

Hourdebaigt, A (SBUC) 1909 I, 1910 W, S, E, I

Hubert, A (ASF) 1906 E, 1907 E, 1908 E, W, 1909 E, W, I

Hueber, A (Lourdes, Toulon) 1990 A 3, NZ 1, 1991 US 2, 1992 I, Arg 1,2, SA 1,2, 1993 E, S, I, W, R 1, SA 1,2, R 2, A 1,2, 1995 [Tg, S (R), I], 2000 It, R

Hutin, R (CASG) 1927 I, S, W

Hyardet, A (Castres) 1995 It, Arg (R)

Ibañez, R (Dax, Perpignan, Castres, Saracens, Wasps) 1996 W 1(R), 1997 It 1(R), R 1, It 2(R), R 2, SA 2(R), 1998 E, S, I, W, Arg 1,2, Fj, Arg 3, A, 1999 I, W 1, E, S, R, WS, Tg (R), NZ 1, W 2, [C, Nm, Fj, Arg, NZ 2, A], 2000 W (R), E (R), S (R), I (R), It (R), R, 2001 S, I, It, W, E, SA 1,2, NZ (R), SA 3, A, Fj, 2002 It (R), W, E, S, I, Arg, A 1(R),2, SA, NZ, C, 2003 E 1, S, I, It, W, R (R), E 2(R),3, [Fj,J(R),S,I,E,NZ(R)], 2005 C(R),Tg, 2006 I,It,E,W,R,SA(R),NZ1(R),2,Arg, 2007 It,I,W1,E1,S,NZ1(R),2(R), E2,3, [Arg 1,Nm(R),I,NZ,E,Arg 2]

Icard, J (SF) 1909 E, W

Iguiniz, E (Bayonne) 1914 E

Ihingoué, D (BEC) 1912 I, S
Imbernon, J-F (Perpignan) 1976 I, W, E, US, A 1, 1977 W, E, S, I, Arg 1,2, NZ 1,2, 1978 E, R, 1979 I, 1981 S, I, W, E, 1982 I, 1983 I, W
Iraçabal, J (Bayonne) 1968 NZ 1,2, SA 1, 1969 S, I, W, R, 1970 S, I, W, E, R, 1971 W, SA 1,2, A 1, 1972 E, W, I 2, A 2, R, 1973 S, NZ, E, W, I, J, 1974 I, W, E, S, Arg 1,2, SA 2(R)
Isaac, H (RCF) 1907 E, 1908 E
Ithurra, E (Biarritz O) 1936 G 1,2, 1937 G
Jacquet, L (Clermont-Auvergne) 2006 NZ2(R),Arg, 2008 S,I(t&R)
Janeczek, T (Tarbes) 1982 Arg 1,2, 1990 R
Janik, K (Toulouse) 1987 R
Janin, D (Bourgoin) 2008 A1(R),2
Jarasse, A (Brive) 1945 B 1
Jardel, J (SB) 1928 I, E
Jauréguy, A (RCF, Toulouse, SF) 1920 S, E, W, I, US, 1922 S, W, 1923 S, W, E, I, 1924 S, W, R, US, 1925 I, NZ, 1926 S, E, W, M, 1927 I, E, 1928 S, A, E, G, W, 1929 I, S, E
Jauréguy, P (Toulouse) 1913 S, SA, W, I
Jauzion, Y (Colomiers, Toulouse) 2001 SA 1,2, NZ, 2002 A 1(R),2(R), 2003 Arg 2, NZ, R, E 2,3, [Fj,S,I,E], 2004 I,It,W,S,E,A,Arg,NZ(t), 2005 W,I,It,SA1,2,A1,2,C,Tg(R),SA3, 2006 R,SA,NZ1,2,Arg, 2007 It,I,W1,E1,S,E3,W2, [Arg 1,Nm(R),I(R),Gg,NZ,E], 2008 It,W,Arg,PI,A3, 2009 I,S,W,E,It, NZ1(R),Sm,NZ3, 2010 S,I,W,It,E
Jeangrand, M-H (Tarbes) 1921 I
Jeanjean, N (Toulouse) 2001 SA 1,2, NZ, SA 3(R), A (R), Fj (R), 2002 It, Arg, A 1
Jeanjean, P (Toulon) 1948 I
Jérôme, G (SF) 1906 NZ, E
Joinel, J-L (Brive) 1977 NZ 1, 1978 R, 1979 I, W, E, S, NZ 1,2, R, 1980 W, E, S, I, SA, 1981 S, I, W, E, R, NZ 1,2, 1982 E, S, I, R, 1983 E, S, I, W, A 1,2, R, 1984 I, W, E, S, NZ 1,2, 1985 S, I, W, Arg 1, 1986 S, I, W, E, R 1, Arg 1,2, A, 1987 [Z]
Jol, M (Biarritz O) 1947 S, I, W, E, 1949 S, I, E, W, Arg 1,2
Jordana, J-L (Pau, Toulouse) 1996 R (R), Arg 1(t),2, W 2, 1997 I (t), W, S (R)
Judas du Souich, C (SCUF) 1911 W, I
Juillet, C (Montferrand, SF) 1995 R 2, Arg, 1999 E, S, WS, NZ 1, [C, Fj, Arg, NZ 2, A], 2000 A, NZ 1,2, 2001 S, I, It, W
Junquas, L (Tyrosse) 1945 B 1,2, W, 1946 B, I, K, W, 1947 S, I, W, E, 1948 S, W
Kaczorowski, D (Le Creusot) 1974 I (R)
Kaempf, A (St Jean-de-Luz) 1946 B
Kayser, B (Leicester) 2008 A1(R),2(R),Arg(R),PI(R),A3(R), 2009 I(R),S(R),W(R),E(R)
Labadie, P (Bayonne) 1952 S, I, SA, W, E, It, 1953 S, I, It, 1954 S, I, NZ, W, E, Arg 2, 1955 S, I, E, W, 1956 I, 1957 I
Labarthète, R (Pau) 1952 S
Labazuy, A (Lourdes) 1952 I, 1954 S, W, 1956 E, 1958 A, W, I, 1959 S, E, It, W
Labit, C (Toulouse) 1999 S, R (R), WS (R), Tg, 2000 R (R), 2002 Arg, A 1(R), 2003 Arg 1,2, NZ (R), R (R), E 3, [Fj(R),J,US,E(R),NZ]
Laborde, C (RCF) 1962 It, R, 1963 R, 1964 SA, 1965 E
Labrousse, T (Brive) 1996 R, SA 1
Lacans, P (Béziers) 1980 SA, 1981 W, E, A 2, R, 1982 W
Lacassagne, H (SBUC) 1906 NZ, 1907 E
Lacaussade, R (Bègles) 1948 A, S
Lacaze, C (Lourdes, Angoulême) 1961 NZ 2,3, A, R, 1962 E, W, I, It, 1963 W, R, 1964 S, NZ, E, 1965 It, R, 1966 S, I, E, W, It, R, 1967 S, E, SA 1,3,4, R, 1968 S, E, W, Cz, NZ 1, 1969 E
Lacaze, H (Périgueux) 1928 I, G, W, 1929 I, W
Lacaze, P (Lourdes) 1958 SA 1,2, 1959 S, E, It, W, I
Lacazedieu, C (Dax) 1923 W, I, 1928 A, I, 1929 S
Lacombe, B (Agen) 1989 B, 1990 A 2
Lacome, M (Pau) 1960 Arg 2
Lacoste, R (Tarbes) 1914 I, W, E
Lacrampe, F (Béziers) 1949 Arg 2
Lacroix, P (Mont-de-Marsan, Agen) 1958 A, 1960 W, I, It, R, Arg 1,2,3, 1961 S, SA, E, W, I, NZ 1,2,3, A, R, 1962 S, E, W, I, R, 1963 S, I, E, W
Lacroix, T (Dax, Harlequins) 1989 A 1(R),2, 1991 W 1(R),2(R), [R, C (R), E], 1992 SA 2, 1993 E, S, I, W, SA 1,2, R 2, A 1,2, 1994 I, W, E, S, C 1, NZ 1,2, C 2, 1995 W, E, S, R 1, [Tg, Iv, S, I, SA, E], 1996 E, S, I, 1997 It 2, R 2, Arg, SA 1,2
Lacroix, T (Albi) 2008 A1(R),2
Lafarge, Y (Montferrand) 1978 R, 1979 NZ 1, 1981 I (R)
Laffitte, R (SCUF) 1910 W, S
Laffont, H (Narbonne) 1926 W
Lafond, A (Bayonne) 1922 E
Lafond, J-B (RCF) 1983 A 1, 1985 Arg 1,2 1986 S, I, W, E, R 1, 1987 I (R), 1988 W, 1989 I, W, E, 1990 W, A 3(R), NZ 2, 1991 S, I, W 1, E, R, US 1, W 2, [R (R), Fj, C, E], 1992 W, E, S, I (R), SA 2, 1993 E, S, I, W
Lagisquet, P (Bayonne) 1983 A 1,2, R, 1984 I, W, NZ 1,2, 1986 R 1(R), Arg 1,2, A, NZ 1, 1987 [S, R, Fj, A, NZ], R, 1988 S, I, W, Arg 1,2,3,4, R, 1989 I, W, E, S, NZ 1,2, B, A 1,2, 1990 W, E, S, I, A 1,2,3, 1991 S, I, US 2, [R]
Lagrange, J-C (RCF) 1966 It
Laharrague, J (Brive, Perpignan, Sale) 2005 W,I,It,SA1,A1,2,C(R), Tg, 2006 R(R),SA,NZ1, 2007 NZ2
Laharrague, N (Perpignan) 2007 NZ1(R),2(R)
Lalande, M (RCF) 1923 S, W, I
Lalanne, F (Mont-de-Marsan) 2000 R
Lamaison, C (Brive, Agen) 1996 SA 1(R),2, 1997 W, E, S, R 1, A 2, It 2, R 2, Arg, SA 1,2, 1998 E, S, I, W, Arg 3(R), A, 1999 R, WS (R), Tg, NZ 1(R), W 2(R), [C (R), Nm, Fj, Arg, NZ 2, A], 2000 W, A, NZ 1,2, 2001 S, I, It, W (R)
Lamboley, G (Toulouse) 2005 S(R),E(R),W(R),I(R),It(R),SA1(R), 2(R),A1,2(R),C(R),Tg,SA3(R), 2007 W1(R), 2010 Arg1(R)
Landreau, F (SF) 2000 A, NZ 1,2, 2001 E (R)
Lane, G (RCF) 1906 NZ, E, 1907 E, 1908 E, W, 1909 E, W, I, 1910 W, E, 1911 S, W, 1912 I, W, E, 1913 S
Langlade, J-C (Hyères) 1990 R, A 1, NZ 1
Lapandry, A (Clermont-Auvergne) 2009 Sm, 2010 W(R),It(R),E(R)
Laperne, D (Dax) 1997 R 1(R)
Laporte, G (Graulhet) 1981 I, W, E, R, NZ 1,2, 1986 S, I, W, E, R 1, Arg 1, A (R), 1987 [R, Z (R), Fj]
Larreguy, G (Bayonne) 1954 It
Larribau, J (Périgueux) 1912 I, S, W, E, 1913 S, 1914 I, E
Larrieu, J (Tarbes) 1920 I, US, 1921 W, 1923 S, W, E, I
Larrieux, M (SBUC) 1927 G 2
Larrue, H (Carmaux) 1960 W, I, It, R, Arg 1,2,3
Lasaosa, P (Dax) 1950 I, 1952 S, I, E, It, 1955 It
Lascubé, G (Agen) 1991 S, I, W 1, E, US 2, W 2, [R, Fj, C, E], 1992 W, E
Lassegue, J-B (Toulouse) 1946 W, 1947 S, I, W, 1948 W, 1949 I, E, W, Arg 1
Lasserre, F (René) (Bayonne, Cognac, Grenoble) 1914 I, 1920 S, 1921 S, W, I, 1922 S, E, W, I, 1923 W, E, 1924 S, I, R, US
Lasserre, J-C (Dax) 1963 It, 1964 S, NZ, E, W, It, I, Fj, 1965 W, It, R, 1966 R, 1967 S
Lasserre, M (Agen) 1967 SA 2,3, 1968 E, W, Cz, NZ 3, A, SA 1,2, 1969 S, I, E, 1970 E, 1971 E, W
Laterrade, G (Tarbes) 1910 E, I, 1911 S, E, I
Laudouar, J (Soustons, SBUC) 1961 NZ 1,2, R, 1962 I, R
Lauga, P (Vichy) 1950 S, I, E, W
Laurent, A (Biarritz O) 1925 NZ, S, W, E, 1926 W
Laurent, J (Bayonne) 1920 S, E, W
Laurent, M (Auch) 1932 G, 1933 G, 1934 G, 1935 G, 1936 G 1
Lauret, W (Biarritz) 2010 SA
Laussucq, C (SF) 1999 S (R), 2000 W (R), S, I
Lavail, G (Perpignan) 1937 G, 1940 B
Lavaud, R (Carcassonne) 1914 I, W
Lavergne, P (Limoges) 1950 S
Lavigne, B (Agen) 1984 R, 1985 E
Lavigne, J (Dax) 1920 E, W
Laziès, H (Auch) 1954 Arg 2, 1955 It, 1956 E, 1957 S
Le Bourhis, R (La Rochelle) 1961 R
Lecointre, M (Nantes) 1952 It
Le Corvec, G (Perpignan) 2007 NZ1
Lecouls, B (Biarritz) 2008 A1,2(R),Arg,PI(R),A3(R), 2009 I
Le Droff, J (Auch) 1963 It, R, 1964 S, NZ, E, 1970 E, R, 1971 S, I
Lefèvre, R (Brive) 1961 NZ 2
Leflamand, L (Bourgoin) 1996 SA 2, 1997 W, E, S, It 2, Arg, SA 1,2(R)
Lefort, J-B (Biarritz O) 1938 G 1
Le Goff, R (Métro) 1938 R, G 2
Legrain, M (SF) 1909 I, 1910 I, 1911 S, E, W, I, 1913 S, SA, E, I, 1914 I, W
Lemeur, Y (RCF) 1993 R 1
Lenient, J-J (Vichy) 1967 R
Lepatey, J (Mazamet) 1954 It, 1955 S, I, E, W

Lepatey, L (Mazamet) 1924 S, I, E
Lescarboura, J-P (Dax) 1982 W, E, S, I, 1983 A 1,2, R, 1984 I, W, E, S, NZ 1,2, R, 1985 E, S, I, W, Arg 1,2, 1986 Arg 2, A, NZ 1, R 2, NZ 2, 1988 S, W, 1990 R
Lesieur, E (SF) 1906 E, 1908 E, W, 1909 E, W, I, 1910 S, E, I, 1911 E, I, 1912 W
Leuvielle, M (SBUC) 1908 W, 1913 S, SA, E, W, 1914 W, E
Levasseur, R (SF) 1925 W, E
Levée, H (RCF) 1906 NZ
Lewis, E W (Le Havre) 1906 E
Lhermet, J-M (Montferrand) 1990 S, I, 1993 R 1
Libaros, G (Tarbes) 1936 G 1, 1940 B
Liebenberg, B (SF) 2003 R (R), E 2(R),3, [US,I(R),NZ(R)], 2004 I(R),US,C,NZ, 2005 S,E
Lièvremont, M (Perpignan, SF) 1995 It, R 2, Arg (R), NZ 2(R), 1996 R, Arg 1(R), SA 2(R), 1997 R 1, A 2(R), 1998 E (R), S, I, W, Arg 1,2, Fj, Arg 3, A, 1999 W 2, [C, Nm, Fj, Arg, NZ 2, A]
Lièvremont, M (Dax) 2008 A1(R),2
Lièvremont, T (Perpignan, SF, Biarritz) 1996 W 2(R), 1998 E, S, I, W, Arg 1,2, Fj, Arg 3, A, 1999 I, W 1, E, W 2, [Nm], 2000 W (R), E (R), S (R), I, It, 2001 E (R), 2004 I(R),It(R),W,S,US,C, 2005 A2,C,Tg(t&R),SA3(R), 2006 S(R),It,E,W
Lira, M (La Voulte) 1962 R, 1963 I, E, W, It, R, 1964 W, It, I, SA, 1965 S, I, R
Llari, R (Carcassonne) 1926 S
Lobies, J (RCF) 1921 S, W, E
Lombard, F (Narbonne) 1934 G, 1937 It
Lombard, T (SF) 1998 Arg 3, A, 1999 I, W 1, S (R), 2000 W, E, S, A, NZ 1, 2001 It, W
Lombarteix, R (Montferrand) 1938 R, G 2
Londios, J (Montauban) 1967 SA 3
Loppy, L (Toulon) 1993 R 2
Lorieux, A (Grenoble, Aix) 1981 A 1, R, NZ 1,2, 1982 W, 1983 A 2, R, 1984 I, W, E, 1985 Arg 1,2(R), 1986 R 2, NZ 2,3, 1987 W, E, [S, Z, Fj, A, NZ], 1988 S, I, W, Arg 1,2,4, 1989 W, A 2
Loury, A (RCF) 1927 E, G 1,2, 1928 S, A, I
Loustau, L (Perpignan) 2004 C
Loustau, M (Dax) 1923 E
Lubin-Lebrère, M-F (Toulouse) 1914 I, W, E, 1920 S, E, W, I, US, 1921 S, 1922 S, E, W, 1924 W, US, 1925 I
Lubrano, A (Béziers) 1972 A 2, 1973 S
Lux, J-P (Tyrosse, Dax) 1967 E, It, W, I, SA 1,2,4, R, 1968 I, E, Cz, NZ 3, A, SA 1,2, 1969 S, I, E, 1970 S, I, W, E, R, 1971 S, I, E, W, A 1,2, 1972 S, I 1, E, W, I 2, A 1,2, R, 1973 S, NZ, E, 1974 I, W, E, S, Arg 1,2, 1975 W
Macabiau, A (Perpignan) 1994 S, C 1
Maclos, P (SF) 1906 E, 1907 E
Magne, O (Dax, Brive, Montferrand, Clermont-Auvergne, London Irish) 1997 W (R), E, S, R 1(R), A 1,2, It 2(R), R 2, Arg (R), 1998 E, S, I, W, Arg 1,2, Fj, Arg 3, A, 1999 I, R, WS, NZ 1, W 2, [C, Nm, Fj, Arg, NZ 2, A], 2000 W, E, S, It, R, A, NZ 1,2, 2001 S, I, It, W, E, SA 1,2, NZ, SA 3, A, Fj, 2002 It, E, S, I, Arg, A 1,2(R), SA, NZ, C, 2003 E 1, S, I, It, W, R, E 2,3(R), [Fj,J,S,I,E,NZ(R)], 2004 I,It,W(R),S,E,A,Arg,NZ, 2005 SA1,2(R),A1, 2006 I,It,E,W(R), 2007 NZ1,2
Magnanou, C (RCF) 1923 E, 1925 W, E, 1926 S, 1929 S, W, 1930 S, I, E, W
Magnol, L (Toulouse) 1928 S, 1929 S, W, E
Magois, H (La Rochelle) 1968 SA 1,2, R
Majérus, R (SF) 1928 W, 1929 I, S, 1930 S, I, E, G, W
Malbet, J-C (Agen) 1967 SA 2,4
Maleig, A (Oloron) 1979 W, E, NZ 2, 1980 W, E, SA, R
Mallier, L (Brive) 1999 R, W 2(R), [C (R)], 2000 I (R), It
Malquier, Y (Narbonne) 1979 S
Malzieu, J (Clermont-Auvergne) 2008 S,It,W,Arg,PI,A3, 2009 I,S(R),W,E,It(R), 2010 I(R),W,It(R),E(R),Arg1
Manterola, T (Lourdes) 1955 It, 1957 R 1
Mantoulan, C (Pau) 1959 I
Marcet, J (Albi) 1925 I, NZ, S, W, E, 1926 I, E
Marchal, J-F (Lourdes) 1979 S, R, 1980 W, S, I
Marconnet, S (SF) 1998 Arg 3, A, 1999 I (R), W 1(R), E, S (R), R, Tg, 2000 A, NZ 1,2, 2001 S, I, It (R), W (R), E, 2002 S (R), Arg (R), A 1,2, SA (R), C (R), 2003 E 1(R), S, I, It, W, Arg 1(t+R),2, NZ, R, E 2,3(t+R), [S,US(R),I,E,NZ], 2004 I,It,W, S,E,A,Arg,NZ, 2005 S,E,W,I,It,SA1,2,A1(R),2(R),C,Tg,SA3(R), 2006 S,I(R),It(R),E,W,R,SA,NZ1,2(R),Arg(R), 2007 It(R),I,W1(R), 2009 W,E,It,NZ1,A,SA(R),Sm,NZ3, 2010 I(R)
Marchand, R (Poitiers) 1920 S, W
Marfaing, M (Toulouse) 1992 R, Arg 1
Marlu, J (Montferrand, Biarritz)) 1998 Fj (R), 2002 S (R), I (R), 2005 E
Marocco, P (Montferrand) 1968 S, I, W, E, R 1, Arg 1,2, A, 1988 Arg 4, 1989 I, 1990 E (R), NZ 1(R), 1991 S, I, W 1, E, US 2, [R, Fj, C, E]
Marot, A (Brive) 1969 R, 1970 S, I, W, 1971 SA 1, 1972 I 2, 1976 A 1
Marquesuzaa, A (RCF) 1958 It, SA 1,2, 1959 S, E, It, W, 1960 S, E, Arg 1
Marracq, H (Pau) 1961 R
Marsh, T (Montferrand) 2001 SA 3, A, Fj, 2002 It, W, E, S, I, Arg, A 1,2, 2003 [Fj,J,S,I,E,NZ], 2004 C,A,Arg,NZ
Martin, C (Lyon) 1909 I, 1910 W, S
Martin, H (SBUC) 1907 E, 1908 W
Martin, J-L (Béziers) 1971 A 2, R, 1972 S, I 1
Martin, L (Pau) 1948 I, A, S, W, E, 1950 S
Martin, R (SF, Bayonne) 2002 E (t+R), S (R), I (R), 2005 SA1(t&R),2,A1,2,C,SA3, 2006 S,I(t&R),R,SA(R),NZ1(R),2,Arg, 2007 E2,W2, [Arg 1,Gg(R),Arg 2(R)], 2009 NZ2(R),A(R)
Martine, R (Lourdes) 1952 S, I, It, 1953 It, 1954 S, I, NZ, W, E, It, Arg 2, 1955 S, I, W, 1958 A, W, It, I, SA 1,2, 1960 S, E, Arg 3, 1961 S, It
Martinez, A (Narbonne) 2002 A 1, 2004 C
Martinez, G (Toulouse) 1982 W, E, S, Arg 1,2, 1983 E, W
Marty, D (Perpignan) 2005 It,C,Tg, 2006 I,It(R),R(R),NZ1(R),Arg(R), 2007 I,W1,E1,S,E2, [Nm,I,Gg,NZ,E,Arg 2], 2008 S,I,E, 2009 SA(R),Sm,NZ3, 2010 S(R),I(R),W(R),It,E(R),SA
Mas, F (Béziers) 1962 R, 1963 S, I, E, W
Mas, N (Perpignan) 2003 NZ, 2005 E,W,I,It, 2007 W1,NZ1,2(R), E2(R),3(R),W2, [Nm(R),Gg(R),Arg 2], 2008 S(R),I,E,It,W,Arg(R), PI,A3, 2009 I(R),S,NZ1(R),2,A(R), SA,Sm(R),NZ3(R), 2010 S,I,W,It,E,SA,Arg1
Maso, J (Perpignan, Narbonne) 1966 It, R, 1967 S, R, 1968 S, W, Cz, NZ 1,2,3, A, R, 1969 S, I, W, 1971 SA 1,2, R, 1972 E, W, A 2, 1973 W, I, J, R
Massare, J (PUC) 1945 B 1,2, W, 1946 B, I, W
Massé, A (SBUC) 1908 W, 1909 E, W, 1910 W, S, E, I
Masse, H (Grenoble) 1937 G
Matheu-Cambas, J (Agen) 1945 W, 1946 B, I, K, W, 1947 S, I, W, E, 1948 I, A, S, W, E, 1949 S, I, E, W, Arg 1,2, 1950 E, W, 1951 S, I
Matiu, L (Biarritz) 2000 W, E
Mauduy, G (Périgueux) 1957 It, R 1,2, 1958 S, E, 1961 W, It
Mauran, J (Castres) 1952 SA, W, E, It, 1953 I, E
Mauriat, P (Lyon) 1907 E, 1908 E, W, 1909 W, I, 1910 W, S, E, I, 1911 S, E, W, I, 1912 I, S, 1913 S, SA, W, I
Maurin, G (ASF) 1906 E
Maury, A (Toulouse) 1925 I, NZ, S, W, E, 1926 S, I, E
Mayssonnié, A (Toulouse) 1908 E, W, 1910 W
Mazars, L (Narbonne, Bayonne) 2007 NZ2, 2010 Arg1
Mazas, L (Colomiers, Biarritz) 1992 Arg, 1996 SA 1
Médard, M (Toulouse) 2008 Arg,PI,A3, 2009 I,S,W,E,It,NZ1, 2,A,SA(R),Sm,NZ3
Mela, A (Albi) 2008 S(R),I,It(R),W(R)
Melville, E (Toulon) 1990 I (R), A 1,2,3, NZ 1, 1991 US 2
Menrath, R (SCUF) 1910 W
Menthiller, Y (Romans) 1964 W, It, SA, R, 1965 E
Merceron, G (Montferrand) 1999 R (R), Tg, 2000 S, I, R, 2001 S (R), W, E, SA 1,2, NZ (R), Fj, 2002 It, W, E, S, I, Arg, A 2, C, 2003 E 1, It (R), W (R), NZ (t+R), R (R), E 3, [Fj(R),J(R),S(R), US,E(R),NZ]
Meret, F (Tarbes) 1940 B
Mericq, S (Agen) 1959 I, 1960 S, E, W, 1961 I
Merle, O (Grenoble, Montferrand) 1993 SA 1,2, R 2, A 1,2, 1994 I, W, E, S, C 1, NZ 1,2, C 2, 1995 W, I, R 1, [Tg, S, I, SA, E], It, R 2, Arg, NZ 1,2, 1996 E, S, R, Arg 1,2, W 2, SA 2, 1997 I, W, E, S, It 1, R 1, A 1,2, It 2, R 2, SA 1(R),2
Mermoz, M (Toulouse, Perpignan) 2008 A2, 2009 S(R),NZ2,A,SA, 2010 SA,Arg1(R)
Merquey, J (Toulon)1950 S, I, E, W
Mesnel, F (RCF) 1986 NZ 2(R),3, 1987 W, E, S, I, [S, Z, Fj, A, NZ], R, 1988 E, Arg 1,2,3,4, R, 1989 I, W, E, S, NZ 1, A 1,2, 1990 E, S, I, A 2,3, NZ 1,2, 1991 S, I, W 1, E, R, US 1,2, W 2, [R, Fj, C, E], 1992 W, E, S, I, SA 1,2, 1993 E (R), W, 1995 I, R 1, [Iv, E]

Mesny, P (RCF, Grenoble) 1979 NZ 1,2, 1980 SA, R, 1981 I, W (R), A 1,2, R, NZ 1,2, 1982 I, Arg 1,2
Meyer, G-S (Périgueux) 1960 S, E, It, R, Arg 2
Meynard, J (Cognac) 1954 Arg 1, 1956 Cz
Mias, L (Mazamet) 1951 S, I, E, W, 1952 I, SA, W, E, It, 1953 S, I, W, It, 1954 S, I, NZ, W, 1957 R 2, 1958 S, E, A, W, I, SA 1,2, 1959 S, It, W, I
Michalak, F (Toulouse) 2001 SA 3(R), A, Fj (R), 2002 It, A 1,2, 2003 It, W, Arg 2(R), NZ, R, E 2, [Fj,J,S,I,E,NZ(R)], 2004 I,W,S,E,A,Arg,NZ, 2005 S(R),E(R),W(R),I(R),It(R),SA1,2,A1,2,C, Tg(R),SA3, 2006 S,I,It,E,W, 2007 E2(R),3, [Arg1(t&R),Nm,I, NZ(R),E(R),Arg 2], 2009 It(R), 2010 S(R),I(R),W(R)
Mignardi, A (Agen) 2007 NZ1,2
Mignoni, P (Béziers, Clermont-Auvergne)) 1997 R 2(R), Arg (t), 1999 R (R), WS, NZ 1, W 2(R), [C, Nm], 2002 W, E (R), I (R), Arg, A 2(R), 2005 S,It(R),C(R), 2006 R, 2007 It,I,W1,E1(R), S,E2,3(R),W2, [Arg 1,Gg,Arg 2(R)]
Milhères, C (Biarritz) 2001 E
Milliand, P (Grenoble) 1936 G 2, 1937 G, It
Millo-Chluski, R (Toulouse) 2005 SA1, 2008 Arg,PI,A3(R), 2009 I(R),S,W(R),NZ1,2,A,SA,Sm(R),NZ3, 2010 SA
Milloud, O (Bourgoin) 2000 R (R), 2001 NZ, 2002 W (R), E (R), 2003 It (R), W (R), Arg 1, R (R), E 2(t+R),3, [J,S(R),US,I(R),E(R)], 2004 US,C(R),A,Arg,NZ(R), 2005 S(R),E(R),W(R),SA1,2(R), A1,2,C(R),Tg,SA3,2006 S(R),I,It,E(R),W(R),NZ1(R),2,Arg, 2007 It,I(R),W1,E1,S,E2,3, [Arg 1,I,Gg,NZ,E]
Minjat, R (Lyon) 1945 B 1
Miorin, H (Toulouse) 1996 R, SA 1, 1997 I, W, E, S, It 1, 2000 It (R), R (R)
Mir, J-H (Lourdes) 1967 R, 1968 I
Mir, J-P (Lourdes) 1967 A
Modin, R (Brive) 1987 [Z]
Moga, A-M-A (Bègles) 1945 B 1,2, W, 1946 B, I, K, W, 1947 S, I, W, E, 1948 I, A, S, W, E, 1949 S, I, E, W, Arg 1,2
Mola, U (Dax, Castres) 1997 S (R), 1999 R (R), WS, Tg (R), NZ 1, W 2, [C, Nm, Fj, Arg (R), NZ 2(R), A (R)]
Momméjat, B (Cahors, Albi) 1958 It, I, SA 1,2, 1959 S, E, It, W, I, 1960 S, E, I, R, 1962 S, E, W, I, It, R, 1963 S, I, W
Moncla, F (RCF, Pau) 1956 Cz, 1957 I, E, W, It, R 1, 1958 SA 1,2, 1959 S, E, It, W, I, 1960 S, E, W, I, It, R, Arg 1,2,3, 1961 S, SA, E, W, It, I, NZ 1,2,3
Moni, C (Nice, SF) 1996 R, 2000 A, NZ 1,2, 2001 S, I, It, W
Monié, R (Perpignan) 1956 Cz, 1957 E
Monier, R (SBUC) 1911 I, 1912 S
Monniot, M (RCF) 1912 W, E
Montade, A (Perpignan) 1925 I, NZ, S, W, 1926 W
Montanella, F (Auch) 2007 NZ1(R)
Montlaur, P (Agen) 1992 E (R), 1994 S (R)
Moraitis, B (Toulon) 1969 E, W
Morel, A (Grenoble) 1954 Arg 2
Morère, J (Toulouse) 1927 E, G 1, 1928 S, A
Moscato, V (Bègles) 1991 R, US 1, 1992 W, E
Mougeot, C (Bègles) 1992 W, E, Arg
Mouniq, P (Toulouse) 1911 S, E, W, I,1912 I, E, 1913 S, SA, E
Moure, H (SCUF) 1908 E
Moureu, P (Béziers) 1920 I, US, 1921 W, E, I, 1922 S, W, I, 1923 S, W, E, I, 1924 S, I, E, W, 1925 E
Mournet, A (Bagnères) 1981 A 1(R)
Mouronval, F (SF) 1909 I
Muhr, A H (RCF) 1906 NZ, E, 1907 E
Murillo, G (Dijon) 1954 It, Arg 1
Nallet, L (Bourgoin, Castres, Racing-Metro) 2000 R, 2001 E, SA 1(R),2(R), NZ, SA3(R), A (R), Fj (R), 2003 NZ, 2005 A2(R),C,Tg(R),SA3, 2006 I(R),It(R),E(R),W(R),R,SA(R),NZ1(R),2, Arg, 2007 It,I,W1,E1,S,E3(R), [Nm,I(R),Gg,Arg 2], 2008 S,I,E,It,W,A1,2,Arg,PI,A3, 2009 I,S,W,E,It,SA,NZ3(R), 2010 S,I,W,It,E,SA,Arg1
Namur, R (Toulon) 1931 E, G
Noble, J-C (La Voulte) 1968 E, W, Cz, NZ 3, A, R
Normand, A (Toulouse) 1957 R 1
Novès, G (Toulouse) 1977 NZ 1,2, R, 1978 W, R, 1979 I, W
Ntamack, E (Toulouse) 1994 W, C 1, NZ 1,2, C 2, 1995 W, I, R 1, [Tg, S, I, SA, E], It, R 2, Arg, NZ 1,2, 1996 E, S, I, W 1, R (R), Arg 1,2, W 2, 1997 I, 1998 Arg 3, 1999 I, W 1, E, S, WS, NZ 1, W 2(R), [C (R), Nm, Fj, Arg, NZ 2, A], 2000 W, E, S, I, It
Ntamack F (Colomiers) 2001 SA 3
Nyanga, Y (Béziers, Toulouse) 2004 US,C, 2005 S(R),E(R),W, I,It,SA1,2,A1(R),2,C(t&R),Tg,SA3, 2006 S,I,It,E,W, 2007 E2(R),3, [Nm,I(R),Gg,Arg 2]
Olibeau, O (Perpignan) 2007 NZ1(R),2(R)
Olive, D (Montferrand) 1951 I, 1952 I
Ondarts, P (Biarritz O) 1986 NZ 3, 1987 W, E, S, I, [S, Z, Fj, A, NZ], R, 1988 E, I, W, Arg 1,2,3,4, R, 1989 I, W, E, NZ 1,2, A 2, 1990 W, E, S, I, R (R), NZ 1,2, 1991 S, I, W 1, E, US 2, W 2, [R, Fj, C, E]
Orso, J-C (Nice, Toulon) 1982 Arg 1,2, 1983 E, S, A 1, 1984 E (R), S, NZ 1, 1985 I (R), W, 1988 I
Othats, J (Dax) 1960 Arg 2,3
Ouedraogo, F (Montpellier) 2007 NZ2(R), 2008 S,I,E(R),It, W,A1,2,Arg(R),PI,A3, 2009 I,S,W,NZ1,2,A,NZ3, 2010 S,I
Ougier, S (Toulouse) 1992 R, Arg 1, 1993 E (R), 1997 It 1
Paco, A (Béziers) 1974 Arg 1,2, R, SA 1,2, 1975 W, E, Arg 1,2, R, 1976 S, I, W, E, US, A 1,2, R, 1977 W, E, S, I, NZ 1,2, R, 1978 E, S, I, W, R, 1979 I, W, E, S, 1980 W
Palat, J (Perpignan) 1938 G 2
Palisson, A (Brive) 2008 A1,2,Arg(R),PI(R),A3(R), 2010 I,W,It,E
Palmié, M (Béziers) 1975 SA 1,2, Arg 1,2, R, 1976 S, I, W, E, US, 1977 W, E, S, I, Arg 1,2, NZ 1,2, R, 1978 E, S, I, W
Paoli, R (see Simonpaoli)
Paparemborde, R (Pau) 1975 SA 1,2, Arg 1,2, R, 1976 S, I, W, E, US, A 1,2, R, 1977 W, E, S, I, Arg 1, NZ 1,2, 1978 E, S, I, W, R, 1979 I, W, E, S, NZ 1,2, R, 1980 W, E, S, SA, R, 1981 S, I, W, E, A 1,2, R, NZ 1,2, 1982 W, I, R, Arg 1,2 1983 E, S, I, W
Papé, P (Bourgoin, Castres, SF) 2004 I,It,W,S,E,C,NZ(R), 2005 I(R),It(R),SA1,2,A1, 2006 NZ1,2, 2007 It(R),I,S(R),NZ1,2, 2008 E, 2009 NZ1,A,Sm, 2010 S,I,Arg1
Pardo, L (Hendaye) 1924 I, E
Pardo, L (Bayonne) 1980 SA, R, 1981 S, I, W, E, A 1, 1982 W, E, S, 1983 A 1(R), 1985 S, I, Arg 2
Pargade, J-H (Lyon U) 1953 It
Pariès, L (Biarritz O) 1968 SA 2, R, 1970 S, I, W, 1975 E, S, I
Parra, M (Bourgoin, Clermont-Auvergne) 2008 S(R),I(R),E,Arg(R), 2009 I(R),S(R),W,E,It,SA(R),Sm,NZ3(R), 2010 S,I,W,It,E,SA,Arg1
Pascalin, P (Mont-de-Marsan) 1950 I, E, W, 1951 S, I, E, W
Pascarel, J-R (TOEC) 1912 W, E, 1913 S, SA, E, I
Pascot, J (Perpignan) 1922 S, E, I, 1923 S, 1926 I, 1927 G 2
Paul, R (Montferrand) 1940 B
Pauthe, G (Graulhet) 1956 E
Pebeyre, E-J (Fumel, Brive) 1945 W, 1946 I, K, W, 1947 S, I, W, E
Pebeyre, M (Vichy, Montferrand) 1970 E, R, 1971 I, SA 1,2, A 1, 1973 W
Péclier, A (Bourgoin) 2004 US,C
Pécune, J (Tarbes) 1974 W, E, S, 1975 Arg 1,2, R, 1976 I, W, E, US
Pédeutour, P (Bègles) 1980 I
Pellissier, L (RCF) 1928 A, I, E, G, W
Pelous, F (Dax, Toulouse) 1995 R 2, Arg, NZ 1,2, 1996 E, S, I, R (R), Arg 1,2, W 2, SA 1,2, 1997 I, W, E, S, It 1, R 1, A 1,2, It 2, R 2, Arg, SA 1,2(R), 1998 E, S, I, W, Arg 1,2, Fj, Arg 3, A, 1999 I, W 1, E, R (R), WS, Tg (R), NZ 1, W 2, [C, Nm, Fj, NZ 2, A], 2000 W, E, S, I, It, A, NZ 1,2, 2001 S, I, It, W, E, 2002 It (R), W (R), E (R), S, I, Arg, A 1,2, SA, NZ, C, 2003 E 1, S, I, It, W, R, E 2,3(R), [Fj,J,S,I,E,NZ(R)], 2004 I,It,W,S,E,US,C,A,Arg,NZ, 2005 S,E,W,I,It,A2, 2006 S,I,It,E,W,R,SA,NZ1, 2007 E2,3,W2(R), [Arg1,Nm(R),Gg(R), NZ,E]
Penaud, A (Brive, Toulouse) 1992 W, E, S, I, R, Arg 1,2, SA 1,2, Arg, 1993 R 1, SA 1,2, R 2, A 1,2, 1994 I, W, E, 1995 NZ 1,2, 1996 S, R, Arg 1,2, W 2, 1997 I, E, R 1, A 2, 2000 W (R), It
Périé, M (Toulon) 1996 E, S, I (R)
Péron, P (RCF) 1975 SA 1,2
Perrier, P (Bayonne) 1982 W, E, S, I (R)
Pesteil, J-P (Béziers) 1975 SA 1, 1976 A 2, R
Petit, C (Lorrain) 1931 W
Peyras, J-B (Bayonne) 2008 A2(R)
Peyrelade, H (Tarbes) 1940 B
Peyrelongue, J (Biarritz) 2004 It,S(R),C(R),A(R),Arg(R),NZ
Peyroutou, G (Périgueux) 1911 S, E
Phliponeau, J-F (Montferrand) 1973 W, I

Piazza, A (Montauban) 1968 NZ 1, A
Picamoles, L (Montpellier, Toulouse) 2008 I(R),E,It,A1,2(t&R), Arg,PI(R),A3(R), 2009 I(R),S(R),E(R),It(R),NZ1,2,SA, 2010 SA(R),Arg1
Picard, T (Montferrand) 1985 Arg 2, 1986 R 1(R), Arg 2
Pierre, J (Bourgoin, Clermont-Auvergne) 2007 NZ1,2, 2010 S(R),I(R),W,It,E,SA(R),Arg1(R)
Pierrot, G (Pau) 1914 I, W, E
Pilon, J (Périgueux) 1949 E, 1950 E
Piqué, J (Pau) 1961 NZ 2,3, A, 1962 S, It, 1964 NZ, E, W, It, I, SA, Fj, R, 1965 S, I, E, W, It
Piquemal, M (Tarbes) 1927 I, S, 1929 I, G, 1930 S, I, E, G, W
Piquiral, E (RCF) 1924 S, I, E, W, R, US, 1925 E, 1926 S, I, E, W, M, 1927 I, S, W, E, G 1,2, 1928 E
Piteu, R (Pau) 1921 S, W, E, I, 1922 S, E, W, I, 1923 E, 1924 E, 1925 I, NZ, W, E, 1926 E
Plantefol, A (RCF) 1967 SA 2,3,4, NZ, R, 1968 E, W, Cz, NZ 2, 1969 E, W
Plantey, S (RCF) 1961 A, 1962 It
Podevin, G (SF) 1913 W, I
Poeydebasque, F (Bayonne) 1914 I, W
Poirier, A (SCUF) 1907 E
Poitrenaud, C (Toulouse) 2001 SA 3, A, Fj, 2003 E 1, S, I, It, W, Arg 1, NZ, E 3, [J,US,E(R),NZ], 2004 E(R),US,C,Arg(R),NZ, 2006 R, 2007 It,I,W1,E1,S,E2,3, [Nm,I,Gg,Arg 2], 2009 I,S, 2010 S,I,W,It,E,SA,Arg1(R)
Pomathios, M (Agen, Lyon U, Bourg) 1948 I, A, S, W, E, 1949 S, I, E, W, Arg 1,2, 1950 S, I, W, 1951 S, I, E, W, 1952 W, E, 1953 S, I, W, 1954 S
Pons, P (Toulouse) 1920 S, E, W, 1921 S, W, 1922 S
Porcu, C (Agen) 2002 Arg (R), A 1,2(R)
Porical, J (Perpignan) 2010 Arg1
Porra, M (Lyon) 1931 I
Porthault, A (RCF) 1951 S, E, W, 1952 I, 1953 S, I, It
Portolan, C (Toulouse) 1986 A, 1989 I, E
Potel, A (Begles) 1932 G
Poux, J-B (Narbonne, Toulouse) 2001 Fj (R), 2002 S, I (R), Arg, A 1(R),2(R), 2003 E 3, [Fj,J,US,NZ], 2007 E2,3,W2(R), [Nm,I(R),Gg,NZ(R),E(R),Arg 2], 2008 E(R),It(R),W(R), 2010 W(R),It(R),E(R),SA(R),Arg1(R)
Prat, J (Lourdes) 1945 B 1,2, W, 1946 B, I, K, W, 1947 S, I, W, E, 1948 I, A, S, W, E, 1949 S, I, E, W, Arg 1,2, 1950 S, I, E, W, 1951 S, E, W, 1952 S, I, SA, W, E, It, 1953 S, I, E, W, It, 1954 S, I, NZ, W, E, It, 1955 S, I, E, W, It
Prat, M (Lourdes) 1951 I, 1952 S, I, SA, W, E, 1953 S, I, E, 1954 I, NZ, W, E, It, 1955 S, I, E, W, It, 1956 I, W, It, Cz, 1957 S, I, W, It, R 1, 1958 A, W, I
Prévost, A (Albi) 1926 M, 1927 I, S, W
Prin-Clary, J (Cavaillon, Brive) 1945 B 1,2, W, 1946 B, I, K, W, 1947 S, I, W
Privat, T (Béziers, Clermont-Auvergne) 2001 SA 3, A, Fj, 2002 It, W, S (R), SA (R), 2003 [NZ], 2005 SA2,A1(R)
Puech, L (Toulouse) 1920 S, E, I, 1921 E, I
Puget, M (Toulouse) 1961 It, 1966 S, I, It, 1967 SA 1,3,4, NZ, 1968 Cz, NZ 1,2, SA 1,2, R, 1969 E, R, 1970 W
Puig, A (Perpignan) 1926 S, E
Pujol, A (SOE Toulouse) 1906 NZ
Pujolle, M (Nice) 1989 B, A 1, 1990 S, I, R, A 1,2, NZ 2
Puricelli, J (Bayonne) 2009 NZ1(R),A,Sm(R),NZ3(R)
Quaglio, A (Mazamet) 1957 R 2, 1958 S, E, A, W, I, SA 1,2, 1959 S, E, It, W, I
Quilis, A (Narbonne) 1967 SA 1,4, NZ, 1970 R, 1971 I
Rabadan, P (SF) 2004 US(R),C(R)
Ramis, R (Perpignan) 1922 E, I, 1923 W
Rancoule, H (Lourdes, Toulon, Tarbes) 1955 E, W, It, 1958 A, W, It, I, SA 1, 1959 S, It, W, 1960 I, It, R, Arg 1,2, 1961 SA, E, W, It, NZ 1,2, 1962 S, E, W, I, It
Rapin, A (SBUC) 1938 R
Raymond, F (Toulouse) 1925 S, 1927 W, 1928 I
Raynal, F (Perpignan) 1935 G, 1936 G 1,2, 1937 G, It
Raynaud, F (Carcassonne) 1933 G
Raynaud, M (Narbonne) 1999 W 1, E (R)
Razat, J-P (Agen) 1962 R, 1963 S, I, R
Rebujent, R (RCF) 1963 E
Revailler, D (Graulhet) 1981 S, I, W, E, A 1,2, R, NZ 1,2, 1982 W, S, I, R, Arg 1
Revillon, J (RCF) 1926 I, E, 1927 S
Ribère, E (Perpignan, Quillan) 1924 I, 1925, I, NZ, S, 1926 S, I, W, M, 1927 I, S, W, E, G 1,2, 1928 S, A, I, E, G, W, 1929 I, E, G, 1930 S, I, E, W, 1931 I, S, W, E, G, 1932 G, 1933 G
Rives, J-P (Toulouse, RCF) 1975 E, S, I, Arg 1,2, R, 1976 S, I, W, E, US, A 1,2, R, 1977 W, E, S, I, Arg 1,2, R, 1978 E, S, I, W, R, 1979 I, W, E, S, NZ 1,2, R, 1980 W, E, S, I, SA, 1981 S, I, W, E, A 2, 1982 W, E, S, I, R, 1983 E, S, I, W, A 1,2, R, 1984 I, W, E, S
Rochon, A (Montferrand) 1936 G 1
Rodrigo, M (Mauléon) 1931 I, W
Rodriguez, L (Mont-de-Marsan, Montferrand, Dax) 1981 A 1,2, R, NZ 1,2, 1982 W, E, S, I, R, 1983 E, S, 1984 I, NZ 1,2, R, 1985 E, S, I, W, 1986 Arg 1, A, R 2, NZ 2,3, 1987 W, E, S, I, [S, Z, Fj, A, NZ], R, 1988 E, S, I, W, Arg 1,2,3,4, R, 1989 I, E, S, NZ 1,2, B, A 1, 1990 W, E, S, I, NZ 1
Rogé, L (Béziers) 1952 It, 1953 E, W, It, 1954 S, Arg 1,2, 1955 S, I, 1956 W, It, E, 1957 S, 1960 S, E
Rollet, J (Bayonne) 1960 Arg 3, 1961 NZ 3, A, 1962 It, 1963 I
Romero, H (Montauban) 1962 S, E, W, I, It, R, 1963 E
Romeu, J-P (Montferrand) 1972 R, 1973 S, NZ, E, W, I, R, 1974 W, E, S, Arg 1,2, R, SA 1,2(R), 1975 W, SA 2, Arg 1,2, R, 1976 S, I, W, E, US, 1977 W, E, S, I, Arg 1,2, NZ 1,2, R
Roques, A (Cahors) 1958 A, W, It, I, SA 1,2, 1959 S, E, W, I, 1960 S, E, W, I, It, Arg 1,2,3, 1961 S, SA, E, W, It, I, 1962 S, E, W, I, It, 1963 S
Roques, J-C (Brive) 1966 S, I, It, R
Rossignol, J-C (Brive) 1972 A 2
Rouan, J (Narbonne) 1953 S, I
Roucariès, G (Perpignan) 1956 S
Rouffia, L (Narbonne) 1945 B 2, W, 1946 W, 1948 I
Rougerie, A (Montferrand, Clermont-Auvergne) 2001 SA 3, A, Fj (R), 2002 It, W, E, S, I, Arg, A 1,2, 2003 E 1, S, I, It, W, Arg 1,2, NZ, R, E 2,3(R), [Fj,J,S,I,E], 2004 US,C,A,Arg,NZ, 2005 S,W,A2,C,Tg,SA3, 2006 I,It,E,W,NZ1,2, 2007 E2,W2, [Arg1,Nm(R),I(R),Gg,Arg 2], 2008 S(R),I,E,It, 2010 S,SA
Rougerie, J (Montferrand) 1973 J
Rougé-Thomas, P (Toulouse) 1989 NZ 1,2
Roujas, F (Tarbes) 1910 I
Roumat, O (Dax) 1989 NZ 2(R), B, 1990 W, E, S, I, R, A 1,2,3, NZ 1,2, 1991 S, I, W 1, E, R, US 1, W 2, [R, Fj, C, E], 1992 W (R), E (R), S, I, SA 1,2, Arg, 1993 E, S, I, W, R 1, SA 1,2, R 2, A 1,2, 1994 I, W, E, C 1, NZ 1,2, C 2, 1995 W, E, S, [Iv, S, I, SA, E], 1996 E, S, I, W 1, Arg 1,2
Rousie, M (Villeneuve) 1931 S, G, 1932 G, 1933 G
Rousset, G (Béziers) 1975 SA 1, 1976 US
Rué, J-B (Agen) 2002 SA (R), C (R), 2003 E 1(R), S (R), It (R), W (R), Arg 1,2(R)
Ruiz, A (Tarbes) 1968 SA 2, R
Rupert, J-J (Tyrosse) 1963 R, 1964 S, Fj, 1965 E, W, It, 1966 S, I, E, W, It, 1967 It, R, 1968 S
Sadourny, J-L (Colomiers) 1991 W 2(R), [C (R)], 1992 E (R), S, I, Arg 1(R),2, SA 1,2, 1993 R 1, SA 1,2, R 2, A 1,2, 1994 I, W, E, S, C 1, NZ 1,2, C 2, 1995 W, E, S, I, R 1, [Tg, S, I, SA, E], It, R 2, Arg, NZ 1,2, 1996 E, S, I, W 1, Arg 1,2, W 2, SA 1,2, 1997 I, W, E, S, It 1, R 1, A 1,2, It 2, R 2, Arg, SA 1,2, 1998 E, S, I, W, 1999 R, Tg, NZ 1(R), 2000 NZ 2, 2001 It, W, E
Sagot, P (SF) 1906 NZ, 1908 E, 1909 W
Sahuc, A (Métro) 1945 B 1,2
Sahuc, F (Toulouse) 1936 G 2
Saint-André, P (Montferrand, Gloucester) 1990 R, A 3, NZ 1,2, 1991 I (R), W 1, E, US 1,2, W 2, [R, Fj, C, E], 1992 W, E, S, I, R, Arg 1,2, SA 1,2, 1993 E, S, I, W, SA 1,2, A 1,2, 1994 I, W, E, S, C 1, NZ 1,2, C 2, 1995 W, E, S, I, R 1, [Tg, Iv, S, I, SA, E], It, R 2, Arg, NZ 1,2, 1996 E, S, I, W 1, R, Arg 1,2, W 2, 1997 It 1,2, R 2, Arg, SA 1,2
Saisset, O (Béziers) 1971 R, 1972 S, I 1, A 1,2, 1973 S, NZ, E, W, I, J, R, 1974 I, Arg 2, SA 1,2, 1975 W
Salas, P (Narbonne) 1979 NZ 1,2, R, 1980 W, E, 1981 A 1, 1982 Arg 2
Salinié, R (Perpignan) 1923 E
Sallefranque, M (Dax) 1981 A 2, 1982 W, E, S
Salut, J (TOEC) 1966 R, 1967 S, 1968 I, E, Cz, NZ 1, 1969 I
Samatan, R (Agen) 1930 S, I, E, G, W, 1931 I, S, W, E, G
Sanac, A (Perpignan) 1952 It, 1953 S, I, 1954 E, 1956 Cz, 1957 S, I, E, W, It
Sangalli, F (Narbonne) 1975 I, SA 1,2, 1976 S, A 1,2, R, 1977 W, E, S, I, Arg 1,2, NZ 1,2

Sanz, H (Narbonne) 1988 Arg 3,4, R, 1989 A 2, 1990 S, I, R, A 1,2, NZ 2, 1991 W 2
Sappa, M (Nice) 1973 J, R, 1977 R
Sarrade, R (Pau) 1929 I
Sarraméa, O (Castres) 1999 R, WS (R), Tg, NZ 1
Saux, J-P (Pau) 1960 W, It, Arg 1,2, 1961 SA, E, W, It, I, NZ 1,2,3, A, 1962 S, E, W, I, It, 1963 S, I, E, It
Savitsky, M (La Voulte) 1969 R
Savy, M (Montferrand) 1931 I, S, W, E, 1936 G 1
Sayrou, J (Perpignan) 1926 W, M, 1928 E, G, W, 1929 S, W, E, G
Scohy, R (BEC) 1931 S, W, E, G
Sébedio, J (Tarbes) 1913 S, E, 1914 I, 1920 S, I, US, 1922 S, E, 1923 S
Séguier, R (Béziers) 1973 J, R
Seigne, L (Agen, Merignac) 1989 B, A 1, 1990 NZ 1, 1993 E, S, I, W, R 1, A 1,2, 1994 S, C 1, 1995 E (R), S
Sella, P (Agen) 1982 R, Arg 1,2, 1983 E, S, I, W, A 1,2, R, 1984 I, W, E, S, NZ 1,2, R, 1985 E, S, I, W, Arg 1,2, 1986 S, I, W, E, R 1, Arg 1,2, A, NZ 1, R 2, NZ 2,3, 1987 W, E, S, I, [S, R, Z (R), Fj, A, NZ], 1988 E, S, I, W, Arg 1,2,3,4, R, 1989 I, W, E, S, NZ 1,2, B, A 1,2, 1990 W, E, S, I, A 1,2,3, 1991 W 1, E, R, US 1,2, W 2, [Fj, C, E], 1992 W, E, S, I, Arg, 1993 E, S, I, W, R 1, SA 1,2, R 2, A 1,2, 1994 I, W, E, S, C 1, NZ 1,2, C 2, 1995 W, E, S, I, [Tg, S, I, SA, E]
Semmartin, J (SCUF) 1913 W, I
Sénal, G (Béziers) 1974 Arg 1,2, R, SA 1,2, 1975 W
Sentilles, J (Tarbes) 1912 W, E, 1913 S, SA
Serin, L (Béziers) 1928 E, 1929 W, E, G, 1930 S, I, E, G, W, 1931 I, W, E
Serre, P (Perpignan) 1920 S, E
Serrière, P (RCF) 1986 A, 1987 R, 1988 E
Servat, W (Toulouse) 2004 I,It,W,S,E,US,C,A,Arg,NZ 2005 S,E(R),W(R),It(R),SA1(R),2, 2008 S,I(R),E(R),W(R), 2009 It(R), NZ1,2,SA,NZ3, 2010 S,I,W,It,E
Servole, L (Toulon) 1931 I, S, W, E, G, 1934 G, 1935 G
Sicart, N (Perpignan) 1922 I
Sillières, J (Tarbes) 1968 R, 1970 S, I, 1971 S, I, E, 1972 E, W
Siman, M (Montferrand) 1948 E, 1949 S, 1950 S, I, E, W
Simon, S (Bègles) 1991 R, US 1
Simonpaoli, R (SF) 1911 I, 1912 I, S
Sitjar, M (Agen) 1964 W, It, I, R, 1965 It, R, 1967 A, E, It, W, I, SA 1,2
Skrela, D (Colomiers, SF, Toulouse) 2001 NZ, 2007 It,I,W1, E1,2,3(R),W2, [Arg 1,Gg(R),Arg 2], 2008 S(R),I,E(R),W,Arg,PI,A3, 2010 SA(R)
Skrela, J-C (Toulouse) 1971 SA 2, A 1,2, 1972 I 1(R), E, W, I 2, A 1, 1973 W, J, R, 1974 W, E, S, Arg 1, R, 1975 W (R), E, S, I, SA 1,2, Arg 1,2, R, 1976 S, I, W, E, US, A 1,2, R, 1977 W, E, S, I, Arg 1,2, NZ 1,2, R, 1978 E, S, I, W
Soler, M (Quillan) 1929 G
Soro, R (Lourdes, Romans) 1945 B 1,2, W, 1946 B, I, K, 1947 S, I, W, E, 1948 I, A, S, W, E, 1949 S, I, E, W, Arg 1,2
Sorondo, L-M (Montauban) 1946 K, 1947 S, I, W, E, 1948 I
Soulette, C (Béziers, Toulouse) 1997 R 2, 1998 S (R), I (R), W (R), Arg 1,2, Fj, 1999 W 2(R), [C (R), Nm (R), Arg, NZ 2, A]
Soulié, E (CASG) 1920 E, I, US, 1921 S, E, I, 1922 E, W, I
Sourgens, J (Bègles) 1926 M
Sourgens, O (Bourgoin) 2007 NZ2
Souverbie, J-M (Bègles) 2000 R
Spanghero, C (Narbonne) 1971 E, W, SA 1,2, A 1,2, R, 1972 S, E, W, I 2, A 1,2, 1974 I, W, E, S, R, SA 1, 1975 E, S, I
Spanghero, W (Narbonne) 1964 SA, Fj, R, 1965 S, I, E, W, It, R, 1966 S, I, E, W, It, R, 1967 S, A, E, SA 1,2,3,4, NZ, 1968 S, I, E, W, NZ 1,2,3, A, SA 1,2, R, 1969 S, I, W, 1970 R, 1971 E, W, SA 1, 1972 E, I 2, A 1,2, R, 1973 S, NZ, E, W, I
Stener, G (PUC) 1956 S, I, E, 1958 SA 1,2
Struxiano, P (Toulouse) 1913 W, I, 1920 S, E, W, I, US
Sutra, G (Narbonne) 1967 SA 2, 1969 W, 1970 S, I
Swierczinski, C (Bègles) 1969 E, 1977 Arg 2
Szarzewski, D (Béziers, SF) 2004 C(R), 2005 I(R),A1,2, SA3, 2006 S,E(R),W(t&R),R(R),SA,NZ1,2(R),Arg(R), 2007 It(R),E2(R), W2,[Arg1(R),Nm,I(R),Gg(R),NZ(R),E(R)], 2008 S(R),I,E,It,W, Arg,PI,A3, 2009 I,S,W,E,It,NZ1(R),2(R),A,SA(R),Sm,NZ3(R), 2010 S(R),I(R),W(R),It(R),E(R),SA,Arg1
Tabacco, P (SF) 2001 SA 1,2, NZ, SA 3, A, Fj, 2003 It (R), W (R), Arg 1, NZ, E 2(R),3, [S(R),US,I(R),NZ], 2004 US, 2005 S
Tachdjian, M (RCF) 1991 S, I, E
Taffary, M (RCF) 1975 W, E, S, I
Taillantou, J (Pau) 1930 I, G, W
Tarricq, P (Lourdes) 1958 A, W, It, I
Tavernier, H (Toulouse) 1913 I
Téchoueyres, W (SBUC) 1994 E, S, 1995 [Iv]
Terreau, M-M (Bourg) 1945 W, 1946 B, I, K, W, 1947 S, I, W, E, 1948 I, A, W, E, 1949 S, Arg 1,2, 1951 S
Theuriet, A (SCUF) 1909 E, W, 1910 S, 1911 W, 1913 E
Thevenot, M (SCUF) 1910 W, E, I
Thierry, R (RCF) 1920 S, E, W, US
Thiers, P (Montferrand) 1936 G 1,2, 1937 G, It, 1938 G 1,2, 1940 B, 1945 B, 1,2
Thiéry, B (Bayonne, Biarritz) 2007 NZ1,2(R), 2008 A1,2
Thion, J (Perpignan, Biarritz) 2003 Arg 1,2, NZ, R, E 2, [Fj,S,I,E], 2004 A,Arg,NZ 2005 S,E,W,I,It,A2,C,Tg,SA3, 2006 S,I,It,E,W,R(R),SA, 2007 It,I(R),W1,E1,S,E2,3,W2, [Arg 1,I,Gg, NZ,E,Arg 2], 2008 E(R),It,W, 2009 E,It(R)
Tignol, P (Toulouse) 1953 S, I
Tilh, H (Nantes) 1912 W, E, 1913 S, SA, E, W
Tillous-Borde, S (Castres) 2008 A1(R),2,PI(R),A3, 2009 I,S,W(R),E(R)
Tolot, J-L (Agen) 1987 [Z]
Tomas, J (Clermont-Auvergne, Montpellier) 2008 It(R),A3(R)
Tordo, J-F (Nice) 1991 US 1(R), 1992 W, E, S, I, R, Arg 1,2, SA 1, Arg, 1993 E, S, I, W, R 1
Torossian, F (Pau) 1997 R 1
Torreilles, S (Perpignan) 1956 S
Tournaire, F (Narbonne, Toulouse) 1995 It, 1996 I, W 1, R, Arg 1,2(R), W 2, SA 1,2, 1997 I, E, S, It 1, R 1, A 1,2, It 2, R 2, Arg, SA 1,2, 1998 E, S, I, W, Arg 1,2, Fj, Arg 3, A, 1999 I, W 1, E, S, R (R), WS, NZ 1, [C, Nm, Fj, Arg, NZ 2, A], 2000 W, E, S, I, It, A (R)
Tourte, R (St Girons) 1940 B
Traille, D (Pau, Biarritz) 2001 SA 3, A, Fj, 2002 It, W, E, S, I, Arg, A 1,2, SA, NZ, C, 2003 E 1, S, I, It, W, Arg, 1,2, NZ, R, E 2, [Fj(R),J,S(R),US,NZ], 2004 I,It,W,S,E, 2005 S,E,W,It(R), SA1(R),2,A1(R), 2006 It,E,W,R,SA,NZ1,2,Arg, 2007 S(R),E2,3, W2(R), [Arg 1,Nm,I,NZ,E], 2008 S,I,E,It(R),W,A1,PI(R),A3(R), 2009 E(R),It,NZ1,2,A,SA,Sm(R),NZ3
Trillo, J (Bègles) 1967 SA 3,4, NZ, R, 1968 S, I, NZ 1,2,3, A, 1969 I, E, W, R, 1970 E, R, 1971 S, I, SA 1,2, A 1,2, 1972 S, A 1,2, R, 1973 S, E
Trinh-Duc, F (Montpellier) 2008 S,I(R),E,It,W(R),A1,2, 2009 W(R),E,It,NZ1,2,SA,Sm,NZ3, 2010 S,I,W,It,E,SA,Arg1
Triviaux, R (Cognac) 1931 E, G
Tucco-Chala, M (PUC) 1940 B
Ugartemendia, J-L (St Jean-de-Luz) 1975 S, I
Vaills, G (Perpignan) 1928 A, 1929 G
Valbon, L (Brive) 2004 US, 2005 S(R), 2006 S,E(R), 2007 NZ1(R)
Vallot, C (SCUF) 1912 S
Van Heerden, A (Tarbes) 1992 E, S
Vannier, M (RCF, Chalon) 1953 W, 1954 S, I, Arg 1,2, 1955 S, I, E, W, It, 1956 S, I, W, It, E, 1957 S, I, E, W, It, R 1,2, 1958 S, E, A, W, It, I, 1960 S, E, W, I, It, R, Arg 1,3, 1961 SA, E, W, It, I, NZ 1, A
Vaquer, F (Perpignan) 1921 S, W, 1922 W
Vaquerin, A (Béziers) 1971 R, 1972 S, I 1, A 1, 1973 S, 1974 W, E, S, Arg 1,2, R, SA 1,2, 1975 W, E, S, I, 1976 US, A 1(R),2, R, 1977 Arg 2, 1979 W, E, 1980 S, I
Vareilles, C (SF) 1907 E, 1908 E, W, 1910 S, E
Varenne, F (RCF) 1952 S
Varvier, T (RCF) 1906 E, 1909 E, W, 1911 E, W, 1912 I
Vassal, G (Carcassonne) 1938 R, G 2
Vaysse, J (Albi) 1924 US, 1926 M
Vellat, E (Grenoble) 1927 I, E, G 1,2, 1928 A
Venditti, D (Bourgoin, Brive) 1996 R, SA 1(R),2, 1997 I, W, E, S, R 1, A 1, SA 2, 2000 W (R), E, S, It (R)
Vergé, L (Bègles) 1993 R 1(R)
Verger, A (SF) 1927 W, E, G 1, 1928 I, E, G, W
Verges, S-A (SF) 1906 NZ, E, 1907 E
Vermeulen, E (Brive, Montferrand, Clermont-Auvergne) 2001 SA 1(R),2(R), 2003 NZ, 2006 NZ1,2,Arg, 2007 W1,S(R), 2008 S,W(R)
Viard, G (Narbonne) 1969 W, 1970 S, R, 1971 S, I
Viars, S (Brive) 1992 W, E, I, R, Arg 1,2, SA 1,2(R), Arg, 1993 R 1, 1994 C 1(R), NZ 1(t), 1995 E (R), [Iv], 1997 R 1(R), A 1(R),2
Vigerie, M (Agen) 1931 W

Vigier, R (Montferrand) 1956 S, W, It, E, Cz, 1957 S, E, W, It, R 1,2, 1958 S, E, A, W, It, I, SA 1,2, 1959 S, E, It, W, I
Vigneau, A (Bayonne) 1935 G
Vignes, C (RCF) 1957 R 1,2, 1958 S, E
Vila, E (Tarbes) 1926 M
Vilagra, J (Vienne) 1945 B 2
Villepreux, P (Toulouse) 1967 It, I, SA 2, NZ, 1968 I, Cz, NZ 1,2,3, A, 1969 S, I, E, W, R, 1970 S, I, W, E, R, 1971 S, I, E, W, A 1,2, R, 1972 S, I 1, E, W, I 2, A 1,2
Viviès, B (Agen) 1978 E, S, I, W, 1980 SA, R, 1981 S, A 1, 1983 A 1(R)
Volot, M (SF) 1945 W, 1946 B, I, K, W
Weller, S (Grenoble) 1989 A 1,2, 1990 A 1, NZ 1
Wolf, J-P (Béziers) 1980 SA, R, 1981 A 2, 1982 E
Yachvili, D (Biarritz) 2002 C (R), 2003 S (R), I, It, W, R (R), E 3, [US,NZ], 2004 I(R), It(R),W(R),S,E, 2005 S(R),E,W,I,It, SA1(R),2,C,Tg, 2006 S(R),I(R),It(R),E,W,SA, NZ1,2(R),Arg, 2007 E1, 2008 E(R),It,W(R),A1,2(R), 2009 NZ1(R),2(R),A, 2010 It(R),SA(R),Arg1(R)
Yachvili, M (Tulle, Brive) 1968 E, W, Cz, NZ 3, A, R, 1969 S, I, R, 1971 E, SA 1,2 A 1, 1972 R, 1975 SA 2
Zago, F (Montauban) 1963 I, E

Richard Heathcote/Getty Images

Sylvain Marconnet became the latest Frenchman through the 80-cap barrier in 2010.

THE IRB/EMIRATES AIRLINE RUGBY PHOTOGRAPH OF THE YEAR 2010

Now in its fifth year, the IRB/Emirates Airline Rugby Photograph of the Year, celebrating superb rugby pictures which capture the 'Spirit of Rugby', continues to flourish.

This year more than 350 entries were received with the shortlist showing rugby played in an icy blizzard in Stockport, England to the sun-baked ground of Kolkata and the drenched turf of Loftus Versfeld in Pretoria, with striking images from Women's Rugby World Cup 2010, the IRB Sevens World Series, Heineken and Vodacom Cups. Tasked with finding the photograph which best illustrates the 'Spirit of Rugby', this year's judging panel had quite a challenge to select the six images you see here which make up the shortlist and, of course, the one winner.

This year's judging panel was: Paul Morgan, editor of the IRB Yearbook and Rugby World magazine; Barry Newcombe, Chair of the Sports Journalists Association; world renowned sports photographer Dave Rogers from Getty Images, Joelle Watkins, Emirates Corporate Communications Manager – UK & Ireland, Andrea Wiggins, IRB communications manager and Jim Drewett, editorial director of Vision Sports Publishing.

The prize for the winner is a trip for two to the Emirates Airline Dubai Rugby Sevens, courtesy of Emirates Airline.

For details of how to enter the 2011 competition, see the back page of this picture section.

THE RUNNERS-UP: IN NO PARTICULAR ORDER

◀ Burning Desire

Lee Warren (Action Images)

Mpho Mbiyozo of South Africa at the Emirates Airline Dubai Rugby Sevens match between South Africa and Australia at The Sevens on December 5, 2009.

▼ Semi's Delight

Michael Paler

Lindsay Morgan and Danielle Meskell celebrate Australia reaching a first-ever Women's Rugby World Cup semi-final following an emphatic 62-0 victory over South Africa at Surrey Sports Park in Guildford.

▲ England's Magnificent Flying Machine

Lissy Tomlinson (Rugbymatters)

Women's Rugby World Cup star England's Maggie Alphonsi – nicknamed 'Maggie the Machine' by pundits – brushes aside Ireland's Niamh Briggs in their opening fixture at Surrey Sports Park in Guildford.

▲ Desperate Stretch

Christiaan Kotze

Vaion Willis of the Blue Bulls tries to place the ball over the try-line during a Vodacom Cup match between the Blue Bulls and Western Province at a drenched Loftus Versfeld in Pretoria, South Africa.

▲ Snow Blizzard

Paul Thomas (Action Images)
Taken at the Heineken Cup Pool Five match between Sale Sharks and Harlequins at Edgeley Park, Stockport, on December 20, 2009. Players from Sale Sharks and Harlequins continue to play on through blizzard snow conditions, while behind the scenes groundstaff struggle to keep the pitch markings visible.

AND THE WINNER IS...

Richard Lane

Taken on April 3, 2010, Bengal Khuki shows a group of girls playing rugby at an orphanage outside Kolkata in India during a trip to coach rugby union to children organised by the England-based charity Rugby Uncle.

Richard Lane says: *"I went to India with Sailen Tudu, the young India international rugby player who moved to England and was playing in Gloucester for Hartpury College. He wanted to return to India to give something back to the kids there as rugby had provided him with such a change of direction in his life. So, a few of us went to Kolkata for two weeks on a coaching trip with him, and one of the places we visited was the Ashalayam orphanage. It was heartbreaking at first, the girls were all orphans who had been rescued from a life as street kids having either lost their parents or their parents just couldn't afford to keep them. The thing that amazed me was how much they loved playing rugby given they had never even seen a rugby ball before! It was hard to coach them as we didn't speak Bengali and they didn't speak English but they played with such joy. It was a very memorable moment for me."*

Bengal Khuki

GEORGIA

GEORGIA'S 2009–10 TEST RECORD

OPPONENTS	DATE	VENUE	RESULT
Argentina Jaguars	14 Nov	H	**Won** 24–22
Italy A	20 Nov	A	**Lost** 7–8
Germany	6 Feb	H	**Won** 77–3
Portugal	13 Feb	A	**Won** 16–10
Spain	27 Feb	H	**Won** 17–9
Romania	13 Mar	A	**Lost** 10–22
Russia	20 Mar	N	**Won** 36–8
Scotland A	11 Jun	N	**Won** 22–21
Italy A	15 Jun	N	**Lost** 3–21
Namibia	20 Jun	N	**Lost** 16–21

GEORGIANS OFF TO THE SUMMIT

By Lúcás Ó'Ceallacháin

AFP

Wins like this one over Spain sent Georgia to Rugby World Cup 2011.

Georgian rugby will long remember the achievements of 2010 – a year which saw them again dominate the European Nations Cup to successfully defend their crown and in the process claim a place at Rugby World Cup 2011 in New Zealand.

The culmination of the two-year European Nations Cup saw Georgia record victories over Germany 77–3, Portugal 16–10 and Spain 17–9 while suffering their first loss of the competition, 22–10 to a Romanian side desperate for victory to keep their own hopes of World Cup qualification alive.

Georgia were already assured of their RWC 2011 place before this defeat in Bucharest, just not the pool they would slot into as either the Europe 1 or Europe 2 qualifier. This meant that the match with rivals Russia would not only determine the European Nations Cup champion, but also this key criteria.

Russia, who were guaranteed their own piece of history with a first Rugby World Cup qualification following a draw against Romania, were coming off some encouraging performances against Canada and Namibia, with a new coaching team in place and significant preparation.

Political issues between the Russian and Georgian governments meant that the title decider was a 'home' game for Georgia at the Akçabaat Fatih Stadium in Trabzon, Turkey. However, the neutral venue did nothing to dampen the atmosphere.

"The stadium was in a beautiful location near the Black Sea, with mountains on one side," recalled Richie Dixon, a former technical advisor to the Georgian Rugby Union (GRU) who would succeed Tim Lane as coach in July 2010.

"It seemed as though thousands of Georgian fans had travelled for the game, which is always Georgia's biggest.

"The game also sparked real interest locally, so much so that I could see people sitting out on their balconies and rooftops to catch a glimpse of the encounter at the stadium!"

A Georgian team packed with players from France's top clubs duly overwhelmed Russia 36–8. A commanding performance full of confidence and experience saw Georgia emerge as comfortable winners to qualify for Rugby World Cup 2011 as Europe 1.

Ilia Zedginidze, the second-row who captained Georgia at RWC 2007 in France, admitted: "It will be a great honour to take part in the Rugby World Cup again.

"For Georgian rugby, still another World Cup appearance means a big surge in popularity, which will bring a fresh wave of children and teenagers into youth rugby teams, another boost for development, another chance to move forward.

"And as regards myself, I am happy to be a part of this process and grateful to everyone who supports us on our way."

Georgia's qualification had been assured a month earlier with victory over Spain at the National Stadium in Tbilisi. Spain did take the lead with a third minute penalty by centre Jaime Nava, but Georgia No 8 Besarion Udesiani crossed for the opening try just after the half hour mark with Merab Kvirikashvili kicking the conversion for a 7–3 half-time advantage.

Five minutes after the restart flanker Lasha Tavartkiladze scored to increase Georgia's advantage, but it was not until 11 minutes from time that prop Goderdzi Shvelidze touched down to enable the home side to breathe easier.

The visitors did have the final say with two more penalties from Nava, but it was Georgia celebrating come the final whistle with qualification confirmed and a successful defence of their European Nations Cup crown within touching distance.

Georgia can now look forward to joining Argentina, England, Scotland and the winners of the cross-continental play-off between Romania and Uruguay – which takes place in November – in Pool B at RWC 2011.

The pool is sure to provide some monumental scrummaging between Los Pumas and the Lelos, who have both turned the scrum into the cornerstone of their play. Davit Zirakishvili against his Clermont team-mate Mario Ledesma will certainly be worth watching out for!

As ever, Georgia struggled throughout the season with managing the release of players from their clubs in France, but since their performance at Rugby World Cup 2007, the players have become more assertive when negotiating release to the national set-up.

"It's always a struggle, but we just have to get on with it. It means we can see new players in action and give more experience to the younger guys," explained Dixon. "As long as our players keep playing rugby the way they do, they will continue to attract interest from overseas."

With World Cup qualification secured, the GRU could afford to use the IRB Nations Cup to blood new players, and they travelled to the Romanian capital Bucharest in June with almost none of their senior internationals.

Despite the absence of so many experienced players, they produced a great performance to defeat defending champions Scotland A 22–21. Defeats to Italy A 21–3 and eventual winners Namibia 21–16 were close games that showed some real promise for the next generation of Georgia-based players.

"What's important now is that we have regular competition for all our players, whether home based or overseas," explained Dixon.

"Government support has meant that we have been able to establish two academies in Georgia at Tbilisi and Kutaisi where the next tier of players get top class coaching and advice on conditioning, nutrition and professional sport. This is part of the GRU's Long-Term Athlete Development (LTAD) and allows us to focus not only on development, but also performance."

The Scot is also excited about regional and domestic competitions. "Rugby is the number one team sport in Georgia, which means the Government has really gotten behind us in terms of support. They have promised funding for the top eight club sides in the country and while the funding available won't be like the salaries that are on offer in France, it will allow players to develop as professional athletes in Georgia and to remain in Georgia.

"What's important is that we have a foundation internationally, but now we need to ensure we have the same domestically. This means putting the right structures in place now to deliver bigger and better results internationally. The GRU has become a highly professionalised organisation and can now tap in to the vast experience of players who have played at World Cups or in the Heineken Cup."

In 2011, there is expected to be even more growth at grassroots level in Georgia, not to mention continued strong performances in the European Nations Cup. However, many will be looking towards the World Cup to see if Dixon's charges can build on their performance in 2007 when the Lelos came within minutes of claiming Ireland's scalp. If they can, then Georgia should pose a real threat to Scotland and the Play-off Winner, be it Romania or Uruguay.

Mike Hewitt/Getty Images

Georgia have benefited from the experience of former Scotland coach Richie Dixon.

GEORGIA INTERNATIONAL RECORDS

MATCH RECORDS UP TO 29TH OCTOBER 2010

WINNING MARGIN

Date	Opponent	Result	Winning Margin
07/04/2007	Czech Republic	98–3	**95**
03/02/2002	Netherlands	88–0	**88**
06/02/2010	Germany	77–3	**74**
26/02/2005	Ukraine	65–0	**65**
12/06/2005	Czech Republic	75–10	**65**

MOST DROP GOALS IN A MATCH

BY THE TEAM

Date	Opponent	Result	DGs
20/10/1996	Russia	29–20	**2**
21/11/1991	Ukraine	19–15	**2**
15/07/1992	Ukraine	15–0	**2**
04/06/1994	Switzerland	22–21	**2**

MOST POINTS IN A MATCH

BY THE TEAM

Date	Opponent	Result	Pts.
07/04/2007	Czech Republic	98–3	**98**
03/02/2002	Netherlands	88–0	**88**
06/02/2010	Germany	77–3	**77**
12/06/2005	Czech Republic	75–10	**75**

MOST POINTS IN A MATCH

BY A PLAYER

Date	Player	Opponent	Pts.
06/02/2010	Merab Kvirikashvili	Germany	**32**
08/03/2003	Pavle Jimsheladze	Russia	**23**
07/04/2007	Merab Kvirikashvili	Czech Republic	**23**
12/06/2005	Malkhaz Urjukashvili	Czech Republic	**20**
28/02/2009	Lasha Malaguradze	Spain	**20**

MOST TRIES IN A MATCH

BY THE TEAM

Date	Opponent	Result	Tries
07/04/2007	Czech Republic	98–3	**16**
03/02/2002	Netherlands	88–0	**14**
23/03/1995	Bulgaria	70–8	**11**
26/02/2005	Ukraine	65–0	**11**
12/06/2005	Czech Republic	75–10	**11**
06/02/2010	Germany	77–3	**11**

MOST TRIES IN A MATCH

BY A PLAYER

Date	Player	Opponent	Tries
23/03/1995	Pavle Jimsheladze	Bulgaria	**3**
23/03/1995	Archil Kavtarashvili	Bulgaria	**3**
12/06/2005	Mamuka Gorgodze	Czech Republic	**3**
07/04/2007	David Dadunashvili	Czech Republic	**3**
07/04/2007	Malkhaz Urjukashvili	Czech Republic	**3**
26/04/2008	Mamuka Gorgodze	Spain	**3**

MOST CONVERSIONS IN A MATCH

BY THE TEAM

Date	Opponent	Result	Cons
06/02/2010	Germany	77–3	**11**
03/02/2002	Netherlands	88–0	**9**
07/04/2007	Czech Republic	98–3	**9**
12/06/2005	Czech Republic	75–10	**7**

MOST CONVERSIONS IN A MATCH

BY A PLAYER

Date	Player	Opponent	Cons
06/02/2010	Merab Kvirikashvili	Germany	**11**
03/02/2002	Pavle Jimsheladze	Netherlands	**9**
07/04/2007	Merab Kvirikashvili	Czech Republic	**9**
12/06/2005	Malkhaz Urjukashvili	Czech Republic	**7**

MOST PENALTIES IN A MATCH

BY THE TEAM

Date	Opponent	Result	Pens
08/03/2003	Russia	23–17	**6**

MOST PENALTIES IN A MATCH BY A PLAYER

Date	Player	Opponent	Pens
08/03/2003	Pavle Jimsheladze	Russia	6

MOST DROP GOALS IN A MATCH BY A PLAYER

Date	Player	Opponent	DGs
15/07/1992	Davit Chavleishvili	Ukraine	2

MOST CAPPED PLAYERS

Player	Caps
Malkhaz Urjukashvili	63
Irakli Abuseridze	62
Grigol Labadze	59
Pavle Jimsheladze	57
Ilia Zedginidze	57

LEADING TRY SCORERS

Player	Tries
Malkhaz Urjukashvili	17
Mamuka Gorgodze	17
Irakli Machkhaneli	15
Ilia Zedginidze	14

LEADING CONVERSIONS SCORERS

Player	Cons
Pavle Jimsheladze	61
Merab Kvirikashvili	50
Malkhaz Urjukashvili	41

LEADING PENALTY SCORERS

Player	Pens
Pavle Jimsheladze	48
Malkhaz Urjukashvili	40
Nugzar Dzagnidze	22
Merab Kvirikashvili	22

LEADING DROP GOAL SCORERS

Player	DGs
Kakha Machitidze	4
Nugzar Dzagnidze	3
Pavle Jimsheladze	3
Lasha Malaguradze	3

LEADING POINTS SCORERS

Player	Pts.
Pavle Jimsheladze	320
Malkhaz Urjukashvili	290
Merab Kvirikashvili	192
Nugzar Dzagnidze	105

GEORGIA INTERNATIONAL PLAYERS

UP TO 29TH OCTOBER 2010

Note: Years given for International Championship matches are for second half of season; eg 1972 means season 1971–72. Years for all other matches refer to the actual year of the match.

V Abashidze 1998 *It, Ukr, I,* 1999 *Tg, Tg,* 2000 *It, Mor, Sp,* 2001 *H, Pt, Rus, Sp, R,* 2006 *J*
N Abdaladze 1997 *Cro, De*
I Abuseridze 2000 *It, Pt, Mor, Sp, H, R,* 2001 *H, Pt, Rus, Sp, R,* 2002 *Pt, Rus, Sp, R, I, Rus,* 2003 *Pt, Rus, CZR, R, It, E, Sa, SA,* 2004 *Rus,* 2005 *Pt, Ukr, R,* 2006 *Rus, R, Pt, Ukr, J, R, Sp, Pt, Pt,* 2007 *R, Rus, CZR, Nm, ESp, ItA, Ar, I, Nm, F,* 2008 *Pt, R, Pt, Rus, Sp,* 2009 *Ger, Pt, Sp, R, Rus, ItA,* 2010 *Pt, Sp, R, Rus*
V Akhvlediani 2007 *CZR*
K Alania 1993 *Lux,* 1994 *Swi,* 1996 *CZR, CZR, Rus,* 1997 *Pt, Pol, Cro, De,* 1998 *It,* 2001 *H, Pt, Sp, F, SA,* 2002 *H, Pt, Rus, Sp, R, I, Rus,* 2003 *Rus,* 2004 *Pt, Sp*
N Andghuladze 1997 *Pol,* 2000 *It, Pt, Mor, Sp, H, R,* 2004 *Sp, Rus, CZR, R*
D Ashvetia 1998 *Ukr,* 2005 *Pt,* 2006 *R,* 2007 *Sp*
K Asieshvili 2008 *ItA,* 2010 *S, ItA, Nm*
G Babunashvili 1992 *Ukr, Ukr, Lat,* 1993 *Rus, Pol, Lux,* 1996 *CZR*
Z Bakuradze 1989 *Z,* 1990 *Z,* 1991 *Ukr, Ukr,* 1993 *Rus, Pol*
D Baramidze 2000 *H*
O Barkalaia 2002 *I,* 2004 *Sp, Rus, CZR, R, Ur, CHL, Rus,* 2005 *Pt, Ukr, R, CZR, CHL,* 2006 *Rus, R, Pt, Ukr, J, Bb, R, Sp,* 2007 *Nm, ItA, I, F,* 2008 *Pt, R, Pt, Rus, Sp, ESp, Ur, ItA,* 2009 *Ger, Sp, R*
D Basilaia 2008 *Pt, R, Pt, CZR, Rus, Sp,* 2009 *Ger, Sp, R, C, US, ItA*
R Belkania 2004 *Sp,* 2005 *CHL,* 2007 *Sp, Rus*
G Beriashvili 1993 *Rus, Pol,* 1995 *Ger*
M Besselia 1991 *Ukr,* 1993 *Rus, Pol,* 1996 *Rus,* 1997 *Pt*
D Bolgashvili 2000 *It, Pt, H, R,* 2001 *H, Pt, Rus, Sp, R, F, SA,* 2002 *H, Pt, Rus, I,* 2003 *Pt, Sp, Rus, CZR, R, E, Sa, SA,* 2004 *Rus, Ur, CHL, Rus,* 2005 *CZR,* 2007 *Sp,* 2010 *ItA*
J Bregvadze 2008 *ESp, ItA,* 2009 *C, IrA,* 2010 *Sp, R, S, Nm*
G Buguianishvili 1996 *CZR, Rus,* 1997 *Pol,* 1998 *It, Rus, I, R,* 2000 *Sp, H, R,* 2001 *H, F, SA,* 2002 *Rus*
D Chavleishvili 1990 *Z, Z,* 1992 *Ukr, Ukr, Lat,* 1993 *Pol, Lux*
M Cheishvili 1989 *Z,* 1990 *Z, Z,* 1995 *H*
D Chichua 2008 *CZR*
I Chikava 1993 *Pol, Lux,* 1994 *Swi,* 1995 *Bul, Mol, H,* 1996 *CZR, CZR,* 1997 *Pol,* 1998 *I*
R Chikvaidze 2004 *Ur, CHL*
L Chikvinidze 1994 *Swi,* 1995 *Bul, Mol, Ger, H,* 1996 *CZR, Rus*
G Chkhaidze 2002 *H, R, I, Rus,* 2003 *Pt, CZR, It, E, SA, Ur,* 2004 *CZR, R,* 2006 *Pt, Ukr,* 2007 *R, Rus, CZR, Nm, ESp, ItA, Ar, I, Nm, F,* 2008 *R, Pt, CZR, Rus, Sp,* 2009 *Ger, Pt, Sp, R, Rus, ItA,* 2010 *Ger, Pt, Sp, R, Rus*
S Chkhenkeli 1997 *Pol*
I Chkhikvadze 2005 *CHL,* 2007 *Sp,* 2008 *Pt, R, Pt, CZR, Rus, ESp, Ur, ItA,* 2009 *Ger, Sp, ItA,* 2010 *Sp, Rus, S, ItA, Nm*
I Chkonia 2007 *ESp, ItA*
D Dadunashvili 2003 *It, E, SA, Ur,* 2004 *Sp, Rus, CZR, R,* 2005 *CHL,* 2007 *Sp, Rus, CZR, Nm, ItA,* 2008 *Pt, R, Pt, CZR, Rus, Sp,* 2009 *C, IrA, US,* 2010 *Sp, S, ItA, Nm*
L Datunashvili 2004 *Sp,* 2005 *Pt, Ukr, R, CZR,* 2006 *Rus, R, Pt, Ukr, J, Bb, CZR, Pt, Pt,* 2007 *R, Rus, Nm, ESp, ItA, I, Nm, F,* 2008 *Pt, Pt,* 2009 *Sp, R, Rus, C, US,* 2010 *Ger, Pt, Sp, R, Rus*
V Didebulidze 1991 *Ukr,* 1994 *Kaz,* 1995 *Bul, Mol,* 1996 *CZR,* 1997 *De,* 1999 *Tg,* 2000 *H,* 2001 *H, Pt, Rus, Sp, R, F, SA,* 2002 *H, Pt, Rus, Sp, R, I, Rus,* 2003 *Pt, Sp, Rus, CZR, R, It, E, Sa, SA,* 2004 *Rus,* 2005 *Pt,* 2006 *R, R,* 2007 *R, Sp, Rus, CZR, Nm, ESp, ItA, Ar, Nm, F*
E Dzagnidze 1992 *Ukr, Ukr, Lat,* 1993 *Rus, Pol,* 1995 *Bul, Mol, Ger, H,* 1998 *I*
N Dzagnidze 1989 *Z,* 1990 *Z, Z,* 1991 *Ukr,* 1992 *Ukr, Ukr, Lat,* 1993 *Rus, Pol,* 1994 *Swi,* 1995 *Ger, H*
T Dzagnidze 2008 *ESp*
D Dzneladze 1992 *Ukr, Lat,* 1993 *Lux,* 1994 *Kaz*
P Dzotsenidze 1995 *Ger, H,* 1997 *Pt, Pol*
G Elizbarashvili 2002 *Rus,* 2003 *Sp,* 2004 *CHL,* 2005 *CZR,* 2006 *Pt, Ukr, J, Bb, CZR, Sp, Pt,* 2007 *R, Sp, Rus, I, F,* 2009 *C, IrA*
O Eloshvili 2002 *H,* 2003 *SA,* 2006 *Bb, CZR,* 2007 *Sp, CZR, Nm, ESp, ItA, I, F*
S Essakia 1999 *Tg, Tg,* 2000 *It, Mor, Sp, H,* 2004 *CZR, R*
M Gagnidze 1991 *Ukr, Ukr*
D Gasviani 2004 *Sp, Rus,* 2005 *CZR, CHL,* 2006 *Ukr, J,* 2007 *Rus, CZR,* 2008 *ESp, Ur, ItA*
A Ghibradze 1992 *Ukr, Ukr, Lat,* 1994 *Swi,* 1995 *Bul, Mol, Ger,* 1996 *CZR*
D Ghudushauri 1989 *Z,* 1991 *Ukr, Ukr*
L Ghvaberidze 2004 *Pt*
R Gigauri 2006 *Ukr, J, Bb, CZR, Sp, Pt, Pt,* 2007 *R, Nm, ESp, ItA, Ar, Nm, F,* 2008 *Pt, R, Pt, Rus, Sp, ESp, Ur,* 2009 *C, IrA, US, ItA,* 2010 *S, ItA, Nm*
A Giorgadze 1996 *CZR,* 1998 *It, Ukr, Rus, R,* 1999 *Tg, Tg,* 2000 *It, Pt, Mor, H, R,* 2001 *H, Pt, Rus, Sp, R, F, SA,* 2002 *H, Pt, Rus, Sp, R, I, Rus,* 2003 *Pt, Sp, Rus, R, It, E, Sa, SA, Ur,* 2005 *Pt, Ukr, R, CZR,* 2006 *Rus, R, Pt, Bb, CZR, Sp, Pt,* 2007 *R, Ar, I, Nm, F,* 2009 *Ger, Pt, Sp,* 2010 *Ger, Pt*
I Giorgadze 2001 *F, SA,* 2003 *Pt, Sp, Rus, R, It, E, Sa, Ur,* 2004 *Rus,* 2005 *Pt, R, CZR,* 2006 *Rus, R, Pt, Bb, CZR, R, Sp, Pt, Pt,* 2007 *R, Sp, Rus, CZR, Ar, Nm, F,* 2008 *R,* 2009 *Ger, Pt, Sp, Rus,* 2010 *Ger, Sp, R, Rus*
M Gorgodze 2003 *Sp, Rus,* 2004 *Pt, Sp, Rus, CZR, R, Ur, CHL, Rus,* 2005 *Pt, Ukr, R, CZR, CHL,* 2006 *Rus, Pt, Bb, CZR, R, Sp, Pt, Pt,* 2007 *Ar, I, Nm,* 2008 *R, Rus, Sp,* 2009 *Ger, Pt, Sp, R, Rus*
E Gueguchadze 1990 *Z, Z*
L Gugava 2004 *Sp, Rus, CZR, Ur, CHL, Rus,* 2005 *Pt, Ukr,* 2006 *Bb, CZR,* 2009 *C, IrA*
I Guiorkhelidze 1998 *R,* 1999 *Tg, Tg*
G Guiunashvili 1989 *Z,* 1990 *Z,* 1991 *Ukr, Ukr,* 1992 *Ukr, Ukr, Lat,* 1993 *Rus, Pol, Lux,* 1994 *Swi,* 1996 *Rus,* 1997 *Pt*
K Guiunashvili 1990 *Z, Z,* 1991 *Ukr, Ukr,* 1992 *Ukr, Ukr, Lat*
B Gujaraidze 2008 *ESp*
S Gujaraidze 2003 *SA, Ur*
I Gundishvili 2002 *I,* 2003 *Pt, Sp, Rus, CZR,* 2008 *ESp, Ur, ItA,* 2009 *C, US*
D Gurgenidze 2007 *Sp, ItA*
A Gusharashvili 1998 *Ukr*
D Iobidze 1993 *Rus, Pol*
E Iovadze 1993 *Lux,* 1994 *Kaz,* 1995 *Bul, Mol, Ger, H,* 2001 *Sp, F, SA,* 2002 *H, Rus, Sp, R, I*
A Issakadze 1989 *Z*
N Iurini 1991 *Ukr,* 1994 *Swi,* 1995 *Ger, H,* 1996 *CZR, CZR, Rus,* 1997 *Pt, Pol, Cro, De,* 1998 *Ukr, Rus,* 2000 *It, Sp, H, R*

S Janelidze 1991 *Ukr, Ukr,* 1993 *Rus,* 1994 *Kaz,* 1995 *Ger,* 1997 *Pt,* 1998 *Ukr, I, R,* 1999 *Tg,* 2000 *R*
R Japarashvili 1992 *Ukr, Ukr, Lat,* 1993 *Pol, Lux,* 1996 *CZR,* 1997 *Pt*
L Javelidze 1997 *Cro,* 1998 *I,* 2001 *H, R, F, SA,* 2002 *H, R,* 2004 *R,* 2005 *Ukr,* 2007 *Sp*
G Jgenti 2004 *Ur,* 2005 *CHL,* 2007 *Sp, CZR, Nm, ESp, ItA,* 2009 *C, IrA, US*
D Jghenti 2004 *CZR, R*
D Jhamutashvili 2005 *CHL*
P Jimsheladze 1995 *Bul, Mol, H,* 1996 *CZR, CZR, Rus,* 1997 *De,* 1998 *It, Ukr, Rus, I, R,* 1999 *Tg, Tg,* 2000 *Pt, Mor, Sp, H, R,* 2001 *H, Pt, Rus, Sp, R, F, SA,* 2002 *H, Pt, Rus, Sp, I, Rus,* 2003 *Pt, Sp, Rus, CZR, R, It, E, Sa, SA, Ur,* 2004 *Rus,* 2005 *R,* 2006 *Rus, R, Pt, Ukr, J, Bb, CZR, Pt, Pt,* 2007 *R, Rus, CZR, Ar*
K Jintcharadze 1993 *Rus, Pol,* 2000 *It, Mor*
D Kacharava 2006 *Ukr, J, R, Sp, Pt,* 2007 *R, Sp, Rus, CZR, Nm, ESp, ItA, I, Nm,* 2008 *Pt, R, Pt, CZR, Rus, Sp,* 2009 *Ger, Pt, Sp, R, Rus, C, IrA, US, ItA,* 2010 *Ger, Pt, Sp, R, Rus*
G Kacharava 2005 *Ukr,* 2006 *J, Bb, CZR, R,* 2007 *Sp,* 2008 *CZR*
G Kakhiani 1995 *Bul, Mol*
V Kakovin 2009 *C, IrA, US,* 2010 *S, ItA, Nm*
V Katsadze 1997 *Pol,* 1998 *It, Ukr, Rus, I, R,* 1999 *Tg, Tg,* 2000 *Pt, Mor, Sp, H, R,* 2001 *H, Pt, Rus, Sp, R,* 2002 *Pt, Rus, Sp, R, I, Rus,* 2003 *Pt, Sp, CZR, R, E, Sa, SA, Ur,* 2004 *Sp,* 2005 *Ukr*
A Kavtarashvili 1994 *Swi,* 1995 *Bul, Mol, Ger,* 1996 *CZR, Rus,* 1997 *Pt, Cro, De,* 1998 *It, Rus, I, R,* 1999 *Tg, Tg,* 2000 *It, H, R,* 2001 *H,* 2003 *SA, Ur*
I Kerauli 1991 *Ukr, Ukr,* 1992 *Ukr, Ukr*
L Khachirashvili 2005 *Ukr*
T Khakhaleishili 1994 *Kaz*
B Khamashuridze 1998 *It, Ukr, Rus, I, R,* 1999 *Tg, Tg,* 2000 *It, Pt, Sp, H, R,* 2001 *Pt, Rus, Sp, R, F, SA,* 2002 *H, Pt, Rus, Sp, R, I, Rus,* 2003 *Pt, CZR, R, It, E, Sa, SA, Ur,* 2004 *Pt, Rus, Rus,* 2005 *Pt, Ukr, CHL,* 2006 *Rus, R, Pt, R, Sp, Pt, Pt,* 2007 *Rus, CZR, ESp, Ar, Nm, F,* 2008 *Pt*
B Khamashuridze 1989 *Z*
M Kharshiladze 1991 *Ukr*
B Khekhelashvili 1999 *Tg, Tg,* 2000 *It, Pt, Mor, Sp, H, R,* 2001 *H, Pt, R, F, SA,* 2002 *H, Pt, Rus, Sp, R, I,* 2003 *Sp, Rus, CZR, R, E, Sa,* 2004 *Sp*
D Khinchagashvili 2003 *Sp, CZR,* 2004 *Pt, Sp, Rus,* 2006 *Bb, CZR, Sp, Pt, Pt,* 2007 *R, Rus, Nm, ESp, ItA, Ar, I, Nm,* 2009 *Ger, Pt, Sp, R, Rus, ItA,* 2010 *Ger, Pt, R, Rus*
L Khmaladze 2008 *ESp, ItA,* 2009 *ItA,* 2010 *S, ItA, Nm*
G Khonelidze 2003 *SA*
G Khositashvili 2008 *ESp, Ur, ItA*
N Khuade 1989 *Z,* 1990 *Z, Z,* 1991 *Ukr, Ukr,* 1993 *Rus, Pol, Lux,* 1994 *Swi,* 1995 *Ger*
Z Khutsishvili 1993 *Lux,* 1994 *Kaz, Swi,* 1995 *Bul,* 1996 *CZR*
A Khvedelidze 1989 *Z,* 1990 *Z, Z,* 1991 *Ukr, Ukr,* 1992 *Ukr, Ukr, Lat,* 1993 *Rus, Pol*
I Kiasashvili 2008 *Pt, CZR, Ur,* 2010 *S, Nm*
D Kiknadze 2004 *Rus,* 2005 *Pt, Ukr*
A Kobakhidze 1997 *Cro,* 1998 *I*
K Kobakhidze 1995 *Ger, H,* 1996 *Rus,* 1997 *Pt,* 1998 *It, Ukr, Rus, I, R,* 1999 *Tg,* 2000 *It*
Z Koberidze 2004 *Ur*
V Kolelishvili 2008 *ItA,* 2010 *S, ItA, Nm*
A Kopaleishvili 2004 *Ur*
A Kopaliani 2003 *It, SA, Ur,* 2004 *Pt,* 2005 *Ukr, R,* 2006 *Rus, R, Ukr, J, Bb, CZR, R, Sp, Pt,* 2007 *R, Sp, Rus, CZR, Ar, I, Nm, F*
G Korkelia 2010 *S, ItA*
D Kubriashvili 2008 *Pt, R, Pt, Rus, Sp,* 2009 *Pt, Sp, R, Rus, ItA,* 2010 *Ger, Pt, Sp*
E Kuparadze 2007 *ESp*
G Kutarashvili 2004 *Pt, Sp, CZR, R,* 2005 *CHL,* 2006 *Rus, R, Pt, Ukr, J, R*
B Kvinikhidze 2002 *R,* 2004 *Pt, Sp, CZR, R,* 2005 *CHL*
M Kvirikashvili 2003 *Pt, Sp, CZR, E, Sa, SA, Ur,* 2004 *Rus, CZR, R, CHL,* 2005 *CZR, CHL,* 2007 *R, Sp, Rus, CZR, Nm, ESp, ItA, Ar, I, Nm, F,* 2008 *Pt, CZR, Rus, Sp,* 2009 *Ger, Pt, R, Rus, C, IrA, US, ItA,* 2010 *Ger, Pt, Sp, R, Rus, ItA, Nm*
G Labadze 1996 *CZR, Rus,* 1997 *Pt, Pol, Cro, De,* 1998 *It, Ukr, Rus, I, R,* 1999 *Tg, Tg,* 2000 *It, Pt, Sp, H, R,* 2001 *H, Pt, Rus, Sp, F, SA,* 2002 *Pt, Rus, Sp, R, Rus,* 2003 *Rus, CZR, R, It, E, Sa,* 2004 *Rus,* 2005 *R,* 2006 *Rus, R, Pt, J, R, Pt, Pt,* 2007 *Rus, Ar, Nm,* 2009 *Ger, Pt, Sp, R, Rus, C, IrA, US,* 2010 *Ger, Pt, Sp, R, Rus*
I Lezhava 1991 *Ukr, Ukr,* 1992 *Ukr,* 1995 *Bul*
Z Lezhava 1991 *Ukr,* 1995 *Ger,* 1996 *CZR, CZR, Rus,* 1997 *Pt, Cro, De,* 1998 *It, Rus, R,* 1999 *Tg*
B Liluashvili 1989 *Z,* 1990 *Z, Z*
L Liluashvili 1997 *Pt*
O Liparteliani 1989 *Z,* 1990 *Z, Z*
S Liparteliani 1991 *Ukr,* 1994 *Kaz, Swi,* 1996 *CZR*
Z Liparteliani 1994 *Kaz, Swi,* 1995 *Bul, Mol, Ger, H*
G Lomgadze 2009 *US*
D Losaberidze 2009 *IrA*
M Lossaberidze 1989 *Z*
K Machitidze 1989 *Z,* 1993 *Rus,* 1995 *Bul, Mol, Ger, H,* 1996 *CZR, CZR, Rus,* 1997 *Pt, Pol, Cro, De,* 1998 *It, Ukr, Rus, R,* 1999 *Tg*
I Machkhaneli 2002 *H, R,* 2003 *It, E, Sa, SA, Ur,* 2004 *Pt, Ur, CHL, Rus,* 2005 *Pt, Ukr, R, CZR, CHL,* 2006 *Rus, R, Pt, Bb, CZR, R, Pt,* 2007 *R, Ar, I, Nm,* 2009 *Ger, Pt, Sp, R, Rus, US, ItA,* 2010 *Ger, Pt, Sp, R, Rus*
M Magrakvelidze 1998 *Ukr,* 2000 *Mor,* 2001 *F,* 2002 *Pt, Sp, R,* 2004 *Rus,* 2005 *Pt, R,* 2006 *Bb, CZR, Pt, Pt,* 2007 *R, CZR, Nm, ESp, ItA, I, F*
I Maisuradze 1997 *Cro,* 1998 *It, Ukr,* 1999 *Tg, Tg,* 2004 *Rus, R,* 2005 *CZR,* 2006 *Bb, CZR, R, Pt, Pt,* 2007 *R, Sp, Rus, CZR, ESp, ItA, I, F*
S Maisuradze 2008 *Pt, CZR, Rus, Sp, ESp, Ur, ItA,* 2009 *IrA, US, ItA,* 2010 *S, Nm*
Z Maisuradze 2004 *Pt, Sp, CZR, Ur, CHL, Rus,* 2005 *Ukr, R,* 2006 *Rus, R, Pt, Ukr, J, Bb, CZR, Sp,* 2007 *Nm, ESp, ItA, Ar, I, F,* 2008 *Pt,* 2009 *C, IrA, US*
L Malaguradze 2008 *Pt, R, Pt, CZR, Rus, Sp, ESp, Ur, ItA,* 2009 *Ger, Pt, Sp, R, Rus, C, IrA, US, ItA,* 2010 *Ger, Pt, Sp, R, Rus*
K Margvelashvili 2003 *It, E, Sa, SA*
M Marjanishvili 1990 *Z, Z,* 1992 *Ukr, Ukr, Lat,* 1993 *Rus, Pol, Lux*
A Matchutadze 1993 *Lux,* 1994 *Kaz,* 1995 *Bul, Mol,* 1997 *Pt, Pol, Cro, De*
Z Matiashvili 2003 *Sp,* 2005 *CHL*
G Mchedlishvili 2008 *CZR*
S Melikidze 2008 *CZR, Sp, ESp, ItA*
L Mgueladze 1992 *Ukr, Ukr*
N Mgueladze 1995 *Bul, Mol, H,* 1997 *Pol*
K Mikautadze 2010 *S, ItA, Nm*
I Modebadze 2003 *SA, Ur,* 2004 *Sp*
S Modebadze 1994 *Kaz,* 1995 *Mol,* 1996 *CZR, CZR, Rus,* 1997 *Pt, Pol, Cro, De,* 1998 *It, Ukr, Rus,* 1999 *Tg,* 2000 *It, Pt,* 2001 *Sp, F, SA,* 2002 *H, Pt, Rus, Sp, R*
A Mtchedlishvili 2004 *Ur, CHL,* 2008 *CZR*
S Mtchedlishvili 2000 *It,* 2007 *Sp*
Z Mtchedlishvili 1995 *Mol,* 1996 *CZR,* 1997 *Cro, De,* 1998 *It, Ukr, Rus, I, R,* 1999 *Tg, Tg,* 2000 *Pt, Mor, Sp, H, R,* 2001 *Rus, Sp, R, F, SA,* 2002 *H, Pt, Rus, I, Rus,* 2003 *Pt, Sp, Rus, CZR, R, It, E, Sa, Ur,* 2004 *Pt, Rus,* 2005 *Pt,* 2006 *J,* 2007 *Rus, CZR, Nm, ESp, ItA, F*
M Mtiulishvili 1991 *Ukr,* 1994 *Kaz,* 1996 *CZR, CZR, Rus,* 1997 *Pt, Pol, Cro, De,* 1998 *It, Ukr, Rus, R,* 2001 *H, Pt, Rus, Sp, R,* 2002 *H, Pt, Rus, Sp, R, I,* 2003 *Rus, CZR, R,* 2004 *Rus, CZR, R*
V Nadiradze 1994 *Kaz, Swi,* 1995 *H,* 1996 *Rus,* 1997 *Pt, De,* 1998 *I, R,* 1999 *Tg,* 2000 *Pt, Mor, Sp, H, R,* 2001 *H, Pt, Rus, Sp, R, F, SA,* 2002 *H, Pt, Rus, Sp, R, I, Rus,* 2003 *Rus, CZR, R, It, E, Sa*
A Natchqebia 1990 *Z, Z*
I Natriashvili 2006 *Ukr, J,* 2007 *ItA,* 2008 *Pt, R, Pt, Rus, Sp,* 2009 *Ger, Pt, Sp, R, Rus, ItA*
I Natriashvili 2008 *ESp, Ur, ItA,* 2009 *C, IrA, US,* 2010 *Ger, R, Rus, ItA, Nm*
N Natroshvili 1992 *Ukr, Ukr, Lat*
G Nemsadze 2005 *CHL,* 2006 *Ukr,* 2007 *Sp,* 2008 *CZR, Sp, ESp, Ur, ItA,* 2009 *IrA, US, ItA,* 2010 *Ger, Pt, R, Rus*
A Nijaradze 2008 *CZR*

I Nikolaenko 1999 *Tg, Tg,* 2000 *It, Mor, Sp, H, R,* 2001 *R, F,* 2003 *Pt, Sp, E, Sa, SA, Ur*
I Ninidze 2004 *Ur, CHL*
M Ninidze 2010 *S, Nm*
D Oboladze 1993 *Rus, Pol, Lux,* 1994 *Swi,* 1995 *Bul, Mol, Ger, H,* 1996 *CZR, CZR, Rus,* 1997 *Pt, Pol,* 1998 *It, Ukr*
T Odisharia 1989 *Z,* 1994 *Kaz*
S Papashvili 2001 *SA,* 2004 *CZR, R,* 2006 *Bb, CZR,* 2007 *Sp*
S Partsikanashvili 1994 *Kaz,* 1996 *CZR, Rus,* 1997 *Pol,* 1999 *Tg, Tg,* 2000 *It, Pt, Mor*
A Peikrishvili 2008 *Pt, Pt,* 2009 *R,* 2010 *Pt, R, Rus*
G Peradze 1991 *Ukr*
Z Peradze 1997 *Pol,* 1998 *Rus*
Z Petriashvili 2009 *C, IrA*
D Pinchukovi 2004 *CZR*
L Pirpilashvili 2004 *Rus, CZR, R, Ur, CHL,* 2005 *Ukr, R, CZR*
G Pirtskhalava 1989 *Z,* 1995 *Ger,* 1996 *CZR, Rus,* 1997 *Pt, Pol*
T Pkhakadze 1989 *Z,* 1990 *Z, Z,* 1993 *Rus, Pol, Lux,* 1994 *Kaz,* 1996 *CZR*
G Rapava-Ruskini 1990 *Z,* 1992 *Ukr, Lat,* 1994 *Kaz,* 1996 *Rus,* 1997 *Pt, Cro, De,* 1998 *It, Ukr, Rus, R,* 1999 *Tg*
T Ratianidze 2000 *It,* 2001 *H, Pt, Sp, R, SA,* 2002 *Pt, Rus, Sp, R, I, Rus,* 2003 *Pt, Sp, Rus, CZR, R*
Z Rekhviashvili 1995 *H,* 1997 *Pt, Pol*
G Rokhvadze 2008 *ItA,* 2009 *C, IrA, US,* 2010 *S, ItA*
S Sakandelidze 1996 *CZR,* 1998 *Ukr*
S Sakvarelidze 2010 *S, ItA*
B Samkharadze 2004 *Pt, Sp, Rus, CZR, R, Ur, CHL,* 2005 *CZR, CHL,* 2006 *Rus, R, Pt, Ukr, Bb, CZR, R, Sp, Pt, Pt,* 2007 *R, Sp, Rus, CZR, Nm, ESp, Ar, I, Nm, F,* 2008 *Pt, R, Pt, Sp, ESp, Ur, ItA,* 2009 *Ger, Sp, R, ItA,* 2010 *Ger, Pt, Sp, R, S, ItA, Nm*
A Sanadze 2004 *CHL*
P Saneblidze 1994 *Kaz*
G Sanikidze 2004 *Ur, CHL*
B Sardanashvili 2004 *CHL*
V Satseradze 1989 *Z,* 1990 *Z,* 1991 *Ukr,* 1992 *Ukr, Ukr, Lat*
E Shanidze 1994 *Swi*
B Sheklashvili 2010 *S, ItA, Nm*
G Shkinin 2004 *CZR, R, CHL,* 2005 *CHL,* 2006 *Rus, R, Ukr, J, R, Sp, Pt, Pt,* 2007 *R, Sp, Rus, CZR, Nm, ESp, ItA, Ar, I, Nm,* 2008 *R, Pt, CZR, Rus, Sp, ESp, Ur, ItA,* 2009 *Pt*
B Shvanguiradze 1990 *Z, Z,* 1992 *Ukr, Ukr, Lat,* 1993 *Rus, Pol, Lux*
G Shvelidze 1998 *I, R,* 1999 *Tg, Tg,* 2000 *It, Pt, Sp, H, R,* 2001 *H, Pt, Sp, F, SA,* 2002 *H, Rus, I, Rus,* 2003 *Pt, Sp, Rus, CZR, R, It, E, Sa, Ur,* 2004 *Rus,* 2005 *Pt, CZR,* 2006 *Rus, R, Pt, R, Sp, Pt, Pt,* 2007 *Ar, I, Nm, F,* 2008 *Pt, R, Pt, CZR, Rus,* 2009 *Ger, Pt, Sp, R, Rus,* 2010 *Sp, R, Rus*
I Sikharulidze 1994 *Kaz*
T Sokhadze 2005 *CZR,* 2006 *Rus, R, Pt, Ukr, J, Pt, Pt,* 2009 *C, IrA*
M Sujashvili 2004 *Pt, Rus,* 2005 *Pt, Ukr, R, CZR,* 2006 *Pt, Ukr, J, Bb, CZR*
S Sultanishvili 1998 *Ukr*
S Sutiashvili 2005 *CHL,* 2006 *Ukr,* 2007 *CZR, Nm, ESp,* 2008 *Pt, R, CZR, Rus,* 2010 *S, ItA, Nm*
P Svanidze 1992 *Ukr*
T Tavadze 1991 *Ukr, Ukr*
L Tavartkiladze 2010 *Ger, Sp, R, Rus, S, ItA, Nm*
N Tchavtchavadze 1998 *It, Ukr,* 2004 *CZR, R, Ur, CHL*
B Tepnadze 1995 *H,* 1996 *CZR,* 1997 *Cro,* 1998 *I, R,* 1999 *Tg*
A Todua 2008 *CZR, Rus, Sp, ESp, Ur, ItA,* 2009 *Sp, R, C, IrA, US, ItA,* 2010 *Ger, Pt, R, Rus, S, ItA, Nm*
P Tqabladze 1993 *Lux,* 1995 *Bul*
L Tsabadze 1994 *Kaz, Swi,* 1995 *Bul, Ger, H,* 1996 *CZR, Rus,* 1997 *Cro, De,* 1998 *It, Rus, I, R,* 1999 *Tg, Tg,* 2000 *Pt, Mor, Sp, R,* 2001 *H, Pt, Rus, Sp, R, F, SA,* 2002 *H, Pt, Rus, Sp, R, I, Rus*
B Tsiklauri 2008 *ItA*
G Tsiklauri 2003 *SA, Ur*
D Tskhvediani 1998 *Ukr*
V Tskitishvili 1994 *Swi,* 1995 *Bul, Mol*
T Turdzeladze 1989 *Z,* 1990 *Z, Z,* 1991 *Ukr,* 1995 *Ger, H*
K Uchava 2002 *Sp,* 2004 *Sp,* 2008 *Pt, R, Pt, Rus, Sp, ESp, Ur, ItA,* 2009 *Ger, Pt, R, C, IrA,* 2010 *S, ItA, Nm*
B Udesiani 2001 *Sp, F,* 2002 *H,* 2004 *Pt, Sp, CZR, R, Rus,* 2005 *Pt, Ukr, R, CZR, CHL,* 2006 *Rus, R, Ukr, J, Bb, CZR, R, Sp, Pt, Pt,* 2007 *R, Rus, CZR, Ar, Nm,* 2008 *CZR, Sp, ESp, Ur, ItA,* 2010 *Ger, Pt, Sp, R, Rus*
M Urjukashvili 1997 *Cro, De,* 1998 *Ukr, Rus, R,* 1999 *Tg, Tg,* 2000 *It, Pt, Mor, Sp,* 2001 *Pt, Rus, Sp, R, F, SA,* 2002 *H, Pt, Sp, R, I, Rus,* 2003 *Pt, Sp, Rus, R, It, E, Sa, Ur,* 2004 *Pt, Rus, Ur, CHL, Rus,* 2005 *Pt, R, CZR,* 2006 *Rus, R, Pt, Ukr, J, R, Sp,* 2007 *Rus, CZR, Nm, ESp, ItA, Ar, I, Nm, F,* 2008 *Sp,* 2009 *R, Rus,* 2010 *Ger, Sp, R, Rus, ItA, Nm*
R Urushadze 1997 *Pol,* 2002 *R,* 2004 *Pt, Rus, Rus,* 2005 *Pt, Ukr, R, CZR, CHL,* 2006 *Rus, R, Pt, Bb, CZR, R, Sp, Pt, Pt,* 2007 *Nm, ESp, ItA, I, Nm, F,* 2008 *Pt, R, Pt, Rus, Sp,* 2009 *Ger, Pt, Sp, R, Rus, C, IrA, US, ItA*
Z Valishvili 2004 *CHL*
D Vartaniani 1991 *Ukr, Ukr,* 1992 *Ukr, Ukr, Lat,* 1997 *Pol,* 2000 *Sp, H, R*
L Vashadze 1991 *Ukr,* 1992 *Ukr, Ukr, Lat*
G Yachvili 2001 *H, Pt, R,* 2003 *Pt, Sp, Rus, CZR, R, It, E, Sa, Ur*
I Zedginidze 1998 *I,* 2000 *It, Pt, Mor, Sp, H, R,* 2001 *H, Pt, Rus, Sp, R,* 2002 *H, Rus, Sp, I, Rus,* 2003 *Pt, Sp, Rus, CZR, R, It, Sa, SA, Ur,* 2004 *Pt, Sp, Rus, CZR, R, Rus,* 2005 *Pt, Ukr, R, CZR,* 2006 *Rus, R, Pt, Ukr, CZR, R, Sp, Pt, Pt,* 2007 *R, Ar, I,* 2009 *Ger, Pt, Sp, Rus, ItA,* 2010 *Ger, Pt, Sp, R, Rus*
T Zibzibadze 2000 *It, Pt, Mor, Sp,* 2001 *H, Pt, Rus, Sp, R, F, SA,* 2002 *H, Pt, Rus, Sp, R, I, Rus,* 2003 *Pt, Sp, Rus, CZR, R, It, E, Sa, Ur,* 2004 *Pt, Sp, Rus, CZR, R, Rus,* 2005 *Pt, Ukr, R, CZR,* 2009 *Ger, Pt, Sp, R,* 2010 *Ger, Pt, Sp, R, Rus, S, ItA, Nm*
D Zirakashvili 2004 *Ur, CHL, Rus,* 2005 *Ukr, R, CZR,* 2006 *Rus, R, Pt, R, Sp, Pt,* 2007 *R, Ar, Nm, F,* 2008 *R,* 2009 *Ger,* 2010 *Ger, Pt, Sp, Rus*

IRELAND

IRELAND'S 2009–10 TEST RECORD

OPPONENTS	DATE	VENUE	RESULT
Australia	15 November	H	**Drew** 20–20
Fiji	21 November	H	**Won** 41–6
South Africa	28 November	H	**Won** 15–10
Italy	6 February	H	**Won** 29–11
France	13 February	A	**Lost** 10–33
England	27 February	A	**Won** 20–16
Wales	13 March	H	**Won** 27–12
Scotland	20 March	H	**Lost** 20–23
New Zealand	12 June	A	**Lost** 28–66
Australia	26 June	A	**Lost** 15–22

REALITY BITES FOR IRISH

By Paul Morgan

Getty Images

Declan Kidney suffered a tough second season in charge of Ireland.

After the nationwide euphoria that had greeted Ireland's Grand Slam in 2009, the new season was always in danger of feeling akin to the morning after the night before and so it proved as Declan Kidney's side surrendered their Six Nations crown to France and at times appeared a shadow of the side that had until recently ruled the European roost.

It was of course far from a cataclysmic fall from grace across the season and they will believe they can come back to the glory days in 2010–11, when they go back to Lansdowne Road (Aviva Stadium).

The autumn internationals yielded a victory over world champions South Africa and a 20–20 draw with the Wallabies in Dublin but subsequent Championship defeats to France and Scotland and a demoralising summer tour of New Zealand and Australia on which they lost all three games, including a heavy 66–28 mauling by the All Blacks in New

Plymouth, left the lingering impression that Ireland were a side who had been unable to build on their historic success the previous year.

After downing Springbok colours in Dublin in November courtesy of five penalties from Jonathan Sexton, the dream of back-to-back Grand Slams died in the Stade de France in their second Six Nations game and although they recovered to beat England and Wales, the Irish signed off in the Six Nations with a 23–20 reverse to Scotland at Croke Park.

"We feel like we've let a lot of people down and that's not a nice feeling," admitted Kidney after the game. "It's hugely disappointing and I can't put into words the way we feel. Like everyone else we wanted to leave Croke Park on a good note.

"You want to win trophies but we didn't this year. These things happen in life. There were so many people depending on us – the supporters and the whole country.

"It's a very disappointing place to be at the moment but these fellas are very resilient. We made mistakes, but we made mistakes trying things. Now we have to work on not making mistakes when the pressure is on. First and foremost it was about winning and trying to get a result, but we tried things that didn't come off. The error count went against us."

Kidney began the season by naming nine uncapped players in his 39-man squad for the autumn internationals and Leinster prop Cian Healy was handed an international debut for Ireland's opener against Australia at Croke Park.

The game was also Brian Driscoll's 100th Test match and the Irish captain marked the occasion in typically heroic style, scoring a late try under the posts which Ronan O'Gara converted to earn the home side a 20–20 draw.

O'Driscoll was later named *Rugby World Magazine's* Player of the Decade, to cap an incredible ten years for the Leinster man.

"We hung on until the death when things weren't going brilliantly for us and that is the mark of a good side," O'Driscoll said after the game. "We gifted them an early try and had to battle our way back into the game. We had to play catch-up and that makes it difficult against a good side like Australia."

Fiji were the next opponents but did not unduly trouble Ireland at the Royal Dublin Society as the home side scored five tries, including a brace from Keith Earls, in a routine 41–6 victory.

Sterner opposition lay ahead in the shape of South Africa the following week. Kidney opted to start with Sexton ahead of O'Gara at fly-half and his faith in the Leinster youngster was amply rewarded as he landed five penalties in a hugely physical 15–10 triumph over the Springboks.

The win completed an unbeaten 2009 for Ireland but the first cracks began to appear in the Six Nations. A comfortable 29–11 score line in their Championship opener against Italy at Croke Park belied what was a disjointed, nervous performance and Kidney's side were put to the sword by the French in Paris seven days later, leaking three tries to Les Bleus, who went on to win the Grand Slam, in a 33–10 defeat.

"Give credit to France, I think they played very well and I would like to compliment them on that," Kidney said after the side's Stade de France mauling. "We went 14 points behind and even though the boys came back at it, we weren't able to make any inroads. They picked us off in the second half with their penalties and drop goals. This is always a very difficult place to come to."

There was however temporary respite against England at Twickenham and Wales in Dublin.

Ireland made most of the running in London and took the lead against the English thanks to an early try from Tommy Bowe. Earls added a second but the home side replied with a try and drop goal and the visitors were indebted to a second Bowe score nine minutes from time to cement a 20–16 win.

"That was an important response after France," said veteran lock Paul O'Connell. "Brian O'Driscoll said yesterday that teams are defined by how they react to losses but we could have picked an easier one to get back on the horse than England at Twickenham, especially as they had their backs to the wall as well.

"I don't think we played outstandingly well but we showed a lot of intensity and a high work-rate. To come back and win the game with eight or nine minutes to go is a good feeling. The guys are very pleased with that."

The visit of Wales to Croke Park also yielded victory. Two tries from Earls and a third from Tomas O'Leary, coupled with a miserly defensive performance, were the highlights as Ireland cantered to a 27–12 win and with a closing clash against Scotland in Dublin lying ahead, Kidney's team still harboured hopes of lifting the Triple Crown and, depending on France's final result against England, possibly the Championship.

As it transpired the French were victorious in Paris but Ireland were themselves ambushed 23–20 by the Scots at Croke Park despite outscoring the visitors by two tries to one. The Triple Crown was gone and Kidney had to be content with finishing the Six Nations as runners-up.

That in itself would have represented a respectable return but there was still the daunting summer tour of New Zealand and Australia to tackle and it was the manner in which his side were manhandled by the All Blacks in particular that will have dismayed Kidney.

Ireland prepared for the tour with a clash with the Barbarians and an under strength side were beaten 29–23 at Thomond Park.

The Test against the New Zealanders saw Kidney recall all the senior players at his disposal but they were powerless to stem the Kiwi tide in New Plymouth. Conrad Smith grabbed the first of the home side's nine tries but the pivotal moment of the match came when No 8 Jamie Heaslip was dismissed in the first-half for an errant knee and the All Blacks duly ran riot.

"It was a horror show," said Kidney after the chastening 66–28 defeat. "We gave away a lot of soft tries and missed tackles. We will have to have a long hard look at that. The players picked themselves up at half-time, you saw that, and we managed to keep the ball a little better in the second half."

A subsequent clash with a strong New Zealand Maori in Rotorua was always going to be a testing midweek fixture ahead of the clash with the Wallabies and so it proved as the Kiwi invitational side continued their Centenary season celebrations with a 31–28 triumph.

Kidney made six changes to the XV that had been demolished by New Zealand for the tour-ending Australia game, handing Ulster No 8 Chris Henry a first cap in place of the suspended Heaslip.

The Irish had not tasted a Test victory Down Under since a 9–3 success in Sydney in 1979 and despite a much-improved performance against the Wallabies in Brisbane they were unable to end their losing sequence.

Ireland shaded the early exchanges and two Sexton penalties gave the visitors an early 6–3 lead only for scrum-half Luke Burgess to strike back for the Australians with a try. Fly-half Quade Cooper added a second try for the home side and at half time, the Wallabies had established a slender 16–15 advantage.

Scoring opportunities were at a premium after the break and two penalties from the boot of Matt Giteau were the only changes to the scoreboard as Australia held out for a 22–15 victory that condemned Ireland to a low key end to the campaign.

"A lot of the players are still on a learning curve," O'Driscoll said. "We had a number of players earning their first caps and it was all good experience, they will take a lot out of it. We haven't managed any victories on this tour and of course that is what you are judged on.

"We wanted to put a bit of pride back into our defensive game as we let ourselves down against New Zealand. Although we had a couple of lapses against Australia, we were fairly solid but the seven-point winning margin probably flattered us. The lads will now enjoy four or five weeks of holidays and try to freshen up for next year."

IRELAND INTERNATIONAL STATISTICS

MATCH RECORDS UP TO 29TH OCTOBER 2010

MOST CONSECUTIVE TEST WINS

10	2002 R,Ru,Gg,A,Fj,Arg,	2003 S1,It1,F,W1
8	2003 Tg, Sm,W2 ,It2, S2, R ,Nm, Arg	
8	2008 Arg, 2009 F, It ,E, S, W ,C, US	
6	1968 S,W,A,	1969 F,E,S
6	2004 SA,US,Arg,	2005 It,S,E

MOST CONSECUTIVE TEST WITHOUT DEFEAT

Matches	Wins	Draws	Period
12	11	1	2008 to 2010
10	10	0	2002 to 2003
8	8	0	2003
7	6	1	1968 to 1969
6	6	0	2004 to 2005

MOST POINTS IN A MATCH

BY THE TEAM

Pts.	Opponents	Venue	Year
83	United States	Manchester (NH)	2000
78	Japan	Dublin	2000
70	Georgia	Dublin	1998
64	Fiji	Dublin	2002
64	Namibia	Sydney	2003
63	Georgia	Dublin	2002
61	Italy	Limerick	2003
61	Pacific Islands	Dublin	2006
60	Romania	Dublin	1986
60	Italy	Dublin	2000
55	Zimbabwe	Dublin	1991
55	United States	Dublin	2004
55	Canada	Limerick	2008
54	Wales	Dublin	2002
53	Romania	Dublin	1998
53	United States	Dublin	1999
51	Italy	Rome	2007
50	Japan	Bloemfontein	1995

BY A PLAYER

Pts.	Player	Opponents	Venue	Year
32	R J R O'Gara	Samoa	Apia	2003
30	R J R O'Gara	Italy	Dublin	2000
26	D G Humphreys	Scotland	Murrayfield	2003
26	D G Humphreys	Italy	Limerick	2003
26	P Wallace	Pacific Islands	Dublin	2006
24	P A Burke	Italy	Dublin	1997
24	D G Humphreys	Argentina	Lens	1999
23	R P Keyes	Zimbabwe	Dublin	1991
23	R J R O'Gara	Japan	Dublin	2000
22	D G Humphreys	Wales	Dublin	2002
21	S O Campbell	Scotland	Dublin	1982
21	S O Campbell	England	Dublin	1983
21	R J R O'Gara	Italy	Rome	2001
21	R J R O'Gara	Argentina	Dublin	2004
21	R J R O'Gara	England	Dublin	2007
20	M J Kiernan	Romania	Dublin	1986
20	E P Elwood	Romania	Dublin	1993
20	S J P Mason	Samoa	Dublin	1996
20	E P Elwood	Georgia	Dublin	1998
20	K G M Wood	United States	Dublin	1999
20	D A Hickie	Italy	Limerick	2003
20	D G Humphreys	United States	Dublin	2004

MOST TRIES IN A MATCH

BY THE TEAM

Tries	Opponents	Venue	Year
13	United States	Manchester (NH)	2000
11	Japan	Dublin	2000
10	Romania	Dublin	1986
10	Georgia	Dublin	1998
10	Namibia	Sydney	2003
9	Fiji	Dublin	2003
8	Western Samoa	Dublin	1988
8	Zimbabwe	Dublin	1991
8	Georgia	Dublin	2002
8	Italy	Limerick	2003
8	Pacific Islands	Dublin	2006
8	Italy	Rome	2007
8	Canada	Limerick	2008
7	Japan	Bloemfontein	1995
7	Romania	Dublin	1998
7	United States	Dublin	1999
7	United States	Dublin	2004
7	Japan	Tokyo	2005

BY A PLAYER

Tries	Player	Opponents	Venue	Year
4	B F Robinson	Zimbabwe	Dublin	1991
4	K G M Wood	United States	Dublin	1999
4	D A Hickie	Italy	Limerick	2003
3	R Montgomery	Wales	Birkenhead	1887
3	J P Quinn	France	Cork	1913
3	E O'D Davy	Scotland	Murrayfield	1930
3	S J Byrne	Scotland	Murrayfield	1953
3	K D Crossan	Romania	Dublin	1986
3	B J Mullin	Tonga	Brisbane	1987
3	M R Mostyn	Argentina	Dublin	1999
3	B G O'Driscoll	France	Paris	2000
3	M J Mullins	United States	Manchester (NH)	2000
3	D A Hickie	Japan	Dublin	2000
3	R A J Henderson	Italy	Rome	2001
3	B G O'Driscoll	Scotland	Dublin	2002
3	K M Maggs	Fiji	Dublin	2002

MOST CONVERSIONS IN A MATCH

BY THE TEAM

Cons	Opponents	Venue	Year
10	Georgia	Dublin	1998
10	Japan	Dublin	2000
9	United States	Manchester (NH)	2000
7	Romania	Dublin	1986
7	Georgia	Dublin	2002
7	Namibia	Sydney	2003
7	United States	Dublin	2004
6	Japan	Bloemfontein	1995
6	Romania	Dublin	1998
6	United States	Dublin	1999
6	Italy	Dublin	2000
6	Italy	Limerick	2003
6	Japan	Tokyo	2005
6	Pacific Islands	Dublin	2006
6	Canada	Limerick	2008

BY A PLAYER

Cons	Player	Opponents	Venue	Year
10	E P Elwood	Georgia	Dublin	1998
10	R J R O'Gara	Japan	Dublin	2000
8	R J R O'Gara	United States	Manchester (NH)	2000
7	M J Kiernan	Romania	Dublin	1986
7	R J R O'Gara	Namibia	Sydney	2003
7	D G Humphreys	United States	Dublin	2004
6	P A Burke	Japan	Bloemfontein	1995
6	R J R O'Gara	Italy	Dublin	2000
6	D G Humphreys	Italy	Limerick	2003
6	D G Humphreys	Japan	Tokyo	2005
6	P Wallace	Pacific Islands	Dublin	2006
5	M J Kiernan	Canada	Dunedin	1987
5	E P Elwood	Romania	Dublin	1999
5	R J R O'Gara	Georgia	Dublin	2002
5	D G Humphreys	Fiji	Dublin	2002
5	D G Humphreys	Romania	Dublin	2005
5	R J R O'Gara	Canada	Limerick	2008
5	J Sexton	Fiji	Dublin	2009

MOST PENALTIES IN A MATCH

BY THE TEAM

Pens	Opponents	Venue	Year
8	Italy	Dublin	1997
7	Argentina	Lens	1999
6	Scotland	Dublin	1982
6	Romania	Dublin	1993
6	United States	Atlanta	1996
6	Western Samoa	Dublin	1996
6	Italy	Dublin	2000
6	Wales	Dublin	2002
6	Australia	Dublin	2002
6	Samoa	Apia	2003
6	Japan	Osaka	2005

BY A PLAYER

Pens	Player	Opponents	Venue	Year
8	P A Burke	Italy	Dublin	1997
7	D G Humphreys	Argentina	Lens	1999
6	S O Campbell	Scotland	Dublin	1982
6	E P Elwood	Romania	Dublin	1993
6	S J P Mason	Western Samoa	Dublin	1996
6	R J R O'Gara	Italy	Dublin	2000
6	D G Humphreys	Wales	Dublin	2002
6	R J R O'Gara	Australia	Dublin	2002

MOST DROPPED GOALS IN A MATCH

BY THE TEAM

Drops	Opponents	Venue	Year
2	Australia	Dublin	1967
2	France	Dublin	1975
2	Australia	Sydney	1979
2	England	Dublin	1981
2	Canada	Dunedin	1987
2	England	Dublin	1993
2	Wales	Wembley	1999
2	New Zealand	Dublin	2001
2	Argentina	Dublin	2004
2	England	Dublin	2005

BY A PLAYER

Drops	Player	Opponents	Venue	Year
2	C M H Gibson	Australia	Dublin	1967
2	W M McCombe	France	Dublin	1975
2	S O Campbell	Australia	Sydney	1979
2	E P Elwood	England	Dublin	1993
2	D G Humphreys	Wales	Wembley	1999
2	D G Humphreys	New Zealand	Dublin	2001
2	R J R O'Gara	Argentina	Dublin	2004
2	R J R O'Gara	England	Dublin	2005

CAREER RECORDS

MOST CAPPED PLAYERS

Caps	Player	Career Span
103	B G O'Driscoll	1999 to 2010
102	J J Hayes	2000 to 2010
99	R J R O'Gara	2000 to 2010
92	M E O'Kelly	1997 to 2009
91	P A Stringer	2000 to 2009
82	G T Dempsey	1998 to 2008
72	D G Humphreys	1996 to 2005
70	K M Maggs	1997 to 2005
70	P J O'Connell	2002 to 2010
69	C M H Gibson	1964 to 1979
68	G E A Murphy	2000 to 2010
66	M J Horan	2000 to 2009
65	S H Easterby	2000 to 2008
65	S P Horgan	2000 to 2009
63	W J McBride	1962 to 1975
63	D P O'Callaghan	2003 to 2010
63	D P Wallace	2000 to 2010
62	A G Foley	1995 to 2005
62	D A Hickie	1997 to 2007
61	J F Slattery	1970 to 1984
59	P S Johns	1990 to 2000
58	P A Orr	1976 to 1987
58	K G M Wood	1994 to 2003
55	B J Mullin	1984 to 1995
54	T J Kiernan	1960 to 1973
54	P M Clohessy	1993 to 2002
52	D G Lenihan	1981 to 1992
51	M I Keane	1974 to 1984

MOST CONSECUTIVE TESTS

Tests	Player	Span
52	W J McBride	1964 to 1975
49	P A Orr	1976 to 1986
43	D G Lenihan	1981 to 1989
39	M I Keane	1974 to 1981
38	P A Stringer	2003 to 2007
37	G V Stephenson	1920 to 1929

MOST TESTS AS CAPTAIN

Tests	Captain	Span
66	B G O'Driscoll	2002 to 2010
36	K G M Wood	1996 to 2003
24	T J Kiernan	1963 to 1973
19	C F Fitzgerald	1982 to 1986
17	J F Slattery	1979 to 1981
17	D G Lenihan	1986 to 1990

MOST POINTS IN TESTS

Pts	Player	Tests	Career
963	R J R O'Gara	99	2000 to 2010
565*	D G Humphreys	72	1996 to 2005
308	M J Kiernan	43	1982 to 1991
296	E P Elwood	35	1993 to 1999
217	S O Campbell	22	1976 to 1984
215	B G O'Driscoll	103	1999 to 2010
158	T J Kiernan	54	1960 to 1973
145	D A Hickie	62	1997 to 2007
113	A J P Ward	19	1978 to 1987

* Humphreys's total includes a penalty try against Scotland in 1999

MOST TRIES IN TESTS

Tries	Player	Tests	Career
40	B G O'Driscoll	103	1999 to 2010
29	D A Hickie	62	1997 to 2007
21	S P Horgan	65	2000 to 2009
19	G T Dempsey	82	1998 to 2008
18	G E A Murphy	68	2000 to 2010
17	B J Mullin	55	1984 to 1995
15	K G M Wood	58	1994 to 2003
15	K M Maggs	70	1997 to 2005
15	T J Bowe	32	2004 to 2010
14	G V Stephenson	42	1920 to 1930
14	R J R O'Gara	99	2000 to 2010
12	K D Crossan	41	1982 to 1992
12	D P Wallace	63	2000 to 2010
11	A T A Duggan	25	1963 to 1972
11	S P Geoghegan	37	1991 to 1996

MOST CONVERSIONS IN TESTS

Cons	Player	Tests	Career
154	R J R O'Gara	99	2000 to 2010
88	D G Humphreys	72	1996 to 2005
43	E P Elwood	35	1993 to 1999
40	M J Kiernan	43	1982 to 1991
26	T J Kiernan	54	1960 to 1973
16	R A Lloyd	19	1910 to 1920
15	S O Campbell	22	1976 to 1984

MOST PENALTY GOALS IN TESTS

Pens	Player	Tests	Career
181	R J R O'Gara	99	2000 to 2010
110	D G Humphreys	72	1996 to 2005
68	E P Elwood	35	1993 to 1999
62	M J Kiernan	43	1982 to 1991
54	S O Campbell	22	1976 to 1984
31	T J Kiernan	54	1960 to 1973
29	A J P Ward	19	1978 to 1987

MOST DROPPED GOALS IN TESTS

Drops	Player	Tests	Career
14	R J R O'Gara	99	2000 to 2010
8	D G Humphreys	72	1996 to 2005
7	R A Lloyd	19	1910 to 1920
7	S O Campbell	22	1976 to 1984
6	C M H Gibson	69	1964 to 1979
6	B J McGann	25	1969 to 1976
6	M J Kiernan	43	1982 to 1991

INTERNATIONAL CHAMPIONSHIP RECORDS

RECORD	DETAIL	SET	
Most points in season	168	in five matches	2000
Most tries in season	17	in five matches	2000
	17	in five matches	2004
	17	in five matches	2007
Highest Score	60	60–13 v Italy	2000
Biggest win	47	60–13 v Italy	2000
Highest score conceded	50	18–50 v England	2000
Biggest defeat	40	6–46 v England	1997
Most appearances	56	C M H Gibson	1964–1979
Most points in matches	527	R J R O'Gara	2000–2010
Most points in season	82	R J R O'Gara	2007
Most points in match	30	R J R O'Gara	v Italy, 2000
Most tries in matches	22	B G O'Driscoll	2000–2010
Most tries in season	5	J E Arigho	1928
	5	B G O'Driscoll	2000
Most tries in match	3	R Montgomery	v Wales, 1887
	3	J P Quinn	v France, 1913
	3	E O'D Davy	v Scotland, 1930
	3	S J Byrne	v Scotland, 1953
	3	B G O'Driscoll	v France, 2000
	3	R A J Henderson	v Italy, 2001
	3	B G O'Driscoll	v Scotland, 2002
Most cons in matches	76	R J R O'Gara	2000–2010
Most cons in season	11	R J R O'Gara	2000
	11	R J R O'Gara	2004
Most cons in match	6	R J R O'Gara	v Italy, 2000
Most pens in matches	105	R J R O'Gara	2000–2010
Most pens in season	17	R J R O'Gara	2006
Most pens in match	6	S O Campbell	v Scotland, 1982
	6	R J R O'Gara	v Italy, 2000
	6	D G Humphreys	v Wales, 2002
Most drops in matches	7	R A Lloyd	1910–1920
Most drops in season	2	on several	Occasions
Most drops in match	2	W M McCombe	v France, 1975
	2	E P Elwood	v England, 1993
	2	D G Humphreys	v Wales, 1999
	2	R J R O'Gara	v England, 2005

MISCELLANEOUS RECORDS

RECORD	HOLDER	DETAIL
Longest Test Career	A J F O'Reilly	1955 to 1970
	C M H Gibson	1964 to 1979
Youngest Test Cap	F S Hewitt	17 yrs 157 days in 1924
Oldest Test Cap	C M H Gibson	36 yrs 195 days in 1979

CAREER RECORDS OF IRELAND INTERNATIONAL PLAYERS (UP TO 29TH OCTOBER 2010)

PLAYER BACKS	DEBUT	CAPS	T	C	P	D	PTS
T J Bowe	2004 v US	32	15	0	0	0	75
G W D'Arcy	1999 v R	49	6	0	0	0	30
K G Earls	2008 v C	10	6	0	0	0	30
L M Fitzgerald	2006 v PI	13	2	0	0	0	10
S P Horgan	2000 v S	65	21	0	0	0	105
D Hurley	2009 v US	1	0	0	0	0	0
R D J Kearney	2007 v Arg	25	5	1	0	0	27
I J Keatley	2009 v C	2	0	4	3	0	17
G E A Murphy	2000 v US	68	18	1	1	1	98
B G O'Driscoll	1999 v A	103	40	0	0	5	215
R J R O'Gara	2000 v S	99	14	154	181	14	963
T G O'Leary	2007 v Arg	18	2	0	0	0	10
E G Reddan	2006 v F	21	0	0	0	0	0
J Sexton	2009 v Fj	8	0	7	17	1	68
A D Trimble	2005 v A	29	8	0	0	0	40
P W Wallace	2006 v SA	22	2	11	7	0	53

FORWARDS							
N A Best	2005 v NZ	18	2	0	0	0	10
R Best	2005 v NZ	39	4	0	0	0	20
T D Buckley	2007 v Arg	19	1	0	0	0	5
T G Court	2009 v It	9	0	0	0	0	0
S Cronin	2009 v Fj	4	0	0	0	0	0
L F M Cullen	2002 v NZ	24	0	0	0	0	0
S P H Ferris	2006 v PI	20	0	0	0	0	0
J P Flannery	2005 v R	36	3	0	0	0	15
J Fogarty	2010 v NZ	1	0	0	0	0	0
J J Hayes	2000 v S	102	2	0	0	0	10
C E Healy	2009 v A	9	0	0	0	0	0
J P R Heaslip	2006 v PI	27	4	0	0	0	20
C Henry	2010 v A	1	0	0	0	0	0
M J Horan	2000 v US	66	6	0	0	0	30
S Jennings	2007 v Arg	9	0	0	0	0	0
D P Leamy	2004 v US	43	2	0	0	0	10
K McLaughlin	2010 v It	1	0	0	0	0	0
J Muldoon	2009 v C	3	0	0	0	0	0
S O'Brien	2009 v Fj	3	0	0	0	0	0
D P O'Callaghan	2003 v W	63	1	0	0	0	5
P J O'Connell	2002 v W	70	6	0	0	0	30
J H O'Connor	2004 v SA	12	1	0	0	0	5
M R O'Driscoll	2001 v R	19	0	0	0	0	0
N Ronan	2009 v C	3	0	0	0	0	0
M R Ross	2009 v C	2	0	0	0	0	0
R Ruddock	2010 v A	1	0	0	0	0	0
D Ryan	2008 v Arg	5	0	0	0	0	0
D Tuohy	2010 v NZ	2	1	0	0	0	5
D Varley	2010 v A	1	0	0	0	0	0
D P Wallace	2000 v Arg	63	12	0	0	0	60

Dave Rogers/Getty Images

In 2010 Paul O'Connell became the latest Ireland player to go through the 70-cap barrier.

IRELAND INTERNATIONAL PLAYERS

UP TO 29TH OCTOBER 2010

Note: Years given for International Championship matches are for second half of season; eg 1972 means season 1971–72. Years for all other matches refer to the actual year of the match. Entries in square brackets denote matches played in RWC Finals.

Abraham, M (Bective Rangers) 1912 E, S, W, SA, 1914 W
Adams, C (Old Wesley), 1908 E, 1909 E, F, 1910 F, 1911 E, S, W, F, 1912 S, W, SA, 1913 W, F, 1914 F, E, S
Agar, R D (Malone) 1947 F, E, S, W, 1948 F, 1949 S, W, 1950 F, E, W
Agnew, P J (CIYMS) 1974 F (R), 1976 A
Ahearne, T (Queen's Coll, Cork) 1899 E
Aherne, L F P (Dolphin, Lansdowne) 1988 E 2, WS, It, 1989 F, W, E, S, NZ, 1990 E, S, F, W (R), 1992 E, S, F, A
Alexander, R (NIFC, Police Union) 1936 E, S, W, 1937 E, S, W, 1938 E, S, 1939 E, S, W
Allen, C E (Derry, Liverpool) 1900 E, S, W, 1901 E, S, W, 1903 S, W, 1904 E, S, W, 1905 E, S, W, NZ, 1906 E, S, W, SA, 1907 S, W
Allen, G G (Derry, Liverpool) 1896 E, S, W, 1897 E, S, 1898 E, S, 1899 E, W
Allen, T C (NIFC) 1885 E, S 1
Allen, W S (Wanderers) 1875 E
Allison, J B (Edinburgh U) 1899 E, S, 1900 E, S, W, 1901 E, S, W, 1902 E, S, W, 1903 S
Anderson, F E (Queen's U, Belfast, NIFC) 1953 F, E, S, W, 1954 NZ, F, E, S, W, 1955 F, E, S, W
Anderson, H J (Old Wesley) 1903 E, S, 1906 E, S
Anderson, W A (Dungannon) 1984 A, 1985 S, F, W, E, 1986 F, S, R, 1987 E, S, F, W, [W, C, Tg, A], 1988 S, F, W, E 1,2, 1989 F, W, E, NZ, 1990 E, S
Andrews, G (NIFC) 1875 E, 1876 E
Andrews, H W (NIFC) 1888 M, 1889 S, W
Archer, A M (Dublin U, NIFC) 1879 S
Arigho, J E (Lansdowne) 1928 F, E, W, 1929 F, E, S, W, 1930 F, E, S, W, 1931 F, E, S, W, SA
Armstrong, W K (NIFC) 1960 SA, 1961 E
Arnott, D T (Lansdowne) 1876 E
Ash, W H (NIFC) 1875 E, 1876 E, 1877 S
Aston, H R (Dublin U) 1908 E, W
Atkins, A P (Bective Rangers) 1924 F
Atkinson, J M (NIFC) 1927 F, A
Atkinson, J R (Dublin U) 1882 W, S
Bagot, J C (Dublin U, Lansdowne) 1879 S, E, 1880 E, S, 1881 S
Bailey, A H (UC Dublin, Lansdowne) 1934 W, 1935 E, S, W, NZ, 1936 E, S, W, 1937 E, S, W, 1938 E, S
Bailey, N (Northampton) 1952 E
Bardon, M E (Bohemians) 1934 E
Barlow, M (Wanderers) 1875 E
Barnes, R J (Dublin U, Armagh) 1933 W
Barr, A (Methodist Coll, Belfast) 1898 W, 1899 S, 1901 E, S
Barry, N J (Garryowen) 1991 Nm 2(R)
Beamish, C E St J (RAF, Leicester) 1933 W, S, 1934 S, W, 1935 E, S, W, NZ, 1936 E, S, W, 1938 W
Beamish, G R (RAF, Leicester) 1925 E, S, W, 1928 F, E, S, W, 1929 F, E, S, W, 1930 F, S, W, 1931 F, E, S, W, SA, 1932 E, S, W, 1933 E, W, S
Beatty, W J (NIFC, Richmond) 1910 F, 1912 F, W
Becker, V A (Lansdowne) 1974 F, W
Beckett, G G P (Dublin U) 1908 E, S, W
Bell, J C (Ballymena, Northampton, Dungannon) 1994 A 1,2, US, 1995 S, It, [NZ, W, F], Fj, 1996 US, S, F, W, E, WS, A, 1997 It 1, F, W, E, S, 1998 Gg, R, SA 3, 1999 F, W, S It (R), A 2, [US (R), A 3(R), R], 2001 R (R), 2003 Tg, Sm, It 2(R)
Bell, R J (NIFC) 1875 E, 1876 E
Bell, W E (Belfast Collegians) 1953 F, E, S, W
Bennett, F (Belfast Collegians) 1913 S
Bent, G C (Dublin U) 1882 W, E
Berkery, P J (Lansdowne) 1954 W, 1955 W, 1956 S, W, 1957 F, E, S, W, 1958 A, E, S
Bermingham, J J C (Blackrock Coll) 1921 E, S, W, F
Best, N A (Ulster) 2005 NZ(R),R, 2006 NZ1,2,A1,SA,A2, 2007 F(R),E(R),S1(R),Arg1, 2(R),S2,It2, [Nm(R),Gg(R),F(R),Arg(t&R)]
Best, R (Ulster) 2005 NZ(R),A(t), 2006 W(R),A1(R),SA,A2,PI(R), 2007 W,F,E,S1,It1, S2(R),It2, [Nm,Gg,Arg(R)], 2008 It,F(R),S(R), W,E,NZ1(R),A,C(R),NZ2,Arg(R), 2009 F(R),It(R),E(R),S,W(R),C, US, 2010 It(R),F(R),E,W,S
Best, S J (Belfast Harlequins, Ulster) 2003 Tg (R), W 2, S 2(R), 2003 [Nm(R)], 2004 W(R),US(R), 2005 J1,2,NZ(R),R, 2006 F(R), W(R),PI(R), 2007 E(R),S1,It1(R),Arg1,2, S2,It2(R), [Nm(R),Gg(R), F(R)]
Bishop, J P (London Irish) 1998 SA, 1,2, Gg, R, SA 3, 1999 F, W, E, S, It, A 1,2, Arg 1, [US, A 3, Arg 2], 2000 E, Arg, C, 2002 NZ 1,2, Fj, Arg, 2003 W 1, E
Blackham, J C (Queen's Coll, Cork) 1909 S, W, F, 1910 E, S, W
Blake-Knox, S E F (NIFC) 1976 E, S, 1977 F (R)
Blayney, J J (Wanderers) 1950 S
Bond, A T W (Derry) 1894 S, W
Bornemann, W W (Wanderers) 1960 E, S, W, SA
Boss, I J (Ulster) 2006 NZ2(R),A1(R),SA(R),A2,PI(R), 2007 F,E(R),Arg1,S2,It2(R), [Gg(R),Arg(R)]
Bowe, T J (Ulster, Ospreys) 2004 US, 2005 J1,2,NZ,A,R, 2006 It,F, 2007 Arg1,S2, 2008 S,W,E,NZ1,A,C,NZ2,Arg, 2009 F,It,E,S,W,A,SA, 2010 It,F,E,W,S,NZ1,A
Bowen, D St J (Cork Const) 1977 W, E, S
Boyd, C A (Dublin U) 1900 S, 1901 S, W
Boyle, C V (Dublin U) 1935 NZ, 1936 E, S, W, 1937 E, S, W, 1938 W, 1939 W
Brabazon, H M (Dublin U) 1884 E, 1885 S 1, 1886 E
Bradley, M J (Dolphin) 1920 W, F, 1922 E, S, W, F, 1923 E, S, W, F, 1925 F, S, W, 1926 F, E, S, W, 1927 F, W
Bradley, M T (Cork Constitution) 1984 A, 1985 S, F, W, E, 1986 F, W, E, S, R, 1987 E, S, F, W, [W, C, Tg, A], 1988 S, F, W, E 1, 1990 W, 1992 NZ 1,2, 1993 S, F, W, E, R, 1994 F, W, E, S, A 1,2, US, 1995 S, F, [NZ]
Bradshaw, G L B (Belfast Collegians) 1903 W
Bradshaw, R M (Wanderers) 1885 E, S 1,2
Brady, A M (UC Dublin, Malone) 1966 S, 1968 E, S, W
Brady, J A (Wanderers) 1976 E, S
Brady, J R (CIYMS) 1951 S, W, 1953 F, E, S, W, 1954 W, 1956 W, 1957 F, E, S, W
Bramwell, T (NIFC) 1928 F
Brand, T N (NIFC) 1924 NZ
Brennan, J I (CIYMS) 1957 S, W
Brennan, T (St Mary's Coll, Barnhall) 1998 SA 1(R),2(R), 1999 F (R), S (R), It, A 2, Arg 1, [US, A 3], 2000 E (R), 2001 W (R), E (R), Sm (R)
Bresnihan, F P K (UC Dublin, Lansdowne, London Irish) 1966 E, W, 1967 A 1, E, S, W, F, 1968 F, E, S, W, A, 1969 F, E, S, W, 1970 SA, F, E, S, W, 1971 F, E, S, W
Brett, J T (Monkstown) 1914 W
Bristow, J R (NIFC) 1879 E
Brophy, N H (Blackrock Coll, UC Dublin, London Irish) 1957 F, E, 1959 E, S, W, F, 1960 F, SA, 1961 S, W, 1962 E, S, W, 1963 E, W, 1967 E, S, W, F, A 2
Brown, E L (Instonians) 1958 F
Brown, G S (Monkstown, United Services) 1912 S, W, SA

Brown, H (Windsor) 1877 E
Brown, T (Windsor) 1877 E, S
Brown, W H (Dublin U) 1899 E
Brown, W J (Malone) 1970 SA, F, S, W
Brown, W S (Dublin U) 1893 S, W, 1894 E, S, W
Browne, A W (Dublin U) 1951 SA
Browne, D (Blackrock Coll) 1920 F
Browne, H C (United Services and RN) 1929 E, S, W
Browne, W F (United Services and Army) 1925 E, S, W, 1926 S, W, 1927 F, E, S, W, A, 1928 E, S
Browning, D R (Wanderers) 1881 E, S
Bruce, S A M (NIFC) 1883 E, S, 1884 E
Brunker, A A (Lansdowne) 1895 E, W
Bryant, C H (Cardiff) 1920 E, S
Buchanan, A McM (Dublin U) 1926 E, S, W, 1927 S, W, A
Buchanan, J W B (Dublin U) 1882 S, 1884 E, S
Buckley, J H (Sunday's Well) 1973 E, S
Buckley, T D (Munster) 2007 Arg1(R),2(R), 2008 It(R),F(R), S(R),W(R),E(R),NZ1(R), A(R),C,NZ2(R), 2009 C,US,Fj(R), 2010 E(R),W(R),S(R),NZ1,A
Bulger, L Q (Lansdowne) 1896 E, S, W, 1897 E, S, 1898 E, S, W
Bulger, M J (Dublin U) 1888 M
Burges, J H (Rosslyn Park) 1950 F, E
Burgess, R B (Dublin U) 1912 SA
Burke, P A (Cork Constitution, Bristol, Harlequins) 1995 E, S, W (R), It, [J], Fj, 1996 US (R), A, 1997 It 1, S (R), 2001 R (R), 2003 S 1(R), Sm (R)
Burkitt, J C S (Queen's Coll, Cork) 1881 E
Burns, I J (Wanderers) 1980 E (R)
Butler, L G (Blackrock Coll) 1960 W
Butler, N (Bective Rangers) 1920 E
Byers, R M (NIFC) 1928 S, W, 1929 E, S, W
Byrne, E (St Mary's Coll) 2001 It (R), F (R), S (R), W (R), E (R), Sm, NZ (R), 2003 A (R), Sm (R)
Byrne, E M J (Blackrock Coll) 1977 S, F, 1978 F, W, E, NZ
Byrne, J S (Blackrock Coll, Leinster, Saracens) 2001 R (R), 2002 W (R), E (R), S (R), It, NZ 2(R), R, Ru (R), Gg, A, Arg, 2003 S 1, It 1, F, W 1, E, A, Tg, Sm, W 2(R), It 2, S2(R), [R(R),Nm(R)], 2004 F,W,E,It,S,SA1,2,3,Arg, 2005 It,S,E,F,W,NZ,A,R
Byrne, N F (UC Dublin) 1962 F
Byrne, S J (UC Dublin, Lansdowne) 1953 S, W, 1955 F
Byron, W G (NIFC) 1896 E, S, W, 1897 E, S, 1898 E, S, W, 1899 E, S, W
Caddell, E D (Dublin U, Wanderers) 1904 S, 1905 E, S, W, NZ, 1906 E, S, W, SA, 1907 E, S, 1908 S, W
Cagney, S J (London Irish) 1925 W, 1926 F, E, S, W, 1927 F, 1928 E, S, W, 1929 F, E, S, W
Caldwell, R (Ulster) 2009 C(R),US(R)
Callan, C P (Lansdowne) 1947 F, E, S, W, 1948 F, E, S, W, 1949 F, E
Cameron, E D (Bective Rangers) 1891 S, W
Campbell, C E (Old Wesley) 1970 SA
Campbell, E F (Monkstown) 1899 S, W, 1900 E, W
Campbell, K P (Ulster) 2005 J1(R),2(R),R
Campbell, S B B (Derry) 1911 E, S, W, F, 1912 F, E, S, W, SA, 1913 E, S, F
Campbell, S O (Old Belvedere) 1976 A, 1979 A 1,2, 1980 E, S, F, W, 1981 F, W, E, S, SA 1, 1982 W, E, S, F, 1983 S, F, W, E, 1984 F, W
Canniffe, D M (Lansdowne) 1976 W, E
Cantrell, J L (UC Dublin, Blackrock Coll) 1976 A, F, W, E, S, 1981 S, SA 1,2, A
Carey, R W (Dungannon) 1992 NZ 1,2
Carney, B B (Munster) 2007 Arg1,2,S2,It2(R)
Carpendale, M J (Monkstown) 1886 S, 1887 W, 1888 W, S
Carr, N J (Ards) 1985 S, F, W, E, 1986 W, E, S, R, 1987 E, S, W
Carroll, C (Bective Rangers) 1930 F
Carroll, R (Lansdowne) 1947 F, 1950 S, W
Casement, B N (Dublin U) 1875 E, 1876 E, 1879 E
Casement, F (Dublin U) 1906 E, S, W
Casey, J C (Young Munster) 1930 S, 1932 E
Casey, P J (UC Dublin, Lansdowne) 1963 F, E, S, W, NZ, 1964 E, S, W, F, 1965 F, E, S
Casey, R E (Blackrock Coll, London Irish) 1999 [A 3(t), Arg 2(R)], 2000 E, US (R), C (R), 2009 C,US
Cave, D M (Ulster) 2009 C,US
Chambers, J (Dublin U) 1886 E, S, 1887 E, S, W
Chambers, R R (Instonians) 1951 F, E, S, W, 1952 F, W
Clancy, T P J (Lansdowne) 1988 W, E 1,2, WS, It, 1989 F, W, E, S
Clarke, A T H (Northampton, Dungannon) 1995 Fj (R), 1996 W, E, WS, 1997 F (R), It 2(R), 1998 Gg (R), R
Clarke, C P (Terenure Coll) 1993 F, W, E, 1998 W, E
Clarke, D J (Dolphin) 1991 W, Nm 1,2, [J, A], 1992 NZ 2(R)
Clarke, J A B (Bective Rangers) 1922 S, W, F, 1923 F, 1924 E, S, W
Clegg, R J (Bangor) 1973 F, 1975 E, S, F, W
Clifford, J T (Young Munster) 1949 F, E, S, W, 1950 F, E, S, W, 1951 F, E, SA, 1952 F, S, W
Clinch, A D (Dublin U, Wanderers) 1892 S, 1893 W, 1895 E, S, W, 1896 E, S, W, 1897 E, S
Clinch, J D (Wanderers, Dublin U) 1923 W, 1924 F, E, S, W, NZ, 1925 F, E, S, 1926 E, S, W, 1927 F, 1928 F, E, S, W, 1929 F, E, S, W, 1930 F, E, S, W, 1931 F, E, S, W, SA
Clohessy, P M (Young Munster) 1993 F, W, E, 1994 F, W, E, S, A 1,2, US, 1995 E, S, F, W, 1996 S, F, 1997 It 2, 1998 F (R), W (R), SA 2(R), Gg, R, SA 3, 1999 F, W, E, S, It, A 1,2 Arg 1, [US, A 3(R)], 2000 E, S, It, F, W, Arg, J, SA, 2001 It, F, R, S, W, E, Sm (R), NZ, 2002 W, E, S, It, F
Clune, J J (Blackrock Coll) 1912 SA, 1913 W, F, 1914 F, E, W
Coffey, J J (Lansdowne) 1900 E, 1901 W, 1902 E, S, W, 1903 E, S, W, 1905 E, S, W, NZ, 1906 E, S, W, SA, 1907 E, 1908 W, 1910 F
Cogan, W St J (Queen's Coll, Cork) 1907 E, S
Collier, S R (Queen's Coll, Belfast) 1883 S
Collins, P C (Lansdowne, London Irish) 1987 [C], 1990 S (R)
Collis, W R F (KCH, Harlequins) 1924 F, W, NZ, 1925 F, E, S, 1926 F
Collis, W S (Wanderers) 1884 W
Collopy, G (Bective Rangers) 1891 S, 1892 S
Collopy, R (Bective Rangers) 1923 E, S, W, F, 1924 F, E, S, W, NZ, 1925 F, E, S, W
Collopy, W P (Bective Rangers) 1914 F, E, S, W, 1921 E, S, W, F, 1922 E, S, W, F, 1923 S, W, F, 1924 F, E, S, W
Combe, A (NIFC) 1875 E
Condon, H C (London Irish) 1984 S (R)
Cook, H G (Lansdowne) 1884 W
Coote, P B (RAF, Leicester) 1933 S
Corcoran, J C (London Irish) 1947 A, 1948 F
Corken, T S (Belfast Collegians) 1937 E, S, W
Corkery, D S (Cork Constitution, Bristol) 1994 A 1,2, US, 1995 E, [NZ, J, W, F], Fj, 1996 US, S, F, W, E, WS, A, 1997 It 1, F, W, E, S, 1998 S, F, W, E, 1999 A 1(R),2(R)
Corley, H H (Dublin U, Wanderers) 1902 E, S, W, 1903 E, S, W, 1904 E, S
Cormac, H S T (Clontarf) 1921 E, S, W
Corrigan, R (Greystones, Lansdowne, Leinster) 1997 C (R), It 2, 1998 S, F, W, E, SA 3(R), 1999 A 1(R),2(R), [Arg 2], 2002 NZ 1,2, R, Ru, Gg, A, Fj (R), Arg, 2003 S 1, It 1, A, Tg, Sm, W 2, It 2, S 2, [R,Arg,A,F], 2004 F,W,E,It,S,SA1,2,3,Arg, 2005 It,S,E,F,W, J1(R),2(R), 2006 F
Costello, P (Bective Rangers) 1960 F
Costello, R A (Garryowen) 1993 S
Costello, V C P (St Mary's Coll, London Irish) 1996 US, F, W, E. WS (R), 1997 C, It 2(R), 1998 S (R), F, W, E, SA 1,2, Gg, R, SA 3, 1999 F, W (R), E, S (R), It, A 1, 2002 R (R), A, Arg, 2003 S 1, It 1, F, E, A, It 2, S 2, [R,Arg,F], 2004 F(R),W(R),It(R), S(R)
Cotton, J (Wanderers) 1889 W
Coulter, H H (Queen's U, Belfast) 1920 E, S, W
Court, T G (Ulster) 2009 It(R),W(t),C,US(R),Fj, 2010 It(R),F(t&R), NZ1(R),A(R)
Courtney, A W (UC Dublin) 1920 S, W, F, 1921 E, S, W, F
Cox, H L (Dublin U) 1875 E, 1876 E, 1877 E, S
Craig, R G (Queen's U, Belfast) 1938 S, W
Crawford, E C (Dublin U) 1885 E, S 1
Crawford, W E (Lansdowne) 1920 E, S, W, F, 1921 E, S, W, F, 1922 E, S, 1923 E, S, W, F, 1924 F, E, W, NZ, 1925 F, E, S, W, 1926 F, E, S, W, 1927 F, E, S, W
Crean, T J (Wanderers) 1894 E, S, W, 1895 E, S, W, 1896 E, S, W
Crichton, R Y (Dublin U) 1920 E, S, W, F, 1921 F, 1922 E, 1923 W, F, 1924 F, E, S, W, NZ, 1925 E, S
Croker, E W D (Limerick) 1878 E
Cromey, G E (Queen's U, Belfast) 1937 E, S, W, 1938 E, S, W, 1939 E, S, W
Cronin, B M (Garryowen) 1995 S, 1997 S
Cronin, S (Connacht) 2009 Fj(R), 2010 W(R),NZ1,A

Cronyn, A P (Dublin U, Lansdowne) 1875 E, 1876 E, 1880 S
Crossan, K D (Instonians) 1982 S, 1984 F, W, E, S, 1985 S, F, W, E, 1986 E, S, R, 1987 E, S, F, W, [W, C, Tg, A], 1988 S, F, W, E 1, WS, It, 1989 W, S, NZ, 1990 E, S, F, W, Arg, 1991 E, S, Nm 2 [Z, J, S], 1992 W
Crotty, D J (Garryowen) 1996 A, 1997 It 1, F, W, 2000 C
Crowe, J F (UC Dublin) 1974 NZ
Crowe, L (Old Belvedere) 1950 E, S, W
Crowe, M P (Lansdowne) 1929 W, 1930 E, S, W, 1931 F, S, W, SA, 1932 S, W, 1933 W, S, 1934 E
Crowe, P M (Blackrock Coll) 1935 E, 1938 E
Cullen, L F M (Blackrock Coll, Leinster, Leicester) 2002 NZ 2(R), R (R), Ru (R), Gg (R), A (R), Fj, Arg (R), 2003 S 1(R), It 1(R), F (R), W 1, Tg, Sm, It 2, 2004 US(R), 2005 J1,2,R, 2007 Arg2, 2009 Fj, 2010 It,F,E(R),W(R)
Cullen, T J (UC Dublin) 1949 F
Cullen, W J (Monkstown and Manchester) 1920 E
Culliton, M G (Wanderers) 1959 E, S, W, F, 1960 E, S, W, F, SA, 1961 E, S, W, F, 1962 S, F, 1964 E, S, W, F
Cummins, W E A (Queen's Coll, Cork) 1879 S, 1881 E, 1882 E
Cunningham, D McC (NIFC) 1923 E, S, W, 1925 F, E, W
Cunningham, M J (UC Cork) 1955 F, E, S, W, 1956 F, S, W
Cunningham, V J G (St Mary's Coll) 1988 E 2, It, 1990 Arg (R), 1991 Nm 1,2, [Z, J(R)], 1992 NZ 1,2, A, 1993 S, F, W, E, R, 1994 F
Cunningham, W A (Lansdowne) 1920 W, 1921 E, S, W, F, 1922 E, 1923 S, W
Cuppaidge, J L (Dublin U) 1879 E, 1880 E, S
Currell, J (NIFC) 1877 S
Curtis, A B (Oxford U) 1950 F, E, S
Curtis, D M (London Irish) 1991 W, E, S, Nm 1,2, [Z, J, S, A], 1992 W, E, S (R), F
Cuscaden, W A (Dublin U, Bray) 1876 E
Cussen, D J (Dublin U) 1921 E, S, W, F, 1922 E, 1923 E, S, W, F, 1926 F, E, S, W, 1927 F, E
Daly, J C (London Irish) 1947 F, E, S, W, 1948 E, S, W
Daly, M J (Harlequins) 1938 E
Danaher, P P A (Lansdowne, Garryowen) 1988 S, F, W, WS, It, 1989 F, NZ (R), 1990 F, 1992 S, F, NZ 1, A, 1993 S, F, W, E, R, 1994 F, W, E, S, A 1,2, US, 1995 E, S, F, W
D'Arcy, G W (Lansdowne, Leinster) 1999 [R (R)], 2002 Fj (R), 2003 Tg (R), Sm (R), W 2(R), 2004 F,W,E,It,S,SA1, 2005 It,NZ, A,R, 2006 It,F,W,S,E,NZ1,2,A1,SA,A2,PI(R), 2007 W,F,E,S1,It1, 2, [Nm,Gg,F,Arg], 2008 It, 2009 F(t&R), It(R),S,W,Fj,SA(R), 2010 It,F,E,W,S,NZ1
Dargan, M J (Old Belvedere) 1952 S, W
Davidson, C T (NIFC) 1921 F
Davidson, I G (NIFC) 1899 E, 1900 S, W, 1901 E, S, W, 1902 E, S, W
Davidson, J C (Dungannon) 1969 F, E, S, W, 1973 NZ, 1976 NZ
Davidson, J W (Dungannon, London Irish, Castres) 1995 Fj, 1996 S, F, W, E, WS, A, 1997 It 1, F, W, E, S, 1998 Gg (R), R (R), SA 3(R), 1999 F, W, E, S, It, A 1,2(R), Arg 1, [US,R (R), Arg 2], 2000 S (R), W (R), US, C, 2001 It (R), S
Davies, F E (Lansdowne) 1892 S, W, 1893 E, S, W
Davis, J L (Monkstown) 1898 E, S
Davis, W J N (Edinburgh U, Bessbrook) 1890 S, W, E, 1891 E, S, W, 1892 E, S, 1895 S
Davison, W (Belfast Academy) 1887 W
Davy, E O'D (UC Dublin, Lansdowne) 1925 W, 1926 F, E, S, W, 1927 F, E, S, W, A, 1928 F, E, S, W, 1929 F, E, S, W, 1930 F, E, S, W, 1931 F, E, S, W, SA, 1932 E, S, W, 1933 E, W, S, 1934 E
Dawson, A R (Wanderers) 1958 A, E, S, W, F, 1959 E, S, W, F, 1960 F, SA, 1961 E, S, W, F, SA, 1962 S, F, W, 1963 F, E, S, W, NZ, 1964 E, S, F
Dawson, K (London Irish) 1997 NZ, C, 1998 S, 1999 [R, Arg 2], 2000 E, S, It, F, W, J, SA, 2001 R, S, W (R), E (R), Sm, 2002 Fj, 2003 Tg, It 2(R), S 2(R)
Dean, P M (St Mary's Coll) 1981 SA 1,2, A, 1982 W, E, S, F, 1984 A, 1985 S, F, W, E, 1986 F, W, R, 1987 E, S, F, W, [W, A], 1988 S, F, W, E 1,2, WS, It, 1989 F, W, E, S
Deane, E C (Monkstown) 1909 E
Deering, M J (Bective Rangers) 1929 W
Deering, S J (Bective Rangers) 1935 E, S, W, NZ, 1936 E, S, W, 1937 E, S
Deering, S M (Garryowen, St Mary's Coll) 1974 W, 1976 F, W, E, S, 1977 W, E, 1978 NZ
De Lacy, H (Harlequins) 1948 E, S
Delany, M G (Bective Rangers) 1895 W
Dempsey, G T (Terenure Coll, Leinster) 1998 Gg (R). SA 3, 1999 F, E, S, It, A 2, 2000 E (R), S, It, F, W, SA, 2001 It, F, S, W, E, NZ, 2002 W, E, S, It, F, NZ 1,2, R, Ru, Gg, A, Arg, 2003 S 1, E (R), A, Sm, W 2(R), It 2, S 2(R),[R,Nm,Arg,A,F], 2004 F,W, E,It,S, SA1,2,3,US(R),Arg, 2005 It(R),S,E,F,W,J1,2,NZ(R),R(R), 2006 E(R),NZ1(R),2(t&R), A1,SA,A2(R),PI, 2007 W,F,E,S1,It1,2, [Nm,Gg,F], 2008 It,F,A(R),NZ2
Dennison, S P (Garryowen) 1973 F, 1975 E, S
Dick, C J (Ballymena) 1961 W, F, SA, 1962 W, 1963 F, E, S, W
Dick, J S (Queen's U, Belfast) 1962 E
Dick, J S (Queen's U, Cork) 1887 E, S, W
Dickson, J A N (Dublin U) 1920 E, W, F
Doherty, A E (Old Wesley) 1974 P (R)
Doherty, W D (Guy's Hospital) 1920 E, S, W, 1921 E, S, W, F
Donaldson, J A (Belfast Collegians) 1958 A, E, S, W
Donovan, T M (Queen's Coll, Cork) 1889 S
Dooley, J F (Galwegians) 1959 E, S, W
Doran, B R W (Lansdowne) 1900 S, W, 1901 E, S, W, 1902 E, S, W
Doran, E F (Lansdowne) 1890 S, W
Doran, G P (Lansdowne) 1899 S, W, 1900 E, S, 1902 S, W, 1903 W, 1904 E
Douglas, A C (Instonians) 1923 F, 1924 E, S, 1927 A, 1928 S
Dowling, I (Munster) 2009 C,US
Downing, A J (Dublin U) 1882 W
Dowse, J C A (Monkstown) 1914 F, S, W
Doyle, J A P (Greystones) 1984 E, S
Doyle, J T (Bective Rangers) 1935 W
Doyle, M G (Blackrock Coll, UC Dublin, Cambridge U, Edinburgh Wands) 1965 F, E, S, W, SA, 1966 F, E, S, W, 1967 A 1, E, S, W, F, A 2, 1968 F, E, S, W, A
Doyle, T J (Wanderers) 1968 E, S, W
Duffy, G W (Harlequins, Connacht) 2004 SA 2(R), 2005 S(R),J1,2, 2007 Arg1,2,S2, [Arg(R)], 2009 C,US
Duggan, A T A (Lansdowne) 1963 NZ, 1964 F, 1966 W, 1967 A 1, S, W, A 2, 1968 F, E, S, W, 1969 F, E, S, W, 1970 SA, F, E, S, W, 1971 F, E, S, W, 1972 F 2
Duggan, W (UC Cork) 1920 S, W
Duggan, W P (Blackrock Coll) 1975 E, S, F, W, 1976 A, F, W, S, NZ, 1977 W, E, S, F, 1978 S, F, W, E, NZ, 1979 E, S, A 1,2, 1980 E, 1981 F, W, E, S, SA 1,2, A, 1982 W, E, S, 1983 S, F, W, E, 1984 F, W, E, S
Duignan, P (Galwegians) 1998 Gg, R
Duncan, W R (Malone) 1984 W, E
Dunlea, F J (Lansdowne) 1989 W, E, S
Dunlop, R (Dublin U) 1889 W, 1890 S, W, E, 1891 E, S, W, 1892 E, S, 1893 W, 1894 W
Dunn, P E F (Bective Rangers) 1923 S
Dunn, T B (NIFC) 1935 NZ
Dunne, M J (Lansdowne) 1929 F, E, S, 1930 F, E, S, W, 1932 E, S, W, 1933 E, W, S, 1934 E, S, W
Dwyer, P J (UC Dublin) 1962 W, 1963 F, NZ, 1964 S, W
Earls, K G (Munster) 2008 C,NZ2(R), 2009 A(R),Fj,SA, 2010 It(R),F,E,W,S
Easterby, S H (Llanelli Scarlets) 2000 S, It, F, W, Arg, US, C, 2001 S, Sm (R), 2002 W, E (R), S (R), It, F, NZ 1,2, R, Ru, Gg, 2003 Tg, Sm, It 2, S 2(t+R), [Nm,Arg,A,F], 2004 F,W,E,It, S,SA1, 2,3,US,Arg, 2005 It,S,E,F,W,NZ,A, 2006 It,F,W,S,E, SA(R), A2(R),PI, 2007 W,F,E,S1,It1,2, [Nm,Gg,F,Arg], 2008 It,S(R), E(R)
Easterby, W G (Ebbw Vale, Ballynahinch, Llanelli, Leinster) 2000 US, C (R), 2001 R (R), S, W (R), Sm (R), 2002 W (R), S (R), R (R), Ru (R), Gg (R), Fj, 2003 S 1(R), It 1(R), Tg, Sm, W 2(R), It 2, S 2(R), [R(R),Nm(R),F(R)], 2004 W(R),It(R),S(R),SA2(R), US, 2005 S(R)
Edwards, H G (Dublin U) 1877 E, 1878 E
Edwards, R W (Malone) 1904 W
Edwards, T (Lansdowne) 1888 M, 1890 S, W, E, 1892 W, 1893 E
Edwards, W V (Malone) 1912 F, E
Egan, J D (Bective Rangers) 1922 S
Egan, J T (Cork Constitution) 1931 F, E, SA
Egan, M S (Garryowen) 1893 E, 1895 S
Ekin, W (Queen's Coll, Belfast) 1888 W, S
Elliott, W R J (Bangor) 1979 S
Elwood, E P (Lansdowne, Galwegians) 1993 W, E, R, 1994 F, W, E, S, A 1,2, 1995 F, W, [NZ, W, F], 1996 US, S, 1997 F, W, E, NZ, C, It 2(R), 1998 F, W, E, SA 1,2, Gg, R, SA 3, 1999 It, Arg 1(R), [US (R), A 3(R), R]
English, M A F (Lansdowne, Limerick Bohemians) 1958 W, F, 1959 E, S, F, 1960 E, S, 1961 S, W, F, 1962 F, W, 1963 E, S, W, NZ
Ennis, F N G (Wanderers) 1979 A 1(R)

Ensor, A H (Wanderers) 1973 W, F, 1974 F, W, E, S, P, NZ, 1975 E, S, F, W, 1976 A, F, W, E, NZ, 1977 E, 1978 S, F, W, E
Entrican, J C (Queen's U, Belfast) 1931 S
Erskine, D J (Sale) 1997 NZ (R), C, It 2
Fagan, G L (Kingstown School) 1878 E
Fagan, W B C (Wanderers) 1956 F, E, S
Farrell, J L (Bective Rangers) 1926 F, E, S, W, 1927 F, E, S, W, A, 1928 F, E, S, W, 1929 F, E, S, W, 1930 F, E, S, W, 1931 F, E, S, W, SA, 1932 E, S, W
Feddis, N (Lansdowne) 1956 E
Feighery, C F P (Lansdowne) 1972 F 1, E, F 2
Feighery, T A O (St Mary's Coll) 1977 W, E
Ferris, H H (Queen's Coll, Belfast) 1901 W
Ferris, J H (Queen's Coll, Belfast) 1900 E, S, W
Ferris, S (Ulster) 2006 PI, 2007 Arg1(R),2,S2, 2008 A(R), C,NZ2(R),Arg, 2009 F,It,E, S,W,A,Fj,SA, 2010 F,E,W,S
Field, M J (Malone) 1994 E, S, A 1(R), 1995 F (R), W (t), It (R), [NZ(t + R), J], Fj, 1996 F (R), W, E, A (R), 1997 F, W, E, S
Finlay, J E (Queen's Coll, Belfast) 1913 E, S, W, 1920 E, S, W
Finlay, W (NIFC) 1876 E, 1877 E, S, 1878 E, 1879 S, E, 1880 S, 1882 S
Finn, M C (UC Cork, Cork Constitution) 1979 E, 1982 W, E, S, F, 1983 S, F, W, E, 1984 E, S, A, 1986 F, W
Finn, R G A (UC Dublin) 1977 F
Fitzgerald, C C (Glasgow U, Dungannon) 1902 E, 1903 E, S
Fitzgerald, C F (St Mary's Coll) 1979 A 1,2, 1980 E, S, F, W, 1982 W, E, S, F, 1983 S, F, W, E, 1984 F, W, A, 1985 S, F, W, E, 1986 F, W, E, S
Fitzgerald, D C (Lansdowne, De La Salle Palmerston) 1984 E, S, 1986 W, E, S, R, 1987 E, S, F, W, [W, C, A], 1988 S, F, W, E 1, 1989 NZ (R), 1990 E, S, F, W, Arg, 1991 F, W, E, S, Nm 1,2, [Z, S, A], 1992 W, S (R)
Fitzgerald, J (Wanderers) 1884 W
Fitzgerald, J J (Young Munster) 1988 S, F, 1990 S, F, W, 1991 F, W, E, S, [J], 1994 A 1,2
Fitzgerald, L M (Leinster) 2006 PI, 2007 Arg2(R), 2008 W(R),E(R),C,NZ2,Arg, 2009 F,It,E,S,W,A
Fitzgibbon, M J J (Shannon) 1992 W, E, S, F, NZ 1,2
Fitzpatrick, J M (Dungannon) 1998 SA 1,2 Gg (R), R (R), SA 3, 1999 F (R), W (R), E (R), It, Arg 1(R), [US (R), A 3, R, Arg 2(t&R)], 2000 S (R), It (R), Arg (R), US, C, SA (t&R), 2001 R (R), 2003 W 1(R), E (R), Tg, W 2(R), It 2(R)
Fitzpatrick, M P (Wanderers) 1978 S, 1980 S, F, W, 1981 F, W, E, S, A, 1985 F (R)
Flannery, J P (Munster) 2005 R(R), 2006 It,F,W,S,E,NZ1,2,A1, 2007 W(R),F(R),E(R), S1(R),It1(R),Arg1,S2,It2(R), [Nm(R),Gg(R), F,Arg], 2008 NZ1,A(R),C,NZ2(R),Arg, 2009 F,It,E,S(R),W,A,Fj, SA, 2010 It,F
Flavin, P (Blackrock Coll) 1997 F (R), S
Fletcher, W W (Kingstown) 1882 W, S, 1883 E
Flood, R S (Dublin U) 1925 W
Flynn, M K (Wanderers) 1959 F, 1960 F, 1962 E, S, F, W, 1964 E, S, W, F, 1965 F, E, S, W, SA, 1966 F, E, S, 1972 F 1, E, F 2, 1973 NZ
Fogarty, J (Leinster) 2010 NZ1(R)
Fogarty, T (Garryowen) 1891 W
Foley, A G (Shannon, Munster) 1995 E, S, F, W, It, [J(t + R)], 1996 A, 1997 It 1, E (R), 2000 E, S, It, F, W, Arg, C, J, SA, 2001 It, F, R, S, W, E, Sm, NZ, 2002 W, E, S, It, F, NZ 1,2, R, Ru, Gg, A, Fj, Arg, 2003 S 1, It 1, F, W 1, E, W 2, [R,A], 2004 F,W,E,It,S, SA1,2,3,US(R),Arg, 2005 It,S,E,F,W
Foley, B O (Shannon) 1976 F, E, 1977 W (R), 1980 F, W, 1981 F, E, S, SA 1,2, A
Forbes, R E (Malone) 1907 E
Forrest, A J (Wanderers) 1880 E, S, 1881 E, S, 1882 W, E, 1883 E, 1885 S 2
Forrest, E G (Wanderers) 1888 M, 1889 S, W, 1890 S, E, 1891 E, 1893 S, W, 1894 E, S, W, 1895 W, 1897 E, S
Forrest, H (Wanderers) 1893 S, W
Fortune, J J (Clontarf) 1963 NZ, 1964 E
Foster, A R (Derry) 1910 E, S, F, 1911 E, S, W, F, 1912 F, E, S, W, 1914 E, S, W, 1921 E, S, W
Francis, N P J (Blackrock Coll, London Irish, Old Belvedere) 1987 [Tg, A], 1988 WS, It, 1989 S, 1990 E, F, W, 1991 E, S, Nm 1,2, [Z, J, S, A], 1992 W, E, S, 1993 F, R, 1994 F, W, E, S, A 1,2, US, 1995 E, [NZ, J, W, F], Fj, 1996 US, S
Franks, J G (Dublin U) 1898 E, S, W
Frazer, E F (Bective Rangers) 1891 S, 1892 S
Freer, A E (Lansdowne) 1901 E, S, W
Fulcher, G M (Cork Constitution, London Irish) 1994 A 2, US, 1995 E (R), S, F, W, It, [NZ, W, F], Fj, 1996 US, S, F, W, E, A, 1997 It 1, W (R), 1998 SA 1(R)
Fulton, J (NIFC) 1895 S, W, 1896 E, 1897 E, 1898 W, 1899 E, 1900 W, 1901 E, 1902 E, S, W, 1903 E, S, W, 1904 E, S
Furlong, J N (UC Galway) 1992 NZ 1,2
Gaffikin, W (Windsor) 1875 E
Gage, J H (Queen's U, Belfast) 1926 S, W, 1927 S, W
Galbraith, E (Dublin U) 1875 E
Galbraith, H T (Belfast Acad) 1890 W
Galbraith, R (Dublin U) 1875 E, 1876 E, 1877 E
Galwey, M J (Shannon) 1991 F, W, Nm 2(R), [J], 1992 E, S, F, NZ 1,2, A, 1993 F, W, E, R, 1994 F, W, E, S, A 1, US (R), 1995 E, 1996 WS, 1998 F (R), 1999 W (R), 2000 E (R), S, It, F, W, Arg, C, 2001 It, F, R, W, E, Sm, NZ, 2002 W, E, S
Ganly, J B (Monkstown) 1927 F, E, S, W, A, 1928 F, E, S, W, 1929 F, S, 1930 F
Gardiner, F (NIFC) 1900 E, S, 1901 E, W, 1902 E, S, W, 1903 E, W, 1904 E, S, W, 1906 E, S, W, 1907 S, W, 1908 S, W, 1909 E, S, F
Gardiner, J B (NIFC) 1923 E, S, W, F, 1924 F, E, S, W, NZ, 1925 F, E, S, W
Gardiner, S (Belfast Albion) 1893 E, S
Gardiner, W (NIFC) 1892 E, S, 1893 E, S, W, 1894 E, S, W, 1895 E, S, W, 1896 E, S, W, 1897 E, S, 1898 W
Garry, M G (Bective Rangers) 1909 E, S, W, F, 1911 E, S, W
Gaston, J T (Dublin U) 1954 NZ, F, E, S, W, 1955 W 1956 F, E
Gavin, T J (Moseley, London Irish) 1949 F, E
Geoghegan, S P (London Irish, Bath) 1991 F, W, E, S, Nm 1, [Z, S, A], 1992 E, S, F, A, 1993 S, F, W, E, R, 1994 F, W, E, S, A 1,2, US, 1995 E, S, F, W, [NZ, J, W, F], Fj, 1996 US, S, W, E
Gibson, C M H (Cambridge U, NIFC) 1964 E, S, W, F, 1965 F, E, S, W, SA, 1966 F, E, S, W, 1967 A 1, E, S, W, F, A 2, 1968 E, S, W, A, 1969 E, S, W, 1970 SA, F, E, S, W, 1971 F, E, S, W, 1972 F 1, E, F 2, 1973 NZ, E, S, W, F, 1974 F, W, E, S, P, 1975 E, S, F, W, 1976 A, F, W, E, S, NZ, 1977 W, E, S, F, 1978 F, W, E, NZ, 1979 S, A 1,2
Gibson, M E (Lansdowne, London Irish) 1979 F, W, E, S, 1981 W (R), 1986 R, 1988 S, F, W, E 2
Gifford, H P (Wanderers) 1890 S
Gillespie, J C (Dublin U) 1922 W, F
Gilpin, F G (Queen's U, Belfast) 1962 E, S, F
Glass, D C (Belfast Collegians) 1958 F, 1960 W, 1961 W, SA
Gleeson, K D (St Mary's Coll, Leinster) 2002 W (R), F (R), NZ 1,2, R, Ru, Gg, A, Arg, 2003 S 1, It 1, F, W 1, E, A, W 2, [R,A,F], 2004 F,W,E,It, 2006 NZ1(R),A1(R), 2007 Arg1,S2(R)
Glennon, B T (Lansdowne) 1993 F (R)
Glennon, J J (Skerries) 1980 E, S, 1987 E, S, F, [W (R)]
Godfrey, R P (UC Dublin) 1954 S, W
Goodall, K G (City of Derry, Newcastle U) 1967 A 1, E, S, W, F, A 2, 1968 F, E, S, W, A, 1969 F, E, S, 1970 SA, F, E, S, W
Gordon, A (Dublin U) 1884 S
Gordon, T G (NIFC) 1877 E, S, 1878 E
Gotto, R P C (NIFC) 1906 SA
Goulding, W J (Cork) 1879 S
Grace, T O (UC Dublin, St Mary's Coll) 1972 F 1, E, 1973 NZ, E, S, W, 1974 E, S, P, NZ, 1975 E, S, F, W, 1976 A, F, W, E, S, NZ, 1977 W, E, S, F, 1978 S
Graham, R I (Dublin U) 1911 F
Grant, E L (CIYMS) 1971 F, E, S, W
Grant, P J (Bective Rangers) 1894 S, W
Graves, C R A (Wanderers) 1934 E, S, W, 1935 E, S, W, NZ, 1936 E, S, W, 1937 E, S, 1938 E, S, W
Gray, R D (Old Wesley) 1923 E, S, 1925 F, 1926 F
Greene, E H (Dublin U, Kingstown) 1882 W, 1884 W, 1885 E, S 2, 1886 E
Greer, R (Kingstown) 1876 E
Greeves, T J (NIFC) 1907 E, S, W, 1909 W, F
Gregg, R J (Queen's U, Belfast) 1953 F, E, S, W, 1954 F, E, S
Griffin, C S (London Irish) 1951 F, E
Griffin, J L (Wanderers) 1949 S, W
Griffiths, W (Limerick) 1878 E
Grimshaw, C (Queen's U, Belfast) 1969 E (R)
Guerin, B N (Galwegians) 1956 S
Gwynn, A P (Dublin U) 1895 W
Gwynn, L H (Dublin U) 1893 S, 1894 E, S, W, 1897 S, 1898 E, S
Hakin, R F (CIYMS) 1976 W, S, NZ, 1977 W, E, F
Hall, R O N (Dublin U) 1884 W
Hall, W H (Instonians) 1923 E, S, W, F, 1924 F, S
Hallaran, C F G T (Royal Navy) 1921 E, S, W, 1922 E, S, W, 1923 E, F, 1924 F, E, S, W, 1925 F, 1926 F, E

Halpin, G F (Wanderers, London Irish) 1990 E, 1991 [J], 1992 E, S, F, 1993 R, 1994 F (R), 1995 It, [NZ, W, F]
Halpin, T (Garryowen) 1909 S, W, F, 1910 E, S, W, 1911 E, S, W, F, 1912 F, E, S
Halvey, E O (Shannon) 1995 F, W, It, [J, W (t), F (R)], 1997 NZ, C (R)
Hamilton, A J (Lansdowne) 1884 W
Hamilton, G F (NIFC) 1991 F, W, E, S, Nm 2, [Z, J, S, A], 1992 A
Hamilton, R L (NIFC) 1926 F
Hamilton, R W (Wanderers) 1893 W
Hamilton, W J (Dublin U) 1877 E
Hamlet, G T (Old Wesley) 1902 E, S, W, 1903 E, S, W, 1904 S, W, 1905 E, S, W, NZ, 1906 SA, 1907 E, S, W, 1908 E, S, W, 1909 E, S, W, F, 1910 E, S, F, 1911 E, S, W, F
Hanrahan, C J (Dolphin) 1926 S, W, 1927 E, S, W, A, 1928 F, E, S, 1929 F, E, S, W, 1930 F, E, S, W, 1931 F, 1932 S, W
Harbison, H T (Bective Rangers) 1984 W (R), E, S, 1986 R, 1987 E, S, F, W
Hardy, G G (Bective Rangers) 1962 S
Harman, G R A (Dublin U) 1899 E, W
Harper, J (Instonians) 1947 F, E, S
Harpur, T G (Dublin U) 1908 E, S, W
Harrison, T (Cork) 1879 S, 1880 S, 1881 E
Harvey, F M W (Wanderers) 1907 W, 1911 F
Harvey, G A D (Wanderers) 1903 E, S, 1904 W, 1905 E, S
Harvey, T A (Dublin U) 1900 W, 1901 S, W, 1902 E, S, W, 1903 E, W
Haycock, P P (Terenure Coll) 1989 E
Hayes, J J (Shannon, Munster) 2000 S, It, F, W, Arg, C, J, SA, 2001 It, F, R, S, W, E, Sm, NZ, 2002 W, E, S, It, F, NZ 1,2, R, Ru, Gg, A, Fj, Arg, 2003 S 1, It 1, F, W 1, E, [R(R),Nm,Arg,A,F], 2004 F,W,E,It,S,SA1,2,3,US,Arg, 2005 It,S,E,F,W,NZ,A,R(R), 2006 It,F,W,S,E,NZ1,2,A1,SA,A2,PI, 2007 W,F,E,S1,It1, S2(R),It2, [Nm,Gg,F,Arg], 2008 It,F,S,W,E,NZ1,A,C(R),NZ2,Arg, 2009 F,It,E,S,W,A,Fj,SA, 2010 It,F,E,W,S
Headon, T A (UC Dublin) 1939 S, W
Healey, P (Limerick) 1901 E, S, W, 1902 E, S, W, 1903 E, S, W, 1904 S
Healy, C E (Leinster) 2009 A,SA, 2010 It,F,E,W,S,NZ1,A
Heaslip, J P R (Leinster) 2006 PI, 2007 Arg1,S2, 2008 It(R),F,S,W,E,NZ1,A,C,NZ2,Arg, 2009 F,It,E,S(R),W,A,Fj,SA, 2010 It,F,E,W,S,NZ1
Heffernan, M R (Cork Constitution) 1911 E, S, W, F
Hemphill, R (Dublin U) 1912 F, E, S, W
Henderson, N J (Queen's U, Belfast, NIFC) 1949 S, W, 1950 F, 1951 F, E, S, W, SA, 1952 F, S, W, E, 1953 F, E, S, W, 1954 NZ, F, E, S, W, 1955 F, E, S, W, 1956 S, W, 1957 F, E, S, W, 1958 A, E, S, W, F, 1959 E, S, W, F
Henderson R A J (London Irish, Wasps, Young Munster) 1996 WS, 1997 NZ, C, 1998 F, W, SA 1(R),2(R), 1999 F (R), E, S (R), It, 2000 S (R), It (R), F, W, Arg, US, J (R), SA, 2001 It, F, 2002 W (R), E (R), F, R (R), Ru (t), Gg (R), 2003 It 1(R),2
Henebrey, G J (Garryowen) 1906 E, S, W, SA, 1909 W, F
Henry, C (Ulster) 2010 A
Heron, A G (Queen's Coll, Belfast) 1901 E
Heron, J (NIFC) 1877 S, 1879 E
Heron, W T (NIFC) 1880 E, S
Herrick, R W (Dublin U) 1886 S
Heuston, F S (Kingstown) 1882 W, 1883 E, S
Hewitt, D (Queen's U, Belfast, Instonians) 1958 A, E, S, F, 1959 S, W, F, 1960 E, S, W, F, 1961 E, S, W, F, 1962 S, F, 1965 W
Hewitt, F S (Instonians) 1924 W, NZ, 1925 F, E, S, 1926 E, 1927 E, S, W
Hewitt, J A (NIFC) 1981 SA 1(R),2(R)
Hewitt, T R (Queen's U, Belfast) 1924 W, NZ, 1925 F, E, S, 1926 F, E, S, W
Hewitt, V A (Instonians) 1935 S, W, NZ, 1936 E, S, W
Hewitt, W J (Instonians) 1954 E, 1956 S, 1959 W, 1961 SA
Hewson, F T (Wanderers) 1875 E
Hickie, D A (St Mary's Coll, Leinster) 1997 W, E, S, NZ, C, It 2, 1998 S, F, W, E, SA 1,2, 2000 S, It, F, W, J, SA, 2001 F, R, S, W, E, NZ, 2002 W, E, S, It, F, R, Ru, Gg, A, 2003 S 1, It 1, F, W 1, E, It 2, S 2, [R,Nm,Arg,A], 2004 SA3,Arg, 2005 It,S,E,F,W, 2006 A2,PI, 2007 W,F,E,S1,It1,2, [Nm,Gg,Arg]
Hickie, D J (St Mary's Coll) 1971 F, E, S, W, 1972 F 1, E
Higgins, J A D (Civil Service) 1947 S, W, A, 1948 F, S, W
Higgins, W W (NIFC) 1884 E, S
Hillary, M F (UC Dublin) 1952 E
Hingerty, D J (UC Dublin) 1947 F, E, S, W
Hinton, W P (Old Wesley) 1907 W, 1908 E, S, W, 1909 E, S, 1910 E, S, W, F, 1911 E, S, W, 1912 F, E, W
Hipwell, M L (Terenure Coll) 1962 E, S, 1968 F, A, 1969 F (R), S (R), W, 1971 F, E, S, W, 1972 F 2
Hobbs, T H M (Dublin U) 1884 S, 1885 E
Hobson, E W (Dublin U) 1876 E
Hogan, N A (Terenure Coll, London Irish) 1995 E, W, [J, W, F], 1996 F, W, E, WS, 1997 F, W, E, It 2
Hogan, P (Garryowen) 1992 F
Hogan, T (Munster, Leinster) 2005 J1(R),2(R), 2007 It1(R),Arg1
Hogg, W (Dublin U) 1885 S 2
Holland, J J (Wanderers) 1981 SA 1,2, 1986 W
Holmes, G W (Dublin U) 1912 SA, 1913 E, S
Holmes, L J (Lisburn) 1889 S, W
Hooks, K J (Queen's U, Belfast, Ards, Bangor) 1981 S, 1989 NZ, 1990 F, W, Arg, 1991 F
Horan, A K (Blackheath) 1920 E, W
Horan, M J (Shannon, Munster) 2000 US (R), 2002 Fj, Arg (R), 2003 S 1(R), It 1(R), F, W 1, E, A, Sm, It 2, S 2, [R,Nm, Arg(t&R),A(R),F(R)], 2004 It(R),S(R),SA1(R),2(t&R), 3(R),US, 2005 It(R),S(R),E(R),F(R),W(R),J1,2,NZ,A,R, 2006 It,W,S,E,NZ1, 2,A1,SA, A2(R), 2007 W,F,E,It1,2, [Nm,Gg,F,Arg], 2008 It,F,S, W,E, NZ1,A,C,NZ2,Arg, 2009 F, It,E,S,W
Horgan, A P (Cork Const, Munster) 2003 Sm, W 2, S 2, 2004 F(R), 2005 J1,2,NZ
Horgan, S P (Lansdowne, Leinster) 2000 S, It, W, Arg, C, J, SA (R), 2001 It, S, W, E, NZ, 2002 S, It, F, A, Fj, Arg, 2003 S 1, [R,Nm,Arg,A,F], 2004 F,W,E,It,S,SA1,2,3,US, Arg, 2005 It,S, E,NZ,A,R, 2006 It,F,W,S,E,NZ1,2,A1,SA,A2,PI, 2007 F,E,S1,It1, [Gg,F, Arg], 2008 S(R),W,E,NZ1,A,C(R), 2009 Fj
Houston, K J (Oxford U, London Irish) 1961 SA, 1964 S, W, 1965 F, E, SA
Howe, T G (Dungannon, Ballymena, Ulster) 2000 US, J, SA, 2001 It, F, R, Sm, 2002 It (R), 2003 Tg, W 2, 2004 F,W,E,SA2
Hughes, R W (NIFC) 1878 E, 1880 E, S, 1881 S, 1882 E, S, 1883 E, S, 1884 E, S, 1885 E, 1886 E
Humphreys, D G (London Irish, Dungannon, Ulster) 1996 F, W, E, WS, 1997 E (R), S, It 2, 1998 S, E (R), SA 2(t + R), R (R), 1999 F, W, E, S, A 1,2, Arg 1, [US, A 3, Arg 2], 2000 E, S (R), F (t&R), W (R), Arg, US (R), C, J (R), SA (R), 2001 It (R), R, S (R), W, E, NZ, 2002 W, E, S, It, F, NZ 1(R),2(R), R (t+R), Ru (R), Gg (R), Fj, 2003 S 1, It 1, F, W 1, E, A, W 2, It 2, S 2(R), [R,Arg,A(R),F(R)], 2004W(R),It(R),S(R),SA2(R),US, 2005 S(R),W(R),J1,2,NZ(R), A(R),R
Hunt, E W F de Vere (Army, Rosslyn Park) 1930 F, 1932 E, S, W, 1933 E
Hunter, D V (Dublin U) 1885 S 2
Hunter, L M (Civil Service) 1968 W, A
Hunter, W R (CIYMS) 1962 E, S, W, F, 1963 F, E, S, 1966 F, E, S
Hurley, D (Munster) 2009 US(t&R)
Hurley, H D (Old Wesley, Moseley) 1995 Fj (t), 1996 WS
Hutton, S A (Malone) 1967 S, W, F, A 2
Ireland J (Windsor) 1876 E, 1877 E
Irvine, H A S (Collegians) 1901 S
Irwin, D G (Queen's U, Belfast, Instonians) 1980 F, W, 1981 F, W, E, S, SA 1,2, A, 1982 W, 1983 S, F, W, E, 1984 F, W, 1987 [Tg, A (R)], 1989 F, W, E, S, NZ, 1990 E, S
Irwin, J W S (NIFC) 1938 E, S, 1939 E, S, W
Irwin, S T (Queen's Coll, Belfast) 1900 E, S, W, 1901 E, W, 1902 E, S, W, 1903 S
Jack, H W (UC Cork) 1914 S, W, 1921 W
Jackman, B J (Leinster) 2005 J1(R),2(R), 2007 Arg1(R),2(R), 2008 It(R),F,S,W(R), E(R)
Jackson, A R V (Wanderers) 1911 E, S, W, F, 1913 W, F, 1914 F, E, S, W
Jackson, F (NIFC) 1923 E
Jackson, H W (Dublin U) 1877 E
Jameson, J S (Lansdowne) 1888 M, 1889 S, W, 1891 W, 1892 E, W, 1893 S
Jeffares, E W (Wanderers) 1913 E, S
Jennings, S (Leicester, Leinster) 2007 Arg 2, 2008 NZ1(R), A,C,NZ2(R), 2010 E(R), W(R),NZ1(R),A
Johns, P S (Dublin U, Dungannon, Saracens) 1990 Arg, 1992 NZ 1,2, A, 1993 S, F, W, E, R, 1994 F, W, E, S, A 1,2, US, 1995 E, S, W, It, [NZ, J, W, F], Fj, 1996 US, S, F, WS, 1997 It 1(R), F, W, E, S, NZ, C, It 2, 1998 S, F, W, E, SA 1,2, Gg, R, SA 3, 1999 F, W, E, S, It, A 1,2, Arg 1, [US, A 3, R], 2000 F (R), J
Johnston, J (Belfast Acad) 1881 S, 1882 S, 1884 S, 1885 S 1,2, 1886 E, 1887 E, S, W
Johnston, M (Dublin U) 1880 E, S, 1881 E, S, 1882 E, 1884 E, S, 1886 E

Johnston, R (Wanderers) 1893 E, W
Johnston, R W (Dublin U) 1890 S, W, E
Johnston, T J (Queen's Coll, Belfast) 1892 E, S, W, 1893 E, S, 1895 E
Johnstone, W E (Dublin U) 1884 W
Johnstone-Smyth, T R (Lansdowne) 1882 E
Kavanagh, J R (UC Dublin, Wanderers) 1953 F, E, S, W, 1954 NZ, S, W, 1955 F, E, 1956 E, S, W, 1957 F, E, S, W, 1958 A, E, S, W, 1959 E, S, W, F, 1960 E, S, W, F, SA, 1961 E, S, W, F, SA, 1962 F
Kavanagh, P J (UC Dublin, Wanderers) 1952 E, 1955 W
Keane, K P (Garryowen) 1998 E (R)
Keane, M I (Lansdowne) 1974 F, W, E, S, P, NZ, 1975 E, S, F, W, 1976 A, F, W, E, S, NZ, 1977 W, E, S, F, 1978 S, F, W, E, NZ, 1979 F, W, E, S, A 1,2, 1980 E, S, F, W, 1981 F, W, E, S, 1982 W, E, S, F, 1983 S, F, W, E, 1984 F, W, E, S
Kearney, R D J (Leinster) 2007 Arg 2, 2008 It(R),F,S,W,E, NZ1, A,C,NZ2,Arg, 2009 F,It,E,S,W,A,Fj,SA, 2010 It,F,W(R),S(R), NZ1,A
Kearney, R K (Wanderers) 1982 F, 1984 A, 1986 F, W
Keatley, I J (Connacht) 2009 C,US
Keeffe, E (Sunday's Well) 1947 F, E, S, W, A, 1948 F
Kelly, H C (NIFC) 1877 E, S, 1878 E, 1879 S, 1880 E, S
Kelly, J C (UC Dublin) 1962 F, W, 1963 F, E, S, W, NZ, 1964 E, S, W, F
Kelly, J P (Cork Constitution) 2002 It, NZ 1,2, R, Ru, Gg, A (R), 2003 It 1, F, A, Tg, Sm, It 2, [R(R),Nm(R),A(R),F]
Kelly, S (Lansdowne) 1954 S, W, 1955 S, 1960 W, F
Kelly, W (Wanderers) 1884 S
Kennedy, A G (Belfast Collegians) 1956 F
Kennedy, A P (London Irish) 1986 W, E
Kennedy, F (Wanderers) 1880 E, 1881 E, 1882 W
Kennedy, F A (Wanderers) 1904 E, W
Kennedy, H (Bradford) 1938 S, W
Kennedy, J M (Wanderers) 1882 W, 1884 W
Kennedy, K W (Queen's U, Belfast, London Irish) 1965 F, E, S, W, SA, 1966 F, E, W, 1967 A 1, E, S, W, F, A 2, 1968 F, A, 1969 F, E, S, W, 1970 SA, F, E, S, W, 1971 F, E, S, W, 1972 F 1, E, F 2, 1973 NZ, E, S, W, F, 1974 F, W, E, S, P, NZ, 1975 F, W
Kennedy, T J (St Mary's Coll) 1978 NZ, 1979 F, W, E (R), A 1,2, 1980 E, S, F, W, 1981 SA 1,2, A
Kenny, P (Wanderers) 1992 NZ 2(R)
Keogh, F S (Bective Rangers) 1964 W, F
Keon, J J (Limerick) 1879 E
Keyes, R P (Cork Constitution) 1986 E, 1991 [Z, J, S, A], 1992 W, E, S
Kidd, F W (Dublin U, Lansdowne) 1877 E, S, 1878 E
Kiely, M D (Lansdowne) 1962 W, 1963 F, E, S, W
Kiernan, M J (Dolphin, Lansdowne) 1982 W (R), E, S, F, 1983 S, F, W, E, 1984 E, S, A, 1985 S, F, W, E, 1986 F, W, E, S, R, 1987 E, S, F, W, [W, C, A], 1988 S, F, W, E 1,2, WS, 1989 F, W, E, S, 1990 E, S, F, W, Arg, 1991 F
Kiernan, T J (UC Cork, Cork Const) 1960 E, S, W, F, SA, 1961 E, S, W, F, SA, 1962 E, W, 1963 F, S, W, NZ, 1964 E, S, 1965 F, E, S, W, SA, 1966 F, E, S, W, 1967 A 1, E, S, W, F, A 2, 1968 F, E, S, W, A, 1969 F, E, S, W, 1970 SA, F, E, S, W, 1971 F, 1972 F 1, E, F 2, 1973 NZ, E, S
Killeen, G V (Garryowen) 1912 E, S, W, 1913 E, S, W, F, 1914 E, S, W
King, H (Dublin U) 1883 E, S
Kingston, T J (Dolphin) 1987 [W, Tg, A], 1988 S, F, W, E 1, 1990 F, W, 1991 [J], 1993 F, W, E, R, 1994 F, W, E, S, 1995 F, W, It, [NZ, J (R), W, F], Fj, 1996 US, S, F
Knox, J H (Dublin U, Lansdowne) 1904 W, 1905 E, S, W, NZ, 1906 E, S, W, 1907 W, 1908 S
Kyle, J W (Queen's U, Belfast, NIFC) 1947 F, E, S, W, A, 1948 F, E, S, W, 1949 F, E, S, W, 1950 F, E, S, W, 1951 F, E, S, W, SA, 1952 F, S, W, E, 1953 F, E, S, W, 1954 NZ, F, 1955 F, E, W, 1956 F, E, S, W, 1957 F, E, S, W, 1958 A, E, S
Lambert, N H (Lansdowne) 1934 S, W
Lamont, R A (Instonians) 1965 F, E, SA, 1966 F, E, S, W, 1970 SA, F, E, S, W
Landers, M F (Cork Const) 1904 W, 1905 E, S, W, NZ
Lane, D J (UC Cork) 1934 S, W, 1935 E, S
Lane, M F (UC Cork) 1947 W, 1949 F, E, S, W, 1950 F, E, S, W, 1951 F, S, W, SA, 1952 F, S, 1953 F, E
Lane, P (Old Crescent) 1964 W
Langan, D J (Clontarf) 1934 W
Langbroek, J A (Blackrock Coll) 1987 [Tg]
Lavery, P (London Irish) 1974 W, 1976 W
Lawlor, P J (Clontarf) 1951 S, SA, 1952 F, S, W, E, 1953 F, 1954 NZ, E, S, 1956 F, E
Lawlor, P J (Bective Rangers) 1935 E, S, W, 1937 E, S, W
Lawlor, P J (Bective Rangers) 1990 Arg, 1992 A, 1993 S
Leahy, K T (Wanderers) 1992 NZ 1
Leahy, M W (UC Cork) 1964 W
Leamy, D P (Munster) 2004 US, 2005 It,J2,NZ,A,R, 2006 It,F,W,S,E,NZ1,2,A1,SA,A2,PI(R), 2007 W,F,E,S1,It1,2, [Nm,Gg, F,Arg], 2008 It,F,S,W,E,NZ1,A, 2009 F(R),It(t&R), E(R),S,W(R), C,US,A(t&R),Fj
Lee, S (NIFC) 1891 E, S, W, 1892 E, S, W, 1893 E, S, W, 1894 E, S, W, 1895 E, W, 1896 E, S, W, 1897 E, 1898 E
Le Fanu, V C (Cambridge U, Lansdowne) 1886 E, S, 1887 E, W, 1888 S, 1889 W, 1890 E, 1891 E, 1892 E, S, W
Lenihan, D G (UC Cork, Cork Const) 1981 A, 1982 W, E, S, F, 1983 S, F, W, E, 1984 F, W, E, S, A, 1985 S, F, W, E, 1986 F, W, E, S, R, 1987 E, S, F, W, [W, C, Tg, A], 1988 S, F, W, E 1,2, WS, It, 1989 F, W, E, S, NZ, 1990 S, F, W, Arg, 1991 Nm 2, [Z, S, A], 1992 W
L'Estrange, L P F (Dublin U) 1962 E
Levis, F H (Wanderers) 1884 E
Lewis, K P (Leinster) 2005 J2(R), 2007 Arg1,2(R)
Lightfoot, E J (Lansdowne) 1931 F, E, S, W, SA, 1932 E, S, W, 1933 E, W, S
Lindsay, H (Dublin U, Armagh) 1893 E, S, W, 1894 E, S, W, 1895 E, 1896 E, S, W, 1898 E, S, W
Little, T J (Bective Rangers) 1898 W, 1899 S, W, 1900 S, W, 1901 E, S
Lloyd, R A (Dublin U, Liverpool) 1910 E, S, 1911 E, S, W, F, 1912 F, E, S, W, SA, 1913 E, S, W, F, 1914 F, E, 1920 E, F
Longwell, G W (Ballymena) 2000 J (R), SA, 2001 F (R), R, S (R), Sm, NZ (R), 2002 W (R), E (R), S (R), It, F, NZ 1,2, R, Ru, Gg, A, Arg, 2003 S 1, It 1, F, E, A, It 2, 2004 It(R)
Lydon, C T J (Galwegians) 1956 S
Lyle, R K (Dublin U) 1910 W, F
Lyle, T R (Dublin U) 1885 E, S 1,2, 1886 E, 1887 E, S
Lynch, J F (St Mary's Coll) 1971 F, E, S, W, 1972 F 1, E, F 2, 1973 NZ, E, S, W, 1974 F, W, E, S, P, NZ
Lynch, L M (Lansdowne) 1956 S
Lytle, J H (NIFC) 1894 E, S, W, 1895 W, 1896 E, S, W, 1897 E, S, 1898 E, S, 1899 S
Lytle, J N (NIFC) 1888 M, 1889 W, 1890 E, 1891 E, S, 1894 E, S, W
Lyttle, V J (Collegians, Bedford) 1938 E, 1939 E, S
McAleese, D R (Ballymena) 1992 F
McAllan, G H (Dungannon) 1896 S, W
Macauley, J (Limerick) 1887 E, S
McBride, W D (Malone) 1988 W, E 1, WS, It, 1989 S, 1990 F, W, Arg, 1993 S, F, W, E, R, 1994 W, E, S, A 1(R), 1995 S, F, [NZ, W, F], Fj (R), 1996 W, E, WS, A, 1997 It 1(R), F, W, E, S
McBride, W J (Ballymena) 1962 E, S, F, W, 1963 F, E, S, W, NZ, 1964 E, S, F, 1965 F, E, S, W, SA, 1966 F, E, S, W, 1967 A 1, E, S, W, F, A 2, 1968 F, E, S, W, A, 1969 F, E, S, W, 1970 SA, F, E, S, W, 1971 F, E, S, W, 1972 F 1, E, F 2, 1973 NZ, E, S, W, F, 1974 F, W, E, S, P, NZ, 1975 E, S, F, W
McCahill, S A (Sunday's Well) 1995 Fj (t)
McCall, B W (London Irish) 1985 F (R), 1986 E, S
McCall, M C (Bangor, Dungannon, London Irish) 1992 NZ 1(R),2, 1994 W, 1996 E (R), A, 1997 It 1, NZ, C, It 2, 1998 S, E, SA 1,2
McCallan, B (Ballymena) 1960 E, S
McCarten, R J (London Irish) 1961 E, W, F
McCarthy, E A (Kingstown) 1882 W
McCarthy, J S (Dolphin) 1948 F, E, S, W, 1949 F, E, S, W, 1950 W, 1951 F, E, S, W, SA, 1952 F, S, W, E, 1953 F, E, S, 1954 NZ, F, E, S, W, 1955 F, E
McCarthy, P D (Cork Const) 1992 NZ 1,2, A, 1993 S, R (R)
MacCarthy, St G (Dublin U) 1882 W
McCarthy, T (Cork) 1898 W
McClelland, T A (Queen's U, Belfast) 1921 E, S, W, F, 1922 E, W, F, 1923 E, S, W, F, 1924 F, E, S, W, NZ
McClenahan, R O (Instonians) 1923 E, S, W
McClinton, A N (NIFC) 1910 W, F
McCombe, W McM (Dublin U, Bangor) 1968 F, 1975 E, S, F, W
McConnell, A A (Collegians) 1947 A, 1948 F, E, S, W, 1949 F, E
McConnell, G (Derry, Edinburgh U) 1912 F, E, 1913 W, F
McConnell, J W (Lansdowne) 1913 S
McCormac, F M (Wanderers) 1909 W, 1910 W, F
McCormick, W J (Wanderers) 1930 E
McCoull, H C (Belfast Albion) 1895 E, S, W, 1899 E
McCourt, D (Queen's U, Belfast) 1947 A

McCoy, J J (Dungannon, Bangor, Ballymena) 1984 W, A, 1985 S, F, W, E, 1986 F, 1987 [Tg], 1988 E 2, WS, It, 1989 F, W, E, S, NZ
McCracken, H (NIFC) 1954 W
McCullen, A (Lansdowne) 2003 Sm
McCullough, M T (Ulster) 2005 J1,2,NZ(R),A(R)
McDermott, S J (London Irish) 1955 S, W
Macdonald, J A (Methodist Coll, Belfast) 1875 E, 1876 E, 1877 S, 1878 E, 1879 S, 1880 E, 1881 S, 1882 E, S, 1883 E, S, 1884 E, S
McDonald, J P (Malone) 1987 [C], 1990 E (R), S, Arg
McDonnell, A C (Dublin U) 1889 W, 1890 S, W, 1891 E
McDowell, J C (Instonians) 1924 F, NZ
McFarland, B A T (Derry) 1920 S, W, F, 1922 W
McGann, B J (Lansdowne) 1969 F, E, S, W, 1970 SA, F, E, S, W, 1971 F, E, S, W, 1972 F 1, E, F 2, 1973 NZ, E, S, W, 1976 F, W, E, S, NZ
McGowan, A N (Blackrock Coll) 1994 US
McGown, T M W (NIFC) 1899 E, S, 1901 S
McGrath, D G (UC Dublin, Cork Const) 1984 S, 1987 [W, C, Tg, A]
McGrath, N F (Oxford U, London Irish) 1934 W
McGrath, P J (UC Cork) 1965 E, S, W, SA, 1966 F, E, S, W, 1967 A 1, A 2
McGrath, R J M (Wanderers) 1977 W, E, F (R), 1981 SA 1,2, A, 1982 W, E, S, F, 1983 S, F, W, E, 1984 F, W
McGrath, T (Garryowen) 1956 W, 1958 F, 1960 E, S, W, F, 1961 SA
McGuinness, C D (St Mary's Coll) 1997 NZ, C, 1998 F, W, E, SA 1,2, Gg, R (R), SA 3, 1999 F, W, E, S
McGuire, E P (UC Galway) 1963 E, S, W, NZ, 1964 E, S, W, F
MacHale, S (Lansdowne) 1965 F, E, S, W, SA, 1966 F, E, S, W, 1967 S, W, F
McHugh, M (St Mary's Coll) 2003 Tg
McIldowie, G (Malone) 1906 SA, 1910 E, S, W
McIlrath, J A (Ballymena) 1976 A, F, NZ, 1977 W, E
McIlwaine, E H (NIFC) 1895 S, W
McIlwaine, E N (NIFC) 1875 E, 1876 E
McIlwaine, J E (NIFC) 1897 E, S, 1898 E, S, W, 1899 E, W
McIntosh, L M (Dublin U) 1884 S
MacIvor, C V (Dublin U) 1912 F, E, S, W, 1913 E, S, F
McIvor, S C (Garryowen) 1996 A, 1997 It 1, S (R)
McKay, J W (Queen's U, Belfast) 1947 F, E, S, W, A, 1948 F, E, S, W, 1949 F, E, S, W, 1950 F, E, S, W, 1951 F, E, S, W, SA, 1952 F
McKee, W D (NIFC) 1947 A, 1948 F, E, S, W, 1949 F, E, S, W, 1950 F, E, 1951 SA
McKeen, A J W (Lansdowne) 1999 [R (R)]
McKelvey, J M (Queen's U, Belfast) 1956 F, E
McKenna, P (St Mary's Coll) 2000 Arg
McKibbin, A R (Instonians, London Irish) 1977 W, E, S, 1978 S, F, W, E, NZ, 1979 F, W, E, S, 1980 E, S
McKibbin, C H (Instonians) 1976 S (R)
McKibbin, D (Instonians) 1950 F, E, S, W, 1951 F, E, S, W
McKibbin, H R (Queen's U, Belfast) 1938 W, 1939 E, S, W
McKinney, S A (Dungannon) 1972 F 1, E, F 2, 1973 W, F, 1974 F, E, S, P, NZ, 1975 E, S, 1976 A, F, W, E, S, NZ, 1977 W, E, S, 1978 S (R), F, W, E
McLaughlin, J H (Derry) 1887 E, S, 1888 W, S
McLaughlin, K (Leinster) 2010 It
McLean, R E (Dublin U) 1881 S, 1882 W, E, S, 1883 E, S, 1884 E, S, 1885 E, S 1
Maclear, B (Cork County, Monkstown) 1905 E, S, W, NZ, 1906 E, S, W, SA, 1907 E, S, W
McLennan, A C (Wanderers) 1977 F, 1978 S, F, W, E, NZ, 1979 F, W, E, S, 1980 E, F, 1981 F, W, E, S, SA 1,2
McLoughlin, F M (Northern) 1976 A
McLoughlin, G A J (Shannon) 1979 F, W, E, S, A 1,2, 1980 E, 1981 SA 1,2, 1982 W, E, S, F, 1983 S, F, W, E, 1984 F
McLoughlin, R J (UC Dublin, Blackrock Coll, Gosforth) 1962 E, S, F, 1963 E, S, W, NZ, 1964 E, S, 1965 F, E, S, W, SA, 1966 F, E, S, W, 1971 F, E, S, W, 1972 F 1, E, F 2, 1973 NZ, E, S, W, F, 1974 F, W, E, S, P, NZ, 1975 E, S, F, W
McMahon, L B (Blackrock Coll, UC Dublin) 1931 E, SA, 1933 E, 1934 E, 1936 E, S, W, 1937 E, S, W, 1938 E, S
McMaster, A W (Ballymena) 1972 F 1, E, F 2, 1973 NZ, E, S, W, F, 1974 F, E, S, P, 1975 F, W, 1976 A, F, W, NZ
McMordie, J (Queen's Coll, Belfast) 1886 S
McMorrow, A (Garryowen) 1951 W
McMullen, A R (Cork) 1881 E, S
McNamara, V (UC Cork) 1914 E, S, W
McNaughton, P P (Greystones) 1978 S, F, W, E, 1979 F, W, E, S, A 1,2, 1980 E, S, F, W, 1981 F
MacNeill, H P (Dublin U, Oxford U, Blackrock Coll, London Irish) 1981 F, W, E, S, A, 1982 W, E, S, F, 1983 S, F, W, E, 1984 F, W, E, A, 1985 S, F, W, E, 1986 F, W, E, S, R, 1987 E, S, F, W, [W, C, Tg, A], 1988 S (R), E 1,2
McQuilkin, K P (Bective Rangers, Lansdowne) 1996 US, S, F, 1997 F (t & R), S
MacSweeney, D A (Blackrock Coll) 1955 S
McVicker, H (Army, Richmond) 1927 E, S, W, A, 1928 F
McVicker, J (Collegians) 1924 F, E, S, W, NZ, 1925 F, E, S, W, 1926 F, E, S, W, 1927 F, E, S, W, A, 1928 W, 1930 F
McVicker, S (Queen's U, Belfast) 1922 E, S, W, F
McWeeney, J P J (St Mary's Coll) 1997 NZ
Madden, M N (Sunday's Well) 1955 E, S, W
Magee, A M (Louis) (Bective Rangers, London Irish) 1895 E, S, W, 1896 E, S, W, 1897 E, S, 1898 E, S, W, 1899 E, S, W, 1900 E, S, W, 1901 E, S, W, 1902 E, S, W, 1903 E, S, W, 1904 W
Magee, J T (Bective Rangers) 1895 E, S
Maggs, K M (Bristol, Bath, Ulster) 1997 NZ (R), C, It 2, 1998 S, F, W, E, SA 1,2, Gg, R (R), SA 3, 1999 F, W, E, S, It, A 1,2, Arg 1, [US, A 3, Arg 2], 2000 E, F, Arg, US (R), C, 2001 It (R), F (R), R, S (R), W, E, Sm, NZ, 2002 W, E, S, R, Ru, Gg, A, Fj, Arg, 2003 S 1, It 1, F, W 1, E, A, W 2, S 2, [R,Nm,Arg,A,F], 2004 F,W(R),E(R),It(R),S(R),SA1(R),2, US, 2005 S,F,W,J1
Maginiss, R M (Dublin U) 1875 E, 1876 E
Magrath, R M (Cork Constitution) 1909 S
Maguire, J F (Cork) 1884 S
Mahoney, J (Dolphin) 1923 E
Malcolmson, G L (RAF, NIFC) 1935 NZ, 1936 E, S, W, 1937 E, S, W
Malone, N G (Oxford U, Leicester) 1993 S, F, 1994 US (R)
Mannion, N P (Corinthians, Lansdowne, Wanderers) 1988 WS, It, 1989 F, W, E, S, NZ, 1990 E, S, F, W, Arg, 1991 Nm 1(R),2, [J], 1993 S
Marshall, B D E (Queen's U, Belfast) 1963 E
Mason, S J P (Orrell, Richmond) 1996 W, E, WS
Massey-Westropp, R H (Limerick, Monkstown) 1886 E
Matier, R N (NIFC) 1878 E, 1879 S
Matthews, P M (Ards, Wanderers) 1984 A, 1985 S, F, W, E, 1986 R, 1987 E, S, F, W, [W, Tg, A], 1988 S, F, W, E 1,2, WS, It, 1989 F, W, E, S, NZ, 1990 E, S, 1991 F, W, E, S, Nm 1 [Z, S, A], 1992 W, E, S
Mattsson, J (Wanderers) 1948 E
Mayne, R B (Queen's U, Belfast) 1937 W, 1938 E, W, 1939 E, S, W
Mayne, R H (Belfast Academy) 1888 W, S
Mayne, T (NIFC) 1921 E, S, F
Mays, K M A (UC Dublin) 1973 NZ, E, S, W
Meares, A W D (Dublin U) 1899 S, W, 1900 E, W
Megaw, J (Richmond, Instonians) 1934 W, 1938 E
Millar, A (Kingstown) 1880 E, S, 1883 E
Millar, H J (Monkstown) 1904 W, 1905 E, S, W
Millar, S (Ballymena) 1958 F, 1959 E, S, W, F, 1960 E, S, W, F, SA, 1961 E, S, W, F, SA, 1962 E, S, F, 1963 F, E, S, W, 1964 F, 1968 F, E, S, W, A, 1969 F, E, S, W, 1970 SA, F, E, S, W
Millar, W H J (Queen's U, Belfast) 1951 E, S, W, 1952 S, W
Miller, E R P (Leicester, Terenure Coll, Leinster) 1997 It 1, F, W, E, NZ, It 2, 1998 S, W (R), Gg, R, 1999 F, W, E (R), S, Arg 1(R), [US (R), A 3(t&R), Arg 2(R)], 2000 US, C (R), SA, 2001 R, W, E, Sm, NZ, 2002 E, S, It (R), Fj (R), 2003 W 1(t+R), Tg, Sm, It 2, S 2, [Nm,Arg(R),A(t&R),F(R)], 2004 SA3(R),US,Arg(R), 2005 It(R),S(R),F(R),W(R), J1(R),2
Miller, F H (Wanderers) 1886 S
Milliken, R A (Bangor) 1973 E, S, W, F, 1974 F, W, E, S, P, NZ, 1975 E, S, F, W
Millin, T J (Dublin U) 1925 W
Minch, J B (Bective Rangers) 1912 SA, 1913 E, S, 1914 E, S
Moffat, J (Belfast Academy) 1888 W, S, M, 1889 S, 1890 S, W, 1891 S
Moffatt, J E (Old Wesley) 1904 S, 1905 E, S, W
Moffett, J W (Ballymena) 1961 E, S
Molloy, M G (UC Galway, London Irish) 1966 F, E, 1967 A 1, E, S, W, F, A 2, 1968 F, E, S, W, A, 1969 F, E, S, W, 1970 F, E, S, W, 1971 F, E, S, W, 1973 F, 1976 A
Moloney, J J (St Mary's Coll) 1972 F 1, E, F 2, 1973 NZ, E, S, W, F, 1974 F, W, E, S, P, NZ, 1975 E, S, F, W, 1976 S, 1978 S, F, W, E, 1979 A 1,2, 1980 S, W
Moloney, L A (Garryowen) 1976 W (R), S, 1978 S (R), NZ
Molony, J U (UC Dublin) 1950 S
Monteith, J D E (Queen's U, Belfast) 1947 E, S, W
Montgomery, A (NIFC) 1895 S

Montgomery, F P (Queen's U, Belfast) 1914 E, S, W
Montgomery, R (Cambridge U) 1887 E, S, W, 1891 E, 1892 W
Moore, C M (Dublin U) 1887 S, 1888 W, S
Moore, D F (Wanderers) 1883 E, S, 1884 E, W
Moore, F W (Wanderers) 1884 W, 1885 E, S 2, 1886 S
Moore, H (Windsor) 1876 E, 1877 S
Moore, H (Queen's U, Belfast) 1910 S, 1911 W, F, 1912 F, E, S, W, SA
Moore, T A P (Highfield) 1967 A 2, 1973 NZ, E, S, W, F, 1974 F, W, E, S, P, NZ
Moore, W D (Queen's Coll, Belfast) 1878 E
Moran, F G (Clontarf) 1936 E, 1937 E, S, W, 1938 S, W, 1939 E, S, W
Morell, H B (Dublin U) 1881 E, S, 1882 W, E
Morgan, G J (Clontarf) 1934 E, S, W, 1935 E, S, W, NZ, 1936 E, S, W, 1937 E, S, W, 1938 E, S, W, 1939 E, S, W
Moriarty, C C H (Monkstown) 1899 W
Moroney, J C M (Garryowen) 1968 W, A, 1969 F, E, S, W
Moroney, R J M (Lansdowne) 1984 F, W, 1985 F
Moroney, T A (UC Dublin) 1964 W, 1967 A 1, E
Morphy, E McG (Dublin U) 1908 E
Morris, D P (Bective Rangers) 1931 W, 1932 E, 1935 E, S, W, NZ
Morrow, J W R (Queen's Coll, Belfast) 1882 S, 1883 E, S, 1884 E, W, 1885 S 1,2, 1886 E, S, 1888 S
Morrow, R D (Bangor) 1986 F, E, S
Mortell, M (Bective Rangers, Dolphin) 1953 F, E, S, W, 1954 NZ, F, E, S, W
Morton, W A (Dublin U) 1888 S
Mostyn, M R (Galwegians) 1999 A 1, Arg 1, [US, A 3, R, Arg 2]
Moyers, L W (Dublin U) 1884 W
Moylett, M M F (Shannon) 1988 E 1
Mulcahy, W A (UC Dublin, Bective Rangers, Bohemians) 1958 A, E, S, W, F, 1959 E, S, W, F, 1960 E, S, W, SA, 1961 E, S, W, SA, 1962 E, S, F, W, 1963 F, E, S, W, NZ, 1964 E, S, W, F, 1965 F, E, S, W, SA
Muldoon, J (Connacht) 2009 C,US, 2010 NZ1
Mullan, B (Clontarf) 1947 F, E, S, W, 1948 F, E, S, W
Mullane, J P (Limerick Bohemians) 1928 W, 1929 F
Mullen, K D (Old Belvedere) 1947 F, E, S, W, A, 1948 F, E, S, W, 1949 F, E, S, W, 1950 F, E, S, W, 1951 F, E, S, W, SA, 1952 F, S, W
Mulligan, A A (Wanderers) 1956 F, E, 1957 F, E, S, W, 1958 A, E, S, F, 1959 E, S, W, F, 1960 E, S, W, F, SA, 1961 W, F, SA
Mullin, B J (Dublin U, Oxford U, Blackrock Coll, London Irish) 1984 A, 1985 S, W, E, 1986 F, W, E, S, R, 1987 E, S, F, W, [W, C, Tg, A], 1988 S, F, W, E 1,2, WS, It, 1989 F, W, E, S, NZ, 1990 E, S, W, Arg, 1991 F, W, E, S, Nm 1,2, [J, S, A], 1992 W, E, S, 1994 US, 1995 E, S, F, W, It, [NZ, J, W, F]
Mullins, M J (Young Munster, Old Crescent) 1999 Arg 1(R), [R], 2000 E, S, It, Arg (t&R), US, C, 2001 It, R, W (R), E (R), Sm (R), NZ (R), 2003 Tg, Sm
Murphy, B J (Munster) 2007 Arg 1(R),2, 2009 C,US
Murphy, C J (Lansdowne) 1939 E, S, W, 1947 F, E
Murphy, G E A (Leicester) 2000 US, C (R), J, 2001 R, S, Sm, 2002 W, E, NZ 1,2, Fj, 2003 S 1(R), It 1, F, W 1, E, A, W 2, It 2(R), S 2, 2004 It,S,SA1,3,US,Arg, 2005 It,S,E, F,W,NZ,A,R, 2006 It,F,W,S,E,NZ1,2,A1(R),SA(R),A2, 2007 W(t&R),F,Arg1 (t&R),2, S2,It2, [Nm(R),Arg], 2008 It,F,S,E,NZ1(R),A(R),Arg, 2009 F(R),It(R),S(R),W(R), 2010 E,W,S,NZ1(R),A(R)
Murphy, J G M W (London Irish) 1951 SA, 1952 S, W, E, 1954 NZ, 1958 W
Murphy, J J (Greystones) 1981 SA 1, 1982 W (R), 1984 S
Murphy, J N (Greystones) 1992 A
Murphy, K J (Cork Constitution) 1990 E, S, F, W, Arg, 1991 F, W (R), S (R), 1992 S, F, NZ 2(R)
Murphy, N A A (Cork Constitution) 1958 A, E, S, W, F, 1959 E, S, W, F, 1960 E, S, W, F, SA, 1961 E, S, W, 1962 E, 1963 NZ, 1964 E, S, W, F, 1965 F, E, S, W, SA, 1966 F, E, S, W, 1967 A 1, E, S, W, F, 1969 F, E, S, W
Murphy, N F (Cork Constitution) 1930 E, W, 1931 F, E, S, W, SA, 1932 E, S, W, 1933 E
Murphy-O'Connor, J (Bective Rangers) 1954 E
Murray, H W (Dublin U) 1877 S, 1878 E, 1879 E
Murray, J B (UC Dublin) 1963 F
Murray, P F (Wanderers) 1927 F, 1929 F, E, S, 1930 F, E, S, W, 1931 F, E, S, W, SA, 1932 E, S, W, 1933 E, W, S
Murtagh, C W (Portadown) 1977 S
Myles, J (Dublin U) 1875 E
Nash, L C (Queen's Coll, Cork) 1889 S, 1890 W, E, 1891 E, S, W
Neely, M R (Collegians) 1947 F, E, S, W
Neill, H J (NIFC) 1885 E, S 1,2, 1886 S, 1887 E, S, W, 1888 W, S
Neill, J McF (Instonians) 1926 F
Nelson, J E (Malone) 1947 A, 1948 E, S, W, 1949 F, E, S, W, 1950 F, E, S, W, 1951 F, E, W, 1954 F
Nelson, R (Queen's Coll, Belfast) 1882 E, S, 1883 S, 1886 S
Nesdale, R P (Newcastle) 1997 W, E, S, NZ (R), C, 1998 F (R), W (R), Gg, SA 3(R), 1999 It, A 2(R), [US (R), R]
Nesdale, T J (Garryowen) 1961 F
Neville, W C (Dublin U) 1879 S, E
Nicholson, P C (Dublin U) 1900 E, S, W
Norton, G W (Bective Rangers) 1949 F, E, S, W, 1950 F, E, S, W, 1951 F, E, S
Notley, J R (Wanderers) 1952 F, S
Nowlan, K W (St Mary's Coll) 1997 NZ, C, It 2
O'Brien, B (Derry) 1893 S, W
O'Brien, B A P (Shannon) 1968 F, E, S
O'Brien, D J (London Irish, Cardiff, Old Belvedere) 1948 E, S, W, 1949 F, E, S, W, 1950 F, E, S, W, 1951 F, E, S, W, SA, 1952 F, S, W, E
O'Brien, K A (Broughton Park) 1980 E, 1981 SA 1(R),2
O'Brien, S (Leinster) 2009 Fj(R),SA(R), 2010 It(R)
O'Brien-Butler, P E (Monkstown) 1897 S, 1898 E, S, 1899 S, W, 1900 E
O'Callaghan, C T (Carlow) 1910 W, F, 1911 E, S, W, F, 1912 F
O'Callaghan, D P (Cork Const, Munster) 2003 W 1(R), Tg (R), Sm (R), W 2(R), It2(R), [R(R),A(t&R)], 2004 F(t&R),W,It, S(t&R), SA2(R),US, 2005 It(R),S(R),W(R),NZ,A,R, 2006 It(R), F(R),W, S(R),E(R),NZ1,2,A1,SA,A2,PI(R), 2007 W,F,E,S1,It1,2, [Nm,Gg, F, Arg], 2008 It,F,S,W,E,NZ1,A,C,NZ2,Arg, 2009 F,It,E,S,W,A, Fj(R),SA, 2010 E,W,S, NZ1,A
O'Callaghan, M P (Sunday's Well) 1962 W, 1964 E, F
O'Callaghan, P (Dolphin) 1967 A 1, E, A 2, 1968 F, E, S, W, 1969 F, E, S, W, 1970 SA, F, E, S, W, 1976 F, W, E, S, NZ
O'Connell, K D (Sunday's Well) 1994 F, E (t)
O'Connell, P (Bective Rangers) 1913 W, F, 1914 F, E, S, W
O'Connell, P J (Young Munster, Munster) 2002 W, It (R), F (R), NZ 1, 2003 E (R), A (R), Tg, Sm, W 2, S 2, [R,Nm,Arg,A,F], 2004 F,W,E,S,SA1,2,3,US,Arg, 2005 It,S,E,F, W, 2006 It,F,S,E, NZ1,2,A1,SA,A2,PI, 2007 W,F,E,S1,2,It2, [Nm,Gg, F,Arg], 2008 S(R), W,E,NZ1,A,C,NZ2,Arg, 2009 F,It,E,S,W,A,Fj, SA, 2010 It,F,E,W,S
O'Connell, W J (Lansdowne) 1955 F
O'Connor, H S (Dublin U) 1957 F, E, S, W
O'Connor, J (Garryowen) 1895 S
O'Connor, J H (Bective Rangers) 1888 M, 1890 S, W, E, 1891 E, S, 1892 E, W, 1893 E, S, 1894 E, S, W, 1895 E, 1896 E, S, W
O'Connor, J H (Wasps) 2004 SA3,Arg, 2005 S,E,F,W,J1,NZ,A,R, 2006 W(R),E(t&R)
O'Connor, J J (Garryowen) 1909 F
O'Connor, J J (UC Cork) 1933 S, 1934 E, S, W, 1935 E, S, W, NZ, 1936 S, W, 1938 S
O'Connor, P J (Lansdowne) 1887 W
O'Cuinneagain, D (Sale, Ballymena) 1998 SA 1,2, Gg (R), R (R), SA 3, 1999 F, W, E, S, It, A 1,2, Arg 1, [US, A 3, R, Arg 2], 2000 E, It (R)
Odbert, R V M (RAF) 1928 F
O'Donnell, R C (St Mary's Coll) 1979 A 1,2, 1980 S, F, W
O'Donoghue, P J (Bective Rangers) 1955 F, E, S, W, 1956 W, 1957 F, E, 1958 A, E, S, W
O'Driscoll, B G (Blackrock Coll, Leinster) 1999 A 1,2, Arg 1, [US, A 3, R (R), Arg 2], 2000 E, S, It, F, W, J, SA, 2001 F, S, W, E, Sm, NZ, 2002 W, E, S, It, F, NZ 1,2, R, Ru, Gg, A, Fj, Arg, 2003 S 1, It 1, F, W 1, E, W 2, It 2, S 2, [R,Nm,Arg,A,F], 2004 W,E,It,S, SA1,2,3,US,Arg, 2005 It,E,F,W, 2006 It,F,W, S,E,NZ1,2,A1,SA,A2,PI, 2007 W,E,S1, It1,S2, [Nm,Gg, F,Arg], 2008 It,F,S,W,NZ1,A,C,NZ2,Arg, 2009 F,It,E,S,W,A,Fj, SA, 2010 It,F,E,W,S,NZ1,A
O'Driscoll, B J (Manchester) 1971 F (R), E, S, W
O'Driscoll, J B (London Irish, Manchester) 1978 S, 1979 A 1,2, 1980 E, S, F, W, 1981 F, W, E, S, SA 1,2, A, 1982 W, E, S, F, 1983 S, F, W, E, 1984 F, W, E, S
O'Driscoll, M R (Cork Const, Munster) 2001 R (R), 2002 Fj (R), 2005 R(R), 2006 W(R),NZ1(R),2(R),A1(R), 2007 E(R),It1, Arg1(t&R),2, 2008 It(R),F(R),S,E(R), 2009 C,US, 2010 NZ1,A
O'Flanagan, K P (London Irish) 1947 A
O'Flanagan, M (Lansdowne) 1948 S
O'Gara, R J R (Cork Const, Munster) 2000 S, It, F, W, Arg (R), US, C (R), J, SA, 2001 It, F, S, W (R), E (R), Sm, 2002 W (R), E (R), S (R), It (t), F (R), NZ 1,2, R, Ru, Gg, A, Arg, 2003 W

1(R), E (R), A (t+R), Tg, Sm, S 2, [R(R),Nm,Arg(R),A,F], 2004 F,W,E,It, S,SA1,2,3,Arg, 2005 It,S,E,F,W,NZ,A,R(R), 2006 It,F, W,S,E,NZ1,2,A1,SA,A2,PI(R), 2007 W,F,E,S1,It1,S2(R),It2, [Nm, Gg,F,Arg], 2008 It,F,S,W,E,NZ1,A,C,NZ2,Arg, 2009 F,It,E,S,W,A, 2010 It,F,E(R),W(R),S(R),NZ1

O'Grady, D (Sale) 1997 It 2

O'Hanlon, B (Dolphin) 1947 E, S, W, 1948 F, E, S, W, 1949 F, E, S, W, 1950 F

O'Hara, P T J (Sunday's Well, Cork Const) 1988 WS (R), 1989 F, W, E, NZ, 1990 E, S, F, W, 1991 Nm 1, [J], 1993 F, W, E, 1994 US

O'Kelly, M E (London Irish, St Mary's Coll, Leinster) 1997 NZ, C, It 2, 1998 S, F, W, E, SA 1,2, Gg, R, SA 3, 1999 A 1(R),2, Arg 1(R), [US (R), A 3, R, Arg 2], 2000 E, S, It, F, W, Arg, US, J, SA, 2001 It, F, S, W, E, NZ, 2002 E, S, It, F, NZ 1(R),2, R, Ru, Gg, A, Fj, Arg, 2003 S 1, It 1, F, W 1, E, A, W 2, S 2, [R, Nm,Arg,A,F], 2004 F,W(R),E,It,S, SA1,2,3,Arg, 2005 It,S,E,F, W,NZ,A, 2006 It,F,W,S,E,SA(R),A2(R),PI, 2007 Arg1,2(R), S2, It2(R), [F(R),Arg(R)], 2008 It,F, 2009 It(R)

O'Leary, A (Cork Constitution) 1952 S, W, E

O'Leary, T G (Munster) 2007 Arg1(R), 2008 NZ2,Arg, 2009 F,It,E,S(R),W,A,Fj(R),SA, 2010 It,F,E,W,S,NZ1,A

O'Loughlin, D B (UC Cork) 1938 E, S, W, 1939 E, S, W

O'Mahony, D W (UC Dublin, Moseley, Bedford) 1995 It, [F], 1997 It 2, 1998 R

O'Mahony, David (Cork Constitution) 1995 It

O'Meara, B T (Cork Constitution) 1997 E (R), S, NZ (R), 1998 S, 1999 [US (R), R (R)], 2001 It (R), 2003 Sm (R), It 2(R)

O'Meara, J A (UC Cork, Dolphin) 1951 F, E, S, W, SA, 1952 F, S, W, E, 1953 F, E, S, W, 1954 NZ, F, E, S, 1955 F, E, 1956 S, W, 1958 W

O'Neill, H O'H (Queen's U, Belfast, UC Cork) 1930 E, S, W, 1933 E, S, W

O'Neill, J B (Queen's U, Belfast) 1920 S

O'Neill, W A (UC Dublin, Wanderers) 1952 E, 1953 F, E, S, W, 1954 NZ

O'Reilly, A J F (Old Belvedere, Leicester) 1955 F, E, S, W, 1956 F, E, S, W, 1957 F, E, S, W, 1958 A, E, S, W, F, 1959 E, S, W, F, 1960 E, 1961 E, F, SA, 1963 F, S, W, 1970 E

Orr, P A (Old Wesley) 1976 F, W, E, S, NZ, 1977 W, E, S, F, 1978 S, F, W, E, NZ, 1979 F, W, E, S, A 1,2, 1980 E, S, F, W, 1981 F, W, E, S, SA 1,2, A, 1982 W, E, S, F, 1983 S, F, W, E, 1984 F, W, E, S, A, 1985 S, F, W, E, 1986 F, S, R, 1987 E, S, F, W, [W, C, A]

O'Shea, C M P (Lansdowne, London Irish) 1993 R, 1994 F, W, E, S, A 1,2, US, 1995 E, S, [J, W, F], 1997 It 1, F, S (R), 1998 S, F, SA 1,2, Gg, R, SA 3, 1999 F, W, E, S, It, A 1, Arg 1, [US, A 3, R, Arg 2], 2000 E

O'Sullivan, A C (Dublin U) 1882 S

O'Sullivan, J M (Limerick) 1884 S, 1887 S

O'Sullivan, P J A (Galwegians) 1957 F, E, S, W, 1959 E, S, W, F, 1960 SA, 1961 E, S, 1962 F, W, 1963 F, NZ

O'Sullivan, W (Queen's Coll, Cork) 1895 S

Owens, R H (Dublin U) 1922 E, S

Parfrey, P (UC Cork) 1974 NZ

Parke, J C (Monkstown) 1903 W, 1904 E, S, W, 1905 W, NZ, 1906 E, S, W, SA, 1907 E, S, W, 1908 E, S, W, 1909 E, S, W, F

Parr, J S (Wanderers) 1914 F, E, S, W

Patterson, C S (Instonians) 1978 NZ, 1979 F, W, E, S, A 1,2, 1980 E, S, F, W

Patterson, R d'A (Wanderers) 1912 F, S, W, SA, 1913 E, S, W, F

Payne, C T (NIFC) 1926 E, 1927 F, E, S, A, 1928 F, E, S, W, 1929 F, E, W, 1930 F, E, S, W

Pedlow, A C (CIYMS) 1953 W, 1954 NZ, F, E, 1955 F, E, S, W, 1956 F, E, S, W, 1957 F, E, S, W, 1958 A, E, S, W, F, 1959 E, 1960 E, S, W, F, SA, 1961 S, 1962 W, 1963 F

Pedlow, J (Bessbrook) 1882 S, 1884 W

Pedlow, R (Bessbrook) 1891 W

Pedlow, T B (Queen's Coll, Belfast) 1889 S, W

Peel, T (Limerick) 1892 E, S, W

Peirce, W (Cork) 1881 E

Phipps, G C (Army) 1950 E, W, 1952 F, W, E

Pike, T O (Lansdowne) 1927 E, S, W, A, 1928 F, E, S, W

Pike, V J (Lansdowne) 1931 E, S, W, SA, 1932 E, S, W, 1933 E, W, S, 1934 E, S, W

Pike, W W (Kingstown) 1879 E, 1881 E, S, 1882 E, 1883 S

Pinion, G (Belfast Collegians) 1909 E, S, W, F

Piper, O J S (Cork Constitution) 1909 E, S, W, F, 1910 E, S, W, F

Polden, S E (Clontarf) 1913 W, F, 1914 F, 1920 F

Popham, I (Cork Constitution) 1922 S, W, F, 1923 F

Popplewell, N J (Greystones, Wasps, Newcastle) 1989 NZ, 1990 Arg, 1991 Nm 1,2, [Z, S, A], 1992 W, E, S, F, NZ 1,2, A, 1993 S, F, W, E, R, 1994 F, W, E, S, US, 1995 E, S, F, W, It, [NZ, J, W, F], Fj, 1996 US, S, F, W, E, A, 1997 It 1, F, W, E, NZ, C, 1998 S (t), F (R)

Potterton, H N (Wanderers) 1920 W

Pratt, R H (Dublin U) 1933 E, W, S, 1934 E, S

Price, A H (Dublin U) 1920 S, F

Pringle, J C (NIFC) 1902 S, W

Purcell, N M (Lansdowne) 1921 E, S, W, F

Purdon, H (NIFC) 1879 S, E, 1880 E, 1881 E, S

Purdon, W B (Queen's Coll, Belfast) 1906 E, S, W

Purser, F C (Dublin U) 1898 E, S, W

Quinlan, A N (Shannon, Munster) 1999 [R (R)], 2001 It, F, 2002 NZ 2(R), Ru (R), Gg (R), A (R), Fj, Arg (R), 2003 S 1(R), It 1(R), F (R), W 1, E (R), A, W 2, [R(R),Nm,Arg], 2004 SA1(R),2(R), 2005 J1,2(t&R), 2007 Arg2,S2(t&R), 2008 C(R),NZ2

Quinlan, D P (Northampton) 2005 J1(R),2

Quinlan, S V J (Blackrock Coll) 1956 F, E, W, 1958 W

Quinn, B T (Old Belvedere) 1947 F

Quinn, F P (Old Belvedere) 1981 F, W, E

Quinn, J P (Dublin U) 1910 E, S, 1911 E, S, W, F, 1912 E, S, W, 1913 E, W, F, 1914 F, E, S

Quinn, K (Old Belvedere) 1947 F, A, 1953 F, E, S

Quinn, M A M (Lansdowne) 1973 F, 1974 F, W, E, S, P, NZ, 1977 S, F, 1981 SA 2

Quirke, J M T (Blackrock Coll) 1962 E, S, 1968 S

Rainey, P I (Ballymena) 1989 NZ

Rambaut, D F (Dublin U) 1887 E, S, W, 1888 W

Rea, H H (Edinburgh U) 1967 A 1, 1969 F

Read, H M (Dublin U) 1910 E, S, 1911 E, S, W, F, 1912 F, E, S, W, SA, 1913 E, S

Reardon, J V (Cork Constitution) 1934 E, S

Reddan, E G (Wasps, Leinster) 2006 F(R), 2007 Arg2,S2(R), [F,Arg], 2008 It,F,S,W,E, NZ1,A(R),C,NZ2(R), 2009 C(R),US(R), Fj, 2010 It(R),F(R), W(R),NZ1(R)

Reid, C (NIFC) 1899 S, W, 1900 E, 1903 W

Reid, J L (Richmond) 1934 S, W

Reid, P J (Garryowen) 1947 A, 1948 F, E, W

Reid, T E (Garryowen) 1953 E, S, W, 1954 NZ, F, 1955 E, S, 1956 F, E, 1957 F, E, S, W

Reidy, C J (London Irish) 1937 W

Reidy, G F (Dolphin, Lansdowne) 1953 W, 1954 F, E, S, W

Richey, H A (Dublin U) 1889 W, 1890 S

Ridgeway, E C (Wanderers) 1932 S, W, 1935 E, S, W

Rigney, B J (Greystones) 1991 F, W, E, S, Nm 1, 1992 F, NZ 1(R),2

Ringland, T M (Queen's U, Belfast, Ballymena) 1981 A, 1982 W, E, F, 1983 S, F, W, E, 1984 F, W, E, S, A, 1985 S, F, W, E, 1986 F, W, E, S, R, 1987 E, S, F, W, [W, C, Tg, A], 1988 S, F, W, E 1

Riordan, W F (Cork Constitution) 1910 E

Ritchie, J S (London Irish) 1956 F, E

Robb, C G (Queen's Coll, Belfast) 1904 E, S, W, 1905 NZ, 1906 S

Robbie, J C (Dublin U, Greystones) 1976 A, F, NZ, 1977 S, F, 1981 F, W, E, S

Robinson, B F (Ballymena, London Irish) 1991 F, W, E, S, Nm 1,2, [Z, S, A], 1992 W, E, S, F, NZ 1,2, A, 1993 W, E, R, 1994 F, W, E, S, A 1,2

Robinson, T T H (Wanderers) 1904 E, S, 1905 E, S, W, NZ, 1906 SA, 1907 E, S, W

Roche, J (Wanderers) 1890 S, W, E, 1891 E, S, W, 1892 W

Roche, R E (UC Galway) 1955 E, S, 1957 S, W

Roche, W J (UC Cork) 1920 E, S, F

Roddy, P J (Bective Rangers) 1920 S, F

Roe, R (Lansdowne) 1952 E, 1953 F, E, S, W, 1954 F, E, S, W, 1955 F, E, S, W, 1956 F, E, S, W, 1957 F, E, S, W

Rolland, A C (Blackrock Coll) 1990 Arg, 1994 US (R), 1995 It (R)

Ronan, N (Munster) 2009 C,US, 2010 A

Rooke, C V (Dublin U) 1891 E, W, 1892 E, S, W, 1893 E, S, W, 1894 E, S, W, 1895 E, S, W, 1896 E, S, W, 1897 E, S

Ross, D J (Belfast Academy) 1884 E, 1885 S 1,2, 1886 E, S

Ross, G R P (CIYMS) 1955 W

Ross, J F (NIFC) 1886 S

Ross, J P (Lansdowne) 1885 E, S 1,2, 1886 E, S

Ross, M R (Harlequins) 2009 C(R),US

Ross, N G (Malone) 1927 F, E

Ross, W McC (Queen's U, Belfast) 1932 E, S, W, 1933 E, W, S, 1934 E, S, 1935 NZ

Ruddock, R (Leinster) 2010 A(R)
Russell, J (UC Cork) 1931 F, E, S, W, SA, 1933 E, W, S, 1934 E, S, W, 1935 E, S, W, 1936 E, S, W, 1937 E, S
Russell, P (Instonians) 1990 E, 1992 NZ 1,2, A
Rutherford, W G (Tipperary) 1884 E, S, 1885 E, S 1, 1886 E, 1888 W
Ryan, D (Munster) 2008 Arg(R), 2009 C(R),US(R), 2010 It(R),F(R)
Ryan, E (Dolphin) 1937 W, 1938 E, S
Ryan, J (Rockwell Coll) 1897 E, 1898 E, S, W, 1899 E, S, W, 1900 S, W, 1901 E, S, W, 1902 E, 1904 E
Ryan, J G (UC Dublin) 1939 E, S, W
Ryan, M (Rockwell Coll) 1897 E, S, 1898 E, S, W, 1899 E, S, W, 1900 E, S, W, 1901 E, S, W, 1903 E, 1904 E, S
Saunders, R (London Irish) 1991 F, W, E, S, Nm 1,2, [Z, J, S, A], 1992 W, 1994 F (t)
Saverimutto, C (Sale) 1995 Fj, 1996 US, S
Sayers, H J M (Lansdowne) 1935 E, S, W, 1936 E, S, W, 1938 W, 1939 E, S, W
Scally, C J (U C Dublin) 1998 Gg (R), R, 1999 S (R), It
Schute, F (Wanderers) 1878 E, 1879 E
Schute, F G (Dublin U) 1912 SA, 1913 E, S
Scott, D (Malone) 1961 F, SA, 1962 S
Scott, R D (Queen's U, Belfast) 1967 E, F, 1968 F, E, S
Scovell, R H (Kingstown) 1883 E, 1884 E
Scriven, G (Dublin U) 1879 S, E, 1880 E, S, 1881 E, 1882 S, 1883 E, S
Sealy, J (Dublin U) 1896 E, S, W, 1897 S, 1899 E, S, W, 1900 E, S
Sexton, J (Leinster) 2009 Fj,SA, 2010 F(R),E,W,S,NZ1(R),A
Sexton, J F (Dublin U, Lansdowne) 1988 E 2, WS, It, 1989 F
Sexton, W J (Garryowen) 1984 A, 1988 S, E 2
Shanahan, T (Lansdowne) 1885 E, S 1,2, 1886 E, 1888 S, W
Shaw, G M (Windsor) 1877 S
Sheahan, F J (Cork Const, Munster) 2000 US (R), 2001 It (R), R, W (R), Sm, 2002 W, E, S, Gg (R), A (t+R), Fj, 2003 S 1(R), It 1(R), 2004 F(R),W(R),It(R),S(R),SA1(R),US, 2005 It(R), S(R),W(R),J1,2, 2006 SA(R),A2(R),PI, 2007 Arg2, [F(t&R)]
Sheehan, M D (London Irish) 1932 E
Sherry, B F (Terenure Coll) 1967 A 1, E, S, A 2, 1968 F, E
Sherry, M J A (Lansdowne) 1975 F, W
Shields, P M (Ballymena) 2003 Sm (R), It 2(R)
Siggins, J A E (Belfast Collegians) 1931 F, E, S, W, SA, 1932 E, S, W, 1933 E, W, S, 1934 E, S, W, 1935 E, S, W, NZ, 1936 E, S, W, 1937 E, S, W
Slattery, J F (UC Dublin, Blackrock Coll) 1970 SA, F, E, S, W, 1971 F, E, S, W, 1972 F 1, E, F 2, 1973 NZ, E, S, W, F, 1974 F, W, E, S, P, NZ, 1975 E, S, F, W, 1976 A, 1977 S, F, 1978 S, F, W, E, NZ, 1979 F, W, E, S, A 1,2, 1980 E, S, F, W, 1981 F, W, E, S, SA 1,2, A, 1982 W, E, S, F, 1983 S, F, W, E, 1984 F
Smartt, F N B (Dublin U) 1908 E, S, 1909 E
Smith, B A (Oxford U, Leicester) 1989 NZ, 1990 S, F, W, Arg, 1991 F, W, E, S
Smith, J H (London Irish) 1951 F, E, S, W, SA, 1952 F, S, W, E, 1954 NZ, W, F
Smith, R E (Lansdowne) 1892 E
Smith, S J (Ballymena) 1988 E 2, WS, It, 1989 F, W, E, S, NZ, 1990 E, 1991 F, W, E, S, Nm 1,2, [Z, S, A], 1992 W, E, S, F, NZ 1,2, 1993 S
Smithwick, F F S (Monkstown) 1898 S, W
Smyth, J T (Queen's U, Belfast) 1920 F
Smyth, P J (Belfast Collegians) 1911 E, S, F
Smyth, R S (Dublin U) 1903 E, S, 1904 E
Smyth, T (Malone, Newport) 1908 E, S, W, 1909 E, S, W, 1910 E, S, W, F, 1911 E, S, W, 1912 E
Smyth, W S (Belfast Collegians) 1910 W, F, 1920 E
Solomons, B A H (Dublin U) 1908 E, S, W, 1909 E, S, W, F, 1910 E, S, W
Spain, A W (UC Dublin) 1924 NZ
Sparrow, W (Dublin U) 1893 W, 1894 E
Spillane, B J (Bohemians) 1985 S, F, W, E, 1986 F, W, E, 1987 F, W, [W, C, A (R)], 1989 E (R)
Spring, D E (Dublin U) 1978 S, NZ, 1979 S, 1980 S, F, W, 1981 W
Spring, R M (Lansdowne) 1979 F, W, E
Spunner, H F (Wanderers) 1881 E, S, 1884 W
Stack, C R R (Dublin U) 1889 S
Stack, G H (Dublin U) 1875 E
Staples, J E (London Irish, Harlequins) 1991 W, E, S, Nm 1,2, [Z, J, S, A], 1992 W, E, NZ 1,2, A, 1995 F, W, It, [NZ], Fj, 1996 US, S, F, A, 1997 W, E, S
Staunton, J W (Garryowen, Wasps) 2001 Sm, 2005 J1(R),2(R), 2006 A1(R), 2007 Arg2
Steele, H W (Ballymena) 1976 E, 1977 F, 1978 F, W, E, 1979 F, W, E, A 1,2
Stephenson, G V (Queen's U, Belfast, London Hosp) 1920 F, 1921 E, S, W, F, 1922 E, S, W, F, 1923 E, S, W, F, 1924 F, E, S, W, NZ, 1925 F, E, S, W, 1926 F, E, S, W, 1927 F, E, S, W, A, 1928 F, E, S, W, 1929 F, E, W, 1930 F, E, S, W
Stephenson, H W V (United Services) 1922 S, W, F, 1924 F, E, S, W, NZ, 1925 F, E, S, W, 1927 A, 1928 E
Stevenson, J (Dungannon) 1888 M, 1889 S
Stevenson, J B (Instonians) 1958 A, E, S, W, F
Stevenson, R (Dungannon) 1887 E, S, W, 1888 M, 1889 S, W, 1890 S, W, E, 1891 W, 1892 W, 1893 E, S, W
Stevenson, T H (Belfast Acad) 1895 E, W, 1896 E, S, W, 1897 E, S
Stewart, A L (NIFC) 1913 W, F, 1914 F
Stewart, J W (Queen's U, Belfast, NIFC) 1922 F, 1924 S, 1928 F, E, S, W, 1929 F, E, S, W
Stoker, E W (Wanderers) 1888 W, S
Stoker, F O (Wanderers) 1886 S, 1888 W, M, 1889 S, 1891 W
Stokes, O S (Cork Bankers) 1882 E, 1884 E
Stokes, P (Garryowen) 1913 E, S, 1914 F, 1920 E, S, W, F, 1921 E, S, F, 1922 W, F
Stokes, R D (Queen's Coll, Cork) 1891 S, W
Strathdee, E (Queen's U, Belfast) 1947 E, S, W, A, 1948 W, F, 1949 E, S, W
Stringer, P A (Shannon, Munster) 2000 S, It, F, W, Arg, C, J, SA, 2001 It, F, R, S (R), W, E, Sm, NZ, 2002 W, E, S, It, F, NZ 1,2, R, Ru, Gg, A, Arg, 2003 S 1, It 1, F, W 1, E, A, W 2, S 2, [R,Nm,Arg,A,F], 2004 F,W,E,It,S,SA1,2,3,US(R),Arg, 2005 It,S,E,F,W, J1,2,NZ,A,R(R), 2006 It,F,W,S,E,NZ1, 2,A1, SA, A2(R),PI, 2007 W,E,S1,It1,2, [Nm,Gg], 2008 It(R),S(R), E(R), NZ1(R),A,C(R), 2009 It(t&R),E(R),S,W(R),C,US
Stuart, C P (Clontarf) 1912 SA
Stuart, I M B (Dublin U) 1924 E, S
Sugars, H S (Dublin U) 1905 NZ, 1906 SA, 1907 S
Sugden, M (Wanderers) 1925 F, E, S, W, 1926 F, E, S, W, 1927 E, S, W, A, 1928 F, E, S, W, 1929 F, E, S, W, 1930 F, E, S, W, 1931 F, E, S, W
Sullivan, D B (UC Dublin) 1922 E, S, W, F
Sweeney, J A (Blackrock Coll) 1907 E, S, W
Symes, G R (Monkstown) 1895 E
Synge, J S (Lansdowne) 1929 S
Taggart, T (Dublin U) 1887 W
Taylor, A S (Queen's Coll, Belfast) 1910 E, S, W, 1912 F
Taylor, D R (Queen's Coll, Belfast) 1903 E
Taylor, J (Belfast Collegians) 1914 E, S, W
Taylor, J W (NIFC) 1879 S, 1880 E, S, 1881 S, 1882 E, S, 1883 E, S
Tector, W R (Wanderers) 1955 F, E, S
Tedford, A (Malone) 1902 E, S, W, 1903 E, S, W, 1904 E, S, W, 1905 E, S, W, NZ, 1906 E, S, W, SA, 1907 E, S, W, 1908 E, S, W
Teehan, C (UC Cork) 1939 E, S, W
Thompson, C (Belfast Collegians) 1907 E, S, 1908 E, S, W, 1909 E, S, W, F, 1910 E, S, W, F
Thompson, J A (Queen's Coll, Belfast) 1885 S 1,2
Thompson, J K S (Dublin U) 1921 W, 1922 E, S, F, 1923 E, S, W, F
Thompson, R G (Lansdowne) 1882 W
Thompson, R H (Instonians) 1951 SA, 1952 F, 1954 NZ, F, E, S, W, 1955 F, S, W, 1956 W
Thornhill, T (Wanderers) 1892 E, S, W, 1893 E
Thrift, H (Dublin U) 1904 W, 1905 E, S, W, NZ, 1906 E, W, SA, 1907 E, S, W, 1908 E, S, W, 1909 E, S, W, F
Tierney, D (UC Cork) 1938 S, W, 1939 E
Tierney, T A (Garryowen) 1999 A 1,2, Arg 1, [US, A 3, R, Arg 2], 2000 E
Tillie, C R (Dublin U) 1887 E, S, 1888 W, S
Todd, A W P (Dublin U) 1913 W, F, 1914 F
Topping, J A (Ballymena) 1996 WS, A, 1997 It 1, F, E, 1999 [R], 2000 US, 2003 A
Torrens, J D (Bohemians) 1938 W, 1939 E, S, W
Trimble, A D (Ulster) 2005 A,R, 2006 F(R),W,S,E,NZ1,2,A1,SA, 2007 W,F(R),E(R),It1(R),Arg1,S2(R),It2, [Nm,F], 2008 It,F,S,W,E, 2009 Fj(R), 2010 It,E(R),NZ1,A
Tucker, C C (Shannon) 1979 F, W, 1980 F (R)
Tuke, B B (Bective Rangers) 1890 E, 1891 E, S, 1892 E, 1894 E, S, W, 1895 E, S
Tuohy, D (Ulster) 2010 NZ1(R),A(t&R)
Turley, N (Blackrock Coll) 1962 E

Tweed, D A (Ballymena) 1995 F, W, It, [J]
Tydings, J J (Young Munster) 1968 A
Tyrrell, W (Queen's U, Belfast) 1910 F, 1913 E, S, W, F, 1914 F, E, S, W
Uprichard, R J H (Harlequins, RAF) 1950 S, W
Varley, D (Munster) 2010 A(R)
Waide, S L (Oxford U, NIFC) 1932 E, S, W, 1933 E, W
Waites, J (Bective Rangers) 1886 S, 1888 M, 1889 W, 1890 S, W, E, 1891 E
Waldron, O C (Oxford U, London Irish) 1966 S, W, 1968 A
Walker, S (Instonians) 1934 E, S, 1935 E, S, W, NZ, 1936 E, S, W, 1937 E, S, W, 1938 E, S, W
Walkington, D B (NIFC) 1887 E, W, 1888 W, 1890 W, E, 1891 E, S, W
Walkington, R B (NIFC) 1875 E, 1876 E, 1877 E, S, 1878 E, 1879 S, 1880 E, S, 1882 E, S
Wall, H (Dolphin) 1965 S, W
Wallace, D P (Garryowen, Munster) 2000 Arg, US, 2001 It, F, R (R), S (R), W, E, NZ, 2002 W, E, S, It, F, 2003 Tg (R), Sm (R), W 2(t+R), S 2, 2004 S,SA1,2, 2005 J2, 2006 It,F,W,S, E,NZ1,2,A1,SA,A2, 2007 W,F,E,S1,It1, [Nm,Gg,F,Arg], 2008 It,F,S,W,E,NZ1, C(R),NZ2,Arg, 2009 F,It,E,S,W,A,SA, 2010 It,F,E,W,S,NZ1
Wallace, Jas (Wanderers) 1904 E, S
Wallace, Jos (Wanderers) 1903 S, W, 1904 E, S, W, 1905 E, S, W, NZ, 1906 W
Wallace, P S (Blackrock Coll, Saracens) 1995 [J], Fj, 1996 US, W, E, WS, A, 1997 It 1, F, W, E, S, NZ, C, 1998 S, F, W, E, SA 1,2, Gg, R, 1999 F, W, E, S, It (R), 1999 A 1,2, Arg 1, [US, A 3, R, Arg 2], 2000 E, US, C (R), 2002 W (R), E (R), S (R), It (R), F (R), NZ 2(R), Ru (R), Gg (R)
Wallace, P W (Ulster) 2006 SA(R),PI, 2007 E(R),Arg1,S2, [Nm(R)], 2008 S(R),E(R), NZ1,A,C(R),NZ2(R), 2009 F,It,E,W(R),A,Fj(R), SA, 2010 It(R),F(t&R),A
Wallace, R M (Garryowen, Saracens) 1991 Nm 1(R), 1992 W, E, S, F, A, 1993 S, F, W, E, R, 1994 F, W, E, S, 1995 W, It, [NZ, J, W], Fj, 1996 US, S, F, WS, 1998 S, F, W, E
Wallace, T H (Cardiff) 1920 E, S, W
Wallis, A K (Wanderers) 1892 E, S, W, 1893 E, W
Wallis, C O'N (Old Cranleighans, Wanderers) 1935 NZ
Wallis, T G (Wanderers) 1921 F, 1922 E, S, W, F
Wallis, W A (Wanderers) 1880 S, 1881 E, S, 1882 W, 1883 S
Walmsley, G (Bective Rangers) 1894 E
Walpole, A (Dublin U) 1888 S, M
Walsh, E J (Lansdowne) 1887 E, S, W, 1892 E, S, W, 1893 E
Walsh, H D (Dublin U) 1875 E, 1876 E
Walsh, J C (UC Cork, Sunday's Well) 1960 S, SA, 1961 E, S, F, SA, 1963 E, S, W, NZ, 1964 E, S, W, F, 1965 F, S, W, SA, 1966 F, S, W, 1967 E, S, W, F, A 2
Ward, A J (Ballynahinch) 1998 F, W, E, SA 1,2, Gg, R, SA 3, 1999 W, E, S, It (R), A 1,2, Arg 1, [US, A 3, R, Arg 2], 2000 F (R), W (t&R), Arg (R), US (R), C, J, SA (R), 2001 It (R), F (R)
Ward, A J P (Garryowen, St Mary's Coll, Greystones) 1978 S, F, W, E, NZ, 1979 F, W, E, S, 1981 W, E, S, A, 1983 E (R), 1984 E, S, 1986 S, 1987 [C, Tg]
Warren, J P (Kingstown) 1883 E
Warren, R G (Lansdowne) 1884 W, 1885 E, S 1,2, 1886 E, 1887 E, S, W, 1888 W, S, M, 1889 S, W, 1890 S, W, E
Watson, R (Wanderers) 1912 SA
Wells, H G (Bective Rangers) 1891 S, W, 1894 E, S
Westby, A J (Dublin U) 1876 E
Wheeler, G H (Queen's Coll, Belfast) 1884 S, 1885 E
Wheeler, J R (Queen's U, Belfast) 1922 E, S, W, F, 1924 E
Whelan, P C (Garryowen) 1975 E, S, 1976 NZ, 1977 W, E, S, F, 1978 S, F, W, E, NZ, 1979 F, W, E, S, 1981 F, W, E
White, M (Queen's Coll, Cork) 1906 E, S, W, SA, 1907 E, W
Whitestone, A M (Dublin U) 1877 E, 1879 S, E, 1880 E, 1883 S
Whitten, I (Ulster) 2009 C,US
Whittle, D (Bangor) 1988 F
Wilkinson, C R (Malone) 1993 S
Wilkinson, R W (Wanderers) 1947 A
Williamson, F W (Dolphin) 1930 E, S, W
Willis, W J (Lansdowne) 1879 E
Wilson, F (CIYMS) 1977 W, E, S
Wilson, H G (Glasgow U, Malone) 1905 E, S, W, NZ, 1906 E, S, W, SA, 1907 E, S, W, 1908 E, S, W, 1909 E, S, W, 1910 W
Wilson, R G (Ulster) 2005 J1
Wilson, W H (Bray) 1877 E, S
Withers, H H C (Army, Blackheath) 1931 F, E, S, W, SA
Wolfe, E J (Armagh) 1882 E
Wood, G H (Dublin U) 1913 W, 1914 F
Wood, B G M (Garryowen) 1954 E, S, 1956 F, E, S, W, 1957 F, E, S, W, 1958 A, E, S, W, F, 1959 E, S, W, F, 1960 E, S, W, F, SA, 1961 E, S, W, F, SA
Wood, K G M (Garryowen, Harlequins) 1994 A 1,2, US, 1995 E, S, [J], 1996 A, 1997 It 1, F, 1997 NZ, It 2, 1998 S, F, W, E, SA 1,2, R (R), SA 3, 1999 F, W, E, S, It (R), A 1,2, Arg 1, [US, A 3, R (R), Arg 2], 2000 E, S, It, F, W, Arg, US, C, J, SA, 2001 It, F, S, W, E, NZ, 2002 F, NZ 1,2, Ru, 2003 W 2, S 2, [R,Nm,Arg,A,F]
Woods, D C (Bessbrook) 1888 M, 1889 S
Woods, N K P J (Blackrock Coll, London Irish) 1994 A 1,2, 1995 E, F, 1996 F, W, E, 1999 W
Wright, R A (Monkstown) 1912 S
Yeates, R A (Dublin U) 1889 S, W
Young, B G (Ulster) 2006 NZ2(R),A1(R),SA(R),A2,PI, 2007 Arg1,2,S2
Young, G (UC Cork) 1913 E
Young, R M (Collegians) 1965 F, E, S, W, SA, 1966 F, E, S, W, 1967 W, F, 1968 W, A, 1969 F, E, S, W, 1970 SA, F, E, S, W, 1971 F, E, S, W

DOUBLE TRIUMPH FOR CORK CON

In recent years, Cork Constitution have earned themselves an unflattering reputation as a side that has failed to translate its undoubted talent into tangible silverware but they laid that myth firmly to rest in 2010 with a famous and first ever league and cup double.

In 2009, the Munster club finished top of the AIB League One table for the fourth consecutive year only to fall to Clontarf in the play-off semi-finals and also reached the AIB Cup final, where they were beaten by Division Two side Ballynahinch in arguably the greatest ever shock in the history of the competition.

Painful memories indeed but 12 months after a season that promised so much but ultimately delivered nothing, Cork Con rebounded in triumphant style to dispatch Garryowen 15–11 in the Cup final at Dubarry Park and then went on complete the fabled double with a 17–10 victory over St Mary's College in the play-off final at Templeville Road.

The first leg of Constitution's trophy haul came in January in the AIB Cup. Ballymena were dispatched 18–9 in the semi-finals before Christmas and Brian Walsh's side were presented with the opportunity to redeem themselves after their catastrophic defeat to Ballynahinch.

They faced Garryowen, victors over Dolphin in the last four, but despite an early try from wing Richie Lane they quickly found themselves behind to their opponents from Limerick courtesy of two penalties from scrum-half Conor Murray and a try from hooker Mike Sherry before half-time.

Worse was to follow when Cork Con second-row Ian Nagle was sent off after unleashing a series of punches at a breakdown minutes before half-time, leaving his team down to 14 men for the rest of the game. But the Leesiders dug deep despite their numerical inferiority and struck the killer blow with a Daragh Lyons try securing their victory and the trophy for the first time since 2006.

"We're very happy with the win, it was a very tough battle," admitted Cork Con captain Evan Ryan. "I suppose Garryowen had the best of the first half, they took their chances very well and they kicked their goals as well.

"At half-time and a man down, we just said we have to keep plugging away, playing our own game and putting pressure on them and luckily enough we got a try out of it. I think our defence at the end was superb.

"It was a great game to watch and that was the common consensus. It was a very good spectacle. It's a competition that is very close to our hearts and it's brilliant to win it again."

Cork Con were now able to focus solely on Division One matters. The competition had a new look after the decision to split the 16 teams into two separate leagues, with the top eight from 2008–09 going into Division One A and the bottom eight into Division One B.

The revamped format was clearly to Cork Con's liking and they were never in danger of failing to reach the play-offs, losing just three times in their 14 league fixtures before getting down to the serious business of knockout rugby. Dolphin stood in their way in the semi-finals but were sent packing with a 31–18 win.

The other last four encounter featured St Mary's College, who had finished second, and Old Belvedere, who reached the play-offs after topping the Division One B table, and after a titanic tussle at Templeville Road, it was St Mary's that emerged 24–23 winners.

The final was as tense as it was entertaining and after the first 40 minutes of frenetic action, the Leesiders were just 3–0 up courtesy of a Jeremy Manning penalty.

The second period was even more dramatic. Manning scrambled over for the first try of the match on 50 minutes but St Mary's came storming back and levelled the scores at 10–10 all deep in second-half injury-time when Gavin Dunne held his nerve to convert Shaun McCarthy's last-gasp try.

The final headed into the dreaded extra-time as it had in 2009 but this time there was to be a decisive, altogether more satisfying result. The previous year Shannon were crowned champions after drawing 19–19 with Clontarf after 120 minutes of play but were awarded the trophy on the basis that they had scored the first try of the match.

This time however neither side seemed willing to rely on the vagaries of the rulebook and Cork Con struck in the dying seconds of the first half of extra-time when wing Cronan Healy finished off a flowing counter-attack. A desperate St Mary's threw the kitchen sink at Walsh's side for the rest of the encounter but Cork Con clung on for victory.

"To be fair, we were hanging on at the end for five or six minutes," admitted Walsh. "Mary's had thrown everything at us, they deserved something from the match and scored a great try and kicked a great conversion.

"The stomach sinks and the heart sinks and you wonder how you're going to get through the next 20 minutes. The spirit of both sides was testament to the value of the league. Two well coached teams played an excellent brand of rugby without a dirty swipe and it was a fitting finale to what has been a great league."

AIB DIVISION ONE 2009–10 RESULTS

2 October, 2009: **Garryowen** 12 **Shannon** 10. 3 October, 2009: **Dolphin** 13 **Cork Constitution** 12, **St Mary's** 24 **Clontarf** 7, **Bohemian** 3 **Blackrock** 8. 10 October, 2009: **Blackrock** 48 **Garryowen** 14, **Clontarf** 19 **Dolphin** 27, **Cork Constitution** 16 **Bohemian** 3, **Shannon** 7 **St Mary's** 12. 24 October, 2009: **Blackrock** 10 **Cork Constitution** 3, **Dolphin** 18 **Shannon** 14, **Garryowen** 3 **St Mary's** 6, **Bohemian** 3 **Clontarf** 8. 31 October, 2009: **Clontarf** 9 **Blackrock** 3, **Cork Constitution** 17 **Garryowen** 13, **Shannon** 38 **Bohemian** 19, **St Mary's** 19 **Dolphin** 10. 14 November, 2009: **Blackrock** 15 **Shannon** 21, **Cork Constitution** 21 **Clontarf** 18, **Bohemian** 25 **St Mary's** 20. 5 December, 2009: **Dolphin** 0 **Bohemian** 3, **Garryowen** 3 **Clontarf** 18, **Shannon** 8 **Cork Constitution** 9, **St Mary's** 25 **Blackrock** 3. 12 December, 2009: **Blackrock** 6 **Dolphin** 12, **Clontarf** 13 **Shannon** 21, **Cork Constitution** 16 **St Mary's** 9, **Bohemian** 5 **Garryowen** 9. 16 January, 2010: **Clontarf** 21 **Bohemian** 12, **Cork Constitution** 18 **Blackrock** 15, **Shannon** 32 **Dolphin** 10, **St Mary's** 14 **Garryowen** 16. 23 January, 2010: **Blackrock** 26 **Clontarf** 13, **Dolphin** 21 **St Mary's** 13, **Garryowen** 6 **Cork Constitution** 6, **Bohemian** 11 **Shannon** 17. 30 January, 2010: **St Mary's** 16 **Shannon** 27. 31 January, 2010: **Dolphin** 17 **Clontarf** 0. 7 February, 2010: **Garryowen** 13 **Dolphin** 12. 20 February, 2010: **Clontarf** 18 **Cork Constitution** 20, **Dolphin** 9 **Garryowen** 21, **Shannon** 3 **Blackrock** 25, **St Mary's** 39 **Bohemian** 12. 6 March, 2010: **Blackrock** 9 **St Mary's** 26, **Clontarf** 14 **Garryowen** 15, **Cork Constitution** 17 **Shannon** 10, **Bohemian** 14 **Dolphin** 32. 27 March, 2010: **Dolphin** 31 **Blackrock** 13, **Garryowen** 13 **Bohemian** 16, **Shannon** 26 **Clontarf** 32, **St Mary's** 24 **Cork Constitution** 20. 3 April, 2010: **Garryowen** 11 **Blackrock** 18, **Bohemian** 5 **Cork Constitution** 33. 10 April, 2010: **Blackrock** 36 **Bohemian** 18, **Clontarf** 24 **St Mary's** 39, **Cork Constitution** 23 **Dolphin** 13, **Shannon** 8 **Garryowen** 9

FINAL TABLE

	P	W	D	L	F	A	BP	PTS
Cork Constitution	14	10	1	3	231	165	4	**46**
St Mary's College	14	9	0	5	286	200	7	**43**
Dolphin	14	8	0	6	225	202	4	**36**
Blackrock	14	7	0	7	235	207	6	**34**
Shannon	14	6	0	8	242	218	10	**34**
Garryowen	14	7	1	6	158	201	4	**34**
Clontarf	14	5	0	9	214	257	4	**24**
Bohemian	14	3	0	11	149	290	4	**16**

SEMI-FINALS

27 April, 2010

St Mary's College 24 **Old Belvedere** 23

Cork Constitution 31 **Dolphin** 18

FINAL

8 May, Templeville Road, Dublin

CORK CONSTITUTION 17 (2G, 1PG)
ST MARY'S COLLEGE 10 (1G, 1PG)

CORK CONSTITUTION: D Lyons; R Lane, S Zebo, E Ryan (captain), C Healy; J Manning, D Williams; M Gately, R Quinn, S Archer, M O'Connell, I Nagle, P O'Mahony, E Leamy, F Cogan **SUBSTITUTIONS:** B Hayes for O'Connell (62 mins); G Murray for Gately (80 mins); B Cuttriss for Nagle (87 mins); A Ryan for Williams (94 mins)
SCORERS *Tries*: Manning, Healy *Conversions*: Lane, Manning *Penalty Goal*: Manning

ST MARY'S COLLEGE: G Dunne; R Doherty, S Grissing, M Sexton, D Fanning; S McCarthy, C McPhillips; J McGrath, Richie Sweeney, Robert Sweeney, S Bradshaw, R Copeland, D Hall, P Nash, H Hogan (captain) **SUBSTITUTIONS:** C McMahon for McGrath (40 mins); G Logan for Bradshaw (56 mins); G Hickie for Richie Sweeney (71 mins); B O'Flanagan for Nash (72 mins); C Quinn for McPhillips (86 mins); C Donohue for Sexton (92 mins); S O'Flanagan for Doherty (94 mins)
SCORERS *Try*: McCarthy *Conversion*: Dunne *Penalty Goal*: Dunne
REFEREE A Rolland (Ireland)

AIB Division Two: Winners: Lansdowne

AIB Division Three: Winners: Queen's University

AIB CUP 2009–10 RESULTS

QUARTER-FINALS: 21 November, 2009: **Ballymena** 20 **Old Belvedere** 19, **Blackrock** 6 **Garryowen** 16. 28 November, 2009: **Cork Constitution** w/o **Queen's University.** 29 November, 2009: **Dolphin** 24 **Galwegians** 10

SEMI-FINALS: 19 December, 2009: **Ballymena** 9 **Cork Constitution** 18, **Dolphin** 9 **Garryowen** 16

FINAL

30 January, Dubarry Park, Athlone

CORK CONSTITUTION 15 (1G, 1T, 1PG)
GARRYOWEN 11 (1T, 2PG)

CORK CONSTITUTION: S Deasy; R Lane, T Gleeson, E Ryan (captain) C Healy; D Lyons, D Williams; M Gately, R Quinn, S Archer, M O'Connell, I Nagle, B Holland, P O'Mahony, F Cogan **SUBSTITUTIONS:** B Hayes for O'Connell (69 mins); A Ryan for Ryan (69 mins); D O'Driscoll for Williams (72 mins); G Murray for Gately (80 mins)
SCORERS *Tries*: Lane, Lyons *Conversion*: Deasy *Penalty Goal*: Deasy

GARRYOWEN: R O'Mahony; I Hanley, C Doyle (captain), K Hartigan, A Gaughan; W Staunton, C Murray; J Harney, M Sherry, D Lavery, F McKenna, E Mackey, P Neville, A Kavanagh, D Sherry **SUBSTITUTIONS:** M Melbourne for Mackey (64 mins); C Hartigan for Kavanagh (69 mins); L Bourke for Gaughan (69 mins); A McCloskey for McKenna (69 mins)
SCORERS *Try*: Sherry *Penalty Goals*: Murray (2)
RED CARD Nagle (36 mins)
REFEREE A Rolland (Ireland)

ITALY

ITALY'S 2009–10 TEST RECORD

OPPONENTS	DATE	VENUE	RESULT
New Zealand	14 Nov	H	**Lost** 6–20
South Africa	21 Nov	H	**Lost** 10–32
Samoa	28 Nov	H	**Won** 24–6
Ireland	06 Feb	A	**Lost** 11–29
England	14 Feb	H	**Lost** 12–17
Scotland	27 Feb	H	**Won** 16–12
France	14 Mar	A	**Lost** 20–46
Wales	20 Mar	A	**Lost** 10–33
South Africa	19 Jun	A	**Lost** 13–29
South Africa	26 Jun	A	**Lost** 11–55

NEW DAWN FOR ITALY

By Gianluca Barca

Clive Mason/Getty Images

Aironi have been a welcome addition to the rugby world.

Times they are a changing and no more so than on the Italian rugby scene. The 2009–10 domestic season marked the end of the game's semi-professional era in the country. In 2009 a number of clubs had been forced to downsize operations due to financial constraints. To avoid the collapse of the whole of the club system and to give the national squad a stronger base, the Italian Federation chose to approach the Magners League proposing two franchises take part in the competition, starting from the 2010–11 season. After a long and drawn out debate, in September 2009, Treviso and Aironi (Viadana plus other clubs from the area) were finally chosen to represent Italy in the Magners League starting one year later.

Twelve months on, Treviso and Aironi were to be the only fully professional teams left in Italy, with the others drifting back into semi-amateur status. The 2009–10 season was therefore a somewhat strange year, the last with the old format of domestic competition. Top players looked to impress as they competed for a contract with one of the two clubs set to be involved in the Magners League and many faced an uncertain future.

In the midst of the changes the national squad's season started with a bang in Milan on November 14 when the Azzurri hosted the All Blacks in the football temple "San Siro", home to both AC and Inter Milan.

The game was widely promoted on Italian TV and in the press, and rugby fever ran high in the country as 80,000 available tickets were snapped up by both rugby fans and newcomers. It was a record attendance for a rugby match in Italy.

On the pitch, the match ended with a ten-minute arm wrestle between the two packs on the New Zealand try line that fired up the crowd but left a bitter taste in the mouth of both sides. Italy, in fact, thought they had done enough to deserve a penalty try which Australian referee Stuart Dickinson did not award, whereas New Zealand coach Graham Henry called for referees to tighten up things in the front row battle.

The All Blacks won 20–6, a result that made the Italian supporters proud of their team; hardly surprising given the average score between the two squads in the previous ten matches had been 62–10.

A week later when Italy travelled to Udine, in the north east of the country, to face World Cup winners South Africa, expectations were high and everybody was waiting for another showdown in the scrum. The Springboks, though, kept the ball away from the forwards and stung Italy with four tries to one to win 32–10. A poor day with the boot for Craig Gower and Luke McLean made the score unflattering for the home side, even if it was Italy's smallest margin of defeat against South Africa since a 40–21 loss in Rome in 1995.

With two honourable defeats against two world giants, the mood of Italian rugby rested on the outcome of the last of the November tests against Samoa, a team Italy had never beaten before. A loss, like the one against the Pacific Islanders a year earlier, would have made Italy's autumn grim. Who cares if you fill Inter Milan's football stadium if you never win a game?

In the run-up to the match the omens were bad. Captain Sergio Parisse injured his knee in training and would be out for the rest of the season. Italy had not only lost their captain, but also their main star and inspiration. Following the Azzurri's missed chances at the posts against South Africa, coach Nick Mallett also made a surprise move, appointing Mirco Bergamasco as the squad's new kicker, a role he had only occasionally filled in his career.

Samoa, however, was a much easier job than expected. Italy's full-back McLean scored his first international try in the first half, while the scrum was awarded a penalty try near the end of the game. Mirco Bergamasco kicked eight points and Italy won 24–6. Mallett could claim another step forward for his team. Not all was rosy however according to the Italian press: rugby experts lamented an old style of play and very limited options in attack, something the new found supporters didn't seem to care about. The three November Tests had attracted some 130,000 fans, the biggest numbers ever. Mallett answered his critics saying that they didn't understand modern rugby. He had cut the margin of defeat against the All Blacks by 50 points since their encounter at Rugby World Cup 2007 – New Zealand won 76–14 – and pointed out that when he coached South Africa in 1999, Italy had lost 101–0 in Durban.

On the eve of the Six Nations, the national coach said that compared with the year before his team was more solid with new options at nine and ten, but had lost its captain "who was for the Azzurri like Richie McCaw and Dan Carter rolled into one for the All Blacks".

In Tito Tebaldi, Mallett had found the scrum-half Italy had been lacking since Alessandro Troncon retired in 2007 and Australian-born Gower, a centre for his club Bayonne, was the much awaited fly-half to marshal the Azzurri back-line. Mallett had also brought into the team the South African lock Quintin Geldenhuys, who had completed his 36-month residency in the country making him eligible to play for the national squad.

With three away matches – Ireland on the opening weekend before France and Wales at the end of the championship – the Six Nations loomed menacingly. At the same time, the Magners League Board's official green light for two Italian teams to take part in the competition was slow to come. Rumours spread that the invitation might be delayed to 2012. The whole country began to doubt if it would ever happen.

On day one in Dublin, Italy lost 29–11 to Ireland, a match which lacked rhythm and momentum. Centre Gonzalo Garcia was sin binned after 30 minutes and the Irish led 23–8 at half-time. The second 40 minutes pleased neither of the two teams.

One week later it was England in Rome, some said a missed chance for the Azzurri, who went down 17–12 at the end of a hard fought battle. Mallett made the point that now people were talking of beating England, a goal that until a couple of seasons before no one would have dreamt of.

It was once again the Scots who would determine the fate of Italy's Six Nations campaign and whether or not they would pick up another wooden spoon. At the Stadio Flaminio it was the Azzurri defence that won the match. Italy made 110 tackles to Scotland's 78 and scored the only try of the game with replacement scrum-half Pablo Canavosio touching down under the posts after a break by centre Gonzalo Canale.

It was Italy's fifth win in the Six Nations against Scotland. Two days later the Magners League officially opened its doors to two Italian clubs starting from the 2010–11 season. The whole country breathed a big sigh of relief.

Job done, with two games to go, the Azzurri reverted back to the old script. In Paris, the French cut their defence to pieces, winning 46–20 after outscoring their visitors by six tries to two. Indiscipline cost centre Garcia an early yellow card in the first quarter of the match with his counterpart David Marty scoring twice in his absence.

Things were not to go much better the following week in Cardiff where Wales won 33–10, a weary Italy collapsing under the Welsh physical assault. It was another nearly but not quite Six Nations' campaign for Italy, whose only scalp remained Scotland.

The 2010 summer tour offered the Azzurri the chance to travel to South Africa during the Football World Cup. Surprisingly, it was the rugby team who outlasted their football counterparts. While the soccer team drew with underdogs New Zealand and bowed out of the tournament after the pool stages, Italian rugby kept closing the gap, with the Azzurri losing 29–13 in the first Test in Witbank, their best-ever score against South Africa. A break by Tebaldi put Parisse over the line in his first match back after injury.

A week later in East London the world champions wasted no time in resetting the balance with a 55–11 win, scoring seven tries to Italy's one. Mallett however could claim his team was slowly but surely moving in the right direction. The squad now had more strength in depth than ever before, with a promising group of youngsters beginning to come through.

On the domestic scene, Treviso and Viadana prepared for the step up to the Magners League by qualifying for the domestic league final for the second consecutive year. Treviso won 16–12, their 15th and last national title. There will not be another for them in the near future as the two finalists no longer compete in the Italian championship.

In the Heineken Cup, for the umpteenth time, neither Treviso nor Viadana managed to go through to the quarter-finals. On day one of the competition, however, Treviso produced one of the most unexpected wins of the tournament by beating French champions Perpignan 9–8. It was the proof that on their day Italian teams could match anyone. The challenge for the two Italian franchises in the Magners League will be to produce that type of performance on a regular basis.

ITALY INTERNATIONAL STATISTICS

MATCH RECORDS UP TO 29TH OCTOBER 2010

WINNING MARGIN

Date	Opponent	Result	Winning Margin
18/05/1994	Czech Republic	104–8	**96**
07/10/2006	Portugal	83–0	**83**
17/06/1993	Croatia	76–11	**65**
19/06/1993	Morocco	70–9	**61**
02/03/1996	Portugal	64–3	**61**

MOST POINTS IN A MATCH BY THE TEAM

Date	Opponent	Result	Pts.
18/05/1994	Czech Republic	104–8	**104**
07/10/2006	Portugal	83–0	**83**
17/06/1993	Croatia	76–11	**76**
19/06/1993	Morocco	70–9	**70**

MOST TRIES IN A MATCH BY THE TEAM

Date	Opponent	Result	Tries
18/05/1994	Czech Republic	104–8	**16**
07/10/2006	Portugal	83–0	**13**
18/11/1998	Netherlands	67–7	**11**
17/06/1993	Croatia	76–11	**11**

MOST CONVERSIONS IN A MATCH BY THE TEAM

Date	Opponent	Result	Cons
18/05/1994	Czech Republic	104–8	**12**
19/06/1993	Morocco	70–9	**10**
17/06/1993	Croatia	76–11	**9**
07/10/2006	Portugal	83–0	**9**

MOST PENALTIES IN A MATCH BY THE TEAM

Date	Opponent	Result	Pens
01/10/1994	Romania	24–6	**8**
10/11/2001	Fiji	66–10	**7**

MOST DROP GOALS IN A MATCH BY THE TEAM

Date	Opponent	Result	DGs
07/10/1990	Romania	29–21	**3**
05/02/2000	Scotland	34–20	**3**
11/07/1973	Transvaal	24–28	**3**

MOST POINTS IN A MATCH BY A PLAYER

Date	Player	Opponent	Pts.
10/11/2001	Diego Dominguez	Fiji	**29**
05/02/2000	Diego Dominguez	Scotland	**29**
01/07/1983	Stefano Bettarello	Canada	**29**
21/05/1994	Diego Dominguez	Netherlands	**28**
20/12/1997	Diego Dominguez	Ireland	**27**

MOST TRIES IN A MATCH BY A PLAYER

Date	Player	Opponent	Tries
19/06/1993	Ivan Francescato	Morocco	**4**
10/10/1937	Renzo Cova	Belgium	**4**

MOST CONVERSIONS IN A MATCH BY A PLAYER

Date	Player	Opponent	Cons
18/05/1994	Luigi Troiani	Czech Republic	**12**
19/06/1993	Gabriel Filizzola	Morocco	**10**
17/06/1993	Luigi Troiani	Croatia	**9**

MOST PENALTIES IN A MATCH BY A PLAYER

Date	Player	Opponent	Pens
01/10/1994	Diego Dominguez	Romania	8
10/11/2001	Diego Dominguez	Fiji	7

MOST DROP GOALS IN A MATCH BY A PLAYER

Date	Player	Opponent	DGs
05/02/2000	Diego Dominguez	Scotland	3
11/07/1973	Rocco Caligiuri	Transvaal	3

MOST CAPPED PLAYERS

Player	Caps
Alessandro Troncon	101
Mauro Bergamasco	84
Marco Bortolami	84
Carlo Checchinato	83
Andrea Lo Cicero	78

LEADING TRY SCORERS

Player	Tries
Marcello Cuttitta	25
Paolo Vaccari	22
Manrico Marchetto	21
Carlo Checchinato	21
Alessandro Troncon	19

LEADING CONVERSIONS SCORERS

Player	Cons
Diego Dominguez	127
Luigi Troiani	57
Stefano Bettarello	46
David Bortolussi	35
Ramiro Pez	33

LEADING PENALTY SCORERS

Player	Pens
Diego Dominguez	209
Stefano Bettarello	106
Luigi Troiani	57
Ramiro Pez	52
Ennio Ponzi	31

LEADING DROP GOAL SCORERS

Player	DGs
Diego Dominguez	19
Stefano Bettarello	15
Ramiro Pez	6
Massimo Bonomi	5
Oscar Collodo	5

LEADING POINT SCORERS

Player	Pts.
Diego Dominguez	983
Stefano Bettarello	483
Luigi Troiani	294
Ramiro Pez	260
David Bortolussi	153

ITALY INTERNATIONAL PLAYERS
UP TO 29TH OCTOBER 2010

Note: Years given for International Championship matches are for second half of season; eg 1972 means season 1971–72. Years for all other matches refer to the actual year of the match.

E Abbiati 1968 *WGe*, 1970 *R*, 1971 *Mor*, *F*, 1972 *Pt*, *Sp*, *Sp*, *Yug*, 1973 *Pt*, *ETv*, 1974 *Leo*
A Agosti 1933 *Cze*
M Aguero 2005 *Tg*, *Ar*, *Fj*, 2006 *Fj*, 2007 *Ur*, *Ar*, *I*, *Pt*, 2008 *A*, *Ar*, *Pl*, 2009 *A*, 2010 *I*, *E*, *S*, *F*, *W*
A Agujari 1967 *Pt*
E Aio 1974 *WGe*
G Aiolfi 1952 *Sp*, *Ger*, *F*, 1953 *F*, 1955 *Ger*, *F*
A Alacevich 1939 *R*
A Albonico 1934 *R*, 1935 *F*, 1936 *Ger*, *R*, 1937 *Ger*, *R*, *Bel*, *Ger*, *F*, 1938 *Ger*
N Aldorvandi 1994 *Sp*, *CZR*, *H*
M Alfonsetti 1994 *F*
E Allevi 1929 *Sp*, 1933 *Cze*
I Aloisio 1933 *Cze*, *Cze*, 1934 *Cat*, *R*, 1935 *Cat*, 1936 *Ger*, *R*
A Altigeri 1973 *Rho*, *WTv*, *Bor*, *NEC*, *Nat*, *Leo*, *FS*, *Tva*, *Cze*, *Yug*, *A*, 1974 *Pt*, *WGe*, 1975 *F*, *E*, *Pol*, *H*, *Sp*, 1976 *F*, *R*, *J*, 1978 *Ar*, *USS*, *Sp*, 1979 *F*, *Pol*, *R*
T Altissimi 1929 *Sp*
V Ambron 1962 *Ger*, *R*, 1963 *F*, 1964 *Ger*, *F*, 1965 *F*, *Cze*, 1966 *F*, *Ger*, *R*, 1967 *Pt*, *R*, 1968 *Pt*, *WGe*, *Yug*, 1969 *Bul*, *Sp*, *Bel*, 1970 *Mad*, *Mad*, *R*, 1971 *Mor*, 1972 *Sp*, *Sp*
R Ambrosio 1987 *NZ*, *USS*, *Sp*, 1988 *F*, *R*, *A*, *I*, 1989 *R*, *Sp*, *Ar*, *Z*, *USS*
B Ancillotti 1978 *Sp*, 1979 *F*, *Pol*, *R*
E Andina 1952 *F*, 1955 *F*
C Angelozzi 1979 *E*, *Mor*, 1980 *Coo*
A Angioli 1960 *Ger*, *F*, 1961 *Ger*, *F*, 1962 *F*, *Ger*, *R*, 1963 *F*
A Angrisiani 1979 *Mor*, *F*, *Pol*, *USS*, *Mor*, 1980 *Coo*, 1984 *Tun*
S Annibal 1980 *Fj*, *Coo*, *Pol*, *Sp*, 1981 *F*, *WGe*, 1982 *R*, *E*, *WGe*, 1983 *F*, *USS*, *Sp*, *Mor*, *F*, *A*, 1984 *F*, 1985 *F*, *Z*, *Z*, 1986 *Tun*, *F*, *Pt*, 1990 *F*
JM Antoni 2001 *Nm*, *SA*
C Appiani 1976 *Sp*, 1977 *Mor*, *Pol*, *Sp*, 1978 *USS*
S Appiani 1985 *R*, 1986 *Pt*, 1988 *A*, 1989 *F*
O Arancio 1993 *Rus*, 1994 *CZR*, *H*, *A*, *A*, *R*, *W*, *F*, 1995 *S*, *I*, *Sa*, *E*, *Ar*, *F*, *R*, *NZ*, *SA*, 1996 *W*, *Pt*, *W*, *A*, *E*, *S*, 1997 *I*, *I*, 1998 *S*, *Geo*, *Ar*, *E*, 1999 *F*, *W*, *I*, *SA*, *E*, *NZ*
D Armellin 1965 *Cze*, 1966 *Ger*, 1968 *Pt*, *WGe*, *Yug*, 1969 *Bul*, *Sp*, *Bel*, *F*
A Arrigoni 1949 *Cze*
G Artuso 1977 *Pol*, *R*, 1978 *Sp*, 1979 *F*, *E*, *NZ*, *Mor*, 1980 *F*, *R*, *JAB*, 1981 *F*, 1982 *F*, *E*, *Mor*, 1983 *F*, *R*, *USS*, *C*, *C*, 1984 *USS*, 1985 *R*, *EngB*, *USS*, *R*, 1986 *Tun*, *F*, *Tun*, 1987 *Pt*, *F*, *R*, *NZ*
E Augeri 1962 *F*, *Ger*, *R*, 1963 *F*
A Autore 1961 *Ger*, *F*, 1962 *F*, 1964 *Ger*, 1966 *Ger*, 1968 *Pt*, *WGe*, *Yug*, 1969 *Bul*, *Sp*, *Bel*, *F*
L Avigo 1959 *F*, 1962 *F*, *Ger*, *R*, 1963 *F*, 1964 *Ger*, *F*, 1965 *F*, *Cze*, 1966 *Ger*, *R*
R Aymonod 1933 *Cze*, 1934 *Cat*, *R*, 1935 *F*
A Azzali 1981 *WGe*, 1982 *F*, *R*, *WGe*, 1983 *F*, *R*, *USS*, *Sp*, *Mor*, *F*, 1984 *F*, *Mor*, *R*, 1985 *R*, *EngB*, *Sp*
S Babbo 1996 *Pt*
A Bacchetti 2009 *I*, *S*
A Balducci 1929 *Sp*
F Baraldi 1973 *Cze*, *Yug*, 1974 *Mid*, *Sus*, *Oxo*, 1975 *E*, *Pol*, *H*, *Sp*, 1976 *F*, *R*, *A*, 1977 *F*, *Mor*, *Cze*
R Baraldi 1971 *R*
A Barattin 1996 *A*, *E*, 1997 *De*
S Barba 1985 *R*, *EngB*, 1986 *E*, *A*, 1987 *Pt*, *F*, *R*, *Ar*, *Fj*, 1988 *R*, *USS*, *A*, 1990 *F*, *Pol*, *Sp*, *H*, *R*, *USS*, 1991 *F*, *R*, *Nm*, *Nm*, *US*, *E*, *USS*, 1992 *Sp*, *F*, *R*, *R*, *S*, 1993 *Sp*, *F*, *Cro*, *Mor*, *Sp*
RJ Barbieri 2006 *J*, *Fj*, *Pt*, 2007 *Ur*, *Ar*, *I*, 2008 *SA*
G Barbini 1978 *USS*
M Barbini 2002 *NZ*, *Sp*, *Ar*, *A*, 2003 *I*, *NZ*, 2004 *F*, *I*, *R*, *J*, *NZ*, *US*, 2005 *W*, *E*, 2007 *I*
N Barbini 1953 *Ger*, *R*, 1954 *Sp*, *F*, 1955 *Ger*, *F*, *Sp*, *Cze*, 1956 *Ger*, 1957 *Ger*, 1958 *R*, 1960 *Ger*, *F*
F Bargelli 1979 *E*, *Sp*, *Mor*, *F*, *Pol*, *USS*, *NZ*, *Mor*, 1980 *F*, *R*, *Fj*, *Sp*, 1981 *F*, *R*
S Barilari 1948 *Cze*, 1953 *Ger*, *R*
M Baroni 1999 *F*, *W*, *I*, *SA*, *SA*, 2000 *C*
V Barzaghi 1929 *Sp*, 1930 *Sp*, 1933 *Cze*
JL Basei 1979 *E*, *Sp*, *Mor*, *F*, *Pol*, *USS*, *NZ*, *Mor*, 1980 *F*, *R*, *Fj*, *JAB*, *Coo*, *USS*, 1981 *R*
A Battagion 1948 *F*, *Cze*
F Battaglini 1948 *F*
M Battaglini 1940 *R*, *Ger*, 1951 *Sp*, 1953 *F*, *R*
A Becca 1937 *R*, 1938 *Ger*, 1939 *R*, 1940 *Ger*
E Bellinazzo 1958 *R*, 1959 *F*, 1960 *Ger*, *F*, 1961 *Ger*, *F*, 1962 *F*, *Ger*, 1964 *Ger*, *F*, 1966 *F*, *Ger*, *R*, 1967 *F*
A Benatti 2001 *Fj*, *SA*, *Sa*, 2002 *W*, 2003 *NZ*
C Bentivoglio 1977 *Pol*
D Beretta 1993 *S*
A Bergamasco 1973 *Bor*, *Tva*, 1977 *Pol*, 1978 *USS*
M Bergamasco 1998 *H*, *E*, 1999 *SA*, *E*, 2000 *Geo*, *S*, *W*, *I*, *E*, *F*, *C*, 2001 *I*, *E*, *F*, *S*, *W*, *Fj*, *SA*, *Sa*, 2002 *F*, *S*, *W*, *I*, *E*, *NZ*, *Sp*, *R*, *A*, 2003 *W*, *I*, *S*, *I*, *Geo*, *NZ*, *Tg*, *W*, 2004 *J*, *C*, *NZ*, 2005 *I*, *W*, *Ar*, *A*, *Ar*, *Fj*, 2006 *I*, *E*, *F*, *J*, *Fj*, *Pt*, *Rus*, *A*, *Ar*, *C*, 2007 *F*, *S*, *W*, *J*, *NZ*, *R*, *Pt*, *S*, 2008 *I*, *E*, *W*, *Ar*, *A*, *Ar*, *Pl*, 2009 *E*, *I*, *S*, *W*, *F*, *A*, *NZ*, *NZ*, *SA*, *Sa*, 2010 *I*, *E*, *S*, *F*, *W*
M Bergamasco 2002 *F*, *S*, *W*, *Ar*, *A*, 2003 *W*, *I*, *E*, *F*, *S*, *S*, *Geo*, *NZ*, *C*, 2004 *E*, *F*, *S*, *I*, *W*, 2005 *I*, *W*, *S*, *Tg*, *Ar*, *Fj*, 2006 *I*, *E*, *F*, *W*, *S*, *J*, *Fj*, *Pt*, *Rus*, *A*, *Ar*, *C*, 2007 *F*, *E*, *S*, *W*, *I*, *J*, *I*, *NZ*, *R*, *S*, 2008 *I*, *E*, *W*, *F*, *S*, *Ar*, *A*, *Ar*, *Pl*, 2009 *E*, *I*, *S*, *W*, *F*, *A*, *NZ*, *NZ*, *SA*, *Sa*, 2010 *I*, *E*, *S*, *F*, *W*, *SA*, *SA*
L Bernabo 1970 *Mad*, *Mad*, *R*, 1972 *Sp*, *Sp*
V Bernabò 2004 *US*, 2005 *Tg*, *Fj*, 2007 *E*, *S*, *W*, *I*, *Ur*, *Ar*, *J*, *I*, *NZ*, *R*, 2010 *W*, *SA*
F Berni 1985 *R*, *Sp*, *Z*, *Z*, 1986 *E*, *A*, 1987 *R*, *NZ*, 1988 *A*, 1989 *F*
D Bertoli 1967 *R*
V Bertolotto 1936 *Ger*, *R*, 1937 *Ger*, *R*, 1942 *R*, 1948 *F*
O Bettarello 1958 *F*, 1959 *F*, 1961 *Ger*
R Bettarello 1953 *Ger*, *R*
S Bettarello 1979 *Pol*, *E*, *Sp*, *F*, *NZ*, *Mor*, 1980 *F*, *R*, *Fj*, *JAB*, *Coo*, *Pol*, *USS*, *Sp*, 1981 *F*, *R*, *USS*, *WGe*, 1982 *F*, *R*, *E*, *WGe*, *Mor*, 1983 *F*, *R*, *USS*, *C*, *Sp*, *Mor*, *F*, *A*, 1984 *F*, *Mor*, *R*, *Tun*, *USS*, 1985 *F*, *R*, *EngB*, *Sp*, *Z*, *USS*, *R*, 1986 *Tun*, *F*, *Pt*, *E*, *A*, *Tun*, *USS*, 1987 *R*, *USS*, *Sp*, 1988 *USS*, *A*
L Bettella 1969 *Sp*, *Bel*, *F*
R Bevilacqua 1937 *Bel*, *Ger*, *F*, 1938 *Ger*, 1939 *Ger*, *R*, 1940 *R*, *Ger*, 1942 *R*
C Bezzi 2003 *W*, *I*, *E*, *F*, *S*, *I*, *NZ*, *W*, 2004 *US*, 2005 *Ar*, *A*
G Biadene 1958 *R*, 1959 *F*
G Bigi 1930 *Sp*, 1933 *Cze*
M Bimbati 1989 *Z*
M Birtig 1998 *H*, 1999 *F*

F Blessano 1975 *F, R, Pol, H, Sp*, 1976 *F, R, J*, 1977 *F, Mor, Pol, R, Cze, R, Sp*, 1978 *F, Ar, Sp*, 1979 *F, Pol, R*
L Boccaletto 1969 *Bul, Bel, F*, 1970 *Cze, Mad, Mad, R*, 1971 *F, R*, 1972 *Pt, Sp, Sp*, 1975 *E*
S Boccazzi 1985 *Z*, 1988 *USS*
R Bocchino 2010 *I, F, W, SA*
M Bocconelli 1967 *R*
M Bollesan 1963 *F*, 1964 *F*, 1965 *F*, 1966 *F, Ger*, 1967 *F, Pt*, 1968 *Pt, WGe, Yug*, 1969 *Bul, Sp, Bel, F*, 1970 *Cze, Mad, Mad, R*, 1971 *Mor, F, R*, 1972 *Pt, Pt, Sp, Sp, Yug*, 1973 *Pt, Rho, WTv, Bor, NEC, Nat, ETv, Leo, FS, Tva, Yug, A*, 1974 *Pt, Mid, Sus, Oxo, WGe, Leo*, 1975 *F, Sp, Cze*
A Bona 1972 *Sp, Yug*, 1973 *Rho, WTv, Bor, NEC, Nat, ETv, Leo, FS, Tva, Cze, Yug, A*, 1974 *Pt, WGe, Leo*, 1975 *F, Sp, R, Cze, E, Pol, H, Sp*, 1976 *F, R, J, A, Sp*, 1977 *F, Mor*, 1978 *Ar, USS, Sp*, 1979 *F, Sp, Mor, F, Pol, USS, NZ, Mor*, 1980 *F, R, Fj, JAB, Pol, Sp*, 1981 *F*
L Bonaiti 1979 *R*, 1980 *Pol*
G Bonati 1939 *Ger, R*
S Bonetti 1972 *Yug*, 1973 *Rho, WTv, Bor, NEC, Nat, ETv, Leo, FS, Tva*, 1974 *Pt, Mid, Sus, Oxo, Leo*, 1975 *F, Sp, R, Cze, E, Pol, H, Sp*, 1976 *R, J, A, Sp*, 1977 *F, Mor, R, Sp*, 1978 *F*, 1979 *F*, 1980 *USS*
S Bonfante 1936 *Ger, R*
G Bonino 1949 *F*
M Bonomi 1988 *F, R*, 1990 *Sp, H, R, USS*, 1991 *F, R, Nm, Nm, E, NZ, USS*, 1992 *R, R*, 1993 *Cro, Mor, Sp, F, S*, 1994 *Sp, R, H, A, A, W*, 1995 *S, I, Sa, F, Ar, R, NZ*, 1996 *W*
S Bordon 1990 *R, USS*, 1991 *Nm, USS*, 1992 *F, R*, 1993 *Sp, F, Pt, Rus, F*, 1994 *R, A, A, R, W, F*, 1995 *I, E, Ar, F, Ar, NZ, SA*, 1996 *W, A, E*, 1997 *I, F*
L Borsetto 1977 *Pol*
V Borsetto 1948 *F, Cze*
M Bortolami 2001 *Nm, SA, Fj, SA, Sa*, 2002 *F, S, W, I, E, NZ, Sp, R, Ar, A*, 2003 *W, I, E, S, Geo, Tg, C*, 2004 *E, F, S, I, W, R, J, C, NZ*, 2005 *I, W, S, E, F, Ar, Ar, A, Tg, Ar, Fj*, 2006 *I, E, F, W, S, J, Fj, Pt, Rus, A, Ar, C*, 2007 *F, E, S, W, I, J, I, NZ, R, Pt*, 2008 *W, F, S, A, Ar, Pl*, 2009 *E, S, W, F, A, A, NZ*, 2010 *I, E, S, F, W, SA, SA*
G Bortolini 1933 *Cze*, 1934 *Cat*
D Bortolussi 2006 *J, Fj, Pt, Rus, Ar, C*, 2007 *Ur, Ar, J, I, NZ, R, Pt, S*, 2008 *I, E*
L Boscaino 1967 *Pt*
L Bossi 1940 *R, Ger*
A Bottacchiara 1991 *NZ, USS*, 1992 *Sp, F, R, R*
G Bottacin 1956 *Cze*
O Bottonelli 1929 *Sp*, 1934 *R*, 1935 *Cat, F*, 1937 *Ger*, 1939 *Ger*
L Bove 1948 *Cze*, 1949 *F, Cze*
O Bracaglia 1939 *R*
M Braga 1958 *R*
L Bricchi 1929 *Sp*, 1930 *Sp*, 1933 *Cze*
L Brighetti 1934 *Cat*
A Brunelli 1969 *Bel*, 1970 *Mad*, 1971 *F*
M Brunello 1988 *I*, 1989 *F*, 1990 *F, Sp, H, R, USS*, 1993 *Pt*
S Brusin 1957 *Ger*
KS Burton 2007 *Ur, Ar*, 2009 *A, NZ*
P Buso 2008 *W*
G Busson 1957 *Ger*, 1958 *R*, 1959 *F*, 1960 *Ger, F*, 1961 *Ger, F*, 1962 *F, Ger*, 1963 *F*
F Caccia-Dominioni 1935 *F*, 1937 *Ger*
C Caione 1995 *R*, 1996 *Pt*, 1997 *F, R, De*, 1998 *Geo, Rus, Cro, Ar, H, E*, 1999 *F, S, SA, Ur, Sp, Fj, Tg, NZ*, 2000 *Sa, Fj, C, R, NZ*, 2001 *I, E, S, Fj*
R Caligiuri 1969 *F*, 1973 *Pt, Rho, WTv, NEC, Nat, ETv, Leo, FS, Tva*, 1975 *E, Pol, H, Sp*, 1976 *F, R, J, A, Sp*, 1978 *F, Ar, USS, Sp*, 1979 *F, Pol, R*
A Caluzzi 1970 *R*, 1971 *Mor, F*, 1972 *Pt, Pt, Sp, Sp*, 1973 *Pt*, 1974 *Oxo, WGe, Leo*
P Camiscioni 1975 *E*, 1976 *R, J, A, Sp*, 1977 *F*, 1978 *F*
M Campagna 1933 *Cze*, 1934 *Cat*, 1936 *Ger, R*, 1937 *Ger, R, Bel*, 1938 *Ger*
G-J Canale 2003 *S, Geo, NZ, Tg, C, W*, 2004 *S, I, W, R, J, C*, 2005 *I, Ar, Ar, A, Tg, Ar, Fj*, 2006 *I, E, F, W, S, A, Ar, C*, 2007 *F, E, S, W, J, I, R, Pt, S*, 2008 *I, E, W, F, S, A*, 2009 *E, I, S, W, F, A, NZ, NZ, Sa*, 2010 *I, E, S, F, W, SA, SA*
PL Canavosio 2005 *A, Tg, Fj*, 2006 *I, E, F, W, S, Fj, Pt, Rus, A, Ar*, 2007 *Ar, J, I, Pt*, 2008 *I, SA, Ar, A, Ar*, 2009 *S, W, F, A*, 2010 *E, S, F, W*
C Cantoni 1956 *Ger, F, Cze*, 1957 *Ger*
L Capitani 1989 *F, R, Sp, Ar, Z, USS*
M Capuzzoni 1993 *Cro*, 1995 *I*
A Caranci 1989 *R*
M Carli 1955 *Sp, Cze*
C Carloni 1935 *F*
D Carpente 2004 *R, J*
T Carraro 1937 *R*
T Casagrande 1977 *R*
U Cassellato 1990 *Sp*, 1992 *R, S*, 1993 *Sp, F, Pt, Cro, Mor, F, S*
R Cassina 1992 *R, S*
A Castellani 1994 *CZR*, 1995 *Ar, R*, 1996 *W, S*, 1997 *Ar, R, De, I*, 1998 *S, W, Geo, Rus, Cro, H, E*, 1999 *F, W, Ur, Sp, Fj, Tg, NZ*
LM Castrogiovanni 2002 *NZ, Sp, R, Ar, A*, 2003 *I, E, F, S, I, Geo, NZ, Tg, C, W*, 2004 *E, F, S, I, W, J*, 2005 *I, W, S, E, F, Ar, A, Ar, Fj*, 2006 *I, E, F, W, S, Pt, Rus, A, Ar, C*, 2007 *F, E, S, J, I, NZ, R, Pt, S*, 2008 *I, E, W, F, S*, 2009 *E, I, S, W, F, NZ, SA, Sa*, 2010 *I, E, S, F, W, SA*
L Catotti 1979 *Pol, E*
Cavelleri 1997 *De*
A Cazzini 1933 *Cze, Cze*, 1934 *Cat, R*, 1935 *Cat, F*, 1936 *Ger, R*, 1937 *Ger, R, Bel, Ger, F*, 1939 *R*, 1942 *R*
G Cecchetto 1955 *F*
A Cecchetto-Milani 1952 *Sp, Ger, F*
G Cecchin 1970 *Cze, R*, 1971 *F, R*, 1972 *Pt*
G Ceccotti 1972 *Pt, Sp*
A Centinari 1930 *Sp*
R Centinari 1935 *F*, 1936 *Ger, R*, 1937 *Bel, F*, 1939 *Ger*
A Cepolino 1999 *Ur, Sp, Fj, Tg, NZ*
L Cesani 1929 *Sp*, 1930 *Sp*, 1935 *Cat, F*
F Ceselin 1989 *F, R*
C Checchinato 1990 *Sp*, 1991 *Nm, Nm, US, NZ, USS*, 1992 *Sp, F, R, S*, 1993 *Pt, Cro, Sp, F, Rus, F, S*, 1994 *Sp, R, CZR, A, A, R, W, F*, 1995 *Sa, F, Ar, R, NZ*, 1996 *W, E*, 1997 *I, F, Ar, R, SA, I*, 1998 *Geo, Rus, Ar, H, E*, 1999 *F, S, SA, SA, Ur, Fj, E, Tg, NZ*, 2000 *Geo, S, W, I, E, F, Sa, Fj*, 2001 *I, E, F, S, W, Nm, SA, Ur, Ar, Fj, SA, Sa*, 2002 *F, S, W, Sp, R*, 2003 *Geo, NZ, Tg, C, W*, 2004 *E, F, I*
G Chechinato 1973 *Cze, Yug, A*, 1974 *WGe, Leo*
G Cherubini 1949 *Cze*, 1951 *Sp*
T Ciccio 1992 *R*, 1993 *Sp, F, Mor, F*
E Cicognani 1940 *Ger*
R Cinelli 1968 *Pt*, 1969 *Sp*
G Cinti 1973 *Rho, WTv, ETv*
F Cioni 1967 *Pt, R*, 1968 *Pt*, 1969 *Bul, Sp, Bel*, 1970 *Cze, Mad, Mad, R*
L Cittadini 2008 *I*, 2010 *SA, SA*
L Clerici 1939 *Ger*
A Colella 1983 *R, USS, C, C, Sp, Mor, F, A, USS*, 1984 *R, Tun, USS*, 1985 *F, R, EngB, Sp, Z, Z, USS, R*, 1986 *Tun, F, Pt, E, A, Tun, USS*, 1987 *Pt, F, Ar, Fj, USS, Sp*, 1988 *F, R, USS*, 1989 *R, Sp, Ar*, 1990 *Pol, R*
O Collodo 1977 *Pol, Cze, R, Sp*, 1978 *F*, 1986 *Pt, E, A, USS*, 1987 *Pt, F, R, NZ, Ar, Fj*
S Colombini 1971 *R*
F Colombo 1933 *Cze*
G Colussi 1957 *F*, 1958 *F*, 1964 *Ger, F*, 1965 *F, Cze*, 1968 *Pt*
C Colusso 1982 *F*
A Comin 1955 *Ger, F, Sp, F, Cze*, 1956 *F, Cze*, 1958 *F*
U Conforto 1965 *Cze*, 1966 *Ger, R*, 1967 *F, R*, 1968 *Pt, WGe, Yug*, 1969 *Bul, Sp, Bel, F*, 1970 *Cze*, 1971 *Mor, F*, 1972 *Yug*, 1973 *Pt*
F Coppio 1993 *F, Pt, Cro, Mor, Sp*
L Cornella 1999 *Sp*
R Corvo 1985 *F, Sp, Z*
U Cossara 1971 *Mor, F, R*, 1972 *Pt, Sp*, 1973 *Pt, Rho, NEC, Nat, Leo, FS, Tva, Cze*, 1975 *F, Sp, R, Cze, E, Pol, H*, 1976 *F, J, A*, 1977 *Pol*
A Costa 1940 *R, Ger*, 1942 *R*
S Costanzo 2004 *R, C, NZ, US*
E Cottafava 1973 *Pt*
R Cova 1937 *Bel, Ger, F*, 1938 *Ger*, 1939 *Ger, R*, 1942 *R*

C Covi 1988 *F, R, USS, A, I,* 1989 *F, R, Sp, Ar, Z, USS,* 1990 *F, Pol, R,* 1991 *F, R, Nm, Nm,* 1996 *E*
F Crepaz 1972 *Pt*
M Crescenzo 1984 *R*
U Crespi 1933 *Cze, Cze,* 1934 *Cat, R,* 1935 *Cat,* 1937 *Ger*
W Cristofoletto 1992 *R,* 1993 *Mor, Sp, F,* 1996 *Pt, A, E, S,* 1997 *I, F, F, Ar, SA, I,* 1998 *S, W, Rus, Ar, E,* 1999 *F, S, W, I, SA, SA, Sp, Fj, E, NZ,* 2000 *E, F*
G Croci 1990 *Sp, H, R, USS,* 1991 *F, R, Nm, US, E, NZ, USS,* 1992 *Sp, F,* 1993 *S,* 1996 *S,* 1997 *I, F, F, Ar, R, SA, I,* 1998 *S, W, Cro*
R Crotti 1993 *S,* 1995 *SA*
L Cuccharelli 1966 *R,* 1967 *R*
G Cucchiella 1973 *A,* 1974 *Sus,* 1979 *Sp, F, Pol, USS, NZ, Mor,* 1980 *F, R, Fj, JAB, Coo,* 1985 *USS, R,* 1986 *Tun, F, Pt, E,* 1987 *Pt, F, Fj*
M Cuttitta 1990 *Pol, R, Sp, H, R, USS,* 1991 *F, Nm, Nm, US, E, NZ, USS,* 1992 *Sp, F, R, R, S,* 1993 *Sp, F, Pt, Cro, Mor, Sp, F, Rus, F, S,* 1994 *Sp, R, CZR, H, A, A, W, F,* 1995 *S, I, Sa, E, Ar, F, Ar, R, NZ, SA,* 1996 *W, Pt, W, E, S,* 1997 *I, F, F, Ar, SA, I,* 1998 *W, Rus, Cro, Ar, H, E,* 1999 *F, S, W,* 2000 *Geo, S, W, I, E*
M Cuttitta 1987 *Pt, F, R, NZ, Ar, Fj, USS, Sp,* 1988 *F, R,* 1989 *Z, USS,* 1990 *Pol, R,* 1991 *F, R, Nm, US, E, NZ, USS,* 1992 *Sp, F, R, R, S,* 1993 *Sp, F, Mor, Sp, F, F,* 1994 *Sp, R, H, A, A, F,* 1995 *S, I, Sa,* 1996 *S,* 1997 *I, F, F, Ar, R, SA, I,* 1998 *S, W, Rus, Cro, Ar,* 1999 *F*
G Dagnini 1949 *F*
D Dal Maso 2000 *Sa, Fj,* 2001 *I, E,* 2004 *J, C, NZ, US,* 2005 *I, W, S, E, F, A*
M Dal Sie 1993 *Pt,* 1994 *R, W, F,* 1995 *F, Ar,* 1996 *A*
A D'Alberton 1966 *F, Ger, R,* 1967 *F, R*
D Daldoss 1979 *Pol, R, E, Sp, Mor*
C D'Alessio 1937 *R, Bel, F,* 1938 *Ger,* 1939 *Ger*
F Dalla Nora 1997 *De*
D Dallan 1997 *De,* 1999 *F, S, W,* 2000 *S, W, I, E, F, C, R, NZ,* 2001 *I, E, F, W, Fj, SA, Sa,* 2002 *F, S, I, E, NZ, Sp, R,* 2003 *W, I, E, F, S, Tg, C, W,* 2004 *E, F, S, I, W, C,* 2006 *J,* 2007 *F, E*
M Dallan 1997 *Ar, R, De, I,* 1998 *Geo, Ar, H, E,* 1999 *SA, SA,* 2000 *S, Sa, C,* 2001 *F, S,* 2003 *Tg, C,* 2004 *E, F, S*
A Danieli 1955 *Ger, F, Sp, F, Cze*
V D'Anna 1993 *Rus*
P Dari 1951 *Sp,* 1952 *Sp, Ger, F,* 1953 *Ger, R,* 1954 *Sp, F*
D Davo 1998 *Geo*
G De Angelis 1934 *Cat, R,* 1935 *Cat, F,* 1937 *R*
E De Anna 1972 *Yug,* 1973 *Cze, A,* 1975 *F, Sp, R, Cze, E, Pol, H, Sp,* 1976 *F, R,* 1978 *Ar, USS, Sp,* 1979 *F, R, Sp, Mor, F, USS, NZ,* 1980 *F, R, Fj, JAB*
R De Bernardo 1980 *USS, Sp,* 1981 *F, R, USS, WGe,* 1982 *R, E,* 1983 *R, USS, C, C, Sp, Mor, F, A, USS,* 1984 *F, USS,* 1985 *R, EngB,* 1988 *I,* 1989 *Ar, Z*
CF De Biase 1987 *Sp,* 1988 *F, A*
G De Carli 1996 *W,* 1997 *R, De,* 1998 *S, Geo, Rus, Ar, H, E,* 1999 *F, I, SA, SA, Ur, Fj,* 2000 *S, Sa, Fj,* 2001 *I, E, W, SA, Ur, Fj, SA, Sa,* 2002 *F, S, W, I, E,* 2003 *W, I, E*
B de Jager 2006 *J*
L De Joanni 1983 *C, Mor, F, A, USS,* 1984 *R, Tun, USS,* 1985 *F, R, EngB, Sp, Z,* 1986 *A, Tun,* 1989 *F, R, Sp, Ar, Z,* 1990 *R*
D De Luca 1998 *Cro*
R De Marchis 1935 *F*
H De Marco 1993 *Pt*
JR de Marigny 2004 *E, F, S, I, W, US,* 2005 *I, W, S,* 2007 *F, E, S, W, I, Ur, J, I, NZ, Pt*
A de Rossi 1999 *Ur, Sp, E,* 2000 *I, E, F, Sa, C, R, NZ,* 2001 *SA, Ur, Ar,* 2002 *I, E, NZ, Sp, R,* 2003 *W, I, E, F, S, I, Geo, Tg, C, W,* 2004 *E, F, S, I, W, R*
C De Rossi 1994 *Sp, H, R*
L De Santis 1952 *Sp*
M De Stefani 1989 *Z*
C De Vecchi 1948 *F*
G Degli Antoni 1963 *F,* 1965 *F,* 1966 *F, Ger, R,* 1967 *F*
G Del Bono 1951 *Sp*
M Del Bono 1960 *Ger, F,* 1961 *Ger, F,* 1962 *F, Ger, R,* 1963 *F,* 1964 *Ger, F*
CA Del Fava 2004 *W, R, J,* 2005 *I, W, S, E, F, Tg, Ar, Fj,* 2006 *I, E, F, W, S, J, Fj, Pt,* 2007 *Ur, Ar, Pt, S,* 2008 *I, E, W, F, S, SA, Ar, A, Ar,* 2009 *I, S, W, F, A, NZ, NZ, SA, Sa,* 2010 *I, S, F, SA*
C Della Valle 1968 *WGe, Yug,* 1969 *F,* 1970 *Mad, Mad,* 1971 *F*
S Dellapè 2002 *F, S, I, E, NZ, Sp, Ar,* 2003 *F, S, S, Geo, Tg, C, W,* 2004 *E, F, S, I, W, C, NZ,* 2005 *I, W, S, E, F, Ar,* 2006 *I, E, W, S, J, Fj, Pt, Rus, A, Ar, C,* 2007 *F, E, S, W, I, J, NZ, R, S,* 2008 *I, E, W, SA, Ar,* 2009 *E, I, S, W, F*
G Delli Ficorilli 1969 *F*
PE Derbyshire 2009 *A,* 2010 *E, F, SA, SA*
A Di Bello 1930 *Sp,* 1933 *Cze, Cze,* 1934 *Cat*
F Di Carlo 1975 *Sp, R, Cze, Sp,* 1976 *F, Sp,* 1977 *Pol, R, Pol,* 1978 *Ar, USS*
B Di Cola 1973 *A*
G Di Cola 1972 *Sp, Sp,* 1973 *A*
F Di Maura 1971 *Mor*
A Di Zitti 1958 *R,* 1960 *Ger,* 1961 *Ger, F,* 1962 *F, Ger, R,* 1964 *Ger, F,* 1965 *F, Cze,* 1966 *F, Ger, R,* 1967 *F, Pt, R,* 1969 *Bul, Sp, Bel,* 1972 *Pt, Sp*
R Dolfato 1985 *F,* 1986 *A,* 1987 *Pt, Fj, USS, Sp,* 1988 *F, R, USS*
D Dominguez 1991 *F, R, Nm, Nm, US, E, NZ, USS,* 1992 *Sp, F, R, S,* 1993 *Sp, F, Rus, F, S,* 1994 *R, H, R, W,* 1995 *S, I, Sa, E, Ar, SA,* 1996 *W, Pt, W, A, E, S,* 1997 *I, F, F, Ar, R, SA, I,* 1998 *S, W, Rus, Ar, H, E,* 1999 *F, S, W, I, Ur, Sp, Fj, E, Tg, NZ,* 2000 *Geo, S, W, I, E, F,* 2001 *F, S, W, Fj, SA, Sa,* 2002 *F, S, I, E, Ar,* 2003 *W, I*
D Donadona 1929 *Sp,* 1930 *Sp*
G Dora 1929 *Sp*
R D'Orazio 1969 *Bul*
M Dotti IV 1939 *R,* 1940 *R, Ger*
F Dotto 1971 *Mor, F,* 1972 *Pt, Pt, Sp*
P Dotto 1993 *Sp, Cro,* 1994 *Sp, R*
J Erasmus 2008 *F, S, SA*
U Faccioli 1948 *F*
A Falancia 1975 *E, Pol*
G Faliva 1999 *SA,* 2002 *NZ, Ar, A*
G Faltiba 1993 *Pt*
G Fanton 1979 *Pol*
P Farina 1987 *F, NZ, Fj*
P Farinelli 1940 *R,* 1949 *F, Cze,* 1951 *Sp,* 1952 *Sp*
T Fattori 1936 *Ger, R,* 1937 *R, Ger, F,* 1938 *Ger,* 1939 *Ger, R,* 1940 *R, Ger*
E Fava 1948 *F, Cze*
P Favaretto 1951 *Sp*
R Favaro 1988 *F, USS, A, I,* 1989 *F, R, Sp, Ar, Z, USS,* 1990 *F, Pol, R, H, R, USS,* 1991 *F, R, Nm, Nm, US, E, NZ, USS,* 1992 *Sp, F, R,* 1993 *Sp, F, Cro, Sp, F,* 1994 *CZR, A, A, R, W, F,* 1995 *S, I, Sa,* 1996 *Pt*
S Favaro 2009 *A, NZ, NZ, SA, Sa,* 2010 *SA*
G Favretto 1948 *Cze,* 1949 *Cze*
A Fedrigo 1972 *Yug,* 1973 *Pt, Rho, WTv, Bor, NEC, Nat, ETv, Leo, FS, Cze, Yug, A,* 1974 *Pt, Mid, Sus, Oxo, WGe, Leo,* 1975 *F, Sp, R, Cze, E, Pol, H, Sp,* 1976 *F, J, A, Sp,* 1977 *F, Pol, R, Cze, R, Sp,* 1978 *F, Ar,* 1979 *Pol, R*
P Fedrigo 1973 *Pt*
P Ferracin 1975 *R, Cze, E, Pol, H, Sp,* 1976 *F,* 1977 *Mor, Pol,* 1978 *USS*
C Festuccia 2003 *W, I, E, F, S, S, I, Geo, NZ, Tg, C, W,* 2004 *E, F, S, I,* 2005 *F, Ar, Ar, A, Tg, Ar,* 2006 *E, F, W, S, Pt, Rus, A, Ar, C,* 2007 *F, E, S, W, I, Ur, Ar, J, NZ, R, S,* 2008 *I, E, W,* 2009 *E, I*
G Figari 1940 *R, Ger,* 1942 *R*
EG Filizzola 1993 *Pt, Mor, Sp, F, Rus, F, S,* 1994 *Sp, CZR, A,* 1995 *R, NZ*
M Finocchi 1968 *Yug,* 1969 *F,* 1970 *Cze, Mad, Mad, R,* 1971 *Mor, R*
G Fornari 1952 *Sp, Ger, F,* 1953 *F, Ger, R,* 1954 *Sp, F,* 1955 *Ger, F, Sp, F, Cze,* 1956 *Ger, F, Cze*
B Francescato 1977 *Cze, R, Sp,* 1978 *F, Sp,* 1979 *F,* 1981 *R*
I Francescato 1990 *R, USS,* 1991 *F, R, US, E, NZ, USS,* 1992 *R, S,* 1993 *Mor, F,* 1994 *Sp, H, R, W, F,* 1995 *S, I, Sa, E, Ar, F, Ar, R, NZ, SA,* 1996 *W, Pt, W, A, E, S,* 1997 *F, F, Ar, R, SA*
N Francescato 1972 *Yug,* 1973 *Rho, WTv, Bor, NEC, Nat, ETv, Leo,* 1974 *Pt,* 1976 *J, A, Sp,* 1977 *F, Mor, Pol, R, R, Sp,* 1978 *F, Ar, USS, Sp,* 1979 *F, R, E, Sp, Mor, F, Pol, USS, NZ,* 1980 *F, R, Fj, JAB, Coo, Pol, USS, Sp,* 1981 *F, R,* 1982 *Mor*

R Francescato 1976 *Sp*, 1978 *Ar*, *USS*, 1979 *Sp*, *F*, *Pol*, *USS*, *NZ*, *Mor*, 1980 *F*, *R*, *Fj*, *JAB*, *Coo*, *Pol*, *USS*, *Sp*, 1981 *F*, *R*, 1982 *WGe*, 1983 *F*, *R*, *USS*, *C*, *C*, *Sp*, *Mor*, *F*, *A*, 1984 *Mor*, *R*, *Tun*, 1985 *F*, *Sp*, *Z*, *USS*, 1986 *Tun*, *F*
G Franceschini 1975 *H*, *Sp*, 1976 *F*, *J*, 1977 *F*, *Pol*, *Pol*, *Cze*, *R*, *Sp*
A Francese 1939 *R*, 1940 *R*
J Francesio 2000 *W*, *I*, *Sa*, 2001 *Ur*
F Frati 2000 *C*, *NZ*, 2001 *I*, *S*
F Frelich 1955 *Cze*, 1957 *F*, *Ger*, 1958 *F*, *R*
M Fumei 1984 *F*
A Fusco 1982 *E*, 1985 *R*, 1986 *Tun*, *F*, *Tun*
E Fusco 1960 *Ger*, *F*, 1961 *F*, 1962 *F*, *Ger*, *R*, 1963 *F*, 1964 *Ger*, *F*, 1965 *F*, 1966 *F*
R Gabanella 1951 *Sp*, 1952 *Sp*
P Gabrielli 1948 *Cze*, 1949 *F*, *Cze*, 1951 *Sp*, 1954 *F*
F Gaetaniello 1975 *H*, 1976 *R*, *A*, *Sp*, 1977 *F*, *Pol*, *R*, *Pol*, *R*, *Sp*, 1978 *Sp*, 1979 *Pol*, *R*, *E*, *Sp*, *Mor*, *F*, *Pol*, *USS*, *NZ*, *Mor*, 1980 *Fj*, *JAB*, *Sp*, 1981 *F*, *R*, *USS*, *WGe*, 1982 *F*, *R*, *E*, *WGe*, *Mor*, 1983 *F*, *R*, *USS*, *C*, *C*, *Sp*
F Gaetaniello 1980 *Sp*, 1982 *E*, 1984 *USS*, 1985 *R*, *Sp*, *Z*, *Z*, *USS*, *R*, 1986 *Pt*, *E*, *A*, *Tun*, *USS*, 1987 *Pt*, *F*, *NZ*, *Ar*, *Fj*, *USS*, *Sp*, 1988 *F*, 1990 *F*, *R*, *Sp*, *H*, 1991 *Nm*, *US*, *E*, *NZ*
A Galante 2007 *Ur*, *Ar*
A Galeazzo 1985 *Sp*, 1987 *Pt*, *R*, *Ar*, *USS*
M Galletto 1972 *Pt*, *Sp*, *Yug*
E Galon 2001 *I*, 2005 *Tg*, *Ar*, *Fj*, 2006 *W*, *S*, *Rus*, 2007 *I*, *Ur*, *Ar*, *I*, *NZ*, *R*, *S*, 2008 *I*, *E*, *W*, *F*, *S*
R Ganzerla 1973 *Bor*, *NEC*
G Garcia 2008 *SA*, *Ar*, *A*, *Ar*, *Pl*, 2009 *E*, *I*, *S*, *A*, *NZ*, *NZ*, *SA*, *Sa*, 2010 *I*, *E*, *S*, *F*, *W*
M Gardin 1981 *USS*, *WGe*, 1982 *Mor*, 1983 *F*, *R*, 1984 *Mor*, *R*, *USS*, 1985 *EngB*, *USS*, *R*, 1986 *Tun*, *F*, *Pt*, *Tun*, *USS*, 1987 *Pt*, *F*, *R*, *NZ*, *Ar*, *Fj*, *USS*, *Sp*, 1988 *R*
JM Gardner 1992 *R*, *S*, 1993 *Rus*, *F*, 1994 *Sp*, *R*, *H*, *F*, 1995 *S*, *I*, *Sa*, *E*, *Ar*, 1996 *W*, 1997 *I*, *F*, *De*, *SA*, *I*, 1998 *S*, *W*
P Gargiullo 1973 *FS*, 1974 *Mid*, *Sus*, *Oxo*
F Garguillo 1972 *Yug*
F Garguilo 1967 *F*, *Pt*, 1968 *Yug*, 1974 *Sus*
S Garozzo 2001 *Ur*, *Ar*, 2002 *Ar*
M Gatto 1967 *Pt*, *R*
G Gattoni 1933 *Cze*, *Cze*
Q Geldenhuys 2009 *A*, *A*, *NZ*, *NZ*, *SA*, *Sa*, 2010 *I*, *E*, *S*, *F*, *W*, *SA*, *SA*
A Gerardo 1968 *Yug*, 1969 *Sp*, 1970 *Cze*, *Mad*, 1971 *R*, 1972 *Sp*
F Geremia 1980 *JAB*, *Pol*
G Geremia 1956 *Cze*
E Gerosa 1952 *Sp*, *Ger*, *F*, 1953 *F*, *Ger*, *R*, 1954 *Sp*
M Gerosa 1994 *CZR*, *A*, *A*, *R*, *W*, 1995 *E*, *Ar*
C Ghezzi 1938 *Ger*, 1939 *Ger*, *R*, 1940 *R*, *Ger*
A Ghini 1981 *USS*, *WGe*, 1982 *F*, *R*, *E*, *Mor*, 1983 *F*, *R*, *C*, *Mor*, *F*, *A*, *USS*, 1984 *F*, *Mor*, *R*, *USS*, 1985 *F*, *R*, *EngB*, *Z*, *Z*, *USS*, 1987 *Fj*, 1988 *R*, *USS*
L Ghiraldini 2006 *J*, *Fj*, 2007 *I*, *J*, *Pt*, 2008 *I*, *E*, *W*, *F*, *S*, *SA*, *Ar*, *A*, *Ar*, *Pl*, 2009 *S*, *W*, *F*, *A*, *A*, *NZ*, *NZ*, *SA*, *Sa*, 2010 *I*, *E*, *S*, *F*, *W*, *SA*, *SA*
S Ghizzoni 1977 *F*, *Mor*, *Pol*, *R*, *Pol*, *Cze*, *R*, *Sp*, 1978 *F*, *Ar*, *USS*, 1979 *F*, *Pol*, *Sp*, *Mor*, *F*, *Pol*, 1980 *R*, *Fj*, *JAB*, *Coo*, *Pol*, *USS*, *Sp*, 1981 *F*, 1982 *F*, *R*, *E*, *WGe*, *Mor*, 1983 *F*, *USS*, *C*, *C*, *Sp*, *Mor*, *F*, *A*, *USS*, 1984 *F*, *Mor*, *R*, *Tun*, *USS*, 1985 *F*, *R*, *EngB*, *Z*, *Z*, *USS*, *R*, 1986 *F*, *E*, *A*, *Tun*, *USS*, 1987 *Pt*, *F*, *R*, *NZ*
M Giacheri 1992 *R*, 1993 *Sp*, *F*, *Pt*, *Rus*, *F*, *S*, 1994 *Sp*, *R*, *CZR*, *H*, *A*, *A*, *F*, 1995 *S*, *I*, *E*, *Ar*, *F*, *Ar*, *R*, *NZ*, *SA*, 1996 *W*, 1998 *Geo*, *Cro*, 1999 *S*, *W*, *I*, *Ur*, *Fj*, *E*, *Tg*, *NZ*, 2001 *Nm*, *SA*, *Ur*, *Ar*, *SA*, 2002 *F*, *S*, *W*, *I*, *E*, *NZ*, *A*, 2003 *E*, *F*, *S*, *I*
G Giani 1966 *Ger*, *R*, 1967 *F*, *Pt*, *R*
G Gini 1968 *Pt*, *WGe*, *Yug*, 1969 *Bul*, *Sp*, *Bel*, *F*, 1970 *Cze*, *Mad*, *Mad*, *R*, 1971 *Mor*, *F*, 1972 *Pt*, *Pt*, 1974 *Mid*, *Oxo*
G Giorgio 1968 *Pt*, *WGe*
M Giovanelli 1989 *Z*, *USS*, 1990 *Pol*, *Sp*, *H*, *R*, *USS*, 1991 *F*, *R*, *Nm*, *E*, *NZ*, *USS*, 1992 *Sp*, *F*, *S*, 1993 *Sp*, *F*, *Pt*, *Cro*, *Mor*, *Sp*, *F*, 1994 *R*, *CZR*, *H*, *A*, *A*, 1995 *F*, *Ar*, *R*, *NZ*, *SA*, 1996 *A*, *E*, *S*, 1997 *F*, *F*, *Ar*, *R*, *SA*, *I*, 1998 *S*, *W*, *Rus*, *Cro*, *Ar*, *H*, *E*, 1999 *S*, *W*, *I*, *SA*, *SA*, *Ur*, *Sp*, *Fj*, *E*, *Tg*, *NZ*, 2000 *Geo*, *S*
E Giugovaz 1965 *Cze*, 1966 *F*
R Giuliani 1951 *Sp*
V Golfetti 1997 *De*
M Gorni 1939 *R*, 1940 *R*, *Ger*
M Goti 1990 *H*
C Gower 2009 *A*, *A*, *NZ*, *NZ*, *SA*, *Sa*, 2010 *I*, *E*, *S*, *F*, *W*, *SA*, *SA*
G Grasselli 1952 *Ger*
G Grespan 1989 *F*, *Sp*, *USS*, 1990 *F*, *R*, 1991 *R*, *NZ*, *USS*, 1992 *R*, *S*, 1993 *Sp*, *F*, *Cro*, *Sp*, *F*, *Rus*, 1994 *Sp*, *CZR*, *R*, *W*
PR Griffen 2004 *E*, *F*, *S*, *I*, *W*, *R*, *J*, *C*, *NZ*, *US*, 2005 *W*, *S*, *F*, *Ar*, *Ar*, *A*, *Tg*, *Ar*, *Fj*, 2006 *I*, *E*, *F*, *W*, *S*, *J*, *Fj*, *Rus*, *A*, *Ar*, *C*, 2007 *F*, *I*, *Ur*, *Ar*, *I*, *NZ*, *R*, *Pt*, 2009 *I*, *S*, *W*, *F*
A Gritti 1996 *Pt*, 1997 *De*, 2000 *Geo*, *S*, *W*, *I*, *E*, *F*, *Sa*, *Fj*, *C*, *R*, *NZ*, 2001 *E*, *F*, *S*, *W*
G Guidi 1996 *Pt*, *E*, 1997 *F*, *Ar*, *R*, 1998 *Cro*
F Gumiero 1997 *De*
M Innocenti 1981 *WGe*, 1982 *F*, *R*, *E*, *WGe*, *Mor*, 1983 *F*, *USS*, *C*, *C*, *Mor*, *F*, *A*, *USS*, 1984 *F*, *Mor*, *Tun*, *USS*, 1985 *F*, *R*, *EngB*, *Sp*, *USS*, *R*, 1986 *Tun*, *F*, *Pt*, *E*, *A*, *Tun*, *USS*, 1987 *Pt*, *F*, *R*, *NZ*, *Ar*, *Fj*, *USS*, *Sp*, 1988 *F*, *R*, *A*
G Intoppa 2004 *R*, *J*, *C*, *NZ*, 2005 *I*, *W*, *E*
C Jannone 1981 *USS*, 1982 *F*, *R*
S Lanfranchi 1949 *F*, *Cze*, 1953 *F*, *Ger*, *R*, 1954 *Sp*, *F*, 1955 *F*, 1956 *Ger*, *Cze*, 1957 *F*, 1958 *F*, 1959 *F*, 1960 *F*, 1961 *F*, 1962 *F*, *Ger*, *R*, 1963 *F*, 1964 *Ger*, *F*
G Lanzi 1998 *Cro*, *Ar*, *H*, *E*, 1999 *Sp*, 2000 *S*, *W*, *I*, 2001 *I*
G Lari 1972 *Yug*, 1973 *Yug*, *A*, 1974 *Pt*, *Mid*, *Sus*, *Oxo*, *Leo*
E Lazzarini 1970 *Cze*, 1971 *Mor*, *F*, *R*, 1972 *Pt*, *Pt*, *Sp*, *Sp*, 1973 *Pt*, *Rho*, *WTv*, *Bor*, *NEC*, *Leo*, *FS*, *Tva*, *Cze*, *Yug*, *A*, 1974 *Pt*, *Mid*, *Sus*, *Oxo*, *WGe*
U Levorato 1956 *Ger*, *F*, 1957 *F*, 1958 *F*, *R*, 1959 *F*, 1961 *Ger*, *F*, 1962 *F*, *Ger*, *R*, 1963 *F*, 1964 *Ger*, *F*, 1965 *F*
A Lijoi 1977 *Pol*, *R*, 1978 *Sp*, 1979 *R*, *Mor*
G Limone 1979 *E*, *Mor*, *USS*, *Mor*, 1980 *JAB*, *Sp*, 1981 *USS*, *WGe*, 1982 *E*, 1983 *USS*
A Lo Cicero 2000 *E*, *F*, *Sa*, *Fj*, *C*, *R*, *NZ*, 2001 *I*, *E*, *F*, *S*, *W*, *Fj*, *SA*, *Sa*, 2002 *F*, *S*, *W*, *Sp*, *R*, *A*, 2003 *F*, *S*, *S*, *I*, *Geo*, *Tg*, *C*, *W*, 2004 *E*, *F*, *S*, *I*, *W*, *R*, *J*, *C*, *NZ*, *US*, 2005 *I*, *W*, *S*, *E*, *F*, *Ar*, *Ar*, *A*, *Tg*, *Ar*, 2006 *E*, *F*, *W*, *S*, *J*, *Fj*, *Pt*, *Rus*, *A*, *Ar*, *C*, 2007 *F*, *E*, *S*, *W*, *Ur*, *Ar*, *J*, *NZ*, *R*, *Pt*, *S*, 2008 *I*, *E*, *W*, *F*, *S*, *Ar*, *Pl*
C Loranzi 1973 *Nat*, *ETv*, *Leo*, *FS*, *Tva*
F Lorigiola 1979 *Sp*, *F*, *Pol*, *USS*, *NZ*, *Mor*, 1980 *F*, *R*, *Fj*, *JAB*, *Pol*, *USS*, *Sp*, 1981 *F*, *R*, *USS*, 1982 *WGe*, 1983 *R*, *USS*, *C*, *Sp*, 1984 *Tun*, 1985 *Sp*, 1986 *Pt*, *E*, *A*, *Tun*, *USS*, 1987 *Pt*, *F*, *R*, *NZ*, *Ar*, 1988 *F*
G Luchini 1973 *Rho*, *Nat*
L Luise 1955 *Ger*, *F*, *Sp*, *F*, *Cze*, 1956 *Ger*, *F*, *Cze*, 1957 *Ger*, 1958 *F*
R Luise III 1959 *F*, 1960 *Ger*, *F*, 1961 *Ger*, *F*, 1962 *F*, *Ger*, *R*, 1965 *F*, *Cze*, 1966 *F*, 1971 *R*, 1972 *Pt*, *Sp*, *Sp*
T Lupini 1987 *R*, *NZ*, *Ar*, *Fj*, *USS*, *Sp*, 1988 *F*, *R*, *USS*, *A*, 1989 *R*
O Maestri 1935 *Cat*, *F*, 1937 *Ger*
R Maffioli 1933 *Cze*, *Cze*, 1934 *Cat*, *R*, 1935 *Cat*, 1936 *Ger*, *R*, 1937 *Ger*, *R*, *Bel*, *Ger*
R Maini 1948 *F*, *Cze*
G Malosti 1953 *F*, 1954 *Sp*, 1955 *F*, 1956 *Ger*, *F*, 1957 *F*, 1958 *F*
G Mancini 1952 *Ger*, *F*, 1953 *F*, *Ger*, *R*, 1954 *Sp*, *F*, 1955 *Cze*, 1956 *Ger*, *F*, *Cze*, 1957 *F*
R Mandelli 2004 *I*, *W*, *R*, *J*, *US*, 2007 *F*, *E*, *Ur*, *Ar*
A Mannato 2004 *US*, 2005 *Ar*, *A*
E Manni 1976 *J*, *A*, *Sp*, 1977 *Mor*
L Manteri 1996 *W*, *A*, *E*, *S*
A Marcato 2006 *J*, *Pt*, 2008 *I*, *E*, *W*, *F*, *S*, *SA*, *Ar*, *A*, *Ar*, *Pl*, 2009 *E*, *S*, *W*, *F*
M Marchetto 1972 *Yug*, 1973 *Pt*, *Cze*, *Yug*, 1974 *Pt*, *Mid*, *Sus*, *WGe*, *Leo*, 1975 *F*, *Sp*, *R*, *Cze*, *E*, *Pol*, *H*, *Sp*, 1976 *F*, *R*, *J*, *A*, *Sp*, 1977 *F*, *Mor*, *Pol*, *R*, *Cze*, *R*, *Sp*, 1978 *F*, *USS*, *Sp*, 1979 *F*, *Pol*, *R*, *E*, *Pol*, *USS*, *NZ*, *Mor*, 1980 *F*, *Coo*, 1981 *USS*
A Marescalchi 1933 *Cze*, 1935 *F*, 1937 *R*
P Mariani 1976 *R*, *A*, *Sp*, 1977 *F*, *Pol*, 1978 *F*, *Ar*, *USS*, *Sp*, 1979 *F*, *Pol*, *R*, *Sp*, *F*, *Pol*, *USS*, *NZ*, *Mor*, 1980 *F*, *R*, *Fj*, *JAB*

P Marini 1949 *F, Cze*, 1951 *Sp*, 1953 *F, Ger, R*, 1955 *Ger*
L Martin 1997 *F, R, De*, 1998 *S, W, Geo, Rus, H, E*, 1999 *F, S, W, I, SA, SA, Ur, Sp, Fj, E*, 2000 *Geo, S, W, I, E, F, Sa, Fj, C, R, NZ*, 2001 *I, E, S, W, SA, Ar, Fj, SA, Sa*, 2002 *F, S*
F Martinenghi 1952 *Sp, Ger*
R Martinez-Frugoni 2002 *NZ, Sp, R*, 2003 *W, I, E, F, S, S, NZ*
G Martini 1965 *F*, 1967 *F*, 1968 *Pt*
R Martini 1959 *F*, 1960 *Ger, F*, 1961 *Ger, F*, 1964 *Ger, F*, 1965 *F*, 1968 *WGe, Yug*
P Masci 1948 *Cze*, 1949 *F, Cze*, 1952 *Sp, Ger, F*, 1953 *F*, 1954 *Sp*, 1955 *F*
M Mascioletti 1977 *Mor, Pol*, 1978 *Ar, USS, Sp*, 1979 *Pol, E, Sp, Mor, F, Pol, USS, NZ, Mor*, 1980 *F, R, Fj*, 1981 *WGe*, 1982 *F, R, WGe*, 1983 *F, R, USS, C, C, Sp, Mor, F, A, USS*, 1984 *F, Mor, Tun*, 1985 *F, R, Z, Z, USS, R*, 1986 *Tun, F, Pt, E, Tun, USS*, 1987 *NZ, Ar, Fj*, 1989 *Sp, Ar, Z, USS*, 1990 *Pol*
A Masi 1999 *Sp*, 2003 *E, F, S, S, I, NZ, Tg, C, W*, 2004 *E, I, W, R, J, C*, 2005 *I, W, S, E, F, Ar, Ar, A*, 2006 *J, Fj, Pt, Rus*, 2007 *F, S, J, NZ, R, Pt, S*, 2008 *I, E, W, F, S, SA, A, Ar, Pl*, 2009 *E, I*, 2010 *I, E, S, F, SA, SA*
L Mastrodomenico 2000 *Sa, C, NZ*, 2001 *Nm, Ar*
I Matacchini 1948 *F, Cze*, 1949 *F, Cze*, 1954 *Sp*, 1955 *Ger, F, Sp, F*
L Mattarolo 1973 *Bor, Nat, ETv, Leo, FS, Tva, Cze*
M Mattei 1967 *R*
R Mattei 1978 *F, USS*
F Mazzantini 1965 *Cze*, 1966 *F*, 1967 *F*
M Mazzantini 2000 *S*, 2001 *S, W*, 2002 *E, NZ*, 2003 *E, F, Geo, NZ, C*
F Mazzariol 1995 *F, Ar, R, NZ*, 1996 *Pt*, 1997 *F, R, De, SA*, 1998 *Geo, Ar, H*, 1999 *F, SA, SA, Sp, E, NZ*, 2000 *Fj, C*, 2001 *Nm, SA, Ur, Ar, Fj, SA*, 2002 *W, NZ, Sp*, 2003 *S, I, NZ, C, W*, 2004 *R*
G Mazzi 1998 *H*, 1999 *SA, SA, Ur, Sp*
N Mazzucato 1995 *SA*, 1996 *Pt, S*, 1997 *I*, 1999 *Sp, E, Tg, NZ*, 2000 *F, Sa, Fj, R*, 2001 *Nm, SA, Ur, Ar*, 2002 *W, I, E, NZ, Sp, R, Ar, A*, 2003 *E, F, S, I, NZ, Tg, W*, 2004 *E, F, S, I, W, R, J*
I Mazzucchelli 1965 *F, Cze*, 1966 *F, Ger, R*, 1967 *F*, 1968 *Pt, WGe*, 1969 *Bul, F*, 1971 *F*, 1972 *Pt, Sp*, 1974 *WGe*, 1975 *F, R, Cze, Pol*, 1976 *F, R*
L McLean 2008 *SA, Ar, Pl*, 2009 *E, I, S, W, F, A, A, NZ, NZ, SA, Sa*, 2010 *I, E, S, F, W, SA, SA*
P Menapace 1996 *Pt*
E Michelon 1969 *Bel, F*, 1970 *Cze, Mad, Mad, R*, 1971 *R*
A Miele 1968 *Yug*, 1970 *Mad*, 1971 *R*, 1972 *Pt, Sp*
GE Milano 1990 *USS*
A Mioni 1955 *Ger, F, F*, 1957 *F*
A Modonesi 1929 *Sp*
L Modonesi 1966 *Ger, R*, 1967 *F, Pt, R*, 1968 *Pt, WGe*, 1970 *Cze, Mad, Mad, R*, 1971 *F*, 1974 *Leo*, 1975 *F, Sp, R, Cze*
N Molari 1957 *F*, 1958 *R*
F Molinari 1973 *NEC*
G Molinari 1948 *F*
P Monfeli 1970 *R*, 1971 *Mor, F*, 1972 *Pt*, 1976 *J, A, Sp*, 1977 *F, R, Cze, R, Sp*, 1978 *F*
JF Montauriol 2009 *E, A*
G Morelli 1988 *I*, 1989 *F, R*
G Morelli 1976 *F*, 1982 *F, R, Mor*, 1983 *R, C, Sp, A, USS*, 1984 *Mor, R, USS*, 1985 *R, EngB, Z, Z, USS, R*, 1986 *Tun, F, E, A, Tun, USS*, 1987 *F, NZ*
G Morelli 1981 *WGe*, 1982 *R, E, Mor*, 1983 *USS*, 1984 *F*
A Moreno 1999 *Tg, NZ*, 2002 *F, S*, 2008 *Ar*
A Moretti 1997 *R*, 1998 *Rus*, 1999 *Ur, Sp, Tg, NZ*, 2002 *E, NZ, Sp, R, Ar, A*, 2005 *Ar*
U Moretti 1933 *Cze*, 1934 *R*, 1935 *Cat*, 1937 *R, Ger, F*, 1942 *R*
A Morimondi 1930 *Sp*, 1933 *Cze*, 1934 *Cat*, 1935 *Cat*
A Moscardi 1993 *Pt*, 1995 *R*, 1996 *S*, 1997 *De*, 1998 *Ar, H, E*, 1999 *F, S, W, I, SA, SA, Ur, Fj, E, Tg, NZ*, 2000 *Geo, S, W, I, E, F, Sa, Fj, C, R, NZ*, 2001 *I, E, F, S, W, Nm, SA, Ur, Ar, Fj, SA, Sa*, 2002 *F, S, W, I, E*
A Muraro 2000 *C, R, NZ*, 2001 *I, E, Nm, SA, Ur, Ar, Fj, SA, Sa*, 2002 *F*
E Nathan 1930 *Sp*
G Navarini 1957 *Ger*, 1958 *R*
M Nicolosi 1982 *R*
C Nieto 2002 *E*, 2005 *Ar, Ar, A, Tg, Ar, Fj*, 2006 *I, E, F, W, J, Fj, A, Ar, C*, 2007 *F, S, W, I, Ar*, 2008 *E, F, S, SA, Ar, A, Ar, Pl*, 2009 *E, I, S, W, F*
A Nisti 1929 *Sp*, 1930 *Sp*
L Nitoglia 2004 *C, NZ, US*, 2005 *I, W, S, E, F, Ar, Tg, Ar, Fj*, 2006 *I, E, F, W, S*
F Ongaro 2000 *C*, 2001 *Nm, SA, Ur, Ar*, 2002 *Ar, A*, 2003 *E, F, S, I, Geo, NZ, Tg, C, W*, 2004 *E, F, S, I, W, R, J, C, NZ, US*, 2005 *I, W, S, E, F, Tg, Ar, Fj*, 2006 *I, E, F, W, S, J, Fj, Pt, Rus, Ar, C*, 2007 *F, S, Ur, Ar, I, NZ, S*, 2008 *F, S, SA, Ar, A, Ar, Pl*, 2009 *E, I, NZ, SA, Sa*, 2010 *I, E, S, F, W, SA, SA*
C Orlandi 1992 *S*, 1993 *Sp, F, Mor, F, Rus, F, S*, 1994 *Sp, CZR, H, A, A, R, W*, 1995 *S, I, Sa, E, Ar, F, Ar, R, NZ, SA*, 1996 *W, Pt, W, A, E, S*, 1997 *I, F, F, Ar, R, SA, I*, 1998 *S, W, Cro*, 2000 *W, F*
S Orlando 2004 *E, S, W, C, NZ, US*, 2005 *E, F, Ar, A*, 2006 *J*, 2007 *Ur, Ar, Pt*
L Orquera 2004 *C, NZ, US*, 2005 *I, W, S, E, F, Ar, Tg*, 2008 *A, Ar*, 2009 *W, F*
A Osti 1981 *F, R, USS*, 1982 *E, Mor*, 1983 *R, C, A, USS*, 1984 *R, USS*, 1985 *F*, 1986 *Tun*, 1988 *R*
S Pace 2001 *SA, Sa*, 2005 *Fj*
S Pace 1977 *Mor*, 1984 *R, Tun*
P Pacifici 1969 *Bul, Sp, F*, 1970 *Cze, Mad, Mad, R*, 1971 *Mor, F*
R Paciucci 1937 *R, Ger, F*
F Paganelli 1972 *Sp*
S Palmer 2002 *Ar, A*, 2003 *I, E, F, S, S, NZ, C, W*, 2004 *I, R*
P Paoletti 1972 *Pt, Sp, Yug*, 1973 *Pt, Rho, WTv, Bor, NEC, Nat, ETv, Leo, FS, Tva*, 1974 *Mid, Oxo, WGe, Leo*, 1975 *F, Sp*, 1976 *R*
T Paoletti 2000 *Geo, S, W, I, E, F, Sa, C, R, NZ*, 2001 *F, Nm, Ur, Ar, Fj, SA*
G Paolin 1929 *Sp*
S Parisse 2002 *NZ, Sp, R, Ar, A*, 2003 *S, I, Geo, NZ, Tg, C, W*, 2004 *E, F, S*, 2005 *I, W, S, E, F, Ar, Ar, A, Tg, Ar, Fj*, 2006 *I, E, F, W, S, Fj, Pt, Rus, A, Ar, C*, 2007 *F, E, S, W, I, J, I, NZ, R, Pt, S*, 2008 *I, E, W, F, S, Ar, A, Ar, Pl*, 2009 *E, I, S, W, F, A, A, NZ, NZ, SA*, 2010 *SA, SA*
E Parmiggiani 1942 *R*, 1948 *Cze*
P Paseli 1929 *Sp*, 1930 *Sp*, 1933 *Cze*
E Passarotto 1975 *Sp*
E Patrizio 2007 *Ur*, 2008 *F, S, SA*
R Pavan 2008 *SA*
A Pavanello 2007 *Ar*, 2009 *SA, Sa*
E Pavanello 2002 *R, Ar, A*, 2004 *R, J, C, NZ, US*, 2005 *Ar, A*
P Pavesi 1977 *Pol*, 1979 *Mor*, 1980 *USS*
M Pavin 1980 *USS*, 1986 *F, Pt, E, A, Tun, USS*, 1987 *Ar*
R Pedrazzi 2001 *Nm, Ar*, 2002 *F, S, W*, 2005 *S, E, F*
P Pedroni 1989 *Z, USS*, 1990 *F, Pol, R*, 1991 *F, R, Nm*, 1993 *Rus, F*, 1994 *Sp, R, CZR, H*, 1995 *I, Sa, E, Ar, F, Ar, R, NZ, SA*, 1996 *W, W*
G Peens 2002 *W, I, E, NZ, Sp, R, Ar, A*, 2003 *E, F, S, S, I, Geo, NZ*, 2004 *NZ*, 2005 *E, F, Ar, Ar, A*, 2006 *Pt, A*
L Pelliccione 1983 *Sp, Mor, F*
L Pelliccione 1977 *Pol*
M Percudani 1952 *F*, 1954 *F*, 1955 *Ger, Sp, F, Cze*, 1956 *Cze*, 1957 *F*, 1958 *R*
F Perrini 1955 *Sp, F, Cze*, 1956 *Ger, F, Cze*, 1957 *F*, 1958 *F*, 1959 *F*, 1962 *R*, 1963 *F*
F Perrone 1951 *Sp*
AR Persico 2000 *S, W, E, F, Sa, Fj*, 2001 *F, S, W, Nm, SA, Ur, Ar, Fj, SA, Sa*, 2002 *F, S, W, I, E, NZ, Sp, R, Ar, A*, 2003 *W, I, E, F, S, I, Geo, Tg, C, W*, 2004 *E, F, S, I, W, R, J, C, NZ*, 2005 *I, W, S, E, F, Ar, Ar, Tg, Ar*, 2006 *I, E*
J Pertile 1994 *R*, 1995 *Ar*, 1996 *W, A, E, S*, 1997 *I, F, SA*, 1998 *Geo, Rus, Cro*, 1999 *S, W, I, SA, SA*
S Perugini 2000 *I, F, Sa, Fj*, 2001 *S, W, Nm, SA, Ur, Ar*, 2002 *W, I*, 2003 *W, S, Geo, NZ, Tg, W*, 2004 *E, F, I, W, C, NZ, US*, 2005 *I, W, S, E, F*, 2006 *I, E, F, W, S, Pt, Rus*, 2007 *F, E, S, W, I, J, I, NZ, Pt, S*, 2008 *I, E, W, F, S, A,*

Ar, *Pl*, 2009 *E*, *I*, *S*, *W*, *F*, *A*, *A*, *NZ*, *NZ*, *SA*, *Sa*, 2010 *I*, *E*, *S*, *F*, *W*, *SA*, *SA*
L Perziano 1993 *Pt*
M Perziano 2000 *NZ*, 2001 *F*, *S*, *W*, *Nm*, *SA*, *Ur*, *Ar*, *Fj*, *SA*
V Pesce 1988 *I*, 1989 *R*
P Pescetto 1956 *Ger*, *Cze*, 1957 *F*
G Petralia 1984 *F*
R Pez 2000 *Sa*, *Fj*, *C*, *R*, *NZ*, 2001 *I*, 2002 *S*, *W*, *E*, *A*, 2003 *I*, *E*, *F*, *S*, *S*, *Geo*, 2005 *Ar*, *A*, *Tg*, *Ar*, *Fj*, 2006 *I*, *E*, *F*, *W*, *S*, *J*, *Fj*, *Pt*, *Rus*, *A*, *Ar*, 2007 *F*, *E*, *S*, *W*, *I*, *J*, *R*, *S*
M Phillips 2002 *F*, *S*, *W*, *I*, *E*, 2003 *W*, *I*, *E*, *F*, *S*, *S*, *I*, *NZ*, *W*
G Pianna 1934 *R*, 1935 *Cat*, *F*, 1936 *Ger*, *R*, 1938 *Ger*
A Piazza 1990 *USS*
F Piccini 1963 *F*, 1964 *Ger*, 1966 *F*
S Picone 2004 *I*, *W*, 2005 *F*, 2006 *E*, *F*, *S*, *J*, *Pt*, *Rus*, *Ar*, *C*, 2008 *E*, *W*, *F*, *S*, *SA*, *Ar*, 2009 *NZ*, *SA*, *Sa*, 2010 *I*, *SA*, *SA*
F Pietroscanti 1987 *USS*, *Sp*, 1988 *A*, *I*, 1989 *F*, *R*, *Sp*, *Ar*, *Z*, *USS*, 1990 *F*, *Pol*, *R*, *H*, 1991 *Nm*, *Nm*, 1992 *Sp*, *F*, *R*, 1993 *Sp*, *Mor*, *Sp*, *F*, *Rus*, *F*
F Pignotti 1968 *WGe*, *Yug*, 1969 *Bul*, *Sp*, *Bel*
C Pilat 1997 *I*, 1998 *S*, *W*, *Geo*, 2000 *E*, *Sa*, 2001 *I*, *W*
MJ Pini 1998 *H*, *E*, 1999 *F*, *Ur*, *Fj*, *E*, *Tg*, *NZ*, 2000 *Geo*, *S*, *W*, *I*, *F*
M Piovan 1973 *Pt*, 1974 *Pt*, *Mid*, *Sus*, *Oxo*, 1976 *A*, 1977 *F*, *Mor*, *R*, 1979 *F*
R Piovan 1996 *Pt*, 1997 *R*, 1998 *Geo*, 2000 *R*, *NZ*
M Piovene 1995 *NZ*
E Piras 1971 *R*
M Pisaneschi 1948 *Cze*, 1949 *Cze*, 1953 *F*, *Ger*, *R*, 1954 *Sp*, *F*, 1955 *Ger*, *F*, *Sp*, *F*, *Cze*
F Pitorri 1948 *Cze*, 1949 *F*
M Pitorri 1973 *NEC*
G Pivetta 1979 *R*, *E*, *Mor*, 1980 *Coo*, *USS*, 1981 *R*, *USS*, *WGe*, 1982 *F*, *R*, *WGe*, *Mor*, 1983 *F*, *USS*, *C*, *Sp*, *Mor*, *F*, *USS*, 1984 *F*, *Mor*, *R*, *Tun*, 1985 *F*, *R*, *Sp*, *Z*, *Z*, 1986 *Pt*, 1987 *Sp*, 1989 *R*, *Sp*, 1990 *F*, *Pol*, *R*, *Sp*, *R*, *USS*, 1991 *F*, *R*, *Nm*, *Nm*, *US*, *E*, *NZ*, *USS*, 1992 *Sp*, *F*, *R*, *R*, 1993 *Cro*, *Mor*, *Sp*
M Platania 1994 *F*, 1995 *F*, *R*, 1996 *Pt*
I Ponchia 1955 *F*, *Sp*, *F*, *Cze*, 1956 *F*, 1957 *Ger*, 1958 *F*
E Ponzi 1973 *Cze*, *A*, 1974 *WGe*, 1975 *F*, *Sp*, *R*, *Cze*, *E*, *Pol*, *H*, *Sp*, 1976 *F*, *R*, *J*, *A*, *Sp*, 1977 *F*, *Mor*, *Pol*, *R*
G Porcellato 1989 *R*
G Porzio 1970 *Cze*, *Mad*, *Mad*
C Possamai 1970 *Cze*, *Mad*, *Mad*
W Pozzebon 2001 *I*, *E*, *F*, *S*, *W*, *Nm*, *SA*, *Ur*, *Ar*, *Fj*, *SA*, *Sa*, 2002 *NZ*, *Sp*, 2004 *R*, *J*, *C*, *NZ*, *US*, 2005 *W*, *E*, 2006 *C*
C Pratichetti 1988 *R*, 1990 *Pol*
M Pratichetti 2004 *NZ*, 2007 *E*, *W*, *I*, *Ur*, *Ar*, *I*, *Pt*, 2008 *SA*, *Ar*, *Ar*, *Pl*, 2009 *E*, *I*, *S*, *W*, *F*, *A*, *NZ*, *SA*, 2010 *W*, *SA*
G Preo 1999 *I*, 2000 *I*, *E*, *Sa*, *Fj*, *R*, *NZ*
P Presutti 1974 *Mid*, *Sus*, *Oxo*, 1977 *Pol*, *Cze*, *R*, *Sp*, 1978 *F*
FP Properzi-Curti 1990 *Pol*, *Sp*, *H*, *R*, 1991 *F*, *Nm*, *Nm*, *US*, *E*, *NZ*, 1992 *Sp*, *F*, *R*, 1993 *Cro*, *Mor*, *F*, *Rus*, *F*, *S*, 1994 *Sp*, *R*, *H*, *A*, *A*, 1995 *S*, *I*, *Sa*, *E*, *Ar*, *NZ*, *SA*, 1996 *W*, *Pt*, *W*, *A*, *E*, 1997 *I*, *F*, *F*, *Ar*, *SA*, 1998 *Ar*, 1999 *S*, *W*, *I*, *SA*, *SA*, *Ur*, *E*, *Tg*, *NZ*, 2001 *F*, *S*, *W*
C Prosperini 1966 *R*, 1967 *F*, *Pt*, *R*
F Pucciarello 1999 *Sp*, *Fj*, *E*, 2002 *S*, *W*, *I*, *E*, *Ar*
G Puglisi 1971 *F*, 1972 *Yug*, 1973 *Cze*
M Pulli 1968 *Pt*, 1972 *Pt*, *Pt*
A Puppo 1972 *Pt*, *Pt*, *Sp*, *Sp*, 1973 *Pt*, *Rho*, *WTv*, *Bor*, *NEC*, *Nat*, *ETv*, *Leo*, *FS*, *Tva*, 1974 *Mid*, *Sus*, *Oxo*, *WGe*, *Leo*, 1977 *R*
I Quaglio 1970 *R*, 1971 *R*, 1972 *Pt*, *Sp*, 1973 *WTv*, *Bor*, *NEC*, *Nat*, *Leo*, *FS*, *Tva*, 1975 *H*, *Sp*, 1976 *F*, *R*
M Quaglio 1984 *Tun*, 1988 *F*, *R*
R Quartaroli 2009 *W*, *F*, *A*
JM Queirolo 2000 *Sa*, *Fj*, 2001 *E*, *F*, *Fj*, 2002 *NZ*, *Sp*, *A*, 2003 *Geo*
P Quintavala 1958 *R*
C Raffo 1929 *Sp*, 1930 *Sp*, 1933 *Cze*, *Cze*, 1937 *R*, *Bel*
G Raineri 1998 *Cro*, *H*, 2000 *Geo*, *Fj*, *R*, *NZ*, 2001 *I*, *E*, *S*, *W*, *Nm*, *SA*, *Ur*, *Ar*, 2002 *W*, *I*, *E*, *NZ*, 2003 *W*, *I*, *E*, *F*, *S*, *Geo*
G Raisi 1956 *Ger*, *F*, 1957 *F*, *Ger*, 1960 *Ger*, 1964 *Ger*, *F*
R Rampazzo 1996 *W*, 1999 *I*
M Ravazzolo 1993 *Cro*, *Sp*, *F*, *F*, *S*, 1994 *Sp*, *R*, *CZR*, *H*, 1995 *S*, *I*, *Sa*, *F*, *Ar*, *NZ*, 1996 *W*, *Pt*, *W*, *A*, 1997 *F*, *Ar*, *R*, *De*, *SA*
A Re Garbagnati 1936 *Ger*, *R*, 1937 *Ger*, *Bel*, *Ger*, *F*, 1938 *Ger*, 1939 *Ger*, *R*, 1940 *R*, *Ger*, 1942 *R*
P Reale 1987 *USS*, *Sp*, 1988 *USS*, *A*, *I*, 1989 *Z*, 1992 *S*
T Reato 2008 *I*, *SA*, *Ar*, *A*, *Ar*, *Pl*, 2009 *E*, *I*, *A*
G Riccardi 1955 *Ger*, *F*, *Sp*, *F*, *Cze*, 1956 *F*, *Cze*
G Ricci 1967 *Pt*, 1969 *Bul*, *Sp*, *Bel*, *F*
G Ricciarelli 1962 *Ger*
L Riccioni 1951 *Sp*, 1952 *Sp*, *Ger*, *F*, 1953 *F*, *Ger*, 1954 *F*
S Rigo 1992 *S*, 1993 *Sp*, *F*, *Pt*
A Rinaldo 1977 *Mor*, *Pol*, *R*, *Cze*
W Rista 1968 *Yug*, 1969 *Bul*, *Sp*, *Bel*, *F*
M Rivaro 2000 *S*, *W*, *I*, 2001 *E*
M Rizzo 2005 *A*, 2008 *SA*
G Rizzoli 1935 *F*, 1936 *Ger*, *R*
C Robazza 1978 *Ar*, *Sp*, 1979 *F*, *Pol*, *R*, *E*, *Sp*, *F*, *Pol*, *USS*, *NZ*, *Mor*, 1980 *F*, *R*, *Fj*, *JAB*, *Coo*, *Pol*, *Sp*, 1981 *F*, *R*, *USS*, *WGe*, 1982 *E*, *WGe*, 1983 *F*, *USS*, *C*, *Mor*, *F*, 1984 *F*, *Tun*, 1985 *F*
KP Robertson 2004 *R*, *J*, *C*, *NZ*, *US*, 2005 *I*, *W*, *S*, *F*, *Ar*, *Ar*, *A*, 2006 *Pt*, *Rus*, 2007 *F*, *E*, *S*, *W*, *I*, *Ur*, *Ar*, *J*, *I*, *NZ*, *R*, *S*, 2008 *I*, *E*, *F*, *S*, *SA*, *Ar*, *A*, *Ar*, *Pl*, 2009 *E*, *I*, *A*, *NZ*, *NZ*, *Sa*, 2010 *I*, *E*, *S*, *F*, *W*, *SA*
A Rocca 1973 *WTv*, *Bor*, *NEC*, 1977 *R*
G Romagnoli 1965 *F*, *Cze*, 1967 *Pt*, *R*
S Romagnoli 1982 *Mor*, 1984 *R*, *Tun*, *USS*, 1985 *F*, *Z*, *Z*, 1986 *Tun*, *Pt*, *A*, *Tun*, *USS*, 1987 *Pt*, *F*, *Fj*
G Romano 1942 *R*
P Romano 1942 *R*
F Roselli 1995 *F*, *R*, 1996 *W*, 1998 *Geo*, *Rus*, *Cro*, *Ar*, *H*, *E*, 1999 *F*, *S*, *W*, *I*, *SA*, *SA*, *Ur*, *Fj*, *Tg*
P Rosi 1948 *F*, *Cze*, 1949 *F*, *Cze*, 1951 *Sp*, 1952 *Ger*, *F*, 1953 *F*, *Ger*, *R*, 1954 *Sp*, *F*
G Rossi 1981 *USS*, *WGe*, 1982 *E*, *WGe*, *Mor*, 1983 *F*, *R*, *USS*, *C*, *C*, *Mor*, *F*, *A*, *USS*, 1984 *Mor*, 1985 *F*, *R*, *EngB*, *Sp*, *Z*, *USS*, *R*, 1986 *Tun*, *F*, *E*, *A*, *Tun*, *USS*, 1987 *R*, *NZ*, *Ar*, *USS*, *Sp*, 1988 *USS*, *A*, *I*, 1989 *F*, *R*, *Sp*, *Ar*, *Z*, *USS*, 1990 *F*, *R*, 1991 *R*
N Rossi 1973 *Yug*, 1974 *Pt*, *Mid*, *Sus*, *Oxo*, *WGe*, *Leo*, 1975 *Sp*, *Cze*, *E*, *H*, 1976 *J*, *A*, *Sp*, 1977 *Cze*, 1980 *USS*
Z Rossi 1959 *F*, 1961 *Ger*, *F*, 1962 *F*, *Ger*, *R*
E Rossini 1948 *F*, *Cze*, 1949 *F*, *Cze*, 1951 *Sp*, 1952 *Ger*
P Rotilio 1997 *De*, 1998 *Geo*
IF Rouyet 2008 *SA*, *Ar*, 2009 *A*, *NZ*, *NZ*, *SA*, *Sa*
B Rovelli 1960 *Ger*, *F*, 1961 *Ger*, *F*
G Rubini 2009 *S*, *W*, *F*, *A*
A Russo 1986 *E*
D Sacca 2003 *I*
R Saetti 1988 *USS*, *I*, 1989 *F*, *R*, *Sp*, *Ar*, *Z*, *USS*, 1990 *F*, *Sp*, *H*, *R*, *USS*, 1991 *R*, *Nm*, *Nm*, *US*, *E*, 1992 *R*
R Saetti 1957 *Ger*, 1958 *F*, *R*, 1959 *F*, 1960 *F*, 1961 *Ger*, *F*, 1964 *Ger*, *F*
A Sagramora 1970 *Mad*, *Mad*, 1971 *R*
E Saibene 1957 *F*, *Ger*
C Salmasco 1965 *F*, 1967 *F*
L Salsi 1971 *Mor*, 1972 *Pt*, *Sp*, *Yug*, 1973 *Pt*, *Rho*, *WTv*, *Nat*, *ETv*, *Leo*, *FS*, *Tva*, *Cze*, *Yug*, *A*, 1974 *Pt*, *Oxo*, *WGe*, *Leo*, 1975 *Sp*, *R*, *Sp*, 1977 *R*, *Pol*, *Cze*, *R*, *Sp*, 1978 *F*
F Salvadego 1985 *Z*
R Salvan 1973 *Yug*, 1974 *Pt*
L Salvati 1987 *USS*, 1988 *USS*, *I*
R Santofadre 1952 *Sp*, *Ger*, *F*, 1954 *Sp*, *F*
F Sartorato 1956 *Ger*, *F*, 1957 *F*
M Savi 2004 *R*, *J*, 2005 *E*
S Saviozzi 1998 *Geo*, *Rus*, *H*, 1999 *W*, *I*, *SA*, *SA*, *Ur*, *Fj*, *Tg*, *NZ*, 2000 *C*, *NZ*, 2002 *NZ*, *Sp*
F Sbaraglini 2009 *S*, *F*, *A*, *NZ*, 2010 *SA*
D Scaglia 1994 *R*, *W*, 1995 *S*, 1996 *W*, *A*, 1999 *W*
E Scalzotto 1974 *Mid*, *Sus*, *Oxo*
A Scanavacca 1997 *De*, 1998 *Geo*, *Cro*, 1999 *Ur*, 2001 *E*, 2002 *Sp*, *R*, 2004 *US*, 2006 *Ar*, *C*, 2007 *F*, *E*, *S*, *I*
R Sciacol 1965 *Cze*
I Scodavolpe 1954 *Sp*
F Screnci 1977 *Cze*, *R*, *Sp*, 1978 *F*, 1979 *Pol*, *R*, *E*, 1982 *F*, 1984 *Mor*

A Selvaggio 1973 *Rho*, *WTv*, *ETv*, *Leo*, *FS*, *Tva*
M Sepe 2006 *J*, *Fj*, 2010 *SA*
D Sesenna 1992 *R*, 1993 *Cro*, *Mor*, *F*, 1994 *R*
G Sessa 1930 *Sp*
G Sessi 1942 *R*
A Sgarbi 2008 *E*, *W*, 2009 *A*, *A*, *SA*
E Sgorbati 1968 *WGe*, *Yug*
E Sgorbati 1933 *Cze*, 1934 *Cat*, *R*, 1935 *Cat*, *F*, 1936 *Ger*, 1937 *Ger*, 1938 *Ger*, 1939 *Ger*, 1940 *R*, *Ger*, 1942 *R*
A Sgorlon 1993 *Pt*, *Mor*, *Sp*, *F*, *Rus*, *F*, *S*, 1994 *CZR*, *R*, *W*, 1995 *S*, *E*, *Ar*, *F*, *Ar*, *R*, *NZ*, *SA*, 1996 *W*, *Pt*, *W*, *A*, *E*, *S*, 1997 *I*, *F*, *F*, *Ar*, *R*, *SA*, *I*, 1998 *S*, *W*, *Rus*, 1999 *F*, *S*, *W*
P Sguario 1958 *R*, 1959 *F*, 1960 *Ger*, *F*, 1961 *Ger*, 1962 *R*
M Silini 1955 *Ger*, *Sp*, *F*, *Cze*, 1956 *Cze*, 1957 *Ger*, 1958 *F*, 1959 *F*
S Silvestri 1954 *F*
U Silvestri 1967 *Pt*, *R*, 1968 *Pt*, *WGe*
U Silvestri 1949 *F*, *Cze*
L Simonelli 1956 *Ger*, *F*, *Cze*, 1958 *F*, 1960 *Ger*, *F*
F Sinitich 1980 *Fj*, *Coo*, *Pol*, *Sp*, 1981 *R*, 1983 *USS*
JW Sole 2005 *Ar*, *Tg*, *Ar*, 2006 *I*, *E*, *F*, *W*, *S*, *J*, *Fj*, *Rus*, *A*, *Ar*, *C*, 2007 *F*, *E*, *I*, *Ur*, *Ar*, *J*, *I*, *R*, *S*, 2008 *I*, *E*, *W*, *F*, *S*, *SA*, *Ar*, *A*, *Ar*, *Pl*, 2009 *E*, *I*, *S*, *W*, *F*, *NZ*, *SA*, *Sa*, 2010 *I*, *E*, *S*, *F*, *W*
F Soncini 1998 *Cro*
F Soro 1965 *Cze*, 1966 *F*, *Ger*, *R*
A Spagnoli 1973 *Rho*
E Speziali 1965 *Cze*
W Spragg 2006 *C*
F Staibano 2006 *J*, *Fj*, 2007 *W*, *I*, *Ur*, *Ar*, 2009 *A*, *A*, *NZ*
MP Stanojevic 2006 *Pt*, *Rus*, *A*, *Ar*, *C*, 2007 *J*, *NZ*
Stefano 1997 *De*
U Stenta 1937 *Bel*, *Ger*, *F*, 1938 *Ger*, 1939 *Ger*, *R*, 1940 *R*, *Ger*, 1942 *R*
P Stievano 1948 *F*, 1952 *F*, 1953 *F*, *Ger*, *R*, 1954 *Sp*, *F*, 1955 *Ger*
S Stocco 1997 *De*, 1998 *Geo*, *H*, 1999 *S*, *I*, 2000 *Fj*
CA Stoica 1997 *I*, *F*, *SA*, *I*, 1998 *S*, *W*, *Rus*, *Cro*, *Ar*, *H*, *E*, 1999 *S*, *W*, *SA*, *SA*, *Ur*, *Sp*, *Fj*, *E*, *Tg*, *NZ*, 2000 *Geo*, *S*, *W*, *I*, *E*, *F*, *Sa*, *Fj*, *C*, *R*, *NZ*, 2001 *I*, *E*, *F*, *S*, *W*, *Fj*, *SA*, *Sa*, 2002 *F*, *S*, *W*, *I*, *E*, *Sp*, *R*, *Ar*, *A*, 2003 *W*, *I*, *S*, *I*, *Geo*, *Tg*, *C*, *W*, 2004 *E*, *F*, *S*, *I*, *W*, *US*, 2005 *S*, *Tg*, *Ar*, 2006 *I*, *E*, *F*, *W*, *S*, 2007 *Ur*, *Ar*
L Tagliabue 1930 *Sp*, 1933 *Cze*, *Cze*, 1934 *Cat*, *R*, 1935 *F*, 1937 *Ger*
S Tartaglini 1948 *Cze*, 1949 *F*, *Cze*, 1951 *Sp*, 1952 *Sp*, *Ger*, *F*, 1953 *F*
A Tassin 1973 *A*
A Taveggia 1954 *F*, 1955 *Ger*, *F*, *Sp*, *F*, 1956 *Ger*, *F*, *Cze*, 1957 *F*, *Ger*, 1958 *F*, *R*, 1959 *F*, 1960 *Ger*, *F*, 1967 *Pt*
D Tebaldi 1985 *Z*, *Z*, 1987 *R*, *Ar*, *Fj*, *USS*, *Sp*, 1988 *F*, *A*, *I*, 1989 *F*, 1990 *F*, *Pol*, *R*, 1991 *Nm*
T Tebaldi 2009 *A*, *A*, *NZ*, *NZ*, *SA*, *Sa*, 2010 *I*, *E*, *S*, *F*, *W*, *SA*, *SA*
T Tedeschi 1948 *F*
G Testoni 1937 *Bel*, 1938 *Ger*, 1942 *R*
C Tinari 1980 *JAB*, *Coo*, *Pol*, *USS*, *Sp*, 1981 *USS*, *WGe*, 1982 *F*, *WGe*, 1983 *R*, *USS*, *C*, *C*, *Sp*, *Mor*, *A*, *USS*, 1984 *Mor*, *R*
M Tommasi 1990 *Pol*, 1992 *R*, *S*, 1993 *Pt*, *Cro*, *Sp*, *F*
G Toniolatti 2008 *A*, 2009 *E*, *I*, *A*, *NZ*
C Torresan 1980 *F*, *R*, *Fj*, *Coo*, *Pol*, *USS*, 1981 *R*, *USS*, 1982 *R*, *Mor*, 1983 *C*, *F*, *A*, *USS*, 1984 *F*, *Mor*, *Tun*, *USS*, 1985 *Z*, *Z*, *USS*
F Tozzi 1933 *Cze*
P Travagli 2004 *C*, *NZ*, 2008 *I*, *E*, *W*, *F*, *S*, *Ar*, *Pl*
L Travini 1999 *SA*, *Ur*, *Sp*, *Fj*, 2000 *I*
F Trebbi 1933 *Cze*, *Cze*
F Trentin 1979 *Mor*, *F*, *Pol*, *USS*, 1981 *R*
M Trevisiol 1988 *F*, *USS*, *A*, *I*, 1989 *F*, *Ar*, *USS*, 1994 *R*
M Trippiteli 1979 *Pol*, 1980 *Pol*, *Sp*, 1981 *F*, *R*, 1982 *F*, *E*, *WGe*, 1984 *Tun*
L Troiani 1985 *R*, 1986 *Tun*, *F*, *Pt*, *A*, *USS*, 1987 *Pt*, *F*, 1988 *R*, *USS*, *A*, *I*, 1989 *Sp*, *Ar*, *Z*, *USS*, 1990 *F*, *Pol*, *R*, *Sp*, *H*, *R*, *USS*, 1991 *F*, *R*, *Nm*, *Nm*, *US*, *E*, 1992 *Sp*, *F*, *R*, *R*, *S*, 1993 *Sp*, *F*, *Cro*, *Rus*, *F*, 1994 *Sp*, *CZR*, *A*, *A*, *F*, 1995 *S*, *E*, *Ar*
A Troncon 1994 *Sp*, *R*, *CZR*, *H*, *A*, *A*, *R*, *W*, *F*, 1995 *S*, *I*, *Sa*, *E*, *Ar*, *F*, *Ar*, *R*, *NZ*, *SA*, 1996 *W*, *W*, *A*, *E*, *S*, 1997 *I*, *F*, *F*, *Ar*, *SA*, *I*, 1998 *S*, *W*, *Geo*, *Rus*, *Ar*, *H*, *E*, 1999 *F*, *S*, *W*, *I*, *Ur*, *Sp*, *Fj*, *E*, *Tg*, *NZ*, 2000 *Geo*, *S*, *W*, *I*, *E*, *F*, *R*, *NZ*, 2001 *I*, *F*, *Nm*, *SA*, *Ur*, *Ar*, *Fj*, *SA*, *Sa*, 2002 *F*, *S*, *W*, *I*, *E*, *Sp*, *R*, *Ar*, *A*, 2003 *W*, *I*, *E*, *F*, *S*, *S*, *I*, *Geo*, *NZ*, *Tg*, *C*, *W*, 2004 *R*, *J*, 2005 *I*, *W*, *S*, *E*, *F*, 2007 *F*, *E*, *S*, *W*, *I*, *J*, *I*, *NZ*, *R*, *Pt*, *S*
G Troncon 1962 *F*, *Ger*, *R*, 1963 *F*, 1964 *Ger*, *F*, 1965 *Cze*, 1966 *F*, *R*, 1967 *F*, 1968 *Yug*, 1972 *Pt*
L Turcato 1952 *Sp*, *Ger*, *F*, 1953 *Ger*, *R*
M Turcato 1949 *F*, 1951 *Sp*
P Vaccari 1991 *Nm*, *Nm*, *US*, *E*, *NZ*, *USS*, 1992 *Sp*, *F*, *R*, *R*, *S*, 1993 *Mor*, *Sp*, *F*, *Rus*, *F*, *S*, 1994 *Sp*, *R*, *CZR*, *H*, *A*, *A*, *R*, *W*, *F*, 1995 *I*, *Sa*, *E*, *Ar*, *F*, *Ar*, *R*, *NZ*, *SA*, 1996 *W*, *W*, *E*, *S*, 1997 *I*, *F*, *F*, *Ar*, *R*, *SA*, *I*, 1998 *S*, *W*, *Cro*, *Ar*, 1999 *Ur*, *Sp*, *E*, *Tg*, *NZ*, 2000 *Geo*, 2001 *Fj*, 2002 *F*, *S*, *Ar*, *A*, 2003 *W*, *I*, *E*, *F*, *S*
V Vagnetti 1939 *R*, 1940 *R*
F Valier 1968 *Yug*, 1969 *F*, 1970 *Cze*, *R*, 1971 *Mor*, *R*, 1972 *Pt*
L Valtorta 1957 *Ger*, 1958 *F*
O Vene 1966 *F*
E Venturi 1983 *C*, 1985 *EngB*, *Sp*, 1986 *Tun*, *Pt*, 1988 *USS*, *A*, 1989 *F*, *R*, *Sp*, *Ar*, *USS*, 1990 *F*, *Pol*, *R*, *Sp*, *H*, *R*, *USS*, 1991 *F*, *R*, *NZ*, *USS*, 1992 *Sp*, *F*, *R*, 1993 *Sp*, *F*
P Vezzani 1973 *Yug*, 1975 *F*, *Sp*, *R*, *Cze*, *E*, *Pol*, *H*, *Sp*, 1976 *F*
F Vialetto 1972 *Yug*
V Viccariotto 1948 *F*
S Vigliano 1937 *R*, *Bel*, *Ger*, *F*, 1939 *R*, 1942 *R*
L Villagra 2000 *Sa*, *Fj*
E Vinci I 1929 *Sp*
P Vinci II 1929 *Sp*, 1930 *Sp*, 1933 *Cze*
F Vinci III 1929 *Sp*, 1930 *Sp*, 1934 *Cat*, *R*, 1935 *Cat*, *F*, 1936 *Ger*, *R*, 1937 *Ger*, *R*, *Ger*, *F*, 1939 *Ger*, *R*, 1940 *Ger*
P Vinci IV 1929 *Sp*, 1930 *Sp*, 1933 *Cze*, *Cze*, 1934 *Cat*, *R*, 1935 *Cat*, *F*, 1937 *Ger*, *Bel*, *Ger*, *F*, 1939 *Ger*
A Visentin 1970 *R*, 1972 *Pt*, *Sp*, 1973 *Rho*, *WTv*, *Bor*, *NEC*, *Nat*, *ETv*, *Leo*, *FS*, *Tva*, *Cze*, *Yug*, *A*, 1974 *Pt*, *Leo*, 1975 *F*, *Sp*, *R*, *Cze*, 1976 *R*, 1978 *Ar*
G Visentin 1935 *Cat*, *F*, 1936 *R*, 1937 *Ger*, *Bel*, *Ger*, *F*, 1938 *Ger*, 1939 *Ger*
T Visentin 1996 *W*
W Visser 1999 *I*, *SA*, *SA*, 2000 *Geo*, *S*, *W*, *I*, *F*, *C*, *R*, *NZ*, 2001 *I*, *E*, *F*, *S*, *W*, *Nm*, *SA*, *Ur*, *Ar*, *Fj*, *SA*, *Sa*
F Vitadello 1985 *Sp*, 1987 *Pt*
C Vitelli 1973 *Cze*, *Yug*, 1974 *Pt*, *Sus*
I Vittorini 1969 *Sp*
RMS Vosawai 2007 *J*, *I*, *NZ*, *R*, *Pt*, 2010 *W*, *SA*
RS Wakarua 2003 *Tg*, *C*, *W*, 2004 *E*, *F*, *S*, *W*, *J*, *C*, *NZ*, 2005 *Fj*
F Williams 1995 *SA*
M Zaffiri 2000 *Fj*, *R*, *NZ*, 2001 *W*, 2003 *S*, 2005 *Tg*, *Fj*, 2006 *W*, *S*, *C*, 2007 *E*, *S*, *W*, *I*
R Zanatta 1954 *Sp*, *F*
G Zanchi 1953 *Ger*, *R*, 1955 *Sp*, *Cze*, 1957 *Ger*
A Zanella 1977 *Mor*
M Zanella 1976 *J*, *Sp*, 1977 *R*, *Pol*, *Cze*, 1978 *Ar*, 1980 *Pol*, *USS*
E Zanetti 1942 *R*
F Zani 1960 *Ger*, *F*, 1961 *Ger*, *F*, 1962 *F*, *R*, 1963 *F*, 1964 *F*, 1965 *F*, 1966 *Ger*, *R*
G Zani 1934 *R*
A Zanni 2005 *Tg*, *Ar*, *Fj*, 2006 *F*, *W*, *S*, *Pt*, *Rus*, *A*, *Ar*, *C*, 2007 *S*, *W*, *I*, *Ur*, *I*, *NZ*, 2008 *I*, *E*, *W*, *F*, *S*, *SA*, *Ar*, *A*, *Pl*, 2009 *E*, *I*, *S*, *W*, *F*, *A*, *A*, *NZ*, *NZ*, *SA*, *Sa*, 2010 *I*, *E*, *S*, *F*, *W*, *SA*, *SA*
C Zanoletti 2001 *Sa*, 2002 *E*, *NZ*, *R*, *Ar*, *A*, 2005 *A*
G Zanon 1981 *F*, *R*, *USS*, *WGe*, 1982 *R*, *E*, *WGe*, *Mor*, 1983 *F*, *R*, *USS*, *C*, *C*, *Sp*, *Mor*, *F*, *A*, *USS*, 1984 *F*, *Mor*, *R*, *USS*, 1985 *F*, *R*, *EngB*, *Sp*, *Z*, *Z*, *USS*, 1986 *USS*, 1987 *R*, *Ar*, *USS*, 1989 *Sp*, *Ar*, 1990 *F*, *Pol*, *R*, *Sp*, *H*, *R*, *USS*, 1991 *Nm*, *US*, *E*
M Zingarelli 1973 *A*
N Zisti 1999 *E*, *NZ*, 2000 *E*, *F*
G Zoffoli 1936 *Ger*, *R*, 1937 *Ger*, *R*, *Ger*, 1938 *Ger*, 1939 *R*
S Zorzi 1985 *R*, 1986 *Tun*, *F*, 1988 *F*, *R*, *USS*, 1992 *R*
A Zucchelo 1956 *Ger*, *F*
C Zucchi 1952 *Sp*, 1953 *F*
L Zuin 1977 *Cze*, 1978 *Ar*, *USS*, *Sp*, 1979 *F*, *Pol*, *R*

JAPAN

JAPAN'S 2009–10 TEST RECORD

OPPONENTS	DATE	VENUE	RESULT
Canada	15 November	H	**Won** 46–8
Canada	21 November	H	**Won** 27–6
Korea	1 May	A	**Won** 71–13
Arabian Gulf	8 May	H	**Won** 60–5
Kazakhstan	15 May	H	**Won** 101–7
Hong Kong	22 May	H	**Won** 94–5
Fiji	12 June	A	**Lost** 8–22
Samoa	19 June	A	**Won** 31–23
Tonga	26 June	A	**Won** 26–23

SCALING THE HEIGHTS

By Rich Freeman

It says something of the standards now expected of the Japanese national team that coach John Kirwan spent more time bemoaning the one that got away than the eight Tests that were won in 2009–10.

"I was at our friend's house for dinner and everyone was saying what a great year we had had," Kirwan said. "But I kept talking about the loss to Fiji. A year ago I would have been absolutely stoked to walk away with one loss from nine Tests, but my personality means I can't believe we lost the Fiji game."

The loss meant Japan was unable to claim the ANZ Pacific Nations Cup title, one of the short-term goals Kirwan has set for his team.

"Our goal has always been to get two wins in the PNC and win the competition," he said. "Our longer term goal is to make the world's top 10."

Fortunately, Kirwan's players have taken the message to heart and they started the year with a bang, overwhelming Canada in back-to-back tests.

A 46–8 win in Sendai was followed by a 27–6 victory in Tokyo as Japan displayed a high-pace game that completely overwhelmed their opponents, coached by Kirwan's former room-mate with the All Blacks, Kieran Crowley.

"Canada was a real test of how we have improved," admitted Kirwan. "It was very important to show people that the team is moving in the right direction and the results showed we are getting better right across the board."

That improvement wasn't exactly on show as Japan got off to a poor start in the HSBC Asian 5 Nations, scoring just 19 points in the opening 40 minutes against Korea before ultimately triumphing 71–13.

But as has been the case every year since the tournament has been in existence, Japan finished the competition with four bonus-point wins from as many games.

With the silverware came the all-important Asian qualification spot at Rugby World Cup 2011, alongside hosts New Zealand, France, Canada and Tonga in Pool A.

"We have qualified for the World Cup so I am very happy," Kirwan said after Japan had brushed aside Hong Kong 94–5 to book their ticket for New Zealand.

"The players have worked very hard and that was our best performance in the competition so far. But it's important we keep growing. I want to show the world how much we have improved and I hope we have the courage to play our style of rugby. I have never taken the field to lose a game and won't in New Zealand and I am sure the players feel the same."

A shell-shocked Hong Kong coach Dai Rees simply said: "We came up against a superb Japan side. They stand alone in Asian rugby."

Kirwan, though, wants Japan to be more than just the best in Asia.

"I believe in a journey," he explained. "If you don't set big goals then you will always underachieve. In 2019 [when Japan hosts the Rugby World Cup] our aim should be to win. Being happy just hosting would be a big mistake."

Kirwan knows the first step on that journey is to get the team into the habit of beating the likes of Fiji, Samoa and Tonga, and the easiest way of doing that is to play mistake-free rugby.

Japan's opening game in the Pacific Nations Cup is always a difficult one as they try to adjust to a physicality, pace and intensity that they never come up against in the A5N.

And so it proved again this year as the Brave Blossoms went down 22–8 to Fiji.

"We lost, they didn't beat us," Kirwan said. "We never gave up so that was a positive. If we can cut down on the individual errors then I think we can be competitive. You can't win a football game with that many errors."

Seven days later, Japan did just that scoring one of the best wins in their history, 31–23 over hosts Samoa in Apia.

"Samoa was the best game we have played," admitted Kirwan. "There were 20 minutes in the second half when we were not so good but we made critical decisions such as [James Arlidge's late] drop goal and we defended very well."

A week later, Japan downed Tonga 26–23 to finish third in the standings, a point behind champions Samoa and Fiji.

"Tonga was very satisfying because we played awfully. But it is the sign of a good team if you can play badly but still grind out a win. In years gone by that was a game we would have lost."

One of the reasons for that win was the ever-improving Top League.

This year's domestic competition was again won by Toshiba Brave Lupus, who beat Sanyo Wild Knights 6–3 in a hard-fought encounter that showed just how physical Japanese rugby has become.

"The Top League is improving every year," said Kirwan. "The different influences with the foreign coaches and the Japanese coaches, who are all getting better, all helps."

That cosmopolitan mix is also evident in the national side, with Takashi Kikutani, Kosuke Endo and Shota Horie having just as much influence on the team as the likes of Shaun Webb and Ryan Nicholas.

Kirwan has already said he will step down after the World Cup, but the team look in good stead to progress on the journey he has started them on.

JAPAN INTERNATIONAL STATISTICS

MATCH RECORDS UP TO 29TH OCTOBER 2010

WINNING MARGIN

Date	Opponent	Result	Winning Margin
06/07/2002	Chinese Taipei	155–3	152
27/10/1998	Chinese Taipei	134–6	128
21/07/2002	Chinese Taipei	120–3	117
03/05/2008	Arabian Gulf	114–6	108
15/05/2010	Kazakhstan	101–7	94

MOST POINTS IN A MATCH
BY THE TEAM

Date	Opponent	Result	Pts.
06/07/2002	Chinese Taipei	155–3	155
27/10/1998	Chinese Taipei	134–6	134
21/07/2002	Chinese Taipei	120–3	120
03/05/2008	Arabian Gulf	114–6	114
15/05/2010	Kazakhstan	101–7	101

MOST TRIES IN A MATCH
BY THE TEAM

Date	Opponent	Result	Tries
06/07/2002	Chinese Taipei	155–3	23
27/10/1998	Chinese Taipei	134–6	20
21/07/2002	Chinese Taipei	120–3	18

MOST CONVERSIONS IN A MATCH
BY THE TEAM

Date	Opponent	Result	Cons
06/07/2002	Chinese Taipei	155–3	20
27/10/1998	Chinese Taipei	134–6	17
21/07/2002	Chinese Taipei	120–3	15
15/05/2010	Kazakhstan	101–7	13

MOST PENALTIES IN A MATCH
BY THE TEAM

Date	Opponent	Result	Pens
08/05/1999	Tonga	44–17	9
08/04/1990	Tonga	28–16	6

MOST DROP GOALS IN A MATCH
BY THE TEAM

Date	Opponent	Result	DGs
15/09/1998	Argentina	44–29	2

MOST POINTS IN A MATCH
BY A PLAYER

Date	Player	Opponent	Pts.
21/07/2002	Toru Kurihara	Chinese Taipei	60
06/07/2002	Daisuke Ohata	Chinese Taipei	40
16/06/2002	Toru Kurihara	Korea	35
08/05/1999	Keiji Hirose	Tonga	34
08/05/2005	Keiji Hirose	Hong Kong	31

MOST TRIES IN A MATCH
BY A PLAYER

Date	Player	Opponent	Tries
06/07/2002	Daisuke Ohata	Chinese Taipei	8
21/07/2002	Toru Kurihara	Chinese Taipei	6
08/05/2005	Daisuke Ohata	Hong Kong	6
27/10/1998	Terunori Masuho	Chinese Taipei	5
01/05/2010	Kosuke Endo	Korea	5

MOST CONVERSIONS IN A MATCH

BY A PLAYER

Date	Player	Opponent	Cons
21/07/2002	Toru Kurihara	Chinese Taipei	15
06/07/2002	Andy Miller	Chinese Taipei	12
16/06/2002	Toru Kurihara	Korea	11
08/05/2005	Keiji Hirose	Hong Kong	11
15/05/2010	Shaun Webb	Kazakhstan	11

MOST PENALTIES IN A MATCH

BY A PLAYER

Date	Player	Opponent	Pens
08/05/1999	Keiji Hirose	Tonga	9
08/04/1990	Takahiro Hosokawa	Tonga	6

MOST DROP GOALS IN A MATCH

BY A PLAYER

Date	Player	Opponent	DGs
15/09/1998	Kensuke Iwabuchi	Argentina	2

MOST CAPPED PLAYERS

Name	Caps
Yukio Motoki	79
Takeomi Ito	62
Daisuke Ohata	58
Hirotoki Onozawa	51

LEADING TRY SCORERS

Name	Tries
Daisuke Ohata	69
Hirotoki Onozawa	40
Terunori Masuho	28
Toru Kurihara	20

LEADING CONVERSIONS SCORERS

Name	Cons
Keiji Hirose	77
Toru Kurihara	71
James Arlidge	52
Ryan Nicholas	45

LEADING PENALTY SCORERS

Name	Pens
Keiji Hirose	76
Toru Kurihara	35
Takahiro Hosokawa	24
James Arlidge	17

LEADING DROP GOAL SCORERS

Name	DGs
Kyohei Morita	5
Yuji Matsuo	2
Katsuhiro Matsuo	2
Keiji Hirose	2
Kensuke Iwabuchi	2

LEADING POINTS SCORERS

Name	Pts.
Keiji Hirose	413
Toru Kurihara	347
Daisuke Ohata	345
Hirotoki Onozawa	200
James Arlidge	183

JAPAN INTERNATIONAL PLAYERS

UP TO 29TH OCTOBER 2010

Note: Years given for International Championship matches are for second half of season; eg 1972 means season 1971–72. Years for all other matches refer to the actual year of the match.

T Adachi 1932 *C, C*
M Aizawa 1984 *Kor*, 1986 *US, C, S, E, Kor*, 1987 *A, NZ, NZ*, 1988 *Kor*
H Akama 1973 *F*, 1975 *A, W*, 1976 *S, E, It, Kor*, 1977 *S*
T Akatsuka 1994 *Fj, SL, M*, 1995 *Tg, NZ*, 2005 *Sp*, 2006 *HK, Kor*
J Akune 2001 *W, C*
M Amino 2000 *Kor, C*, 2003 *Rus, AuA, Kor, E, E, S, Fj, US*
E Ando 2006 *AG, Kor, Geo, Tg, Sa, JAB, Fj*, 2007 *HK, Fj, Tg, Sa, JAB, It*
D Anglesey 2002 *Tg, Tai, Tai*
T Aoi 1959 *BCo, BCo*, 1963 *BCo*
S Aoki 1989 *S*, 1990 *Fj*, 1991 *US, C*, 1993 *W*
Y Aoki 2007 *Kor, AuA, JAB*, 2008 *Kor, Kaz, HK, AuA, Tg, Fj, Sa, US, US*, 2009 *Kaz, Sin, Sa, JAB, Tg, Fj*
S Arai 1959 *BCo, BCo*
JA Arlidge 2007 *Kor*, 2008 *Kor, AG, Kaz, HK, AuA, Tg, Fj, M, Sa*, 2009 *Sa, JAB, Tg, Fj, C, C*, 2010 *Kor, AG, Kaz, HK, Fj, Sa, Tg*
G Aruga 2006 *HK, Kor*, 2007 *Kor, HK, AuA, Sa, JAB, It, Fj, C*, 2008 *Kor, HK*, 2009 *C, C*
K Aruga 1974 *NZU*, 1975 *A, A, W, W*, 1976 *S, E, It, Kor*
R Asano 2003 *AuA, AuA, F, Fj*, 2005 *Ar, HK, Kor, R, C, I, I, Sp*, 2006 *Kor, Geo, Tg, It, HK, Kor*, 2007 *Kor, It, W*
M Atokawa 1969 *HK*, 1970 *Tha, BCo*, 1971 *E, E*
H Atou 1976 *BCo*
T Baba 1932 *C*
GTM Bachop 1999 *C, Tg, Sa, Fj, Sp, Sa, W, Ar*
I Basiyalo 1997 *HK, US, US, C, HK*
D Bickle 1996 *HK, HK, C, US, US, C*
KCC Chang 1930 *BCo*, 1932 *C, C*
T Chiba 1930 *BCo*
M Chida 1980 *Kor*, 1982 *HK, C, C, Kor*, 1983 *W*, 1984 *F, F, Kor*, 1985 *US, I, I, F, F*, 1986 *US, C, S, E, Kor*, 1987 *US, E*
H Daimon 2004 *S, W*
K Endo 2004 *It*, 2006 *AG, Kor, Geo, Tg, It, JAB, Fj*, 2007 *HK, Fj, Tg, AuA, Sa, It, Fj, W, C*, 2008 *AuA, Tg, Fj, M, US, US*, 2009 *C, C*, 2010 *Kor, AG, Kaz, HK, Fj, Sa, Tg*
J Enomoto 2005 *Sp*
R Enomoto 1959 *BCo, BCo*
B Ferguson 1993 *W*, 1994 *Fj, Fj, HK, Tai, M, Kor*, 1995 *Tg, Tg, R, W, I, NZ*, 1996 *HK, HK, C, US, US, C*
K Fijii 2000 *Sa*
S Fuchigami 2000 *I*, 2002 *Rus, Tai*, 2003 *US, Rus*
A Fuji 1959 *BCo, BCo*
M Fujii 1930 *BCo*
M Fujikake 1993 *W*, 1994 *HK, SL, M*, 1995 *Tg*
T Fujimoto-Kamohara 1969 *HK*, 1970 *BCo*, 1971 *E, E*, 1972 *HK*, 1973 *W*
N Fujita 2010 *Kor, AG, Kaz*
T Fujita 1980 *H, F*, 1983 *W*, 1984 *F, F, Kor*, 1985 *US, I, I, F, F*, 1986 *US, C, S, E*, 1987 *US, E, A, NZ, NZ*, 1989 *S*, 1990 *Fj, Tg, Kor, Sa*, 1991 *US, US, I*
M Fujiwara 1973 *W*, 1974 *NZU*, 1975 *A, A, W, W*, 1976 *S, E, It*, 1977 *S*, 1978 *F, Kor*, 1979 *HK, E*, 1980 *H, F*
K Fukumuro 1990 *Kor*
K Fukuoka 2000 *Fj*
S Fukuoka 1990 *Kor*
R Fukurodate 1976 *BCo, Kor*, 1979 *E, E*, 1980 *H, F, Kor*
T Fumihara 2000 *I*
T Goda 1990 *Fj, Tg, Kor, Sa, US, Kor*, 1991 *US*, 1994 *SL, M*, 1995 *Tg*
WR Gordon 1997 *HK, C, US, US*, 1998 *C, US, HK, HK, US, C*, 1999 *C, Sa, Fj, Sp, Sa, W, Ar*
A Goromaru 2005 *Ur, R, C, I*, 2009 *Kaz, HK, Kor, Sin, JAB, C*
S Goto 2005 *Ur, Ar, Kor, R, C, I, I*, 2006 *HK*
M Hagimoto 1987 *E*
T Hagiwara-Maekawa 1930 *BCo*
K Hamabe 1996 *C, US, US, C, Kor*, 1997 *HK, C, US, US, C*, 2001 *Sa, C*
T Haneda 1994 *Tai, SL, M*, 1995 *Tg*
S Hara 1970 *BCo*, 1971 *E, E*, 1973 *W, F*, 1974 *NZU, SL*, 1975 *A, W*, 1976 *E*
T Harada 1959 *BCo*
S Hasegawa 1997 *HK*, 1998 *C, US, HK, HK, US, C, Ar, Kor, Tai, HK, Kor*, 1999 *C, Tg, Sa, Fj, US, Sa, W*, 2000 *Fj, US, Tg, Sa, C*, 2001 *W, W, Sa, C*, 2002 *Tg, Kor, Tai, Kor*, 2003 *US, AuA, E, S, F, Fj, US*
K Hatakeyama 2008 *US, US*, 2009 *HK, Sin, Sa, JAB, Tg, Fj, C, C*, 2010 *Kor, Kaz, Sa, Tg*
T Hatakeyama 1976 *It, Kor*, 1977 *S*, 1978 *F, Kor*, 1979 *HK, E, E*
T Hayashi 1980 *F*, 1982 *C, C, Kor*, 1983 *W*, 1984 *F, F*, 1985 *US, I, I, F, F*, 1986 *US, C, S, E, Kor*, 1987 *US, E, A, NZ, NZ*, 1990 *Tg, Sa*, 1991 *US, C, HK, S, I, Z*, 1992 *HK*
T Hayashi 1989 *S*
T Higashida 1983 *W*
T Hirai 1980 *Kor*, 1982 *HK*
S Hirao 1983 *W*, 1984 *F, F*, 1985 *US, I, I*, 1986 *US, C, S, E*, 1987 *US, E, A, NZ, NZ*, 1988 *Kor*, 1989 *S*, 1990 *Fj, Tg, Kor, US, Kor*, 1991 *US, C, HK, S, I, Z*, 1995 *R, W, I*
S Hirao 1932 *C, C*
T Hirao 1998 *Kor*, 1999 *Tg, Sa, W*, 2001 *Tai, Sa, C*, 2004 *Kor, Rus, C, It*
H Hirashima 2008 *US, US*, 2009 *Kaz, Kor, Sa, JAB, Tg, Fj, C, C*, 2010 *Kor, AG, Kaz, HK, Fj, Sa, Tg*
T Hirata 2000 *US, C*
J Hiratsuka 1999 *US*
K Hirose 1994 *Tai, Kor*, 1995 *Tg, NZ*, 1996 *HK, HK, C, US, US, Kor*, 1998 *HK, HK, US, C, Kor, Tai, HK, Kor*, 1999 *C, Tg, Sa, Fj, US, Sp, Sa, W, Ar*, 2000 *Fj, US, Kor, C, I*, 2003 *AuA, AuA, Kor, E, E, S*, 2005 *HK, I, Sp*
T Hirose 1988 *Kor*
T Hirose 2007 *HK*
E Hirotsu 1995 *Tg*
Y Hisadomi 2002 *Rus*, 2003 *Rus, AuA, Kor, E*, 2004 *Kor, C, It, S, R*, 2005 *Sp*, 2006 *AG, Kor, Geo, Tg, It, Sa, JAB, Fj, HK, Kor*
M Hohokabe 1978 *F, Kor*
RK Holani 2008 *Kaz, HK, AuA, Fj, M, Sa, US, US*, 2010 *HK, Fj, Sa, Tg*
K Honjo 1982 *C, C*, 1985 *US, I, F*
K Horaguchi 1979 *E, E*, 1980 *F*, 1982 *HK, C, C, Kor*, 1983 *W*, 1984 *F*, 1985 *US, I, I, F, F*, 1987 *US, E*
S Horie 2009 *C, C*, 2010 *Kor, Kaz, HK, Fj, Sa, Tg*
M Horikoshi 1988 *Kor*, 1989 *S*, 1990 *Fj, Tg, Kor, US, Kor*, 1991 *US, C, HK, I, Z*, 1992 *HK*, 1993 *Ar, Ar*, 1994 *Tai, Kor*, 1995 *Tg, R, W, I*, 1997 *C*, 1998 *C, US, Tai, HK, Kor*
S Hoshino 1975 *W*, 1976 *S*, 1978 *Kor*, 1979 *HK*

T Hosokawa 1990 *Tg, Kor, Sa, US,* 1991 *US, S, I, Z,* 1993 *Ar, Ar*
S Iburi 1972 *HK*
M Iguchi 1973 *F,* 1974 *NZU,* 1975 *A, A, W*
H Ijyuin 1932 *C, C*
W Ikeda 2004 *Kor, Rus, C, It, S, R, W,* 2005 *Sp,* 2006 *AG, Geo, Tg, It, JAB, Fj*
Y Ikeda 1980 *Kor,* 1983 *W,* 1984 *F, F*
Y Ikegaya 2008 *AG, HK, M*
H Ikuta 1987 *US, A, NZ*
K Imaizumi 1988 *Kor,* 1994 *Fj, HK,* 1996 *US,* 1997 *C, US, US, C*
k Imakoma 1988 *Kor*
K Imamura 1959 *BCo, BCo*
R Imamura 1959 *BCo, BCo*
Y Imamura 2006 *AG, Geo, It, Sa, Fj,* 2007 *HK, Fj, Tg, AuA, Sa, JAB, It, Fj, W, C,* 2008 *AG, Kaz, HK, AuA, M,* 2009 *Kaz, Kor, Sin, Sa, JAB, Tg, Fj*
R Imazato 1969 *HK,* 1970 *Tha, BCo,* 1971 *E, E,* 1972 *HK,* 1973 *W, F,* 1975 *A, A, W, W,* 1976 *S, E, It*
T Inokuchi 2007 *It, A, W,* 2008 *AG, HK, AuA, M*
Y Inose 2008 *AG, Kaz, AuA, Tg, M, Sa*
M Inoue 1982 *C, C, Kor*
M Irie 2008 *US*
R Ishi 1999 *Sp*
K Ishii 1986 *S*
J Ishiyama 1980 *H, F, Kor,* 1982 *HK, C, Kor,* 1983 *W,* 1985 *US, I, I, F, F*
K Ishizuka 1963 *BCo*
T Ishizuka 1974 *NZU, SL,* 1975 *A, W, W,* 1978 *F, Kor,* 1979 *HK, E, E,* 1980 *H, F, Kor,* 1982 *HK, C, C, Kor*
H Ito 2004 *Kor, Rus*
M Ito 2000 *Tg, Sa, Kor, C, I,* 2004 *Kor, C,* 2006 *AG, Kor, Geo, Tg, Sa, Fj, HK, Kor*
M Ito 1969 *HK*
T Ito 1996 *HK, HK, C, US, US, C, Kor,* 1997 *HK, C, US, US,* 1998 *C, US, HK, HK, US, C, Ar, Kor, Tai, HK, Kor,* 1999 *Tg, Sa, Fj, US, Sp, Sa, W, Ar,* 2000 *I,* 2001 *Kor, W, Sa, C,* 2002 *Rus, Tg, Kor, Tai, Kor, Tai,* 2003 *US, Rus, AuA, AuA, Kor, E, E, S, F, Fj, US,* 2004 *Kor, Rus, C, It,* 2005 *Ur, Ar, R, C, I, Sp*
T Ito 1963 *BCo,* 1969 *HK,* 1970 *Tha, BCo,* 1971 *E,* 1972 *HK,* 1973 *W, F,* 1974 *NZU*
T Ito 1980 *H, F,* 1982 *HK, C, Kor*
K Iwabuchi 1997 *HK, C, US, US, C, HK,* 1998 *C, US, Ar, Tai, HK,* 1999 *C,* 2001 *Tai, W, W, Sa,* 2002 *Tg, Kor, Tai, Kor*
Y Iwama 2000 *US, Tg, Sa, Kor, C,* 2001 *Tai*
H Iwashita 1930 *BCo*
Y Izawa 1970 *Tha, BCo,* 1971 *E, E,* 1972 *HK,* 1973 *W, F,* 1974 *NZU,* 1975 *A, A, W,* 1976 *S, E, It*
K Izawa-Nakamura 1994 *Tai, SL, M,* 1995 *Tg, Tg, I, NZ,* 1996 *US, Kor,* 1997 *HK, C, US, US, C, HK,* 1998 *Ar, Kor, Tai, HK, Kor*
JW Joseph 1999 *C, Tg, Sa, Fj, US, Sp, Sa, W, Ar*
H Kajihara 1989 *S,* 1990 *Fj, Tg, Kor, Sa, US, Kor,* 1991 *US, US, HK, S, I, Z,* 1993 *Ar, Ar,* 1994 *Fj, Fj, M, Kor,* 1995 *Tg, R, W, I, NZ,* 1996 *HK, HK, C, US, US, C, Kor,* 1997 *C*
S Kaleta 1992 *HK,* 1993 *Ar, Ar, W*
K Kamata 1970 *BCo*
T Kanai 2009 *Kaz, HK, Sin, JAB, Fj*
F Kanaya 1980 *F,* 1982 *HK, C, C,* 1983 *W,* 1984 *F, F, Kor,* 1985 *US*
R Kanazawa 2010 *AG, Sa, Tg*
Kanbara 1971 *E*
H Kaneshiro 1993 *Ar*
H Kano 1974 *SL,* 1982 *Kor*
T Kasahara 1932 *C, C*
K Kasai 1999 *C,* 2005 *Ar, HK, Kor, R, C, I, I,* 2006 *AG, Tg*
Y Kasai 1985 *F, F*
Y Katakura 1959 *BCo*
A Kato 2001 *Tai*
H Kato 1993 *Ar, Ar*
D Katsuno 2002 *Kor*
T Katsuraguchi 1970 *Tha*
H Kawachi 1980 *H, Kor,* 1982 *C,* 1983 *W,* 1984 *F, F, Kor*
K Kawachi 1984 *Kor*
R Kawai 2000 *I*
N Kawamata 2008 *US,* 2009 *HK, Kor, C, C,* 2010 *HK, Fj, Sa, Tg*
K Kawasaki 1963 *BCo*
M Kawasaki 1970 *Tha*
T Kawasaki 2000 *US, Tg*
Y Kawase 1983 *W,* 1985 *US, I, I, F,* 1986 *Kor,* 1987 *A*
T Kikutani 2005 *Sp,* 2006 *AG, Kor, Geo, Tg, It, Sa, JAB, Fj, Kor,* 2008 *Kor, AG, AuA, Tg, Fj, Sa, US, US,* 2009 *Kaz, HK, Kor, Sin, Sa, JAB, Tg, Fj, C, C,* 2010 *Kor, AG, Fj, Sa, Tg*
CW Kim 2007 *W, C*
K Kimura 1996 *C*
T Kimura 1984 *F, F, Kor,* 1985 *US,* 1986 *E, Kor,* 1987 *E, A, NZ*
T Kinashita 2002 *Tg, Kor*
T Kinoshita 1932 *C, C*
H Kiso 2001 *Kor, Tai,* 2003 *AuA, AuA, Kor, E, E, S, Fj, US,* 2004 *S, R, W,* 2005 *HK, I, Sp,* 2006 *AG, Kor, Geo, It, Sa, JAB, Fj, HK, Kor,* 2007 *Kor, Fj, AuA, A, W, C,* 2008 *US*
T Kitagawa 2005 *Sp,* 2006 *AG, Kor, Tg, Sa, JAB,* 2008 *Kor, AG, Kaz, HK, AuA, Tg, Fj, M, Sa, US, US,* 2009 *Kaz, Kor, Sa, JAB, Tg, Fj, C, C,* 2010 *Kor, AG, HK, Fj, Sa, Tg*
T Kitagawa 2006 *HK,* 2007 *HK, A*
Y Kitagawa 2007 *Kor,* 2009 *HK, Kor, Sin, JAB*
T Kitahara 1978 *Kor,* 1979 *HK*
H Kitajima 1963 *BCo*
T Kitano 1930 *BCo,* 1932 *C, C*
S Kitaoka 1959 *BCo*
T Kizu 2009 *C,* 2010 *AG*
H Kobayashi 1983 *W,* 1984 *F, Kor,* 1985 *I, F,* 1986 *Kor*
I Kobayashi 1975 *A, A, W, W,* 1976 *BCo, S, E, It, Kor,* 1977 *S,* 1978 *F, Kor,* 1979 *HK, E, E*
K Kobayashi 1959 *BCo, BCo*
K Koizumi 1997 *US, C, HK,* 2000 *Fj, US, Tg, Sa, C,* 2001 *W, C,* 2002 *Tg, Tai*
J Komura 1992 *HK,* 1998 *Kor,* 2000 *Kor, C*
GN Konia 2003 *US, AuA, AuA, F, Fj, US*
K Konishi 1986 *US, Kor*
Y Konishi 1980 *F, Kor,* 1982 *HK, Kor,* 1983 *W,* 1984 *F, F, Kor,* 1985 *US, I, I, F, F,* 1986 *US, C, S, E, Kor,* 1987 *NZ*
M Koshiyama 1984 *F, F, Kor,* 1985 *US, I, I,* 1986 *C, Kor,* 1987 *NZ, NZ*
T Kouda 1988 *Kor*
O Koyabu 1974 *SL*
K Kubo 2000 *I,* 2001 *Kor, W, Sa, C,* 2002 *Rus, Kor, Tai, Kor, Kor,* 2003 *US, Rus, E, F, Fj,* 2004 *Kor, C, It*
K Kubota 2004 *S, R, W*
T Kudo-Nakayama 1979 *E*
T Kumagae 2004 *Kor, Rus, C, It, S, R, W,* 2005 *Ur, Ar, Kor, R, C, I, I, Sp,* 2006 *AG, Kor, Geo, It, Sa, Fj,* 2007 *HK, Fj, AuA, Sa, A*
N Kumagai 1977 *S,* 1978 *F,* 1979 *HK*
M Kunda 1990 *Sa, US, Kor,* 1991 *C, HK, S, I, Z,* 1992 *HK,* 1993 *Ar, Ar, W,* 1994 *Fj, Fj, HK, Tai, Kor,* 1995 *Tg, R, W, I, NZ,* 1996 *HK, HK, C,* 1997 *HK, C, US, US,* 1998 *C, HK, HK, US, C, Ar, Kor, HK, Kor,* 1999 *Sa, Fj, US, Sp, Sa, W, Ar*
S Kurihara 1986 *S, E,* 1987 *E*
S Kurihara 1974 *SL*
T Kurihara 2000 *Fj, US, Tg, Sa, Kor, C,* 2001 *Kor, W, W, Sa, C,* 2002 *Rus, Tg, Kor, Tai, Kor, Tai,* 2003 *US, Rus, AuA, AuA, E, E, S, F, Fj, US*
M Kurokawa 1998 *Tai, HK, Kor,* 2000 *Fj, Tg, Sa, Kor, C*
T Kurosaka 1970 *BCo,* 1974 *SL,* 1975 *A, A, W, W*
M Kusatsu 1963 *BCo*
T Kusumi 2007 *A, W,* 2008 *Kor*
E Kutsuki 1985 *F,* 1986 *US, C, S, E,* 1987 *US, E, A, NZ, NZ,* 1989 *S,* 1990 *Fj, Tg, Kor, Sa, US, Kor,* 1991 *US, US, C, HK, S, I, Z,* 1992 *HK,* 1993 *W,* 1994 *Fj, Fj, HK*
S Latu 1993 *W,* 1994 *Fj, Fj, HK, Tai, SL, Kor,* 1995 *Tg, R, W, I*
S Latu 1987 *US, A, NZ, NZ,* 1989 *S,* 1990 *Fj, Tg, Kor, Sa, US, Kor,* 1991 *US, C, HK, S, I, Z,* 1992 *HK,* 1993 *Ar, Ar,* 1994 *Fj, Fj, HK, Tai, Kor,* 1995 *Tg, Tg, R, W, I, NZ*
MG Leitch 2008 *US, US,* 2009 *Kaz, HK, Kor, Sa, JAB, C, C,* 2010 *HK, Fj, Tg*

CED Loamanu 2005 *Ur, HK*, 2007 *Kor, Fj, Tg, Sa, JAB, It, Fj, W, C*, 2008 *AuA, Tg, Fj, M, Sa*
ET Luaiufi 1990 *Fj, Kor, US, Kor*, 1991 *US, US, C, HK, S, I, Z*
T Madea 1991 *US, C, HK*, 1994 *SL, M*, 1995 *Tg*
P Mafileo 2008 *US*
S Makabe 2009 *C*, 2010 *Kaz*
HAW Makiri 2005 *Ur, Ar, HK, Kor, R, I, I*, 2006 *AG, Tg, Sa, JAB*, 2007 *Kor, Tg, AuA, Sa, JAB, It, A, Fj, W, C*, 2008 *AuA, Tg, Fj, M, Sa*
M Mantani 1969 *HK*, 1970 *Tha, BCo*, 1971 *E, E*, 1972 *HK*
G Marsh 2007 *AuA, Sa, JAB*
T Masuho 1991 *US, C, HK, S, I, Z*, 1993 *Ar, Ar*, 1994 *Fj, Fj, Tai, SL, Kor*, 1995 *Tg, W*, 1996 *HK, C, US, US, C*, 1997 *HK, C, US, C, HK*, 1998 *C, US, HK, HK, US, C, Ar, Kor, Tai, HK*, 1999 *C, US, Sp, Sa*, 2000 *Fj, US, Tg, Sa, Kor, C*, 2001 *Kor, W, Sa, C*
Y Masutome 1986 *Kor*
K Matsubara 1930 *BCo*
T Matsubara 1932 *C, C*
Y Matsubara 2004 *Kor, Rus, C, It*, 2005 *Sp*, 2006 *AG, Kor, Geo, Tg, It, Sa, JAB, Fj, Kor*, 2007 *Kor, Fj, Tg, Sa, JAB, It, Fj, W, C*
T Matsuda 1992 *HK*, 1993 *W*, 1994 *Fj, HK, Tai, Kor*, 1995 *Tg, R, W, I, NZ*, 1996 *HK, HK, C, US, US, C, Kor*, 1998 *US, HK, HK, US, C, Ar, Kor, Tai, HK, Kor*, 1999 *C, Fj, US, Sp, Sa, Ar*, 2001 *Kor, Tai, W*, 2003 *US, AuA, Kor, E, S, Fj, US*
J Matsumoto 1977 *S*, 1978 *F*, 1980 *H*, 1982 *C, C*
T Matsunaga 1985 *F, F*
Y Matsunobu 1963 *BCo*
H Matsuo 2003 *AuA, AuA, Kor, E, E*
H Matsuo 1994 *SL*
K Matsuo 1986 *US, C, S, E, Kor*, 1987 *E, NZ*, 1988 *Kor*, 1990 *Tg, Kor, Sa, US*, 1991 *US, HK, S, I, Z*, 1993 *Ar, Ar*, 1994 *Fj, Fj, HK, M*, 1995 *Tg*
Y Matsuo 1974 *SL*, 1976 *BCo, E, It, Kor*, 1977 *S*, 1979 *HK, E, E*, 1982 *HK, C, C*, 1983 *W*, 1984 *F, F, Kor*
S Matsuoka 1963 *BCo*, 1970 *Tha*
K Matsushita 2008 *US, US*, 2010 *AG, HK, Fj, Sa, Tg*
F Mau 2004 *Rus, C, It, S, R, W*
AF McCormick 1996 *HK, HK, US*, 1997 *HK, C, US, US, C, HK*, 1998 *C, US, HK, Ar, Kor, Tai, HK*, 1999 *C, Tg, Sa, Fj, US, Sp, Sa, W, Ar*
R Miki 1999 *Sp*, 2002 *Tg, Tai, Kor, Tai, Kor*, 2004 *S, R, W*
A Miller 2002 *Rus, Kor, Tai, Kor, Tai*, 2003 *Kor, S, F, Fj, US*
S Miln 1998 *C, US, HK, HK, US*
Y Minamikawa 1976 *BCo*, 1978 *F, Kor*, 1979 *HK, E, E*, 1980 *H, F, Kor*, 1982 *HK, C, C, Kor*
M Mishima 1930 *BCo*, 1932 *C, C*
T Miuchi 2002 *Rus, Kor, Kor, Tai, Kor*, 2003 *US, Rus, AuA, Kor, E, E, S, F, Fj, US*, 2004 *Rus, C, It, S, R, W*, 2005 *Ur, Ar, HK, Kor, R, C, I, I*, 2006 *HK, Kor*, 2007 *Kor, HK, Fj, Tg, Sa, It, Fj, W, C*, 2008 *Kor, AG, Kaz, HK, AuA, Tg, Fj, Sa*
S Miura 1963 *BCo*
K Miyai 1959 *BCo, BCo*, 1963 *BCo*
K Miyaji 1969 *HK*
K Miyajima 1959 *BCo, BCo*
H Miyaji-Yoshizawa 1930 *BCo*
T Miyake 2005 *Sp*, 2006 *Sa, JAB, Fj*
K Miyamoto 1986 *S, E*, 1987 *US, E, A*, 1988 *Kor*, 1991 *I*
K Miyata 1971 *E, E*, 1972 *HK*
M Miyauchi 1975 *W*, 1976 *It, Kor*
K Mizobe 1997 *C*
K Mizoguchi 1997 *C*
K Mizube 1997 *HK*
H Mizuno 2004 *R*, 2005 *HK, Kor, R, C, I*, 2006 *AG, Geo, Tg, It, Sa, JAB*
M Mizutani 1970 *Tha*, 1971 *E*
N Mizuyama 2008 *Tg, M, Sa, US*
S Mori 1974 *NZU, SL*, 1975 *A, A, W, W*, 1976 *BCo, S, E, It, Kor*, 1977 *S*, 1978 *F*, 1979 *HK, E, E*, 1980 *H, F, Kor*
K Morioka 1982 *Kor*
K Morita 2004 *C, It*, 2005 *Ur, Ar, Kor, R, C, I*
A Moriya 2006 *Tg, It, Sa, JAB, Fj*, 2008 *AG, Kaz*
Y Motoki 1991 *US, US, C*, 1992 *HK*, 1993 *Ar, Ar*, 1994 *Fj, Fj, Tai, SL, Kor*, 1995 *Tg, Tg, R, W, I, NZ*, 1996 *HK, HK, C, US, US, C, Kor*, 1997 *HK, C, US, US, C, HK*, 1998 *C, US, HK, HK, US, C, Ar, Kor, HK, Kor*, 1999 *C, Tg, Sa, Fj, US, Sp, Sa, W, Ar*, 2001 *W, W, Sa, C*, 2002 *Rus, Tg, Kor, Tai, Kor, Tai, Kor*, 2003 *Kor, E, E, S, Fj, US*, 2004 *Kor, Rus, C, It, S, R, W*, 2005 *Ur, Ar, HK, Kor, R, C, I, I*
K Motoyoshi 2001 *Tai*
S Mukai 1985 *I, I, F*, 1986 *US, C, E, Kor*, 1987 *US, A, NZ, NZ*
M Mukoyama 2004 *Kor, C, It, S, R, W*
K Muraguchi 1976 *S, Kor*
D Murai 1985 *I, I, F, F*, 1987 *E*
K Murata 1963 *BCo*
W Murata 1991 *US, S*, 1995 *Tg, NZ*, 1996 *HK, HK, C, US, US, C, Kor*, 1997 *HK, C, US, US, HK*, 1998 *HK, HK, US, C, Ar, Kor, Kor*, 1999 *US, W*, 2001 *W, W, Sa*, 2002 *Rus, Tg, Kor, Tai, Kor, Tai*, 2003 *US, AuA, E*, 2005 *Ur, Ar, Kor, I, I*
Y Murata 1971 *E, E*, 1972 *HK*, 1973 *W*, 1974 *NZU, SL*
M Nagai 1988 *Kor*
Y Nagatomo 1993 *W*, 1994 *Fj, HK, SL, M*, 1995 *Tg*, 1996 *US, US*, 1997 *C*
Y Nagatomo 2010 *Kor, AG, Kaz*
M Nakabayashi 2005 *HK, Kor, R, I*
T Nakai 2005 *Ur, HK, C, I, I, Sp*, 2006 *AG, Kor, Geo, Tg, It, Fj*
T Nakamichi 1996 *HK, HK, US, US, C*, 1998 *Ar, Kor*, 1999 *C, Sa, Fj, Sp, W, Ar*, 2000 *Fj, US, Tg*
N Nakamura 1998 *C, US, HK, HK, US, C, Ar, Kor, Tai, HK, Kor*, 1999 *C, Tg, Sa, Fj, US, Sp, W, Ar*, 2000 *I*
S Nakamura 2009 *Kaz, Sin*, 2010 *AG, Kaz, HK, Fj*
S Nakashima 1989 *S*, 1990 *Fj, Tg, Kor, Sa, US*, 1991 *US, US, C, HK, S*
T Nakayama 1976 *BCo*, 1978 *F*, 1979 *E*, 1980 *H*, 1982 *C, C*
Y Nakayama 2008 *Kor, AG, Kaz, HK, Tg*, 2009 *HK, Kor, Sin, Tg, Fj*
H Namba 2000 *Fj, US, Tg, Sa, Kor, C, I*, 2001 *Tai, W, W, C*, 2002 *Rus, Tg, Kor, Tai, Kor*, 2003 *US, Rus, AuA, AuA, Kor, E, E, F*
R Nicholas 2008 *Kor, Kaz, HK, AuA, Tg, Fj, Sa, US, US*, 2009 *HK, Kor, Sa, JAB, Tg, Fj, C, C*, 2010 *Kor, Kaz, HK, Fj, Sa, Tg*
H Nishida 1994 *Fj*
S Nishigaki 1932 *C, C*
T Nishiura 2004 *W*, 2006 *HK, Kor*, 2007 *Kor, Fj, Tg, Sa, It, Fj, W, C*, 2008 *Kor, HK, AuA, Tg, Fj, Sa*
H Nishizumi 1963 *BCo*
M Niwa 1932 *C*
I Nogami 1932 *C*
T Nozawa 2000 *Tg, Sa, Kor, C*
M Oda 2000 *US, Tg, Sa, Kor, I*
H Ogasawara 1969 *HK*, 1970 *Tha, BCo*, 1971 *E, E*, 1973 *F*, 1974 *NZU*, 1975 *A, A, W, W*, 1977 *S*
K Oguchi 1997 *US, C, HK*, 1998 *Tai*, 1999 *Sa, Ar*, 2000 *Fj, Tg, Sa, Kor*
K Ohara 1998 *Kor, Tai*, 2000 *Kor, C, I*
D Ohata 1996 *Kor*, 1997 *HK, C, US*, 1998 *HK, C, Ar, Kor, HK*, 1999 *C, Tg, Sa, Fj, US, Sp, Sa, W, Ar*, 2000 *Fj, US, Kor, C, I*, 2002 *Rus, Kor, Tai, Kor, Tai, Kor*, 2003 *US, Rus, AuA, AuA, Kor, E, E, S, F, Fj, US*, 2004 *Kor, Rus, C, It*, 2005 *Ur, Ar, HK, Kor, R, C, I, I*, 2006 *AG, Kor, Geo, Tg, HK, Kor*
K Ohigashi 1973 *W, F*, 1974 *NZU, SL*
K Ohigashi 2004 *Kor, Rus, C*, 2007 *Kor, HK, AuA, JAB*
K Ohotsuka 1959 *BCo*
S Oikawa 1980 *H*
E Okabe 1963 *BCo*
Y Okada 1932 *C, C*
M Okidoi 1987 *A, NZ, NZ*
N Okubo 1999 *Tg, Sa, Fj, US, Sp, Sa, W, Ar*, 2000 *Fj, US, Tg, Sa, Kor, C*, 2002 *Rus, Tg, Kor, Tai, Kor, Tai*, 2003 *US, Rus, S, F, Fj, US*, 2004 *S, R, W*
T Omata 1970 *BCo*
S Onishi 2000 *Fj, US, Tg, Sa, Kor, C*, 2001 *Kor, Tai, W, C*, 2005 *Sp*, 2006 *AG, Kor, Geo, Tg, It, JAB, HK, Kor*, 2007 *HK, Tg, AuA, Sa, JAB, It, Fj, W, C*, 2008 *Kor, AG, HK, M, Sa*

H Ono 2004 *Kor, Rus, C, S*, 2005 *Ar, Kor, I*, 2006 *Kor, Geo, It, Sa, JAB, Fj, HK, Kor*, 2007 *Kor, Fj, Tg, Sa, JAB, It, Fj, W, C*, 2008 *Kor, AG, AuA, Tg, Fj, US*, 2009 *HK, Sin, Sa, JAB, Tg, C, C*, 2010 *Kor, Kaz, HK, Fj, Sa, Tg*
K Ono 2007 *Kor, AuA, JAB, It, A*
S Ono 1932 *C, C*
H Onozawa 2001 *W, Sa, C*, 2002 *Rus, Kor, Tai, Kor*, 2003 *Rus, AuA, AuA, Kor, E, E, S, F, Fj, US*, 2004 *Kor, Rus, C, It*, 2005 *Ur, Ar, HK, Kor, R, C, I, Sp*, 2006 *HK, Kor*, 2007 *Kor, Tg, AuA, JAB, A, Fj, W, C*, 2008 *Kor, AG, Kaz, HK, AuA, Tg, Fj, Sa*, 2009 *Kaz, HK, Kor, Sa, Tg, C, C*, 2010 *Fj, Sa, Tg*
S Onuki 1984 *F, F, Kor*, 1985 *US, I, I, F, F*, 1986 *US, C, S, E, Kor*, 1987 *US, E*
PD O'Reilly 2005 *Kor*, 2006 *JAB, Fj, HK, Kor*, 2007 *It, Fj, C*, 2009 *Kaz, C, C*
G Ota 1930 *BCo*
O Ota 1986 *US, S*, 1989 *S*, 1990 *Fj, Tg, Kor, Sa, US, Kor*, 1991 *US, C, HK, S, I, Z*, 1992 *HK*, 1993 *Ar, Ar, W*, 1994 *Fj, HK, Tai, Kor*, 1995 *Tg, R, W, I, NZ*
T Otao 2004 *W*, 2009 *Kaz, HK, Kor, Sin, JAB, Tg*
L Oto 1992 *HK*, 1995 *R, W, I, NZ*, 1996 *C*, 1997 *C, HK*
M Oto 1972 *HK*
N Oto 2001 *Kor, Tai, W, Sa*, 2005 *Sp*, 2006 *Kor, Tg, It, Sa, JAB, Fj*, 2007 *A*
K Otukolo 2005 *HK, Kor, C*
F Ouchi 1991 *US*
H Ouchi 1990 *Kor*, 1993 *Ar, W*, 1994 *HK*
N Owashi 1992 *HK*
M Oyabu 1998 *Kor*
A Oyagi 1983 *W*, 1984 *F, F, Kor*, 1985 *US, I, I, F, F*, 1986 *US, C*, 1987 *US, E, NZ, NZ*, 1988 *Kor*, 1989 *S*, 1990 *Fj, Tg, Kor, Sa, US, Kor*, 1991 *US, C, I, Z*
J Oyamada 1997 *HK, US*
A Ozaki 2008 *Kor, AG, HK*
M Ozaki 1963 *BCo*, 1969 *HK*
H Ozeki 1996 *HK, HK, US, C, Kor*
A Parker 2002 *Rus, Tg, Kor, Tai, Kor, Tai*, 2003 *US, Rus, AuA, AuA, Kor, E, E, S, F, Fj, US*, 2004 *It*
R Parkinson 2003 *Rus, AuA, E, S, Fj*, 2005 *Ur, Ar, HK, I, I*
D Quate 2009 *C*
BB Robins 2007 *Kor, Fj, Tg, AuA, Sa, JAB, It, Fj, W, C*, 2008 *Kor, AG, Kaz, HK, AuA, Tg, Fj, M, Sa, US, US*, 2009 *Kaz*
K Sagawa 1977 *S*
Y Saito 2001 *Tai, W, W, Sa, C*, 2002 *Rus, Kor, Tai, Kor*, 2003 *Kor, E, E, US*, 2004 *Kor*
M Sakamoto 1978 *F, Kor*, 1980 *Kor*
M Sakata 1994 *SL, M*, 1996 *C, US, US, C, Kor*, 1997 *US, US, C, HK*, 1998 *US, HK, Tai*, 1999 *C, Tg, US, Sp, Sa, W, Ar*, 2001 *W, W, Sa, C*, 2002 *Rus, Tg, Kor, Tai, Kor*, 2003 *US, Rus, AuA, S, F, Fj*
Y Sakata 1969 *HK*, 1970 *Tha, BCo*, 1971 *E, E*, 1972 *HK*
Y Sakuraba 1986 *S, E*, 1987 *A, NZ, NZ*, 1988 *Kor*, 1992 *HK*, 1993 *Ar, Ar, W*, 1994 *Fj, HK, Tai, SL, Kor*, 1995 *Tg, R, W, I, NZ*, 1996 *HK, Kor*, 1997 *C, US, C, HK*, 1998 *C, US, HK, HK, US, C, Ar, Kor, Tai, HK, Kor*, 1999 *C, Tg, Sa, Fj, W, Ar*
L Samurai Vatuvei 2001 *Kor, Tai, W, W, Sa, C*, 2002 *Rus, Tg, Kor, Kor, Tai*, 2003 *US, Rus, AuA*, 2004 *Kor, Rus, C, It*, 2006 *HK, Kor*, 2007 *It, A, C*
T Saruta 1969 *HK*
M Sasada 1976 *BCo, E, It, Kor*, 1977 *S*, 1979 *HK, E*
Y Sasada 1973 *W, F*
T Sasaki 2007 *HK, Fj, Tg, AuA, JAB, A*
K Sato 1996 *US, US, C*, 1997 *C*
T Sato 2005 *Sp*, 2006 *AG, Kor, Geo, Tg, Sa, Fj*, 2007 *Kor, AuA*
T Sato 2008 *Kor, AG, Kaz, HK*
T Sato 2008 *AG, Kaz, HK*
Y Sato 1994 *Fj, SL, M*, 1995 *Tg*, 1996 *C*
T Sawaguchi 2002 *Kor*
K Sawaki 1998 *Ar, Tai, Kor*, 1999 *Sa*, 2004 *S*, 2006 *HK, Kor*
K Segawa 1982 *HK*
K Sejimo 1980 *H, F*, 1982 *HK, C, C, Kor*
K Shibata 1972 *HK*, 1973 *W*, 1974 *SL*, 1975 *A*, 1976 *BCo, S, E*
M Shichinohe 2002 *Tai, Kor*
S Shiga 1959 *BCo, BCo*
F Shimazaki 1970 *Tha, BCo*, 1971 *E, E*, 1972 *HK*, 1973 *W, F*
S Shimizu 1996 *Kor*
S Shimizu 1930 *BCo*
M Shimoji 1979 *HK*
S Shimomura 2004 *S, R*, 2007 *HK*
M Shimosono 1970 *Tha*, 1971 *E, E*, 1972 *HK*, 1973 *F*
Y Shinomiya 2003 *US, AuA, Kor*
K Shinozuka 2008 *Kor, AG, Kaz, HK, M*
K Shomen 2002 *Kor*, 2006 *Kor*
G Smith 1998 *C, US, HK, HK, US, C, Ar, Kor, HK*, 1999 *C, Tg, Sa, Fj, US, Sa, W, Ar*
T Soma 2005 *Sp*, 2006 *AG, Kor, Geo, Tg, It*, 2007 *Kor, HK, Fj, Tg, AuA, Sa, JAB, It, Fj, W, C*, 2008 *Kor, Kaz, AuA, Tg, Fj, M, Sa*
Y Sonoda 2000 *Fj, US, Tg*, 2001 *Tai, W, C*, 2002 *Rus, Kor*, 2003 *US, Rus, AuA, Kor, E, E, S, F, Fj, US*
H Sugarwara 2000 *Fj, US, Tg, I*, 2001 *Tai, W*
T Sugata 1998 *Kor*
H Suzuki 1930 *BCo*
G Tachikawa 1999 *C, Tg*, 2005 *Ur, Ar, Kor, R, C, I, I, Sp*, 2007 *Kor, Fj, Tg*, 2010 *Kor, Kaz, HK*
H Taione 1986 *US, C, S*, 1988 *Kor*
K Taira 2007 *Kor, Fj, AuA, A, Fj, W, C*, 2008 *Tg, Fj, US*, 2009 *HK, Sin, Sa, JAB, Fj, C*, 2010 *Kor, Kaz, HK, Fj*
H Takafumi 1999 *Fj*
S Takagi 2005 *Ur, HK, R, I, I*
H Takahashi 2005 *Ur, Ar, Kor, C, I*
K Takahashi 1990 *Fj, Sa, Kor*, 1991 *US, US, C*, 1992 *HK*, 1993 *Ar, Ar, W*, 1994 *Fj, HK, SL, M*, 1995 *Tg, W, NZ*, 1996 *HK, HK, C*, 1997 *US, C, HK*
T Takata 1974 *NZU*, 1975 *A, A, W, W*, 1976 *BCo, S, E, It, Kor*, 1977 *S*
K Takayangi 2001 *Kor, Tai*
K Takei 2004 *It*, 2006 *AG, Kor, Geo, It, Fj*
T Takeyama 1994 *Tai, M, Kor*, 1995 *Tg*
M Takura 1989 *S*, 1990 *Fj, Tg, Kor, Sa, US*, 1991 *US, HK, S, I, Z*, 1994 *Fj, Tai, Kor*, 1995 *Tg, R, I*
H Tamura 1998 *HK, US, C, Ar, Kor, Tai, HK, Kor*, 1999 *C*
F Tanaka 2008 *AG, HK, AuA, Tg, Fj, Sa, US, US*, 2009 *Kaz, HK, Sin, Sa, Tg, Fj*, 2010 *Kor, Kaz, HK, Fj, Sa, Tg*
K Tanaka 2004 *S, R, W*
N Tanaka 1974 *SL*, 1975 *A, W*, 1976 *BCo, S, E*, 1977 *S*, 1980 *F, Kor*, 1982 *HK, Kor*
S Tanaka 1959 *BCo, BCo*
N Tanifuji 1979 *HK, E, E*, 1982 *C, C*, 1983 *W*, 1984 *F, Kor*, 1985 *US*
Y Tanigawa 1969 *HK*
T Taniguchi 2006 *Tg, It, JAB*, 2008 *Kor, Kaz, HK, AuA, Tg, Fj, M, US*
H Tanuma 1996 *Kor*, 1997 *HK, C, US, US, HK*, 1998 *C, US, HK*, 1999 *Sa, Fj, US, Sp, Sa, W, Ar*, 2000 *Fj, US, Tg, Sa, Kor, C, I*, 2001 *Kor, Tai, W, W, Sa, C*, 2002 *Kor*, 2003 *AuA, E, F*
J Tarrant 2009 *Kaz, HK, Kor, Sa, JAB, Tg, Fj*
M Tatsukawa 2000 *Sa*
T Taufa 2009 *Kaz, Kor, Sin, Sa, JAB, Tg, Fj, C, C*, 2010 *Kor, AG, Kaz, HK, Fj, Sa, Tg*
N Taumoefolau 1985 *F, F*, 1986 *US, C, S, E, Kor*, 1987 *US, E, A, NZ*, 1988 *Kor*, 1989 *S*, 1990 *Fj*
T Terai 1969 *HK*, 1970 *Tha*, 1971 *E, E*, 1972 *HK*, 1973 *W, F*, 1974 *NZU*, 1975 *A, W, W*, 1976 *S, E, It, Kor*
S Teramura 1930 *BCo*
LM Thompson 2007 *HK, Fj, Tg, Sa, JAB, It, Fj, W, C*, 2008 *M, Sa, US, US*, 2009 *Kaz, Kor, Sa, Tg, Fj*, 2010 *Kor, AG, Kaz, HK, Fj, Sa, Tg*
R Thompson 1998 *C, US, HK, HK, US, C*
Z Toba-Nakajima 1930 *BCo*, 1932 *C*
K Todd 2000 *Fj, Sa, I*
H Tominaga 1959 *BCo, BCo*
K Tomioka 2008 *US, US*, 2009 *Kor, Sin, Sa, JAB*
T Tomioka 2005 *I, I*
T Toshi 1932 *C, C*
H Toshima 1980 *H, F*, 1982 *HK, C, C*, 1984 *F, F, Kor*
M Toyoda 2008 *US*
N Toyoda 1982 *HK*

S Toyoda 1974 *SL*
T Toyoda 1978 *Kor*
M Toyota 2009 *Sin, Sa, Tg, Fj*, 2010 *Kor, AG, Kaz, HK*
K Toyoyama 1976 *BCo*, 1979 *E, E*, 1980 *H*
M Toyoyama 2000 *Fj, US, Sa, C*, 2001 *Kor, W, W, Sa, C*, 2002 *Rus, Kor, Tai, Kor, Tai*, 2003 *US, Rus, AuA, Kor, E, E, S, Fj, US*
M Tsuchida 1985 *F*
T Tsuchiya 1959 *BCo, BCo*
E Tsuji 1980 *Kor*, 1982 *Kor*
T Tsuji 2003 *S, Fj, US*, 2005 *HK, R, C*, 2006 *Kor*
Y Tsujimoto 2001 *Kor*
K Tsukagoshi 2002 *Kor*, 2005 *Ur, Ar, HK, Kor, R, C, I, I*
S Tsukda 2001 *Kor, C*, 2002 *Tg, Tai, Kor, Tai, Kor*, 2003 *AuA, E*
T Tsuyama 1976 *BCo, Kor*
P Tuidraki 1997 *HK, C*, 1998 *C, US, HK, HK, US, C, Tai*, 1999 *Tg, Sa, Fj, Sa, W, Ar*, 2000 *I*, 2001 *Tai, W, W*
A Tupuailei 2009 *C, C*, 2010 *Kor, AG, Kaz, HK, Fj, Sa, Tg*
M Uchida 1969 *HK*
A Ueda 1975 *W*, 1978 *Kor*, 1979 *E, E*
S Ueki 1963 *BCo*
N Ueyama 1973 *F*, 1974 *NZU, SL*, 1975 *A, A, W, W*, 1976 *BCo, E, It, Kor*, 1978 *F*, 1980 *Kor*
H Ujino 1976 *BCo*, 1977 *S*, 1978 *F, Kor*, 1979 *HK, E, E*, 1980 *H, Kor*, 1982 *HK, Kor*
Y Uryu 2000 *Sa*, 2001 *Kor*
S Vatuvei 2010 *Kor, AG, Kaz, Sa*
K Wada 1997 *HK, US, US, C, HK*
K Wada 2010 *AG, Kaz, Fj, Tg*
S Wada 1930 *BCo*
T Wada 1975 *A*, 1976 *S*, 1979 *E, E*
J Washington 2005 *Ur, Ar, HK, Kor, R, C, I*
M Washiya 2000 *Kor, C*
H Watanabe 1990 *Sa*
T Watanabe 2002 *Kor*
Y Watanabe 1996 *HK, HK*, 1998 *C, US, HK, Ar, Kor, Tai, HK*, 1999 *C, Tg, US, Sp, Sa*, 2000 *Fj, US*, 2003 *Rus, AuA, AuA, E, S*, 2004 *Kor*, 2005 *HK, R, C*, 2007 *HK, Fj, Tg, Sa, JAB, A, W*
S Webb 2008 *AG, Kaz, HK, AuA, Tg, Fj, M, Sa, US, US*, 2009 *Kaz, Kor, Sa, Tg, Fj, C, C*, 2010 *Kor, Kaz, HK, Fj, Sa, Tg*
IM Williams 1993 *W*
T Yagai 1930 *BCo*
T Yajima 1978 *Kor*, 1979 *E*
K Yamada 1963 *BCo*
T Yamaguchi 2004 *S, R, W*
Y Yamaguchi 1970 *Tha, BCo*, 1971 *E, E*, 1972 *HK*
E Yamamoto 2001 *Kor, W*, 2002 *Tg, Kor*
I Yamamoto 1973 *W*
M Yamamoto 2002 *Rus, Kor, Tai, Kor*, 2003 *Rus, AuA, AuA, Kor, E, E, Fj, US*, 2004 *Kor, Rus, C, S, R, W*, 2006 *Sa, JAB, Fj*, 2007 *HK, Fj, AuA, JAB, A*
M Yamamoto 2004 *C, S, W*, 2006 *HK, Kor*, 2007 *HK, Fj, Tg, AuA, Sa*
T Yamamoto 1988 *Kor*, 1989 *S*, 1990 *Fj*
R Yamamura 2002 *Tg, Tai, Tai*, 2003 *AuA, F*, 2004 *Kor, Rus, C, It, S, R, W*, 2005 *Ur, Ar, HK, Kor, R, C, I, I, Sp*, 2006 *Kor, Geo, It, Sa, JAB, Fj, HK, Kor*, 2007 *Kor, Tg, AuA, Sa, JAB, It, A, Fj, W, C*
R Yamanaka 2010 *AG*
T Yamaoka 2004 *It, S, R, W*, 2005 *Sp*, 2006 *AG, Kor, Geo, Tg, It, Sa, JAB, Fj*
H Yamashita 2009 *Kaz, HK, Kor, Sin, Sa, JAB, Tg, Fj*
O Yamashita 1974 *SL*
M Yasuda 1984 *F*
N Yasuda 2000 *Kor, I*
Y Yasue 2009 *HK, Kor*
T Yasui 1976 *S, E*, 1977 *S*, 1978 *F, Kor*, 1979 *HK, E*
K Yasumi 1986 *C*, 1987 *US, NZ*
Y Yatomi 2006 *Kor*, 2007 *HK, Fj, Tg, AuA, Sa, JAB, A, Fj*, 2009 *Kaz, Kor, JAB, C*
O Yatsuhashi 1996 *US, C*, 1998 *US, HK, HK, US, C, Ar, Tai, Kor*, 2000 *Kor, C*
A Yokoi 1969 *HK*, 1970 *Tha, BCo*, 1971 *E*, 1972 *HK*, 1973 *W, F*
A Yoshida 1995 *R, W, I, NZ*, 1996 *C, US, C, Kor*, 1997 *US, HK*, 1999 *Sa*, 2000 *Fj, US, Tg, Sa, Kor, C*
H Yoshida 2001 *Sa, C*, 2002 *Tg, Tai*, 2004 *R, W*, 2006 *AG, Kor, Geo, Tg, Sa, JAB, Fj, HK, Kor*
H Yoshida 2008 *Kor, AG, Kaz, M*, 2009 *Kaz, HK, Sin*
J Yoshida 1973 *W, F*
M Yoshida 1974 *NZU*, 1975 *A, A, W*, 1976 *BCo, S, E, It, Kor*, 1977 *S*, 1978 *F, Kor*
T Yoshida 2002 *Tg, Tai, Kor*, 2003 *E*
T Yoshida 2007 *Kor, Fj, Tg, Sa, It, Fj, W, C*, 2008 *Kor, Kaz, AuA, Tg, M, Sa, US*, 2009 *Kor, Sa, JAB, C, C*, 2010 *AG, HK, Sa*
Y Yoshida 1988 *Kor*, 1989 *S*, 1990 *Fj, Tg, Kor, Sa, US, Kor*, 1991 *US, US, C, HK, S, I, Z*, 1992 *HK*, 1993 *Ar, Ar, W*, 1994 *Fj, Fj, HK, Tai, M, Kor*, 1995 *Tg, Tg, R, I, NZ*, 1996 *HK*
K Yoshinaga 1986 *Kor*, 1987 *US, A, NZ*, 1990 *Sa*
K Yoshino 1973 *W*
T Yoshino 1985 *US, I, I, F, F*, 1986 *Kor*, 1987 *NZ*
H Yuhara 2010 *Kor, AG, HK, Fj*

NAMIBIA

NAMIBIA'S 2009–10 TEST RECORD

OPPONENTS	DATE	VENUE	RESULT
Portugal	7 Nov	A	**Won** 12–9
Tunisia	14 Nov	A	**Won** 18–13
Tunisia	28 Nov	H	**Won** 22–10
Russia	23 Jan	H	**Lost** 15–30
Romania	11 Jun	A	**Won** 21–17
Scotland A	15 June	N	**Won** 23–20
Georgia	20 Jun	N	**Won** 21–16

OUT TO PROVE A POINT

By Helge Schutz

Namibia may have qualified for a fourth successive Rugby World Cup by beating Tunisia 40–23 on aggregate in the Africa Cup final last November, but it is their success at the IRB Nations Cup seven months later which could be a watershed moment for rugby in the country.

No-one had mentioned Namibia as a title contender when they arrived in the Romanian capital Bucharest for the six-team tournament in June, perhaps not surprising after failing to win a match on their previous Nations Cup appearance in 2007.

However Namibia, under new coach Johan Diergaardt, were determined to make a point and rose to the occasion with some fantastic displays to claim the trophy for the first time in their history with an unbeaten record.

In the opening match, Namibia came from behind to beat hosts Romania 21–17 thanks to an extraordinary try by right wing Llewellyn Winkler, who sidestepped and dummied his way through a bewildered defence for the killer blow at the death.

Four days later defending champions Scotland A were overcome 23–20 with Namibia's exciting back-line catching the eye as scrum-half Eugene Jantjies pulled the strings. The outstanding Jantjies crossed for Namibia's opening try at the Stadionul National Arcul de Triumf, before hooker Shaun Esterhuizen and flanker Tinus du Plessis also touched down to put their side on course for another victory.

Scotland A were not about to relinquish their crown without a fight and closed to within three points with ten minutes remaining. Namibia, though, survived wave after wave of Scottish attacks to add another scalp to their efforts in Bucharest.

"This was a truly great game and I would like to thank the players for their commitment and hard work," Diergaardt said afterwards. "They've done a great job and showed courage and character and we would like also to thank God, because I think luck was again on our side. Though, I would say we fairly deserved to win the game, we also needed some luck too and it was ours."

The final match saw Namibia face Georgia and again have to come from behind after trailing the European Nations Cup champions 13–0 at half-time, thanks in no small part to the tremendous physicality and cast-iron defence of the Lelos. A couple of injuries to key players derailed Georgia a little and Namibia pounced with tries from captain Jacques Burger and full-back Chrysander Botha securing a 26–21 win.

"We tried to work hard as a team and the work ethic was better than theirs," said Burger, who then had to endure a nervous wait with his team-mates to learn Italy A's fate against Romania before Namibia were confirmed as Nations Cup champions.

"We knew from the beginning it would be hard and physical and we decided to keep playing. In the last 40 minutes we started to close the gap and capitalise on their mistakes and that was the game."

Diergaardt praised the team's character after the match. "This is not the end, it's just the beginning as this team has a lot of potential to become a great team. We are thankful for what we have."

The first signs of this potential had been evident the previous November, when Namibia beat Portugal 12–9 in the build up to their crucial Rugby World Cup 2011 qualifiers with Tunisia. In five previous encounters, the home side had always come out on top, a sequence Namibia brought to an end with an 18–13 win in Tunis. The increasingly influential Botha had got Namibia off to a dream start with a third-minute try, but they needed Emile Wessels' late penalty to make certain of the victory.

A fortnight later at the Hage Geingob Stadium in Windhoek, Namibia followed that historic win with a 22–10 triumph to secure their place at RWC 2011 as Africa 1 alongside defending champions South Africa, Fiji, Wales and Samoa in Pool D.

The victory was far from plain sailing as Tunisia led 10–9 at half-time, only for a Du Plessis try and the accurate boot of Wessels to seal a win which was greeted with elation from fans and players alike after the match. The relief was understandable, as it meant Tunisia, not Namibia, would enter the cross-continental play-off for another shot at qualification.

Coach John Williams, though, admitted he had expected nothing less than for Namibia to qualify for the World Cup in New Zealand. A fourth successive Rugby World Cup is an achievement for a country with only 800 rugby players, but Namibia are yet to win on the World Cup stage. Williams, though, was adamant that this spell can be broken in 2011.

"Anything is possible," he insisted. "As long as you believe that you can achieve it, I honestly believe that. Even when we went to the 2007 World Cup I believed and I told the players that we will beat Ireland. (Namibia eventually lost 32–17 after coming within 10 points of the Irish)."

That victory over Tunisia was, however, the last time that Williams led Namibia as he had announced his resignation before the match to join the South African rugby franchise the Falcons. His assistant Diergaardt took over at the helm and some of Williams' belief was evident among the squad during the Nations Cup.

Next on the horizon for Namibia is the Africa Cup and a European tour with matches against Portugal and Spain, both vital elements of Diegaardt's preparations for RWC 2011.

Another key development tool was Namibia's participation in South Africa's Vodacom Cup competition for the first time in eight years, following successful negotiations between the Namibia Rugby Union (NRU) and the South African Rugby Union.

The NRU used the competition to groom locally based players in preparation for the World Cup, and although the 'Welwitschias' finished second last in their group after only winning one match, they picked up invaluable experience against tough opposition.

They started off with three successive Vodacom Cup defeats, before hitting top gear with a great 66–35 victory against the Falcons in Windhoek in March. Left wing Heini Bock scored three tries while full-back Botha had a haul of 19 points, consisting of a try and seven conversions.

The Welwitschias lost their final group matches, 58–34 to the Blue Bulls on April 10 and 51–20 to the Golden Lions a week later. Botha, though, finished the competition as the third highest point scorer with a total of 80 points, at an average of 11.42 points per match, while he was joint sixth on the try-scoring list with five.

The next generation of Namibian players, meanwhile, also suffered disappointment after missing out on qualification for the IRB Junior World Rugby Trophy 2011 following a 25–19 loss to Zimbabwe in the final of the African qualifier in Abidjan, Ivory Coast, on 30 July.

On the domestic front, Wanderers returned to the summit of Namibian club rugby after beating defending champions Rehoboth 35–22 to win the MTC Premier League rugby trophy on September 18.

In a titanic battle at the Hage Geingob Stadium, the match was still wide open when Rehoboth held a 22–21 lead midway through the second half. However, Wanderers attacked relentlessly and tries by flanker Alberto Engelbrecht and No 8 PJ van Lill in the final 10 minutes saw them ease to victory.

The win ended a barren spell for the former powerhouses of Namibian club rugby, who last won the Premier League title in 2006.

The NRU also expanded its efforts to develop women's rugby during 2010, having introduced the sport on a trial basis the year before. A women's league was introduced for the first time with five teams competing throughout the country, Reho Pandas beating Western Suburbs 19–10 in the final.

NAMIBIA INTERNATIONAL STATISTICS

MATCH RECORDS UP TO 29TH OCTOBER 2010

WINNING MARGIN

Date	Opponent	Result	Winning Margin
15/06/2002	Madagascar	112–0	**112**
21/04/1990	Portugal	86–9	**77**
27/05/2006	Kenya	82–12	**70**
26/05/2007	Zambia	80–10	**70**

MOST POINTS IN A MATCH
BY THE TEAM

Date	Opponent	Result	Pts.
15/06/2002	Madagascar	112–0	**112**
21/04/1990	Portugal	86–9	**86**
31/08/2003	Uganda	82–13	**82**
27/05/2006	Kenya	82–12	**82**

MOST TRIES IN A MATCH
BY THE TEAM

Date	Opponent	Result	Tries
15/06/2002	Madagascar	112–0	**18**
21/04/1990	Portugal	86–9	**16**
17/10/1999	Germany	79–13	**13**

MOST CONVERSIONS IN A MATCH
BY THE TEAM

Date	Opponent	Result	Cons
15/06/2002	Madagascar	112–0	**11**
21/04/1990	Portugal	86–9	**11**
31/08/2003	Uganda	82–13	**11**
27/05/2006	Kenya	82–12	**11**

MOST PENALTIES IN A MATCH
BY THE TEAM

Date	Opponent	Result	Pens
22/06/1991	Italy	33–19	**5**
23/01/1998	Portugal	36–19	**5**
30/06/1990	France A	20–25	**5**
28/11/2009	Tunisia	22–10	**5**

MOST DROP GOALS IN A MATCH
BY THE TEAM

1 on 7 Occasions

MOST POINTS IN A MATCH
BY A PLAYER

Date	Player	Opponent	Pts.
06/07/1993	Jaco Coetzee	Kenya	**35**
26/05/2007	Justinus van der Westhuizen	Zambia	**33**
27/06/2009	Chrysander Botha	Cote D'Ivoire	**29**
21/04/1990	Moolman Olivier	Portugal	**26**
15/06/2002	Riaan van Wyk	Madagascar	**25**

MOST TRIES IN A MATCH
BY A PLAYER

Date	Player	Opponent	Tries
21/04/1990	Gerhard Mans	Portugal	**6**
15/06/2002	Riaan van Wyk	Madagascar	**5**
16/05/1992	Eden Meyer	Zimbabwe	**4**
16/08/2003	Melrick Africa	Kenya	**4**

MOST CONVERSIONS IN A MATCH

BY A PLAYER

Date	Player	Opponent	Cons
21/04/1990	Moolman Olivier	Portugal	11
27/05/2006	Morne Schreuder	Kenya	11
26/05/2007	Justinus van der Westhuizen	Zambia	9
31/08/2003	Rudi van Vuuren	Uganda	8
04/07/1993	Jaco Coetzee	Arabian Gulf	8

MOST PENALTIES IN A MATCH

BY A PLAYER

Date	Player	Opponent	Pens
22/06/1991	Jaco Coetzee	Italy	5
23/01/1998	Rudi van Vuuren	Portugal	5
30/06/1990	Shaun McCulley	France A	5
28/11/2009	Emile Wessels	Tunisia	5

MOST DROP GOALS IN A MATCH

BY A PLAYER

1 on 7 Occasions

MOST CAPPED PLAYERS

Name	Caps
Herman Lindvelt	32
Hugo Horn	31
Hugo Horn	28
Casper Derks	28

LEADING TRY SCORERS

Name	Tries
Gerhard Mans	27
Eden Meyer	21
Melrick Africa	12

LEADING CONVERSIONS SCORERS

Name	Cons
Jaco Coetzee	84
Morne Schreuder	36
Rudi van Vuuren	26
Emile Wessels	14

LEADING PENALTY SCORERS

Name	Pens
Jaco Coetzee	46
Emile Wessels	21
Morne Schreuder	18
Rudi van Vuuren	14

LEADING DROP GOAL SCORERS

Name	DGs
Jaco Coetzee	3

LEADING POINTS SCORERS

Name	Points.
Jaco Coetzee	344
Morne Schreuder	146
Gerhard Mans	118
Rudi van Vuuren	109
Eden Meyer	98

NAMIBIA INTERNATIONAL PLAYERS

UP TO 29TH OCTOBER 2010

Note: Years given for International Championship matches are for second half of season; eg 1972 means season 1971–72. Years for all other matches refer to the actual year of the match.

MJ Africa 2003 *Sa, Ken, Uga, Ar, I, A,* 2005 *Mad, Mor,* 2006 *Ken, Tun, Ken, Tun, Mor, Mor,* 2007 *Za, Geo, ArA, R, Uga, SA, I, F, Ar, Geo*
W Alberts 1991 *Sp, Pt, It, It, Z, Z, I, I, Z, Z, Z,* 1995 *Z,* 1996 *Z, Z*
H Amakali 2005 *Mad*
J Augustyn 1991 *Z,* 1998 *Iv, Mor, Z*
RS Bardenhorst 2007 *Geo, ArA, R*
J Barnard 1990 *Z, Pt, W, W, F, F,* 1991 *Sp, Pt, It, It, Z, Z, I, I, Z, Z, Z,* 1992 *Z, Z*
D Beukes 2000 *Z, Ur,* 2001 *Z, Z*
E Beukes 1990 *Z, F, WGe*
J Beukes 1994 *Z, Mor,* 1995 *Z*
AJ Blaauw 1996 *Z, Z,* 1997 *Tg, Z,* 1998 *Pt, Tun, Z, Iv, Mor, Z,* 1999 *Z, Fj, F, C, Ger,* 2000 *SA23, Z, SA23, Z, Ur,* 2001 *SA23, SA23, It,* 2003 *Ar, I, A, R,* 2004 *Mor*
J Bock 2005 *Mad, Mor,* 2009 *Iv, Iv,* 2010 *R, S, Geo*
JH Bock 2005 *Mad, Mor,* 2006 *Ken, Tun, Ken, Tun, Mor, Mor,* 2007 *Za, ArA, R, SA, I, F, Ar, Geo,* 2009 *Pt, Tun,* 2010 *R, Geo*
J Booysen 2003 *Sa, Ken, Ar, A,* 2007 *Uga*
M Booysen 1993 *W, AG, Z,* 1994 *Rus, Z, HK,* 1996 *Z, Z*
LW Botes 2006 *Ken, Mor,* 2007 *Za, Geo, ArA, R, Uga, SA, F*
CA Botha 2008 *Z,* 2009 *Iv, Iv, Pt, Tun, Tun,* 2010 *Rus, R, S, Geo*
HP Botha 2000 *SA23, Z, SA23, Z, Ur*
H Breedt 1997 *Z,* 1998 *Tun, Z*
H Brink 1992 *Z, Z,* 1993 *W, Ken, Z,* 1994 *Rus, Z, Iv, Mor, HK*
J Britz 1996 *Z*
E Buitenbag 2010 *Rus*
B Buitendag 1990 *W, W, F, F, WGe, EngB,* 1991 *Sp, Pt, It, It, Z, Z, I, I, Z, Z, Z,* 1992 *Z, Z,* 1993 *W, AG, Ken, Z*
J Burger 2004 *Za, Ken, Z, Mor,* 2006 *Tun, Tun, Mor, Mor,* 2007 *Za, Geo, ArA, R, SA, I, F, Ar, Geo,* 2008 *Z,* 2009 *Iv, Iv, Pt, Tun, Tun,* 2010 *R, S, Geo*
B Calitz 1995 *Z*
C Campbell 2008 *Z*
DJ Coetzee 1990 *Pt, W, F, F, WGe,* 1991 *Sp, Pt, It, It, Z, Z, I, I, Z, Z, Z,* 1992 *Z, Z,* 1993 *W, AG, Ken, Z,* 1994 *Z, Iv, Mor, HK,* 1995 *Z, Z*
JC Coetzee 1990 *W*
M Couw 2006 *Ken*
B Cronjé 1994 *Rus*
J Dames 1997 *Z,* 1998 *Tun, Z*
D de Beer 2000 *Z*
S de Beer 1995 *Z,* 1997 *Tg, Z,* 1998 *Tun, Z, Iv, Mor, Z,* 1999 *Ger*
AD de Klerk 2009 *Iv, Iv*
CJ De Koe 2010 *Geo*
DP de la Harpe 2010 *Rus, R, S, Geo*
S de la Harpe 2010 *S*
H de Waal 1990 *Z, Pt*
N de Wet 2000 *Ur*
R Dedig 2004 *Mor, Za, Ken, Z, Mor*
CJH Derks 1990 *Z, Pt, W, W, F, F, WGe, EngB,* 1991 *Sp, Pt, It, It, Z, Z, I, I, Z, Z, Z,* 1992 *Z, Z,* 1993 *W, AG, Z,* 1994 *Rus, Z, Iv, Mor, HK*
J Deysel 1990 *Z, Pt, W, W, EngB,* 1991 *Sp, Pt, It, It, Z, Z, I, I, Z, Z, Z,* 1992 *Z*
V Dreyer 2002 *Z,* 2003 *Ar, I*
J Drotsky 2006 *Ken,* 2008 *Sen*
I du Plessis 2005 *Mor,* 2009 *Tun*
M du Plessis 2001 *Z,* 2005 *Mor*
N du Plessis 1993 *Ken,* 1994 *Rus,* 1995 *Z*
O Du Plessis 2008 *Sen*
T du Plessis 2006 *Ken, Tun, Mor, Mor,* 2007 *Geo, R, Uga, SA, I, F, Ar, Geo,* 2008 *Sen, Z,* 2009 *Iv, Iv, Pt, Tun, Tun,* 2010 *R, S, Geo*
P du Plooy 1992 *Z, Z,* 1994 *Z, Mor, HK*
S du Rand 2007 *Geo, ArA, R, Uga*
JA du Toit 2007 *Za, Geo, ArA, R, Uga, SA, I, F, Geo,* 2008 *Sen, Z,* 2009 *Pt, Tun, Tun,* 2010 *Rus, R, S, Geo*
N du Toit 2002 *Tun,* 2003 *Sa, Ar, I, A, R*
V du Toit 1990 *Pt, W, W, F*
JH Duvenhage 2000 *SA23, Z, SA23, Z,* 2001 *SA23, SA23, It, Z, Z,* 2002 *Mad,* 2003 *Sa, Uga, Ar, I, R,* 2007 *Za, ArA, R, Uga*
A Engelbrecht 2000 *SA23, Z*
J Engelbrecht 1990 *WGe,* 1994 *Rus, Z, Iv, Mor, HK,* 1995 *Z, Z*
N Engelbrecht 1996 *Z*
H Engels 1990 *F, WGe*
E Erasmus 1997 *Tg, Z*
G Esterhuizen 2008 *Sen, Z*
N Esterhuizen 2006 *Ken, Tun, Mor,* 2007 *Za, Geo, ArA, R, Uga, SA, I, F, Ar, Geo,* 2008 *Z,* 2009 *Iv, Iv, Pt, Tun, Tun,* 2010 *Rus, R, S, Geo*
SF Esterhuizen 2008 *Z,* 2009 *Iv, Iv, Pt, Tun, Tun,* 2010 *Rus, R, S, Geo*
D Farmer 1997 *Tg, Z,* 1998 *Pt, Iv, Mor, Z,* 1999 *Z, Fj, Ger*
F Fisch 1999 *Z, Ger*
TR Forbes 2010 *Rus*
S Furter 1999 *Z, Fj, F, C, Ger,* 2001 *SA23, SA23, It,* 2002 *Mad, Z, Tun, Tun,* 2003 *Sa, Ken, Uga, Ar, I, A, R,* 2004 *Mor,* 2006 *Ken, Tun, Ken*
E Gaoab 2005 *Mad, Mor*
I Gaya 2004 *Za, Ken*
J Genis 2000 *SA23, Z, SA23, Z, Ur,* 2001 *Z*
N Genis 2006 *Mor*
R Gentz 2001 *It*
R Glundeung 2006 *Ken*
CJ Goosen 1991 *Sp, Pt, It, It,* 1993 *W*
D Gouws 1997 *Z,* 2000 *SA23, Z, SA23, Z, Ur,* 2001 *SA23, SA23, It, Z, Z*
T Gouws 2003 *Ken, Uga,* 2004 *Za, Ken,* 2006 *Ken, Tun*
A Graham 2001 *SA23, SA23, It, Z, Z,* 2002 *Mad, Tun,* 2003 *Ken, Uga, I,* 2004 *Mor*
A Greeff 1997 *Tg*
D Grobelaar 2008 *Z*
DP Grobler 2001 *Z,* 2002 *Mad, Tun, Tun,* 2003 *Sa, Ken, Uga, Ar, I, A, R,* 2004 *Mor, Za, Ken, Z, Mor,* 2006 *Ken, Tun, Ken,* 2007 *Za, Geo, ArA, R, SA, Ar*
HJ Grobler 1990 *Z, Pt, W, W, F, F, WGe, EngB,* 1991 *Sp, Pt, It, It, Z, Z, I, I, Z, Z, Z,* 1992 *Z, Z*
T Grünewald 1990 *Z*
D Grunschloss 2003 *A, R*
F Hartung 1996 *Z, Z*
RJ Herridge 2009 *Pt, Tun, Tun*
L Holtzhausen 1997 *Tg, Z,* 1998 *Pt, Tun, Z, Iv, Mor, Z,* 1999 *Ger*
F Horn 2005 *Mad, Mor,* 2006 *Ken*
H Horn 1997 *Tg,* 1998 *Pt, Iv, Mor, Z,* 1999 *Z, Fj, F, C, Ger,* 2001 *SA23, SA23, It,* 2002 *Mad, Z, Tun,* 2003 *Sa,* 2007 *Za, Geo, R, Uga, SA, I, F, Ar, Geo,* 2008 *Sen, Z,* 2009 *Iv, Iv, Tun, Tun,* 2010 *Rus*
K Horn 1997 *Tg,* 1998 *Pt*
Q Hough 1995 *Z, Z,* 1997 *Z,* 1998 *Pt, Tun, Z, Iv, Mor, Z,* 1999 *Z, Fj, F, C*

D Husselman 1993 *AG*, 1994 *Z*, *Mor*, 2002 *Mad*, *Z*, *Tun*, 2003 *Sa*, *Ar*, *I*, *A*
JJ Husselman 2004 *Za*, *Ken*
E Isaacs 1993 *Ken*, 1994 *Iv*
P Isaacs 2000 *SA23*, *Z*, *SA23*, *Z*, *Ur*, 2001 *Z*, *Z*, 2003 *A*, 2005 *Mad*, *Mor*
E Izaacs 1998 *Pt*, 1999 *Z*, *Ger*, 2000 *Z*, *SA23*, *Z*, *Ur*, 2001 *SA23*, *SA23*, *It*, *Z*, *Z*, 2002 *Mad*, *Z*, *Tun*, *Tun*, 2003 *Sa*, *Ken*, *Ar*, *A*, *R*
M Jacobs 1999 *Z*, *Fj*, *F*, *Ger*
E Jansen 2006 *Ken*
EA Jantjies 2006 *Ken*, *Tun*, *Ken*, *Tun*, 2007 *Za*, *Geo*, *ArA*, *R*, *Uga*, *SA*, *I*, *F*, *Ar*, *Geo*, 2008 *Sen*, *Z*, 2009 *Iv*, *Iv*, *Pt*, *Tun*, *Tun*, 2010 *Rus*, *R*, *S*, *Geo*
R Jantjies 1994 *HK*, 1995 *Z*, *Z*, 1996 *Z*, 1997 *Z*, 1998 *Pt*, *Tun*, *Iv*, *Mor*, *Z*, 1999 *Z*, *Fj*, *F*, *C*, 2000 *SA23*, *Z*, *SA23*, *Z*
M Jeary 2003 *Uga*, 2004 *Ken*, *Z*, *Mor*
R Jeary 2000 *SA23*, *SA23*, *Z*, *Ur*
D Jeffrey 1990 *F*
J Jenkins 2002 *Mad*, *Tun*, 2003 *Ken*
D Kamonga 2004 *Mor*, *Za*, *Ken*, *Z*, *Mor*, 2007 *Uga*, *Geo*
M Kapitako 2000 *Z*, *SA23*, *Z*, 2001 *It*, *Z*, *Z*, 2003 *Uga*, 2004 *Za*, 2006 *Tun*
M Katjiuanjo 2005 *Mad*, *Mor*
M Kazombiaze 2006 *Ken*, *Tun*
U Kazombiaze 2006 *Ken*, *Tun*, *Mor*, *Mor*, 2007 *Za*, *ArA*, *Uga*, *SA*, *I*, *F*, *Ar*, *Geo*, 2008 *Sen*, *Z*, 2009 *Iv*, *Iv*, *Pt*, *Tun*, *Tun*, 2010 *Rus*, *S*, *Geo*
DPW Koen 2006 *Tun*
H Koll 2009 *Pt*, *Tun*, 2010 *Rus*, *R*, *S*, *Geo*
A Kotze 1991 *Sp*, *Z*, *Z*, *I*, *I*, 1993 *W*, *AG*, *Z*
D Kotze 1993 *W*, *AG*, *Ken*, *Z*, 1994 *Rus*, *HK*
J Kotze 1995 *Z*, *Z*, 1996 *Z*, *Z*, 2000 *SA23*, *Z*, *SA23*, *Z*, 2001 *SA23*, *SA23*, *It*, *Z*, *Z*, 2002 *Mad*, *Z*, *Tun*, *Tun*, 2004 *Za*, *Ken*, *Z*, *Mor*
P Kotze 2001 *SA23*, *SA23*, *It*
P Kotze 1996 *Z*
L Kotzee 2008 *Z*
JL Kruger 2001 *SA23*, *It*, *Z*, *Z*
R Kruger 2003 *Ken*, *Uga*, 2005 *Mad*, *Mor*
R Kruger 2004 *Mor*, *Za*, *Ken*, *Mor*
SO Lambert 2000 *SA23*, *Z*, *Ur*, 2001 *SA23*, *SA23*, *It*, *Z*, *Z*, 2003 *Ken*, *Uga*, 2004 *Mor*, 2005 *Mad*, 2006 *Ken*, *Tun*, *Ken*
B Langenhoven 2007 *SA*, *I*, *F*, *Ar*, *Geo*, 2008 *Sen*, *Z*, 2009 *Pt*, *Tun*, *Tun*, 2010 *Rus*
G Lensing 2002 *Mad*, *Z*, *Tun*, *Tun*, 2003 *Sa*, *Ar*, *I*, *A*, *R*, 2004 *Mor*, 2006 *Ken*, *Mor*, *Mor*, 2007 *ArA*, *R*, *SA*, *I*, *F*, *Ar*, *Geo*, 2009 *Iv*, *Iv*, *Tun*, *Tun*
C Lesch 2005 *Mad*, *Mor*
HD Lindvelt 1998 *Iv*, *Z*, 1999 *F*, *C*, *Ger*, 2001 *It*, *Z*, *Z*, 2002 *Mad*, *Z*, *Tun*, *Tun*, 2003 *Sa*, *Ken*, *Uga*, *Ar*, *I*, *A*, 2004 *Mor*, *Za*, *Ken*, *Z*, *Mor*, 2006 *Ken*, *Tun*, *Mor*, *Mor*, 2007 *Za*, *Geo*, *ArA*, *SA*, *F*, *Ar*
J Lombaard 1996 *Z*
H Loots 1990 *Z*
J Losper 2005 *Mor*
S Losper 1990 *Z*, *Pt*, *W*, *W*, *F*, *F*, *WGe*, *EngB*, 1991 *Sp*, *Pt*, *It*, *It*, *Z*, *Z*, *I*, *I*, *Z*, *Z*, *Z*
TC Losper 2007 *Za*, *Geo*, *ArA*, *R*, *Uga*, *SA*, *I*, *F*, 2008 *Sen*
W Lötter 1990 *Z*
RC Loubser 1999 *F*, 2005 *Mad*, *Mor*
O Louw 1993 *Ken*, *Z*, 1994 *Z*, *Iv*, 1996 *Z*
W Ludwig 2001 *SA23*
M MacKenzie 2004 *Mor*, 2006 *Ken*, *Tun*, 2007 *Uga*, *I*, *F*, *Ar*
B Malgas 1991 *Z*, *Z*, *Z*, 1993 *W*, *AG*, *Ken*, *Z*, 1994 *Rus*, *Z*, *Iv*, *Mor*, *HK*, 1995 *Z*, *Z*, 1996 *Z*
G Mans 1990 *Z*, *Pt*, *W*, *W*, *F*, *EngB*, 1991 *Sp*, *Pt*, *It*, *It*, *Z*, *Z*, *I*, *I*, *Z*, *Z*, *Z*, 1992 *Z*, *Z*, 1993 *W*, *AG*, *Ken*, *Z*, 1994 *Rus*, *Z*, *Iv*, *Mor*, *HK*
M Marais 1992 *Z*, 1993 *W*, *AG*, *Z*
W Maritz 1990 *Z*, *EngB*, 1991 *Z*, *Z*, *I*, *I*, *Z*, *Z*, *Z*
S McCulley 1990 *W*, *W*, *F*, *WGe*
E Meyer 1991 *Sp*, *Pt*, *It*, *It*, *Z*, *Z*, *I*, *I*, *Z*, *Z*, *Z*, 1992 *Z*, *Z*, 1993 *W*, 1994 *Z*, *Iv*, *Mor*, *HK*, 1995 *Z*, *Z*, 1996 *Z*
H Meyer 2004 *Za*, *Ken*, *Z*, *Mor*
JM Meyer 2003 *Ken*, *Uga*, *Ar*, *I*, *R*, 2006 *Ken*, *Tun*, *Tun*, *Mor*, *Mor*, 2007 *Uga*, *SA*, *I*, *F*, *Ar*, *Geo*
P Meyer 2005 *Mad*
DA Mouton 1999 *Z*, *Fj*, *Ger*, 2000 *SA23*, *Z*, *SA23*, *Z*, *Ur*, 2001 *SA23*, 2002 *Mad*, *Z*, *Tun*, 2003 *Sa*, *Ken*, *Uga*, *Ar*, *I*, *A*, *R*, 2004 *Mor*, 2005 *Mad*, *Mor*, 2006 *Tun*, *Ken*, *Tun*, *Mor*, 2007 *Ar*, 2008 *Sen*
H Mouton 2000 *Z*
P Mouton 2005 *Mad*, *Mor*
H Neethling 1993 *Ken*
G Nel 2006 *Mor*, *Mor*
S Nell 2000 *SA23*, *Z*, *SA23*, *Z*
J Nienaber 1998 *Pt*, *Tun*, *Z*, *Mor*, *Z*
J Nieuwenhuis 2007 *Za*, *Geo*, *ArA*, *R*, *Uga*, *SA*, *I*, *F*, *Geo*, 2008 *Sen*, *Z*, 2009 *Iv*, *Iv*, *Tun*, *Tun*, 2010 *R*, *S*, *Geo*
E O'Callaghan 2010 *R*, *S*, *Geo*
J Olivier 1999 *Z*, *Fj*, *Ger*, 2000 *SA23*, *Z*, *Z*, *Ur*
M Olivier 1990 *Pt*, *F*, *EngB*
LT Oosthuizen 1990 *Z*, *Pt*, *W*, *W*, *F*, *F*, *WGe*, *EngB*
J Opperman 1999 *Z*, *Fj*, *F*, *C*, *Ger*
T Opperman 2002 *Mad*, *Z*
WJ Otto 1993 *AG*, *Z*, 1994 *Rus*
R Pedro 1998 *Z*, 1999 *Ger*, 2000 *Ur*, 2001 *SA23*, *SA23*, *It*, *Z*, *Z*, 2003 *Sa*, *Ken*, *Uga*, *Ar*, *I*, *A*, *R*, 2004 *Mor*
D Philander 2008 *Sen*, 2009 *Iv*, *Iv*, *Pt*, *Tun*, *Tun*, 2010 *Rus*
F Pienaar 2006 *Ken*
D Pieters 2008 *Sen*
L Plaath 2001 *SA23*, *SA23*, *It*, *Z*, *Z*
CJ Powell 2001 *SA23*, *It*, *Z*, *Z*, 2002 *Mad*, *Z*, *Tun*, *Tun*, 2003 *Sa*, *Ken*, *Uga*, *Ar*, *I*, *R*, 2004 *Mor*, *Ken*, *Z*, *Mor*, 2006 *Ken*, *Tun*, *Tun*, *Mor*, *Mor*, 2007 *Za*, *Geo*, *ArA*, *R*, *Ar*, *Geo*
JH Redelinghuys 2006 *Ken*, *Tun*, *Mor*, 2007 *Za*, *Geo*, *R*, *Uga*, *SA*, *I*, *F*, *Ar*, *Geo*, 2008 *Sen*, *Z*, 2009 *Iv*, *Iv*, *Pt*, *Tun*, 2010 *Rus*, *R*, *S*, *Geo*
C Redlinghaus 2001 *SA23*, *SA23*, *It*
H Reinders 1996 *Z*
G Rich 1993 *W*
C Roets 1995 *Z*
P Rossouw 2004 *Za*, *Ken*, *Z*, *Mor*, 2005 *Mad*, *Mor*, 2006 *Mor*, *Mor*, 2007 *Za*, *Geo*, *ArA*, *R*
A Samuelson 1995 *Z*, 1996 *Z*, *Z*, 1997 *Tg*, *Z*, 1998 *Pt*, *Tun*, *Z*, *Iv*, *Mor*, *Z*, 1999 *Z*, *Fj*, *F*, *C*, *Ger*
M Schreuder 2002 *Mad*, *Z*, *Tun*, *Tun*, 2003 *Sa*, *Ken*, *Uga*, *I*, *A*, *R*, 2004 *Mor*, *Za*, *Ken*, *Z*, *Mor*, 2006 *Ken*, *Ken*, 2007 *Ar*, *Geo*
C Schumacher 1995 *Z*, 1997 *Z*
JH Senekal 1998 *Iv*, *Mor*, *Z*, 1999 *Z*, *Fj*, *F*, *C*, *Ger*, 2002 *Mad*, *Z*, 2003 *Sa*, *Ken*, *Uga*, *Ar*, *I*, *A*, *R*, 2005 *Mad*, 2006 *Ken*, *Mor*, *Mor*, 2007 *Geo*, *ArA*, *R*, *Uga*, *I*, *Ar*, *Geo*
A Skinner 1990 *Z*, *Pt*, *W*, *W*, *F*, *F*, *WGe*, *EngB*
G Smit 1990 *F*
E Smith 1998 *Tun*, *Iv*, *Mor*, *Z*, 1999 *Fj*, *F*, *C*, 2002 *Mad*
P Smith 1993 *Ken*, 1994 *Iv*, 1995 *Z*, *Z*
S Smith 1990 *Pt*, *W*, *W*, *F*, *EngB*, 1992 *Z*, *Z*, 1993 *W*, *AG*, *Ken*, *Z*, 1994 *Rus*, *Z*, *Iv*, *Mor*, *HK*, 1996 *Z*
W Smith 2002 *Mad*, *Z*, *Tun*
D Snyders 2003 *Uga*, 2005 *Mad*
H Snyman 1990 *F*, *F*, 1991 *Sp*, *Pt*, *It*, *It*, *Z*, *Z*, *I*, *I*, *Z*, *Z*, *Z*, 1992 *Z*, *Z*, 1993 *W*, *AG*, *Ken*, *Z*, 1994 *Z*, *Iv*, *Mor*, *HK*, 1995 *Z*, *Z*, 1996 *Z*, *Z*
M Snyman 1994 *Rus*, *Z*, *Iv*, *Mor*, *HK*
D Spangenberg 2005 *Mad*, *Mor*
A Steenkamp 1994 *Iv*, *Mor*
C Steenkamp 2007 *Uga*
T Steenkamp 1992 *Z*, *Z*, 1993 *Ken*, 1994 *Rus*, *Iv*, 1995 *Z*, 1996 *Z*, 1998 *Pt*, *Tun*, *Z*
P Steyn 1996 *Z*, *Z*, 1997 *Tg*, *Z*, 1998 *Pt*, *Tun*, *Z*, *Iv*, *Mor*, 1999 *Z*, *Fj*, *F*, *C*
A Stoop 1990 *Z*, *Pt*, *W*, *EngB*, 1991 *Sp*, *Pt*, *It*, *It*, *Z*, *I*, *I*, *Z*
L Stoop 1994 *Iv*
G Suze 2005 *Mad*
N Swanepoel 2003 *Ken*, *Ar*, *I*, *A*, *R*, 2004 *Mor*, *Za*, *Ken*, *Z*, *Mor*
H Swart 1995 *Z*, 1996 *Z*, 1997 *Tg*, *Z*, 1998 *Pt*, *Tun*, *Z*
JL Swart 1990 *F*, *WGe*
BM Swartz 1990 *W*, *W*, *F*, *F*, *WGe*, *EngB*
R Theart 1998 *Pt*
J Theron 1998 *Iv*, *Mor*, *Z*, 1999 *Fj*, *F*, *C*, *Ger*, 2004 *Mor*
RHR Thompson 2004 *Za*, *Ken*, *Mor*, 2005 *Mad*, 2006 *Ken*, *Tun*, *Ken*, *Tun*, *Mor*, *Mor*
D Tredoux 2001 *Z*
H Undveld 2006 *Ken*
L van Coller 1993 *AG*, *Ken*, 1994 *Rus*, *Iv*
GE van der Berg 2005 *Mor*, 2006 *Ken*, *Tun*, *Tun*, *Mor*
L van der Linde 2006 *Tun*

A van der Merwe 1990 *Pt, W, W, F, F, WGe, EngB*, 1991 *Sp, Pt, It, It, Z, Z, I, I, Z, Z, Z*, 1992 *Z, Z*
D van der Merwe 1990 *WGe*
S van der Merwe 1997 *Tg, Z*, 1998 *Iv, Mor, Z*, 1999 *Z, Fj, F, C*, 2002 *Z, Tun, Tun*, 2003 *Sa, Ken, Ar, I, A, R*, 2004 *Za, Ken, Z, Mor*, 2006 *Tun, Mor*
J van der Westhuizen 2007 *Za, Geo*
L van Dyk 1998 *Tun, Z, Iv, Mor, Z*, 1999 *Fj, F, C, Ger*, 2002 *Mad*
JA van Lill 2002 *Mad, Tun, Tun*, 2003 *Sa, Ar, I, A, R*, 2004 *Mor*, 2006 *Tun*, 2007 *Za, ArA*
PJ van Lill 2006 *Ken*, 2008 *Sen, Z*, 2009 *Iv, Pt, Tun, Tun*, 2010 *Rus, R, S, Geo*
RE van Neel 2010 *Rus*
F van Rensburg 1995 *Z*, 1996 *Z, Z*, 1997 *Tg*, 1998 *Tun, Z*, 1999 *Z, Fj, F, C, Ger*, 2000 *Z*, 2001 *It, Z, Z*
SJ van Rensburg 1998 *Z, Iv, Mor, Z*, 1999 *Z, Fj, F, Ger*, 2000 *Z, Ur*
S van Rooi 2003 *Uga, A*, 2004 *Mor*, 2005 *Mor*
A van Rooyen 1991 *Sp, Pt, It, It, I*, 1992 *Z, Z*
M van Rooyen 1996 *Z*, 1998 *Pt, Tun, Z, Mor, Z*, 1999 *Z, F, C*
C van Schalkwyk 1993 *AG, Z*
A Van Tonder 1995 *Z*
CJ van Tonder 2002 *Tun*, 2003 *Sa, Ken, Uga, I, A, R*, 2004 *Mor, Za, Ken, Z, Mor*, 2006 *Ken, Ken*, 2007 *Za*
JH van Tonder 2004 *Mor, Ken, Z, Mor*, 2006 *Ken, Tun*, 2007 *Uga, SA, I, F, Ar, Geo*, 2008 *Z*, 2009 *Iv, Iv, Pt, Tun*
N van Vuuren 1993 *AG*
RJ van Vuuren 1997 *Tg, Z*, 1998 *Pt, Tun, Z*, 1999 *Z, Ger*, 2000 *SA23, Z, SA23, Z, Ur*, 2002 *Mad, Z*, 2003 *Ken, Uga, R*
A van Wyk 1993 *W, Ken*, 1994 *Iv, HK*
G van Wyk 1999 *Z, Fj, F, C*, 2000 *Z, SA23, Z, Ur*, 2001 *It*
L van Wyk 2004 *Mor*
M van Wyk 2009 *Iv, Iv, Pt*, 2010 *Rus, S, Geo*
R van Wyk 2002 *Mad, Z, Tun, Tun*, 2003 *Sa*, 2004 *Mor, Za, Ken, Z, Mor*
R van Wyk 2004 *Za, Ken, Z, Mor*
J van Zyl 2008 *Sen*
R van Zyl 1997 *Tg, Z*, 1998 *Tun, Z, Iv, Mor, Z*
WP van Zyl 2007 *SA, I, F, Ar, Geo*, 2008 *Z*, 2009 *Iv, Iv, Pt, Tun, Tun*, 2010 *R, S, Geo*
T Venter 2003 *Uga*, 2004 *Mor*, 2008 *Z*, 2009 *Iv, Iv, Pt, Tun, Tun*, 2010 *Rus*
D Vermaak 1998 *Z*
JJ Vermaak 1990 *Pt*, 1994 *Rus*, 1996 *Z*
A Vermeulen 2010 *Rus*
B Vermeulen 1995 *Z*
D Vermeulen 1996 *Z, Z*, 1997 *Tg, Z*, 1998 *Pt*
G Vermeulen 1990 *EngB*, 1991 *Z*
M Visser 2007 *Za, Geo, ArA, R, Uga, SA, Ar, Geo*, 2009 *Iv, Iv, Pt, Tun, Tun*, 2010 *Rus, R, S, Geo*
P von Wielligh 1991 *It, Z*, 1992 *Z*, 1993 *AG, Z*, 1994 *Iv, Mor*, 1995 *Z*, 1996 *Z*
B Walters 2009 *Pt*
G Walters 2008 *Z*, 2009 *Iv*, 2010 *R, Geo*
W Wentzel 1991 *Sp, Z, Z*
E Wessels 2002 *Tun, Tun*, 2003 *Sa, Ar, I, A, R*, 2006 *Tun, Mor, Mor*, 2007 *SA, I, F*, 2009 *Iv, Pt, Tun, Tun*, 2010 *Rus*
L Winkler 2008 *Z*, 2009 *Iv, Iv*, 2010 *Rus, R, S, Geo*
RC Witbooi 2004 *Za, Z*, 2005 *Mor*, 2006 *Ken, Tun, Ken*, 2007 *Za, Geo, R, Uga, I, F, Geo*, 2008 *Sen*
J Wohler 2005 *Mad, Mor*
J Zaayman 1997 *Tg, Z*, 1998 *Pt, Tun, Z, Iv, Mor, Z*, 1999 *Z, Fj, F, C, Ger*

Dave Rogers/Getty Images

Namibia will be back at the Rugby World Cup in 2011.

NEW ZEALAND

NEW ZEALAND'S 2009–10 TEST RECORD

OPPONENTS	DATE	VENUE	RESULT
Australia	31 Oct	N	**Won** 32–19
Wales	7 Nov	A	**Won** 19–12
Italy	14 Nov	A	**Won** 20–6
England	21 Nov	A	**Won** 19–6
France	28 Nov	A	**Won** 39–12
Ireland	12 June	H	**Won** 66–28
Wales	19 June	H	**Won** 42–9
Wales	26 June	H	**Won** 29–10
South Africa	10 July	H	**Won** 32–12
South Africa	17 July	H	**Won** 31–17
Australia	31 July	A	**Won** 49–28
Australia	7 Aug	H	**Won** 20–10
South Africa	21 Aug	A	**Won** 29–22
Australia	11 Sep	A	**Won** 23–22

ALL BLACKS BACK TO BRILLIANT BEST

By Iain Spragg

Dave Rogers/Getty Images

There was no stopping New Zealand in the Tri–Nations.

When Graham Henry sat down with his coaching staff of Steve Hansen and Wayne Smith to plot the All Blacks' penultimate Test campaign before Rugby World Cup 2011 is staged in New Zealand, he had some rather radical advice from a group of his senior players to digest.

The suggestion was that the three senior coaches swap their jobs within the All Black set-up. After six years of the same coaching regime, the players believed the self-imposed changes would reinvigorate the side and Henry agreed with them. Hansen relinquished his forwards remit to become the new backs coach, Smith took on responsibility for the defence while Henry himself remained as head coach but also became responsible for the New Zealand forwards.

"If you're a bit nervous about it, it brings the best out of you," said Henry after the decision to overhaul his backroom set-up. "It's good for me to have that challenge. I've got energy, I'm excited about that opportunity and I'll be using a lot of the knowledge of the forward pack to help. We discussed it at some length and the reason behind it and the players are excited."

It was a brave, innovative decision but 12 months later, it had reaped handsome rewards as New Zealand completed a perfect season with 14 wins in 14 Tests, reclaiming the Tri–Nations title in the process with a series of dominant displays against their southern hemisphere rivals.

Henry's gamble had proved to be nothing of the sort and the Kiwis could look ahead to the World Cup with a renewed and wholly justified sense of confidence.

The first instalment of the New Zealanders' season was the traditional tour of Europe and Henry named four uncapped players, fly-half Mike Delany, wing Zac Guildford who graduated from the IRB Junior World Championship last year, full-back Ben Smith and utility back Tamati Ellison, in his 33-strong squad.

As had happened 12 months earlier, the tour actually began with a Bledisloe Cup clash with Australia on neutral territory. The previous year Hong Kong had hosted the game but this time Tokyo was the setting as the old rivals crossed swords and the All Blacks sealed a 32–19 victory over the Wallabies thanks mainly to Dan Carter's 22-point haul. It was their seventh win on the bounce over the Australians.

Their first game in Europe was against Wales in Cardiff but Henry was deprived of the services of Sitiveni Sivivatu and Tony Woodcock after both players were cited and handed one-week bans for misdemeanours in the Bledisloe Cup clash.

Wales were looking to end a 56-year drought against the tourists and while it was probably a closer encounter than Henry and his troops would have wished for, New Zealand scored the only try of the match through Andrew Hore and eventually emerged narrow 19–12 winners.

"It was a highly competitive Test match between two good sides," said Henry after victory over the side he coached between 1998 and 2002. "Our guys have come a long way to play here and they did well under those circumstances."

Italy proved characteristically stubborn opponents in the next match in front of 80,000 in the San Siro Stadium, a record for a rugby match in the country, but even though the All Blacks were below strength they had enough quality to subdue the Azzurri and claim a 20–6 win.

Unsurprisingly, Henry recalled 13 of his frontline players for the clash with the English at Twickenham the following week and the All Blacks needed all of their experience and power as Martin Johnson's side briefly threatened to derail the tour.

Carter and Jonny Wilkinson traded first-half penalties to leave the game finely balanced at the break and it needed a beautifully-worked

Jimmy Cowan try after the restart to finally the break the home side's resistance.

"We're happy to get the win but parts of our game definitely need to improve," said Carter, who overtook Andrew Mehrtens as New Zealand's all-time Test points scorer at Twickenham. "It's never easy here so we'll take that and work on the bits that need working on during the week. Defensively we're very sound, we pride ourselves on it, it's definitely something for the boys to be proud of but attacking, we need to work on holding on to the ball, building phases and being composed."

The All Blacks may have been shackled for long periods at HQ but they ran riot seven days later against the French in Marseille, running in five unanswered tries for a 39–12 triumph and a 100% record on the European leg of their campaign.

Before returning home, the All Blacks faced the Barbarians at Twickenham and were beaten 25–18 courtesy of a Bryan Habana hat-trick but since the NZRFU did not award caps for the game, the team's unblemished Test record remained intact.

The following summer Ireland and Wales were on New Zealand soil but the former offered very little resistance in New Plymouth as Henry's team ran in nine tries, including two each for Conrad Smith, Cowan and Sam Whitelock, in a surprisingly one-sided 66–28 romp after Jamie Heaslip's early red card.

Wales provided marginally sterner opposition seven days later in Dunedin but the All Blacks were determined to mark the last-ever Test match held at Carisbrook in style after 102 years of loyal service and Carter helped himself to 27 points as the tourists were beaten 42–9.

The gulf between the two sides was significantly narrower in the second Test in Hamilton however. New Zealand were restricted to two tries at the Waikato Stadium and had their own defence breached by Jamie Roberts, but it was too little too late and the home side were 29–10 winners.

Henry revealed his ruthless streak when he axed four players from the team that beat Wales for his squad for the subsequent Tri–Nations, but it was difficult to argue with his decision as the All Blacks kicked off the tournament with a 32–12 demolition of the Springboks at Eden Park. The All Blacks outscored the South Africans four tries to nil and in the process ended a three-match losing sequence against the reigning world champions.

"I was pretty proud of the way the guys made really good decisions and we built the pressure and took our chances," said captain Richie McCaw. "Whether to kick or carry, the guys looked at what was in front of them. You can have a go in your own half as long as you look after the ball and do the little things right."

The New Zealanders repeated the trick against the same opposition in Wellington a week later with a 31–17, bonus point victory and they already had a firm grip on the Tri–Nations.

That grip became a stranglehold after a dominant display against the Australians in Melbourne in their next game as full-back Mils Muliaina scored two of the All Blacks seven tries in a 49–28 triumph.

The Wallabies made the trip across the Tasman Sea for the return match in Christchurch in early August and while there was no repeat of the rout in Melbourne, New Zealand took another inexorable step towards the Tri–Nations title with a 20–10 triumph thanks to tries from Muliaina and Smith.

Their penultimate game of the campaign was against South Africa at the rechristened FNB Stadium in Soweto and some 95,000 supporters, the largest crowd for a Test match in South Africa for more than half a century, thronged the ground as the Springboks looked to exact revenge for their two recent defeats to the All Blacks.

It was also John Smit's 100th Test for South Africa but it was heartbreak for both the Springbok captain and his team as Richie McCaw and replacement wing Israel Dagg grabbed late tries for the All Blacks to snatch a 29–22 win. The result meant New Zealand were confirmed as Tri–Nations champions for a record 10th time.

"They don't get any bigger than that," said Henry. "It was a huge Test match, played in front of that crowd in that stadium. I just felt so proud of what they've achieved. The character, backed by their guts and togetherness was superb. So I think it was a very special win by the All Blacks today, an outstanding result and something we will never forget as far as we're concerned."

Already crowned champions, New Zealand were in no mood to surrender their unbeaten Test record in their final game against the Australians in Sydney but as they had done in Soweto, they left it late and were heavily indebted to a last-gasp try from No 8 Kieran Read to secure a dramatic 23–22 victory at ANZ Stadium.

"When you get in situations like that out there the key is to be composed and keep believing in what you're doing," said McCaw, who led the All Blacks out for the 52nd time in his career to surpass Sean Fitzpatrick as the most capped All Black captain in history. "We trained all week how we wanted to play and perhaps the first 50 minutes we didn't execute it and we were behind on the scoreboard. It's not rocket science at all. It's just everyone being on the same page and doing it well I think."

NEW ZEALAND INTERNATIONAL STATISTICS

MATCH RECORDS UP TO 29TH OCTOBER 2010

MOST CONSECUTIVE TEST WINS

17 1965 SA 4, 1966 BI 1, 2, 3, 4, 1967 A, E, W, F, S, 1968 A 1, 2, F 1, 2, 3, 1969 W 1, 2
15 2005 A 1, SA 2, A 2, W, I ,E, S, 2006 I 1, 2, Arg, A 1, SA 1, A 2, 3, SA 2
15 2009 A 3, 4, W, It E, F 3, 2010 I 1, W 1, 2, SA 1, 2, A 1, 2, SA 3, A 3
12 1988 A 3, 1989 F 1, 2, Arg 1, 2, A, W, I, 1990 S 1, 2, A 1, 2

MOST CONSECUTIVE TESTS WITHOUT DEFEAT

Matches	Wins	Draws	Periods
23	22	1	1987 to 1990
17	17	0	1965 to 1969
17	15	2	1961 to 1964
15	15	0	2005 to 2006
15	15	0	2009 to 2010

MOST POINTS IN A MATCH

BY THE TEAM

Pts	Opponents	Venue	Year
145	Japan	Bloemfontein	1995
108	Portugal	Lyons	2007
102	Tonga	Albany	2000
101	Italy	Huddersfield	1999
101	Samoa	N Plymouth	2008
93	Argentina	Wellington	1997
91	Tonga	Brisbane	2003
91	Fiji	Albany	2005
85	Romania	Toulouse	2007
76	Italy	Marseilles	2007
74	Fiji	Christchurch	1987
73	Canada	Auckland	1995
71	Fiji	Albany	1997
71	Samoa	Albany	1999

BY A PLAYER

Pts	Player	Opponents	Venue	Year
45	S D Culhane	Japan	Bloemfontein	1995
36	T E Brown	Italy	Huddersfield	1999
33	C J Spencer	Argentina	Wellington	1997
33	A P Mehrtens	Ireland	Dublin	1997
33	D W Carter	British/Irish	Wellington	2005
33	N J Evans	Portugal	Lyons	2007
32	T E Brown	Tonga	Albany	2000
30	M C G Ellis	Japan	Bloemfontein	1995
30	T E Brown	Samoa	Albany	2001
29	A P Mehrtens	Australia	Auckland	1999
29	A P Mehrtens	France	Paris	2000
29	L R MacDonald	Tonga	Brisbane	2003
29	D W Carter	Canada	Hamilton	2007

MOST TRIES IN A MATCH

BY THE TEAM

Tries	Opponents	Venue	Year
21	Japan	Bloemfontein	1995
16	Portugal	Lyons	2007
15	Tonga	Albany	2000
15	Fiji	Albany	2005
15	Samoa	N Plymouth	2008
14	Argentina	Wellington	1997
14	Italy	Huddersfield	1999
13	U S A	Berkeley	1913
13	Tonga	Brisbane	2003
13	Romania	Toulouse	2007
12	Italy	Auckland	1987
12	Fiji	Christchurch	1987

BY A PLAYER

Tries	Player	Opponents	Venue	Year
6	M C G Ellis	Japan	Bloemfontein	1995
5	J W Wilson	Fiji	Albany	1997
4	D McGregor	England	Crystal Palace	1905
4	C I Green	Fiji	Christchurch	1987
4	J A Gallagher	Fiji	Christchurch	1987
4	J J Kirwan	Wales	Christchurch	1988
4	J T Lomu	England	Cape Town	1995
4	C M Cullen	Scotland	Dunedin	1996
4	J W Wilson	Samoa	Albany	1999
4	J M Muliaina	Canada	Melbourne	2003
4	S W Sivivatu	Fiji	Albany	2005

MOST CONVERSIONS IN A MATCH

BY THE TEAM

Cons	Opponents	Venue	Year
20	Japan	Bloemfontein	1995
14	Portugal	Lyons	2007
13	Tonga	Brisbane	2003
13	Samoa	N Plymouth	2008
12	Tonga	Albany	2000
11	Italy	Huddersfield	1999
10	Fiji	Christchurch	1987
10	Argentina	Wellington	1997
10	Romania	Toulouse	2007
9	Canada	Melbourne	2003
9	Italy	Marseilles	2007
9	Ireland	N Plymouth	2010
8	Italy	Auckland	1987
8	Wales	Auckland	1988
8	Fiji	Albany	1997
8	Italy	Hamilton	2003
8	Fiji	Albany	2005

BY A PLAYER

Cons	Player	Opponents	Venue	Year
20	S D Culhane	Japan	Bloemfontein	1995
14	N J Evans	Portugal	Lyons	2007
12	T E Brown	Tonga	Albany	2000
12	L R MacDonald	Tonga	Brisbane	2003
11	T E Brown	Italy	Huddersfield	1999
10	G J Fox	Fiji	Christchurch	1987
10	C J Spencer	Argentina	Wellington	1997
9	D W Carter	Canada	Melbourne	2003
8	G J Fox	Italy	Auckland	1987
8	G J Fox	Wales	Auckland	1988
8	A P Mehrtens	Italy	Hamilton	2002

MOST DROPPED GOALS IN A MATCH

BY THE TEAM

Drops	Opponent	Venue	Year
3	France	Christchurch	1986

BY A PLAYER

Drops	Player	Opponents	Venue	Year
2	O D Bruce	Ireland	Dublin	1978
2	F M Botica	France	Christchurch	1986
2	A P Mehrtens	Australia	Auckland	1995

MOST PENALTIES IN A MATCH

BY THE TEAM

Pens	Opponents	Venue	Year
9	Australia	Auckland	1999
9	France	Paris	2000
7	Western Samoa	Auckland	1993
7	South Africa	Pretoria	1999
7	South Africa	Wellington	2006
7	Australia	Auckland	2007
6	British/Irish Lions	Dunedin	1959
6	England	Christchurch	1985
6	Argentina	Wellington	1987
6	Scotland	Christchurch	1987
6	France	Paris	1990
6	South Africa	Auckland	1994
6	Australia	Brisbane	1996
6	Ireland	Dublin	1997
6	South Africa	Cardiff	1999
6	Scotland	Murrayfield	2001
6	South Africa	Christchurch	2004
6	Australia	Sydney	2004
6	South Africa	Dunedin	2008
6	Australia	Tokyo	2009

BY A PLAYER

Pens	Player	Opponents	Venue	Year
9	A P Mehrtens	Australia	Auckland	1999
9	A P Mehrtens	France	Paris	2000
7	G J Fox	Western Samoa	Auckland	1993
7	A P Mehrtens	South Africa	Pretoria	1999
7	D W Carter	South Africa	Wellington	2006
7	D W Carter	Australia	Auckland	2007
6	D B Clarke	British/Irish Lions	Dunedin	1959
6	K J Crowley	England	Christchurch	1985
6	G J Fox	Argentina	Wellington	1987
6	G J Fox	Scotland	Christchurch	1987
6	G J Fox	France	Paris	1990
6	S P Howarth	South Africa	Auckland	1994
6	A P Mehrtens	Australia	Brisbane	1996
6	A P Mehrtens	Ireland	Dublin	1997
6	A P Mehrtens	South Africa	Cardiff	1999
6	A P Mehrtens	Scotland	Murrayfield	2001
6	D W Carter	South Africa	Dunedin	2008
6	D W Carter	Australia	Tokyo	2009

CAREER RECORDS

MOST CAPPED PLAYERS

Caps	Player	Career Span
92	S B T Fitzpatrick	1986 to 1997
89	J M Muliaina	2003 to 2010
89	R H McCaw	2001 to 2010
81	J W Marshall	1995 to 2005
80	K F Mealamu	2002 to 2010
79	I D Jones	1990 to 1999
74	J F Umaga	1997 to 2005
74	D W Carter	2003 to 2010
70	A P Mehrtens	1995 to 2004
69	T D Woodcock	2002 to 2010
67	C R Jack	2001 to 2007
66	G M Somerville	2000 to 2008
66	J T Rokocoko	2003 to 2010
63	J J Kirwan	1984 to 1994
63	J T Lomu	1994 to 2002
62	R M Brooke	1992 to 1999
62	D C Howlett	2000 to 2007
62	R So'oialo	2002 to 2009
61	A J Williams	2002 to 2008
60	C W Dowd	1993 to 2001
60	J W Wilson	1993 to 2001
59	A D Oliver	1997 to 2007
58	G W Whetton	1981 to 1991
58	Z V Brooke	1987 to 1997
58	C M Cullen	1996 to 2002
57	B T Kelleher	1999 to 2007
56	O M Brown	1992 to 1998
56	L R MacDonald	2000 to 2008
55	C E Meads	1957 to 1971
55	F E Bunce	1992 to 1997
55	M N Jones	1987 to 1998

MOST CONSECUTIVE TESTS

Tests	Player	Career span
63	S B T Fitzpatrick	1986 to 1995
51	C M Cullen	1996 to 2000
49	R M Brooke	1995 to 1999
41	J W Wilson	1996 to 1999
40	G W Whetton	1986 to 1991

MOST TESTS AS CAPTAIN

Tests	Player	Career span
52	R H McCaw	2004 to 2010
51	S B T Fitzpatrick	1992 to 1997
30	W J Whineray	1958 to 1965
23	R D Thorne	2002 to 2007
22	T C Randell	1998 to 2002
21	J F Umaga	2004 to 2005
19	G N K Mourie	1977 to 1982
18	B J Lochore	1966 to 1970
17	A G Dalton	1981 to 1985

MOST POINTS IN TESTS

Points	Player	Tests	Career
1118	D W Carter	74	2003 to 2010
967	A P Mehrtens	70	1995 to 2004
645	G J Fox	46	1985 to 1993
291	C J Spencer	35	1997 to 2004
245	D C Howlett	62	2000 to 2007
236	C M Cullen	58	1996 to 2002
234	J W Wilson	60	1993 to 2001
230	J T Rokocoko	66	2003 to 2010
207	D B Clarke	31	1956 to 1964
201	A R Hewson	19	1981 to 1984
185	J T Lomu	63	1994 to 2002
185*	J F Umaga	74	1997 to 2005

* Umaga's haul includes a penalty try

MOST TRIES IN TESTS

Tries	Player	Tests	Career
49	D C Howlett	62	2000 to 2007
46	C M Cullen	58	1996 to 2002
46	J T Rokocoko	66	2003 to 2010
44	J W Wilson	60	1993 to 2001
37	J T Lomu	63	1994 to 2002
37*	J F Umaga	74	1997 to 2005
35	J J Kirwan	63	1984 to 1994
29	J M Muliaina	89	2003 to 2010
28	D W Carter	74	2003 to 2010
27	S W Sivivatu	43	2005 to 2009
24	J W Marshall	81	1995 to 2005
20	F E Bunce	55	1992 to 1997
20*	R H McCaw	89	2001 to 2010

* Umaga and McCaw's hauls each include a penalty try

MOST CONVERSIONS IN TESTS

Cons	Player	Tests	Career
192	D W Carter	74	2003 to 2010
169	A P Mehrtens	70	1995 to 2004
118	G J Fox	46	1985 to 1993
49	C J Spencer	35	1997 to 2004
43	T E Brown	18	1999 to 2001
33	D B Clarke	31	1956 to 1964
32	S D Culhane	6	1995 to 1996

MOST PENALTY GOALS IN TESTS

Penalties	Player	Tests	Career
196	D W Carter	74	2003 to 2010
188	A P Mehrtens	70	1995 to 2004
128	G J Fox	46	1985 to 1993
43	A R Hewson	19	1981 to 1984
41	C J Spencer	35	1997 to 2004
38	D B Clarke	31	1956 to 1964
24	W F McCormick	16	1965 to 1971

MOST DROPPED GOALS IN TESTS

Drops	Player	Tests	Career
10	A P Mehrtens	70	1995 to 2004
7	G J Fox	46	1985 to 1993
5	D B Clarke	31	1956 to 1964
5	M A Herewini	10	1962 to 1967
5	O D Bruce	14	1976 to 1978

TRI-NATIONS RECORDS

RECORD	DETAIL	HOLDER	SET
Most points in season	184	in six matches	2010
Most tries in season	22	in six matches	2010
Highest Score	55	55–35 v S Africa (h)	1997
Biggest win	37	43–6 v Australia (h)	1996
Highest score conceded	46	40–46 v S Africa (a)	2000
Biggest defeat	21	7–28 v Australia (a)	1999
Most appearances	40	J M Muliaina	2003 to 2010
Most points in matches	426	D W Carter	2003 to 2010
Most points in season	99	D W Carter	2006
Most points in match	29	A P Mehrtens	v Australia (h) 1999
Most tries in matches	16	C M Cullen	1996 to 2002
Most tries in season	7	C M Cullen	2000
Most tries in match	3	J T Rokocoko	v Australia (a) 2003
	3	D C Howlett	v Australia (h) 2005
Most cons in matches	54	D W Carter	2003 to 2010
Most cons in season	14	D W Carter	2006
Most cons in match	4	C J Spencer	v S Africa (h) 1997
	4	A P Mehrtens	v Australia (a) 2000
	4	A P Mehrtens	v S Africa (a) 2000
	4	C J Spencer	v S Africa (a) 2003
	4	D W Carter	v S Africa (a) 2006
	4	D W Carter	v Australia (a) 2008
	4	D W Carter	v Australia (a) 2010
Most pens in matches	94	D W Carter	2003 to 2010
Most pens in season	21	D W Carter	2006
Most pens in match	9	A P Mehrtens	v Australia (h) 1999

MISCELLANEOUS RECORDS

RECORD	HOLDER	DETAIL
Longest Test Career	E Hughes/C E Meads	1907–21/1957–71
Youngest Test Cap	J T Lomu	19 yrs 45 days in 1994
Oldest Test Cap	E Hughes	40 yrs 123 days in 1921

CAREER RECORDS OF NEW ZEALAND INTERNATIONAL PLAYERS (UP TO 29TH OCTOBER 2010)

PLAYER	DEBUT	CAPS	T	C	P	D	PTS
BACKS							
D W Carter	2003 v W	74	28	192	196	2	1118
Q J Cowan	2004 v It	41	5	0	0	0	25
A W Cruden	2010 v I	6	1	0	0	0	5
I J A Dagg	2010 v I	6	2	0	0	0	10
M P Delany	2009 v It	1	0	0	0	0	0
S R Donald	2008 v E	19	1	13	20	0	91
A M Ellis	2006 v E	14	2	0	0	0	10
T E Ellison	2009 v It	1	0	0	0	0	0
H E Gear	2008 v A	2	0	0	0	0	0
R L Gear	2004 v PI	19	11	0	0	0	55
Z R Guildford	2009 v W	4	0	0	0	0	0
C S Jane	2008 v A	21	5	0	0	0	25
R D Kahui	2008 v E	11	5	0	0	0	25
B G Leonard	2007 v F	13	2	0	0	0	10
C L McAlister	2005 v BI	30	7	26	22	0	153
L T C Masaga	2009 v It	1	0	0	0	0	0
A S Mathewson	2010 v A	1	0	0	0	0	0
J M Muliaina	2003 v E	89	29	0	0	0	145
M A Nonu	2003 v E	52	16	0	0	0	80
R M N Ranger	2010 v W	3	1	0	0	0	5
J T Rokocoko	2003 v E	66	46	0	0	0	230
S W Sivivatu	2005 v Fj	43	27	0	0	0	135
C R Slade	2010 v A	1	0	0	0	0	0
B R Smith	2009 v It	1	0	0	0	0	0
C G Smith	2004 v It	41	17	0	0	0	85
B J Stanley	2010 v I	3	0	0	0	0	0
I Toeava	2005 v S	26	6	0	0	0	30
A S M Tuitavake	2008 v I	6	1	0	0	0	5
P A T Weepu	2004 v W	44	6	6	5	0	57
R N Wulf	2008 v E	4	0	0	0	0	0

FORWARDS

I F "John" Afoa	2005 v I	25	0	0	0	0	0
A F Boric	2008 v E	16	1	0	0	0	5
W W V Crockett	2009 v It	3	0	0	0	0	0
A P de Malmanche	2009 v It	5	0	0	0	0	0
T J S Donnelly	2009 v A	13	0	0	0	0	0
J J Eaton	2005 v I	15	1	0	0	0	5
B R Evans	2009 v F	2	0	0	0	0	0
R A Filipo	2007 v C	4	0	0	0	0	0
C R Flynn	2003 v C	12	3	0	0	0	15
B J Franks	2010 v I	7	1	0	0	0	5
O T Franks	2009 v It	17	0	0	0	0	0
A K Hore	2002 v E	47	5	0	0	0	25
J Kaino	2006 v I	33	4	0	0	0	20
T D Latimer	2009 v F	5	0	0	0	0	0
S T Lauaki	2005 v Fj	17	3	0	0	0	15
R H McCaw	2001 v I	89	20*	0	0	0	100
J L Mackintosh	2008 v S	1	0	0	0	0	0
K F Mealamu	2002 v W	80	10	0	0	0	50
L J Messam	2008 v S	5	1	0	0	0	5
K J O'Neill	2008 v SA	1	0	0	0	0	0
K J Read	2008 v S	25	3	0	0	0	15
I B Ross	2009 v F	8	2	0	0	0	10
R So'oialo	2002 v W	62	6	0	0	0	30
A J Thomson	2008 v I	17	1	0	0	0	5
B C Thorn	2003 v W	46	3	0	0	0	15
N S Tialata	2005 v W	43	2	0	0	0	10
V V J Vito	2010 v I	6	0	0	0	0	0
G B Whitelock	2009 v It	1	1	0	0	0	5
S L Whitelock	2010 v I	8	2	0	0	0	10
A J Williams	2002 v E	61	7	0	0	0	35
T D Woodcock	2002 v W	69	7	0	0	0	35

* McCaw's figures include a penalty try awarded against Ireland in 2008.

NEW ZEALAND INTERNATIONAL PLAYERS

UP TO 29TH OCTOBER 2010

Note: Years given for International Championship matches are for second half of season; eg 1972 means season 1971–72. Years for all other matches refer to the actual year of the match. Entries in square brackets denote matches played in RWC Finals.

Abbott, H L (Taranaki) 1906 F
Afoa, I F (Auckland) 2005 I, S, 2006 E(R), 2008 I1, SA2, A1(R), 2(R), SA3(R), A3(R), S, I2(t&R), W(R), E3(R), 2009 F1(R) , 2(R), It1, SA2(R), A2(R), SA3(R), A3(R), 4(R), It2(R), E(R), 2010 SA3(R), A3(R)
Aitken, G G (Wellington) 1921 SA 1, 2
Alatini, P F (Otago) 1999 F 1(R), [It, SA 3(R)], 2000 Tg, S 1, A 1, SA 1, A 2, SA 2, It, 2001 Sm, Arg 1, F, SA 1, A 1, SA 2, A 2
Allen, F R (Auckland) 1946 A 1, 2, 1947 A 1, 2, 1949 SA 1, 2
Allen, M R (Taranaki, Manawatu) 1993 WS (t), 1996 S 2 (t), 1997 Arg 1(R), 2(R), SA 2(R), A 3(R), E 2, W (R)
Allen, N H (Counties) 1980 A 3, W
Alley, G T (Canterbury) 1928 SA 1, 2, 3
Anderson, A (Canterbury) 1983 S, E, 1984 A 1, 2, 3, 1987 [Fj]
Anderson, B L (Wairarapa-Bush) 1986 A 1
Anesi, S R (Waikato) 2005 Fj(R)
Archer, W R (Otago, Southland) 1955 A 1, 2, 1956 SA 1, 3
Argus, W G (Canterbury) 1946 A 1, 2, 1947 A 1, 2
Arnold, D A (Canterbury) 1963 I, W, 1964 E, F
Arnold, K D (Waikato) 1947 A 1, 2
Ashby, D L (Southland) 1958 A 2
Asher, A A (Auckland) 1903 A
Ashworth, B G (Auckland) 1978 A 1, 2
Ashworth, J C (Canterbury, Hawke's Bay) 1978 A 1, 2, 3, 1980 A 1, 2, 3, 1981 SA 1, 2, 3, 1982 A 1, 2, 1983 BI 1, 2, 3, 4, A, 1984 F 1, 2, A 1, 2, 3, 1985 E 1, 2, A
Atiga, B A C (Auckland) 2003 [Tg(R)]
Atkinson, H (West Coast) 1913 A 1
Avery, H E (Wellington) 1910 A 1, 2, 3
Bachop, G T M (Canterbury) 1989 W, I, 1990 S 1, 2, A 1, 2, 3, F 1, 2, 1991 Arg 1, 2, A 1, 2, [E, US, C, A, S], 1992 Wld 1, 1994 SA 1, 2, 3, A, 1995 C, [I, W, S, E, SA], A 1, 2
Bachop, S J (Otago) 1994 F 2, SA 1, 2, 3, A
Badeley, C E O (Auckland) 1921 SA 1, 2
Baird, J A S (Otago) 1913 A 2
Ball, N (Wellington) 1931 A, 1932 A 2, 3, 1935 W, 1936 E
Barrett, J (Auckland) 1913 A 2, 3
Barry, E F (Wellington) 1934 A 2
Barry, L J (North Harbour) 1995 F 2
Bates, S P (Waikato) 2004 It(R)
Batty, G B (Wellington, Bay of Plenty) 1972 W, S, 1973 E 1, I, F, E 2, 1974 A 1, 3, I, 1975 S, 1976 SA 1, 2, 3, 4, 1977 BI 1
Batty, W (Auckland) 1930 BI 1, 3, 4, 1931 A
Beatty, G E (Taranaki) 1950 BI 1
Bell, R H (Otago) 1951 A 3, 1952 A 1, 2
Bellis, E A (Wanganui) 1921 SA 1, 2, 3
Bennet, R (Otago) 1905 A
Berghan, T (Otago) 1938 A 1, 2, 3
Berry, M J (Wairarapa-Bush) 1986 A 3(R)
Berryman, N R (Northland) 1998 SA 2(R)
Bevan, V D (Wellington) 1949 A 1, 2, 1950 BI 1, 2, 3, 4
Birtwistle, W M (Canterbury) 1965 SA 1, 2, 3, 4, 1967 E, W, S
Black, J E (Canterbury) 1977 F 1, 1979 A, 1980 A 3
Black, N W (Auckland) 1949 SA 3
Black, R S (Otago) 1914 A 1
Blackadder, T J (Canterbury) 1998 E 1(R), 2, 2000 Tg, S 1, 2, A 1, SA 1, A 2, SA 2, F 1, 2, It
Blair, B A (Canterbury) 2001 S (R), Arg 2, 2002 E, W
Blake, A W (Wairarapa) 1949 A 1
Blowers, A F (Auckland) 1996 SA 2(R), 4(R), 1997 I, E 1(R), W (R), 1999 F 1(R), SA 1, A 1(R), SA 2, A 2(R), [It]
Boggs, E G (Auckland) 1946 A 2, 1949 SA 1
Bond, J G (Canterbury) 1949 A 2
Booth, E E (Otago) 1906 F, 1907 A 1, 3
Boric, A F (North Harbour) 2008 E1(R), 2(R), SA2, A2(R), SA3(R), Sm, A3(R), 4(R), S, E3(R), 2009 It2, E(R), F3(R), 2010 I1, W1, A3(R)
Boroevich, K G (Wellington) 1986 F 1, A 1, F 3(R)
Botica, F M (North Harbour) 1986 F 1, A 1, 2, 3, F 2, 3, 1989 Arg 1(R)
Bowden, N J G (Taranaki) 1952 A 2
Bowers, R G (Wellington) 1954 I, F
Bowman, A W (Hawke's Bay) 1938 A 1, 2, 3
Braid, D J (Auckland) 2002 W, 2003 [C(R), Tg], 2008 A1
Braid, G J (Bay of Plenty) 1983 S, E
Bremner, S G (Auckland, Canterbury) 1952 A 2, 1956 SA 2
Brewer, M R (Otago, Canterbury) 1986 F 1, A 1, 2, 3, F 2, 3, 1988 A 1, 1989 A, W, I, 1990 S 1, 2, A 1, 2, 3, F 1, 2, 1992 I 2, A 1, 1994 F 1, 2, SA 1, 2, 3, A, 1995 C, [I, W, E, SA], A 1, 2
Briscoe, K C (Taranaki) 1959 BI 2, 1960 SA 1, 2, 3, 4, 1963 I, W, 1964 E, S
Brooke, R M (Auckland) 1992 I 2, A 1, 2, 3, SA, 1993 BI 1, 2, 3, A, WS, 1994 SA 2, 3, 1995 C, [J, S, E, SA], A 1, 2, It, F 1, 2, 1996 WS, S 1, 2, A 1, SA 1, A 2, SA 2, 3, 4, 5, 1997 Fj, Arg 1, 2, A 1, SA 1, A 2, SA 2, A 3, I, E 1, W, E 2, 1998 E 1, 2, A 1, SA 1, A 2, SA 2, A 3, 1999 WS, F 1, SA 1, A 1, SA 2, A 2, [Tg, E, It (R), S, F 2]
Brooke, Z V (Auckland) 1987 [Arg], 1989 Arg 2(R), 1990 A 1, 2, 3, F 1(R), 1991 Arg 2, A 1, 2, [E, It, C, A, S], 1992 A 2, 3, SA, 1993 BI 1, 2, 3(R), WS (R), S, E, 1994 F 2, SA 1, 2, 3, A, 1995 [J, S, E, SA], A 1, 2, It, F 1, 2, 1996 WS, S 1, 2, A 1, SA 1, A 2, SA 2, 3, 4, 5, 1997 Arg 1, 2, A 1, SA 1, A 2, SA 2, A 3, I, E 1, W, E 2
Brooke-Cowden, M (Auckland) 1986 F 1, A 1, 1987 [W]
Broomhall, S R (Canterbury) 2002 SA 1(R), 2(R), E, F
Brown, C (Taranaki) 1913 A 2, 3
Brown, O M (Auckland) 1992 I 2, A 1, 2, 3, SA, 1993 BI 1, 2, 3, A, S, E, 1994 F 1, 2, SA 1, 2, 3, A, 1995 C, [I, W, S, E, SA], A 1, 2, It, F 1, 2, 1996 WS, S 1, 2, A 1, SA 1, A 2, SA 2, 3, 4, 5, 1997 Fj, Arg 1, 2, A 1, SA 1, A 2, SA 2, A 3, I, E 1, W, E 2, 1998 E 1, 2, A 1, SA 1, A 2, SA 2
Brown, R H (Taranaki) 1955 A 3, 1956 SA 1, 2, 3, 4, 1957 A 1, 2, 1958 A 1, 2, 3, 1959 BI 1, 3, 1961 F 1, 2, 3, 1962 A 1
Brown, T E (Otago) 1999 WS, F 1(R), SA 1(R), A 1(R), 2(R), [E (R), It, S (R)], 2000 Tg, S 2(R), A 1(R), SA 1(R), A 2(R), 2001 Sm, Arg 1(R), F, SA 1, A 1
Brownlie, C J (Hawke's Bay) 1924 W, 1925 E, F
Brownlie, M J (Hawke's Bay) 1924 I, W, 1925 E, F, 1928 SA 1, 2, 3, 4
Bruce, J A (Auckland) 1914 A 1, 2
Bruce, O D (Canterbury) 1976 SA 1, 2, 4, 1977 BI 2, 3, 4, F 1, 2, 1978 A 1, 2, I, W, E, S
Bryers, R F (King Country) 1949 A 1
Budd, T A (Southland) 1946 A 2, 1949 A 2
Bullock-Douglas, G A H (Wanganui) 1932 A 1, 2, 3, 1934 A 1, 2
Bunce, F E (North Harbour) 1992 Wld 1, 2, 3, I 1, 2, A 1, 2, 3, SA, 1993 BI 1, 2, 3, A, WS, S, E, 1994 F 1, 2, SA 1, 2, 3, A, 1995 C, [I, W, S, E, SA], A 1, 2, It, F 1, 2, 1996 WS, S 1, 2, A1, SA 1, A 2, SA 2, 3, 4, 5, 1997 Fj, Arg 1, 2, A 1, SA 1, A 2, SA 2, A 3, I, E 1, W, E 2
Burgess, G A J (Auckland) 1981 SA 2
Burgess, G F (Southland) 1905 A
Burgess, R E (Manawatu) 1971 BI 1, 2, 3, 1972 A 3, W, 1973 I, F
Burke, P S (Taranaki) 1955 A 1, 1957 A 1, 2
Burns, P J (Canterbury) 1908 AW 2, 1910 A 1, 2, 3, 1913 A 3
Bush, R G (Otago) 1931 A

Bush, W K (Canterbury) 1974 A 1, 2, 1975 S, 1976 I, SA, 2, 4, 1977 BI 2, 3, 4(R), 1978 I, W, 1979 A
Buxton, J B (Canterbury) 1955 A 3, 1956 SA 1
Cain, M J (Taranaki) 1913 US, 1914 A 1, 2, 3
Callesen, J A (Manawatu) 1974 A 1, 2, 3, 1975 S
Cameron, D (Taranaki) 1908 AW 1, 2, 3
Cameron, L M (Manawatu) 1980 A 3, 1981 SA 1(R), 2, 3, R
Carleton, S R (Canterbury) 1928 SA 1, 2, 3, 1929 A 1, 2, 3
Carrington, K R (Auckland) 1971 BI 1, 3, 4
Carter, D W (Canterbury) 2003 W, F, A 1(R), [It, C, Tg, SA(R), F(R)], 2004 E1, 2, PI, A1, SA1, A2, It, W, F, 2005 Fj, BI1, 2, SA1, A1, W, E, 2006 Arg, A1, SA1, A2, 3, SA2, 3, E, F1, 2, W, 2007 F1, C, SA1, A1, SA2, A2, [It, S, F], 2008 I1, E1, 2, SA1, 2, A1, 2, SA3, Sm, A3, 4, S(R), I2, W, E3, 2009 A2, SA3, A3, 4, W, E, F3, 2010 I1, W1, 2, SA1, 2, A1, 2, SA3
Carter, M P (Auckland) 1991 A 2, [It, A], 1997 Fj (R), A 1(R), 1998 E 2(R), A 2
Casey, S T (Otago) 1905 S, I, E, W, 1907 A 1, 2, 3, 1908 AW 1
Cashmore, A R (Auckland) 1996 S 2(R), 1997 A 2(R)
Catley, E H (Waikato) 1946 A 1, 1947 A 1, 2, 1949 SA 1, 2, 3, 4
Caughey, T H C (Auckland) 1932 A 1, 3, 1934 A 1, 2, 1935 S, I, 1936 E, A 1, 1937 SA 3
Caulton, R W (Wellington) 1959 BI 2, 3, 4, 1960 SA 1, 4, 1961 F 2, 1963 E 1, 2, I, W, 1964 E, S, F, A 1, 2, 3
Cherrington, N P (North Auckland) 1950 BI 1
Christian, D L (Auckland) 1949 SA 4
Clamp, M (Wellington) 1984 A 2, 3
Clark, D W (Otago) 1964 A 1, 2
Clark, W H (Wellington) 1953 W, 1954 I, E, S, 1955 A 1, 2, 1956 SA 2, 3, 4
Clarke, A H (Auckland) 1958 A 3, 1959 BI 4, 1960 SA 1
Clarke, D B (Waikato) 1956 SA 3, 4, 1957 A 1, 2, 1958 A 1, 3, 1959 BI 1, 2, 3, 4, 1960 SA 1, 2, 3, 4, 1961 F 1, 2, 3, 1962 A 1, 2, 3, 4, 5, 1963 E 1, 2, I, W, 1964 E, S, F, A 2, 3
Clarke, E (Auckland) 1992 Wld 2, 3, I 1, 2, 1993 BI 1, 2, S (R), E, 1998 SA 2, A 3
Clarke, I J (Waikato) 1953 W, 1955 A 1, 2, 3, 1956 SA 1, 2, 3, 4, 1957 A 1, 2, 1958 A 1, 3, 1959 BI 1, 2, 1960 SA 2, 4, 1961 F 1, 2, 3, 1962 A 1, 2, 3, 1963 E 1, 2
Clarke, R L (Taranaki) 1932 A 2, 3
Cobden, D G (Canterbury) 1937 SA 1
Cockerill, M S (Taranaki) 1951 A 1, 2, 3
Cockroft, E A P (South Canterbury) 1913 A 3, 1914 A 2, 3
Codlin, B W (Counties) 1980 A 1, 2, 3
Collins, A H (Taranaki) 1932 A 2, 3, 1934 A 1
Collins, J (Wellington) 2001 Arg 1, 2003 E (R), W, F, SA 1, A 1, SA 2, A 2, [It, W, SA, A, F], 2004 E2(R), Arg, PI(R), A1(R), SA1, It, F, 2005 Fj, BI1, 2, 3, SA1, A1, SA2, W, E, 2006 Arg, A1, 2, 3, SA2(R), 3, F1, 2, W, 2007 F2, C, SA1, A1, SA2(R), A2, [It, Pt, R, F]
Collins, J L (Poverty Bay) 1964 A 1, 1965 SA 1, 4
Colman, J T H (Taranaki) 1907 A 1, 2, 1908 AW 1, 3
Connor, D M (Auckland) 1961 F 1, 2, 3, 1962 A 1, 2, 3, 4, 5, 1963 E 1, 2, 1964 A 2, 3
Conway, R J (Otago, Bay of Plenty) 1959 BI 2, 3, 4, 1960 SA 1, 3, 4, 1965 SA 1, 2, 3, 4
Cooke, A E (Auckland, Wellington) 1924 I, W, 1925 E, F, 1930 BI 1, 2, 3, 4
Cooke, R J (Canterbury) 1903 A
Cooksley, M S B (Counties, Waikato) 1992 Wld 1, 1993 BI 2, 3(R), A, 1994 F 1, 2, SA 1, 2, A, 2001 A 1(R), SA 2(t&R)
Cooper, G J L (Auckland, Otago) 1986 F 1, A 1, 2, 1992 Wld 1, 2, 3, I 1
Cooper, M J A (Waikato) 1992 I 2, SA (R), 1993 BI 1(R), 3(t), WS (t), S, 1994 F 1, 2
Corner, M M N (Auckland) 1930 BI 2, 3, 4, 1931 A, 1934 A 1, 1936 E
Cossey, R R (Counties) 1958 A 1
Cottrell, A I (Canterbury) 1929 A 1, 2, 3, 1930 BI 1, 2, 3, 4, 1931 A, 1932 A 1, 2, 3
Cottrell, W D (Canterbury) 1968 A 1, 2, F 2, 3, 1970 SA 1, 1971 BI 1, 2, 3, 4
Couch, M B R (Wairarapa) 1947 A 1, 1949 A 1, 2
Coughlan, T D (South Canterbury) 1958 A 1
Cowan, Q J (Southland) 2004 It(R), 2005 W(R), I(R), S(R), 2006 I1(R), SA1(R), A2(R), SA2(R), 3, 2008 E1(R), 2(R), SA1(R), A1(t&R), 2, SA3, Sm, A3, 4, I2, W, E3, 2009 F1, 2, A1, SA2, A2, SA3, A3, 4, W(R), It2(R), E, F3, 2010 I1, W1, 2, SA1, 2(R), A1, SA3, A3(R)
Creighton, J N (Canterbury) 1962 A 4
Cribb, R T (North Harbour) 2000 S 1, 2, A 1, SA 1, A 2, SA 2, F 1, 2, It, 2001 Sm, F, SA 1, A 1, SA 2, A 2
Crichton, S (Wellington) 1983 S, E
Crockett, W W V (Canterbury) 2009 It1, W, It2
Cross, T (Canterbury) 1904 BI, 1905 A
Crowley, K J (Taranaki) 1985 E 1, 2, A, Arg 1, 2, 1986 A 3, F 2, 3, 1987 [Arg], 1990 S 1, 2, A 1, 2, 3, F 1, 2, 1991 Arg 1, 2, [A]
Crowley, P J B (Auckland) 1949 SA 3, 4, 1950 BI 1, 2, 3, 4
Cruden, A W (Manawatu) 2010 I1(R), W1(R), 2(R), SA2(R), A1(R), 3
Culhane, S D (Southland) 1995 [J], It, F 1, 2, 1996 SA 3, 4
Cullen C M (Manawatu, Central Vikings, Wellington) 1996 WS, S 1, 2, A 1, SA 1, A 2, SA 2, 3, 4, 5, 1997 Fj, Arg 1, 2, A 1, SA 1, A 2, SA 2, A 3, I, E 1, W, E 2, 1998 E 1, 2, A 1, SA 1, A 2, SA 2, A 3, 1999 WS, F 1, SA 1, A 1, SA 2, A 2, [Tg, E, It (R), S, F 2, SA 3], 2000 Tg, S 1, 2, A 1, SA 1, A 2, SA 2, F 1, 2, It, 2001 A 2(R), 2002 It, Fj, A 1, SA 1, A 2, F
Cummings, W (Canterbury) 1913 A 2, 3
Cundy, R T (Wairarapa) 1929 A 2(R)
Cunningham, G R (Auckland) 1979 A, S, E, 1980 A 1, 2
Cunningham, W (Auckland) 1905 S, I, 1906 F, 1907 A 1, 2, 3, 1908 AW 1, 2, 3
Cupples, L F (Bay of Plenty) 1924 I, W
Currie, C J (Canterbury) 1978 I, W
Cuthill, J E (Otago) 1913 A 1, US
Dagg, I J A (Hawke's Bay) 2010 I1, W1, SA2(R), A1(R), SA3(R), A3
Dalley, W C (Canterbury) 1924 I, 1928 SA 1, 2, 3, 4
Dalton, A G (Counties) 1977 F 2, 1978 A 1, 2, 3, I, W, E, S, 1979 F 1, 2, S, 1981 S 1, 2, SA 1, 2, 3, R, F 1, 2, 1982 A 1, 2, 3, 1983 BI 1, 2, 3, 4, A, 1984 F 1, 2, A 1, 2, 3, 1985 E 1, 2, A
Dalton, D (Hawke's Bay) 1935 I, W, 1936 A 1, 2, 1937 SA 1, 2, 3, 1938 A 1, 2
Dalton, R A (Wellington) 1947 A 1, 2
Dalzell, G N (Canterbury) 1953 W, 1954 I, E, S, F
Davie, M G (Canterbury) 1983 E (R)
Davies, W A (Auckland, Otago) 1960 SA 4, 1962 A 4, 5
Davis, K (Auckland) 1952 A 2, 1953 W, 1954 I, E, S, F, 1955 A 2, 1958 A 1, 2, 3
Davis, L J (Canterbury) 1976 I, 1977 BI 3, 4
Davis, W L (Hawke's Bay) 1967 A, E, W, F, S, 1968 A 1, 2, F 1, 1969 W 1, 2, 1970 SA 2
Deans, I B (Canterbury) 1988 W 1, 2, A 1, 2, 3, 1989 F 1, 2, Arg 1, 2, A
Deans, R G (Canterbury) 1905 S, I, E, W, 1908 AW 3
Deans, R M (Canterbury) 1983 S, E, 1984 A 1(R), 2, 3
Delamore, G W (Wellington) 1949 SA 4
Delany, M P (Bay of Plenty) 2009 It 2
De Malmanche, A P (Waikato) 2009 It1(R), A3(R), 2010 I1(R), W1(R), 2(R)
Dermody, C (Southland) 2006 I1, 2, E(R)
Devine, S J (Auckland) 2002 E, W 2003 E (R), W, F, SA 1, A 1(R), [C, SA(R), F]
Dewar, H (Taranaki) 1913 A 1, US
Diack, E S (Otago) 1959 BI 2
Dick, J (Auckland) 1937 SA 1, 2, 1938 A 3
Dick, M J (Auckland) 1963 I, W, 1964 E, S, F, 1965 SA 3, 1966 BI 4, 1967 A, E, W, F, 1969 W 1, 2, 1970 SA 1, 4
Dixon, M J (Canterbury) 1954 I, E, S, F, 1956 SA 1, 2, 3, 4, 1957 A 1, 2
Dobson, R L (Auckland) 1949 A 1
Dodd, E H (Wellington) 1905 A
Donald, A J (Wanganui) 1983 S, E, 1984 F 1, 2, A 1, 2, 3
Donald, J G (Wairarapa) 1921 SA 1, 2
Donald, Q (Wairarapa) 1924 I, W, 1925 E, F
Donald, S R (Waikato) 2008 E1(R), 2(R), A2(R), SA3(R), Sm(R), A3(R), 4, S, I2(R), 2009 F1, 2, A1, SA1, 2, A2(R), SA3, A4(R), It2(R), F3(R)
Donaldson, M W (Manawatu) 1977 F 1, 2, 1978 A 1, 2, 3, I, E, S, 1979 F 1, 2, A, S (R), 1981 SA 3(R)
Donnelly, T J S (Otago) 2009 A3, 4, W(R), It2, E, F3, 2010 W2, SA1, 2, A1, 2, SA3, A3
Dougan, J P (Wellington) 1972 A 1, 1973 E 2
Dowd, C W (Auckland) 1993 BI 1, 2, 3, A, WS, S, E, 1994 SA 1(R), 1995 C, [I, W, J, E, SA], A 1, 2, It, F 1, 2, 1996 WS, S 1, 2, A 1, SA 1, A 2, SA 2, 3, 4, 5, 1997 Fj, Arg 1, 2, A 1, SA 1, A 2, SA 2, A 3, I, E 1, W, 1998 E 1, 2, A 1, SA 1, A

2, 3(R), 1999 SA 2(R), A 2(R), [Tg (R), E, It, S, F 2, SA 3], 2000 Tg, S 1(R), 2(R), A 1(R), SA 1(R), A 2(R)
Dowd, G W (North Harbour) 1992 I 1(R)
Downing, A J (Auckland) 1913 A 1, US, 1914 A 1, 2, 3
Drake, J A (Auckland) 1986 F 2, 3, 1987 [Fj, Arg, S, W, F], A
Duff, R H (Canterbury) 1951 A 1, 2, 3, 1952 A 1, 2, 1955 A 2, 3, 1956 SA 1, 2, 3, 4
Duggan, R J L (Waikato) 1999 [It (R)]
Duncan, J (Otago) 1903 A
Duncan, M G (Hawke's Bay) 1971 BI 3(R), 4
Duncan, W D (Otago) 1921 SA 1, 2, 3
Dunn, E J (North Auckland) 1979 S, 1981 S 1
Dunn, I T W (North Auckland) 1983 BI 1, 4, A
Dunn, J M (Auckland) 1946 A 1
Earl, A T (Canterbury) 1986 F 1, A 1, F 3(R), 1987 [Arg], 1989 W, I, 1991 Arg 1(R), 2, A 1, [E (R), US, S], 1992 A 2, 3(R)
Eastgate, B P (Canterbury) 1952 A 1, 2, 1954 S
Eaton, J J (Taranaki) 2005 I, E(t), S(R), 2006 Arg, A1, 2(R), 3, SA3(R), F1(R), 2(R), 2009 A1(R), SA1(R), A3(R), 4(R), W
Elliott, K G (Wellington) 1946 A 1, 2
Ellis, A M (Canterbury) 2006 E(R), F2(R), 2007 [Pt(R), R], 2008 I1, E1, 2, SA1, 2, A1, S(R), 2009 It2, E(R), F3(R)
Ellis, M C G (Otago) 1993 S, E, 1995 C, [I (R), W, J, S, SA (R)]
Ellison, T E (Wellington) 2009 It 2
Elsom, A E G (Canterbury) 1952 A 1, 2, 1953 W, 1955 A 1, 2, 3
Elvidge, R R (Otago) 1946 A 1, 2, 1949 SA 1, 2, 3, 4, 1950 BI 1, 2, 3
Erceg, C P (Auckland) 1951 A 1, 2, 3, 1952 A 1
Evans, B R (Hawke's Bay) 2009 F1(R), 2(R)
Evans, D A (Hawke's Bay) 1910 A 2
Evans, N J (North Harbour, Otago) 2004 E1(R), 2, Arg, PI(R), 2005 I, S, 2006 F2(R), W(R), 2007 F1(R), 2, SA2(R), A2(R), [Pt, S(R), R, F(R)]
Eveleigh, K A (Manawatu) 1976 SA 2, 4, 1977 BI 1, 2
Fanning, A H N (Canterbury) 1913 A 3
Fanning, B J (Canterbury) 1903 A, 1904 BI
Farrell, C P (Auckland) 1977 BI 1, 2
Fawcett, C L (Auckland) 1976 SA 2, 3
Fea, W R (Otago) 1921 SA 3
Feek, G E (Canterbury) 1999 WS (R), A 1(R), SA 2, [E (t), It], 2000 F 1, 2, It, 2001 I, S
Filipo, R A (Wellington) 2007 C, SA1(R), A1(R), 2008 S(R)
Finlay, B E L (Manawatu) 1959 BI 1
Finlay, J (Manawatu) 1946 A 1
Finlayson, I (North Auckland) 1928 SA 1, 2, 3, 4, 1930 BI 1, 2
Fitzgerald, J T (Wellington) 1952 A 1
Fitzpatrick, B B J (Wellington) 1953 W, 1954 I, F
Fitzpatrick, S B T (Auckland) 1986 F 1, A 1, F 2, 3, 1987 [It, Fj, Arg, S, W, F], A, 1988 W 1, 2, A 1, 2, 3, 1989 F 1, 2, Arg 1, 2, A, W, I, 1990 S 1, 2, A 1, 2, 3, F 1, 2, 1991 Arg 1, 2, A 1, 2, [E, US, It, C, A, S], 1992 Wld 1, 2, 3, I 1, 2, A 1, 2, 3, SA, 1993 BI 1, 2, 3, A, WS, S, E, 1994 F 1, 2, SA 1, 2, 3, A, 1995 C, [I, W, S, E, SA], A 1, 2, It, F 1, 2, 1996 WS, S 1, 2, A 1, SA 1, A 2, SA 2, 3, 4, 5, 1997 Fj, Arg 1, 2, A 1, SA 1, A 2, SA 2, A 3, W (R)
Flavell, T V (North Harbour, Auckland) 2000 Tg, S 1(R), A 1(R), SA 1, 2(t), F 1(R), 2(R), It, 2001 Sm, Arg 1, F, SA 1, A 1, SA 2, A 2, 2006 I1(R), 2, 2007 F1(R), 2(R), C, SA1, A1
Fleming, J K (Wellington) 1979 S, E, 1980 A 1, 2, 3
Fletcher, C J C (North Auckland) 1921 SA 3
Flynn, C R (Canterbury) 2003 [C(R), Tg], 2004 It(R), 2008 S(R), I2(R), 2009 It2, F3(R), 2010 SA1(R), 2(R), A1(R), 2(R), 3(R)
Fogarty, R (Taranaki) 1921 SA 1, 3
Ford, B R (Marlborough) 1977 BI 3, 4, 1978 I, 1979 E
Forster, S T (Otago) 1993 S, E, 1994 F 1, 2, 1995 It, F 1
Fox, G J (Auckland) 1985 Arg 1, 1987 [It, Fj, Arg, S, W, F], A, 1988 W 1, 2, A 1, 2, 3, 1989 F 1, 2, Arg 1, 2, A, W, I, 1990 S 1, 2, A 1, 2, 3, F 1, 2, 1991 Arg 1, 2, A 1, 2, [E, It, C, A], 1992 Wld 1, 2(R), A 1, 2, 3, SA, 1993 BI 1, 2, 3, A, WS
Francis, A R H (Auckland) 1905 A, 1907 A 1, 2, 3, 1908 AW 1, 2, 3, 1910 A 1, 2, 3
Francis, W C (Wellington) 1913 A 2, 3, 1914 A 1, 2, 3
Franks, B J (Tasman) 2010 I1, W1, SA1(R), 2(R), A1(R), 2(R), SA3
Franks, O T (Canterbury) 2009 It1(R), A1(R), SA1(R), 2, A2, SA3, W(R), E, F3(R), 2010 I1, W1, 2(t&R), SA1, 2, A1, 2, 3
Fraser, B G (Wellington) 1979 S, E, 1980 A 3, W, 1981 S 1, 2, SA 1, 2, 3, R, F 1, 2, 1982 A 1, 2, 3, 1983 BI 1, 2, 3, 4, A, S, E, 1984 A 1
Frazer, H F (Hawke's Bay) 1946 A 1, 2, 1947 A 1, 2, 1949 SA 2
Fryer, F C (Canterbury) 1907 A 1, 2, 3, 1908 AW 2
Fuller, W B (Canterbury) 1910 A 1, 2
Furlong, B D M (Hawke's Bay) 1970 SA 4
Gallagher, J A (Wellington) 1987 [It, Fj, S, W, F], A, 1988 W 1, 2, A 1, 2, 3, 1989 F 1, 2, Arg 1, 2, A, W, I
Gallaher, D (Auckland) 1903 A, 1904 BI, 1905 S, E, W, 1906 F
Gard, P C (North Otago) 1971 BI 4
Gardiner, A J (Taranaki) 1974 A 3
Gear, H E (Wellington) 2008 A4, 2009 A3(R)
Gear, R L (North Harbour, Nelson Bays, Tasman) 2004 PI, It, 2005 BI1(R), 2, 3, SA1, A1, SA2, W, S, 2006 Arg, A1, 2, SA2, 3(R), E, W, 2007 C(R), A1
Geddes, J H (Southland) 1929 A 1
Geddes, W McK (Auckland) 1913 A 2
Gemmell, B McL (Auckland) 1974 A 1, 2
George, V L (Southland) 1938 A 1, 2, 3
Gibbes, J B (Waikato) 2004 E1, 2, Arg(R), PI, A1, 2, SA2, 2005 BI2(R)
Gibson, D P E (Canterbury) 1999 WS, F 1, SA 1, A 1, SA 2, A 2, [Tg (R), E (R), It, S (R), F 2(R)], 2000 F 1, 2, 2002 It, I 1(R), 2(R), Fj, A 2(R), SA 2(R)
Gilbert, G D M (West Coast) 1935 S, I, W, 1936 E
Gillespie, C T (Wellington) 1913 A 2
Gillespie, W D (Otago) 1958 A 3
Gillett, G A (Canterbury, Auckland) 1905 S, I, E, W, 1907 A 2, 3, 1908 AW 1, 3
Gillies, C C (Otago) 1936 A 2
Gilray, C M (Otago) 1905 A
Glasgow, F T (Taranaki, Southland) 1905 S, I, E, W, 1906 F, 1908 AW 3
Glenn, W S (Taranaki) 1904 BI, 1906 F
Goddard, M P (South Canterbury) 1946 A 2, 1947 A 1, 2, 1949 SA 3, 4
Going, S M (North Auckland) 1967 A, F, 1968 F 3, 1969 W 1, 2, 1970 SA 1(R), 4, 1971 BI 1, 2, 3, 4, 1972 A 1, 2, 3, W, S, 1973 E 1, I, F, E 2, 1974 I, 1975 S, 1976 I (R), SA 1, 2, 3, 4, 1977 BI 1, 2
Gordon, S B (Waikato) 1993 S, E
Graham, D J (Canterbury) 1958 A 1, 2, 1960 SA 2, 3, 1961 F 1, 2, 3, 1962 A 1, 2, 3, 4, 5, 1963 E 1, 2, I, W, 1964 E, S, F, A 1, 2, 3
Graham, J B (Otago) 1913 US, 1914 A 1, 3
Graham, W G (Otago) 1979 F 1(R)
Grant, L A (South Canterbury) 1947 A 1, 2, 1949 SA 1, 2
Gray, G D (Canterbury) 1908 AW 2, 1913 A 1, US
Gray, K F (Wellington) 1963 I, W, 1964 E, S, F, A 1, 2, 3, 1965 SA 1, 2, 3, 4, 1966 BI 1, 2, 3, 4, 1967 W, F, S, 1968 A 1, F 2, 3, 1969 W 1, 2
Gray, W N (Bay of Plenty) 1955 A 2, 3, 1956 SA 1, 2, 3, 4
Green, C I (Canterbury) 1983 S (R), E, 1984 A 1, 2, 3, 1985 E 1, 2, A, Arg 1, 2, 1986 A 2, 3, F 2, 3, 1987 [It, Fj, S, W, F], A
Grenside, B A (Hawke's Bay) 1928 SA 1, 2, 3, 4, 1929 A 2, 3
Griffiths, J L (Wellington) 1934 A 2, 1935 S, I, W, 1936 A 1, 2, 1938 A 3
Guildford, Z R (Hawke's Bay) 2009 W, E, 2010 I1(R), W2
Guy, R A (North Auckland) 1971 BI 1, 2, 3, 4
Haden, A M (Auckland) 1977 BI 1, 2, 3, 4, F 1, 2, 1978 A 1, 2, 3, I, W, E, S, 1979 F 1, 2, A, S, E, 1980 A 1, 2, 3, W, 1981 S 2, SA 1, 2, 3, R, F 1, 2, 1982 A 1, 2, 3, 1983 BI 1, 2, 3, 4, A, 1984 F 1, 2, 1985 Arg 1, 2
Hadley, S (Auckland) 1928 SA 1, 2, 3, 4
Hadley, W E (Auckland) 1934 A 1, 2, 1935 S, I, W, 1936 E, A 1, 2
Haig, J S (Otago) 1946 A 1, 2
Haig, L S (Otago) 1950 BI 2, 3, 4, 1951 A 1, 2, 3, 1953 W, 1954 E, S
Hales, D A (Canterbury) 1972 A 1, 2, 3, W
Hamilton, D C (Southland) 1908 AW 2
Hamilton, S E (Canterbury) 2006 Arg, SA1
Hammett, M G (Canterbury) 1999 F 1(R), SA 2(R), [It, S (R), SA 3], 2000 Tg, S 1(R), 2(t&R), A 1(R), SA 1(R), A 2(R), SA 2(R), F 2(R), It (R), 2001 Arg 1(t), 2002 It (R), I 1, 2, A 1, SA 1, 2(R), 2003 SA 1(R), A 1(R), SA 2, [It(R), C, W(R), SA(R), F(R)]
Hammond, I A (Marlborough) 1952 A 2
Harper, E T (Canterbury) 1904 BI, 1906 F
Harding, S (Otago) 2002 Fj
Harris, P C (Manawatu) 1976 SA 3
Hart, A H (Taranaki) 1924 I
Hart, G F (Canterbury) 1930 BI 1, 2, 3, 4, 1931 A, 1934 A 1, 1935 S, I, W, 1936 A 1, 2
Harvey, B A (Wairarapa-Bush) 1986 F 1
Harvey, I H (Wairarapa) 1928 SA 4

Harvey, L R (Otago) 1949 SA 1, 2, 3, 4, 1950 BI 1, 2, 3, 4
Harvey, P (Canterbury) 1904 BI
Hasell, E W (Canterbury) 1913 A 2, 3
Hayman, C J (Otago) 2001 Sm (R), Arg 1, F (R), A 1(R), SA 2(R), A 2(R), 2002 F (t), W, 2004 E1, 2, PI, A1, 2, SA2, It, W(R), F, 2005 BI1, SA1, A1, SA2, A2, W, E, 2006 I1, 2, A1, SA1, A2, 3, SA3, E, F1, 2, W, 2007 F1, 2, SA1, A1, SA2, A2, [It, Pt(R), S, F]
Hayward, H O (Auckland) 1908 AW 3
Hazlett, E J (Southland) 1966 BI 1, 2, 3, 4, 1967 A, E
Hazlett, W E (Southland) 1928 SA 1, 2, 3, 4, 1930 BI 1, 2, 3, 4
Heeps, T R (Wellington) 1962 A 1, 2, 3, 4, 5
Heke, W R (North Auckland) 1929 A 1, 2, 3
Hemi, R C (Waikato) 1953 W, 1954 I, E, S, F, 1955 A 1, 2, 3, 1956 SA 1, 3, 4, 1957 A 1, 2, 1959 BI 1, 3, 4
Henderson, P (Wanganui) 1949 SA 1, 2, 3, 4, 1950 BI 2, 3, 4
Henderson, P W (Otago) 1991 Arg 1, [C], 1992 Wld 1, 2, 3, I 1, 1995 [J]
Herewini, M A (Auckland) 1962 A 5, 1963 I, 1964 S, F, 1965 SA 4, 1966 BI 1, 2, 3, 4, 1967 A
Hewett, D N (Canterbury) 2001 I (R), S (R), Arg 2, 2002 It (R), I 1, 2, A 1, SA 1, A 2, SA 2, 2003 E, F, SA 1, A 1, SA 2, A 2, [It, Tg(R), W, SA, A, F]
Hewett, J A (Auckland) 1991 [It]
Hewitt, N J (Southland) 1995 [I (t), J], 1996 A 1(R), 1997 SA 1(R), I, E 1, W, E 2, 1998 E 2(t + R)
Hewson, A R (Wellington) 1981 S 1, 2, SA 1, 2, 3, R, F 1, 2, 1982 A 1, 2, 3, 1983 BI 1, 2, 3, 4, A, 1984 F 1, 2, A 1
Higginson, G (Canterbury, Hawke's Bay) 1980 W, 1981 S 1, SA 1, 1982 A 1, 2, 1983 A
Hill, D W (Waikato) 2006 I2(R)
Hill, S F (Canterbury) 1955 A 3, 1956 SA 1, 3, 4, 1957 A 1, 2, 1958 A 3, 1959 BI 1, 2, 3, 4
Hines, G R (Waikato) 1980 A 3
Hobbs, M J B (Canterbury) 1983 BI 1, 2, 3, 4, A, S, E, 1984 F 1, 2, A 1, 2, 3, 1985 E 1, 2, A, Arg 1, 2, 1986 A 2, 3, F 2, 3
Hoeft, C H (Otago) 1998 E 2(t + R), A 2(R), SA 2, A 3, 1999 WS, F 1, SA 1, A 1, 2, [Tg, E, S, F 2, SA 3(R)], 2000 S 1, 2, A 1, SA 1, A 2, SA 2, 2001 Sm, Arg 1, F, SA 1, A 1, SA 2, A 2, 2003 W, [C, F(R)]
Holah, M R (Waikato) 2001 Sm, Arg 1(t&R), F (R), SA 1(R), A 1(R), SA 2(R), A 2(R), 2002 It, I 2(R), A 2(t), E, F, W (R), 2003 W, F (R), A 1(R), SA 2, [It(R), C, Tg(R), W(R), SA(t&R), A(R), F(t&R)], 2004 E1(R), 2, Arg(R), PI, A1, SA1, A2, SA2, 2005 BI3(R), A1(R), 2006 I1, SA3(t)
Holder, E C (Buller) 1934 A 2
Hook, L S (Auckland) 1929 A 1, 2, 3
Hooper, J A (Canterbury) 1937 SA 1, 2, 3
Hopkinson, A E (Canterbury) 1967 S, 1968 A 2, F 1, 2, 3, 1969 W 2, 1970 SA 1, 2, 3
Hore, A K (Taranaki) 2002 E, F, 2004 E1(t), 2(R), Arg, A1(t), 2005 W(R), I(R), S(R), 2006 I2(R), Arg(R), A1(R), SA1(R), A2(R), SA3, E(R), F2(R), W(R), 2007 F1(R), C, SA2(R), [Pt, S(R), R(R), F(R)], 2008 I1, E1, 2, SA1, 2, A1, 2, SA3, Sm, A3, 4, 2009 F1, A1, SA1, 2, A2, SA3, A3, 4, W, E, F3
Hore, J (Otago) 1930 BI 2, 3, 4, 1932 A 1, 2, 3, 1934 A 1, 2, 1935 S, 1936 E
Horsley, R H (Wellington) 1960 SA 2, 3, 4
Hotop, J (Canterbury) 1952 A 1, 2, 1955 A 3
Howarth, S P (Auckland) 1994 SA 1, 2, 3, A
Howlett, D C (Auckland) 2000 Tg (R), F 1, 2, It, 2001 Sm, Arg 1(R), F (R), SA 1, A 1, 2, I, S, Arg 2, 2002 It, I 1, 2(R), Fj, A 1, SA 1, A 2, SA 2, E, F, W, 2003 E, W, F, SA 1, A 1, SA 2, A 2, [It, C(R), Tg, W, SA, A, F], 2004 E1, A1, SA1, A2, SA2, W, F, 2005 Fj, BI1, A2, I, E, 2006 I1, 2, SA1, A3, SA3, 2007 F2(R), C, SA2, A2, [It, S, R(R)]
Hughes, A M (Auckland) 1949 A 1, 2, 1950 BI 1, 2, 3, 4
Hughes, E (Southland, Wellington) 1907 A 1, 2, 3, 1908 AW 1, 1921 SA 1, 2
Hunter, B A (Otago) 1971 BI 1, 2, 3
Hunter, J (Taranaki) 1905 S, I, E, W, 1906 F, 1907 A 1, 2, 3, 1908 AW 1, 2, 3
Hurst, I A (Canterbury) 1973 I, F, E 2, 1974 A 1, 2
Ieremia, A (Wellington) 1994 SA 1, 2, 3, 1995 [J], 1996 SA 2(R), 5(R), 1997 A 1(R), SA 1(R), A 2, SA 2, A 3, I, E 1, 1999 WS, F 1, SA 1, A 1, SA 2, A 2, [Tg, E, S, F 2, SA 3], 2000 Tg, S 1, 2, A 1, 2, SA 2
Ifwersen, K D (Auckland) 1921 SA 3
Innes, C R (Auckland) 1989 W, I, 1990 A 1, 2, 3, F 1, 2, 1991 Arg 1, 2, A 1, 2, [E, US, It, C, A, S]
Innes, G D (Canterbury) 1932 A 2
Irvine, I B (North Auckland) 1952 A 1
Irvine, J G (Otago) 1914 A 1, 2, 3
Irvine, W R (Hawke's Bay, Wairarapa) 1924 I, W, 1925 E, F, 1930 BI 1
Irwin, M W (Otago) 1955 A 1, 2, 1956 SA 1, 1958 A 2, 1959 BI 3, 4, 1960 SA 1
Jack, C R (Canterbury, Tasman) 2001 Arg 1(R), SA 1(R), 2, A 2, I, S, Arg 2, 2002 I 1, 2, A 1, SA 1, A 2, SA 2, 2003 E, W, F, SA 1, A 1, SA 2(R), A 2, [It, C, SA, A, F], 2004 E1, 2, Arg, PI, A1, SA1, A2, SA2, It, W, F, 2005 Fj(R), BI1, 2, 3, SA1, A1, SA2, A2, W, E, S, 2006 I1, 2, A1, SA1, A2, 3, SA2(R), 3, E, F2, 2007 F1, 2, A1, SA2, A2, [It, Pt, S(R), R(R), F(R)]
Jackson, E S (Hawke's Bay) 1936 A 1, 2, 1937 SA 1, 2, 3, 1938 A 3
Jaffray, J L (Otago, South Canterbury) 1972 A 2, 1975 S, 1976 I, SA 1, 1977 BI 2, 1979 F 1, 2
Jane, C S (Wellington) 2008 A4(R), S(R), 2009 F1, 2, It1(R), A1, SA3(R), A3, 4, W, It2, F3, 2010 I1, W1, 2, SA1, 2, A1, 2, SA3, A3
Jarden, R A (Wellington) 1951 A 1, 2, 1952 A 1, 2, 1953 W, 1954 I, E, S, F, 1955 A 1, 2, 3, 1956 SA 1, 2, 3, 4
Jefferd, A C R (East Coast) 1981 S 1, 2, SA 1
Jessep, E M (Wellington) 1931 A, 1932 A 1
Johnson, L M (Wellington) 1928 SA 1, 2, 3, 4
Johnston, W (Otago) 1907 A 1, 2, 3
Johnstone, B R (Auckland) 1976 SA 2, 1977 BI 1, 2, F 1, 2, 1978 I, W, E, S, 1979 F 1, 2, S, E
Johnstone, C R (Canterbury) 2005 Fj(R), BI2(R), 3(R)
Johnstone, P (Otago) 1949 SA 2, 4, 1950 BI 1, 2, 3, 4, 1951 A 1, 2, 3
Jones, I D (North Auckland, North Harbour) 1990 S 1, 2, A 1, 2, 3, F 1, 2, 1991 Arg 1, 2, A 1, 2, [E, US, It, C, A, S], 1992 Wld 1, 2, 3, I 1, 2, A 1, 2, 3, SA, 1993 BI 1, 2(R), 3, WS, S, E, 1994 F 1, 2, SA 1, 3, A, 1995 C, [I, W, S, E, SA], A 1, 2, It, F 1, 2, 1996 WS, S 1, 2, A 1, SA 1, A 2, SA 2, 3, 4, 5, 1997 Fj, Arg 1, 2, A 1, SA 1, A 2, SA 2, A 3, I, E 1, W, E 2, 1998 E 1, 2, A 1, SA 1, A 2, 3(R), 1999 F 1(R), [It, S (R)]
Jones, M G (North Auckland) 1973 E 2
Jones, M N (Auckland) 1987 [It, Fj, S, F], A, 1988 W 1, 2, A 2, 3, 1989 F 1, 2, Arg 1, 2, 1990 F 1, 2, 1991 Arg 1, 2, A 1, 2, [E, US, S], 1992 Wld 1, 3, I 2, A 1, 3, SA, 1993 BI 1, 2, 3, A, WS, 1994 SA 3(R), A, 1995 A 1(R), 2, It, F 1, 2, 1996 WS, S 1, 2, A 1, SA 1, A 2, SA 2, 3, 4, 5, 1997 Fj, 1998 E 1, A 1, SA 1, A 2
Jones, P F H (North Auckland) 1954 E, S, 1955 A 1, 2, 1956 SA 3, 4, 1958 A 1, 2, 3, 1959 BI 1, 1960 SA 1
Joseph, H T (Canterbury) 1971 BI 2, 3
Joseph, J W (Otago) 1992 Wld 2, 3(R), I 1, A 1(R), 3, SA, 1993 BI 1, 2, 3, A, WS, S, E, 1994 SA 2(t), 1995 C, [I, W, J (R), S, SA (R)]
Kahui, R D (Waikato) 2008 E2, A1, 2, SA3, Sm, A3, S, W, 2010 W1(R), 2, SA1(R)
Kaino, J (Auckland) 2006 I1(R), 2, 2008 I1, E1, SA1, 2, A1, 2, SA3, Sm, A3, 4, I2, W, E3, 2009 F2, It1, A1, SA1, 2, A2, SA3, W, E(R), F3, 2010 I1, W2, SA1, 2, A1, 2, SA3, A3(R)
Karam, J F (Wellington, Horowhenua) 1972 W, S, 1973 E 1, I, F, 1974 A 1, 2, 3, I, 1975 S
Katene, T (Wellington) 1955 A 2
Kearney, J C (Otago) 1947 A 2, 1949 SA 1, 2, 3
Kelleher, B T (Otago, Waikato) 1999 WS (R), SA 1(R), A 2(R), [Tg (R), E (R), It, F 2], 2000 S 1, A 1(R), 2(R), It (R), 2001 Sm, F (R), A 1(R), SA 2, A 2, I, S, 2002 It, I 2(R), Fj, SA 1(R), 2(R), 2003 F (R), [A(R)], 2004 Arg, PI(R), SA1(R), 2(R), It, W(R), F, 2005 Fj, BI1(R), 2, 3, SA1, W, E, 2006 I1, 2, A1, 2, 3, SA3(R), E, F1(R), 2, W, 2007 F2, C, SA1, A1, 2, [It, S, F]
Kelly, J W (Auckland) 1949 A 1, 2
Kember, G F (Wellington) 1970 SA 4
Ketels, R C (Counties) 1980 W, 1981 S 1, 2, R, F 1
Kiernan, H A D (Auckland) 1903 A
Kilby, F D (Wellington) 1932 A 1, 2, 3, 1934 A 2
Killeen, B A (Auckland) 1936 A 1
King, R M (Waikato) 2002 W
King, R R (West Coast) 1934 A 2, 1935 S, I, W, 1936 E, A 1, 2, 1937 SA 1, 2, 3, 1938 A 1, 2, 3
Kingstone, C N (Taranaki) 1921 SA 1, 2, 3
Kirk, D E (Auckland) 1985 E 1, 2, A, Arg 1, 1986 F 1, A 1, 2, 3, F 2, 3, 1987 [It, Fj, Arg, S, W, F], A
Kirkpatrick, I A (Canterbury, Poverty Bay) 1967 F, 1968 A 1(R), 2, F 1, 2, 3, 1969 W 1, 2, 1970 SA 1, 2, 3, 4, 1971 BI 1, 2, 3, 4, 1972 A 1, 2, 3, W, S, 1973 E 1, I, F, E 2, 1974 A 1, 2, 3, I 1975 S, 1976 I, SA 1, 2, 3, 4, 1977 BI 1, 2, 3, 4

Kirton, E W (Otago) 1967 E, W, F, S, 1968 A 1, 2, F 1, 2, 3, 1969 W 1, 2, 1970 SA 2, 3
Kirwan, J J (Auckland) 1984 F 1, 2, 1985 E 1, 2, A, Arg 1, 2, 1986 F 1, A 1, 2, 3, F 2, 3, 1987 [It, Fj, Arg, S, W, F], A, 1988 W 1, 2, A 1, 2, 3, 1989 F 1, 2, Arg 1, 2, A, 1990 S 1, 2, A 1, 2, 3, F 1, 2, 1991 Arg 2, A 1, 2, [E, It, C, A, S], 1992 Wld 1, 2(R), 3, I 1, 2, A 1, 2, 3, SA, 1993 BI 2, 3, A, WS, 1994 F 1, 2, SA 1, 2, 3
Kivell, A L (Taranaki) 1929 A 2, 3
Knight, A (Auckland) 1934 A 1
Knight, G A (Manawatu) 1977 F 1, 2, 1978 A 1, 2, 3, E, S, 1979 F 1, 2, A, 1980 A 1, 2, 3, W, 1981 S 1, 2, SA 1, 3, 1982 A 1, 2, 3, 1983 BI 1, 2, 3, 4, A, 1984 F 1, 2, A 1, 2, 3, 1985 E 1, 2, A, 1986 A 2, 3
Knight, L G (Poverty Bay) 1977 BI 1, 2, 3, 4, F 1, 2
Koteka, T T (Waikato) 1981 F 2, 1982 A 3
Kreft, A J (Otago) 1968 A 2
Kronfeld, J A (Otago) 1995 C, [I, W, S, E, SA], A 1, 2(R) 1996 WS, S 1, 2, A 1, SA 1, A 2, SA 2, 3, 4, 5, 1997 Fj, Arg 1, 2, A 1, SA 1, A 2, SA 2, A 3, I (R), E 1, W, E 2, 1998 E 1, 2, A 1, SA 1, 2 A 3, 1999 WS, F 1, SA 1, A 1, SA 2, A 2, [Tg, E, S, F 2, SA 3], 2000 Tg, S 1(R), 2, A 1(R), SA 1, A 2, SA 2
Laidlaw, C R (Otago, Canterbury) 1964 F, A 1, 1965 SA 1, 2, 3, 4, 1966 BI 1, 2, 3, 4, 1967 E, W, S, 1968 A 1, 2, F 1, 2, 1970 SA 1, 2, 3
Laidlaw, K F (Southland) 1960 SA 2, 3, 4
Lambert, K K (Manawatu) 1972 S (R), 1973 E 1, I, F, E 2, 1974 I, 1976 SA 1, 3, 4, 1977 BI 1, 4
Lambourn, A (Wellington) 1934 A 1, 2, 1935 S, I, W, 1936 E, 1937 SA 1, 2, 3, 1938 A 3
Larsen, B P (North Harbour) 1992 Wld 2, 3, I 1, 1994 F 1, 2, SA 1, 2, 3, A (t), 1995 [I, W, J, E(R)], It, F 1, 1996 S 2(t), SA 4(R)
Latimer, T D (Bay of Plenty) 2009 F1(R), 2, It1, 2, F3(R)
Lauaki, S T (Waikato) 2005 Fj(R), BI1(R), 2(R), 3, A2, I, S, 2007 [It(R), Pt, S(R), R], 2008 E1(R), 2(R), SA1(R), 2(R), A1(R), Sm(R)
Laulala, C D E (Canterbury) 2004 W, 2006 I2
Le Lievre, J M (Canterbury) 1962 A 4
Lee, D D (Otago) 2002 E (R), F
Lendrum, R N (Counties) 1973 E 2
Leonard, B G (Waikato) 2007 F1(R), 2(R), SA2(R), A2(R), [It(R), Pt, S(R), R(R), F(R)], 2009 It1, SA1, A3(R), W
Leslie, A R (Wellington) 1974 A 1, 2, 3, I, 1975 S, 1976 I, SA 1, 2, 3, 4
Leys, E T (Wellington) 1929 A 3
Lilburne, H T (Canterbury, Wellington) 1928 SA 3, 4, 1929 A 1, 2, 3, 1930 BI 1, 4, 1931 A, 1932 A 1, 1934 A 2
Lindsay, D F (Otago) 1928 SA 1, 2, 3
Lineen, T R (Auckland) 1957 A 1, 2, 1958 A 1, 2, 3, 1959 BI 1, 2, 3, 4, 1960 SA 1, 2, 3
Lister, T N (South Canterbury) 1968 A 1, 2, F 1, 1969 W 1, 2, 1970 SA 1, 4, 1971 BI 4
Little, P F (Auckland) 1961 F 2, 3, 1962 A 2, 3, 5, 1963 I, W, 1964 E, S, F
Little, W K (North Harbour) 1990 S 1, 2, A 1, 2, 3, F 1, 2, 1991 Arg 1, 2, A 1, [It, S], 1992 Wld 1, 2, 3, I 1, 2, A 1, 2, 3, SA, 1993 BI 1, WS (R), 1994 SA 2(R), A, 1995 C, [I, W, S, E, SA], A 1, 2, It, F 1, 2, 1996 S 2, A 1, SA 1, A 2, SA 2, 3, 4, 5, 1997 W, E 2, 1998 E 1, A 1, SA 1, A 2
Loader, C J (Wellington) 1954 I, E, S, F
Lochore, B J (Wairarapa) 1964 E, S, 1965 SA 1, 2, 3, 4, 1966 BI 1, 2, 3, 4, 1967 A, E, W, F, S, 1968 A 1, F 2, 3, 1969 W 1, 2, 1970 SA 1, 2, 3, 4, 1971 BI 3
Loe, R W (Waikato, Canterbury) 1987 [It, Arg], 1988 W 1, 2, A 1, 2, 3, 1989 F 1, 2, Arg 1, 2, A, W, I, 1990 S 1, 2, A 1, 2, 3, F 1, 2, 1991 Arg 1, 2, A 1, 2, [E, It, C, A, S], 1992 Wld 1, 2, 3, I 1, A 1, 2, 3, SA, 1994 F 1, 2, SA 1, 2, 3, A, 1995 [J, S, SA (R)], A 2(t), F 2(R)
Lomu, J T (Counties Manukau, Wellington) 1994 F 1, 2, 1995 [I, W, S, E, SA], A 1, 2, It, F 1, 2, 1996 WS, S 1, A 1, SA 1, A 2, 1997 E 1, W, E 2, 1998 E 1, 2, A 1(R), SA 1, A 2, SA 2, A 3, 1999 WS (R), SA 1(R), A 1(R), SA 2(R), A 2(R), [Tg, E, It, S, F 2, SA 3], 2000 Tg, S 1, 2, A 1, SA 1, A 2, SA 2, F 1, 2001 Arg 1, F, SA 1, A 1, SA 2, A 2, I, S, Arg 2, 2002 It (R), I 1(R), 2, Fj, SA 1(R), E, F, W
Long, A J (Auckland) 1903 A
Loveridge, D S (Taranaki) 1978 W, 1979 S, E, 1980 A 1, 2, 3, W, 1981 S 1, 2, SA 1, 2, 3, R, F 1, 2, 1982 A 1, 2, 3, 1983 BI 1, 2, 3, 4, A, 1985 Arg 2
Lowen, K R (Waikato) 2002 E
Lucas, F W (Auckland) 1924 I, 1925 F, 1928 SA 4, 1930 BI 1, 2, 3, 4
Lunn, W A (Otago) 1949 A 1, 2
Lynch, T W (South Canterbury) 1913 A 1, 1914 A 1, 2, 3
Lynch, T W (Canterbury) 1951 A 1, 2, 3
McAlister, C L (North Harbour) 2005 BI3, SA1(R), A1(R), SA2(R), A2(R), 2006 I1, 2, SA1(R), A3, SA2, F1, W, 2007 F2, C, SA1(R), A1, SA2, A2, [It, S, R, F], 2009 F1(R), 2(R), It1, SA1(R), 2(R), A2, It2, F3(R)
McAtamney, F S (Otago) 1956 SA 2
McCahill, B J (Auckland) 1987 [Arg, S (R), W (R)], 1989 Arg 1(R), 2(R), 1991 A 2, [E, US, C, A]
McCaw, R H (Canterbury) 2001 I, S, Arg 2, 2002 I 1, 2, A 1, SA 1, A 2, SA 2, 2003 E, F, SA 1, A 1, 2, [It, C(R), Tg(R), W, SA, A, F], 2004 E1, Arg, It, W, F, 2005 Fj, BI1, 2, SA1, A1, SA2, A2, W(R), I, S, 2006 I1, 2, A1, SA1, A2, 3, SA2, 3, E, F1, 2, W, 2007 F1, 2, C(R), SA1, A1, SA2, A2, [It, S, R(R), F], 2008 I1, E1, 2, A2, SA3, A3, 4, S(R), I2, W, E3, 2009 A1, SA1, 2, A2, SA3, A3, 4, W, E, F3, 2010 I1, W1, 2, SA1, 2, A1, 2, SA3, A3
McCaw, W A (Southland) 1951 A 1, 2, 3, 1953 W, 1954 F
McCool, M J (Wairarapa-Bush) 1979 A
McCormick, W F (Canterbury) 1965 SA 4, 1967 E, W, F, S, 1968 A 1, 2, F 1, 2, 3, 1969 W 1, 2, 1970 SA 1, 2, 3, 1971 BI 1
McCullough, J F (Taranaki) 1959 BI 2, 3, 4
McDonald, A (Otago) 1905 S, I, E, W, 1907 A 1, 1908 AW 1, 1913 A 1, US
Macdonald, A J (Auckland) 2005 W(R), S
Macdonald, H H (Canterbury, North Auckland) 1972 W, S, 1973 E 1, I, F, E 2, 1974 I, 1975 S, 1976 I, SA 1, 2, 3
MacDonald, L R (Canterbury) 2000 S 1(R), 2(R), SA 1(t), 2(R), 2001 Sm, Arg 1, F, SA 1(R), A 1(R), SA 2, A 2, I, S, 2002 I 1, 2, Fj (R), A 2(R), SA 2, 2003 A 2(R), [It(R), C, Tg, W, SA, A, F], 2005 BI1, 2(R), SA1, 2, A2, W(R), I, E(R), S(R), 2006 Arg, A1, SA1, A2, 3(R), SA2, F1, 2, 2007 F1, 2, C(R), SA1(R), [It, Pt(R), S, F], 2008 I1(R), E1(R), 2, SA1(R), 2(R)
McDonnell, J M (Otago) 2002 It, I 1(R), 2(R), Fj, SA 1(R), A 2(R), E, F
McDowell, S C (Auckland, Bay of Plenty) 1985 Arg 1, 2, 1986 A 2, 3, F 2, 3, 1987 [It, Fj, S, W, F], A, 1988 W 1, 2, A 1, 2, 3, 1989 F 1, 2, Arg 1, 2, A, W, I, 1990 S 1, 2, A 1, 2, 3, F 1, 2, 1991 Arg 1, 2, A 1, 2, [E, US, It, C, A, S], 1992 Wld 1, 2, 3, I 1, 2
McEldowney, J T (Taranaki) 1977 BI 3, 4
MacEwan, I N (Wellington) 1956 SA 2, 1957 A 1, 2, 1958 A 1, 2, 3, 1959 BI 1, 2, 3, 1960 SA 1, 2, 3, 4, 1961 F 1, 2, 3, 1962 A 1, 2, 3, 4
McGrattan, B (Wellington) 1983 S, E, 1985 Arg 1, 2, 1986 F 1, A 1
McGregor, A J (Auckland) 1913 A 1, US
McGregor, D (Canterbury, Southland) 1903 A, 1904 BI, 1905 E, W
McGregor, N P (Canterbury) 1924 W, 1925 E
McGregor, R W (Auckland) 1903 A, 1904 BI
McHugh, M J (Auckland) 1946 A 1, 2, 1949 SA 3
McIntosh, D N (Wellington) 1956 SA 1, 2, 1957 A 1, 2
McKay, D W (Auckland) 1961 F 1, 2, 3, 1963 E 1, 2
McKechnie, B J (Southland) 1977 F 1, 2, 1978 A 2(R), 3, W (R), E, S, 1979 A, 1981 SA 1(R), F 1
McKellar, G F (Wellington) 1910 A 1, 2, 3
McKenzie, R J (Wellington) 1913 A 1, US, 1914 A 2, 3
McKenzie, R McC (Manawatu) 1934 A 1, 1935 S, 1936 A 1, 1937 SA 1, 2, 3, 1938 A 1, 2, 3
McLachlan, J S (Auckland) 1974 A 2
McLaren, H C (Waikato) 1952 A 1
McLean, A L (Bay of Plenty) 1921 SA 2, 3
McLean, H F (Wellington, Auckland) 1930 BI 3, 4, 1932 A 1, 2, 3, 1934 A 1, 1935 I, W, 1936 E
McLean, J K (King Country, Auckland) 1947 A 1, 1949 A 2
McLeod, B E (Counties) 1964 A 1, 2, 3, 1965 SA 1, 2, 3, 4, 1966 BI 1, 2, 3, 4, 1967 E, W, F, S, 1968 A 1, 2, F 1, 2, 3, 1969 W 1, 2, 1970 SA 1, 2
McLeod, S J (Waikato) 1996 WS, S 1, 1997 Fj (R), Arg 2(t + R), I (R), E 1(R), W (t), E 2(R), 1998 A 1, SA 1(R)
McMinn, A F (Wairarapa, Manawatu) 1903 A, 1905 A
McMinn, F A (Manawatu) 1904 BI
McMullen, R F (Auckland) 1957 A 1, 2, 1958 A 1, 2, 3, 1959 BI 1, 2, 3, 1960 SA 2, 3, 4
McNab, J R (Otago) 1949 SA 1, 2, 3, 1950 BI 1, 2, 3

McNaughton, A M (Bay of Plenty) 1971 BI 1, 2, 3
McNeece, J (Southland) 1913 A 2, 3, 1914 A 1, 2, 3
McPhail, B E (Canterbury) 1959 BI 1, 4
Macpherson, D G (Otago) 1905 A
MacPherson, G L (Otago) 1986 F 1
MacRae, I R (Hawke's Bay) 1966 BI 1, 2, 3, 4, 1967 A, E, W, F, S, 1968 F 1, 2, 1969 W 1, 2, 1970 SA 1, 2, 3, 4
McRae, J A (Southland) 1946 A 1(R), 2
McWilliams, R G (Auckland) 1928 SA 2, 3, 4, 1929 A 1, 2, 3, 1930 BI 1, 2, 3, 4
Mackintosh, J L (Southland) 2008 S
Mackrell, W H C (Auckland) 1906 F
Macky, J V (Auckland) 1913 A 2
Maguire, J R (Auckland) 1910 A 1, 2, 3
Mahoney, A (Bush) 1935 S, I, W, 1936 E
Mains, L W (Otago) 1971 BI 2, 3, 4, 1976 I
Major, J (Taranaki) 1967 A
Maka, I (Otago) 1998 E 2(R), A 1(R), SA 1(R), 2
Maling, T S (Otago) 2002 It, I 2(R), Fj, A 1, SA 1, A 2, SA 2, 2004 Arg, A1, SA1, 2
Manchester, J E (Canterbury) 1932 A 1, 2, 3, 1934 A 1, 2, 1935 S, I, W, 1936 E
Mannix, S J (Wellington) 1994 F 1
Marshall, J W (Southland, Canterbury) 1995 F 2, 1996 WS, S 1, 2, A 1, SA 1, A 2, SA 2, 3, 4, 5, 1997 Fj, Arg 1, 2, A 1, SA 1, A 2, SA 2, A 3, I, E 1, W, E 2, 1998 A 1, SA 1, A 2, SA 2, A 3, 1999 WS, F 1, SA 1, A 1, SA 2, A 2, [Tg, E, S, F 2(R), SA 3], 2000 Tg, S 2, A 1, SA 1, A 2, SA 2, F 1, 2, It, 2001 Arg 1, F, SA 1, A 1, 2(R), 2002 I 1, 2, Fj (R), A 1, SA 1, A 2, SA 2, 2003 E, SA 1(R), A 1, SA 2, A 2, [It, Tg, W, SA, A], 2004 E1, 2, PI, A1, SA1, A2, SA2, 2005 Fj(R), BI1, 2(R), 3(R)
Masaga, L T C (Counties Manukau) 2009 It1
Masoe, M C (Taranaki, Wellington) 2005 W, E, 2006Arg, A1(R), SA1(R), A2(R), 3(R), SA2, E, F2(R), 2007 F1, 2(R), C, A1(R), SA2(R), [It(R), Pt, S, R, F(R)]
Mason, D F (Wellington) 1947 A 2(R)
Masters, R R (Canterbury) 1924 I, W, 1925 E, F
Mataira, H K (Hawke's Bay) 1934 A 2
Matheson, J D (Otago) 1972 A 1, 2, 3, W, S
Mathewson, A S (Wellington) 2010 A2(R)
Mauger, A J D (Canterbury) 2001 I, S, Arg 2, 2002 It (R), I 1, 2, Fj, A 1, SA 1, A 2, SA 2, 2003 SA 1, A 1, SA 2, A 2, [W, SA, A, F], 2004 SA2(R), It(R), W, F(R), 2005 Fj, BI1, 2, SA1, A1, SA2, A2, I, E, 2006 I1, 2, A1, 2, SA3, E, 2007 F1, C, SA1, A1, [It(R), Pt, R]
Max, D S (Nelson) 1931 A, 1934 A 1, 2
Maxwell, N M C (Canterbury) 1999 WS, F 1, SA 1, A 1, SA 2, A 2, [Tg, E, S, F 2, SA 3], 2000 S 1, 2, A 1, SA 1(R), A 2, SA 2, F 1, 2, It (R), 2001 Sm, Arg 1, F, SA 1, A 1, SA 2, A2, I, S, Arg 2, 2002 It, I 1, 2, Fj, 2004 It, F
Mayerhofler, M A (Canterbury) 1998 E 1, 2, SA 1, A 2, SA 2, A 3
Meads, C E (King Country) 1957 A 1, 2, 1958 A 1, 2, 3, 1959 BI 2, 3, 4, 1960 SA 1, 2, 3, 4, 1961 F 1, 2, 3, 1962 A 1, 2, 3, 5, 1963 E 1, 2, I, W, 1964 E, S, F, A 1, 2, 3, 1965 SA 1, 2, 3, 4, 1966 BI 1, 2, 3, 4, 1967 A, E, W, F, S, 1968 A 1, 2, F 1, 2, 3, 1969 W 1, 2, 1970 SA 3, 4, 1971 BI 1, 2, 3, 4
Meads, S T (King Country) 1961 F 1, 1962 A 4, 5, 1963 I, 1964 A 1, 2, 3, 1965 SA 1, 2, 3, 4, 1966 BI 1, 2, 3, 4
Mealamu, K F (Auckland) 2002 W, 2003 E (R), W, F (R), SA 1, A 1, SA 2(R), A 2, [It, W, SA, A, F], 2004 E1, 2, PI, A1, SA1, A2, SA2, W, F(R), 2005 Fj(R), BI1, 2, 3, SA1, A1, SA2, A2, I, E, 2006 I1, 2, A1, 2, 3, SA2(R), E, F1(R), 2, 2007 F1, 2(R), SA1(R), A1(R), SA2, A2(R), [It, Pt(R), R], 2008 I1(R), E1(t&R), 2(t&R), SA1(R), 2(R), A1(R), 2(R), SA3(R), Sm(R), A3(R), 4(R), S, I2, W, E3, 2009 F1(R), 2, It1, A1(R), SA1(R), 2(R), 2010 I1, W1, 2, SA1, 2, A1, 2, SA3, A3
Meates, K F (Canterbury) 1952 A 1, 2
Meates, W A (Otago) 1949 SA 2, 3, 4, 1950 BI 1, 2, 3, 4
Meeuws, K J (Otago, Auckland) 1998 A 3, 1999 WS, F 1, SA 1, A 1, SA 2, A 2, [Tg, It (R), S (R), F 2(R), SA 3], 2000 Tg (R), S 2, A 1, SA 1, A 2, SA 2, 2001 Arg 2, 2002 It, Fj, E, F, W (R), 2003 W, F (R), SA 1(R), A 1(R), SA 2, [It(R), C, Tg, W(R), SA(R), A(R)], 2004 E1, 2, PI, A1, SA1, A2, SA2
Mehrtens, A P (Canterbury) 1995 C, [I, W, S, E, SA], A 1, 2, 1996 WS, S 1, 2, A 1, SA 1, A 2, SA 2, 5, 1997 Fj, SA 2(R), I, E 1, W, E 2, 1998 E 1, 2, A 1, SA 1(R), A 2, SA 2, A 3, 1999 F 1, SA 1, A 1, SA 2, A 2, [Tg, E, S, F 2, SA 3], 2000 S 1, 2, A 1, SA 1, A 2, SA 2, F 1, 2, It (R), 2001 Arg 1, A 1(R), SA 2, A 2, I, S, Arg 2, 2002 It, I 1, 2, Fj (R), A 1, SA 1, A 2, SA 2, E (R), F, W, 2004 E2(R), Arg, A2(R), SA2
Messam, L J (Waikato) 2008 S, 2009 F1, It2, 2010 SA1(R), 2(R)
Metcalfe, T C (Southland) 1931 A, 1932 A 1
Mexted, G G (Wellington) 1950 BI 4
Mexted, M G (Wellington) 1979 S, E, 1980 A 1, 2, 3, W, 1981 S 1, 2, SA 1, 2, 3, R, F 1, 2, 1982 A 1, 2, 3, 1983 BI 1, 2, 3, 4, A, S, E, 1984 F 1, 2, A 1, 2, 3, 1985 E 1, 2, A, Arg 1, 2
Mika, B M (Auckland) 2002 E (R), F, W (R)
Mika, D G (Auckland) 1999 WS, F 1, SA 1(R), A 1, 2, [It, SA 3(R)]
Mill, J J (Hawke's Bay, Wairarapa) 1924 W, 1925 E, F, 1930 BI 1
Milliken, H M (Canterbury) 1938 A 1, 2, 3
Milner, H P (Wanganui) 1970 SA 3
Mitchell, N A (Southland, Otago) 1935 S, I, W, 1936 E, A 2, 1937 SA 3, 1938 A 1, 2
Mitchell, T W (Canterbury) 1976 SA 4(R)
Mitchell, W J (Canterbury) 1910 A 2, 3
Mitchinson, F E (Wellington) 1907 A 1, 2, 3, 1908 AW 1, 2, 3, 1910 A 1, 2, 3, 1913 A 1(R), US
Moffitt, J E (Wellington) 1921 SA 1, 2, 3
Moore, G J T (Otago) 1949 A 1
Moreton, R C (Canterbury) 1962 A 3, 4, 1964 A 1, 2, 3, 1965 SA 2, 3
Morgan, J E (North Auckland) 1974 A 3, I, 1976 SA 2, 3, 4
Morris, T J (Nelson Bays) 1972 A 1, 2, 3
Morrison, T C (South Canterbury) 1938 A 1, 2, 3
Morrison, T G (Otago) 1973 E 2(R)
Morrissey, P J (Canterbury) 1962 A 3, 4, 5
Mourie, G N K (Taranaki) 1977 BI 3, 4, F 1, 2, 1978 I, W, E, S, 1979 F 1, 2, A, S, E, 1980 W, 1981 S 1, 2, F 1, 2, 1982 A 1, 2, 3
Muliaina, J M (Auckland, Waikato) 2003 E (R), W, F, SA 1, A 1, SA 2, A 2, [It, C, Tg, W, SA, A, F], 2004 E1, 2, Arg, PI, A1, SA1, A2, SA2, It, W, F, 2005 Fj, BI1(R), 2, 3, SA1, A1, SA2, A2, W, E, 2006 I1, 2, A1, SA1, A2, 3, SA2, 3, E, F1(R), 2, W, 2007 C, SA1, A1, SA2, A2, [It, Pt, F], 2008 I1, E1, 2(t), SA1, 2, A1, 2, SA3, Sm, A3, I2, W, E3, 2009 F1, 2, It1, A1, SA1, 2, A2, SA3, A3, 4, W, It2(R), E, F3, 2010 W2, SA1, 2, A1, 2, SA3, A3
Muller, B L (Taranaki) 1967 A, E, W, F, 1968 A 1, F 1, 1969 W 1, 1970 SA 1, 2, 4, 1971 BI 1, 2, 3, 4
Mumm, W J (Buller) 1949 A 1
Murdoch, K (Otago) 1970 SA 4, 1972 A 3, W
Murdoch, P H (Auckland) 1964 A 2, 3, 1965 SA 1, 2, 3
Murray, H V (Canterbury) 1913 A 1, US, 1914 A 2, 3
Murray, P C (Wanganui) 1908 AW 2
Myers, R G (Waikato) 1978 A 3
Mynott, H J (Taranaki) 1905 I, W, 1906 F, 1907 A 1, 2, 3, 1910 A 1, 3
Nathan, W J (Auckland) 1962 A 1, 2, 3, 4, 5, 1963 E 1, 2, W, 1964 F, 1966 BI 1, 2, 3, 4, 1967 A
Nelson, K A (Otago) 1962 A 4, 5
Nepia, G (Hawke's Bay, East Coast) 1924 I, W, 1925 E, F, 1929 A 1, 1930 BI 1, 2, 3, 4
Nesbit, S R (Auckland) 1960 SA 2, 3
Newby, C A (North Harbour) 2004 E2(t), SA2(R), 2006 I2(R)
Newton, F (Canterbury) 1905 E, W, 1906 F
Nicholls, H E (Wellington) 1921 SA 1
Nicholls, M F (Wellington) 1921 SA 1, 2, 3, 1924 I, W, 1925 E, F, 1928 SA 4, 1930 BI 2, 3
Nicholson, G W (Auckland) 1903 A, 1904 BI, 1907 A 2, 3
Nonu, M A (Wellington) 2003 E, [It(R), C, Tg(R)], 2004 It(R), W(R), F(R), 2005 BI2(R), W(R), I, S(R), 2006 I1, E, F1(R), 2, W(R), 2007 F1(R), 2(R), 2008 I1, E1, 2, SA1, 2, A1, 2, SA3, Sm, A3, 4(R), S, I2, W, E3, 2009 F1, 2, It1, A1, SA1, 2, A2(t&R), SA3, A3, 4, W, E, F3, 2010 SA1, 2, A1, 2, SA3, A3
Norton, R W (Canterbury) 1971 BI 1, 2, 3, 4, 1972 A 1, 2, 3, W, S, 1973 E 1, I, F, E 2, 1974 A 1, 2, 3, I, 1975 S, 1976 I, SA 1, 2, 3, 4, 1977 BI 1, 2, 3, 4
O'Brien, J G (Auckland) 1914 A 1
O'Callaghan, M W (Manawatu) 1968 F 1, 2, 3
O'Callaghan, T R (Wellington) 1949 A 2
O'Donnell, D H (Wellington) 1949 A 2
O'Halloran, J D (Wellington) 2000 It (R)
Old, G H (Manawatu) 1981 SA 3, R (R), 1982 A 1(R)
O'Leary, M J (Auckland) 1910 A 1, 3, 1913 A 2, 3
Oliver, A D (Otago) 1997 Fj (t), 1998 E 1, 2, A 1, SA 1, A 2, SA 2, A 3, 1999 WS, F 1, SA 1, A 1, SA 2, A 2, [Tg, E, S, F 2, SA 3(R)], 2000 Tg (R), S 1, 2, A 1, SA 1, A 2, SA 2, F

1, 2, It, 2001 Sm, Arg 1, F, SA 1, A 1, SA 2, A 2, I, S, Arg 2, 2003 E, F, 2004 It, F, 2005 W, S, 2006 Arg, SA1, 2, 3(R), F1, W, 2007 F2, SA1, A1, 2, [It(R), Pt(R), S, F]
Oliver, C J (Canterbury) 1929 A 1, 2, 1934 A 1, 1935 S, I, W, 1936 E
Oliver, D J (Wellington) 1930 BI 1, 2
Oliver, D O (Otago) 1954 I, F
Oliver, F J (Southland, Otago, Manawatu) 1976 SA 4, 1977 BI 1, 2, 3, 4, F 1, 2, 1978 A 1, 2, 3, I, W, E, S, 1979 F 1, 2, 1981 SA 2
O'Neill, K J (Canterbury) 2008 SA2(R)
Orr, R W (Otago) 1949 A 1
Osborne, G M (North Harbour) 1995 C, [I, W, J, E, SA], A 1, 2, F 1(R), 2, 1996 SA 2, 3, 4, 5, 1997 Arg 1(R), A 2, 3, I, 1999 [It]
Osborne, W M (Wanganui) 1975 S, 1976 SA 2(R), 4(R), 1977 BI 1, 2, 3, 4, F 1(R), 2, 1978 I, W, E, S, 1980 W, 1982 A 1, 3
O'Sullivan, J M (Taranaki) 1905 S, I, E, W, 1907 A 3
O'Sullivan, T P A (Taranaki) 1960 SA 1, 1961 F 1, 1962 A 1, 2
Page, J R (Wellington) 1931 A, 1932 A 1, 2, 3, 1934 A 1, 2
Palmer, B P (Auckland) 1929 A 2, 1932 A 2, 3
Parker, J H (Canterbury) 1924 I, W, 1925 E
Parkhill, A A (Otago) 1937 SA 1, 2, 3, 1938 A 1, 2, 3
Parkinson, R M (Poverty Bay) 1972 A 1, 2, 3, W, S, 1973 E 1, 2
Paterson, A M (Otago) 1908 AW 2, 3, 1910 A 1, 2, 3
Paton, H (Otago) 1910 A 1, 3
Pene, A R B (Otago) 1992 Wld 1(R), 2, 3, I 1, 2, A 1, 2(R), 1993 BI 3, A, WS, S, E, 1994 F 1, 2(R), SA 1(R)
Phillips, W J (King Country) 1937 SA 2, 1938 A 1, 2
Philpott, S (Canterbury) 1991 [It (R), S (R)]
Pickering, E A R (Waikato) 1958 A 2, 1959 BI 1, 4
Pierce, M J (Wellington) 1985 E 1, 2, A, Arg 1, 1986 A 2, 3, F 2, 3, 1987 [It, Arg, S, W, F], A, 1988 W 1, 2, A 1, 2, 3, 1989 F 1, 2, Arg 1, 2, A, W, I
Pokere, S T (Southland, Auckland) 1981 SA 3, 1982 A 1, 2, 3, 1983 BI 1, 2, 3, 4, A, S, E, 1984 F 1, 2, A 2, 3, 1985 E 1, 2, A
Pollock, H R (Wellington) 1932 A 1, 2, 3, 1936 A 1, 2
Porter, C G (Wellington) 1925 F, 1929 A 2, 3, 1930 BI 1, 2, 3, 4
Preston, J P (Canterbury, Wellington) 1991 [US, S], 1992 SA (R), 1993 BI 2, 3, A, WS, 1996 SA 4(R), 1997 I (R), E 1(R)
Procter, A C (Otago) 1932 A 1
Purdue, C A (Southland) 1905 A
Purdue, E (Southland) 1905 A
Purdue, G B (Southland) 1931 A, 1932 A 1, 2, 3
Purvis, G H (Waikato) 1991 [US], 1993 WS
Purvis, N A (Otago) 1976 I
Quaid, C E (Otago) 1938 A 1, 2
Ralph, C S (Auckland, Canterbury) 1998 E 2, 2002 It, I 1, 2, A 1, SA 1, A 2, SA 2, 2003 E, A 1(R), [C, Tg, SA(R), F(t&R)]
Ranby, R M (Waikato) 2001 Sm (R)
Randell, T C (Otago) 1997 Fj, Arg 1, 2, A 1, SA 1, A 2, SA 2, A 3, I, E 1, W, E 2, 1998 E 1, 2, A 1, SA 1, A 2, SA 2, A 3, 1999 WS, F 1, SA 1, A 1, SA 2, A 2, [Tg, E, It, S, F 2, SA 3], 2000 Tg, S 1, 2(R), A 1, SA 1, A 2, SA 2, F 2(R), It (R), 2001 Arg 1, F, SA 1, A 1, SA 2, A 2, 2002 It, Fj, E, F, W
Ranger, R M N (Northland) 2010 W2(R), SA2, A3(R)
Rangi, R E (Auckland) 1964 A 2, 3, 1965 SA 1, 2, 3, 4, 1966 BI 1, 2, 3, 4
Rankin, J G (Canterbury) 1936 A 1, 2, 1937 SA 2
Rawlinson, G P (North Harbour) 2006 I1, 2(R), SA2, 2007 SA1
Read, K J (Canterbury) 2008 S, I2(R), E3(R), 2009 F1, 2, It1, A1(R), SA1(R), 2(R),A2, SA3, A3, 4(R), W, E, F3, 2010 I1, W1, 2, SA1, 2, A1, 2, SA3, A3
Reedy, W J (Wellington) 1908 AW 2, 3
Reid, A R (Waikato) 1952 A 1, 1956 SA 3, 4, 1957 A 1, 2
Reid, H R (Bay of Plenty) 1980 A 1, 2, W, 1983 S, E, 1985 Arg 1, 2, 1986 A 2, 3
Reid, K H (Wairarapa) 1929 A 1, 3
Reid, S T (Hawke's Bay) 1935 S, I, W, 1936 E, A 1, 2, 1937 SA 1, 2, 3
Reihana, B T (Waikato) 2000 F 2, It
Reside, W B (Wairarapa) 1929 A 1
Rhind, P K (Canterbury) 1946 A 1, 2
Richardson, J (Otago, Southland) 1921 SA 1, 2, 3, 1924 I, W, 1925 E, F
Rickit, H (Waikato) 1981 S 1, 2
Riechelmann, C C (Auckland) 1997 Fj (R), Arg 1(R), A 1(R), SA 2(t), I (R), E 2(t)
Ridland, A J (Southland) 1910 A 1, 2, 3
Roberts, E J (Wellington) 1914 A 1, 2, 3, 1921 SA 2, 3
Roberts, F (Wellington) 1905 S, I, E, W, 1907 A 1, 2, 3, 1908 AW 1, 3, 1910 A 1, 2, 3
Roberts, R W (Taranaki) 1913 A 1, US, 1914 A 1, 2, 3
Robertson, B J (Counties) 1972 A 1, 3, S, 1973 E 1, I, F, 1974 A 1, 2, 3, I, 1976 I, SA 1, 2, 3, 4, 1977 BI 1, 3, 4, F 1, 2, 1978 A 1, 2, 3, W, E, S, 1979 F 1, 2, A, 1980 A 2, 3, W, 1981 S 1, 2
Robertson, D J (Otago) 1974 A 1, 2, 3, I, 1975 S, 1976 I, SA 1, 3, 4, 1977 BI 1
Robertson, S M (Canterbury) 1998 A 2(R), SA 2(R), A 3(R), 1999 [It (R)], 2000 Tg (R), S 1, 2(R), A 1, SA 1(R), 2(R), F 1, 2, It, 2001 I, S, Arg 2, 2002 I 1, 2, Fj (R), A 1, SA 1, A 2, SA 2
Robilliard, A C C (Canterbury) 1928 SA 1, 2, 3, 4
Robinson, C E (Southland) 1951 A 1, 2, 3, 1952 A 1, 2
Robinson, K J (Waikato) 2002 E, F (R), W, 2004 E1, 2, PI, 2006 E, W, 2007 SA2, A2, [R, F]
Robinson, M D (North Harbour) 1998 E 1(R), 2001 S (R), Arg 2
Robinson, M P (Canterbury) 2000 S 2, SA 1, 2002 It, I 2, A 1, SA 1, E (t&R), F, W (R)
Rokocoko, J T (Auckland) 2003 E, W, F, SA 1, A 1, SA 2, A 2, [It, W, SA, A, F], 2004 E1, 2, Arg, PI, A1, SA1, A2, SA2, It, W, F, 2005 SA1(R), A1, SA2, A2, W, E(R), S, 2006 I1, 2, A1, 2, 3, SA3, E, F1, 2, 2007 F1, 2, SA1, A1, SA2, A2, [Pt, R, F], 2008 S, I2, W, E3, 2009 F1, 2, It1, SA1, 2, A2, SA3, A3, 2010 I1, W1, SA1, A1, 2, SA3
Rollerson, D L (Manawatu) 1980 W, 1981 S 2, SA 1, 2, 3, R, F 1(R), 2
Roper, R A (Taranaki) 1949 A 2, 1950 BI 1, 2, 3, 4
Ross, I B (Canterbury) 2009 F1, 2, It1, A1, SA1, 2, A2, SA3
Rowley, H C B (Wanganui) 1949 A 2
Rush, E J (North Harbour) 1995 [W (R), J], It, F 1, 2, 1996 S 1(R), 2, A 1(t), SA 1(R)
Rush, X J (Auckland) 1998 A 3, 2004 E1, 2, PI, A1, SA1, A2, SA2
Rutledge, L M (Southland) 1978 A 1, 2, 3, I, W, E, S, 1979 F 1, 2, A, 1980 A 1, 2, 3
Ryan, J (Wellington) 1910 A 2, 1914 A 1, 2, 3
Ryan, J A C (Otago) 2005 Fj, BI3(R), A1(R), SA2(R), A2(R), W, S, 2006 F1, W(R)
Sadler, B S (Wellington) 1935 S, I, W, 1936 A 1, 2
Salmon, J L B (Wellington) 1981 R, F 1, 2(R)
Savage, L T (Canterbury) 1949 SA 1, 2, 4
Saxton, C K (South Canterbury) 1938 A 1, 2, 3
Schuler, K J (Manawatu, North Harbour) 1990 A 2(R), 1992 A 2, 1995 [I (R), J]
Schuster, N J (Wellington) 1988 A 1, 2, 3, 1989 F 1, 2, Arg 1, 2, A, W, I
Schwalger, J E (Wellington) 2007 C, 2008 I1(R)
Scott, R W H (Auckland) 1946 A 1, 2, 1947 A 1, 2, 1949 SA 1, 2, 3, 4, 1950 BI 1, 2, 3, 4, 1953 W, 1954 I, E, S, F
Scown, A I (Taranaki) 1972 A 1, 2, 3, W (R), S
Scrimshaw, G (Canterbury) 1928 SA 1
Seear, G A (Otago) 1977 F 1, 2, 1978 A 1, 2, 3, I, W, E, S, 1979 F 1, 2, A
Seeling, C E (Auckland) 1904 BI, 1905 S, I, E, W, 1906 F, 1907 A 1, 2, 1908 AW 1, 2, 3
Sellars, G M V (Auckland) 1913 A 1, US
Senio, K (Bay of Plenty) 2005 A2(R)
Shaw, M W (Manawatu, Hawke's Bay) 1980 A 1, 2, 3(R), W, 1981 S 1, 2, SA 1, 2, R, F 1, 2, 1982 A 1, 2, 3, 1983 BI 1, 2, 3, 4, A, S, E, 1984 F 1, 2, A 1, 1985 E 1, 2, A, Arg 1, 2, 1986 A 3
Shelford, F N K (Bay of Plenty) 1981 SA 3, R, 1984 A 2, 3
Shelford, W T (North Harbour) 1986 F 2, 3, 1987 [It, Fj, S, W, F], A, 1988 W 1, 2, A 1, 2, 3, 1989 F 1, 2, Arg 1, 2, A, W, I, 1990 S 1, 2
Siddells, S K (Wellington) 1921 SA 3
Simon, H J (Otago) 1937 SA 1, 2, 3
Simpson, J G (Auckland) 1947 A 1, 2, 1949 SA 1, 2, 3, 4, 1950 BI 1, 2, 3
Simpson, V L J (Canterbury) 1985 Arg 1, 2
Sims, G S (Otago) 1972 A 2
Sivivatu, S W (Waikato) 2005 Fj, BI1, 2, 3, I, E, 2006 SA2, 3, E(R), F1, 2, W, 2007 F1, 2, C, SA1, A1(R), [It, S, R, F], 2008 I1, E1, 2, SA1, 2, A1, 2, SA3, A3, 4, I2, W, E3, 2009 A1, SA1, 2, A2, SA3, A4, It2, E, F3
Skeen, J R (Auckland) 1952 A 2
Skinner, K L (Otago, Counties) 1949 SA 1, 2, 3, 4, 1950 BI 1, 2, 3, 4, 1951 A 1, 2, 3, 1952 A 1, 2, 1953 W, 1954 I, E, S, F, 1956 SA 3, 4

Skudder, G R (Waikato) 1969 W 2
Slade, C R (Canterbury) 2010 A3(R)
Slater, G L (Taranaki) 2000 F 1(R), 2(R), It (R)
Sloane, P H (North Auckland) 1979 E
Smith, A E (Taranaki) 1969 W 1, 2, 1970 SA 1
Smith, B R (Otago) 2009 It 2
Smith, B W (Waikato) 1984 F 1, 2, A 1
Smith, C G (Wellington) 2004 It, F, 2005 Fj(R), BI3, W, S, 2006 F1, W, 2007 SA2(R), [Pt, S, R(R)], 2008 I1, E1, SA1, 2, A1(R), 2, SA3, Sm, A3, 4, I2, E3, 2009 F2, A1, SA1, 2, A2, 4, W, E, F3, 2010 I1, W1, SA1, 2, A1, 2, SA3, A3
Smith, G W (Auckland) 1905 S, I
Smith, I S T (Otago, North Otago) 1964 A 1, 2, 3, 1965 SA 1, 2, 4, 1966 BI 1, 2, 3
Smith, J B (North Auckland) 1946 A 1, 1947 A 2, 1949 A 1, 2
Smith, R M (Canterbury) 1955 A 1
Smith, W E (Nelson) 1905 A
Smith, W R (Canterbury) 1980 A 1, 1982 A 1, 2, 3, 1983 BI 2, 3, S, E, 1984 F 1, 2, A 1, 2, 3, 1985 E 1, 2, A, Arg 2
Snow, E M (Nelson) 1929 A 1, 2, 3
Solomon, F (Auckland) 1931 A, 1932 A 2, 3
Somerville, G M (Canterbury) 2000 Tg, S 1, SA 2(R), F 1, 2, It, 2001 Sm, Arg 1(R), F, SA 1, A 1, SA 2, A 2, I, S, Arg 2(t+R), 2002 I 1, 2, A 1, SA 1, A 2, SA 2, 2003 E, F, SA 1, A 1, SA 2(R), A 2, [It, Tg, W, SA, A, F], 2004 Arg, SA1, A2(R), SA2(R), It(R), W, F(R), 2005 Fj, BI1(R)2, 3, SA1(R), A1(R), SA2(R), A2(R), 2006 Arg, A1(R), SA1(R), A2(R), 3(R), SA2, 2007 [Pt, R], 2008 E1, 2, SA1, A1, 2, SA3, Sm, A3, 4(R)
Sonntag, W T C (Otago) 1929 A 1, 2, 3
So'oialo, R (Wellington) 2002 W, 2003 E, SA 1(R), [It(R), C, Tg, W(t)], 2004 W, F, 2005 Fj, BI1, 2, 3, SA1, A1, SA2, A2, W, I(R), E, 2006 I1, 2, A1, SA1, A2, 3, SA3, E(R), F1, 2, W, 2007 F1(R), 2, SA1, A1, SA2, A2, [It, Pt(R), S, F], 2008 I1, E1, 2, SA1, 2, A1, 2, SA3, Sm, A3, 4, I2, W, E3, 2009 A1, SA1, 2, A2(R), 3(R), 4, It2
Speight, M W (Waikato) 1986 A 1
Spencer, C J (Auckland) 1997 Arg 1, 2, A 1, SA 1, A 2, SA 2, A 3, E 2(R), 1998 E 2(R), A 1(R), SA 1, A 3(R), 2000 F 1(t&R), It, 2002 E, 2003 E, W, F, SA 1, A 1, SA 2, A 2, [It, C, Tg, W, SA, A, F], 2004 E1, 2, PI, A1, SA1, A2
Spencer, J C (Wellington) 1905 A, 1907 A 1(R)
Spiers, J E (Counties) 1979 S, E, 1981 R, F 1, 2
Spillane, A P (South Canterbury) 1913 A 2, 3
Stanley, B J (Auckland) 2010 I1, W1, 2
Stanley, J T (Auckland) 1986 F 1, A 1, 2, 3, F 2, 3, 1987 [It, Fj, Arg, S, W, F], A, 1988 W 1, 2, A 1, 2, 3, 1989 F 1, 2, Arg 1, 2, A, W, I, 1990 S 1, 2
Stead, J W (Southland) 1904 BI, 1905 S, I, E, 1906 F, 1908 AW 1, 3
Steel, A G (Canterbury) 1966 BI 1, 2, 3, 4, 1967 A, F, S, 1968 A 1, 2
Steel, J (West Coast) 1921 SA 1, 2, 3, 1924 W, 1925 E, F
Steele, L B (Wellington) 1951 A 1, 2, 3
Steere, E R G (Hawke's Bay) 1930 BI 1, 2, 3, 4, 1931 A, 1932 A 1
Steinmetz, P C (Wellington) 2002 W (R)
Stensness, L (Auckland) 1993 BI 3, A, WS, 1997 Fj, Arg 1, 2, A 1, SA 1
Stephens, O G (Wellington) 1968 F 3
Stevens, I N (Wellington) 1972 S, 1973 E 1, 1974 A 3
Stewart, A J (Canterbury, South Canterbury) 1963 E 1, 2, I, W, 1964 E, S, F, A 3
Stewart, J D (Auckland) 1913 A 2, 3
Stewart, K W (Southland) 1973 E 2, 1974 A 1, 2, 3, I, 1975 S, 1976 I, SA 1, 3, 1979 S, E, 1981 SA 1, 2
Stewart, R T (South Canterbury, Canterbury) 1928 SA 1, 2, 3, 4, 1930 BI 2
Stohr, L B (Taranaki) 1910 A 1, 2, 3
Stone, A M (Waikato, Bay of Plenty) 1981 F 1, 2, 1983 BI 3(R), 1984 A 3, 1986 F 1, A 1, 3, F 2, 3
Storey, P W (South Canterbury) 1921 SA 1, 2
Strachan, A D (Auckland, North Harbour) 1992 Wld 2, 3, I 1, 2, A 1, 2, 3, SA, 1993 BI 1, 1995 [J, SA (t)]
Strahan, S C (Manawatu) 1967 A, E, W, F, S, 1968 A 1, 2, F 1, 2, 3, 1970 SA 1, 2, 3, 1972 A 1, 2, 3, 1973 E 2
Strang, W A (South Canterbury) 1928 SA 1, 2, 1930 BI 3, 4, 1931 A
Stringfellow, J C (Wairarapa) 1929 A 1(R), 3
Stuart, K C (Canterbury) 1955 A 1
Stuart, R C (Canterbury) 1949 A 1, 2, 1953 W, 1954 I, E, S, F
Stuart, R L (Hawke's Bay) 1977 F 1(R)
Sullivan, J L (Taranaki) 1937 SA 1, 2, 3, 1938 A 1, 2, 3
Sutherland, A R (Marlborough) 1970 SA 2, 4, 1971 BI 1, 1972 A 1, 2, 3, W, 1973 E 1, I, F
Svenson, K S (Wellington) 1924 I, W, 1925 E, F
Swain, J P (Hawke's Bay) 1928 SA 1, 2, 3, 4
Tanner, J M (Auckland) 1950 BI 4, 1951 A 1, 2, 3, 1953 W
Tanner, K J (Canterbury) 1974 A 1, 2, 3, I, 1975 S, 1976 I, SA 1
Taumoepeau, S (Auckland) 2004 It, 2005 I(R), S
Taylor, G L (Northland) 1996 SA 5(R)
Taylor, H M (Canterbury) 1913 A 1, US, 1914 A 1, 2, 3
Taylor, J M (Otago) 1937 SA 1, 2, 3, 1938 A 1, 2, 3
Taylor, M B (Waikato) 1979 F 1, 2, A, S, E, 1980 A 1, 2
Taylor, N M (Bay of Plenty, Hawke's Bay) 1977 BI 2, 4(R), F 1, 2, 1978 A 1, 2, 3, I, 1982 A 2
Taylor, R (Taranaki) 1913 A 2, 3
Taylor, W T (Canterbury) 1983 BI 1, 2, 3, 4, A, S, 1984 F 1, 2, A 1, 2, 1985 E 1, 2, A, Arg 1, 2, 1986 A 2, 1987 [It, Fj, S, W, F], A, 1988 W 1, 2
Tetzlaff, P L (Auckland) 1947 A 1, 2
Thimbleby, N W (Hawke's Bay) 1970 SA 3
Thomas, B T (Auckland, Wellington) 1962 A 5, 1964 A 1, 2, 3
Thomson, A J (Otago) 2008 I1(t&R), E2, SA1, 2, A2(R), SA3(R), Sm, A4(t&R), S, 2009 F1, SA3(R), A3, 4, W(R), E, 2010 W1(R), 2(R)
Thomson, H D (Wellington) 1908 AW 1
Thorn, B C (Canterbury, Tasman) 2003 W (R), F (R), SA 1(R), A 1(R), SA 2, [It, C, Tg, W, SA(R), A(R), F(R)], 2008 I1, E1, 2, SA1, A1, 2, SA3, A3, 4, I2, W, E3, 2009 F1, 2, It1, A1, SA1, 2, A2, SA3, A3, 4, W, E, F3, 2010 I1, W1, 2, SA1, 2, A1, 2, SA3, A3
Thorne, G S (Auckland) 1968 A 1, 2, F 1, 2, 3, 1969 W 1, 1970 SA 1, 2, 3, 4
Thorne, R D (Canterbury) 1999 SA 2(R), [Tg, E, S, F 2, SA 3], 2000 Tg, S 2, A 2(R), F 1, 2, 2001 Sm, Arg 1, F, SA 1, A 1, I, S, Arg 2, 2002 It, I 1, 2, Fj, A 1, SA 1, A2, SA 2, 2003 E, W, F, SA 1, A 1, SA 2, A 2, [It, C, Tg, W, SA, A, F], 2006 SA1, 2, E, W(R), 2007 F1, C, SA2, [S, R]
Thornton, N H (Auckland) 1947 A 1, 2, 1949 SA 1
Tialata, N S (Wellington) 2005 W, E(t), S(R), 2006 I1(R), 2(R), Arg(R), SA1, 2, 3(R), F1(R), 2(R), W, 2007 F1(R), 2(R), C, A1(R), SA2(R), [It(t&R), Pt, S(R), R], 2008 I1, E1, 2, SA1(R), 2(R), Sm(R), A4, S(R), I2, W, E3, 2009 F1, 2, A1, SA1, A3, 4, W, It2, F3, 2010 I1(R), W2
Tiatia, F I (Wellington) 2000 Tg (R), It
Tilyard, J T (Wellington) 1913 A 3
Timu, J K R (Otago) 1991 Arg 1, A 1, 2, [E, US, C, A], 1992 Wld 2, I 2, A 1, 2, 3, SA, 1993 BI 1, 2, 3, A, WS, S, E, 1994 F 1, 2, SA 1, 2, 3, A
Tindill, E W T (Wellington) 1936 E
Toeava, I (Auckland) 2005 S, 2006 Arg, A1(t&R), A3, SA2(R), 2007 F1, 2, SA1, 2, A2, [It(R), Pt, S(R), R, F(R)], 2008 SA3(R), Sm(R), A4, S, I2(R), E3(R), 2009 F1, 2(R), It1, SA3(R), A3
Tonu'u, O F J (Auckland) 1997 Fj (R), A 3(R), 1998 E 1, 2, SA 1(R)
Townsend, L J (Otago) 1955 A 1, 3
Tremain, K R (Canterbury, Hawke's Bay) 1959 BI 2, 3, 4, 1960 SA 1, 2, 3, 4, 1961 F 2, 3 1962 A 1, 2, 3, 1963 E 1, 2, I, W, 1964 E, S, F, A 1, 2, 3, 1965 SA 1, 2, 3, 4, 1966 BI 1, 2, 3, 4, 1967 A, E, W, S, 1968 A 1, F 1, 2, 3
Trevathan, D (Otago) 1937 SA 1, 2, 3
Tuck, J M (Waikato) 1929 A 1, 2, 3
Tuiali'i, M M (Auckland) 2004 Arg, A2(R), SA2(R), It, W, 2005 I, E(R), S(R), 2006 Arg
Tuigamala, V L (Auckland) 1991 [US, It, C, S], 1992 Wld 1, 2, 3, I 1, A 1, 2, 3, SA, 1993 BI 1, 2, 3, A, WS, S, E
Tuitavake, A S M (North Harbour) 2008 I1, E1, A1, 2(R), Sm, S
Tuitupou, S (Auckland) 2004 E1(R), 2(R), Arg, SA1(R), A2(R), SA2, 2006 Arg, SA1, 2(R)
Turner, R S (North Harbour) 1992 Wld 1, 2(R)
Turtill, H S (Canterbury) 1905 A
Twigden, T M (Auckland) 1980 A 2, 3
Tyler, G A (Auckland) 1903 A, 1904 BI, 1905 S, I, E, W, 1906 F
Udy, D K (Wairarapa) 1903 A
Umaga, J F (Wellington) 1997 Fj, Arg 1, 2, A 1, SA 1, 2, 1999 WS, F 1, SA 1, A 1, SA 2, A 2, [Tg, E, S, F 2, SA 3], 2000 Tg, S 1, 2, A 1, SA 1, A 2, SA 2, F 1, 2, It, 2001 Sm, Arg 1, F, SA 1, A 1, SA 2, A 2, I, S, Arg 2, 2002 I 1, Fj, SA 1(R), A 2, SA 2, E, F, W, 2003 E, W, F, SA 1, A 1, SA 2, A

2, [It], 2004 E1, 2, Arg, PI, A1, SA1, A2, SA2, It, F, 2005 Fj, BI1, 2, 3, SA1, A1, SA2, A2, W, E, S
Urbahn, R J (Taranaki) 1959 BI 1, 3, 4
Urlich, R A (Auckland) 1970 SA 3, 4
Uttley, I N (Wellington) 1963 E 1, 2
Vidiri, J (Counties Manukau) 1998 E 2(R), A 1
Vincent, P B (Canterbury) 1956 SA 1, 2
Vito, V V J (Wellington) 2010 I1(R), W1, A1(R), 2(R), SA3(R), A3
Vodanovich, I M H (Wellington) 1955 A 1, 2, 3
Wallace, W J (Wellington) 1903 A, 1904 BI, 1905 S, I, E, W, 1906 F, 1907 A 1, 2, 3, 1908 AW 2
Waller, D A G (Wellington) 2001 Arg 2(t)
Walsh, P T (Counties) 1955 A 1, 2, 3, 1956 SA 1, 2, 4, 1957 A 1, 2, 1958 A 1, 2, 3, 1959 BI 1, 1963 E 2
Ward, R H (Southland) 1936 A 2, 1937 SA 1, 3
Waterman, A C (North Auckland) 1929 A 1, 2
Watkins, E L (Wellington) 1905 A
Watt, B A (Canterbury) 1962 A 1, 4, 1963 E 1, 2, W, 1964 E, S, A 1
Watt, J M (Otago) 1936 A 1, 2
Watt, J R (Wellington) 1958 A 2, 1960 SA 1, 2, 3, 4, 1961 F 1, 3, 1962 A 1, 2
Watts, M G (Taranaki) 1979 F 1, 2, 1980 A 1, 2, 3(R)
Webb, D S (North Auckland) 1959 BI 2
Weepu, P A T (Wellington) 2004 W, 2005 SA1(R), A1, SA2, A2, I, E(R), S, 2006 Arg, A1(R), SA1, A3(R), SA2, F1, W(R), 2007 F1, C(R), SA1(R), A1(R), SA2, 2008 A2(R), SA3(R), Sm(R), A3(R), 4(R), S, I2(R), W(R), E3(R), 2009 F1(R), 2(R), It1(R), A1(R), SA1(R), 2(R), 2010 I1(R), W1(R), 2(R) , SA1(R), 2, A1(R), 2, SA3(R), A3
Wells, J (Wellington) 1936 A 1, 2
West, A H (Taranaki) 1921 SA 2, 3
Whetton, A J (Auckland) 1984 A 1(R), 3(R), 1985 A (R), Arg 1(R), 1986 A 2, 1987 [It, Fj, Arg, S, W, F], A, 1988 W 1, 2, A 1, 2, 3, 1989 F 1, 2, Arg 1, 2, A, 1990 S 1, 2, A 1, 2, 3, F 1, 2, 1991 Arg 1, [E, US, It, C, A]
Whetton, G W (Auckland) 1981 SA 3, R, F 1, 2, 1982 A 3, 1983 BI 1, 2, 3, 4, 1984 F 1, 2, A 1, 2, 3, 1985 E 1, 2, A, Arg 2, 1986 A 2, 3, F 2, 3, 1987 [It, Fj, Arg, S, W, F], A, 1988 W 1, 2, A 1, 2, 3, 1989 F 1, 2, Arg 1, 2, A, W, I, 1990 S 1, 2, A 1, 2, 3, F 1, 2, 1991 Arg 1, 2, A 1, 2, [E, US, It, C, A, S]
Whineray, W J (Canterbury, Waikato, Auckland) 1957 A 1, 2, 1958 A 1, 2, 3, 1959 BI 1, 2, 3, 4, 1960 SA 1, 2, 3, 4, 1961 F 1, 2, 3, 1962 A 1, 2, 3, 4, 5, 1963 E 1, 2, I, W, 1964 E, S, F, 1965 SA 1, 2, 3, 4
White, A (Southland) 1921 SA 1, 1924 I, 1925 E, F
White, H L (Auckland) 1954 I, E, F, 1955 A 3
White, R A (Poverty Bay) 1949 A 1, 2, 1950 BI 1, 2, 3, 4, 1951 A 1, 2, 3, 1952 A 1, 2, 1953 W, 1954 I, E, S, F, 1955 A 1, 2, 3, 1956 SA 1, 2, 3, 4
White, R M (Wellington) 1946 A 1, 2, 1947 A 1, 2
Whitelock, G B (Canterbury) 2009 It1(R)
Whitelock, S L (Canterbury) 2010 I1(R), W1(R), 2(R), SA1(R), 2(R), A1(R), 2(R), SA3(R)
Whiting, G J (King Country) 1972 A 1, 2, S, 1973 E 1, I, F
Whiting, P J (Auckland) 1971 BI 1, 2, 4, 1972 A 1, 2, 3, W, S, 1973 E 1, I, F, 1974 A 1, 2, 3, I, 1976 I, SA 1, 2, 3, 4
Williams, A J (Auckland, Tasman) 2002 E, F, W, 2003 E, W, F, SA 1, A 1, SA 2, A 2, [Tg, W, SA, A, F], 2004 SA1(R), A2, It(R), W, F(R), 2005 Fj, BI1, 2, 3, SA1, A1, SA2, A2, I, E, 2006 Arg, A1(R), SA1, A2, 3(R), SA2, 3, F1, 2, W, 2007 F1, 2, [It, Pt, S, F], 2008 I1, E1, 2, SA1, 2, A1, 2, SA3, Sm, A3, 4, S, I2, W, E3
Williams, B G (Auckland) 1970 SA 1, 2, 3, 4, 1971 BI 1, 2, 4, 1972 A 1, 2, 3, W, S, 1973 E 1, I, F, E 2, 1974 A 1, 2, 3, I, 1975 S, 1976 I, SA 1, 2, 3, 4, 1977 BI 1, 2, 3, 4, F 1, 1978 A 1, 2, 3, I (R), W, E, S
Williams, G C (Wellington) 1967 E, W, F, S, 1968 A 2
Williams, P (Otago) 1913 A 1
Williment, M (Wellington) 1964 A 1, 1965 SA 1, 2, 3, 1966 BI 1, 2, 3, 4, 1967 A
Willis, R K (Waikato) 1998 SA 2, A 3, 1999 SA 1(R), A 1(R), SA 2(R), A 2(R), [Tg (R), E (R), It, F 2(R), SA 3], 2002 SA 1(R)
Willis, T E (Otago) 2002 It, Fj, SA 2(R), A 2, SA 2
Willocks, C (Otago) 1946 A 1, 2, 1949 SA 1, 3, 4
Wilson, B W (Otago) 1977 BI 3, 4, 1978 A 1, 2, 3, 1979 F 1, 2, A
Wilson, D D (Canterbury) 1954 E, S
Wilson, H W (Otago) 1949 A 1, 1950 BI 4, 1951 A 1, 2, 3
Wilson, J W (Otago) 1993 S, E, 1994 A, 1995 C, [I, J, S, E, SA], A 1, 2, It, F 1, 1996 WS, S 1, 2, A 1, SA 1, A 2, SA 2, 3, 4, 5, 1997 Fj, Arg 1, 2, A 1, SA 1, A 2, SA 2, A 3, I, E 1, W, E 2, 1998 E 1, 2, A 1, SA 1, A 2, SA 2, A 3, 1999 WS, F 1, SA 1, A 1, SA 2, A 2, [Tg, E, It, S, F 2, SA 3], 2001 Sm, Arg 1, F, SA 1, A 1, SA 2
Wilson, N A (Wellington) 1908 AW 1, 2, 1910 A 1, 2, 3, 1913 A 2, 3, 1914 A 1, 2, 3
Wilson, N L (Otago) 1951 A 1, 2, 3
Wilson, R G (Canterbury) 1979 S, E
Wilson, S S (Wellington) 1977 F 1, 2, 1978 A 1, 2, 3, I, W, E, S, 1979 F 1, 2, A, S, E, 1980 A 1, W, 1981 S 1, 2, SA 1, 2, 3, R, F 1, 2, 1982 A 1, 2, 3, 1983 BI 1, 2, 3, 4, A, S, E
Witcombe, D J C (Auckland) 2005 Fj, BI1(R), 2(R), SA1(R), A1(R)
Wolfe, T N (Wellington, Taranaki) 1961 F 1, 2, 3, 1962 A 2, 3, 1963 E 1
Wood, M E (Canterbury, Auckland) 1903 A, 1904 BI
Woodcock, T D (North Harbour) 2002 W, 2004 E1(t&R), 2(t&R), Arg, W, F, 2005 Fj, BI1, 2, 3, SA1, A1, SA2, A2, W(R), I, E, 2006 Arg, A1, 2, 3, SA2(R), 3, E, F1, 2, W(R), 2007 F1, 2, SA1, A1, SA2, A2, [It, Pt(R), S, F], 2008 E2(R), SA1, 2, A1, 2, SA3, Sm, A3, 4, I2, W, E3, 2009 F1, 2, It1(R), A1, SA1, 2, A2, SA3, A3, 4, E, F3, 2010 W1(R), 2, SA1, 2, A1, 2, SA3, A3
Woodman, F A (North Auckland) 1981 SA 1, 2, F 2
Wrigley, E (Wairarapa) 1905 A
Wright, T J (Auckland) 1986 F 1, A 1, 1987 [Arg], 1988 W 1, 2, A 1, 2, 3, 1989 F 1, 2, Arg 1, 2, A, W, I, 1990 S 1, 2, A 1, 2, 3, F 1, 2, 1991 Arg 1, 2, A 1, 2, [E, US, It, S]
Wulf, R N (North Harbour) 2008 E2, SA1, 2, Sm(R)
Wylie, J T (Auckland) 1913 A 1, US
Wyllie, A J (Canterbury) 1970 SA 2, 3, 1971 BI 2, 3, 4, 1972 W, S, 1973 E 1, I, F, E 2
Yates, V M (North Auckland) 1961 F 1, 2, 3
Young, D (Canterbury) 1956 SA 2, 1958 A 1, 2, 3, 1960 SA 1, 2, 3, 4, 1961 F 1, 2, 3, 1962 A 1, 2, 3, 5, 1963 E 1, 2, I, W, 1964 E, S, F

ROMANIA

ROMANIA'S 2009–10 TEST RECORD

OPPONENTS	DATE	VENUE	RESULT
Italy A	13 November	A	**Lost** 6–33
Fiji	28 November	H	**Lost** 18–29
Germany	13 February	H	**Won** 67–5
Russia	27 February	A	**Drew** 21–21
Georgia	13 March	H	**Won** 22–10
Portugal	20 March	A	**Won** 20–9
Spain	27 March	H	**Won** 48–3
Ukraine	22 May	A	**Won** 33–3
Ukraine	5 June	H	**Won** 61–7
Namibia	11 June	H	**Won** 21–17
Argentina Jaguars	15 June	H	**Won** 24–8
Italy A	20 June	H	**Won** 27–22
Tunisia	17 July	H	**Won** 56–13

THE RECOVERY BEGINS

By Chris Thau

AFP

Former All Black Steve McDowall – seen here at the opening of Rugby World Cup 2007 – is helping Romania in their quest to return to the top table of international rugby.

A year ago an out-of sorts Romania, beaten in succession by Russia, Georgia and Portugal, were very much in the doldrums, all but out of Rugby World Cup 2011 contention and seemingly with little prospect of even making the play-offs.

But that was 2009. The impetus for recovery came from the new FRR President Alin Petrache, a former Romanian No 8 and captain, who made World Cup qualification his main priority in the aftermath of a 22–21 defeat by Portugal in Bucharest in March 2009.

He approached many of the Romanian stars resident in France, some of whom he had played with, and asked them to support his crusade. They responded to his call to arms wholeheartedly and the Romanian clans gathered for the IRB Nations Cup 2009 to try to regroup for the second half of the European Nations Cup, which doubled as the region's qualifying process for RWC 2011.

A change in the coaching personnel with the experienced Serge Lairle – a former Toulouse prop and forwards coach – taking over helped alter the outlook and eventually transform Romania's fortunes.

Romania showed their potential against a gifted France A side and the ton of self belief and confidence from that Nations Cup encounter was what they so badly needed when the ENC resumed with the Oaks in the unaccustomed position of fourth behind Georgia, Russia and Portugal.

They resumed their campaign in February 2010 in Constanta and, without any of their French-based stars, overwhelmed Germany 67–5. A fortnight later, also on the Black Sea in the Russian city of Sochi, Romania snatched a valuable 21–21 draw with Russia which kept their hopes of qualifying for RWC 2011 via the play-offs alive.

The match, which Romania could have won, gave them a timely injection of confidence. Two weeks later the Romanian renaissance gathered momentum and credibility with a solid yet unspectacular 22–10 win over Georgia in Bucharest.

While Georgia swept past Russia 36–8 on neutral soil in Turkey to be crowned ENC champions and take the Europe 1 qualification spot, Romania continued their revival with a 20–9 win over Portugal in Lisbon and then beat Spain 48–3 to secure the crucial third place behind RWC 2011 qualified Georgia and Russia.

By this time the Romanian Federation had had a change of heart and appointed former All Black prop Steve McDowall and Romanian legend Romeo Gontineac as the new coaches.

The first assignment for this new duo was the home and away play-off with Ukraine to establish Europe's representative in the cross-continental play-off to determine the 20th and final qualifier for RWC 2011.

"Although we scored nearly 100 points on aggregate (Romania won 33–3 in Kiev and 61–7 in Botosani), the matches against Ukraine were crucial for us in our attempt to create a dialogue with the players and also to introduce ourselves and our methods to them," explained McDowall, the first foreign coach to move his family permanently to Romania, a clear sign of confidence in the team and in Romanian rugby.

"This is a huge job for which one needs 100% concentration, something we ask the players to give. I could not have given the 100% concentration without having the family around. It is as simple as that.

"I have been working with the boys as their fitness and conditioning coach for the past two years, so I know them pretty well. But we came with a new approach, based on solution finding and decision-making. It is like Sudoku, finding the right number to go in the right place. Encouraging them to read the game and choose instantaneously the right option: anticipate, action and reaction.

"Working with Romeo is a bonus because he is not only a very competent coach, but he is also trilingual in Romanian, French and

English and we could discuss things and communicate with the team much easier. Mind you my Romanian has improved a bit during the last couple of years!

"Despite the comfort of the final scoreline, the Ukrainian nut was far more difficult to crack than some people thought. We achieved our objective, but more significantly the boys started to believe in what we were trying to do."

The IRB Nations Cup, held for a fourth consecutive year in Bucharest, provided the coaches with an additional opportunity to continue the process and in this respect the last gasp 21–17 defeat by Namibia in the opening match proved a bonus in the attempt to reshape and more significantly re-educate the Romanian team.

This is how, having correctly identified the Argentine set-pieces as their main strength, the Romanians managed to overcome the Jaguars 24–8, their first ever win against an Argentine selection.

"All the mental preparation and the new approach has given the team to confidence to win," said Gontineac. "I hope this self-belief and ability to react to the game as it evolves in front of you will become a feature of our approach to matches. We agree on a blueprint which enables us to play from the same hymnsheet but players have considerable freedom to take decisions as the game evolved. The belief in our ability will help us to play better and understand each other better."

After the forward battle against the Jaguars, Romania surprised Italy A with their expansive style. They attempted and succeeded to play a new-look game in which the forwards revert to their role of ball suppliers and the backs are given opportunities to run, rather than spend all day defending and kicking the ball.

The Italians dominated the set piece, but credit should be given to the Romanian pack, led by captain and player of the tournament Sorin Socol and Ovidiu Tonita, who played their hearts out. In the end it was the remarkable accuracy of Romania's recognised kicker Dan Dumbrava, which was the difference in a tense finale.

The next stage in Romania's march towards respectability was a play-off against Tunisia in Buzau in July. Led by flanker Stelian Burcea and with fly half Dumbrava having a great day with the boot, Romania subdued the lively, never say-die Tunisians to win 56–13.

This win set up a home and away play-off with Uruguay, the conquerors of Kazakhstan, in November to fill the one remaining place at RWC 2011. Four years ago Uruguay lost out to Portugal for the final place, but if Romania can cap their fight back and take their place alongside Argentina, England, Scotland and Georgia in Pool B it will be a dream outcome for them.

ROMANIA INTERNATIONAL STATISTICS

MATCH RECORDS UP TO 29TH OCTOBER 2010

WINNING MARGIN

Date	Opponent	Result	Winning Margin
21/09/1976	Bulgaria	100–0	**100**
19/03/2005	Ukraine	97–0	**97**
13/04/1996	Portugal	92–0	**92**
17/11/1976	Morocco	89–0	**89**
19/04/1996	Belgium	83–5	**78**

MOST POINTS IN A MATCH

BY THE TEAM

Date	Opponent	Result	Points
21/09/1976	Bulgaria	100–0	**100**
19/03/2005	Ukraine	97–0	**97**
13/04/1996	Portugal	92–0	**92**
17/11/1976	Morocco	89–0	**89**

BY A PLAYER

Date	Player	Opponent	Points
5/10/2002	Ionut Tofan	Spain	**30**
13/04/1996	Virgil Popisteanu	Portugal	**27**
04/02/2001	Petre Mitu	Portugal	**27**
13/04/1996	Ionel Rotaru	Portugal	**25**

MOST TRIES IN A MATCH

BY THE TEAM

Date	Opponent	Result	Tries
17/11/1976	Morocco	89–0	**17**
21/10/1951	East Germany	64–26	**16**
19/03/2005	Ukraine	97–0	**15**
16/04/1978	Spain	74–3	**14**

BY A PLAYER

Date	Name	Opponent	Tries
30/04/1972	Gheorghe Rascanu	Morocco	**5**
18/10/1986	Cornel Popescu	Portugal	**5**
13/04/1996	Ionel Rotaru	Portugal	**5**

MOST CONVERSIONS IN A MATCH

BY THE TEAM

Date	Opponent	Result	Cons
3/04/1996	Portugal	92–0	**12**
19/03/2005	Ukraine	97–0	**11**
04/10/1997	Belgium	83–13	**10**

BY A PLAYER

Date	Player	Opponent	Cons
13/04/1996	Virgil Popisteanu	Portugal	**12**
04/10/1997	Serban Guranescu	Belgium	**10**
19/03/2005	Dan Dumbrava	Ukraine	**8**
22/03/2008	Florin Vlaicu	Czech Republic	**8**

MOST PENALTIES IN A MATCH

BY THE TEAM

Date	Opponent	Result	Pens
14/05/1994	Italy	26–12	**6**
04/02/2001	Portugal	47–0	**6**

BY A PLAYER

Date	Player	Opponent	Pens
14/05/1994	Neculai Nichitean	Italy	**6**
04/02/2001	Petre Mitu	Portugal	**6**

MOST DROP GOALS IN A MATCH

BY THE TEAM

Date	Opponent	Result	DGs
29/10/1967	West Germany	27–5	**4**
14/11/1965	West Germany	9–8	**3**
17/10/1976	Poland	38–8	**3**
03/10/1990	Spain	19–6	**3**

BY A PLAYER

Date	Name	Opponent	DGs
29/10/1967	Valeriu Irimescu	West Germany	**3**
17/10/1976	Dumitru Alexandru	Poland	**3**

MOST CAPPED PLAYERS

Name	Caps
Adrian Lungu	**77**
Romeo Gontineac	**75**
Gabriel Brezoianu	**71**
Florica Morariu	**70**

LEADING TRY SCORERS

Name	Tries
Petre Motrescu	**33**
Gabriel Brezoianu	**28**
Florica Morariu	**26**
Mihai Vusec	**22**

LEADING CONVERSIONS SCORERS

Name	Cons
Dan Dumbrava	**56**
Petre Mitu	**53**
Ionut Tofan	**51**
Florin Vlaicu	**40**

LEADING PENALTY SCORERS

Name	Pens
Neculai Nichitean	**54**
Petre Mitu	**53**
Dan Dumbrava	**48**
Ionut Tofan	**46**

LEADING DROP GOAL SCORERS

Name	DGs
Dumitru Alexandru	**13**
Neculai Nichitean	**10**
Valeriu Irimescu	**10**
Gelu Ignat	**7**

LEADING POINTS SCORERS

Name	Points
Petre Mitu	**335**
Ionut Tofan	**315**
Dan Dumbrava	**274**
Neculai Nichitean	**246**
Dumitru Alexandru	**240**

ROMANIA INTERNATIONAL PLAYERS

UP TO 29TH OCTOBER 2010

Note: Years given for International Championship matches are for second half of season; eg 1972 means season 1971–72. Years for all other matches refer to the actual year of the match.

A Achim 1974 *Pol*, 1976 *Pol, Mor*
M Adascalitei 2007 *Rus*, 2009 *Pt, Ur, F, ItA*
M Aldea 1979 *USS, W, Pol, F*, 1980 *It, USS, I, F*, 1981 *It, Sp, USS, S, NZ, F*, 1982 *WGe, It, USS, Z, Z, F*, 1983 *Mor, WGe, It, USS, Pol, W, USS, F*, 1984 *It, S, F*, 1985 *E, USS*
C Alexandrescu 1934 *It*
D Alexandru 1974 *Pol*, 1975 *Sp, JAB*, 1976 *Sp, USS, Bul, Pol, F, Mor*, 1977 *Sp, It, F, Pol, F*, 1978 *Cze, Sp*, 1979 *It, Sp, USS, W, F*, 1980 *It, I, Pol, F*, 1981 *Sp, USS, S, NZ, F*, 1982 *Z*, 1983 *It, USS, Pol, W*, 1984 *It, S, F, Sp*, 1985 *E*, 1987 *It, USS, Z, S, USS, F*, 1988 *USS*
N Anastasiade 1927 *Cze*, 1934 *It*
V Anastasiade 1939 *It*
I Andrei 2003 *W, I, Ar, Nm*, 2004 *CZR, Pt, Sp, Rus, Geo, It, W, J, CZR*, 2005 *Rus, US, S, Pt*, 2006 *CZR*, 2007 *Pt*, 2008 *Sp, Pt, Rus*
I Andriesi 1937 *It, H, Ger*, 1938 *F, Ger*, 1939 *It*, 1940 *It*
E Apjoc 1996 *Bel*, 2000 *It*, 2001 *Pt*
D Armasel 1924 *F, US*
A Atanasiu 1970 *It, F*, 1971 *It, Mor, F*, 1972 *Mor, Cze, WGe*, 1973 *Sp, Mor, Ar, Ar, WGe*, 1974 *Pol*
I Bacioiu 1976 *USS, Bul, Pol, F, Mor*
N Baciu 1964 *Cze, EGe*, 1967 *It, F*, 1968 *Cze, Cze, F*, 1969 *Pol, WGe, F*, 1970 *It*, 1971 *It, Mor, F*, 1972 *Mor, Cze, WGe*, 1973 *Ar, Ar*, 1974 *Cze, EGe*
B Balan 2003 *Pt, Sp, Geo*, 2004 *W*, 2005 *Rus, Ukr, J, US, S, Pt*, 2006 *Geo, Pt, Ukr, Rus, F, Geo, Sp, S*, 2007 *Sp, ESp, ItA, Nm, It, S, Pt, NZ*, 2009 *Fj*, 2010 *Ger, Rus*
D Balan 1983 *F*
PV Balan 1998 *H, Pol, Ukr, Ar, Geo, I*, 1999 *F, S, A, US, I*, 2000 *Mor, H, Pt, Sp, Geo, F, It*, 2001 *Pt, Sp, H, Rus, Geo, I, E*, 2002 *Pt, Sp, H, Rus, Geo, Sp, S*, 2003 *CZR, F, W, I, Nm*, 2004 *It, W, J, CZR*, 2005 *Geo, C, I*, 2006 *Geo, Pt, F, Geo, Sp, S*, 2007 *Geo*, 2009 *Ur, F*
L Balcan 1963 *Bul, EGe, Cze*
F Balmus 2000 *Mor, H, Pt*
S Bals 1927 *F, Ger, Cze*
G Baltaretu 1965 *WGe, F*
C Barascu 1957 *F*
M Baraulea 2004 *CZR, Pt, Geo*
A Barbu 1958 *WGe, It*, 1959 *EGe, Pol, Cze, EGe*, 1960 *F*
A Barbuliceanu 2008 *Rus, ESp*, 2009 *Sp, Ger, Rus, Geo, Pt*
S Bargaunas 1971 *It, Mor*, 1972 *F*, 1974 *Cze*, 1975 *It*
S Barsan 1934 *It*, 1936 *F, It*, 1937 *It, H, F, Ger*, 1938 *F, Ger*, 1939 *It*, 1940 *It*, 1942 *It*
RC Basalau 2007 *Pt*, 2008 *Geo, Pt, Rus, CZR, Ur, Rus, ESp*, 2010 *ItA, Tun*
CD Beca 2009 *Sp, Ger, Rus, Geo, Pt*
E Beches 1979 *It, Sp, USS*, 1982 *WGe, It*, 1983 *Pol*
M Bejan 2001 *I, W*, 2002 *Pt*, 2003 *Geo, CZR*, 2004 *It*
C Beju 1936 *F, It, Ger*
G Bentia 1919 *US, F*, 1924 *F, US*
V Bezarau 1995 *Ar, F, It*
R Bezuscu 1985 *It*, 1987 *F*
G Bigiu 2007 *Pt*, 2008 *Geo, Sp, Pt, Rus, CZR, Ur, Rus*
M Blagescu 1952 *EGe, EGe*, 1953 *It*, 1955 *Cze*, 1957 *F, Cze, Bel, F*
G Blasek 1937 *It, H, F, Ger*, 1940 *It*, 1942 *It*
A Bogheanu 1980 *Mor*
D Boldor 1988 *It, Sp, US, USS, USS, W*, 1989 *It, E, Sp, Z*

A Boroi 1975 *Sp*
P Bors 1975 *JAB*, 1976 *Sp*, 1977 *It*, 1980 *It*, *USS*, *I*, *Pol*, *F*, 1981 *It*, *Sp*, *USS*, *S*, *NZ*, *F*, 1982 *WGe*, 1983 *Mor*, *WGe*, *It*, *USS*, 1984 *It*
IC Botezatu 2009 *Ger*, *Rus*, *Geo*, *ItA*, 2010 *Ger*, *Rus*, *Ukr*, *Ukr*, *Nm*, *ArJ*
D Bozian 1997 *Bel*, 1998 *H*, *Pol*, *Ukr*
V Brabateanu 1919 *US*, *F*
M Braga 1970 *It*, *F*
C Branescu 1994 *It*, *E*, 1997 *F*
I Bratulescu 1927 *Ger*, *Cze*
G Brezoianu 1996 *Bel*, 1997 *F*, 1998 *H*, *Pol*, *Ukr*, *Ar*, *Geo*, *I*, 1999 *F*, *S*, *A*, *US*, *I*, 2000 *H*, *Pt*, *Sp*, *Geo*, *F*, *It*, 2001 *Sp*, *Rus*, *Geo*, *I*, *W*, *E*, 2002 *Pt*, *Sp*, *H*, *Rus*, *Geo*, *I*, *It*, *Sp*, *W*, *S*, 2003 *Pt*, *Sp*, *Rus*, *Geo*, *CZR*, *F*, *W*, *I*, *A*, *Ar*, *Nm*, 2005 *Rus*, *Ukr*, *J*, *US*, *S*, *Pt*, *C*, *I*, 2006 *CZR*, *Pt*, *Ukr*, *Rus*, *F*, *Geo*, *Sp*, *S*, 2007 *Geo*, *Sp*, *CZR*, *ESp*, *ItA*, *Nm*, *It*, *S*, *NZ*
V Brici 1991 *NZ*, 1992 *USS*, *F*, *It*, 1993 *Tun*, *F*, *Sp*, *I*, 1994 *Sp*, *Ger*, *Rus*, *It*, *W*, *It*, *E*, 1995 *F*, *S*, *J*, *J*, *SA*, *A*, 1996 *Pt*, *F*, 1997 *WalA*, *F*
TE Brinza 1990 *It*, *USS*, 1991 *C*, 1992 *It*, *Ar*, 1993 *Pt*, *Tun*, *F*, *F*, *I*, 1994 *Sp*, *Ger*, *It*, *W*, *It*, *E*, 1995 *F*, *S*, *J*, *J*, *SA*, *A*, 1996 *Pt*, *F*, *Pol*, 1997 *WalA*, *F*, *W*, *Ar*, *F*, *It*, 1998 *Ukr*, 1999 *A*, *US*, *I*, 2000 *H*, *Geo*, 2002 *H*
I Bucan 1976 *Bul*, 1977 *Sp*, 1978 *Cze*, 1979 *F*, 1980 *It*, *USS*, *I*, *Pol*, *F*, 1981 *It*, *Sp*, *USS*, *S*, *NZ*, *F*, 1982 *WGe*, *It*, *USS*, *Z*, *Z*, *F*, 1983 *Mor*, *WGe*, *It*, *USS*, *Pol*, *W*, *USS*, *F*, 1984 *It*, *S*, *F*, *Sp*, 1985 *E*, *Tun*, *USS*, *USS*, *It*, 1986 *Pt*, *S*, *F*, *Pt*, 1987 *It*, *USS*, *Z*, *S*, *USS*, *F*
M Bucos 1972 *Mor*, *Cze*, *WGe*, 1973 *Sp*, 1975 *JAB*, *Pol*, *F*, 1976 *H*, *It*, *Sp*, *USS*, *Bul*, *Pol*, *F*, *Mor*, 1977 *Sp*, *It*, *F*, *Pol*, *It*, *F*, 1978 *Pol*, *F*, 1979 *W*, 1980 *It*, *Mor*
P Buda 1953 *It*, 1955 *Cze*, 1957 *F*, *Cze*
C Budica 1974 *Cze*, *EGe*, *Cze*
S Burcea 2006 *F*, 2007 *ESp*, *ItA*, *Nm*, *Rus*, *Pt*, 2008 *Geo*, *Pt*, *CZR*, *Ur*, *Rus*, *ESp*, 2009 *Sp*, *Ger*, *Rus*, *Geo*, *Pt*, *ItA*, *Fj*, 2010 *Ger*, *Rus*, *Geo*, *Pt*, *Ukr*, *Ukr*, *Nm*, *ArJ*, *ItA*, *Tun*
M Burghelea 1974 *Cze*, *EGe*, *F*, 1975 *It*
S Burlescu 1936 *F*, *It*, *Ger*, 1938 *F*, *Ger*, 1939 *It*
M Butugan 2003 *Pt*
VN Calafeteanu 2004 *J*, 2005 *Ukr*, 2006 *CZR*, *Pt*, *Ukr*, *F*, *Sp*, *S*, 2007 *Geo*, *Sp*, *CZR*, *ESp*, *ItA*, *Nm*, *It*, *S*, *Pt*, *NZ*, 2008 *Geo*, *Sp*, *Pt*, *CZR*, 2009 *Ger*, *Geo*, *Pt*, *Ur*, *F*, *ItA*, *ItA*, *Fj*, 2010 *Ger*, *Rus*, *Tun*
A Caligari 1951 *EGe*, 1953 *It*
S Caliman 1958 *EGe*, 1960 *Pol*, *EGe*, *Cze*
P Calistrat 1940 *It*, 1942 *It*
Ion Camenita 1939 *It*
CF Caplescu 2007 *Sp*, *CZR*, *Rus*, *Pt*, 2008 *Rus*, *CZR*, *Ur*
C Capmare 1983 *Pol*, 1984 *It*
N Capusan 1960 *F*, 1961 *Pol*, *Cze*, *EGe*, *F*, 1962 *Cze*, *EGe*, *Pol*, *It*
R Capusan 1963 *Bul*, *EGe*, *Cze*
G Caracostea 1919 *US*, *F*
G Caragea 1980 *I*, *Pol*, *F*, 1981 *It*, *Sp*, *USS*, *S*, *NZ*, *F*, 1982 *WGe*, *It*, *USS*, *Z*, *Z*, *F*, 1983 *Mor*, *WGe*, *It*, *USS*, *Pol*, *W*, *F*, 1984 *F*, *Sp*, 1985 *E*, *Tun*, 1986 *S*, *F*, *Tun*, *Tun*, *Pt*, *F*, *I*, 1988 *It*, *Sp*, *US*, *USS*, 1989 *E*
C Carp 1989 *Z*, *Sa*, *USS*
D Carpo 2007 *ItA*, 2008 *Sp*, *Pt*, *Rus*, *CZR*, *Ur*, *Rus*, *ESp*, 2009 *Sp*, *Ger*, *Rus*, *Geo*, *Pt*, *Ur*, *F*, 2010 *Ger*, *Rus*, *Geo*, *Pt*, *Sp*, *ArJ*, *ItA*, *Tun*
GA Catuna 2009 *ItA*
I Cazan 2010 *ItA*, *Tun*
G Celea 1963 *EGe*
D Chiriac 1999 *S*, *A*, *I*, 2001 *H*
G Chiriac 1996 *Bel*, 2001 *Pt*, *Rus*, 2002 *Sp*, *H*, *Rus*, *Geo*, *I*, *Sp*, *W*, *S*, 2003 *Sp*, *Rus*, *Geo*, *F*, *W*, *I*, *A*, *Ar*, *Nm*
R Chiriac 1952 *EGe*, 1955 *Cze*, 1957 *F*, *Bel*, *F*, 1958 *Sp*, *WGe*, 1960 *F*, 1961 *Pol*, *EGe*, *Cze*, *EGe*, *F*, 1962 *Cze*, *EGe*, *Pol*, *It*, *F*, 1963 *Bul*, *EGe*, *Cze*, *F*, 1964 *Cze*, *EGe*, *WGe*, *F*
M Chiricencu 1980 *It*, *Pol*
S Chirila 1989 *Sp*, *S*, 1990 *F*, *H*, *Sp*, *It*, *USS*, 1991 *It*
V Chirita 1999 *S*
G Cilinca 1993 *Pt*
N Cioarec 1974 *Pol*, 1976 *It*, 1979 *Pol*
P Ciobanel 1961 *Pol*, *EGe*, *Cze*, *EGe*, *F*, 1962 *Cze*, *EGe*, *Pol*, *It*, *F*, 1963 *F*, 1964 *Cze*, *EGe*, *WGe*, *F*, 1965 *WGe*, *F*, 1966 *Cze*, *It*, *F*, 1967 *F*, 1968 *Cze*, *Cze*, *F*, 1969 *Pol*, *WGe*, *Cze*, *F*, 1970 *F*, 1971 *F*
I Ciobanu 1952 *EGe*
M Ciobanu 1949 *Cze*, 1951 *EGe*
R Cioca 1994 *Sp*, *Ger*, *Rus*, *It*, *It*, *E*, 1995 *S*, *J*, 1996 *Bel*
I Ciofu 2000 *It*, 2003 *Pt*
ML Ciolacu 1998 *Ukr*, *Ar*, *Geo*, *I*, 1999 *F*, 2001 *Sp*, *H*, *Rus*, *Geo*, *W*, *E*
S Ciorascu 1988 *US*, *USS*, *USS*, *F*, *W*, 1989 *It*, *E*, *Sp*, *Z*, *Sa*, *USS*, *S*, 1990 *It*, *F*, *H*, *Sp*, *USS*, 1991 *It*, *NZ*, *S*, *F*, *C*, *Fj*, 1992 *Sp*, *It*, *It*, *Ar*, 1994 *Ger*, *Rus*, *It*, *W*, 1995 *F*, *S*, *J*, *C*, *SA*, *A*, 1996 *F*, 1997 *F*, *It*, 1999 *F*
M Ciornei 1972 *WGe*, *F*, 1973 *Ar*, *Ar*, *WGe*, *F*, 1974 *Mor*, *Pol*, *EGe*, *F*, *Cze*, 1975 *It*, *Sp*
SE Ciuntu 2007 *NZ*, *Rus*, *Pt*, 2008 *Geo*, *Sp*, *Pt*, *Rus*, *CZR*, *Ur*, *ESp*, 2009 *Sp*, *Ger*, *Rus*, *Geo*, *Pt*, *Ur*, *F*, *ItA*, *Fj*, 2010 *Ger*, *Geo*, *Pt*, *Sp*, *Ukr*, *Ukr*, *Nm*, *ArJ*, *ItA*, *Tun*
C Cocor 1940 *It*, 1949 *Cze*
M Codea 1998 *Ukr*, 2001 *E*
L Codoi 1980 *I*, *Pol*, 1984 *F*, 1985 *Tun*, *USS*
C Cojocariu 1990 *It*, *F*, *H*, *Sp*, *It*, *USS*, 1991 *It*, *NZ*, *F*, *S*, *F*, *C*, *Fj*, 1992 *Sp*, *It*, *USS*, *F*, *Ar*, 1993 *Pt*, *F*, *F*, *I*, 1994 *Sp*, *Ger*, *Rus*, *It*, *W*, *It*, *E*, 1995 *F*, *S*, *J*, *J*, *C*, *SA*, *A*, *Ar*, *F*, *It*, 1996 *F*
L Colceriu 1991 *S*, *Fj*, 1992 *Sp*, *It*, *It*, 1993 *I*, 1994 *Sp*, *Ger*, *Rus*, *It*, *W*, *It*, 1995 *F*, *J*, *J*, *C*, *SA*, *A*, 1997 *WalA*, *F*, *W*, *Bel*, *Ar*, *F*, *It*, 1998 *Pol*, *Ukr*
D Coliba 1987 *USS*, *F*
M Coltuneac 2002 *Sp*, *W*, *S*
T Coman 1984 *Sp*, 1986 *F*, *Tun*, *Tun*, *I*, 1988 *Sp*, *US*, *USS*, *USS*, 1989 *It*, 1992 *F*
C Constantin 2001 *Pt*, 2002 *Geo*, *W*
F Constantin 1972 *Mor*, *Cze*, *WGe*, 1973 *Ar*, *Ar*, *WGe*, 1980 *Mor*, 1982 *It*
I Constantin 1971 *Mor*, 1972 *WGe*, 1973 *Ar*, *Ar*, *WGe*, *F*, 1974 *Mor*, *Pol*, *Sp*, *F*, *Cze*, 1975 *It*, *Sp*, *JAB*, *Pol*, *F*, 1976 *H*, *It*, *Sp*, *USS*, *Bul*, *Pol*, 1977 *It*, *F*, 1978 *Pol*, *F*, 1979 *It*, *Sp*, *USS*, *W*, *Pol*, *F*, 1980 *It*, *USS*, *I*, *Pol*, *F*, 1981 *It*, *Sp*, *USS*, *S*, *NZ*, *F*, 1982 *WGe*, *It*, *USS*, *Z*, *Z*, 1983 *WGe*, *USS*, 1985 *It*
L Constantin 1983 *USS*, *F*, 1984 *It*, *S*, *F*, *Sp*, 1985 *E*, *It*, *Tun*, *USS*, *USS*, *It*, 1986 *Pt*, *S*, *F*, *Tun*, *Tun*, *Pt*, *F*, *I*, 1987 *It*, *USS*, *Z*, *F*, *S*, *USS*, *F*, 1991 *It*, *NZ*, *F*
LT Constantin 1985 *USS*
S Constantin 1980 *Mor*, 1982 *Z*, *Z*, 1983 *Pol*, *W*, *USS*, *F*, 1984 *S*, *F*, 1985 *USS*, 1986 *Pt*, *S*, *F*, *Tun*, 1987 *It*, *Z*, *S*
T Constantin 1992 *USS*, *F*, *It*, 1993 *Pt*, *F*, *Sp*, 1996 *Pt*, 1997 *It*, 1999 *F*, *US*, *I*, 2000 *Pt*, *Sp*, *Geo*, *F*, 2002 *Rus*, *Geo*
T Constantin 1985 *USS*
N Copil 1985 *USS*, *It*, 1986 *S*
D Coravu 1968 *F*
N Cordos 1958 *EGe*, 1961 *EGe*, 1963 *Bul*, *Cze*, 1964 *Cze*, *EGe*
V Cornel 1977 *F*, 1978 *Cze*, *Sp*
G Corneliu 1980 *Mor*, *USS*, 1982 *WGe*, *It*, *Z*, *Z*, 1986 *Tun*, *Pt*, *F*, 1993 *I*, 1994 *W*
G Corneliu 1976 *USS*, *Bul*, 1977 *F*, 1979 *It*, 1981 *S*, 1982 *Z*
M Corneliu 1979 *USS*
F Corodeanu 1997 *WalA*, *F*, *W*, 1998 *H*, *Pol*, *Ar*, *Geo*, 1999 *F*, *S*, *A*, *US*, *I*, 2000 *H*, *Sp*, *Geo*, *F*, *It*, 2001 *Pt*, *Sp*, *H*, *Rus*, *Geo*, *I*, *E*, 2002 *Pt*, *Sp*, *Rus*, *Geo*, *It*, *Sp*, *W*, *S*, 2003 *Sp*, 2005 *Geo*, *J*, *US*, *S*, *Pt*, *C*, *I*, 2006 *Geo*, *CZR*, *Pt*, *Geo*, *Sp*, *S*, 2007 *Geo*, *ESp*, *ItA*, *Nm*, *It*, *S*, *Pt*, *NZ*, 2008 *Ur*, *Rus*, *ESp*, 2009 *Sp*, *Ger*, *Rus*, *Pt*
Coste 2007 *Pt*, 2008 *Geo*, *Sp*, *Pt*, *Rus*, *CZR*, *Ur*, 2009 *Sp*, *Rus*, *Geo*, *Pt*, *F*, 2010 *Ukr*
L Costea 1994 *E*, 1995 *S*, *J*, *J*, *Ar*, *F*, 1997 *WalA*, *F*
L Coter 1957 *F*, *Cze*, 1959 *EGe*, *Pol*, *Cze*, 1960 *F*
F Covaci 1936 *Ger*, 1937 *H*, *F*, *Ger*, 1940 *It*, 1942 *It*
C Cratunescu 1919 *US*, *F*
N Crissoveloni 1936 *F*, *It*, 1937 *H*, *F*, *Ger*, 1938 *F*, *Ger*
S Cristea 1973 *Mor*
C Cristoloveanu 1952 *EGe*
G Crivat 1938 *F*, *Ger*
V Csoma 1983 *WGe*
D Curea 2005 *Rus*, *Ukr*, *J*, *US*, *S*, *Pt*
V Daiciulescu 1966 *Cze*, *F*, 1967 *It*, *Pol*, 1968 *F*, 1969 *Pol*
A Damian 1934 *It*, 1936 *F*, *It*, *Ger*, 1937 *It*, 1938 *F*, *Ger*, 1939 *It*, 1949 *Cze*

G Daraban 1969 *Cze*, 1972 *Mor, Cze, WGe, F*, 1973 *Sp, Mor, Ar, Ar*, 1974 *Cze, EGe, F, Cze*, 1975 *It, Sp, JAB, Pol, F*, 1976 *H, It, Sp, USS, Bul, Pol, F, Mor*, 1977 *Sp, It, F*, 1978 *Cze, Sp, Pol, F*, 1982 *F*, 1983 *Mor, WGe, It, USS, W*
CR Dascalu 2006 *Ukr, F, Geo, Sp, S*, 2007 *Sp, CZR, ESp, NZ, Rus, Pt*, 2008 *Geo, Rus, Ur, Rus, ESp*, 2009 *Sp, Rus, Geo, Ur, ItA, ItA*, 2010 *Ger, Rus, Geo, Sp, Ukr, Ukr, Nm*
V David 1984 *Sp*, 1986 *Pt, S, F, Tun*, 1987 *USS, Z, F*, 1992 *USS*
S Demci 1998 *Ar*, 2001 *H, Rus, Geo, I, W*
R Demian 1959 *EGe*, 1960 *F*, 1961 *Pol, EGe, Cze, EGe, F*, 1962 *Cze, Pol, It, F*, 1963 *Bul, EGe, Cze, F*, 1964 *WGe, F*, 1965 *WGe, F*, 1966 *Cze, It, F*, 1967 *It, Pt, Pol, WGe, F*, 1968 *Cze, F*, 1969 *Pol, WGe, F*, 1971 *It, Mor*
E Denischi 1949 *Cze*, 1952 *EGe, EGe*
I Diaconu 1942 *It*
C Diamandi-Telu 1938 *Ger*, 1939 *It*
ND Dima 1999 *A, US, I*, 2000 *H, Pt, Geo, F, It*, 2001 *Sp, H, Rus, Geo, W, E*, 2002 *Pt, Sp, Rus, W, S*, 2004 *CZR, Pt, Sp, Rus, Geo*, 2009 *ItA, ItA*, 2010 *Ger, Geo, Pt, Sp, Nm, ArJ*
TI Dimofte 2004 *It, W, CZR*, 2005 *C, I*, 2006 *Geo, CZR, Pt, Ukr, Rus, F, Geo, Sp, S*, 2007 *ESp, ItA, Nm, It, S, Pt, NZ, Rus, Pt*, 2008 *Geo, Sp, Pt, Rus, CZR, Ur, Rus, ESp*, 2009 *Sp, Ger, Rus, Geo, Pt, Ur, F, ItA, Fj*, 2010 *Ger, Rus, Geo, Pt, Sp, Ukr, Ukr, Nm, ItA, Tun*
C Dinescu 1934 *It*, 1936 *F, It, Ger*, 1937 *It, H, F, Ger*, 1938 *F, Ger*, 1940 *It*, 1942 *It*
C Dinu 1965 *WGe, F*, 1966 *Cze, It, F*, 1967 *It, Pt, Pol, WGe*, 1968 *F*, 1969 *Pol, WGe, Cze, F*, 1970 *It, F*, 1971 *Mor, F*, 1972 *Mor, Cze, WGe, F*, 1973 *Sp, Mor, Ar, Ar, WGe, F*, 1974 *Mor, Pol, Sp, Cze, F, Cze*, 1975 *It, Sp*, 1976 *H, It, Sp, Pol, F, Mor*, 1977 *Sp, It, F, Pol, It, F*, 1978 *Sp, Pol, F*, 1979 *Sp, USS, W, Pol*, 1980 *I, Pol, F*, 1981 *It, Sp, USS, NZ, F*, 1982 *F*, 1983 *Mor, WGe, It, USS*
F Dinu 2000 *Mor, H*
G Dinu 1990 *It, F, H, Sp, It, USS*, 1991 *It, S, F, C, Fj*, 1992 *Sp, It, USS, F, It*, 1993 *F*
G Dinu 1975 *Pol*, 1979 *It, Sp*, 1983 *Pol, USS*
F Dobre 2001 *E*, 2004 *W, CZR*, 2007 *Pt*, 2008 *CZR*
I Dobre 1951 *EGe*, 1952 *EGe*, 1953 *It*, 1955 *Cze*, 1957 *Cze, Bel, F*, 1958 *Sp*
I Doja 1986 *Tun, Pt, F, I*, 1988 *F, W*, 1989 *Sp, Z, Sa, S*, 1990 *It*, 1991 *It, NZ, F, C*, 1992 *Sp*
V Doja 1997 *Bel*, 1998 *Pol, Geo, I*
A Domocos 1989 *Z, Sa, USS*
I Dorutiu 1957 *Cze, Bel, F*, 1958 *Sp, WGe*
A Draghici 1919 *US*
C Dragnea 1995 *F*, 1996 *Pol*, 1997 *WalA, F, Bel, Ar, F, It*, 1998 *H, Pol*, 1999 *F*, 2000 *F*
I Dragnea 1985 *Tun*
S Dragnea 2002 *S*
M Dragomir 1996 *Bel*, 1997 *Bel*, 1998 *H, Pol, Ukr, Geo, I*, 2001 *I, W, E*
M Dragomir 2001 *H, Geo*, 2002 *I*
V Dragomir 1964 *Cze, EGe*, 1966 *It*, 1967 *Pol, WGe*
G Dragomirescu 1919 *F*
G Dragomirescu-Rahtopol 1963 *Bul, EGe, Cze, F*, 1964 *Cze, EGe, WGe, F*, 1965 *WGe, F*, 1966 *Cze*, 1967 *It, Pt, Pol, WGe, F*, 1968 *Cze, Cze, F*, 1969 *Pol, WGe, Cze, F*, 1970 *It, F*, 1971 *It, Mor*, 1972 *Mor, Cze, WGe, F*, 1973 *WGe, F*
N Dragos 1995 *Ar, It*, 1997 *WalA, F, Ar, F, It*, 1998 *H, Pol, Ukr, Ar, Geo, I*, 1999 *F, S*, 2000 *Sp, Geo, F*
CS Draguceanu 1994 *Sp, Ger, Rus, It, W, It, E*, 1995 *S, J, Ar, F, It*, 1996 *Bel*, 1997 *W, Bel, Ar, F, It*, 1998 *H, Pol, Ukr, Ar, Geo, I*, 1999 *S, A, US, I*, 2000 *Mor, H, Pt, Sp, Geo, F, It*
C Dragulescu 1969 *Cze*, 1970 *F*, 1971 *It*, 1972 *Cze*
G Drobota 1960 *Pol, Cze*, 1961 *EGe, EGe, F*, 1962 *Cze, EGe, Pol, F*, 1964 *Cze, EGe, F*
D Dumbrava 2002 *W*, 2003 *Sp, Rus, Geo, CZR, F, W, I, A, Nm*, 2004 *CZR, Pt, Sp, Rus, Geo, It, J, CZR*, 2005 *Rus, Geo, Ukr, J, US, S, Pt, C*, 2006 *Geo, Pt, Rus*, 2007 *Sp, CZR, Pt, Rus, Pt*, 2008 *Sp, Pt, Rus, CZR, Ur, Rus, ESp*, 2009 *Fj*, 2010 *Geo, Pt, Sp, Ukr, Ukr, Nm, ArJ, ItA, Tun*
H Dumitras 1984 *It*, 1985 *E, It, USS*, 1986 *Pt, F, I*, 1987 *It, USS, Z, S, USS, F*, 1988 *It, Sp, US, USS, USS, F, W*, 1989 *It, E, Z, Sa, USS, S*, 1990 *It, F, H, Sp, USS*, 1991 *It, NZ, F, S, F, C, Fj*, 1992 *Sp, USS, F, Ar*, 1993 *Pt, Tun, F, Sp, F, I*
I Dumitras 2002 *H*, 2006 *Geo, CZR, Ukr, Rus, F*, 2007 *Geo, Sp, CZR, ESp, ItA, Nm, It, S, Pt, NZ*, 2009 *Ur, F, ItA, ItA, Fj*, 2010 *Ger, Rus, Geo, Pt, Sp*
E Dumitrescu 1953 *It*, 1958 *Sp, WGe*
G Dumitrescu 1988 *It, Sp, F, W*, 1989 *It, E, Sp, Z, Sa, USS, S*, 1990 *It, F, H, Sp, It, USS*, 1991 *It, NZ, F*, 1997 *It*
L Dumitrescu 1997 *Bel, Ar*, 2001 *W*
G Dumitriu 1937 *H, F, Ger*
D Dumitru 2009 *Ur, F, ItA, ItA, Fj*
G Dumitru 1973 *Sp, Mor, Ar, Ar, WGe, F*, 1974 *Mor, Sp, Cze, EGe, F*, 1975 *JAB, Pol, F*, 1976 *H, It, Sp*, 1977 *Sp, Pol, F*, 1978 *Cze, Sp, Pol, F*, 1979 *It, Sp, USS, W, Pol, F*, 1980 *It, Mor, USS, I, Pol, F*, 1981 *It, Sp, USS, S, NZ, F*, 1982 *WGe, It, USS, Z, Z, F*, 1983 *Mor, WGe, It, USS, Pol, USS, F*, 1984 *It, S, F*, 1985 *E, It, Tun, USS*, 1986 *F, I*, 1987 *USS, F, S, USS, F*
M Dumitru 1990 *F, H, Sp, It, USS*, 1991 *NZ, F, F, C*, 1992 *F*, 1993 *F, Sp, F*
M Dumitru 1997 *WalA*, 1998 *Ar*, 1999 *F*, 2000 *Mor, H, Pt, Sp, Geo, F*, 2002 *H*, 2003 *Sp*
M Dumitru 2002 *Pt, Sp, H, I*
S Dumitru 2004 *It*, 2005 *Rus, Ukr, US, S, Pt*
R Durbac 1968 *Cze*, 1969 *WGe, Cze*, 1970 *It, F*, 1971 *It, Mor, F*, 1972 *WGe, F*, 1973 *Ar, Ar, WGe, F*, 1974 *Mor, Pol, Sp, Cze, EGe, F, Cze*, 1975 *It, Sp, JAB, Pol, F*
A Duta 1973 *Ar*
R Eckert 1927 *F, Ger, Cze*
I Enache 1977 *It*
M Ezaru 2000 *Pt, Geo, F*
V Falcusanu 1974 *Sp, Cze*
G Fantaneanu 1934 *It*, 1936 *F, It, Ger*, 1937 *It, H, F, Ger*
C Fercu 2005 *C, I*, 2006 *Geo, CZR, Pt, Ukr, Rus, F, Geo, Sp*, 2007 *Geo, Sp, CZR, ESp, ItA, Nm, It, S, Pt*, 2008 *Geo, Sp, Pt, Rus, CZR, Ur, Rus, ESp*, 2009 *Sp, Ger, Rus, Pt, Ur, F*, 2010 *Ger, Rus, Geo, Pt, Sp, Ukr, Nm, ArJ, ItA, Tun*
C Florea 1937 *It, F, Ger*
G Florea 1981 *S, NZ, F*, 1982 *WGe, It, USS, Z, Z*, 1984 *Sp*, 1985 *USS*, 1986 *Pt, F*
S Florea 2000 *It*, 2001 *Sp, Geo, I, E*, 2002 *It, Sp, W*, 2003 *Sp, Rus, Geo, CZR, A, Ar, Nm*, 2007 *Sp, CZR, S, NZ*, 2009 *Sp, Ger*, 2010 *Rus, Ukr, Ukr, Nm*
I Florescu 1957 *F, Cze*
M Florescu 1995 *F*
P Florescu 1967 *It, Pt, Pol, WGe, F*, 1968 *Cze, Cze, F*, 1969 *Pol, WGe, Cze, F*, 1971 *Mor*, 1973 *Sp, Mor, Ar, Ar*, 1974 *Cze, EGe, F*
P Florian 1927 *F*, 1934 *It*
T Florian 1927 *F, Ger*
V Flutur 1994 *Ger*, 1995 *J, J, C, SA, A, Ar, F, It*, 1996 *Bel, Pol*, 1997 *WalA, F*
M Foca 1992 *It, USS, It, Ar*, 1993 *Pt, Tun, F*
C Fugigi 1964 *Cze*, 1969 *Cze*, 1972 *Mor, Cze, WGe, F*, 1973 *Sp, Ar, Ar, WGe, F*, 1974 *Mor, Sp, Cze, EGe*, 1975 *It, Sp, JAB*
C Fugigi 1992 *Ar*
R Fugigi 1995 *It*, 1996 *Pt, F, Pol*, 1998 *Ukr, Ar, I*, 1999 *S, I*
S Fuicu 1976 *H*, 1980 *USS, I, Pol, F*, 1981 *It, Sp, USS, S, NZ, F*, 1982 *Z, Z, F*, 1983 *Mor, WGe, It, USS, W*, 1984 *It*
N Fulina 1988 *F, W*, 1989 *It, E, Sp, Sa, USS*, 1990 *It, F, H, Sp, USS*, 1991 *NZ, C, Fj*, 1992 *It, It*, 1993 *Pt, F, Sp, F, I*, 1994 *Sp, Ger, Rus, It, W, It*
C Gal 2005 *I*, 2006 *Geo, CZR, Pt, S*, 2007 *Geo, CZR, ESp, ItA, Nm, It, S, NZ, Rus, Pt*, 2008 *Geo, Sp, Pt, Rus*, 2009 *Ger, Pt, ItA, ItA, Fj*, 2010 *Geo, Pt, Sp, Ukr, Ukr, Nm, ArJ, ItA, Tun*
S Galan 1985 *It, It*
I Garlesteanu 1924 *F, US*, 1927 *F, Cze*
A Gealapu 1994 *It, E*, 1995 *F, S, J, J, C, SA, A, Ar, F, It*, 1996 *Pt, F, Pol*
C Gheara 2004 *CZR, Sp, Rus, Geo*
C Gheorghe 1992 *It*, 1993 *Tun, F, Sp*, 1994 *Sp, Ger, Rus, E*
G Ghera 2010 *Ger*
D Gherasim 1959 *Cze*

V Ghiata 1951 *EGe*
S Ghica 1937 *H, F,* 1942 *It*
V Ghioc 2000 *It,* 2001 *Pt, Sp, Rus, Geo, I, W, E,* 2002 *Pt, Sp, H, W, S,* 2003 *CZR, Ar,* 2004 *It, W, CZR,* 2005 *Ukr, J, S,* 2008 *Pt*
N Ghiondea 1949 *Cze,* 1951 *EGe*
D Ghiuzelea 1951 *EGe,* 1952 *EGe, EGe,* 1953 *It,* 1955 *Cze,* 1957 *Cze*
A Girbu 1992 *Ar,* 1993 *Tun, Sp, F, I,* 1994 *Sp,* 1995 *Ar, F, It,* 1996 *Pt, F, Pol,* 1997 *WalA, F, Ar, F, It,* 1998 *H, Pol, Geo, I*
L Giucal 2009 *Sp, Ger*
M Giucal 1985 *It, Tun, USS, It,* 1986 *Pt, F, Tun*
A Giugiuc 1963 *Bul, EGe, Cze,* 1964 *Cze, EGe,* 1966 *Cze*
V Giuglea 1986 *S, Tun*
I Glavan 1942 *It*
RS Gontineac 1995 *F, S, J, J, C, SA, A,* 1996 *Pt, F, Pol,* 1997 *F, W, Ar, F, It,* 1998 *H, Pol, Ukr, Ar, Geo, I,* 1999 *F, S, A, US, I,* 2000 *H, Sp, Geo, F,* 2001 *Rus, Geo,* 2002 *Pt, Sp, Rus, Geo, I, It, Sp, W, S,* 2003 *Pt, Sp, Geo, CZR, F, W, I, A, Ar, Nm,* 2004 *CZR, Pt, Rus, Geo, It, W, J, CZR,* 2005 *Geo, C,* 2006 *Geo, Pt, Ukr, Rus, F, Geo, Sp, S,* 2007 *Geo, Sp, It, S, Pt, NZ,* 2008 *ESp*
A Gorcioaia 2009 *Ger*
G Graur 1958 *It,* 1959 *EGe, Pol, Cze, EGe,* 1960 *Pol, EGe, Cze,* 1961 *EGe,* 1962 *EGe, It*
E Grigore 1982 *WGe,* 1984 *Sp,* 1985 *E, Tun,* 1987 *It, USS, Z, F, S*
V Grigorescu 1936 *F, It, Ger,* 1939 *It*
M Guramare 1982 *WGe, It,* 1983 *Mor, WGe,* 1988 *Sp*
A Guranescu 1991 *S, F,* 1992 *USS, It,* 1993 *Pt, Tun, I,* 1994 *Ger, Rus, It, W, E,* 1995 *SA, A, Ar, F, It*
S Guranescu 1997 *W, Bel, Ar,* 2001 *Sp, H, Rus, I*
A Hariton 1973 *Mor, Ar, Ar,* 1978 *Cze, Sp*
T Hell 1958 *EGe*
CN Hildan 1998 *H, Pol, Geo,* 1999 *S*
L Hodorca 1984 *It,* 1985 *Tun,* 1986 *Pt, S, F, Tun, Tun, I,* 1987 *It, Z,* 1988 *F*
M Holban 1980 *Mor,* 1982 *F,* 1985 *It, USS,* 1986 *Pt, I*
J Hussar 1919 *US*
D Iacob 1996 *Bel,* 2001 *Pt, Sp, H, Geo, W*
ML Iacob 1997 *W, Bel, Ar, F, It,* 1999 *S*
Ianus 2009 *Sp,* 2010 *Ukr, Nm, ItA, Tun*
P Ianusevici 1974 *Pol, Cze, EGe, Cze,* 1975 *It,* 1976 *USS, Bul, Pol, F, Mor,* 1977 *Sp, Pol, It, F,* 1978 *F*
I Iconomu 1919 *US, F*
M Iconomu 1919 *US, F*
N Ifrim 1937 *F, Ger*
G Ignat 1986 *Pt, S, F, Tun,* 1988 *It, Sp, US, USS, USS, F, W,* 1989 *It, E, Sp, S,* 1990 *It, F, H, Sp,* 1991 *It, NZ,* 1992 *Sp, It, USS, F*
V Ilca 1987 *F*
I Ilie 1952 *EGe, EGe,* 1953 *It,* 1955 *Cze,* 1957 *F, Cze, Bel, F,* 1958 *It,* 1959 *EGe*
M Iliescu 1961 *EGe,* 1963 *Bul, EGe, Cze, F,* 1965 *WGe, F,* 1967 *WGe*
T Ioan 1937 *H, F, Ger*
V Ioan 1927 *Ger, Cze,* 1937 *It*
F Ion 1991 *S,* 1992 *Sp,* 1993 *F*
G Ion 1984 *Sp,* 1986 *F, I,* 1988 *USS, F, W,* 1989 *It, E, Sp, Sa, USS, S,* 1990 *It, F, H, Sp, It, USS,* 1991 *It, NZ, F, S, F, C, Fj,* 1992 *Sp, It, USS, F, Ar,* 1993 *Pt, F, Sp, F,* 1994 *Sp, It, W, It,* 1997 *WalA*
P Ion 2003 *Ar,* 2004 *It,* 2005 *Rus, Ukr, J, US, S,* 2006 *Geo, CZR, Pt, Ukr, Rus, F, Geo, S,* 2007 *Geo, Sp, CZR, ESp, ItA, Pt, NZ, Rus,* 2008 *Geo, Sp, Rus, Ur, Rus, ESp,* 2009 *Sp, Ger, Rus, Geo, Pt, Ur, F, ItA, ItA, Fj,* 2010 *Ger, Rus, Geo, Pt*
V Ion 1980 *Mor, USS,* 1982 *Z, Z, F,* 1983 *Mor, It, USS, W, USS, F,* 1984 *S,* 1985 *It,* 1987 *It, USS, Z, F, S*
A Ionescu 1958 *EGe, It,* 1959 *EGe, Pol, Cze,* 1960 *Pol, EGe, Cze,* 1961 *Pol, Cze, EGe, F,* 1962 *EGe, It, F,* 1963 *F,* 1964 *Cze, EGe, F,* 1965 *WGe,* 1966 *Cze, It, F*
D Ionescu 1949 *Cze,* 1951 *EGe,* 1952 *EGe, EGe,* 1953 *It,* 1955 *Cze,* 1957 *F, Cze, F,* 1958 *Sp, It*
G Ionescu 1934 *It,* 1936 *F, It, Ger,* 1937 *It, F,* 1938 *F, Ger,* 1940 *It,* 1942 *It*
G Ionescu 1949 *Cze*
M Ionescu 1972 *Mor,* 1976 *USS, Bul, Pol, F,* 1977 *It, F, Pol, It, F,* 1978 *Cze, Sp, Pol, F,* 1979 *It, Sp, USS, W, Pol, F,* 1980 *I,* 1981 *NZ,* 1983 *USS*
R Ionescu 1968 *Cze, Cze,* 1971 *F*
S Ionescu 1936 *It, Ger,* 1937 *It*
V Ionescu 1993 *Tun, F,* 1994 *Rus,* 1998 *Ukr*
V Ionescu 1992 *It*
F Ionita 1974 *Sp,* 1978 *Pol, F*
P Iordachescu 1957 *F, Cze, Bel, F,* 1958 *Sp, WGe, EGe, It,* 1959 *EGe, Pol, Cze, EGe,* 1960 *Pol, EGe, Cze,* 1961 *EGe,* 1963 *F,* 1964 *Cze, EGe, WGe,* 1965 *WGe, F,* 1966 *Cze*
M Iordan 1980 *Mor*
P Iordanescu 1949 *Cze*
V Iorgulescu 1967 *WGe,* 1968 *Cze, F,* 1969 *Pol, WGe, Cze,* 1970 *It, F,* 1971 *F,* 1973 *Ar, Ar*
V Irimescu 1960 *F,* 1961 *Pol, Cze, EGe, F,* 1962 *Cze, EGe, Pol, It, F,* 1963 *F,* 1964 *F,* 1965 *WGe, F,* 1966 *Cze, It, F,* 1967 *It, Pt, Pol, WGe, F,* 1968 *Cze, Cze, F,* 1969 *Pol, WGe, Cze, F,* 1970 *It, F,* 1971 *F*
I Irimia 1936 *F, It, Ger,* 1937 *It, H, Ger,* 1938 *F, Ger,* 1939 *It,* 1940 *It*
G Irisescu 1993 *Sp*
A Iulian 2003 *CZR*
VM Ivan 2010 *Geo, Pt, Sp, Ukr, Ukr, Tun*
I Ivanciuc 1991 *Fj,* 1994 *E,* 1995 *J, C, SA, A*
I Jipescu 1927 *F*
C Kramer 1955 *Cze,* 1958 *Sp, WGe, It,* 1960 *Pol, EGe, Cze*
T Krantz 1940 *It,* 1942 *It*
C Kurtzbauer 1939 *It*
C Lapusneanu 1934 *It*
MA Lazar 2008 *CZR, Ur, Rus, ESp,* 2009 *Geo,* 2010 *Geo, Pt, Sp, Tun*
MV Lemnaru 2009 *Sp, Rus*
G Leonte 1984 *S, F,* 1985 *E, It, USS,* 1987 *It, USS, Z, S, USS, F,* 1988 *It, Sp, US, USS, USS, F, W,* 1989 *It, E, Sp, Z, Sa, USS, S,* 1990 *It, F, H, Sp, It,* 1991 *It, NZ, F, S, F, C,* 1992 *USS, F, It, Ar,* 1993 *Tun, F, Sp, F, I,* 1994 *Sp, Ger, Rus, It, W, It,* 1995 *F, S, J, J, C, SA, A*
M Leuciuc 1987 *F*
T Luca 1995 *Ar, F, It,* 1996 *F*
V Lucaci 1996 *Bel*
V Lucaci 2009 *Fj,* 2010 *Sp, Ukr*
A Lungu 1980 *It, USS,* 1981 *It, Sp, USS, S, NZ, F,* 1982 *WGe, It, USS, Z, Z, F,* 1983 *Mor, WGe, It, USS, Pol, W, USS, F,* 1984 *It, S, F, Sp,* 1985 *E, It, Tun, USS, USS, It,* 1986 *Pt, S, F, Tun, Tun, Pt, F, I,* 1987 *It, USS, Z, F, S, USS, F,* 1988 *It, Sp, US, USS, USS, F, W,* 1989 *It, E, Sp, Z, Sa, USS, S,* 1990 *It, F, It,* 1991 *It, NZ, F, S, F, C, Fj,* 1992 *Sp, It, USS, F, Ar,* 1995 *A*
R Lungu 2002 *Pt, H, It, Sp, W,* 2003 *Pt*
A Lupu 2006 *S*
C Lupu 1998 *Pol, I,* 1999 *F,* 2000 *Mor, It,* 2001 *Pt, H, Rus, W,* 2002 *H, Rus*
S Luric 1951 *EGe,* 1952 *EGe, EGe,* 1953 *It,* 1955 *Cze*
V Luscal 1958 *Sp, WGe, EGe*
F Macaneata 1983 *USS*
M Macovei 2006 *Ukr, Rus,* 2007 *Geo, Rus, Pt,* 2008 *Geo, Rus, CZR, Ur, Rus, ESp,* 2009 *Rus, Geo, ItA,* 2010 *Ger, Geo, Sp, Ukr*
V Maftei 1995 *Ar, F, It,* 1996 *Bel,* 1997 *WalA, W, F,* 1998 *Ar,* 2001 *Pt, Sp, H, Geo, I,* 2002 *Pt, Sp, Rus, Geo, I, It, Sp, S,* 2003 *Pt, Geo, CZR, F, W, I, A, Ar, Nm,* 2004 *Pt, Sp, Rus, Geo, W, J, CZR,* 2005 *Rus, Geo, Ukr, C, I,* 2006 *CZR*
G Malancu 1976 *H, It, USS, Bul*
A Man 1988 *US, USS, USS*
D Manoileanu 1949 *Cze*
DG Manole 2009 *Ger*
G Manole 1959 *Pol,* 1960 *Pol, EGe, Cze*
AV Manta 1996 *Bel,* 1997 *F,* 1998 *Ar, Geo, I,* 2000 *F,* 2001 *Pt, Sp, Rus, Geo,* 2002 *Sp, H, Rus, I, It, Sp,* 2003 *Pt, Rus,* 2005 *C, I,* 2006 *Geo, CZR, Pt, Geo,* 2007 *It, S, NZ,* 2009 *Pt, Ur, F, ItA,* 2010 *Rus, Pt, Ukr, Tun*
H Manu 1919 *US, F,* 1927 *F, Ger*
N Marascu 1919 *F,* 1924 *F, US,* 1927 *F, Cze*
A Marasescu 1927 *F, Ger,* 1936 *It, Ger*
E Marculescu 1936 *F, It, Ger,* 1937 *It,* 1939 *It,* 1940 *It*
A Marghescu 1980 *Pol,* 1981 *It,* 1983 *W, USS, F,* 1984 *S, F, Sp,* 1985 *E*

I Marica 1972 *WGe, F*, 1973 *Sp, Mor, WGe, F*, 1974 *Mor, Sp, Cze, EGe, F, Cze*, 1975 *It, Sp*
A Marin 1978 *Cze, Sp, Pol*, 1979 *F*, 1980 *Pol*, 1982 *USS*, 1983 *Pol*, 1984 *Sp*, 1985 *USS, It*, 1986 *Pt*, 1987 *USS, Z*
A Marin 2008 *CZR*
N Marin 1991 *Fj*, 1992 *Sp, It*, 1993 *F, I*, 1995 *Ar, F, It*
A Marinache 1949 *Cze*, 1951 *EGe*, 1952 *EGe, EGe*, 1955 *Cze*, 1957 *F, Bel, F*, 1960 *F*, 1961 *Pol, EGe, Cze, EGe, F*, 1962 *Cze, Pol*
V Marinescu 1967 *Pt, WGe*, 1968 *Cze*, 1969 *Cze, F*
F Marioara 1994 *E*, 1996 *Pol*, 1998 *Geo, I*
S Maris 2010 *Ukr, Ukr, Nm, ArJ, ItA, Tun*
A Mateescu 1959 *EGe, Pol, Cze, EGe*, 1960 *Pol, EGe, Cze*, 1962 *EGe, Pol*, 1963 *Bul, EGe, Cze*, 1964 *Cze, EGe*, 1965 *WGe, F*, 1966 *F*, 1970 *It, F*, 1973 *Sp, WGe, F*, 1974 *Mor, Pol, Sp*
A Mateiescu 1934 *It*, 1936 *F, Ger*
R Mavrodin 1998 *Geo, I*, 1999 *F, A, US, I*, 2000 *H, Pt, Sp, Geo, F, It*, 2002 *Pt, Sp, H, I, It, Sp, W*, 2003 *I, A, Ar, Nm*, 2004 *Pt, Sp, Rus, Geo, W, J, CZR*, 2005 *Rus, J, US, S, Pt*, 2006 *Ukr, Rus, F, Geo, Sp, S*, 2007 *Geo, ESp, ItA, Nm, It, S, Pt, NZ*, 2009 *Ur*
F Maxim 2007 *Rus*
G Mazilu 1958 *Sp, WGe*, 1959 *EGe, Pol, Cze*
S Mehedinti 1951 *EGe*, 1953 *It*
G Melinte 1958 *EGe, It*
P Mergisescu 1960 *Pol, EGe, Cze*
C Mersoiu 2000 *Mor, Pt*, 2001 *I*, 2002 *S*, 2003 *Pt, Sp, Geo, CZR, F, W*, 2004 *CZR, Pt, Sp, Rus, It, W, J, CZR*, 2005 *Rus, Geo, Ukr, I*, 2006 *CZR, Pt, Geo, Sp*, 2007 *Geo, Sp, CZR, Rus, Pt*, 2008 *Geo, Sp, Pt, Rus, CZR, Ur, Rus, ESp*, 2009 *Geo*
A Miclescu 1971 *Mor*
S Mihailescu 1919 *F*, 1924 *F, US*, 1927 *F*
D Mihalache 1973 *Mor*
M Mihalache 2007 *Pt*, 2008 *Geo, Sp, Rus*
V Mihalascu 1967 *Pol, WGe*
A Mitocaru 1992 *Ar*, 1993 *Pt, Sp, F*
P Mitu 1996 *Bel, Pol*, 1997 *W, Bel, Ar, It*, 1998 *H, Pol, Ukr, Ar, Geo, I*, 1999 *F, S, A, US, I*, 2000 *H, Pt, Sp, Geo, It*, 2001 *Pt, Sp, H, Rus*, 2002 *Pt, Sp, H, Rus, Geo, Sp, W, S*, 2003 *Geo*, 2005 *I*, 2006 *Geo*, 2009 *Sp, Ger, Rus, Pt*
M Miu 2003 *Pt, Sp*
V Mladin 1955 *Cze*, 1957 *Bel, F*, 1958 *Sp, WGe, It*, 1959 *EGe*, 1960 *F*
S Mocanu 1996 *Bel*, 1998 *H, Pol, Ukr*, 2000 *Mor, Pt*
T Moldoveanu 1937 *F, Ger*, 1938 *F, Ger*, 1939 *It*, 1940 *It*
O Morariu 1984 *Sp*, 1985 *Tun*
V Morariu 1952 *EGe, EGe*, 1953 *It*, 1955 *Cze*, 1957 *F, Cze, Bel, F*, 1959 *EGe*, 1960 *F*, 1961 *Pol, Cze, EGe, F*, 1962 *Cze, EGe, Pol, It, F*, 1963 *F*, 1964 *WGe, F*
C Moscu 1934 *It*, 1937 *It*
M Mot 1980 *Mor*, 1982 *It, USS, Z*, 1985 *It, It*, 1986 *F, Tun*, 1988 *US, USS*
M Motoc 1988 *US*, 1989 *S*
P Motrescu 1973 *Mor, Ar, Ar*, 1974 *Mor, Pol, Sp, Cze*, 1975 *JAB, Pol, F*, 1976 *H, It, Sp, Bul, Pol, F, Mor*, 1977 *Sp, It, F, Pol, It, F*, 1978 *Cze, Sp, Pol, F*, 1979 *It, Sp, USS, W, Pol*, 1980 *It, Mor*
B Munteanu 2000 *It*
IC Munteanu 1940 *It*, 1942 *It*
M Munteanu 1973 *WGe, F*, 1974 *Mor, Sp, Cze, EGe, F, Cze*, 1975 *It, Sp, JAB, Pol, F*, 1976 *H, It, Sp, Pol, Mor*, 1978 *Pol, F*, 1979 *It, Sp, W, Pol*, 1980 *It, I, Pol, F*, 1981 *It, Sp, USS, S, NZ, F*, 1982 *F*, 1983 *Mor, WGe, It, USS, Pol, W, USS, F*, 1984 *It, S, F*, 1985 *USS*, 1986 *S, Tun, Pt, F*, 1988 *It, Sp*
T Munteanu 2003 *CZR*, 2004 *CZR*
F Murariu 1976 *H, USS, Bul, Pol, F, Mor*, 1977 *Sp, It, F, Pol, It, F*, 1978 *Cze, Sp, Pol, F*, 1979 *It, Sp, USS, W, Pol, F*, 1980 *It, I, Pol, F*, 1981 *USS, NZ*, 1982 *USS, Z, Z, F*, 1983 *Mor, WGe, It, USS, Pol, W, F*, 1984 *It, S, F, Sp*, 1985 *E, It, Tun, USS, USS, It*, 1986 *Pt, S, F, Tun*, 1987 *It, USS, Z, S, USS, F*, 1988 *It, Sp, US, USS, USS, F, W*, 1989 *It, E, Sp, Z*
D Musat 1974 *Sp, Cze, EGe, Cze*, 1975 *It, JAB, Pol, F*, 1976 *Mor*, 1980 *Mor*
M Nache 1980 *Mor*
M Nagel 1958 *EGe*, 1960 *Pol, EGe, Cze*
R Nanu 1952 *EGe, EGe*, 1953 *It*, 1955 *Cze*, 1957 *F, Bel, F*
V Nastase 1985 *Tun, USS*, 1986 *Tun, Pt, F, I*
D Neaga 1988 *It, Sp, USS, F, W*, 1989 *It, E, Sp, Z, Sa, USS, S*, 1990 *It, F, H, Sp, USS*, 1991 *It, F, S, F, C, Fj*, 1993 *Tun, F, Sp, I*, 1994 *Sp, Ger, Rus, It, W, It, E*, 1995 *F, S, J, J, C*, 1996 *Pt, F*
I Neagu 1972 *Mor, Cze*
E Necula 1987 *It, F*
P Nedelcovici 1924 *F*
C Nedelcu 1964 *Cze, EGe*
M Nedelcu 1993 *Pt, Tun, F*, 1994 *Sp, It*, 1995 *Ar, F, It*
V Nedelcu 1996 *Pol*, 1997 *WalA, F, W, Ar, F*, 1998 *H, Pol, Ukr, Ar*, 2000 *H*, 2001 *I, W, E*, 2002 *Rus, Geo*
I Negreci 1994 *E*, 1995 *F, J, C, SA, A, Ar, F, It*
I Nemes 1924 *F, US*, 1927 *Ger, Cze*
N Nere 2006 *CZR*, 2007 *CZR, Rus, Pt*, 2008 *Sp, Pt, Rus*, 2009 *Sp, Ger, Rus, Geo, Pt*
G Nica 1964 *Cze, EGe, WGe*, 1966 *It, F*, 1967 *Pol, F*, 1969 *Pol, WGe, Cze, F*, 1970 *It, F*, 1971 *It, Mor, F*, 1972 *Mor, Cze, WGe, F*, 1973 *Sp, Mor, Ar, Ar, WGe, F*, 1974 *Mor, Pol, Sp, Cze, EGe, F, Cze*, 1975 *It, Sp, JAB, Pol, F*, 1976 *H, It, Sp, USS, Bul, Pol, F, Mor*, 1977 *Sp, It, F, Pol, It, F*, 1978 *Pol, F*
N Nichitean 1990 *It, Sp, It, USS*, 1991 *It, F, F, C, Fj*, 1992 *USS, It, Ar*, 1993 *Pt, Tun, F, Sp*, 1994 *Sp, Ger, Rus, It, W, It*, 1995 *F, S, J, J, C*, 1997 *WalA, F*
G Nicola 1927 *F, Ger, Cze*
C Nicolae 2003 *Pt, Rus*, 2006 *Sp*, 2007 *ItA, Nm, Pt, Rus*, 2009 *Geo, Pt, Ur, F, ItA, Fj*, 2010 *Pt, Ukr, Nm, ArJ, Tun*
M Nicolae 2003 *I, A*
N Nicolau 1940 *It*
M Nicolescu 1969 *Pol, WGe, Cze, F*, 1971 *It, Mor, F*, 1972 *Mor, Cze, WGe, F*, 1973 *Sp, Mor, Ar, Ar, WGe, F*, 1974 *Mor, Cze, EGe, F, Cze*, 1975 *It, Sp, Pol, F*
P Niculescu 1958 *It*, 1959 *EGe, Cze*
V Niculescu 1938 *F, Ger*
F Nistor 1986 *Tun*
V Nistor 1959 *EGe, Pol, EGe*
M Oblomenco 1967 *It, Pt, WGe, F*
G Olarasu 2000 *Mor, H*
M Olarasu 2000 *Mor*
V Onutu 1967 *It, Pt, Pol, WGe, F*, 1968 *Cze*, 1969 *F*, 1971 *It, Mor*
N Oprea 2000 *It*, 2001 *Pt, Sp, H, Rus, Geo, I, W, E*
F Opris 1986 *F, Tun, Tun, Pt, F, I*, 1987 *F*
G Oprisor 2004 *W, J, CZR*, 2005 *Rus, Ukr, J, US, S, Pt*
T Oroian 1988 *F, W*, 1989 *It, E, Sp, Z, USS*, 1990 *Sp, It*, 1993 *Pt, Tun, F, Sp, I*, 1994 *Sp, Ger, Rus, It, W, It, E*, 1995 *F, S, J, J, C*
M Ortelecan 1972 *Mor, Cze, WGe, F*, 1974 *Pol*, 1976 *It, Sp, USS, Bul, F*, 1977 *Sp, It, F, Pol, It, F*, 1978 *Cze, Sp*, 1979 *F*, 1980 *USS*
A Palosanu 1952 *EGe, EGe*, 1955 *Cze*, 1957 *F, Cze*
E Pana 1937 *F, Ger*
M Paraschiv 1975 *Sp, JAB, Pol, F*, 1976 *H, It, Sp, USS, Bul, F, Mor*, 1977 *Sp, It, Pol, F*, 1978 *Cze, Sp, Pol, F*, 1979 *It, Sp, W*, 1980 *It, I, F*, 1981 *It, USS, S, NZ, F*, 1982 *WGe, It, USS, Z, Z, F*, 1983 *Mor, WGe, It, USS, Pol, W, USS, F*, 1984 *It, S, F*, 1985 *E, It, Tun, USS, USS, It*, 1986 *Pt, S, Tun*, 1987 *It, USS, Z, F, S, USS, F*
G Parcalabescu 1940 *It*, 1942 *It*, 1949 *Cze*, 1951 *EGe*, 1952 *EGe, EGe*, 1953 *It*, 1955 *Cze*, 1957 *Cze, Bel, F*, 1958 *It*, 1959 *EGe, Pol, Cze*, 1960 *Pol, EGe, Cze*
G Pasache 2001 *E*
V Pascu 1983 *It, Pol, W, USS, F*, 1984 *It*, 1985 *USS*, 1986 *Pt, S, F, Tun, I*, 1987 *F*, 1988 *It*
C Patrichi 1993 *Pt, Tun*
A Pavlovici 1972 *Mor, Cze*
A Penciu 1955 *Cze*, 1957 *F, Cze, Bel, F*, 1958 *Sp, WGe, EGe, It*, 1959 *EGe, Pol, Cze, EGe*, 1960 *F*, 1961 *Pol, EGe, Cze, EGe, F*, 1962 *Cze, EGe, Pol, It, F*, 1963 *Bul, Cze, F*, 1964 *WGe, F*, 1965 *WGe, F*, 1966 *It, F*, 1967 *F*
I Peter 1973 *Sp, Mor*
AA Petrache 1998 *H, Pol*, 1999 *F, S, A, US, I*, 2000 *Mor, H, Pt, Sp, Geo, F*, 2001 *W, E*, 2002 *Pt, Sp, H, Rus, I, It, Sp, W, S*, 2003 *Pt, Sp, Rus*, 2004 *It, W, J, CZR*
CC Petre 2001 *E*, 2002 *Pt, Sp, H, Rus, Geo, I, It, Sp, W, S,*

2003 *Pt, Rus, Geo, CZR, F, W, I, A, Ar, Nm*, 2004 *CZR, Pt, Sp, Rus, Geo, It, W, J, CZR*, 2005 *Rus, Geo, Ukr, J, US, S, Pt, C, I*, 2006 *Geo, CZR, Pt, Ukr, Rus, F, Geo, Sp, S*, 2007 *Geo, Sp, CZR, ESp, ItA, Nm, It, S, Pt, NZ*, 2008 *Sp, Rus*, 2009 *Ger, Pt, Ur, F, ItA, ItA*, 2010 *Ger, Rus, Geo, Pt, Sp, Tun*
SA Petrichei 2002 *I, S*, 2003 *Sp, Rus, Geo, CZR, F, W, I, Ar, Nm*, 2004 *Pt, Sp, Rus, Geo*, 2007 *ESp, Nm*, 2009 *Ur, ItA, ItA, Fj*
P Petrisor 1985 *It*, 1987 *USS*
H Peuciulescu 1927 *F*
M Picoiu 2001 *Pt, H*, 2002 *Pt, Sp, H, Rus, I, It, Sp, W*
C Pinghert 1996 *Bel*
I Pintea 1974 *Pol*, 1976 *Pol, F, Mor*, 1977 *Sp, It, F, Pol, It, F*, 1979 *It, Sp, USS, W, Pol, F*, 1980 *It, USS*
D Piti 1987 *USS, F*, 1988 *It, Sp, US*, 1991 *S*
A Plotschi 1985 *It, Tun*, 1987 *S*
Plumea 1927 *Ger*
S Podarescu 1979 *Pol, F*, 1980 *USS*, 1982 *WGe, It, USS, F*, 1983 *Mor, WGe, USS, F*, 1984 *It*, 1985 *E, It*
C Podea 2001 *Geo, I*, 2002 *I, It, Sp, W*, 2003 *Pt, Sp, Rus, F, A*
R Polizu 1919 *US*
A Pop 1970 *It*, 1971 *It, Mor*, 1972 *Mor, Cze, F*, 1973 *WGe, F*, 1974 *Mor, Pol, Sp, EGe, F, Cze*, 1975 *It, Sp, JAB, Pol, F*
D Popa 1993 *Tun, F, Sp*
D Popa 1994 *Ger*
I Popa 1934 *It*, 1936 *F, It, Ger*, 1937 *H, F*, 1938 *F, Ger*, 1939 *It*, 1940 *It*, 1942 *It*
M Popa 1962 *EGe*
N Popa 1952 *EGe*
V Poparlan 2007 *Nm, Pt*, 2008 *Geo, Sp, Pt, Ur, Rus, ESp*, 2009 *Sp, Ger, Rus, Geo*
A Popean 1999 *S*, 2001 *Pt, H*
C Popescu 1986 *Tun, Pt, F*
CD Popescu 1997 *Bel*, 2003 *CZR, F, W, I, A, Ar, Nm*, 2004 *CZR, Pt, Sp, Rus, Geo, J, CZR*, 2005 *Rus, S, Pt, C*, 2006 *CZR, Ukr, Rus, F, Geo, Sp, S*, 2007 *Geo, Sp, CZR, ESp, ItA, Nm, It, Pt*, 2009 *Ur, F, ItA*, 2010 *Geo, Pt, Sp, Ukr, Ukr, ArJ, ItA, Tun*
I Popescu 1958 *EGe*
I Popescu 2001 *Pt, Sp, H, Rus, Geo*
C Popescu-Colibasi 1934 *It*
V Popisteanu 1996 *Pt, F, Pol*
F Popovici 1973 *Sp, Mor*
N Postolache 1972 *WGe, F*, 1973 *Sp, Mor, WGe, F*, 1974 *Mor, Pol, Sp, EGe, F, Cze*, 1975 *It, Sp, Pol, F*, 1976 *H, It*
C Preda 1961 *Pol, Cze*, 1962 *EGe, F*, 1963 *Bul, EGe, Cze, F*, 1964 *Cze, EGe, WGe, F*
NF Racean 1988 *USS, USS, F, W*, 1989 *It, E, Z, Sa, USS*, 1990 *H, Sp, It, USS*, 1991 *NZ, F, F, C, Fj*, 1992 *Sp, It, USS, F, It, Ar*, 1993 *Pt, Tun, F, Sp*, 1994 *Ger, Rus, It, W*, 1995 *F, S, J, J, C, SA, A*
A Radoi 2008 *CZR*, 2009 *ItA, Fj*, 2010 *Sp, Ukr, Ukr, Nm, ArJ, ItA, Tun*
M Radoi 1995 *F*, 1996 *Pt, Pol*, 1997 *WalA, F, W, Bel, Ar, F, It*, 1998 *H, Pol, Ukr*
P Radoi 1980 *Mor*
T Radu 1991 *NZ*
C Raducanu 1985 *It*, 1987 *It, USS, Z, F, S*, 1989 *It, E, Sp, Z*
A Radulescu 1980 *USS, Pol*, 1981 *It, Sp, USS, S, F*, 1982 *WGe, It, USS, Z, Z*, 1983 *Pol, W, USS, F*, 1984 *It, S, F, Sp*, 1985 *E, USS*, 1988 *It, Sp, US, USS, USS, F, W*, 1989 *It, E, Sa, USS*, 1990 *It, F, H, Sp, It, USS*
T Radulescu 1958 *Sp, WGe*, 1959 *EGe, Pol, Cze, EGe*, 1963 *Bul, EGe, Cze*, 1964 *F*, 1965 *WGe, F*, 1966 *Cze*
D Rascanu 1972 *WGe, F*
G Rascanu 1966 *It, F*, 1967 *It, Pt, Pol, WGe, F*, 1968 *Cze, Cze, F*, 1969 *Pol, WGe, Cze, F*, 1970 *It, F*, 1971 *It, Mor, F*, 1972 *Mor, Cze, WGe, F*, 1974 *Sp*
C Ratiu 2003 *CZR*, 2005 *J, US, S, Pt, C, I*, 2006 *CZR, Pt, Ukr, Rus, F, Geo, Sp, S*, 2007 *Sp, CZR, ESp, It, S, Pt, NZ, Rus, Pt*, 2009 *Geo, Pt*, 2010 *Sp*
I Ratiu 1992 *It*
S Rentea 2000 *Mor*
I Roman 1976 *Bul*
C Rosu 1993 *I*
I Rotaru 1995 *J, C, Ar, It*, 1996 *Pt, F, Pol*, 1997 *W, Bel, Ar, F*
L Rotaru 1999 *F, A, I*
N Rus 2007 *Rus*
VS Rus 2007 *Rus, Pt*, 2008 *Geo, Pt, Rus*, 2009 *F, ItA, Fj*
M Rusu 1959 *EGe*, 1960 *F*, 1961 *Pol, Cze*, 1962 *Cze, EGe, Pol, It, F*, 1963 *Bul, EGe, Cze, F*, 1964 *WGe, F*, 1965 *WGe, F*, 1966 *Cze, It, F*, 1967 *It, Pt, Pol*
V Rusu 1960 *Pol, EGe, Cze*, 1961 *EGe, F*, 1962 *Cze, EGe, Pol, It, F*, 1964 *Cze, EGe, WGe, F*, 1965 *WGe*, 1966 *It, F*, 1967 *WGe*, 1968 *Cze*
I Sadoveanu 1939 *It*, 1942 *It*
AA Salageanu 1995 *Ar, F, It*, 1996 *Pt, F, Pol*, 1997 *W, Bel, F*
V Samuil 2000 *It*, 2001 *Pt, E*, 2002 *Pt, Sp, Geo*
C Sasu 1989 *Z*, 1991 *It, NZ, F, S, F, C, Fj*, 1993 *I*
C Sauan 1999 *S, A, US, I*, 2000 *It*, 2002 *Geo, I, It, Sp*, 2003 *Pt, Rus, Geo, CZR, F, W, I, A, Ar, Nm*, 2004 *CZR, Pt, Sp, Rus, Geo, It, W, J, CZR*, 2005 *Rus, Geo, Ukr, J, US, S, Pt*, 2006 *Rus*, 2007 *Geo*
G Sava 1989 *Z, S*, 1990 *H, Sp, It, USS*, 1991 *It, F, S, F, C*, 1992 *Sp*
I Sava 1959 *EGe, Pol, Cze, EGe*, 1960 *F*, 1961 *Pol, EGe, Cze, EGe, F*, 1962 *Cze, Pol, It, F*
C Scarlat 1976 *H, Sp*, 1977 *F*, 1978 *Cze, Sp*, 1979 *It, Sp, USS, W, Pol, F*, 1980 *It, USS*, 1982 *USS*
R Schmettau 1919 *US, F*
V Sebe 1960 *Pol, EGe, Cze*
I Seceleanu 1992 *It, USS, F, It, Ar*, 1993 *Pt, Tun, F, Sp, F*
S Seceleanu 1986 *Pt, F, I*, 1990 *It*
E Septar 1996 *Bel, Pol*, 1997 *WalA, W*, 1998 *Pol, Ukr, I*, 1999 *F, S, A, US, I*, 2000 *It*
B Serban 1989 *Sa, USS, S*, 1990 *It*, 1992 *It, USS*
C Serban 1964 *Cze, EGe, WGe*, 1967 *Pol*, 1968 *Cze, F*, 1969 *Pol, WGe, Cze, F*, 1970 *It, F*, 1971 *It, Mor, F*, 1972 *F*, 1973 *WGe, F*, 1974 *Mor*
M Serbu 1967 *It*
E Sfetescu 1924 *F, US*, 1927 *Cze*
E Sfetescu 1934 *It*, 1936 *F, Ger*, 1937 *It*
G Sfetescu 1927 *F, Ger*
M Sfetescu 1924 *F, US*, 1927 *Ger, Cze*
N Sfetescu 1927 *F, Ger, Cze*
G Simion 1998 *H*
G Simion 1919 *US*
I Simion 1976 *H, It, Sp*, 1979 *Pol, F*, 1980 *F*
ML Sirbe 2008 *CZR*, 2010 *Ukr, Ukr, Nm, ArJ, Tun*
L Sirbu 1996 *Pt*, 2000 *Mor, H, Pt, Geo, F*, 2001 *H, Rus, Geo, I, W, E*, 2002 *Pt, Sp, H, Rus, I, It, S*, 2003 *Pt, Sp, CZR, F, W, I, A, Ar, Nm*, 2004 *Pt, Sp, Rus, Geo, It, W, CZR*, 2005 *Rus, Geo, Ukr, J, US, S, Pt, C*, 2006 *Geo, Pt, Ukr, Rus, F, Geo, Sp*, 2007 *Geo, ItA, It, S, Pt, NZ*, 2009 *Ur, F, ItA, ItA, Fj*, 2010 *Ger, Rus, Geo, Pt, Sp, Nm, ArJ, ItA*
M Slobozeanu 1936 *F*, 1937 *H, F, Ger*, 1938 *F, Ger*
OS Slusariuc 1993 *Tun*, 1995 *J, J, C*, 1996 *Pt, F*, 1997 *Bel, Ar, F*, 1998 *H, Ar, Geo, I*, 1999 *F, S, A*
S Soare 2001 *I, W*, 2002 *Geo*
S Soare 1924 *F, US*
M Socaciu 2000 *It*, 2001 *I, W, E*, 2002 *It, W, S*, 2003 *Pt, Sp, Rus, Geo, CZR, F, W, I, A, Nm*, 2004 *CZR, Pt, Sp, Rus, Geo, It, W, J, CZR*, 2005 *Rus, Geo, Ukr, J, US, Pt, C, I*, 2006 *CZR*
S Socol 2001 *Sp, H, Rus, Geo*, 2002 *Pt, It, Sp, W*, 2003 *Sp, Rus, Geo, F, W, I, A, Ar, Nm*, 2004 *CZR, Pt, Sp, Rus, Geo*, 2005 *Rus, Geo, Ukr, C, I*, 2006 *Geo, CZR, Pt, Ukr, Rus, F, Geo, Sp, S*, 2007 *Geo, Sp, CZR, It, S, Pt, NZ*, 2009 *Ur, F, ItA, Fj*, 2010 *Ger, Rus, Geo, Pt, Sp, Ukr, Ukr, Nm, ArJ, ItA*
N Soculescu 1949 *Cze*, 1951 *EGe*, 1952 *EGe, EGe*, 1953 *It*, 1955 *Cze*
N Soculescu 1927 *Ger*
V Soculescu 1927 *Cze*
GL Solomie 1992 *Sp, F, It, Ar*, 1993 *Pt, Tun, F, Sp, F, I*, 1994 *Sp, Ger, W, It, E*, 1995 *F, S, J, J, C, SA, A, Ar, F, It*, 1996 *Pt, F, Pol*, 1997 *WalA, F, W, Bel, Ar, F, It*, 1998 *H, Pol, Ukr, Ar, Geo, I*, 1999 *S, A, US, I*, 2000 *Sp, F, It*, 2001 *Sp, H, Rus*
C Stan 1990 *H, USS*, 1991 *It, F, S, F, C, Fj*, 1992 *Sp, It, It, Ar*, 1996 *Pt, Bel, F, Pol*, 1997 *WalA, F, W, Bel*, 1998 *Ar, Geo*, 1999 *F, S, A, US, I*
A Stanca 1996 *Pt, Pol*
R Stanca 1997 *F*, 2003 *Sp, Rus*, 2009 *Geo, Pt*
A Stanciu 1958 *EGe, It*

G Stanciu 1958 *EGe, It*
C Stanescu 1957 *Bel*, 1958 *WGe*, 1959 *EGe*, 1960 *F*, 1961 *Pol, EGe, Cze*, 1962 *Cze, It, F*, 1963 *Bul, EGe, Cze, F*, 1964 *WGe, F*, 1966 *Cze, It*
C Stefan 1951 *EGe*, 1952 *EGe*
E Stoian 1927 *Cze*
E Stoica 1973 *Ar, Ar*, 1974 *Cze*, 1975 *Sp, Pol, F*, 1976 *Sp, USS, Bul, F, Mor*, 1977 *Sp, It, F, Pol, It, F*, 1978 *Cze, Sp, Pol, F*, 1979 *It, Sp, USS, W, Pol, F*, 1980 *It, USS, I, Pol, F*, 1981 *It, Sp, USS, S, NZ, F*, 1982 *WGe, It, USS, Z, Z, F*
G Stoica 1963 *Bul, Cze*, 1964 *WGe*, 1966 *It, F*, 1967 *Pt, F*, 1968 *Cze, Cze, F*, 1969 *Pol*
I Stroe 1986 *Pt*
E Suciu 1976 *Bul, Pol*, 1977 *It, F, It*, 1979 *USS, Pol, F*, 1981 *Sp*
M Suciu 1968 *F*, 1969 *Pol, WGe, Cze*, 1970 *It, F*, 1971 *It, Mor, F*, 1972 *Mor, F*
O Sugar 1983 *It*, 1989 *Z, Sa, USS, S*, 1991 *NZ, F*
K Suiogan 1996 *Bel*
F Surugiu 2008 *Ur, Rus, ESp*, 2010 *Ukr, Ukr, Nm, ArJ, ItA*
D Talaba 1996 *Bel*, 1997 *F, It*
C Tanase 1938 *F, Ger*, 1939 *It*, 1940 *It*
A Tanasescu 1919 *F*, 1924 *F, US*
N Tanoviceanu 1937 *It, H, F*, 1939 *It*
I Tarabega 1934 *It*, 1936 *It*
F Tasca 2008 *Ur, Rus, ESp*, 2009 *Sp, Ger, Rus, Geo, Pt*
V Tata 1971 *F*, 1973 *Ar, Ar*
CF Tatu 2003 *Ar*, 2004 *CZR, Pt, Sp, Rus, Geo, It, W*, 2005 *Ukr, J*
I Tatucu 1973 *Sp, Mor*, 1974 *Cze, F*
D Teleasa 1971 *It*, 1973 *Sp, Ar, Ar*
D Tenescu 1951 *EGe*
I Teodorescu 2001 *I, W, E*, 2002 *Pt, Sp, S*, 2003 *Pt, Sp, Rus, W, I, A, Ar, Nm*, 2004 *CZR, Pt, Sp, Rus, Geo, W, J, CZR*, 2005 *Rus, Geo, Ukr, J, US, S, Pt, C, I*, 2006 *Geo, CZR, Pt, Ukr, F, Geo, S*, 2007 *ESp, ItA*
I Teodorescu 1958 *Sp, WGe, EGe, It*, 1960 *Pol, EGe, Cze*, 1963 *Bul, EGe, Cze*, 1965 *WGe, F*
A Teofilovici 1957 *F, Cze, Bel, F*, 1958 *Sp, WGe*, 1959 *EGe*, 1960 *F*, 1961 *Pol, EGe, Cze, EGe, F*, 1962 *Cze, Pol, It, F*, 1963 *Bul, EGe, Cze, F*, 1964 *WGe*
O Tepurica 1985 *USS*
M Tibuleac 1957 *Bel, F*, 1959 *Pol, Cze*, 1966 *Cze*, 1967 *It, Pt, Pol, WGe*, 1968 *Cze, Cze*
G Ticlean 1919 *F*
M Tigora 2004 *CZR*
A Tinca 1987 *USS, F*
VM Tincu 2002 *Pt, Sp, H, Rus, Geo, I, It, Sp, S*, 2003 *Pt, Sp, Rus, Geo, F, W*, 2004 *Sp*, 2005 *Geo, Ukr, C, I*, 2006 *Geo, CZR, F, S*, 2007 *Geo, Sp, CZR, ESp, ItA, Nm, It, S, Pt, NZ*, 2008 *Geo*, 2009 *F, ItA, ItA*, 2010 *Ger, Rus, Geo, Pt*
M Toader 1982 *WGe*, 1984 *Sp*, 1985 *E, It, Tun, USS*, 1986 *S, F, Tun, Tun, Pt, F, I*, 1987 *It, USS, Z, F, S, USS, F*, 1988 *F, W*, 1989 *It, E, Sp, Sa, USS, S*, 1990 *It, F, It*
P Toderasc 2000 *It*, 2001 *Pt, Rus, Geo, W, E*, 2002 *H, Rus, Geo, I, It, Sp, W, S*, 2003 *Sp, Rus, Geo, CZR, F, W, I, A, Ar, Nm*, 2004 *CZR, Pt, Sp, Rus, Geo, It, J, CZR*, 2005 *J, US, S, Pt, C, I*, 2006 *Geo, Pt, Ukr, Sp*, 2007 *Geo, ESp, ItA, Nm, It, S*, 2009 *ItA, Fj*
IR Tofan 1997 *Bel, Ar, F, It*, 1998 *H, Ar*, 1999 *I*, 2000 *Mor, Sp, Geo*, 2001 *Pt, Sp, H, Geo, I, W, E*, 2002 *Pt, Sp, H, Rus, Geo, I, It, Sp, W, S*, 2003 *Pt, Sp, Rus, Geo, CZR, F, W, I, A, Ar, Nm*, 2004 *Sp, Geo, It, W, J*, 2005 *Rus, Geo, Ukr, J, US, I*, 2006 *Geo, CZR, Pt, Geo, Sp, S*, 2007 *Geo, ESp, ItA, Nm, S*
S Tofan 1985 *USS, It*, 1986 *Tun, Pt, F, I*, 1987 *It, USS, Z, F, S, USS, F*, 1988 *It, Sp, US, USS*, 1991 *NZ*, 1992 *Ar*, 1993 *Pt*, 1994 *It, E*
O Tonita 2000 *Mor, H, Pt, Sp, F*, 2001 *Pt, Sp, H, Rus, Geo, I*, 2002 *Sp, It, Sp, W*, 2003 *Rus, Geo, F, W, I, A, Ar, Nm*, 2004 *Sp, Rus, Geo, It*, 2005 *Rus, Pt, C, I*, 2006 *Geo, Pt, Geo, Sp, S*, 2007 *Sp, CZR, It, S, Pt, NZ*, 2009 *Ur, F, ItA, ItA, Fj*, 2010 *Ger, Rus, Geo, Pt, Nm, ArJ, ItA*
Traian 1942 *It*
N Tranca 1992 *Sp*
B Tudor 2003 *CZR, A*
F Tudor 1924 *F, US*
M Tudor 1924 *F, US*
AM Tudori 2003 *F, W, I, A, Ar, Nm*, 2004 *Sp, Rus, Geo, W, J, CZR*, 2005 *Rus, Geo, Ukr, J, US, S, Pt*, 2006 *Geo, CZR, Ukr, Rus, F*, 2007 *Sp, CZR, ESp, ItA, Nm, It, S, Pt*, 2009 *Geo, Ur, ItA*
D Tudosa 1999 *S*, 2002 *Geo, I, It*, 2003 *Pt, W*
T Tudose 1977 *It*, 1978 *Cze, Sp, Pol, F*, 1979 *It, Sp, USS*, 1980 *USS*
V Tufa 1985 *USS*, 1986 *Pt, S*, 1990 *It*, 1991 *F*, 1995 *F, S, J, J, SA, A*, 1996 *Pt, F, Pol*
D Tunaru 1985 *It*
V Turlea 1974 *Sp*, 1975 *JAB, Pol, F*, 1977 *Pol*
C Turut 1937 *H*, 1938 *F*
I Tutuianu 1960 *Pol, EGe*, 1963 *Bul, EGe, Cze*, 1964 *Cze, EGe, WGe*, 1965 *WGe, F*, 1966 *Cze, It, F*, 1967 *Pt, Pol, WGe, F*, 1968 *Cze, Cze, F*, 1969 *Pol, WGe, Cze, F*, 1970 *It, F*, 1971 *F*
G Tutunea 1992 *Sp*
M Ungur 1996 *Bel*
V Ungureanu 1979 *It*
V Urdea 1979 *F*
SF Ursache 2009 *ItA*, 2010 *Ukr, Nm*
V Ursache 2004 *It, W, CZR*, 2005 *S, C*, 2006 *Geo, Ukr, Rus, F, S*, 2007 *Geo, Sp, CZR, ESp, ItA, Nm, Pt, NZ, Rus*, 2008 *Pt, Rus, CZR, Rus*, 2009 *ItA, Fj*, 2010 *Ger, Rus, Geo, Pt, Sp, Ukr, Ukr, Nm, ArJ, ItA, Tun*
R Vacioiu 1977 *It, F, It*
E Valeriu 1949 *Cze*, 1952 *EGe*
M Vardala 1924 *F, US*
N Vardela 1927 *F, Ger*
G Varga 1976 *It, USS, Bul, Pol, F, Mor*, 1977 *Sp, It, F, Pol*, 1978 *Sp*
N Varta 1958 *EGe*
G Varzaru 1980 *Mor, I, Pol, F*, 1981 *It, Sp, USS, F*, 1983 *Mor, WGe, It, USS, F*, 1984 *S, F*, 1985 *Tun, USS*, 1986 *F*, 1988 *It, Sp, US, USS, USS*
Z Vasluianu 1989 *Sp, Z, Sa*
P Veluda 1967 *It, Pt, Pol, WGe, F*, 1968 *Cze, Cze*
R Veluda 1949 *Cze*, 1952 *EGe*
N Veres 1986 *Tun, Pt*, 1987 *F, USS, F*, 1988 *It, Sp, USS*
M Vidrascu 1919 *US, F*
P Vidrascu 1919 *US*, 1924 *F, US*, 1927 *Cze*
M Vioreanu 1994 *E*, 1998 *H, Pol, Ukr, Ar, Geo, I*, 1999 *F, S, A, US, I*, 2000 *Mor, Pt, Sp, Geo, F*, 2001 *Geo*, 2002 *Rus, Geo, I, It, Sp*, 2003 *Sp, Rus, F, I, A, Ar, Nm*
A Visan 1949 *Cze*
D Vlad 2005 *US, S, C, I*, 2006 *Rus*, 2007 *Sp, CZR, It, Rus, Pt*, 2008 *Sp, CZR*
G Vlad 1991 *C, Fj*, 1992 *Sp, It, USS, F, It, Ar*, 1993 *Pt, F, I*, 1994 *Sp, Ger, Rus, It, W, It, E*, 1995 *F, C, SA, A, Ar, It*, 1996 *Pt, F*, 1997 *W, Ar, F, It*, 1998 *Ar*
V Vlad 1980 *Mor*
FA Vlaicu 2006 *Ukr, F, Geo, Sp, S*, 2007 *Geo, Sp, CZR, ESp, ItA, Nm, S, NZ, Pt*, 2008 *Geo, Pt, Rus, CZR, Ur*, 2009 *Sp, Ger, Rus, Geo, Pt, Ur, F, ItA, ItA, Fj*, 2010 *Ger, Rus, Geo, Sp, Ukr, Ukr, ArJ, ItA, Tun*
C Vlasceanu 2000 *Mor, Pt, Sp, Geo, F*
B Voicu 2003 *CZR*, 2004 *CZR, Pt, Sp, Rus, It, J*, 2005 *J, Pt*
M Voicu 1979 *Pol*
M Voicu 2002 *Pt*
V Voicu 1951 *EGe*, 1952 *EGe, EGe*, 1953 *It*, 1955 *Cze*
R Voinov 1985 *It*, 1986 *Pt, S, F, Tun*
P Volvoreanu 1924 *US*
G Vraca 1919 *US, F*
M Vusec 1959 *EGe, Pol, Cze, EGe*, 1960 *F*, 1961 *Pol, EGe, Cze, EGe, F*, 1962 *Cze, EGe, Pol, It, F*, 1963 *Bul, EGe, Cze, F*, 1964 *WGe, F*, 1965 *WGe, F*, 1966 *It, F*, 1967 *It, Pt, Pol, WGe, F*, 1968 *Cze, Cze, F*, 1969 *Pol, F*
RL Vusec 1998 *Geo, I*, 1999 *F, S, A, US, I*, 2000 *Mor, H, Pt, Sp, F*, 2002 *H, Rus, I*
F Wirth 1934 *It*
I Zafiescu 1979 *W, Pol, F*
M Zafiescu 1980 *Mor*, 1986 *I*
D Zamfir 1949 *Cze*
B Zebega 2004 *CZR, Pt, Rus, Geo, It, W, CZR*, 2005 *Rus, Ukr, US, S*, 2006 *Ukr, Sp*, 2007 *Rus, Pt*, 2008 *Geo, Pt, Rus, CZR, Ur*, 2010 *Ger, Sp, Ukr, Ukr, Nm, ArJ*
D Zlatoianu 1958 *Sp, WGe, EGe, It*, 1959 *EGe*, 1960 *Pol, EGe, Cze*, 1961 *EGe, EGe, F*, 1964 *Cze, EGe*, 1966 *Cze*

RUSSIA

RUSSIA'S 2009–10 TEST RECORD

OPPONENTS	DATE	VENUE	RESULT
Canada	28 Nov	A	**Lost** 6–22
Namibia	23 Jan	A	**Won** 30–15
Portugal	6 Feb	H	**Won** 14–10
Spain	13 Feb	A	**Won** 38–20
Romania	27 Feb	H	**Drew** 21–21
Germany	13 Mar	H	**Won** 48–11
Georgia	20 Mar	N	**Lost** 8–36
USA	5 Jun	A	**Lost** 22–39
England Saxons	9 Jun	N	**Lost** 17–49
Uruguay	19 Jun	N	**Won** 38–19

THE BEAR STARTS TO ROAR

By Lúcás Ó'Ceallacháin

Mike Stobe/Getty Images

Russia had plenty to celebrate in 2010, including their first-ever World Cup qualification.

Never will a 21–21 draw with Romania have been so rapturously celebrated as on 27 February 2010, when the result was enough to secure Russia a deserved place at Rugby World Cup 2011 in New Zealand, a first chance to sample the sport's global showpiece.

These have been quite a remarkable 12 months for Russia in both the 15-man game and in Sevens, where the sport's newly acquired Olympic status opened up exciting new avenues for the future.

In the short term, Russia's Rugby World Cup qualification was a remarkable first for a developing nation and they can look forward to Pool C matches on the biggest stage of all against Australia, Ireland, Italy and the USA.

Over and above this excellence in 15s, the inclusion of Rugby Sevens in the sporting programme for the 2016 Olympic Games in Brazil has added the catalyst that Russian rugby needed both domestically and internationally, part of what Executive Vice President Howard Thomas calls the "the perfect wave".

Thomas has previously been involved with Sale Sharks and Premier Rugby, the umbrella organisation of England's top flight, so is no stranger to the professional game.

"Qualification is enormous for Russia. The players have achieved history and this will inspire the next generation," said a very proud Thomas after the Romania game.

"Russia understands, the government understands the stature of the sport and for the national team to be able to perform on that stage will be significant . . . we want to set a pathway to become a major rugby playing nation.

"We have got a detailed Strategic Plan and so far I think we are doing a good job of sticking to it. It is challenging and we want to be a top 12 rugby playing nation by 2015 and we want to reach the quarter-final of Rugby World Cup 2019."

Russia took another massive step forward when the IRB Council awarded Rugby World Cup Sevens 2013 to Moscow on the back of a compelling bid by the Rugby Union of Russia (RUR), spearheaded by Union President Vyacheslav Kopiev and Thomas.

"The success of our bid is due in no small part to our partnership with the City of Moscow, who have an impressive infrastructure and budget for hosting major international sporting events," Thomas explained.

"Government support has been fundamental to all the recent success of Russian rugby. The RWC Sevens will allow the RUR to showcase rugby at its best and be an excellent development tool to push rugby forward all over Russia.

"The legacy programme will be a major boost to rugby all over Russia, not just Moscow, as we intend to host a week-long festival for youth teams, culminating in a finals day with the RWC Sevens finals."

Kopiev added that the Union is "committed to host the best ever Rugby World Cup Sevens tournament and to further promote rugby within Russia and Eastern Europe, creating a permanent foundation for long term growth.

"We also believe that we can create new rugby enthusiasts who can become lifelong devotees of the sport, both on and off the field, and we sincerely foresee a vision whereby rugby met Russia, Russia embraced rugby and the sport of rugby felt richer for the experience."

The successful bid for Rugby World Cup Sevens 2013 was mirrored by some excellent results by the Russian team on the IRB Sevens World

Marc Piscotty/Getty Images

Steve Diamond has been a key part of the Russian rugby revolution.

Series. The eye-catching performances of several players had fans around the world sitting up and taking note of the so-called 'sleeping giants' and one player who brought a real spark was wing Vasily Artemyev, whose tries helped inspire Shield and Bowl final performances in Dubai and George, South Africa, early in the season.

The bulk of that team went on to compete at the Churchill Cup, where the Russians showed that their RWC qualification was no fluke with excellent tries against USA and the England Saxons and a convincing victory over Uruguay, but their graduation also made room for a number of younger players to enter the fray and gain big match experience at the final two IRB Sevens legs in London and Edinburgh.

And on the last day of the season it was those younger starlets who won the Shield at fortress Murrayfield to match the sterling efforts of their more celebrated countrymen earlier in the season. Their performances brought recognition in the media and within the sport that Russia had arrived as a competitive force on the world stage.

"The IRB Sevens World Series will be a stepping stone for a big performance at the Rugby World Cup Sevens at home in Moscow in 2013, as well as a realistic shot at qualifying for the Olympic Games in Rio in 2016," said Thomas. More regular competition on the circuit certainly bodes well for 2016.

And while Pavel Baronovskiy was making steady progress as head coach in Sevens, the coaching personnel in the 15-a-side game raised a level, Nikolai Nerush taking over as coach and also fortunate to count on the support of Director of Rugby Steve Diamond, who made the trip from England with Thomas, ensuring that the approach altered across the board.

For the first time, much of the preparation for the European Nations Cup happened in Canada and South Africa. There were more international fixtures with notable wins against Namibia and many of Russia's clubs spent time in Ireland and the UK playing pre-season games.

The enhanced professionalism of the staff was also reflected in the players, the likes of lock Kyril Kulemin of Castres in France bringing a new approach to the national team, while Artemyev's Sevens form translated seamlessly to the longer form of the Game. The muscular wing is potentially now all set for a mouth-watering World Cup pool clash against former team-mate and room-mate Luke Fitzgerald, the Russian having learned his trade in Ireland at Blackrock College and then at Leinster's Academy.

Crucially, however, Diamond and Nerush have their feet firmly on the ground and recognise the scale of the challenge ahead, both in the immediate and distant future. While Russia produced excellent performances to gain automatic World Cup qualification, the European Nations Cup still eluded them, again outmuscled by arch rivals Georgia in front of a 7,000-strong partisan crowd in the Turkish city of Trabzon.

In European Sevens, Russia again hosted the FIRA finale in Moscow and put in some great performances, but relinquished their crown to Portugal, finishing third overall. All valuable ammunition for future team talks.

"The team performed admirably in Turkey in a very hostile environment," said Thomas. "While Georgia were clear winners on the day, I believe the bravery, courage and passion that this team played with will be of huge importance for the trip to New Zealand in 2011. The loss hurt, but it will only make the team stronger and hungrier."

It is within the junior ranks, though, that Russia's latent potential lies and there too progress is slowly being made.

The hosting of the IRB Junior World Rugby Trophy (JWRT) 2010 was a dress rehearsal for Russia both on and off the field. The global rugby community was keen to see how Russia would handle an international rugby tournament and, with strong support from the City of Moscow, the test was passed comfortably, showing that Russia is fully on track to host a successful RWC Sevens in 2013.

On the field even bigger challenges awaited with Russia's Under-20s automatically qualifying as hosts but lacking the same experience as their opponents. As a result, there was little expectation heaped on the team, but in front of their home fans they surprised many with gutsy performances to finish an extremely creditable third.

"The best thing about hosting the Junior World Rugby Trophy is that we increased our talent pool at this level and at least three or four players did enough to have the senior team coaches considering them for the trip to New Zealand in 2011. The success of the team ignited a belief at this level that Russia is a country with a bright rugby future," enthused Thomas.

While the international year has been one of wonder for Russian rugby, there has also been plenty to smile about domestically. The Russian Super League continues to go from strength to strength with clubs becoming more competitive, particularly Imperia, Slava, Fili and Spartak.

The national competition came to a thrilling climax in 2009–10 when the home and away play-off couldn't separate arch rivals VVA Podmoskovje (Moscow region) and Enisei STM (Krasnoyarsk). A third game was needed before the Moscow club VVA finally emerged winners and the same club also went on to win the European Club Sevens Championship.

"Both clubs provide the bulk of the national team's players and it's no surprise that their successes and experiences have brought a more professional and competitive edge to their clubs," said Thomas.

Russia will be competing amongst the top countries at the Rugby World Cup and it is hard to imagine how anything they do will top 2010, but one thing is certain – the world will be watching when Russia lines up against USA on the 15 September in Taranaki for the clash of the titans.

The success of 2010 will spur Russia on in 2011, but their losses against Georgia in the ENC and the surrendering of their Sevens crown to Portugal will provide even more motivation for the squad as they bid to make a real statement on the grandest stage of all.

"Qualification for the 2011 World Cup is really important, and not just to get there," said Diamond.

"We don't want to get beaten 100–0 by the sides once we get there, the strategic plan is to go and be competitive against similar nations.

"There would be no bigger fixture in Russia on TV than the former USSR playing the USA. Living here for 18 months, you realise it [Russia] is such a nationalist country where when the national team of any sport shows any promise, then the whole country gets behind them."

Mark Wieland/Getty Images

Russia, here with Yury Gostyuzhev winning a lineout in London, see Sevens as a key part of their development.

SAMOA

SAMOA'S 2009–10 TEST RECORD

OPPONENTS	DATE	VENUE	RESULT
Wales	13 Nov	A	**Lost** 13–17
France	21 Nov	A	**Lost** 5–43
Italy	28 Nov	A	**Lost** 6–24
Tonga	12 June	H	**Won** 24–23
Japan	19 June	H	**Lost** 23–31
Fiji	26 June	H	**Won** 31–9

SAMOA IN SEVENS HEAVEN

By Jeremy Duxbury

Ethan Miller/Getty Images

Samoa enjoyed a sensational year in Sevens with trophy after trophy coming their way.

Samoa's unparalleled success in the IRB Sevens World Series in 2009–10 seems to have led to a change in stance from the Samoa Rugby Union in the way the top Sevens players fit into the Test picture.

In previous years, the Samoa Sevens team was basically kept apart from the Manu Samoa 15s side with only a handful of local players making the transition.

Under new coach Stephen Betham, Samoa achieved some outstanding results in the IRB Sevens World Series, during which they won four of the eight tournaments and finished runners-up twice – see pages 47–52 for a full review.

Perhaps, even more remarkable was the way they defeated Gordon Tietjens's New Zealand in six consecutive tournaments. And this was on the back of a winless 2008–09 season when Samoa only once reached the semi-final stages and finished a lowly seventh in the table.

When so many of this Sevens side began to appear in the Manu Samoa team, it was a clear sign that Betham and national 15s coach Fuimaono Titimaea Tafua had struck a very beneficial working relationship.

"I had put that Sevens side together when I was Samoa Sevens coach in 2006," Tafua said. "So I knew those players well."

Even more satisfying was that these national stars of the shorter code became the key players when Samoa claimed their first-ever ANZ Pacific Nations Cup in June – for full review see pages 557–560.

Pesamino scored a try against Tonga on his Test debut, then repeated the feat in the surprise loss to Japan and in the all-important victory over Fiji.

With the Samoans needing to beat Fiji by more than 12 points and secure a bonus point to take the title, Fiji kept things reasonably tight and trailed just 14–9 with a little over 10 minutes left to play.

Then up stepped another Samoa Sevens star, loose forward Alafoti Faosiliva, with a brace of tries in three minutes. And deep into stoppage time, Sevens playmaker Uale Mai added the icing with a fifth Samoan try to stun Fiji 31–9 and record the second-highest winning margin over their neighbours.

Other key Sevens players in the Samoan victory included fly-half Lolo Lui and flanker Ofisa Treviranus, defying the sometimes pushed theory that the two codes are growing apart.

Though Manu Samoa had only edged Tonga 24–23 in the opening PNC game, they had dominated much of the match and only some poor goal-kicking and a couple of breakaway tries from the visitors had kept the game close.

Tries from Pesamino and Exeter's new half-back Junior Poluleuligaga, plus a penalty try, were just enough to avoid what would have been an embarrassing home defeat at Apia Park as Samoa hosted the region's premier tournament for the first time. Tonga have not beaten Samoa in Apia since 1980.

In Samoa's next match, played as a double-header with Tonga-Fiji kicking off a couple of hours earlier, Japan raced to a shock 25–6 lead at half-time with Ryan Nicholas enjoying a cracker of a match. The inside centre went over for two tries as some smart inter-passing and through kicks unzipped the Samoan defence.

The hosts pegged one back in the second half when London Irish No 8 George Stowers powered over for a try. Pesamino's flash down the wing brought the score to 28–16 with 10 minutes to play, but Japan fly-half James Arlidge connected nicely with a late dropped goal to give the Brave Blossoms some breathing space.

Loose forward Joe Tekori of Castres grabbed a late score for Samoa, and though it wasn't enough to give his side a bonus point, it did reduce their target in the deciding match against Fiji.

The subsequent win over the Flying Fijians provided a dramatic finish to the tournament. Faosiliva scored two tries in quick succession having only been on the field for a matter of minutes to give Samoa a huge shot in the arm after what had been a mediocre 12 months of 15 rugby.

After losing all three Tests in the 2009 European tour, the Samoans slumped to their worst-ever finish in May's IRB Pacific Rugby Cup.

In the IRB Junior World Championship in June, Samoa lost all five matches to finish in 12th and last place, which means they get relegated to the Junior World Rugby Trophy in 2011. This was particularly surprising after strong seventh–place finishes in both 2008 and 2009.

Even the Manusina women's side were convincingly beaten 87–0 at home by Australia's Wallaroos in their Oceania qualifier for Women's Rugby World Cup 2010.

"On the tour to Europe, we had wanted to win one game against a Tier One team," explained head coach Tafua, not an unreasonable target considering their record against Wales and Italy.

They very nearly achieved that aim in the opening match against the Welsh at the Millennium Stadium, the site of their famous 38–31 victory at the 1999 Rugby World Cup.

Bolstered with Europe-based professionals like 'IRB/Emirates Airline Rugby Photograph of the Year' subject Seilala Mapusua, Sale's hulking wing Anitele'a Tuilagi and his big brother Henry of Perpignan, Tafua's team rocked Wales once more.

In the end, Wales did well to repel wave after wave of Samoan attack in the closing stages and hang on for a nail-biting 17–13 win.

After this promising start to the tour, Tafua was hardly expecting the next result – a one-sided 43–5 defeat against France in front of a 68,000-strong Parisian crowd.

Samoa trailed 33–0 at the break, and at the final whistle had only a Tekori try to their credit.

And so onto Ascoli Piceno to face Italy, a team they had never lost to and one that had not beaten anyone in almost 18 months.

But against the formbook, Nick Mallett's team produced a solid all-round performance to win 24–6 and end a 13-match run of defeats. Italy scored two tries and kept their try-line intact, while full-back Titi Esau collected Samoa's only points with two kicks at goal.

So Samoa trudged back to the Pacific Islands without a win to show for their efforts and a miserable total of just 24 points from three matches. Not quite what the doctor had ordered.

Their next task of note was the IRB Pacific Rugby Cup, a tournament that Samoa had more or less dominated since its inception in 2006 as part of the IRB's high-performance investments for second tier unions.

In the first four years of the PRC, one Samoan team had always reached the final and had won the competition in 2006 and 2007, while neither of the Samoan teams – Upolu or Savai'i – had finished outside the top three since 2006.

Hosted by Fiji for the first time in a more condensed format, both Samoan teams struggled to find form and neither managed to record a win against a team from a different country until the fourth round.

The 2006 champions Savai'i Samoa eventually finished in fourth place thanks to a late flurry of points against the Tau'uta Reds of Tonga.

Upolu Samoa, the 2007 champions who had reached the previous three finals, were left languishing in fifth spot.

"The PRC didn't go well for us," Tafua said. "It was all our local players, many going overseas for the first time. We started poorly and just didn't recover."

"As for the Pacific Nations Cup, we didn't play that well against Tonga yet picked up a win; and the players didn't really learn from their mistakes when we faced Japan."

"Yes, we got the win against Fiji to win the tournament, but I think we still have a lot of work to do before the World Cup."

Tafua said they will have trials in Auckland ahead of November's tour to Japan, Ireland, England and Scotland, so that the selectors can get a better look at the Samoans playing in the ITM Cup in New Zealand.

The Test against Japan in Tokyo falls outside the IRB window, so it will likely be a very different Samoan line-up from the subsequent three matches and will feature more locally-based players.

The setting up of the SRU's High Performance Unit four years ago has certainly increased the percentage of local players in the Manu Samoa squad.

"And that is where the current Samoa Sevens team came from," Tafua said. "They have been together for four seasons now, which is a big factor in their success."

The former national skipper hopes to have his World Cup squad together for the whole of the 2011 Pacific Nations Cup, and is also eyeing a one-off Test with the Wallabies.

Playing in the so-called RWC group of death with South Africa, Wales, Fiji and Namibia, the Samoans will need to make full use of every warm-up game that comes their way.

And there is now no doubt that the Samoan Sevens boys, who all started in the SRU's High Performance Unit in Apia, will become a key factor in deciding whether the Manu can repeat their World Cup achievements of 1991 and 1995 when they reached the quarter-finals.

SAMOA INTERNATIONAL STATISTICS

MATCH RECORDS UP TO 29TH OCTOBER 2010

WINNING MARGIN

Date	Opponent	Result	Winning Margin
11/07/2009	PNG	115–7	**108**
08/04/1990	Korea	74–7	**67**
18/07/2009	PNG	73–12	**61**
10/06/2000	Japan	68–9	**59**
29/06/1997	Tonga	62–13	**49**

MOST POINTS IN A MATCH

BY THE TEAM

Date	Opponent	Result	Pts.
11/07/2009	PNG	115–7	**115**
08/04/1990	Korea	74–7	**74**
18/07/2009	PNG	73–12	**73**
10/06/2000	Japan	68–9	**68**
29/06/1997	Tonga	62–13	**62**

MOST TRIES IN A MATCH

BY THE TEAM

Date	Opponent	Result	Tries
11/07/2009	PNG	115–7	**17**
08/04/1990	Korea	74–7	**13**
18/07/2009	PNG	73–12	**11**

MOST CONVERSIONS IN A MATCH

BY THE TEAM

Date	Opponent	Result	Cons
11/07/2009	PNG	115–7	**15**
18/07/2009	PNG	73–12	**9**
08/04/1990	Korea	74–7	**8**

MOST PENALTIES IN A MATCH

BY THE TEAM

Date	Opponent	Result	Pens
29/05/2004	Tonga	24–14	8

MOST DROP GOALS IN A MATCH

BY THE TEAM

1 on 9 Occasions

MOST POINTS IN A MATCH

BY A PLAYER

Date	Player	Opponent	Pts.
11/07/2009	Gavin Williams	PNG	**30**
29/05/2004	Roger Warren	Tonga	**24**
03/10/1999	Silao Leaega	Japan	**23**
08/04/1990	Andy Aiolupo	Korea	**23**
08/07/2000	Toa Samania	Italy	**23**

MOST TRIES IN A MATCH

BY A PLAYER

Date	Player	Opponent	Tries
28/05/1991	Tupo Fa'amasino	Tonga	**4**
10/06/2000	Elvis Seveali'I	Japan	**4**
02/07/2005	Alesana Tuilagi	Tonga	**4**
11/07/2009	Esera Lauina	PNG	**4**

MOST CONVERSIONS IN A MATCH

BY A PLAYER

Date	Player	Opponent	Cons
11/07/2009	Gavin Williams	PNG	**10**
18/07/2009	Titi Jnr Esau	PNG	**9**
08/04/1990	Andy Aiolupo	Korea	**8**

MOST PENALTIES IN A MATCH

BY A PLAYER

Date	Player	Opponent	Pens
29/05/2004	Roger Warren	Tonga	**8**

MOST DROP GOALS IN A MATCH

BY A PLAYER

1 on 9 Occasions

MOST CAPPED PLAYERS

Name	Caps
Brian Lima	65
To'o Vaega	60
Semo Sititi	59
Opeta Palepoi	42
Steve So'oialo	38

LEADING PENALTY SCORERS

Name	Pens
Darren Kellett	35
Earl Va'a	31
Silao Leaega	31
Roger Warren	29
Andy Aiolupo	24

LEADING TRY SCORERS

Name	Tries
Brian Lima	31
Semo Sititi	17
Afato So'oialo	15
To'o Vaega	15
Rolagi Koko	12

LEADING DROP GOAL SCORERS

Name	DGs
Darren Kellett	2
Roger Warren	2
Steve Bachop	2

LEADING CONVERSIONS SCORERS

Name	Cons
Andy Aiolupo	35
Earl Va'a	33
Silao Leaega	26
Tanner Vili	21
Gavin Williams	18

LEADING POINTS SCORERS

Name	Pts.
Earl Va'a	184
Andy Aiolupo	172
Silao Leaega	160
Darren Kellett	155
Brian Lima	150

SAMOA INTERNATIONAL PLAYERS

UP TO 29TH OCTOBER 2010

Note: Years given for International Championship matches are for second half of season; eg 1972 means season 1971–72. Years for all other matches refer to the actual year of the match.

A'ati 1932 *Tg*
JT Afoa 2010 *Tg*, *J*
Agnew 1924 *Fj*, *Fj*
S Ah Fook 1947 *Tg*
F Ah Long 1955 *Fj*
Ah Mu 1932 *Tg*
Ah Sue 1928 *Fj*
T Aialupo 1986 *W*
F Aima'asu 1981 *Fj*, 1982 *Fj*, *Fj*, *Fj*, *Tg*, 1988 *Tg*, *Fj*
AA Aiolupo 1983 *Tg*, 1984 *Fj*, *Tg*, 1985 *Fj*, *Tg*, *Tg*, 1986 *Fj*, *Tg*, 1987 *Fj*, *Tg*, 1988 *Tg*, *Fj*, *I*, *W*, 1989 *Fj*, *WGe*, *Bel*, *R*, 1990 *Kor*, *Tg*, *J*, *Tg*, *Fj*, 1991 *W*, *A*, *Ar*, *S*, 1992 *Tg*, *Fj*, 1993 *Tg*, *Fj*, *S*, *NZ*, 1994 *Tg*, *W*, *A*
A Aiono 2009 *PNG*
Aitofele 1924 *Fj*, *Fj*, 1928 *Fj*
P Alalatoa 1986 *W*
V Alalatoa 1988 *I*, *W*, 1989 *Fj*, 1991 *Tg*, *W*, *A*, *Ar*, *S*, 1992 *Tg*, *Fj*
P Alauni 2009 *PNG*
R Ale 1997 *M*, *Tg*, *Fj*, 1999 *J*, *Ar*, *W*, *S*
A Alelupo 1994 *Fj*
T Aleni 1982 *Tg*, 1983 *Tg*, 1985 *Tg*, 1986 *W*, *Fj*, *Tg*, 1987 *Fj*
S Alesana 1979 *Tg*, *Fj*, 1980 *Tg*, 1981 *Fj*, *Fj*, 1982 *Fj*, *Tg*, 1983 *Tg*, *Fj*, 1984 *Fj*, *Tg*, 1985 *Fj*, *Tg*
T Allen 1924 *Fj*, *Fj*
K Anufe 2009 *JAB*, *Tg*
L Aoelua 2008 *NZ*
T Aoese 1981 *Fj*, *Fj*, 1982 *Fj*, *Fj*, *Fj*, *Tg*, 1983 *Tg*
J Apelu 1985 *Tg*
F Asi 1963 *Fj*, *Fj*, *Tg*
F Asi 1975 *Tg*, *Tg*
SP Asi 1999 *S*, 2000 *Fj*, *J*, *Tg*, *C*, *It*, *US*, *W*, *S*, 2001 *Tg*, *Fj*, *NZ*, *Fj*, *Tg*, *Fj*
Atiga 1924 *Fj*
S Ati'ifale 1979 *Tg*, 1980 *Tg*, 1981 *Fj*, *Fj*
J Atoa 1975 *Tg*, *Tg*, 1981 *Fj*
SJ Bachop 1991 *Tg*, *Fj*, *W*, *A*, *Ar*, *S*, 1998 *Tg*, *Fj*, 1999 *J*, *C*, *F*, *NZ*, *US*, *Fj*, *J*, *Ar*, *W*, *S*
C Betham 1955 *Fj*
ML Birtwistle 1991 *Fj*, *W*, *A*, *Ar*, *S*, 1993 *Fj*, *NZ*, 1994 *Tg*, *W*, *Fj*, *A*, 1996 *I*
W Brame 2009 *JAB*, *J*, *Fj*
FE Bunce 1991 *W*, *A*, *Ar*, *S*
CH Capper 1924 *Fj*
J Cavanagh 1955 *Fj*, *Fj*, *Fj*
J Clarke 1997 *Tg*, 1998 *A*, 1999 *US*, *Fj*, *J*
A Collins 2005 *S*, *Ar*

A Cortz 2007 *Fj*
G Cowley 2005 *S, Ar*, 2006 *JAB, J, Tg*
T Cowley 2000 *J, C, It*
L Crichton 2006 *Fj, Tg*, 2007 *Fj, JAB, AuA, SA, J, Tg, SA, Tg, E, US*
O Crichton 1988 *Tg*
O Crichton 1955 *Fj, Fj, Fj*, 1957 *Tg, Tg*
T Curtis 2000 *Fj, J, Tg, C, It, US*
H Ekeroma 1972 *Tg, Tg*
G Elisara 2003 *I, Nm*
S Enari 1975 *Tg, Tg*
S Epati 1972 *Tg*
T Esau 2009 *PNG, PNG, F, It*
K Ese 1947 *Tg*
S Esera 1981 *Fj*
L Eves 1957 *Tg, Tg*
H Fa'afili 2008 *Fj, AuA, M, Tg, J*, 2009 *J, Tg, Fj, PNG, W, F, It*
T Fa'afou 2007 *Fj*
P Fa'alogo 1963 *Fj*
Fa'amaile 1947 *Tg*
T Fa'amasino 1988 *W*, 1989 *Bel, R*, 1990 *Kor, Tg, J, Tg, Fj*, 1991 *Tg, Fj, A*, 1995 *It, Ar, E, SA, Fj, Tg*, 1996 *NZ, M, Tg, Fj*
JS Fa'amatuainu 2005 *S, Ar*, 2006 *JAB*, 2008 *Fj, AuA, J*, 2009 *JAB, J, Tg, Fj, PNG, W, F, It*
S Fa'aofo 1990 *Tg*
Fa'asalele 1957 *Tg, Tg*
F Fa'asau 1963 *Fj, Tg*
M Fa'asavalu 2002 *SA*, 2003 *I, Nm, Ur, Geo, E, SA*
V Faasua 1987 *Fj*, 1988 *Tg, Fj, W*
S Fa'asua 2000 *W*
F Fa'asuaga 1947 *Tg*
L Fa'atau 2000 *Fj, Tg, C, US*, 2001 *I, It*, 2002 *Fj, Tg, Fj, Tg, SA*, 2003 *I, Ur, E, SA*, 2004 *Tg, S, Fj*, 2005 *A, Tg, Tg, Fj, S, E, Ar*, 2006 *JAB, J, Fj, Tg*, 2007 *Fj, JAB, AuA, SA, J, Tg, SA, US*
K Faiva'ai 1998 *Tg, Fj, A*, 1999 *J, C, Tg, NZ, US, Fj*
L Falaniko 1990 *Tg, Fj*, 1991 *Tg*, 1993 *Tg, Fj, S, NZ*, 1995 *SA, It, Ar, E, SA, Fj, Tg, S, E*, 1996 *NZ, M*, 1999 *US, Fj, W, S*
E Fale 2008 *Tg*
S Fale 1955 *Fj*
A Faleata 1960 *M, M*
S Fanolua 1990 *Tg, Fj*, 1991 *Tg, Fj*
TL Fanolua 1996 *NZ, Fj*, 1997 *Tg*, 1998 *Tg, Fj, A*, 1999 *W, S*, 2000 *J, Tg, C, It, US*, 2001 *Tg, Fj, NZ, Fj, Tg, J, Fj*, 2002 *Fj*, 2003 *Nm, Ur, Geo, E*, 2005 *A, Tg, Fj, Fj*
R Fanuatanu 2003 *I, Geo*
M Faoagali 1999 *J, C*
A Faosilivia 2006 *J, Tg*, 2008 *M, Tg, NZ*, 2010 *Tg, J, Fj*
DS Farani 2005 *Tg, Fj, S, E, Ar*, 2006 *J, Fj, Tg*
J Fatialofa 2008 *M*, 2009 *F*
M Fatialofa 1996 *Tg*
PM Fatialofa 1988 *I, W*, 1989 *Bel, R*, 1990 *Kor, Tg, J*, 1991 *Tg, Fj, W, A, Ar, S*, 1992 *Tg, Fj*, 1993 *Tg, Fj, S, NZ*, 1994 *Tg, W, Fj, A*, 1995 *SA, It, Ar, E, SA, Fj, Tg, S, E*, 1996 *NZ, M, Fj*
Fatu 1947 *Tg*
E Feagai 1963 *Fj, Tg*
S Feagai 1963 *Fj, Fj*
D Feaunati 2003 *Nm, Ur, Geo, E, SA*, 2006 *JAB*
I Fea'unati 1996 *I*, 1997 *M, Tg*, 1999 *Tg, NZ, Fj, Ar*, 2000 *Fj, J, Tg, C, It, US*, 2006 *JAB, Fj, Tg*
M Fepuleai 1957 *Tg*
V Fepuleai 1988 *W*, 1989 *Fj, WGe, R*
I Fesuiai'i 1985 *Fj, Tg*
T Fetu 1960 *M, M*
S Fiaola 1960 *M, M*
JA Filemu 1995 *S, E*, 1996 *NZ, M, Tg, Fj, I*, 1997 *M, Fj*, 1999 *J, C, Tg, F, NZ*, 2000 *Fj, J, Tg, C, It, US*, 2001 *Tg, Fj, Tg, J*
F Fili 2003 *I, Nm*, 2009 *W, F*
F Filisoa 2005 *Tg*
Filivaa 1928 *Fj*
T Fong 1983 *Tg, Fj*, 1984 *Fj, Tg*, 1986 *W, Fj, Tg*, 1987 *Fj, Tg*
S Fretton 1947 *Tg*
Fruean 1932 *Tg*
J Fruean 1972 *Tg*, 1975 *Tg, Tg*
S Fruean 1955 *Fj, Fj*
P Fuatai 1988 *Tg, Fj*, 1989 *Fj, WGe, R*
S Fuatai 1972 *Tg*
T Fuga 1999 *F, NZ, US*, 2000 *Fj, J, Tg, C, It, US*, 2007 *SA, Tg*
E Fuimaono-Sapolu 2005 *S, E, Ar*, 2006 *Fj, Tg*, 2007 *SA, E, US*, 2008 *Fj, AuA, M, Tg, J*, 2009 *JAB, J, Fj, PNG, PNG, F, It*
T Gage 1960 *M, M*
T Galuvao 1972 *Tg*
N George 2004 *Tg, Fj*
C Glendinning 1999 *J, C, Tg, F, NZ, US, Fj, J, W, S*, 2000 *Fj, J, Tg, C, It, US*, 2001 *Tg, Fj, NZ, Fj, Tg, Fj*
A Grey 1957 *Tg, Tg*
I Grey 1985 *Fj, Tg*
P Grey 1975 *Tg, Tg*, 1979 *Tg, Fj*, 1980 *Tg*
G Harder 1995 *SA, It, Ar, SA*
Hellesoe 1932 *Tg*
J Helleur 2010 *Tg, J, Fj*
M Hewitt 1955 *Fj, Fj*
J Huch 1982 *Fj, Fj*, 1986 *Fj, Tg*
J Hunt 1957 *Tg, Tg*
A Ieremia 1992 *Tg, Fj*, 1993 *Tg, Fj, S, NZ*
Iese 1928 *Fj*
I Imo 1924 *Fj*
T Imo 1955 *Fj, Fj, Fj*, 1957 *Tg, Tg*
A Ioane 1957 *Tg, Tg, Tg*
E Ioane 1990 *Tg, Fj*, 1991 *Tg, Fj, S*
T Iona 1975 *Tg*
T Iosua 2006 *JAB, J*
Iupati 1924 *Fj*
M Iupeli 1988 *Tg, Fj, I, W*, 1989 *Fj, WGe, R*, 1993 *Tg, S, NZ*, 1994 *Tg, W, Fj, A*, 1995 *SA, E*
S Iuta 1947 *Tg*
T Jensen 1987 *Tg*, 1989 *Bel*
CAI Johnston 2005 *A, Tg, Fj, S, E, Ar*, 2006 *Fj, Tg*, 2007 *JAB, AuA, SA, J, Tg, SA, Tg, E, US*, 2008 *Fj, AuA, M, J*, 2009 *JAB, J, Tg, Fj, PNG, W, F, It*, 2010 *J, Fj*
J Johnston 2008 *AuA, M, Tg, J*
MN Jones 1986 *W*
S Kalapu 1957 *Tg*, 1960 *M*
D Kaleopa 1990 *Kor, Tg, J*, 1991 *A*, 1992 *Fj*, 1993 *Tg, Fj, S*
S Kaleta 1994 *Tg, W*, 1995 *S, E*, 1996 *NZ, M*, 1997 *Tg, Fj*
T Kali 1975 *Tg, Tg*
L Kamu 1955 *Fj, Fj, Fj*
MG Keenan 1991 *W, A, Ar*, 1992 *Tg, Fj*, 1993 *NZ*, 1994 *Tg, W, Fj, A*
JR Keil 2007 *JAB*, 2010 *J*
F Kelemete 1984 *Fj, Tg*, 1985 *Tg*, 1986 *W*
DK Kellet 1993 *Tg, Fj, S, NZ*, 1994 *Tg, W, Fj, A*, 1995 *It, Ar, Fj, Tg, S, E*
DA Kerslake 2005 *Tg, Fj, Tg, Fj*, 2006 *J, Tg*, 2007 *Fj, JAB, AuA, SA, J, Tg*
A Koko 1999 *J*
R Koko 1983 *Tg, Fj, Fj*, 1984 *Fj, Tg*, 1985 *Fj, Tg, Tg*, 1986 *W, Fj, Tg*, 1987 *Fj, Tg*, 1988 *Tg, Fj, I, W*, 1989 *WGe, R*, 1993 *Tg, S, NZ*, 1994 *Tg*
M Krause 1984 *Tg*, 1986 *W*
H Kruse 1963 *Fj, Fj, Tg*
JA Kuoi 1987 *Fj, Tg*, 1988 *I, W*, 1990 *Kor, Tg*
B Laban 1955 *Fj*, 1957 *Tg, Tg*
SL Lafaiali'I 2001 *Tg, Fj, NZ, Tg*, 2002 *Fj, Tg, Fj, Tg, SA*, 2003 *I, Nm, Ur, Geo, E, SA*, 2004 *Tg, S, Fj*, 2005 *A, S, E*, 2007 *Fj, JAB, J, Tg, Tg, US*
I Laga'aia 1975 *Tg, Tg*, 1979 *Tg, Fj*
F Lalomilo 2001 *I, It*
PR Lam 1991 *W, Ar, S*, 1994 *W, Fj, A*, 1995 *SA, Ar, E, SA, Fj, Tg, S, E*, 1996 *NZ, M, Tg, Fj, I*, 1997 *M, Tg, Fj*, 1998 *Tg, Fj, A*, 1999 *J, C, Tg, F, NZ, US, Fj, J, Ar, W, S*
F Lameta 1990 *Tg, Fj*
S Lameta 1982 *Fj*
Latai 1928 *Fj*
G Latu 1994 *Tg, W, Fj, A*, 1995 *SA, Ar, E, SA, Fj, Tg*
E Lauina 2008 *Fj, AuA, M, Tg, J, NZ*, 2009 *JAB, J, Tg, Fj, PNG, PNG*
M Lautau 1985 *Fj*
S Leaega 1997 *M, Tg, Fj*, 1999 *J, J, Ar, W, S*, 2001 *Tg, Fj, NZ, Fj, Tg, Fj, I, It*, 2002 *Fj, SA*
K Lealamanua 2000 *Fj, J, Tg, C, It*, 2001 *NZ, Fj, Tg, J, Fj*, 2002 *Fj, Fj, Tg, SA*, 2003 *I, Nm, Ur, Geo, E, SA*, 2004 *Tg, S, Fj*, 2005 *S, E*, 2007 *SA, Tg, E, US*
GE Leaupepe 1995 *SA, Ar, E, Fj, Tg, S, E*, 1996 *NZ, M, Tg, Fj, I*, 1997 *Tg, Fj*, 1998 *Tg, A*, 1999 *J, C, Tg, F, NZ, US, Fj, J, Ar, W*, 2005 *A*
S Leaupepe 1979 *Tg, Fj*, 1980 *Tg*
P Leavai 1990 *J*
A Leavasa 1979 *Tg, Fj*, 1980 *Tg*
P Leavasa 1955 *Fj, Fj, Fj*, 1957 *Tg, Tg, Tg*
PL Leavasa 1993 *Tg, Fj, S*, 1995 *It, Ar, E, S, E*, 1996 *NZ, M, Tg, Fj, I*, 1997 *M, Tg, Fj*, 2002 *Tg, Fj, Tg, SA*
S Leavasa 1955 *Fj, Fj, Fj*, 1957 *Tg*
T Leiasamaivao 1993 *Tg, S, NZ*, 1994 *Tg, W, Fj*, 1995 *SA, It, Ar, E, SA, S, E*, 1996 *NZ, M, Tg, Fj, I*, 1997 *M, Tg, Fj*
N Leleimalefaga 2007 *Fj, US*
S Lemalu 2003 *Ur, Geo, E*, 2004 *Tg, S, Fj*, 2008 *M, Tg, J, NZ*
S Lemamea 1988 *I, W*, 1989 *Fj, WGe, Bel, R*, 1990 *J*, 1992 *Tg, Fj*, 1995 *E, SA, Fj, Tg*
D Lemi 2004 *Tg, S, Fj*, 2005 *Tg, Fj, Tg, Fj*, 2007 *Fj, JAB, AuA, SA, J, Tg, SA, Tg, E, US*, 2008 *Fj, AuA, M, Tg, J*, 2009 *W, F, It*, 2010 *Tg, J, Fj*
DA Leo 2005 *A, Tg, Fj, Tg, Fj, S, E, Ar*, 2006 *JAB, J, Fj, Tg*, 2007 *AuA, SA, J, Tg, SA, Tg, E*, 2008 *AuA, M, Tg, J*, 2009 *J, Fj, PNG*
M Leota 2000 *Fj, Tg, C*
P Leota 1990 *Kor, Tg, J*
T Leota 1997 *Tg, Fj*, 1998 *Tg, Fj, A*, 1999 *J, C, Tg, F, Fj, J, Ar, W, S*, 2000 *Fj, J*, 2001 *Tg, Fj, NZ, Fj, J, Fj*, 2002 *Fj, Tg, Fj, Tg, SA*, 2003 *I*, 2005 *A*
A Le'u 1987 *Fj, Tg*, 1989 *WGe, R*, 1990 *Kor, J, Tg, Fj*, 1993 *Tg, Fj, S, NZ*, 1996 *I*
T Leupolu 2001 *I, It*, 2002 *Fj, Tg, Fj, Tg, SA*, 2003 *I, Nm, SA*, 2004 *Tg, S, Fj*, 2005 *Ar*, 2007 *AuA*
R Levasa 2008 *NZ*, 2009 *J, PNG*, 2010 *J, Fj*
FH Levi 2007 *Fj, JAB, AuA, SA, J, Tg*, 2008 *Fj, AuA, M, J, NZ*, 2009 *JAB, J, Tg, Fj, PNG, W, F, It*, 2010 *Tg, J, Fj*
A Liaina 1963 *Fj, Fj, Tg*
S Liaina 1963 *Fj, Fj, Tg*
P Lilomaiava 1993 *NZ*
BP Lima 1991 *Tg, Fj, W, A, Ar, S*, 1992 *Tg, Fj*, 1993 *Fj, S, NZ*, 1994 *Tg, W, Fj, A*, 1995 *SA, It, Ar, E, SA, Fj, Tg, S, E*, 1996 *NZ, M, Tg, Fj*, 1997 *M, Fj*, 1998 *Tg, Fj, A*, 1999 *Tg, F, NZ, US, J, Ar, W, S,*

2000 *C, It, US*, 2001 *Fj, Tg, Fj, I, It*, 2002 *Fj, Tg*, 2003 *I, Nm, Ur, Geo, E, SA*, 2004 *Tg, S, Fj*, 2005 *A, Fj*, 2006 *JAB, J, Fj*, 2007 *Fj, JAB, Tg, SA, E*
F Lima 1981 *Fj*
M Lima 1982 *Fj, Fj*
M Lome 1957 *Tg, Tg, Tg*, 1963 *Fj*
M Luafalealo 1999 *J*, 2000 *It, US*, 2001 *Tg, Fj, NZ, Fj, J, Fj*
E Lua'iufi 1987 *Fj, Tg*, 1988 *Tg, Fj*
Lui 1928 *Fj*, 1932 *Tg*
L Lui 2004 *Fj*, 2005 *Tg, Fj, Ar*, 2006 *JAB, J, Tg*, 2007 *Tg, Tg, E, US*, 2009 *JAB, J, Tg, Fj, PNG, PNG, W, F*, 2010 *Tg, J, Fj*
M Lupeli 1993 *Fj*
A Macdonald 1924 *Fj, Fj*, 1928 *Fj*, 1932 *Tg*
M Magele 2009 *PNG*
T Magele 1988 *Tg*
U Mai 2008 *AuA, M, Tg, J, NZ*, 2009 *JAB, J, Fj, PNG, PNG, W, F, It*, 2010 *Tg, J, Fj*
F Mailei 1963 *Fj, Tg*
M Makesi 1960 *M, M*
F Malele 1979 *Tg, Fj*, 1980 *Tg*
J Maligi 2000 *W, S*
P Maligi 1982 *Fj, Tg*, 1983 *Tg, Fj*, 1984 *Fj, Tg*, 1985 *Fj, Tg, Tg*, 1986 *Fj, Tg*
L Malo 1979 *Fj*
J Mamea 2000 *W, S*
L Mano 1988 *Fj, I, W*
C Manu 2002 *Fj, Tg, Tg, SA*
S Mapusua 2006 *JAB, J, Fj, Tg*, 2007 *JAB, AuA, SA, J, Tg, Tg, E, US*, 2009 *Tg, Fj, W, F, It*
P Mareko 1979 *Fj*
K Mariner 2005 *Ar*
M Mata'afa 1947 *Tg*
P Matailina 1957 *Tg, Tg, Tg*
O Matauiau 1996 *Tg, Fj*, 1999 *Ar, W, S*, 2000 *It, W, S*
K Mavaega 1985 *Tg*
M McFadyen 1957 *Tg*, 1960 *M, M*
K McFall 1983 *Fj*
J Meafou 2007 *Tg, SA, E*, 2008 *NZ*
L Mealamu 2000 *W, S*
I Melei 1972 *Tg*
C Meredith 1928 *Fj*, 1932 *Tg*
J Meredith 2001 *I, It*, 2002 *Fj, Tg, Fj, Tg, SA*, 2003 *I, Nm, Ur, Geo, E, SA*, 2004 *Tg, S, Fj*, 2005 *A, Tg, Fj, Fj*
J Meredith 1960 *M*, 1963 *Fj, Fj, Tg*
O Meredith 1947 *Tg*
A Mika 2000 *S*
D Mika 1994 *W, A*
MAN Mika 1995 *SA, It, Ar, E, SA, S, E*, 1997 *Tg, Fj*, 1999 *Tg, F, NZ, J, Ar, W*
S Mika 2004 *Fj*, 2005 *A, Tg, Fj, Tg, Fj*
S Mikaele 2008 *NZ*, 2009 *PNG, PNG*
P Misa 2000 *W, S*
S Moala 2008 *Fj*
F Moamanu 1989 *WGe*
S Moamanu 1985 *Fj*, 1986 *Fj, Tg*
M Moke 1990 *Kor, Tg, J, Tg, Fj*
Moli 1928 *Fj*
P Momoisea 1972 *Tg, Tg*
H Moors 1924 *Fj, Fj*
R Moors 1994 *Tg*
Mose 1932 *Tg*
S Motoi 1984 *Tg*
F Motusagu 2000 *Tg, It*, 2005 *A*
L Mulipola 2009 *PNG*
L Mulipola 2009 *F, It*
P Neenee 1987 *Fj, Tg*, 1991 *Tg, Fj*
O Nelson 1955 *Fj, Fj, Fj*, 1957 *Tg, Tg*
N Ngapaku 2000 *J, C, US*
F Nickel 1957 *Tg*, 1960 *M, M*
N Nifo 2009 *PNG*
Nimmo 1957 *Tg*
T Nu'uali'itia 1994 *Tg, A*, 1995 *SA, It, Ar, E, SA*, 1996 *NZ*
A Olive 2008 *Tg*
F Otto 2010 *Tg, Fj*
FJP Palaamo 1998 *Tg, Fj, A*, 1999 *J, C, F, NZ, US, Fj*, 2007 *Fj, E*, 2009 *JAB, Fj, PNG, PNG*
S Pala'amo 1955 *Fj, Fj, Fj*, 1957 *Tg*
A Palamo 1979 *Tg, Fj*, 1980 *Tg*, 1981 *Fj, Fj*, 1982 *Fj, Fj, Fj, Tg*
LN Palamo 1979 *Tg, Fj*, 1981 *Fj, Fj*, 1982 *Fj, Fj, Fj, Tg*, 1984 *Fj, Tg*, 1985 *Tg*, 1986 *W, Fj, Tg*
T Palamo 1972 *Tg*
O Palepoi 1998 *Tg, Fj, A*, 1999 *J, F, NZ, US, Fj, J, Ar*, 2000 *J, C, It, US, W*, 2001 *Tg, Fj, NZ, Fj, Tg, J, Fj, I, It*, 2002 *Fj, Tg, Fj, Tg, SA*, 2003 *I, Nm, Ur, Geo, E, SA*, 2004 *Tg, S*, 2005 *A, Tg, Fj, Tg, Fj*
Panapa 1932 *Tg*
M Papali'I 1955 *Fj, Fj*
P Papali'I 1924 *Fj, Fj*
PJ Paramore 1991 *Tg, Fj, A*, 1992 *Fj*, 1994 *Tg*, 1995 *SA, It, Ar, SA, Fj, Tg*, 1996 *I*, 1997 *M, Tg, Fj*, 1998 *Tg, Fj, A*, 1999 *J, Ar, W*, 2001 *Tg, Fj, NZ, Fj, Tg, J, Fj*
J Parkinson 2005 *A, Tg*
T Pati 1997 *Tg*
M Patolo 1986 *W, Fj, Tg*
HV Patu 1995 *S, E*, 1996 *I*, 2000 *W, S*
O Patu 1980 *Tg*
T Patu 1979 *Tg, Fj*, 1980 *Tg*, 1981 *Fj, Fj*
P Paul 1955 *Fj, Fj, Fj*
M Paulino 2008 *NZ*
P Paulo 1989 *Bel*, 1990 *Tg, Fj*
A Perelini 1991 *Tg, Fj, W, A, Ar, S*, 1992 *Tg, Fj*, 1993 *NZ*
Al Perenise 2010 *Tg, J, Fj*
S Perez 1963 *Fj, Fj, Tg*
MS Pesamino 2009 *PNG, PNG*, 2010 *Tg, J, Fj*
N Petaia 1963 *Fj*
Petelo 1932 *Tg*
T Petelo 1985 *Fj*
P Petia 2003 *Nm*
O Pifeleti 1987 *Fj*
Pio 1928 *Fj*
GT Pisi 2010 *Tg, Fj*
S Po Ching 1990 *Kor, Tg*, 1991 *Tg*
S Poching 2000 *W, S*, 2001 *Tg*
AJ Polu 2007 *JAB, SA, J, Tg, SA, Tg, E, US*, 2008 *M, NZ*, 2009 *JAB, J, Tg, Fj, W, F, It*, 2010 *Tg, J*
P Poulos 2003 *Ur, Geo, E, SA*
Poutoa 1928 *Fj*
E Puleitu 1995 *SA, E*
M Pulusila 1960 *M, M*
S Punivalu 1981 *Fj, Fj*, 1982 *Fj, Fj, Fj*, 1983 *Tg, Fj*
JEP Purdie 2007 *Fj, SA, J, Tg, SA, Tg, E, US*
I Railey 1924 *Fj, Fj*
D Rasmussen 2003 *I, Ur, Geo, E, SA*, 2004 *Tg, S, Fj*
R Rasmussen 1997 *Tg*
B Reidy 1995 *SA, Fj, Tg*, 1996 *NZ, M, Tg, Fj, I*, 1997 *M*, 1998 *Fj, A*, 1999 *Tg, F, NZ, US, Fj, J, Ar, W, S*
K Roberts 1972 *Tg*
F Ropati 1982 *Fj, Fj, Fj*, 1984 *Fj, Tg*
R Ropati 2003 *SA*, 2008 *NZ*
W Ryan 1983 *Fj*, 1985 *Tg*
E Sa'aga 1924 *Fj, Fj*, 1932 *Tg*
S Sae 1975 *Tg*
PD Saena 1988 *Tg, Fj, I*, 1989 *Fj, Bel, R*, 1990 *Kor, Tg, J, Tg, Fj*, 1991 *Tg, Fj*, 1992 *Tg, Fj*, 1993 *Tg, Fj*
L Sagaga 1963 *Fj, Tg*
K Saifoloi 1979 *Tg, Fj*, 1980 *Tg*, 1982 *Fj, Fj*, 1984 *Fj, Tg*
P Saili 1957 *Tg, Tg, Tg*
M Salanoa 2005 *Tg, Fj*, 2006 *JAB, J, Fj, Tg*, 2007 *Fj, JAB, AuA, SA, J, Tg, Tg*, 2008 *AuA*
M Salavea 2010 *Tg, Fj*
T Salesa 1979 *Tg, Fj*, 1980 *Tg*, 1981 *Fj, Fj*, 1982 *Fj, Fj, Fj, Tg*, 1983 *Tg, Fj, Fj*, 1984 *Fj, Tg*, 1985 *Fj, Tg, Tg*, 1986 *Fj, Tg*, 1987 *Fj, Tg*, 1988 *Tg, Fj, I*, 1989 *Fj, WGe, R*
G Salima 2008 *Fj, AuA, M*
T Samania 1994 *W, Fj, A*, 1996 *NZ, M*, 2000 *Fj, J, C, It*, 2001 *Tg*
D Sanft 2006 *JAB, J*
Q Sanft 2000 *W, S*
L Sasi 1982 *Fj, Tg*, 1983 *Tg, Fj*, 1984 *Fj, Tg*, 1985 *Tg*, 1986 *W, Fj, Tg*, 1987 *Fj, Tg*, 1988 *Tg, Fj*
B Sasulu 2008 *Fj, AuA*
N Sasulu 2008 *AuA*
S Sauila 1989 *Bel*
L Savai'inaea 1957 *Tg, Tg*
J Schaafhausen 1947 *Tg*
W Schaafhausen 1947 *Tg*
P Schmidt 1989 *Fj, WGe*
P Schmidt 1980 *Tg*, 1985 *Tg*
R Schmidt 1979 *Tg*, 1980 *Tg*
D Schuster 1982 *Tg*, 1983 *Tg, Fj, Fj*
H Schuster 1989 *Fj*, 1990 *Kor, Tg, J*
J Schuster 1985 *Fj, Tg, Tg*
M Schuster 2000 *S*, 2004 *Tg, S, Fj*
NSJ Schuster 1993 *S*, 1999 *Tg, F, US*
P Schuster 1975 *Tg, Tg*
MM Schwalger 2000 *W, S*, 2001 *It*, 2003 *Nm, Ur, Geo, E*, 2005 *S, E, Ar*, 2006 *JAB, J, Fj, Tg*, 2007 *Fj, JAB, SA, Tg, SA, Tg, E, US*, 2008 *Fj*, 2009 *JAB, J, Tg, Fj, PNG, W, F, It*, 2010 *Tg, J, Fj*
Sefo 1932 *Tg*
E Sefo 1984 *Fj*
T Sefo 1987 *Tg*, 1988 *I*
P Segi 2001 *Fj, NZ, Fj, Tg, J, I, It*, 2002 *Fj, Tg, Fj, Tg*
K Seinafo 1992 *Tg*
F Selesele 2010 *Tg, J*
S Semeane 2009 *It*
J Senio 2004 *Tg, S, Fj*, 2005 *Tg, Fj, Tg, Fj*, 2006 *JAB, J, Fj, Tg*
U Setu 2010 *Tg*
T Seumanutafa 1981 *Fj*
E Seveali'I 2000 *Fj, J, Tg, C*, 2001 *Tg, NZ, J, Fj, It*, 2002 *Fj, Tg, Fj, Tg, SA*, 2005 *E*, 2007 *SA, J, Tg, SA, Tg, US*
F Sililoto 1980 *Tg*, 1981 *Fj, Fj*, 1982 *Fj, Fj, Fj*
Simaile 1928 *Fj*
Simanu 1928 *Fj*, 1932 *Tg*
A Simanu 1975 *Tg, Tg*, 1981 *Fj*
Sinaumea 1924 *Fj*
F Sini 1995 *SA, Ar, E, SA*
K Sio 1988 *Tg, Fj, I, W*, 1989 *Fj, WGe, R*, 1990 *J, Tg, Fj*, 1992 *Tg, Fj*, 1993 *NZ*, 1994 *Tg*
T Sio 1990 *Tg*, 1992 *Fj*
P Sioa 1981 *Fj, Fj*

P Sione 1960 *M, M*
S Sititi 1999 *J, C, F, J, W, S,* 2000 *Fj, J, Tg, C, US,* 2001 *Tg, Fj, NZ, Fj, Tg, J, Fj, I, It,* 2002 *Fj, Tg, Fj, Tg, SA,* 2003 *I, Nm, Ur, Geo, E, SA,* 2004 *Tg, S, Fj,* 2005 *A, Fj, Tg, Fj, S, E, Ar,* 2006 *JAB, J, Fj, Tg,* 2007 *Fj, JAB, AuA, SA, J, Tg, SA, Tg, E, US,* 2008 *Fj, AuA, M, Tg, J, NZ,* 2009 *J, PNG, PNG*
F Siu 1975 *Tg, Tg*
P Siu 1963 *Fj, Fj, Tg*
E Skelton 2009 *J, Tg, PNG, PNG*
S Skelton 1982 *Fj*
C Slade 2006 *J, Fj, Tg,* 2008 *Fj, AuA, M, Tg, NZ*
R Slade 1972 *Tg*
S Smith 1995 *S, E,* 1996 *Tg, Fj,* 1999 *C, Tg, F, NZ*
P Solia 1955 *Fj, Fj*
I Solipo 1981 *Fj*
F Solomona 1985 *Tg*
A So'oialo 1996 *I,* 1997 *M, Tg, Fj,* 1998 *Tg,* 1999 *Tg, F, NZ, US, Fj, J, Ar,* 2000 *Tg, It,* 2001 *Tg, Fj, NZ, Fj, Tg, J, I*
S So'oialo 1998 *Tg, Fj,* 1999 *NZ, US, Fj, J, Ar, W, S,* 2000 *W, S,* 2001 *Tg, Fj, NZ, Fj, J, Fj, I,* 2002 *Tg, Fj, Tg, SA,* 2003 *I, Nm, Ur, Geo, E, SA,* 2004 *Tg, S, Fj,* 2005 *E,* 2007 *Fj, JAB, AuA, SA, J, Tg, E, US*
F So'olefai 1999 *C, Tg,* 2000 *W, S,* 2001 *Tg, Fj, NZ, Fj, J*
L Sosene 1960 *M*
V Stet 1963 *Fj*
A Stewart 2005 *A, Tg*
G Stowers 2001 *I,* 2008 *Fj, AuA, M, Tg, J, NZ,* 2009 *JAB, J, Tg, Fj, PNG, W, It,* 2010 *Tg, J, Fj*
R Stowers 2008 *Fj*
T Stowers 1960 *M*
F Sua 1982 *Fj, Fj, Fj, Tg,* 1983 *Tg, Fj,* 1984 *Fj,* 1985 *Fj, Tg, Tg,* 1986 *Fj, Tg,* 1987 *Fj*
P Swepson 1957 *Tg*
S Ta'ala 1996 *Tg, Fj, I,* 1997 *M, Tg, Fj,* 1998 *Tg, Fj, A,* 1999 *J, C, Tg, US, Fj, J, Ar, W, S,* 2001 *J*
T Taega 1997 *Fj*
PI Taele 2005 *Tg, Fj, E, Ar,* 2006 *JAB, J, Fj, Tg,* 2010 *J*
D Tafeamalii 2000 *W, S*
D Tafua 1981 *Fj, Fj,* 1982 *Fj, Fj, Fj, Tg,* 1983 *Tg, Fj,* 1985 *Fj, Tg, Tg,* 1986 *W, Fj, Tg,* 1987 *Tg,* 1989 *Fj, WGe, R*
L Tafunai 2004 *Tg, Fj,* 2005 *Tg, Fj, Tg, Fj, S, Ar,* 2008 *AuA, M, Tg, J, NZ*
TDL Tagaloa 1990 *Kor, Tg, J, Tg, Fj,* 1991 *W, A, Ar, S*
S Tagicakibau 2003 *Nm, Ur, Geo, E, SA,* 2004 *Tg, S, Fj,* 2005 *S, E, Ar,* 2007 *Tg,* 2009 *JAB, J, Tg, Fj*
Tagimanu 1924 *Fj*
I Taina 2005 *Tg, Fj, Tg, Fj, S*
F Taiomaivao 1989 *Bel*
L Talapo'o 1960 *M, M*
F Talapusi 1979 *Tg, Fj,* 1980 *Tg*
F Talapusi 2005 *A, Fj, Tg, Fj*
Tamalua 1932 *Tg*
F Tanoa'i 1996 *Tg, Fj*
S Tanuko 1987 *Tg*
P Tapelu 2002 *SA*
V Tasi 1981 *Fj,* 1982 *Fj, Fj, Fj, Tg,* 1983 *Tg, Fj,* 1984 *Fj, Tg*
S Tatupu 1990 *Tg,* 1993 *Tg, Fj, NZ,* 1995 *It, Ar, E, SA, Fj, Tg*
N Tauafao 2005 *A, Tg, Fj, Tg, Fj, S, Ar,* 2007 *Fj,* 2008 *Fj, AuA, Tg, J, NZ,* 2009 *J, Fj, PNG, PNG*
S Taulafo 2009 *W, F, It,* 2010 *Tg, Fj*
I Tautau 1985 *Fj, Tg,* 1986 *W*
T Tavita 1984 *Fj, Tg*
H Tea 2008 *Fj, AuA, Tg, J, NZ,* 2009 *PNG*
I Tekori 2007 *JAB, AuA, SA, J, SA, Tg, E, US,* 2009 *JAB, Tg, Fj, W, F,* 2010 *Tg, J, Fj*
AT Telea 1995 *S, E,* 1996 *NZ, M, Tg, Fj*
E Telea 2008 *Fj*
S Telea 1989 *Bel*
A Teo 1947 *Tg*
F Teo 1955 *Fj*
V Teo 1957 *Tg, Tg*
KG Thompson 2007 *Fj, JAB, AuA, SA, Tg, SA, Tg, E, US,* 2008 *M, Tg, J,* 2009 *W, F, It,* 2010 *Tg, Fj*
H Thomson 1947 *Tg*
A Tiatia 2001 *Tg, Fj, NZ, Fj, Tg, J, Fj*
R Tiatia 1972 *Tg*
S Tilialo 1972 *Tg*
M Timoteo 2009 *Tg, F, It*
F Tipi 1998 *Fj, A,* 1999 *J, C, F, NZ, Fj*
F Toala 1998 *Fj,* 1999 *J, C, S,* 2000 *W, S*
L Toelupe 1979 *Fj*
P Toelupe 2008 *Fj, AuA, J, NZ*
T Tofaeono 1989 *Fj, Bel*
A Toleafoa 2000 *W, S,* 2002 *SA*
K Toleafoa 1955 *Fj, Fj*
PL Toleafoa 2006 *JAB, J, Fj*
K Tole'afoa 1998 *Tg, A,* 1999 *Ar*
F Toloa 1979 *Tg,* 1980 *Tg*
S Toloia 1975 *Tg*
R Tolufale 2008 *NZ,* 2009 *PNG*
J Tomuli 2001 *I, It,* 2002 *Fj, Tg, Fj, Tg, SA,* 2003 *I, Nm, Ur, Geo, E, SA,* 2006 *JAB, J*
L Tone 1998 *Tg, Fj, A,* 1999 *J, C, Tg, F, NZ, US, J, Ar, W, S,* 2000 *Fj, J, Tg, C, It, US, S,* 2001 *NZ, Fj, Tg, J, Fj*
S Tone 2000 *W*
Toni 1924 *Fj,* 1928 *Fj*
OFJ Tonu'u 1992 *Tg,* 1993 *Tg, Fj, S, NZ*
F To'omalatai 1989 *Bel*
PS To'omalatai 1985 *Fj, Tg,* 1986 *W, Fj, Tg,* 1988 *Tg, Fj, I, W,* 1989 *Fj, WGe, Bel, R,* 1990 *Kor, Tg, J, Tg, Fj,* 1991 *Tg, Fj, W, A, Ar, S,* 1992 *Tg, Fj,* 1993 *Fj, S,* 1994 *A,* 1995 *Fj*
O Treviranus 2009 *JAB, J, Tg, Fj, PNG, PNG, W, F, It,* 2010 *J, Fj*
Tualai 1924 *Fj, Fj*
I Tualaulelei 1963 *Fj, Fj, Tg*
F Tuatagaloa 1957 *Tg*
K Tuatagaloa 1963 *Fj, Fj, Tg,* 1972 *Tg*
S Tuatagaloa 1975 *Tg*
V Tuatagaloa 1963 *Fj, Tg*
Tufele 1924 *Fj*
D Tuiavi'I 2003 *I, Nm, Ur, E, SA*
VL Tuigamala 1996 *Fj, I,* 1997 *M, Tg, Fj,* 1998 *Tg, Fj, A,* 1999 *F, NZ, US, Fj, J, Ar, W, S,* 2000 *Fj, J, Tg, US,* 2001 *J, Fj, I, It*
AF Tuilagi 2005 *Tg, Fj, Tg, Fj, S, Ar,* 2006 *J, Tg,* 2007 *Fj, JAB, AuA, SA, J,* 2008 *AuA, M, Tg, J,* 2009 *W*
AT Tuilagi 2002 *Fj, Tg, SA,* 2005 *A, Tg, Fj, Tg, Fj, S, E,* 2007 *AuA, SA, J, Tg, SA, Tg, E, US,* 2009 *JAB*
F Tuilagi 1992 *Tg,* 1994 *W, Fj, A,* 1995 *SA, SA, Fj,* 2000 *W, S,* 2001 *Fj, NZ, Tg,* 2002 *Fj, Tg, Fj, Tg, SA*
H Tuilagi 2002 *Fj, Tg, Fj, Tg,* 2007 *SA, E,* 2008 *J,* 2009 *W, F, It*
T Tuisaula 1947 *Tg*
R Tuivaiti 2004 *Fj*
A Tunupopo 1963 *Fj*
P Tupa'i 2005 *A, Tg, S, E, Ar*
A Tupou 2008 *NZ,* 2009 *PNG*
S Tupuola 1982 *Fj, Fj, Fj, Tg,* 1983 *Tg, Fj,* 1985 *Tg,* 1986 *Fj, Tg,* 1987 *Fj, Tg,* 1988 *W,* 1989 *R*
P Tu'uau 1972 *Tg, Tg,* 1975 *Tg, Tg*
Tuvale 1928 *Fj*
D Tyrrell 2000 *Fj, J, C,* 2001 *It,* 2002 *Fj, Tg, SA,* 2003 *I, Nm, Ur, Geo, E, SA*
S Uati 1988 *Tg, Fj*
T Ugapo 1988 *Tg, Fj, I, W,* 1989 *Fj, WGe, Bel*
U Ulia 2004 *Tg, S, Fj,* 2005 *Ar,* 2006 *JAB, J, Fj, Tg,* 2007 *Fj, JAB, AuA, Tg, Tg, US*
J Ulugia 1985 *Fj, Tg*
M Umaga 1995 *SA, It, Ar, E, SA,* 1998 *Tg, Fj, A,* 1999 *Tg, F, NZ, US, Fj*
S Urika 1960 *M, M*
A Utu'utu 1979 *Tg, Fj*
L Utu'utu 1975 *Tg*
E Va'a 1996 *I,* 1997 *M, Fj,* 1998 *A,* 1999 *Tg, NZ, Fj, J, W, S,* 2001 *Tg, Fj, NZ, Fj, Tg, J, Fj, I,* 2002 *Fj, Tg, Fj, Tg, SA,* 2003 *I, Nm, Ur, Geo, E, SA*
JH Va'a 2005 *A, Fj, Tg, Fj, S, E, Ar,* 2006 *Fj, Tg,* 2007 *JAB, AuA, SA, J, Tg, SA,* 2009 *JAB, J, Tg, Fj, W, It*
MT Vaea 1991 *Tg, Fj, W, A, Ar, S,* 1992 *Fj,* 1995 *S*
K Vaega 1982 *Fj, Tg,* 1983 *Fj*
TM Vaega 1986 *W,* 1989 *WGe, Bel, R,* 1990 *Kor, Tg, J, Tg, Fj,* 1991 *Tg, Fj, W, A, Ar, S,* 1992 *Tg, Fj,* 1993 *Tg, Fj, S, NZ,* 1994 *Tg, W, Fj, A,* 1995 *SA, It, Ar, E, SA, Fj, Tg, S, E,* 1996 *NZ, M, Tg, Fj, I,* 1997 *M, Tg,* 1998 *Fj, A,* 1999 *J, C, F, NZ, Fj, J, Ar, W, S,* 2000 *Fj, J, Tg, C, It, US,* 2001 *Fj, Tg, J, Fj, I*
A Vaeluaga 2000 *W, S,* 2001 *Tg, Fj, Tg, J, Fj, I,* 2007 *JAB, AuA, SA, J, SA, E, US*
F Vagaia 1972 *Tg*
K Vai 1987 *Fj, Tg,* 1989 *Bel*
S Vaifale 1989 *R,* 1990 *Kor, Tg, J, Tg, Fj,* 1991 *Tg, Fj, W, Ar, S,* 1992 *Tg, Fj,* 1993 *S, NZ,* 1994 *Tg, W, Fj, A,* 1995 *SA, It, SA, Fj, S, E,* 1996 *NZ, M, Tg,* 1997 *Tg, Fj*
S Vaili 2001 *I, It,* 2002 *Fj, Tg, Fj, Tg,* 2003 *Geo,* 2004 *Tg, S, Fj*
L Vailoaloa 2005 *A*
T Vaise 1960 *M, M*
S Vaisola Sefo 2007 *US*
T Veiru 2000 *W, S*
M Vili 1957 *Tg*
M Vili 1975 *Tg, Tg*
M Vili 1960 *M, M*
T Vili 1999 *C, Tg, US, Ar,* 2000 *Fj, J, Tg, C, It, US,* 2001 *Tg, Fj, J, Fj, I, It,* 2003 *Ur, Geo, E, SA,* 2004 *Tg, S, Fj,* 2005 *A, Tg, Fj, S, E,* 2006 *J, Fj, Tg*
K Viliamu 2001 *I, It,* 2002 *Fj, SA,* 2003 *I, Ur, Geo, E, SA,* 2004 *S*
T Viliamu 1947 *Tg*
Visesio 1932 *Tg*
FV Vitale 1994 *W, Fj, A,* 1995 *Fj, Tg*
F Vito 1972 *Tg,* 1975 *Tg, Tg*
M von Dincklage 2004 *S*
R Warren 2004 *Tg, S,* 2005 *Tg, Fj, Tg, Fj, S, Ar,* 2008 *Fj, M, Tg, J, NZ*
S Wendt 1955 *Fj, Fj, Fj*
AF Williams 2009 *JAB, J, Fj, PNG, PNG, F, It,* 2010 *J*
DR Williams 1988 *I, W,* 1995 *SA, It, E*
G Williams 2007 *Fj, JAB, AuA, SA, SA, Tg,* 2008 *M, Tg, J,* 2009 *JAB, J, Tg, Fj, PNG, PNG, W, It,* 2010 *J*
H Williams 2001 *Tg, Tg, J*
P Williams 2010 *Tg, J, Fj*
P Young 1988 *I,* 1989 *Bel*

SCOTLAND

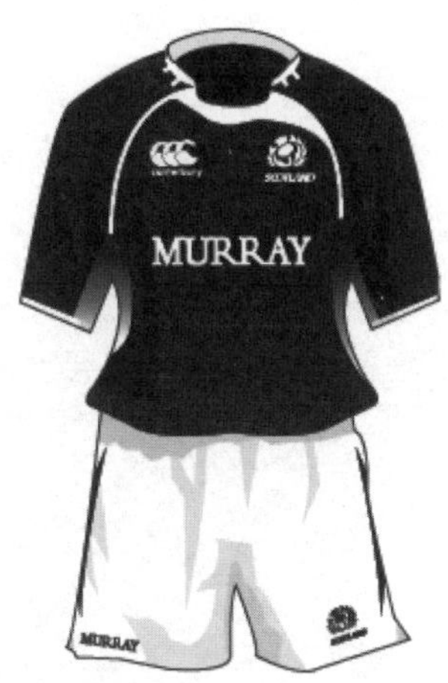

SCOTLAND'S 2009–10 TEST RECORD

OPPONENTS	DATE	VENUE	RESULT
Fiji	14 November	H	**Won** 23–10
Australia	21 November	H	**Won** 9–8
Argentina	28 November	H	**Lost** 6–9
France	7 February	H	**Lost** 9–18
Wales	13 February	A	**Lost** 24–31
Italy	27 February	A	**Lost** 12–16
England	13 March	H	**Drew** 15–15
Ireland	20 March	A	**Won** 23–20
Argentina	12 June	A	**Won** 24–16
Argentina	19 June	A	**Won** 13–9

ROBINSON MASTERMINDS REVIVAL

By Iain Spragg

Getty Images

Scotland ended the season on a massive high with an historic win in Argentina.

Englishmen may not be traditionally renowned for their popularity north of the border but the Scottish rugby fraternity was more than happy to make an exception for Taunton-born Andy Robinson after the first 12 months of his reign as the country's new head coach.

Appointed as Frank Hadden's successor in June 2009, Robinson inherited a beleaguered side that had claimed a meagre three Six Nations wins in three previous, hugely disappointing seasons but the manner in which he galvanised his new charges probably surpassed the expectations of even the most optimistic Scottish supporter.

The former Bath, England and Edinburgh coach began his tenure by leading the Scotland A side to victory in the IRB Nations Cup in Romania, the country's first piece of international silverware in a decade, but the best was yet to come in the form of a win against Australia at Murrayfield in the autumn internationals, a lionhearted if last-gasp triumph over the Irish in the Championship at Croke Park, and, arguably most significantly, victory in the two-Test series against the Pumas in Argentina in the summer.

At the very least, Robinson had comprehensively halted Scotland's recent decline and with a record of five wins in ten Tests from a campaign that culminated in three successive victories away from the familiar surroundings of Murrayfield, it was a season which suggested a bright future.

"The environment the coach has created has been top class and it's an environment in which we feel we can improve and become a top-class team," said captain Chris Cusiter after the side's 23–20 victory over Ireland in Dublin, which came courtesy of a Dan Parks' penalty late in the game.

"To beat Ireland away for the first time in years is fantastic, a reward for all the effort. It was a significant step to take to go on and win and that was a really pleasing facet of the game.

"The squad has kept believing that we could win these games and our performances have been consistent and very high standard. We have proved we can compete and we have managed to beat Ireland, who are one of the form teams in Europe."

Fresh from the Scotland second string's success in Romania, Robinson embarked on his first season at the helm by naming a squad of 32 for the autumn internationals with three uncapped players – Worcester's Alex Grove, Edinburgh's Alan MacDonald and Glasgow Warriors' Richie Vernon – and his first Test in charge saw the Fijians dispatched 23–10 at Murrayfield with tries from Johnnie Beattie and Graeme Morrison.

A week later the Scots went in search of their first victory over the Wallabies in 27 years and, despite conceding the lion's share of possession and territory, they emerged 9–8 winners courtesy of Phil Godman's two penalties and a Chris Paterson drop goal.

"I thought it was a tremendous performance, the most courageous from a team I have ever been involved in," said Robinson. "The guys knew what this was about. It was an incredible effort and credit to all of them. At half-time I was very confident. At 6–3 up I thought that this was going to be our day."

The following weekend Scotland were beaten 9–6 by Argentina, extending the Pumas' winning sequence at Murrayfield to 19 years, but despite the setback Robinson's team looked ahead to the impending Six Nations with renewed confidence.

Initially, however, their Championship campaign appeared to be following a depressingly familiar script.

The opening game against the French at Murrayfield was a one-sided affair despite a final scoreline of 18–9 in favour of Les Bleus. Scotland had once again begun the tournament with defeat and there was further heartbreak in store in Cardiff six days later as they fell victim to a spectacular fightback by the home side.

Scotland ran riot in the early exchanges in the Millennium Stadium and inside the opening 20 minutes John Barclay and Max Evans had both scored tries, one of which was converted by Paterson in his 100th Test, and the visitors were firmly in the ascendency.

The second half however was the stuff of nightmares. A Lee Byrne try began the Welsh revival and Scotland suddenly found themselves reduced to 13 men in the final 10 minutes after Scott Lawson and Godman were both yellow carded. A Stephen Jones penalty in the 79th minute that followed Godman's dismissal levelled the scores at 24–24 but worse was to come when Shane Williams danced over the line at the death to deny Scotland their first victory in Cardiff for eight years.

The match was unfortunately marred by a serious injury to Thom Evans, a neck injury that resulted in the end of a promising career in the game.

Robinson made four changes to his starting XV for the trip to Rome to play Italy with Hugo Southwell and Simon Danielli replacing Paterson and Rory Lamont in the backs but the changes in personnel had little effect on Scotland's fortunes as the side slumped to a 16–12 defeat in an error-strewn performance.

With three losses in three games, the memories of what had been an encouraging autumn were fading fast but just as they appeared to be on the verge of imploding, Robinson's side turned the corner.

England were the next opponents in Edinburgh and against Robinson's compatriots, the home side suddenly found their feet. Scotland dominated the first half and led 9–6 at the break and although the match eventually ended in a 15–15 stalemate and no tries for either side, the sequence of defeats had come to an end.

"We're learning and what you saw was an improvement from Italy," Robinson said. "I thought we played positive rugby, I thought we moved England around and, credit to their defence, they held up well.

"I thought we created opportunities and I thought the way we tried to play with the counter-attack and some of the attacking plays we put on were very good. The players took another step forward and I'm really looking forward to Ireland next week."

Scotland knew they would be the reluctant recipients of the wooden spoon if they lost in Dublin but if there were any nerves in the camp before the Croke Park clash, they were not in evidence during the match. A Beattie try and nine points from the boot of Parks gave the Scots a 14–7 half-time lead but Ireland rallied after the break and with the final whistle looming, the score stood at 20–20. There was however time for one last score and it went to Scotland when Parks landed a sensational penalty from the touchline.

"You make your own luck and I am really pleased at how the team approached the game," Robinson said after his team had denied Ireland the Triple Crown and condemned Italy to last in the Championship table. "It went to the wire. We had a couple of chances, we scored a try – it makes a real difference, because you get the five points.

"We kept our composure right through to the end and I was really pleased with the set piece. We put the Irish line under some pressure. Ireland played really well at the start and I thought at one stage it was going to be a 30-pointer, but we held on."

An intimidating summer tour of Argentina lay ahead but in the first Test in Tucuman, Scotland maintained the resolute form they had shown in the latter stages of the Six Nations and a haul of 24 points from Parks was enough to give the visitors a 24–16 victory as they became the first team to beat the Pumas at the Estadio Monumental Jose Fierro.

Robinson made just one change for the second Test in Mar del Plata, bringing in Danielli for Nick de Luca on the wing and Scotland were on the verge of recording their first ever series victory in the southern hemisphere.

The return clash was as fiercely contested as the first Test but Scotland battled their way to a half-time lead of 10–6 courtesy of Jim Hamilton's converted try, his first in international rugby, and a Parks penalty.

The second half saw the Pumas reply with a penalty from Martin Rodriguez but there was to be just one more score in the game and that went to the visitors when Parks landed his second penalty from the Argentinean 10 metre line. Scotland were 13–9 winners and for the first time since 1982, they had won three Tests in succession on the road.

"It is a special and a great feeling," Robinson said as he reflected on his first season as head coach. "We'll enjoy this moment. It's the first time, certainly since I've been involved, that we've won two games away. It's very pleasing,"

"Some days you go and win ugly, some days you go and win through courage. I think today we won with courage. It gives everybody belief in what we are trying to do."

SCOTLAND INTERNATIONAL STATISTICS

MATCH RECORDS UP TO 29TH OCTOBER 2010

MOST CONSECUTIVE TEST WINS

6 1925 F,W,I,E, 1926 F,W
6 1989 Fj, R, 1990 I,F,W,E

MOST CONSECUTIVE TESTS WITHOUT DEFEAT

Matches	Wins	Draws	Period
9	6*	3	1885 to 1887
6	6	0	1925 to 1926
6	6	0	1989 to 1990
6	4	2	1877 to 1880
6	5	1	1983 to 1984

** includes an abandoned match*

MOST POINTS IN A MATCH

BY THE TEAM

Pts	Opponents	Venue	Year
100	Japan	Perth	2004
89	Ivory Coast	Rustenburg	1995
65	United States	San Francisco	2002
60	Zimbabwe	Wellington	1987
60	Romania	Hampden Park	1999
56	Portugal	Saint Etienne	2007
55	Romania	Dunedin	1987
53	United States	Murrayfield	2000
51	Zimbabwe	Murrayfield	1991
49	Argentina	Murrayfield	1990
49	Romania	Murrayfield	1995

BY A PLAYER

Pts	Player	Opponents	Venue	Year
44	A G Hastings	Ivory Coast	Rustenburg	1995
40	C D Paterson	Japan	Perth	2004
33	G P J Townsend	United States	Murrayfield	2000
31	A G Hastings	Tonga	Pretoria	1995
27	A G Hastings	Romania	Dunedin	1987
26	K M Logan	Romania	Hampden Park	1999
24	B J Laney	Italy	Rome	2002
24	D A Parks	Argentina	Tucumán	2010
23	G Ross	Tonga	Murrayfield	2001
21	A G Hastings	England	Murrayfield	1986
21	A G Hastings	Romania	Bucharest	1986
21	C D Paterson	Wales	Murrayfield	2007

MOST TRIES IN A MATCH

BY THE TEAM

Tries	Opponents	Venue	Year
15	Japan	Perth	2004
13	Ivory Coast	Rustenburg	1995
12	Wales	Raeburn Place	1887
11	Zimbabwe	Wellington	1987
10	United States	San Francisco	2002
9	Romania	Dunedin	1987
9	Argentina	Murrayfield	1990

BY A PLAYER

Tries	Player	Opponents	Venue	Year
5	G C Lindsay	Wales	Raeburn Place	1887
4	W A Stewart	Ireland	Inverleith	1913
4	I S Smith	France	Inverleith	1925
4	I S Smith	Wales	Swansea	1925
4	A G Hastings	Ivory Coast	Rustenburg	1995

MOST CONVERSIONS IN A MATCH

BY THE TEAM

Cons	Opponents	Venue	Year
11	Japan	Perth	2004
9	Ivory Coast	Rustenburg	1995
8	Zimbabwe	Wellington	1987
8	Romania	Dunedin	1987
8	Portugal	Saint Etienne	2007

BY A PLAYER

Cons	Player	Opponents	Venue	Year
11	C D Paterson	Japan	Perth	2004
9	A G Hastings	Ivory Coast	Rustenburg	1995
8	A G Hastings	Zimbabwe	Wellington	1987
8	A G Hastings	Romania	Dunedin	1987

MOST PENALTIES IN A MATCH

BY THE TEAM

Penalties	Opponents	Venue	Year
8	Tonga	Pretoria	1995
7	Wales	Murrayfield	2007
6	France	Murrayfield	1986
6	Italy	Murrayfield	2005
6	Ireland	Murrayfield	2007
6	Italy	Saint Etienne	2007
6	Argentina	Tucumán	2010

BY A PLAYER

Pens	Player	Opponents	Venue	Year
8	A G Hastings	Tonga	Pretoria	1995
7	C D Paterson	Wales	Murrayfield	2007
6	A G Hastings	France	Murrayfield	1986
6	C D Paterson	Italy	Murrayfield	2005
6	C D Paterson	Ireland	Murrayfield	2007
6	C D Paterson	Italy	Saint Etienne	2007
6	D A Parks	Argentina	Tucumán	2010

MOST DROPPED GOALS IN A MATCH

BY THE TEAM

Drops	Opponents	Venue	Year
3	Ireland	Murrayfield	1973
2	on several	occasions	

BY A PLAYER

Drops	Player	Opponents	Venue	Year
2	R C MacKenzie	Ireland	Belfast	1877
2	N J Finlay	Ireland	Glasgow	1880
2	B M Simmers	Wales	Murrayfield	1965
2	D W Morgan	Ireland	Murrayfield	1973
2	B M Gossman	France	Parc des Princes	1983
2	J Y Rutherford	New Zealand	Murrayfield	1983
2	J Y Rutherford	Wales	Murrayfield	1985
2	J Y Rutherford	Ireland	Murrayfield	1987
2	C M Chalmers	England	Twickenham	1995
2	D A Parks	Wales	Cardiff	2010
2	D A Parks	Argentina	Tucumán	2010

CAREER RECORDS

MOST CAPPED PLAYERS

Caps	Player	Career Span
100	C D Paterson	1999 to 2010
87	S Murray	1997 to 2007
82	G P J Townsend	1993 to 2003
77	J P R White	2000 to 2009
75	G C Bulloch	1997 to 2005
71	S B Grimes	1997 to 2005
70	K M Logan	1992 to 2003
66	S M Taylor	2000 to 2009
65	S Hastings	1986 to 1997
64	M R L Blair	2002 to 2010
64	N J Hines	2000 to 2010
61	A G Hastings	1986 to 1995
61	G W Weir	1990 to 2000
61	T J Smith	1997 to 2005
60	C M Chalmers	1989 to 1999
60	B W Redpath	1993 to 2003
54	H F G Southwell	2004 to 2010
53	A R Henderson	2001 to 2008
53	D A Parks	2004 to 2010
52	J M Renwick	1972 to 1984
52	C T Deans	1978 to 1987
52	A G Stanger	1989 to 1998
52	A P Burnell	1989 to 1999
52	C P Cusiter	2004 to 2010
51	A R Irvine	1972 to 1982
51	G Armstrong	1988 to 1999

MOST CONSECUTIVE TESTS

Tests	Player	Span
49	A B Carmichael	1967 to 1978
44	C D Paterson	2004 to 2008
40	H F McLeod	1954 to 1962
37	J M Bannerman	1921 to 1929
35	A G Stanger	1989 to 1994

MOST TESTS AS CAPTAIN

Tests	Captain	Span
25	D M B Sole	1989 to 1992
21	B W Redpath	1998 to 2003
20	A G Hastings	1993 to 1995
19	J McLauchlan	1973 to 1979
19	J P R White	2005 to 2008
16	R I Wainwright	1995 to 1998
15	M C Morrison	1899 to 1904
15	A R Smith	1957 to 1962
15	A R Irvine	1980 to 1982

MOST POINTS IN TESTS

Points	Player	Tests	Career
752	C D Paterson	100	1999 to 2010
667	A G Hastings	61	1986 to 1995
273	A R Irvine	51	1972 to 1982
220	K M Logan	70	1992 to 2003
210	P W Dods	23	1983 to 1991
172	D A Parks	53	2004 to 2010
166	C M Chalmers	60	1989 to 1999
164	G P J Townsend	82	1993 to 2003
141	B J Laney	20	2001 to 2004
123	D W Hodge	26	1997 to 2002
106	A G Stanger	52	1989 to 1998

MOST TRIES IN TESTS

Tries	Player	Tests	Career
24	I S Smith	32	1924 to 1933
24	A G Stanger	52	1989 to 1998
22	C D Paterson	100	1999 to 2010
17	A G Hastings	61	1986 to 1995
17	A V Tait	27	1987 to 1999
17	G P J Townsend	82	1993 to 2003
15	I Tukalo	37	1985 to 1992
13	K M Logan	70	1992 to 2003
12	A R Smith	33	1955 to 1962

MOST CONVERSIONS IN TESTS

Cons	Player	Tests	Career
87	C D Paterson	100	1999 to 2010
86	A G Hastings	61	1986 to 1995
34	K M Logan	70	1992 to 2003
26	P W Dods	23	1983 to 1991
25	A R Irvine	51	1972 to 1982
19	D Drysdale	26	1923 to 1929
17	B J Laney	20	2001 to 2004
15	D W Hodge	26	1997 to 2002
14	F H Turner	15	1911 to 1914
14	R J S Shepherd	20	1995 to 1998

MOST PENALTY GOALS IN TESTS

Penalties	Player	Tests	Career
153	C D Paterson	100	1999 to 2010
140	A G Hastings	61	1986 to 1995
61	A R Irvine	51	1972 to 1982
50	P W Dods	23	1983 to 1991
33	D A Parks	53	2004 to 2010
32	C M Chalmers	60	1989 to 1999
29	K M Logan	70	1992 to 2003
29	B J Laney	20	2001 to 2004
21	M Dods	8	1994 to 1996
21	R J S Shepherd	20	1995 to 1998

MOST DROPPED GOALS IN TESTS

Drops	Player	Tests	Career
12	J Y Rutherford	42	1979 to 1987
11	D A Parks	53	2004 to 2010
9	C M Chalmers	60	1989 to 1999
7	I R McGeechan	32	1972 to 1979
7	G P J Townsend	82	1993 to 2003
6	D W Morgan	21	1973 to 1978
5	H Waddell	15	1924 to 1930

Graham Stuart/AFP/Getty Images

Chris Paterson, the only Scot with 100 caps.

INTERNATIONAL CHAMPIONSHIP RECORDS

RECORD	DETAIL	HOLDER	SET
Most points in season	120	in four matches	1999
Most tries in season	17	in four matches	1925
Highest Score	38	38–10 v Ireland	1997
Biggest win	28	31–3 v France	1912
	28	38–10 v Ireland	1997
Highest score conceded	51	16–51 v France	1998
Biggest defeat	40	3–43 v England	2001
Most appearances	50	C D Paterson	2000–2010
Most points in matches	372	C D Paterson	2000–2010
Most points in season	65	C D Paterson	2007
Most points in match	24	B J Laney	v Italy, 2002
Most tries in matches	24	I S Smith	1924–1933
Most tries in season	8	I S Smith	1925
Most tries in match	5	G C Lindsay	v Wales, 1887
Most cons in matches	32	C D Paterson	2000–2010
Most cons in season	11	K M Logan	1999
Most cons in match	5	F H Turner	v France, 1912
	5	J W Allan	v England, 1931
	5	R J S Shepherd	v Ireland, 1997
Most pens in matches	90	C D Paterson	2000–2010
Most pens in season	16	C D Paterson	2007
Most pens in match	7	C D Paterson	v Wales, 2007
Most drops in matches	8	J Y Rutherford	1979–1987
	8	C M Chalmers	1989–1998
	8	D A Parks	2004–2010
Most drops in season	5	D A Parks	2010
Most drops in match	2	on several	Occasions

MISCELLANEOUS RECORDS

RECORD	HOLDER	DETAIL
Longest Test Career	W C W Murdoch	1935 to 1948
Youngest Test Cap	N J Finlay	17 yrs 36 days in 1875*
Oldest Test Cap	J McLauchlan	37 yrs 210 days in 1979

* C Reid, also 17 yrs 36 days on debut in 1881, was a day *older* than Finlay, having lived through an extra leap-year day.

CAREER RECORDS OF SCOTLAND INTERNATIONAL PLAYERS (UP TO 29TH OCTOBER 2010)

PLAYER	DEBUT	CAPS	T	C	P	D	PTS
BACKS							
M R L Blair	2002 v C	64	5	0	0	0	25
B J Cairns	2008 v Arg	7	1	0	0	0	5
C P Cusiter	2004 v W	52	3	0	0	0	15
S C J Danielli	2003 v It	26	6	0	0	0	30
N J de Luca	2008 v F	19	0	0	0	0	0
M B Evans	2008 v C	13	2	0	0	0	10
T H Evans	2008 v Arg	10	1	0	0	0	5
P J Godman	2005 v R	23	1	12	14	0	71
A Grove	2009 v Fj	3	0	0	0	0	0
R P Lamont	2005 v W	23	6	0	0	0	30
S F Lamont	2004 v Sm	47	7	0	0	0	35
R G.M.Lawson	2006 v A	20	0	0	0	0	0
G A Morrison	2004 v A	25	3	0	0	0	15
D A Parks	2004 v W	53	4	10	33	11	172
C D Paterson	1999 v Sp	100	22	87	153	3	752
H F G Southwell	2004 v Sm	54	8	0	0	0	40
N Walker	2002 v R	15	4	0	0	0	20
S L Webster	2003 v I	37	8	0	0	0	40
FORWARDS							
J A Barclay	2007 v NZ	20	2	0	0	0	10
J W Beattie	2006 v R	14	3	0	0	0	15
K D R Brown	2005 v R	37	3	0	0	0	15
D A Callam	2006 v R	11	1	0	0	0	5
G Cross	2009 v W	2	0	0	0	0	0
A G Dickinson	2007 v NZ	18	0	0	0	0	0
R W Ford	2004 v A	40	2	0	0	0	10
R J Gray	2010 v F	3	0	0	0	0	0
D W H Hall	2003 v W	30	1	0	0	0	5
J L Hamilton	2006 v R	29	1	0	0	0	5
N J Hines	2000 v NZ	64	2	0	0	0	10
A Hogg	2004 v W	48	10	0	0	0	50
A F Jacobsen	2002 v C	47	0	0	0	0	0
A D Kellock	2004 v A	27	0	0	0	0	0

S Lawson	2005 v R	22	2	0	0	0	10
M J Low	2009 v F	8	0	0	0	0	0
A R MacDonald	2009 v Arg	4	0	0	0	0	0
S J MacLeod	2004 v A	22	0	0	0	0	0
E A Murray	2005 v R	32	2	0	0	0	10
M L Mustchin	2008 v Arg	5	0	0	0	0	0
R M Rennie	2008 v I	1	0	0	0	0	0
A K Strokosch	2006 v A	17	1	0	0	0	5
S M Taylor	2000 v US	66	6	0	0	0	30
K Traynor	2009 v Fj	3	0	0	0	0	0
R J Vernon	2009 v Fj	3	0	0	0	0	0
J P R White	2000 v E	77	4	0	0	0	20

Marty Melville/Getty Images

Richie Vernon is a star of the future, making his Test debut in 2009.

SCOTLAND INTERNATIONAL PLAYERS

MATCH RECORDS UP TO 29TH OCTOBER 2010

Note: Years given for International Championship matches are for second half of season; eg 1972 means season 1971–72. Years for all other matches refer to the actual year of the match. Entries in square brackets denote matches played in RWC Finals.

Abercrombie, C H (United Services) 1910 I, E, 1911 F, W, 1913 F, W
Abercrombie, J G (Edinburgh U) 1949 F, W, I, 1950 F, W, I, E
Agnew, W C C (Stewart's Coll FP) 1930 W, I
Ainslie, R (Edinburgh Inst FP) 1879 I, E, 1880 I, E, 1881 E, 1882 I, E
Ainslie, T (Edinburgh Inst FP) 1881 E, 1882 I, E, 1883 W, I, E, 1884 W, I, E, 1885 W, I 1,2
Aitchison, G R (Edinburgh Wands) 1883 I
Aitchison, T G (Gala) 1929 W, I, E
Aitken, A I (Edinburgh Inst FP) 1889 I
Aitken, G G (Oxford U) 1924 W, I, E, 1925 F, W, I, E, 1929 F
Aitken, J (Gala) 1977 E, I, F, 1981 F, W, E, I, NZ 1,2, R, A, 1982 E, I, F, W, 1983 F, W, E, NZ, 1984 W, E, I, F, R
Aitken, R (London Scottish) 1947 W
Allan, B (Glasgow Acads) 1881 I
Allan, J (Edinburgh Acads) 1990 NZ 1, 1991, W, I, R, [J, I, WS, E, NZ]
Allan, J L (Melrose) 1952 F, W, I, 1953 W
Allan, J L F (Cambridge U) 1957 I, E
Allan, J W (Melrose) 1927 F, 1928 I, 1929 F, W, I, E, 1930 F, E, 1931 F, W, I, E, 1932 SA, W, I, 1934 I, E
Allan, R C (Hutchesons' GSFP) 1969 I
Allardice, W D (Aberdeen GSFP) 1947 A, 1948 F, W, I, 1949 F, W, I, E
Allen, H W (Glasgow Acads) 1873 E
Anderson, A H (Glasgow Acads) 1894 I
Anderson, D G (London Scottish) 1889 I, 1890 W, I, E, 1891 W, E, 1892 W, E
Anderson, E (Stewart's Coll FP) 1947 I, E
Anderson, J W (W of Scotland) 1872 E
Anderson, T (Merchiston Castle School) 1882 I
Angus, A W (Watsonians) 1909 W, 1910 F, W, E, 1911 W, I, 1912 F, W, I, E, SA, 1913 F, W, 1914 E, 1920 F, W, I, E
Anton, P A (St Andrew's U) 1873 E
Armstrong, G (Jedforest, Newcastle) 1988 A, 1989 W, E, I, F, Fj, R, 1990 I, F, W, E, NZ 1,2, Arg, 1991 F, W, E, I, R, [J, I, WS, E, NZ], 1993 I, F, W, E, 1994 E, I, 1996 NZ, 1,2, A, 1997 W, SA (R), 1998 It, I, F, W, E, SA (R), 1999 W, E, I, F, Arg, R, [SA, U, Sm, NZ]
Arneil, R J (Edinburgh Acads, Leicester and Northampton) 1968 I, E, A, 1969 F, W, I, E, SA, 1970 F, W, I, E, A, 1971 F, W, I, E (2[1C]), 1972 F, W, E, NZ
Arthur, A (Glasgow Acads) 1875 E, 1876 E
Arthur, J W (Glasgow Acads) 1871 E, 1872 E
Asher, A G G (Oxford U) 1882 I, 1884 W, I, E, 1885 W, 1886 I, E
Auld, W (W of Scotland) 1889 W, 1890 W
Auldjo, L J (Abertay) 1878 E
Bain, D McL (Oxford U) 1911 E, 1912 F, W, E, SA, 1913 F, W, I, E, 1914 W, I
Baird, G R T (Kelso) 1981 A, 1982 E, I, F, W, A 1,2, 1983 I, F, W, E, NZ, 1984 W, E, I, F, A, 1985 I, W, E, 1986 F, W, E, I, R, 1987 E, 1988 I
Balfour, A (Watsonians) 1896 W, I, E, 1897 E
Balfour, L M (Edinburgh Acads) 1872 E
Bannerman, E M (Edinburgh Acads) 1872 E, 1873 E
Bannerman, J M (Glasgow HSFP) 1921 F, W, I, E, 1922 F, W, I, E, 1923 F, W, I, E, 1924 F, W, I, E, 1925 F, W, I, E, 1926 F, W, I, E, 1927 F, W, I, E, A, 1928 F, W, I, E, 1929 F, W, I, E
Barclay, J A (Glasgow Warriors) 2007 [NZ], 2008 F,W,Arg 2,NZ,SA,C, 2009 W,F,It,I, Fj,A, 2010 F,W,It,E,I,Arg 1,2
Barnes, I A (Hawick) 1972 W, 1974 F (R), 1975 E (R), NZ, 1977 I, F, W
Barrie, R W (Hawick) 1936 E
Bearne, K R F (Cambridge U, London Scottish) 1960 F, W
Beattie, J A (Hawick) 1929 F, W, 1930 W, 1931 F, W, I, E, 1932 SA, W, I, E, 1933 W, E, I, 1934 I, E, 1935 W, I, E, NZ, 1936 W, I, E
Beattie, J R (Glasgow Acads) 1980 I, F, W, E, 1981 F, W, E, I, 1983 F, W, E, NZ, 1984 E (R), R, A, 1985 I, 1986 F, W, E, I, R, 1987 I, F, W, E
Beattie, J W (Glasgow Warriors) 2006 R,PI, 2007 F, 2008 Arg 1, 2009 Fj,A,Arg, 2010 F,W,It,E,I,Arg 1,2
Beattie, R S (Newcastle, Bristol) 2000 NZ 1,2(R), Sm (R), 2003 E(R), It(R), I 2, [J(R),US,Fj]
Bedell-Sivright, D R (Cambridge U, Edinburgh U) 1900 W, 1901 W, I, E, 1902 W, I, E, 1903 W, I, 1904 W, I, E, 1905 NZ, 1906 W, I, E, SA, 1907 W, I, E, 1908 W, I
Bedell-Sivright, J V (Cambridge U) 1902 W
Begbie, T A (Edinburgh Wands) 1881 I, E
Bell, D L (Watsonians) 1975 I, F, W, E
Bell, J A (Clydesdale) 1901 W, I, E, 1902 W, I, E
Bell, L H I (Edinburgh Acads) 1900 E, 1904 W, I
Berkeley, W V (Oxford U) 1926 F, 1929 F, W, I
Berry, C W (Fettesian-Lorettonians) 1884 I, E, 1885 W, I 1, 1887 I, W, E, 1888 W, I
Bertram, D M (Watsonians) 1922 F, W, I, E, 1923 F, W, I, E, 1924 W, I, E
Beveridge, G (Glasgow) 2000 NZ 2(R), US (R), Sm (R), 2002 Fj(R), 2003 W 2, 2005 R(R)
Biggar, A G (London Scottish) 1969 SA, 1970 F, I, E, A, 1971 F, W, I, E (2[1C]), 1972 F, W
Biggar, M A (London Scottish) 1975 I, F, W, E, 1976 W, E, I, 1977 I, F, W, 1978 I, F, W, E, NZ, 1979 W, E, I, F, NZ, 1980 I, F, W, E
Birkett, G A (Harlequins, London Scottish) 1975 NZ
Bishop, J M (Glasgow Acads) 1893 I
Bisset, A A (RIE Coll) 1904 W
Black, A W (Edinburgh U) 1947 F, W, 1948 E, 1950 W, I, E
Black, W P (Glasgow HSFP) 1948 F, W, I, E, 1951 E
Blackadder, W F (W of Scotland) 1938 E
Blaikie, C F (Heriot's FP) 1963 I, E, 1966 E, 1968 A, 1969 F, W, I, E
Blair, M R L (Edinburgh) 2002 C, US, 2003 F(t+R), W 1(R), SA 2(R), It 2, I 2, [US], 2004 W(R),E(R),It(R),F(R),I(R),Sm(R),A1(R), 3(R),J(R),A4(R),SA(R),2005 I(t&R),It(R),W(R),E,R,Arg, Sm(R), NZ(R), 2006 F,W,E,I,It(R),SA 1,2,R,PI(R),A, 2007 I2,SA, [Pt,R,It, Arg], 2008 F,W,I,E,It,Arg 1,2,NZ,SA,C, 2009 W,F,It,I,E,Fj(R), 2010 W(R),It(R), I(R),Arg 1(R),2(R)
Blair, P C B (Cambridge U) 1912 SA, 1913 F, W, I, E
Bolton, W H (W of Scotland) 1876 E
Borthwick, J B (Stewart's Coll FP) 1938 W, I
Bos, F H ten (Oxford U, London Scottish) 1959 E, 1960 F, W, SA, 1961 F, SA, W, I, E, 1962 F, W, I, E, 1963 F, W, I, E
Boswell, J D (W of Scotland) 1889 W, I, 1890 W, I, E, 1891 W, I, E, 1892 W, I, E, 1893 I, E, 1894 I, E
Bowie, T C (Watsonians) 1913 I, E, 1914 I, E
Boyd, G M (Glasgow HSFP) 1926 E
Boyd, J L (United Services) 1912 E, SA
Boyle, A C W (London Scottish) 1963 F, W, I
Boyle, A H W (St Thomas's Hospital, London Scottish) 1966 A, 1967 F, NZ, 1968 F, W, I

Brash, J C (Cambridge U) 1961 E
Breakey, R W (Gosforth) 1978 E
Brewis, N T (Edinburgh Inst FP) 1876 E, 1878 E, 1879 I, E, 1880 I, E
Brewster, A K (Stewart's-Melville FP) 1977 E, 1980 I, F, 1986 E, I, R
Brotherstone, S J (Melrose, Brive, Newcastle) 1999 I (R), 2000 F, W, E, US, A, Sm, 2002 C (R)
Brown, A H (Heriot's FP) 1928 E, 1929 F, W
Brown, A R (Gala) 1971 E (2[1C]), 1972 F, W, E
Brown, C H C (Dunfermline) 1929 E
Brown, D I (Cambridge U) 1933 W, E, I
Brown, G L (W of Scotland) 1969 SA, 1970 F, W (R), I, E, A, 1971 F, W, I, E (2[1C]), 1972 F, W, E, NZ, 1973 E (R), P, 1974 W, E, I, F, 1975 I, F, W, E, A, 1976 F, W, E, I
Brown, J A (Glasgow Acads) 1908 W, I
Brown, J B (Glasgow Acads) 1879 I, E, 1880 I, E, 1881 I, E, 1882 I, E, 1883 W, I, E, 1884 W, I, E, 1885 I 1,2, 1886 W, I, E
Brown, K D R (Borders, Glasgow Warriors) 2005 R,Sm(R),NZ(R), 2006 SA 1(R),2(R), R,PI,A, 2007 E,W,It,I1,2(R),SA, [Pt(R),R(R), NZ,It(R),Arg(R)], 2008 F(R),W,I,E(R), It(R),Arg 1(R),2(R), 2009 W(R),F(R),It(R),E(R), 2010 F,W,It,E,I,Arg 1,2
Brown, P C (W of Scotland, Gala) 1964 F, NZ, W, I, E, 1965 I, E, SA, 1966 A, 1969 I, E, 1970 W, E, 1971 F, W, I, E (2[1C]), 1972 F, W, E, NZ, 1973 F, W, I, E, P
Brown, T G (Heriot's FP) 1929 W
Brown, W D (Glasgow Acads) 1871 E, 1872 E, 1873 E, 1874 E, 1875 E
Brown, W S (Edinburgh Inst FP) 1880 I, E, 1882 I, E, 1883 W, E
Browning, A (Glasgow HSFP) 1920 I, 1922 F, W, I, 1923 W, I, E
Bruce, C R (Glasgow Acads) 1947 F, W, I, E, 1949 F, W, I, E
Bruce, N S (Blackheath, Army and London Scottish) 1958 F, A, I, E, 1959 F, W, I, E, 1960 F, W, I, E, SA, 1961 F, SA, W, I, E, 1962 F, W, I, E, 1963 F, W, I, E, 1964 F, NZ, W, I, E
Bruce, R M (Gordonians) 1947 A, 1948 F, W, I
Bruce-Lockhart, J H (London Scottish) 1913 W, 1920 E
Bruce-Lockhart, L (London Scottish) 1948 E, 1950 F, W, 1953 I, E
Bruce-Lockhart, R B (Cambridge U and London Scottish) 1937 I, 1939 I, E
Bryce, C C (Glasgow Acads) 1873 E, 1874 E
Bryce, R D H (W of Scotland) 1973 I (R)
Bryce, W E (Selkirk) 1922 W, I, E, 1923 F, W, I, E, 1924 F, W, I, E
Brydon, W R C (Heriot's FP) 1939 W
Buchanan, A (Royal HSFP) 1871 E
Buchanan, F G (Kelvinside Acads and Oxford U) 1910 F, 1911 F, W
Buchanan, J C R (Stewart's Coll FP) 1921 W, I, E, 1922 W, I, E, 1923 F, W, I, E, 1924 F, W, I, E, 1925 F, I
Buchanan-Smith, G A E (London Scottish, Heriot's FP) 1989 Fj (R), 1990 Arg
Bucher, A M (Edinburgh Acads) 1897 E
Budge, G M (Edinburgh Wands) 1950 F, W, I, E
Bullmore, H H (Edinburgh U) 1902 I
Bulloch, A J (Glasgow) 2000 US, A, Sm, 2001 F (t+R), E
Bulloch, G C (West of Scotland, Glasgow) 1997 SA, 1998 It, I, F, W, E, Fj, A 1, SA, 1999 W, E, It, I, F, Arg, [SA, U, Sm, NZ], 2000 It, I, W (R), NZ 1,2, A (R), Sm (R), 2001 F, W, E, It, I, Tg, Arg, NZ, 2002 E, It, I, F, W, C, US, R, SA, Fj, 2003 I 1, F, W 1, E, It 1, SA 1,2, It 2(R), W2, I 2, [US,F,Fj,A], 2004 W,E,It,F,I,Sm,A1,2,3,J,A4,SA, 2005 F,I,It,W,E
Burnell, A P (London Scottish, Montferrand) 1989 E, I, F, Fj, R, 1990 I, F, W, E, Arg, 1991 F, W, E, I, R, [J, Z, I, WS, E, NZ], 1992 E, I, F, W, 1993 I, F, W, E, NZ, 1994 W, E, I, F, Arg 1,2, SA, 1995 [Iv, Tg (R), F (R)], WS, 1998 E, SA, 1999 W, E, It, I, F, Arg, [Sp, Sm (R), NZ]
Burnet, P J (London Scottish and Edinburgh Acads) 1960 SA
Burnet, W (Hawick) 1912 E
Burnet, W A (W of Scotland) 1934 W, 1935 W, I, E, NZ, 1936 W, I, E
Burnett, J N (Heriot's FP) 1980 I, F, W, E
Burns, G G (Watsonians, Edinburgh) 1999 It (R), 2001 Tg (R), NZ (R), 2002 US (R)
Burrell, G (Gala) 1950 F, W, I, 1951 SA
Cairns, A G (Watsonians) 1903 W, I, E, 1904 W, I, E, 1905 W, I, E, 1906 W, I, E
Cairns, B J (Edinburgh) 2008 Arg 1,2,NZ,SA,C, 2009 W,Arg
Calder, F (Stewart's-Melville FP) 1986 F, W, E, I, R, 1987 I, F, W, E, [F, Z, R, NZ], 1988 I, F, W, E, 1989 W, E, I, F, R, 1990 I, F, W, E, NZ 1,2, 1991 R, [J, I, WS, E, NZ]
Calder, J H (Stewart's-Melville FP) 1981 F, W, E, I, NZ 1,2, R, A, 1982 E, I, F, W, A 1,2, 1983 I, F, W, E, NZ, 1984 W, E, I, F, A, 1985 I, F, W
Callam, D A (Edinburgh) 2006 R(R),PI(R),A, 2007 E,W,It,I1,F(R),SA, [NZ], 2008 F
Callander, G J (Kelso) 1984 R, 1988 I, F, W, E, A
Cameron, A (Glasgow HSFP) 1948 W, 1950 I, E, 1951 F, W, I, E, SA, 1953 I, E, 1955 F, W, I, E, 1956 F, W, I
Cameron, A D (Hillhead HSFP) 1951 F, 1954 F, W
Cameron, A W C (Watsonians) 1887 W, 1893 W, 1894 I
Cameron, D (Glasgow HSFP) 1953 I, E, 1954 F, NZ, I, E
Cameron, N W (Glasgow U) 1952 E, 1953 F, W
Campbell, A J (Hawick) 1984 I, F, R, 1985 I, F, W, E, 1986 F, W, E, I, R, 1988 F, W, A
Campbell, G T (London Scottish) 1892 W, I, E, 1893 I, E, 1894 W, I, E, 1895 W, I, E, 1896 W, I, E, 1897 I, 1899 I, 1900 E
Campbell, H H (Cambridge U, London Scottish) 1947 I, E, 1948 I, E
Campbell, J A (W of Scotland) 1878 E, 1879 I, E, 1881 I, E
Campbell, J A (Cambridge U) 1900 I
Campbell, N M (London Scottish) 1956 F, W
Campbell, S J (Dundee HSFP) 1995 C, I, F, W, E, R, [Iv, NZ (R)], WS (t), 1996 I, F, W, E, 1997 A, SA, 1998 Fj (R), A 2(R)
Campbell-Lamerton, J R E (London Scottish) 1986 F, 1987 [Z, R(R)]
Campbell-Lamerton, M J (Halifax, Army, London Scottish) 1961 F, SA, W, I, 1962 F, W, I, E, 1963 F, W, I, E, 1964 I, E, 1965 F, W, I, E, SA, 1966 F, W, I, E
Carmichael, A B (W of Scotland) 1967 I, NZ, 1968 F, W, I, E, A, 1969 F, W, I, E, SA, 1970 F, W, I, E, A, 1971 F, W, I, E (2[1C]), 1972 F, W, E, NZ, 1973 F, W, I, E, P, 1974 W, E, I, F, 1975 I, F, W, E, NZ, A, 1976 F, W, E, I, 1977 E, I (R), F, W, 1978 I
Carmichael, J H (Watsonians) 1921 F, W, I
Carrick, J S (Glasgow Acads) 1876 E, 1877 E
Cassels, D Y (W of Scotland) 1880 E, 1881 I, 1882 I, E, 1883 W, I, E
Cathcart, C W (Edinburgh U) 1872 E, 1873 E, 1876 E
Cawkwell, G L (Oxford U) 1947 F
Chalmers, C M (Melrose) 1989 W, E, I, F, Fj, 1990 I, F, W, E, NZ 1,2, Arg, 1991 F, W, E, I, R, [J, Z (R), I, WS, E, NZ], 1992 E, I, F, W, A 1,2, 1993 I, F, W, E, NZ, 1994 W, SA, 1995 C, I, F, W, E, R, [Iv, Tg, F, NZ], WS, 1996 A, It, 1997 W, I, F, A (R), SA, 1998 It, I, F, W, E, 1999 Arg (R)
Chalmers, T (Glasgow Acads) 1871 E, 1872 E, 1873 E, 1874 E, 1875 E, 1876 E
Chambers, H F T (Edinburgh U) 1888 W, I, 1889 W, I
Charters, R G (Hawick) 1955 W, I, E
Chisholm, D H (Melrose) 1964 I, E, 1965 E, SA, 1966 F, I, E, A, 1967 F, W, NZ, 1968 F, W, I
Chisholm, R W T (Melrose) 1955 I, E, 1956 F, W, I, E, 1958 F, W, A, I, 1960 SA
Church, W C (Glasgow Acads) 1906 W
Clark, R L (Edinburgh Wands, Royal Navy) 1972 F, W, E, NZ, 1973 F, W, I, E, P
Clauss, P R A (Oxford U) 1891 W, I, E, 1892 W, E, 1895 I
Clay, A T (Edinburgh Acads) 1886 W, I, E, 1887 I, W, E, 1888 W
Clunies-Ross, A (St Andrew's U) 1871 E
Coltman, S (Hawick) 1948 I, 1949 F, W, I, E
Colville, A G (Merchistonians, Blackheath) 1871 E, 1872 E
Connell, G C (Trinity Acads and London Scottish) 1968 E, A, 1969 F, E, 1970 F
Cooper, M McG (Oxford U) 1936 W, I
Corcoran, I (Gala) 1992 A 1(R)
Cordial, I F (Edinburgh Wands) 1952 F, W, I, E
Cotter, J L (Hillhead HSFP) 1934 I, E
Cottington, G S (Kelso) 1934 I, E, 1935 W, I, 1936 E
Coughtrie, S (Edinburgh Acads) 1959 F, W, I, E, 1962 W, I, E, 1963 F, W, I, E
Couper, J H (W of Scotland) 1896 W, I, 1899 I
Coutts, F H (Melrose, Army) 1947 W, I, E
Coutts, I D F (Old Alleynians) 1951 F, 1952 E
Cowan, R C (Selkirk) 1961 F, 1962 F, W, I, E
Cowie, W L K (Edinburgh Wands) 1953 E
Cownie, W B (Watsonians) 1893 W, I, E, 1894 W, I, E, 1895 W, I, E
Crabbie, G E (Edinburgh Acads) 1904 W
Crabbie, J E (Edinburgh Acads, Oxford U) 1900 W, 1902 I, 1903 W, I, 1904 E, 1905 W
Craig, A (Orrell, Glasgow) 2002 C, US, R, SA, Fj, 2003 I 1, F(R),

W 1(R), E, It 1, SA 1,2, W 2, I 2, [J,US,F], 2004 A3(R), 2005 F,I,It,W,E
Craig, J B (Heriot's FP) 1939 W
Craig, J M (West of Scotland, Glasgow) 1997 A, 2001 W (R), E (R), It
Cramb, R I (Harlequins) 1987 [R(R)], 1988 I, F, A
Cranston, A G (Hawick) 1976 W, E, I, 1977 E, W, 1978 F (R), W, E, NZ, 1981 NZ 1,2
Crawford, J A (Army, London Scottish) 1934 I
Crawford, W H (United Services, RN) 1938 W, I, E, 1939 W, E
Crichton-Miller, D (Gloucester) 1931 W, I, E
Crole, G B (Oxford U) 1920 F, W, I, E
Cronin, D F (Bath, London Scottish, Bourges, Wasps) 1988 I, F, W, E, A, 1989 W, E, I, F, Fj, R, 1990 I, F, W, E, NZ 1,2, 1991 F, W, E, I, R, [Z], 1992 A 2, 1993 I, F, W, E, NZ, 1995 C, I, F, [Tg, F, NZ], WS, 1996 NZ 1,2, A, It, 1997 F (R), 1998 I, F, W, E
Cross, G (Edinburgh) 2009 W, 2010 E(R)
Cross, M (Merchistonians) 1875 E, 1876 E, 1877 I, E, 1878 E, 1879 I, E, 1880 I, E
Cross, W (Merchistonians) 1871 E, 1872 E
Cumming, R S (Aberdeen U) 1921 F, W
Cunningham, G (Oxford U) 1908 W, I, 1909 W, E, 1910 F, I, E, 1911 E
Cunningham, R F (Gala) 1978 NZ, 1979 W, E
Currie, L R (Dunfermline) 1947 A, 1948 F, W, I, 1949 F, W, I, E
Cusiter, C P (Borders, Perpignan, Glasgow Warriors) 2004 W,E,It,F,I,Sm,A1,2,3,J,A4, SA,2005 F,I,It,W,Arg(R),Sm,NZ, 2006 F(R),W(R),E(R),I(R),It,R(R),PI, 2007 E,W,It, I1,F(R),I2(R), [R(R),NZ, It(R),Arg(R)], 2008 F(R),W(R),I(R), 2009 W(R),F(R),It(R), I(R),E(R), Fj,A,Arg, 2010 F,W,It,E,I
Cuthbertson, W (Kilmarnock, Harlequins) 1980 I, 1981 W, E, I, NZ 1,2, R, A, 1982 E, I, F, W, A 1,2, 1983 I, F, W, NZ, 1984 W, E, A
Dalgleish, A (Gala) 1890 W, E, 1891 W, I, 1892 W, 1893 W, 1894 W, I
Dalgleish, K J (Edinburgh Wands, Cambridge U) 1951 I, E, 1953 F, W
Dall, A K (Edinburgh) 2003 W 2(R)
Dallas, J D (Watsonians) 1903 E
Danielli, S C J (Bath, Borders, Ulster) 2003 It 2, W 2, [J(R),US,Fj,A], 2004 W, E,It, F,I,2005 F,I, 2008 W(R),It,Arg 1, 2009 F,It,I,E,Fj,A, 2010 It,E(R),I(R),Arg 2
Davidson, J A (London Scottish, Edinburgh Wands) 1959 E, 1960 I, E
Davidson, J N G (Edinburgh U) 1952 F, W, I, E, 1953 F, W, 1954 F
Davidson, J P (RIE Coll) 1873 E, 1874 E
Davidson, R S (Royal HSFP) 1893 E
Davies, D S (Hawick) 1922 F, W, I, E, 1923 F, W, I, E, 1924 F, E, 1925 W, I, E, 1926 F, W, I, E, 1927 F, W, I
Dawson, J C (Glasgow Acads) 1947 A, 1948 F, W, 1949 F, W, I, 1950 F, W, I, E, 1951 F, W, I, E, SA, 1952 F, W, I, E, 1953 E
Deans, C T (Hawick) 1978 F, W, E, NZ, 1979 W, E, I, F, NZ, 1980 I, F, 1981 F, W, E, I, NZ 1,2, R, A, 1982 E, I, F, W, A 1,2, 1983 I, F, W, E, NZ, 1984 W, E, I, F, A, 1985 I, F, W, E, 1986 F, W, E, I, R, 1987 I, F, W, E, [F, Z, R, NZ]
Deans, D T (Hawick) 1968 E
Deas, D W (Heriot's FP) 1947 F, W
De Luca, N J (Edinburgh) 2008 F,W,I(t&R),Arg 2(R),NZ,SA,C, 2009 F(R),It(R),I(R), E(R),Fj(R),A(R),Arg(R), 2010 It(R),E,I,Arg 1,2(R)
Dewey, R E (Edinburgh, Ulster) 2006 R, 2007 E(R),W,It,I1,F,I2,SA, [Pt,R,NZ(R),It,Arg]
Dick, L G (Loughborough Colls, Jordanhill, Swansea) 1972 W (R), E, 1974 W, E, I, F, 1975 I, F, W, E, NZ, A, 1976 F, 1977 E
Dick, R C S (Cambridge U, Guy's Hospital) 1934 W, I, E, 1935 W, I, E, NZ, 1936 W, I, E, 1937 W, 1938 W, I, E
Dickinson, A G (Gloucester) 2007 [NZ], 2008 E(R),It(R),Arg 1(R),2(t&R),NZ(R), SA(R),C(R), 2009 W(t&R),F,It(R),I,E, 2010 F,W,It(R),I(R),Arg 2(R)
Dickson, G (Gala) 1978 NZ, 1979 W, E, I, F, NZ, 1980 W, 1981 F, 1982 W (R)
Dickson, M R (Edinburgh U) 1905 I
Dickson, W M (Blackheath, Oxford U) 1912 F, W, E, SA, 1913 F, W, I
Di Rollo, M P (Edinburgh) 2002 US (R), 2005 R,Arg,Sm,NZ, 2006 F,E,I,It,SA 1,2, R,PI, A, 2007 E,W,It,I1,F(R), [Pt,NZ]
Dobson, J (Glasgow Acads) 1911 E, 1912 F, W, I, E, SA
Dobson, J D (Glasgow Acads) 1910 I
Dobson, W G (Heriot's FP) 1922 W, I, E
Docherty, J T (Glasgow HSFP) 1955 F, W, 1956 E, 1958 F, W, A, I, E
Dods, F P (Edinburgh Acads) 1901 I
Dods, J H (Edinburgh Acads) 1895 W, I, E, 1896 W, I, E, 1897 I, E
Dods, M (Gala, Northampton) 1994 I (t), Arg 1,2, 1995 WS, 1996 I, F, W, E
Dods, P W (Gala) 1983 I, F, W, E, NZ, 1984 W, E, I, F, R, A, 1985 I, F, W, E, 1989 W, E, I, F, 1991 I (R), R, [Z, NZ (R)]
Donald, D G (Oxford U) 1914 W, I
Donald, R L H (Glasgow HSFP) 1921 W, I, E
Donaldson, W P (Oxford U, W of Scotland) 1893 I, 1894 I, 1895 E, 1896 I, E, 1899 I
Don-Wauchope, A R (Fettesian-Lorettonians) 1881 E, 1882 E, 1883 W, 1884 W, I, E, 1885 W, I 1,2, 1886 W, I, E, 1888 I
Don-Wauchope, P H (Fettesian-Lorettonians) 1885 I 1,2, 1886 W, 1887 I, W, E
Dorward, A F (Cambridge U, Gala) 1950 F, 1951 SA, 1952 W, I, E, 1953 F, W, E, 1955 F, 1956 I, E, 1957 F, W, I, E
Dorward, T F (Gala) 1938 W, I, E, 1939 I, E
Douglas, B A F (Borders) 2002 R, SA, Fj, 2003 I 1, F, W 1, E, It 1, SA 1,2, It 2, W 2, [J,US(t&R),F(R),Fj,A], 2004 W,E,It,F,I,Sm, A1,2,3,A4(R),SA(R),2005 F(R),I(R),It(R), W(R),E(R),R,Arg, NZ, 2006 F,W,E,I,It,SA 1,2(R)
Douglas, G (Jedforest) 1921 W
Douglas, J (Stewart's Coll FP) 1961 F, SA, W, I, E, 1962 F, W, I, E, 1963 F, W, I
Douty, P S (London Scottish) 1927 A, 1928 F, W
Drew, D (Glasgow Acads) 1871 E, 1876 E
Druitt, W A H (London Scottish) 1936 W, I, E
Drummond, A H (Kelvinside Acads) 1938 W, I
Drummond, C W (Melrose) 1947 F, W, I, E, 1948 F, I, E, 1950 F, W, I, E
Drybrough, A S (Edinburgh Wands, Merchistonians) 1902 I, 1903 I
Dryden, R H (Watsonians) 1937 E
Drysdale, D (Heriot's FP) 1923 F, W, I, E, 1924 F, W, I, E, 1925 F, W, I, E, 1926 F, W, I, E, 1927 F, W, I, E, A, 1928 F, W, I, E, 1929 F
Duff, P L (Glasgow Acads) 1936 W, I, 1938 W, I, E, 1939 W
Duffy, H (Jedforest) 1955 F
Duke, A (Royal HSFP) 1888 W, I, 1889 W, I, 1890 W, I
Dunbar, J P A (Leeds) 2005 F(R), It(R)
Duncan, A W (Edinburgh U) 1901 W, I, E, 1902 W, I, E
Duncan, D D (Oxford U) 1920 F, W, I, E
Duncan, M D F (W of Scotland) 1986 F, W, E, R, 1987 I, F, W, E, [F, Z, R, NZ], 1988 I, F, W, E, A, 1989 W
Duncan, M M (Fettesian-Lorettonians) 1888 W
Dunlop, J W (W of Scotland) 1875 E
Dunlop, Q (W of Scotland) 1971 E (2[1C])
Dykes, A S (Glasgow Acads) 1932 E
Dykes, J C (Glasgow Acads) 1922 F, E, 1924 I, 1925 F, W, I, 1926 F, W, I, E, 1927 F, W, I, E, A, 1928 F, I, 1929 F, W, I
Dykes, J M (Clydesdale, Glasgow HSFP) 1898 I, E, 1899 W, E, 1900 W, I, 1901 W, I, E, 1902 E
Edwards, D B (Heriot's FP) 1960 I, E, SA
Edwards, N G B (Harlequins, Northampton) 1992 E, I, F, W, A 1, 1994 W
Elgie, M K (London Scottish) 1954 NZ, I, E, W, 1955 F, W, I, E
Elliot, C (Langholm) 1958 E, 1959 F, 1960 F, 1963 E, 1964 F, NZ, W, I, E, 1965 F, W, I
Elliot, M (Hawick) 1895 W, 1896 E, 1897 I, E, 1898 I, E
Elliot, T (Gala) 1905 E
Elliot, T (Gala) 1955 W, I, E, 1956 F, W, I, E, 1957 F, W, I, E, 1958 W, A, I
Elliot, T G (Langholm) 1968 W, A, 1969 F, W, 1970 E
Elliot, W I D (Edinburgh Acads) 1947 F, W, E, A, 1948 F, W, I, E, 1949 F, W, I, E, 1950 F, W, I, E, 1951 F, W, I, E, SA, 1952 F, W, I, E, 1954 NZ, I, E, W
Ellis, D G (Currie) 1997 W, E, I, F
Emslie, W D (Royal HSFP) 1930 F, 1932 I
Eriksson, B R S (London Scottish) 1996 NZ 1, A, 1997 E
Evans, H L (Edinburgh U) 1885 I 1,2
Evans, M B (Glasgow Warriors) 2008 C(R), 2009 W(R),F,It,I,E, 2010 F,W(t&R),It,E,I,Arg 1,2
Evans, T H (Glasgow Warriors) 2008 Arg 1,NZ,SA, 2009 F,It,I,E,Arg, 2010 F,W
Ewart, E N (Glasgow Acads) 1879 E, 1880 I, E
Fahmy, E C (Abertillery) 1920 F, W, I, E
Fairley, I T (Kelso, Edinburgh) 1999 It, I (R), [Sp (R)]
Fasson, F H (London Scottish, Edinburgh Wands) 1900 W, 1901 W, I, 1902 W, E

Fell, A N (Edinburgh U) 1901 W, I, E, 1902 W, E, 1903 W, E
Ferguson, J H (Gala) 1928 W
Ferguson, W G (Royal HSFP) 1927 A, 1928 F, W, I, E
Fergusson, E A J (Oxford U) 1954 F, NZ, I, E, W
Finlay, A B (Edinburgh Acads) 1875 E
Finlay, J F (Edinburgh Acads) 1871 E, 1872 E, 1874 E, 1875 E
Finlay, N J (Edinburgh Acads) 1875 E, 1876 E, 1878 E, 1879 I, E, 1880 I, E, 1881 I, E
Finlay, R (Watsonians) 1948 E
Fisher, A T (Waterloo, Watsonians) 1947 I, E
Fisher, C D (Waterloo) 1975 NZ, A, 1976 W, E, I
Fisher, D (W of Scotland) 1893 I
Fisher, J P (Royal HSFP, London Scottish) 1963 E, 1964 F, NZ, W, I, E, 1965 F, W, I, E, SA, 1966 F, W, I, E, A, 1967 F, W, I, E, NZ, 1968 F, W, I, E
Fleming, C J N (Edinburgh Wands) 1896 I, E, 1897 I
Fleming, G R (Glasgow Acads) 1875 E, 1876 E
Fletcher, H N (Edinburgh U) 1904 E, 1905 W
Flett, A B (Edinburgh U) 1901 W, I, E, 1902 W, I
Forbes, J L (Watsonians) 1905 W, 1906 I, E
Ford, D St C (United Services, RN) 1930 I, E, 1931 E, 1932 W, I
Ford, J R (Gala) 1893 I
Ford, R W (Borders, Glasgow, Edinburgh) 2004 A3(R), 2006 W(R),E(R),PI(R),A(R), 2007 E(R),W(R),It(R),I1(R),F,I2,SA, [Pt(R),R, It,Arg], 2008 F,W,I,E,Arg 1,2, NZ,SA,C, 2009 W,F,It,I,E,Fj,A,Arg, 2010 F,W,It,E,I,Arg 1,2
Forrest, J E (Glasgow Acads) 1932 SA, 1935 E, NZ
Forrest, J G S (Cambridge U) 1938 W, I, E
Forrest, W T (Hawick) 1903 W, I, E, 1904 W, I, E, 1905 W, I
Forsayth, H H (Oxford U) 1921 F, W, I, E, 1922 W, I, E
Forsyth, I W (Stewart's Coll FP) 1972 NZ, 1973 F, W, I, E, P
Forsyth, J (Edinburgh U) 1871 E
Foster, R A (Hawick) 1930 W, 1932 SA, I, E
Fox, J (Gala) 1952 F, W, I, E
Frame, J N M (Edinburgh U, Gala) 1967 NZ, 1968 F, W, I, E, 1969 W, I, E, SA, 1970 F, W, I, E, A, 1971 F, W, I, E (2[1C]), 1972 F, W, E, 1973 P (R)
France, C (Kelvinside Acads) 1903 I
Fraser, C F P (Glasgow U) 1888 W, 1889 W
Fraser, J W (Edinburgh Inst FP) 1881 E
Fraser, R (Cambridge U) 1911 F, W, I, E
French, J (Glasgow Acads) 1886 W, 1887 I, W, E
Frew, A (Edinburgh U) 1901 W, I, E
Frew, G M (Glasgow HSFP) 1906 SA, 1907 W, I, E, 1908 W, I, E, 1909 W, I, E, 1910 F, W, I, 1911 I, E
Friebe, J P (Glasgow HSFP) 1952 E
Fullarton, I A (Edinburgh) 2000 NZ 1(R),2, 2001 NZ (R), 2003 It 2(R), I 2(t), 2004 Sm(R), A1(R),2
Fulton, A K (Edinburgh U, Dollar Acads) 1952 F, 1954 F
Fyfe, K C (Cambridge U, Sale, London Scottish) 1933 W, E, 1934 E, 1935 W, I, E, NZ, 1936 W, E, 1939 I
Gallie, G H (Edinburgh Acads) 1939 W
Gallie, R A (Glasgow Acads) 1920 F, W, I, E, 1921 F, W, I, E
Gammell, W B B (Edinburgh Wands) 1977 I, F, W, 1978 W, E
Geddes, I C (London Scottish) 1906 SA, 1907 W, I, E, 1908 W, E
Geddes, K I (London Scottish) 1947 F, W, I, E
Gedge, H T S (Oxford U, London Scottish, Edinburgh Wands) 1894 W, I, E, 1896 E, 1899 W, E
Gedge, P M S (Edinburgh Wands) 1933 I
Gemmill, R (Glasgow HSFP) 1950 F, W, I, E, 1951 F, W, I
Gibson, W R (Royal HSFP) 1891 I, E, 1892 W, I, E, 1893 W, I, E, 1894 W, I, E, 1895 W, I, E
Gilbert-Smith, D S (London Scottish) 1952 E
Gilchrist, J (Glasgow Acads) 1925 F
Gill, A D (Gala) 1973 P, 1974 W, E, I, F
Gillespie, J I (Edinburgh Acads) 1899 E, 1900 W, E, 1901 W, I, E, 1902 W, I, 1904 I, E
Gillies, A C (Watsonians) 1924 W, I, E, 1925 F, W, E, 1926 F, W, 1927 F, W, I, E
Gilmour, H R (Heriot's FP) 1998 Fj
Gilray, C M (Oxford U, London Scottish) 1908 E, 1909 W, E, 1912 I
Glasgow, I C (Heriot's FP) 1997 F (R)
Glasgow, R J C (Dunfermline) 1962 F, W, I, E, 1963 I, E, 1964 I, E, 1965 W, I
Glen, W S (Edinburgh Wands) 1955 W
Gloag, L G (Cambridge U) 1949 F, W, I, E
Godman, P J (Edinburgh) 2005 R(R),Sm(R),NZ(R), 2006 R,PI(R),A(t&R), 2007 W,It, 2008 Arg 2,NZ,SA,C, 2009 W,F,It,I,E,Fj,A,Arg, 2010 F,W(R),E(R)
Goodfellow, J (Langholm) 1928 W, I, E
Goodhue, F W J (London Scottish) 1890 W, I, E, 1891 W, I, E, 1892 W, I, E
Gordon, R (Edinburgh Wands) 1951 W, 1952 F, W, I, E, 1953 W
Gordon, R E (Royal Artillery) 1913 F, W, I
Gordon, R J (London Scottish) 1982 A 1,2
Gore, A C (London Scottish) 1882 I
Gossman, B M (W of Scotland) 1980 W, 1983 F, W
Gossman, J S (W of Scotland) 1980 E (R)
Gowans, J J (Cambridge U, London Scottish) 1893 W, 1894 W, E, 1895 W, I, E, 1896 I, E
Gowlland, G C (London Scottish) 1908 W, 1909 W, E, 1910 F, W, I, E
Gracie, A L (Harlequins) 1921 F, W, I, E, 1922 F, W, I, E, 1923 F, W, I, E, 1924 F
Graham, G (Newcastle) 1997 A (R), SA (R), 1998 I, F (R), W (R), 1999 F (R), Arg (R), R, [SA, U, Sm, NZ (R)], 2000 I (R), US, A, Sm, 2001 I (R), Tg (R), Arg (R), NZ (R), 2002 E (R), It (R), I (R), F (R), W (R)
Graham, I N (Edinburgh Acads) 1939 I, E
Graham, J (Kelso) 1926 I, E, 1927 F, W, I, E, A, 1928 F, W, I, E, 1930 I, E, 1932 SA, W
Graham, J H S (Edinburgh Acads) 1876 E, 1877 I, E, 1878 E, 1879 I, E, 1880 I, E, 1881 I, E
Grant, D (Hawick) 1965 F, E, SA, 1966 F, W, I, E, A, 1967 F, W, I, E, NZ, 1968 F
Grant, D M (East Midlands) 1911 W, I
Grant, M L (Harlequins) 1955 F, 1956 F, W, 1957 F
Grant, T O (Hawick) 1960 I, E, SA, 1964 F, NZ, W
Grant, W St C (Craigmount) 1873 E, 1874 E
Gray, C A (Nottingham) 1989 W, E, I, F, Fj, R, 1990 I, F, W, E, NZ 1,2, Arg, 1991 F, W, E, I, [J, I, WS, E, NZ]
Gray, D (W of Scotland) 1978 E, 1979 I, F, NZ, 1980 I, F, W, E, 1981 F
Gray, G L (Gala) 1935 NZ, 1937 W, I, E
Gray, R J (Glasgow Warriors) 2010 F(R),W(R),I(R)
Gray, S D (Borders, Northampton) 2004 A3, 2008 NZ(R),SA(R), C(R), 2009 W(R),It(R), I(R),E
Gray, T (Northampton, Heriot's FP) 1950 E, 1951 F, E
Greenlees, H D (Leicester) 1927 A, 1928 F, W, 1929 I, E, 1930 E
Greenlees, J R C (Cambridge U, Kelvinside Acads) 1900 I, 1902 W, I, E, 1903 W, I, E
Greenwood, J T (Dunfermline and Perthshire Acads) 1952 F, 1955 F, W, I, E, 1956 F, W, I, E, 1957 F, W, E, 1958 F, W, A, I, E, 1959 F, W, I
Greig, A (Glasgow HSFP) 1911 I
Greig, L L (Glasgow Acads, United Services) 1905 NZ, 1906 SA, 1907 W, 1908 W, I
Greig, R C (Glasgow Acads) 1893 W, 1897 I
Grieve, C F (Oxford U) 1935 W, 1936 E
Grieve, R M (Kelso) 1935 W, I, E, NZ, 1936 W, I, E
Grimes, S B (Watsonians, Newcastle) 1997 A (t+R), 1998 I (R), F (R), W (R), E (R), Fj, A 1, 2, 1999 W (R), E, It, I, F, Arg, R, [SA, U, Sm (R), NZ (R)], 2000 It, I, F (R), W, US, A, Sm (R), 2001 F (R), W (R), E (R), It, I (R), Tg, Arg, NZ, 2002 E, It, I, F (R), W (R), C, US, R, SA, Fj, 2003 I 1, F, W 1, E(R), It 1(R), W 2, I 2, [J,US,F,Fj,A], 2004 W,E,It,F, I,Sm,A1,J,A4,SA, 2005 F,I,It,W,E(R)
Grove, A (Worcester) 2009 Fj,A,Arg
Gunn, A W (Royal HSFP) 1912 F, W, I, SA, 1913 F
Hall, A J A (Glasgow) 2002 US (R)
Hall, D W H (Edinburgh, Glasgow Warriors) 2003 W 2(R), 2005 R(R),Arg,Sm(R), NZ(R), 2006 F,E,I,It(R),SA 1(R),2,R,PI,A, 2007 E,W,It,I1,F(R), 2008 Arg 2(R),NZ(R), SA(R),C(R), 2009 W(R),F(R), It(R),I(R),E(R),Fj(R),A(R),Arg(R)
Hamilton, A S (Headingley) 1914 W, 1920 F
Hamilton, C P (Newcastle) 2004 A2(R), 2005 R,Arg,Sm,NZ
Hamilton, H M (W of Scotland) 1874 E, 1875 E
Hamilton, J L (Leicester, Edinburgh) 2006 R(R),A(R), 2007 E,W,It(R),I1(R),F(R),I2, SA, [R,NZ(R),It,Arg], 2008 F,W,I(R),NZ,SA, C, 2009 W,F,I,E, 2010 W,It,E,I,Arg 1,2
Hannah, R S M (W of Scotland) 1971 I
Harrower, P R (London Scottish) 1885 W
Hart, J G M (London Scottish) 1951 SA
Hart, T M (Glasgow U) 1930 W, I
Hart, W (Melrose) 1960 SA
Harvey, L (Greenock Wands) 1899 I
Hastie, A J (Melrose) 1961 W, I, E, 1964 I, E, 1965 E, SA, 1966 F, W, I, E, A, 1967 F, W, I, NZ, 1968 F, W

Hastie, I R (Kelso) 1955 F, 1958 F, E, 1959 F, W, I
Hastie, J D H (Melrose) 1938 W, I, E
Hastings, A G (Cambridge U, Watsonians, London Scottish) 1986 F, W, E, I, R, 1987 I, F, W, E, [F, Z, R, NZ], 1988 I, F, W, E, A, 1989 Fj, R, 1990 I, F, W, E, NZ 1,2, Arg, 1991 F, W, E, I, [J, I, WS, E, NZ], 1992 E, I, F, W, A 1, 1993 I, F, W, E, NZ, 1994 W, E, I, F, SA, 1995 C, I, F, W, E, R, [Iv, Tg, F, NZ]
Hastings, S (Watsonians) 1986 F, W, E, I, R, 1987 I, F, W, [R], 1988 I, F, W, A, 1989 W, E, I, F, Fj, R, 1990 I, F, W, E, NZ 1,2, Arg, 1991 F, W, E, I, [J, Z, I, WS, E, NZ], 1992 E, I, F, W, A 1,2, 1993 I, F, W, E, NZ, 1994 E, I, F, SA, 1995 W, E, R (R), [Tg, F, NZ], 1996 I, F, W, E, NZ 2, It, 1997 W, E (R)
Hay, B H (Boroughmuir) 1975 NZ, A, 1976 F, 1978 I, F, W, E, NZ, 1979 W, E, I, F, NZ, 1980 I, F, W, E, 1981 F, W, E, I, NZ 1,2
Hay, J A (Hawick) 1995 WS
Hay-Gordon, J R (Edinburgh Acads) 1875 E, 1877 I, E
Hegarty, C B (Hawick) 1978 I, F, W, E
Hegarty, J J (Hawick) 1951 F, 1953 F, W, I, E, 1955 F
Henderson, A R (Glasgow Warriors) 2001 I (R), Tg (R), NZ (R), 2002 It, I, US (R), 2003 SA 1,2, It 2, I 2, [US,F,Fj,A], 2004 W,E(t&R),It(R),F,I,Sm,A1,2,3,J,A4,SA, 2005 W(R),R, Arg, Sm,NZ, 2006 F,W,E,I,It,SA 1,2,PI,A, 2007 E,It(R),I1(R),F,I2,SA,[NZ, It(R),Arg(R)], 2008 F,W,I,It(R)
Henderson, B C (Edinburgh Wands) 1963 E, 1964 F, I, E, 1965 F, W, I, E, 1966 F, W, I, E
Henderson, F W (London Scottish) 1900 W, I
Henderson, I C (Edinburgh Acads) 1939 I, E, 1947 F, W, E, A, 1948 I, E
Henderson, J H (Oxford U, Richmond) 1953 F, W, I, E, 1954 F, NZ, I, E, W
Henderson, J M (Edinburgh Acads) 1933 W, E, I
Henderson, J Y M (Watsonians) 1911 E
Henderson, M M (Dunfermline) 1937 W, I, E
Henderson, N F (London Scottish) 1892 I
Henderson, R G (Newcastle Northern) 1924 I, E
Hendrie, K G P (Heriot's FP) 1924 F, W, I
Hendry, T L (Clydesdale) 1893 W, I, E, 1895 I
Henriksen, E H (Royal HSFP) 1953 I
Hepburn, D P (Woodford) 1947 A, 1948 F, W, I, E, 1949 F, W, I, E
Heron, G (Glasgow Acads) 1874 E, 1875 E
Hill, C C P (St Andrew's U) 1912 F, I
Hilton, D I W (Bath, Glasgow) 1995 C, I, F, W, E, R, [Tg, F, NZ], WS, 1996 I, F, W, E, NZ 1,2, A, It, 1997 W, A, SA, 1998 It, I (R), F, W, E, A 1,2, SA (R), 1999 W (R), E (R), It (R), I (R), F, R (R), [SA (R), U (R), Sp], 2000 It (R), F (R), W (R), 2002 SA(R)
Hines, N J (Edinburgh, Glasgow, Perpignan, Leinster) 2000 NZ 2(R), 2002 C, US, R(R), SA(R), Fj(R), 2003 W 1(R), E, It 1, SA 1,2, It 2, W 2(R), I 2, [US,F(R),Fj,A], 2004 E(R), It(R),F(R),I(R), A3,J,A4,SA,2005 F(R),I(R),It(R),W(R),E, 2006 E(R),I,It,SA 1,2, R,PI, 2007 W(R),It,I1,F,I2,SA, [Pt,R,It,Arg], 2008 F,W,I,E,It,NZ, SA,C, 2009 I(R),E(R),Fj,A, Arg, 2010 F,It(R),E(R)
Hinshelwood, A J W (London Scottish) 1966 F, W, I, E, A, 1967 F, W, I, E, NZ, 1968 F, W, I, E, A, 1969 F, W, I, SA, 1970 F, W
Hinshelwood, B G (Worcester) 2002 C (R), R(R), SA(R), Fj, 2003 It 2, [J,US(R),Fj(R), A(R)], 2004 W,E,It,Sm,A1,2,J,A4,SA, 2005 It(R)
Hodge D W (Watsonians, Edinburgh) 1997 F (R), A, SA (t+R), 1998 A 2(R), SA, 1999 W, Arg, R, [Sp, Sm (R)], 2000 F (R), W, E, NZ 1,2, US (R), Sm (R), 2001 F (R), W, E, It, I (R), 2002 E, W (R), C, US
Hodgson, C G (London Scottish) 1968 I, E
Hogg, A (Edinburgh) 2004 W,E(R),It,F(R),I,Sm,A1,2,3,J,A4,SA, 2005 F,I,It,W,E,R,Arg, Sm,NZ, 2006 F,W,E,I,It,SA 1,2, 2007 E(R), W(R),It(R),I1(R), F,I2,SA(t&R), [Pt,R,It, Arg], 2008 W(R),I,E,It,Arg 1,2,NZ,SA, 2009 W
Hogg, C D (Melrose) 1992 A 1,2, 1993 NZ (R), 1994 Arg 1,2
Hogg, C G (Boroughmuir) 1978 F (R), W (R)
Holmes, S D (London Scottish) 1998 It, I, F
Holms, W F (RIE Coll) 1886 W, E, 1887 I, E, 1889 W, I
Horsburgh, G B (London Scottish) 1937 W, I, E, 1938 W, I, E, 1939 W, I, E
Howie, D D (Kirkcaldy) 1912 F, W, I, E, SA, 1913 F, W
Howie, R A (Kirkcaldy) 1924 F, W, I, E, 1925 W, I, E
Hoyer-Millar, G C (Oxford U) 1953 I
Huggan, J L (London Scottish) 1914 E
Hume, J (Royal HSFP) 1912 F, 1920 F, 1921 F, W, I, E, 1922 F
Hume, J W G (Oxford U, Edinburgh Wands) 1928 I, 1930 F
Hunter, F (Edinburgh U) 1882 I
Hunter, I G (Selkirk) 1984 I (R), 1985 F (R), W, E
Hunter, J M (Cambridge U) 1947 F
Hunter, M D (Glasgow High) 1974 F
Hunter, W J (Hawick) 1964 F, NZ, W, 1967 F, W, I, E
Hutchison, W R (Glasgow HSFP) 1911 E
Hutton, A H M (Dunfermline) 1932 I
Hutton, J E (Harlequins) 1930 E, 1931 F
Inglis, H M (Edinburgh Acads) 1951 F, W, I, E, SA, 1952 W, I
Inglis, J M (Selkirk) 1952 E
Inglis, W M (Cambridge U, Royal Engineers) 1937 W, I, E, 1938 W, I, E
Innes, J R S (Aberdeen GSFP) 1939 W, I, E, 1947 A, 1948 F, W, I, E
Ireland, J C H (Glasgow HSFP) 1925 W, I, E, 1926 F, W, I, E, 1927 F, W, I, E
Irvine, A R (Heriot's FP) 1972 NZ, 1973 F, W, I, E, P, 1974 W, E, I, F, 1975 I, F, W, E, NZ, A, 1976 F, W, E, I, 1977 E, I, F, W, 1978 I, F, E, NZ, 1979 W, E, I, F, NZ, 1980 I, F, W, E, 1981 F, W, E, I, NZ 1,2, R, A, 1982 E, I, F, W, A 1,2
Irvine, D R (Edinburgh Acads) 1878 E, 1879 I, E
Irvine, R W (Edinburgh Acads) 1871 E, 1872 E, 1873 E, 1874 E, 1875 E, 1876 E, 1877 I, E, 1878 E, 1879 I, E, 1880 I, E
Irvine T W (Edinburgh Acads) 1885 I 1,2, 1886 W, I, E, 1887 I, W, E, 1888 W, I, 1889 I
Jackson, K L T (Oxford U) 1933 W, E, I, 1934 W
Jackson, T G H (Army) 1947 F, W, E, A, 1948 F, W, I, E, 1949 F, W, I, E
Jackson, W D (Hawick) 1964 I, 1965 E, SA, 1968 A, 1969 F, W, I, E
Jacobsen, A F (Edinburgh) 2002 C (R), US, 2003 I 2, 2004 It,F,I,A3,J,A4,SA, 2005 R,Arg(R),Sm, 2006 R(R),PI(R),A(R), 2007 E(R),W(R),It(t&R),I1(R),F(R), I2,SA(R), [Pt], 2008 F,W,I,E,It,Arg 1,2,NZ,SA,C, 2009 W,F,It,Fj,A,Arg, 2010 F(R),W(R),It,E,I,Arg 1,2
Jamieson, J (W of Scotland) 1883 W, I, E, 1884 W, I, E, 1885 W, I 1,2
Jardine, I C (Stirling County) 1993 NZ, 1994 W, E (R), Arg 1,2, 1995 C, I, F, [Tg, F (t & R), NZ (R)], 1996 I, F, W, E, NZ 1,2, 1998 Fj
Jeffrey, J (Kelso) 1984 A, 1985 I, E, 1986 F, W, E, I, R, 1987 I, F, W, E, [F, Z, R], 1988 I, W, A, 1989 W, E, I, F, Fj, R, 1990 I, F, W, E, NZ 1,2, Arg, 1991 F, W, E, I, [J, I, WS, E, NZ]
Johnston, D I (Watsonians) 1979 NZ, 1980 I, F, W, E, 1981 R, A, 1982 E, I, F, W, A 1,2, 1983 I, F, W, NZ, 1984 W, E, I, F, R, 1986 F, W, E, I, R
Johnston, H H (Edinburgh Collegian FP) 1877 I, E
Johnston, J (Melrose) 1951 SA, 1952 F, W, I, E
Johnston, W C (Glasgow HSFP) 1922 F
Johnston, W G S (Cambridge U) 1935 W, I, 1937 W, I, E
Joiner, C A (Melrose, Leicester) 1994 Arg 1,2, 1995 C, I, F, W, E, R, [Iv, Tg, F, NZ], 1996 I, F, W, E, NZ 1, 1997 SA, 1998 It, I, A 2(R), 2000 NZ 1(R),2, US (R)
Jones, P M (Gloucester) 1992 W (R)
Junor, J E (Glasgow Acads) 1876 E, 1877 I, E, 1878 E, 1879 E, 1881 I
Keddie, R R (Watsonians) 1967 NZ
Keith, G J (Wasps) 1968 F, W
Keller, D H (London Scottish) 1949 F, W, I, E, 1950 F, W, I
Kellock, A D (Edinburgh, Glasgow Warriors) 2004 A3(t&R), 2005 R(R),Arg(R), Sm(R),NZ(R), 2006 F,W,E,It(R),SA 1(R),2,PI(R),A, 2007 E, 2008 Arg 1(t&R),2(R), 2009 It,Fj,A,Arg, 2010 F,W,It,E,I, Arg 1,2
Kelly, R F (Watsonians) 1927 A, 1928 F, W, E
Kemp, J W Y (Glasgow HSFP) 1954 W, 1955 F, W, I, E, 1956 F, W, I, E, 1957 F, W, I, E, 1958 F, W, A, I, E, 1959 F, W, I, E, 1960 F, W, I, E, SA
Kennedy, A E (Watsonians) 1983 NZ, 1984 W, E, A
Kennedy, F (Stewart's Coll FP) 1920 F, W, I, E, 1921 E
Kennedy, N (W of Scotland) 1903 W, I, E
Ker, A B M (Kelso) 1988 W, E
Ker, H T (Glasgow Acads) 1887 I, W, E, 1888 I, 1889 W, 1890 I, E
Kerr, D S (Heriot's FP) 1923 F, W, 1924 F, 1926 I, E, 1927 W, I, E, 1928 I, E
Kerr, G (Leeds, Borders, Glasgow, Edinburgh) 2003 I 1(R), F(R), W 1(R), E(R), SA 1,2, W 2, [J(R),US,F], 2004 W(R),E(R),It(R),F(R), I(R),J,A4,SA, 2005 F,I,It,W,E,Arg,Sm(R), NZ, 2006 F,W,E,I,It,SA 1,2,R,PI,A, 2007 E,W,It,I1,F,SA, [Pt(R),R,NZ(R),It,Arg], 2008 F(R), W(R),I(R)
Kerr, G C (Old Dunelmians, Edinburgh Wands) 1898 I, E, 1899 I, W, E, 1900 W, I, E
Kerr, J M (Heriot's FP) 1935 NZ, 1936 I, E, 1937 W, I

Kerr, R C (Glasgow) 2002 C, US, 2003 W 2
Kerr, W (London Scottish) 1953 E
Kidston, D W (Glasgow Acads) 1883 W, E
Kidston, W H (W of Scotland) 1874 E
Kilgour, I J (RMC Sandhurst) 1921 F
King, J H F (Selkirk) 1953 F, W, E, 1954 E
Kininmonth, P W (Oxford U, Richmond) 1949 F, W, I, E, 1950 F, W, I, E, 1951 F, W, I, E, SA, 1952 F, W, I, 1954 F, NZ, I, E, W
Kinnear, R M (Heriot's FP) 1926 F, W, I
Knox, J (Kelvinside Acads) 1903 W, I, E
Kyle, W E (Hawick) 1902 W, I, E, 1903 W, I, E, 1904 W, I, E, 1905 W, I, E, NZ, 1906 W, I, E, 1908 E, 1909 W, I, E, 1910 W
Laidlaw, A S (Hawick) 1897 I
Laidlaw, F A L (Melrose) 1965 F, W, I, E, SA, 1966 F, W, I, E, A, 1967 F, W, I, E, NZ, 1968 F, W, I, A, 1969 F, W, I, E, SA, 1970 F, W, I, E, A, 1971 F, W, I
Laidlaw, R J (Jedforest) 1980 I, F, W, E, 1981 F, W, E, I, NZ 1,2, R, A, 1982 E, I, F, W, A 1,2, 1983 I, F, W, E, NZ, 1984 W, E, I, F, R, A, 1985 I, F, 1986 F, W, E, I, R, 1987 I, F, W, E, [F, R, NZ], 1988 I, F, W, E
Laing, A D (Royal HSFP) 1914 W, I, E, 1920 F, W, I, 1921 F
Lambie, I K (Watsonians) 1978 NZ (R), 1979 W, E, NZ
Lambie, L B (Glasgow HSFP) 1934 W, I, E, 1935 W, I, E, NZ
Lamond, G A W (Kelvinside Acads) 1899 W, E, 1905 E
Lamont, R P (Glasgow, Sale, Toulon) 2005 W,E,R,Arg,Sm, 2007 E(R),I1(R),F(R),I2, SA, [Pt,R,It,Arg], 2008 F,I,E,SA,C, 2009 Fj,A,Arg, 2010 W
Lamont, S F (Glasgow, Northampton, Llanelli Scarlets) 2004 Sm,A1,2,3,J,A4,SA, 2005 F,I,It,W,E,R,Arg,Sm,NZ, 2006 F,W,E,I, It,SA1,R,PI,A, 2007 E,W,It,I1,F,I2,[Pt,R,It,Arg], 2008 NZ, 2009 W,Fj,A,Arg, 2010 F,W,It,E,I,Arg 1,2
Laney, B J (Edinburgh) 2001 NZ, 2002 E, It, I, F, W, C, US, R, SA, Fj, 2003 I 1, F, SA 2(R), It 2(R), W 2, 2004 W,E,It,I(R)
Lang, D (Paisley) 1876 E, 1877 I
Langrish, R W (London Scottish) 1930 F, 1931 F, W, I
Lauder, W (Neath) 1969 I, E, SA, 1970 F, W, I, A, 1973 F, 1974 W, E, I, F, 1975 I, F, NZ, A, 1976 F, 1977 E
Laughland, I H P (London Scottish) 1959 F, 1960 F, W, I, E, 1961 SA, W, I, E, 1962 F, W, I, E, 1963 F, W, I, 1964 F, NZ, W, I, E, 1965 F, W, I, E, SA, 1966 F, W, I, E, 1967 E
Lawrie, J R (Melrose) 1922 F, W, I, E, 1923 F, W, I, E, 1924 W, I, E
Lawrie, K G (Gala) 1980 F (R), W, E
Lawson, A J M (Edinburgh Wands, London Scottish) 1972 F (R), E, 1973 F, 1974 W, E, 1976 E, I, 1977 E, 1978 NZ, 1979 W, E, I, F, NZ, 1980 W (R)
Lawson, R G M (Gloucester) 2006 A(R), 2007 E(R),W(R),It(R),I1(R), F,SA(R), [Pt(R), NZ(R)], 2008 E(R),Arg 1(R),2(R),NZ(R),SA(R),C(R), 2009 A(R),Arg(R), 2010 E(R), Arg 1,2
Lawson, S (Glasgow, Sale, Gloucester) 2005 R,Arg(R),Sm,NZ, 2006 F(R),W,I(R),It,SA 1,2(R),R(R), 2007 [Pt,R(R),NZ,Arg(R)], 2008 It(R), 2010 F(R),W(R),E(R),I(R),Arg1(R), 2(R)
Lawther, T H B (Old Millhillians) 1932 SA, W
Ledingham, G A (Aberdeen GSFP) 1913 F
Lee, D J (London Scottish, Edinburgh) 1998 I (R), F, W, E, Fj, A 1,2, SA, 2001 Arg, 2004 It(R),F,I(R)
Lees, J B (Gala) 1947 I, A, 1948 F, W, E
Leggatt, H T O (Watsonians) 1891 W, I, E, 1892 W, I, 1893 W, E, 1894 I, E
Lely, W G (Cambridge U, London Scottish) 1909 I
Leslie, D G (Dundee HSFP, W of Scotland, Gala) 1975 I, F, W, E, NZ, A, 1976 F, W, E, I, 1978 NZ, 1980 E, 1981 W, E, I, NZ 1,2, R, A, 1982 E, 1983 I, F, W, E, 1984 W, E, I, F, R, 1985 F, W, E
Leslie, J A (Glasgow, Northampton) 1998 SA, 1999 W, E, It, I, F, [SA], 2000 It, F, W, US, A, Sm, 2001 F, W, E, It, I, Tg, Arg, NZ, 2002 F, W
Leslie, M D (Glasgow, Edinburgh) 1998 SA (R), 1999 W, E, It, I, F, R, [SA, U, Sm, NZ], 2000 It, I, F, W, E, NZ 1,2, 2001 F, W, E, It, 2002 It (R), I (R), F, W, R, SA, Fj(R), 2003 I 1, F, SA 1(R), 2 (R), It 2(R), W 2, [J(R),US(R)]
Liddell, E H (Edinburgh U) 1922 F, W, I, 1923 F, W, I, E
Lind, H (Dunfermline) 1928 I, 1931 F, W, I, E, 1932 SA, W, E, 1933 W, E, I, 1934 W, I, E, 1935 I, 1936 E
Lindsay, A B (London Hospital) 1910 I, 1911 I
Lindsay, G C (London Scottish) 1884 W, 1885 I 1, 1887 W, E
Lindsay-Watson, R H (Hawick) 1909 I
Lineen, S R P (Boroughmuir) 1989 W, E, I, F, Fj, R, 1990 I, F, W, E, NZ 1,2, Arg, 1991 F, W, E, I, R, [J, Z, I, E, NZ], 1992 E, I, F, W, A 1,2
Little, A W (Hawick) 1905 W
Logan, K M (Stirling County, Wasps) 1992 A 2, 1993 E (R), NZ (t), 1994 W, E, I, F, Arg 1,2, SA, 1995 C, I, F, W, E, R, [Iv, Tg, F, NZ], WS, 1996 W (R), NZ 1,2, A, It, 1997 W, E, I, F, A, 1998 I, F, SA (R), 1999 W, E, It, I, F, Arg, R, [SA, U, Sm, NZ], 2000 It, I, F, Sm, 2001 F, W, E, It, 2002 I (R), F (R), W, 2003 I 1, F, W 1, E, It 1, SA 1,2, It 2, I 2, [J,US(R),F,Fj,A]
Logan, W R (Edinburgh U, Edinburgh Wands) 1931 E, 1932 SA, W, I, 1933 W, E, I, 1934 W, I, E, 1935 W, I, E, NZ, 1936 W, I, E, 1937 W, I, E
Longstaff, S L (Dundee HSFP, Glasgow) 1998 F (R), W, E, Fj, A 1,2 1999 It (R), I (R), Arg (R), R, [U (R), Sp], 2000 It, I, NZ 1
Lorraine, H D B (Oxford U) 1933 W, E, I
Loudoun-Shand, E G (Oxford U) 1913 E
Low, M J (Glasgow Warriors) 2009 F(R),E(R),Fj,A,Arg, 2010 F,Arg 1,2
Lowe, J D (Heriot's FP) 1934 W
Lumsden, I J M (Bath, Watsonians) 1947 F, W, A, 1949 F, W, I, E
Lyall, G G (Gala) 1947 A, 1948 F, W, I, E
Lyall, W J C (Edinburgh Acads) 1871 E
Mabon, J T (Jedforest) 1898 I, E, 1899 I, 1900 I
Macarthur, J P (Waterloo) 1932 E
MacCallum, J C (Watsonians) 1905 E, NZ, 1906 W, I, E, SA, 1907 W, I, E, 1908 W, I, E, 1909 W, I, E, 1910 F, W, I, E, 1911 F, I, E, 1912 F, W, I, E
McClung, T (Edinburgh Acads) 1956 I, E, 1957 W, I, E, 1959 F, W, I, 1960 W
McClure, G B (W of Scotland) 1873 E
McClure, J H (W of Scotland) 1872 E
McCowan, D (W of Scotland) 1880 I, E, 1881 I, E, 1882 I, E, 1883 I, E, 1884 I, E
McCowat, R H (Glasgow Acads) 1905 I
McCrae, I G (Gordonians) 1967 E, 1968 I, 1969 F (R), W, 1972 F, NZ
McCrow, J W S (Edinburgh Acads) 1921 I
Macdonald, A E D (Heriot's FP) 1993 NZ
MacDonald, A R (Edinburgh) 2009 Arg, 2010 W(t&R),E(R),I(t)
McDonald, C (Jedforest) 1947 A
Macdonald, D C (Edinburgh U) 1953 F, W, 1958 I, E
Macdonald, D S M (Oxford U, London Scottish, W of Scotland) 1977 E, I, F, W, 1978 I, W, E
Macdonald, J D (London Scottish, Army) 1966 F, W, I, E, 1967 F, W, I, E
Macdonald, J M (Edinburgh Wands) 1911 W
Macdonald, J S (Edinburgh U) 1903 E, 1904 W, I, E, 1905 W
Macdonald, K R (Stewart's Coll FP) 1956 F, W, I, 1957 W, I, E
Macdonald, R (Edinburgh U) 1950 F, W, I, E
McDonald, W A (Glasgow U) 1889 W, 1892 I, E
Macdonald, W G (London Scottish) 1969 I (R)
MacDougall, B (Borders) 2006 W, SA2(R)
Macdougall, J B (Greenock Wands, Wakefield) 1913 F, 1914 I, 1921 F, I, E
McEwan, M C (Edinburgh Acads) 1886 E, 1887 I, W, E, 1888 W, I, 1889 W, I, 1890 W, I, E, 1891 W, I, E, 1892 E
MacEwan, N A (Gala, Highland) 1971 F, W, I, E (2[1C]), 1972 F, W, E, NZ, 1973 F, W, I, E, P, 1974 W, E, I, F, 1975 W, E
McEwan, W M C (Edinburgh Acads) 1894 W, E, 1895 W, E, 1896 W, I, E, 1897 I, E, 1898 I, E, 1899 I, W, E, 1900 W, E
MacEwen, R K G (Cambridge U, London Scottish) 1954 F, NZ, I, W, 1956 F, W, I, E, 1957 F, W, I, E, 1958 W
Macfadyen, D J H (Glasgow) 2002 C (R), US, 2004 Sm,A1,2,3,J,A4,SA, 2006 SA 1,2(R)
Macfarlan, D J (London Scottish) 1883 W, 1884 W, I, E, 1886 W, I, 1887 I, 1888 I
McFarlane, J L H (Edinburgh U) 1871 E, 1872 E, 1873 E
McGaughey, S K (Hawick) 1984 R
McGeechan, I R (Headingley) 1972 NZ, 1973 F, W, I, E, P, 1974 W, E, I, F, 1975 I, F, W, E, NZ, A, 1976 F, W, E, I, 1977 E, I, F, W, 1978 I, F, W, NZ, 1979 W, E, I, F
McGlashan, T P L (Royal HSFP) 1947 F, I, E, 1954 F, NZ, I, E, W
MacGregor, D G (Watsonians, Pontypridd) 1907 W, I, E
MacGregor, G (Cambridge U) 1890 W, I, E, 1891 W, I, E, 1893 W, I, E, 1894 W, I, E, 1896 E
MacGregor, I A A (Hillhead HSFP, Llanelli) 1955 I, E, 1956 F, W, I, E, 1957 F, W, I
MacGregor, J R (Edinburgh U) 1909 I
McGuinness, G M (W of Scotland) 1982 A 1,2, 1983 I, 1985 I, F, W, E
McHarg, A F (W of Scotland, London Scottish) 1968 I, E, A, 1969 F, W, I, E, 1971 F, W, I, E (2[1C]), 1972 F, E, NZ, 1973 F,

W, I, E, P, 1974 W, E, I, F, 1975 I, F, W, E, NZ, A, 1976 F, W, E, I, 1977 E, I, F, W, 1978 I, F, W, NZ, 1979 W, E

McIlwham, G R (Glasgow Hawks, Glasgow, Bordeaux-Bègles) 1998 Fj, A 2(R), 2000 E (R), NZ 2(R), US (R), A (R), Sm (R), 2001 F (R), W (R), E (R), It (R), 2003 SA 2(R), It 2(R), W 2(R), I 2, [A(R)]

McIndoe, F (Glasgow Acads) 1886 W, I

MacIntyre, I (Edinburgh Wands) 1890 W, I, E, 1891 W, I, E

McIvor, D J (Edinburgh Acads) 1992 E, I, F, W, 1993 NZ, 1994 SA

Mackay, E B (Glasgow Acads) 1920 W, 1922 E

McKeating, E (Heriot's FP) 1957 F, W, 1961 SA, W, I, E

McKelvey, G (Watsonians) 1997 A

McKendrick, J G (W of Scotland) 1889 I

Mackenzie, A D G (Selkirk) 1984 A

Mackenzie, C J G (United Services) 1921 E

Mackenzie, D D (Edinburgh U) 1947 W, I, E, 1948 F, W, I

Mackenzie, D K A (Edinburgh Wands) 1939 I, E

Mackenzie, J M (Edinburgh U) 1905 NZ, 1909 W, I, E, 1910 W, I, E, 1911 W, I

McKenzie, K D (Stirling County) 1994 Arg 1,2, 1995 R, [Iv], 1996 I, F, W, E, NZ 1,2, A, It, 1998 A 1(R), 2

Mackenzie, R C (Glasgow Acads) 1877 I, E, 1881 I, E

Mackie, G Y (Highland) 1975 A, 1976 F, W, 1978 F

MacKinnon, A (London Scottish) 1898 I, E, 1899 I, W, E, 1900 E

Mackintosh, C E W C (London Scottish) 1924 F

Mackintosh, H S (Glasgow U, W of Scotland) 1929 F, W, I, E, 1930 F, W, I, E, 1931 F, W, I, E, 1932 SA, W, I, E

MacLachlan, L P (Oxford U, London Scottish) 1954 NZ, I, E, W

Maclagan, W E (Edinburgh Acads) 1878 E, 1879 I, E, 1880 I, E, 1881 I, E, 1882 I, E, 1883 W, I, E, 1884 W, I, E, 1885 W, I 1,2, 1887 I, W, E, 1888 W, I, 1890 W, I, E

McLaren, A (Durham County) 1931 F

McLaren, E (London Scottish, Royal HSFP) 1923 F, W, I, E, 1924 F

McLaren, J G (Bourgoin, Glasgow, Bordeaux-Bègles, Castres) 1999 Arg, R, [Sp, Sm], 2000 It (R), F, E, NZ 1, 2001 F, W, E (R), I, Tg, Arg, NZ, 2002 E, It, I, F, W, 2003 W 1, E, It 1, SA 1(R), It 2, I 2(R), [J,F(R),Fj(t&R),A(R)]

McLauchlan, J (Jordanhill) 1969 E, SA, 1970 F, W, 1971 F, W, I, E (2[1C]), 1972 F, W, E, NZ, 1973 F, W, I, E, P, 1974 W, E, I, F, 1975 I, F, W, E, NZ, A, 1976 F, W, E, I, 1977 W, 1978 I, F, W, E, NZ, 1979 W, E, I, F, NZ

McLean, D I (Royal HSFP) 1947 I, E

Maclennan, W D (Watsonians) 1947 F, I

MacLeod, D A (Glasgow U) 1886 I, E

MacLeod, G (Edinburgh Acads) 1878 E, 1882 I

McLeod, H F (Hawick) 1954 F, NZ, I, E, W, 1955 F, W, I, E, 1956 F, W, I, E, 1957 F, W, I, E, 1958 F, W, A, I, E, 1959 F, W, I, E, 1960 F, W, I, E, SA, 1961 F, SA, W, I, E, 1962 F, W, I, E

MacLeod, K G (Cambridge U) 1905 NZ, 1906 W, I, E, SA,1907 W, I, E, 1908 I, E

MacLeod, L M (Cambridge U) 1904 W, I, E, 1905 W, I, NZ

MacLeod, S J (Borders, Llanelli Scarlets, Edinburgh) 2004 A3,J(t&R),A4(R),SA(R), 2006 F(R),W(R),E,SA2(R), 2007 I2(R), [Pt(R),R(R),NZ,It(R),Arg(R)], 2008 F(R),W(R),I,E,It,Arg 1,2, 2010 Arg 2(t&R)

Macleod, W M (Fettesian-Lorettonians, Edinburgh Wands) 1886 W, I

McMillan, K H D (Sale) 1953 F, W, I, E

MacMillan, R G (London Scottish) 1887 W, I, E, 1890 W, I, E, 1891 W, E, 1892 W, I, E, 1893 W, E, 1894 W, I, E, 1895 W, I, E, 1897 I, E

MacMyn, D J (Cambridge U, London Scottish) 1925 F, W, I, E, 1926 F, W, I, E, 1927 E, A, 1928 F

McNeil, A S B (Watsonians) 1935 I

McPartlin, J J (Harlequins, Oxford U) 1960 F, W, 1962 F, W, I, E

Macphail, J A R (Edinburgh Acads) 1949 E, 1951 SA

Macpherson, D G (London Hospital) 1910 I, E

Macpherson, G P S (Oxford U, Edinburgh Acads) 1922 F, W, I, E, 1924 W, E, 1925 F, W, E, 1927 F, W, I, E, 1928 F, W, E, 1929 I, E, 1930 F, W, I, E, 1931 W, E, 1932 SA, E

Macpherson, N C (Newport) 1920 W, I, E, 1921 F, E, 1923 I, E

McQueen, S B (Waterloo) 1923 F, W, I, E

Macrae, D J (St Andrew's U) 1937 W, I, E, 1938 W, I, E, 1939 W, I, E

Madsen, D F (Gosforth) 1974 W, E, I, F, 1975 I, F, W, E, 1976 F, 1977 E, I, F, W, 1978 I

Mair, N G R (Edinburgh U) 1951 F, W, I, E

Maitland, G (Edinburgh Inst FP) 1885 W, I 2

Maitland, R (Edinburgh Inst FP) 1881 E, 1882 I, E, 1884 W, 1885 W

Maitland, R P (Royal Artillery) 1872 E

Malcolm, A G (Glasgow U) 1888 I

Manson, J J (Dundee HSFP) 1995 E (R)

Marsh, J (Edinburgh Inst FP) 1889 W, I

Marshall, A (Edinburgh Acads) 1875 E

Marshall, G R (Selkirk) 1988 A (R), 1989 Fj, 1990 Arg, 1991 [Z]

Marshall, J C (London Scottish) 1954 F, NZ, I, E, W

Marshall, K W (Edinburgh Acads) 1934 W, I, E, 1935 W, I, E, 1936 W, 1937 E

Marshall, T R (Edinburgh Acads) 1871 E, 1872 E, 1873 E, 1874 E

Marshall, W (Edinburgh Acads) 1872 E

Martin, H (Edinburgh Acads, Oxford U) 1908 W, I, E, 1909 W, E

Masters, W H (Edinburgh Inst FP) 1879 I, 1880 I, E

Mather, C G (Edinburgh, Glasgow) 1999 R (R), [Sp, Sm (R)], 2000 F (t), 2003 [F,Fj,A], 2004 W,E,F

Maxwell, F T (Royal Engineers) 1872 E

Maxwell, G H H P (Edinburgh Acads, RAF, London Scottish) 1913 I, E, 1914 W, I, E, 1920 W, E, 1921 F, W, I, E, 1922 F, E

Maxwell, J M (Langholm) 1957 I

Mayer, M J M (Watsonians, Edinburgh) 1998 SA, 1999 [SA (R), U, Sp, Sm, NZ], 2000 It, I

Mein, J (Edinburgh Acads) 1871 E, 1872 E, 1873 E, 1874 E, 1875 E

Melville, C L (Army) 1937 W, I, E

Menzies, H F (W of Scotland) 1893 W, I, 1894 W, E

Metcalfe, G H (Glasgow Hawks, Glasgow) 1998 A 1,2, 1999 W, E, It, I, F, Arg, R, [SA, U, Sm, NZ], 2000 It, I, F, W, E, 2001 I, Tg, 2002 E, It, I, F, W (R), C, US, 2003 I 1, F, W 1, E, It 1, SA 1,2, W 2, I 2, [US,F,Fj,A]

Metcalfe, R (Northampton, Edinburgh) 2000 E, NZ 1,2, US (R), A (R), Sm, 2001 F, W, E

Methuen, A (London Scottish) 1889 W, I

Michie, E J S (Aberdeen U, Aberdeen GSFP) 1954 F, NZ, I, E, 1955 W, I, E, 1956 F, W, I, E, 1957 F, W, I, E

Millar, J N (W of Scotland) 1892 W, I, E, 1893 W, 1895 I, E

Millar, R K (London Scottish) 1924 I

Millican, J G (Edinburgh U) 1973 W, I, E

Milne, C J B (Fettesian-Lorettonians, W of Scotland) 1886 W, I, E

Milne, D F (Heriot's FP) 1991 [J(R)]

Milne, I G (Heriot's FP, Harlequins) 1979 I, F, NZ, 1980 I, F, 1981 NZ 1,2, R, A, 1982 E, I, F, W, A 1,2, 1983 I, F, W, E, NZ, 1984 W, E, I, F, A, 1985 F, W, E, 1986 F, W, E, I, R, 1987 I, F, W, E, [F, Z, NZ], 1988 A, 1989 W, 1990 NZ 1,2

Milne, K S (Heriot's FP) 1989 W, E, I, F, Fj, R, 1990 I, F, W, E, NZ 2, Arg, 1991 F, W (R), E, [Z], 1992 E, I, F, W, A 1, 1993 I, F, W, E, NZ, 1994 W, E, I, F, SA, 1995 C, I, F, W, E, [Tg, F, NZ]

Milne, W M (Glasgow Acads) 1904 I, E, 1905 W, I

Milroy, E (Watsonians) 1910 W, 1911 E, 1912 W, I, E, SA, 1913 F, W, I, E, 1914 I, E

Mitchell, G W E (Edinburgh Wands) 1967 NZ, 1968 F, W

Mitchell, J G (W of Scotland) 1885 W, I 1,2

Moffat, J S D (Edinburgh, Borders) 2002 R, SA, Fj(R), 2004 A3

Moir, C C (Northampton) 2000 W, E, NZ 1

Moncreiff, F J (Edinburgh Acads) 1871 E, 1872 E, 1873 E

Monteith, H G (Cambridge U, London Scottish) 1905 E, 1906 W, I, E, SA, 1907 W, I, 1908 E

Monypenny, D B (London Scottish) 1899 I, W, E

Moodie, A R (St Andrew's U) 1909 E, 1910 F, 1911 F

Moore, A (Edinburgh Acads) 1990 NZ 2, Arg, 1991 F, W, E

Morgan, D W (Stewart's-Melville FP) 1973 W, I, E, P, 1974 I, F, 1975 I, F, W, E, NZ, A, 1976 F, W, 1977 I, F, W, 1978 I, F, W, E

Morrison, G A (Glasgow Warriors) 2004 A1(R),2(R),3,J(R),A4(R), SA(R), 2008 W(R),E,It,Arg 1,2, 2009 W,F,It,I,E,Fj,A, 2010 F,W,It, E,I,Arg 1,2

Morrison, I R (London Scottish) 1993 I, F, W, E, 1994 W, SA, 1995 C, I, F, W, E, R, [Tg, F, NZ]

Morrison, M C (Royal HSFP) 1896 W, I, E, 1897 I, E, 1898 I, E, 1899 I, W, E, 1900 W, E, 1901 W, I, E, 1902 W, I, E, 1903 W, I, 1904 W, I, E

Morrison, R H (Edinburgh U) 1886 W, I, E

Morrison, W H (Edinburgh Acads) 1900 W

Morton, D S (W of Scotland) 1887 I, W, E, 1888 W, I, 1889 W, I, 1890 I, E

Mowat, J G (Glasgow Acads) 1883 W, E
Mower, A L (Newcastle) 2001 Tg, Arg, NZ, 2002 It, 2003 I 1, F, W 1, E, It 1, SA 1,2, W 2, I 2
Muir, D E (Heriot's FP) 1950 F, W, I, E, 1952 W, I, E
Munnoch, N M (Watsonians) 1952 F, W, I
Munro, D S (Glasgow High Kelvinside) 1994 W, E, I, F, Arg 1,2, 1997 W (R)
Munro, P (Oxford U, London Scottish) 1905 W, I, E, NZ, 1906 W, I, E, SA, 1907 I, E, 1911 F, W, I
Munro, R (St Andrew's U) 1871 E
Munro, S (Ayr, W of Scotland) 1980 I, F, 1981 F, W, E, I, NZ 1,2, R, 1984 W
Munro, W H (Glasgow HSFP) 1947 I, E
Murdoch, W C W (Hillhead HSFP) 1935 E, NZ, 1936 W, I, 1939 E, 1948 F, W, I, E
Murray, C A (Hawick, Edinburgh) 1998 E (R), Fj, A 1,2, SA, 1999 W, E, It, I, F, Arg, [SA, U, Sp, Sm, NZ], 2000 NZ 2, US, A, Sm, 2001 F, W, E, It (R), Tg, Arg
Murray, E A (Glasgow, Northampton) 2005 R(R), 2006 R,Pl,A, 2007 E,W,It,I1,F,I2,SA, [Pt,R,It,Arg], 2008 F,W,I,E,It,Arg 1,2,NZ,SA,C, 2009 It,I,E, 2010 W,It,E,I
Murray, G M (Glasgow Acads) 1921 I, 1926 W
Murray, H M (Glasgow U) 1936 W, I
Murray, K T (Hawick) 1985 I, F, W
Murray, R O (Cambridge U) 1935 W, E
Murray, S (Bedford, Saracens, Edinburgh) 1997 A, SA, 1998 It, Fj, A 1,2, SA, 1999 W, E, It, I, F, Arg, R, [SA, U, Sm, NZ], 2000 It, I, F, W, E, NZ 1, US, A, Sm, 2001 F, W, E, It, I, Tg, Arg, NZ, 2002 E, It, I, F, W, R, SA, 2003 I 1, F, W 1, E, It 1, SA 1,2, It 2, W 2, [J,F,A(R)], 2004 W,E,It,F,I,Sm,A1,2, 2005 F,I,It,W,E,R, Arg,Sm,NZ, 2006 F,W,I,It,SA1,R,Pl,A, 2007 E(t&R),W,It,I1, F,SA(R),[Pt,NZ]
Murray, W A K (London Scottish) 1920 F, I, 1921 F
Mustchin, M L (Edinburgh) 2008 Arg 1,2,NZ(R),SA(R),C(R)
Napier, H M (W of Scotland) 1877 I, E, 1878 E, 1879 I, E
Neill, J B (Edinburgh Acads) 1963 E, 1964 F, NZ, W, I, E, 1965 F
Neill, R M (Edinburgh Acads) 1901 E, 1902 I
Neilson, G T (W of Scotland) 1891 W, I, E, 1892 W, E, 1893 W, 1894 W, I, 1895 W, I, E, 1896 W, I, E
Neilson, J A (Glasgow Acads) 1878 E, 1879 E
Neilson, R T (W of Scotland) 1898 I, E, 1899 I, W, 1900 I, E
Neilson, T (W of Scotland) 1874 E
Neilson, W (Merchiston Castle School, Cambridge U, London Scottish) 1891 W, E, 1892 W, I, E, 1893 I, E, 1894 E, 1895 W, I, E, 1896 I, 1897 I, E
Neilson, W G (Merchistonians) 1894 E
Nelson, J B (Glasgow Acads) 1925 F, W, I, E, 1926 F, W, I, E, 1927 F, W, I, E, 1928 I, E, 1929 F, W, I, E, 1930 F, W, I, E, 1931 F, W, I
Nelson, T A (Oxford U) 1898 E
Nichol, J A (Royal HSFP) 1955 W, I, E
Nichol, S A (Selkirk) 1994 Arg 2(R)
Nicol, A D (Dundee HSFP, Bath, Glasgow) 1992 E, I, F, W, A 1,2, 1993 NZ, 1994 W, 1997 A, SA, 2000 I (R), F, W, E, NZ 1,2, 2001 F, W, E, I (R), Tg, Arg, NZ
Nimmo, C S (Watsonians) 1920 E
Ogilvy, C (Hawick) 1911 I, E, 1912 I
Oliver, G H (Hawick) 1987 [Z], 1990 NZ 2(R), 1991 [Z]
Oliver, G K (Gala) 1970 A
Orr, C E (W of Scotland) 1887 I, E, W, 1888 W, I, 1889 W, I, 1890 W, I, E, 1891 W, I, E, 1892 W, I, E
Orr, H J (London Scottish) 1903 W, I, E, 1904 W, I
Orr, J E (W of Scotland) 1889 I, 1890 W, I, E, 1891 W, I, E, 1892 W, I, E, 1893 I, E
Orr, J H (Edinburgh City Police) 1947 F, W
Osler, F L (Edinburgh U) 1911 F, W
Park, J (Royal HSFP) 1934 W
Parks, D A (Glasgow Warriors) 2004 W(R),E(R),F(R),I, Sm (t&R),A1,2,3,J,A4,SA, 2005 F,I,It, W,R,Arg,Sm,NZ, 2006 F,W,E,I,It(R),SA1,Pl,A, 2007 E,I1,F,I2(R),SA(R), [Pt,R,NZ(R), It,Arg], 2008 F,W,I(R),E(R),It,Arg 1,2(R),NZ(R),SA(t),C(R), 2010 W,It,E,I,Arg 1,2
Paterson, C D (Edinburgh, Gloucester) 1999 [Sp], 2000 F, W, E, NZ 1,2, US, A, Sm, 2001 F, W, E, It, I, NZ, 2002 E, It, I, F, W, C, US, R, SA, Fj, 2003 I 1, F, W 1, E, It 1, SA 1,2, It 2(R), W 2(R), I 2, [J,US,F,Fj,A], 2004 W,E,It,F,I,Sm,A3,J,A4,SA,2005 F,I,It,W,E, R,Arg,Sm,NZ, 2006 F,W,E,I,It,SA 1,2,R(R),Pl,A, 2007 E,W,It,I1,F,I2,SA,[Pt(R),R,NZ, It,Arg], 2008 F(R),W,I,E,It,Arg 1,2,NZ,SA, 2009 W(R),F(R),It(t&R),I,E,Fj(R),A(R), Arg(R), 2010 F,W
Paterson, D S (Gala) 1969 SA, 1970 I, E, A, 1971 F, W, I, E (2[1C]), 1972 W
Paterson, G Q (Edinburgh Acads) 1876 E
Paterson, J R (Birkenhead Park) 1925 F, W, I, E, 1926 F, W, I, E, 1927 F, W, I, E, A, 1928 F, W, I, E, 1929 F, W, I, E
Patterson, D (Hawick) 1896 W
Patterson, D W (West Hartlepool) 1994 SA, 1995 [Tg]
Pattullo, G L (Panmure) 1920 F, W, I, E
Paxton, I A M (Selkirk) 1981 NZ 1,2, R, A, 1982 E, I, F, W, A 1,2, 1983 I, E, NZ, 1984 W, E, I, F, 1985 I (R), F, W, E, 1986 W, E, I, R, 1987 I, F, W, E, [F, Z, R, NZ], 1988 I, E, A
Paxton, R E (Kelso) 1982 I, A 2(R)
Pearson, J (Watsonians) 1909 I, E, 1910 F, W, I, E, 1911 F, 1912 F, W, SA, 1913 I, E
Pender, I M (London Scottish) 1914 E
Pender, N E K (Hawick) 1977 I, 1978 F, W, E
Penman, W M (RAF) 1939 I
Peterkin, W A (Edinburgh U) 1881 E, 1883 I, 1884 W, I, E, 1885 W, I 1,2
Peters, E W (Bath) 1995 C, I, F, W, E, R, [Tg, F, NZ], 1996 I, F, W, E, NZ 1,2, A, It, 1997 A, SA, 1998 W, E, Fj, A 1,2, SA, 1999 W, E, It, I
Petrie, A G (Royal HSFP) 1873 E, 1874 E, 1875 E, 1876 E, 1877 I, E, 1878 E, 1879 I, E, 1880 I, E
Petrie, J M (Glasgow) 2000 NZ 2, US, A, Sm, 2001 F, W, It (R), I (R), Tg, Arg, 2002 F (t), W (R), C, R(R), Fj, 2003 F(t+R), W 1(R), SA 1(R), 2 (R), It 2, W 2, I 2(R), [J,US,F(t&R),A(R)], 2004 It(R),I(R),Sm(R),A1(R),2(t&R),3(R),J,A4,SA(R), 2005 F,I,It,W,E(R), R, 2006 F(R), W(R),I(R),SA 2
Philip, T K (Edinburgh) 2004 W,E,It,F,I
Philp, A (Edinburgh Inst FP) 1882 E
Pinder, S J (Glasgow) 2006 SA 1(R),2(R)
Pocock, E I (Edinburgh Wands) 1877 I, E
Pollock, J A (Gosforth) 1982 W, 1983 E, NZ, 1984 E (R), I, F, R, 1985 F
Polson, A H (Gala) 1930 E
Pountney, A C (Northhampton) 1998 SA, 1999 W (t+R), E (R), It (t+R), I (R), F, Arg, [SA, U, Sm, NZ], 2000 It, I, F, W, E, US,A, Sm, 2001 F, W, E, It, I, 2002 E, I, F, W, R, SA, Fj
Proudfoot, M C (Melrose, Glasgow) 1998 Fj, A 1,2, 2003 I 2(R)
Purdie, W (Jedforest) 1939 W, I, E
Purves, A B H L (London Scottish) 1906 W, I, E, SA, 1907 W, I, E, 1908 W, I, E
Purves, W D C L (London Scottish) 1912 F, W, I, SA, 1913 I, E
Rea, C W W (W of Scotland, Headingley) 1968 A, 1969 F, W, I, SA, 1970 F, W, I, A, 1971 F, W, E (2[1C])
Redpath, B W (Melrose, Narbonne, Sale) 1993 NZ (t), 1994 E (t), F, Arg 1,2, 1995 C, I, F, W, E, R, [Iv, F, NZ], WS, 1996 I, F, W, E. A (R), It, 1997 E, I, F, 1998 Fj, A 1,2, SA, 1999 R (R), [U (R), Sp], 2000 It, I, US, A, Sm, 2001 F (R), E (R), It, I, 2002 E, It, I, F, W, R, SA, Fj, 2003 I 1, F, W 1, E, It 1, SA 1,2, [J,US(R),F,Fj,A]
Reed, A I (Bath, Wasps) 1993 I, F, W, E, 1994 E, I, F, Arg 1,2, SA, 1996 It, 1997 W, E, I, F, 1999 It (R), F (R), [Sp]
Reid, C (Edinburgh Acads) 1881 I, E, 1882 I, E, 1883 W, I, E, 1884 W, I, E, 1885 W, I 1,2, 1886 W, I, E, 1887 I, W, E, 1888 W, I
Reid, J (Edinburgh Wands) 1874 E, 1875 E, 1876 E, 1877 I, E
Reid, J M (Edinburgh Acads) 1898 I, E, 1899 I
Reid, M F (Loretto) 1883 I, E
Reid, R E (Glasgow) 2001 Tg (R), Arg
Reid, S J (Boroughmuir, Leeds, Narbonne) 1995 WS, 1999 F, Arg, [Sp], 2000 It (t), F, W, E (t)
Reid-Kerr, J (Greenock Wand) 1909 E
Relph, W K L (Stewart's Coll FP) 1955 F, W, I, E
Rennie, R M (Edinburgh) 2008 I(R)
Renny-Tailyour, H W (Royal Engineers) 1872 E
Renwick, J M (Hawick) 1972 F, W, E, NZ, 1973 F, 1974 W, E, I, F, 1975 I, F, W, E, NZ, A, 1976 F, W, E (R), 1977 I, F, W, 1978 I, F, W, E, NZ, 1979 W, E, I, F, NZ, 1980 I, F, W, E, 1981 F, W, E, I, NZ 1,2, R, A, 1982 E, I, F, W, 1983 I, F, W, E, 1984 R
Renwick, W L (London Scottish) 1989 R
Renwick, W N (London Scottish, Edinburgh Wands) 1938 E, 1939 W
Richardson, J F (Edinburgh Acads) 1994 SA
Ritchie, G (Merchistonians) 1871 E
Ritchie, G F (Dundee HSFP) 1932 E
Ritchie, J M (Watsonians) 1933 W, E, I, 1934 W, I, E
Ritchie, W T (Cambridge U) 1905 I, E
Robb, G H (Glasgow U) 1881 I, 1885 W

Roberts, G (Watsonians) 1938 W, I, E, 1939 W, E
Robertson, A H (W of Scotland) 1871 E
Robertson, A W (Edinburgh Acads) 1897 E
Robertson, D (Edinburgh Acads) 1875 E
Robertson, D D (Cambridge U) 1893 W
Robertson, I (London Scottish, Watsonians) 1968 E, 1969 E, SA, 1970 F, W, I, E, A
Robertson, I P M (Watsonians) 1910 F
Robertson, J (Clydesdale) 1908 E
Robertson, K W (Melrose) 1978 NZ, 1979 W, E, I, F, NZ, 1980 W, E, 1981 F, W, E, I, R, A, 1982 E, I, F, A 1,2, 1983 I, F, W, E, 1984 E, I, F, R, A, 1985 I, F, W, E, 1986 I, 1987 F (R), W, E, [F, Z, NZ], 1988 E, A, 1989 E, I, F
Robertson, L (London Scottish United Services) 1908 E, 1911 W, 1912 W, I, E, SA, 1913 W, I, E
Robertson, M A (Gala) 1958 F
Robertson, R D (London Scottish) 1912 F
Robson, A (Hawick) 1954 F, 1955 F, W, I, E, 1956 F, W, I, E, 1957 F, W, I, E, 1958 W, A, I, E, 1959 F, W, I, E, 1960 F
Rodd, J A T (United Services, RN, London Scottish) 1958 F, W, A, I, E, 1960 F, W, 1962 F, 1964 F, NZ, W, 1965 F, W, I
Rogerson, J (Kelvinside Acads) 1894 W
Roland, E T (Edinburgh Acads) 1884 I, E
Rollo, D M D (Howe of Fife) 1959 E, 1960 F, W, I, E, SA, 1961 F, SA, W, I, E, 1962 F, W, E, 1963 F, W, I, E, 1964 F, NZ, W, I, E, 1965 F, W, I, E, SA, 1966 F, W, I, E, A, 1967 F, W, E, NZ, 1968 F, W, I
Rose, D M (Jedforest) 1951 F, W, I, E, SA, 1953 F, W
Ross, A (Kilmarnock) 1924 F, W
Ross, A (Royal HSFP) 1905 W, I, E, 1909 W, I
Ross, A R (Edinburgh U) 1911 W, 1914 W, I, E
Ross, E J (London Scottish) 1904 W
Ross, G (Edinburgh, Leeds) 2001 Tg, 2002 R, SA, Fj(R), 2003 I 1, W 1(R), SA 2(R), It 2, I 2, [J], 2004 Sm,A1(R), 2(R),J(R), SA(R),2005 It(R),W(R),E, 2006 F(R),W(R),E(R),I(R),It, SA 1(R),2
Ross, G T (Watsonians) 1954 NZ, I, E, W
Ross, I A (Hillhead HSFP) 1951 F, W, I, E
Ross, J (London Scottish) 1901 W, I, E, 1902 W, 1903 E
Ross, K I (Boroughmuir FP) 1961 SA, W, I, E, 1962 F, W, I, E, 1963 F, W, E
Ross, W A (Hillhead HSFP) 1937 W, E
Rottenburg, H (Cambridge U, London Scottish) 1899 W, E, 1900 W, I, E
Roughead, W N (Edinburgh Acads, London Scottish) 1927 A, 1928 F, W, I, E, 1930 I, E, 1931 F, W, I, E, 1932 W
Rowan, N A (Boroughmuir) 1980 W, E, 1981 F, W, E, I, 1984 R, 1985 I, 1987 [R], 1988 I, F, W, E
Rowand, R (Glasgow HSFP) 1930 F, W, 1932 E, 1933 W, E, I, 1934 W
Roxburgh, A J (Kelso) 1997 A, 1998 It, F (R), W, E, Fj, A 1(R),2(R)
Roy, A (Waterloo) 1938 W, I, E, 1939 W, I, E
Russell, R R (Saracens, London Irish) 1999 R, [U (R), Sp, Sm (R), NZ (R)], 2000 I (R), 2001 F (R), 2002 F (R), W (R), 2003 W 1(R), It 1(R), SA 1 (R), 2 (R), It 2, I 2(R), [J,F(R),Fj(t),A(R)] , 2004 W(R),E(R),F(R),I(R),J(R),A4(R),SA(R), 2005 It(R)
Russell, W L (Glasgow Acads) 1905 NZ, 1906 W, I, E
Rutherford, J Y (Selkirk) 1979 W, E, I, F, NZ, 1980 I, F, E, 1981 F, W, E, I, NZ 1,2, A, 1982 E, I, F, W, A 1,2, 1983 E, NZ, 1984 W, E, I, F, R, 1985 I, F, W, E, 1986 F, W, E, I, R, 1987 I, F, W, E, [F]
Sampson, R W F (London Scottish) 1939 W, 1947 W
Sanderson, G A (Royal HSFP) 1907 W, I, E, 1908 I
Sanderson, J L P (Edinburgh Acads) 1873 E
Schulze, D G (London Scottish) 1905 E, 1907 I, E, 1908 W, I, E, 1909 W, I, E, 1910 W, I, E, 1911 W
Scobie, R M (Royal Military Coll) 1914 W, I, E
Scotland, K J F (Heriot's FP, Cambridge U, Leicester) 1957 F, W, I, E, 1958 E, 1959 F, W, I, E, 1960 F, W, I, E, 1961 F, SA, W, I, E, 1962 F, W, I, E, 1963 F, W, I, E, 1965 F
Scott, D M (Langholm, Watsonians) 1950 I, E, 1951 W, I, E, SA, 1952 F, W, I, 1953 F
Scott, J M B (Edinburgh Acads) 1907 E, 1908 W, I, E, 1909 W, I, E, 1910 F, W, I, E, 1911 F, W, I, 1912 W, I, E, SA, 1913 W, I, E
Scott, J S (St Andrew's U) 1950 E
Scott, J W (Stewart's Coll FP) 1925 F, W, I, E, 1926 F, W, I, E, 1927 F, W, I, E, A, 1928 F, W, E, 1929 E, 1930 F
Scott, M (Dunfermline) 1992 A 2
Scott, R (Hawick) 1898 I, 1900 I, E
Scott, S (Edinburgh, Borders) 2000 NZ 2 (R), US (t+R), 2001 It (R), I (R), Tg (R), NZ (R), 2002 US (R), R(R), Fj(R), 2004 Sm(R), A1(R)
Scott, T (Langholm, Hawick) 1896 W, 1897 I, E, 1898 I, E, 1899 I, W, E, 1900 W, I, E
Scott, T M (Hawick) 1893 E, 1895 W, I, E, 1896 W, E, 1897 I, E, 1898 I, E, 1900 W, I
Scott, W P (W of Scotland) 1900 I, E, 1902 I, E, 1903 W, I, E, 1904 W, I, E, 1905 W, I, E, NZ, 1906 W, I, E, SA, 1907 W, I, E
Scoular, J G (Cambridge U) 1905 NZ, 1906 W, I, E, SA
Selby, J A R (Watsonians) 1920 W, I
Shackleton, J A P (London Scottish) 1959 E, 1963 F, W, 1964 NZ, W, 1965 I, SA
Sharp, A V (Bristol) 1994 E, I, F, Arg 1,2 SA
Sharp, G (Stewart's FP, Army) 1960 F, 1964 F, NZ, W
Shaw, G D (Sale) 1935 NZ, 1936 W, 1937 W, I, E, 1939 I
Shaw, I (Glasgow HSFP) 1937 I
Shaw, J N (Edinburgh Acads) 1921 W, I
Shaw, R W (Glasgow HSFP) 1934 W, I, E, 1935 W, I, E, NZ, 1936 W, I, E, 1937 W, I, E, 1938 W, I, E, 1939 W, I, E
Shedden, D (W of Scotland) 1972 NZ, 1973 F, W, I, E, P, 1976 W, E, I, 1977 I, F, W, 1978 I, F, W
Shepherd, R J S (Melrose) 1995 WS, 1996 I, F, W, E, NZ 1,2, A, It, 1997 W, E, I, F, SA, 1998 It, I, W (R), Fj (t), A 1,2
Shiel, A G (Melrose, Edinburgh) 1991 [I (R), WS], 1993 I, F, W, E, NZ, 1994 Arg 1,2, SA, 1995 R, [Iv, F, NZ], WS, 2000 I, NZ 1(R),2
Shillinglaw, R B (Gala, Army) 1960 I, E, SA, 1961 F, SA
Simmers, B M (Glasgow Acads) 1965 F, W, 1966 A, 1967 F, W, I, 1971 F (R)
Simmers, W M (Glasgow Acads) 1926 W, I, E, 1927 F, W, I, E, A, 1928 F, W, I, E, 1929 F, W, I, E, 1930 F, W, I, E, 1931 F, W, I, E, 1932 SA, W, I, E
Simpson, G L (Kirkcaldy, Glasgow) 1998 A 1,2, 1999 Arg (R), R, [SA, U, Sm, NZ], 2000 It, I, NZ 1(R), 2001 I, Tg (R), Arg (R), NZ
Simpson, J W (Royal HSFP) 1893 I, E, 1894 W, I, E, 1895 W, I, E, 1896 W, I, 1897 E, 1899 W, E
Simpson, R S (Glasgow Acads) 1923 I
Simson, E D (Edinburgh U, London Scottish) 1902 E, 1903 W, I, E, 1904 W, I, E, 1905 W, I, E, NZ, 1906 W, I, E, 1907 W, I, E
Simson, J T (Watsonians) 1905 NZ, 1909 W, I, E, 1910 F, W, 1911 I
Simson, R F (London Scottish) 1911 E
Sloan, A T (Edinburgh Acads) 1914 W, 1920 F, W, I, E, 1921 F, W, I, E
Sloan, D A (Edinburgh Acads, London Scottish) 1950 F, W, E, 1951 W, I, E, 1953 F
Sloan, T (Glasgow Acads, Oxford U) 1905 NZ, 1906 W, SA, 1907 W, E, 1908 W, 1909 I
Smeaton, P W (Edinburgh Acads) 1881 I, 1883 I, E
Smith, A R (Oxford U) 1895 W, I, E, 1896 W, I, 1897 I, E, 1898 I, E, 1900 I, E
Smith, A R (Cambridge U, Gosforth, Ebbw Vale, Edinburgh Wands) 1955 W, I, E, 1956 F, W, I, E, 1957 F, W, I, E, 1958 F, W, A, I, 1959 F, W, I, E, 1960 F, W, I, E, SA, 1961 F, SA, W, I, E, 1962 F, W, I, E
Smith, C J (Edinburgh) 2002 C, US (R), 2004 Sm(t&R),A1(R),2(R),3(R),J(R), 2005 Arg(R),Sm,NZ(R), 2006 F(R),W(R),E(R), I(R),It(R),SA 1(R),2,R(R), 2007 I2(R), [R(R), NZ,It(R),Arg(R)], 2008 E(R),It(R)
Smith, D W C (London Scottish) 1949 F, W, I, E, 1950 F, W, I, 1953 I
Smith, E R (Edinburgh Acads) 1879 I
Smith, G K (Kelso) 1957 I, E, 1958 F, W, A, 1959 F, W, I, E, 1960 F, W, I, E, 1961 F, SA, W, I, E
Smith, H O (Watsonians) 1895 W, 1896 W, I, E, 1898 I, E, 1899 W, I, E, 1900 E, 1902 E
Smith, I R (Gloucester, Moseley) 1992 E, I, W, A 1,2, 1994 E (R), I, F, Arg 1,2, 1995 [Iv], WS, 1996 I, F, W, E, NZ 1,2, A, It, 1997 E, I, F, A, SA
Smith, I S (Oxford U, Edinburgh U) 1924 W, I, E, 1925 F, W, I, E, 1926 F, W, I, E, 1927 F, I, E, 1929 F, W, I, E, 1930 F, W, I, 1931 F, W, I, E, 1932 SA, W, I, E, 1933 W, E, I
Smith I S G (London Scottish) 1969 SA, 1970 F, W, I, E, 1971 F, W, I
Smith, M A (London Scottish) 1970 W, I, E, A

THE COUNTRIES

Smith, R T (Kelso) 1929 F, W, I, E, 1930 F, W, I
Smith, S H (Glasgow Acads) 1877 I, 1878 E
Smith, T J (Gala) 1983 E, NZ, 1985 I, F
Smith T J (Watsonians, Dundee HSFP, Glasgow, Brive, Northampton) 1997 E, I, F, 1998 SA, 1999 W, E, It, I, Arg, R, [SA, U, Sm, NZ], 2000 It, I, F, W, E, NZ 1,2, US, A, Sm, 2001 F, W, E, It, I, Tg, Arg, NZ, 2002 E, It, I, F, W, R, SA, Fj, 2003 I 1, F, W 1, E, It 1,2, [J,US,F,Fj,A], 2004 W,E,Sm,A1,2,2005 F,I,It,W,E
Sole, D M B (Bath, Edinburgh Acads) 1986 F, W, 1987 I, F, W, E, [F, Z, R, NZ], 1988 I, F, W, E, A, 1989 W, E, I, F, Fj, R, 1990 I, F, W, E, NZ 1,2, Arg, 1991 F, W, E, I, R, [J, I, WS, E, NZ], 1992 E, I, F, W, A 1,2
Somerville, D (Edinburgh Inst FP) 1879 I, 1882 I, 1883 W, I, E, 1884 W
Southwell, H F G (Edinburgh, Stade Français) 2004 Sm(t&R),A1,2,3(R),J,A4,SA,2005 F,I,It,W,E,R(R),Arg(R),Sm(R),NZ, 2006 F,W,E,I,It,SA 1,2, 2006 R,Pl(t&R),A(R), 2007 E,W,It,I1,SA(R), [Pt(R),R(R),NZ,It(R),Arg(R)], 2008 F(R),W,I,E,It,Arg 2,NZ(R),SA(R), 2009 W,F,It,E(R), 2010 F(R),It,E,I,Arg 1,2
Speirs, L M (Watsonians) 1906 SA, 1907 W, I, E, 1908 W, I, E, 1910 F, W, E
Spence, K M (Oxford U) 1953 I
Spencer, E (Clydesdale) 1898 I
Stagg, P K (Sale) 1965 F, W, E, SA, 1966 F, W, I, E, A, 1967 F, W, I, E, NZ, 1968 F, W, I, E, A, 1969 F, W, I (R), SA, 1970 F, W, I, E, A
Stanger, A G (Hawick) 1989 Fj, R, 1990 I, F, W, E, NZ 1,2, Arg, 1991 F, W, E, I, R, [J, Z, I, WS, E, NZ], 1992 E, I, F, W, A 1,2, 1993 I, F, W, E, NZ, 1994 W, E, I, F, SA, 1995 R, [Iv], 1996 NZ 2, A, It, 1997 W, E, I, F, A, SA, 1998 It, I (R), F, W, E
Stark, D A (Boroughmuir, Melrose, Glasgow Hawks) 1993 I, F, W, E, 1996 NZ 2(R), It (R), 1997 W (R), E, SA
Steel, J F (Glasgow) 2000 US, A, 2001 I, Tg, NZ
Steele, W C C (Langholm, Bedford, RAF, London Scottish) 1969 E, 1971 F, W, I, E (2[1C]), 1972 F, W, E, NZ, 1973 F, W, I, E, 1975 I, F, W, E, NZ (R), 1976 W, E, I, 1977 E
Stephen, A E (W of Scotland) 1885 W, 1886 I
Steven, P D (Heriot's FP) 1984 A, 1985 F, W, E
Steven, R (Edinburgh Wands) 1962 I
Stevenson, A K (Glasgow Acads) 1922 F, 1923 F, W, E
Stevenson, A M (Glasgow U) 1911 F
Stevenson, G D (Hawick) 1956 E, 1957 F, 1958 F, W, A, I, E, 1959 W, I, E, 1960 W, I, E, SA, 1961 F, SA, W, I, E, 1963 F, W, I, 1964 E, 1965 F
Stevenson, H J (Edinburgh Acads) 1888 W, I, 1889 W, I, 1890 W, I, E, 1891 W, I, E, 1892 W, I, E, 1893 I, E
Stevenson, L E (Edinburgh U) 1888 W
Stevenson, R C (London Scottish) 1897 I, E, 1898 E, 1899 I, W, E
Stevenson, R C (St Andrew's U) 1910 F, I, E, 1911 F, W, I
Stevenson, W H (Glasgow Acads) 1925 F
Stewart, A K (Edinburgh U) 1874 E, 1876 E
Stewart, A M (Edinburgh Acads) 1914 W
Stewart, B D (Edinburgh Acads, Edinburgh) 1996 NZ 2, A, 2000 NZ 1,2
Stewart, C A R (W of Scotland) 1880 I, E
Stewart, C E B (Kelso) 1960 W, 1961 F
Stewart, J (Glasgow HSFP) 1930 F
Stewart, J L (Edinburgh Acads) 1921 I
Stewart M J (Northampton) 1996 It, 1997 W, E, I, F, A, SA, 1998 It, I, F, W, Fj (R), 2000 It, I, F, W, E, NZ 1(R), 2001 F, W, E, It, I, Tg, Arg, NZ, 2002 E, It, I, F, W, C, US, R(R)
Stewart, M S (Stewart's Coll FP) 1932 SA, W, I, 1933 W, E, I, 1934 W, I, E
Stewart, W A (London Hospital) 1913 F, W, I, 1914 W
Steyn, S S L (Oxford U) 1911 E, 1912 I
Strachan, G M (Jordanhill) 1971 E (C) (R), 1973 W, I, E, P
Strokosch, A K (Edinburgh, Gloucester) 2006 A(R), 2008 I,E,It,Arg 1,2,C, 2009 F,It,I,E,Fj,A,Arg, 2010 It(R),Arg 1(R),2(R)
Stronach, R S (Glasgow Acads) 1901 W, E, 1905 W, I, E
Stuart, C D (W of Scotland) 1909 I, 1910 F, W, I, E, 1911 I, E
Stuart, L M (Glasgow HSFP) 1923 F, W, I, E, 1924 F, 1928 E, 1930 I, E
Suddon, N (Hawick) 1965 W, I, E, SA, 1966 A, 1968 E, A, 1969 F, W, I, 1970 I, E, A
Sutherland, W R (Hawick) 1910 W, E, 1911 F, E, 1912 F, W, E, SA, 1913 F, W, I, E, 1914 W
Swan, J S (Army, London Scottish, Leicester) 1953 E, 1954 F, NZ, I, E, W, 1955 F, W, I, E, 1956 F, W, I, E, 1957 F, W, 1958 F
Swan, M W (Oxford U, London Scottish) 1958 F, W, A, I, E, 1959 F, W, I
Sweet, J B (Glasgow HSFP) 1913 E, 1914 I
Symington, A W (Cambridge U) 1914 W, E
Tait, A V (Kelso, Newcastle, Edinburgh) 1987 [F(R), Z, R, NZ], 1988 I, F, W, E, 1997 I, F, A, 1998 It, I, F, W, E, SA, 1999 W (R), E, It, I, F, Arg, R, [A, U, NZ]
Tait, J G (Edinburgh Acads) 1880 I, 1885 I 2
Tait, P W (Royal HSFP) 1935 E
Taylor, E G (Oxford U) 1927 W, A
Taylor, R C (Kelvinside-West) 1951 W, I, E, SA
Taylor, S M (Edinburgh, Stade Français) 2000 US, A, 2001 E, It, I, NZ (R), 2002 E, It, I, F, W, C, US, R, SA, Fj, 2003 I 1, F, W 1, E, It 1, SA 1,2, It 2, I 2, [J,US,F,Fj,A], 2004 W,E,It,F,I, 2005 It,W,E,Arg,Sm,NZ, 2006 F,W,E,I,It,Pl,A, 2007 E,W,It,I1,F,I2, [Pt,R, It,Arg], 2008 E,It,C, 2009 W,F,It,I,E
Telfer, C M (Hawick) 1968 A, 1969 F, W, I, E, 1972 F, W, E, 1973 W, I, E, P, 1974 W, E, I, 1975 A, 1976 F
Telfer, J W (Melrose) 1964 F, NZ, W, I, E, 1965 F, W, I, 1966 F, W, I, E, 1967 W, I, E, 1968 E, A, 1969 F, W, I, E, SA, 1970 F, W, I
Tennent, J M (W of Scotland) 1909 W, I, E, 1910 F, W, E
Thom, D A (London Scottish) 1934 W, 1935 W, I, E, NZ
Thom, G (Kirkcaldy) 1920 F, W, I, E
Thom, J R (Watsonians) 1933 W, E, I
Thomson, A E (United Services) 1921 F, W, E
Thomson, A M (St Andrew's U) 1949 I
Thomson, B E (Oxford U) 1953 F, W, I
Thomson, F M A (Glasgow Warriors) 2007 I2(t&R),SA(R), [NZ(R)], 2008 F(R),W(R), I(R),E(R),It
Thomson, I H M (Heriot's FP, Army) 1951 W, I, 1952 F, W, I, 1953 I, E
Thomson, J S (Glasgow Acads) 1871 E
Thomson, R H (London Scottish, PUC) 1960 I, E, SA, 1961 F, SA, W, I, E, 1963 F, W, I, E, 1964 F, NZ, W
Thomson, W H (W of Scotland) 1906 SA
Thomson, W J (W of Scotland) 1899 W, E, 1900 W
Timms, A B (Edinburgh U, Edinburgh Wands) 1896 W, 1900 W, I, 1901 W, I, E, 1902 W, E, 1903 W, E, 1904 I, E, 1905 I, E
Tod, H B (Gala) 1911 F
Tod, J (Watsonians) 1884 W, I, E, 1885 W, I 1,2, 1886 W, I, E
Todd, J K (Glasgow Acads) 1874 E, 1875 E
Tolmie, J M (Glasgow HSFP) 1922 E
Tomes, A J (Hawick) 1976 E, I, 1977 E, 1978 I, F, W, E, NZ, 1979 W, E, I, F, NZ, 1980 F, W, E, 1981 F, W, E, I, NZ 1,2, R, A, 1982 E, I, F, W, A 1,2, 1983 I, F, W, 1984 W, E, I, F, R, A, 1985 W, E, 1987 I, F, E (R), [F, Z, R, NZ]
Torrie, T J (Edinburgh Acads) 1877 E
Townsend, G P J (Gala, Northampton, Brive, Castres, Borders) 1993 E (R), 1994 W, E, I, F, Arg 1,2, 1995 C, I, F, W, E, WS, 1996 I, F, W, E, NZ 1,2, A, It, 1997 W, E, I, F, A, SA, 1998 It, I, F, W, E, Fj, A 1,2, SA (R), 1999 W, E, It, I, F, [SA, U, Sp (R), Sm, NZ], 2000 It, I, F, W, E, NZ 1,2, US, A, Sm, 2001 F, It, I, Arg, NZ, 2002 E, It, I, F, W, R(R), SA(R), Fj, 2003 I 1(R), F, W 1, E, It 1, SA 1,2, W 2, [J(R),US,F,Fj,A]
Traynor, K (Edinburgh) 2009 Fj(R),A(R),Arg(R)
Tukalo, I (Selkirk) 1985 I, 1987 I, F, W, E, [F, Z, R, NZ], 1988 F, W, E, A, 1989 W, E, I, F, Fj, 1990 I, F, W, E, NZ 1, 1991 I, R, [J, Z, I, WS, E, NZ], 1992 E, I, F, W, A 1,2
Turk, A S (Langholm) 1971 E (R)
Turnbull, D J (Hawick) 1987 [NZ], 1988 F, E, 1990 E (R), 1991 F, W, E, I, R, [Z], 1993 I, F, W, E, 1994 W
Turnbull, F O (Kelso) 1951 F, SA
Turnbull, G O (W of Scotland) 1896 I, E, 1897 I, E, 1904 W
Turnbull, P (Edinburgh Acads) 1901 W, I, E, 1902 W, I, E
Turner, F H (Oxford U, Liverpool) 1911 F, W, I, E, 1912 F, W, I, E, SA, 1913 F, W, I, E, 1914 I, E
Turner, J W C (Gala) 1966 W, A, 1967 F, W, I, E, NZ, 1968 F, W, I, E, A, 1969 F, 1970 E, A, 1971 F, W, I, E (2[1C])
Usher, C M (United Services, Edinburgh Wands) 1912 E, 1913 F, W, I, E, 1914 E, 1920 F, W, I, E, 1921 W, E, 1922 F, W, I, E
Utterson, K N (Borders) 2003 F, W 1, E(R)
Valentine, A R (RNAS, Anthorn) 1953 F, W, I
Valentine, D D (Hawick) 1947 I, E
Veitch, J P (Royal HSFP) 1882 E, 1883 I, 1884 W, I, E, 1885 I 1,2, 1886 E

Vernon, R J (Glasgow Warriors) 2009 Fj(R),A(R),Arg(R)
Villar, C (Edinburgh Wands) 1876 E, 1877 I, E
Waddell, G H (London Scottish, Cambridge U) 1957 E, 1958 F, W, A, I, E, 1959 F, W, I, E, 1960 I, E, SA, 1961 F, 1962 F, W, I, E
Waddell, H (Glasgow Acads) 1924 F, W, I, E, 1925 I, E, 1926 F, W, I, E, 1927 F, W, I, E, 1930 W
Wade, A L (London Scottish) 1908 E
Wainwright, R I (Edinburgh Acads, West Hartlepool, Watsonians, Army, Dundee HSFP) 1992 I (R), F, A 1,2, 1993 NZ, 1994 W, E, 1995 C, I, F, W, E, R, [Iv, Tg, F, NZ], WS, 1996 I, F, W, E, NZ 1,2, 1997 W, E, I, F, SA, 1998 It, I, F, W, E, Fj, A 1,2
Walker, A (W of Scotland) 1881 I, 1882 E, 1883 W, I, E
Walker, A W (Cambridge U, Birkenhead Park) 1931 F, W, I, E, 1932 I
Walker, J G (W of Scotland) 1882 E, 1883 W
Walker, M (Oxford U) 1952 F
Walker, N (Borders, Ospreys) 2002 R, SA, Fj, 2007 W(R),It(R),F,I2(R),SA, [R(R),NZ], 2008 F,W,I,E,C
Wallace, A C (Oxford U) 1923 F, 1924 F, W, E, 1925 F, W, I, E, 1926 F
Wallace, W M (Cambridge U) 1913 E, 1914 W, I, E
Wallace, M I (Glasgow High Kelvinside) 1996 A, It, 1997 W
Walls, W A (Glasgow Acads) 1882 E, 1883 W, I, E, 1884 W, I, E, 1886 W, I, E
Walter, M W (London Scottish) 1906 I, E, SA, 1907 W, I, 1908 W, I, 1910 I
Walton, P (Northampton, Newcastle) 1994 E, I, F, Arg 1,2, 1995 [Iv], 1997 W, E, I, F, SA (R), 1998 I, F, SA, 1999 W, E, It, I, F (R), Arg, R, [SA (R), U (R), Sp]
Warren, J R (Glasgow Acads) 1914 I
Warren, R C (Glasgow Acads) 1922 W, I, 1930 W, I, E
Waters, F H (Cambridge U, London Scottish) 1930 F, W, I, E, 1932 SA, W, I
Waters, J A (Selkirk) 1933 W, E, I, 1934 W, I, E, 1935 W, I, E, NZ, 1936 W, I, E, 1937 W, I, E
Waters, J B (Cambridge U) 1904 I, E
Watherston, J G (Edinburgh Wands) 1934 I, E
Watherston, W R A (London Scottish) 1963 F, W, I
Watson, D H (Glasgow Acads) 1876 E, 1877 I, E
Watson, W S (Boroughmuir) 1974 W, E, I, F, 1975 NZ, 1977 I, F, W, 1979 I, F
Watt, A G J (Glasgow High Kelvinside) 1991 [Z], 1993 I, NZ, 1994 Arg 2(t & R)
Watt, A G M (Edinburgh Acads) 1947 F, W, I, A, 1948 F, W
Weatherstone, T G (Stewart's Coll FP) 1952 E, 1953 I, E, 1954 F, NZ, I, E, W, 1955 F, 1958 W, A, I, E, 1959 W, I, E
Webster, S L (Edinburgh) 2003 I 2(R), 2004 W(R),E,It,F,I,Sm,A1,2, 2005 It,NZ(R), 2006 F(R), W(R), E(R), I(R),It(R),SA 1(R),2,R,PI,A, 2007 W(R),I2,SA, [Pt,R,NZ,It,Arg], 2008 F,I,E,It,Arg 1(R),2,C, 2009 W
Weir, G W (Melrose, Newcastle) 1990 Arg, 1991 R, [J, Z, I, WS, E, NZ], 1992 E, I, F, W, A 1,2, 1993 I, F, W, E, NZ, 1994 W (R), E, I, F, SA, 1995 F (R), W, E, R, [Iv, Tg, F, NZ], WS, 1996 I, F, W, E, NZ 1,2, A, It (R), 1997 W, E, I, F, 1998 It, I, F, W, E, SA, 1999 W, Arg (R), R (R), [SA (R), Sp, Sm, NZ], 2000 It (R), I (R), F
Welsh, R (Watsonians) 1895 W, I, E, 1896 W
Welsh, R B (Hawick) 1967 I, E
Welsh, W B (Hawick) 1927 A, 1928 F, W, I, 1929 I, E, 1930 F, W, I, E, 1931 F, W, I, E, 1932 SA, W, I, E, 1933 W, E, I
Welsh, W H (Edinburgh U) 1900 I, E, 1901 W, I, E, 1902 W, I, E
Wemyss, A (Gala, Edinburgh Wands) 1914 W, I, 1920 F, E, 1922 F, W, I
West, L (Edinburgh U, West Hartlepool) 1903 W, I, E, 1905 I, E, NZ, 1906 W, I, E
Weston, V G (Kelvinside Acads) 1936 I, E
White, D B (Gala, London Scottish) 1982 F, W, A 1,2, 1987 W, E, [F, R, NZ], 1988 I, F, W, E, A, 1989 W, E, I, F, Fj, R, 1990 I, F, W, E, NZ 1,2, 1991 F, W, E, I, R, [J, Z, I, WS, E, NZ], 1992 E, I, F, W
White, D M (Kelvinside Acads) 1963 F, W, I, E
White, J P R (Glasgow, Sale, Clermont-Auvergne) 2000 E, NZ 1,2, US (R), A (R), Sm, 2001 F (R), I, Tg, Arg, NZ, 2002 E, It, I, F, W, C, US, SA(R), Fj, 2003 F(R), W 1, E, It 1, SA 1,2, It 2, [J,US(R),F,Fj(R),A], 2004 W(R),E,It,F,I,Sm,A1,2,J(R), A4(R),SA, 2005 F,I,E,Arg,Sm,NZ, 2006 F,W,E,I,It,SA 1,2,R, 2007 I2,SA, [Pt,R,It,Arg], 2008 F,W,E(R), It(R),NZ,SA, 2009 W,F,It,I,E,Fj (R),A(R),Arg(R)
White, T B (Edinburgh Acads) 1888 W, I, 1889 W
Whittington, T P (Merchistonians) 1873 E
Whitworth, R J E (London Scottish) 1936 I
Whyte, D J (Edinburgh Wands) 1965 W, I, E, SA, 1966 F, W, I, E, A, 1967 F, W, I, E
Will, J G (Cambridge U) 1912 F, W, I, E, 1914 W, I, E
Wilson, A W (Dunfermline) 1931 F, I, E
Wilson, A W (Glasgow) 2005 R(R)
Wilson, G A (Oxford U) 1949 F, W, E
Wilson, G R (Royal HSFP) 1886 E, 1890 W, I, E, 1891 I
Wilson, J H (Watsonians) 1953 I
Wilson, J S (St Andrew's U) 1931 F, W, I, E, 1932 E
Wilson, J S (United Services, London Scottish) 1908 I, 1909 W
Wilson, R (London Scottish) 1976 E, I, 1977 E, I, F, 1978 I, F, 1981 R, 1983 I
Wilson, R L (Gala) 1951 F, W, I, E, SA, 1953 F, W, E
Wilson, R W (W of Scotland) 1873 E, 1874 E
Wilson, S (Oxford U, London Scottish) 1964 F, NZ, W, I, E, 1965 W, I, E, SA, 1966 F, W, I, A, 1967 F, W, I, E, NZ, 1968 F, W, I, E
Wood, A (Royal HSFP) 1873 E, 1874 E, 1875 E
Wood, G (Gala) 1931 W, I, 1932 W, I, E
Woodburn, J C (Kelvinside Acads) 1892 I
Woodrow, A N (Glasgow Acads) 1887 I, W, E
Wotherspoon, W (W of Scotland) 1891 I, 1892 I, 1893 W, E, 1894 W, I, E
Wright, F A (Edinburgh Acads) 1932 E
Wright, H B (Watsonians) 1894 W
Wright, K M (London Scottish) 1929 F, W, I, E
Wright, P H (Boroughmuir) 1992 A 1,2, 1993 F, W, E, 1994 W, 1995 C, I, F, W, E, R, [Iv, Tg, F, NZ], 1996 W, E, NZ 1
Wright, R W J (Edinburgh Wands) 1973 F
Wright, S T H (Stewart's Coll FP) 1949 E
Wright, T (Hawick) 1947 A
Wyllie, D S (Stewart's-Melville FP) 1984 A, 1985 W (R), E, 1987 I, F, [F, Z, R, NZ], 1989 R, 1991 R, [J (R), Z], 1993 NZ (R), 1994 W (R), E, I, F
Young, A H (Edinburgh Acads) 1874 E
Young, E T (Glasgow Acads) 1914 E
Young, R G (Watsonians) 1970 W
Young, T E B (Durham) 1911 F
Young, W B (Cambridge U, London Scottish) 1937 W, I, E, 1938 W, I, E, 1939 W, I, E, 1948 E

CURRIE HEAT UP TO WIN MARATHON TITLE RACE

By Iain Spragg

It was the longest, most disrupted Premiership campaign in recent memory. The deluge of snow that suffocated Scotland for much of December and January ensured the season was prolonged by two months as the weather made a mockery of the fixture list but when the games were finally completed, it was Currie who emerged as champions.

For the Balerno side, it was a second title success in the space of four years but perhaps more impressively, a triumph of self-belief over outside expectation after many had dismissed them as potential relegation candidates following their mediocre, mid-table finish the previous season.

Currie lost just once during the entire league campaign, but were hounded all the way by defending champions Ayr and it was not until they overcame Glasgow Hawks 55–21 at Burnbrae in early May that their coronation as champions was confirmed.

"People outside of Currie were saying we had already won the league, but nobody at the club was saying that," said coach Ally Donaldson after the decisive win against the Hawks. "There's always doubt in your mind.

"It has been a long tough slog but the players have been outstanding. We've trained in public parks, we've trained after clearing snow off the pitch and we've even had the players putting down frost covers.

"They're a brilliant bunch of guys and they deserve an enormous amount of credit. You read online comments about Currie buying a team, but our playing budget will be one of the lowest in the leagues. These guys are all there for the right reasons, and it is not the money."

Ironically for such an elongated season, the title was arguably settled by just four pivotal games as Currie and Ayr left the other ten sides in the division languishing behind them in what was a two-horse race and although the newly-crowned champions tasted only a solitary defeat, Ayr themselves were just beaten just twice.

The first of these two crucial reverses came in early October when the Alloway-based side travelled to newly-promoted Dundee in a game played in a gale force wind. The contest was as keenly-fought as the conditions were atrocious but it was finally settled by the two fly-halves – Ayr's No

10 Frazier Climo missing a late penalty chance and then watching on as his opposite number Barry Jones landed his own attempt two minutes later to give Dundee a 24–22 triumph.

"We played poorly in the first half, we did not produce the rugby we are capable of and the decision-making was poor" admitted Ayr coach Kenny Murray. "But remember that we lost away at Selkirk at the same time last season and bounced back. It will be a big week in training but I'm confident we will bounce back again before we play Melrose next week."

His side did indeed recover from the setback but at the same time Currie were stringing together a ten-match winning sequence of their own and when the two sides finally crossed swords at Millbrae in early November the defending champions desperately needed a win.

At Dundee, Climo had been the unwitting villain when he failed to land the three points that could have turned the match but this time he was the undisputed hero with three penalties and a conversion of his own try for a haul of 16 points that gave Ayr a timely 21–7 triumph. Currie remained on top of the table but only on points difference.

The onset of a harsh winter threw the competition into temporary chaos but as the snow finally began to thaw in the New Year, the title race heated up. It remained a straight shootout between the new-found 'big two' and with none of the other teams able to take points from them, the season effectively boiled down to Ayr's trip to Malleny Park to face Currie in early May.

The game was fittingly close as the title contenders slugged it out and only two tries were scored – one for Ayr wing Cammy Taylor and the reply, five minutes later, from Currie flanker Jamie Thomson – and so it was the home side's greater accuracy with the boot that sealed a 16–13 victory that all but assured them of the title.

Mathematically, Currie needed two points from their final league game against the Hawks to wrap up the silverware and knew a win, draw or loss with the prerequisite two losing points would suffice but a fatal defeat was never realistically on the cards against their Glaswegian opponents.

Wing Wille Moala scorched over inside the opening minute and a deluge of tries followed from Andrew Binikos, John Cox (2), James Johnstone, Jamie Thomson, Neil Scobie and a second from Moala to complete a comprehensive win and give Currie only their second league title in the club's history.

"When we won the league four years ago we did it with a team that was coming towards the end of its time together," coach Donaldson said after the match. "We got a bit of criticism about the way we played then because it was more forward-oriented. This is a more rounded team and it's also a younger team as there are only two guys over 30 in it.

"This is a team that I hope can go on and improve. We have four guys in the Scotland Under-20s and the average age of the front row is 22. The future does look bright for us."

There was, however, considerable consolation for Ayr in the shape of the Scottish Cup, which saw the team shake of the impending disappointment of surrendering their Premiership crown by beating Melrose in the final at Murrayfield in March.

It was to be a seven-try thriller but despite Melrose dominating the early exchanges, it was Ayr who drew first blood when Jonathan Crossan charged down an attempted clearance for the first five-pointer of the contest.

The Borders side wasted no time in responding through Ben Allen, but Ayr's Gordon Reid bulldozed his way over shortly before the break to give his side a slender 17–13 advantage.

The second period ebbed and flowed as neither side seemed capable of delivering the knockout blow, but just as it seemed the match could well be decided by a hard-earned penalty or scrambled drop goal, Ayr cut loose and two tries inside the final ten minutes from wings Taylor and Andy Wilson finally quelled the Melrose resistance and gave Murray's team a 36–23 win.

"We had 200 folk having breakfast at the club this morning and took about 12 buses through I think, and the supporters were great out there," said Murray after lifting the trophy. "The boys showed true grit and I'm really proud of them. Up to the last two scores in the final ten minutes, I thought it could have gone either way but we took our chances, pressed on and got the tries. We tired a little towards the end but that's what happens when you play so many matches in a short space of time."

For Melrose, defeat was a particularly bitter pill to swallow having narrowly lost to Heriots in the final 12 months earlier. It was the club's third successive appearance in the final but despite only claiming one win in three attempts, coach Craig Chalmers refused to dwell on another disappointing trip to Murrayfield for his side.

"Our performance was just not there today," Chalmers admitted. "Full credit to Ayr, they took the chance when it came their way. It was closer than the score suggests but Ayr were far more composed with them at the right times, so full credit to them, they deserved to win."

"We didn't play anywhere near as well as we did against Currie in the semi-final despite the fact that we knew we had to reach that level to have any chance of winning. We were still in the game with ten minutes to go, but after that we lost the plot and started to throw crazy passes. I hate losing but you just have to get on with it and try and get back to the final next year."

SCOTTISH HYDRO ELECTRIC PREMIERSHIP 2009–10 RESULTS

29 August 2009: **Ayr** 37 **Heriots** 21, **West** 18 **Watsonians** 22, **Selkirk** 24 **Boroughmuir** 29, **Stewart's** 21 **Edinburgh** 39, **Melrose** 22 **Glasgow** 20, **Currie** 41 **Dundee** 18. 5 September: **Watsonians** 16 **Ayr** 22, **Dundee** 31 **Melrose** 36, **Glasgow** 46 **Stewart's** 0, **Edinburgh** 33 **Selkirk** 10, **Boroughmuir** 37 **West** 20, **Heriots** 15 **Currie** 28. 12 September: **Heriots** 33 **Watsonians** 41, **Ayr** 31 **Boroughmuir** 13, **West** 26 **Edinburgh** 34, **Selkirk** 20 **Glasgow** 52, **Stewart's** 5 **Dundee** 47, **Currie** 26 **Melrose** 20. 18 September: **Glasgow** 20 **West** 22. 19 September: **Edinburgh** 18 **Ayr** 25, **Boroughmuir** 10 **Heriots** 26, **Melrose** 29 **Stewart's** 6, **Dundee** 27 **Selkirk** 19, **Watsonians** 15 **Currie** 43. 26 September: **Watsonians** 11 **Boroughmuir** 26, **Heriots** 34 **Edinburgh** 24 **Ayr** 32 **Glasgow** 25, **West** 25 **Dundee** 37, **Selkirk** 22 **Melrose** 45, **Currie** 49 **Stewart's** 17. 3 October: **Dundee** 24 **Ayr** 22, **Glasgow** 15 **Heriots** 24, **Edinburgh** 7 **Watsonians** 17, **Stewart's** 22 **Selkirk** 30, **Melrose** 44 **West** 7, **Boroughmuir** 14 **Currie** 46. 10 October: **Boroughmuir** 34 **Edinburgh** 40, **Watsonians** 14 **Glasgow** 33, **Heriots** 17 **Dundee** 24, **Ayr** 34 **Melrose** 15, **West** 31 **Stewart's** 24, **Currie** 88 **Selkirk** 3. 16 October: **Currie** 48 **Edinburgh** 21. 17 October: **Stewart's** 13 **Ayr** 31, **Melrose** 37 **Heriots** 28, **Dundee** 41 **Watsonians** 15, **Glasgow** 21 **Boroughmuir** 17, **Selkirk** 27 **West** 20. 24 October: **Edinburgh** 12 **Glasgow** 43, **Boroughmuir** 26 **Dundee** 25, **Watsonians** 27 **Melrose** 42, **Heriots** 24 **Stewart's** 21, **Ayr** 47 **Selkirk** 17, **Currie** 56 **West** 18. 31 October: **West** 26 **Ayr** 34, **Stewart's** 20 **Watsonians** 13, **Melrose** 35 **Boroughmuir** 13, **Dundee** 15 **Edinburgh** 24, **Selkirk** 30 **Heriots** 12, **Currie** 59 **Glasgow** 6. 7 November: **Edinburgh** 14 **Melrose** 17, **Heriots** 21 **West** 24, **Glasgow** 10 **Dundee** 33, **Boroughmuir** 29 **Stewart's** 18, **Watsonians** 30 **Selkirk** 30, **Ayr** 21 **Currie** 7. 13 November: **Currie** 28 **Heriots** 3, **Selkirk** 21 **Edinburgh** 6. 14 November: **Melrose** 43 **Dundee** 9, **West** 34 **Boroughmuir** 24, **Ayr** 26 **Watsonians** 5. 15 November: **Stewart's** 18 **Glasgow** 24. 21 November: **Watsonians** 7 **West** 13. 27 November: **Boroughmuir** 24 **Selkirk** 32. 28 November: **Edinburgh** 20 **Stewart's** 25, **Dundee** 13 **Currie** 22. 29 November: **Glasgow** 15 **Melrose** 15. 5 December: **Edinburgh** 26 **West** 3, **Melrose** 17 **Currie** 26, **Watsonians** 13 **Heriots** 39, **Boroughmuir** 6 **Ayr** 13. 12 December: **Heriots** 40 **Boroughmuir** 14, **Stewart's** 12 **Melrose** 34, **West** 17 **Glasgow** 42, **Ayr** 53 **Edinburgh** 20 **Selkirk** 18 **Dundee** 10, **Currie** 48 **Watsonians** 23. 19 December: **Melrose** 14 **Selkirk** 14. 16 January 2010: **Edinburgh** 12 **Boroughmuir** 29, **Dundee** 13 **Heriots** 8, **Stewart's** 33 **West** 44. 23 January: **Ayr** 66 **Stewart's** 15, **Heriots** 28 **Melrose** 16, **West** 34 **Selkirk** 25, **Edinburgh** 5 **Currie** 29, **Watsonians** 16 **Dundee** 13, **Boroughmuir** 8 **Glasgow** 19. 30 January: **Stewart's** 22 **Heriots** 53. 12 February: **Watsonians** 3 Edinburgh 7. 13 February: **West** 20 **Melrose** 18, **Dundee** 52 **Stewart's** 5. 20 February: **Heriots** 44 **Selkirk** 20, **Watsonians** 26 **Stewart's** 13, **Boroughmuir** 32 **Melrose** 26, **Edinburgh** 19 **Dundee** 40. 27 February: **Dundee** 20 **West** 0. 3 March: **Stewart's** 7 **Currie** 75. 6 March: **Dundee** 32 **Glasgow** 33, **Melrose** 34 **Edinburgh** 13, **Stewart's** 3 **Boroughmuir** 38, **Selkirk** 34 **Watsonians** 14, **West** 33 **Heriots** 49. 20 March: **Glasgow** 23 **Edinburgh** 21, **Boroughmuir** 19 **Watsonians** 23. 27 March: **Selkirk** 49 **Stewart's** 3, **Dundee** 43 **Boroughmuir** 11. 3 April: **Glasgow** 33 **Watsonians** 22. 9 April: **Glasgow** 17 **Ayr** 32. 13 April: **Ayr** 34 **West** 28. 17 April: **Glasgow** 37 **Selkirk** 21, **Edinburgh** 6 **Heriots** 21, **Ayr** 39 **Dundee** 20, **Melrose** 18 **Watsonians** 20, **West** 12 **Currie** 63. 20 April: **Currie** 57 **Boroughmuir** 14. 24 April: **Heriots** 25 **Glasgow** 21, **Melrose** 23 **Ayr** 36, **Selkirk** 22 **Currie** 42. 1 May: **Currie** 16 **Ayr** 13. 6 May: **Heriots** 17 **Ayr** 19. 8 May: **Glasgow** 21 **Currie** 55.

FINAL TABLE

	P	W	D	L	F	A	BP	PTS
Currie	22	21	0	21	952	318	17	**101**
Ayr	21	19	0	2	667	362	16	**92**
Melrose	22	12	2	8	600	453	15	**67**
Dundee	22	12	0	10	587	454	15	**63**
Heriots	22	12	0	10	580	496	12	**60**
Glasgow	22	12	1	9	576	521	10	**60**
Selkirk	21	8	2	11	488	633	8	**44**
Boroughmuir	22	8	0	14	467	599	11	**43**
West	22	8	0	14	475	697	11	**43**
Watsonians	22	7	1	14	393	578	9	**39**
Edinburgh	22	7	0	15	421	569	9	**37**
Stewarts	22	2	0	20	323	849	5	**13**

SCOTTISH HYDRO ELECTRIC PREMIERSHIP TWO Winners: Stirling County
SCOTTISH HYDRO ELECTRIC PREMIERSHIP THREE Winners: Hillhead/Jordanhill
SCOTTISH HYDRO ELECTRIC NATIONAL ONE Winners: Dalziel
SCOTTISH HYDRO ELECTRIC NATIONAL TWO Winners: Greenock Wanderers
SCOTTISH HYDRO ELECTRIC NATIONAL THREE Winners: Allan Glen's

SCOTTISH HYDRO ELECTRIC NATIONAL CUP 2009–10 RESULTS

QUARTER-FINALS

Ayr 32 **Gala** 0

Perthshire 12 **Melrose** 24

Howe of Fife 7 **Currie** 75

Stirling County 14 **Heriots** 34

SEMI-FINALS

Melrose 31 **Currie** 8

Ayr 23 **Heriots** 14

FINAL

24 April, 2010, Murrayfield, Edinburgh

MELROSE 23 (2G, 3PG)
AYR 36 (4G, 1PG, 1T)

MELROSE: F Thomson; C Anderson, J Murray, J King, B Allen; S Wight (captain), R Chrystie; K Cooney, W Mitchell, R Higgins, G Dodds, G Elder, J Dalziel, G Runciman, R Miller. *Substitutions:* N Beavon for Cooney (32 mins); S McCormick for Chrystie (54 mins); L Gibson for Mitchell (58 mins); Cooney for Beavon (63 mins); S Johnson for G Dodds (63 mins); A Dodds for Thomson (64 mins); N McTaggart for Runciman (68 mins).

SCORERS: *Tries:* Allen, Murray *Conversions:* Wight (2) *Penalty Goals:* Wight (3)

AYR: G Anderson; C Taylor, R Curle, M Stewart, A Wilson; F Climo, J Hunter; G Reid, S Fenwick, G Sykes, S Sutherland, D Kelly (captain), J Crossan, A Dunlop, J Crossan. *Substitutions:* AJ Macfarlane for Hunter (44 mins); G Tippett for Crossan (50 mins); S Adair for Sykes (68 mins); Crossan for Tippett (69 mins).

SCORERS: *Tries:* Crossan, Reid, Sutherland, Taylor, Wilson *Conversions:* Climo (4) *Penalty Goal:* Climo

REFEREE: I Heard (Gala)

SOUTH AFRICA

SOUTH AFRICA'S 2009–10 TEST RECORD

OPPONENTS	DATE	VENUE	RESULT
France	13 Nov	A	**Lost** 13–20
Italy	21 Nov	A	**Won** 32–10
Ireland	28 Nov	A	**Lost** 10–15
Wales	5 June	A	**Won** 34–31
France	12 June	H	**Won** 42–17
Italy	19 June	H	**Won** 29–13
Italy	26 June	H	**Won** 55–11
New Zealand	10 July	A	**Lost** 12–32
New Zealand	17 July	A	**Lost** 17–31
Australia	24 July	A	**Lost** 13–30
New Zealand	21 Aug	H	**Lost** 22–29
Australia	28 Aug	H	**Won** 44–31
Australia	4 Sep	H	**Lost** 39–41

SPRINGBOKS IN TOUGH TIMES

By Iain Spragg

Gallo Images

South Africa suffered an incredibly tough end to their season losing 39–41 to Australia.

Peter de Villiers was never a universally popular choice when he succeeded Jake White as Springbok coach in 2008. His appointment dramatically polarised opinion in the politically-charged atmosphere of South African rugby but his critics were forced to bide their time when he guided the team to a cathartic series victory over the British & Irish Lions in the summer of 2009.

He followed that considerable achievement with the Tri-Nations title in the same year and after what had been a difficult initial few months in the job, it seemed De Villier's position was no longer the subject of any serious debate.

That, however, was before the Springboks' disappointing 2009–10 campaign in which they won just six of their 13 Tests, surrendering their Tri-Nations title with barely a whimper. Adding to their woes, De Villiers himself made a series of very public gaffes that were manna from heaven to his detractors.

South Africa closed their season with a 41–39 defeat by Australia in the Free State Stadium in Bloemfontein condemning the Springboks to last place in the Tri-Nations table, and almost as soon as the final whistle blew, De Villiers' critics pounced.

White, the man who had masterminded their Rugby World Cup 2007 triumph, offered to coach the side again on a caretaker basis while South Africa's Sport and Recreation minister, Reverend Makhenkesi Stofile, called for De Villiers to appoint a spokesman to avoid any further verbal faux pas.

The pressure was intense and although SARU president Oregan Hoskins tried to calm the deluge of speculation with a statement backing the under-fire coach, the sense that De Villiers was back to square one in terms of public popularity was palpable.

What was to prove an annus horribilis for the coach and his players began in November when he named his squad for the tour of Europe. Back row forwards Juan Smith and Pierre Spies were both ruled out with injury while centre Jean de Villiers and full-back Francois Steyn missed the tour because of overseas club commitments as De Villiers named nine uncapped players for the trip.

"We're number one in the world and we seriously want to stay there," he said. "We are looking ahead so we can stay number one for many years. We don't want to be caught with our pants down when the first-stringers all leave the scene at the same time.

"There's still life after the 2011 World Cup and we want to leave a legacy for whoever takes over. It will be make or break for some of these new players and I want to see whether they have reached their ceiling or whether they can still grow."

The tour, however, did not begin auspiciously. A warm-up game with Leicester at Welford Road had been organised and the Tigers caught the Springboks cold, claiming a famous 22–17 victory over the tourists.

South Africa then crossed the Channel to face France still licking their wounds and there was little respite to be found in Toulouse as Les Bleus extended their unbeaten home record against the Springboks to 12 years with a 20–13 triumph.

Another warm-up fixture with a Guinness Premiership side was next up and just as Leicester had before them, Saracens produced a sensational display to topple De Villiers's side as they emerged from their clash at Wembley 24–23 winners.

The tour was in danger of meltdown but the Springboks steeled themselves and ran in four tries through Bryan Habana, Jaque Fourie, Fourie du Preez and Wynand Olivier in the Test against Italy in Udine to record a comfortable 32–10 victory and steady the collective nerves.

The three-Test tour concluded against Six Nations champions Ireland at their temporary home of Croke Park. The coach made wholesale changes to his front row for the game, recalling props BJ Botha and Tendai Mtawarira at the expense of Adriaan Strauss and Wian du Preez and switching captain John Smit back to hooker.

South Africa were certainly competitive up front as a result but paid a heavy price for their indiscipline as Ireland fly-half Johnny Sexton landed five penalties. Schalk Burger scored the only try in Dublin, but it was not enough to avert a 15–10 defeat and the Springboks' European tour ended as it had begun – in defeat.

Six months later, South Africa returned to the northern hemisphere for a one-off Test with Wales in the Millennium Stadium and despite De Villiers being forced to field a much-changed starting XV, the Springboks escaped from Cardiff with a tense 34–31 win.

It was then back to South Africa for a clash with France and a two-Test series against Italy before the Tri-Nations, and in the familiar surroundings of home, the team enjoyed its best phase of the season in terms of results.

France were ruthlessly dispatched 42–17 in Cape Town courtesy of two Gio Aplon tries, and although the Springboks were far more subdued in the first Test in Witbank against the Italians, they still ran in four tries through Habana, his 37th Test try, flanker Francois Louw, Morné Steyn and Zane Kirchner to record a 29–13 victory.

The second Test against the Azzurri in East London saw the South Africans recapture some of the verve that had been in evidence in early 2009 and their seven-try rout, including a record-equalling 38th Test score for Habana on his 60th Springbok appearance, resulted in what should have been a morale-boosting 55–11 triumph.

In truth, however, their Tri-Nations challenge began badly and De Villiers' side failed to recover from the early setbacks. Being forced to play their opening three games on the road did not help but throughout the tournament, the defending champions looked a shadow of their former selves.

They began against New Zealand in Auckland and the visitors were powerless to stem the tide at Eden Park as the All Blacks ran in four tries and South Africa had to rely on Steyn's boot for all of their points in a 32–12 defeat.

A week later the two teams squared up again in Wellington and although they did conjure up a much-needed try from Danie Rossouw, they again conceded four as the All Blacks ran out 31–17 winners. A 30–13 defeat to Australia at Suncorp Stadium in Brisbane the following week ensured the team returned to South Africa with three defeats from three contests.

"It's not a good start for us at all," conceded Smit after the game. "When you go away from home, you've got to try to get some points and we haven't done so. We've got a lot of work to do back home.

"I think when you have a good season, it's harder the next season and you've got to work even harder so we've got to make sure we do that work so we can get some pride back at home. It's nice to get home but we're also disappointed we're not taking any points back."

That pride was evident for the first of their three home fixtures but it was not enough to prevent a fourth consecutive defeat as the All Blacks staged a dramatic second-half fightback in Soweto to claim a heartbreaking 29–22 win.

The match was Smit's 100th Test but he and his side were unable to mark the occasion with a victory the record 95,000-strong crowd at the FNB Stadium craved, despite Burger crashing over for the opening try of the contest. Steyn's trusty boot kept the scoreboard ticking over but just as South Africa seemed poised to break their Tri-Nations duck, New Zealand went over twice in the closing three minutes to snatch victory from the jaws of defeat.

With just two games remaining, De Villiers' side were facing the humiliating prospect of a Tri-Nations whitewash. They did, though, avoid that particular fate next time out by beating Australia 44–31 at Loftus Versfeld in Pretoria.

The game was Victor Matfield's 100th International for South Africa and while Smit had been unable to celebrate his own century of caps the previous week, the big lock did get the result the landmark merited as Smith, Gurthro Steenkamp, Spies, Frans Steyn and JP Pietersen all crossed the whitewash.

"I think the guys wanted to do it for themselves, do it for Victor and do it for their country," De Villiers said after the team's face-saving victory. "So that on its own was obviously enough motivation for them to go out there and play.

"I was worried when we gave them those early tries, especially in the state we were in, the confidence being low. So to give them a start like that it took really a lot of heart and character to come back and win a game a like this."

The final instalment of the 2010 Tri-Nations was staged in Bloemfontein and the euphoria South Africa had experienced at the final whistle in Pretoria quickly turned to despair in the Free State Stadium as the Wallabies recorded their first win on the high veldt since 1963 and ensured the Springboks finished the season on a low ebb.

The game was a thoroughbred classic with three tries to South Africa and five to the visitors but it was ultimately the booming boot of Australia's Kurtley Beale that decided the contest, landing a superb 55-metre penalty with the last kick to seal a dramatic 41–39 triumph.

South Africa had been beaten for the seventh time in 13 Tests and as Rugby World Cup 2011 looms larger, the memories of the side's unquestioned achievements in 2009 were fading rapidly.

SOUTH AFRICA INTERNATIONAL STATISTICS

MATCH RECORDS UP TO 29TH OCTOBER 2010

MOST CONSECUTIVE TEST WINS

17 1997 A2,It, F 1,2, E,S, 1998 I 1,2,W 1,E 1, A 1,NZ 1,2, A 2, W 2, S, I 3

15 1994 Arg 1,2, S, W 1995 WS, A, R, C, WS, F, NZ, W, It, E, 1996 Fj

MOST CONSECUTIVE TESTS WITHOUT DEFEAT

Matches	Wins	Draws	Period
17	17	0	1997 to 1998
16	15	1	1994 to 1996
15	12	3	1960 to 1963

MOST POINTS IN A MATCH

BY THE TEAM

Pts	Opponent	Venue	Year
134	Uruguay	E London	2005
105	Namibia	Cape Town	2007
101	Italy	Durban	1999
96	Wales	Pretoria	1998
74	Tonga	Cape Town	1997
74	Italy	Port Elizabeth	1999
72	Uruguay	Perth	2003
68	Scotland	Murrayfield	1997
64	USA	Montpellier	2007
63	Argentina	Johannesburg	2008
62	Italy	Bologna	1997
61	Australia	Pretoria	1997

BY A PLAYER

Pts	Player	Opponent	Venue	Year
35	P C Montgomery	Namibia	Cape Town	2007
34	J H de Beer	England	Paris	1999
31	P C Montgomery	Wales	Pretoria	1998
31	M Steyn	N Zealand	Durban	2009
30	T Chavhanga	Uruguay	E London	2005
29	G S du Toit	Italy	Port Elizabeth	1999
29	P C Montgomery	Samoa	Paris	2007
28	G K Johnson	W Samoa	Johannesburg	1995
26	J H de Beer	Australia	Pretoria	1997
26	P C Montgomery	Scotland	Murrayfield	1997
26	M Steyn	Italy	East London	2010
25	J T Stransky	Australia	Bloemfontein	1996
25	C S Terblanche	Italy	Durban	1999

MOST TRIES IN A MATCH

BY THE TEAM

Tries	Opponent	Venue	Year
21	Uruguay	E London	2005
15	Wales	Pretoria	1998
15	Italy	Durban	1999
15	Namibia	Cape Town	2007
12	Tonga	Cape Town	1997
12	Uruguay	Perth	2003
11	Italy	Port Elizabeth	1999
10	Ireland	Dublin	1912
10	Scotland	Murrayfield	1997

BY A PLAYER

Tries	Player	Opponent	Venue	Year
6	T Chavhanga	Uruguay	E London	2005
5	C S Terblanche	Italy	Durban	1999
4	C M Williams	W Samoa	Johannesburg	1995
4	P W G Rossouw	France	Parc des Princes	1997
4	C S Terblanche	Ireland	Bloemfontein	1998
4	B G Habana	Samoa	Paris	2007
4	J L Nokwe	Australia	Johannesburg	2008

MOST CONVERSIONS IN A MATCH

BY THE TEAM

Cons	Opponent	Venue	Year
13	Italy	Durban	1999
13	Uruguay	E London	2005
12	Namibia	Cape Town	2007
9	Scotland	Murrayfield	1997
9	Wales	Pretoria	1998
9	Argentina	Johannesburg	2008
8	Italy	Port Elizabeth	1999
8	USA	Montpellier	2007
7	Scotland	Murrayfield	1951
7	Tonga	Cape Town	1997
7	Italy	Bologna	1997
7	France	Parc des Princes	1997
7	Italy	Genoa	2001
7	Samoa	Pretoria	2002
7	Samoa	Brisbane	2003
7	England	Bloemfontein	2007
7	Italy	East London	2010

BY A PLAYER

Cons	Player	Opponent	Venue	Year
12	P C Montgomery	Namibia	Cape Town	2007
9	P C Montgomery	Wales	Pretoria	1998
9	A D James	Argentina	Johannesburg	2008
8	P C Montgomery	Scotland	Murrayfield	1997
8	G S du Toit	Italy	Port Elizabeth	1999
8	G S du Toit	Italy	Durban	1999
7	A O Geffin	Scotland	Murrayfield	1951
7	J M F Lubbe	Tonga	Cape Town	1997
7	H W Honiball	Italy	Bologna	1997
7	H W Honiball	France	Parc des Princes	1997
7	A S Pretorius	Samoa	Pretoria	2002
7	J N B van der Westhuyzen	Uruguay	E London	2005
7	P C Montgomery	England	Bloemfontein	2007

MOST PENALTIES IN A MATCH

BY THE TEAM

Pens	Opponent	Venue	Year
8	Scotland	Port Elizabeth	2006
8	N Zealand	Durban	2009
7	France	Pretoria	1975
7	France	Cape Town	2006
7	Australia	Cape Town	2009
6	Australia	Bloemfontein	1996
6	Australia	Twickenham	1999
6	England	Pretoria	2000
6	Australia	Durban	2000
6	France	Johannesburg	2001
6	Scotland	Johannesburg	2003
6	N Zealand	Bloemfontein	2009
6	Australia	Bloemfontein	2010

BY A PLAYER

Pens	Player	Opponent	Venue	Year
8	M Steyn	N Zealand	Durban	2009
7	P C Montgomery	Scotland	Port Elizabeth	2006
7	P C Montgomery	France	Cape Town	2006
7	M Steyn	Australia	Cape Town	2009
6	G R Bosch	France	Pretoria	1975
6	J T Stransky	Australia	Bloemfontein	1996
6	J H de Beer	Australia	Twickenham	1999
6	A J J van Straaten	England	Pretoria	2000
6	A J J van Straaten	Australia	Durban	2000
6	P C Montgomery	France	Johannesburg	2001
6	L J Koen	Scotland	Johannesburg	2003
6	M Steyn	Australia	Bloemfontein	2010

MOST DROPPED GOALS IN A MATCH

BY THE TEAM

Drops	Opponent	Venue	Year
5	England	Paris	1999
4	England	Twickenham	2006
3	S America	Durban	1980
3	Ireland	Durban	1981
3	Scotland	Murrayfield	2004

BY A PLAYER

Drops	Player	Opponent	Venue	Year
5	J H de Beer	England	Paris	1999
4	A S Pretorius	England	Twickenham	2006
3	H E Botha	S America	Durban	1980
3	H E Botha	Ireland	Durban	1981
3	J N B van der Westhuyzen	Scotland	Murrayfield	2004
2	B L Osler	N Zealand	Durban	1928
2	H E Botha	NZ Cavaliers	Cape Town	1986
2	J T Stransky	N Zealand	Johannesburg	1995
2	J H de Beer	N Zealand	Johannesburg	1997
2	P C Montgomery	N Zealand	Cardiff	1999
2	F P L Steyn	Australia	Cape Town	2007

CAREER RECORDS

MOST CAPPED PLAYERS

Caps	Player	Career Span
102	P C Montgomery	1997 to 2008
102	J W Smit	2000 to 2010
101	V Matfield	2001 to 2010
89	J H van der Westhuizen	1993 to 2003
80	J P du Randt	1994 to 2007
77	M G Andrews	1994 to 2001
68	J P Botha	2002 to 2010
66	A G Venter	1996 to 2001
66	B G Habana	2004 to 2010
65	J H Smith	2003 to 2010
65	C J van der Linde	2002 to 2010
64	B J Paulse	1999 to 2007
63	J de Villiers	2002 to 2010
63	S W P Burger	2003 to 2010
62	J Fourie	2003 to 2010
55	P F du Preez	2004 to 2009
54	A-H le Roux	1994 to 2002
54	D J Rossouw	2003 to 2010
52	J C van Niekerk	2001 to 2010
51	P A van den Berg	1999 to 2007
47	J T Small	1992 to 1997
47	E R Januarie	2005 to 2010
43	J Dalton	1994 to 2002
43	P W G Rossouw	1997 to 2003
43	R Pienaar	2006 to 2010
42	G H Teichmann	1995 to 1999
42	R B Skinstad	1997 to 2007
40	A D James	2001 to 2010

MOST CONSECUTIVE TESTS

Tests	Player	Span
46	J W Smit	2003 to 2007
39	G H Teichmann	1996 to 1999
28	V Matfield	2008 to 2010
26	A H Snyman	1996 to 1998
26	A N Vos	1999 to 2001
25	S H Nomis	1967 to 1972
25	A G Venter	1997 to 1999
25	A-H le Roux	1998 to 1999

MOST TESTS AS CAPTAIN

Tests	Captain	Span
76	J W Smit	2003 to 2010
36	G H Teichmann	1996 to 1999
29	J F Pienaar	1993 to 1996
22	D J de Villiers	1965 to 1970
18	C P J Krigé	1999 to 2003
16	A N Vos	1999 to 2001
15	M du Plessis	1975 to 1980
12	R B Skinstad	2001 to 2007
11	J F K Marais	1971 to 1974
11	V Matfield	2007 to 2010

MOST POINTS IN TESTS

Pts	Player	Tests	Career
893	P C Montgomery	102	1997 to 2008
312	H E Botha	28	1980 to 1992
269	M Steyn	21	2009 to 2010
240	J T Stransky	22	1993 to 1996
221	A J J van Straaten	21	1999 to 2001
190	J H van der Westhuizen	89	1993 to 2003
190	B G Habana	66	2004 to 2010
181	J H de Beer	13	1997 to 1999
171	A S Pretorius	31	2002 to 2007
156	H W Honiball	35	1993 to 1999
150	J Fourie	62	2003 to 2010
148	A D James	40	2001 to 2010
145	L J Koen	15	2000 to 2003
135*	B J Paulse	64	1999 to 2007
130	P J Visagie	25	1967 to 1971

* includes a penalty try

MOST TRIES IN TESTS

Tries	Player	Tests	Career
38	J H van der Westhuizen	89	1993 to 2003
38	B G Habana	66	2004 to 2010
30	J Fourie	62	2003 to 2010
27*	B J Paulse	64	1999 to 2007
25	P C Montgomery	94	1997 to 2008
21	P W G Rossouw	43	1997 to 2003
20	J T Small	47	1992 to 1997
19	D M Gerber	24	1980 to 1992
19	C S Terblanche	37	1998 to 2003
19	J de Villiers	63	2002 to 2010
14	C M Williams	27	1993 to 2000

* includes a penalty try

MOST CONVERSIONS IN TESTS

Cons	Player	Tests	Career
153	P C Montgomery	102	1997 to 2008
50	H E Botha	28	1980 to 1992
38	H W Honiball	35	1993 to 1999
33	J H de Beer	13	1997 to 1999
33	M Steyn	21	2009 to 2010
31	A S Pretorius	31	2002 to 2007
30	J T Stransky	22	1993 to 1996
26	A D James	40	2001 to 2010
25	G S du Toit	14	1998 to 2006
23	A J J van Straaten	21	1999 to 2001
23	L J Koen	15	2000 to 2003
20	P J Visagie	25	1967 to 1971

MOST PENALTY GOALS IN TESTS

Pens	Player	Tests	Career
148	P C Montgomery	102	1997 to 2008
56	M Steyn	21	2009 to 2010
55	A J J van Straaten	21	1999 to 2001
50	H E Botha	28	1980 to 1992
47	J T Stransky	22	1993 to 1996
31	L J Koen	15	2000 to 2003
27	J H de Beer	13	1997 to 1999
26	A D James	40	2001 to 2010
25	H W Honiball	35	1993 to 1999
25	A S Pretorius	31	2002 to 2007
23	G R Bosch	9	1974 to 1976
19	P J Visagie	25	1967 to 1971

MOST DROPPED GOALS IN TESTS

Drops	Player	Tests	Career
18	H E Botha	28	1980 to 1992
8	J H de Beer	13	1997 to 1999
8	A S Pretorius	31	2002 to 2007
6	P C Montgomery	102	1997 to 2008
5	J D Brewis	10	1949 to 1953
5	P J Visagie	25	1967 to 1971
5	M Steyn	21	2009 to 2010
4	B L Osler	17	1924 to 1933

TRI-NATIONS RECORDS

RECORD	DETAIL		SET
Most points in season	158	in six matches	2009
Most tries in season	18	in four matches	1997
Highest Score	61	61–22 v Australia (h)	1997
Biggest win	45	53–8 v Australia (h)	2008
Highest score conceded	55	35–55 v N Zealand (a)	1997
Biggest defeat	49	0–49 v Australia (a)	2006
Most appearances	42	V Matfield	2001 to 2010
Most points in matches	210	P C Montgomery	1997 to 2008
Most points in season	95	M Steyn	2009
Most points in match	31	M Steyn	v N Zealand (h),2009
Most tries in matches	9	J Fourie	2005 to 2010
Most tries in season	4	J L Nokwe	2008
Most tries in match	4	J L Nokwe	v Australia (h) 2008
Most cons in matches	26	P C Montgomery	1997 to 2008
Most cons in season	12	J H de Beer	1997
Most cons in match	6	J H de Beer	v Australia (h),1997
Most pens in matches	43	P C Montgomery	1997 to 2008
Most pens in season	23	M Steyn	2009
Most pens in match	8	M Steyn	v N Zealand (h),2009

MISCELLANEOUS RECORDS

RECORD	HOLDER	DETAIL
Longest Test Career	J P du Randt	1994-2007
Youngest Test Cap	A J Hartley	18 yrs 18 days in 1891
Oldest Test Cap	J N Ackermann	37 yrs 34 days in 2007

CAREER RECORDS OF SOUTH AFRICA INTERNATIONAL PLAYERS (UP TO 29TH OCTOBER 2010)

PLAYER BACKS	DEBUT	CAPS	T	C	P	D	PTS
G G Aplon	2010 v W	9	2	0	0	0	10
B A Basson	2010 v W	2	0	0	0	0	0
J L de Jongh	2010 v W	6	1	0	0	0	5
J de Villiers	2002 v F	63	19	0	0	0	95
P F du Preez	2004 v I	55	13	0	0	0	65
J Fourie	2003 v U	62	30	0	0	0	150
B G Habana	2004 v E	66	38	0	0	0	190
F Hougaard	2009 v It	5	0	0	0	0	0
A A Jacobs	2001 v It	30	7	0	0	0	35
A D James	2001 v F	40	3	26	26	1	148
C A Jantjes	2001 v It	24	4	1	0	0	22
E R Januarie	2005 v U	47	5	0	0	0	25
Z Kirchner	2009 v BI	10	1	0	0	0	5
W M Murray	2007 v Sm	3	0	0	0	0	0
A Z Ndungane	2006 v A	11	1	0	0	0	5
O M Ndungane	2008 v It	7	2	0	0	0	10
J L Nokwe	2008 v Arg	4	5	0	0	0	25
W Olivier	2006 v S	32	1	0	0	0	5
R Pienaar	2006 v NZ	43	6	13	17	0	107
J-P R Pietersen	2006 v A	36	12	0	0	0	60
F P L Steyn	2006 v I	39	6	5	16	3	97
M Steyn	2009 v BI	21	4	33	56	5	269
FORWARDS							
A Bekker	2008 v W	24	1	0	0	0	5
B J Botha	2006 v NZ	25	1	0	0	0	5
J P Botha	2002 v F	68	7	0	0	0	35
S B Brits	2008 v It	3	0	0	0	0	0
H W Brüssow	2008 v E	13	1	0	0	0	5
S W P Burger	2003 v Gg	63	13	0	0	0	65
P D Carstens	2002 v S	9	0	0	0	0	0
J R Deysel	2009 v It	1	0	0	0	0	0

B W du Plessis	2007 v A	32	5	0	0	0	25
J N du Plessis	2007 v A	20	1	0	0	0	5
W H du Preez	2009 v It	1	0	0	0	0	0
A J Hargreaves	2010 v W	2	0	0	0	0	0
R Kankowski	2007 v W	16	1	0	0	0	5
L-F P Louw	2010 v W	7	2	0	0	0	10
B G Maku	2010 v It	1	0	0	0	0	0
V Matfield	2001 v It	101	6	0	0	0	30
T Mtawarira	2008 v W	22	1	0	0	0	5
B V Mujati	2008 v W	12	0	0	0	0	0
G J Muller	2006 v S	23	0	0	0	0	0
D J Potgieter	2009 v I	6	1	0	0	0	5
M C Ralepelle	2006 v NZ	17	0	0	0	0	0
D J Rossouw	2003 v U	54	8	0	0	0	40
J W Smit	2000 v C	102	6	0	0	0	30
J H Smith	2003 v S	65	11	0	0	0	55
P J Spies	2006 v A	37	7	0	0	0	35
G G Steenkamp	2004 v S	31	5	0	0	0	25
J A Strauss	2008 v A	7	0	0	0	0	0
C J van der Linde	2002 v S	65	4	0	0	0	20
P R van der Merwe	2010 v F	6	1	0	0	0	5
J C van Niekerk	2001 v NZ	52	10	0	0	0	50
L A Watson	2007 v Sm	10	0	0	0	0	0

SOUTH AFRICA INTERNATIONAL PLAYERS

UP TO 29TH OCTOBER 2010

Note: Years given for International Championship matches are for second half of season; eg 1972 means season 1971–72. Years for all other matches refer to the actual year of the match. Entries in square brackets denote matches played in RWC Finals.

Ackermann, D S P (WP) 1955 BI 2,3,4, 1956 A 1,2, NZ 1,3, 1958 F 2
Ackermann, J N (NT, BB, N) 1996 Fj, A 1, NZ 1, A 2, 2001 F 2(R), It 1, NZ 1(R), A 1, 2006 I, E1,2, 2007 Sm, A2
Aitken, A D (WP) 1997 F 2(R), E, 1998 I 2(R), W 1(R), NZ 1,2(R), A 2(R)
Albertyn, P K (SWD) 1924 BI 1,2,3,4
Alexander, F A (GW) 1891 BI 1,2
Allan, J (N) 1993 A 1(R), Arg 1,2(R), 1994 E 1,2, NZ 1,2,3, 1996 Fj, A 1, NZ 1, A 2, NZ 2
Allen, P B (EP) 1960 S
Allport, P H (WP) 1910 BI 2,3
Anderson, J W (WP) 1903 BI 3
Anderson, J H (WP) 1896 BI 1,3,4
Andrew, J B (Tvl) 1896 BI 2
Andrews, E P (WP) 2004 I1,2,W1(t&R),PI,NZ1,A1,NZ2, A2,W2,I3,E, 2005 F1,A2, NZ2(t),Arg(R),F3(R), 2006 S1,2,F,A1(R),NZ1(t), 2007 A2(R),NZ2(R)
Andrews, K S (WP) 1992 E, 1993 F 1,2, A 1(R), 2,3, Arg 1(R), 2, 1994 NZ 3
Andrews, M G (N) 1994 E 2, NZ 1,2,3, Arg 1,2, S, W, 1995 WS, [A, WS, F, NZ], W, It, E, 1996 Fj, A 1, NZ 1, A 2, NZ 2,3,4,5, Arg 1,2, F 1,2, W, 1997 Tg (R), BI 1,2, NZ 1, A 1, NZ 2, A 2, It, F 1,2, E, S, 1998 I 1,2, W 1, E 1, A 1, NZ 1,2, A 2, W 2, S, I 3, E 2, 1999 NZ 1,2(R), A 2(R), [S, U, E, A 3, NZ 3], 2000 A 2, NZ 2, A 3, Arg, I, W, E 3, 2001 F 1,2, It 1, NZ 1, A 1,2, NZ 2, F 3, E
Antelme, J G M (Tvl) 1960 NZ 1,2,3,4, 1961 F
Apsey, J T (WP) 1933 A 4,5, 1938 BI 2
Aplon, G G (WP) 2010 W1,F,It 1,2,NZ1(R),2(R),A1,NZ3, A3(R)
Ashley, S (WP) 1903 BI 2
Aston, F T D (Tvl) 1896 BI 1,2,3,4
Atherton, S (N) 1993 Arg 1,2, 1994 E 1,2, NZ 1,2,3, 1996 NZ 2
Aucamp, J (WT) 1924 BI 1,2
Baard, A P (WP) 1960 I
Babrow, L (WP) 1937 A 1,2, NZ 1,2,3
Badenhorst, C (OFS) 1994 Arg 2, 1995 WS (R)
Bands, R E (BB) 2003 S 1,2, Arg (R), A 1, NZ 1, A 2, NZ 2, [U,E,Sm(R),NZ(R)]
Barnard, A S (EP) 1984 S Am 1,2, 1986 Cv 1,2
Barnard, J H (Tvl) 1965 S, A 1,2, NZ 3,4
Barnard, R W (Tvl) 1970 NZ 2(R)
Barnard, W H M (NT) 1949 NZ 4, 1951 W
Barry, D W (WP) 2000 C, E 1,2, A 1(R), NZ 1, A 2, 2001 F 1,2, US (R), 2002 W 2, Arg, Sm, NZ 1, A 1, NZ 2, A 2, 2003 A 1, NZ 1, A 2, [U,E,Sm,NZ], 2004 PI,NZ1,A1,NZ2, A2,W2,I3,E,Arg(t), 2005 F1,2,A1, NZ2,W(R),F3(R), 2006 F
Barry, J (WP) 1903 BI 1,2,3
Bartmann, W J (Tvl, N) 1986 Cv 1,2,3,4, 1992 NZ, A, F, 1,2
Basson, B A (GW) 2010 W1(R),It 1(R)
Bastard, W E (N) 1937 A 1, NZ 1,2,3, 1938 BI 1,3
Bates, A J (WT) 1969 E, 1970 NZ 1,2, 1972 E
Bayvel, P C R (Tvl) 1974 BI 2,4, F 1,2, 1975 F 1,2, 1976 NZ 1,2,3,4
Beck, J J (WP) 1981 NZ 2(R), 3(R), US
Bedford, T P (N) 1963 A 1,2,3,4, 1964 W, F, 1965 I, A 1,2, 1968 BI 1,2,3,4, F 1,2, 1969 A 1,2,3,4, S, E, 1970 I, W, 1971 F 1,2
Bekker, A (WP) 2008 W1,2(R),It(R),NZ1(R),2(t&R), A1(t&R),Arg(R),NZ3,A2,3,W3(R),S(R),E(R), 2009 BI 1(R),2(R),NZ2(R),A1(R),2(R),F(t&R),It,I, 2010It2,NZ1(R), 2(R)
Bekker, H J (WP) 1981 NZ 1,3
Bekker, H P J (NT) 1952 E, F, 1953 A 1,2,3,4, 1955 BI 2,3,4, 1956 A 1,2, NZ 1,2,3,4
Bekker, M J (NT) 1960 S
Bekker, R P (NT) 1953 A 3,4
Bekker, S (NT) 1997 A 2(t)
Bennett, R G (Border) 1997 Tg (R), BI 1(R), 3, NZ 1, A 1, NZ 2
Bergh, W F (SWD) 1931 W, I, 1932 E, S, 1933 A 1,2,3,4,5, 1937 A 1,2, NZ 1,2,3, 1938 BI 1,2,3
Bestbier, A (OFS) 1974 F 2(R)
Bester, J J N (WP) 1924 BI 2,4
Bester, J L A (WP) 1938 BI 2,3
Beswick, A M (Bor) 1896 BI 2,3,4
Bezuidenhout, C E (NT) 1962 BI 2,3,4
Bezuidenhout, C J (MP) 2003 NZ 2(R), [E,Sm,NZ]
Bezuidenhout, N S E (NT) 1972 E, 1974 BI 2,3,4, F 1,2, 1975 F 1,2, 1977 Wld
Bierman, J N (Tvl) 1931 I
Bisset, W M (WP) 1891 BI 1,3
Blair, R (WP) 1977 Wld
Bobo, G (GL, WP) 2003 S 2(R), Arg, A 1(R), NZ 2, 2004 S(R), 2008 It
Boome, C S (WP) 1999 It 1,2, W, NZ 1(R), A 1, NZ 2, A 2, 2000 C, E 1,2, 2003 S 1(R),2(R), Arg (R), A 1(R), NZ 1(R), A 2, NZ 2(R), [U(R),Gg,NZ(R)]
Bosch, G R (Tvl) 1974 BI 2, F 1,2, 1975 F 1,2, 1976 NZ 1,2,3,4
Bosman, H M (FS) 2005 W,F3, 2006 A1(R)
Bosman, N J S (Tvl) 1924 BI 2,3,4
Botha, B J (N, Ulster) 2006 NZ2(R),3,A3, I(R),E1,2, 2007 E1,Sm,A1,NZ1,Nm(R), S(t&R), [Sm(R),E1,Tg(R), US], 2008 W2, 2009 It(R),I, 2010 W1,F,It 2(R),NZ1(R), 2(R),A1
Botha, D S (NT) 1981 NZ 1
Botha, G van G (BB) 2005 A3(R), F3(R), 2007 E1(R),2(R),Sm(R),A1(R),NZ1,A2, NZ2(R),Nm,S, [Tg]
Botha, H E (NT) 1980 S Am 1,2, BI 1,2,3,4, S Am 3,4, F, 1981 I 1,2, NZ 1,2,3, US, 1982 S Am 1,2, 1986 Cv 1,2,3,4, 1989 Wld 1,2, 1992 NZ, A, F 1,2, E
Botha, J A (Tvl) 1903 BI 3
Botha, J P (BB) 2002 F, 2003 S 1,2, A 1, NZ 1, A 2(R), [U,E,Gg,Sm,NZ], 2004 I1,PI, NZ1,A1,NZ2,A2, W2,I3,E,S,Arg, 2005 A1,2,3,NZ1,A4,NZ2,Arg,W,F3, 2007 E1,2,A1, NZ1,Nm,S, [Sm,E1,Tg,US(R),Fj, Arg,E2],W, 2008 W1,2,It,NZ1,2,A1,Arg,W3,S,E, 2009 BI 1,2,NZ1,2,A1,2,3,NZ3,F,It, 2010 It 1,2,NZ1
Botha, J P F (NT) 1962 BI 2,3,4

Botha, P H (Tvl) 1965 A 1,2
Boyes, H C (GW) 1891 BI 1,2
Brand, G H (WP) 1928 NZ 2,3, 1931 W, I, 1932 E, S, 1933 A 1,2,3,4,5, 1937 A 1,2, NZ 2,3, 1938 BI 1
Bredenkamp, M J (GW) 1896 BI 1,3
Breedt, J C (Tvl) 1986 Cv 1,2,3,4, 1989 Wld 1,2, 1992 NZ, A
Brewis, J D (NT) 1949 NZ 1,2,3,4, 1951 S, I, W, 1952 E, F, 1953 A 1
Briers, T P D (WP) 1955 BI 1,2,3,4, 1956 NZ 2,3,4
Brink D J (WP) 1906 S, W, E
Brink, R (WP) 1995 [R, C]
Brits, S B (WP) 2008 It(R),NZ2(R),A1
Britz, G J J (FS, WP) 2004 I1(R),2(R),W1(R),PI,A1, NZ2,A2(R),I3(t),S(t&R),Arg(R), 2005 U, 2006 E2(R), 2007 NZ2(R)
Britz, W K (N) 2002 W 1
Brooks, D (Bor) 1906 S
Brosnihan, W (GL, N) 1997 A 2, 2000 NZ 1(t+R), A 2(t+R), NZ 2(R), A 3(R), E 3(R)
Brown, C B (WP) 1903 BI 1,2,3
Brüssow, H W (FS) 2008 E(R), 2009 BI 1,2(R),3, NZ1,2,A1,2,3,NZ3,F,It,I
Brynard, G S (WP) 1965 A 1, NZ 1,2,3,4, 1968 BI 3,4
Buchler, J U (Tvl) 1951 S, I, W, 1952 E, F, 1953 A 1,2,3,4, 1956 A 2
Burdett, A F (WP) 1906 S, I
Burger, J M (WP) 1989 Wld 1,2
Burger, M B (NT) 1980 BI 2(R), S Am 3, 1981 US (R)
Burger, S W P (WP) 1984 E 1,2, 1986 Cv 1,2,3,4
Burger, S W P (WP) 2003 [Gg(R),Sm(R),NZ(R)], 2004 I1,2,W1,PI,NZ1,A1,NZ2,A2, W2,I3,E, 2005 F1,2, A1,2(R),3(R),NZ1,A4,NZ2,Arg(R),W,F3, 2006 S1,2, 2007 E1,2, A1,NZ1,Nm,S, [Sm,US,Fj,Arg,E2],W, 2008 It(R),NZ1,2,A1,NZ3,A2,3,W3,S,E, 2009 BI 2,A2(R),3(R),NZ3,F,I, 2010 F,It 2,NZ1,2,A1,NZ3,A2,3
Burger, W A G (Bor) 1906 S, I, W, 1910 BI 2
Carelse, G (EP) 1964 W, F, 1965 I, S, 1967 F 1,2,3, 1968 F 1,2, 1969 A 1,2,3,4, S
Carlson, R A (WP) 1972 E
Carolin, H W (WP) 1903 BI 3, 1906 S, I
Carstens, P D (NS) 2002 S, E, 2006 E1(t&R),2(R), 2007 E1,2(t&R),Sm(R), 2009 BI 1(R),3(t)
Castens, H H (WP) 1891 BI 1
Chavhanga, T (WP) 2005 U, 2007 NZ2(R), 2008 W1,2
Chignell, T W (WP) 1891 BI 3
Cilliers, G D (OFS) 1963 A 1,3,4
Cilliers, N V (WP) 1996 NZ 3(t)
Claassen, J T (WT) 1955 BI 1,2,3,4, 1956 A 1,2, NZ 1,2,3,4, 1958 F 1,2, 1960 S, NZ 1,2,3, W, I, 1961 E, S, F, I, A 1,2, 1962 BI 1,2,3,4
Claassen, W (N) 1981 I 1,2, NZ 2,3, US, 1982 S Am 1,2
Claassens, M (FS) 2004 W2(R),S(R),Arg(R), 2005 Arg(R),W,F3, 2007 A2(R),NZ2(R)
Clark, W H G (Tvl) 1933 A 3
Clarkson, W A (N) 1921 NZ 1,2, 1924 BI 1
Cloete, H A (WP) 1896 BI 4
Cockrell, C H (WP) 1969 S, 1970 I, W
Cockrell, R J (WP) 1974 F 1,2, 1975 F 1,2, 1976 NZ 1,2, 1977 Wld, 1981 NZ 1,2(R), 3, US
Coetzee, D (BB) 2002 Sm, 2003 S 1,2, Arg, A 1, NZ 1, A 2, NZ 2, [U,E,Sm(R),NZ(R)], 2004 S(R),Arg(R), 2006 A1(R)
Coetzee, J H H (WP) 1974 BI 1, 1975 F 2(R), 1976 NZ 1,2,3,4
Conradie, J H (WP) 2002 W 1,2, Arg (R), Sm, NZ 1, A 1, NZ 2(R), A 2(R), S, E, 2004 W1(R),PI,NZ2,A2, 2005 Arg, 2008 W1,2(R),NZ1(R)
Cope, D K (Tvl) 1896 BI 2
Cotty, W (GW) 1896 BI 3
Crampton, G (GW) 1903 BI 2
Craven, D H (WP) 1931 W, I, 1932 S, 1933 A 1,2,3,4,5, 1937 A 1,2, NZ 1,2,3, 1938 BI 1,2,3,
Cronjé, G (BB) 2003 NZ 2, 2004 I2(R),W1(R)
Cronjé, J (BB, GL) 2004 I1,2,W1,PI,NZ1,A1,NZ2(R), A2(t&R),S(t&R),Arg, 2005 U,F1,2,A1,3,NZ1(R),2(t),Arg, W,F3, 2006 S2(R),F(R),A1(t&R),NZ1,A2,NZ2,A3(R), I(R),E1, 2007 A2(R),NZ2,Nm
Cronje, P A (Tvl) 1971 F 1,2, A 1,2,3, 1974 BI 3,4
Crosby, J H (Tvl) 1896 BI 2
Crosby, N J (Tvl) 1910 BI 1,3
Currie, C (GW) 1903 BI 2
D'Alton, G (WP) 1933 A 1
Dalton, J (Tvl, GL, Falcons) 1994 Arg 1(R), 1995 [A, C], W, It, E, 1996 NZ 4(R),5, Arg 1,2, F 1,2, W, 1997 Tg (R), BI 3, NZ 2, A 2, It, F 1,2, E, S, 1998 I 1,2, W 1, E 1, A 1, NZ 1,2, A 2, W 2, S, I 3, E 2, 2002 W 1,2, Arg, NZ 1, A 1, NZ 2, A 2, F, E
Daneel, G M (WP) 1928 NZ 1,2,3,4, 1931 W, I, 1932 E, S
Daneel, H J (WP) 1906 S, I, W, E
Davidson, C D (N) 2002 W 2(R), Arg, 2003 Arg, NZ 1(R), A 2
Davids, Q (WP) 2002 W 2, Arg (R), Sm (R), 2003 Arg, 2004 I1(R),2,W1,PI(t&R), NZ1(R)
Davison, P M (EP) 1910 BI 1
De Beer, J H (OFS) 1997 BI 3, NZ 1, A 1, NZ 2, A 2, F 2(R), S, 1999 A 2, [S, Sp, U, E, A 3]
De Bruyn, J (OFS) 1974 BI 3
De Jongh, H P K (WP) 1928 NZ 3
De Jongh, J L (WP) 2010 W1,F(R),It 1(R),2,A1(R),NZ3
De Klerk, I J (Tvl) 1969 E, 1970 I, W
De Klerk, K B H (Tvl) 1974 BI 1,2,3(R), 1975 F 1,2, 1976 NZ 2(R), 3,4, 1980 S Am 1,2, BI 2, 1981 I 1,2
De Kock, A N (GW) 1891 BI 2
De Kock, D (Falcons) 2001 It 2(R), US
De Kock, J S (WP) 1921 NZ 3, 1924 BI 3
De Kock, N A (WP) 2001 It 1, 2002 Sm (R), NZ 1(R),2, A 2, F, 2003 [U(R),Gg,Sm(R),NZ(R)]
Delport, G M (GL, Worcester) 2000 C (R), E 1(t+R), A 1, NZ 1, A 2, NZ 2, A 3, Arg, I, W, 2001 F 2, It 1, 2003 A 1, NZ 2, [U,E,Sm,NZ]
Delport, W H (EP) 1951 S, I, W, 1952 E, F, 1953 A 1,2,3,4
De Melker, S C (GW) 1903 BI 2, 1906 E
Devenish, C E (GW) 1896 BI 2
Devenish, G St L (Tvl) 1896 BI 2
Devenish, G E (Tvl) 1891 BI 1
De Villiers, D I (Tvl) 1910 BI 1,2,3
De Villiers, D J (WP, Bol) 1962 BI 2,3, 1965 I, NZ 1,3,4, 1967 F 1,2,3,4, 1968 BI 1,2,3,4, F 1,2, 1969 A 1,4, E, 1970 I, W, NZ 1,2,3,4
De Villiers, H A (WP) 1906 S, W, E
De Villiers, H O (WP) 1967 F 1,2,3,4, 1968 F 1,2, 1969 A 1,2,3,4, S, E, 1970 I, W
De Villiers, J (WP, Munster) 2002 F, 2004 PI,NZ1,A1, NZ2,A2,W2(R),E, 2005 U,F1,2,A1,2,3,NZ1,A4,NZ2, Arg,W,F3, 2006 S1,NZ2,3,A3,I,E1,2, 2007 E1,2,A1, NZ1,Nm, [Sm], 2008 W1,2,It,NZ1,2,A1,Arg,NZ3,A2,3, W3,S,E, 2009 BI 1,2,NZ1,2,A1,2,3,NZ3, I(R), 2010 F(t&R),It1,2,NZ1,2,3,A2,3
De Villiers, P du P (WP) 1928 NZ 1,3,4, 1932 E, 1933 A 4, 1937 A 1,2, NZ 1
Devine, D (Tvl) 1924 BI 3, 1928 NZ 2
De Vos, D J J (WP) 1965 S, 1969 A 3, S
De Waal, A N (WP) 1967 F 1,2,3,4
De Waal, P J (WP) 1896 BI 4
De Wet, A E (WP) 1969 A 3,4, E
De Wet, P J (WP) 1938 BI 1,2,3
Deysel, J R (NS) 2009 It(R)
Dinkelmann, E E (NT) 1951 S, I, 1952 E, F, 1953 A 1,2
Dirksen, C W (NT) 1963 A 4, 1964 W, 1965 I, S, 1967 F 1,2,3,4, 1968 BI 1,2
Dlulane, V T (MP) 2004 W2(R)
Dobbin, F J (GW) 1903 BI 1,2, 1906 S, W, E, 1910 BI 1, 1912 S, I, W
Dobie, J A R (Tvl) 1928 NZ 2
Dormehl, P J (WP) 1896 BI 3,4
Douglass, F W (EP) 1896 BI 1
Drotské, A E (OFS) 1993 Arg 2, 1995 [WS (R)], 1996

A 1(R), 1997 Tg, BI 1,2,3(R), NZ 1, A 1, NZ 2(R), 1998 I 2(R), W 1(R), I 3(R), 1999 It 1,2, W, NZ 1, A 1, NZ 2, A 2, [S, Sp (R), U, E, A 3, NZ 3]
Dryburgh, R G (WP) 1955 BI 2,3,4, 1956 A 2, NZ 1,4, 1960 NZ 1,2
Duff, B R (WP) 1891 BI 1,2,3
Duffy, B A (Bor) 1928 NZ 1
Du Plessis, B W (NS) 2007 A2(t&R),NZ2,Nm(R),S(R),[Sm(R),E1(R),US(R),Arg(R), E2(t)],W(R), 2008 W1(R),2(R),It,NZ1(R),2,Arg,NZ3,A2, 3,W3,S, 2009 BI 1,2,3(R),NZ1, 2,A1,2,3,NZ3,F,I(R)
Du Plessis, C J (WP) 1982 S Am 1,2, 1984 E 1,2, S Am 1,2, 1986 Cv 1,2,3,4, 1989 Wld 1,2
Du Plessis, D C (NT) 1977 Wld, 1980 S Am 2
Du Plessis, F (Tvl) 1949 NZ 1,2,3
Du Plessis, J N (FS, NS) 2007 A2,NZ2, [Fj,Arg(t&R)], W, 2008 A3(R),E, 2009 NZ1(t), 2(R),A1(R),2(R), NZ3(R), 2010 W1(R),F(R),It 1,2,NZ1,3,A2,3
Du Plessis, M (WP) 1971 A 1,2,3, 1974 BI 1,2, F 1,2, 1975 F 1,2, 1976 NZ 1,2,3,4, 1977 Wld, 1980 S Am 1,2, BI 1,2,3,4, S Am 4, F
Du Plessis, M J (WP) 1984 S Am 1,2, 1986 Cv 1,2,3,4, 1989 Wld 1,2
Du Plessis, N J (WT) 1921 NZ 2,3, 1924 BI 1,2,3
Du Plessis, P G (NT) 1972 E
Du Plessis, T D (NT) 1980 S Am 1,2
Du Plessis, W (WP) 1980 S Am 1,2, BI 1,2,3,4, S Am 3,4, F, 1981 NZ 1,2,3, 1982 S Am 1,2
Du Plooy, A J J (EP) 1955 BI 1
Du Preez, F C H (NT) 1961 E, S, A 1,2, 1962 BI 1,2,3,4, 1963 A 1, 1964 W, F, 1965 A 1,2, NZ 1,2,3,4, 1967 F 4, 1968 BI 1,2,3,4, F 1,2, 1969 A 1,2, S, 1970 I, W, NZ 1,2,3,4, 1971 F 1,2, A 1,2,3
Du Preez, G J D (GL) 2002 Sm (R), A 1(R)
Du Preez, J G H (WP) 1956 NZ 1
Du Preez, P F (BB) 2004 I1,2,W1,PI(R),NZ1,A1, NZ2(R),A2(R),W2,I3,E,S,Arg, 2005 U(R),F1,2(R), A1(R),2(R),3,NZ1(R),A4(R), 2006 S1,2,F,A1(R),NZ1, A2,NZ2,3,A3, 2007 Nm,S, [Sm,E1,US,Fj,Arg,E2], 2008 Arg(R),NZ3,A2,3,W3, 2009 BI 1,2,3,NZ1, 2,A1,2,3, NZ3,F,It,I
Du Preez, R J (N) 1992 NZ, A, 1993 F 1,2, A 1,2,3
Du Preez, W H (FS) 2009 It
Du Rand, J A (R, NT) 1949 NZ 2,3, 1951 S, I, W, 1952 E, F, 1953 A 1,2,3,4, 1955 BI 1,2,3,4, 1956 A 1,2, NZ 1,2,3,4
Du Randt, J P (OFS, FS) 1994 Arg 1,2, S, W, 1995 WS, [A, WS, F, NZ], 1996 Fj, A 1, NZ 1, A 2, NZ 2,3,4, 1997 Tg, BI 1,2,3, NZ 1, A 1, NZ 2, A 2, It, F 1,2, E, S, 1999 NZ 1, A 1, NZ 2, A 2, [S, Sp (R), U, E, A 3, NZ 3], 2004 I1,2,W1,PI,NZ1,A1,NZ2,A2, W2,I3,E, S(R),Arg(R), 2005 U(R),F1,A1,NZ1,A4,NZ2, Arg,W(R),F3, 2006 S1,2,F,A1,NZ1,A2, NZ2,3,A3, 2007 Sm,NZ1,Nm,S, [Sm,E1,US,Fj,Arg,E2]
Du Toit, A F (WP) 1928 NZ 3,4
Du Toit, B A (Tvl) 1938 BI 1,2,3
Du Toit, G S (GW, WP) 1998 I 1, 1999 It 1,2, W (R), NZ 1,2, 2004 I1,W1(R),A1(R), S(R),Arg, 2006 S1(R),2(R),F(R)
Du Toit, P A (NT) 1949 NZ 2,3,4, 1951 S, I, W, 1952 E, F
Du Toit, P G (WP) 1981 NZ 1, 1982 S Am 1,2, 1984 E 1,2
Du Toit, P S (WP) 1958 F 1,2, 1960 NZ 1,2,3,4, W, I, 1961 E, S, F, I, A 1,2
Duvenhage, F P (GW) 1949 NZ 1,3
Edwards, P (NT) 1980 S Am 1,2
Ellis, J H (SWA) 1965 NZ 1,2,3,4, 1967 F 1,2,3,4, 1968 BI 1,2,3,4, F 1,2, 1969 A 1,2,3,4, S, 1970 I, W, NZ 1,2,3,4, 1971 F 1,2, A 1,2,3, 1972 E, 1974 BI 1,2,3,4, F 1,2, 1976 NZ 1
Ellis, M C (Tvl) 1921 NZ 2,3, 1924 BI 1,2,3,4
Els, W W (OFS) 1997 A 2(R)
Engelbrecht, J P (WP) 1960 S, W, I, 1961 E, S, F, A 1,2, 1962 BI 2,3,4, 1963 A 2,3, 1964 W, F, 1965 I, S, A 1,2, NZ 1,2,3,4, 1967 F 1,2,3,4, 1968 BI 1,2, F 1,2, 1969 A 1,2
Erasmus, F S (NT, EP) 1986 Cv 3,4, 1989 Wld 2
Erasmus, J C (OFS, GL) 1997 BI 3, A 2, It, F 1,2, S, 1998 I 1,2, W 1, E 1, A 1, NZ 2, A 2, S, W 2, I 3, E 2, 1999 It 1,2, W, A 1, NZ 2, A 2, [S, U, E, A 3, NZ 3], 2000 C, E 1, A 1, NZ 1,2, A 3, 2001 F 1,2
Esterhuizen, G (GL) 2000 NZ 1(R),2, A 3, Arg, I, W (R), E 3(t)
Etlinger, T E (WP) 1896 BI 4
Ferreira, C (OFS) 1986 Cv 1,2
Ferreira, P S (WP) 1984 S Am 1,2
Ferris, H H (Tvl) 1903 BI 3
Fleck R F (WP) 1999 It 1,2, NZ 1(R), A 1, NZ 2(R), A 2, [S, U, E, A 3, NZ 3], 2000 C, E 1,2, A 1, NZ 1, A 2, NZ 2, A 3, Arg, I, W, E 3, 2001 F 1(R),2, It 1, NZ 1, A 1,2, 2002 S, E
Floors, L (FS) 2006 E2
Forbes, H H (Tvl) 1896 BI 2
Fortuin, B A (FS) 2006 I, 2007 A2
Fourie, C (EP) 1974 F 1,2, 1975 F 1,2
Fourie, J (GL, WP) 2003 [U,Gg,Sm(R),NZ(R)], 2004 I2,E(R),S,Arg, 2005 U(R),F2(R), A1(R),2,3,NZ1,A4, NZ2,Arg,W,F3, 2006 S1,A1,NZ1,A2,NZ2,3,A3, 2007 Sm(R),A1, NZ1,Nm,S, [Sm,E1,US,Fj,Arg,E2],W, 2008 Arg(R),W3(R),S(R),E(R), 2009 BI 1(R), 2(R),3,NZ1, 2,A1,2,3,NZ3,F,It,I, 2010 W1,F,It2,NZ1,2,A1,2,3
Fourie, T T (SET) 1974 BI 3
Fourie, W L (SWA) 1958 F 1,2
Francis, J A J (Tvl) 1912 S, I, W, 1913 E, F
Frederickson, C A (Tvl) 1974 BI 2, 1980 S Am 1,2
Frew, A (Tvl) 1903 BI 1
Froneman, D C (OFS) 1977 Wld
Froneman, I L (Bor) 1933 A 1
Fuls, H T (Tvl, EP) 1992 NZ (R), 1993 F 1,2, A 1,2,3, Arg 1,2
Fry, S P (WP) 1951 S, I, W, 1952 E, F, 1953 A 1,2,3,4, 1955 BI 1,2,3,4
Fynn, E E (N) 2001 F 1, It 1(R)
Fyvie, W (N) 1996 NZ 4(t & R), 5(R), Arg 2(R)
Gage, J H (OFS) 1933 A 1
Gainsford, J L (WP) 1960 S, NZ 1,2,3,4, W, I, 1961 E, S, F, A 1,2, 1962 BI 1,2,3,4, 1963 A 1,2,3,4, 1964 W, F, 1965 I, S, A 1,2, NZ 1,2,3,4, 1967 F 1,2,3
Garvey, A C (N) 1996 Arg 1,2, F 1,2, W, 1997 Tg, BI 1,2,3(R), A 1(t), It, F 1,2, E, S, 1998 I 1,2, W 1, E1, A 1, NZ 1,2 A 2, W 2, S, I 3, E 2, 1999 [Sp]
Geel, P J (OFS) 1949 NZ 3
Geere, V (Tvl) 1933 A 1,2,3,4,5
Geffin, A O (Tvl) 1949 NZ 1,2,3,4, 1951 S, I, W
Geldenhuys, A (EP) 1992 NZ, A, F 1,2
Geldenhuys, S B (NT) 1981 NZ 2,3, US, 1982 S Am 1,2, 1989 Wld 1,2
Gentles, T A (WP) 1955 BI 1,2,4, 1956 NZ 2,3, 1958 F 2
Geraghty, E M (Bor) 1949 NZ 4
Gerber, D M (EP, WP) 1980 S Am 3,4, F, 1981 I 1,2, NZ 1,2,3, US, 1982 S Am 1,2, 1984 E 1,2, S Am 1,2, 1986 Cv 1,2,3,4, 1992 NZ, A, F 1,2, E
Gerber, H J (WP) 2003 S 1,2
Gerber, M C (EP) 1958 F 1,2, 1960 S
Gericke, F W (Tvl) 1960 S
Germishuys, J S (OFS, Tvl) 1974 BI 2, 1976 NZ 1,2,3,4, 1977 Wld, 1980 S Am 1,2, BI 1,2,3,4, S Am 3,4, F, 1981 I 1,2, NZ 2,3, US
Gibbs, B (GW) 1903 BI 2
Goosen, C P (OFS) 1965 NZ 2
Gorton, H C (Tvl) 1896 BI 1
Gould, R L (N) 1968 BI 1,2,3,4
Grant, P J (WP) 2007 A2(R),NZ2(R), 2008 W1(t&R), It(R),A1(R)
Gray, B G (WP) 1931 W, 1932 E, S, 1933 A 5
Greeff, W W (WP) 2002 Arg (R), Sm, NZ 1, A 1, NZ 2, A 2, F, S, E, 2003 [U,Gg]
Greenwood, C M (WP) 1961 I
Greyling, P J F (OFS) 1967 F 1,2,3,4, 1968 BI 1, F 1,2, 1969 A 1,2,3,4, S, E, 1970 I, W, NZ 1,2,3,4, 1971 F 1,2, A 1,2,3, 1972 E
Grobler, C J (OFS) 1974 BI 4, 1975 F 1,2

Guthrie, F H (WP) 1891 BI 1,3, 1896 BI 1
Habana, B G (GL, BB, WP) 2004 E(R),S,Arg, 2005 U,F1,2,A1,2,3,NZ1,A4,NZ2, Arg,W,F3, 2006 S2,F,A1,NZ1,A2,NZ2,3, I, E1,2, 2007 E1,2, S, [Sm,E1,Tg(R),US, Fj,Arg,E2], W, 2008 W1,2,It,NZ1,2, A1,NZ3,W3,S,E, 2009 BI 1,2,NZ1,2,A1,2,3,NZ3, F,It,I, 2010 F,It 1,2,NZ1,2,A1,NZ3,A2,3
Hahn, C H L (Tvl) 1910 BI 1,2,3
Hall, D B (GL) 2001 F 1,2, NZ 1, A 1,2, NZ 2, It 2, E, US, 2002 Sm, NZ 1,2, A 2
Halstead, T M (N) 2001 F 3, It 2, E, US (R), 2003 S 1,2
Hamilton, F (EP) 1891 BI 1
Hargreaves, A J (NS) 2010 W1(R),It 1(R)
Harris, T A (Tvl) 1937 NZ 2,3, 1938 BI 1,2,3
Hartley, A J (WP) 1891 BI 3
Hattingh, H (NT) 1992 A (R), F 2(R), E, 1994 Arg 1,2
Hattingh, L B (OFS) 1933 A 2
Heatlie, B H (WP) 1891 BI 2,3, 1896 BI 1,4, 1903 BI 1,3
Hendricks, M (Bol) 1998 I 2(R), W 1(R)
Hendriks, P (Tvl) 1992 NZ, A, 1994 S, W, 1995 [A, R, C], 1996 A 1, NZ 1, A 2, NZ 2,3,4,5
Hepburn, T B (WP) 1896 BI 4
Heunis, J W (NT) 1981 NZ 3(R), US, 1982 S Am 1,2, 1984 E 1,2, S Am 1,2, 1986 Cv 1,2,3,4, 1989 Wld 1,2
Hill, R A (R) 1960 W, I, 1961 I, A 1,2, 1962 BI 4, 1963 A 3
Hills, W G (NT) 1992 F 1,2, E, 1993 F 1,2, A 1
Hirsch, J G (EP) 1906 I, 1910 BI 1
Hobson, T E C (WP) 1903 BI 3
Hoffman, R S (Bol) 1953 A 3
Holton, D N (EP) 1960 S
Honiball, H W (N) 1993 A 3(R), Arg 2, 1995 WS (R), 1996 Fj, A 1, NZ 5, Arg 1,2, F 1,2, W, 1997 Tg, BI 1,2,3(R), NZ 1(R), A 1(R), NZ 2, A 2, It, F 1,2, E, 1998 W 1(R), E 1, A 1, NZ 1,2, A 2, W 2, S, I 3, E 2, 1999 [A 3(R), NZ 3]
Hopwood, D J (WP) 1960 S, NZ 3,4, W, 1961 E, S, F, I, A 1,2, 1962 BI 1,2,3,4, 1963 A 1,2,4, 1964 W, F, 1965 S, NZ 3,4
Hougaard, D J (BB) 2003 [U(R),E(R),Gg,Sm,NZ], 2007 Sm,A2,NZ2
Hougaard, F (BB) 2009 It(R), 2010 A1(R),NZ3,A2,3
Howe, B F (Bor) 1956 NZ 1,4
Howe-Browne, N R F G (WP) 1910 BI 1,2,3
Hugo, D P (WP) 1989 Wld 1,2
Human, D C F (WP) 2002 W 1,2, Arg (R), Sm (R)
Hurter, M H (NT) 1995 [R, C], W, 1996 Fj, A 1, NZ 1,2,3,4,5, 1997 NZ 1,2, A 2
Immelman, J H (WP) 1913 F
Jackson, D C (WP) 1906 I, W, E
Jackson, J S (WP) 1903 BI 2
Jacobs, A A (Falcons, NS) 2001 It 2(R), US, 2002 W 1(R), Arg, Sm (R), NZ 1(t+R), A 1(R), F, S, E (R), 2008 W1,2,NZ1,2,Arg,NZ3,A2,3,W3,S,E, 2009 BI 1,2,NZ2(R),A1(R), 2(R),3(R),NZ3(R),F,It
James, A D (N, Bath) 2001 F 1,2, NZ 1, A 1,2, NZ 2, 2002 F (R), S, E, 2006 NZ1,A2,NZ2,3(R),E1, 2007 E1,2,A1,NZ1,Nm,S, [Sm,E1,US,Fj,Arg,E2], 2008 W1,2,NZ1,2,A1,Arg,NZ3,A2,3, 2010 It1,2(R),NZ1(R), A1(R),2(R)
Jansen, E (OFS) 1981 NZ 1
Jansen, J S (OFS) 1970 NZ 1,2,3,4, 1971 F 1,2, A 1,2,3, 1972 E
Jantjes, C A (GL, WP) 2001 It 1, A 1,2, NZ 2, F 3, It 2, E, US, 2005 Arg,W, 2007 W(R), 2008 W1,2,It,NZ1,2(R),A1,Arg,NZ3(R),A2,3,W3,S,E
Januarie, E R (GL, WP) 2005 U,F2,A1,2,3(R),NZ1,A4, NZ2, 2006 S1(R),2(R),F(R),A1, I,E1,2, 2007 E1,2,Sm, Nm(R), [Sm(R),Tg], W, 2008 W2,It,NZ1,2,A1,Arg, NZ3(R),A2(R), 3(R),W3(R),S,E, 2009 BI 1(R),NZ1(R), 2(R),A1(R),2(R),NZ3(R), 2010 W1,F,It 1,2,NZ1, 2,3(R)
Jennings, C B (Bor) 1937 NZ 1
Johnson, G K (Tvl) 1993 Arg 2, 1994 NZ 3, Arg 1, 1995 WS, [R, C, WS]
Johnstone, P G A (WP) 1951 S, I, W, 1952 E, F, 1956 A 1, NZ 1,2,4
Jones, C H (Tvl) 1903 BI 1,2
Jones, P S T (WP) 1896 BI 1,3,4
Jordaan, N (BB) 2002 E (R)
Jordaan, R P (NT) 1949 NZ 1,2,3,4
Joubert, A J (OFS, N) 1989 Wld 1(R), 1993 A 3, Arg 1, 1994 E 1,2, NZ 1,2(R), 3, Arg 2, S, W, 1995 [A, C, WS, F, NZ], W, It, E, 1996 Fj, A 1, NZ 1,3,4,5, Arg 1,2, F 1,2, W, 1997 Tg, BI 1,2, A 2
Joubert, M C (Bol, WP) 2001 NZ 1, 2002 W 1,2, Arg (R), Sm, NZ 1, A1, NZ 2, A 2, F (R), 2003 S 2, Arg, A 1, 2004 I1,2,W1,PI,NZ1,A1,NZ2,A2,W2,I3,E,S,Arg, 2005 U,F1,2, A1
Joubert, S J (WP) 1906 I, W, E
Julies, W (Bol, SWD, GL) 1999 [Sp], 2004 I1,2,W1, S,Arg, 2005 A2(R),3(t), 2006 F(R), 2007 Sm, [Tg]
Kahts, W J H (NT) 1980 BI 1,2,3, S Am 3,4, F, 1981 I 1,2, NZ 2, 1982 S Am 1,2
Kaminer, J (Tvl) 1958 F 2
Kankowski, R (NS) 2007 W, 2008 W2(R),It,A1(R), W3(R),S(R),E(R), 2009 BI3, NZ3(R),F,It, 2010 W1(R),It 1(R) ,NZ2(R),A1,3(R)
Kayser, D J (EP, N) 1999 It 2(R), A 1(R), NZ 2, A 2, [S, Sp (R), U, E, A 3], 2001 It 1(R), NZ 1(R), A 2(R), NZ 2(R)
Kebble, G R (N) 1993 Arg 1,2, 1994 NZ 1(R), 2
Kelly, E W (GW) 1896 BI 3
Kempson, R B (N, WP, Ulster) 1998 I 2(R), W 1, E 1, A 1, NZ 1,2 A 2, W 2, S, I 3, E 2, 1999 It 1,2, W, 2000 C, E 1,2, A 1, NZ 1, A 2,3, Arg, I, W, E 3, 2001 F 1,2(R), NZ 1, A 1,2, NZ 2, 2003 S 1(R),2(R), Arg, A 1(R), NZ 1(R), A 2
Kenyon, B J (Bor) 1949 NZ 4
Kipling, H G (GW) 1931 W, I, 1932 E, S, 1933 A 1,2,3,4,5
Kirchner, Z (BB) 2009 BI 3,F,It,I, 2010 W1(R),F,It1, NZ1,2,A1
Kirkpatrick, A I (GW) 1953 A 2, 1956 NZ 2, 1958 F 1, 1960 S, NZ 1,2,3,4, W, I, 1961 E, S, F
Knight, A S (Tvl) 1912 S, I, W, 1913 E, F
Knoetze, F (WP) 1989 Wld 1,2
Koch, A C (Bol) 1949 NZ 2,3,4, 1951 S, I, W, 1952 E, F, 1953 A 1,2,4, 1955 BI 1,2,3,4, 1956 A 1, NZ 2,3, 1958 F 1,2, 1960 NZ 1,2
Koch, H V (WP) 1949 NZ 1,2,3,4
Koen, L J (GL, BB) 2000 A 1, 2001 It 2, E, US, 2003 S 1,2, Arg, A 1, NZ 1, A 2, NZ 2, [U,E,Sm(R),NZ(R)]
Kotze, G J M (WP) 1967 F 1,2,3,4
Krantz, E F W (OFS) 1976 NZ 1, 1981 I 1,
Krige, C P J (WP) 1999 It 2, W, NZ 1, 2000 C (R), E 1(R),2, A 1(R), NZ 1, A 2, NZ 2, A 3, Arg, I, W, E 3, 2001 F 1,2, It 1(R), A 1(t+R), It 2(R), E (R), 2002 W 2, Arg, Sm, NZ 1, A 1, NZ 2, A 2, F, S, E, 2003 Arg, A 1, NZ 1, A 2, NZ 2, [E,Sm,NZ]
Krige, J D (WP) 1903 BI 1,3, 1906 S, I, W
Kritzinger, J L (Tvl) 1974 BI 3,4, F 1,2, 1975 F 1,2, 1976 NZ 4
Kroon, C M (EP) 1955 BI 1
Kruger, P E (Tvl) 1986 Cv 3,4
Kruger, R J (NT, BB) 1993 Arg 1,2, 1994 S, W, 1995 WS, [A, R, WS, F, NZ], W, It, E, 1996 Fj, A 1, NZ 1, A 2, NZ 2,3,4,5, Arg 1,2, F 1,2, W, 1997 Tg, BI 1,2, NZ 1, A 1, NZ 2, 1999 NZ 2, A 2(R), [Sp, NZ 3(R)]
Kruger, T L (Tvl) 1921 NZ 1,2, 1924 BI 1,2,3,4, 1928 NZ 1,2
Kuhn, S P (Tvl) 1960 NZ 3,4, W, I, 1961 E, S, F, I, A 1,2, 1962 BI 1,2,3,4, 1963 A 1,2,3, 1965 I, S
Labuschagne, J J (GL) 2000 NZ 1(R), 2002 W 1,2, Arg, NZ 1, A 1, NZ 2, A2, F, S, E
La Grange, J B (WP) 1924 BI 3,4
Larard, A (Tvl) 1896 BI 2,4
Lategan, M T (WP) 1949 NZ 1,2,3,4, 1951 S, I, W, 1952 E, F, 1953 A 1,2
Laubscher, T G (WP) 1994 Arg 1,2, S, W, 1995 It, E
Lawless, M J (WP) 1964 F, 1969 E (R), 1970 I, W

Ledger, S H (GW) 1912 S, I, 1913 E, F
Leonard, A (WP, SWD) 1999 A 1, [Sp]
Le Roux, A H (OFS, N) 1994 E 1, 1998 I 1,2, W 1(R), E 1(R), A 1(R), NZ 1(R),2(R), A 2(R), W 2(R), S (R), I 3(R), E 2(t+R), 1999 It 1(R),2(R), W (R), NZ 1(R), A 1(R), NZ 2(R), A 2(R), [S(R), Sp, U (R), E (R), A 3(R), NZ 3(R)], 2000 E 1(t+R),2(R), A 1(R),2(R), NZ 2, A 3(R), Arg (R), I (t), W (R), E 3(R), 2001 F 1(R),2, It 1, NZ 1(R), A 1(R),2(R), NZ 2(R), F 3, It 2, E, US (R), 2002 W 1(R),2(R), Arg, NZ 1(R), A 1(R), NZ 2(R), A 2(R)
Le Roux, H P (Tvl) 1993 F 1,2, 1994 E 1,2, NZ 1,2,3, Arg 2, S, W, 1995 WS [A, R, C (R), WS, F, NZ], W, It, E, 1996 Fj, NZ 2, Arg 1,2, F 1,2, W
Le Roux, J H S (Tvl) 1994 E 2, NZ 1,2
Le Roux, M (OFS) 1980 BI 1,2,3,4, S Am 3,4, F, 1981 I 1
Le Roux, P A (WP) 1906 I, W, E
Little, E M (GW) 1891 BI 1,3
Lobberts, H (BB) 2006 E1(R), 2007 NZ2(R)
Lochner, G P (WP) 1955 BI 3, 1956 A 1,2, NZ 1,2,3,4, 1958 F 1,2
Lochner, G P (EP) 1937 NZ 3, 1938 BI 1,2
Lockyear, R J (GW) 1960 NZ 1,2,3,4, 1960 I, 1961 F
Lombard, A C (EP) 1910 BI 2
Lombard, F (FS) 2002 S, E
Lötter, D (Tvl) 1993 F 2, A 1,2
Lotz, J W (Tvl) 1937 A 1,2, NZ 1,2,3, 1938 BI 1,2,3
Loubscher, R I P (EP, N) 2002 W 1, 2003 S 1, [U(R),Gg]
Loubser, J A (WP) 1903 BI 3, 1906 S, I, W, E, 1910 BI 1,3
Lourens, M J (NT) 1968 BI 2,3,4
Louw, F H (WP) 2002 W 2(R), Arg, Sm
Louw, J S (Tvl) 1891 BI 1,2,3
Louw, L-F P (WP) 2010 W1,F,It 1,2,NZ1,2,3(R)
Louw, M J (Tvl) 1971 A 2,3
Louw, M M (WP) 1928 NZ 3,4, 1931 W, I, 1932 E, S, 1933 A 1,2,3,4,5, 1937 A 1,2, NZ 2,3, 1938 BI 1,2,3
Louw, R J (WP) 1980 S Am 1,2, BI 1,2,3,4 S Am 3,4, F, 1981 I 1,2, NZ 1,3, 1982 S Am 1,2, 1984 E 1,2, S Am 1,2
Louw, S C (WP) 1933 A 1,2,3,4,5, 1937 A 1, NZ 1,2,3, 1938 BI 1,2,3
Lubbe, E (GW) 1997 Tg, BI 1
Luyt, F P (WP) 1910 BI 1,2,3, 1912 S, I, W, 1913 E
Luyt, J D (EP) 1912 S, W, 1913 E, F
Luyt, R R (W P) 1910 BI 2,3, 1912 S, I, W, 1913 E, F
Lyons, D J (EP) 1896 BI 1
Lyster, P J (N) 1933 A 2,5, 1937 NZ 1
McCallum, I D (WP) 1970 NZ 1,2,3,4, 1971 F 1,2, A 1,2,3, 1974 BI 1,2
McCallum, R J (WP) 1974 BI 1
McCulloch, J D (GW) 1913 E, F
MacDonald, A W (R) 1965 A 1, NZ 1,2,3,4
Macdonald, D A (WP) 1974 BI 2
Macdonald, I (Tvl) 1992 NZ, A, 1993 F 1, A 3, 1994 E 2, 1995 WS (R)
McDonald, J A J (WP) 1931 W, I, 1932 E, S
McEwan, W M C (Tvl) 1903 BI 1,3
McHardy, E E (OFS) 1912 S, I, W, 1913 E, F
McKendrick, J A (WP) 1891 BI 3
Maku, B G (BB) 2010 It1(R)
Malan, A S (Tvl) 1960 NZ 1,2,3,4, W, I, 1961 E, S, F, 1962 BI 1, 1963 A 1,2,3, 1964 W, 1965 I, S
Malan, A W (NT) 1989 Wld 1,2, 1992 NZ, A, F 1,2, E
Malan, E (NT) 1980 BI 3(R), 4
Malan, G F (WP) 1958 F 2, 1960 NZ 1,3,4, 1961 E, S, F, 1962 BI 1,2,3, 1963 A 1,2,4, 1964 W, 1965 A 1,2, NZ 1,2
Malan, P (Tvl) 1949 NZ 4
Mallett, N V H (WP) 1984 S Am 1,2
Malotana, K (Bor) 1999 [Sp]
Mans, W J (WP) 1965 I, S
Marais, C F (WP) 1999 It 1(R),2(R), 2000 C, E 1,2, A 1, NZ 1, A 2, NZ 2, A 3, Arg (R), W (R)
Marais, F P (Bol) 1949 NZ 1,2, 1951 S, 1953 A 1,2
Marais, J F K (WP) 1963 A 3, 1964 W, F, 1965 I, S, A 2, 1968 BI, 1,2,3,4, F 1,2, 1969 A 1,2,3,4, S, E, 1970 I, W, NZ 1,2,3,4, 1971 F 1,2, A 1,2,3, 1974 BI 1,2,3,4, F 1,2
Maré, D S (Tvl) 1906 S
Marsberg, A F W (GW) 1906 S, W, E
Marsberg, P A (GW) 1910 BI 1
Martheze, W C (GW) 1903 BI 2, 1906 I, W
Martin, H J (Tvl) 1937 A 2
Matfield, V (BB) 2001 It 1(R), NZ 1, A 2, NZ 2, F 3, It 2, E, US, 2002 W 1, Sm, NZ 1, A 1, NZ 2(R), 2003 S 1,2, Arg, A 1, NZ 1, A 2, NZ 2, [U,E,Sm,NZ], 2004 I1,2,W1,NZ2, A2,W2,I3,E,S,Arg, 2005 F1,2,A1,2,3, NZ1,A4,NZ2,Arg,W,F3, 2006 S1,2,F,A1,NZ1,A2, NZ2,3,A3, 2007 E1,2,A1,NZ1,Nm,S, [Sm,E1,Tg(R), US,Fj,Arg,E2], 2008 W1(R),2,It, NZ1,2,A1,Arg,NZ3, A2,3,W3,S,E, 2009 BI 1,2,3,NZ1,2,A1,2,3,NZ3, F,It(R),I, 2010 W1, F,It 1,NZ1,2,A1,NZ3,A2,3
Mellet, T B (GW) 1896 BI 2
Mellish, F W (WP) 1921 NZ 1,3, 1924 BI 1,2,3,4
Mentz, H (N) 2004 I1,W1(R)
Merry, J (EP) 1891 BI 1
Metcalf, H D (Bor) 1903 BI 2
Meyer, C du P (WP) 1921 NZ 1,2,3
Meyer, P J (GW) 1896 BI 1
Meyer, W (OFS, GL) 1997 S (R), 1999 It 2, NZ 1(R), A 1(R), 2000 C (R), E 1, NZ 1(R),2(R), Arg, I, W, E 3, 2001 F 1(R),2, It 1, F 3(R), It 2, E, US (t+R), 2002 W 1,2, Arg, NZ 1,2, A 2, F
Michau, J M (Tvl) 1921 NZ 1
Michau, J P (WP) 1921 NZ 1,2,3
Millar, W A (WP) 1906 E, 1910 BI 2,3, 1912 I, W, 1913 F
Mills, W J (WP) 1910 BI 2
Moll, T (Tvl) 1910 BI 2
Montini, P E (WP) 1956 A 1,2
Montgomery, P C (WP, Newport, N, Perpignan) 1997 BI 2,3, NZ 1, A 1, NZ 2, A 2, F 1,2, E, S, 1998 I 1,2, W 1, E 1, A 1, NZ 1,2, A 2, W 2, S, I 3, E 2, 1999 It 1,2, W, NZ 1, A 1, NZ 2, A 2, [S, U, E, A 3, NZ 3], 2000 C, E 1,2, A 1, NZ 1, A 2(R), Arg, I, W, E 3, 2001 F 1, 2(t), It 1, NZ 1, F 3(R), It 2(R), 2004 I2,W1,PI,NZ1,A1,NZ2,A2,W2,I3,E,S, 2005 U,F1,2,A1, 2,3,NZ1,A4,NZ2,Arg,W,F3, 2006 S1,2,F,A1,NZ1,A2, NZ2, 2007 E1,2,Sm(R),A1,NZ1,Nm,S, [Sm,E1,Tg(R), US,Fj,Arg,E2], 2008 W1(R),2(R),NZ1(R),2, Arg(R),NZ3, A2(R),3(R)
Moolman, L C (NT) 1977 Wld, 1980 S Am 1,2, BI 1,2,3,4, S Am 3,4, F, 1981 I 1,2, NZ 1,2,3, US, 1982 S Am 1,2, 1984 S Am 1,2, 1986 Cv 1,2,3,4
Mordt, R H (Z-R, NT) 1980 S Am 1,2, BI 1,2,3,4, S Am 3,4, F, 1981 I 2, NZ 1,2,3, US, 1982 S Am 1,2, 1984 S Am 1,2
Morkel, D A (Tvl) 1903 BI 1
Morkel, D F T (Tvl) 1906 I, E, 1910 BI 1,3, 1912 S, I, W, 1913 E, F
Morkel, H J (WP) 1921 NZ 1
Morkel, H W (WP) 1921 NZ 1,2
Morkel, J A (WP) 1921 NZ 2,3
Morkel, J W H (WP) 1912 S, I, W, 1913 E, F
Morkel, P G (WP) 1912 S, I, W, 1913 E, F, 1921 NZ 1,2,3
Morkel, P K (WP) 1928 NZ 4
Morkel, W H (WP) 1910 BI 3, 1912 S, I, W, 1913 E, F, 1921 NZ 1,2,3
Morkel, W S (Tvl) 1906 S, I, W, E
Moss, C (N) 1949 NZ 1,2,3,4
Mostert, P J (WP) 1921 NZ 1,2,3, 1924 BI 1,2,4, 1928 NZ 1,2,3,4, 1931 W, I, 1932 E, S
Mtawarira, T (NS) 2008 W2,It,A1(R),Arg,NZ3,A2,3,W3,S,E, 2009 BI 1,2,3,NZ1,2,A1, 2,3,NZ3,F,It(R),I
Muir, D J (WP) 1997 It, F 1,2, E, S
Mujati, B V (WP) 2008 W1,It(R),NZ1(R),2(t),A1(R),Arg(R),NZ3(R),A2(R),3, W3(t), S(R),E(R)
Mulder, J C (Tvl, GL) 1994 NZ 2,3, S, W, 1995 WS,

[A, WS, F, NZ], W, It, E, 1996 Fj, A 1, NZ 1, A 2, NZ 2,5, Arg 1,2, F 1,2, W, 1997 Tg, BI 1, 1999 It 1(R),2, W, NZ 1, 2000 C(R), A 1, E 3, 2001 F 1, It 1
Muller, G H (WP) 1969 A 3,4, S, 1970 W, NZ 1,2,3,4, 1971 F 1,2, 1972 E, 1974 BI 1,3,4
Muller, G J (NS) 2006 S1(R),NZ1(R),A2,NZ2,3,A3, I(R),E1,2, 2007 E1(R),2(R),Sm(R), A1(R),NZ1(R),A2, NZ2,Nm(R), [Sm(R),E1(R),Fj(t&R),Arg(t&R)],W, 2009 BI 3
Muller, G P (GL) 2003 A 2, NZ 2, [E,Gg(R),Sm,NZ]
Muller, H L (OFS) 1986 Cv 4(R), 1989 Wld 1(R)
Muller, H S V (Tvl) 1949 NZ 1,2,3,4, 1951 S, I, W, 1952 E, F, 1953 A 1,2,3,4
Muller, L J J (N) 1992 NZ, A
Muller, P G (N) 1992 NZ, A, F 1,2, E, 1993 F 1,2, A 1,2,3, Arg 1,2, 1994 E 1,2, NZ 1, S, W, 1998 I 1,2, W 1, E 1, A 1, NZ 1,2, A 2, 1999 It 1, W, NZ 1, A 1, [Sp, E, A 3, NZ 3]
Murray, W M (N) 2007 Sm,A2,NZ2
Myburgh, F R (EP) 1896 BI 1
Myburgh, J L (NT) 1962 BI 1, 1963 A 4, 1964 W, F, 1968 BI 1,2,3, F 1,2, 1969 A 1,2,3,4, E, 1970 I, W, NZ 3,4
Myburgh, W H (WT) 1924 BI 1
Naude, J P (WP) 1963 A 4, 1965 A 1,2, NZ 1,3,4, 1967 F 1,2,3,4, 1968 BI 1,2,3,4
Ndungane, A Z (BB) 2006 A1,2,NZ2,3,A3, E1,2, 2007 E2,Nm(R), [US],W(R)
Ndungane, O M (NS) 2008 It,NZ1,A3, 2009 BI 3,A3,NZ3, 2010 W1
Neethling, J B (WP) 1967 F 1,2,3,4, 1968 BI 4, 1969 S, 1970 NZ 1,2
Nel, J A (Tvl) 1960 NZ 1,2, 1963 A 1,2, 1965 A 2, NZ 1,2,3,4, 1970 NZ 3,4
Nel, J J (WP) 1956 A 1,2, NZ 1,2,3,4, 1958 F 1,2
Nel, P A R O (Tvl) 1903 BI 1,2,3
Nel, P J (N) 1928 NZ 1,2,3,4, 1931 W, I, 1932 E, S, 1933 A 1,3,4,5, 1937 A 1,2, NZ 2,3
Nimb, C F (WP) 1961 I
Nokwe, J L (FS) 2008 Arg,A2,3, 2009 BI 3
Nomis, S H (Tvl) 1967 F 4, 1968 BI 1,2,3,4, F 1,2, 1969 A 1,2,3,4, S, E, 1970 I, W, NZ 1,2,3,4, 1971 F 1,2, A 1,2,3, 1972 E
Nykamp, J L (Tvl) 1933 A 2
Ochse, J K (WP) 1951 I, W, 1952 E, F, 1953 A 1,2,4
Oelofse, J S A (Tvl) 1953 A 1,2,3,4
Oliver, J F (Tvl) 1928 NZ 3,4
Olivier, E (WP) 1967 F 1,2,3,4, 1968 BI 1,2,3,4, F 1,2, 1969 A 1,2,3,4, S, E
Olivier, J (NT) 1992 F 1,2, E, 1993 F 1,2 A 1,2,3, Arg 1, 1995 W, It (R), E, 1996 Arg 1,2, F 1,2, W
Olivier, W (BB) 2006 S1(R),2,F,A1,NZ1,A2,NZ2(R),3,A3, I(R), E1,2, 2007 E1,2,NZ1(R),A2,NZ2, [E1(R),Tg, Arg(R)],W(R), 2009 BI 3,NZ1(R),2(R),F(R),It(R),I, 2010 F,It2(R) ,NZ1,2,A1
Olver, E (EP) 1896 BI 1
Oosthuizen, J J (WP) 1974 BI 1, F 1,2, 1975 F 1,2, 1976 NZ 1,2,3,4
Oosthuizen, O W (NT, Tvl) 1981 I 1(R), 2, NZ 2,3, US, 1982 S Am 1,2, 1984 E 1,2
Osler, B L (WP) 1924 BI 1,2,3,4, 1928 NZ 1,2,3,4, 1931 W, I, 1932 E, S, 1933 A 1,2,3,4,5
Osler, S G (WP) 1928 NZ 1
Otto, K (NT, BB) 1995 [R, C (R), WS (R)], 1997 BI 3, NZ 1, A 1, NZ 2, It, F 1,2, E, S, 1998 I 1,2, W 1, E 1, A 1, NZ 1,2, A 2, W 2, S, I 3, E 2, 1999 It 1, W, NZ 1, A 1, [S (R), Sp, U, E, A 3, NZ 3], 2000 C, E 1,2, A 1
Oxlee, K (N) 1960 NZ 1,2,3,4, W, I, 1961 S, A 1,2, 1962 BI 1,2,3,4, 1963 A 1,2,4, 1964 W, 1965 NZ 1,2
Pagel, G L (WP) 1995 [A (R), R, C, NZ (R)], 1996 NZ 5(R)
Parker, W H (EP) 1965 A 1,2
Partridge, J E C (Tvl) 1903 BI 1
Paulse, B J (WP) 1999 It 1,2, NZ 1, A 1,2(R), [S (R), Sp, NZ 3], 2000 C, E 1,2, A 1, NZ 1, A 2, NZ 2, A 3, Arg, W, E 3, 2001 F 1,2, It 1, NZ 1, A 1,2, NZ 2, F 3, It 2, E, 2002 W 1,2, Arg, Sm (R), A 1, NZ 2, A 2, F, S, E, 2003 [Gg], 2004 I1,2,W1,PI,NZ1,A1, NZ2,A2,W2,I3,E, 2005 A2,3,NZ1,A4,F3, 2006 S1,2,A1(R),NZ1,3(R),A3(R), 2007 A2,NZ2
Payn, C (N) 1924 BI 1,2
Pelser, H J M (Tvl) 1958 F 1, 1960 NZ 1,2,3,4, W, I, 1961 F, I, A 1,2
Pfaff, B D (WP) 1956 A 1
Pickard, J A J (WP) 1953 A 3,4, 1956 NZ 2, 1958 F 2
Pienaar, J F (Tvl) 1993 F 1,2, A 1,2,3, Arg 1,2, 1994 E 1,2, NZ 2,3, Arg 1,2, S, W, 1995 WS, [A, C, WS, F, NZ], W, It, E, 1996 Fj, A 1, NZ 1, A 2, NZ 2
Pienaar, R (NS) 2006 NZ2(R),3(R),A3(R), I(t), E1(R), 2007 E1(R),2(R),Sm(R),A1, NZ1,A2,NZ2,Nm(R),S(R), [E1(t&R),Tg,US(R),Arg(R)],W, 2008 W1(R),It(R),NZ2(R), A1(R),3(R),W3,S,E, 2009 BI 1,2,3(R),NZ1,A1(R),2,3, It(R),I(R), 2010 W1,F(R),It 1(R), 2(R),NZ1(R),2(R),A1
Pienaar, Z M J (OFS) 1980 S Am 2(R), BI 1,2,3,4, S Am 3,4, F, 1981 I 1,2, NZ 1,2,3
Pietersen, J-P R (NS) 2006 A3, 2007 Sm,A1,NZ1,A2, NZ2,Nm,S, [Sm,E1,Tg,US(R),Fj, Arg,E2],W, 2008 NZ2,A1,Arg,NZ3,A2,W3,S,E, 2009 BI 1,2,NZ1,2,A1, 2,F,It,I, 2010 NZ3,A2,3
Pitzer, G (NT) 1967 F 1,2,3,4, 1968 BI 1,2,3,4, F 1,2, 1969 A 3,4
Pope, C F (WP) 1974 BI 1,2,3,4, 1975 F 1,2, 1976 NZ 2,3,4
Potgieter, D J (BB) 2009 I(t), 2010 W1,F(t&R),It 1,2(R),A1(R)
Potgieter, H J (OFS) 1928 NZ 1,2
Potgieter, H L (OFS) 1977 Wld
Powell, A W (GW) 1896 BI 3
Powell, J M (GW) 1891 BI 2, 1896 BI 3, 1903 BI 1,2
Prentis, R B (Tvl) 1980 S Am 1,2, BI 1,2,3,4, S Am 3,4, F, 1981 I 1,2
Pretorius, A S (GL) 2002 W 1,2, Arg, Sm, NZ 1, A 1, NZ 2, F, S (R), E, 2003 NZ 1(R), A 1, 2005 A2,3, NZ1,A4,NZ2,Arg, 2006 NZ2(R),3,A3, I, E1(t&R),2, 2007 S(R), [Sm(R), E1(R),Tg,US(R),Arg(R)],W
Pretorius, J C (GL) 2006 I, 2007 NZ2
Pretorius, N F (Tvl) 1928 NZ 1,2,3,4
Prinsloo, J (Tvl) 1958 F 1,2
Prinsloo, J (NT) 1963 A 3
Prinsloo, J P (Tvl) 1928 NZ 1
Putter, D J (WT) 1963 A 1,2,4
Raaff, J W E (GW) 1903 BI 1,2, 1906 S, W, E, 1910 BI 1
Ralepelle, M C (BB) 2006 NZ2(R), E2(R), 2008 E(t&R), 2009 BI 3,NZ1(R),2(R), A2(R),NZ3(R), 2010 W1(R),F(R),It 1,2(R) ,NZ1(R),2(R),A1(R),2(R),3(R)
Ras, W J de Wet (OFS) 1976 NZ 1(R), 1980 S Am 2(R)
Rautenbach, S J (WP) 2002 W 1(R),2(t+R), Arg (R), Sm, NZ 1(R), A 1, NZ 2(R), A 2(R), 2003 [U(R),Gg,Sm,NZ], 2004 W1,NZ1(R)
Reece-Edwards, H (N) 1992 F 1,2, 1993 A 2
Reid, A (WP) 1903 BI 3
Reid, B C (Bor) 1933 A 4
Reinach, J (OFS) 1986 Cv 1,2,3,4
Rens, I J (Tvl) 1953 A 3,4
Retief, D F (NT) 1955 BI 1,2,4, 1956 A 1,2, NZ 1,2,3,4
Reyneke, H J (WP) 1910 BI 3
Richards, A R (WP) 1891 BI 1,2,3
Richter, A (NT) 1992 F 1,2, E, 1994 E 2, NZ 1,2,3, 1995 [R, C, WS (R)]
Riley, N M (ET) 1963 A 3
Riordan, C A (Tvl) 1910 BI 1,2
Robertson, I W (R) 1974 F 1,2, 1976 NZ 1,2,4
Rodgers, P H (NT, Tvl) 1989 Wld 1,2, 1992 NZ, F 1,2
Rogers, C D (Tvl) 1984 E 1,2, S Am 1,2
Roos, G D (WP) 1910 BI 2,3
Roos, P J (WP) 1903 BI 3, 1906 I, W, E
Rosenberg, W (Tvl) 1955 BI 2,3,4, 1956 NZ 3, 1958 F 1
Rossouw, C L C (Tvl, N) 1995 WS, [R, WS, F, NZ], 1999 NZ 2(R), A 2(t), [Sp, NZ 3(R)]
Rossouw, D H (WP) 1953 A 3, 4
Rossouw, D J (BB) 2003 [U,Gg,Sm(R),NZ], 2004

E(R),S,Arg, 2005 U,F1,2,A1,W(R), F3(R), 2006 S1,2, F,A1,I,E1,2, 2007 E1,Sm,A1(R),NZ1,S, [Sm,E1,Tg,Fj, Arg,E2], 2008 W1(t&R),NZ3(R),A3(R),S(R),E, 2009 BI 1(R),2(R),NZ1(R),2(R),A1(R),3(R),NZ3(R), F(R),It,I, 2010 W1,F,NZ1(R),2,A1,NZ3(t&R),A2(R),3

Rossouw, P W G (WP) 1997 BI 2,3, NZ 1, A 1, NZ 2(R), A 2(R), It, F 1,2, E, S, 1998 I 1,2, W 1, E 1, A 1, NZ 1,2, A 2, W 2, S, I 3, E 2, 1999 It 1, W, NZ 1, A 1(R), NZ 2, A 2, [S, U, E, A 3], 2000 C, E 1,2, A 2, Arg (R), I, W, 2001 F 3, US, 2003 Arg

Rousseau, W P (WP) 1928 NZ 3,4

Roux, F du T (WP) 1960 W, 1961 A 1,2, 1962 BI 1,2,3,4, 1963 A 2, 1965 A 1,2, NZ 1,2,3,4, 1968 BI 3,4, F 1,2 1969 A 1,2,3,4, 1970 I, NZ 1,2,3,4

Roux, J P (Tvl) 1994 E 2, NZ 1,2,3, Arg 1, 1995 [R, C, F (R)], 1996 A 1(R), NZ 1, A 2, NZ 3

Roux, O A (NT) 1969 S, E, 1970 I, W, 1972 E, 1974 BI 3,4

Roux, W G (BB) 2002 F (R), S, E

Russell, R B (MP, N) 2002 W 1(R),2, Arg, A 1(R), NZ 2(R), A 2, F, E (R), 2003 Arg (R), A 1(R), NZ 1, A 2(R), 2004 I2(t&R),W1,NZ1(R),W2(R),Arg(R), 2005 U(R),F2(R), A1(t),Arg(R),W(R), 2006 F

Samuels, T A (GW) 1896 BI 2,3,4

Santon, D (Bol) 2003 A 1(R), NZ 1(R), A 2(t), [Gg(R)]

Sauermann, J T (Tvl) 1971 F 1,2, A 1, 1972 E, 1974 BI 1

Schlebusch, J J J (OFS) 1974 BI 3,4, 1975 F 2

Schmidt, L U (NT) 1958 F 2, 1962 BI 2

Schmidt, U L (NT, Tvl) 1986 Cv 1,2,3,4, 1989 Wld 1,2, 1992 NZ, A, 1993 F 1,2, A 1,2,3, 1994 Arg 1,2, S, W

Schoeman, J (WP) 1963 A 3,4, 1965 I, S, A 1, NZ 1,2

Scholtz, C P (WP, Tvl) 1994 Arg 1, 1995 [R, C, WS]

Scholtz, H (FS) 2002 A 1(R), NZ 2(R), A 2(R), 2003 [U(R),Gg]

Scholtz, H H (WP) 1921 NZ 1,2

Schutte, P J W (Tvl) 1994 S, W

Scott, P A (Tvl) 1896 BI 1,2,3,4

Sendin, W D (GW) 1921 NZ 2

Sephaka, L D (GL) 2001 US, 2002 Sm, NZ 1, A 1, NZ 2, A 2, F, 2003 S 1,2, A 1, NZ 1, A 2(t+R), NZ 2, [U,E(t&R),Gg], 2005 F2,A1,2(R),W, 2006 S1(R),NZ3(t&R),A3(R), I

Serfontein, D J (WP) 1980 BI 1,2,3,4, S Am 3,4, F, 1981 I 1,2, NZ 1,2,3, US, 1982 S Am 1,2, 1984 E 1,2, S Am 1,2

Shand, R (GW) 1891 BI 2,3

Sheriff, A R (Tvl) 1938 BI 1,2,3

Shimange, M H (FS, WP) 2004 W1(R),NZ2(R),A2(R), W2(R), 2005 U(R),A1(R),2(R),Arg(R), 2006 S1(R)

Shum, E H (Tvl) 1913 E

Sinclair, D J (Tvl) 1955 BI 1,2,3,4

Sinclair, J H (Tvl) 1903 BI 1

Skene, A L (WP) 1958 F 2

Skinstad, R B (WP, GL, N) 1997 E (t), 1998 W 1(R), E 1(t), NZ 1(R),2(R), A 2(R), W 2(R), S, I 3, E 2, 1999 [S, Sp (R), U, E, A 3], 2001 F 1(R),2(R), It 1, NZ 1, A 1,2, NZ 2, F 3, It 2, E, 2002 W 1,2, Arg, Sm, NZ 1, A 1, NZ 2, A 2, 2003 Arg (R), 2007 E2(t&R),Sm,NZ1, A2, [E1(R),Tg,US(R),Arg(R)]

Slater, J T (EP) 1924 BI 3,4, 1928 NZ 1

Smal, G P (WP) 1986 Cv 1,2,3,4, 1989 Wld 1,2

Small, J T (Tvl, N, WP) 1992 NZ, A, F 1,2, E, 1993 F 1,2, A 1,2,3, Arg 1,2, 1994 E 1,2, NZ 1,2,3(t), Arg 1, 1995 WS, [A, R, F, NZ], W, It, E (R), 1996 Fj, A 1, NZ 1, A 2, NZ 2, Arg 1,2, F 1,2, W, 1997 Tg, BI 1, NZ 1(R), A 1(R), NZ 2, A 2, It, F 1,2, E, S

Smit, F C (WP) 1992 E

Smit, J W (NS, Clermont-Auvergne) 2000 C (t), A 1(R), NZ 1(t+R), A 2(R), NZ 2(R), A 3(R), Arg, I, W, E 3, 2001 F 1,2, It 1, NZ 1(R), A 1(R),2(R), NZ 2(R), F 3(R), It 2, E, US (R), 2003 [U(R),E(t&R),Gg,Sm,NZ], 2004 I1,2,W1,PI,NZ1,A1,NZ2,A2,W2,I3,E,S,Arg, 2005 U,F1,2,A1,2,3,NZ1,A4,NZ2,Arg,W,F3, 2006 S1,2, F,A1,NZ1,A2,NZ2,3,A3, I, E1,2, 2007 E1,2,Sm,A1, [Sm,E1,Tg(R),US,Fj,Arg,E2],W, 2008 W1,2,NZ1, W3,S,E, 2009 BI 1,2,3,NZ1,2,A1,2,3,NZ3,F,It,I, 2010 W1,F,It 2,NZ1, 2,A1,NZ3,A2,3

Smith, C M (OFS) 1963 A 3,4, 1964 W, F, 1965 A 1,2, NZ 2

Smith, C W (GW) 1891 BI 2, 1896 BI 2,3

Smith, D (GW) 1891 BI 2

Smith D J (Z-R) 1980 BI 1,2,3,4

Smith, G A C (EP) 1938 BI 3

Smith, J H (FS) 2003 S 1(R),2(R), A 1, NZ 1, A 2, NZ 2, [U,E,Sm,NZ], 2004 W2, 2005 U(R),F2(R),A2,3, NZ1,A4,NZ2,Arg,W,F3, 2006 S1,2,F,A1,NZ1,A2, I, E2, 2007 E1,2, A1,Nm,S, [Sm,E1,Tg(t&R),US,Fj, Arg,E2],W, 2008 W1,2,It,NZ1,2,A1,Arg,NZ3,A2,3, W3,S, 2009 BI 1,2,3,NZ1,2,A1,2,3, 2010 NZ3,A2,3

Smith, P F (GW) 1997 S (R), 1998 I 1(t),2, W 1, NZ 1(R),2(R), A 2(R), W 2, 1999 NZ 2

Smollan, F C (Tvl) 1933 A 3,4,5

Snedden, R C D (GW) 1891 BI 2

Snyman, A H (NT, BB, N) 1996 NZ 3,4, Arg 2(R), W (R), 1997 Tg, BI 1,2,3, NZ 1, A 1, NZ 2, A 2, It, F 1,2, E, S, 1998 I 1,2, W 1, E 1, A 1, NZ 1,2, A 2, W 2, S, I 3, E 2, 1999 NZ 2, 2001 NZ 2, F 3, US, 2002 W 1, 2003 S 1, NZ 1, 2006 S1,2

Snyman, D S L (WP) 1972 E, 1974 BI 1,2(R), F 1,2, 1975 F 1,2, 1976 NZ 2,3, 1977 Wld

Snyman, J C P (OFS) 1974 BI 2,3,4

Sonnekus, G H H (OFS) 1974 BI 3, 1984 E 1,2

Sowerby, R S (N) 2002 Sm (R)

Spies, J J (NT) 1970 NZ 1,2,3,4

Spies, P J (BB) 2006 A1,NZ2,3,A3, I, E1, 2007 E1(R),2,A1, 2008 W1,2,A1,Arg,NZ3, A2,3,W3,S,E, 2009 BI 1,2,3(R),NZ1,2,A1,2,3,NZ3, 2010 F,It 1,2,NZ1,2,A1,NZ3,A2,3

Stander, J C J (OFS) 1974 BI 4(R), 1976 NZ 1,2,3,4

Stapelberg, W P (NT) 1974 F 1,2

Starke, J J (WP) 1956 NZ 4

Starke, K T (WP) 1924 BI 1,2,3,4

Steenekamp, J G A (Tvl) 1958 F 1

Steenkamp, G G (FS, BB) 2004 S,Arg, 2005 U,F2(R), A2,3,NZ1(R),A4(R), 2007 E1(R), 2,A1,[Tg,Fj(R)], 2008 W1,2(R),NZ1,2,A1,W3(R),S(R), 2009 BI 1(R),3(R), 2010 F,It 1,2, NZ1,2,A1,NZ3,A2,3

Stegmann, A C (WP) 1906 S, I

Stegmann, J A (Tvl) 1912 S, I, W, 1913 E, F

Stewart, C (WP) 1998 S, I 3, E 2

Stewart, D A (WP) 1960 S, 1961 E, S, F, I, 1963 A 1,3,4, 1964 W, F, 1965 I

Steyn, F P L (NS, Racing Metro) 2006 I,E1,2, 2007 E1(R),2(R),Sm,A1(R),NZ1(R),S, [Sm(R),E1,Tg(R),US, Fj,Arg,E2],W, 2008 W2(R),It,NZ1(R),2(R),A1,NZ3(R), A2(R), W3(R),S(R),E(R), 2009 BI 1,2,3(t&R),NZ1,2, A1,2(R),3(R),NZ3, 2010 W1,A2,3

Steyn, M (BB) 2009 BI 1(t&R),2(R),3,NZ1(R),2,A1,2,3, NZ3,F,It,I, 2010 F,It 1,2, NZ1,2,A1,NZ3,A2,3

Stofberg, M T S (OFS, NT, WP) 1976 NZ 2,3, 1977 Wld, 1980 S Am 1,2, BI 1,2,3,4, S Am 3,4, F, 1981 I 1,2, NZ 1,2, US, 1982 S Am 1,2, 1984 E 1,2

Strachan, L C (Tvl) 1932 E, S, 1937 A 1,2, NZ 1,2,3, 1938 BI 1,2,3

Stransky, J T (N, WP) 1993 A 1,2,3, Arg 1, 1994 Arg 1,2, 1995 WS, [A, R (t), C, F, NZ], W, It, E, 1996 Fj (R), NZ 1, A 2, NZ 2,3,4,5(R)

Straeuli, R A W (Tvl) 1994 NZ 1, Arg 1,2, S, W, 1995 WS, [A, WS, NZ (R)], E (R)

Strauss, C P (WP) 1992 F 1,2, E, 1993 F 1,2, A 1,2,3, Arg 1,2, 1994 E 1, NZ 1,2, Arg 1,2

Strauss, J A (WP) 1984 S Am 1,2

Strauss, J A (FS) 2008 A1(R),Arg(R),NZ3(R),A2(R),3(R), 2009 F(R),It

Strauss, J H P (Tvl) 1976 NZ 3,4, 1980 S Am 1

Strauss, S S F (GW) 1921 NZ 3

Strydom, C F (OFS) 1955 BI 3, 1956 A 1,2, NZ 1,4, 1958 F 1,

Strydom, J J (Tvl, GL) 1993 F 2, A 1,2,3, Arg 1,2, 1994 E 1, 1995 [A, C, F, NZ], 1996 A 2(R), NZ 2(R), 3,4, W (R), 1997 Tg, BI 1,2,3, A 2

Strydom, L J (NT) 1949 NZ 1,2

Styger, J J (OFS) 1992 NZ (R), A, F 1,2, E, 1993 F 2(R), A 3(R)
Suter, M R (N) 1965 I, S
Swanepoel, W (OFS, GL) 1997 BI 3(R), A 2(R), F 1(R), 2, E, S, 1998 I 2(R), W 1(R), E 2(R), 1999 It 1,2(R), W, A 1, [Sp, NZ 3(t)], 2000 A 1, NZ 1, A 2, NZ 2, A 3
Swart, J (WP) 1996 Fj, NZ 1(R), A 2, NZ 2,3,4,5, 1997 BI 3(R), It, S (R)
Swart, J J N (SWA) 1955 BI 1
Swart, I S (Tvl) 1993 A 1,2,3, Arg 1, 1994 E 1,2, NZ 1,3, Arg 2(R), 1995 WS, [A, WS, F, NZ], W, 1996 A 2
Taberer, W S (GW) 1896 BI 2
Taylor, O B (N) 1962 BI 1
Terblanche, C S (Bol, N) 1998 I 1,2, W 1, E 1, A 1, NZ 1,2, A 2, W 2, S, I 3, E 2, 1999 It 1(R),2, W, A 1, NZ 2(R), [Sp, E (R), A 3(R), NZ 3], 2000 E 3, 2002 W 1,2, Arg, Sm, NZ 1, A 1,2(R), 2003 S 1,2, Arg, A 1, NZ 1, A 2, NZ 2, [Gg]
Teichmann, G H (N) 1995 W, 1996 Fj, A 1, NZ 1, A 2, NZ 2,3,4,5, Arg 1,2, F 1,2, W, 1997 Tg, BI 1,2,3, NZ 1, A 1, NZ 2, A 2, It, F 1,2 E, S, 1998 I 1,2, W 1, E 1, A 1, NZ 1,2, A 2, W 2, S, I 3, E 2, 1999 It 1, W, NZ 1
Theron, D F (GW) 1996 A 2(R), NZ 2(R), 5, Arg 1,2, F 1,2, W, 1997 BI 2(R), 3, NZ 1(R), A 1, NZ 2(R)
Theunissen, D J (GW) 1896 BI 3
Thompson, G (WP) 1912 S, I, W
Tindall, J C (WP) 1924 BI 1, 1928 NZ 1,2,3,4
Tobias, E G (SARF, Bol) 1981 I 1,2, 1984 E 1,2, S Am 1,2
Tod, N S (N) 1928 NZ 2
Townsend, W H (N) 1921 NZ 1
Trenery, W E (GW) 1891 BI 2
Tromp, H (NT) 1996 NZ3,4, Arg 2(R), F 1(R)
Truter, D R (WP) 1924 BI 2,4
Truter, J T (N) 1963 A 1, 1964 F, 1965 A 2
Turner, F G (EP) 1933 A 1,2,3, 1937 A 1,2, NZ 1,2,3, 1938 BI 1,2,3
Twigge, R J (NT) 1960 S
Tyibilika, S (N) 2004 S,Arg, 2005 U,A2,Arg, 2006 NZ1,A2,NZ2
Ulyate, C A (Tvl) 1955 BI 1,2,3,4, 1956 NZ 1,2,3
Uys, P de W (NT) 1960 W, 1961 E, S, I, A 1,2, 1962 BI 1,4, 1963 A 1,2, 1969 A 1(R), 2
Uys, P J (Pumas) 2002 S
Van Aswegen, H J (WP) 1981 NZ 1, 1982 S Am 2(R)
Van Biljon, L (N) 2001 It 1(R), NZ 1, A 1,2, NZ 2, F 3, It 2(R), E (R), US, 2002 F (R), S, E (R), 2003 NZ 2(R)
Van Broekhuizen, H D (WP) 1896 BI 4
Van Buuren, M C (Tvl) 1891 BI 1
Van de Vyver, D F (WP) 1937 A 2
Van den Berg, D S (N) 1975 F 1,2, 1976 NZ 1,2
Van den Berg, M A (WP) 1937 A 1, NZ 1,2,3
Van den Berg, P A (WP, GW, N) 1999 It 1(R),2, NZ 2, A 2, [S, U (t+R), E (R), A 3(R), NZ 3(R)], 2000 E 1(R), A 1, NZ 1, A 2, NZ 2(R), A 3(t+R), Arg, I, W, E 3, 2001 F 1(R),2, A 2(R), NZ 2(R), US, 2004 NZ1, 2005 U,F1,2,A1(R),2(R),3(R),4(R),Arg(R), F3(R), 2006 S2(R),A1(R),NZ1,A2(R),NZ2(R),A3(R), I, E1(R),2(R), 2007 Sm,A2(R), NZ2,Nm(t&R),S(R), [Tg,US],W(R)
Van den Bergh, E (EP) 1994 Arg 2(t & R)
Van der Linde, A (WP) 1995 It, E, 1996 Arg 1(R), 2(R), F 1(R), W (R), 2001 F 3(R)
Van der Linde, C J (FS, Leinster) 2002 S (R), E(R), 2004 I1(R),2(R),PI(R),A1(R), NZ2(t&R),A2(R),W2(R), I3(R),E(t&R),S,Arg, 2005 U,F1(R),2,A1(R),3,NZ1,A4, NZ2, Arg,W,F3, 2006 S2(R),F(R),A1,NZ1,A2,NZ2, I, E1,2, 2007 E1(R),2,A1(R),NZ1(R), A2,NZ2,Nm,S, [Sm,E1(R),Tg,US(R),Arg,E2],W, 2008 W1(t&R),It, NZ1,2,A1,Arg,NZ3, A2, 2009 F(R),I(t), 2010 W1, It1(R) ,NZ2,A1(t&R),NZ3(R),A2(R),3(R)
Van der Merwe, A J (Bol) 1955 BI 2,3,4, 1956 A 1,2, NZ 1,2,3,4, 1958 F 1, 1960 S, NZ 2
Van der Merwe, A V (WP) 1931 W
Van der Merwe, B S (NT) 1949 NZ 1
Van der Merwe, H S (NT) 1960 NZ 4, 1963 A 2,3,4, 1964 F
Van der Merwe, H S (GL) 2007 W(t+R)
Van der Merwe, J P (WP) 1970 W
Van der Merwe, P R (SWD, WT, GW) 1981 NZ 2,3, US, 1986 Cv 1,2, 1989 Wld 1
Van der Merwe, P R (BB) 2010 F(R),It 2(R),A1(R),NZ3, A2,3(R)
Vanderplank, B E (N) 1924 BI 3,4
Van der Schyff, J H (GW) 1949 NZ 1,2,3,4, 1955 BI 1
Van der Watt, A E (WP) 1969 S (R), E, 1970 I
Van der Westhuizen, J C (WP) 1928 NZ 2,3,4, 1931 I
Van der Westhuizen, J H (WP) 1931 I, 1932 E, S
Van der Westhuizen, J H (NT, BB) 1993 Arg 1,2, 1994 E 1,2(R), Arg 2, S, W, 1995 WS, [A, C (R), WS, F, NZ], W, It, E, 1996 Fj, A 1,2(R), NZ 2,3(R), 4,5, Arg 1,2, F 1,2, W, 1997 Tg, BI 1,2,3, NZ 1, A 1, NZ 2, A 2, It, F 1, 1998 I 1,2, W 1, E 1, A 1, NZ 1,2, A 2, W 2, S, I 3, E 2, 1999 NZ 2, A 2, [S, Sp (R), U, E, A 3, NZ 3], 2000 C, E 1,2, A 1(R), NZ 1(R), A 2(R), Arg, I, W, E 3, 2001 F 1,2, It 1(R), NZ 1, A 1,2, NZ 2, F 3, It 2, E, US (R), 2003 S 1,2, A 1, NZ 1, A 2(R), NZ 2, [U,E,Sm,NZ]
Van der Westhuyzen, J N B (MP, BB) 2000 NZ 2(R), 2001 It 1(R), 2003 S 1(R),2, Arg, A 1, 2003 [E,Sm, NZ], 2004 I1,2,W1,PI,NZ1,A1,NZ2,A2,W2,I3,E,S,Arg, 2005 U,F1,2, A1,4(R),NZ2(R), 2006 S1,2,F,A1
Van Druten, N J V (Tvl) 1924 BI 1,2,3,4, 1928 NZ 1,2,3,4
Van Heerden, A J (Tvl) 1921 NZ 1,3
Van Heerden, F J (WP) 1994 E 1,2(R), NZ 3, 1995 It, E, 1996 NZ 5(R), Arg 1(R),2(R), 1997 Tg, BI 2(t+R), 3(R), NZ 1(R),2(R), 1999 [Sp]
Van Heerden, J L (NT, Tvl) 1974 BI 3,4, F 1,2, 1975 F 1,2, 1976 NZ 1,2,3,4, 1977 Wld, 1980 BI 1,3,4, S Am 3,4, F
Van Heerden, J L (BB) 2003 S 1,2, A 1, NZ 1, A 2(t), 2007 A2,NZ2,S(R), [Sm(R),E1,Tg,US,Fj(R),E2(R)]
Van Jaarsveld, C J (Tvl) 1949 NZ 1
Van Jaarsveldt, D C (R) 1960 S
Van Niekerk, J A (WP) 1928 NZ 4
Van Niekerk, J C (GL, WP, Toulon) 2001 NZ 1(R), A 1(R), NZ 2(t+R), F 3(R), It2, US, 2002 W 1(R),2(R), Arg (R), Sm, NZ 1, A 1, NZ 2, A 2, F, S, E, 2003 A 2, NZ 2, [U,E, Gg,Sm], 2004 NZ1(R),A1(t),NZ2,A2, W2,I3,E,S,Arg(R), 2005 U(R),F2(R),A1(R),2,3, NZ1,A4, NZ2, 2006 S1,2,F,A1,NZ1(R),A2(R), 2008 It(R),NZ1, 2,Arg(R),A2(R), 2010 W1
Van Reenen, G L (WP) 1937 A 2, NZ 1
Van Renen, C G (WP) 1891 BI 3, 1896 BI 1,4
Van Renen, W (WP) 1903 BI 1,3
Van Rensburg, J T J (Tvl) 1992 NZ, A, E, 1993 F 1,2, A 1, 1994 NZ 2
Van Rooyen, G W (Tvl) 1921 NZ 2,3
Van Ryneveld, R C B (WP) 1910 BI 2,3
Van Schalkwyk, D (NT) 1996 Fj (R), NZ 3,4,5, 1997 BI 2,3, NZ 1, A 1
Van Schoor, R A M (R) 1949 NZ 2,3,4, 1951 S, I, W, 1952 E, F, 1953 A 1,2,3,4
Van Straaten, A J J (WP) 1999 It 2(R), W, NZ 1(R), A 1, 2000 C, E 1,2, NZ 1, A 2, NZ 2, A 3, Arg (R), I (R), W, E 3, 2001 A 1,2, NZ 2, F 3, It 2, E
Van Vollenhoven, K T (NT) 1955 BI 1,2,3,4, 1956 A 1,2, NZ 3
Van Vuuren, T F (EP) 1912 S, I, W, 1913 E, F
Van Wyk, C J (Tvl) 1951 S, I, W, 1952 E, F, 1953 A 1,2,3,4, 1955 BI 1
Van Wyk, J F B (NT) 1970 NZ 1,2,3,4, 1971 F 1,2, A 1,2,3, 1972 E, 1974 BI 1,3,4, 1976 NZ 3,4
Van Wyk, S P (WP) 1928 NZ 1,2
Van Zyl, B P (WP) 1961 I
Van Zyl, C G P (OFS) 1965 NZ 1,2,3,4
Van Zyl, D J (WP) 2000 E 3(R)
Van Zyl, G H (WP) 1958 F 1, 1960 S, NZ 1,2,3,4, W, I, 1961 E, S, F, I, A 1,2, 1962 BI 1,3,4
Van Zyl, H J (Tvl) 1960 NZ 1,2,3,4, I, 1961 E, S, I, A 1,2
Van Zyl, P J (Bol) 1961 I
Veldsman, P E (WP) 1977 Wld

Venter, A G (OFS) 1996 NZ 3,4,5, Arg 1,2, F 1,2, W, 1997 Tg, BI 1,2,3, NZ 1, A 1, NZ 2, It, F 1,2, E, S, 1998 I 1,2, W 1, E 1, A 1, NZ 1,2, A 2, W 2, S (R), I 3(R), E 2(R), 1999 It 1,2(R), W (R), NZ 1, A 1, NZ 2, A 2, [S, U, E, A 3, NZ 3], 2000 C, E 1,2, A 1, NZ 1, A 2, NZ 2, A 3, Arg, I, W, E 3, 2001 F 1, It 1, NZ 1, A 1,2, NZ 2, F 3(R), It 2(R), E (t+R), US (R)
Venter, A J (N) 2000 W (R), E 3(R), 2001 F 3, It 2, E, US, 2002 W 1,2, Arg, NZ 1(R),2, A 2, F, S (R), E, 2003 Arg, 2004 PI,NZ1,A1,NZ2(R),A2,I3,E, 2006 NZ3,A3
Venter, B (OFS) 1994 E 1,2, NZ 1,2,3, Arg 1,2, 1995 [R, C, WS (R), NZ (R)], 1996 A 1, NZ 1, A 2, 1999 A 2, [S, U]
Venter, F D (Tvl) 1931 W, 1932 S, 1933 A 3
Versfeld, C (WP) 1891 BI 3
Versfeld, M (WP) 1891 BI 1,2,3
Vigne, J T (Tvl) 1891 BI 1,2,3
Viljoen, J F (GW) 1971 F 1,2, A 1,2,3, 1972 E
Viljoen, J T (N) 1971 A 1,2,3
Villet, J V (WP) 1984 E 1,2
Visagie, I J (WP) 1999 It 1, W, NZ 1, A 1, NZ 2, A 2, [S, U, E, A 3, NZ 3], 2000 C, E 2, A 1, NZ 1, A 2, NZ 2, A 3, 2001 NZ 1, A 1,2, NZ 2, F 3, It 2(R), E (t+R), US, 2003 S 1(R),2(R), Arg
Visagie, P J (GW) 1967 F 1,2,3,4, 1968 BI 1,2,3,4, F 1,2, 1969 A 1,2,3,4, S, E, 1970 NZ 1,2,3,4, 1971 F 1,2, A 1,2,3
Visagie, R G (OFS, N) 1984 E 1,2, S Am 1,2, 1993 F 1
Visser, J de V (WP) 1981 NZ 2, US
Visser, M (WP) 1995 WS (R)
Visser, P J (Tvl) 1933 A 2
Viviers, S S (OFS) 1956 A 1,2, NZ 2,3,4
Vogel, M L (OFS) 1974 BI 2(R)
Von Hoesslin, D J B (GW) 1999 It 1(R),2, W (R), NZ 1, A 1(R)
Vos, A N (GL) 1999 It 1(t+R),2, NZ 1(R),2(R), A 2, [S (R), Sp, E (R), A 3(R), NZ 3], 2000 C, E 1,2, A 1, NZ 1, A 2, NZ 2, A 3, Arg, I, W, E 3, 2001 F 1,2, It 1, NZ 1, A 1,2, NZ 2, F 3, It 2, E, US
Wagenaar, C (NT) 1977 Wld
Wahl, J J (WP) 1949 NZ 1
Walker, A P (N) 1921 NZ 1,3, 1924 BI 1,2,3,4
Walker, H N (OFS) 1953 A 3, 1956 A 2, NZ 1,4
Walker, H W (Tvl) 1910 BI 1,2,3
Walton, D C (N) 1964 F, 1965 I, S, NZ 3,4, 1969 A 1,2, E
Wannenburg, P J (BB) 2002 F (R), E, 2003 S 1,2, Arg, A 1(t+R), NZ 1(R), 2004 I1,2, W1,PI(R), 2006 S1(R),F,NZ2(R),3,A3, 2007 Sm(R),NZ1(R),A2,NZ2
Waring, F W (WP) 1931 I, 1932 E, 1933 A 1,2,3,4,5
Watson, L A (WP) 2007 Sm, 2008 W1,2,It,NZ1(R), 2(R),Arg,NZ3(R),A2(R),3(t&R)
Wegner, N (WP) 1993 F 2, A 1,2,3
Wentzel, M van Z (Pumas) 2002 F (R), S
Wessels, J J (WP) 1896 BI 1,2,3
Whipp, P J M (WP) 1974 BI 1,2, 1975 F 1, 1976 NZ 1,3,4, 1980 S Am 1,2
White, J (Bor) 1931 W, 1933 A 1,2,3,4,5, 1937 A 1,2, NZ 1,2
Wiese, J J (Tvl) 1993 F 1, 1995 WS, [R, C, WS, F, NZ], W, It, E, 1996 NZ 3(R), 4(R), 5, Arg 1,2, F 1,2, W
Willemse, A K (GL) 2003 S 1,2, NZ 1, A 2, NZ 2, [U,E,Sm,NZ], 2004 W2,I3, 2007 E1, 2(R),Sm,A1, NZ1,Nm,S(R), [Tg]
Williams, A E (GW) 1910 BI 1
Williams, A P (WP) 1984 E 1,2
Williams, C M (WP, GL) 1993 Arg 2, 1994 E 1,2, NZ 1,2,3, Arg 1,2, S, W, 1995 WS, [WS, F, NZ], It, E, 1998 A 1(t), NZ 1(t), 2000 C (R), E 1(t),2(R), A 1(R), NZ 2, A 3, Arg, I, W (R)
Williams, D O (WP) 1937 A 1,2, NZ 1,2,3, 1938 BI 1,2,3
Williams, J G (NT) 1971 F 1,2, A 1,2,3, 1972 E, 1974 BI 1,2,4, F 1,2, 1976 NZ 1,2
Wilson, L G (WP) 1960 NZ 3,4, W, I, 1961 E, F, I, A 1,2, 1962 BI 1,2,3,4, 1963 A 1,2,3,4, 1964 W, F, 1965 I, S, A 1,2, NZ 1,2,3,4
Wolmarans, B J (OFS) 1977 Wld
Wright, G D (EP, Tvl) 1986 Cv 3,4, 1989 Wld 1,2, 1992 F 1,2, E
Wyness, M R K (WP) 1962 BI 1,2,3,4, 1963 A 2
Zeller, W C (N) 1921 NZ 2,3
Zimerman, M (WP) 1931 W, I, 1932 E, S

TONGA

TONGA'S 2009–10 TEST RECORD

OPPONENTS	DATE	VENUE	RESULT
Ireland A	13 Nov	A	**Lost** 19–48
Scotland A	20 Nov	A	**Lost** 7–38
Portugal	28 Nov	A	**Won** 24–19
Samoa	12 June	A	**Lost** 23–24
Fiji	19 June	N	**Lost** 38–41
Japan	26 June	N	**Lost** 23–26
Chile	29 Sept	A	**Won** 32–30

EYEING STABILITY AND GROWTH

Sweeping changes in Tonga in early 2010 have demonstrated that the Union is implementing the measures that will deliver not only a competitive team at Rugby World Cup 2011, but the building blocks for future growth and stability.

The nation that has helped produce such rugby greats as Viliami (Willie) Ofahengaue and Jonah Lomu has experienced challenging times in recent years, struggling to assemble its best team and going through continual changes of administration.

However, under the guidance of the IRB, an exciting new dawn began in February 2010 when the newly formed Tonga Rugby Union Authority was appointed to oversee the national administration of the game for a period of two years as a result of the administrative and governance difficulties experienced by the Tongan Rugby Football Union.

The TRUA Board includes significant administrative experience with former IRB vice chairman Bob Tuckey, who was appointed chairman, and the other directors being Fakahau Valu, 'Aminiasi Kefu, Takitoa Taumoepeau and Tapu Panuve.

Tuckey, a Queenslander who also chaired the Australian Rugby Union from 2001 to 2005, has been a long-time friend of Pacific Island rugby, and his influence has already seen important signs of growth.

"Since the 2007 Rugby World Cup, Tonga has not had a single Test against a Tier 1 nation. I think this has been, and remains, one of our biggest problems," Tuckey said.

With the IRB committed to the global competitiveness of the Game, matches were arranged in November 2010 against Italy A and the French Barbarians in addition to participation in the Americas Rugby Championship in order to boost competition.

Though Tonga finished bottom of the ANZ Pacific Nations Cup standings for the third consecutive year after losing all three matches under new head coach Isitolo Maka, they somehow scored more points than any of their opponents. Tonga claimed four bonus points, losing all three games by less than three points. They also had the best attacking record in the competition, averaging 28 points per match, while Kurt Morath was the top point scorer with 41.

Playing all their games in the Samoan capital Apia, Tonga lost their opener against the hosts 24–23 before throwing away a 28-point lead to lose 41–38 to Fiji. In their final Test, they led Japan for nearly the entire match before conceding a last gasp penalty try with hooker Aleki Lutui in the sin-bin to fall 26–23.

The Tongan disappointment was clear to see, but they were heartened by the closeness of the scores, knowing that their young players would gain plenty from the experience. While only one of the Tongan back-line – half-back Mahe Fangupo – was playing his rugby domestically, 10 of the 17 forwards were based in the kingdom and had risen quickly through the ranks thanks to TRUA's new development programme.

At the same time as the senior side were in PNC action, Tonga's next generation were in Argentina at the IRB Junior World Championship. Tonga ultimately finished 11th, beating Samoa 23–3 to safeguard their place in the 2011 tournament.

In the IRB Pacific Rugby Cup 2010, Tautahi Gold had been the early pace setters and led the competition after three rounds with wins over countrymen the Tau'uta Reds, Savai'i Samoa and the Fiji Barbarians. However, defeats by Fiji Warriors and Upolu Samoa saw them miss out on the final. Tautahi Gold ultimately finished third with Tau'uta Reds last.

"There was no A programme in place when we started," Tuckey said. "So we organised a two-match tour of Fiji in April against the Fiji Warriors, and later we were fortunate to enter the IRB's Americas Rugby Championship to play against the A sides from Argentina, USA and Canada in October."

En route to Córdoba for the Americas Rugby Championship, the Ikale Tahi stopped off in Santiago for a first ever Test against Chile, a match they edged 32–30.

Tuckey is confident that this development work will widen the pool of players for coach Maka and his selectors to choose from.

While several new faces are expected to emerge before RWC 2011, one man in particular has already shown his class – No 8 Sione Kalamafoni, who made his Test debut in 2007 at age 18 and has just returned to the fold after two years doing missionary work for his church.

Another important initiative undertaken by Tuckey and his Board is the advance of women's rugby in the kingdom.

"With Rugby Sevens entering the Olympics in 2016, I can foresee a huge growth in Sevens tournaments worldwide," Tuckey said. "Our academy coach Josh Taumalolo has also taken up the role of coach of our women's Sevens team, who will make their first outing to Borneo and Malaysia in October after four weekends of coaching clinics with our HPU staff."

"In the build-up to the 2011 Rugby World Cup we hope to line up a total of six Test matches and four A matches. And having just opened our first Licensed Training Centre in Nuku'alofa, I'm pleased to be able to say that rugby in Tonga is looking quite stable."

TONGA INTERNATIONAL STATISTICS

MATCH RECORDS UP TO 30TH SEPTEMBER 2010

WINNING MARGIN

Date	Opponent	Result	Winning Margin
21/03/2003	Korea	119–0	**119**
08/07/2006	Cook Islands	90–0	**90**
01/01/1979	Solomon Islands	92–3	**89**
10/02/2007	Korea	83–3	**80**
15/03/2003	Korea	75–0	**75**

MOST POINTS IN A MATCH

BY THE TEAM

Date	Opponent	Result	Pts.
21/03/2003	Korea	119–0	**119**
01/01/1979	Solomon Islands	92–3	**92**
08/07/2006	Cook Islands	90–0	**90**
06/12/2002	Papua New Guinea	84–12	**84**
10/02/2007	Korea	83–3	**83**

MOST TRIES IN A MATCH

BY THE TEAM

Date	Opponent	Result	Tries
21/03/2003	Korea	119–0	**17**
08/07/2006	Cook Islands	90–0	**14**
10/02/2007	Korea	83–3	**13**
24/06/2006	Cook Islands	77–10	**13**

MOST CONVERSIONS IN A MATCH

BY THE TEAM

Date	Opponent	Result	Cons
21/03/2003	Korea	119–0	**17**
08/07/2006	Cook Islands	90–0	**10**

MOST PENALTIES IN A MATCH

BY THE TEAM

Date	Opponent	Result	Pens
10/11/2001	Scotland	20–43	**5**
28/06/2008	Samoa	15–20	**5**

MOST DROP GOALS IN A MATCH

BY A PLAYER

Date	Opponent	Result	DGS
	8 Matches		**1**

MOST POINTS IN A MATCH

BY A PLAYER

Date	Player	Opponent	Pts.
21/03/2003	Pierre Hola	Korea	**39**
10/02/2007	Fangatapu Apikotoa	Korea	**28**
04/05/1999	Sateki Tu'ipulotu	Korea	**27**
21/03/2003	Benhur Kivalu	Korea	**25**
06/12/2002	Pierre Hola	Papua New Guinea	**24**

MOST TRIES IN A MATCH

BY A PLAYER

Date	Player	Opponent	Tries
21/03/2003	Benhur Kivalu	Korea	**5**
24/06/2006	Viliami Hakalo	Cook Islands	**3**
08/07/2006	Tevita Vaikona	Cook Islands	**3**
05/07/1997	Siua Taumalolo	Cook Islands	**3**
28/03/1999	Siua Taumalolo	Georgia	**3**
04/05/1999	Jonny Koloi	Korea	**3**

MOST CONVERSIONS IN A MATCH

BY A PLAYER

Date	Player	Opponent	Cons
21/03/2003	Pierre Hola	Korea	17
08/07/2006	Fangatapu Apikotoa	Cook Islands	9
10/02/2007	Fangatapu Apikotoa	Korea	9
06/12/2002	Pierre Hola	Papua New Guinea	9
05/07/1997	Kusitafu Tonga	Cook Islands	9

MOST PENALTIES IN A MATCH

BY A PLAYER

Date	Player	Opponent	Pens
25/05/2001	Kusitafu Tonga	Fiji	4
10/11/2001	Sateki Tu'ipulotu	Scotland	4
19/02/1995	Sateki Tu'ipulotu	Japan	4
23/07/2005	Fangatapu Apikotoa	Samoa	4
16/09/2007	Pierre Hola	Samoa	4

MOST DROP GOALS IN A MATCH

BY A PLAYER

Date	Player	Opponent	DGS
	8 Matches		1

MOST CAPPED PLAYERS

Name	Caps
'Elisi Vunipola	41
Benhur Kivalu	38
Pierre Hola	37
Manu Vunipola	35
Fe'ao Vunipola	32

LEADING TRY SCORERS

Name	Tries
Siua Taumalolo	12
Fepikou Tatafu	11
Benhur Kivalu	10

LEADING CONVERSIONS SCORERS

Name	Cons
Pierre Hola	65
Sateki Tu'ipulotu	33
Fangatapu 'Apikotoa	30
Kusitafu Tonga	25

LEADING PENALTY SCORERS

Name	Pens
Pierre Hola	35
Sateki Tu'ipulotu	32
Siua Taumalolo	12
Tomasi Lovo	12

LEADING DROP GOAL SCORERS

Name	DGs
Pierre Hola	3

LEADING POINTS SCORERS

Name	Pts.
Pierre Hola	289
Sateki Tu'ipulotu	190
Siua Taumalolo	108
Fangatapu 'Apikotoa	99

TONGA INTERNATIONAL PLAYERS
UP TO 30TH SEPTEMBER 2010

Note: Years given for International Championship matches are for second half of season; eg 1972 means season 1971–72. Years for all other matches refer to the actual year of the match.

I Afeaki 1995 *F, S, Iv*, 1997 *Fj*, 2001 *S, W*, 2002 *J, Fj, Sa, Fj*, 2003 *Kor, Kor, I, Fj, Fj, It, C*, 2004 *Sa, Fj*, 2005 *It*, 2007 *Sa, SA, E*
P Afeaki 1983 *Fj, Sa*
S Afeaki 2002 *Fj, Fj, PNG, PNG*, 2003 *Kor, Kor, I, Fj, It, W, NZ*
V Afeaki 1997 *Sa*, 2002 *Sa, Fj*
J Afu 2008 *M, J, AuA, Sa, Fj*, 2009 *Fj, Sa, J*
T Afu Fifita 1924 *Fj, Fj, Fj*
A Afu Fungavaka 1982 *Sa*, 1984 *Fj, Fj*, 1985 *Fj*, 1986 *W, Fj, Fj*, 1987 *C, W, I, Sa, Fj*
S 'Aho 1974 *S, W*
T Ahoafi 2007 *AuA, Sa*
P Ahofono 1990 *Sa*
K Ahota'e'iloa 1999 *Sa, F, Fj*, 2000 *C, Fj, J*
M Ahota'e'iloa 2009 *IrA, S*, 2010 *Sa, Fj, J*
S Aisake 1934 *Fj*
M Akau'ola 1934 *Fj*
P 'Ake 1926 *Fj, Fj, Fj*
A Alatini 2001 *S*, 2002 *J, Fj*, 2003 *I, Fj*
M Alatini 1969 *M*, 1972 *Fj, Fj*, 1973 *M, A, A, Fj*, 1974 *S, W, C*, 1975 *M*, 1977 *Fj*
PF Alatini 1995 *Sa*
S Alatini 1994 *Sa, Fj*, 1998 *Sa, Fj*, 2000 *NZ, US*
S Alatini 1977 *Fj*, 1979 *NC, M, E*
T Alatini 1932 *Fj*
V 'Alipate 1967 *Fj*, 1968 *Fj, Fj, Fj*, 1969 *M*
A Amone 1987 *W, I, Sa, Fj*
A Amore 1988 *Fj*
T Anitoni 1995 *J, Sa, Fj*, 1996 *Sa, Fj*
V Anitoni 1990 *Sa*
F Apikotoa 2004 *Sa, Fj*, 2005 *Fj, Sa, Fj, Sa, It, F*, 2006 *Coo, Coo*, 2007 *Kor, AuA, J, JAB*, 2008 *M, J, AuA, Sa, Fj*, 2009 *Fj, J, JAB*, 2010 *Fj*
T Apitani 1947 *Fj, Fj*
S Asi 1987 *C*
T Asi 1996 *Sa*
H 'Asi 2000 *C*
S Ata 1928 *Fj*
S Atiola 1987 *Sa, Fj*, 1988 *Fj, Fj*, 1989 *Fj, Fj*, 1990 *Fj, J*
K Bakewa 2002 *PNG, PNG*, 2003 *Fj*
O Beba 1932 *Fj, Fj, Fj*
O Blake 1983 *M, M*, 1987 *Sa, Fj*, 1988 *Sa, Fj, Fj*
T Bloomfield 1973 *M, A, A, Fj*, 1986 *W*
D Briggs 1997 *W*
J Buloka 1932 *Fj, Fj*
D Edwards 1998 *A*, 1999 *Geo, Geo, Kor, US, Sa, F, Fj, C, NZ, It, E*
T Ete'aki 1984 *Fj*, 1986 *W, Fj, Fj*, 1987 *C, W, I*, 1990 *Fj, J, Sa, Kor, Sa*, 1991 *Sa*
U Fa'a 1994 *Sa, W*, 1995 *J*, 1998 *Sa, A, Fj*
L Fa'aoso 2004 *Sa, Fj*, 2005 *Fj, Sa, Fj, Sa*, 2007 *US, E*, 2009 *IrA, S, Pt*
P Fa'apoi 1963 *Fj*
V Fa'aumu 1986 *Fj, Fj*
T Fainga'anuku 1999 *NZ, It, E*, 2000 *C, Fj, J, NZ*, 2001 *Fj, Sa, Fj, Sa*
S Faka 'osi'folau 1997 *Z, Nm, SA, Fj, Sa, Coo, W*, 1998 *A, Fj*, 1999 *Geo, Kor, Fj*, 2001 *Sa*
P Fakalelu 2005 *It*, 2006 *Coo, Coo*, 2009 *Sa, J, JAB, S*
J Fakalolo 1926 *Fj, Fj, Fj*
P Fakana 1963 *Fj, Fj*
F Fakaongo 1993 *S, Fj*, 1995 *Iv, Sa, Fj*, 2000 *Fj, J, NZ, Sa*, 2001 *S, W*, 2002 *J, Fj, Sa*
V Fakatou 1998 *Sa, A, Fj*, 1999 *Kor, NZ*
V Fakatulolo 1975 *M*
S Fakaua 2005 *Sa*
P Faka'ua 1967 *Fj, Fj, Fj*, 1968 *Fj, Fj, Fj*, 1969 *M, M*, 1972 *Fj*
N Fakauho 1977 *Fj, Fj*
P Fakava 1988 *Sa, Fj*
FP Faletau 1999 *Geo, Kor, Kor, J, US, Sa, F, Fj, C*
K Faletau 1988 *Sa, Fj*, 1989 *Fj, Fj*, 1990 *Sa*, 1991 *Fj*, 1992 *Fj*, 1997 *Nm, SA, Fj, Sa, Coo, W*, 1999 *Sa, F, Fj, C*
M Fanga'uta 1982 *Fj*
K Fangupo 2009 *IrA, S, Pt*
MU Fangupo 2009 *Sa, J, JAB, IrA*, 2010 *J*
F Faotusa 1990 *Sa*
LAH Fatafehi 2009 *Fj, Sa, JAB, IrA, S, Pt*, 2010 *Sa, Fj, J*
IT Fatani 1992 *Fj*, 1993 *Sa, S, Fj, A, Fj*, 1997 *Fj, Coo*, 1999 *Geo, Kor, Kor, J, US, Sa, F, Fj, C, NZ, It, E*, 2000 *C, Fj, J, NZ, Sa, US*
O Faupula 1924 *Fj, Fj, Fj*
AOM Feao 2010 *Sa, Fj*
S Fe'ao 1995 *F, S*
SL Fekau 1983 *M, M*
K Feke 1988 *Fj, Fj*, 1989 *Fj*, 1990 *Fj, Sa*
SH Fekitoa 2010 *Sa, J*
T Feleola 1934 *Fj*
M Felise 1987 *W, I*
I Fenukitau 1993 *Sa, S, Fj, A, Fj*, 1994 *Sa, Fj*, 1995 *J, J, F, S*, 2002 *J, Fj, Sa*, 2003 *It, W, NZ, C*
Fetu'ulele 1967 *Fj*
K Fielea 1987 *C, W, I, Sa, Fj*, 1990 *J, Sa, Kor, Sa*, 1991 *Sa*
L Fifita 1934 *Fj*
P Fifita 1983 *Fj*
P Fifita 2003 *C*
S Fifita 1974 *S, W, C*, 1975 *M*
T Fifita 1982 *Sa*, 1984 *Fj, Fj*, 1986 *W, Fj, Fj*, 1987 *C, W, I*, 1991 *Sa, Fj, Fj*
T Fifita 2001 *Fj, Fj*, 2003 *Fj*, 2006 *J*, 2008 *M, J, AuA*
V Fifita 1982 *Fj*
V Fifita 2005 *F*
F Filikitonga 1990 *Fj, Sa*
L Fililava 1960 *M*
M Filimoehala 1968 *Fj*, 1974 *W, C*, 1975 *M, M*
OAML Filipine 2000 *C*, 2006 *J, Fj, Coo, Sa*, 2007 *US, SA*, 2008 *M, J, AuA*
M Filise 1986 *Fj, Fj*
T Filise 2001 *Fj, Fj, S, W*, 2002 *Sa, Fj*, 2004 *Sa, Fj*, 2005 *Fj, Sa, Fj, Sa*, 2007 *Fj, Sa, E*
S Filo 2004 *Sa, Fj*, 2009 *IrA, S*
I Finau 1987 *Sa, Fj*, 1990 *Fj, J, Sa*
M Finau 1979 *NC, M, E, Sa*, 1980 *Sa*, 1984 *Fj*
M Finau 2007 *AuA*, 2008 *J*, 2009 *Fj, J, JAB*, 2010 *J*
S Finau 1998 *Sa*, 1999 *Geo, Sa, F, Fj, C, E*, 2001 *Fj, Fj, S*, 2005 *It, F*
S Finau 1989 *Fj, Fj*, 1990 *Fj, J, Sa, Kor, Sa*
S Finau 1924 *Fj, Fj, Fj*, 1926 *Fj, Fj, Fj*
T Finau 1967 *Fj*
T Finau 1924 *Fj, Fj, Fj*
V Finau 1987 *Sa, Fj*
I Fine 2007 *Kor, AuA, JAB, Sa*
K Fine 1987 *C, W, I*, 1988 *Fj*
L Fineanganofo 1924 *Fj, Fj, Fj*
J Finisi 1932 *Fj, Fj, Fj*

S Finisi 1928 *Fj*
P Fisi'iahi 1992 *Sa*
K Fisilau 1999 *J, US*, 2000 *C*, 2005 *Fj, Sa, It*
S Fisilau 2010 *Sa, Fj, J*
K Fokofuka 1995 *Sa*
K Folea 1991 *Fj*
S Foliaki 1973 *A, A*, 1977 *Fj*
Fololisi 1991 *Fj*
U Fono 2009 *IrA, S*
V Fono 2005 *Sa, Fj, It, F*
H Fonua 1973 *M, A, A, Fj*, 1974 *S, W, C*
O Fonua 2009 *Fj, Sa, S, Pt*
S Fonua 1928 *Fj, Fj, Fj*
SO Fonua 2002 *Sa, Sa*, 2003 *It, W, NZ, C*, 2007 *Kor, AuA, J, JAB, Fj, Sa*
T Fonua 2007 *Kor*
K Fotu 1990 *Fj, Sa, Kor, Sa*
L Fotu 1991 *Sa*, 1992 *Fj*, 1993 *S, Fj*
R Fotu 1979 *M*, 1983 *Fj, Sa*
S Fotu 1968 *Fj, Fj, Fj*, 1969 *M, M*
S Fotu 1947 *Fj*
TK Fotu 1987 *C*, 1988 *Sa, Fj*, 1989 *Fj*, 1990 *J*
P Fua'ava 1985 *Fj*
T Fuataimi 1928 *Fj*, 1932 *Fj, Fj, Fj*
F Fukofuka 1926 *Fj, Fj, Fj*, 1928 *Fj*
SM Fukofuka 2010 *Sa, Fj*
T Fukofuka 1993 *Fj*, 1995 *J, J, F, S, Iv, Fj*
A Fungavaka 1982 *Fj*
L Fusimalohi 1987 *Fj*, 1988 *Fj*, 1990 *J, Sa*
W Gibbons 2002 *PNG*, 2003 *Fj*
F Hafoka 1932 *Fj, Fj, Fj*
I Hafoka 1928 *Fj, Fj*, 1932 *Fj, Fj, Fj*, 1934 *Fj*
K Hafoka 1967 *Fj, Fj*, 1968 *Fj, Fj, Fj*
M Hafoka 1977 *Fj, Fj*, 1979 *M*, 1980 *Sa*
S Hafoka 1997 *W*
T Hafoka 1987 *Fj*
WM Hafu 2009 *IrA, S*
VA Hakalo 2006 *J, Coo, Sa*
S Hala 1999 *Geo, Geo, Kor*, 2002 *J, Fj, Sa, Sa, Fj*, 2003 *Kor, Kor*
H Halaeua 2010 *Fj, J*
M Halafatu 1989 *Fj*
KM Halafihi 2010 *Sa, J*
T Halafihi 1982 *Sa, Fj*, 1983 *Sa*, 1985 *Fj*
S Halahingano 1924 *Fj, Fj, Fj*
T Halaifonua 2009 *Fj, J, JAB*
A Halangahu 2007 *Kor*
C Halangi 2002 *Fj*
T Halasika 1988 *Fj, Fj*
C Hala'ufia 2000 *C*, 2001 *Fj, Sa, Fj, Sa, W*, 2002 *Sa*, 2004 *Sa, Fj*, 2005 *Fj, Fj, Sa, It, F*, 2006 *J, Fj, Coo, Sa, Coo*, 2007 *JAB, Fj*, 2009 *Fj*
S Hala'ufia 1977 *Fj*, 1979 *NC, M, E, Sa*, 1981 *Fj*
L Halavatau 1982 *Sa, Fj*
T Haumono 1924 *Fj, Fj, Fj*, 1926 *Fj, Fj, Fj*, 1928 *Fj*, 1932 *Fj, Fj, Fj*
D Havea 2000 *NZ, US*
S Havea 2004 *Sa, Fj*, 2005 *Fj, Sa, Fj, Sa, It, F*, 2006 *J, Fj, Coo, Sa*, 2007 *Kor, JAB, Fj, Sa, US, SA*, 2008 *M, J, AuA, Sa, Fj*
T Havea 1924 *Fj, Fj, Fj*
AP Havili 2000 *C, Fj, J, Sa, US*, 2001 *Fj, Sa, Fj*, 2007 *AuA, J, JAB, US, SA, E*
M Havili 1987 *Sa*, 1988 *Fj*
P Havili 1981 *Fj, Fj, Fj*
KP Hehea 2006 *J, Fj, JAB, Coo, Sa, Coo*, 2007 *US, Sa, SA, E*, 2008 *Sa, Fj*, 2009 *IrA, S, Pt*
SE Hehepoto 1972 *Fj*, 1973 *M, A, A, Fj*
M Hekeheke 1986 *Fj, Fj*, 1988 *Fj*
Helehele 1985 *Fj*
T Helu 1967 *Fj, Fj*
WFU Helu 2010 *Fj, J*
O Hiko 1979 *E*
RP Hola 1998 *Sa, A, Fj*, 2001 *W*, 2002 *J, Fj, Sa, Sa, Fj, PNG, PNG*, 2003 *Kor, Kor, I, Fj, It, W, NZ, C*, 2005 *Fj*, 2006 *J, Fj, JAB, Coo, Sa, Coo*, 2007 *Sa, US, Sa, SA, E*, 2008 *J, Sa, Fj*, 2009 *Sa, J, JAB, IrA, S, Pt*
S Hola 1979 *Fj*
L Hopoate 1986 *W*
V Hosea 1967 *Fj, Fj*
F Hufanga 1973 *M*
S Hufanga 2003 *Fj, W, NZ, C*, 2004 *Sa, Fj*, 2005 *It, F*, 2006 *J, Fj, JAB*, 2007 *Fj, US, Sa, SA, E*, 2008 *AuA, Sa*, 2009 *IrA, S, Pt*
F Ika 1988 *Sa, Fj, Fj, Fj*, 1989 *Fj, Fj*
S Ika 2008 *M, J, AuA*, 2009 *Sa, J, JAB*
M Ilolahia 1947 *Fj*
Inoke 1947 *Fj*
K 'Inoke 1967 *Fj, Fj, Fj*, 1968 *Fj, Fj, Fj*, 1969 *M, M*, 1972 *Fj*, 1973 *A*, 1975 *M*
K 'Iongi 1967 *Fj, Fj, Fj*, 1968 *Fj, Fj, Fj*, 1969 *M, M*, 1972 *Fj*, 1973 *M, A, Fj*
T 'Isitolo 1995 *Iv, Sa, Fj*
M Kafatolu 2002 *J, Fj, Sa*
T Kaho 1973 *A*
J Kaihau 1932 *Fj, Fj*
P Kaihau 1975 *M*, 1977 *Fj, Fj, Fj*
S Kaihau 1934 *Fj*
M Kaihea 1999 *Geo, Kor, Kor, J, Sa, F*
L Kainga 1928 *Fj, Fj*
L Kaiqa 1928 *Fj*
'A Kaitu'u 2000 *C*
J Kalaivalu 1996 *Sa*
SM Kalamafoni 2007 *Kor, AuA, J, JAB, Fj, Sa*, 2010 *Sa, Fj, J*
N Kalaniuvalu 1963 *Fj*
R Kapeli 1992 *Sa, Fj*, 1993 *Fj, A*
S Kapeli 2005 *Sa*
T Kapeli 1982 *Sa*
PF Kata 2009 *Pt*, 2010 *Sa, Fj, J*
FKM Katoa 2009 *J, JAB*
L Katoa 1996 *Sa, Fj*, 1997 *Nm, Fj, Sa*
P Katoa 1977 *Fj, Fj, Fj*, 1979 *NC, M, E, Sa, Fj*, 1981 *Fj, Fj, Fj*
P Katoa 1924 *Fj*
T Kaufana 1947 *Fj*
T Kaufusi 2007 *Kor, AuA, J, JAB, Fj, Sa*, 2009 *Sa, JAB*
L Kauhalaniua 1984 *Fj*
E Kauhenga 2002 *Sa, Fj*, 2003 *Fj*, 2006 *J*, 2007 *SA*, 2008 *M, J, AuA*, 2009 *Sa, J, JAB, IrA, S, Pt*
S Kava 1967 *Fj*
T Kavapalu 1967 *Fj*, 1968 *Fj, Fj, Fj*, 1969 *M, M*, 1972 *Fj*, 1973 *M, A, Fj*, 1974 *W*, 1975 *M, M*
A Kefu 1926 *Fj, Fj, Fj*, 1928 *Fj, Fj*
F Kefu 1972 *Fj, Fj*, 1973 *A*, 1974 *W, C*, 1975 *M*
M Kefu 1959 *Fj*, 1960 *M*, 1963 *Fj, Fj*
E Kelemeni 1967 *Fj, Fj, Fj*
K Kioa 1959 *Fj*, 1960 *M*
P Kiole 1977 *Fj, Fj, Fj*, 1979 *M, E, Fj*, 1980 *Sa*
S Kiole 2005 *Fj, Fj, Sa*, 2007 *AuA, J, JAB, Fj, Sa*, 2008 *Fj*
FT Kitekei'aho 1987 *C, W, I*
T kitekei'aho 1979 *Fj*
BH Kivalu 1998 *Sa, A*, 1999 *Geo, Geo, Kor, Sa, F, Fj, C, NZ, It, E*, 2000 *C, Fj, J, NZ, Sa, US*, 2002 *J, Sa, Sa, Fj, PNG, PNG*, 2003 *Kor, Kor, Fj, Fj, It, W, NZ, C*, 2004 *Sa, Fj*, 2005 *Fj, Sa, Fj, Sa*
T Kolo 1993 *A*, 1995 *Sa, Fj*
C Koloi 1999 *US*
S Koloi 1998 *Sa, Fj*, 1999 *Geo, Geo, Kor, Kor, J, C, NZ, It, E*, 2000 *NZ, Sa, US*, 2001 *Sa*
E Koloto 1986 *W*
F Lagilagi 1991 *Fj*
Jione Laiseni 1932 *Fj, Fj*
E Langi 2003 *NZ*
F Langi 1990 *Fj, J*
P Langi 1986 *W, Fj*
F Lani 1986 *Fj*
T Latailakepa 1992 *Sa, Fj*, 1993 *Sa*
K Latu 1987 *Fj*
O Latu 2006 *J, Fj, JAB, Coo, Sa, Coo*, 2007 *Kor, AuA, J, JAB, Fj, Sa, US, Sa, SA, E*, 2008 *M, J, AuA, Sa, Fj*, 2009 *Fj, Sa, J*
P Latu 1994 *W*, 1995 *J, J, F, S, Iv, Sa, Fj*
S Latu 1984 *Fj, Fj*
S Latu 1992 *Fj*, 1993 *Fj, A*
S Latu 1972 *Fj*, 1973 *M, A, A, Fj*, 1974 *S, W, C*, 1975 *M, M*
U Latu 1997 *W*, 1998 *Sa*, 2002 *PNG, PNG*, 2003 *Kor, Kor, I, It, W, NZ, C*
U Latufeku 1959 *Fj*, 1960 *M*, 1963 *Fj*, 1968 *Fj, Fj, Fj*
P Latukefu 1995 *J, J, S, Iv, Sa, Fj*, 1998 *A, Fj*
T Latukefu 1967 *Fj, Fj, Fj*, 1968 *Fj, Fj, Fj*
M Latunipulu 1926 *Fj, Fj, Fj*
F Latusela 2003 *Kor, Kor*
F Lauei 1985 *Fj*

H Lavaka 1996 *Sa*, 1997 *SA*, *Fj*, *Sa*, *Coo*, *W*, 2003 *I*, *Fj*, *Fj*, *It*, *W*, *NZ*, *C*
K Lavaka 1996 *Fj*
M Lavaka 1993 *S*, *Fj*, *A*, *Fj*
S Lavaka 2008 *J*
T Lavaki 1990 *J*, *Kor*, 1993 *S*
F Lavemai 1984 *Fj*, *Fj*, 1985 *Fj*, 1986 *W*
M Lavulo 1979 *E*
T Lea'aetoa 2002 *PNG*, *PNG*, 2003 *Kor*, *Kor*, *I*, *It*, *W*, *NZ*, *C*, 2005 *It*, *F*, 2006 *J*, *Fj*, *JAB*, *Coo*, *Sa*, *Coo*, 2008 *M*, *J*, *AuA*, *Sa*, *Fj*
J Leba 1932 *Fj*, *Fj*, *Fj*
G Leger 2001 *S*, *W*, 2002 *J*, *Fj*, *Sa*, *Sa*, *Fj*, 2003 *Kor*, *Kor*, *I*, *Fj*, *It*, *NZ*, *C*
T Leger 1967 *Fj*, *Fj*
T Leha 1983 *M*, *M*
S Leilani 1981 *Fj*, 1983 *Fj*, *Sa*
FVMH Lemoto 2007 *Fj*
S Lepa 1928 *Fj*, *Fj*
A Liava'a 1979 *E*, 1981 *Fj*, *Fj*, *Fj*, 1983 *Fj*, *Sa*, *M*, *M*, 1984 *Fj*, *Fj*, 1985 *Fj*, 1987 *C*, *W*, *I*
S Liava'a 1979 *M*, *E*, 1981 *Fj*, *Fj*
V Likio 1947 *Fj*, *Fj*
L Lile 2002 *Fj*, 2003 *Fj*
VF Lilo 2007 *Kor*, *J*, *JAB*, *US*, *Sa*, *SA*, *E*, 2008 *M*, *J*, *AuA*, *Sa*, *Fj*, 2009 *Fj*, *Sa*, *J*, *JAB*, *IrA*, *S*, *Pt*, 2010 *Sa*, *Fj*, *J*
J Lino 1926 *Fj*, *Fj*, *Fj*
M Liongitau 1924 *Fj*, *Fj*, *Fj*
S Lisala 2005 *Sa*, *Fj*
S Lo'amanu 1926 *Fj*, *Fj*, *Fj*, 1928 *Fj*, *Fj*, *Fj*
L Lokotui 2001 *W*
S Lolo 1993 *Sa*
T Lolo'ahea 1987 *Sa*, 1990 *J*, *Sa*, *Kor*, *Sa*, 1991 *Sa*, *Fj*, *Fj*
L Lolohea 2007 *JAB*
P Lolohea 1983 *M*, *M*
K Lomu 1979 *Fj*
W Lose 1995 *F*, *S*, *Iv*
L Loto'ahea 1994 *Sa*
T Loto'ahea 1987 *Fj*, 1988 *Fj*, *Fj*, 1989 *Fj*, *Fj*, 1993 *S*, *Fj*, 1994 *W*, *Fj*
T Lovo 1982 *Sa*, 1986 *W*, *Fj*, *Fj*, 1987 *Sa*, 1988 *Fj*, 1989 *Fj*, *Fj*, 1990 *Sa*
S Lu'au 2007 *AuA*
I Lupina 1969 *M*, 1972 *Fj*
T Lutua 1990 *Kor*, 1992 *Fj*, 1994 *Sa*, *W*, *Fj*, 1995 *J*, *J*, *Iv*
V Lutua 1981 *Fj*, *Fj*, *Fj*, 1987 *W*, *I*, 1988 *Fj*, *Fj*
A Lutui 1999 *Geo*, *J*, *Sa*, *F*, 2001 *Fj*, *Fj*, *S*, *W*, 2004 *Sa*, *Fj*, 2005 *Fj*, *Sa*, *Fj*, *Sa*, 2006 *Fj*, *JAB*, 2007 *AuA*, *J*, *JAB*, *Fj*, *Sa*, *US*, *Sa*, *SA*, *E*, 2010 *Sa*, *Fj*, *J*
F Ma'afa 1981 *Fj*, *Fj*
F Ma'afu 1985 *Fj*, 1986 *Fj*, *Fj*, 1988 *Sa*, *Fj*, *Fj*, *Fj*
P Ma'afu 1979 *M*, *E*, *Sa*, *Fj*, 1980 *Sa*, 1981 *Fj*, *Fj*, 1983 *M*, *M*
P Ma'afu 1959 *Fj*, 1960 *M*, 1963 *Fj*
T Ma'afu 1983 *M*, *M*
V Ma'ake 1973 *M*, *A*, *A*, *Fj*, 1974 *S*, *W*, *C*, 1975 *M*, *M*, 1977 *Fj*, *Fj*, *Fj*, 1979 *NC*, *M*, *E*, *Sa*, *Fj*, 1980 *Sa*
I Ma'asi 2009 *Fj*, *Sa*, *J*
V Ma'asi 1997 *W*, 2000 *C*, *J*, *Sa*, *US*, 2001 *Fj*, *Fj*, *Sa*, *S*, *W*, 2002 *J*, *Fj*, *Sa*, *Sa*, 2003 *I*, *Fj*, *Fj*, *It*, *W*, *NZ*, *C*, 2005 *Fj*, *Sa*, *It*, *F*, 2008 *M*, *J*, *AuA*, *Sa*, *Fj*, 2009 *Fj*, *Sa*
S Mafana 1959 *Fj*, 1960 *M*, 1963 *Fj*, *Fj*
A Mafi 1995 *Iv*
F Mafi 1993 *A*, *Fj*, 1994 *Sa*, *W*, *Fj*, 1995 *J*, *J*, *F*, 1996 *Sa*, *Fj*, 1998 *Sa*, *A*, 1999 *Geo*, *Geo*, *Kor*, *J*, *US*, *NZ*, *It*, *E*
S Mafi 1969 *M*, *M*, 1972 *Fj*, *Fj*, *Fj*, 1973 *M*, *A*, *A*, *Fj*, 1974 *S*, *W*, *C*, 1975 *M*, *M*
S Mafi 1988 *Fj*, 1989 *Fj*, 1990 *Fj*, *Kor*, 1993 *Sa*
S Mafi 2010 *Sa*, *Fj*, *J*
S Mafile'o 1995 *Iv*, *Sa*, *Fj*, 1997 *Z*, *Nm*, *SA*, 2002 *J*, 2003 *Kor*, *Kor*, *I*, *Fj*
R Mahe 2005 *Sa*, *It*, *F*, 2006 *Fj*, *JAB*, *Coo*, *Coo*, 2007 *Kor*, 2009 *IrA*
S Mahe 1981 *Fj*, *Fj*, *Fj*
F Mahoni 1993 *Sa*, *A*, *Fj*, 1995 *J*, *J*, *F*, *Sa*, *Fj*, 1996 *Sa*, *Fj*, 1999 *Geo*, *J*
A Mailangi 2010 *J*
F Mailangi 1968 *Fj*, *Fj*, *Fj*, 1969 *M*
F Mailangi 1928 *Fj*, *Fj*
L Mailangi 1959 *Fj*, 1960 *M*, 1963 *Fj*, *Fj*
M Maile 2008 *AuA*
P Mailefihi 1979 *E*, 1982 *Fj*
AK Mailei 2002 *J*, *Fj*, *Sa*, *Sa*, *Fj*, *PNG*, *PNG*, 2003 *Kor*, *Kor*, 2010 *Sa*, *J*
A Ma'ilei 2005 *Fj*, *Sa*, *F*
T Mak 1988 *Fj*
A Maka 2005 *F*
F Maka 2007 *US*, *Sa*, *SA*, *E*
L Maka 1997 *Z*, 1999 *Geo*, *J*, *US*, *F*, *NZ*, *It*, *E*, 2000 *C*, *Fj*, *J*, *NZ*, *US*, 2002 *J*, *Sa*, *Fj*, 2003 *Kor*, *Kor*
P Maka 1985 *Fj*
T Maka 1979 *NC*, *Sa*, 1981 *Fj*, *Fj*
V Maka 1983 *Fj*, *Sa*, 1984 *Fj*, *Fj*
H Makahoi 1974 *C*, 1975 *M*, *M*, 1977 *Fj*, *Fj*, *Fj*, 1979 *Sa*, *Fj*, 1980 *Sa*
S Makalo 1975 *M*
M Makasini 2005 *Fj*, *Sa*, *Fj*, *Sa*
T Makisi 1983 *M*, *M*, 1989 *Fj*, *Fj*
Malu 1947 *Fj*
M Malu 1979 *NC*, *Sa*
MV Malupo 2009 *Sa*, *JAB*
L Manako 2000 *NZ*, *Sa*
T Manako 1995 *J*, *J*
T Manako 2000 *J*
C Manu 1987 *Sa*, *Fj*, 1989 *Fj*, *Fj*
E Manu 1996 *Sa*, *Fj*, 1999 *Kor*, *J*, *US*
F Manukia 1993 *A*, *Fj*, 1994 *Sa*, *W*, *Fj*, 1995 *J*, *J*
M Manukia 1993 *Sa*, *S*, *Fj*, *A*, *Fj*, 1994 *Fj*
T Mapa 1967 *Fj*, *Fj*
P Mapakaitolo 1977 *Fj*, *Fj*
P Mapakaitolo 2009 *Fj*, *J*
S Martens 1998 *A*, *Fj*, 1999 *Geo*, *Geo*, *Kor*, *Kor*, *J*, *US*, *Sa*, *F*, *Fj*, *C*, *NZ*, *It*, *E*, 2001 *S*, *W*, 2002 *Fj*, *Sa*, *Sa*, *Fj*, 2003 *Kor*, *Kor*, *It*, *W*, *NZ*, *C*, 2009 *Fj*, *Sa*, *J*
S Masi 1989 *Fj*
F Masila 1990 *J*, 1991 *Fj*, 1993 *Sa*, *S*, *A*, *Fj*, 1994 *W*, 1995 *F*, *Fj*, 1998 *Sa*, *A*
Masili 1991 *Fj*
SK Masima 2005 *Fj*
T Matakaiongo 1997 *W*
S Matangi 2000 *J*, *Sa*, 2001 *Fj*, *Sa*, 2002 *Fj*, *PNG*, 2004 *Sa*, *Fj*
S Matapule 1973 *M*, 1975 *M*
SH Mata'u 2007 *AuA*, 2008 *J*
S Mateaki 1928 *Fj*, *Fj*
K Ma'u 1981 *Fj*, 1983 *Fj*, *Sa*, *M*, 1984 *Fj*, *Fj*
T Ma'u 1947 *Fj*, *Fj*
V Ma'u 1947 *Fj*
O Misa 2004 *Sa*, *Fj*
S Misa 1926 *Fj*, *Fj*, *Fj*
S Moa 1928 *Fj*
U Moa 1998 *A*, *Fj*, 1999 *Geo*
V Moa 1993 *Sa*, *S*, 1998 *Sa*
F Moala 1982 *Sa*, *Fj*, 1983 *Fj*, *Sa*, *M*, *M*, 1984 *Fj*, *Fj*, 1985 *Fj*
F Moala 1982 *Sa*, 1983 *Sa*, 1985 *Fj*
F Moala 1963 *Fj*, *Fj*, 1968 *Fj*, *Fj*, *Fj*
K Moala 1959 *Fj*, 1960 *M*, 1963 *Fj*, 1967 *Fj*, *Fj*
M Moala 1986 *W*, *Fj*, *Fj*
M Moala 2004 *Sa*, *Fj*, 2009 *IrA*, *S*, *Pt*
P Moala 1982 *Sa*, 1986 *W*, *Fj*, *Fj*, 1987 *Sa*, *Fj*
P Moala 1981 *Fj*, *Fj*, *Fj*
S Moala 1988 *Fj*
T Moala 1972 *Fj*
V Moala'eua 1977 *Fj*, *Fj*, *Fj*, 1979 *NC*, *M*, *Sa*, *Fj*, 1981 *Fj*, *Fj*
V Moeaki 1934 *Fj*
Mofuike 1986 *Fj*
S Mohi 1986 *W*, *Fj*, *Fj*, 1987 *C*, *W*, *I*
S Moimoi 2001 *W*
S Moli 1992 *Fj*
F Molitika 2000 *C*, *J*, 2001 *Fj*, *Sa*, *S*, 2005 *It*, *F*
MK Molitika 1997 *Nm*, *SA*, *Fj*, *Sa*, *Coo*, *W*, 2000 *NZ*, *Sa*, *US*, 2001 *S*, 2005 *It*, 2006 *Fj*, *JAB*, *Coo*, *Sa*, 2007 *E*
DW Morath 2010 *Sa*, *Fj*
K Morath 2009 *IrA*, *S*, *Pt*, 2010 *Sa*, *Fj*, *J*
S Moto'apuaka 1980 *Sa*, 1987 *C*
K Motu'apuaka 1972 *Fj*
S Motu'apuaka 1969 *M*, *M*, 1972 *Fj*
S Motu'apuka 1979 *Fj*
S Motuliki 1967 *Fj*
Mounga 1947 *Fj*
E Mo'ungaloa 1924 *Fj*, *Fj*, *Fj*
F Muller 1967 *Fj*, 1968 *Fj*, *Fj*, *Fj*, 1969 *M*, *M*, 1972 *Fj*, *Fj*

S Na'a Tovo 1924 *Fj, Fj, Fj*
T Na'aniumotu 2006 *J, JAB, Coo, Sa, Coo*
F Naitoko 2005 *Sa*
S Napa'a 1934 *Fj*
S Nau 2000 *C, Fj, J*, 2001 *Fj*, 2003 *Fj*, 2005 *It, F*, 2006 *JAB, Coo, Sa*
N Naufahu 2001 *Fj, Sa, Fj, W*, 2002 *J, Sa, Sa, Fj, PNG, PNG*, 2003 *Kor, Kor, I, W, C*
S Nauvai 1960 *M*
T Ngaluafe 1974 *S, W, C*, 1975 *M, M*
J Ngauamo 2003 *Kor, I, Fj, It, C*, 2005 *It*
MM Ngauamo 2002 *PNG, PNG*, 2003 *Kor, I, Fj, It, W, NZ, C*, 2005 *F*, 2006 *Fj, JAB*, 2008 *Sa, Fj*
S Ngauamo 1997 *Coo*, 1998 *A*
T Nisa 1991 *Fj*, 1992 *Fj*
U Niuila 1990 *Sa*
S Nuku 1981 *Fj, Fj, Fj*, 1984 *Fj, Fj*
L Ofa 1983 *Fj, Sa, M, M*, 1984 *Fj*
A Olosoni 2010 *Sa, Fj, J*
I Omani 1928 *Fj*, 1932 *Fj, Fj, Fj*
M 'Otai 1995 *J, J, F, S, Iv*
M 'Ota'ota 2000 *C*, 2005 *Fj, Sa, Fj*
H Paea 2007 *Kor*
L Pahulu 1973 *A, Fj*, 1974 *S*
V Pahulu 1967 *Fj, Fj, Fj*, 1968 *Fj, Fj, Fj*, 1969 *M, M*, 1973 *M*
P Palavi 1924 *Fj, Fj, Fj*
U Palavi 1960 *M*, 1963 *Fj, Fj*
J Pale 2001 *S, W*, 2002 *J, Fj, Sa, Sa, Fj*, 2003 *Fj*
M Pale 1998 *A*, 1999 *Geo*, 2002 *J, Fj*, 2006 *J, Coo, Sa*
SW Palei 2009 *J, JAB*
S Palenapa 1990 *Fj, J, Sa, Kor, Sa*, 1996 *Sa, Fj*
D Palu 2002 *PNG, PNG*, 2003 *Kor, Kor, I, Fj, C*, 2006 *J, JAB, Coo*, 2007 *AuA, J, JAB*
P Palu 1979 *NC*, 1981 *Fj*
TM Palu 2008 *M, J, AuA*
S Panelapa 1988 *Fj*
H Pau'u 1983 *Fj, Sa*
T Pau'u 1992 *Fj*
J Payne 2002 *PNG, PNG*, 2003 *Kor, Kor, I, Fj, It, W, NZ, C*
D Penisini 1997 *Nm, Coo*, 1999 *Geo, Kor, C*
'O Pepa 1928 *Fj, Fj, Fj*
H Petelo 1982 *Fj*
H Pierra 2005 *Sa*
O Pifeleti 1983 *Fj, Sa, M, M*, 1984 *Fj, Fj*, 1985 *Fj*, 1989 *Fj, Fj*, 1990 *Sa*, 1991 *Sa, Fj, Fj*
S Piukala 2008 *AuA*
T Piukala 1934 *Fj*
H Pohiva 1997 *W*, 1998 *Sa, Fj*
VV Pola 2010 *Fj*
THN Pole 2007 *Kor, AuA, J, JAB, Fj, Sa, US, Sa, E*, 2008 *M, Sa, Fj*, 2009 *Fj, Sa, J*
S Pone 2008 *M, AuA, Sa, Fj*
S Pongi 1990 *Sa*
SE Poteki 2007 *Kor*
VT Poteki 2007 *Kor*, 2008 *M*
S Pouanga 1947 *Fj, Fj*
E Pou'uhila 1988 *Fj*
ST Puloka 1928 *Fj, Fj*, 1934 *Fj*
K Pulu 2002 *Fj, PNG, PNG*, 2003 *Kor, Kor, I, Fj, It, W, NZ*, 2005 *Fj, Sa, Fj, Sa*, 2006 *J*, 2007 *US, Sa, SA, E*, 2008 *Fj*, 2009 *Sa, J*
M Pulumu 1979 *NC, Sa, Fj*, 1980 *Sa*, 1981 *Fj, Fj, Fj*
T Pulumufila 1974 *S, W, C*
H Saafi 2000 *NZ*
T Samiu 1947 *Fj*
Sanilaita 1981 *Fj*
S Satui 2009 *S, Pt*
A Saulala 1991 *Fj*
C Schaumkel 1992 *Sa, Fj*, 1997 *SA, Fj*
S Selupe 1963 *Fj, Fj*, 1967 *Fj, Fj*, 1969 *M, M*, 1972 *Fj*, 1973 *M, A, Fj*
S Selupe 1967 *Fj*, 1969 *M*, 1972 *Fj*
S Selupe 1924 *Fj, Fj, Fj*, 1928 *Fj*
T Siale 1997 *Nm, Sa*
M Sifa 1947 *Fj*
S Sika 1968 *Fj, Fj, Fj*, 1969 *M, M*
AH Sikalu 2007 *AuA, J*, 2010 *Sa, Fj*
T Sime 1963 *Fj*
T Sitanilei 1932 *Fj*
J Sitoa 1998 *A*
E Siua 2009 *Pt*
T Soaiti 1932 *Fj, Fj, Fj*
T Soane 1982 *Sa, Fj*, 1983 *Fj, Sa*, 1984 *Fj, Fj*, 1985 *Fj*
L Stanley 1985 *Fj*
L Susimalofi 1989 *Fj*
L Tafa 2007 *J*
S Tahaafe 1987 *C*
P Taholo 1983 *M*
S Tai 1997 *W*, 1998 *A*
U Tai 1969 *M*, 1972 *Fj*
E Taione 1999 *It, E*, 2000 *Fj, J*, 2001 *S, W*, 2005 *F*, 2006 *JAB, Sa*, 2007 *Fj, Sa, US, Sa, SA, E*, 2008 *M, Sa, Fj*, 2009 *Fj*
K Take 1989 *Fj*
E Talakai 1993 *Sa, S, Fj, Fj*, 1995 *S, Iv, Sa, Fj*
H Taliai 1934 *Fj*
P Tanginoa 1995 *Fj*, 1997 *W*, 1998 *Sa, A*, 1999 *Geo*
T Tanginoa 2007 *AuA, J*
F Taniela 1982 *Fj*
I Tapueluelu 1990 *Fj, J, Sa, Sa*, 1993 *Sa, S*, 1999 *Kor, Kor, J, US, NZ, It, E*
F Tatafu 1996 *Fj*, 1997 *Z, Nm, Fj, Sa, Coo, W*, 1999 *Geo, Kor, Kor, J, Sa, Fj, C, NZ, E*, 2002 *J, Fj, Sa, PNG, PNG*
S Tatafu 1967 *Fj*
T Tatafu 1963 *Fj*
V Tau 1999 *US*
A Taufa 1993 *A*, 1995 *J, J, F, S*
A Taufa 2010 *Sa, Fj, J*
E Taufa 2007 *Sa*, 2008 *M, J, AuA, Sa, Fj*
I Taufa 1972 *Fj*
S Taufa 1984 *Fj*
S Taufa 2005 *Fj, Sa, Fj, Sa*
T Taufa 1990 *Fj*
T Taufahema 1998 *Sa, A, Fj*, 1999 *Sa, F, NZ, It*, 2000 *C, Fj, J, NZ, Sa*, 2001 *Fj, Sa, Fj, S, W*
M Taufateau 1983 *M, M*, 1984 *Fj*, 1987 *Fj*
V Taufatofua 1926 *Fj, Fj, Fj*
A Ta'ufo'ou 1997 *Nm, SA, Fj, Sa, Coo*
E Ta'ufo'ou 2000 *C, Fj, J, NZ, Sa, US*
N Taufo'ou 1996 *Sa, Fj*, 1997 *Nm, SA, Fj, Sa, Coo, W*, 1998 *Sa, A, Fj*, 1999 *Geo, Kor, F, Fj, NZ, It, E*, 2000 *NZ, Sa, US*
E Taukafa 2002 *PNG, PNG*, 2003 *Kor, Kor, Fj, Fj, It, W, NZ, C*, 2005 *Fj, Sa, It, F*, 2006 *J, Fj, Coo, Sa, Coo*, 2007 *US, Sa, SA, E*, 2008 *Sa, Fj*
S Taukapo 2005 *Sa*
P Taukolo 1982 *Sa, Fj*
P Taula 2009 *Fj, JAB, IrA, S, Pt*, 2010 *Sa, Fj, J*
S Taumalolo 1996 *Sa, Fj*, 1997 *Z, Nm, SA, Coo, W*, 1999 *Geo, Geo, Sa, F, Fj, C, NZ*, 2000 *NZ, Sa, US*, 2001 *Fj, Sa, S, W*, 2006 *J*, 2007 *JAB, Fj, Sa*
P Taumiuvao 1986 *Fj*
N Taumoefolau 1979 *NC, E, Sa, Fj*
P Taumoepeau 1928 *Fj, Fj, Fj*
T Taumoepeau 1999 *Geo, Kor, Kor, J, US, NZ, E*, 2000 *Fj, J, NZ, Sa, US*, 2001 *Fj, Sa, Sa, S, W*, 2002 *J, Fj, Sa*, 2006 *J, Fj, JAB, Coo, Sa, Coo*, 2007 *AuA, J, Fj, Sa*
T Taumoepeau 1988 *Fj*
V Taumoepeau 1994 *Sa, W*, 1995 *Sa, Fj*
P Taumoua 2007 *J*
S Taupeaafe 1994 *W, Fj*, 1998 *Sa, A, Fj*, 1999 *Kor, J, NZ, It, E*, 2000 *NZ, US*, 2001 *Fj, Sa*
F Tautau'a 2007 *Kor*
S Tavo 1959 *Fj*, 1960 *M*, 1963 *Fj, Fj*, 1967 *Fj, Fj, Fj*, 1968 *Fj, Fj, Fj*, 1969 *M, M*
M Te Pou 1998 *A, Fj*, 1999 *Geo, Geo, Kor, Kor, J, US, F, NZ, It*, 2001 *S, W*
Telanisi 1967 *Fj*
S Telefoni 2008 *M, J, AuA, Sa, Fj*, 2009 *IrA, Pt*
Teri 1991 *Fj*
Teutau 1991 *Fj*
SLN Timani 2008 *J, AuA*, 2009 *Fj, JAB*
D Tiueti 1997 *Fj, Sa, W*, 1999 *Geo, Geo, Kor, Sa, F, Fj, C, NZ, It, E*, 2000 *C, Fj, J, NZ, Sa, US*, 2001 *S, W*
T Tofua 1924 *Fj, Fj, Fj*, 1926 *Fj, Fj, Fj*
T Toga 1968 *Fj*
T Tohi 1997 *Nm, SA*
T Toke 2007 *Kor, J, JAB, Fj, Sa, US, Sa*, 2008 *M, AuA*, 2009 *Fj, JAB, IrA*, 2010 *Sa, Fj, J*
V Toloke 1995 *J, Sa, Fj*, 1996 *Sa, Fj*, 1999 *Geo, Geo, Kor, Kor, US, NZ, E*, 2000 *NZ, Sa, US*, 2002 *J, Sa*
M Toma 1988 *Sa, Fj, Fj*, 1991 *Sa, Fj, Fj*

G Tonga 1997 *Z, W*
K Tonga 1996 *Fj*, 1997 *Nm, SA, Fj, Sa, Coo*, 1999 *Geo, Geo, Kor*, 2001 *Fj, Sa*
K Tonga 2003 *Fj, C*, 2004 *Sa, Fj*, 2005 *Fj, Fj*
K Tonga 1947 *Fj, Fj*
M Tonga 2001 *Fj, Sa, Fj, Sa*, 2003 *Kor, Kor*
M Tonga 1947 *Fj, Fj*
P Tonga 1973 *A*
S Tonga 2005 *Sa, Fj, Sa*
T Tonga 1990 *Sa*
S Tonga Simiki 1924 *Fj*, 1926 *Fj, Fj, Fj*
H Tonga'uiha 2005 *Fj, Sa, Sa*, 2006 *J, Fj, JAB, Coo, Sa, Coo*, 2007 *Kor, AuA, J, JAB, Fj, Sa, E*, 2008 *M, J, Sa, Fj*, 2009 *Fj, Sa, J*
SL Tonga'uiha 2005 *It, F*, 2007 *JAB, US, Sa, SA, E*
'O Topeni 2000 *J*
J Tuamoheloa 2003 *Fj*
S Tuamoheloa 2003 *Fj, C*, 2005 *Fj*
T Tuavao 1986 *Fj*
N Tufui 1990 *Fj, J, Sa, Sa*, 1992 *Fj*, 1994 *Fj*, 1995 *S, Iv*
S Tufui 1926 *Fj, Fj, Fj*, 1928 *Fj, Fj, Fj*, 1932 *Fj, Fj, Fj*, 1934 *Fj*
TH Tu'ifua 2003 *Fj, It, W, NZ*, 2006 *J, Fj, JAB, Coo, Sa*, 2007 *Fj, Sa, US, Sa, SA, E*
S Tu'ihalamaka 1999 *Kor, Kor, J, US*, 2001 *Sa, Fj*
P Tui'halamaka 1972 *Fj*, 1973 *M, A, A, Fj*, 1974 *S, C*, 1975 *M, M*, 1977 *Fj, Fj*, 1979 *NC*, 1981 *Fj, Fj, Fj*, 1987 *C*
Tu'ikolovatu 1983 *Fj*
T Tu'ineua 1992 *Fj*, 1993 *Sa, S, Fj, A, Fj*
E Tu'ipolotu 1926 *Fj, Fj, Fj*, 1928 *Fj, Fj*
S Tu'ipolotu 1981 *Fj*
S Tu'ipolotu 1947 *Fj, Fj*
K Tuipulotu 1994 *Fj*, 1997 *Fj, Sa, Coo*
K Tu'ipulotu 1994 *W*, 1997 *SA, Fj, Coo, W*, 1999 *Kor, Kor, J, US, Fj, It, E*, 2000 *Fj, J*, 2001 *Fj*
M Tu'ipulotu 1977 *Fj, Fj, Fj*
P Tu'ipulotu 1979 *Sa*, 1980 *Sa*
S Tu'ipulotu 1993 *Fj*, 1994 *Sa, W, Fj*, 1995 *J, J, F, S, Iv*, 1999 *Kor, F, Fj, C, It, E*, 2001 *S*, 2003 *Fj, Fj, It, NZ*
SM Tu'ipulotu 1997 *W*, 1998 *Sa, A*, 1999 *Sa, F, NZ, E*, 2000 *C, NZ, Sa, US*, 2001 *Fj, Fj, Sa*, 2005 *Fj, Sa, It, F*, 2006 *J, Fj, JAB, Coo, Sa*, 2007 *US, Sa, SA, E*, 2008 *M, J, AuA, Sa*
V Tu'ipulotu 1977 *Fj, Fj, Fj*, 1979 *M, E, Fj*
J Tu'itavake 1932 *Fj*
L Tu'itavake 1959 *Fj*, 1960 *M*, 1963 *Fj, Fj*
P Tu'itavake 1995 *Fj*
I Tuivai 1993 *Sa*
K Tuivailala 1987 *Sa*, 1988 *Sa, Fj, Fj*, 1989 *Fj, Fj*, 1990 *Fj, J, Sa, Kor*, 1991 *Fj*
K Tuivailala 1988 *Fj*
M Tuku'aho 1979 *Fj*
M Tuku'aho 1979 *NC, Sa*, 1980 *Sa*, 1982 *Sa*
T Tulia 2003 *Kor, Kor, I, Fj*, 2004 *Sa, Fj*, 2005 *Fj, Sa*
A Tulikaki 1993 *S*
S Tulikifanga 1997 *SA, Fj, Sa, Coo*
S Tunufa'i 1934 *Fj*
F Tupi 1973 *A, A, Fj*, 1974 *S, W*, 1975 *M, M*
H Tupou 1982 *Sa, Fj*, 1983 *M, M*, 1984 *Fj, Fj*, 1987 *C, W, I*
IM Tupou 2006 *Coo, Coo*, 2007 *Kor, AuA, J, JAB, US, Sa, SA*, 2008 *J*, 2009 *Fj, Sa, JAB*
J Tupou 1994 *Fj*
M Tupou 2005 *Fj, Fj, Sa*
P Tupou 1984 *Fj*, 1986 *W*, 1988 *Fj*
S Tupou 1975 *M*
M Tu'ungafasi 1986 *W, Fj*, 1987 *W, I*
L Tu'uta 1928 *Fj, Fj*
T Tu'utu Kakato 1987 *C, W, I*, 1990 *Sa, Kor*, 1991 *Sa, Fj*, 1992 *Fj*
A Uasi 1993 *S*, 1994 *Sa, Fj*
L Uhatafe 1987 *Sa, Fj*
V Uhi 1997 *Z, Nm, SA, Fj, Sa, Coo*
S Ula 1959 *Fj*, 1960 *M*, 1963 *Fj, Fj*
L Ulufonua 2002 *PNG*, 2003 *Kor, Kor, Fj*
T Unga 1934 *Fj*
S Vaea 1974 *S, W, C*, 1975 *M*, 1977 *Fj, Fj*
S Vaea 1928 *Fj, Fj, Fj*
L Vaeno 1986 *Fj*
S Vaeno 1991 *Sa*
S Va'enuku 2003 *Fj, It, W, NZ*, 2004 *Sa, Fj*, 2005 *Sa, Fj, Sa, It*, 2007 *AuA, Sa*
T Va'enuku 1991 *Sa, Fj*, 1992 *Sa, Fj*, 1993 *S, Fj, A, Fj*, 1994 *Sa, W, Fj*, 1995 *F, S, Iv*
U Va'enuku 1995 *F, S, Iv*
L Va'eono 1987 *W*
L Vaeuo 1985 *Fj*
S Vaha'akolo 1990 *J, Kor*
S Vahafolau 2007 *J, Fj, Sa*, 2008 *Sa, Fj*, 2009 *IrA, S, Pt*
N Vahe 1977 *Fj, Fj*
S Vai 1981 *Fj, Fj*, 1988 *Sa, Fj*
A Vaihu 1975 *M*
T Vaikona 2006 *J, Fj, JAB, Coo*
H Vaingalo 1988 *Fj*
T Vaioleti 2005 *F*
SFK Vaiomounga 2009 *S, Pt*, 2010 *Sa, Fj, J*
L Vaipulu 1987 *C*
JW Vaka 2004 *Sa, Fj*, 2005 *Sa*, 2007 *US, Sa, SA, E*, 2009 *Fj, Sa, J, JAB, IrA, S*
PM Vakaloa 2009 *IrA, Pt*
P Vakamalolo 1993 *Sa*
I Vaka'uta 1959 *Fj*, 1963 *Fj, Fj*
S Vaka'uta 1924 *Fj, Fj, Fj*
V Vaka'uta 1959 *Fj*, 1960 *M*
V Vake 1932 *Fj*
VL Vaki 2001 *Fj, Sa, Fj, Sa, S, W*, 2002 *J, Fj, Sa, Sa, Fj*, 2003 *Fj, Fj, It, W, NZ, C*, 2005 *Fj, Sa, It, F*, 2006 *JAB, Coo, Sa, Coo*, 2007 *US, Sa, SA, E*, 2008 *Fj*
Valeli 1947 *Fj*
F Valu 1973 *M, A, A, Fj*, 1974 *S, W, C*, 1975 *M, M*, 1977 *Fj, Fj, Fj*, 1979 *NC, M, E, Sa, Fj*, 1980 *Sa*, 1981 *Fj*, 1983 *Fj, Sa, M, M*, 1987 *C, W, I*
V Vanisi 1969 *M, M*
L Vano 1986 *Fj*
A Vasi 1993 *Fj*
I Vave 1973 *A, A, Fj*, 1974 *S, C*
T Vave 1993 *A*
M Vea 1992 *Fj*
S Veehala 1987 *Sa, Fj*, 1988 *Fj, Fj*, 1989 *Fj*, 1990 *J, Kor*, 1991 *Sa, Fj, Fj*
J Vikilani 1932 *Fj, Fj*
T Vikilani 1992 *Fj*, 1994 *Sa, W*
T Viliame 1979 *M*
O Vitelefi 1986 *W*
F Vuna 1977 *Fj, Fj, Fj*, 1979 *NC, M, Sa*, 1981 *Fj*
V Vuni 1932 *Fj, Fj, Fj*, 1934 *Fj*
A Vunipola 1982 *Fj*
E Vunipola 1990 *Fj, Kor*, 1993 *Sa, S, Fj, A, Fj*, 1994 *Sa, W*, 1995 *J, J, F, S, Iv*, 1996 *Sa, Fj*, 1997 *Z*, 1999 *Geo, Geo, Kor, Kor, J, F, Fj, NZ, It, E*, 2000 *C, Fj, J, NZ, Sa, US*, 2001 *Fj, Sa, Fj, Sa, S*, 2004 *Sa, Fj*, 2005 *F*
F Vunipola 1988 *Fj*, 1991 *Sa, Fj, Fj*, 1994 *Sa, W, Fj*, 1995 *J, J, F, S, Iv, Sa, Fj*, 1996 *Sa, Fj*, 1997 *SA, Fj, Coo*, 1998 *Sa, Fj*, 1999 *Geo, Kor, Kor, Fj, C, NZ, E*, 2000 *NZ, Sa, US*, 2001 *Sa*
K Vunipola 1982 *Sa, Fj*, 1983 *Fj, Sa, M, M*
M Vunipola 1987 *W, Sa*, 1988 *Sa, Fj, Fj, Fj*, 1989 *Fj, Fj*, 1990 *Kor*, 1991 *Fj, Fj*, 1992 *Sa*, 1993 *Sa, S, Fj, A, Fj*, 1994 *Sa, W*, 1995 *J, J, F, S, Sa, Fj*, 1996 *Sa, Fj*, 1997 *Nm, SA, Coo*, 1999 *Geo, Kor, Kor, US, Fj*
S Vunipola 1977 *Fj*, 1981 *Fj*, 1982 *Sa*
V Vunipola 1982 *Fj*
VS Vunipola 2004 *Sa, Fj*, 2005 *It*
S Vunipoli 1960 *M*, 1963 *Fj*
B Woolley 1998 *Sa, Fj*, 1999 *Geo, Geo, Kor, J, US, Sa, C, It*

USA

USA'S 2009–10 TEST RECORD

OPPONENTS	DATE	VENUE	RESULT
Uruguay	14 Nov	A	**Won** 27–22
Uruguay	21 Nov	H	**Won** 27–6
Russia	5 Jun	H	**Won** 39–22
England Saxons	13 Jun	H	**Lost** 9–32
France A	19 Jun	H	**Lost** 10–24

OPPORTUNITY KNOCKS FOR USA

By Alex Goff

For the first time in several years, the USA national team began a new calendar year untroubled by instability. Coach Eddie O'Sullivan had taken charge early in 2009 and was building on the plans he'd set in place. The team had qualified for Rugby World Cup 2011, and had a busy schedule to look forward to. It was a far cry from the coach changeovers, sparse schedules and uncertainty of previous years.

The 2010 season really started in November, when the USA played a home-and-away series with Uruguay to claim the Americas 2 qualification place at the World Cup.

After losing to Canada it was on to Montevideo, where a seemingly insurmountable lead almost disappeared as Uruguay stormed back in a game when captain Todd Clever said "the top four inches let us down".

The team didn't play the clock well and kept committing penalties, which Jeronimo Etcheverry punished to cut the deficit to 27–22.

The Eagles did a better job a week later in Florida to hand O'Sullivan a 27–6 victory as a birthday present. Hayden Smith led a gritty forward effort and Clever scored two crowd-pleasing tries to put Los Teros away.

"Now we can plan for the next 18 months," said a slightly relieved O'Sullivan. "It gives us the opportunity to really put some things in place."

USA can now look forward to Pool C matches with Australia, Ireland, Italy and Russia at Rugby World Cup 2011 in New Zealand. O'Sullivan recognises the difficulty of taking on the Wallabies, and the expected media stampede on the rematch with his home country Ireland, but the Russians and Italians are clearly targeted by the Eagles for World Cup wins.

"If we win two, we've got automatic qualification for the next one," O'Sullivan said. "It's certainly going to be difficult, but we think it's reasonable to target games we can reasonably expect to win. We've got the chance now to build through the year going into the World Cup."

So with the plan in place for 2010 and 2011, O'Sullivan looked to make a few changes, dropping some long-time veterans for young guns, and giving some opportunities for some promising gridiron crossovers.

The results were mixed. The Eagles rebounded from a poor first half to defeat Russia 39–22 in June's Churchill Cup – an important result against a team they hadn't seen since 2004 and one they will meet again at RWC 2011 – but faltered against the England Saxons to lose 32–9. In the Plate Final against France A, they let scoring opportunities slide and lost 24–10 in a game they felt they could have won.

But winning one and losing two didn't tell the whole story. Their captain and best player Clever missed the Churchill Cup with a shoulder injury. Starting lock Hayden Smith was also out. O'Sullivan was testing new players in almost every position, and yet they were as competitive as they have ever been.

"We've got a very young squad," said Nigel Melville, the CEO and President of Rugby Operations for USA Rugby. "If you look at the whole of it, the strategy with Eddie has been for him to work with a group of young coaches and young players who could go through to the World Cup.

"The main thing is we've had steady improvement which I think was very, very important."

With only the Churchill Cup and November tours in which to play Test matches, players get much of their international exposure on the IRB Sevens World Series. USA Sevens coach Al Caravelli had hoped to field a consistent squad through the 2009–2010 season, but injuries and professional contracts made that tough. As a result the season started off roughly, the worries starting to mount after Wellington, where the USA again left without any Series' points. But signs of promise could be seen in winning their final two matches, including a dramatic Shield Final win over Tonga.

And so to Las Vegas.

The players were thrilled at the new location, the fans embraced the Las Vegas party atmosphere, and coaches worried about keeping their players' heads in the game.

Vegas turned out to be the perfect location for an IRB Sevens tournament, and it also proved to be the place where the USA Sevens team found its rhythm, winning the Bowl Final.

That tournament led to bigger things, as the USA made the Adelaide Sevens final in Australia, losing to eventual Series champions Samoa 38–10. Caravelli had to make more changes going into the final two tournaments of the year, but his team had again shown their potential. In this coming season, stability in the squad will be key.

"We've used Sevens as a development tool and it's done very well," Melville added. "A lot of good players have come out of that programme – Chris Wyles, Kevin Swiryn, Z Ngwenya. It's a great way to get players to develop their skills and play in an international environment, but with the Pan-Am Games and Olympics coming up, the question is whether we continue to use it as a development tool."

Clearly the United States Olympic Committee sees the USA Women's

Sevens programme as one capable of winning a medal, so it was frustrating for everyone to see that programme do little in 2010.

Coach Sue Parker took a young team to Dubai in December 2009, and then new coach Ric Suggitt took a split squad to Las Vegas in February, where they tellingly lost to China in the final. That was it. Suggitt spent the rest of the year scouring the country for young talent and new blood.

All the resources for women's international rugby in the USA went to the fifteens team for Women's Rugby World Cup 2010. Drawn in a tough pool with Kazakhstan, Ireland and hosts England, the Women's Eagles knew they needed the right preparation to challenge for a top four spot.

For the first time the players received a per diem, and entered the World Cup full of confidence. They duly overwhelmed Kazakhstan 51–0 in their opening Pool C match, only to then fall foul of Ireland in a must-win game, unable to retain possession and going down 22–12.

After that a competitive performance against England – the USA was the only team to score two tries against the hosts in a 37–10 defeat – was somewhat anti-climactic, failing to make the top four.

American rugby players are nothing if not resilient and they bounced back impressively in the play-off stages, edging Canada 23–20 for fifth place.

Domestically the Women's Premier League was launched in the fall of 2009, with eight of the top clubs in the nation playing each other. Following that model, somewhat, is the College Premier League.

Frustrated with lack of regular, high-level competition, and confident that college sports is what American fans want to see, the collegiate teams pushed for a national league. In the spring of 2011 they will get it, as 31 teams will play in a national competition.

In June 2010 the company that puts on the USA Sevens tournament started a Sevens Collegiate Rugby Championship. The event drew 16 university teams and was broadcast live on NBC. That single event has started a massive growth in collegiate Sevens teams and tournaments, riding the Olympic wave.

Domestically, New York Athletic Club recorded their third Super League championship with a last-minute victory over San Francisco Golden Gate. The University of California reclaimed the national collegiate title they lost to BYU a year before. Penn State won their second straight women's college title, beating Stanford, the six straight final between the rivals.

At the youth level the game continues to grow quickly, and the success in getting the Sevens Collegiate Rugby Championship on television – and NBC also securing broadcast rights for the 2011 World Cup – means rugby will be on the minds of many Americans in 2011.

USA INTERNATIONAL STATISTICS

MATCH RECORDS UP TO 29TH OCTOBER 2010

WINNING MARGIN

Date	Opponent	Result	Winning Margin
01/07/2006	Barbados	91–0	**91**
06/07/1996	Japan	74–5	**69**
07/11/1989	Uruguay	60–3	**57**
12/03/1994	Bermuda	60–3	**57**

MOST POINTS IN A MATCH

BY THE TEAM

Date	Opponent	Result	Pts.
01/07/2006	Barbados	91–0	**91**
06/07/1996	Japan	74–5	**74**
17/05/2003	Japan	69–27	**69**
12/04/2003	Spain	62–13	**62**
08/04/1998	Portugal	61–5	**61**

MOST TRIES IN A MATCH

BY THE TEAM

Date	Opponent	Result	Tries
01/07/2006	Barbados	91–0	**13**
17/05/2003	Japan	69–27	**11**
07/11/1989	Uruguay	60–3	**11**
06/07/1996	Japan	74–5	**11**

MOST CONVERSIONS IN A MATCH

BY THE TEAM

Date	Opponent	Result	Cons
01/07/2006	Barbados	91–0	**13**
07/11/1989	Uruguay	60–3	**8**
06/07/1996	Japan	74–5	**8**

MOST PENALTIES IN A MATCH

BY THE TEAM

Date	Opponent	Result	Pens
18/09/1996	Canada	18–23	**6**

MOST DROP GOALS IN A MATCH

BY THE TEAM

Date	Player	Opponent	DGS
	16 Matches		**1**

MOST POINTS IN A MATCH

BY A PLAYER

Date	Player	Opponent	Pts.
07/11/1989	Chris O'Brien	Uruguay	**26**
31/05/2004	Mike Hercus	Russia	**26**
01/07/2006	Mike Hercus	Barbados	**26**
12/03/1994	Chris O'Brien	Bermuda	**25**
06/07/1996	Matt Alexander	Japan	**24**

MOST TRIES IN A MATCH

BY A PLAYER

Date	Player	Opponent	Tries
06/07/1996	Vaea Anitoni	Japan	**4**
07/06/1997	Brian Hightower	Japan	**4**
08/04/1998	Vaea Anitoni	Portugal	**4**

MOST CONVERSIONS IN A MATCH

BY A PLAYER

Date	Player	Opponent	Cons
01/07/2006	Mike Hercus	Barbados	13
06/07/1996	Matt Alexander	Japan	8
07/11/1989	Chris O'Brien	Uruguay	7
17/05/2003	Mike Hercus	Japan	7

MOST PENALTIES IN A MATCH

BY A PLAYER

Date	Player	Opponent	Pens
18/09/1996	Matt Alexander	Canada	6
21/09/1996	Matt Alexander	Uruguay	5
02/10/1993	Chris O'Brien	Australia	5
20/10/2003	Mike Hercus	Scotland	5
22/05/1999	Kevin Dalzell	Fiji	5
09/06/1984	Ray Nelson	Canada	5

MOST DROP GOALS IN A MATCH

BY THE TEAM

Date	Player	Opponent	DGS
	16 Players		1

MOST CAPPED PLAYERS

Name	Caps
Luke Gross	62
Mike MacDonald	58
Alec Parker	55
Dave Hodges	53

LEADING TRY SCORERS

Name	Tries
Vaea Anitoni	26
Philip Eloff	10
Riaan van Zyl	10
Paul Emerick	10

LEADING CONVERSIONS SCORERS

Name	Cons
Mike Hercus	90
Matt Alexander	45
Chris O'Brien	24
Grant Wells	14

LEADING PENALTY SCORERS

Name	Pens
Mike Hercus	76
Matt Alexander	55
Mark Williams	35

LEADING DROP GOAL SCORERS

Name	DGs
Mike Hercus	4

LEADING POINTS SCORERS

Name	Pts.
Mike Hercus	465
Matt Alexander	286
Chris O'Brien	144
Mark Williams	143
Vaea Anitoni	130

USA INTERNATIONAL PLAYERS
UP TO 29TH OCTOBER 2010

Note: Years given for International Championship matches are for second half of season; eg. 1972 means season 1971–72. Years for all other matches refer to the actual year of the match.

M Alexander 1995 *C*, 1996 *I*, *C*, *HK*, *J*, *HK*, *J*, *Ar*, *C*, *Ur*, 1997 *W*, *C*, *HK*, *J*, *J*, *HK*, *C*, *W*, *W*, 1998 *Pt*, *Sp*, *J*, *HK*, *C*
AE Allen 1912 *A*
S Allen 1996 *J*, 1997 *HK*, *J*, *J*, *C*, *W*, *W*
T Altemeier 1978 *C*
D Anderson 2002 *S*
B Andrews 1978 *C*, 1979 *C*
VN Anitoni 1992 *C*, 1994 *C*, *Ar*, *Ar*, *I*, 1995 *C*, 1996 *I*, *C*, *C*, *HK*, *J*, *HK*, *J*, *Ar*, *C*, *Ur*, 1997 *W*, *C*, *J*, *HK*, *C*, *W*, *W*, 1998 *Pt*, *Sp*, *J*, *HK*, *C*, *C*, *J*, *HK*, *Fj*, *Ar*, *C*, *Ur*, 1999 *Tg*, *Fj*, *J*, *C*, *Sa*, *E*, *I*, *R*, *A*, 2000 *Fj*, *Sa*
J Arrell 1912 *A*
S Auerbach 1976 *A*
CA Austin 1912 *A*, 1913 *NZ*
M Aylor 2006 *IrA*, *M*, *C*, *Bar*, *Ur*, *Ur*, 2007 *S*, *C*, *Sa*, *SA*, 2008 *IrA*
A Bachelet 1993 *C*, *A*, 1994 *Ber*, *C*, *Ar*, *Ar*, *I*, 1995 *C*, 1996 *I*, *C*, *C*, *HK*, *J*, *HK*, *J*, *Ar*, *C*, 1997 *W*, *C*, *HK*, *J*, *J*, *HK*, *C*, *W*, *W*, 1998 *Pt*, *Sp*, *J*, *HK*, *C*, *C*, *J*
R Bailey 1979 *C*, 1980 *NZ*, 1981 *C*, *SA*, 1982 *C*, 1983 *C*, *A*, 1987 *Tun*, *C*, *J*, *E*
B Barnard 2006 *IrA*, *M*, *Bar*, *C*
I Basauri 2007 *S*, *E*, *Tg*, 2008 *Ur*, *J*, *J*
D Bateman 1982 *C*, *E*, 1983 *A*, 1985 *J*, *C*
P Bell 2006 *IrA*, *M*, *C*, *Bar*, *C*, *Ur*, *Ur*
W Bernhard 1987 *Tun*
C Biller 2009 *I*, *W*, *ArJ*, *E*, *Geo*, *C*, *C*, 2010 Rus, *E*
TW Billups 1993 *C*, *A*, 1994 *Ber*, *C*, *Ar*, *Ar*, *I*, 1995 *C*, 1996 *I*, *C*, *C*, *HK*, *HK*, *J*, *Ar*, *C*, *Ur*, 1997 *W*, *C*, *HK*, *HK*, *W*, *W*, 1998 *Pt*, *Sp*, *J*, *HK*, *C*, *C*, *J*, *HK*, *Fj*, *Ar*, *C*, *Ur*, 1999 *Tg*, *Fj*, *J*, *C*, *Sa*, *E*, *I*, *R*, *A*
RR Blasé 1913 *NZ*
A Blom 1998 *Sp*, *J*, *HK*, *C*, *C*, *HK*, *Fj*, *Ar*, *Ur*, 1999 *Sa*, 2000 *J*, *C*, *I*
H Bloomfield 2007 *E*, *Tg*, *SA*, 2008 *E*, *C*
R Bordley 1976 *A*, *F*, 1977 *C*, *E*, 1978 *C*
J Boyd 2008 *IrA*, 2009 *I*, *ArJ*
S Bracken 1994 *Ar*, 1995 *C*
G Brackett 1976 *A*, *F*, 1977 *E*
N Brendel 1983 *A*, 1984 *C*, 1985 *J*, *C*, 1987 *Tun*, *E*
D Briley 1979 *C*, 1980 *W*, *C*, *NZ*
J Buchholz 2001 *C*, 2002 *S*, 2003 *Sp*, *E*, *Ar*, *Fj*, *J*, *F*, 2004 *C*
B Burdette 2006 *Ur*, *Ur*, 2007 *E*, *S*, *C*, *E*, *Tg*, *Sa*, *SA*
J Burke 2000 *C*, *I*
JR Burke 1990 *C*, *J*, 1991 *J*, *J*, *S*, *C*, *F*, *NZ*, 1992 *C*
J Burkhardt 1983 *C*, 1985 *C*
E Burlingham 1980 *NZ*, 1981 *C*, *SA*, 1982 *C*, *E*, 1983 *C*, *A*, 1984 *C*, 1985 *C*, 1986 *J*, 1987 *Tun*, *C*, *J*, *E*
Cabrol 1920 *F*
C Campbell 1993 *C*, *A*, 1994 *Ber*, *C*, *Ar*
D Care 1998 *Pt*, *J*, *C*
M Carlson 1987 *W*, *C*
DB Carroll 1913 *NZ*
L Cass 1913 *NZ*
M Caulder 1984 *C*, 1985 *C*, 1989 *C*
R Causey 1977 *C*, 1981 *C*, *SA*, 1982 *C*, *E*, 1984 *C*, 1986 *J*, 1987 *E*
W Chai 1993 *C*
D Chipman 1976 *A*, 1978 *C*
JE Clark 1979 *C*, 1980 *C*
J Clarkson 1986 *J*, 1987 *Tun*, *C*, *J*, *E*
J Clayton 1999 *C*, *R*, *A*, 2000 *J*, *C*, *I*, *Fj*, *Tg*, *Sa*, *S*, *W*
N Cleaveland 1924 *F*
T Clever 2003 *Ar*, 2005 *C*, *R*, *W*, *ArA*, *C*, 2006 *IrA*, *M*, *C*, *Bar*, *C*, *Ur*, *Ur*, 2007 *E*, *S*, *C*, *E*, *Tg*, *Sa*, *SA*, 2008 *E*, *IrA*, *C*, *Ur*, *J*, *J*, 2009 *ArJ*, *E*, *Geo*, *C*, *C*, *Ur*, *Ur*
R Cooke 1979 *C*, 1980 *W*, *C*, *NZ*, 1981 *C*, *SA*
B Corcoran 1989 *Ur*, *Ar*, 1990 *Ar*
J Coulson 1999 *A*
M Crick 2007 *E*, *S*, *C*, 2008 *E*, *IrA*, *C*, *Ur*, *J*, *J*
R Crivellone 1983 *C*, 1986 *C*, 1987 *C*
K Cross 2003 *Sp*, *Sp*, *J*, *C*, *E*, *E*, *Ar*, *C*, *Fj*, *S*, 2004 *C*, *Rus*
C Culpepper 1977 *E*, 1978 *C*
C Curtis 1997 *C*, *HK*, *J*, 1999 *Sa*, 2001 *Ar*
P Dahl 2009 *I*, *W*, *E*
B Daily 1989 *Ur*, *Ar*, 1990 *Ar*, *C*, *A*, *J*, 1991 *J*, *J*, *S*, *F*, *F*, *It*
K Dalzell 1996 *Ur*, 1998 *Sp*, *C*, *HK*, *C*, *Ur*, 1999 *Tg*, *Fj*, *J*, *C*, *Sa*, *E*, *I*, *R*, *A*, 2000 *J*, *C*, *I*, *Fj*, *Tg*, *Sa*, *S*, *W*, 2001 *C*, *E*, *SA*, 2002 *S*, *C*, *C*, *CHL*, *Ur*, 2003 *Sp*, *Sp*, *J*, *C*, *E*, *C*, *Ur*, *Fj*, *S*, *J*, *F*
P Danahy 2009 *ArJ*, *Ur*, 2010 *Rus*, *E*
WP Darsie 1913 *NZ*
Davies 1920 *F*
G De Bartolo 2008 *E*, *C*, *Ur*, *J*, *J*, 2009 *W*, *ArJ*
D de Groot 1924 *F*
MG de Jong 1990 *C*, 1991 *J*, *J*, *S*, *C*, *F*, *F*, *It*, *E*
M Deaton 1983 *A*, 1984 *C*, 1985 *J*
M Delai 1996 *I*, *HK*, *J*, 1997 *HK*, 1998 *HK*, 2000 *J*, *C*, *I*, *Fj*, *Tg*, *Sa*, *S*, *W*, 2001 *C*, *Ar*, *Ur*
RH Devereux 1924 *F*
D Dickson 1986 *J*, 1987 *A*
G Dixon 1924 *F*
Doe 1924 *F*
C Doherty 1987 *W*
Doi 1920 *F*
D Dorsey 2001 *SA*, 2002 *S*, *C*, *C*, *CHL*, *Ur*, *CHL*, *Ur*, 2003 *Sp*, *Sp*, *J*, *C*, *E*, *Ar*, *C*, *Ur*, *Fj*, *S*, *J*, *F*, 2004 *C*, *Rus*, *M*, *C*, *F*
G Downes 1992 *HK*
B Doyle 2008 *E*, *IrA*, *C*
R Duncanson 1977 *E*
P Eloff 2000 *J*, *C*, *I*, *Fj*, *Tg*, *Sa*, *S*, *W*, 2001 *C*, *Ar*, *Ur*, *E*, *SA*, 2002 *S*, *C*, *CHL*, *Ur*, 2003 *Sp*, *Sp*, *J*, *C*, *E*, *C*, *Ur*, *Fj*, *S*, *J*, *F*, 2006 *Bar*, *C*, *Ur*, *Ur*, 2007 *Tg*, *Sa*, *SA*
P Emerick 2003 *Sp*, *E*, *Ar*, *C*, *Ur*, *Fj*, *S*, *J*, 2004 *M*, *C*, *F*, *I*, *It*, 2005 *C*, *R*, *W*, *ArA*, *C*, 2006 *C*, *Bar*, *C*, *Ur*, *Ur*, 2007 *S*, *C*, *E*, 2008 *E*, *IrA*, *C*, *Ur*, *J*, *J*, 2009 *E*, *Geo*, *C*, *C*, *Ur*, *Ur*, 2010 *Rus*, *E*, *F*
TV Enosa 2009 *ArJ*, *E*
BE Erb 1912 *A*
C Erskine 2006 *C*, *Ur*, *Ur*, 2007 *E*, *Tg*, *Sa*, *SA*, 2008 *Ur*, *J*, *J*
V Esikia 2006 *IrA*, *M*, *Bar*, *C*, *Ur*, *Ur*, 2007 *E*, *E*, *Tg*, *Sa*, *SA*, 2008 *E*, *IrA*
J Everett 1984 *C*, 1985 *J*, 1986 *J*, *C*, 1987 *Tun*, *J*, *E*
W Everett 1985 *J*, 1986 *J*, *C*
M Fabling 1995 *C*
M Fanucchi 1979 *C*, 1980 *W*
R Farley 1989 *I*, *Ur*, *Ar*, 1990 *Ar*, *C*, *A*, *J*, 1991 *J*, *J*, *S*, *C*, *F*, *F*, *It*, *E*, 1992 *C*

P Farner 1999 *Tg, Fj, J, C,* 2000 *J, C, I, Fj, Tg, Sa, S, W,* 2002 *C, C, CHL, Ur, CHL, Ur*
L Farrish 1924 *F*
D Fee 2002 *C, C, CHL, Ur, CHL, Ur,* 2003 *Sp, Sp, J, C, E, C, Ur, Fj, S, J, F,* 2004 *C, Rus, M, C, F, I, It,* 2005 *C, R, W, ArA, C*
O Fifita 2000 *Fj, Tg, Sa, S, W,* 2001 *C, Ar, Ur, E, SA,* 2002 *C, C,* 2003 *Sp, E, E, Ar, S*
S Finkel 1981 *C,* 1983 *C, A,* 1986 *C,* 1987 *A, E*
AW Flay 1990 *J,* 1991 *J, J, S, F, It, E*
R Flynn 2000 *C, I, Fj, Tg, Sa, W,* 2001 *C, Ar*
J Fowler 1980 *W, C, NZ,* 1981 *C, SA,* 1982 *C, E*
W Fraumann 1976 *F,* 1977 *E*
A Freeman 1995 *C,* 1996 *I*
M French 2005 *W, ArA,* 2006 *IrA, M, Ur, Ur,* 2007 *E, C*
B Furrow 1998 *C, C, J, HK*
JJ Gagiano 2008 *Ur, J, J,* 2009 *I, W, ArJ, E, Geo, C, C, Ur, Ur,* 2010 Rus, *E, F*
M Gale 1992 *C*
FJ Gard 1912 *A,* 1913 *NZ*
B Geraghty 1993 *C*
J Gillam 2000 *Tg*
D Gillies 1998 *Ar,* 1999 *Tg*
G Glasscock 1913 *NZ*
D Gonzalez 1990 *A,* 1993 *C*
G Goodman 1992 *C*
J Gouws 2003 *E, E, Ar, C, Ur, S, F,* 2004 *I, It*
E Graft 1924 *F*
J Grant 1981 *SA*
R Grant 2000 *Tg*
S Gray 1976 *F,* 1977 *E,* 1979 *C,* 1980 *W, NZ,* 1981 *SA*
R Green 1994 *I,* 1995 *C,* 1996 *I, C, C, HK, J, HK, J,* 1998 *Fj, Ar*
M Griffin 2003 *Sp, J, E,* 2004 *Rus, C, F,* 2005 *C, R*
J Grobler 1996 *Ar, C, Ur,* 1997 *C, J, J,* 1998 *J, Fj, C, Ur,* 1999 *Fj, J, C, Sa, E, I, R, A,* 2000 *J, C, I, Tg, Sa, S, W,* 2001 *C, Ar, Ur, E, SA,* 2002 *C, CHL, Ur*
L Gross 1996 *I, C, C, HK, J, HK, J, C, Ur,* 1997 *C, HK, J, J, HK, C, W, W,* 1998 *Pt, Sp, J, HK, C, C, J, HK, Fj, Ar, C, Ur,* 1999 *Tg, Fj, J, C, Sa, E, I, R, A,* 2000 *Fj, Tg, Sa, S, W,* 2001 *C, Ar, E, SA,* 2002 *S, C,* 2003 *Sp, Sp, J, C, E, E, Ar, C, Ur, Fj, S, J, F*
D Guest 1976 *F,* 1977 *C*
I Gunn 1982 *E*
EB Hall 1913 *NZ*
M Halliday 1977 *E,* 1978 *C,* 1980 *W, C,* 1982 *C, E*
C Hansen 2005 *C,* 2006 *IrA, M, C*
J Hanson 1977 *C, E,* 1980 *W, C,* 1981 *C,* 1983 *C, A*
PR Harrigan 1912 *A*
J Hartman 1983 *A,* 1984 *C*
J Hartman 2005 *C, ArA*
M Hawkins 2010 *Rus*
C Hawley 2009 *ArJ, E, Geo,* 2010 *E*
W Hayward 1991 *J, C*
GM Hein 1987 *Tun, C, J, A, E, W, C,* 1988 *R, USS,* 1989 *I, C, Ur, Ar,* 1990 *Ar, A,* 1991 *J, F, F, It, NZ, E,* 1992 *HK,* 1993 *C, A,* 1994 *Ber*
R Helu 1981 *C, SA,* 1982 *C, E,* 1983 *C, A,* 1985 *J, C,* 1987 *Tun, C, J, A*
B Henderson 1977 *C*
M Hercus 2002 *S, C, C, CHL, Ur, CHL, Ur,* 2003 *Sp, Sp, J, C, Ur, Fj, S, J, F,* 2004 *C, Rus, M, C, F, I, It,* 2005 *C, R, W, ArA, C,* 2006 *Bar, C, Ur, Ur,* 2007 *E, Tg, Sa, SA,* 2008 *E, IrA, C, Ur, J, J,* 2009 *I, W, E, Geo, C, C, Ur, Ur*
SJ Hiatt 1993 *A,* 1998 *Ar, C*
KG Higgins 1985 *J, C,* 1986 *J, C,* 1987 *Tun, C, J, A, E, W, C,* 1988 *C, R, USS,* 1989 *I, C, Ur, Ar,* 1990 *Ar, A, J,* 1991 *J, J, S, C, F, It, E*
B Hightower 1997 *W, J, HK, C, W, W,* 1998 *Fj, C, Ur,* 1999 *Tg, Fj, J, C, Sa, I, R, A*
D Hobson 1991 *J*
M Hobson 2005 *R*
D Hodges 1996 *Ur,* 1997 *W, W,* 1998 *Pt, Sp, J, HK, C, J, HK, Fj, Ar, C, Ur,* 1999 *Tg, Fj, J, C, Sa, E, I, R, A,* 2000 *J, C, I, Fj, Tg, Sa, S, W,* 2001 *C, Ar, Ur, E, SA,* 2002 *S, C, C, CHL, Ur, CHL, Ur,* 2003 *Sp, J, C, E, Fj, S, J, F,* 2004 *M, C, F*
C Hodgson 2002 *S, C, CHL, CHL,* 2003 *Sp, Sp, J, C, E, C,* 2004 *C, Rus*
J Hollings 1979 *C,* 1980 *NZ*
J Holtzman 1995 *C,* 1997 *HK, J,* 1998 *Ar*
J Hopkins 1996 *HK*
D Horton 1986 *C,* 1987 *A, C*
B Horwath 1984 *C,* 1985 *J, C,* 1986 *C,* 1987 *A, W,* 1990 *J*
B Hough 1991 *C,* 1992 *HK,* 1994 *Ar*
B Howard 1998 *HK, Fj, Ar,* 1999 *Sa*
B Howard 2010 *E*
C Howard 1980 *NZ*
J Hullinger 2006 *IrA, C, Bar, Ur, Ur*
FW Hyland 1924 *F*
M Inns 1985 *J, C,* 1986 *C*
R Isaac 1989 *C, Ar*
D Jablonski 1977 *C,* 1978 *C,* 1979 *C,* 1980 *W*
DW James 1990 *C, A,* 1993 *C, A,* 1994 *Ber, C, Ar, Ar, I*
WL Jefferson 1985 *J, C,* 1986 *C,* 1987 *W, C,* 1989 *I*
J Jellaco 1982 *C, E*
D Jenkinson 1984 *C,* 1985 *C,* 1986 *J*
N Johnson 2009 *I, W, E, Geo, C, C, Ur,* 2010 *Rus, F*
PW Johnson 1987 *C, A, W, C,* 1988 *C, R, USS,* 1989 *I, C, Ar,* 1990 *A,* 1991 *F, F, NZ,* 1992 *HK, C*
W Johnson 2009 *I, W, Ur, Ur*
S Jones 2005 *ArA,* 2006 *Ur*
G Judge 1991 *C,* 1992 *HK*
M Kane 2000 *J, I, Fj,* 2004 *M, C, F,* 2005 *ArA, C*
J Kelleher 1978 *C,* 1979 *C*
T Kelleher 2000 *C, I,* 2001 *C, Ar, Ur*
J Keller 1992 *HK, C*
J Kelly 2006 *M, C, Bar*
S Kelso 1977 *C, E,* 1978 *C*
D Kennedy 1997 *HK,* 1998 *Pt, Sp, J, HK*
J Keyter 2000 *W,* 2001 *SA,* 2002 *S, C, C, CHL, Ur, CHL, Ur,* 2003 *C, E, Ar, C, Ur, S, F*
F Khasigian 1976 *A*
K Khasigian 1998 *Ar,* 1999 *J, E, I, R, A,* 2000 *J, C, I, Fj, Sa, S, W,* 2001 *C, Ar, Ur, E, SA,* 2002 *S, C, C, CHL, Ur, CHL, Ur,* 2003 *Sp, Sp, J, C, E, Ar, C, Ur, Fj, S, J, F*
EN King 1912 *A,* 1913 *NZ*
K Kjar 2001 *Ar, SA,* 2002 *S, C, C, CHL, Ur, CHL,* 2003 *E, E, Ar, S, J,* 2005 *ArA, C,* 2006 *C,* 2007 *E, S, C*
T Klein 1976 *A,* 1977 *C,* 1978 *C*
S Klerck 2003 *Ar, Ur, J,* 2004 *C, Rus, M, C, I, It*
T Kluempers 1996 *J,* 2000 *W,* 2001 *C, Ar, Ur*
A Knowles 1913 *NZ*
Knutson 1988 *USS*
D La Prevotte 2010 *E*
CD Labounty 1998 *C, J*
A Lakomskis 2002 *CHL, Ur,* 2004 *I, It*
G Lambert 1981 *C, SA,* 1982 *C, E,* 1984 *C,* 1985 *C,* 1987 *Tun, C, J, A, E,* 1988 *C, R, USS,* 1989 *C, Ur, Ar,* 1990 *Ar*
S Laporta 1989 *Ur, Ar*
M Laulaupealu 2008 *E, IrA, C*
SC Lavalla 2009 *ArJ,* 2010 *Rus, E, F*
S Lawrence 2006 *C, Bar, C, Ur, Ur*
R Le Clerc 1998 *C, Ur*
B Le May 2008 *J,* 2009 *E*
PW LeClerc 1996 *HK, J,* 1997 *W, J, HK, C,* 1998 *C,* 1999 *Tg, Fj, J, C, Sa*
R Lehner 1995 *C,* 1996 *C, C, HK, J, HK, J, Ar, C,* 1997 *W, C, J, J, HK, C, W, W,* 1998 *Pt, Sp, J, HK, C, C, Ar, Ur,* 1999 *Tg, Fj, J, Sa, E, I, R,* 2000 *J, C, I, Fj, Tg, Sa*
O Lentz 2006 *IrA, M, Bar,* 2007 *E, Tg, Sa, SA*
J Lett 2008 *E, IrA, C*
WN Leversee 1988 *R,* 1989 *I, Ur,* 1990 *Ar, C, A, J,* 1991 *J, J, S, F, It,* 1994 *Ar, I,* 1996 *Ar*
R Lewis 1990 *C,* 1991 *S*
M L'Huillier 1999 *E, A*
R Liddington 2003 *Ar, C, S,* 2004 *Rus, M, C*
J Lik 2005 *C, R, ArA*
S Lipman 1988 *C, R, USS,* 1990 *C, J,* 1991 *F, It, NZ, E*
C Lippert 1989 *C, Ur, Ar,* 1990 *Ar, C, A, J,* 1991 *J, S, C, F, F, It, NZ,* 1993 *A,* 1994 *Ber, C, Ar, Ar, I,* 1996 *HK, J, Ar, C, Ur,* 1997 *C, HK, J, J, HK, W, W,* 1998 *J, HK, C, C, J, HK*
M Liscovitz 1977 *C, E,* 1978 *C*

R Lockerem 1996 *C, Ur*
J Lombard 1977 *C, E*, 1979 *C*
C Long 2003 *Sp*
J Lopez 1978 *C*
I Loveseth 1983 *A*
RA Lumkong 1994 *Ber, C, Ar, Ar, I*, 1996 *C, C, HK, J, HK, J, Ar, C, Ur*, 1997 *W*, 1998 *Pt, Sp, J, HK, C, C, J, HK, Fj, C, Ur*, 1999 *E, R, A*
D Lyle 1994 *I*, 1995 *C*, 1996 *I, C, C, HK, J, HK, J*, 1997 *W, C, HK, J, J, HK, C, W, W*, 1999 *Tg, Fj, J, C, Sa, E, I, R*, 2000 *S, W*, 2001 *C, Ar, E, SA*, 2002 *CHL, Ur*, 2003 *Sp, Sp, J, C, E, C, Ur, Fj, S, J, F*
M MacDonald 2000 *Fj*, 2001 *C, Ar, Ur, E, SA*, 2002 *S, C, C, CHL, Ur, CHL, Ur*, 2003 *Sp, Sp, J, C, E, E, C, Ur, Fj, S, J, F*, 2004 *C, Rus, F, I, It*, 2005 *C, R, W, ArA, C*, 2006 *IrA, C, Bar, C, Ur, Ur*, 2007 *S, C, E, Tg, Sa, SA*, 2008 *E, IrA, C, Ur, J, J*, 2009 *I, W, ArJ, Geo, C, C*
C Mackay 2008 *J*, 2009 *I, W, ArJ*
A Magleby 2000 *W*, 2001 *Ar, Ur, E*
A Malifa 2009 *I, W, ArJ, E, Geo, C*
V Malifa 2007 *E, S, C, E, SA*, 2008 *IrA, C, Ur, J, J*, 2009 *Ur, Ur*, 2010 *Rus, E, F*
P Malloy 1995 *C*
C Manelli 1924 *F*
L Manga 1986 *J*, 1989 *Ar*, 1991 *J, C, NZ, E*, 1992 *HK, C*
M Mangan 2005 *C, R, W, ArA, C*, 2006 *IrA, M, C, Bar, C, Ur*, 2007 *E, S, C, E, Tg, SA*
J McBride 1998 *Pt, Sp, C, Fj, Ar, C, Ur*, 2000 *J, C, I, Tg, Sa*
B McClenahan 2009 *W, ArJ, E, Ur*
T McCormack 1989 *Ur, Ar*, 1990 *Ar, C*
G McDonald 1989 *I*, 1996 *I, C*
A McGarry 2002 *S, CHL*
JL McKim 1912 *A*, 1913 *NZ*
M McLeod 1997 *J, HK, C*
T Meek 2006 *IrA, M, C, Bar*
Mehan 1920 *F*
H Mexted 2006 *Bar, Ur, Ur*, 2007 *E, S, C, E, Sa*
J Meyersieck 1982 *C*, 1983 *C, A*, 1985 *J*, 1986 *C*
J Mickel 1986 *C*
K Miles 1982 *C, E*
C Miller 2002 *CHL, Ur*
MM Mitchell 1913 *NZ*
M Moeakiola 2007 *E, Tg, Sa, SA*, 2008 *E, IrA, C, Ur, J, J*, 2009 *I, W, ArJ, E, Geo, C, C, Ur, Ur*, 2010 *Rus, F*
E Momson 1912 *A*
B Monroe 1985 *C*
A Montgomery 1986 *C*, 1987 *W, C*, 1988 *C*, 1989 *I, C*
LM Morris 1912 *A*
B Morrison 1979 *C*, 1980 *W*
C Morrow 1997 *W, C, HK, C, W, W*, 1998 *Pt, C, C*, 1999 *Tg, C, E*
T Moser 1980 *W*
N Mottram 1990 *Ar, J*, 1991 *J, S, C, F, NZ, E*, 1992 *C*
F Mounga 1998 *C, J, HK, Fj, C, Ur*, 1999 *Sa, E, I, R, A*, 2003 *Sp, J*, 2004 *F, I, It*, 2005 *R*, 2007 *E, C, Sa*
Muldoon 1920 *F*
D Murphy 1976 *F*
J Naivalu 2000 *Sa, S, W*, 2001 *C, Ur, E*, 2004 *C, Rus, M, C, F*
J Naqica 2001 *E, SA*, 2002 *S, C, C, CHL, Ur*, 2003 *Ar*
J Nash 2006 *M, C*
RB Nelson 1983 *C, A*, 1984 *C*, 1985 *C*, 1986 *J*, 1987 *C, J, A, E*, 1988 *R, USS*, 1989 *I, Ur, Ar*, 1990 *Ar, C, A, J*, 1991 *J, S, C, F, F, It, E*
T Ngwenya 2007 *E, Tg, Sa, SA*, 2008 *IrA, C, Ur, J, J*, 2009 *Geo, C, C, Ur, Ur*, 2010 *Rus, E, F*
C Nicolau 2002 *C*, 2003 *J, C, E*
S Niebauer 1976 *A*, 1979 *C*, 1980 *W, C, NZ*, 1981 *C, SA*, 1982 *C, E*
D Niu 1999 *Tg, Fj, J, C, E, I, R, A*
RM Noble 1912 *A*
CP O'Brien 1988 *C, R, USS*, 1989 *I, C, Ur, Ar*, 1990 *Ar, A, J*, 1991 *S, C, F, F, NZ, E*, 1992 *HK*, 1993 *C, A*, 1994 *Ber*
T O'Brien 1980 *NZ*, 1983 *C, A*
M O'Donnell 1976 *F*
C Okezie 1979 *C*, 1980 *C, NZ*, 1981 *C*, 1982 *C, E*
JT O'Neill 1920 *F*, 1924 *F*
M Ording 1976 *A, F*, 1977 *E*, 1978 *C*
M Ormsby 1983 *C*
A Osborne 2007 *C*
C Osentowski 2004 *It*, 2005 *C, R, W*, 2006 *IrA, M, C, Bar, C, Ur, Ur*, 2007 *E, S, C, E, Tg, Sa, SA*
K Oxman 1976 *A*
S Paga 1998 *C, C*, 1999 *C, Sa, E, I, R, A*, 2002 *CHL, Ur, CHL, Ur*, 2003 *J*, 2004 *C, Rus, F*
T Palamo 2007 *SA*, 2008 *J*
M Palefau 2005 *C, R, W, ArA, C*, 2006 *IrA, M, C*, 2007 *E, S*, 2008 *E*
AF Paoli 1982 *E*, 1983 *C*, 1985 *J*, 1986 *J, C*, 1987 *C, J, A, W, C*, 1988 *C, R, USS*, 1989 *I, C, Ur, Ar*, 1991 *J, F, It*
A Parker 1996 *HK, J, HK, J, Ar, C, Ur*, 1997 *W*, 1998 *Pt, Sp, J, HK, C, C, J, HK, Fj*, 1999 *Fj, C, Sa, E, I, R, A*, 2002 *CHL, Ur, CHL, Ur*, 2003 *Sp, Sp, C, E, C, Ur, Fj, S, F*, 2004 *C, Rus, C, I, It*, 2005 *W*, 2006 *C, Ur, Ur*, 2007 *E, Tg, Sa, SA*, 2008 *Ur, J*, 2009 *Geo, C, C, Ur, Ur*
D Parks 1980 *C*
E Parthmore 1977 *E*
J Patrick 1920 *F*, 1924 *F*
D Payne 2007 *S, SA*
SB Peart 1912 *A*, 1913 *NZ*
J Peter 1987 *W, C*
L Peters 2010 *E*
T Petersen 1993 *C*
M Petri 2007 *SA*, 2008 *E, IrA, C, Ur, J, J*, 2009 *I, W, E, Geo, C, C, Ur, Ur*, 2010 *Rus, E, F*
A Petruzzella 2004 *M, C, F, I*, 2005 *W, ArA, C*, 2006 *IrA, M, Bar*
MD Pidcock 1991 *C, NZ, E*
ST Pittman 2008 *Ur, J*, 2009 *ArJ, E, Geo, C, C*, 2010 *Rus, E, F*
D Power 2009 *ArJ*
M Purcell 1980 *W*, 1981 *C, SA*, 1982 *C, E*, 1983 *C, A*, 1984 *C*, 1986 *J, C*, 1987 *Tun, C, J, E*
T Purpura 2010 Rus, *E*
J Pye 2005 *ArA, C*
P Quinn 2007 *E*, 2008 *Ur, J, J*
JA Ramage 1913 *NZ*
RR Randell 1993 *A*, 1994 *Ber, C, Ar, I*, 1995 *C*, 1996 *I, HK, J, Ar, C*, 1997 *C*
J Raven 1998 *C, J*
E Reed 1999 *A*, 2001 *Ur, E, SA*, 2002 *S, C, C*
AM Ridnell 1987 *A*, 1988 *C, R, USS*, 1991 *J, S, C, F, F, It, NZ, E*, 1992 *HK*, 1993 *C*
J Rissone 1996 *I, C, C, HK, Ur*
WL Rogers 1924 *F*
R Rosser 2006 *Ur, Ur*
V Rouse 2010 *Rus, E*
D Rowe 2005 *R, W*
A Russell 2006 *C, Ur*
A Ryland 2005 *C, R, W, C*
R Samaniego 1992 *HK*
AM Sanborn 1912 *A*
L Sanft 1996 *J*
J Santos 1995 *C*, 1996 *C, C, HK*
A Satchwell 2002 *S*, 2003 *Ur*
A Saulala 1997 *C, HK, C, W, W*, 1998 *Pt, Sp, HK, C, J, HK*, 1999 *Tg, Fj, J, C, Sa, E, A*, 2000 *Fj, Tg*
M Saunders 1987 *Tun, C, J, A, E, W, C*, 1988 *C, R, USS*, 1989 *I, C*
MH Sawicki 1990 *Ar, J*, 1991 *J, F, NZ*
MA Scharrenberg 1993 *A*, 1994 *Ber, C, Ar, Ar*, 1995 *C*, 1996 *I, J, HK, J, Ar, C, Ur*, 1997 *W, C, HK, J, J, HK, C, W, W*, 1998 *Pt, Sp, J, HK, C, C, Ar, C, Ur*, 1999 *Tg, Fj, J, C, Sa, I, R, A*
KL Schaupp 1912 *A*
J Scheitlin 1979 *C*
CJ Schlereth 1993 *C*, 1994 *I*, 1998 *J*
Schmidt 1920 *F*
G Schneeweis 1976 *A*, 1977 *E*
B Schoener 2006 *IrA, M, C*
RS Scholtz 1920 *F*, 1924 *F*
E Schram 1993 *A*, 1994 *Ber, C, Ar, Ar*, 1996 *J, Ar*
J Schraml 1991 *C*, 1992 *HK*, 1993 *C*
K Schubert 2000 *J, C, I, Fj, Tg, Sa*, 2001 *C, Ar, Ur, E, SA,*

2002 *S, C, C, CHL, Ur, CHL, Ur,* 2003 *Sp, Sp, J, C, E, Ar, C, Ur, Fj, S, J, F,* 2004 *C, Rus, M, C, F, I, It,* 2005 *C, R, W, ArA, C,* 2006 *IrA, M, C, Bar, C,* 2008 *IrA, C*
RE Schurfeld 1992 *HK, C,* 1993 *A,* 1994 *Ber, C*
T Scott 1976 *F*
T Selfridge 1976 *A, F,* 1977 *C,* 1980 *W, C*
D Shanagher 1980 *NZ,* 1981 *C, SA,* 1982 *C, E,* 1984 *C,* 1985 *J,* 1986 *J,* 1987 *W*
R Shaw 2008 *IrA, C*
P Sheehy 1991 *NZ, E,* 1992 *HK, C*
M Sherlock 1977 *C*
M Sherman 2003 *E, Ar, F,* 2004 *Rus,* 2005 *C, W, ArA*
W Shiflet 1983 *C, A,* 1985 *J,* 1987 *A*
K Shuman 1997 *HK, J, J, W,* 1998 *J, HK, C, C, J, Ar,* 1999 *Tg, Fj, J, E, I, R, A,* 2000 *J, C, I, Fj, Tg, Sa, S, W,* 2001 *Ar, Ur, E, SA*
M Siano 1989 *I, C, Ur, Ar*
J Sifa 2008 *Ur, J,* 2009 *I, W, ArJ, E, Ur, Ur,* 2010 *Rus, F*
MK Sika 1993 *C, A,* 1994 *Ber, C, Ar, Ar, I,* 1996 *C, C, J, HK, J, Ar, C, Ur,* 1997 *J, W*
S Sika 2003 *Fj, J, F,* 2004 *M, C, F, I, It,* 2005 *W, C,* 2006 *IrA, M,* 2007 *S, C, E, Tg, Sa, SA,* 2008 *IrA, C, Ur,* 2009 *Geo, C*
C Slaby 2008 *E, C*
C Slater 1920 *F,* 1924 *F*
H Smith 2008 *Ur, J, J,* 2009 *I, W, E, Geo, C, C, Ur, Ur*
M Smith 1988 *C*
T Smith 1980 *C,* 1981 *C, SA,* 1982 *E*
WL Smith 1912 *A*
B Smoot 1992 *C*
J Sprague 2009 *Ur, Ur*
M Stanaway 1997 *C, HK, J, C,* 1998 *HK*
L Stanfill 2005 *C,* 2006 *C,* 2007 *E, S, C, E, Tg, Sa, SA,* 2008 *E, IrA,* 2009 *I, W, ArJ, E, Geo, C, C, Ur, Ur,* 2010 *Rus, E, F*
D Steinbauer 1992 *C,* 1993 *C*
J Stencel 2006 *C*
D Stephenson 1976 *A, F,* 1977 *C*
I Stevens 1998 *C*
P Still 2000 *S, W,* 2001 *C, Ar, Ur, E, SA*
HR Stolz 1913 *NZ*
W Stone 1976 *F*
D Straehley 1983 *C,* 1984 *C*
G Sucher 1998 *C, J, HK, Fj, C, Ur,* 1999 *Tg, Fj, J, C, Sa, E, I, R, A*
A Suniula 2008 *J,* 2010 *Rus, E*
R Suniula 2009 *I, W, E, C, C*
B Surgener 2001 *SA,* 2002 *C, Ur,* 2003 *Sp, E, E,* 2004 *C, F, I, It,* 2005 *W*
E Swanson 1976 *A*
C Sweeney 1976 *A, F,* 1977 *C, E*
M Swiderski 1976 *A*
K Swiryn 2009 *I, W, C, C, Ur, Ur*
B Swords 1980 *W, C, NZ*
KR Swords 1985 *J, C,* 1986 *C,* 1987 *Tun, C, J, A, W, C,* 1988 *C, R, USS,* 1989 *I, C, Ur, Ar,* 1990 *Ar, C, A, J,* 1991 *J, J, S, C, F, F, It, NZ, E,* 1992 *C,* 1993 *C, A,* 1994 *Ber, C, Ar, Ar*
TK Takau 1994 *Ar, Ar, I,* 1996 *C, C, HK, J, HK,* 1997 *C, HK, J, HK, W, W,* 1998 *Sp, HK, C, C, J, HK, Ur,* 1999 *E, I, R, A*
R Tardits 1993 *A,* 1994 *Ber, C, Ar, Ar, I,* 1995 *C,* 1996 *I, C, C, J, Ar,* 1997 *W, C,* 1998 *Sp, HK, Fj,* 1999 *Tg, Fj, J, C, Sa, I, R*
J Tarpoff 2002 *S, C, C, CHL,* 2003 *Sp, Sp, C, E, E,* 2006 *IrA, M, C, Bar*
P Thiel 2009 *Ur, Ur,* 2010 *Rus, E, F*
Tilden 1920 *F*
M Timoteo 2000 *Tg,* 2001 *C, Ar, Ur, SA,* 2002 *S, C, C, CHL, Ur, CHL,* 2003 *Sp, Sp, J, E, Ar, C, F,* 2004 *C, Rus, M, C, F, I, It,* 2005 *C, R,* 2006 *IrA, M, C, Bar*
A Tuilevuka 2006 *IrA, M, C,* 2009 *I, W, ArJ, E, Geo, C, Ur, Ur,* 2010 *Rus*
A Tuipulotu 2004 *C, Rus, M, C, I, It,* 2005 *C, R, W,* 2006 *C, Bar, C, Ur, Ur,* 2007 *E, S, C, Tg, Sa,* 2008 *E*
CE Tunnacliffe 1991 *F, NZ, E,* 1992 *HK*
JC Urban 1913 *NZ*
T Usasz 2009 *I, W, ArJ, E, Geo, C, C, Ur, Ur,* 2010 Rus, *E*
Vaka 1987 *C*
AC Valentine 1924 *F*
J Van der Geissen 2008 *E, C, Ur, J, J,* 2009 *I, W, E, Geo, C, C, Ur, Ur,* 2010 *Rus, E, F*
M van der Molen 1992 *C*
R van Zyl 2003 *Sp, Sp, J, C, E, C, Ur, Fj, S, J, F,* 2004 *C, F*
Vidal 1920 *F*
F Viljoen 2004 *Rus, M, C, F, I, It,* 2005 *C, R, W, ArA, C,* 2006 *IrA, M, C, Ur, Ur,* 2007 *E, S, C*
T Vinick 1986 *C,* 1987 *A, E*
J Vitale 2006 *C, Ur,* 2007 *E,* 2008 *IrA*
BG Vizard 1986 *J, C,* 1987 *Tun, C, J, A, E, W, C,* 1988 *C, R, USS,* 1989 *I, C,* 1990 *C, A,* 1991 *J, J, S, C, F, It*
C Vogl 1996 *C, C,* 1997 *W, C, HK, J, J, HK, C,* 1998 *HK, Fj, Ar*
G Voight 1913 *NZ*
J Waasdorp 2003 *J, E, Ar, Ur, J, F,* 2004 *C, Rus, M, C, F, I, It,* 2005 *C, ArA, C*
D Wack 1976 *F,* 1977 *C,* 1978 *C,* 1980 *C*
B Waite 1976 *F*
J Walker 1996 *I, C, HK, J, Ar, C, Ur,* 1997 *W, J, HK, C, W, W,* 1998 *Sp, J, HK, C, C, J, HK, Ar, C, Ur,* 1999 *Tg, J*
Wallace 1920 *F*
L Walton 1980 *C, NZ,* 1981 *C, SA*
A Ward 1980 *NZ,* 1983 *C*
B Warhurst 1983 *C, A,* 1984 *C,* 1985 *J, C,* 1986 *J,* 1987 *Tun, C, J*
M Waterman 1992 *C*
J Welch 2008 *J, J,* 2009 *I, Geo, C*
G Wells 2000 *J, C, I, Fj, Tg, Sa, S, W,* 2001 *C, Ar, Ur, E*
T Whelan 1982 *E,* 1987 *C,* 1988 *C, R, USS*
EA Whitaker 1990 *J,* 1991 *F, F, It, NZ*
B Wiedemer 2007 *E,* 2008 *E, IrA, C*
L Wilfley 2000 *I, Tg, W,* 2001 *Ar, Ur, SA,* 2002 *S, C, C, CHL, Ur, CHL, Ur,* 2003 *Sp, Sp, J, C, E, E, S*
JP Wilkerson 1991 *E,* 1993 *A,* 1994 *C,* 1996 *C, Ur,* 1997 *W, C, HK, J, J, C, W, W,* 1998 *Pt, Sp, J, HK*
B Williams 1988 *C, R, USS,* 1989 *C,* 1992 *C*
C Williams 1990 *C, A, J,* 1991 *J, S, C*
D Williams 2004 *C, Rus, M, C, F, I, It,* 2005 *ArA,* 2006 *Ur, Ur,* 2007 *E, C*
MA Williams 1987 *W, C,* 1988 *C, R, USS,* 1989 *I, Ur, Ar,* 1990 *Ar, C, A,* 1991 *J, J, F, F, It, NZ, E,* 1992 *HK,* 1994 *C, Ar, Ar, I,* 1996 *I, C, C, HK,* 1997 *W,* 1998 *Fj, Ar, Ur,* 1999 *Tg, J, C, Sa, E, I*
G Wilson 1978 *C,* 1980 *W, C,* 1981 *C, SA*
Winston 1920 *F*
Wrenn 1920 *F*
M Wyatt 2003 *Ar, C, Ur, J, F,* 2004 *C, Rus, M, C, F, I, It,* 2005 *W, ArA, C,* 2006 *C*
C Wyles 2007 *E, S, C, E, Tg, Sa, SA,* 2008 *E, IrA, C, Ur, J, J,* 2009 *I, W, Geo, C, C, Ur, Ur,* 2010 *Rus, F*
D Younger 2000 *J, C, I, Fj*
S Yungling 1997 *HK, W*
R Zenker 1987 *W, C*

WALES

WALES' 2009–10 TEST RECORD

OPPONENTS	DATE	VENUE	RESULT
New Zealand	7 November	H	**Lost** 12–19
Samoa	13 November	H	**Won** 17–13
Argentina	21 November	H	**Won** 33–16
Australia	28 November	H	**Lost** 12–33
England	6 February	A	**Lost** 17–30
Scotland	13 February	H	**Won** 31–24
France	26 February	H	**Lost** 20–26
Ireland	13 March	A	**Lost** 12–27
Italy	20 March	H	**Won** 33–10
South Africa	5 June	H	**Lost** 31–34
New Zealand	19 June	A	**Lost** 9–42
New Zealand	26 June	A	**Lost** 10–29

WALES FAIL TO MAKE PROGRESS

By Paul Morgan

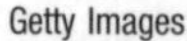
Getty Images

Wales coach Warren Gatland endured a frustrating 12 months.

If international rugby is a results business, Wales coach Warren Gatland will reflect on the 2009–10 campaign as one in which his talented side failed to deliver on a frustratingly regular basis, falling significantly short of expectations both in the Six Nations and on their subsequent summer tour of New Zealand.

In their 12 games, Wales claimed victory a mere four times. Two wins were recorded in the autumn against Samoa and Argentina and two more against Scotland and Italy in the Championship but when they were presented with the challenge of the bigger beasts in the international rugby jungle, Wales were overpowered.

There were close calls. The All Blacks escaped from the Millennium Stadium in November with a 19–12 triumph, and could have been beaten on a different day, while the Springboks were visibly relieved to get out of jail with a 34–31 victory in Cardiff in June but the harsh reality was

Tom Shaw/Getty Images

Shane Williams danced his way to a dramatic win over Scotland.

Wales failed to claim a major European or Tri-Nations scalp throughout the campaign.

"This season has been frustrating," Gatland conceded after Wales closed the Six Nations with a face-saving 33–10 victory over Italy in Cardiff. "We haven't reached our potential and we've let games slip. We feel our final position doesn't reflect where we are right now.

"In some games this season we've let ourselves down and been behind and had to chase. But we were under pressure going into the Italy game so it was an excellent result. We created chances and it was nice to have the half-time lead. We have lots to work on but we showed what we're capable of today."

The season began with Gatland naming a 29-man squad for the autumn internationals. There was no gentle opener for Wales with New Zealand the first opponents at the Millennium Stadium and the coach named his strongest XV for the clash, selecting Ospreys prop Paul James at tighthead in place of the injured Adam James.

It was a tight, occasionally tense encounter in Cardiff. Stephen Jones and Daniel Carter exchanged two first-half penalties apiece but the All Blacks struck what proved to be a decisive blow after the break when hooker Andrew Hore crashed over for the only try of the match and despite Jones landing a fourth penalty, Wales were

Phil Walter/Getty Images

Wales battled bravely in New Zealand, regaining some pride in the second Test.

beaten 19–12 and their 56-year wait for victory over the Kiwis continued.

"For us, it's about learning to play at the highest level, making sure for 80 minutes that we switch on and nail critical moments," Gatland admitted. "There are fine things as a team we hammer in at training but we must carry them into the game and keep developing.

"In the changing rooms afterwards the players were gutted and maybe previously they would have been happy with that scoreline. We think we are closing the gap to the top sides and it was a good performance, but the challenge for us is to improve on that and it is important we keep improving through the rest of this series."

Wales did briefly improve in terms of results, albeit against more modest opposition, and although their 17–13 win over the Samoans was not without drama and anxiety, their 33–16 victory over Argentina in Cardiff was a four-try feast in which the home side were full of verve and vigour. Wing Shane Williams helped himself to second-half brace and in the process joined Test rugby's exclusive 50-try club.

"We are happy," said Wales captain Ryan Jones after only a third win in the last seven meetings against the Pumas. "The boys stood proud, we defended superbly and we've got two wins out of three in this autumn campaign. It is about dusting ourselves off now for next weekend against Australia. We made a few errors but we are improving. We did more things right than we did wrong."

A back injury ruled Jones out of the Wallabies game with Gethin Jenkins temporarily assuming the captaincy but there was no dream bow for the Wales skipper as Australia ran riot in attack, scoring tries through Digby Ioane, James Horwill, David Pocock and Tatafu Polota–Nau in a commanding 33–12 win. The home side could muster just four penalties in reply as they slumped to the second heaviest defeat of Gatland's 22-match reign as head coach.

Wales regrouped for the Six Nations and Gatland took the brave decision to name 17-year-old Ospreys wing Tom Prydie and 19-year-old Neath wing Kristian Phillips in his squad for the tournament.

Neither made the 22 for the Championship opener with England at Twickenham and they were perhaps fortunate to miss what was an indisciplined performance in London which saw Alun Wyn Jones sin binned for a first-half trip on Dylan Hartley. England took full advantage of their numerical superiority to race into a 20–3 lead and Wales never recovered.

Their 30–17 defeat was the worst possible start to the Six Nations but Wales bounced back against Scotland in Cardiff in their next game. It was however far from a routine victory as the home side had to battle back from a stunning opening salvo by the Scots and it required a last-gasp try from Williams to seal a dramatic 31–24 win.

France were the next visitors to the Millennium Stadium and again Wales were painfully slow out of the blocks as Les Bleus raced into a 20–0 lead. Another fightback ensued but this time Gatland's side left themselves too much ground to make up despite tries from Leigh Halfpenny and another from the prolific Williams and France emerged 26–20 winners.

Two successive defeats became three a fortnight later against the Irish at Croke Park. Another yellow card, this time shown to Lee Byrne, again proved fatal as Ireland scored twice with the visitors down to 14 men and Wales were eventually beaten 27–12.

"We are very disappointed," Gatland conceded. "The yellow card was very costly in the game. We haven't learned our lesson from England and, from a coaching point of view that is very frustrating. We did create some chances and opportunities but we tried to force things a little too much. We need to keep our patience and work on accuracy. But Ireland were very good and very clinical. We had more territory and possession but turnovers were costly for us."

Gatland handed Prydie his Test debut for the final Championship fixture against Italy, making him Wales' youngest ever international, at 18 years and 25 days. The teenager did not score but Wales still signed off with a 33–10 win that at least ensured the team finished above the Azzurri and Scotland in the final standings.

With the two-Test series against the All Blacks looming, Wales entertained South Africa at the Millennium Stadium in June in a pre-tour warm-up but they boarded the plane for New Zealand on the back of a 34–31 reverse and the opportunity for only a second victory over the Springboks in 104 years had slipped by.

The first Test against the Kiwis in June was also the final Test match at Carisbrook and the All Blacks ensured they bid goodbye to the famous old stadium in appropriate style with a convincing 42–9 win in which Wales were unable to breach the home side's defence.

Gatland made two changes for the second Test, opting to start with Dan Biggar at fly-half ahead of Stephen Jones, while Jonathan Davies replaced the injured Andrew Bishop in the midfield, and it was undoubtedly a far more accomplished Welsh display in Hamilton.

The hosts established a 13–3 half-time lead with a try from centre Cory Jane but the visitors refused to capitulate and a Roberts score after the break applied a degree of pressure only for substitute Aaron Cruden to grab a late try for New Zealand to record a final 29–10 scoreline that flattered the Kiwis.

Wales had lost again but there were some crumbs of comfort, not least the fact their 19-point losing deficit equalled their best previous effort on New Zealand soil – the 19–0 defeat in Christchurch back in 1969.

"The effort was huge," said scrum-half Mike Phillips. "Our defence was much better and they didn't look like scoring at times. It's just disappointing we didn't take one or two chances and didn't push them even harder.

"It's been disappointing to lose two games but I think we have to be positive looking forward and there have been a lot of positives. We're closing the gap and there is certainly a victory within us against these types of teams.

"I think we matched them in so many areas in the last two games and I think it's just a mental thing about really going out on the field believing that we're good enough as individual players and as a team collectively. And I think there's a bright future ahead of Wales around the corner and there's definitely a victory within us."

WALES INTERNATIONAL STATISTICS

MATCH RECORDS UP TO 29TH OCTOBER 2010

MOST CONSECUTIVE TEST WINS

11 1907 I, 1908 E,S,F,I,A, 1909 E,S,F,I, 1910 F
10 1999 F1,It,E,Arg 1,2,SA,C,F2,Arg 3,J
8 1970 F, 1971 E,S,I,F, 1972 E,S,F
8 2004 J, 2005 E,It,F,S,I,US,C

MOST CONSECUTIVE TESTS WITHOUT DEFEAT

Matches	Wins	Draws	Period
11	11	0	1907 to 1910
10	10	0	1999 to 1999
8	8	0	1970 to 1972
8	8	0	2004 to 2005

MOST POINTS IN A MATCH

BY THE TEAM

Pts	Opponents	Venue	Year
102	Portugal	Lisbon	1994
98	Japan	Cardiff	2004
81	Romania	Cardiff	2001
77	U S A	Hartford	2005
72	Japan	Cardiff	2007
70	Romania	Wrexham	1997
66	Romania	Cardiff	2004
64	Japan	Cardiff	1999
64	Japan	Osaka	2001
61	Canada	Cardiff	2006
60	Italy	Treviso	1999
60	Canada	Toronto	2005
58	Fiji	Cardiff	2002
57	Japan	Bloemfontein	1995
55	Japan	Cardiff	1993

BY A PLAYER

Pts.	Player	Opponents	Venue	Year
30	N R Jenkins	Italy	Treviso	1999
29	N R Jenkins	France	Cardiff	1999
28	N R Jenkins	Canada	Cardiff	1999
28	N R Jenkins	France	Paris	2001
28	G L Henson	Japan	Cardiff	2004
27	N R Jenkins	Italy	Cardiff	2000
27	C Sweeney	U S A	Hartford	2005
26	S M Jones	Romania	Cardiff	2001
24	N R Jenkins	Canada	Cardiff	1993
24	N R Jenkins	Italy	Cardiff	1994
24	G L Henson	Romania	Wrexham	2003
23	A C Thomas	Romania	Wrexham	1997
23	N R Jenkins	Argentina	Llanelli	1998
23	N R Jenkins	Scotland	Murrayfield	2001
22	N R Jenkins	Portugal	Lisbon	1994
22	N R Jenkins	Japan	Bloemfontein	1995
22	N R Jenkins	England	Wembley	1999
22	S M Jones	Canada	Cardiff	2002
22	J W Hook	England	Cardiff	2007
22	D R Biggar	Canada	Toronto	2009

MOST TRIES IN A MATCH

BY THE TEAM

Tries	Opponents	Venue	Year
16	Portugal	Lisbon	1994
14	Japan	Cardiff	2004
11	France	Paris	1909
11	Romania	Wrexham	1997
11	Romania	Cardiff	2001
11	U S A	Hartford	2005
11	Japan	Cardiff	2007
10	France	Swansea	1910
10	Japan	Osaka	2001
10	Romania	Cardiff	2004
9	France	Cardiff	1908
9	Japan	Cardiff	1993
9	Japan	Cardiff	1999
9	Japan	Tokyo	2001
9	Canada	Toronto	2005
9	Canada	Cardiff	2006

BY A PLAYER

Tries	Player	Opponents	Venue	Year
4	W Llewellyn	England	Swansea	1899
4	R A Gibbs	France	Cardiff	1908
4	M C R Richards	England	Cardiff	1969
4	I C Evans	Canada	Invercargill	1987
4	N Walker	Portugal	Lisbon	1994
4	G Thomas	Italy	Treviso	1999
4	S M Williams	Japan	Osaka	2001
4	T G L Shanklin	Romania	Cardiff	2004
4	C L Charvis	Japan	Cardiff	2004

MOST CONVERSIONS IN A MATCH

BY THE TEAM

Cons	Opponents	Venue	Year
14	Japan	Cardiff	2004
11	Portugal	Lisbon	1994
11	U S A	Hartford	2005
10	Romania	Cardiff	2001
8	France	Swansea	1910
8	Japan	Cardiff	1999
8	Romania	Cardiff	2004
8	Canada	Cardiff	2006
7	France	Paris	1909
7	Japan	Osaka	2001
7	Japan	Cardiff	2007

BY A PLAYER

Cons	Player	Opponents	Venue	Year
14	G L Henson	Japan	Cardiff	2004
11	N R Jenkins	Portugal	Lisbon	1994
11	C Sweeney	U S A	Hartford	2005
10	S M Jones	Romania	Cardiff	2001
8	J Bancroft	France	Swansea	1910
8	N R Jenkins	Japan	Cardiff	1999
8	J Hook	Canada	Cardiff	2006
7	S M Jones	Japan	Osaka	2001
7	S M Jones	Romania	Cardiff	2004
6	J Bancroft	France	Paris	1909
6	G L Henson	Romania	Wrexham	2003
6	C Sweeney	Canada	Toronto	2005

MOST PENALTIES IN A MATCH

BY THE TEAM

Pens	Opponents	Venue	Year
9	France	Cardiff	1999
8	Canada	Cardiff	1993
7	Italy	Cardiff	1994
7	Canada	Cardiff	1999
7	Italy	Cardiff	2000
6	France	Cardiff	1982
6	Tonga	Nuku'alofa	1994
6	England	Wembley	1999
6	Canada	Cardiff	2002
6	England	Cardiff	2009
6	Canada	Toronto	2009

BY A PLAYER

Pens	Player	Opponents	Venue	Year
9	N R Jenkins	France	Cardiff	1999
8	N R Jenkins	Canada	Cardiff	1993
7	N R Jenkins	Italy	Cardiff	1994
7	N R Jenkins	Canada	Cardiff	1999
7	N R Jenkins	Italy	Cardiff	2000
6	G Evans	France	Cardiff	1982
6	N R Jenkins	Tonga	Nuku'alofa	1994
6	N R Jenkins	England	Wembley	1999
6	S M Jones	Canada	Cardiff	2002
6	D R Biggar	Canada	Toronto	2009

MOST DROPPED GOALS IN A MATCH

BY THE TEAM

Drops	Opponents	Venue	Year
3	Scotland	Murrayfield	2001
2	Scotland	Swansea	1912
2	Scotland	Cardiff	1914
2	England	Swansea	1920
2	Scotland	Swansea	1921
2	France	Paris	1930
2	England	Cardiff	1971
2	France	Cardiff	1978
2	England	Twickenham	1984
2	Ireland	Wellington	1987
2	Scotland	Cardiff	1988
2	France	Paris	2001

BY A PLAYER

Drops	Player	Opponents	Venue	Year
3	N R Jenkins	Scotland	Murrayfield	2001
2	J Shea	England	Swansea	1920
2	A Jenkins	Scotland	Swansea	1921
2	B John	England	Cardiff	1971
2	M Dacey	England	Twickenham	1984
2	J Davies	Ireland	Wellington	1987
2	J Davies	Scotland	Cardiff	1988
2	N R Jenkins	France	Paris	2001

MOST CAPPED PLAYERS

Caps	Player	Career Span
100	Gareth Thomas	1995 to 2007
95	M E Williams	1996 to 2010
94	C L Charvis	1996 to 2007
92	G O Llewellyn	1989 to 2004
91	S M Jones	1998 to 2010
87	N R Jenkins	1991 to 2002
74	D J Peel	2001 to 2010
74	G D Jenkins	2002 to 2010
73	S M Williams	2000 to 2010
72	I C Evans	1987 to 1998
66	T G L Shanklin	2001 to 2010
64	A R Jones	2003 to 2010
63	I M Gough	1998 to 2010
59	R Howley	1996 to 2002
58	G R Jenkins	1991 to 2000
58	J Thomas	2003 to 2010
57	D J Jones	2001 to 2009
55	J P R Williams	1969 to 1981
54	R N Jones	1986 to 1995
53	G O Edwards	1967 to 1978
53	I S Gibbs	1991 to 2001
52	L S Quinnell	1993 to 2002
52	M Taylor	1994 to 2005
51	D Young	1987 to 2001

MOST CONSECUTIVE TESTS

Tests	Player	Span
53	G O Edwards	1967 to 1978
43	K J Jones	1947 to 1956
39	G Price	1975 to 1983
38	T M Davies	1969 to 1976
33	W J Bancroft	1890 to 1901

MOST TESTS AS CAPTAIN

Tests	Captain	Span
28	I C Evans	1991 to 1995
26	R P Jones	2008 to 2010
22	R Howley	1998 to 1999
22	C L Charvis	2002 to 2004
21	Gareth Thomas	2003 to 2007
19	J M Humphreys	1995 to 2003
18	A J Gould	1889 to 1897
14	D C T Rowlands	1963 to 1965
14	W J Trew	1907 to 1913

MOST POINTS IN TESTS

Points	Player	Tests	Career
1049	N R Jenkins	87	1991 to 2002
815	S M Jones	91	1998 to 2010
304	P H Thorburn	37	1985 to 1991
255	S M Williams	73	2000 to 2010
232	J W Hook	43	2006 to 2010
211	A C Thomas	23	1996 to 2000
200	Gareth Thomas	100	1995 to 2007
166	P Bennett	29	1969 to 1978
157	I C Evans	72	1987 to 1998

MOST TRIES IN TESTS

Tries	Player	Tests	Career
51	S M Williams	73	2000 to 2010
40	Gareth Thomas	100	1995 to 2007
33	I C Evans	72	1987 to 1998
22	C L Charvis	94	1996 to 2007
20	G O Edwards	53	1967 to 1978
20	T G R Davies	46	1966 to 1978
20	T G L Shanklin	66	2001 to 2010
18	G R Williams	44	2000 to 2005
17	R A Gibbs	16	1906 to 1911
17	J L Williams	17	1906 to 1911
17	K J Jones	44	1947 to 1957

MOST CONVERSIONS IN TESTS

Cons	Player	Tests	Career
132	S M Jones	91	1998 to 2010
130	N R Jenkins	87	1991 to 2002
43	P H Thorburn	37	1985 to 1991
38	J Bancroft	18	1909 to 1914
34	J W Hook	43	2006 to 2010
30	A C Thomas	23	1996 to 2000
29	G L Henson	31	2001 to 2009
25	C Sweeney	35	2003 to 2007
20	W J Bancroft	33	1890 to 1901
20	I R Harris	25	2001 to 2004

MOST PENALTY GOALS IN TESTS

Penalties	Player	Tests	Career
235	N R Jenkins	87	1991 to 2002
166	S M Jones	91	1998 to 2010
70	P H Thorburn	37	1985 to 1991
36	P Bennett	29	1969 to 1978
35	S P Fenwick	30	1975 to 1981
35	J W Hook	43	2006 to 2010
32	A C Thomas	23	1996 to 2000
22	G Evans	10	1981 to 1983

MOST DROPPED GOALS IN TESTS

Drops	Player	Tests	Career
13	J Davies	32	1985 to 1997
10	N R Jenkins	87	1991 to 2002
8	B John	25	1966 to 1972
7	W G Davies	21	1978 to 1985

INTERNATIONAL CHAMPIONSHIP RECORDS

RECORD	DETAIL		SET
Most points in season	151	in five matches	2005
Most tries in season	21	in four matches	1910
Highest Score	49	49–14 v France	1910
Biggest win	39	47–8 v Italy	2008
Highest score conceded	60	26–60 v England	1998
Biggest defeat	51	0–51 v France	1998
Most appearances	51	M E Williams	1998–2010
Most points in matches	445	S M Jones	2000–2010
Most points in season	74	N R Jenkins	2001
Most points in match	28	N R Jenkins	v France, 2001
Most tries in matches	20	S M Williams	2000–2010
Most tries in season	6	M C R Richards	1969
	6	S M Williams	2008
Most tries in match	4	W Llewellyn	v England, 1899
	4	M C R Richards	v England, 1969
Most cons in matches	67	S M Jones	2000–2010
Most cons in season	12	S M Jones	2005
Most cons in match	8	J Bancroft	v France, 1910
Most pens in matches	94	S M Jones	2000–2010
Most pens in season	16	P H Thorburn	1986
	16	N R Jenkins	1999
Most pens in match	7	N R Jenkins	v Italy, 2000
Most drops in matches	8	J Davies	1985–1997
Most drops in season	5	N R Jenkins	2001
Most drops in match	3	N R Jenkins	v Scotland, 2001

MISCELLANEOUS RECORDS

RECORD	HOLDER	DETAIL
Longest Test Career	G O Llewellyn	1989 to 2004
Youngest Test Cap	T W J Prydie	18 yrs 25 days in 2010
Oldest Test Cap	T H Vile	38 yrs 152 days in 1921

CAREER RECORDS OF WALES INTERNATIONAL PLAYERS (UP TO 29TH OCTOBER 2010)

PLAYER	DEBUT	CAPS	T	C	P	D	PTS
BACKS							
D R Biggar	2008 v C	6	0	7	10	0	44
A M Bishop	2008 v SA	11	0	0	0	0	0
L M Byrne	2005 v NZ	35	8	0	0	0	40
G J Cooper	2001 v It	46	9	0	0	0	45
C D Czekaj	2005 v C	7	2	0	0	0	10
J J V Davies	2009 v C	7	2	0	0	0	10
S L Halfpenny	2008 v SA	17	7	0	8	0	59
W T M Harries	2010 v NZ	1	0	0	0	0	0
G L Henson	2001 v J	31	3	29	18	1	130
J W Hook	2006 v Arg	43	10	34	35	3	232
T James	2007 v E	9	2	0	0	0	10
M A Jones	2001 v E	47	13	0	0	0	65
S M Jones	1998 v SA	91	7	132	166	6	815
T D Knoyle	2010 v NZ	1	0	0	0	0	0
D J Peel	2001 v J	74	5	0	0	0	25
W M Phillips	2003 v R	42	4	0	0	0	20
T W J Prydie	2010 v It	4	1	0	0	0	5
R S Rees	2010 v E	5	0	0	0	0	0
J H Roberts	2008 v S	24	2	0	0	0	10
M Roberts	2008 v C	3	0	0	0	0	0
T G L Shanklin	2001 v J	66	20	0	0	0	100
S M Williams	2000 v F	73	51	0	0	0	255
FORWARDS							
H Bennett	2003 v I	34	0	0	0	0	0
L C Charteris	2004 v SA	22	0	0	0	0	0
B S Davies	2009 v S	13	0	0	0	0	0
G L Delve	2006 v S	11	1	0	0	0	5
Ian Evans	2006 v Arg	16	1	0	0	0	5
I A R Gill	2010 v I	1	0	0	0	0	0
I M Gough	1998 v SA	63	1	0	0	0	5
R Hibbard	2006 v Arg	9	0	0	0	0	0
P James	2003 v R	13	0	0	0	0	0
W James	2007 v E	4	0	0	0	0	0
G D Jenkins	2002 v R	74	3	0	0	0	15
A R Jones	2003 v E	64	2	0	0	0	10

A-W Jones	2006 v Arg	40	5	0	0	0	25
D A R Jones	2002 v Fj	42	2	0	0	0	10
D J Jones	2001 v A	57	0	0	0	0	0
D L Jones	2000 v Sm	10	0	0	0	0	0
R P Jones	2004 v SA	43	2*	0	0	0	10
E T Lewis-Roberts	2008 v C	1	0	0	0	0	0
D J Lydiate	2009 v Arg	2	0	0	0	0	0
R J McCusker	2010 v SA	3	0	0	0	0	0
C Mitchell	2009 v C	4	0	0	0	0	0
S Morgan	2007 v A	1	0	0	0	0	0
A Powell	2008 v SA	14	0	0	0	0	0
M Rees	2005 v US	39	2	0	0	0	10
R Sowden-Taylor	2005 v It	8	0	0	0	0	0
G M Thomas	2001 v J	24	4	0	0	0	20
J Thomas	2003 v A	58	7	0	0	0	35
S Warburton	2009 v US	7	0	0	0	0	0
G J Williams	2003 v It	9	0	0	0	0	0
M E Williams	1996 v Bb	95	14	0	0	1	73
J V Yapp	2005 v E	16	0	0	0	0	0

* Ryan Jones's figures include a penalty try awarded against Canada in 2006

WALES INTERNATIONAL PLAYERS

MATCH RECORDS UP TO 29TH OCTOBER 2010

Note: Years given for International Championship matches are for second half of season; eg 1972 means season 1971–72. Years for all other matches refer to the actual year of the match. Entries in square brackets denote matches played in RWC Finals.

Ackerman, R A (Newport, London Welsh) 1980 NZ, 1981 E, S, A, 1982 I, F, E, S, 1983 S, I, F, R, 1984 S, I, F, E, A, 1985 S, I, F, E, Fj
Alexander, E P (Llandovery Coll, Cambridge U) 1885 S, 1886 E, S, 1887 E, I
Alexander, W H (Llwynypia) 1898 I, E, 1899 E, S, I, 1901 S, I
Allen, A G (Newbridge) 1990 F, E, I
Allen, C P (Oxford U, Beaumaris) 1884 E, S
Andrews, F (Pontypool) 1912 SA, 1913 E, S, I
Andrews, F G (Swansea) 1884 E, S
Andrews, G E (Newport) 1926 E, S, 1927 E, F, I
Anthony, C T (Swansea, Newport, Gwent Dragons) 1997 US 1(R),2(R), C (R), Tg (R), 1998 SA 2, Arg, 1999 S, I (R), 2001 J 1,2, I (R), 2002 I, F, It, E, S, 2003 R (R)
Anthony, L (Neath) 1948 E, S, F
Appleyard, R C (Swansea) 1997 C, R, Tg, NZ, 1998 It, E (R), S, I, F
Arnold, P (Swansea) 1990 Nm 1, 2, Bb, 1991 E, S, I, F 1, A, [Arg, A], 1993 F (R), Z 2, 1994 Sp, Fj, 1995 SA, 1996 Bb (R)
Arnold, W R (Swansea) 1903 S
Arthur, C S (Cardiff) 1888 I, M, 1891 E
Arthur, T (Neath) 1927 S, F, I, 1929 E, S, F, I, 1930 E, S, I, F, 1931 E, S, F, I, SA, 1933 E, S
Ashton, C (Aberavon) 1959 E, S, I, 1960 E, S, I, 1962 I
Attewell, S L (Newport) 1921 E, S, F
Back, M J (Bridgend) 1995 F (R), E (R), S, I
Badger, O (Llanelli) 1895 E, S, I, 1896 E
Baker, A (Neath) 1921 I, 1923 E, S, F, I
Baker, A M (Newport) 1909 S, F, 1910 S
Bancroft, J (Swansea) 1909 E, S, F, I, 1910 F, E, S, I, 1911 E, F, I, 1912 E, S, I, 1913 I, 1914 E, S, F
Bancroft, W J (Swansea) 1890 S, E, I, 1891 E, S, I, 1892 E, S, I, 1893 E, S, I, 1894 E, S, I, 1895 E, S, I, 1896 E, S, I, 1897 E, 1898 I, E, 1899 E, S, I, 1900 E, S, I, 1901 E, S, I
Barlow, T M (Cardiff) 1884 I
Barrell, R J (Cardiff) 1929 S, F, I, 1933 I
Bartlett, J D (Llanelli) 1927 S, 1928 E, S
Bassett, A (Cardiff) 1934 I, 1935 E, S, I, 1938 E, S
Bassett, J A (Penarth) 1929 E, S, F, I, 1930 E, S, I, 1931 E, S, F, I, SA, 1932 E, S, I
Bateman, A G (Neath, Richmond, Northampton) 1990 S, I, Nm 1,2, 1996 SA, 1997 US, S, F, E, R, NZ, 1998 It, E, S, I, 1999 S, Arg 1,2, SA, C, [J, A (R)], 2000 It, E, S, I, Sm, US, SA, 2001 E (R), It (t), R, I, Art (R), Tg
Bater, J (Ospreys) 2003 R (R)
Bayliss, G (Pontypool) 1933 S
Bebb, D I E (Carmarthen TC, Swansea) 1959 E, S, I, F, 1960 E, S, I, F, SA, 1961 E, S, I, F, 1962 E, S, F, I, 1963 E, F, NZ, 1964 E, S, F, SA, 1965 E, S, I, F, 1966 F, A, 1967 S, I, F, E
Beckingham, G (Cardiff) 1953 E, S, 1958 F
Bennett, A M (Cardiff) 1995 [NZ] SA, Fj
Bennett, H (Ospreys) 2003 I 2(R), S 2(R), [C(R),Tg(R)], 2004 S(R),F(R),Arg 1(R),2, SA1(R), 2006 Arg 2,PI(R), 2007 E2, [J(R)],SA, 2008 E,S,It(R),F, 2009 S(R),E(R),F(R), It,I(R), NZ(R),Sm,Arg(R),A(R), 2010 E(R),S(R),F,I(R),It(R),NZ1(R), 2(R)
Bennett, I (Aberavon) 1937 I
Bennett, P (Cardiff Harlequins) 1891 E, S, 1892 S, I
Bennett, P (Llanelli) 1969 F (R), 1970 SA, S, F, 1972 S (R), NZ, 1973 E, S, I, F, A, 1974 S, I, F, E, 1975 S (R), I, 1976 E, S, I, F, 1977 I, F, E, S, 1978 E, S, I, F
Bergiers, R T E (Cardiff Coll of Ed, Llanelli) 1972 E, S, F, NZ, 1973 E, S, I, F, A, 1974 E, 1975 I
Bevan, G W (Llanelli) 1947 E
Bevan, J A (Cambridge U) 1881 E
Bevan, J C (Cardiff, Cardiff Coll of Ed) 1971 E, S, I, F, 1972 E, S, F, NZ, 1973 E, S
Bevan, J D (Aberavon) 1975 F, E, S, A
Bevan, S (Swansea) 1904 I
Beynon, B (Swansea) 1920 E, S
Beynon, G E (Swansea) 1925 F, I
Bidgood, R A (Newport) 1992 S, 1993 Z 1,2, Nm, J (R)
Biggar, D R (Ospreys) 2008 C(R), 2009 C,US(R),Sm, 2010 NZ1(R),2
Biggs, N W (Cardiff) 1888 M, 1889 I, 1892 I, 1893 E, S, I, 1894 E, I
Biggs, S H (Cardiff) 1895 E, S, 1896 S, 1897 E, 1898 I, E, 1899 S, I, 1900 I
Birch, J (Neath) 1911 S, F
Birt, F W (Newport) 1911 E, S, 1912 E, S, I, SA, 1913 E
Bishop, A M (Ospreys) 2008 SA2(R),C,A(R), 2009 S(R),C,US, Arg(R),A(R), 2010 I(R),It(R),NZ1
Bishop, D J (Pontypool) 1984 A
Bishop, E H (Swansea) 1889 S
Blackmore, J H (Abertillery) 1909 E
Blackmore, S W (Cardiff) 1987 I, [Tg (R), C, A]
Blake, J (Cardiff) 1899 E, S, I, 1900 E, S, I, 1901 E, S, I
Blakemore, R E (Newport) 1947 E
Bland, A F (Cardiff) 1887 E, S, I, 1888 S, I, M, 1890 S, E, I
Blyth, L (Swansea) 1951 SA, 1952 E, S
Blyth, W R (Swansea) 1974 E, 1975 S (R), 1980 F, E, S, I
Boobyer, N (Llanelli) 1993 Z 1(R),2, Nm, 1994 Fj, Tg, 1998 F, 1999 It (R)
Boon, R W (Cardiff) 1930 S, F, 1931 E, S, F, I, SA, 1932 E, S, I, 1933 E, I
Booth, J (Pontymister) 1898 I
Boots, J G (Newport) 1898 I, E, 1899 I, 1900 E, S, I, 1901 E, S, I, 1902 E, S, I, 1903 E, S, I, 1904 E
Boucher, A W (Newport) 1892 E, S, I, 1893 E, S, I, 1894 E, 1895 E, S, I, 1896 E, I, 1897 E
Bowcott, H M (Cardiff, Cambridge U) 1929 S, F, I, 1930 E, 1931 E, S, 1933 E, I
Bowdler, F A (Cross Keys) 1927 A, 1928 E, S, I, F, 1929 E, S, F, I, 1930 E, 1931 SA, 1932 E, S, I, 1933 I
Bowen, B (S Wales Police, Swansea) 1983 R, 1984 S, I, F, E, 1985 Fj, 1986 E, S, I, F, Fj, Tg, WS, 1987 [C, E, NZ], US, 1988 E, S, I, F, WS, 1989 S, I
Bowen, C A (Llanelli) 1896 E, S, I, 1897 E
Bowen, D H (Llanelli) 1883 E, 1886 E, S, 1887 E
Bowen, G E (Swansea) 1887 S, I, 1888 S, I
Bowen, W (Swansea) 1921 S, F, 1922 E, S, I, F
Bowen, Wm A (Swansea) 1886 E, S, 1887 E, S, I, 1888 M, 1889 S, I, 1890 S, E, I, 1891 E, S
Brace, D O (Llanelli, Oxford U) 1956 E, S, I, F, 1957 E, 1960 S, I, F, 1961 I
Braddock, K J (Newbridge) 1966 A, 1967 S, I
Bradshaw, K (Bridgend) 1964 E, S, I, F, SA, 1966 E, S, I, F
Brew, A (Newport Gwent Dragons, Ospreys) 2007 I(R),A2,E2
Brew, N R (Gwent Dragons) 2003 R

Brewer, T J (Newport) 1950 E, 1955 E, S
Brice, A B (Aberavon) 1899 E, S, I, 1900 E, S, I, 1901 E, S, I, 1902 E, S, I, 1903 E, S, I, 1904 E, S, I
Bridges, C J (Neath) 1990 Nm 1,2, Bb, 1991 E (R), I, F 1, A
Bridie, R H (Newport) 1882 I
Britton, G R (Newport) 1961 S
Broster, B G J (Saracens) 2005 US(R),C
Broughton, A S (Treorchy) 1927 A, 1929 S
Brown, A (Newport) 1921 I
Brown, J (Cardiff) 1925 I
Brown, J A (Cardiff) 1907 E, S, I, 1908 E, S, F, 1909 E
Brown, M (Pontypool) 1983 R, 1986 E, S, Fj (R), Tg, WS
Bryant, D J (Bridgend) 1988 NZ 1,2, WS, R, 1989 S, I, F, E
Bryant, J (Celtic Warriors) 2003 R (R)
Buchanan, D A (Llanelli) 1987 [Tg, E, NZ, A], 1988 I
Buckett, I M (Swansea) 1994 Tg, 1997 US 2, C
Budgett, N J (Ebbw Vale, Bridgend) 2000 S, I, Sm (R), US, SA, 2001 J 1(R),2, 2002 I, F, It, E, S
Burcher, D H (Newport) 1977 I, F, E, S
Burgess, R C (Ebbw Vale) 1977 I, F, E, S, 1981 I, F, 1982 F, E, S
Burnett, R (Newport) 1953 E
Burns, J (Cardiff) 1927 F, I
Bush, P F (Cardiff) 1905 NZ, 1906 E, SA, 1907 I, 1908 E, S, 1910 S, I
Butler, E T (Pontypool) 1980 F, E, S, I, NZ (R), 1982 S, 1983 E, S, I, F, R, 1984 S, I, F, E, A
Byrne, L M (Llanelli Scarlets, Ospreys) 2005 NZ(R),Fj,SA, 2006 E(t&R),S(t&R),I,It,F,Arg1,2,PI,2007F1,A1,E2,2008 E,S,It,I,F,SA3,NZ,A, 2009 S,E,F,It,I, 2010 E,S,F,I,It, SA1,NZ1,2
Cale, W R (Newbridge, Pontypool) 1949 E, S, I, 1950 E, S, I, F
Cardey, M D (Llanelli) 2000 S
Carter, A J (Newport) 1991 E, S
Cattell, A (Llanelli) 1883 E, S
Challinor, C (Neath) 1939 E
Charteris, L C (Newport Gwent Dragons) 2004 SA2(R),R, 2005 US,C,NZ(R),Fj, 2007 SA(R), 2008 C,NZ(R), 2009 S(R),F (R),It,I(R),US(R),NZ,Sm,Arg,A, 2010 E,F(R),I,It
Charvis, C L (Swansea, Tarbes, Newcastle, Newport Gwent Dragons) 1996 A 3(R), SA, 1997 US, S, I, F, 1998 It (R), E, S, I, F, Z (R), SA 1,2, Arg, 1999 S, I, F 1, It, E, Arg 1, SA, F 2, [Arg 3, A], 2000 F, It (R), E, S, I, Sm, US, SA, 2001 E, S, F, It, R, I, Arg, Tg, A, 2002 E (R), S, SA 1,2, R, Fj, C, NZ, 2003 It, E 1(R), S 1(R), I 1, F,A, NZ, E 2, S 2, [C, Tg,It,NZ,E], 2004 S,F,E,It,Arg 1,2,SA1,2,R,NZ,J, 2005 US,C,NZ,SA,A, 2006 E,S,I,It, 2007 A1,2,E2,Arg(R),F2(R), [C(t&R),A,J,Fj],SA
Clapp, T J S (Newport) 1882 I, 1883 E, S, 1884 E, S, I, 1885 E, S, 1886 S, 1887 E, S, I, 1888 S, I
Clare, J (Cardiff) 1883 E
Clark, S S (Neath) 1882 I, 1887 I
Cleaver, W B (Cardiff) 1947 E, S, F, I, A, 1948 E, S, F, I, 1949 I, 1950 E, S, I, F
Clegg, B G (Swansea) 1979 F
Clement, A (Swansea) 1987 US (R), 1988 E, NZ 1, WS (R), R, 1989 NZ, 1990 S (R), I (R), Nm 1,2, 1991 S (R), A (R), F 2, [WS, A], 1992 I, F, E, S, 1993 I (R), F, J, C, 1994 S, I, F, Sp, C (R), Tg, WS, It, SA, 1995 F, E, [J, NZ, I]
Clement, W H (Llanelli) 1937 E, S, I, 1938 E, S, I
Cobner, T J (Pontypool) 1974 S, I, F, E, 1975 F, E, S, I, A, 1976 E, S, 1977 F, E, S, 1978 E, S, I, F, A 1
Cockbain, B J (Celtic Warriors, Ospreys) 2003 R, [C,It,NZ,E], 2004 S,I,F,E,Arg 1,2,SA2,NZ, 2005 E,It,F,S,I,US,C(R),NZ,Fj, 2007 F1(t&R),A1
Coldrick, A P (Newport) 1911 E, S, I, 1912 E, S, F
Coleman, E O (Newport) 1949 E, S, I
Coles, F C (Pontypool) 1960 S, I, F
Collins, J E (Aberavon) 1958 A, E, S, F, 1959 E, S, I, F, 1960 E, 1961 F
Collins, R G (S Wales Police, Cardiff, Pontypridd) 1987 E (R), I, [I, E, NZ], US, 1988 E, S, I, F, R, 1990 E, S, I, 1991 A, F 2, [WS], 1994 C, Fj, Tg, WS, R, It, SA, 1995 F, E, S, I
Collins, T J (Mountain Ash) 1923 I
Conway-Rees, J (Llanelli) 1892 S, 1893 E, 1894 E
Cook, T (Cardiff) 1949 S, I
Cooper, G J (Bath, Celtic Warriors, Newport Gwent Dragons, Gloucester, Cardiff Blues) 2001 It, J 1,2, 2003 E 1, S 1, I 1, F(R), A, NZ, E 2, [C,Tg,It(t&R),NZ,E], 2004 S,I,F,E, It,R(R),NZ(R), J, 2005 E(R), It(R),F(R),NZ(R),Fj,SA,A, 2006 E(R),PI(R), 2007 A1(R), E2, [J(R)], 2008 SA1,2,3,NZ,A,2009 C,US(R),NZ,Arg, 2010 E,S
Cooper, V L (Llanelli) 2002 C, 2003 I 2(R), S 2
Cope, W (Cardiff, Blackheath) 1896 S
Copsey, A H (Llanelli) 1992 I, F, E, S, A, 1993 E, S, I, J, C, 1994 E (R), Pt, Sp (R), Fj, Tg, WS (R)
Cornish, F H (Cardiff) 1897 E, 1898 I, E, 1899 I
Cornish, R A (Cardiff) 1923 E, S, 1924 E, 1925 E, S, F, 1926 E, S, I, F
Coslett, T K (Aberavon) 1962 E, S, F
Cowey, B T V (Welch Regt, Newport) 1934 E, S, I, 1935 E
Cresswell, B R (Newport) 1960 E, S, I, F
Cummins, W (Treorchy) 1922 E, S, I, F
Cunningham, L J (Aberavon) 1960 E, S, I, F, 1962 E, S, F, I, 1963 NZ, 1964 E, S, I, F, SA
Czekaj, C D (Cardiff Blues) 2005 C, 2006 Arg 1(R), 2007 I,S,A1,2, 2009 C
Dacey, M (Swansea) 1983 E, S, I, F, R, 1984 S, I, F, E, A, 1986 Fj, Tg, WS, 1987 F (R), [Tg]
Daniel, D J (Llanelli) 1891 S, 1894 E, S, I, 1898 I, E, 1899 E, I
Daniel, L T D (Newport) 1970 S
Daniels, P C T (Cardiff) 1981 A, 1982 I
Darbishire, G (Bangor) 1881 E
Dauncey, F H (Newport) 1896 E, S, I
Davey, C (Swansea) 1930 F, 1931 E, S, F, I, SA, 1932 E, S, I, 1933 E, S, 1934 E, S, I, 1935 E, S, I, NZ, 1936 S, 1937 E, I, 1938 E, I
David, R J (Cardiff) 1907 I
David, T P (Llanelli, Pontypridd) 1973 F, A, 1976 I, F
Davidge, G D (Newport) 1959 F, 1960 S, I, F, SA, 1961 E, S, I, 1962 F
Davies, A (Cambridge U, Neath, Cardiff) 1990 Bb (R), 1991 A, 1993 Z 1,2, J, C, 1994 Fj, 1995 [J, I]
Davies, A C (London Welsh) 1889 I
Davies, A E (Llanelli) 1984 A
Davies, B (Llanelli) 1895 E, 1896 E
Davies, B (Llanelli Scarlets) 2006 I(R)
Davies, B S (Cardiff Blues) 2009 S(R),It(R),C,NZ(R),Sm(R), 2010 E(t&R),S(R),F,I,It, SA1,NZ1,2
Davies, C (Cardiff) 1947 S, F, I, A, 1948 E, S, F, I, 1949 F, 1950 E, S, I, F, 1951 E, S, I
Davies, C (Llanelli) 1988 WS, 1989 S, I (R), F
Davies, C A H (Llanelli, Cardiff) 1957 I, 1958 A, E, S, I, 1960 SA, 1961 E
Davies, C H (Swansea, Llanelli) 1939 S, I, 1947 E, S, F, I
Davies, C L (Cardiff) 1956 E, S, I
Davies, C R (Bedford, RAF) 1934 E
Davies, D B (Llanelli) 1907 E
Davies, D B (Llanelli) 1962 I, 1963 E, S
Davies, D E G (Cardiff) 1912 E, F
Davies, D G (Cardiff) 1923 E, S
Davies, D H (Neath) 1904 S
Davies, D H (Bridgend) 1921 I, 1925 I
Davies, D H (Aberavon) 1924 E
Davies, D I (Swansea) 1939 E
Davies, D J (Neath) 1962 I
Davies, D M (Somerset Police) 1950 E, S, I, F, 1951 E, S, I, F, SA, 1952 E, S, I, F, 1953 I, F, NZ, 1954 E
Davies, E (Maesteg) 1919 NZA
Davies, E G (Cardiff) 1928 F, 1929 E, 1930 S
Davies, E P (Aberavon) 1947 A, 1948 I
Davies, G (Swansea) 1900 E, S, I, 1901 E, S, I, 1905 E, S, I
Davies, G (Cambridge U, Pontypridd) 1947 S, A, 1948 E, S, F, I, 1949 E, S, F, 1951 E, S
Davies, H (Swansea) 1898 I, E, 1901 S, I
Davies, H (Bridgend) 1984 S, I, F, E
Davies, H G (Llanelli) 1921 F, I, 1925 F
Davies, H J (Neath) 1912 E, S
Davies, H J (Newport) 1924 S
Davies, H J (Cambridge U, Aberavon) 1959 E, S
Davies, H S (Treherbert) 1923 I
Davies, I T (Llanelli) 1914 S, F, I
Davies, J (Neath, Llanelli, Cardiff) 1985 E, Fj, 1986 E, S, I, F, Fj, Tg, WS, 1987 F, E, S, I, [I, Tg (R), C, E, NZ, A], 1988 E, S, I, F, NZ 1,2, WS, R, 1996 A 3, 1997 US (t), S (R), F (R), E
Davies, Rev J A (Swansea) 1913 S, F, I, 1914 E, S, F, I
Davies, J D (Neath, Richmond) 1991 I, F 1, 1993 F (R), Z 2, J, C, 1994 S, I, F, E, Pt, Sp, C, WS, R, It, SA, 1995 F, E, [J, NZ, I] SA, 1996 It, E, S, I, F 1, A 1, Bb, F 2, It, 1998 Z, SA 1
Davies, J H (Aberavon) 1923 I
Davies, J J V (Scarlets) 2009 C,US,Sm(R),Arg,A, 2010 NZ1(R),2
Davies, L (Swansea) 1939 S, I
Davies, L (Bridgend) 1966 E, S, I

Davies, L B (Neath, Cardiff, Llanelli) 1996 It, E, S, I, F 1, A 1, Bb, F 2, It (R), 1997 US 1,2, C, R, Tg, NZ (R), 1998 E (R), I, F, 1999 C, 2001 I, 2003 It
Davies, L M (Llanelli) 1954 F, S, 1955 I
Davies, M (Swansea) 1981 A, 1982 I, 1985 Fj
Davies, Mefin (Pontypridd, Celtic Warriors, Gloucester) 2002 SA 2(R), R, Fj, 2003 It, S 1(R), I 1(R), F, A(R), NZ(R), I 2, R, [Tg,NZ(R),E(R)], 2004 S,F,It(R),Arg 1,2(R),SA1, 2(R),R,NZ,J, 2005 E,It,F,S,I,C(R),NZ,SA(R),A(t), 2006 S(R),I(R),It(R),F(R), 2007 A2
Davies, M J (Blackheath) 1939 S, I
Davies, N G (London Welsh) 1955 E
Davies, N G (Llanelli) 1988 NZ 2, WS, 1989 S, I, 1993 F, 1994 S, I, E, Pt, Sp, C, Fj, Tg (R), WS, R, It, 1995 E, S, I, Fj, 1996 E, S, I, F 1, A 1,2, Bb, F 2, 1997 E
Davies, P T (Llanelli) 1985 E, Fj, 1986 E, S, I, F, Fj, Tg, WS, 1987 F, E, I, [Tg, C, NZ], 1988 WS, R, 1989 S, I, F, E, NZ, 1990 F, E, S, 1991 I, F 1, A, F 2, [WS, Arg, A], 1993 F, Z 1, Nm, 1994 S, I, F, E, C, Fj (R), WS, R, It, 1995 F, I
Davies, R H (Oxford U, London Welsh) 1957 S, I, F, 1958 A, 1962 E, S
Davies, S (Swansea) 1992 I, F, E, S, A, 1993 E, S, I, Z 1(R),2, Nm, J, 1995 F, [J, I], 1998 I (R), F
Davies, T G R (Cardiff, London Welsh) 1966 A, 1967 S, I, F, E, 1968 E, S, 1969 S, I, F, NZ 1,2, A, 1971 E, S, I, F, 1972 E, S, F, NZ, 1973 E, S, I, F, A, 1974 S, F, E, 1975 F, E, S, I, 1976 E, S, I, F, 1977 I, F, E, S, 1978 E, S, I, A 1,2
Davies, T J (Devonport Services, Swansea, Llanelli) 1953 E, S, I, F, 1957 E, S, I, F, 1958 A, E, S, F, 1959 E, S, I, F, 1960 E, SA, 1961 E, S, F
Davies, T M (London Welsh, Swansea) 1969 S, I, F, E, NZ 1,2, A, 1970 SA, S, E, I, F, 1971 E, S, I, F, 1972 E, S, F, NZ, 1973 E, S, I, F, A, 1974 S, I, F, E, 1975 F, E, S, I, A, 1976 E, S, I, F
Davies, W (Cardiff) 1896 S
Davies, W (Swansea) 1931 SA, 1932 E, S, I
Davies, W A (Aberavon) 1912 S, I
Davies, W G (Cardiff) 1978 A 1,2, NZ, 1979 S, I, F, E, 1980 F, E, S, NZ, 1981 E, S, A, 1982 I, F, E, S, 1985 S, I, F
Davies, W T H (Swansea) 1936 I, 1937 E, I, 1939 E, S, I
Davis, C E (Newbridge) 1978 A 2, 1981 E, S
Davis, M (Newport) 1991 A
Davis, W E N (Cardiff) 1939 E, S, I
Dawes, S J (London Welsh) 1964 I, F, SA, 1965 E, S, I, F, 1966 A, 1968 I, F, 1969 E, NZ 2, A, 1970 SA, S, E, I, F, 1971 E, S, I, F
Day, H C (Newport) 1930 S, I, F, 1931 E, S
Day, H T (Newport) 1892 I, 1893 E, S, 1894 S, I
Day, T B (Swansea) 1931 E, S, F, I, SA, 1932 E, S, I, 1934 S, I, 1935 E, S, I
Deacon, J T (Swansea) 1891 I, 1892 E, S, I
Delahay, W J (Bridgend) 1922 E, S, I, F, 1923 E, S, F, I, 1924 NZ, 1925 E, S, F, I, 1926 E, S, I, F, 1927 S
Delaney, L (Llanelli) 1989 I, F, E, 1990 E, 1991 F 2, [WS, Arg, A], 1992 I, F, E
Delve, G L (Bath, Gloucester) 2006 S(R),I(R),Arg 1(R),2(R), 2008 S(R),It(R),I(R),SA1(R),2, 2010 I,It(R)
Devereux, D B (Neath) 1958 A, E, S
Devereux, J A (S Glamorgan Inst, Bridgend) 1986 E, S, I, F, Fj, Tg, WS, 1987 F, E, S, I, [I, C, E, NZ, A], 1988 NZ 1,2, R, 1989 S, I
Diplock, R S (Bridgend) 1988 R
Dobson, G A (Cardiff) 1900 S
Dobson, T (Cardiff) 1898 I, E, 1899 E, S
Donovan, A J (Swansea) 1978 A 2, 1981 I (R), A, 1982 E, S
Donovan, R E (S Wales Police) 1983 F (R)
Douglas, M H J (Llanelli) 1984 S, I, F
Douglas, W M (Cardiff) 1886 E, S, 1887 E, S
Dowell, W H (Newport) 1907 E, S, I, 1908 E, S, F, I
Durston, A P R (Bridgend) 2001 J 1,2
Dyke, J C M (Penarth) 1906 SA
Dyke, L M (Penarth, Cardiff) 1910 I, 1911 S, F, I
Edmunds, D A (Neath) 1990 I (R), Bb
Edwards, A B (London Welsh, Army) 1955 E, S
Edwards, B O (Newport) 1951 I
Edwards, D (Glynneath) 1921 E
Edwards, G O (Cardiff, Cardiff Coll of Ed) 1967 F, E, NZ, 1968 E, S, I, F, 1969 S, I, F, E, NZ 1,2, A, 1970 SA, S, E, I, F, 1971 E, S, I, F, 1972 E, S, F, NZ, 1973 E, S, I, F, A, 1974 S, I, F, E, 1975 F, E, S, I, A, 1976 E, S, I, F, 1977 I, F, E, S, 1978 E, S, I, F
Eidman, I H (Cardiff) 1983 S, R, 1984 I, F, E, A, 1985 S, I, Fj, 1986 E, S, I, F
Elliott, J (Cardiff) 1894 I, 1898 I, E
Elsey, W J (Cardiff) 1895 E
Emyr, Arthur (Swansea) 1989 E, NZ, 1990 F, E, S, I, Nm 1,2, 1991 F 1,2, [WS, Arg, A]
Evans, A (Pontypool) 1924 E, I, F
Evans, B (Llanelli) 1933 E, S, 1936 E, S, I, 1937 E
Evans, B R (Swansea, Cardiff Blues) 1998 SA 2(R), 1999 F 1, It, E, Arg 1,2, C, [J (R), Sm (R), A (R)], 2000 Sm, US, 2001 J 1(R), 2002 SA 1,2, R(R), Fj, C, NZ, 2003 It, E 1, S 1, I 2, R, 2004 F(R),E(t),It(R)
Evans, B S (Llanelli) 1920 E, 1922 E, S, I, F
Evans, C (Pontypool) 1960 E
Evans, D (Penygraig) 1896 S, I, 1897 E, 1898 E
Evans, D B (Swansea) 1926 E
Evans, D B (Swansea) 1933 S
Evans, D D (Cheshire, Cardiff U) 1934 E
Evans, D J (Scarlets) 2009 C,US
Evans, D P (Llanelli) 1960 SA
Evans, D W (Cardiff) 1889 S, I, 1890 E, I, 1891 E
Evans, D W (Oxford U, Cardiff, Treorchy) 1989 F, E, NZ, 1990 F, E, S, I, Bb, 1991 A (R), F 2(R), [A (R)], 1995 [J (R)]
Evans, E (Llanelli) 1937 E, 1939 S, I
Evans, F (Llanelli) 1921 S
Evans, G (Cardiff) 1947 E, S, F, I, A, 1948 E, S, F, I, 1949 E, S, I
Evans, G (Maesteg) 1981 S (R), I, F, A, 1982 I, F, E, S, 1983 F, R
Evans, G D (Llanelli Scarlets) 2006 PI(R)
Evans, G L (Newport) 1977 F (R), 1978 F, A 2(R)
Evans, G R (Cardiff) 1889 S
Evans, G R (Llanelli) 1998 SA 1, 2003 I 2, S 2, [NZ]
Evans, H I (Swansea) 1922 E, S, I, F
Evans, Ian (Ospreys) 2006 Arg 1,2,A,C,NZ, 2007 [J(R),Fj],SA, 2008 E(R),S,It,F(R), SA1(R),2(R),3,NZ
Evans, I (London Welsh) 1934 S, I
Evans, I C (Llanelli, Bath) 1987 F, E, S, I, [I, C, E, NZ, A], 1988 E, S, I, F, NZ 1,2, 1989 I, F, E, 1991 E, S, I, F 1, A, F 2, [WS, Arg, A], 1992 I, F, E, S, A, 1993 E, S, I, F, J, C, 1994 S, I, E, Pt, Sp, C, Fj, Tg, WS, R, 1995 E, S, I, [J, NZ, I], SA, Fj, 1996 It, E, S, I, F 1, A 1,2, Bb, F 2, A 3, SA, 1997 US, S, I, F, 1998 It
Evans, I L (Llanelli) 1991 F 2(R)
Evans, J (Llanelli) 1896 S, I, 1897 E
Evans, J D (Cardiff) 1958 I, F
Evans, J E (Llanelli) 1924 S
Evans, J H (Pontypool) 1907 E, S, I
Evans, J R (Newport) 1934 E
Evans, J W (Blaina) 1904 E
Evans, O J (Cardiff) 1887 E, S, 1888 S, I
Evans, P D (Llanelli) 1951 E, F
Evans, R (Bridgend) 1963 S, I, F
Evans, R L (Llanelli) 1993 E, S, I, F, 1994 S, I, F, E, Pt, Sp, C, Fj, WS, R, It, SA, 1995 F, [NZ, I (R)]
Evans, R T (Newport) 1947 F, I, 1950 E, S, I, F, 1951 E, S, I, F
Evans, S (Swansea, Neath) 1985 F, E, 1986 Fj, Tg, WS, 1987 F, E, [I, Tg]
Evans, T D (Swansea) 1924 I
Evans, T G (London Welsh) 1970 SA, S, E, I, 1972 E, S, F
Evans, T H (Llanelli) 1906 I, 1907 E, S, I, 1908 I, A, 1909 E, S, F, I, 1910 F, E, S, I, 1911 E, S, F, I
Evans, T P (Swansea) 1975 F, E, S, I, A, 1976 E, S, I, F, 1977 I
Evans, T W (Llanelli) 1958 A
Evans, V (Neath) 1954 I, F, S
Evans, W F (Rhymney) 1882 I, 1883 S
Evans, W G (Brynmawr) 1911 I
Evans, W H (Llwynypia) 1914 E, S, F, I
Evans, W J (Pontypool) 1947 S
Evans, W R (Bridgend) 1958 A, E, S, I, F, 1960 SA, 1961 E, S, I, F, 1962 E, S, I
Everson, W A (Newport) 1926 S
Faulkner, A G (Pontypool) 1975 F, E, S, I, A, 1976 E, S, I, F, 1978 E, S, I, F, A 1,2, NZ, 1979 S, I, F
Faull, J (Swansea) 1957 I, F, 1958 A, E, S, I, F, 1959 E, S, I, 1960 E, F
Fauvel, T J (Aberavon) 1988 NZ 1(R)
Fear, A G (Newport) 1934 S, I, 1935 S, I
Fender, N H (Cardiff) 1930 I, F, 1931 E, S, F, I
Fenwick, S P (Bridgend) 1975 F, E, S, A, 1976 E, S, I, F, 1977 I, F, E, S, 1978 E, S, I, F, A 1,2, NZ, 1979 S, I, F, E, 1980 F, E, S, I, NZ, 1981 E, S
Finch, E (Llanelli) 1924 F, NZ, 1925 F, I, 1926 F, 1927 A, 1928 I
Finlayson, A A J (Cardiff) 1974 I, F, E
Fitzgerald, D (Cardiff) 1894 S, I
Ford, F J V (Welch Regt, Newport) 1939 E
Ford, I R (Newport) 1959 E, S
Ford, S P (Cardiff) 1990 I, Nm 1,2, Bb, 1991 E, S, I, A

Forster, J A (Newport Gwent Dragons) 2004 Arg 1
Forward, A (Pontypool, Mon Police) 1951 S, SA, 1952 E, S, I, F
Fowler, I J (Llanelli) 1919 NZA
Francis, D G (Llanelli) 1919 NZA, 1924 S
Francis, P W (Maesteg) 1987 S
Funnell, J S (Ebbw Vale) 1998 Z (R), SA 1
Fury, W L (London Irish) 2008 SA1(R),2(R)
Gabe, R T (Cardiff, Llanelli) 1901 I, 1902 E, S, I, 1903 E, S, I, 1904 E, S, I, 1905 E, S, I, NZ, 1906 E, I, SA, 1907 E, S, I, 1908 E, S, F, I
Gale, N R (Swansea, Llanelli) 1960 I, 1963 E, S, I, NZ, 1964 E, S, I, F, SA, 1965 E, S, I, F, 1966 E, S, I, F, A, 1967 E, NZ, 1968 E, 1969 NZ 1(R),2, A
Gallacher, I S (Llanelli) 1970 F
Garrett, R M (Penarth) 1888 M, 1889 S, 1890 S, E, I, 1891 S, I, 1892 E
Geen, W P (Oxford U, Newport) 1912 SA, 1913 E, I
George, E E (Pontypridd, Cardiff) 1895 S, I, 1896 E
George, G M (Newport) 1991 E, S
Gething, G I (Neath) 1913 F
Gibbs, A (Newbridge) 1995 I, SA, 1996 A 2, 1997 US 1,2, C
Gibbs, I S (Neath, Swansea) 1991 E, S, I, F 1, A, F 2, [WS, Arg, A], 1992 I, F, E, S, A, 1993 E, S, I, F, J, C, 1996 It, A 3, SA, 1997 US, S, I, F, Tg, NZ, 1998 It, E, S, SA 2, Arg, 1999 S, I, F 1, It, E, C, F 2, [Arg 3, J, Sm, A], 2000 I, Sm, US, SA, 2001 E, S, F, It
Gibbs, R A (Cardiff) 1906 S, I, 1907 E, S, 1908 E, S, F, I, 1910 F, E, S, I, 1911 E, S, F, I
Giles, R (Aberavon) 1983 R, 1985 Fj (R), 1987 [C]
Gill, I A R (Saracens) 2010 I(R)
Girling, B E (Cardiff) 1881 E
Goldsworthy, S J (Swansea) 1884 I, 1885 E, S
Gore, J H (Blaina) 1924 I, F, NZ, 1925 E
Gore, W (Newbridge) 1947 S, F, I
Gough, I M (Newport, Pontypridd, Newport Gwent Dragons, Ospreys) 1998 SA 1, 1999 S, 2000 F, It (R), E (R), S, I, Sm, US, SA, 2001 E, S, F, It, Tg, A, 2002 I (R), F (R), It, S, 2003 R, 2005 It(R),US(R),SA,A, 2006 E,S,I,It,F,Arg 1,2,A,C,NZ, 2007 I,S(R),F1,It,E1, Arg,F2, [C,A,Fj(R)], 2008 E,S,It,I,F,SA1,2,3(R), C,A, 2009 S,E,F,I,C(R),US, 2010 I(R), It(R)
Gould, A J (Newport) 1885 E, S, 1886 E, S, 1887 E, S, I, 1888 S, 1889 I, 1890 S, E, I, 1892 E, S, I, 1893 E, S, I, 1894 E, S, 1895 E, S, I, 1896 E, S, I, 1897 E
Gould, G H (Newport) 1892 I, 1893 S, I
Gould, R (Newport) 1882 I, 1883 E, S, 1884 E, S, I, 1885 E, S, 1886 E, 1887 E, S
Graham, T C (Newport) 1890 I, 1891 S, I, 1892 E, S, 1893 E, S, I, 1894 E, S, 1895 E, S
Gravell, R W R (Llanelli) 1975 F, E, S, I, A, 1976 E, S, I, F, 1978 E, S, I, F, A 1,2, NZ, 1979 S, I, 1981 I, F, 1982 F, E, S
Gray, A J (London Welsh) 1968 E, S
Greenslade, D (Newport) 1962 S
Greville, H G (Llanelli) 1947 A
Griffin, Dr J (Edinburgh U) 1883 S
Griffiths, C R (Llanelli) 1979 E (R)
Griffiths, D (Llanelli) 1888 M, 1889 I
Griffiths, G (Llanelli) 1889 I
Griffiths, G M (Cardiff) 1953 E, S, I, F, NZ, 1954 I, F, S, 1955 I, F, 1957 E, S
Griffiths, J (Swansea) 2000 Sm (R)
Griffiths, J L (Llanelli) 1988 NZ 2, 1989 S
Griffiths, M (Bridgend, Cardiff, Pontypridd) 1988 WS, R, 1989 S, I, F, E, NZ, 1990 F, E, Nm 1,2, Bb, 1991 I, F 1,2, [WS, Arg, A], 1992 I, F, E, S, A, 1993 Z 1,2, Nm, J, C, 1995 F (R), E, S, I, [J, I], 1998 SA 1
Griffiths, V M (Newport) 1924 S, I, F
Gronow, B (Bridgend) 1910 F, E, S, I
Gwilliam, J A (Cambridge U, Newport) 1947 A, 1948 I, 1949 E, S, I, F, 1950 E, S, I, F, 1951 E, S, I, SA, 1952 E, S, I, F, 1953 E, I, F, NZ, 1954 E
Gwynn, D (Swansea) 1883 E, 1887 S, 1890 E, I, 1891 E, S
Gwynn, W H (Swansea) 1884 E, S, I, 1885 E, S
Hadley, A M (Cardiff) 1983 R, 1984 S, I, F, E, 1985 F, E, Fj, 1986 E, S, I, F, Fj, Tg, 1987 S (R), I, [I, Tg, C, E, NZ, A], US, 1988 E, S, I, F
Halfpenny, S L (Cardiff Blues) 2008 SA3,C,NZ, 2009 S,E,F,NZ,Sm,Arg,A, 2010 E(R),S,F,I,SA1,NZ1,2
Hall, I (Aberavon) 1967 NZ, 1970 SA, S, E, 1971 S, 1974 S, I, F
Hall, M R (Cambridge U, Bridgend, Cardiff) 1988 NZ 1(R),2, WS, R, 1989 S, I, F, E, NZ, 1990 F, E, S, 1991 A, F 2, [WS, Arg, A], 1992 I, F, E, S, A, 1993 E, S, I, 1994 S, I, F, E, Pt, Sp, C, Tg, R, It, SA, 1995 F, S, I, [J, NZ, I]
Hall, W H (Bridgend) 1988 WS
Hancock, F E (Cardiff) 1884 I, 1885 E, S, 1886 S
Hannan, J (Newport) 1888 M, 1889 S, I, 1890 S, E, I, 1891 E, 1892 E, S, I, 1893 E, S, I, 1894 E, S, I, 1895 E, S, I
Harding, A F (London Welsh) 1902 E, S, I, 1903 E, S, I, 1904 E, S, I, 1905 E, S, I, NZ, 1906 E, S, I, SA, 1907 I, 1908 E, S
Harding, C T (Newport) 1888 M, 1889 S, I
Harding, G F (Newport) 1881 E, 1882 I, 1883 E, S
Harding, R (Swansea, Cambridge U) 1923 E, S, F, I, 1924 I, F, NZ, 1925 F, I, 1926 E, I, F, 1927 E, S, F, I, 1928 E
Harries, W T M (Newport Gwent Dragons) 2010 NZ2(R)
Harris, C A (Aberavon) 1927 A
Harris, D J E (Pontypridd, Cardiff) 1959 I, F, 1960 S, I, F, SA, 1961 E, S
Harris, I R (Cardiff) 2001 Arg, Tg, A, 2002 I, It (R), E, S (R), Fj(R), C(R), NZ(R), 2003 It, E 1(R), S 1(R), I 1(R), F, I 2, S 2, [C,Tg,It,E], 2004 S,I,F,It
Hathway, G F (Newport) 1924 I, F
Havard, Rev W T (Llanelli) 1919 NZA
Hawkins, F J (Pontypridd) 1912 I, F
Hayward, B I (Ebbw Vale) 1998 Z (R), SA 1
Hayward, D J (Newbridge) 1949 E, F, 1950 E, S, I, F, 1951 E, S, I, F, SA, 1952 E, S, I, F
Hayward, D J (Cardiff) 1963 E, NZ, 1964 S, I, F, SA
Hayward, G (Swansea) 1908 S, F, I, A, 1909 E
Hellings, D (Llwynypia) 1897 E, 1898 I, E, 1899 S, I, 1900 E, I, 1901 E, S
Henson, G L (Swansea, Ospreys) 2001 J 1(R), R, 2003 NZ(R), R, 2004 Arg 1,2,SA1,2,R,NZ,J, 2005 E,It,F,S,I, 2006 I(R),F(R),A,NZ(R), 2007 A1(t&R),2(R),SA, 2008 E,S,It,I,F, 2009 F(R),It,I
Herrerá, R C (Cross Keys) 1925 S, F, I, 1926 E, S, I, F, 1927 E
Hiams, H (Swansea) 1912 I, F
Hibbard, R (Ospreys) 2006 Arg 1(R),2(R), 2007 A1(R),2(R), 2008 SA1(R),2,C, 2009 C,US(R)
Hickman, A (Neath) 1930 E, 1933 S
Hiddlestone, D D (Neath) 1922 E, S, I, F, 1924 NZ
Hill, A F (Cardiff) 1885 S, 1886 E, S, 1888 S, I, M, 1889 S, 1890 S, I, 1893 E, S, I, 1894 E, S, I
Hill, S D (Cardiff) 1993 Z 1,2, Nm, 1994 I (R), F, SA, 1995 F, SA, 1996 A 2, F 2(R), It, 1997 E
Hinam, S (Cardiff) 1925 I, 1926 E, S, I, F
Hinton, J T (Cardiff) 1884 I
Hirst, G L (Newport) 1912 S, 1913 S, 1914 E, S, F, I
Hodder, W (Pontypool) 1921 E, S, F
Hodges, J J (Newport) 1899 E, S, I, 1900 E, S, I, 1901 E, S, 1902 E, S, I, 1903 E, S, I, 1904 E, S, 1905 E, S, I, NZ, 1906 E, S, I
Hodgson, G T R (Neath) 1962 I, 1963 E, S, I, F, NZ, 1964 E, S, I, F, SA, 1966 S, I, F, 1967 I
Hollingdale, B G (Swansea) 1912 SA, 1913 E
Hollingdale, T H (Neath) 1927 A, 1928 E, S, I, F, 1930 E
Holmes, T D (Cardiff) 1978 A 2, NZ, 1979 S, I, F, E, 1980 F, E, S, I, NZ, 1981 A, 1982 I, F, E, 1983 E, S, I, F, 1984 E, 1985 S, I, F, E, Fj
Hook, J W (Ospreys) 2006 Arg 1(R),2,A(R),PI, C,NZ(R), 2007 I,S,F1,It,E1,A1,2,Arg,F2,[C,A(R),J,Fj],SA, 2008 E,S,It(R),I(R), F,SA1(R),2,3(R),C,NZ(R), 2009 S(R),F(R),It,NZ,Sm,Arg,A, 2010 E,S,F,I,It,SA1
Hopkin, W H (Newport) 1937 S
Hopkins, K (Cardiff, Swansea) 1985 E, 1987 F, E, S, [Tg, C (R)], US
Hopkins, P L (Swansea) 1908 A, 1909 E, I, 1910 E
Hopkins, R (Maesteg) 1970 E (R)
Hopkins, T (Swansea) 1926 E, S, I, F
Hopkins, W J (Aberavon) 1925 E, S
Horsman, C L (Worcester) 2005 NZ(R),Fj,SA,A, 2006 PI, 2007 I,F1,It,E1,A2(R),E2, F2, [J,Fj]
Howarth, S P (Sale, Newport) 1998 SA 2, Arg, 1999 S, I, F 1, It, E, Arg 1,2, SA, C, F 2, [Arg 3, J, Sm, A], 2000 F, It, E
Howells, B (Llanelli) 1934 E
Howells, W G (Llanelli) 1957 E, S, I, F
Howells, W H (Swansea) 1888 S, I
Howley, R (Bridgend, Cardiff) 1996 E, S, I, F 1, A 1,2, Bb, F 2, It, A 3, SA, 1997 US, S, I, F, E, Tg (R), NZ, 1998 It, E, S, I, F, Z, SA 2, Arg, 1999 S, I, F 1, It, E, Arg 1,2, SA, C, F 2, [Arg 3, J, Sm, A], 2000 F, It, E, Sm, US, SA, 2001 E, S, F, R, I, Arg, Tg, A, 2002 I, F, It, E, S
Hughes, D (Newbridge) 1967 NZ, 1969 NZ 2, 1970 SA, S, E, I

Hughes, G (Penarth) 1934 E, S, I
Hughes, H (Cardiff) 1887 S, 1889 S
Hughes, K (Cambridge U, London Welsh) 1970 I, 1973 A, 1974 S
Hullin, W G (Cardiff) 1967 S
Humphreys, J M (Cardiff, Bath) 1995 [NZ, I], SA, Fj, 1996 It, E, S, I, F 1, A 1,2, Bb, It, A 3, SA, 1997 S, I, F, E, Tg (R), NZ (R), 1998 It (R), E (R), S (R), I (R), F (R), SA 2, Arg, 1999 S, Arg 2(R), SA (R), C, [J (R)], 2003 E 1, I 1
Hurrell, R J (Newport) 1959 F
Hutchinson, F O (Neath) 1894 I, 1896 S, I
Huxtable, R (Swansea) 1920 F, I
Huzzey, H V P (Cardiff) 1898 I, E, 1899 E, S, I
Hybart, A J (Cardiff) 1887 E
Ingledew, H M (Cardiff) 1890 I, 1891 E, S
Isaacs, I (Cardiff) 1933 E, S
Jackson, T H (Swansea) 1895 E
James, C R (Llanelli) 1958 A, F
James, D (Swansea) 1891 I, 1892 S, I, 1899 E
James, D M (Cardiff) 1947 A, 1948 E, S, F, I
James, D R (Treorchy) 1931 F, I
James, D R (Bridgend, Pontypridd, Llanelli Scarlets) 1996 A 2(R), It, A 3, SA, 1997 I, Tg (R), 1998 F (R), Z, SA 1,2, Arg, 1999 S, I, F 1, It, E, Arg 1,2, SA, F 2, [Arg 3, Sm, A], 2000 F, It (R), I (R), Sm (R), US, SA, 2001 E, S, F, It, R, I, 2002 I, F, It, E, S (R), NZ(R), 2005 SA,A, 2006 I,F, 2007 E2,Arg, [J]
James, E (Swansea) 1890 S, 1891 I, 1892 S, I, 1899 E
James, J B (Bridgend) 1968 E
James, P (Ospreys) 2003 R, 2009 NZ,Sm,Arg,A, 2010 E,S,F,I, It(t&R),SA1,NZ1,2
James, T (Cardiff Blues) 2007 E2(R),SA(R), 2008 SA2(R), 2009 C,US,Sm,Arg(R),A(R), 2010 E
James, T O (Aberavon) 1935 I, 1937 S
James, W (Gloucester) 2007 E2,Arg(R),F2(R), [J]
James, W J (Aberavon) 1983 E, S, I, F, R, 1984 S, 1985 S, I, F, E, Fj, 1986 E, S, I, F, Fj, Tg, WS, 1987 E, S, I
James, W P (Aberavon) 1925 E, S
Jarman, H (Newport) 1910 E, S, I, 1911 E
Jarrett, K S (Newport) 1967 E, 1968 E, S, 1969 S, I, F, E, NZ 1,2, A
Jarvis, L (Cardiff) 1997 R (R)
Jeffery, J J (Cardiff Coll of Ed, Newport) 1967 NZ
Jenkin, A M (Swansea) 1895 I, 1896 E
Jenkins, A E (Llanelli) 1920 E, S, F, I, 1921 S, F, 1922 F, 1923 E, S, F, I, 1924 NZ, 1928 S, I
Jenkins, D M (Treorchy) 1926 E, S, I, F
Jenkins, D R (Swansea) 1927 A, 1929 E
Jenkins, E (Newport) 1910 S, I
Jenkins, E M (Aberavon) 1927 S, F, I, A, 1928 E, S, I, F, 1929 F, 1930 E, S, I, F, 1931 E, S, F, I, SA, 1932 E, S, I
Jenkins, G D (Pontypridd, Celtic Warriors, Cardiff Blues) 2002 R, NZ(R), 2003 E 1(R), S 1(R), I 1, F, A, NZ, I 2(R), E 2, [C,Tg,It(R),NZ(R),E(R)], 2004 S(R),I(R),F,E,It,Arg 1(R),2(R), SA1,2(R),R,NZ,J, 2005 E,It,F,S,I, 2006 E(R),S(R),I(R),It(R),F (R),A,C, NZ(R), 2007 I,S(R),F1,It,E1,2(R),Arg(R),F2(R), [C,A,J (R),Fj],SA, 2008 E(R),S(R),It, I,F,SA1,2,3,NZ,A, 2009 S,E,F,It (R),I,NZ, Sm,Arg,A, 2010 S(R),It
Jenkins, G R (Pontypool, Swansea) 1991 F 2, [WS (R), Arg, A], 1992 I, F, E, S, A, 1993 C, 1994 S, I, F, E, Pt, Sp, C, Tg, WS, R, It, SA, 1995 F, E, S, I, [J], SA (R), Fj (t), 1996 E (R), 1997 US, US 1, C, 1998 S, I, F, Z, SA 1(R), 1999 I (R), F 1, It, E, Arg 1,2, SA, F 2, [Arg 3, J, Sm, A], 2000 F, It, E, S, I, Sm, US, SA
Jenkins, J C (London Welsh) 1906 SA
Jenkins, J L (Aberavon) 1923 S, F
Jenkins, L H (Mon TC, Newport) 1954 I, 1956 E, S, I, F
Jenkins, N R (Pontypridd, Cardiff) 1991 E, S, I, F 1, 1992 I, F, E, S, 1993 E, S, I, F, Z 1,2, Nm, J, C, 1994 S, I, F, E, Pt, Sp, C, Tg, WS, R, It, SA, 1995 F, E, S, I, [J, NZ, I], SA, Fj, 1996 F 1, A 1,2, Bb, F 2, It, A 3(R), SA, 1997 S, I, F, E, Tg, NZ, 1998 It, E, S, I, F, SA 2, Arg, 1999 S, I, F 1, It, E, Arg 1,2, SA, C, F 2, [Arg 3, J, Sm, A], 2000 F, It, E, I (R), Sm (R), US (R), SA, 2001 E, S, F, It, 2002 SA 1(R),2(R), R
Jenkins, V G J (Oxford U, Bridgend, London Welsh) 1933 E, I, 1934 S, I, 1935 E, S, NZ, 1936 E, S, I, 1937 E, 1938 E, S, 1939 E
Jenkins, W J (Cardiff) 1912 I, F, 1913 S, I
John, B (Llanelli, Cardiff) 1966 A, 1967 S, NZ, 1968 E, S, I, F, 1969 S, I, F, E, NZ 1,2, A, 1970 SA, S, E, I, 1971 E, S, I, F, 1972 E, S, F
John, D A (Llanelli) 1925 I, 1928 E, S, I
John, D E (Llanelli) 1923 F, I, 1928 E, S, I
John, E R (Neath) 1950 E, S, I, F, 1951 E, S, I, F, SA, 1952 E, S, I, F, 1953 E, S, I, F, NZ, 1954 E
John G (St Luke's Coll, Exeter) 1954 E, F
John, J H (Swansea) 1926 E, S, I, F, 1927 E, S, F, I
John, P (Pontypridd) 1994 Tg, 1996 Bb (t), 1997 US (R), US 1,2, C, R, Tg, 1998 Z (R), SA 1
John, S C (Llanelli, Cardiff) 1995 S, I, 1997 E (R), Tg, NZ (R), 2000 F (R), It (R), E (R), Sm (R), SA (R), 2001 E (R), S (R), Tg (R), A, 2002 I, F, It (R), S (R)
Johnson, T A W (Cardiff) 1921 E, F, I, 1923 E, S, F, 1924 E, S, NZ, 1925 E, S, F
Johnson, W D (Swansea) 1953 E
Jones , A E (SEE Emyr)
Jones, A H (Cardiff) 1933 E, S
Jones, A M (Llanelli Scarlets) 2006 E(t&R),S(R)
Jones, A R (Ospreys) 2003 E 2(R), S 2, [C(R),Tg(R),It,NZ,E], 2004 S,I,Arg 1,2,SA1, 2,R,NZ,J(t&R), 2005 E,It,F,S,I,US,NZ,Fj(R),SA (t&R),A(R), 2006 E,S,I,It,F,Arg 1,2, A,PI(R),C,NZ, 2007 S, It(R),E1(R),A1,Arg, [C,A], 2008 E,S,I,F,SA1,3,NZ,A, 2009 S,E,F,I, 2010 E,S,F,I,It,SA1,NZ1,2
Jones, A W (Mountain Ash) 1905 I
Jones, A-W (Ospreys) 2006 Arg 1,2,PI,C(R),NZ(R), 2007 I,S,F1,It,E1,2,Arg,F2, [C,A,J,Fj],SA, 2008 E,I,F,SA1,2,3,NZ,A, 2009 S,E,F,It,I,NZ,Sm,Arg,A, 2010 E,S, SA1(R),NZ1,2
Jones, B J (Newport) 1960 I, F
Jones, B L (Devonport Services, Llanelli) 1950 E, S, I, F, 1951 E, S, SA, 1952 E, I, F
Jones, C (Harlequins) 2007 A1(R),2
Jones, C W (Cambridge U, Cardiff) 1934 E, S, I, 1935 E, S, I, NZ, 1936 E, S, I, 1938 E, S, I
Jones, C W (Bridgend) 1920 E, S, F
Jones, D (Aberavon) 1897 E
Jones, D (Treherbert) 1902 E, S, I, 1903 E, S, I, 1905 E, S, I, NZ, 1906 E, S, SA
Jones, D (Neath) 1927 A
Jones, D (Cardiff) 1994 SA, 1995 F, E, S, [J, NZ, I], SA, Fj, 1996 It, E, S, I, F 1, A 1,2, Bb, It, A 3
Jones, D A R (Llanelli Scarlets) 2002 Fj, C, NZ, 2003 It(R), E 1, S 1, I 1, F, NZ, E 2, [C,Tg,It,NZ(R),E], 2004 S,I,F,E,It,Arg 2,SA1,2,R,NZ,J, 2005 E,Fj, 2006 F(R), 2008 SA1, 2(R),C,NZ (R),A(R), 2009 S,E(R), F(R),It,I,C,US,NZ(R)
Jones, D C J (Swansea) 1947 E, F, I, 1949 E, S, I, F
Jones, D J (Neath, Ospreys) 2001 A (R), 2002 I (R), F (R), 2003 I 2, S 2,[C,It], 2004 S,E,It,Arg1,2,SA1(R),2,R(R),NZ(t&R),J, 2005 US,C,NZ,SA,A, 2006 E,S,I,It,F,Arg 1,2, A(R),PI,C(R),NZ, 2007 I(R),S,F1(R),It(R),E1(R),Arg,F2, [C(R),A(R),J,Fj(R)],SA(R), 2008 E,S,It(R),I(R),F(t&R),SA1(R),2(R), 2009 C,US,NZ(R), Arg(R), A(R)
Jones, D K (Llanelli, Cardiff) 1962 E, S, F, I, 1963 E, F, NZ, 1964 E, S, SA, 1966 E, S, I, F
Jones, D L (Newport) 1926 E, S, I, F, 1927 E
Jones, D L (Ebbw Vale, Celtic Warriors, Cardiff Blues) 2000 Sm, 2003 R (R), 2004 SA1, 2008 S(R),It(R), 2009 C,US, 2010 F,SA1,NZ2(R)
Jones, D P (Pontypool) 1907 I
Jones, E H (Swansea, Neath) 1930 I, F
Jones, E L (Llanelli) 1930 F, 1933 E, S, I, 1935 E
Jones, E L (Llanelli) 1939 S
Jones, G (Ebbw Vale) 1963 S, I, F
Jones, G (Llanelli) 1988 NZ 2, 1989 F, E, NZ, 1990 F
Jones, G G (Cardiff) 1930 S, 1933 I
Jones, G H (Bridgend) 1995 SA
Jones, H (Penygraig) 1902 S, I
Jones, H (Neath) 1904 I
Jones, H J (Neath) 1929 E, S
Jones, I C (London Welsh) 1968 I
Jones, I E (Llanelli) 1924 E, S, 1927 S, F, I, A, 1928 E, S, I, F, 1929 E, S, F, I, 1930 E, S
Jones, J (Aberavon) 1901 E
Jones, J (Bedwellty) (Abertillery) 1914 E, S, F, I
Jones, J (Swansea) 1924 F
Jones, J (Aberavon) 1919 NZA, 1920 E, S, 1921 S, F, I
Jones, J A (Cardiff) 1883 S
Jones, J P (Tuan) (Pontypool) 1913 S
Jones, J P (Jack) (Pontypool) 1908 A, 1909 E, S, F, I, 1910 F, E, 1912 E, F, 1913 F, I, 1920 F, I, 1921 E
Jones, K D (Cardiff) 1960 SA, 1961 E, S, I, 1962 E, F, 1963 E, S, I, NZ
Jones, K J (Newport) 1947 E, S, F, I, A, 1948 E, S, F, I, 1949 E, S, I, F, 1950 E, S, I, F, 1951 E, S, I, F, SA, 1952 E, S, I, F,

WALES

1953 E, S, I, F, NZ, 1954 E, I, F, S, 1955 E, S, I, F, 1956 E, S, I, F, 1957 S
Jones, K P (Ebbw Vale) 1996 Bb, F 2, It, A 3, 1997 I (R), E, 1998 S, I, F (R), SA 1
Jones, K W J (Oxford U, London Welsh) 1934 E
Jones, Matthew (Ospreys) 2005 C(R)
Jones, M A (Neath, Ebbw Vale) 1987 S, 1988 NZ 2(R), 1989 S, I, F, E, NZ, 1990 F, E, S, I, Nm 1,2, Bb, 1998 Z
Jones, M A (Llanelli Scarlets) 2001 E (R), S, J 1, 2002 R, Fj, C, NZ, 2003 It, I 1, A, NZ, E 2, [C,Tg,It,E], 2006 E,S,I,It,Arg 1,2,PI,C,NZ, 2007 S,F1,It,E1,Arg,F2, [C,A,Fj], SA, 2008 E,It,I,F,SA1,2,C,A, 2009 E,It,I,US
Jones, P E R (Newport) 1921 S
Jones, P L (Newport) 1912 SA, 1913 E, S, F, 1914 E, S, F, I
Jones, R (Llwynypia) 1901 I
Jones, R (Northampton) 1926 E, S, F
Jones, R (London Welsh) 1929 E
Jones, R B (Cambridge U) 1933 E, S
Jones, R E (Coventry) 1967 F, E, 1968 S, I, F
Jones, R G (Llanelli, Cardiff) 1996 It, E, S, I, F 1, A 1, 1997 US (R), S (R), US 1,2, R, Tg, NZ
Jones, R H (Swansea) 1901 I, 1902 E, 1904 E, S, I, 1905 E, 1908 F, I, A, 1909 E, S, F, I, 1910 F, E
Jones, R L (Llanelli) 1993 Z 1,2, Nm, J, C
Jones, R N (Swansea) 1986 E, S, I, F, Fj, Tg, WS, 1987 F, E, S, I, [I, Tg, E, NZ, A], US, 1988 E, S, I, F, NZ 1, WS, R, 1989 I, F, E, NZ, 1990 F, E, S, I, 1991 E, S, F 2, [WS, Arg, A], 1992 I, F, E, S, A, 1993 E, S, I, 1994 I (R), Pt, 1995 F, E, S, I, [NZ, I]
Jones, R P (Ospreys) 2004 SA2,NZ(R),J, 2005 E(R),F,S,I,US, 2006 A,C,NZ, 2007 I,S, F1,It,E1, 2008 E,S,It,I,F,SA1,2,3, C,NZ,A, 2009 E,F,It(R),I,C,US,NZ,Sm,Arg, 2010 E,S, F,It, SA1,NZ1,2
Jones, S (Neath, Newport Gwent Dragons) 2001 J 1(R), 2004 SA2,R(R),NZ(R),J(R)
Jones, S M (Llanelli Scarlets, Clermont Auvergne) 1998 SA 1(R), 1999 C (R), [J (R)], 2000 It (R), S, I, 2001 E, F (R), J 1,2, R, I, Arg, Tg, A, 2002 I, F, It, S, SA 1,2, R(R), Fj, C, NZ, 2003 S 1, I 1, F, A, NZ, E 2, [Tg,It(R),NZ,E], 2004 S,I,F,E,It,SA2,R,NZ, 2005 E,It,F,S,I,NZ,SA,A, 2006 E,S,I,It,F,A,NZ, 2007 I,S,F1,It, [C(R),A,J,Fj], 2008 S(R),It,I, F(R),SA1,2,3,NZ,A, 2009 S,E,F,It(R),I,NZ,Arg,A, 2010 E,S,F,I,It,SA1,NZ1,2(R)
Jones, S T (Pontypool) 1983 S, I, F, R, 1984 S, 1988 E, S, F, NZ 1,2
Jones, T (Newport) 1922 E, S, I, F, 1924 E, S
Jones, T B (Newport) 1882 I, 1883 E, S, 1884 S, 1885 E, S
Jones, T I (Llanelli) 1927 A, 1928 E, S, I, F
Jones, W (Cardiff) 1898 I, E
Jones, W D (Llanelli) 1948 E
Jones, W H (Llanelli) 1934 S, I
Jones, W I (Llanelli, Cambridge U) 1925 E, S, F, I
Jones, W J (Llanelli) 1924 I
Jones, W K (Cardiff) 1967 NZ, 1968 E, S, I, F
Jones, W R (Swansea) 1927 A, 1928 F
Jones-Davies, T E (London Welsh) 1930 E, I, 1931 E, S
Jones-Hughes, J (Newport) 1999 [Arg 3(R), J], 2000 F
Jordan, H M (Newport) 1885 E, S, 1889 S
Joseph, W (Swansea) 1902 E, S, I, 1903 E, S, I, 1904 E, S, 1905 E, S, I, NZ, 1906 E, S, I, SA
Jowett, W F (Swansea) 1903 E
Judd, S (Cardiff) 1953 E, S, I, F, NZ, 1954 E, F, S, 1955 E, S
Judson, T H (Llanelli) 1883 E, S
Kedzlie, Q D (Cardiff) 1888 S, I
Keen, L (Aberavon) 1980 F, E, S, I
Knight, P (Pontypridd) 1990 Nm 1,2, Bb (R), 1991 E, S
Knill, F M D (Cardiff) 1976 F (R)
Knoyle, T D (Scarlets) 2010 NZ1(R)
Lamerton, A E H (Llanelli) 1993 F, Z 1,2, Nm, J
Lane, S M (Cardiff) 1978 A 1(R),2, 1979 I (R), 1980 S, I
Lang, J (Llanelli) 1931 F, I, 1934 S, I, 1935 E, S, I, NZ, 1936 E, S, I, 1937 E
Law, V J (Newport) 1939 I
Lawrence, S D (Bridgend) 1925 S, I, 1926 S, I, F, 1927 E
Legge, W S G (Newport) 1937 I, 1938 I
Leleu, J (London Welsh, Swansea) 1959 E, S, 1960 F, SA
Lemon, A W (Neath) 1929 I, 1930 S, I, F, 1931 E, S, F, I, SA, 1932 E, S, I, 1933 I
Lewis, A J L (Ebbw Vale) 1970 F, 1971 E, I, F, 1972 E, S, F, 1973 E, S, I, F
Lewis, A L P (Cardiff) 1996 It, E, S, I, A 2(t), 1998 It, E, S, I, F, SA 2, Arg, 1999 F 1(R), E (R), Arg 1(R),2(R), SA (R), C (R), [J (R), Sm (R), A (R)], 2000 Sm (R), US (R), SA (R), 2001 F (R), J 1,2, 2002 R(R)
Lewis, B R (Swansea, Cambridge U) 1912 I, 1913 I
Lewis, C P (Llandovery) 1882 I, 1883 E, S, 1884 E, S
Lewis, D H (Cardiff) 1886 E, S
Lewis, E J (Llandovery) 1881 E
Lewis, E W (Llanelli, Cardiff) 1991 I, F 1, A, F 2, [WS, Arg, A], 1992 I, F, S, A, 1993 E, S, I, F, Z 1,2, Nm, J, C, 1994 S, I, F, E, Pt, Sp, Fj, WS, R, It, SA, 1995 E, S, I, [J, I], 1996 It, E, S, I, F 1
Lewis, G (Pontypridd, Swansea) 1998 SA 1(R), 1999 It (R), Arg 2, C, [J], 2000 F (R), It, S, I, Sm, US (t+R), 2001 F (R), J 1,2, R, I
Lewis, G W (Richmond) 1960 E, S
Lewis, H (Swansea) 1913 S, F, I, 1914 E
Lewis, J G (Llanelli) 1887 I
Lewis, J M C (Cardiff, Cambridge U) 1912 E, 1913 S, F, I, 1914 E, S, F, I, 1921 I, 1923 E, S
Lewis, J R (S Glam Inst, Cardiff) 1981 E, S, I, F, 1982 F, E, S
Lewis, M (Treorchy) 1913 F
Lewis, P I (Llanelli) 1984 A, 1985 S, I, F, E, 1986 E, S, I
Lewis, R A (Abertillery) 1966 E, S, I, F, A, 1967 I
Lewis, T W (Cardiff) 1926 E, 1927 E, S
Lewis, W (Llanelli) 1925 F
Lewis, W H (London Welsh, Cambridge U) 1926 I, 1927 E, F, I, A, 1928 F
Lewis-Roberts, E T (Sale) 2008 C(R)
Llewellyn, D S (Ebbw Vale, Newport) 1998 SA 1(R), 1999 F 1(R), It (R), [J (R)]
Llewellyn, G D (Neath) 1990 Nm 1,2, Bb, 1991 E, S, I, F 1, A, F 2
Llewellyn, G O (Neath, Harlequins, Ospreys, Narbonne) 1989 NZ, 1990 E, S, I, 1991 E, S, A (R), 1992 I, F, E, S, A, 1993 E, S, I, F, Z 1,2, Nm, J, C, 1994 S, I, F, E, Pt, Sp, C, Tg, WS, R, It, SA, 1995 F, E, S, I, [J, NZ, I], 1996 It, E, S, I, F 1, A 1,2, Bb, F 2, It, A 3, SA, 1997 US, S, I, F, E, US 1,2, NZ, 1998 It, E, 1999 C (R), [Sm], 2002 E (R), SA 1,2, R(R), Fj, C, NZ, 2003 E 1(R), S 1(R), I 1, F, A, NZ, I 2, S 2(R), [C,Tg,It,E(R)], 2004 S, F(R),E(R),It,Arg 1,2,SA1,R,NZ
Llewellyn, P D (Swansea) 1973 I, F, A, 1974 S, E
Llewellyn, W (Llwynypia) 1899 E, S, I, 1900 E, S, I, 1901 E, S, I, 1902 E, S, I, 1903 I, 1904 E, S, I, 1905 E, S, I, NZ
Llewelyn, D B (Newport, Llanelli) 1970 SA, S, E, I, F, 1971 E, S, I, F, 1972 E, S, F, NZ
Lloyd, A (Bath) 2001 J 1
Lloyd, D J (Bridgend) 1966 E, S, I, F, A, 1967 S, I, F, E, 1968 S, I, F, 1969 S, I, F, E, NZ 1, A, 1970 F, 1972 E, S, F, 1973 E, S
Lloyd, D P M (Llanelli) 1890 S, E, 1891 E, I
Lloyd, E (Llanelli) 1895 S
Lloyd, G L (Newport) 1896 I, 1899 S, I, 1900 E, S, 1901 E, S, 1902 S, I, 1903 E, S, I
Lloyd, R (Pontypool) 1913 S, F, I, 1914 E, S, F, I
Lloyd, T (Maesteg) 1953 I, F
Lloyd, T J (Neath) 1909 F, 1913 F, I, 1914 E, S, F, I
Loader, C D (Swansea) 1995 SA, Fj, 1996 F 1, A 1,2, Bb, F 2, It, A 3, SA, 1997 US, S, I, F, E, US 1, R, Tg, NZ
Lockwood, T W (Newport) 1887 E, S, I
Long, E C (Swansea) 1936 E, S, I, 1937 E, S, 1939 S, I
Luscombe, H N (Newport Gwent Dragons, Harlequins) 2003 S 2(R), 2004 Arg 1,2,SA1,2,R,J, 2005 E,It,S(t&R), 2006 E,S,I,It,F, 2007 I
Lydiate, D J (Newport Gwent Dragons) 2009 Arg(R),A
Lyne, H S (Newport) 1883 S, 1884 E, S, I, 1885 E
McBryde, R C (Swansea, Llanelli, Neath, Llanelli Scarlets) 1994 Fj, SA (t), 1997 US 2, 2000 I (R), 2001 E, S, F, It, R, I, Arg, Tg, A, 2002 I, F, It, E, S (R), SA 1,2, C, NZ, 2003 A, NZ, E 2, S 2, [C,It,NZ,E], 2004 I,E,It, 2005 It(R),F(R),S(R),I(R)
McCall, B E W (Welch Regt, Newport) 1936 E, S, I
McCarley, A (Neath) 1938 E, S, I
McCusker, R J (Scarlets) 2010 SA1(R),NZ1(R),2(R)
McCutcheon, W M (Swansea) 1891 S, 1892 E, S, 1893 E, S, I, 1894 E
McIntosh, D L M (Pontypridd) 1996 SA, 1997 E (R)
Madden, M (Llanelli) 2002 SA 1(R), R, Fj(R), 2003 I 1(R),F(R)
Maddock, H T (London Welsh) 1906 E, S, I, 1907 E, S, 1910 F
Maddocks, K (Neath) 1957 E
Main, D R (London Welsh) 1959 E, S, I, F
Mainwaring, H J (Swansea) 1961 F
Mainwaring, W T (Aberavon) 1967 S, I, F, E, NZ, 1968 E
Major, W C (Maesteg) 1949 F, 1950 S

Male, B O (Cardiff) 1921 F, 1923 S, 1924 S, I, 1927 E, S, F, I, 1928 S, I, F
Manfield, L (Mountain Ash, Cardiff) 1939 S, I, 1947 A, 1948 E, S, F, I
Mann, B B (Cardiff) 1881 E
Mantle, J T (Loughborough Colls, Newport) 1964 E, SA
Margrave, F L (Llanelli) 1884 E, S
Marinos, A W N (Newport, Gwent Dragons)) 2002 I (R), F, It, E, S, SA 1,2, 2003 R
Marsden-Jones, D (Cardiff) 1921 E, 1924 NZ
Martin, A J (Aberavon) 1973 A, 1974 S, I, 1975 F, E, S, I, A, 1976 E, S, I, F, 1977 I, F, E, S, 1978 E, S, I, F, A 1,2, NZ, 1979 S, I, F, E, 1980 F, E, S, I, NZ, 1981 I, F
Martin, W J (Newport) 1912 I, F, 1919 NZA
Mason, J E (Pontypridd) 1988 NZ 2(R)
Mathews, Rev A A (Lampeter) 1886 S
Mathias, R (Llanelli) 1970 F
Matthews, C M (Bridgend) 1939 I
Matthews, J (Cardiff), 1947 E, A, 1948 E, S, F, 1949 E, S, I, F, 1950 E, S, I, F, 1951 E, S, I, F
May, P S (Llanelli) 1988 E, S, I, F, NZ 1,2, 1991 [WS]
Meek, N N (Pontypool) 1993 E, S, I
Meredith, A (Devonport Services) 1949 E, S, I
Meredith, B V (St Luke's Coll, London Welsh, Newport) 1954 I, F, S, 1955 E, S, I, F, 1956 E, S, I, F, 1957 E, S, I, F, 1958 A, E, S, I, 1959 E, S, I, F, 1960 E, S, F, SA, 1961 E, S, I, 1962 E, S, F, I
Meredith, C C (Neath) 1953 S, NZ, 1954 E, I, F, S, 1955 E, S, I, F, 1956 E, I, 1957 E, S
Meredith, J (Swansea) 1888 S, I, 1890 S, E
Merry, J A (Pill Harriers) 1912 I, F
Michael, G M (Swansea) 1923 E, S, F
Michaelson, R C B (Aberavon, Cambridge U) 1963 E
Millar, W H (Mountain Ash) 1896 I, 1900 E, S, I, 1901 E, S, I
Mills, F M (Swansea, Cardiff) 1892 E, S, I, 1893 E, S, I, 1894 E, S, I, 1895 E, S, I, 1896 E
Mitchell, C (Ospreys) 2009 C(R),US(R),Sm(R), 2010 NZ2(R)
Moon, R H StJ B (Llanelli) 1993 F, Z 1,2, Nm, J, C, 1994 S, I, F, E, Sp, C, Fj, WS, R, It, SA, 1995 E (R), 2000 S, I, Sm (R), US (R), 2001 E (R), S (R)
Moore, A P (Cardiff) 1995 [J], SA, Fj, 1996 It
Moore, A P (Swansea) 1995 SA (R), Fj, 1998 S, I, F, Z, SA 1, 1999 C, 2000 S, I, US (R), 2001 E (R), S, F, It, J 1,2, R, I, Arg, Tg, A, 2002 F, It, E, S
Moore, S J (Swansea, Moseley) 1997 C, R, Tg
Moore, W J (Bridgend) 1933 I
Morgan, C H (Llanelli) 1957 I, F
Morgan, C I (Cardiff) 1951 I, F, SA, 1952 E, S, I, 1953 S, I, F, NZ, 1954 E, I, S, 1955 E, S, I, F, 1956 E, S, I, F, 1957 E, S, I, F, 1958 E, S, I, F
Morgan, C S (Cardiff Blues) 2002 I, F, It, E, S, SA 1,2, R(R), 2003 F, 2005 US
Morgan, D (Swansea) 1885 S, 1886 E, S, 1887 E, S, I, 1889 I
Morgan, D (Llanelli) 1895 I, 1896 E
Morgan, D E (Llanelli) 1920 I, 1921 E, S, F
Morgan, D R R (Llanelli) 1962 E, S, F, I, 1963 E, S, I, F, NZ
Morgan, E (Swansea) 1914 E, S, F, I
Morgan, E (London Welsh) 1902 E, S, I, 1903 I, 1904 E, S, I, 1905 E, S, I, NZ, 1906 E, S, I, SA, 1908 F
Morgan, F L (Llanelli) 1938 E, S, I, 1939 E
Morgan, G R (Newport) 1984 S
Morgan, H J (Abertillery) 1958 E, S, I, F, 1959 I, F, 1960 E, 1961 E, S, I, F, 1962 E, S, F, I, 1963 S, I, F, 1965 E, S, I, F, 1966 E, S, I, F, A
Morgan, H P (Newport) 1956 E, S, I, F
Morgan, J L (Llanelli) 1912 SA, 1913 E
Morgan, K A (Pontypridd, Swansea, Newport Gwent Dragons) 1997 US 1,2, C, R, NZ, 1998 S, I, F, 2001 J 1,2, R, I, Arg, Tg, A, 2002 I, F, It, E, S, SA 1,2, 2003 E 1, S 1, [C,It], 2004 J(R), 2005 E(R),It(R),F,S,I,US,C,NZ,Fj, 2006 A,PI, NZ, 2007 I,S,It,E1,Arg,F2, [C,A(R),J]
Morgan, M E (Swansea) 1938 E, S, I, 1939 E
Morgan, N H (Newport) 1960 S, I, F
Morgan, P E J (Aberavon) 1961 E, S, F
Morgan, P J (Llanelli) 1980 S (R), I, NZ (R), 1981 I
Morgan, S (Cardiff Blues) 2007 A2(R)
Morgan, T (Llanelli) 1889 I
Morgan, W G (Cambridge U) 1927 F, I, 1929 E, S, F, I, 1930 I, F
Morgan, W I (Swansea) 1908 A, 1909 E, S, F, I, 1910 F, E, S, I, 1911 E, F, I, 1912 S
Morgan, W L (Cardiff) 1910 S
Moriarty, R D (Swansea) 1981 A, 1982 I, F, E, S, 1983 E, 1984 S, I, F, E, 1985 S, I, F, 1986 Fj, Tg, WS, 1987 [I, Tg, C (R), E, NZ, A]
Moriarty, W P (Swansea) 1986 I, F, Fj, Tg, WS, 1987 F, E, S, I, [I, Tg, C, E, NZ, A], US, 1988 E, S, I, F, NZ 1
Morley, J C (Newport) 1929 E, S, F, I, 1930 E, I, 1931 E, S, F, I, SA, 1932 E, S, I
Morris, D R (Neath, Swansea, Leicester) 1998 Z, SA 1(R),2(R), 1999 S, I, It (R), 2000 US, SA, 2001 E, S, F, It, Arg, Tg, A, 2004 Arg 1(R),2(R),SA1(R)
Morris, G L (Swansea) 1882 I, 1883 E, S, 1884 E, S
Morris, H T (Cardiff) 1951 F, 1955 I, F
Morris, J I T (Swansea) 1924 E, S
Morris, M S (S Wales Police, Neath) 1985 S, I, F, 1990 I, Nm 1,2, Bb, 1991 I, F 1, [WS (R)], 1992 E
Morris, R R (Swansea, Bristol) 1933 S, 1937 S
Morris, S (Cross Keys) 1920 E, S, F, I, 1922 E, S, I, F, 1923 E, S, F, I, 1924 E, S, F, NZ, 1925 E, S, F
Morris, W (Llanelli) 1896 S, I, 1897 E
Morris, W D (Neath) 1967 F, E, 1968 E, S, I, F, 1969 S, I, F, E, NZ 1,2, A, 1970 SA, S, E, I, F, 1971 E, S, I, F, 1972 E, S, F, NZ, 1973 E, S, I, A, 1974 S, I, F, E
Morris, W G H (Abertillery) 1919 NZA, 1920 F, 1921 I
Morris, W J (Newport) 1965 S, 1966 F
Morris, W J B (Pontypool) 1963 S, I
Moseley, K (Pontypool, Newport) 1988 NZ 2, R, 1989 S, I, 1990 F, 1991 F 2, [WS, Arg, A]
Murphy, C D (Cross Keys) 1935 E, S, I
Mustoe, L (Cardiff) 1995 Fj, 1996 A 1(R),2, 1997 US 1,2, C, R (R), 1998 E (R), I (R), F (R)
Nash, D (Ebbw Vale) 1960 SA, 1961 E, S, I, F, 1962 F
Newman, C H (Newport) 1881 E, 1882 I, 1883 E, S, 1884 E, S, 1885 E, S, 1886 E, 1887 E
Nicholas, D L (Llanelli) 1981 E, S, I, F
Nicholas, T J (Cardiff) 1919 NZA
Nicholl, C B (Cambridge U, Llanelli) 1891 I, 1892 E, S, I, 1893 E, S, I, 1894 E, S, 1895 E, S, I, 1896 E, S, I
Nicholl, D W (Llanelli) 1894 I
Nicholls, E G (Cardiff) 1896 S, I, 1897 E, 1898 I, E, 1899 E, S, I, 1900 S, I, 1901 E, S, I, 1902 E, S, I, 1903 I, 1904 E, 1905 I, NZ, 1906 E, S, I, SA
Nicholls, F E (Cardiff Harlequins) 1892 I
Nicholls, H C W (Cardiff) 1958 I
Nicholls, S H (Cardiff) 1888 M, 1889 S, I, 1891 S
Norris, C H (Cardiff) 1963 F, 1966 F
Norster, R L (Cardiff) 1982 S, 1983 E, S, I, F, 1984 S, I, F, E, A, 1985 S, I, F, E, Fj, 1986 Fj, Tg, WS, 1987 F, E, S, I, [I, C, E], US, 1988 E, S, I, F, NZ 1, WS, 1989 F, E
Norton, W B (Cardiff) 1882 I, 1883 E, S, 1884 E, S, I
Oakley, R L (Gwent Dragons) 2003 I 2, S 2(R)
O'Connor, A (Aberavon) 1960 SA, 1961 E, S, 1962 F, I
O'Connor, R (Aberavon) 1957 E
O'Neil, W (Cardiff) 1904 S, I, 1905 E, S, I, 1907 E, I, 1908 E, S, F, I
O'Shea, J P (Cardiff) 1967 S, I, 1968 S, I, F
Oliver, G (Pontypool) 1920 E, S, F, I
Osborne, W T (Mountain Ash) 1902 E, S, I, 1903 E, S, I
Ould, W J (Cardiff) 1924 E, S
Owen, A D (Swansea) 1924 E
Owen, G D (Newport) 1955 I, F, 1956 E, S, I, F
Owen, M J (Pontypridd, Newport Gwent Dragons) 2002 SA 1,2, R, C(R), NZ(R), 2003 It, I 2, S 2, 2004 S(R),I(R),F,E,It,Arg 1,2,SA2,R,NZ,J, 2005 E,It,F,S,I,NZ,Fj,SA,A, 2006 E,S,I,It,F,PI, 2007 A1(R),2,E2, [C(R),A(R),J(R),Fj(R)]
Owen, R M (Swansea) 1901 I, 1902 E, S, I, 1903 E, S, I, 1904 E, S, I, 1905 E, S, I, NZ, 1906 E, S, I, SA, 1907 E, S, 1908 F, I, A, 1909 E, S, F, I, 1910 F, E, 1911 E, S, F, I, 1912 E, S
Packer, H (Newport) 1891 E, 1895 S, I, 1896 E, S, I, 1897 E
Palmer, F C (Swansea) 1922 E, S, I
Parfitt, F C (Newport) 1893 E, S, I, 1894 E, S, I, 1895 S, 1896 S, I
Parfitt, S A (Swansea) 1990 Nm 1(R), Bb
Parker, D S (Swansea) 1924 I, F, NZ, 1925 E, S, F, I, 1929 F, I, 1930 E
Parker, E T (Swansea) 1919 NZA, 1920 E, S, I, 1921 E, S, F, I, 1922 E, S, I, F, 1923 E, S, F
Parker, S T (Pontypridd, Celtic Warriors, Newport Gwent Dragons, Ospreys) 2002 R, Fj, C, NZ, 2003 E 2, [C,It,NZ], 2004 S,I,Arg 1,2,SA1,2,NZ, 2005 Fj,SA,A, 2006 PI,C,NZ, 2007 A1,2,F2(t&R), [C,A],SA, 2008 E,S(R),It(R),SA1

Parker, W J (Swansea) 1899 E, S
Parks, R D (Pontypridd, Celtic Warriors) 2002 SA 1(R), Fj(R), 2003 I 2, S 2
Parsons, G (Newport) 1947 E
Pascoe, D (Bridgend) 1923 F, I
Pask, A E I (Abertillery) 1961 F, 1962 E, S, F, I, 1963 E, S, I, F, NZ, 1964 E, S, I, F, SA, 1965 E, S, I, F, 1966 E, S, I, F, A, 1967 S, I
Payne, G W (Army, Pontypridd) 1960 E, S, I
Payne, H (Swansea) 1935 NZ
Peacock, H (Newport) 1929 S, F, I, 1930 S, I, F
Peake, E (Chepstow) 1881 E
Pearce, P G (Bridgend) 1981 I, F, 1982 I (R)
Pearson, T W (Cardiff, Newport) 1891 E, I, 1892 E, S, 1894 S, I, 1895 E, S, I, 1897 E, 1898 I, E, 1903 E
Peel, D J (Llanelli Scarlets, Sale) 2001 J 2(R), R (R), Tg (R), 2002 I (R), It (R), E (R), S (R), SA 1,2, R, Fj, C, NZ, 2003 It, S 1(R), I 1(R), F, NZ(R), I 2, S 2, [C(R),Tg(R),It,NZ(R),E(R)], 2004 S(R),I(R),F(R),E(R),It(R),Arg 1,2,SA1,2,R,NZ, 2005 E,It,F,S,I, 2006 E,S,I,It,A,C,NZ, 2007 I,S,F1,It,E1,Arg,F2, [C,A,Fj],SA, 2008 S(R),It, SA3(R),C(R),NZ(R), 2009 S(R),E(R),F(R),C(R), US,Sm,Arg(R),A, 2010 I(R),It(R)
Pegge, E V (Neath) 1891 E
Perego, M A (Llanelli) 1990 S, 1993 F, Z 1, Nm (R), 1994 S, I, F, E, Sp
Perkins, S J (Pontypool) 1983 S, I, F, R, 1984 S, I, F, E, A, 1985 S, I, F, E, Fj, 1986 E, S, I, F
Perrett, F L (Neath) 1912 SA, 1913 E, S, F, I
Perrins, V C (Newport) 1970 SA, S
Perry, W J (Neath) 1911 E
Phillips, A J (Cardiff) 1979 E, 1980 F, E, S, I, NZ, 1981 E, S, I, F, A, 1982 I, F, E, S, 1987 [C, E, A]
Phillips, B (Aberavon) 1925 E, S, F, I, 1926 E
Phillips, D H (Swansea) 1952 F
Phillips, H P (Newport) 1892 E, 1893 E, S, I, 1894 E, S
Phillips, H T (Newport) 1927 E, S, F, I, A, 1928 E, S, I, F
Phillips, K H (Neath) 1987 F, [I, Tg, NZ], US, 1988 E, NZ 1, 1989 NZ, 1990 F, E, S, I, Nm 1,2, Bb, 1991 E, S, I, F 1, A
Phillips, L A (Newport) 1900 E, S, I, 1901 S
Phillips, R D (Neath) 1987 US, 1988 E, S, I, F, NZ 1,2, WS, 1989 S, I
Phillips, W D (Cardiff) 1881 E, 1882 I, 1884 E, S, I
Phillips, W M (Llanelli Scarlets, Cardiff Blues, Ospreys) 2003 R, 2004 Arg 1(R),2(R), J(R), 2005 US,C,NZ,Fj(R),SA(R), 2006 S(R),It(R),F,Arg 1,2,PI,C(R),NZ(R), 2007 I(R), F1(R),E1(R),A1,2, F2(R), [C(R),A(R),J,Fj(R)],SA(R), 2008 E,S,It(R),I,F, 2009 S,E,F,It,I, 2010 It,SA1,NZ1,2
Pickering, D F (Llanelli) 1983 E, S, I, F, R, 1984 S, I, F, E, A, 1985 S, I, F, E, Fj, 1986 E, S, I, F, Fj, 1987 F, E, S
Plummer, R C S (Newport) 1912 S, I, F, SA, 1913 E
Pook, T R (Newport) 1895 S
Popham, A J (Leeds, Llanelli Scarlets) 2003 A (R), I 2, R, S 2, [Tg,NZ], 2004 I(R),It(R),SA1,J(R), 2005 C,Fj(R), 2006 E(R),It(R),F, Arg 1,2,PI,NZ(R), 2007 I, S,F1,It,E1,2(R),Arg,F2, [C,A(t),J,Fj], SA(R), 2008 E(R)
Powell, A (Cardiff Blues) 2008 SA3,C(R),NZ,A, 2009 S,E,F,It,NZ,Sm,Arg,A, 2010 E,S
Powell, G (Ebbw Vale) 1957 I, F
Powell, J (Cardiff) 1923 I
Powell, J A (Cardiff) 1906 I
Powell, R D (Cardiff) 2002 SA 1(R),2(R), C(R)
Powell, R W (Newport) 1888 S, I
Powell, W C (London Welsh) 1926 S, I, F, 1927 E, F, I, 1928 S, I, F, 1929 E, S, F, I, 1930 S, I, F, 1931 E, S, F, I, SA, 1932 E, S, I, 1935 E, S, I
Powell, W J (Cardiff) 1920 E, S, F, I
Price, B (Newport) 1961 I, F, 1962 E, S, 1963 E, S, F, NZ, 1964 E, S, I, F, SA, 1965 E, S, I, F, 1966 E, S, I, F, A, 1967 S, I, F, E, 1969 S, I, F, NZ 1,2, A
Price, G (Pontypool) 1975 F, E, S, I, A, 1976 E, S, I, F, 1977 I, F, E, S, 1978 E, S, I, F, A 1,2, NZ, 1979 S, I, F, E, 1980 F, E, S, I, NZ, 1981 E, S, I, F, A, 1982 I, F, E, S, 1983 E, I, F
Price, M J (Pontypool, RAF) 1959 E, S, I, F, 1960 E, S, I, F, 1962 E
Price, R E (Weston-s-Mare) 1939 S, I
Price, T G (Llanelli) 1965 E, S, I, F, 1966 E, A, 1967 S, F
Priday, A J (Cardiff) 1958 I, 1961 I
Pritchard, C C (Newport, Pontypool) 1904 S, I, 1905 NZ, 1906 E, S
Pritchard, C C (Pontypool) 1928 E, S, I, F, 1929 E, S, F, I
Pritchard, C M (Newport) 1904 I, 1905 E, S, NZ, 1906 E, S, I, SA, 1907 E, S, I, 1908 E, 1910 F, E
Proctor, W T (Llanelli) 1992 A, 1993 E, S, Z 1,2, Nm, C, 1994 I, C, Fj, WS, R, It, SA, 1995 S, I, [NZ], Fj, 1996 It, E, S, I, A 1,2, Bb, F 2, It, A 3, 1997 E(R), US 1,2, C, R, 1998 E (R), S, I, F, Z, 2001 A
Prosser, D R (Neath) 1934 S, I
Prosser, F J (Cardiff) 1921 I
Prosser, G (Pontypridd) 1995 [NZ]
Prosser, I G (Neath) 1934 E, S, I, 1935 NZ
Prosser, T R (Pontypool) 1956 S, F, 1957 E, S, I, F, 1958 A, E, S, I, F, 1959 E, S, I, F, 1960 E, S, I, F, SA, 1961 I, F
Prothero, G J (Bridgend) 1964 S, I, F, 1965 E, S, I, F, 1966 E, S, I, F
Pryce-Jenkins, T J (London Welsh) 1888 S, I
Prydie, T W J (Ospreys) 2010 It,SA1,NZ1,2
Pugh, C H (Maesteg) 1924 E, S, I, F, NZ, 1925 E, S
Pugh, J D (Neath) 1987 US, 1988 S (R), 1990 S
Pugh, P (Neath) 1989 NZ
Pugh, R (Ospreys) 2005 US(R)
Pugsley, J (Cardiff) 1910 E, S, I, 1911 E, S, F, I
Pullman, J J (Neath) 1910 F
Purdon, F T (Newport) 1881 E, 1882 I, 1883 E, S
Quinnell, D L (Llanelli) 1972 F (R), NZ, 1973 E, S, A, 1974 S, F, 1975 E (R), 1977 I (R), F, E, S, 1978 E, S, I, F, A 1, NZ, 1979 S, I, F, E, 1980 NZ
Quinnell, J C (Llanelli, Richmond, Cardiff) 1995 Fj, 1996 A 3(R), 1997 US (R), S (R), I (R), E (R), 1998 SA 2, Arg, 1999 I, F 1, It, E, Arg 1,2, SA, C, F 2, [Arg 3, J, A], 2000 It, E, 2001 S (R), F (R), It (R), J 1,2, R (R), I (R), Arg, 2002 I, F
Quinnell, L S (Llanelli, Richmond) 1993 C, 1994 S, I, F, E, Pt, Sp, C, WS, 1997 US, S, I, F, E, 1998 It, E, S (R), Z, SA 2, Arg, 1999 S, I, F 1, It, E, Arg 1,2, SA, C, F 2, [Arg 3, Sm, A], 2000 F, It, E, Sm, US, SA, 2001 E, S, F, It, Arg, Tg, A, 2002 I, F, It, E, R, C(R)
Radford, W J (Newport) 1923 I
Ralph, A R (Newport) 1931 F, I, SA, 1932 E, S, I
Ramsay, S (Treorchy) 1896 E, 1904 E
Randall, R J (Aberavon) 1924 I, F
Raybould, W H (London Welsh, Cambridge U, Newport) 1967 S, I, F, E, NZ, 1968 I, F, 1970 SA, E, I, F (R)
Rayer, M A (Cardiff) 1991 [WS (R), Arg, A (R)], 1992 E (R), A, 1993 E, S, I, Z 1, Nm, J (R), 1994 S (R), I (R), F, E, Pt, C, Fj, WS, R, It
Rees, A (Maesteg) 1919 NZA
Rees, A (Maesteg) 1962 E, S, F
Rees, A M (London Welsh) 1934 E, 1935 E, S, I, NZ, 1936 E, S, I, 1937 E, S, I, 1938 E, S
Rees, B I (London Welsh) 1967 S, I, F
Rees, C F W (London Welsh) 1974 I, 1975 A, 1978 NZ, 1981 F, A, 1982 I, F, E, S, 1983 E, S, I, F
Rees, D (Swansea) 1900 E, 1903 E, S, 1905 E, S
Rees, D (Swansea) 1968 S, I, F
Rees, E B (Swansea) 1919 NZA
Rees, H E (Neath) 1979 S, I, F, E, 1980 F, E, S, I, NZ, 1983 E, S, I, F
Rees, H T (Cardiff) 1937 S, I, 1938 E, S, I
Rees, J (Swansea) 1920 E, S, F, I, 1921 E, S, I, 1922 E, 1923 E, F, I, 1924 E
Rees, J I (Swansea) 1934 E, S, I, 1935 S, NZ, 1936 E, S, I, 1937 E, S, I, 1938 E, S, I
Rees, L M (Cardiff) 1933 I
Rees, M (Llanelli Scarlets) 2005 US, 2006 Arg 1,A,C,NZ(R), 2007 I(R),S(t&R),F1,It, E1,A1,Arg,F2, [C,A,Fj], 2008 E(R),S(R),It,I, F(R),SA1,3,NZ,A, 2009 S,E,F,It(R),I,NZ, Sm(R),Arg,A, 2010 I,It,SA1,NZ1,2
Rees, P (Llanelli) 1947 F, I
Rees, P M (Newport) 1961 E, S, I, 1964 I
Rees, R (Swansea) 1998 Z
Rees, R S (Cardiff Blues) 2010 E(R),S(R),F,I,NZ2(R)
Rees, T A (Llandovery) 1881 E
Rees, T E (London Welsh) 1926 I, F, 1927 A, 1928 E
Rees, T J (Newport) 1935 S, I, NZ, 1936 E, S, I, 1937 E, S
Rees-Jones, G R (Oxford U, London Welsh) 1934 E, S, 1935 I, NZ, 1936 E
Reeves, F C (Cross Keys) 1920 F, I, 1921 E
Reynolds, A D (Swansea) 1990 Nm 1,2(R), 1992 A (R)
Rhapps, J (Penygraig) 1897 E
Rice-Evans, W (Swansea) 1890 S, 1891 E, S
Richards, D S (Swansea) 1979 F, E, 1980 F, E, S, I, NZ, 1981 E, S, I, F, 1982 I, F, 1983 E, S, I, R (R)
Richards, E G (Cardiff) 1927 S
Richards, E I (Cardiff) 1925 E, S, F

Richards, E S (Swansea) 1885 E, 1887 S
Richards, H D (Neath) 1986 Tg (R), 1987 [Tg, E (R), NZ]
Richards, K H L (Bridgend) 1960 SA, 1961 E, S, I, F
Richards, M C R (Cardiff) 1968 I, F, 1969 S, I, F, E, NZ 1,2, A
Richards, R (Aberavon) 1913 S, F, I
Richards, R C (Cross Keys) 1956 F
Richards, T B (Swansea)1960 F
Richards, T L (Maesteg) 1923 I
Richards, W C (Pontypool) 1922 E, S, I, F, 1924 I
Richardson, S J (Aberavon) 1978 A 2(R), 1979 E
Rickards, A R (Cardiff) 1924 F
Ring, J (Aberavon) 1921 E
Ring, M G (Cardiff, Pontypool) 1983 E, 1984 A, 1985 S, I, F, 1987 I, [I, Tg, A], US, 1988 E, S, I, F, NZ 1,2, 1989 NZ, 1990 F, E, S, I, Nm 1,2, Bb, 1991 E, S, I, F 1,2, [WS, Arg, A]
Ringer, J (Bridgend) 2001 J 1(R),2(R)
Ringer, P (Ebbw Vale, Llanelli) 1978 NZ, 1979 S, I, F, E, 1980 F, E, NZ
Roberts, C R (Neath) 1958 I, F
Roberts, D E A (London Welsh) 1930 E
Roberts, E (Llanelli) 1886 E, 1887 I
Roberts, E J (Llanelli) 1888 S, I, 1889 I
Roberts, G J (Cardiff) 1985 F (R), E, 1987 [I, Tg, C, E, A]
Roberts, H M (Cardiff) 1960 SA, 1961 E, S, I, F, 1962 S, F, 1963 I
Roberts, J (Cardiff) 1927 E, S, F, I, A, 1928 E, S, I, F, 1929 E, S, F, I
Roberts, J H (Cardiff Blues) 2008 S,SA1,2,3,C(R),NZ,A, 2009 S,E,F,It,I(R),NZ,Sm, Arg,A, 2010 E,S,F,I,It,SA1,NZ1,2
Roberts, M (Scarlets) 2008 C, 2009 NZ(R),A(t&R)
Roberts, M G (London Welsh) 1971 E, S, I, F, 1973 I, F, 1975 S, 1979 E
Roberts, T (Newport, Risca) 1921 S, F, I, 1922 E, S, I, F, 1923 E, S
Roberts, W (Cardiff) 1929 E
Robins, J D (Birkenhead Park) 1950 E, S, I, F, 1951 E, S, I, F, 1953 E, I, F
Robins, R J (Pontypridd) 1953 S, 1954 F, S, 1955 E, S, I, F, 1956 E, F, 1957 E, S, I, F
Robinson, I R (Cardiff) 1974 F, E
Robinson, J P (Cardiff Blues) 2001 J 1(R),2(R), Arg (R), Tg (R), A, 2002 I, Fj(R), C, NZ, 2003 A, NZ, I 2, S 2, 2006 Arg 1,2, 2007 I,S,F1(R),A1,2,Arg(t&R),F2,[J]
Robinson, M F D (Swansea) 1999 S, I, F 1, Arg 1
Robinson, N J (Cardiff Blues) 2003 I 2, R, 2004 Arg 1(R),2,SA1, 2005 US,C,NZ(R),Fj, 2006 S(R),Arg 1,2, 2009 US
Rocyn-Jones, D N (Cambridge U) 1925 I
Roderick, W B (Llanelli) 1884 I
Rogers, P J D (London Irish, Newport, Cardiff) 1999 F 1, It, E, Arg 1,2, SA, C, F 2, [Arg 3, J, Sm, A], 2000 F, It, E, S, I, SA
Rosser, M A (Penarth) 1924 S, F
Rowland, E M (Lampeter) 1885 E
Rowlands, C F (Aberavon) 1926 I
Rowlands, D C T (Pontypool) 1963 E, S, I, F, NZ, 1964 E, S, I, F, SA, 1965 E, S, I, F
Rowlands, G (RAF, Cardiff) 1953 NZ, 1954 E, F, 1956 F
Rowlands, K A (Cardiff) 1962 F, I, 1963 I, 1965 I, F
Rowles, G A (Penarth) 1892 E
Rowley, M (Pontypridd) 1996 SA, 1997 US, S, I, F, R
Roy, W S (Cardiff) 1995 [J (R)]
Russell, S (London Welsh) 1987 US
Samuel, D (Swansea) 1891 I, 1893 I
Samuel, J (Swansea) 1891 I
Samuel, T F (Mountain Ash) 1922 S, I, F
Scourfield, T B (Torquay Athletic) 1930 F
Scrine, F G (Swansea) 1899 E, S, 1901 I
Selley, T J (Llanelli Scarlets) 2005 US(R)
Shanklin, J L (London Welsh) 1970 F, 1972 NZ, 1973 I, F
Shanklin, T G L (Saracens, Cardiff Blues) 2001 J 2, 2002 F, It, SA 1(R),2(R),R, Fj, 2003 It, E 1, S 1, I 1, F(t+R), A, NZ, S 2, [Tg,NZ], 2004 I(R),F(R),E,It(R),Arg 1(R),2, SA1,2(R),R,NZ,J, 2005 E,It,F,S,I, 2006 A,C,NZ, 2007 S(R),F1,It,E1,2,Arg, [C,A,J(R), Fj],SA, 2008 E(R),S,It,I,F,SA1,2,3,C,NZ,A, 2009 S,E,F,It(R),I,NZ,Sm, 2010 It(R)
Shaw, G (Neath) 1972 NZ, 1973 E, S, I, F, A, 1974 S, I, F, E, 1977 I, F
Shaw, T W (Newbridge) 1983 R
Shea, J (Newport) 1919 NZA, 1920 E, S, 1921 E
Shell, R C (Aberavon) 1973 A (R)
Sidoli, R A (Pontypridd, Celtic Warriors, Cardiff Blues) 2002 SA 1(R),2(R),R, Fj, NZ, 2003 It, E 1, S 1, I 1, F, A, NZ, E 2, [C(R), Tg,It(R),NZ,E], 2004 I,It(R), 2005 E,It,F,S,I,C,NZ,Fj(R),SA,A, 2006 E,S,I,It,F,PI,C(R), 2007 I(t&R),S,A1,2,E2
Simpson, H J (Cardiff) 1884 E, S, I
Sinkinson, B D (Neath) 1999 F 1, It, E, Arg 1,2, SA, F 2, [Arg 3, J, Sm, A], 2000 F, It, E, 2001 R (R), I, Arg (R), Tg, A, 2002 It (R)
Skrimshire, R T (Newport) 1899 E, S, I
Skym, A (Llanelli) 1928 E, S, I, F, 1930 E, S, I, F, 1931 E, S, F, I, SA, 1932 E, S, I, 1933 E, S, I, 1935 E
Smith, J S (Cardiff) 1884 E, I, 1885 E
Smith, R (Ebbw Vale) 2000 F (R)
Sowden-Taylor, R (Cardiff Blues) 2005 It(R),C(R),NZ(R), 2007 A2(R),SA, 2008 C, 2009 C,US
Sparks, B A (Neath) 1954 I, 1955 E, F, 1956 E, S, I, 1957 S
Spiller, W (Cardiff) 1910 S, I, 1911 E, S, F, I, 1912 E, F, SA, 1913 E
Spratt, J P (Ospreys) 2009 C(R),US(R)
Squire, J (Newport, Pontypool) 1977 I, F, 1978 E, S, I, F, A 1, NZ, 1979 S, I, F, E, 1980 F, E, S, I, NZ, 1981 E, S, I, F, A, 1982 I, F, E, 1983 E, S, I, F
Stadden, W J (Cardiff) 1884 I, 1886 E, S, 1887 I, 1888 S, M, 1890 S, E
Stephens, C (Bridgend) 1998 E (R), 2001 J 2(R)
Stephens, C J (Llanelli) 1992 I, F, E, A
Stephens, G (Neath) 1912 E, S, I, F, SA, 1913 E, S, F, I, 1919 NZA
Stephens, I (Bridgend) 1981 E, S, I, F, A, 1982 I, F, E, S, 1984 I, F, E, A
Stephens, Rev J G (Llanelli) 1922 E, S, I, F
Stephens, J R G (Neath) 1947 E, S, F, I, 1948 I, 1949 S, I, F, 1951 F, SA, 1952 E, S, I, F, 1953 E, S, I, F, NZ, 1954 E, I, 1955 E, S, I, F, 1956 S, I, F, 1957 E, S, I, F
Stock, A (Newport) 1924 F, NZ, 1926 E, S
Stoddart, M L (Llanelli Scarlets) 2007 SA, 2008 SA1(R),C
Stone, P (Llanelli) 1949 F
Strand-Jones, J (Llanelli) 1902 E, S, I, 1903 E, S
Sullivan, A C (Cardiff) 2001 Arg, Tg
Summers, R H B (Haverfordwest) 1881 E
Sutton, S (Pontypool, S Wales Police) 1982 F, E, 1987 F, E, S, I, [C, NZ (R), A]
Sweeney, C (Pontypridd, Celtic Warriors, Newport Gwent Dragons) 2003 It(R), E 1, NZ(R), I 2, S 2, [C,It,NZ(t&R),E(t)], 2004 I(R),F(R),E(R),It(R),Arg 1,SA1(R),2(R), R(R),J, 2005 It(R),F(t),S(R),US,C,NZ,Fj(R),SA(t&R),A(R), 2006 PI,C(R), 2007 S(t), A2(R),E2,F2(R), [J(R)],SA(R)
Sweet-Escott, R B (Cardiff) 1891 S, 1894 I, 1895 I
Tamplin, W E (Cardiff) 1947 S, F, I, A, 1948 E, S, F
Tanner, H (Swansea, Cardiff) 1935 NZ, 1936 E, S, I, 1937 E, S, I, 1938 E, S, I, 1939 E, S, I, 1947 E, S, F, I, 1948 E, S, F, I, 1949 E, S, I, F
Tarr, D J (Swansea, Royal Navy) 1935 NZ
Taylor, A R (Cross Keys) 1937 I, 1938 I, 1939 E
Taylor, C G (Ruabon) 1884 E, S, I, 1885 E, S, 1886 E, S, 1887 E, I
Taylor, H T (Cardiff) 1994 Pt, C, Fj, Tg, WS (R), R, It, SA, 1995 E, S, [J, NZ, I], SA, Fj, 1996 It, E, S, I, F 1, A 1,2, It, A 3
Taylor, J (London Welsh) 1967 S, I, F, E, NZ, 1968 I, F, 1969 S, I, F, E, NZ 1, A, 1970 F, 1971 E, S, I, F, 1972 E, S, F, NZ, 1973 E, S, I, F
Taylor, M (Pontypool, Swansea, Llanelli Scarlets, Sale) 1994 SA, 1995 F, E, SA (R), 1998 Z, SA 1,2, Arg, 1999 I, F 1, It, E, Arg 1,2, SA, F 2, [Arg 3, J, Sm, A], 2000 F, It, E, S, Sm, US, 2001 E, S, F, It, 2002 S, SA 1,2, 2003 E 1, S 1, I 1, F, A, NZ, E 2, [C(R),Tg, NZ,E], 2004 F,E,It,R(R), 2005 I,US,C,NZ
Thomas, A C (Bristol, Swansea) 1996 It, E, S, I, F 2(R), SA, 1997 US, S, I, F, US 1,2, C, R, NZ (t), 1998 It, E, S (R), Z, SA 1, 2000 Sm, US, SA (R)
Thomas, A R F (Newport) 1963 NZ, 1964 E
Thomas, A G (Swansea, Cardiff) 1952 E, S, I, F, 1953 S, I, F, 1954 E, I, F, 1955 S, I, F
Thomas, B (Neath, Cambridge U) 1963 E, S, I, F, NZ, 1964 E, S, I, F, SA, 1965 E, 1966 E, S, I, 1967 NZ, 1969 S, I, F, E, NZ 1,2
Thomas, B M G (St Bart's Hospital) 1919 NZA, 1921 S, F, I, 1923 F, 1924 E
Thomas, C J (Newport) 1888 I, M, 1889 S, I, 1890 S, E, I, 1891 E, I
Thomas, C R (Bridgend) 1925 E, S
Thomas, D J (Swansea) 1904 E, 1908 A, 1910 E, S, I, 1911 E, S, F, I, 1912 E
Thomas, D J (Swansea) 1930 S, I, 1932 E, S, I, 1933 E, S, 1934 E, 1935 E, S, I
Thomas, D L (Neath) 1937 E
Thomas, D L (Aberavon) 1961 I
Thomas, E (Newport) 1904 S, I, 1909 S, F, I, 1910 F
Thomas, E J R (Mountain Ash) 1906 SA, 1908 F, I, 1909 S

Thomas, G (Newport) 1888 M, 1890 I, 1891 S
Thomas, G (Bridgend, Cardiff, Celtic Warriors, Toulouse, Cardiff Blues) 1995 [J, NZ, I], SA, Fj, 1996 F 1, A 1,2, Bb, F 2, It, A 3, 1997 US, S, I, F, E, US 1,2, C, R, Tg, NZ, 1998 It, E, S, I, F, SA 2, Arg, 1999 F 1(R), It, E, Arg 2, SA, F 2, [Arg 3, J (R), Sm, A], 2000 F, It, E, S, I, US (R), SA, 2001 E, F, It, J 1,2, R, Arg, Tg, A, 2002 E, R, Fj, C, NZ, 2003 It, E 1, S 1, I 1, F, I 2, E 2, [C,It,NZ(R),E], 2004 S,I,F,E,It,SA2,R,NZ, 2005 E,It,F, NZ,SA,A, 2006 E,S,A,C, 2007 It(t&R),E1,A1,2,E2,Arg,F2, [C(R),A,Fj]
Thomas, G M (Bath, Ospreys, Llanelli Scarlets, Newport Gwent Dragons) 2001 J 1,2, R, I (R), Arg, Tg (R), A (R), 2002 S (R), SA 2(R),R(R), 2003 It(R), E 1, S 1, F, E 2(R), R, 2006 Arg 1,2,PI, 2007 I(t&R),A1,2, 2010 NZ1,2
Thomas, H M (Llanelli) 1912 F
Thomas, H W (Swansea) 1912 SA, 1913 E
Thomas, H W (Neath) 1936 E, S, I, 1937 E, S, I
Thomas, I (Bryncethin) 1924 E
Thomas, I D (Ebbw Vale, Llanelli Scarlets) 2000 Sm, US (R), SA (R), 2001 J 1,2, R, I, Arg (R), Tg, 2002 It, E, S, SA 1,2, Fj, C, NZ, 2003 It, E 1, S 1, I 1, F, A, NZ, E 2, [Tg,NZ,E], 2004 I,F, 2007 A1,2,E2
Thomas, J (Swansea, Ospreys) 2003 A, NZ(R), E 2(R), R, [It(R),NZ,E], 2004 S(t&R),I, F,E,Arg 2(R),SA1(R),R(t&R),J, 2005 E(R),It,F(R),S(R),US,C,NZ, 2006 It(R),F(R),A, PI(R),C,NZ, 2007 S(R),F1(R),It(R),E1(R),A1,2,Arg,F2,[C,A],SA, 2008 E,S,It,I,F, SA1, 2, 2009 It,Sm(R),Arg(R),A(R), 2010 E(R),S,F,I,It,SA1,NZ1, 2
Thomas, J D (Llanelli) 1954 I
Thomas, L C (Cardiff) 1885 E, S
Thomas, M C (Newport, Devonport Services) 1949 F, 1950 E, S, I, F, 1951 E, S, I, F, SA, 1952 E, S, I, F, 1953 E, 1956 E, S, I, F, 1957 E, S, 1958 E, S, I, F, 1959 I, F
Thomas, N (Bath) 1996 SA (R), 1997 US 1(R),2, C (R), R, Tg, NZ, 1998 Z, SA 1
Thomas, R (Swansea) 1900 E, S, I, 1901 E
Thomas, R (Pontypool) 1909 F, I, 1911 S, F, 1912 E, S, SA, 1913 E
Thomas, R C C (Swansea) 1949 F, 1952 I, F, 1953 S, I, F, NZ, 1954 E, I, F, S, 1955 S, I, 1956 E, S, I, 1957 E, 1958 A, E, S, I, F, 1959 E, S, I, F
Thomas, R L (London Welsh) 1889 S, I, 1890 I, 1891 E, S, I, 1892 E
Thomas, R M (Newport Gwent Dragons) 2006 Arg 2(R), 2007 E2(R),SA, 2008 It,SA2,C, 2009 It
Thomas, S (Llanelli) 1890 S, E, 1891 I
Thomas, S G (Llanelli) 1923 E, S, F, I
Thomas, T R (Cardiff Blues) 2005 US(R),C,NZ(R),Fj,SA,A, 2006E,S,I,It,F,PI,C(R),NZ, 2007 I,S,F1(R),It(R),E1(R),2(R),F2(R), [C(R),A(R),J,Fj(R)],SA(R), 2008 SA2(R)
Thomas, W D (Llanelli) 1966 A, 1968 S, I, F, 1969 E, NZ 2, A, 1970 SA, S, E, I, F, 1971 E, S, I, F, 1972 E, S, F, NZ, 1973 E, S, I, F, 1974 E
Thomas, W G (Llanelli, Waterloo, Swansea) 1927 E, S, F, I, 1929 E, 1931 E, S, SA, 1932 E, S, I, 1933 E, S, I
Thomas, W H (Llandovery Coll, Cambridge U) 1885 S, 1886 E, S, 1887 E, S, 1888 S, I, 1890 E, I, 1891 S, I
Thomas, W J (Cardiff) 1961 F, 1963 F
Thomas, W J L (Llanelli, Cardiff) 1995 SA, Fj, 1996 It, E, S, I, F 1, 1996 Bb (R), 1997 US
Thomas, W L (Newport) 1894 S, 1895 E, I
Thomas, W T (Abertillery) 1930 E
Thompson, J F (Cross Keys) 1923 E
Thorburn, P H (Neath) 1985 F, E, Fj, 1986 E, S, I, F, 1987 F, [I, Tg, C, E, NZ, A], US, 1988 S, I, F, WS, R (R), 1989 S, I, F, E, NZ, 1990 F, E, S, I, Nm 1,2, Bb, 1991 E, S, I, F 1, A
Titley, M H (Bridgend, Swansea) 1983 R, 1984 S, I, F, E, A, 1985 S, I, Fj, 1986 F, Fj, Tg, WS, 1990 F, E
Towers, W H (Swansea) 1887 I, 1888 M
Travers, G (Pill Harriers, Newport) 1903 E, S, I, 1905 E, S, I, NZ, 1906 E, S, I, SA, 1907 E, S, I, 1908 E, S, F, I, A, 1909 E, S, I, 1911 S, F, I
Travers, W H (Newport) 1937 S, I, 1938 E, S, I, 1939 E, S, I, 1949 E, S, I, F
Treharne, E (Pontypridd) 1881 E, 1883 E
Trew, W J (Swansea) 1900 E, S, I, 1901 E, S, 1903 S, 1905 S, 1906 S, 1907 E, S, 1908 E, S, F, I, A, 1909 E, S, F, I, 1910 F, E, S, 1911 E, S, F, I, 1912 S, 1913 S, F
Trott, R F (Cardiff) 1948 E, S, F, I, 1949 E, S, I, F
Truman, W H (Llanelli) 1934 E, 1935 E
Trump, L C (Newport) 1912 E, S, I, F
Turnbull, B R (Cardiff) 1925 I, 1927 E, S, 1928 E, F, 1930 S
Turnbull, M J L (Cardiff) 1933 E, I
Turner, P (Newbridge) 1989 I (R), F, E
Uzzell, H (Newport) 1912 E, S, I, F, 1913 S, F, I, 1914 E, S, F, I, 1920 E, S, F, I
Uzzell, J R (Newport) 1963 NZ, 1965 E, S, I, F
Vickery, W E (Aberavon) 1938 E, S, I, 1939 E
Vile, T H (Newport) 1908 E, S, 1910 I, 1912 I, F, SA, 1913 E, 1921 S
Vincent, H C (Bangor) 1882 I
Voyle, M J (Newport, Llanelli, Cardiff) 1996 A 1(t), F 2, 1997 E, US 1,2, C, Tg, NZ, 1998 It, E, S, I, F, Arg (R), 1999 S (R), I (t), It (R), SA (R), F 2(R), [J, A (R)], 2000 F (R)
Wakeford, J D M (S Wales Police) 1988 WS, R
Waldron, R G (Neath) 1965 E, S, I, F
Walker, N (Cardiff) 1993 I, F, J, 1994 S, F, E, Pt, Sp, 1995 F, E, 1997 US 1,2, C, R (R), Tg, NZ, 1998 E
Waller, P D (Newport) 1908 A, 1909 E, S, F, I, 1910 F
Walne, N J (Richmond, Cardiff) 1999 It (R), E (R), C
Walters, N (Llanelli) 1902 E
Wanbon, R (Aberavon) 1968 E
Warburton, S (Cardiff Blues) 2009 US(R),Sm,A(R), 2010 S(R),I(R),It,SA1
Ward, W S (Cross Keys) 1934 S, I
Warlow, D J (Llanelli) 1962 I
Waters, D R (Newport) 1986 E, S, I, F
Waters, K (Newbridge) 1991 [WS]
Watkins, D (Newport) 1963 E, S, I, F, NZ, 1964 E, S, I, F, SA, 1965 E, S, I, F, 1966 E, S, I, F, 1967 I, F, E
Watkins, E (Neath) 1924 E, S, I, F
Watkins, E (Blaina) 1926 S, I, F
Watkins, E V (Cardiff) 1935 NZ, 1937 S, I, 1938 E, S, I, 1939 E, S
Watkins, H V (Llanelli) 1904 S, I, 1905 E, S, I, 1906 E
Watkins, I J (Ebbw Vale) 1988 E (R), S, I, F, NZ 2, R, 1989 S, I, F, E
Watkins, L (Oxford U, Llandaff) 1881 E
Watkins, M J (Newport) 1984 I, F, E, A
Watkins, M J (Llanelli Scarlets) 2003 It(R), E 1(R), S 1(R), I 1(R), R, S 2, 2005 US(R),C(R),Fj,SA(R),A, 2006 E,S,I,It,F,Arg 1,2(R)
Watkins, S J (Newport, Cardiff) 1964 S, I, F, 1965 E, S, I, F, 1966 E, S, I, F, A, 1967 S, I, F, E, NZ, 1968 E, S, 1969 S, I, F, E, NZ 1, 1970 E, I
Watkins, W R (Newport) 1959 F
Watts, D (Maesteg) 1914 E, S, F, I
Watts, J (Llanelli) 1907 E, S, I, 1908 E, S, F, I, A, 1909 S, F, I
Watts, W H (Newport) 1892 E, S, I, 1893 E, S, I, 1894 E, S, I, 1895 E, I, 1896 E
Watts, W J (Llanelli) 1914 E
Weatherley, D J (Swansea) 1998 Z
Weaver, D S (Swansea) 1964 E
Webb, A (Jim) (Abertillery) 1907 S, 1908 E, S, F, I, A, 1909 E, S, F, I, 1910 F, E, S, I, 1911 E, S, F, I, 1912 E, S
Webb, J (Newport) 1888 M, 1889 S
Webbe, G M C (Bridgend) 1986 Tg (R), WS, 1987 F, E, S, [Tg], US, 1988 F (R), NZ 1, R
Webster, R E (Swansea) 1987 [A], 1990 Bb, 1991 [Arg, A], 1992 I, F, E, S, A, 1993 E, S, I, F
Wells, G T (Cardiff) 1955 E, S, 1957 I, F, 1958 A, E, S
Westacott, D (Cardiff) 1906 I
Wetter, J J (Newport) 1914 S, F, I, 1920 E, S, F, I, 1921 E, 1924 I, NZ
Wetter, W H (Newport) 1912 SA, 1913 E
Wheel, G A D (Swansea) 1974 I, E (R), 1975 F, E, I, A, 1976 E, S, I, F, 1977 I, E, S, 1978 E, S, I, F, A 1,2, NZ, 1979 S, I, 1980 F, E, S, I, 1981 E, S, I, F, A, 1982 I
Wheeler, P J (Aberavon) 1967 NZ, 1968 E
Whitefoot, J (Cardiff) 1984 A (R), 1985 S, I, F, E, Fj, 1986 E, S, I, F, Fj, Tg, WS, 1987 F, E, S, I, [I, C]
Whitfield, J J (Newport) 1919 NZA, 1920 E, S, F, I, 1921 E, 1922 E, S, I, F, 1924 S, I
Whitson, G K (Newport) 1956 F, 1960 S, I
Wilkins, G (Bridgend) 1994 Tg
Williams, A (Ospreys, Bath) 2003 R (R), 2005 v US(R),C(R), 2006 Arg 2(R), 2007 A2(R)
Williams, B (Llanelli) 1920 S, F, I
Williams, B H (Neath, Richmond, Bristol) 1996 F 2, 1997 R, Tg, NZ, 1998 It, E, Z (R), SA 1, Arg (R), 1999 S (R), I, It (R), 2000 F (R), It (R), E (t+R), 2001 R (R), I (R), Tg (R), A (R), 2002 I (R), F (R), It (R), E (R), S
Williams, B L (Cardiff) 1947 E, S, F, I, A, 1948 E, S, F, I, 1949 E, S, I, 1951 I, SA, 1952 S, 1953 E, S, I, F, NZ, 1954 S, 1955 E

Williams, B R (Neath) 1990 S, I, Bb, 1991 E, S
Williams, C (Llanelli) 1924 NZ, 1925 E
Williams, C (Aberavon, Swansea) 1977 E, S, 1980 F, E, S, I, NZ, 1983 E
Williams, C D (Cardiff, Neath) 1955 F, 1956 F
Williams, D (Ebbw Vale) 1963 E, S, I, F, 1964 E, S, I, F, SA, 1965 E, S, I, F, 1966 E, S, I, A, 1967 F, E, NZ, 1968 E, 1969 S, I, F, E, NZ 1,2, A, 1970 SA, S, E, I, 1971 E, S, I, F
Williams, D (Llanelli) 1998 SA 1(R)
Williams, D A (Bridgend, Swansea) 1990 Nm 2(R), 1995 Fj (R)
Williams, D B (Newport, Swansea) 1978 A 1, 1981 E, S
Williams, E (Neath) 1924 NZ, 1925 F
Williams, E (Aberavon) 1925 E, S
Williams, F L (Cardiff) 1929 S, F, I, 1930 E, S, I, F, 1931 F, I, SA, 1932 E, S, I, 1933 I
Williams, G (London Welsh) 1950 I, F, 1951 E, S, I, F, SA, 1952 E, S, I, F, 1953 NZ, 1954 E
Williams, G (Bridgend) 1981 I, F, 1982 E (R), S
Williams, G J (Bridgend, Cardiff Blues) 2003 It(R), E 1(R), S 1, F(R), E 2(R), 2009 C(R),US, 2010 E,S
Williams, G M (Aberavon) 1936 E, S, I
Williams, G P (Bridgend) 1980 NZ, 1981 E, S, A, 1982 I
Williams, G R (Cardiff Blues) 2000 I, Sm, US, SA, 2001 S, F, It, R (R), I (R), Arg, Tg (R), A (R), 2002 F (R), It (R), E (R), S, SA 1,2, R, Fj, C, NZ, 2003 It, E 1, S 1, I 1, F, A, NZ, E 2, [Tg,It(R)], 2004 S,I,F,E,It,Arg1,R,J, 2005 F(R),S,US,C
Williams, H R (Llanelli) 1954 S, 1957 F, 1958 A
Williams, J F (London Welsh) 1905 I, NZ, 1906 S, SA
Williams, J J (Llanelli) 1973 F (R), A, 1974 S, I, F, E, 1975 F, E, S, I, A, 1976 E, S, I, F, 1977 I, F, E, S, 1978 E, S, I, F, A 1,2, NZ, 1979 S, I, F, E
Williams, J L (Cardiff) 1906 SA, 1907 E, S, I, 1908 E, S, I, A, 1909 E, S, F, I, 1910 I, 1911 E, S, F, I
Williams, J L (Blaina) 1920 E, S, F, I, 1921 S, F, I
Williams, J P R (London Welsh, Bridgend) 1969 S, I, F, E, NZ 1,2, A, 1970 SA, S, E, I, F, 1971 E, S, I, F, 1972 E, S, F, NZ, 1973 E, S, I, F, A, 1974 S, I, F, 1975 F, E, S, I, A, 1976 E, S, I, F, 1977 I, F, E, S, 1978 E, S, I, F, A 1,2, NZ, 1979 S, I, F, E, 1980 NZ, 1981 E, S
Williams, L H (Cardiff) 1957 S, I, F, 1958 E, S, I, F, 1959 E, S, I, 1961 F, 1962 E, S
Williams, M E (Pontypridd, Cardiff Blues) 1996 Bb, F 2, It (t), 1998 It, E, Z, SA 2, Arg, 1999 S, I, C, J, [Sm], 2000 E (R), 2001 E, S, F, It, 2002 I, F, It, E, S, SA 1,2, Fj, C, NZ, 2003 It, E 1, S 1, I 1, F, A, NZ, E 2, [C,Tg(R),It,E(R)], 2004 S,I, F(t&R), E(R),It, SA2(t&R),R(R),NZ(R),J(R), 2005 E,It,F,S,I,Fj,SA,A, 2006 E,S,I,It,F,A,C,NZ, 2007 I,S, F1,It,E1,Arg,F2, [C,A,J,Fj], 2008 E,S,It,I,F,SA3,NZ,A, 2009 S,E,F,I,NZ,Arg,A, 2010 E,S,F,I
Williams, M T (Newport) 1923 F
Williams, O (Llanelli) 1947 E, S, A, 1948 E, S, F, I
Williams, O L (Bridgend) 1990 Nm 2
Williams, R D G (Newport) 1881 E
Williams, R F (Cardiff) 1912 SA, 1913 E, S, 1914 I
Williams, R H (Llanelli) 1954 I, F, S, 1955 S, I, F, 1956 E, S, I, 1957 E, S, I, F, 1958 A, E, S, I, F, 1959 E, S, I, F, 1960 E
Williams, S (Llanelli) 1947 E, S, F, I, 1948 S, F
Williams, S A (Aberavon) 1939 E, S, I
Williams, S M (Neath, Cardiff, Northampton) 1994 Tg, 1996 E (t), A 1,2, Bb, F 2, It, A 3, SA, 1997 US, S, I, F, E, US 1,2(R), C, R (R), Tg (R), NZ (t+R), 2002 SA 1,2, R, Fj(R), 2003 It, E 1, S 1, F(R)
Williams, S M (Neath, Ospreys) 2000 F (R), It, E, S, I, Sm, SA (R), 2001 J 1,2, I, 2003 R, [NZ,E], 2004 S,I,F,E,It,Arg 1,2,SA1,2, NZ,J, 2005 E,It,F,S,I,NZ,Fj,SA,A, 2006 E,S, It,F,Arg 1,2,A,PI(R), C,NZ, 2007 F1,It,E1,F2, [C,A,J,Fj], 2008 E,S,It,I,F,SA 1,2,3,NZ,A, 2009 S,F,It,I,NZ,Arg,A, 2010 E,S,F,I,It
Williams, T (Pontypridd) 1882 I
Williams, T (Swansea) 1888 S, I
Williams, T (Swansea) 1912 I, 1913 F, 1914 E, S, F, I
Williams, T (Swansea) 1921 F
Williams, T G (Cross Keys) 1935 S, I, NZ, 1936 E, S, I, 1937 S, I
Williams, W A (Crumlin) 1927 E, S, F, I
Williams, W A (Newport) 1952 I, F, 1953 E
Williams, W E O (Cardiff) 1887 S, I, 1889 S, 1890 S, E
Williams, W H (Pontymister) 1900 E, S, I, 1901 E
Williams, W L T (Llanelli, Cardiff) 1947 E, S, F, I, A, 1948 I, 1949 E
Williams, W O G (Swansea, Devonport Services) 1951 F, SA, 1952 E, S, I, F, 1953 E, S, I, F, NZ, 1954 E, I, F, S, 1955 E, S, I, F, 1956 E, S, I
Williams, W P J (Neath) 1974 I, F
Williams-Jones, H (S Wales Police, Llanelli) 1989 S (R), 1990 F (R), I, 1991 A, 1992 S, A, 1993 E, S, I, F, Z 1, Nm, 1994 Fj, Tg, WS (R), It (t), 1995 E (R)
Willis, W R (Cardiff) 1950 E, S, I, F, 1951 E, S, I, F, SA, 1952 E, S, 1953 S, NZ, 1954 E, I, F, S, 1955 E, S, I, F
Wiltshire, M L (Aberavon) 1967 NZ, 1968 E, S, F
Windsor, R W (Pontypool) 1973 A, 1974 S, I, F, E, 1975 F, E, S, I, A, 1976 E, S, I, F, 1977 I, F, E, S, 1978 E, S, I, F, A 1,2, NZ, 1979 S, I, F
Winfield, H B (Cardiff) 1903 I, 1904 E, S, I, 1905 NZ, 1906 E, S, I, 1907 S, I, 1908 E, S, F, I, A
Winmill, S (Cross Keys) 1921 E, S, F, I
Wintle, M E (Llanelli) 1996 It
Wintle, R V (London Welsh) 1988 WS (R)
Wooller, W (Sale, Cambridge U, Cardiff) 1933 E, S, I, 1935 E, S, I, NZ, 1936 E, S, I, 1937 E, S, I, 1938 S, I, 1939 E, S, I
Wyatt, C P (Llanelli) 1998 Z (R), SA 1(R),2, Arg, 1999 S, I, F 1, It, E, Arg 1,2, SA, C (R), F 2, [Arg 3, J (R), Sm, A], 2000 F, It, E, US, SA, 2001 E, R, I, Arg (R), Tg (R), A (R), 2002 I, It (R), E, S (R), 2003 A(R), NZ(t+R), E 2, [Tg(R),NZ(R)]
Wyatt, G (Pontypridd, Celtic Warriors) 1997 Tg, 2003 R (R)
Wyatt, M A (Swansea) 1983 E, S, I, F, 1984 A, 1985 S, I, 1987 E, S, I
Yapp, J V (Cardiff Blues) 2005 E(R),It(R),F(R),S(R),I(R),C(R),Fj, 2006 Arg 1(R), 2008 C,NZ(R), 2009 S(R),It,C,US, 2010 SA1(R),NZ1(R)
Young, D (Swansea, Cardiff) 1987 [E, NZ], US, 1988 E, S, I, F, NZ 1,2, WS, R, 1989 S, NZ, 1990 F, 1996 A 3, SA, 1997 US, S, I, F, E, R, NZ, 1998 It, E, S, I, F, 1999 I, E (R), Arg 1(R),2(R), SA, C (R), F 2, [Arg 3, J, Sm, A], 2000 F, It, E, S, I, 2001 E, S, F, It, R, I, Arg
Young, G A (Cardiff) 1886 E, S
Young, J (Harrogate, RAF, London Welsh) 1968 S, I, F, 1969 S, I, F, E, NZ 1, 1970 E, I, F, 1971 E, S, I, F, 1972 E, S, F, NZ, 1973 E, S, I, F
Young, P (Gwent Dragons) 2003 R (R)

ALL BLACKS' UNIQUE DOUBLE

By Iain Spragg

The 2009–10 campaign ushered in a new era for the club game in Wales with the advent of play-offs at the end of the season but there was still a distinctly familiar feeling to proceedings as Neath reasserted their dominance in the Principality by winning both the Premiership title and the subsequent, inaugural Premiership Play-Off Final.

The Welsh All Blacks had claimed the 'traditional' league and cup double in 2008 but two years on they made history by landing the 'new' double. It could have been an unprecedented treble had they successfully defended their SWALEC Cup crown but they crashed out of that particular competition in the third round in January to The Wanderers.

The season began with Neath looking to restore their reputation as top dogs in the Premiership after their four-year reign as champions had been ended by Cardiff and they were quickly out of the blocks with nine wins in their opening 11 games.

It soon became apparent Swansea were to be their only serious challengers, but victories home and away against the All Whites proved crucial and by mid-April they were already on the verge of recapturing their title. The only obstacle was the unfortunate Bedwas, who were overwhelmed 109–21 at the Gnoll to ensure the Welsh All Blacks lifted the trophy in considerable style to give Patrick Horgan his first piece of silverware as Neath coach.

A series of knockout games between the top eight sides then ensued but rather than throw up a surprise protagonist for the inaugural Premiership Play-Off Final, it was Neath and Swansea – the two strongest sides in the regular season – who battled their way through to compete in the ground breaking clash at Cardiff Arms Park at the end of May.

The match, played in searing heat in the capital, was predictably fierce between two of the oldest adversaries. Neath drew first blood when they exploited some weak defence to score two tries through Kevin Farrell and Ashley James but man-of-the-match James Dixon kept Swansea in contention with the boot.

A third try for Horgan's team stretched Neath's lead but the All Whites came roaring back with a converted Hanno Dirksen try and it needed a late Arwel Thomas penalty to level the scores at 22–22. There was, however, time for one last moment of drama when Dirksen seemed certain to score his second and snatch victory only to fumble the ball and the opportunity evaporate.

The play-off rules dictated the winners would be decided by tries scored and not by extra-time, so by virtue of their three scores to Swansea's one, Neath were crowned champions.

"We were hoping to close a momentous season with a second trophy and just managed to do so," said Horgan after the final whistle. "I think we have been the best team in the league this year and at three tries to one, we deserved it.

"This tournament is about the top eight playing it out and I think we've been the best team throughout the campaign and we've won two trophies and other people haven't got any.

"It was always going to be tight because Swansea have got some quality. Our two wins over them during the regular season were also hard-fought affairs. It has been a hard season, we completed our regular fixture list a month ago and the players have done well to stick it out."

The SWALEC Cup produced an archetypal David and Goliath clash as Llanelli, bidding to lift the trophy for a record-breaking 14th time as well as gain redemption for narrowly losing the 2009 final to Neath, fought through to face Carmarthen Quins, who were appearing in the final for the first time in the club's history.

The dreamers amongst the crowd were praying for a Quins victory but it was not to be as the Scarlets showed their greater experience on the big stage and tries from Daniel Newton and Ben Morgan gave Llanelli a comfortable cushion.

To their credit, Carmarthen rallied in the second half and caused a degree of anxiety in the Llanelli ranks when Jamie Davies crashed over in the 63rd minute but it was too little, too late and the side in red held out for a 20–8 victory and a place in the record books.

"This latest cup success took away last year's sick feeling against Neath," said Llanelli head of rugby Anthony Buchanan. "We can be very proud of the lads, there is no better feeling than taking the cup back to Llanelli. This group wanted to be part of Llanelli's rich cup history and I'm chuffed for them it was achieved against a gritty side like Carmarthen.

"This is a continuous journey for the young players in this side as we present them with the opportunities to show their skills, be competitive and keep improving as well as experiencing the ups and downs of winning and losing. Winning this trophy is a huge plus for the region. It's good for these players and the performance augurs well for the region going forward as some of these guys look to step up to the Scarlets squad."

PRINCIPALITY PREMIERSHIP 2009–10 RESULTS

29 August 2009: **Bedwas** 15 **Neath** 34, **Cardiff** 29 **Swansea** 35, **Llanelli** 47 **Cross Keys** 16, **Newport** 36 **Carmarthen** 6, **Pontypool** 25 **Aberavon** 38, **Pontypridd** 36 **Llandovery** 21, **Wanderers** 27 **Ebbw Vale** 23. 5 September: **Aberavon** 21 **Wanderers** 22, **Bedwas** 30 **Llanelli** 23, **Carmarthen** 17 **Pontypridd** 13, **Cross Keys** 30 **Pontypool** 23, **Ebbw Vale** 3 **Cardiff** 30, **Llandovery** 19 **Neath** 35, **Swansea** 38 **Newport** 6. 12 September: **Bedwas** 26 **Swansea** 58, **Carmarthen** 22 **Neath** 25, **Cross Keys** 27 **Aberavon** 35, **Llanelli** 12 **Llandovery** 10, **Newport** 22 **Ebbw Vale** 13, **Pontypool** 15 **Pontypridd** 48, **Wanderers** 15 **Cardiff** 20. 18 September: **Ebbw Vale** 3 **Pontypridd** 28, **Wanderers** 25 **Newport** 19. 19 September: **Aberavon** 44 **Bedwas** 18, **Cardiff** 32 **Cross Keys** 32, **Llandovery** 24 **Carmarthen** 23, **Pontypool** 17 **Neath** 39, **Swansea** 53 **Llanelli** 19. 22 September: **Cardiff** 22 **Neath** 20, **Llanelli** 30 **Aberavon** 12, **Newport** 13 **Pontypridd** 6. 26 September: **Cardiff** 20 **Llandovery** 25 **Carmarthen** 33 **Wanderers** 37, **Llanelli** 37 **Pontypool** 11, **Neath** 41 **Ebbw Vale** 7, **Newport** 46 **Bedwas** 15, **Pontypridd** 37 **Cross Keys** 19, **Swansea** 36 **Aberavon** 36. 3 October: **Bedwas** 13 **Pontypridd** 20, **Carmarthen** 26 **Aberavon** 11, **Cross Keys** 20 **Newport** 8, **Ebbw Vale** 25 **Llanelli** 19, **Llandovery** 28 **Swansea** 41, **Pontypool** 10 **Cardiff** 38, **Wanderers** 33 **Neath** 24. 10 October: **Aberavon** 46 **Ebbw Vale** 7, **Bedwas** 35 **Pontypool** 31, **Cardiff** 27 **Carmarthen** 16, **Neath** 24 **Cross Keys** 13, **Newport** 27 **Llandovery** 18, **Wanderers** 28 **Llanelli** 30 **Pontypridd** 24 **Swansea** 11. 17 October: **Cardiff** 29 **Bedwas** 22, **Ebbw Vale** 12 **Cross Keys** 36, **Llandovery** 52 **Aberavon** 34, **Newport** 53 **Pontypool** 14, **Swansea** 27 **Neath** 31, **Wanderers** 12 **Pontypridd** 18 **Carmarthen** 10 **Llanelli** 18. 24 October: **Aberavon** 32 **Llanelli** 32, **Bedwas** 21 **Ebbw Vale** 3, **Carmarthen** 24 **Swansea** 33, **Cross Keys** 17 **Wanderers** 19, **Pontypool** 21 **Llandovery** 68, **Pontypridd** 21 **Newport** 20. 25 October: **Neath** 27 **Cardiff** 39. 31 October: **Aberavon** 20 **Newport** 27, **Cardiff** 12 **Pontypridd** 20, **Cross Keys** 20 **Bedwas** 13, **Ebbw Vale** 22 **Llandovery** 24, **Llanelli** 26 **Neath** 28, **Pontypool** 10 **Carmarthen** 40, **Wanderers** 12 **Swansea** 28. 6 November: **Aberavon** 17 **Cross Keys** 9. 7 November: **Bedwas** 28 **Wanderers** 9, **Carmarthen** 41 **Ebbw Vale** 3, **Newport** 23 **Cardiff** 17. 14 November: **Cross Keys** 25 **Carmarthen** 8, **Ebbw Vale** 14 **Swansea** 7, **Newport** 23 **Llanelli** 17, **Wanderers** 15 **Pontypool** 10. 5 December: **Aberavon** 10 **Pontypridd** 3, **Carmarthen** 18 **Bedwas** 0, **Llandovery** 13 **Wanderers** 6, **Llanelli** 10 **Cardiff** 16, **Neath** 21 **Newport** 13, **Pontypool** 14 **Ebbw Vale** 9, **Swansea** 16 **Cross Keys** 8. 12 December: **Cross Keys** 37 **Llandovery** 8, **Neath** 10 **Llanelli** 25, **Newport** 28 **Aberavon** 21, **Pontypridd** 20 **Cardiff** 21, **Swansea** 36 **Pontypool** 24. 19 December: **Neath** 25 **Llandovery** 20. 26 December: **Swansea** 15 **Bedwas** 13, **Cardiff** 0 **Wanderers** 26, **Llandovery** 16 **Llanelli** 16, **Neath** 36 **Aberavon** 33. 2 January 2010: **Neath** 64 **Pontypool** 6, **Llanelli** 18 **Swansea** 31. 23 January: **Bedwas** 6 **Newport** 24, **Llandovery** 5 **Cardiff** 45, **Wanderers** 17 **Cross Keys** 20. 27 January: **Cross Keys** 11 **Pontypridd.** 30 January: **Aberavon** 12 **Neath** 29, **Llanelli** 25 **Pontypridd** 13, **Swansea** 33 **Llandovery** 28. 4 February: **Llanelli** 49 **Ebbw Vale** 3. 5 February: **Newport** 45 **Cross Keys** 19, **Cardiff** 30 **Pontypool** 5. 6 February: **Pontypridd** 46 **Bedwas** 7, **Aberavon** 30 **Carmarthen** 22, **Neath** 48 **Wanderers** 17. 12 February: **Llandovery** 42 **Pontypool** 10, **Swansea** 32 **Carmarthen** 11. 14 February: **Ebbw Vale** 23 **Bedwas** 6. 17 February: **Pontypridd** 49 **Pontypool** 5. 23 February:

Llanelli 30 **Bedwas** 3. 27 February: **Bedwas** 35 **Cross Keys** 12, **Carmarthen** 25 **Pontypool** 15, **Llandovery** 36 **Ebbw Vale** 0, **Swansea** 63 **Wanderers** 10. 2 March: **Ebbw Vale** 15 **Aberavon** 19, **Wanderers** 6 **Carmarthen** 9. 3 March: **Newport** 43 **Swansea** 9. 6 March: **Ebbw Vale** 8 **Carmarthen** 13, **Llandovery** 19 **Cross Keys** 16, **Pontypool** 27 **Swansea** 24, **Wanderers** 17 **Bedwas** 24. 9 March: **Cardiff** 32 **Ebbw Vale** 0, **Neath** 36 **Carmarthen** 22. 10 March: **Llanelli** 34 **Wanderers** 21. 12 March: **Cross Keys** 10 **Neath** 27, **Pontypool** 44 **Bedwas** 29, **Swansea** 37 **Pontypridd** 15. 13 March: **Carmarthen Quins** 9 **Cardiff** 16, **Llandovery** 27 **Newport** 37. 16 March: **Llandovery** 33 **Pontypridd** 17. 17 March: **Llanelli** 24 **Carmarthen** 19. 19 March: **Aberavon** 23 **Llandovery** 5, **Bedwas** 21 **Cardiff** 17, **Neath** 23 **Swansea** 6, **Pontypridd** 32 **Wanderers** 7. 21 March: **Cross Keys** 17 **Ebbw Vale** 16. 23 March: **Aberavon** 14 **Swansea** 26. 26 March: **Ebbw Vale** 13 **Newport** 16. 27 March: **Pontypool** 15 **Cross Keys** 13. 30 March: **Carmarthen** 17 **Llandovery** 6, **Cross Keys** 29 **Llanelli** 10. 31 March: **Cardiff** 19 **Newport** 17, **Pontypridd** 27 **Ebbw Vale** 6, **Wanderers** 10 **Aberavon** 12. 3 April: **Aberavon** 23 **Cardiff** 10, **Carmarthen** 13 **Cross Keys** 10, **Llandovery** 19 **Bedwas** 16, **Llanelli** 30 **Newport** 27, **Neath** 48 **Pontypridd** 23, **Pontypool** 26 **Wanderers** 6, **Swansea** 26 **Ebbw Vale** 5. 6 April: **Newport** 23 **Wanderers** 17, **Pontypool** 27 **Llanelli** 26. 7 April: **Cross Keys** 16 **Cardiff** 17, **Pontypridd** 42 **Carmarthen** 27. 10 April: **Bedwas** 28 **Carmarthen** 30, **Cardiff** 24 **Llanelli** 42, **Cross Keys** 20 **Swansea** 25, **Ebbw Vale** 22 **Pontypool** 12, **Pontypridd** 28 **Aberavon** 28, **Wanderers** 17 **Llandovery** 36, **Newport** 27 **Neath** 24. 13 April: **Pontypridd** 36 **Neath** 51, **Cardiff** 31 **Aberavon** 31. 14 April: **Pontypool** 20 **Newport** 15, **Bedwas** 35 **Llandovery** 34. 17 April: **Aberavon** 60 **Pontypool** 27, **Ebbw Vale** 36 **Wanderers** 30, **Neath** 109 **Bedwas** 21. 20 April: **Bedwas** 36 **Aberavon** 37, **Carmarthen** 14 **Newport** 47, **Ebbw Vale** 21 **Neath** 48. 21 April: **Swansea** 34 **Cardiff** 19, **Pontypridd** 48 **Llanelli** 14.

FINAL TABLE

	P	W	D	L	F	A	BP	PTS
Neath	26	21	0	5	927	532	20	**104**
Swansea	26	19	1	6	780	527	18	**96**
Newport	26	18	0	8	685	470	14	**86**
Pontypridd	26	16	1	9	682	486	15	**81**
Aberavon	26	14	4	8	709	617	13	**77**
Llanelli	26	14	2	10	668	565	17	**77**
Cardiff	26	15	2	9	612	507	11	**75**
Llandovery	26	12	1	13	636	621	10	**60**
Carmarthen	26	11	0	15	515	562	8	**52**
Cross Keys	26	9	1	16	502	550	9	**47**
Bedwas	26	8	0	18	516	792	12	**44**
Wanderers	26	7	0	19	461	662	12	**40**
Pontypool	26	7	0	19	464	891	8	**36**
Ebbw Vale	26	5	0	21	312	687	8	**28**

PRINCIPALITY PREMIERSHIP PLAY-OFF CHAMPIONSHIP

ROUND ONE

27 April, 2010

Neath 34 **Pontypridd** 3
Aberavon 18 **Llandovery** 35
Swansea 60 **Newport** 19

29 April, 2010

Llanelli 14 **Cardiff** 9

ROUND TWO

3 May, 2010

Pontypridd 21 **Llandovery** 12

11 May, 2010

Newport 48 **Llanelli** 35

ROUND THREE

13 May, 2010

Neath 26 **Llandovery** 18.

17 May, 2010

Swansea 31 **Newport** 17

FINAL TABLE

22 May 2010, Arms Park, Cardiff

NEATH 22 (2G, 1PG, 1T) SWANSEA 22 (1G, 5PG)

**Neath win 3–1 on try count*

NEATH: G King; K James, N Brew, S Thomas, A Jenkins; A Thomas (captain), K Farrell; A V Lott, A James, M Jones, E Evans, N Edwards, G Gravell, L Evans, A Whitney. *Substitutions:* E Lewis for L Evans (temp 25 to 33 mins); A Bramwell for Jenkins (47 mins); P Sidoli for Edwards (64 mins); A Littlehales for A James (71 mins); T James for Farrell (72 mins); M Collins for L Evans (78 mins).

SCORERS: *Tries:* Farrell, James, Whitney *Conversions:* Thomas (2) *Penalty Goal:* Thomas

SWANSEA: N Thomas; E Walker, H Dirksen, D Watts, N Jones; J Dixon, R Wells; T Evans, S Baldwin, L May, J Goode, S Kiley (captain), L Jones, S Jones, B Lewis. *Substitutions:* D Blyth for Goode (temp 14 to 18 mins); O Phillips for Baldwin (temp 44 to 66 mins); A Clatworthy for Evans (59 mins); A Thomas for Watts (61 mins); S Lewis for B Lewis (70 mins).

SCORERS: *Try:* Dirksen *Conversion:* Dixon *Penalty Goals:* Dixon (5)

REFEREE: D Jones (Pontllanfraith)

LEAGUE ONE EAST

Winners: UWIC

LEAGUE ONE WEST

Winners: Tonmawr

LEAGUE ONE NORTH

Winners: Nant Conwy

LEAGUE TWO EAST

Winners: Gilfach Goch

LEAGUE TWO WEST

Winners: Maesteg

LEAGUE THREE EAST

Winners: Fleur de Lys

LEAGUE THREE SOUTH EAST

Winners: Tylorstown

LEAGUE THREE SOUTH WEST

Winners: Skewen

LEAGUE THREE WEST

Winners: Newcastle Emlyn

LEAGUE FOUR EAST

Winners: Risca

LEAGUE FOUR SOUTH EAST

Winners: Dowlais

LEAGUE FOUR SOUTH WEST

Winners: Aberavon Green Stars

LEAGUE FOUR WEST

Winners: Tumble

LEAGUE FIVE EAST

Winners: Oakdale

LEAGUE FIVE SOUTH EAST

Winners: Barry

LEAGUE FIVE SOUTH CENTRAL

Winners: Bridgend Sports Club

LEAGUE FIVE SOUTH WEST

Winners: Birchgrove

LEAGUE FIVE WEST

Winners: Neyland

LEAGUE SIX EAST

Winners: Beaufort

LEAGUE SIX SOUTH EAST

Winners: Hafodyrynys

LEAGUE SIX CENTRAL

Winners: Glyncoch

LEAGUE SIX WEST

Winners: Tregaron

SWALEC CUP 2009–10 RESULTS

QUARTER-FINALS

30 March, 2009

Bedwas 24 **Cardiff** 34

Wanderers 26 **Carmarthen** 31

Pontypridd 41 **Aberavon** 16

Tonmawr 16 **Llanelli** 26

SEMI-FINALS

20 April, 2009

Carmarthen 41 **Pontypridd** 12

Llanelli 46 **Cardiff** 25

FINAL

8 May 2010, Millennium Stadium, Cardiff

LLANELLI 20 (2G, 2PG) CARMARTHEN 8 (1PG, 1)

LLANELLI: D Newton; D Ford, N Reynolds, S Williams, C Keenan; S Shingler, G Davies; S Hopkins, C Hawkins (captain), J Corsi, N White, J Galley, A Powell, B Morgan, D Eager. *Substitutions:* J Lewis for Newton (46 mins); J James for Davies (73 mins); C Jones for Corsi (73 mins); E Siggery for Galley (77 mins); S Martin for Williams (80 mins); R Lawrence for Hawkins (80 mins).

SCORERS: *Tries:* Newton, Morgan *Conversions:* Shingler (2) *Penalty Goals:* Shingler (2)

YELLOW CARD: Ford (51 mins)

CARMARTHEN: A Rees; R Carter, A Banfield, T Davies (captain), J Davies; G Cull, S Martens; A Beaujeau, R Wilkes, K Jones, G Evans, M Morgan, A Thomas, S Timani, E Lloyd. *Substitutions:* C Jones for Timani (57 mins); J Garland for Banfield (77 mins); R Richards for Martens (77 mins); M Monoghan for Beaujean (77 mins); C Kelly for Wilkes (77 mins).

SCORERS: *Try:* Davies *Penalty Goal:* Cull

YELLOW CARDS: Wilkes (30 mins), Morgan (81 mins)

REFEREE: T Hayes (Wales)

an All Blacks side who haven't lost on this tour is pretty special. We understand the Barbarians ethos and rugby is all about friendship."

In May 2010, the Baa–Baas faced England at Twickenham looking for a repeat of their victory 12 months earlier but Martin Johnson's side were in no mood for further embarrassment and ran out 35–26 victors.

England had established a 32–7 advantage early in the second half but Baa–Baa tries from David Smith, Census Johnston and Paul Sackey had English alarm bells ringing in the final quarter and ensured the crowd enjoyed a grandstand finish.

The Barbarians' season ended in Limerick in June with a game against an experimental Ireland side at Thomond Park and it proved to be a victorious send-off as they survived a powerful second-half surge by the home side to record a 29–23 win.

The Baa–Baas included veteran Irish second row Malcolm O'Kelly in the XV in what was his final senior appearance of a long and distinguished career and he enjoyed a fitting send-off as Xavier Rush and George Smith crossed to give the visitors a 21–3 lead. Kiwi prop Cedric Heymans bulldozed over after the break to stretch the advantage and although the Irish rallied with a Tony Buckley score, it was not enough to overhaul the Baa–Baas.

For New Zealand Maori, the game's other great invitational team, 2010 was their Centenary season and they faced a daunting three-match schedule against the New Zealand Barbarians, Ireland and England to celebrate their first 100 years of rugby.

"The guys are aware that it's a big year for us," said Maori coach Jamie Joseph as he announced his 26-man squad including 12 debutants for the Barbarians clash. "It's a big year for their families, their whanau and for Maoridom in general.

"These three games are about celebrating Maori rugby but, having said that, the guys are also playing for All Blacks places. If I create the right environment for them to excel, then I'll be pretty happy."

The clash with the New Zealand Barbarians was staged in Whangarei in mid-June and the Maori raced into an early lead courtesy of a Luke McAlister penalty and tries in quick succession from Stephen Brett and captain Liam Messam but the Baa–Baas responded with two tries of their own from No 8 Peter Saili and Ben Smith.

The momentum was now with the New Zealand Barbarians and they took the lead for the first time in the match when prop Jamie Mackintosh crashed over shortly after the restart. Three more tries followed in a pulsating encounter but when Colin Slade landed a penalty three minutes from time, giving the Baa–Baas a 31–30 lead, the Maori challenge appeared to have subsided.

That was until wing Hosea Gear sliced open the defence with a superbly-timed run for his side's fifth try, which was converted by McAlister, and the Maori recorded a dramatic 37–31 win.

Six days later Ireland were the opposition in Rotorua and as they had done against the New Zealand Baa–Baas, the Maori were the quickest out of the blocks and inside the opening 14 minutes Gear and Dwayne Sweeney had both breached the Irish defence but they paid a heavy price for repeated indiscipline with Jonathan Sexton punishing them with six penalties to make it 18–18 at the break.

The second half saw Ireland take the lead with a Paddy Wallace score but substitute Karl Lowe made a significant contribution from the bench with a third try for the home side and the Maori held on for a 31–28 victory, although Sexton did have a 73rd-minute opportunity to level the scores with an unsuccessful penalty.

"It's awesome, the boys really dug in for 80 minutes and showed their character towards the end there," said captain Messam. "It is 100 years and I think we celebrated it in the right way."

The Centenary celebrations climaxed with the clash against England in Napier, arguably the sternest test of the three-match series, and All Black coach Graham Henry was among the crowd to run the rule over the Maori ahead of the Tri-Nations.

England were fresh from beating the Wallabies in Sydney and although only wing Chris Ashton was retained from the XV that downed Australia for the McLean Park clash, the confidence in the English squad was evident as they surged into a 13–0 lead with two Charlie Hodgson penalties and a Steffon Armitage try.

The home side responded with scores from Gear and Messam but England were proving irresistible in the first period and tries from Danny Care and Ashton before the break gave the visitors a 28–17 half time advantage.

The Maori were in real danger of closing their Centenary season with defeat but emerged for the second 40 minutes rejuvenated and were indebted to the irrepressible Gear, who completed his hat-trick, and Willie Ripia, who landed two penalties and by the time the final whistle sounded, they had emerged 35–28 winners.

Victory however was tinged with anxiety. Captain Messam revealed after the match that the squad were unsure what, if any, fixtures would be arranged for the side for next season and as the first 100 years of Maori rugby ended in triumph, a question mark lingered about the side's immediate future.

"It's a shame if they do lose this team, but all we can do is go out there and perform," Messam said. "I thought there were some awesome tries, not just in this game, but in the last two games as well. If we do our job, then hopefully the rest will take care of itself."

BRITISH & IRISH LIONS INTERNATIONAL STATISTICS

UP TO 29TH OCTOBER 2010

MATCH RECORDS

MOST CONSECUTIVE TEST WINS

6	1891	*SA* 1,2,3,	1896 *SA* 1,2,3
3	1899	*A* 2,3,4	
3	1904	*A* 1,2,3	
3	1950	*A* 1,2,	1955 *SA* 1
3	1974	*SA* 1,2,3	

MOST CONSECUTIVE TESTS WITHOUT DEFEAT

Matches	Wins	Draws	Period
6	6	0	1891 to 1896
6	4	2	1971 to 1974

MOST POINTS IN A MATCH

BY THE TEAM

Pts	Opponents	Venue	Year
31	Australia	Brisbane	1966
29	Australia	Brisbane	2001
28	S Africa	Pretoria	1974
28	S Africa	Johannesburg	2009
26	S Africa	Port Elizabeth	1974
25	S Africa	Cape Town	1997
25	Argentina	Cardiff	2005
25	S Africa	Pretoria	2009
24	Australia	Sydney	1950
24	Australia	Sydney	1959

BY A PLAYER

Pts	Player	Opponents	Venue	Year
20	J P Wilkinson	Argentina	Cardiff	2005
20	S M Jones	S Africa	Pretoria	2009
18	A J P Ward	S Africa	Cape Town	1980
18	A G Hastings	N Zealand	Christchurch	1993
18	J P Wilkinson	Australia	Sydney	2001
17	T J Kiernan	S Africa	Pretoria	1968
16	B L Jones	Australia	Brisbane	1950

MOST TRIES IN A MATCH

BY THE TEAM

Tries	Opponents	Venue	Year
5	Australia	Sydney	1950
5	S Africa	Johannesburg	1955
5	Australia	Sydney	1959
5	Australia	Brisbane	1966
5	S Africa	Pretoria	1974

BY A PLAYER

Tries	Player	Opponents	Venue	Year
2	A M Bucher	Australia	Sydney	1899
2	W Llewellyn	Australia	Sydney	1904
2	C D Aarvold	N Zealand	Christchurch	1930
2	J E Nelson	Australia	Sydney	1950
2	M J Price	Australia	Sydney	1959
2	M J Price	N Zealand	Dunedin	1959
2	D K Jones	Australia	Brisbane	1966
2	T G R Davies	N Zealand	Christchurch	1971
2	J J Williams	S Africa	Pretoria	1974
2	J J Williams	S Africa	Port Elizabeth	1974
2	T Croft	S Africa	Durban	2009
2	S M Williams	S Africa	Johannesburg	2009

MOST CONVERSIONS IN A MATCH

BY THE TEAM

Cons	Opponents	Venue	Year
5	Australia	Brisbane	1966
4	S Africa	Johannesburg	1955
3	Australia	Sydney	1950
3	Australia	Sydney	1959
3	Australia	Brisbane	2001
3	S Africa	Durban	2009

BY A PLAYER

Cons	Player	Opponents	Venue	Year
5	S Wilson	Australia	Brisbane	1966
4	A Cameron	S Africa	Johannesburg	1955
3	J P Wilkinson	Australia	Brisbane	2001
3	S M Jones	S Africa	Durban	2009

MOST PENALTIES IN A MATCH

BY THE TEAM

Pens	Opponents	Venue	Year
6	N Zealand	Christchurch	1993
6	Argentina	Cardiff	2005
5	S Africa	Pretoria	1968
5	S Africa	Cape Town	1980
5	Australia	Sydney	1989
5	S Africa	Cape Town	1997
5	S Africa	Durban	1997
5	S Africa	Pretoria	2009

BY A PLAYER

Pens	Player	Opponents	Venue	Year
6	A G Hastings	N Zealand	Christchurch	1993
6	J P Wilkinson	Argentina	Cardiff	2005
5	T J Kiernan	S Africa	Pretoria	1968
5	A J P Ward	S Africa	Cape Town	1980
5	A G Hastings	Australia	Sydney	1989
5	N R Jenkins	S Africa	Cape Town	1997
5	N R Jenkins	S Africa	Durban	1997
5	S M Jones	S Africa	Pretoria	2009

MOST DROPPED GOALS IN A MATCH

BY THE TEAM

Drops	Opponents	Venue	Year
2	S Africa	Port Elizabeth	1974

BY A PLAYER

Drops	Player	Opponents	Venue	Year
2	P Bennett	S Africa	Port Elizabeth	1974

CAREER RECORDS

MOST CAPPED PLAYERS

Caps	Player	Career Span
17	W J McBride	1962 to 1974
13	R E G Jeeps	1955 to 1962
12	C M H Gibson	1966 to 1971
12	G Price	1977 to 1983
10	A J F O'Reilly	1955 to 1959
10	R H Williams	1955 to 1959
10	G O Edwards	1968 to 1974

MOST CONSECUTIVE TESTS

Tests	Player	Span
15	W J McBride	1966 to 1974
12	C M H Gibson	1966 to 1971
12	G Price	1977 to 1983

MOST TESTS AS CAPTAIN

Tests	Captain	Span
6	A R Dawson	1959
6	M O Johnson	1997 to 2001

MOST POINTS IN TESTS

Points	Player	Tests	Career
67	J P Wilkinson	6	2001 to 2005
66	A G Hastings	6	1989 to 1993
53	S M Jones	6	2005 to 2009
44	P Bennett	8	1974 to 1977
41	N R Jenkins	4	1997 to 2001
35	T J Kiernan	5	1962 to 1968
30	S Wilson	5	1966
30	B John	5	1968 to 1971

MOST TRIES IN TESTS

Tries	Player	Tests	Career
6	A J F O'Reilly	10	1955 to 1959
5	J J Williams	7	1974 to 1977
4	W Llewellyn	4	1904
4	M J Price	5	1959

MOST CONVERSIONS IN TESTS

Cons	Player	Tests	Career
7	J P Wilkinson	6	2001 to 2005
7	S M Jones	6	2005 to 2009
6	S Wilson	5	1966
4	J F Byrne	4	1896
4	C Y Adamson	4	1899
4	B L Jones	3	1950
4	A Cameron	2	1955

MOST PENALTY GOALS IN TESTS

Penalties	Player	Tests	Career
20	A G Hastings	6	1989 to 1993
16	J P Wilkinson	6	2001 to 2005
13	N R Jenkins	4	1997 to 2001
12	S M Jones	6	2005 to 2009
11	T J Kiernan	5	1962 to 1968
10	P Bennett	8	1974 to 1977
7	S O Campbell	7	1980 to 1983

MOST DROPPED GOALS IN TESTS

Drops	Player	Tests	Career
2	P F Bush	4	1904
2	D Watkins	6	1966
2	B John	5	1968 to 1971
2	P Bennett	8	1974 to 1977
2	C R Andrew	5	1989 to 1993

SERIES RECORDS

RECORD	HOLDER	DETAIL
Most team points		79 in S Africa 1974
Most team tries		10 in S Africa 1955 & 1974
Most points by player	N R Jenkins	41 in S Africa 1997
Most tries by player	W Llewellyn	4 in Australia 1904
	J J Williams	4 in S Africa 1974

MAJOR TOUR RECORDS

RECORD	DETAIL	YEAR	PLACE
Most team points	842	1959	Australia, NZ & Canada
Most team tries	165	1959	Australia, NZ & Canada
Highest score & biggest win	116–10	2001	v W Australia President's XV
Most individual points	188 by B John	1971	Australia & N Zealand
Most individual tries	22 by A J F O'Reilly	1959	Australia, NZ & Canada
Most points in match	37 by A G B Old	1974 v SW Districts	Mossel Bay, S Africa
Most tries in match	6 by D J Duckham	1971 v W Coast/Buller	Greymouth, N Zealand
	6 by J J Williams	1974 v SW Districts	Mossel Bay, S Africa

MISCELLANEOUS RECORDS

RECORD	HOLDER	DETAIL
Longest Test Career	W J McBride	13 seasons, 1962–1974
Youngest Test Cap	A J F O'Reilly	19 yrs 91 days in 1955
Oldest Test Cap	N A Back	36 yrs 160 days in 2005

BRITISH & IRISH LIONS INTERNATIONAL PLAYERS
UP TO 29TH OCTOBER 2010

From 1891 onwards.
* Indicates that the player was uncapped at the time of his first Lions Test but was subsequently capped by his country.

Aarvold, C D (Cambridge U, Blackheath and England) 1930 NZ 1,2,3,4, A
Ackerman, R A (London Welsh and Wales) 1983 NZ 1,4 (R)
Ackford, P J (Harlequins and England) 1989 A 1,2,3
Adamson, C Y (Durham City) 1899 A 1,2,3,4
Alexander, R (NIFC and Ireland) 1938 SA 1,2,3
Andrew, C R (Wasps and England) 1989 A 2,3, 1993 NZ 1,2,3
Arneil, R J (Edinburgh Acads and Scotland) 1968 SA 1,2,3,4
Archer, H A (Guy's H and *England) 1908 NZ 1,2,3
Ashcroft, A (Waterloo and England) 1959 A 1, NZ 2
Aston, R L (Cambridge U and England) 1891 SA 1,2,3
Ayre-Smith, A (Guy's H) 1899 A 1,2,3,4
Back, N A (Leicester and England) 1997 SA 2(R),3, 2001 A 2,3, 2005 NZ 1
Bainbridge, S J (Gosforth and England) 1983 NZ 3,4
Baird, G R T (Kelso and Scotland) 1983 NZ 1,2,3,4
Baker, A M (Newport and Wales) 1910 SA 3
Baker, D G S (Old Merchant Taylors' and England) 1955 SA 3,4
Balshaw, I R (Bath and England) 2001 A 1(R),2(R),3(R)
Bassett, J A (Penarth and Wales) 1930 NZ 1,2,3,4, A
Bateman, A G (Richmond and Wales) 1997 SA 3(R)
Bayfield, M C (Northampton and England) 1993 NZ 1,2,3
Beamish, G R (Leicester, RAF and Ireland) 1930 NZ 1,2,3,4,A
Beattie, J R (Glasgow Acads and Scotland) 1983 NZ 2(R)
Beaumont, W B (Fylde and England) 1977 NZ 2,3,4, 1980 SA 1,2,3,4
Bebb, D I E (Swansea and Wales) 1962 SA 2,3, 1966 A 1,2, NZ 1,2,3,4
Bedell-Sivright, D R (Cambridge U and Scotland) 1904 A 1
Bell, S P (Cambridge U) 1896 SA 2,3,4
Belson, F C (Bath) 1899 A 1
Bennett, P (Llanelli and Wales) 1974 SA 1,2,3,4, 1977 NZ 1,2,3,4
Bentley, J (Newcastle and England) 1997 SA 2,3
Bevan, J C (Cardiff Coll of Ed, Cardiff and Wales) 1971 NZ 1
Bevan, T S (Swansea and Wales) 1904 A 1,2,3, NZ
Black, A W (Edinburgh U and Scotland) 1950 NZ 1,2
Black, B H (Oxford U, Blackheath and England) 1930 NZ 1,2,3,4, A
Blakiston, A F (Northampton and England) 1924 SA 1,2,3,4
Bowcott, H M (Cambridge U, Cardiff and Wales) 1930 NZ 1,2,3,4, A
Bowe, T J (Ospreys and Ireland) 2009 SA 1,2,3
Boyd, C A (Dublin U and *Ireland) 1896 SA 1
Boyle, C V (Dublin U and Ireland) 1938 SA 2,3
Brand, T N (NIFC and *Ireland) 1924 SA 1,2
Bresnihan, F P K (UC Dublin and Ireland) 1968 SA 1,2,4
Bromet, E (Cambridge U) 1891 SA 2,3
Bromet, W E (Oxford U and England) 1891 SA 1,2,3
Brophy, N H (UC Dublin and Ireland) 1962 SA 1,4
Brown, G L (W of Scotland and Scotland) 1971 NZ 3,4, 1974 SA 1,2,3, 1977 NZ 2,3,4
Bucher, A M (Edinburgh Acads and Scotland) 1899 A 1,3,4
Budge, G M (Edinburgh Wands and Scotland) 1950 NZ 4
Bulger, L Q (Lansdowne and Ireland) 1896 SA 1,2,3,4
Bulloch, G C (Glasgow and Scotland) 2001 A l(t), 2005 NZ 3(R)
Burcher, D H (Newport and Wales) 1977 NZ 3
Burnell, A P (London Scottish and Scotland) 1993 NZ 1
Bush, P F (Cardiff and *Wales) 1904 A 1,2,3, NZ
Butterfield, J (Northampton and England) 1955 SA 1,2,3,4
Byrne, J F (Moseley and England) 1896 SA 1,2,3,4
Byrne, J S (Leinster and Ireland) 2005 Arg, NZ 1,2(R),3
Byrne, L M (Ospreys and Wales) 2009 SA 1
Calder, F (Stewart's-Melville FP and Scotland) 1989 A 1,2,3
Calder, J H (Stewart's-Melville FP and Scotland) 1983 NZ 3
Cameron, A (Glasgow HSFP and Scotland) 1955 SA 1,2
Campbell, S O (Old Belvedere and Ireland) 1980 SA 2(R),3,4, 1983 NZ 1,2,3,4
Campbell-Lamerton, M J (Halifax, Army and Scotland) 1962 SA 1,2,3,4, 1966 A 1,2, NZ 1,3
Carey, W J (Oxford U) 1896 SA 1,2,3,4
Carleton, J (Orrell and England) 1980 SA 1,2,4, 1983 NZ 2,3,4
Carling, W D C (Harlequins and England) 1993 NZ 1
Catt, M J (Bath and England) 1997 SA 3
Cave, W T C (Cambridge U and *England) 1903 SA 1,2,3
Chalmers, C M (Melrose and Scotland) 1989 A 1
Chapman, F E (Westoe, W Hartlepool and *England) 1908 NZ 3
Charvis, C L (Swansea and Wales) 2001 A 1(R),3(R)
Clarke, B B (Bath and England) 1993 NZ 1,2,3
Clauss, P R A (Oxford U and Scotland) 1891 SA 1,2,3
Cleaver, W B (Cardiff and Wales) 1950 NZ 1,2,3
Clifford, T (Young Munster and Ireland) 1950 NZ 1,2,3, A 1,2
Clinch, A D (Dublin U and Ireland) 1896 SA 1,2,3,4
Cobner, T J (Pontypool and Wales) 1977 NZ 1,2,3
Colclough, M J (Angoulême and England) 1980 SA 1,2,3,4, 1983 NZ 1,2,3,4
Collett, G F (Cheltenham) 1903 SA 1,2,3
Connell, G C (Trinity Acads and Scotland) 1968 SA 4
Cookson, G (Manchester) 1899 A 1,2,3,4
Cooper, G J (Newport Gwent Dragons and Wales) 2005 Arg
Corry, M E (Leicester and England) 2001 A 1,2(t+R),3, 2005 Arg, NZ 1,2(R),3(R)
Cotton, F E (Loughborough Colls, Coventry and England) 1974 SA 1,2,3,4, 1977 NZ 2,3,4
Coulman, M J (Moseley and England) 1968 SA 3
Cove-Smith, R (Old Merchant Taylors' and England) 1924 SA 1,2,3,4
Cowan, R C (Selkirk and Scotland) 1962 SA 4
Crean, T J (Wanderers and Ireland) 1896 SA 1,2,3,4
Croft, T R (Leicester and England) 2009 SA 1,2,3(t&R)
Cromey, G E (Queen's U, Belfast and Ireland) 1938 SA 3
Crowther, S N (Lennox) 1904 A 1,2,3, NZ
Cueto, M J (Sale and England) 2005 NZ 3
Cunningham, W A (Lansdowne and Ireland) 1924 SA 3
Cusiter, C P (Borders and Scotland) 2005 Arg (R)
Dallaglio, L B N (Wasps and England) 1997 SA 1,2,3
Dancer, G T (Bedford) 1938 SA 1,2,3
D'Arcy, G (Leinster and Ireland) 2005 Arg

Davey, J (Redruth and England) 1908 NZ 1
Davidson, I G (NIFC and Ireland) 1903 SA 1
Davidson, J W (London Irish and Ireland) 1997 SA 1,2,3
Davies, C (Cardiff and Wales) 1950 NZ 4
Davies, D M (Somerset Police and Wales) 1950 NZ 3,4, A 1
Davies, D S (Hawick and Scotland) 1924 SA 1,2,3,4
Davies, H J (Newport and Wales) 1924 SA 2
Davies, T G R (Cardiff, London Welsh and Wales) 1968 SA 3, 1971 NZ 1,2,3,4
Davies, T J (Llanelli and Wales) 1959 NZ 2,4
Davies, T M (London Welsh, Swansea and Wales) 1971 NZ 1,2,3,4, 1974 SA 1,2,3,4
Davies, W G (Cardiff and Wales) 1980 SA 2
Davies, W P C (Harlequins and England) 1955 SA 1,2,3
Dawes, S J (London Welsh and Wales) 1971 NZ 1,2,3,4
Dawson, A R (Wanderers and Ireland) 1959 A 1,2, NZ 1,2,3,4
Dawson, M J S (Northampton, Wasps and England) 1997 SA 1,2,3, 2001 A 2(R),3, 2005 NZ 1(R),3(R)
Dibble, R (Bridgwater Albion and England) 1908 NZ 1,2,3
Dixon, P J (Harlequins and England) 1971 NZ 1,2,4
Dobson, D D (Oxford U and England) 1904 A 1,2,3, NZ
Dodge, P W (Leicester and England) 1980 SA 3,4
Dooley, W A (Preston Grasshoppers and England) 1989 A 2,3
Doran, G P (Lansdowne and Ireland) 1899 A 1,2
Down, P J (Bristol and *England) 1908 NZ 1,2,3
Doyle, M G (Blackrock Coll and Ireland) 1968 SA 1
Drysdale, D (Heriot's FP and Scotland) 1924 SA 1,2,3,4
Duckham, D J (Coventry and England) 1971 NZ 2,3,4
Duggan, W P (Blackrock Coll and Ireland) 1977 NZ 1,2,3,4
Duff, P L (Glasgow Acads and Scotland) 1938 SA 2,3
Easterby, S H (Llanelli Scarlets and Ireland) 2005 NZ 2,3
Edwards, G O (Cardiff and Wales) 1968 SA 1,2, 1971 NZ 1,2,3,4, 1974 SA 1,2,3,4
Edwards, R W (Malone and Ireland) 1904 A 2,3, NZ
Ellis, H A (Leicester and England) 2009 SA 3(R)
Evans, G (Maesteg and Wales) 1983 NZ 3,4
Evans, G L (Newport and Wales) 1977 NZ 2,3,4
Evans, I C (Llanelli and Wales) 1989 A 1,2,3, 1993 NZ 1,2 3, 1997 SA 1
Evans, R T (Newport and Wales) 1950 NZ 1,2,3,4, A 1,2
Evans, T P (Swansea and Wales) 1977 NZ 1
Evans, W R (Cardiff and Wales) 1959 A 2, NZ 1,2,3
Evers, G V (Moseley) 1899 A 2,3,4
Farrell, J L (Bective Rangers and Ireland) 1930 NZ 1,2,3,4,A
Faull, J (Swansea and Wales) 1959 A 1, NZ 1,3,4
Fenwick, S P (Bridgend and Wales) 1977 NZ 1,2,3,4
Fitzgerald, C F (St Mary's Coll and Ireland) 1983 NZ 1,2,3,4
Fitzgerald, L M (Leinster and Ireland) 2009 SA 2
Flutey, R J (Wasps and England) 2009 SA 3
Ford, R W (Edinburgh and Scotland) 2009 SA 3(R)
Foster, A R (Queen's U, Belfast and Ireland) 1910 SA 1,2
Francombe, J S (Manchester) 1899 A 1
Gabe, R T (Cardiff and Wales) 1904 A 1,2,3, NZ
Gibbs, I S (Swansea and Wales) 1993 NZ 2,3, 1997 SA 1,2,3
Gibbs, R A (Cardiff and Wales) 1908 NZ 1,2
Gibson, C M H (Cambridge U, NIFC and Ireland) 1966 NZ 1,2,3,4, 1968 SA 1(R),2,3,4, 1971 NZ 1,2,3,4
Gibson, G R (Northern and England) 1899 A 1,2,3,4
Gibson, T A (Cambridge U and *England) 1903 SA 1,2,3
Giles, J L (Coventry and England) 1938 SA 1,3
Gillespie, J I (Edinburgh Acads and Scotland) 1903 SA 1,2,3
Gould, J H (Old Leysians) 1891 SA 1
Gravell, R W R (Llanelli and Wales) 1980 SA 1(R),2,3,4
Graves, C R A (Wanderers and Ireland) 1938 SA 1,3
Gray, H G S (Scottish Trials) 1899 A 1,2
Greenwood, J T (Dunfermline and Scotland) 1955 SA 1,2,3,4
Greenwood, W J H (Harlequins and England) 2005 NZ 1(R),3
Greig, L L (US and *Scotland) 1903 SA 1,2,3
Grewcock, D J (Bath and England) 2001 A 1,2,3, 2005 Arg, NZ 1(R)
Grieve, C F (Oxford U and Scotland) 1938 SA 2,3
Griffiths, G M (Cardiff and Wales) 1955 SA 2,3,4
Griffiths, V M (Newport and Wales) 1924 SA 3,4
Guscott, J C (Bath and England) 1989 A 2,3, 1993 NZ 1,2,3, 1997 SA 1,2,3
Hall, M R (Bridgend and Wales) 1989 A 1
Hammond, J (Cambridge U, Blackheath) 1891 SA 1,2,3, 1896 SA 2,4
Hancock, P F (Blackheath and England) 1891 SA 1,2,3, 1896 SA 1,2,3,4
Hancock, P S (Richmond and *England) 1903 SA 1,2,3
Handford, F G (Manchester and England) 1910 SA 1,2,3
Harding, A F (London Welsh and Wales) 1904 A 1,2,3, NZ, 1908 NZ 1,2,3
Harding, R (Cambridge U, Swansea and Wales) 1924 SA 2,3,4
Harris, S W (Blackheath and England) 1924 SA 3,4
Harrison, E M (Guy's H) 1903 SA 1
Hastings, A G (London Scottish, Watsonians and Scotland) 1989 A 1,2,3, 1993 NZ 1,2,3
Hastings, S (Watsonians and Scotland) 1989 A 2,3
Hay, B H (Boroughmuir and Scotland) 1980 SA 2,3,4
Hayes, J J (Munster and Ireland) 2005 Arg, 2009 SA 3(R)
Hayward, D J (Newbridge and Wales) 1950 NZ 1,2,3
Healey, A S (Leicester and England) 1997 SA 2(R),3(R)
Heaslip, J P R (Leinster and Ireland) 2009 SA 1,2,3
Henderson, N J (Queen's U, Belfast, NIFC and Ireland) 1950 NZ3
Henderson, R A J (Wasps and Ireland) 2001 A 1,2,3
Henderson, R G (Northern and Scotland) 1924 SA 3,4
Hendrie, K G P (Heriot's FP and Scotland) 1924 SA 2
Henson, G L (Neath-Swansea Ospreys and Wales) 2005 NZ 2
Hewitt, D (Queen's U, Belfast, Instonians and Ireland) 1959 A 1,2, NZ 1,3,4, 1962 SA 4
Hickie, D A (Leinster and Ireland) 2005 Arg
Higgins, R (Liverpool and England) 1955 SA 1
Hill, R A (Saracens and England) 1997 SA 1,2, 2001 A 1,2, 2005 NZ 1
Hind, G R (Guy's H and *England) 1908 NZ 2,3
Hinshelwood, A J W (London Scottish and Scotland) 1966 NZ 2,4, 1968 SA 2
Hodgson, J McD (Northern and *England) 1930 NZ 1,3
Holmes, T D (Cardiff and Wales) 1983 NZ 1
Hopkins, R (Maesteg and Wales) 1971 NZ 1(R)
Horgan, S P (Leinster and Ireland) 2005 Arg (R),NZ 1(R),2(R),3(R)
Horrocks-Taylor, J P (Leicester and England) 1959 NZ 3
Horton, A L (Blackheath and England) 1968 SA 2,3,4
Howard, W G (Old Birkonians) 1938 SA 1
Howie, R A (Kirkcaldy and Scotland) 1924 SA 1,2,3,4
Howley, R (Cardiff and Wales) 2001 A 1,2
Hulme, F C (Birkenhead Park and England) 1904 A 1
Irvine, A R (Heriot's FP and Scotland) 1974 SA 3,4, 1977 NZ 1,2,3,4, 1980 SA 2,3,4
Irwin, D G (Instonians and Ireland) 1983 NZ 1,2,4
Isherwood, G A M (Old Alleynians, Sale) 1910 SA 1,2,3
Jackett, E J (Falmouth, Leicester and England) 1908 NZ 1,2,3
Jackson, F S (Leicester) 1908 NZ 1
Jackson, P B (Coventry and England) 1959 A 1,2, NZ 1,3,4
James, D R (Llanelli and Wales) 2001 A 1,2,3
Jarman, H (Newport and Wales) 1910 SA 1,2,3
Jarman, J W (Bristol and *England) 1899 A 1,2,3,4
Jeeps, R E G (Northampton and *England) 1955 SA 1,2,3,4, 1959 A 1,2, NZ 1,2,3, 1962 SA 1,2,3,4
Jenkins, G D (Cardiff Blues and Wales) 2005 NZ 1,2,3, 2009 SA 1,2
Jenkins, N R (Pontypridd, Cardiff and Wales) 1997 SA 1,2,3, 2001 A 2(R)
Jenkins, V G J (Oxford U, London Welsh and Wales) 1938 SA 1
John, B (Cardiff and Wales) 1968 SA 1, 1971 NZ 1,2,3,4
John, E R (Neath and Wales) 1950 NZ 1,2,3,4, A 1,2

Johnson, M O (Leicester and England) 1993 NZ 2,3, 1997 SA 1,2,3, 2001 A 1,2,3
Johnston, R (Wanderers and Ireland) 1896 SA 1,2,3
Jones, A R (Ospreys and Wales) 2009 SA 1(R),2
Jones, A-W (Ospreys and Wales) 2009 SA 1,2(R),3(R)
Jones, B L (Devonport Services, Llanelli and Wales) 1950 NZ 4, A 1,2
Jones, D K (Llanelli, Cardiff and Wales) 1962 SA 1,2,3, 1966 A 1,2, NZ 1
Jones, E L (Llanelli and *Wales) 1938 SA 1,3
Jones, I E (Llanelli and Wales) 1930 NZ 1,2,3,4, A
Jones, J P "Jack" (Newport and *Wales) 1908 NZ 1,2,3, 1910 SA 1,2,3
Jones J P "Tuan" (Guy's H and *Wales) 1908 NZ 2,3
Jones K D (Cardiff and Wales) 1962 SA 1,2,3,4
Jones K J (Newport and Wales) 1950 NZ 1,2,4
Jones R N (Swansea and Wales) 1989 A 1,2,3
Jones, R P (Neath-Swansea Ospreys and Wales) 2005 NZ 1(R),2,3
Jones, S M (Clermont Auvergne, Llanelli Scarlets and Wales) 2005 NZ 1,2(R),3, 2009 SA 1,2,3
Jones S T (Pontypool and Wales) 1983 NZ 2,3,4
Judkins, W (Coventry) 1899 A 2,3,4
Kay, B J (Leicester and England) 2005 Arg (R),NZ 1
Keane, M I (Lansdowne and Ireland) 1977 NZ 1
Kearney, R D J (Leinster and Ireland) 2009 SA 1(R),2,3
Kennedy, K W (CIYMS, London Irish and Ireland) 1966 A 1,2, NZ 1,4
Kiernan, M J (Dolphin and Ireland) 1983 NZ 2,3,4
Kiernan, T J (Cork Const and Ireland) 1962 SA 3, 1968 SA 1,2,3,4
Kininmonth, P W (Oxford U, Richmond and Scotland) 1950 NZ 1,2,4
Kinnear, R M (Heriot's FP and *Scotland) 1924 SA1,2,3,4
Kyle, J W (Queen's U, Belfast, NIFC and Ireland) 1950 NZ 1,2,3,4, A 1,2
Kyrke, G V (Marlborough N) 1908 NZ 1
Laidlaw, F A L (Melrose and Scotland) 1966 NZ 2,3
Laidlaw, R J (Jedforest and Scotland) 1983 NZ 1(R),2,3,4
Lamont, R A (Instonians and Ireland) 1966 NZ 1,2,3,4
Lane, M F (UC Cork and Ireland) 1950 NZ 4, A 2
Larter, P J (Northampton, RAF and England) 1968 SA 2
Laxon, H (Cambridge U) 1908 NZ 1
Leonard, J (Harlequins and England) 1993 NZ 2,3, 1997 SA 1(R), 2001 A 1(R),2(R)
Lewis, R A (Abertillery and Wales) 1966 NZ 2,3,4
Lewsey, O J (Wasps and England) 2005 NZ 1,2,3
Llewellyn, W (Llwynypia, Newport and Wales) 1904 A 1,2,3, NZ
Lynch, J F (St Mary's Coll and Ireland) 1971 NZ 1,2,3,4
McBride, W J (Ballymena and Ireland) 1962 SA 3,4, 1966 NZ 2,3,4, 1968 SA 1,2,3,4, 1971 NZ 1,2,3,4, 1974 SA 1,2,3,4
Macdonald, R (Edinburgh U and Scotland) 1950 NZ 1, A 2
McEvedy, P F (Guy's H) 1904 A 2,3, NZ, 1908 NZ 2,3
McFadyean, C W (Moseley and England) 1966 NZ 1,2,3,4
McGeechan, I R (Headingley and Scotland) 1974 SA 1,2,3,4, 1977 NZ 1,2,3(R),4
McGown, T M W (NIFC and Ireland) 1899 A 1,2,3,4
McKay, J W (Queen's U, Belfast and Ireland) 1950 NZ 1,2,3,4, A 1,2
McKibbin, H R (Queen's U, Belfast and Ireland) 1938 SA 1,2,3
Mackie, O G (Wakefield Trinity and *England) 1896 SA 1,2,3,4
Maclagan, W E (London Scottish and Scotland) 1891 SA 1,2,3
McLauchlan, J (Jordanhill and Scotland) 1971 NZ 1,2,3,4, 1974 SA 1,2,3,4
McLeod, H F (Hawick and Scotland) 1959 A 1,2, NZ 1,2,3,4
McLoughlin, R J (Gosforth, Blackrock Coll and Ireland) 1966 A 1,2, NZ,4
Macmillan, R G (London Scottish and Scotland) 1891 SA 1,2,3
MacNeill, H P (Oxford U and Ireland) 1983 NZ 1,2,4 (R)
Macpherson, N C (Newport and Scotland) 1924 SA 1,2,3,4
Macrae, D J (St Andrew's U and Scotland) 1938 SA 1
McVicker, J (Collegians and Ireland) 1924 SA 1,3,4
Magee, A M (Bective R and Ireland) 1896 SA 1,2,3,4
Magee, J M (Bective R) 1896 SA 2,4
Marques, R W D (Harlequins and England) 1959 A 2, NZ 2
Marsden-Jones, D (London Welsh and Wales) 1924 SA 1,2
Marshall, H (Blackheath and *England) 1891 SA 2,3
Martin, A J (Aberavon and Wales) 1977 NZ 1
Martelli, E (Dublin U) 1899 A 1
Martindale, S A (Kendal and England) 1930 A
Massey, B F (Hull and ER) 1904 A 3
Matthews, J (Cardiff and Wales) 1950 NZ 1,2,3,4, A 1,2
Maxwell, R B (Birkenhead Park) 1924 SA 1
Mayfield, W E (Cambridge U) 1891 SA 2,3
Mayne, R B (Queen's U, Belfast and Ireland) 1938 SA 1,2,3
Meares, A W D (Dublin U and *Ireland) 1896 SA 3,4
Mears, L A (Bath and England) 2009 SA 1
Meredith, B V (Newport and Wales) 1955 SA 1,2,3,4, 1962 SA 1,2,3,4
Meredith, C C (Neath and Wales) 1955 SA 1,2,3,4
Millar, S (Ballymena and Ireland) 1959 A 1,2, NZ 2, 1962 SA 1,2,3,4, 1968 SA 1,2
Miller, E R P (Leicester and England) 1997 SA 2(R)
Milliken, R A (Bangor and Ireland) 1974 SA 1,2,3,4
Milne, K S (Heriot's FP and Scotland) 1993 NZ 1
Mitchell, W G (Richmond and England) 1891 SA 1,2,3
Monye, Y C C (Harlequins and England) 2009 SA 1,3
Moody, L W (Leicester and England) 2005 Arg, NZ 2,3
Moore, B C (Nottingham, Harlequins and England) 1989 A 1,2,3, 1993 NZ 2,3
Morgan, C I (Cardiff and Wales) 1955 SA 1,2,3,4
Morgan, D W (Stewart's-Melville FP and Scotland) 1977 NZ 3(R),4
Morgan, E (London Welsh, Guy's H and Wales) 1904 A 1,2,3, NZ
Morgan, E (Swansea and *Wales) 1908 NZ 2,3
Morgan, G J (Clontarf and Ireland) 1938 SA 3
Morgan, H J (Abertillery and Wales) 1959 NZ.3,4, 1962 SA 2,3
Morgan, M E (Swansea and Wales) 1938 SA 1,2
Morgan, W L (Cardiff and *Wales) 1908 NZ 2,3
Morley, J C (Newport and Wales) 1930 NZ 1,2,3
Morris, C D (Orrell and England) 1993 NZ 1,2,3
Morris, D R (Swansea and Wales) 2001 A 3(R)
Morrison, M C (Royal HSFP and Scotland) 1903 SA 1,2,3
Mortimer, W (Marlborough N and *England) 1896 SA 1,2,3,4
Mulcahy, W A (UC Dublin and Ireland) 1959 A 1, NZ 4, 1962 SA 1,2,3,4
Mullen, K D (Old Belvedere and Ireland) 1950 NZ 1,2, A 2
Mulligan, A A (Wanderers, London Irish and Ireland) 1959 NZ 4
Mullin, B J (London Irish and Ireland) 1989 A 1
Mullineux, M (Blackheath) 1896 SA 1, 1899 A 1
Mullins, R C (Oxford U) 1896 SA 1,3
Murphy, G E A (Leicester and Ireland) 2005 Arg, NZ 3
Murphy, N A A (Cork Const and Ireland) 1959 A 2, NZ 1,2,4, 1966 A 1,2, NZ 2,3
Murray, P F (Wanderers and Ireland) 1930 NZ 1,2,4, A
Neale, M E (Bristol, Blackheath and *England) 1910 SA 1,2,3
Neary, A (Broughton Park and England) 1977 NZ 4
Neill, R M (Edinburgh Acads and Scotland) 1903 SA 2,3
Nelson, J E (Malone and Ireland) 1950 NZ 3,4, A 1,2
Nicholls, E G (Cardiff and Wales) 1899 A 1,2,3,4
Nicholson, B E (Harlequins and England) 1938 SA 2
Nicholson, E T (Birkenhead Park and *England) 1899 A 3,4
Norris, C H (Cardiff and Wales) 1966 NZ 1,2,3
Norster, R L (Cardiff and Wales) 1983 NZ 1,2, 1989 A 1
Novis, A L (Blackheath and England) 1930 NZ 2,4, A
O'Brien, A B (Guy's H) 1904 A 1,2,3, NZ
O'Callaghan, D P (Munster and Ireland) 2005 Arg, NZ 2,3, 2009 SA 1(R)
O'Connell, P J (Munster and Ireland) 2005 NZ 1,2,3, 2009 SA 1,2,3

O'Donnell, R C (St Mary's Coll and Ireland) 1980 SA I
O'Driscoll, B G (Blackrock Coll, Leinster and Ireland) 2001 A 1,2,3, 2005 NZ 1, 2009 SA 1,2
O'Driscoll, J B (London Irish and Ireland) 1980 SA 1,2,3,4, 1983 NZ 2,4
O'Gara, R J R (Munster and Ireland) 2005 NZ 3(R), 2009 SA 2(R)
O'Neill, H O'H (Queen's U, Belfast and Ireland) 1930 NZ 1,2,3,4, A
O'Reilly, A J F (Old Belvedere and Ireland) 1955 SA 1,2,3,4, 1959 A 1,2, NZ 1,2,3,4
Oldham, W L (Coventry and England) 1908 NZ 1
Orr, P A (Old Wesley and Ireland) 1977 NZ 1
O'Shea, J P (Cardiff and Wales) 1968 SA 1
Owen, M J (Newport Gwent Dragons and Wales) 2005 Arg
Parker, D S (Swansea and Wales) 1930 NZ 1,2,3,4, A
Pask, A E I (Abertillery and Wales) 1962 SA 1,2,3, 1966 A 1,2, NZ 1,3,4
Patterson, C S (Instonians and Ireland) 1980 SA 1,2,3
Patterson, W M (Sale and *England) 1959 NZ 2
Paxton, I A M (Selkirk and Scotland) 1983 NZ 1,2,3,4
Pedlow, A C (CIYMS and Ireland) 1955 SA 1,4
Peel, D J (Llanelli Scarlets and Wales) 2005 NZ 1,2,3
Perry, M B (Bath and England) 2001 A 1,2,3
Phillips, W M (Ospreys and Wales) 2009 SA 1,2,3
Pillman, C H (Blackheath and England) 1910 SA 2,3
Piper, O J S (Cork Const and Ireland) 1910 SA 1
Poole, H (Cardiff) 1930 NZ 3
Popplewell, N J (Greystones and Ireland) 1993 NZ 1,2,3
Preece, I (Coventry and England) 1950 NZ 1
Prentice, F D (Leicester and England) 1930 NZ 2, A
Price, B (Newport and Wales) 1966 A 1,2, NZ 1,4
Price, G (Pontypool and Wales) 1977 NZ 1,2,3,4, 1980 SA 1,2,3,4, 1983 NZ 1,2,3,4
Price, M J (Pontypool and Wales) 1959 A 1,2, NZ 1,2,3
Prosser, T R (Pontypool and Wales) 1959 NZ,4
Pullin, J V (Bristol and England) 1968 SA 2,3,4, 1971 NZ 1,2,3,4
Quinnell, D L (Llanelli and *Wales) 1971 NZ. 3, 1977 NZ 2,3, 1980 SA 1,2
Quinnell, L S (Llanelli and Wales) 2001 A 1,2,3
Ralston, C W (Richmond and England) 1974 SA 4
Reed, A I (Bath and Scotland) 1993 NZ 1
Rees, H E (Neath and *Wales) 1977 NZ 4
Rees, M (Llanelli Scarlets and Wales) 2009 SA 1(R),2,3
Reeve, J S R (Harlequins and England) 1930 NZ 1,3,4, A
Regan, M P (Bristol and England) 1997 SA 3
Reid, T E (Garryowen and Ireland) 1955 SA 2,3
Renwick, J M (Hawick and Scotland) 1980 SA 1
Rew, H (Blackheath, Army and England) 1930 NZ 1,2,3,4
Reynolds, F J (Old Cranleighans and England) 1938 SA 1,2
Richards, D (Leicester and England) 1989 A 1,2,3, 1993 NZ 1,2,3
Richards, D S (Swansea and Wales) 1980 SA 1
Richards, M C R (Cardiff and Wales) 1968 SA 1,3,4
Richards, T J (Bristol and Australia) 1910 SA 1,2
Rimmer, G (Waterloo and England) 1950 NZ 3
Ringland, T M (Ballymena and Ireland) 1983 NZ 1
Risman, A B W (Loughborough Colls and England) 1959 A 1,2, NZ 1,4
Ritson, J A S (Northern and *England) 1908 NZ 1
Robbie, J C (Greystones and Ireland) 1980 SA 4
Roberts, J H (Cardiff Blues and Wales) 2009 SA 1,2
Robins, J D (Birkenhead Park and Wales) 1950 NZ 1,2,3, A 1,2
Robins, R J (Pontypridd and Wales) 1955 SA 1,2,3,4
Robinson, J T (Sale and England) 2001 A 1,2,3, 2005 NZ 1,2
Rodber, T A K (Northampton and England) 1997 SA 1,2
Rogers, D P (Bedford and England) 1962 SA 1,4
Rogers, R J (Bath) 1904 NZ
Rotherham, A (Cambridge U and *England) 1891 SA 1,2,3
Rowlands, K A (Cardiff and Wales) 1962 SA 1,2,4
Rowntree, G C (Leicester and England) 2005 Arg, NZ 2(t+R),3(R)
Rutherford, D (Gloucester and England) 1966 A 1
Rutherford, J Y (Selkirk and Scotland) 1983 NZ 3
Saunders, S M (Guy's H) 1904 A 1,2
Savage, K F (Northampton and England) 1968 SA 1,2,3,4
Scotland, K J F (Cambridge U, Heriot's FP and Scotland) 1959 A 1,2, NZ 1,3,4
Scott, W P (West of Scotland and Scotland) 1903 SA 1,2,3
Sealy, J (Dublin U and *Ireland) 1896 SA 1,2,3,4
Sharp, R A W (Oxford U, Redruth and England) 1962 SA 3,4
Shaw, S D (Wasps and England) 2009 SA 2,3
Sheridan, A J (Sale and England) 2009 SA 2(t&R),3
Simpson, C (Cambridge U) 1891 SA 1
Skrimshire, R T (Newport and Wales) 1903 SA 1,2,3
Slattery, J F (Blackrock Coll and Ireland) 1974 SA 1,2,3,4
Slemen, M A C (Liverpool and England) 1980 SA 1
Smith, A R (Edinburgh Wands, London Scottish and Scotland) 1962 SA 1,2,3
Smith, D F (Richmond and England) 1910 SA 1,2,3
Smith, D W C (London Scottish and Scotland) 1950 A 1
Smith, G K (Kelso and Scotland) 1959 A 1,2, NZ 1,3
Smith, I S (Oxford U, London Scottish and Scotland) 1924 SA 1,2
Smith, O J (Leicester and England) 2005 Arg
Smith, T J (Watsonians, Northampton and Scotland) 1997 SA 1,2,3, 2001 A 1,2,3
Smith, T W (Leicester) 1908 NZ 2,3
Smyth, R S (Dublin U and Ireland) 1903 SA 1,2,3
Smyth, T (Malone, Newport and Ireland) 1910 SA 2,3
Sole, D M B (Edinburgh Acads and Scotland) 1989 A 1,2,3
Spong, R S (Old Millhillians and England) 1930 NZ 1,2,3,4, A
Spoors, J A (Bristol) 1910 SA 1,2,3
Squire, J (Newport, Pontypool and Wales) 1977 NZ 4, 1980 SA 1,2,3,4, 1983 NZ 1
Squires, P J (Harrogate and England) 1977 NZ 1
Stagg, P K (Oxford U, Sale and Scotland) 1968 SA 1,3,4
Stanger-Leathes, C F (Northern and *England) 1904 A 1
Steele, W C C (Bedford, RAF and Scotland) 1974 SA 1,2
Stephens, I (Bridgend and Wales) 1983 NZ 1
Stephens, J R G (Neath and Wales) 1950 A 1,2
Stevenson, R C (St Andrew's U and Scotland) 1910 SA 1,2,3
Stimpson, T R G (Newcastle and England) 1997 SA 3(R)
Stout, F M (Gloucester and England) 1899 A 1,2,3,4, 1903 SA 1,2,3
Surtees, A A (Cambridge U) 1891 SA 1,2,3
Swannell, B I (Northampton and *Australia) 1899 A 2,3,4, 1904 A 1,2,3, NZ
Tait, A V (Newcastle and Scotland) 1997 SA 1,2
Tanner, H (Swansea and Wales) 1938 SA 2
Taylor, A R (Cross Keys and Wales) 1938 SA 1,2
Taylor, J (London Welsh and Wales) 1971 NZ 1,2,3,4
Taylor, R B (Northampton and England) 1968 SA 1,2,3,4
Teague, M C (Gloucester, Moseley and England) 1989 A 2,3, 1993 NZ 2(t)
Tedford, A (Malone and Ireland) 1903 SA 1,2,3
Telfer, J W (Melrose and Scotland) 1966 A 1,2, NZ 1,2,4, 1968 SA 2,3,4
Thomas, G (Toulouse and Wales) 2005 NZ 1,2,3
Thomas, M C (Devonport Services, Newport and Wales) 1950 NZ 2,3, A 1, 1959 NZ 1
Thomas, R C C (Swansea and Wales) 1955 SA 3,4
Thomas, W D (Llanelli and *Wales) 1966 NZ 2,3, 1968 SA 3(R),4, 1971 NZ 1,2,4 (R)
Thompson, C E K (Lancashire) 1899 A 2,3,4
Thompson, R (Cambridge U) 1891 SA 1,2,3
Thompson, R H (Instonians, London Irish and Ireland) 1955 SA 1,2,4
Thompson, S G (Northampton and England) 2005 Arg (R), NZ 1(R),2
Timms, A B (Edinburgh U and Scotland) 1899 A 2,3,4
Todd, A F (Blackheath and *England) 1896 SA 1,2,3,4
Townsend, G P J (Northampton and Scotland) 1997 SA 1,2
Trail, D H (Guy's H) 1904 A 1,2,3, NZ
Travers, W H (Newport and Wales) 1938 SA 2,3
Tucker, C C (Shannon and Ireland) 1980 SA 3,4

Turner, J W C (Gala and Scotland) 1968 SA 1,2,3,4
Underwood, R (RAF, Leicester and England) 1989 A 1,2,3, 1993 NZ 1,2,3
Underwood, T (Newcastle and England) 1997 SA 3
Unwin, E J (Rosslyn Park, Army and England) 1938 SA 1,2
Uttley, R M (Gosforth and England) 1974 SA 1,2,3,4
Vassall, H H (Blackheath and England) 1908 NZ 1,2,3
Vickery, P J (Gloucester, Wasps and England) 2001 A 1,2,3, 2009 SA 1,3
Vile, T H (Newport and *Wales) 1904 A 2,3, NZ
Voyce, A T (Gloucester and England) 1924 SA 3,4
Waddell, G H (Cambridge U, London Scottish and Scotland) 1962 SA 1,2
Waddell, H (Glasgow Acads and Scotland) 1924 SA 1,2,4
Wainwright, R I (Watsonians and Scotland) 1997 SA 3
Walker, E F (Lennox) 1903 SA 2,3
Walker, S (Instonians and Ireland) 1938 SA 1,2,3
Wallace, D P (Munster and Ireland) 2009 SA 1,2,3(R)
Wallace, Jos (Wanderers and Ireland) 1903 SA 1,2,3
Wallace, P S (Saracens and Ireland) 1997 SA 1,2,3
Wallace, W (Percy Park) 1924 SA 1
Waller, P D (Newport and Wales) 1910 SA 1,2,3
Ward, A J P (Garryowen and Ireland) 1980 SA 1
Waters, J A (Selkirk and Scotland) 1938 SA 3
Watkins, D (Newport and Wales) 1966 A 1,2, NZ 1,2,3,4
Watkins, S J (Newport and Wales) 1966 A 1,2, NZ 3
Webb, J (Abertillery and Wales) 1910 SA 1,2,3
Welsh, W B (Hawick and Scotland) 1930 NZ 4
Weston, M P (Richmond, Durham City and England) 1962 SA 1,2,3,4, 1966 A 1,2
Wheeler, P J (Leicester and England) 1977 NZ 2,3,4, 1980 SA 1,2,3,4
White, D B (London Scottish and Scotland) 1989 A 1
White, J M (Leicester and England) 2005 Arg (R),NZ 1,2,3
Whitley, H (Northern and *England) 1924 SA 1,3,4
Whittaker, T S (Lancashire) 1891 SA 1,2,3
Wilkinson, J P (Newcastle and England) 2001 A 1,2,3, 2005 Arg, NZ 1,2
Willcox, J G (Oxford U, Harlequins and England) 1962 SA 1,2,4
Williams, B L (Cardiff and Wales) 1950 NZ 2,3,4, A 1,2
Williams, C (Swansea and Wales) 1980 SA 1,2,3,4
Williams, D (Ebbw Vale and Wales) 1966 A 1,2, NZ 1,2,4
Williams, D B (Cardiff and *Wales) 1977 NZ 1,2,3
Williams, J F (London Welsh and Wales) 1908 NZ 3
Williams, J J (Llanelli and Wales) 1974 SA 1,2,3,4, 1977 NZ 1,2,3
Williams, J L (Cardiff and Wales) 1908 NZ 1,2
Williams, J P R (London Welsh and Wales) 1971 NZ 1,2,3,4, 1974 SA 1,2,3,4
Williams, M E (Cardiff Blues and Wales) 2005 NZ 3(R), 2009 SA 1(R),2(R),3
Williams, R H (Llanelli and Wales) 1955 SA 1,2,3,4, 1959 A 1,2, NZ 1,2,3,4
Williams, S H (Newport and *England) 1910 SA 1,2,3
Williams, S M (Ospreys and Wales) 2005 Arg, NZ 2, 2009 SA 2(R),3
Williams, W O G (Swansea and Wales) 1955 SA 1,2,3,4
Willis, W R (Cardiff and Wales) 1950 NZ 4, A 1,2
Wilson, S (London Scottish and Scotland) 1966 A 2, NZ 1,2,3,4
Windsor, R W (Pontypool and Wales) 1974 SA 1,2,3,4, 1977 NZ 1
Winterbottom, P J (Headingley, Harlequins and England) 1983 NZ 1,2,3,4, 1993 NZ, 1,2,3
Wood, B G M (Garryowen and Ireland) 1959 NZ 1,3
Wood, K B (Leicester) 1910 SA 1,3
Wood, K G M (Harlequins and Ireland) 1997 SA 1,2, 2001 A 1,2,3
Woodward, C R (Leicester and England) 1980 SA 2,3
Worsley, J P R (Wasps and England) 2009 SA3
Wotherspoon, W (Cambridge U and Scotland) 1891 SA 1
Young, A T (Cambridge U, Blackheath and England) 1924 SA 2
Young, D (Cardiff and Wales) 1989 A 1,2,3
Young, J (Harrogate, RAF and Wales) 1968 SA 1
Young, J R C (Oxford U, Harlequins and England) 1959 NZ 2
Young, R M (Queen's U, Belfast, Collegians and Ireland) 1966 A 1,2, NZ 1, 1968 SA 3

Cross-Border Tournaments

TOULOUSE CLAIM FOURTH TITLE

By Bruce Reihana

Dave Rogers/Getty Images

Toulouse capture their fourth Heineken Cup in Edinburgh.

I don't think many people could argue that Toulouse were not worthy champions of Europe and although the final against Biarritz wasn't a classic in terms of running rugby, it was right up there in terms of intensity and drama and, I believe, a great advert for the Heineken Cup.

There's no doubt about it, Toulouse are a formidable side and they will be among the favourites for the trophy again in the new season. They were beaten just once throughout the tournament when the Blues narrowly managed to turn them over in Cardiff in round three back in December but that result aside, they were dominant.

They've got plenty of experienced Test players in the ranks but collectively, their defence was superb and that ultimately laid the platform for their success. Out wide they possess a cutting edge with the likes of Vincent Clerc and Yannick Jauzion and in the pack they've got the wise old heads with players like William Servat and Thierry Dusautoir and that kind of personnel gave them a great balance.

Winning the final set Toulouse apart as the only club to lift the Heineken Cup four times and you've got to admire that level of consistency over the last 15 years of the competition. They've also lost two finals and they've got that big-match experience in spades, which is invaluable when you're challenging for trophies at this level.

Overall, I thought the quality of the tournament was really high. I felt the likes of Toulouse, Leinster and hopefully us at Northampton played some good, adventurous stuff and in most of the fixtures I believe there was no shortage of attacking intent. Defences are still incredibly tough to break down when you have the best sides in Europe locking horns, but I felt most sides in the competition were approaching the matches with a positive mindset and a willingness to take a few risks in search of tries.

It was, of course, France's year. The national team were the undisputed top dogs in the Six Nations, winning the Grand Slam and the Top 14 clubs followed suit in the Heineken Cup. They got four teams through to the quarter-finals, they saw off the Irish challenge of Leinster and Munster in the semi-finals and it was the first all-French final since Toulouse beat Stade Français five years ago.

French rugby looks in rude health, doesn't it?

I think there was a degree of soul searching outside France, asking why they were so dominant. Was it the salary cap in the Premiership? Was it the growing exodus of players across the Channel?

Perhaps these were factors but I believe these periods of one country domination come in natural cycles. The Irish provinces were the teams to beat before Toulouse took the crown and they themselves ended a period when English teams won the final four times in five seasons.

Saying that, I've got to admit I was surprised Northampton were the only Premiership team to reach the last eight. It was a fantastic experience for everyone at the club but I wouldn't have predicted we would be the only English representatives in the quarter-finals.

If I had one theory on why the rest of the English clubs struggled, it would be the demands of the Premiership. I can't speak from first-hand experience but I get the impression the teams who compete in the Top

14 and the Magners League are able to give a greater focus to the Heineken Cup while the Premiership sides cannot afford to ease up domestically and that can have a knock on effect when it comes to performing in Europe.

The likes of Gloucester, Leicester and Sale all came pretty close to making the last eight and maybe with a bit more luck it could have been a different story. I'm sure the English teams will come again.

It was also close but no cigar for Edinburgh and Glasgow. The Scotland national team made some big strides forward, so the SRU would surely have been hoping that one of the two regional sides could have claimed an elusive quarter-final place. It didn't happen but with Saints having drawn Edinburgh in the group stages of the Heineken Cup in 2010–11, I'm expecting a couple of tough games.

The Irish fell at the semis but I'm sure they will be a force to be reckoned with again and after two titles for Munster and another for Leinster in the space of four seasons, it was always going to be difficult to sustain such a consistent level of success.

The Ospreys were the only Welsh region to make it through to the knockout stages, only to be beaten in a thriller by Biarritz. Dan Biggar had a chance with a late drop goal to win it for the Ospreys but it wasn't to be and they crashed out. It was the third year in a row they lost at the quarter-final stage and some people argue that with the quality of players they have that's a disappointing return. Personally, I think they're a great team to watch and their time will come if they front up.

For Northampton, it was a rewarding and exciting season and although we were all disappointed to be knocked out, there's no disgrace in losing to Munster at Thomond Park. I've run out at more grounds than I can remember over the years but Thomond Park really is one of the most ferocious but fantastic places to play. The atmosphere really was electric.

We had Munster on the back foot at half-time but were a bit sloppy in our defence after the restart and they punished us. You just can't afford those kind of mistakes in big games like that but we will learn from the experience and hopefully come back stronger and more street wise as a result.

The coaching team of Jim Mallinder, Paul Grayson and Dorian West have got a clear plan for future of the team and keep emphasising how we have to keep taking steps forward together as a squad. I think we achieved that in the Heineken Cup and with the likes of Chris Ashton, Ben Foden and Phil Dowson all maturing, I hope we can make a bigger impact next season.

The debate about the merits of the Heineken Cup and Super 14 never goes away. It's been eight years since I played in the old Super 12 for the Chiefs, so I'm not sure if I'm the best person to make comparisons, but I have to say I prefer to watch the Heineken Cup.

The key issue for me is the interpretation of the breakdown. I found the way the breakdown laws are implemented in Super 14 rugby very frustrating and I believe that a much fairer fight for the ball is allowed in the Heineken Cup.

I also think the Super 14 is lacking a bit of the fluency it was famed for a few years ago while the Heineken Cup has become a quicker product. I'm obviously biased but for me the Heineken Cup produces a more attractive brand of rugby right now.

HEINEKEN CUP 2009–10 RESULTS

ROUND ONE

9 October, 2009

Ulster 26 **Bath** 12

Leinster 9 **London Irish** 12

Leinster 9 **London Irish** 12

10 October, 2009

Blues 20 **Harlequins** 6

Treviso 9 **Perpignan** 8

Stade Français 31 **Edinburgh** 7

Scarlets 24 **Brive** 12

Glasgow 18 **Biarritz** 22

Clermont Auvergne 36 **Viadana** 18

Northampton 31 **Munster** 27

11 October, 2009

Leicester 32 **Ospreys** 32

Toulouse 36 **Sale** 17

ROUND TWO

16 October, 2009

Dragons 22 **Glasgow** 14

Sale 27 **Blues** 26

Perpignan 29 **Northampton** 13

17 October, 2009

Munster 41 **Treviso** 10

Viadana 11 **Leicester** 46

Biarritz 42 **Gloucester** 15

London Irish 25 **Scarlets** 27

Edinburgh 17 **Ulster** 13

Brive 13 **Leinster** 36

Harlequins 19 **Toulouse** 23

18 October, 2008

Ospreys 25 **Clermont Auvergne** 24

Bath 27 **Stade Français** 29

ROUND THREE

11 December, 2009	
Glasgow 33 **Gloucester** 11	**Munster** 24 **Perpignan** 23
12 December, 2009	
Ulster 23 **Stade Français** 13	**Blues** 15 **Toulouse** 9
Viadana 7 **Ospreys** 62	**Scarlets** 7 **Leinster** 32
Northampton 30 **Treviso** 18	**Brive** 3 **London Irish** 36
13 December, 2008	
Harlequins 19 **Sale** 29	**Bath** 16 **Edinburgh** 9
Biarritz 49 **Dragons** 13	**Clermont Auvergne** 40-30 **Leicester**

ROUND FOUR

19 December, 2009	
Edinburgh 9 **Bath** 6	**London Irish** 34 **Brive** 13
Dragons 8 **Biarritz** 26	**Treviso** 18 **Northampton** 21
Ospreys 45 **Viadana** 19	**Leinster** 39 **Scarlets** 7
Toulouse 23 **Blues** 7	**Leicester** 20 **Clermont Auvergne** 15
20 December, 2009	
Gloucester 19 **Glasgow** 6	**Stade Français** 29 **Ulster** 16
Sale 21 **Harlequins** 17	**Perpignan** 14 **Munster** 37

ROUND FIVE

15 January, 2010	
Glasgow 29 **Dragons** 25	**Ulster** 21 **Edinburgh** 13
16 January, 2010	
Leicester 47 **Viadana** 8	**Blues** 36 **Sale** 19
Treviso 7 **Munster** 44	**Clermont Auvergne** 27 **Ospreys** 7
Stade Français 15 **Bath** 13	**Leinster** 27 **Brive** 10
Gloucester 23 **Biarritz** 8	
17 January, 2010	
Scarlets 31 **London Irish** 22	**Toulouse** 33 **Harlequins** 21
Northampton 34 **Perpignan** 0	

ROUND SIX

22 January, 2010	
Munster 12 **Northampton** 9	**Perpignan** 34 **Treviso** 6
23 January, 2010	
Ospreys 17 **Leicester** 12	**Edinburgh** 9 **Stade Français** 7
Viadana 20 **Clermont Auvergne** 59	**London Irish** 11 **Leinster** 11
Bath 10 **Ulster** 28	**Brive** 17 **Scarlets** 20
24 January, 2009	
Dragons 23 **Gloucester** 32	**Harlequins** 20 **Blues** 45
Biarritz 41 **Glasgow** 20	**Sale** 13 **Toulouse** 19

GROUP TABLES

POOL ONE

	P	W	D	L	F	A	BP	PTS
Munster	6	5	0	1	185	94	4	24
Northampton	6	4	0	2	138	104	3	19
Perpignan	6	2	0	4	108	123	3	11
Treviso	6	1	0	5	68	178	1	5

POOL FOUR

	P	W	D	L	F	A	BP	PTS
Stade Français	6	4	0	2	124	95	2	18
Ulster	6	4	0	2	127	94	1	17
Edinburgh	6	3	0	3	64	94	1	13
Bath	6	1	0	5	84	116	3	7

POOL TWO

	P	W	D	L	F	A	BP	PTS
Biarritz	6	5	0	1	188	97	3	23
Gloucester	6	4	0	2	119	129	1	17
Glasgow	6	2	0	4	120	140	1	9
Dragons	6	1	0	5	108	169	2	6

POOL FIVE

	P	W	D	L	F	A	BP	PTS
Toulouse	6	5	0	1	143	92	3	23
Blues	6	4	0	2	149	104	2	18
Sale	6	3	0	3	126	153	2	14
Harlequins	6	0	0	6	102	171	2	2

POOL THREE

	P	W	D	L	F	A	BP	PTS
Clermont	6	4	0	2	201	120	5	21
Ospreys	6	4	1	1	188	121	2	20
Leicester	6	3	1	2	187	123	4	18
Viadana	6	0	0	6	83	295	0	0

POOL SIX

	P	W	D	L	F	A	BP	PTS
Leinster	6	4	1	1	154	60	4	22
Scarlets	6	4	0	2	116	147	1	17
London Irish	6	3	1	2	140	94	3	17
Brive	6	0	0	6	68	177	1	1

QUARTER-FINALS

9 April, 2010	
Leinster 29 **Clermont Auvergne** 28	
10 April, 2010	
Biarritz 29 **Ospreys** 28	**Munster** 33 **Northampton** 19
11 April, 2010	
Toulouse 42 **Stade Français** 16	

SEMI-FINALS

1 May 2010, Stade Ernest Wallon, Toulouse

TOULOUSE 26 (2G, 4PG)
LEINSTER 16 (1G, 3PG)

TOULOUSE: C Poitrenaud; V Clerc, F Fritz, Y Jauzion, C Heymans; D Skrela, B Kelleher; D Human, W Servat, B Lecouls, R Millo-Chluski, P Albacete, J Bouilhou, T Dusautoir (captain), S Sowerby. *Substitutions:* M Medard for Heymans (41 mins); J-B Poux for Lecouls (43 mins); Y Montes for Human (71 mins); L Picamoles for Millo-Chluski (72 mins); J-B Elissalde for Skrela (73 mins); V Lacombe for Servat (74 mins).

SCORERS: *Tries:* Jauzion, Skrela *Conversions:* Skrela (2) *Penalty Goals:* Skrela (4)

LEINSTER: R Kearney; S Horgan, B O'Driscoll, G D'Arcy, I Nacewa; S Berne, E Reddan; C Healy, J Fogarty, S Wright, L Cullen (captain), N Hines, K McLaughlin, S Jennings, J Heaslip. *Substitutions:* CJ Van der Linde for Healy (30 mins); S Keogh for Jennings (51 mins); Healy for Wright (56 mins); M O'Kelly for McLaughlin (66 mins).

SCORERS: *Try:* Heaslip *Conversion:* Berne *Penalty Goals:* Berne (2), Kearney

REFEREE: N Owens (Wales)

2 May 2010, Estadio Anoeta, San Sebastian

BIARRITZ (6PG) 18 MUNSTER 7 (1G)

BIARRITZ: I Balshaw; T Ngwenya, A Mignardi, A Erinle, J-B Gobelet; K Hunt, D Yachvili; E Coetzee, B August, C Johnstone, J Thion (captain), T Hall, M Lund, W Lauret, I Harinordoquy. *Substitutions:* M Carizza for Hall (temp, 2-5 mins); J Peyrelongue for Erinle (47 mins); F Barcella for Coetzee (61 mins); F Faure for Harinordoquy (68 mins); Carizza for Hall (70 mins); P Bidabe for Gobelet (82 mins).

SCORERS: *Penalty Goals:* Yachvili (6)

MUNSTER: P Warwick; D Hurley, K Earls, J De Villiers, L Mafi; R O'Gara (captain), T O'Leary; M Horan, J Flannery, J Hayes, D O'Callaghan, M O'Driscoll, A Quinlan, D Wallace, J Coughlan. *Substitutions:* A Buckley for Hayes (58 mins); N Williams for Coughlan (64 mins); J Brugnaut for Horan (76 mins); N Ronan for Quinlan (77 mins); P Stringer for O'Leary (79 mins); S Deasy for Hurley (81 mins); T Gleeson for Warwick (83 mins); D Varley for Flannery (83 mins).

SCORERS: *Try:* Earls *Conversion:* O'Gara

REFEREE: D Pearson (England)

FINAL

22 May 2010, Stade de France, Paris

BIARRITZ 19 (1G, 4PG) TOULOUSE 21 (4PG, 3DG)

BIARRITZ: I Balshaw; T Ngwenya, K Hunt, A Mignardi, J-B Gobelet; J Peyrelongue, D Yachvili; E Coetzee, B August, C Johnstone, J Thion (captain), T Hall, M Lund, W Lauret, I Harinordoquy. *Substitutions:* F Barcella for Coetzee (50 mins); P Bidade for Gobelet (60 mins); M Carizza for Hall (61 mins); F Faure for Lauret (61 mins); R Terrain for August (71 mins); V Courrent for Yachvili (74 mins).

SCORERS: *Try:* Hunt *Conversion:* Courrent *Penalty Goals:* Yachvili (4)

TOULOUSE: C Poitrenaud; V Clerc, F Fritz, Y Jauzion, M Medard; D Skrela, B Kelleher; J-B Poux, W Servat, B Lecouls, R Millo-Chluski, P Albacete, J Bouilhou, T Dusautoir (captain), S Sowerby. *Substitutions:* Y Maestri for Millo-Chluski (59 mins); D Human for Poux (63 mins); C Johnston for Lecouls (66 mins); C Heymans for Poitrenaud (71 mins); Y David for Fritz (75 mins); L Picamoles for Sowerby (75 mins); Vernet Basualdo for Servat (76 mins).

SCORERS: *Penalty Goals:* Skrela (3) Fritz *Drop Goals:* Skrela (2), Fritz

YELLOW CARD: Albacete (51 mins)

REFEREE: W Barnes (England)

BLUES END WALES' DROUGHT

By Iain Spragg

Cardiff Blues won a pulsating Amin Challenge Cup final against Toulon.

It had been a long, arduous and at times heartbreaking wait but after a decade-and-a-half of Welsh sweat and tears, Cardiff Blues finally drew a line under the Principality's failure to win a European club trophy with a superb 28–21 victory over Toulon in Marseille in the final of the Amlin Challenge Cup.

Ironically, the team only found themselves in the second tier competition after the ERC ruled that the three runners-up in the Heineken Cup that failed to reach the quarter-finals would be parachuted into the knockout stages of the Challenge Cup but no-one at the Blues, or probably throughout Wales, was perturbed by their circuitous route to glory.

There of course had been near misses for Welsh sides in the past. The 'old' Cardiff had made it to the final of the inaugural Heineken Cup in 1996 only to fall to Biarritz in extra-time. And in 2002, Pontypridd were finalists in the Challenge Cup but were ambushed by the Sale Sharks and a year later Caerphilly reached the final of the briefly-mourned European Shield competition but were comfortably outgunned by Castres.

This time however there was to be no valiant failure. Toulon may have raced into a 13–6 lead at half-time in the vociferous surroundings of the Stade Vélodrome but the Blues were not to be denied their moment of history and tries from Jamie Roberts, Leigh Halfpenny and Bradley Davies after the break, coupled with some resolute tackling in the closing minutes, ensured a Welsh club finally got its name on the European honours' board.

"It's great for everyone involved, the players, the coaches and the travelling fans as well," said Roberts after the final whistle. "It was really outstanding. The final whistle was my abiding memory. They tried to run it out of defence, Chris [Czekaj] ripped the ball off their player and that feeling when Richie [Rees] kicked it out, was absolutely incredible. It's definitely a notch up from the EDF Cup win last year and hopefully we can build on this next year."

"I think that ten minute spell of defence at the end won us the game. It was incredible and everyone really put their bodies on the line and kept them out. I know we leaked a try at the end, but that ten minutes won us the game. I didn't touch a ball in the first half. We struggled a bit in the line-out and we couldn't get any platform, but managed to get hold of the ball in the second half and it was great to score a try."

The group stages of the tournament saw Wasps, Newcastle, Toulon and Bourgoin top their groups with five wins from their six pool games but Irish province Connacht were undoubtedly the most impressive side to qualify, reaching the quarter-finals unbeaten and ensuring home advantage in the last four.

The five were joined by the Blues, Scarlets and Gloucester and the quarter-finals games were underway.

The first saw Connacht maintain their impressive form with a 23–20 win over Bourgoin in Galway courtesy of three late penalties from substitute Miah Nikora while later the same day Toulon stormed into the last four with a five-try, 38–12 demolition of Scarlets.

The following day Wasps made mincemeat of Premiership rivals Gloucester in a one-sided contest, thanks largely to a Tom Varndell hat-trick, but their 42–26 victory was comfortably eclipsed by the Blues 55–20 destruction away to Newcastle.

The semi-finals were staged three weeks later and the first saw Toulon travel to Ireland to face Connacht. The home side made the more positive start to proceedings but a Mafileo Kefu try just before half-time and 14 points from Jonny Wilkinson were decisive and the French side emerged 19–12 winners despite a spirited late rally from their Magners League opponents.

"It was a really tough match," admitted Toulon No 8 and Man-of-the-Match Juan Martin Fernandez Lobbe. "Connacht played a great game with great defence and managed to ruin our line-out, which made it hard for us to get ball there. We are just glad we managed to hold them at the end and get the win. It will be lovely to play the final in Marseille."

Cardiff were the visitors to Adams Park for the second semi-final and

Dave Rogers/Getty Images

Not even Jonny Wilkinson could stop Toulon falling at the final hurdle.

the reward of facing Toulon in the final and the two sides produced a gripping contest that was not settled until the final whistle.

The first-half set the tone with three penalties from Dave Walder for the home side to a Halfpenny try and a penalty to the visitors and as both sides emerged for the second period, Wasps were clinging onto a precarious 9–8 lead. The turning point came when prop Gethin Jenkins charged over for a second try for the Welshmen and although Walder landed a fifth penalty to reduce the arrears to 18–15, he missed with one late, last chance to take the game into extra-time and Cardiff had ended Wasps' 16-match unbeaten run at home in Europe.

"Credit to the Blues, we gave them a couple of soft penalties but they took their chances and a try count of 2–0 suggests they probably deserved to win," conceded Wasps director of rugby Tony Hanks. "Their senior players really stepped up."

"I thought we were quite controlled and played smart in the first half. But we just didn't have enough of the ball and lacked field position to launch any meaningful attacks. We were desperate to make the final and it is a pretty empty feeling right now. We have got to make sure we learn from this."

Toulon had national if not exactly home advantage as they and Cardiff decamped to the south of France and Marseille for the final and although Blues supporters were outnumbered by their counterparts, hopes remained high of a famous day for Welsh rugby.

The two teams traded a couple of penalties apiece in the opening half hour but the first big moment came four minutes before the break when Kiwi centre Sonny Bill Williams beat three Cardiff defenders for the first try of the match, which was converted by Wilkinson.

The Blues now had their backs firmly to the wall as they retreated to the dressing room but were on level terms ten minutes after the restart when Roberts danced over from close range following a menacing attack and the match suddenly began to swing in their favour.

Fifteen minutes later the 'away' side had their second try after a delicate overhead pass from back rower Xavier Rush gave Halfpenny just enough room to touch down in the corner and the fightback was in full swing.

Strains of 'Bread of Heaven' began echoing around the Stade Vélodrome and Cardiff responded with a third try as lock Davies utilised all his bulk and power to charge over from short range and with a successful conversion from full-back Ben Blair, they were 12 points to the good.

Toulon had just ten minutes to rescue themselves and score the two converted tries that would have secured victory but despite intense pressure, they could only muster an unconverted try from substitute Thomas Sourice.

Cardiff had joined the exclusive list of European champions and for the first time since club rugby went continental in the 1990s, Wales could boast a winning team.

"It must have been a great game to watch, in the first half we were hanging in by our toenails," Blues coach Dai Young said. "But we showed guts and determination and when we had the chances we struck. We had confidence in our own ability and knew if we got enough ball in the right areas and went through the phases, the opportunities would come.

"The attitude was excellent and we could have chucked the towel in at some stages. It is another sign of how far we're moving forward as a region. I'm really pleased for all the players, they put the work in and they deserve all the plaudits and we're really going to enjoy tonight."

Getty Images

Connacht staged a sensational cup campaign, losing to Toulon in a compelling semi-final.

EUROPEAN CHALLENGE CUP 2009–10 RESULTS

ROUND ONE	
8 October, 2009	
Worcester 17 **Montpellier** 22	
9 October	
Castres 17 **Toulon** 33	**Albi** 7 **Montauban** 17
Bayonne 61 **Roma** 3	**Connacht** 46 **Olympus** 6
Bourgoin 29 **Leeds** 19	
10 October	
Bucharest 21 **Parma** 9	**Padova** 27 **Newcastle** 29
11 October	
Wasps 18 **Racing** 13	**Saracens** 36 **Rovigo** 12
ROUND TWO	
15 October	
Toulon 31 **Saracens** 23	
16 October	
Montpellier 19 **Connacht** 22	**Montauban** 27 **Padova** 10
17 October	
Bucharest 19 **Bourgoin** 21	**Olympus** 5 **Worcester** 38
Rovigo 11 **Castres** 76	**Racing** 16 **Bayonne** 20
Roma 0 **Wasps** 57	
18 October	
Leeds 37 **Parma** 13	**Newcastle** 45 **Albi** 3
ROUND THREE	
10 December	
Newcastle 17 **Montauban** 6	
11 December	
Castres 9 **Saracens** 2	**Montpellier** 57 **Olympus** 24
Toulon 73 **Rovigo** 3	
12 December	
Bucharest 6 **Leeds** 10	**Wasps** 22 **Bayonne** 18
Parma 14 **Bourgoin** 9	**Worcester** 21 **Connacht** 26
Padova 16 **Albi** 35	**Racing** 62 **Roma** 0
ROUND FOUR	
17 December	
Bayonne 3 **Wasps** 12	**Bourgoin** 31 **Parma** 10

18 December

Connacht 19 **Worcester** 9

Montauban 24 **Newcastle** 19

19 December

Roma 3 **Racing** 53

Saracens 18 **Castres** 14

Olympus 6 **Montpellier** 42

20 December

Albi 38 **Padova** 16

Leeds 47 **Bucharest** 0

Rovigo 7 **Toulon** 30

ROUND FIVE

14 January, 2010

Bourgoin 33 **Bucharest** 15

Wasps 50 **Roma** 16

Saracens 28 **Toulon** 9

15 January

Castres 47 **Rovigo** 0

Albi 14 **Newcastle** 16

Connacht 20 **Montpellier** 10

16 January

Parma 16 **Leeds** 38

Worcester 54 **Olympus** 3

Padova 23 **Montauban** 31

Bayonne 27 **Racing** 14

ROUND SIX

21 January

Racing 19 **Wasps** 17

22 January

Montauban 27 **Albi** 20

Newcastle 20 **Padova** 3

Montpellier 8 **Worcester** 3

23 January

Parma 16 **Bucharest** 9

Olympus 0 **Connacht** 66

Roma 6 **Bayonne** 55

Toulon 30 **Castres** 5

Rovigo 8 **Saracens** 56

24 January

Leeds 9 **Bourgoin** 18

GROUP TABLES

POOL ONE

	P	W	D	L	F	A	BP	PTS
Bourgoin	6	5	0	1	141	86	3	23
Leeds	6	4	0	2	160	82	3	19
Parma	6	2	0	4	78	145	0	8
Bucharest	6	1	0	5	70	136	3	7

POOL TWO

	P	W	D	L	F	A	BP	PTS
Connacht	6	6	0	0	199	63	2	26
Montpellier	6	4	0	2	158	92	3	19
Worcester	6	2	0	4	140	83	5	13
Madrid	6	0	0	6	44	303	0	0

POOL THREE

	P	W	D	L	F	A	BP	PTS
Toulon	6	5	0	1	218	88	3	23
Saracens	6	5	0	1	184	83	2	22
Castres	6	2	0	4	173	127	3	11
Rovigo	6	0	0	6	41	318	0	0

POOL FOUR

	P	W	D	L	F	A	BP	PTS
Wasps	6	5	0	1	176	69	3	23
Bayonne	6	4	0	2	184	73	3	19
Racing	6	3	0	3	177	85	4	16
Roma	6	0	0	6	28	338	0	0

POOL FIVE

	P	W	D	L	F	A	BP	PTS
Newcastle	6	5	0	1	146	77	3	23
Montauban	6	5	0	1	132	96	1	21
Albi	6	2	0	4	117	137	4	12
Petrarca	6	0	0	6	95	180	1	1

Getty Images

London Wasps racked up 23 points in the pool stages but lost in the semis.

QUARTER-FINALS

10 April	
Connacht 23 **Bourgoin** 20	**Toulon** 38 **Scarlets** 12
11 April	
Wasps 42 **Gloucester** 26	**Newcastle** 20 **Cardiff** 55

SEMI-FINALS

30 April, Sportsground, Galway

CONNACHT 12 (4PG)
TOULON 19 (1G, 3PG, 1DG)

CONNACHT: G Duffy; T Nathan, N Ta'auso, A Wynne, F Carr; I Keatley, F Murphy; B Wilkinson, S Cronin, J Hagan, M Swift, M McCarthy, J Muldoon (captain), J O'Connor, G Naoupu

SUBSTITUTIONS: B Tuohy for Nathan (19 mins); R Morris for Hagan (40 mins); R Loughney for Wilkinson (48 mins); M Nikora for Keatley (54 mins); M McComish for McCarthy (58 mins); B Upton for Swift (59 mins); C O'Loughlin for Murphy (69 mins)

SCORERS *Penalty Goals*: Keatley (4)

TOULON: L Rooney; G Lovobalavu, M Kefu, T May, C Marienval; J Wilkinson, M Henjak (captain); S Taumoepeau, P Fitzgerald, T Leaaetoa, J Suta, E Lozada, J van Niekerk, T Sourice, J Fernandez Lobbe

SUBSTITUTIONS: S Bruno for Fitzgerald (54 mins); O Missoup for Sourice (54 mins); S Williams for Wilkinson (58 mins); B Basteres for Taumoepeau (59 mins); T Ryan for Leaaetoa (64 mins); K Chesney for Lozada (64 mins); P Mignoni for Henjak (68 mins); F Auelua for Fernandez Lobbe (79 mins)

SCORERS *Try*: Kefu *Conversion*: Wilkinson *Penalty Goals*: Wilkinson (3) *Drop Goal*: Wilkinson

REFEREE W Barnes (England)

1 May, Adams Park, Wycombe

WASPS 15 (5PG) CARDIFF 18 (1G, 2PG, 1T)

WASPS: M Van Gisbergen; P Sackey, B Jacobs, D Waldouck, D Lemi; D Walder, J Simpson; T Payne, R Webber, P Vickery, S Shaw, G Skivington, J Worsley, T Rees (captain), D Ward–Smith

SUBSTITUTIONS: T Lindsay for Webber (temp 36–41 mins); Z Taulafo for Payne (48 mins); S Betsen for Rees (60 mins); D Cirpiani for Van Gisbergen (70 mins)

SCORERS *Penalty Goals*: Walder (5)

CARDIFF: B Blair; L Halfpenny, C Laulala, J Roberts, C Czekaj; C Sweeney, D Allinson; G Jenkins, T Rhys Thomas, T Filise, D Jones, P Tito (captain), M Molitika, M Williams, X Rush

SUBSTITUTIONS: B Davies for Tito (54 mins); S Andrews for Filise (54 mins); G Williams for Rhys Thomas (78 mins)

SCORERS *Tries*: Halfpenny, Jenkins *Conversion*: Blair *Penalty Goals*: Blair (2)

YELLOW CARDS Shaw (54 mins), Andrews (73 mins)

REFEREE R Poite (France)

FINAL

23 May, Stade Vélodrome, Marseille

TOULON 21 (1G, 3PG, 1T)
CARDIFF 28 (2G, 3PG, 1T)

TOULON: C Marienval; G Lovobalavu, T May, S Williams, J Sinzelle; J Wilkinson, M Henjak; S Taumoepeau, P Fitzgerald, D Kubriashvili, E Lozada, R Skeate, J van Niekerk (captain), F Auelua, J Fernandez Lobbe

SUBSTITUTIONS: S Bruno for Fitzgerald (temp 34 to 40 mins); T Ryan for Kubriashvili (40 mins); M Kefu for Wilkinson (46 mins); J Suta for Lozada (51 mins); P Mignoni for Henjak (56 mins); L Emmanuelli for Taumoepeau (56 mins); Bruno for Fitzgerald (56 mins); T Sourice for Auelua (65 mins); T Umaga for Sinzelle (67 mins)

SCORERS *Tries*: Williams, Sourice *Conversion*: Wilkinson *Penalty Goals*: Wilkinson (2) May

CARDIFF BLUES: B Blair; L Halfpenny, C Laulala, J Roberts, C Czekaj; C Sweeney, R Rees; G Jenkins (captain), R Thomas, T Filise, D Jones, B Davies, M Molitika, X Rush, M Williams

SUBSTITUTIONS: J Yapp for Jenkins (40 mins); G Williams for Thomas (45 mins); P Tito for Jones (50 mins); S Andrews for Filise (56 mins); S Warburton for Molitika (60 mins); D Hewitt for Laulala (78 mins)

SCORERS *Tries*: Roberts, Halfpenny, B Davies *Conversions*: Blair (2) *Penalty Goals*: Blair (3)

REFEREE A Rolland (Ireland)

SAXONS RECLAIM CROWN

By Iain Spragg

Mike Stobe/Getty Images

England Saxons are delighted to get their hands back on the Churchill Cup.

England's second string travelled to America for the eighth instalment of the Churchill Cup shorn, as ever, of some 44 players who were otherwise engaged on the senior team's summer tour of Australia and New Zealand but they still proved too strong for all opponents in the States as they emphatically won back their status as the tournament's top dogs.

The Saxons had been deposed as champions 12 months earlier when they were comprehensively outplayed by Ireland A in a heavy 49–22 defeat in Denver but they returned to winning ways a year later as they overcame a stubborn Canada side 38–18 in the final at the Red Bull Stadium in New Jersey.

For England it was a record fifth Cup triumph in eight years and after winning the inaugural competition in 2003 under the guise of England A, beating the USA in the final in Vancouver, it was also a personal triumph for Saxons coach Stuart Lancaster, who once again had limited time to mould his makeshift squad into a cohesive, winning unit.

"It's a fantastic achievement," said Lancaster after the final. "Three weeks ago we met in a Heathrow hotel with disappointed players who had not made the senior tour and young players who came in straight from the Premiership and collectively to put all that together and form a team is great, I'm really proud.

"I'd like to think that the players have enjoyed it. They're working with different players and different coaches and learning different ways to play. That's what international rugby is all about, we want to make sure these players have enough room to grow and develop so when they make the step to the senior stage they're ready."

The group phase of the tournament produced just one perceived surprise result as Canada beat France A 33–27 in Pool B but other than the Canucks' morale-boosting victory, the games went as expected and England duly faced Canada in the Cup final, while hosts America played Les Bleus' second string in the Plate final and Russia and Uruguay contested the Bowl match.

The Cup clash saw the Saxons impose themselves on Canada in the early stages and they were rewarded for their initial dominance with tries from Nick Abendanon and Alex Goode, both of which were converted by fly-half Stephen Myler.

The well-drilled Canucks however refused to buckle under the pressure and hauled themselves back into contention with tries from Matt Evans and Chauncey O'Toole to make it a real contest. England knew they had a game on their hands but ultimately their big-match experience told and second-half scores from John Clarke and Luke Narraway sealed what may have appeared a comfortable 38–18 win but had in reality been a testing examination of the Saxons' credentials.

"This is my third Churchill Cup campaign and my first win," back rower Narraway said after the final. "Last year against Ireland we had a talented squad but something obviously didn't work. Full credit to the lads, they have worked hard and we played some exciting football and it was a great to be a part of. We took the foot off the pedal but all credit to Canada, they are a really good side. They came back at us but we had enough talent and energy in the tank to win the game."

The Plate final presented France A with the opportunity to put the disappointment of failing to reach the Cup game behind them but they were made to work extremely hard by the USA for their eventual 24–10 victory.

The French drew first blood with a try inside the first 10 minutes from wing Julien Arias but the home crowd were cheering vociferously when second row Scott Lavalla crashed over on the half-hour mark to level the scores at 7–7, rounding off a superb counter attack by the Eagles.

Prop Jacques Forestier rumbled over for France's second try just before the break but the second half was so keenly fought that a solitary penalty apiece were the only scores until late on when Arias delivered the coup de grace with his second try.

"It was not a pretty match but very tough," admitted France team manager Fabien Pelous. "We are happy to have played in this tournament and although we would have liked to play in the big final, at least we have something to show from the competition."

For hosts America, defeat was a disappointment but coach Eddie O'Sullivan was determined to remain upbeat.

"The scoreline is a bit harsh when compared to how close this match was," he said. "I'm very proud of this whole team and how they fought until the end. Playing a team of this calibre is a big challenge and their level of play was definitely lifted to the next level. They made France fight for everything and I'm happy with the heart they showed today."

Both Russia and Uruguay went into the Bowl final looking for their first wins of the tournament but the match was effectively decided in the opening 13 minutes as the Bears launched a devastating opening salvo that stunned their South American opponents.

Russian wing Vasily Artemyev scored the game's opening try but it was the two tries from flanker Victor Gresev that really did the damage as he ripped through gaping holes in the Uruguayan defence and with little more than ten minutes on the clock, the Bears were 19 points clear.

The Teros replied with a try from full-back Ivo Dugonjic but Russia underlined their superiority moments before half-time when centre Alexey Makovetskiy stormed over and as the two teams headed for the dressing room, the Bears had established a 26–5 lead.

The second period followed a similar pattern to the first and any thoughts of a Uruguay comeback were quickly dispelled when Bears scrum-half Alexander Yanyushkin scampered over a minute after the restart.

To their credit, the Teros finished the match strongly, outscoring the Russians two tries to one in the closing 20 minutes, but the damage had already been done and the Bears were 38–19 victors.

"We have come a long way in 18 months but the goal setting is going well and over the next 18, as we head towards the World Cup, we will get better," said Steve Diamond, the Russian director of rugby. "The Churchill Cup has been great. The Russians have had a big eye opener about how to prepare for a top competition. It's good to play at the highest level and they have learnt that they need to prepare fully for each game."

CHURCHILL CUP 2010 RESULTS

GROUP PHASE

5 June, Infinity Park, Colorado	
Canada 48	**Uruguay** 6
USA 39	**Russia** 22
9 June, Infinity Park, Colorado	
England Saxons 49	**Russia** 17
10 June, Infinity Park, Colorado	
France A 43	**Uruguay** 10
13 June, Infinity Park, Colorado	
USA 9	**England Saxons** 32
Canada 33	**France A** 27

GROUP TABLES

POOL A

	P	W	D	L	F	A	BP	Pts
Canada	2	2	0	0	81	33	1	**9**
France A	2	1	0	1	70	43	2	**6**
Uruguay	2	0	0	2	16	91	0	**0**

POOL B

	P	W	D	L	F	A	BP	Pts
England Saxons	2	2	0	0	81	26	2	**10**
USA	2	1	0	1	48	54	1	**5**
Russia	2	0	0	2	39	88	0	**0**

CHURCHILL CUP FINAL

19 June, Red Bull Arena, New Jersey

ENGLAND SAXONS 38 (3G, 4PG, 1T) CANADA 18 (1PG, 3T)

ENGLAND SAXONS: A Goode; J Simpson–Daniel, J Clarke, A Allen, N Abendanon; S Myler, L Dickson; N Wood, A Titterrell, A Corbiserio, J Hudson, G Skivington (captain), T Wood, A Saull, L Narraway

SUBSTITUTIONS: G Kitchener for Hudson (47 mins); K Myall for Wood (57 mins); Corbiserio for Wood (59 mins); D Bell for Corbisiero (60 mins); M Young for Dickson (62 mins); T Varndell for Simpson–Daniel (62 mins); R Vickers for Titterrell (66 mins); O Smith for Clarke (66 mins)

SCORERS *Tries*: Abendanon, Goode, Clarke, Narraway *Conversions*: Myler (3) *Penalty Goals*: Myler (4)

CANADA: J Pritchard; C Hearn, DTH van der Merwe, P Mackenzie, J Mensah–Coker; M Evans, S White; D Wooldridge, P Riordan (captain), A Tiedemann, L Tait, B Erichsen, C O'Toole, A Kleeberger, A Carpenter

SUBSTITUTIONS: T Hotson for Erichsen (47 mins); R Smith for Pritchard (47 mins); N Dala for Carpenter (49 mins); J Marshall for Wooldridge (53 mins), R Hamilton for Riordan (57 mins); Erichsen for Kleeberger (69 mins); E Wilson for White (69 mins); C Braid for Evans (72 mins)

SCORERS *Tries*: Evans, O'Toole, Smith *Penalty Goal*: Hearn

REFEREE J Garces (France)

CHURCHILL CUP PLATE FINAL

19 June, Red Bull Arena, New Jersey

USA 10 (1G, 1PG) FRANCE A 24 (3G, 1PG)

USA: C Wyles; T Ngwenya, A Tuilevuka, J Sifa, P Emerick; N Malifa, M Petri; M Moeakiola, P Thiel, S Pittman, J Van Der Giessen (captain), S Lavalla, L Stanfill, JJ Gagiano, N Johnson

SUBSTITUTIONS: A Suniula for Sifa (53 mins); T Purpura for Moeakiola (59 mins); T Usasz for Petri (59 mins); P Danahy for Johnson (59 mins); C Biller for Thiel (65 mins); D LaPrevotte for Gagiano (70 mins); V Rouse for Tuilevuka (79 mins)

SCORERS *Try*: Lavalla *Conversion*: Malifa *Penalty Goal*: Malifa

FRANCE A: M Medard; Y Audrin, H Chavancy, R Cabannes, J Arias; L Beauxis, J Dupuy; Y Forestier, B Kayser (captain), R Slimani, Y Maestri, G Villececa, JP Perez, S Nicolas, A Battut

SUBSTITUTIONS: J Schuster for Slimani (44 mins); J Wisniewski for Medard (55 mins); F Cazenave for Dupuy (55 mins); JP Genevois for Kayser (64 mins); J Suta for Maestri (71 mins); F Faure for Battut (71 mins); S for Forestier (71 mins); A Plante for Audrin (75 mins)

SCORERS *Tries*: Arias (2), Forestier *Conversions*: Beauxis (3) *Penalty Goal* Beauxis

REFEREE C Pollock (New Zealand)

CHURCHILL CUP BOWL FINAL

19 June, Red Bull Arena, New Jersey

RUSSIA 38 (4G, 2T) URUGUAY 19 (2G, 1T)

RUSSIA: I Klyuchnikov; I Kuzin, M Babaev, A Makovetskiy, V Artemyev; Y Kushnarev, A Yanyushkin; S Popov, V Korshunov (captain), A Travkin, A Voytov, A Fatakhov, V Gresev, K Kushnarev, N Medkov

SUBSTITUTIONS: A Khrokin for Travkin (47 mins); A Korobeynikov for Klyuchnikov (64 mins); A Shakirov for Yanyushkin (66 mins); V Botvinnikov for Popov (66 mins); S Sergeev for Kushnarev (66 mins); E Matveev for Korshunov (78 mins); S Trishin for Makovetskiy (79 mins)

SCORERS *Tries*: Artemyev, Gresev (2), Makovetskiy, Yanyushkin, Medkov

CONVERSIONS: Kushnarev (4)

URUGUAY: I Dugonjic; L Leivas, JM Llovet, J De Freitas, G Mieres; E Caffera, M Martinez; A Corral, C Arboleya (captain), P Lemoine , JP Horta, D Magno, S Deicas, I Grignola, M Fonseca

SUBSTITUTIONS: M Braun for Deicas (21 mins); N Morales for Caffera (43 mins); JP Rombys for Lemoine (46 mins); N Martinez for Mieres (66 mins); JP Ruffalini for Corral (66 mins); N Badano for Magno (79 mins)

SCORERS *Tries*: Dugonjic, M Martinez, N Martinez *Conversions*: J De Freitas, Morales

REFEREE C Damasco (Italy)

Mike Stobe/Getty Images

Russia were welcome guests at the Churchill Cup, here celebrating their Bowl win.

CROSS-BORDER TOURNAMENTS

SAINTS BREAK DOMESTIC DUCK

By Iain Spragg

Getty Images

Northampton Saints put their names on a new trophy, the LV= Cup.

Northampton finally added a piece of major domestic silverware to the Franklin's Gardens trophy cabinet after beating Gloucester in a high-scoring and hugely entertaining LV= Cup final, giving the club's coaching team of Jim Mallinder and Dorian West their third knockout tournament triumph in little more than two years.

The Saints failed to win a single significant competition during the game's long gone amateur era but since the advent of professionalism, the team famously lifted the Heineken Cup in 2000. In 2008, they completed a National League One and National Trophy double following the disappointment of relegation from the Premiership and 12 months on they were again celebrating after winning the European Challenge Cup final.

A big domestic trophy however had still eluded them but that finally changed when the LV= Cup (Anglo-Welsh Cup) reached what proved to be a crowd-pleasing climax at Worcester's Sixways as the Saints edged out the valiant Cherry and Whites 30–24 in a five-try thriller.

"Cup finals are all about winning, and you would take 3–0 in a final," admitted director of rugby Mallinder. "But it is obviously more encouraging when you can play like that. There were two teams who wanted to play rugby and it was a good advert for the game. It shows how far the side has progressed and it was great for our fans. It was special.

"We have talked about being in three competitions but it is pointless being involved in three competitions and you come away with nothing. We were not going to come away with nothing this season. We are building as a team, that's what successful teams need, they need to be around each other to enjoy each other's company and play a good game like we have today."

The tournament's four qualifying groups kicked off in early November and in Pool One, it was Saracens who narrowly emerged victorious. The London club won two of its four games but so too did Leicester and it was Sarries who progressed to the semi-finals because they had gained two bonus points to the Tigers' one.

In a new structure that guaranteed each side four matches, teams didn't face those in their pool.

It was even tighter in Pool Two. Gloucester and Scarlets were both to finish level on points but going into the final round of matches the Welsh side still had their destiny in their own hands, only for them to lose at home to the Blues and the Englishmen completed a remarkable, victorious recovery at Harlequins. The Cherry and Whites went through on number of tries scored.

In Pool Three, Cardiff saw off the stubborn challenge of second-place Wasps to reach the last four while in Pool Four, Northampton were totally dominant in wins over Dragons, Bath and Leeds.

The first of the semi-finals pitted the Blues against Gloucester at the Cardiff City Stadium with the West Country side looking for revenge for their 50–12 humiliation in last season's Anglo-Welsh final and they exacted it in the Welsh capital despite coming out second best in the early exchanges.

Cardiff led 10–3 in the first-half thanks chiefly to a try from Casey Laulala but the visitors began what was to prove an irresistible comeback shortly before the break when Freddie Burns struck. The second period witnessed a fine individual display from England wing James Simpson-Daniel, who ripped the Blues defence to shreds with a fine hat-trick, and Gloucester booked their place in the final with a 29–18 win.

"We are delighted to have got through to another final," said Gloucester captain Mike Tindall. "The Blues have been a problem team for us in the past and it's nice to register a victory against them. I suppose it was revenge."

The other last-four clash saw Saracens head north to play Northampton at Franklin's Gardens for a clash that was nothing if not ill-tempered. There were a total of five yellow cards brandished by the referee during the match but without doubt the most significant was that shown to Saracens prop Richard Skuse, who was sin binned just before half-time for not rolling away.

At the time of his temporary dismissal, the visitors had built up a slender but significant 12–11 lead but Northampton ruthlessly exploited their numerical advantage either side of the break with two tries and a penalty to establish a 24–12 platform. The game eventually finished 31–20 to the Saints and Sarries were out.

"In the second half, we were playing down the slope and we knew if we could put some phases together we could open them up," Mallinder said. "We still like to play and we moved the ball well when we had the opportunity. I'm delighted with the win. The final is going to be a hard game because Gloucester have improved massively since the start of the season and they will go in fancying themselves to beat us."

In contrast, Saracens director of rugby Brendan Venter was left to reflect on his side's expensive indiscipline. "It was stupid and cost us the points after half-time. That was hugely significant. We were leading by a point and 10 minutes later, they have scored 13 points. It killed the game for us."

The final was switched from its traditional home at Twickenham to Sixways but any fears the two sets of fans harboured that the sense of occasion would suffer were dispelled as both sides served up a breathless encounter that ebbed and flowed for 80 minutes.

The enforced absence of Northampton quartet Ben Foden, Chris Ashton, Dylan Hartley and Euan Murray and Gloucester's Tindall, Gareth Delve and Marco Bortolami on Six Nations duty was unfortunate but the players who were on show did not disappoint.

The lead changed five times in total once the scoring got underway and it was the Cherry and Whites who drew first blood when Akapusi

Qera crashed over from short range. Soane Tonga'uiha replied for the Saints after a characteristically fluid counter attacking thrust from inside their own-half and when James Downey added a second try under the posts, which was converted by the impeccable Stephen Myler, Northampton had established a 20–14 lead by the time the half-time whistle sounded.

The neutral may have justifiably predicted a Saints procession in the second period but it was Gloucester who struck first after the restart with a penalty try, the referee punishing the Northampton front row for collapsing three metres out from the line.

The resulting routine conversion put the Cherry and Whites 21–20 ahead but sadly for their supporters, it was the team's last significant score and within three minutes, Northampton were in front with a sniping run and try from Lee Dickson, which was again converted by Myler.

Myler added his second penalty to finish the match with 15 points and a 100% record and although Nicky Robinson slotted three points late on, it was not enough to deny the Saints their moment of glory.

For Gloucester, defeat was their fourth successive failure in a final since they won the Anglo-Welsh competition seven years ago and although head coach Bryan Redpath acknowledged his side had at least done themselves justice at Sixways, he also insisted the club should not get used to defeat in the big games.

"It's never easy losing in finals but I can't question our performance or effort," said Redpath. "But our ball retention was poor from our back line throughout the game and that enabled them to relieve the pressure. It's not as bad as the Cardiff game last year in the EDF final but it doesn't ease the hurt when you lose a final."

"It was a great game of rugby and we have no excuses even though we could easily have won it. I'm just very disappointed to have lost a cup final but we must now focus on trying to qualify for the Heineken Cup through the Premiership."

For victorious Northampton, victory booked their place in the following season's Heineken Cup and kept them on course for what ultimately proved to be an unsuccessful Treble challenge.

"There has been a lot of talk this season about the quality or lack of quality in the Premiership but what an advert for the English game that was," Mallinder said as Northampton's celebrations began in earnest. "For us, it is an important step to get some silverware and to show how much we have progressed as a club in recent seasons. But it was a very close game and we had to defend superbly at times to keep Gloucester out."

GROUP TABLES

POOL ONE

	P	W	D	L	F	A	BP	Pts
Saracens	4	2	0	2	83	69	2	10
Leicester	4	2	0	2	84	82	1	9
Sale	4	1	0	3	57	83	2	6
Ospreys	4	1	0	3	68	97	1	5

POOL THREE

	P	W	D	L	F	A	BP	Pts
Blues	4	3	0	1	120	84	3	15
Wasps	4	3	0	1	67	55	1	13
Harlequins	4	2	1	1	79	67	1	11
Worcester	4	2	0	2	73	64	1	9

POOL TWO

	P	W	D	L	F	A	BP	Pts
Gloucester	4	2	0	2	87	81	3	11
Scarlets	4	2	1	1	88	83	1	11
London Irish	4	1	0	3	54	70	2	6
Newcastle	4	0	0	4	41	105	2	2

POOL FOUR

	P	W	D	L	F	A	BP	Pts
Northampton	4	4	0	0	81	45	0	16
Dragons	4	3	0	1	103	79	0	12
Bath	4	2	0	2	94	75	1	9
Leeds Carnegie	4	1	0	3	53	93	1	5

SEMI-FINALS

14 March, City Stadium, Cardiff

CARDIFF 18 (1G, 2PG, 1T)
GLOUCESTER 29 (3G, 1PG, 1T)

CARDIFF: B Blair; T James, C Laulala, D Hewitt, C Czekaj; C Sweeney, G Cooper; F Filise, T R Thomas, S Andrews, S Morgan, P Tito (captain), A Powell, B White, X Rush

SUBSTITUTIONS: G Evans for Hewitt (temp 22 to 29 mins); A Petorius for Morgan (65 mins); M Molitika for Powell (65 mins); D Allinson for Cooper (69 mins); Evans for Hewitt (78 mins)

SCORERS *Tries*: Laulala, Sweeney *Conversion*: Blair *Penalty Goals*: Blair (2)

GLOUCESTER: F Burns; J Simpson–Daniel, M Tindall (captain), E Fuimaono–Sapolu, L Vainikolo; N Robinson, D Lewis; N Wood, O Azam, P Doran–Jones, W James, A Brown, P Buxton, A Qera, J Boer

SUBSTITUTIONS: A Eustace for Boer (40 mins); P Capdevielle for Doran–Jones (44 mins); A Dickinson for Wood (62 mins); T Molenaar for Fuimaono–Sapolu (62 mins); J Pasqualin for Lewis (65 mins); D Dawidiuk for Azam (71 mins); A Hazell for Qera (73 mins); T Voyce for Robinson (78 mins)

SCORERS *Tries*: Burns, Simpson–Daniel (3) *Conversions*: Robinson (3) *Penalty Goal*: Robinson

YELLOW CARD White (53 mins)

REFEREE G Clancy (Ireland)

14 March, Franklin's Gardens, Northampton

NORTHAMPTON 31 (1G, 3PG, 3T)
SARACENS 20 (5PG, 1T)

NORTHAMPTON: B Reihana; C Ashton, J Clarke, J Downey, P Diggin; S Geraghty, L Dickson; S Tonga'uiha, B Sharman, B Mujati, I Fernández Lobbe, P Dowson (captain), N Best, R Wilson

SUBSTITUTIONS: A Dickens for Dickson (66 mins); S Myler for Downey (71 mins); R Dreyer for Tonga'uiha (71 mins); A Long for Sharman (71 mins); J Cannon for Fernández Lobbe (71 mins); M Easter for Dowson (71 mins)

SCORERS *Tries*: Dowson, Mujati, Diggin, Best *Conversion*: Geraghty *Penalty Goals*: Geraghty (3)

SARACENS: A Goode; R Penney, K Ratuvou, B Barritt, C Wyles; D Hougaard, N de Kock; K Lealamanua, S Brits, R Skuse, H Smith, M Botha, J Burger, A Saull, E Joubert (captain, sin-bin, 21–31)

SUBSTITUTIONS: T Mercey for Lealamanua (11 mins); E Reynecke for Brits (41 mins); R Haughton for Wyles (42 mins); A Brown for Saull (temp 43 to 50 mins); G Jackson for Hougaard (50 mins); J Marshall for de Kock (50 mins); T Ryder for Smith (53 mins); J Melck for Saull (53 mins); A Brown for Mercey (60 mins)

SCORERS *Tries*: Melck *Penalty Goals*: Hougaard (4), Jackson

YELLOW CARDS Joubert (21 mins), Skuse (40 mins), Dreyer (71 mins), Kruger (73 mins), Botha (75 mins)

REFEREE R Poite (France)

FINAL

21 March, Sixways, Worcester

NORTHAMPTON 30 (3G, 3PG)
GLOUCESTER 24 (1G, 4PG, 1G)

NORTHAMPTON: S Geraghty; P Diggin, J Clarke, J Downey, B Reihana; S Myler, L Dickson; S Tonga'uiha, B Sharman, B Mujati, C Lawes, J Kruger, P Dowson, N Best, R Wilson

SUBSTITUTIONS: A Long for Sharman (62 mins); M Easter for Lawes (70 mins); J Ansbro for Clarke (74 mins)

SCORERS *Tries*: Tonga'uiha, Downey, Dickson *Conversions*: Myler (3) *Penalty Goals*: Myler (3)

GLOUCESTER: F Burns; J Simpson–Daniel, T Molenaar, E Fuimaono–Sapolu, L Vainikolo; N Robinson, R Lawson; N Wood, O Azam, P Capdevielle, W James, A Brown, P Buxton, A Qera, A Eustace

SUBSTITUTIONS: A Satala for Brown (37 mins); C Sharples for Molenaar (41 mins); T Voyce for Burns (63 mins); D Lewis for Lawson (69 mins); A Hazell for Qera (69 mins); D Dawidiuk for Ozam (74 mins)

SCORERS *Tries*: Qera, Penalty try *Conversion*: Robinson *Penalty Goals*: Robinson (4)

REFEREE A Lewis (Ireland)

BULLS CONTINUE DOMINANCE

Gallo Images

There was no stopping the Bulls in the Super 14.

The Bulls charged their way to a magnificent third Super Rugby title in four seasons, beating compatriots the Stormers in a hugely symbolic final staged at the Orlando Stadium in Soweto and in the process brought down the curtain on five hugely entertaining years of Super 14 rugby.

The southern hemisphere's premier provincial tournament will be expanded to 15 teams in 2011 with the admission of the Melbourne

Rebels, but the Bulls ensured they will be remembered as the dominant force of the 14-team incarnation of the competition with a 25–17 victory over the Stormers in front of 36,000 vuvuzela-blowing supporters.

The symbolism of the second all South African final was obvious. Soweto remains a predominantly black, football area but the Orlando Stadium made the majority white rugby crowd who descended on the ground feel immediately at home as the two sides produced an enthralling clash.

Making their debut in a Super Rugby final, the Stormers breached the Bulls defence twice in the second half through wing Bryan Habana and scrum-half Ricky Januarie but the indefatigable boot of Morné Steyn proved the difference between the two sides. The Springbok fly-half converted Francois Hougaard's superb first-half try and landed six penalties under the watchful eye of South Africa President Jacob Zuma to ensure the Bulls retained their Super 14 crown.

His personal haul of 20 points took Steyn to 263 for the 2010 tournament, a new individual record for the competition and meant the Bulls joined New Zealand's Blues and the Crusaders before them as the only sides to claim back-to-back titles.

"I'd like to thank all our fans for coming out here from Pretoria and everyone in Soweto who supported us," said victorious Bulls captain Victor Matfield. "It's an awesome day and a special one for us. I think here in Soweto, with all the vuvuzelas, this is a great day for our country which we will remember for a long, long time.

"I'm not sure about their guys, but for us, we knew what was coming. The guys were really looking forward to it and they showed that tonight. They came out firing and started well. The boys played some good stuff and with the support behind us, it was just brilliant."

The 2010 Super 14 kicked off in early February and from the outset it was evident that the Bulls would once again be the side to beat. They opened their account with a 51–34 triumph away to the Chiefs and recorded a second successive half century of points eight days later with a 50–32 demolition of the Brumbies at Loftus Versfeld. The champions narrowly missed out on a third 50-pointer next up against the Waratahs, beating the Sydney-based side 48–38, but the deluge of points in their three opening games was a potent statement of intent.

In fact, it was not until early April and after six straight victories that Frans Ludeke's free-scoring side tasted defeat. It came against the Blues in Auckland as Isaia Toeava and Joe Rokocoko scored the crucial tries for the home side and the South African side's run of 12 straight Super Rugby victories spanning the 2009 and 2010 campaigns was at an end.

As the Bulls forged ahead to finish first in the final table, it quickly became a simple question of which three other sides would join them in the knockout stages.

It was eventually to be the Stormers, two-time runners-up the Waratahs and the Crusaders, the seven-time champions, who booked their place in the last four courtesy of a 40–22 victory over the Brumbies in Christchurch in their final game of the regular season to deny the Reds a place in the last four.

The first semi-final saw the Bulls entertain the Crusaders at the Orlando Stadium and although the Kiwis broke through the South African lines three times through captain Richie McCaw, Sean Maitland and Sam Whitelock, they were overwhelmed by 24 points from Steyn's deadly boot, a superior Bulls scrum and scores by Pierre Spies, Zane Kirchner and Fourie du Preez in a 39–24 defeat.

"This is a very good Bulls team and we gave them a head start," McCaw conceded after the game. "We came back strongly in the second half but were not clinical enough when we had them under pressure and that has been the story of our season.

"You've got to take those high balls, it was obvious that sort of tactic to put us under pressure was going to be there. It's those little mistakes in your own half that you cannot afford. A good team like the Bulls will make you pay for it."

The match was Matfield's 100th game for the Bulls and victory against the visitors ensured his side had the opportunity to defend their Super 14 title in the final.

"This ranks among the most memorable experiences of my rugby career, coming to Soweto, reaching 100 appearances and defeating a great Crusaders team," Matfield said. "We realised that starting slowly and giving our opponents a 15-point lead would be suicidal and so we set out to take control from the kick-off and it worked. Resting our top players last weekend also worked in our favour."

The second semi-final saw the Waratahs follow the Crusaders to South Africa to tackle the Stormers at Newlands and again it was the home side who emerged victorious.

The game was not quite the feast of rugby that the first semi had been and there was just one try in the 80 minutes, scored by the Stormers centre Juan de Jongh. The Waratahs tried valiantly to find a way through the Stormers defence but despite their efforts could muster just a single penalty and a drop goal from Berrick Barnes as they went down 25–6.

"Our defence was excellent," said Stormers coach Allister Coetzee. "It just goes to show how systems can win matches. We pitched up physically and the work rate was good and when you have those two attributes working for you, it is very hard for the opposition to cut your defence."

For the Australians, defeat was their third reverse at the semi-final stage and having also finished runners-up in 2005 and 2008, their wait for a Super Rugby title continued.

"I thought the Stormers were particularly good at the physical contact," admitted coach Chris Hickey. "We felt we were playing off the back foot for a lot of the night. I thought that was significant, and probably there was a period of time in the first 10 minutes of the second half when we conceded six or seven penalties that gave all the momentum to the Stormers."

The final at the end of May was only the second time two teams from the Rainbow Nation had met at the business end of the tournament. In 2007, the Bulls had dramatically triumphed 20–19 over the Sharks in Durban in arguably the tournament's greatest ever final and although the 2010 showpiece game could not quite hit the same heights, it was nonetheless a superb match and worthy of the occasion.

The ever-reliable Steyn landed three first-half penalties to give the Bulls an early advantage and the home side looked to have decisively asserted their authority when Hougaard dashed over in the 25th minute after an incisive break by the superb Du Preez. Steyn converted and the Bulls led 16–0.

The Stormers rallied with a Peter Grant penalty before the break and minutes after the restart they were back in the game when Habana raced away for an interception score and his third try in three appearances in Super Rugby finals.

The scoreboard now read 16–10 to the Bulls but the Stormers' recovery was strangled by Steyn's phenomenal kicking as he landed three unanswered penalties to re-establish a 15-point cushion. There was a brief glimmer of hope for the side from Cape Town when Januarie burrowed over from close range but it was too little, too late as the Bulls clinically wound down the clock and the celebrations began.

"I must make a special mention of Victor Matfield and Fourie du Preez," said Ludeke after the final whistle. "Those two players, for Bulls rugby, they're really special guys. Their rugby intelligence and the way they lead from the front is amazing. It's great to have them there and hopefully we can keep them for many years. There is a long legacy of pride in playing for the Bulls. The jersey means something to the players.

"The start we had was really important. Obviously those high balls worked nicely in the beginning. There were some turnovers and the guys capitalised on that. The second half Bryan almost turned the game on its head, but the guys kept their cool and in the end we won."

SUPER 14 2010 RESULTS

12 February: **Blues** 20 **Hurricanes** 34, **Force** 15 **Brumbies** 24, **Cheetahs** 34 **Bulls** 51. 13 February: **Crusaders** 32 **Highlanders** 17, **Reds** 28 **Waratahs** 30, **Lions** 13 **Stormers** 26, **Sharks** 18 **Chiefs** 19. 19 February: **Highlanders** 15 **Blues** 19, **Reds** 41 **Crusaders** 20, **Sharks** 20 **Cheetahs** 25, **Lions** 65 **Chiefs** 72. 20 February: **Hurricanes** 47 **Force** 22, **Bulls** 50 **Brumbies** 32, **Stormers** 27 **Waratahs** 6. 26 February: **Crusaders** 35 **Sharks** 6, **Stormers** 17 **Brumbies** 19. 27 February: **Hurricanes** 33 **Lions** 18, **Reds** 18 **Blues** 27, **Force** 19 **Chiefs** 37, **Cheetahs** 24 **Highlanders** 31, **Bulls** 48 **Waratahs** 38. 5 March: **Chiefs** 18 **Reds** 23, **Brumbies** 24 **Lions** 13. 6 March: **Crusaders** 33 **Blues** 20, **Waratahs** 25 **Sharks** 21, **Stormers** 33 **Highlanders** 0, **Cheetahs** 28 **Hurricanes** 12. 12 March: **Chiefs** 19 **Crusaders** 26, **Waratahs** 73 **Lions** 12. March 13: **Brumbies** 24 **Sharks** 22, **Bulls** 50 **Highlanders** 35, **Stormers** 37 **Hurricanes** 13. March 14: **Reds** 50 **Force** 10. March 19: **Blues** 39 **Brumbies** 34, **Bulls** 19 **Hurricanes** 18. March 20: **Crusaders** 46 **Lions** 19, **Highlanders** 16 **Sharks** 30, **Force** 10 **Waratahs** 14, **Stormers** 21 **Cheetahs** 8. March 26: **Highlanders** 39 **Lions** 29, **Brumbies** 30 **Chiefs** 23, **Cheetahs** 10 **Reds** 31. March 27: **Hurricanes** 26 **Sharks** 29, **Waratahs** 39 **Blues** 32, **Force** 15 **Bulls** 28. 2 April: **Hurricanes** 26 **Crusaders** 26, **Force** 16 **Stormers** 15. April 3: **Blues** 32 **Bulls** 17, **Chiefs** 27 **Highlanders** 21, **Waratahs** 40 **Cheetahs** 17, **Sharks** 30 **Reds** 28. 9 April: **Chiefs** 19 **Bulls** 33. 10 April: **Highlanders** 27 **Force** 41, **Blues** 21 **Stormers** 33, **Crusaders** 20 **Waratahs** 13, **Brumbies** 61 **Cheetahs** 15, **Lions** 26 **Reds** 41. 16 April: **Chiefs** 15 **Stormers** 49, **Brumbies** 13 **Hurricanes** 23. 17 April: **Blues** 38 **Force** 17, **Crusaders** 45 **Cheetahs** 6, **Reds** 19 **Bulls** 12, **Lions** 28 **Sharks** 32. 23 April: **Chiefs** 25 **Cheetahs** 25, **Reds** 16 **Stormers** 13, **Force** 24 **Crusaders** 16. 24 April: **Highlanders** 31 **Hurricanes** 33, **Waratahs** 19 **Brumbies** 12, **Bulls** 51 **Lions** 11, **Sharks** 23 **Blues** 10. 30 April: **Highlanders** 26 **Waratahs** 10, **Stormers** 42 **Crusaders** 14. 1 May: **Hurricanes** 33 **Chiefs** 27, **Brumbies** 32 **Reds** 12, **Cheetahs** 36 **Blues** 32, **Lions** 12 **Force** 33, **Bulls** 27 **Sharks** 19. 7 May: **Hurricanes** 44 **Reds** 21, **Bulls** 40 **Crusaders** 35. 8 May: **Chiefs** 19 **Waratahs** 46, **Brumbies** 31 **Highlanders** 3, **Lions** 14 **Blues** 56, **Cheetahs** 29 **Force** 14, **Sharks** 20 **Stormers** 14. 14 May: **Crusaders** 40 **Brumbies** 22, **Waratahs** 32 **Hurricanes** 16, **Sharks** 27 **Force** 22. 15 May: **Blues** 30 **Chiefs** 20, **Reds** 38 **Highlanders** 36, **Cheetahs** 59 **Lions** 10, **Stormers** 38 **Bulls** 10.

FINAL TABLE

	P	W	D	L	F	A	BP	PTS
Bulls	13	10	0	3	436	345	7	**47**
Stormers	13	9	0	4	365	171	8	**44**
Waratahs	13	9	0	4	385	288	7	**43**
Crusaders	13	8	1	4	388	295	7	**41**
Reds	13	8	0	5	366	308	7	**39**
Brumbies	13	8	0	5	358	291	5	**37**
Blues	13	7	0	6	376	333	9	**37**
Hurricanes	13	7	1	5	358	323	7	**37**
Sharks	13	7	0	6	297	299	5	**33**
Cheetahs	13	5	1	7	316	393	4	**26**
Chiefs	13	4	1	8	340	418	8	**26**
Highlanders	13	3	0	10	297	397	7	**19**
Force	13	4	0	9	258	364	3	**19**
Lions	13	0	0	13	270	585	5	**5**

SEMI-FINALS

22 May, Orlando Stadium, Soweto

BULLS 39 (3G, 6PG)
CRUSADERS 24 (3G, 1PG)

BULLS: Z Kirchner; J van der Westhuyzen, J Pretorius, W Olivier, F Hougaard; M Steyn, F du Preez; G Steemkamp, G Botha, W Kruger, D Rossouw, V Matfield (captain), D Stegmann, D Potgieter, P Spies

SUBSTITUTIONS: F Van der Merwe for Rossouw (temp 53 to 59 mins); P Wannenburg for Potgieter (56 mins); Van der Merwe for Rossouw (62 mins); S Dippenaar for van der Westhuyzen (65 mins); D Kuün for Stegmann (66 mins); B Maku for Botha (69 mins); B Roux for Kruger (70 mins); JL Potgieter for Olivier (74 mins)

SCORERS *Tries*: Spies, Kirchner, Du Preez *Conversions*: Steyn (3) *Penalty Goals*: Steyn (6)

CRUSADERS: C Slade; S Maitland, R Fruean, D Bowden, Z Guildford; D Carter, A Ellis; O Franks, T Paulo, B Franks, B Thorn, S Whitelock, G Whitelock, R McCaw (captain), K Read

SUBSTITUTIONS: T Waldrom for G Whitelock (50 mins); W Crockett for Franks (56 mins); C Jack for Thorn (57 mins); T Bateman for Fruean (58 mins); K Fotuali'i for Ellis (66 mins); J Payne for Slade (74 mins); D Perrin for Paulo (74 mins)

SCORERS *Tries*: McCaw, Maitland, S Whitelock *Conversions*: Carter (3) *Penalty Goals*: Carter

REFEREE S Dickinson (Australia)

22 May, Newlands, Cape Town

STORMERS 25 (1G, 6PG) WARATAHS 6 (1PG, 1DG)

STORMERS: J Pietersen; G Aplon, J Fourie, J De Jongh, B Habana; P Grant, D Duvenage; W Blaauw, T Liebenberg, B Harris, A Fondse, A Bekkes, S Burger (captain), F Louw, D Vermeulen

SUBSTITUTIONS: A van Zyl for Fondse (62 mins), D Fourie for Liebenberg (67 mins); E Guinazu for Blaauw (67 mins); R Januarie for Duvenage (68 mins); P Louw for Burger (73 mins); T Whitehead for J Fourie (74 mins), W de Waal for Grant (74 mins)

SCORERS *Tries*: De Jongh *Conversion*: Grant *Penalty Goals*: Grant (6)

WARATAHS: K Beale; L Turner, R Horne, T Carter, D Mitchell; B Barnes, L Burgess; D Palmer, T Polotoa–Nau, A Baxter, D Mumm, K Douglas, P McCutcheon, P Waugh (captain), B Mowen

SUBSTITUTIONS: D Dennis for McCutcheon (temp 35 to 40 mins); J Tilse for Palmer (42 mins); Dennis for McCutcheon (63 mins); R Sidey for Horne (73 mins); J Holmes for Burgess (73 mins); D Fitzpatrick for Polotoa–Nau (77 mins); D Halangahu for Beale (78 mins).

SCORERS *Penalty Goal*: Barnes *Drop Goal*: Barnes

REFEREE Mark Lawrence (South Africa)

FINAL

29 May, Orlando Stadium, Soweto

BULLS 25 (1G, 6PG)
STORMERS 17 (2G, 1PG)

BULLS: Z Kirchner; G van den Heever, J Pretorius, W Olivier, F Hougaard; M Steyn, F du Preez; G Steenkamp, G Botha, W Kruger, D Rossouw, V Matfield (captain), D Stegmann, D Potgieter, P Spies

SUBSTITUTIONS: van der Westhuyzen for van den Heever (9 mins); F van der Merwe for Rossouw (55 mins); P Wannenburg for Potgieter (58 mins); B Maku for Botha (72 mins); B Roux for Kruger (73 mins); D Kuün for Stegmann (73 mins); JL Potgieter for Pretorious (76 mins).

SCORERS *Try*: Hougaard *Conversion*: Steyn *Penalty Goals*: Steyn (6)

STORMERS: J Pietersen; G Aplon, J Fourie, J de Jongh, B Habana; P Grant, D Duvenage; W Blaauw, T Liebenberg, B Harris, A Fondse, A Bekker, S Burger (captain); F Louw, D Vermeulen

SUBSTITUTIONS: A van Zyl for Bekker (temp 4 to 16 mins); T Whitehead for de Jongh (23 minutes); JC Kritzinger for Blauuw (55 mins); van Zyl for Fondse (55 mins); D Fourie for Liebenberg (61 mins); R Januarie for Duvenage (65 mins); P Louw for Harris (77 mins).

SCORERS *Tries*: Habana, Januarie *Conversions*: Grant (2) *Penalty Goal*: Grant

REFEREE C Joubert (South Africa)

Stu Forster/Getty Images

A delighted Ryan Jones led the Ospreys to the Magners League title.

WALES CLAIM CELTIC GLORY

By Cardiff Blues' Tom Shanklin

Although there's always a very healthy and often fierce rivalry between the Blues and the Ospreys in any competition the two teams are involved in, I have to congratulate them on winning the Magners League after their victory over Leinster in the Grand Final. The Ospreys deserve a lot of credit for going over to Dublin and winning at the RDS.

Finals are pressure cooker occasions when there is so much at stake and to face Leinster in their own backyard and come away with the win was a fantastic achievement. It was an incredibly ferocious atmosphere over in Ireland and I think the Ospreys' win was as much about their mental strength as a unit as it was the undoubted talent in the team.

Season after season, you see sides winning trophies because they are mentally tough. The margins at this level are very small indeed and the difference is so often which of the two sides can cope with the pressure at the critical moments.

The Ospreys have had their critics in the past who have labelled them chokers, but they proved they do have the big-match mentality over in Dublin.

I think their perceived problems have chiefly come in the Heineken Cup in recent seasons and it's easy to forget that they have now won the Magners League three times in the last five years, which is an impressive record. It's certainly not an accident, is it?

It was a star-studded final when you look at the two starting XVs. The majority of the personnel on show at the RDS were fully-fledged

Test players and that underlines the strength of the competition at the moment and why it is so difficult to win it.

The Magners League has really matured since its introduction. I wouldn't say it was weak at the beginning but it is now a real battleground and every year it gets tougher and tougher to genuinely challenge for the silverware.

There is always a lot of debate about where the competition ranks in terms of importance in the rugby calendar and while I cannot speak for the other clubs and provinces, for the Blues it is our number one priority at the start of each season. It's our bread and butter and although we were delighted to win the Amlin Challenge Cup, the Magners League is always our first target.

It is the same with the Heineken Cup, which grabs the headlines but is also a bonus rather than something that we focus on first.

I think it's important for any side to prove itself regularly in its domestic competition.

It was the first year of the newly introduced play-offs and Grand Final and although I was genuinely happy to see a Welsh side lifting the trophy, I'm really not a big fan of the new format.

Rugby League pioneered the play-off format in Britain with the Super League and a lot of other sports have adopted it but I'm not convinced it's the right way to go. For me, league competitions should be decided by a side's consistency for the duration of a campaign and should not come down to the lottery of 80 minutes at the end of the year.

I understand play-offs are good in terms of revenue and it's good for broadcasters. I'm sure the supporters enjoy the big day out for the final as well, even if their side is beaten, but I believe a league should be settled by league results and nothing else. It's probably an old-fashioned view.

It also undermines the genuine knockout competitions and blurs the lines between league and cup rugby.

Saying that, justice was served in the sense the two teams that finished first and second in the table made it to the final, but I'm sure some of the Leinster boys will have sat in their dressing room after the final whistle thinking they had been robbed because they had finished three points clear of the Ospreys and won two more games.

Yes, all the teams kicked off the new season in the knowledge there would be play-offs but I know I would be disgruntled if the Blues had finished top but we eventually didn't lift the trophy because we had been beaten in the play-off final.

It was an enjoyable but ultimately frustrating campaign from a Blues perspective. We eventually finished fifth and lost out to Munster by a single point for the fourth and final play-off spot. We were very strong in the second half of the season but paid a heavy price for a really sluggish start in the competition.

We were bottom of the table after losing our opening three games to Edinburgh, Munster and Connacht and although we ended the sequence when we beat Scarlets 19–15 at home, we were beaten by the Warriors next time out and, to be honest, really struggling. We bounced back after Christmas but it was too little, too late to overhaul Munster.

We seem to have developed an unwanted habit of starting the season poorly and it's something we need to rectify because you leave yourselves a mountain to climb if you are so slow out of the blocks.

Looking at the Magners from a country-by-country viewpoint, it was obviously a good year for Wales while Ireland and Scotland will feel it was a case of could do better.

The expectations of the Irish provinces is sky high these days in the wake of the success the Ireland team has enjoyed and the trophies the provinces have claimed over the last few years. It's a huge challenge to repeat that level of success season after season and although Leinster and Munster both finished in the top four, Ulster and Connacht found themselves off the pace.

For me, it was a solid season for Scotland with the Warriors making the semi-finals and Edinburgh finishing sixth, three points adrift of us. You could make the argument both sides over-performed when you consider the modest Scottish player base in terms of numbers. It's a constant challenge for both sides.

As I said before, the Ospreys' victory in the final was a great advert for the Welsh regions even though Scarlets and the Dragons finished in the bottom half of the table. I think it was further evidence of how the regional system has developed and how the sides are improving.

The Ospreys, in particular, continue to build and have a very clear game plan that serves them very well.

In terms of the stars of the tournament and individual performances, I was very impressed with Tommy Bowe and James Hook.

Bowe scored one of the Ospreys' two tries in the final and Hook got one in the semi-final against the Warriors but they were superb all through the season. Both of them are real box office players and they produced the goods exactly when it mattered.

I've also got to give a mention to Xavier Rush and Ceri Sweeney for the Blues. Xavier was just so consistent and tireless for us all year while Ceri came into the side after sitting on the bench early on and made a big difference to the way we were playing and the results we achieved.

MAGNERS LEAGUE 2009–10 RESULTS

4 September, 2009: **Connacht** 12 **Ospreys** 19, **Blues** 21 **Edinburgh** 22, **Warriors** 22 **Munster** 9. 5 September: **Scarlets** 18 **Leinster** 16. 6 September: **Dragons** 23 **Ulster** 6. 11 September: **Munster** 24 **Blues** 13, **Edinburgh** 62 **Connacht** 13. 12 September: **Ospreys** 16 **Ulster** 20, **Leinster** 23 **Dragons** 14. 13 September: **Warriors** 19 **Scarlets** 11. 18 September: **Connacht** 18 **Blues** 16, **Ospreys** 11 **Leinster** 18, **Dragons** 30 **Warriors** 19, **Ulster** 13 **Edinburgh** 16. 19 September: **Scarlets** 20 **Munster** 22. 25 September: **Warriors** 16 **Ospreys** 26, **Connacht** 6 **Ulster** 30. 26 September: **Blues** 19 **Scarlets** 15, **Edinburgh** 19 **Leinster** 21. 27 September: **Munster** 27 **Dragons** 3. 2 October: **Ulster** 45 **Scarlets** 24. 3 October: **Dragons** 23 **Connacht** 10, **Blues** 5 **Warriors** 21, **Leinster** 30 **Munster** 0. 4 October: **Ospreys** 31 **Edinburgh** 10. 23 October: **Scarlets** 18 **Dragons** 3, **Warriors** 34 **Connacht** 20, **Edinburgh** 12 **Munster** 7. 24 October: **Ulster** 16 **Leinster** 14, **Blues** 20 **Ospreys** 12. 30 October: **Connacht** 16 **Scarlets** 10, **Ospreys** 9 **Warriors** 9. 31 October: **Munster** 24 **Ulster** 10, **Leinster** 23 **Blues** 6. 1 November: **Edinburgh** 8 **Dragons** 9. 4 December: **Scarlets** 16 **Edinburgh** 17, **Ulster** 13 **Warriors** 25. 5 December: **Ospreys** 19 **Munster** 14. 6 December: **Blues** 21 **Connacht** 9, **Dragons** 30 **Leinster** 14. 26 December: **Scarlets** 14 **Ospreys** 21, **Leinster** 15 **Ulster** 3, **Munster** 35 **Connacht** 3. 27 December: **Warriors** 25 **Edinburgh** 12, **Blues** 42 **Dragons** 13. 31 December: **Dragons** 9 **Scarlets** 14. 1 January, 2010: **Ospreys** 26 **Blues** 0. 2 January: **Edinburgh** 15 **Warriors** 22, **Ulster** 15 **Munster** 10. 9 January: **Edinburgh** 21 **Blues** 12. 19 February: **Ulster** 22 **Dragons** 22, **Warriors** 7 **Blues** 30, **Munster** 19 **Edinburgh** 12. 20 February: **Leinster** 27 **Scarlets** 14. 21 February: **Ospreys** 19 **Connacht** 17. 5 March: **Scarlets** 25 **Ulster** 8, **Connacht** 19 **Warriors** 19. 6 March: **Dragons** 31 **Munster** 22. 7 March: **Edinburgh** 33 **Ospreys** 17, Cardiff 20 **Leinster** 29. 17 March: **Connacht** 16 **Dragons** 3. 18 March: **Leinster** 20 **Warriors** 14, **Munster** 23 **Scarlets** 17. 26 March: **Blues** 19 **Ulster** 9, **Edinburgh** 24 **Scarlets** 20, **Munster** 27 **Warriors** 19. 27 March: **Leinster** 17 **Connacht** 14, **Dragons** 28 **Ospreys** 20. 2 April: **Connacht** 22 **Edinburgh** 21, **Ospreys** 27 **Scarlets** 19, **Munster** 15 **Leinster** 16. 3 April: **Ulster** 24 **Blues** 33. 4 April: **Warriors** 27 **Dragons** 19. 13 April: **Ulster** 27 **Ospreys** 38. 16 April: **Warriors** 25 **Ulster** 18, **Leinster** 20 **Ospreys** 16. 17 April: **Scarlets** 16 **Blues** 39. 18 April: **Connacht** 12 **Munster** 18, **Dragons** 49 **Edinburgh** 28. 21 April: **Connacht** 27 **Leinster** 13. 23 April: **Dragons** 14 **Blues** 20, **Warriors** 30 **Leinster** 6. 24 April: **Munster** 11 **Ospreys** 15. 25 April: **Scarlets** 58 **Connacht** 10, **Edinburgh** 25 **Ulster** 37. 7 May: **Ospreys** 42 **Dragons** 10, **Scarlets** 32 **Warriors** 37, **Ulster** 41 **Connacht** 10. 9 May: **Blues** 13 **Munster** 12, **Leinster** 37 **Edinburgh** 28.

FINAL TABLE

	P	W	D	L	F	A	BP	PTS
Leinster	18	13	0	5	359	295	3	**55**
Ospreys	18	11	1	6	384	298	6	**52**
Warriors	18	11	2	5	390	321	3	**51**
Munster	18	9	0	9	319	282	9	**45**
Blues	18	10	0	8	349	315	4	**44**
Edinburgh	18	8	0	10	385	391	9	**41**
Dragons	18	8	1	9	333	378	5	**39**
Ulster	18	7	1	10	357	370	6	**36**
Scarlets	18	5	0	13	361	382	9	**29**
Connacht	18	5	1	12	254	459	4	**26**

SEMI-FINALS

14 May, Liberty Stadium, Swansea

OSPREYS 20 (2G, 2PG) GLASGOW 5 (1T)

OSPREYS: L Byrne; T Bowe, A Bishop, J Hook, S Williams; D Biggar, M Phillips; P James, H Bennett, A Jones, A W Jones, J Thomas, J Collins, M Holah, R Jones (captain).

SUBSTITUTIONS: F Tiatia for Jones (56 mins); N Walker for Bishop (56 mins); I Gough for Collins (61 mins); R Bevington for Jones (71 mins); E Shervington for Bennett (78 mins); J Nutbrown for Phillips (78 mins).

SCORERS *Tries*: S Williams, Hook *Conversions*: Biggar (2) *Penalty Goals*: Biggar (2)

GLASGOW: B Stortoni; R Dewey, M Evans, G Morrison, DTH van der Merwe; D Parks, M McMillan; E Kalman, F Thomson, M Low, T Barker, A Kellock (captain), K Brown, J Barclay, J Beattie.

SUBSTITUTIONS: K Tkachuk for Kalman (17mins); C Shaw for Stortoni (40 mins); D Turner for Kellock (56 mins); H O'Hare for Dewey (56 mins); J Eddie for Barker (66 mins); P McArthur for Thomson (71 mins); Kalman for Low (78 mins).

SCORERS *Try*: Thomson

REFEREE G Clancy (Ireland)

15 May, RDS, Dublin

LEINSTER 16 (1G, 3PG) MUNSTER 6 (1PG, 1DG)

LEINSTER: R Kearney; S Horgan, B O'Driscoll, G D'Arcy, I Nacewa; J Sexton, E Reddan; C Healy, J Fogarty, S Wright, N Hines, M O'Kelly, K McLaughlin, S Jennings (captain), J Heaslip.

SUBSTITUTIONS: CJ van der Linde for Wright (46 mins); R Strauss for Fogarty (72 mins); Wright for Healy (74 mins); T Hogan for Hines (79 mins).

SCORERS *Try*: Kearney *Conversion*: Sexton *Penalty Goals*: Sexton (3)

MUNSTER: P Warwick; D Howlett, K Earls, J de Villiers, L Mafi; R O'Gara (captain), T O'Leary; M Horan, D Varley, J Hayes; D O'Callaghan, M O'Driscoll; A Quinlan, N Ronan, N Williams.

SUBSTITUTIONS: D Wallace for Williams (53 mins); D Ryan for Hayes (56 mins); D Hurley for de Villiers (60 mins); J Coughlan for Ronan (61 mins); P Stringer for O'Leary (65 mins)

SCORERS *Penalty Goal*: O'Gara *Drop Goal*: O'Gara.

YELLOW CARD Horgan (13 mins)

REFEREE N Owens (Wales)

GRAND FINAL

29 May, RDS, Dublin

LEINSTER 12 (4PG) OSPREYS 17 (2G, 1PG)

LEINSTER: R Kearney; S Horgan; B O'Driscoll, G D'Arcy; I Nacewa; J Sexton, E Reddan; S Wright, J Fogarty, CJ van der Linde, N Hines, M O'Kelly, K McLaughlin, S Jennings (captain), J Heaslip.

SUBSTITUTIONS: S Keogh for McLaughlin (30mins); T Hogan for Keogh (42 mins); C Healy for van der Linde (48 mins), R Strauss for Jennings (67 mins).

SCORERS *Penalty Goals*: Sexton (4)

OSPREYS: L Byrne; T Bowe, A Bishop, J Hook; S Williams; D Biggar, M Phillips; P James, H Bennett, A Jones, Alun Wyn–Jones, J Thomas, J Collins, M Holah, R Jones (captain).

SUBSTITUTIONS: I Gough for Thomas (62 mins); F Tiatia for R Jones (67 mins), N Walker for Williams (71 mins).

SCORERS *Tries*: Bowe, Byrne *Conversions*: Biggar (2) *Penalty Goal*: Biggar

REFEREE C White (English)

DRAMATIC WIN FOR SAMOA

By Tom Chick

Bruce Southwick/Zoomfiji/www.oceaniarugby.com

Samoa celebrate a sensational rugby double.

The ANZ Pacific Nations Cup crowned its first champion from outside New Zealand this year as Samoa dramatically overcame the odds to snatch the title from Fiji's grasp on home soil with a thrilling 41–38 victory.

With all but the opening match between Fiji and Japan being hosted in Apia, it was Samoa who capitalised on the absence of defending champions, the Junior All Blacks, and saved their best performance of the tournament for when it mattered in a dramatic finale.

A new name was always set to be etched onto the PNC trophy in the fifth instalment of the tournament and for the first time since its inception none of the three representative sides from Australia or New Zealand (Junior All Blacks, New Zealand Maori and Australia A) participated.

But with a first ever IRB Sevens World Series title already secured, this triumph was another feather in the cap of Samoan rugby in 2010. Fittingly, many of the Sevens winning squad starred for Fuimaono Tafua's team throughout the tournament and crucially in the title decider against the favourites, Fiji, who themselves had a 100% record heading into the match.

Having narrowly beaten Tonga 24–23 in the opening match, the hosts suffered just their second ever defeat to HSBC Asian 5 Nations champions Japan and their first in the history of the PNC, losing 31–23 in the second week of the competition. The defeat left them needing a try-scoring bonus point and winning margin of more than 13 points against Fiji to win the PNC for the first time.

Joe Tekori put the Samoans on course after 16 minutes, scoring the first try of the match, before the home crowd erupted when Mikaele Pesamino demonstrated why he was named IRB Sevens Player of the Year in the 22nd minute, chipping over the Fijian defence and showing great speed to collect and score.

With just 15 minutes to go, however, it looked as if Samoa would fall short in their quest for a first PNC title as Fiji gradually clawed their way back into the match and reduced the deficit to 14–9 thanks to three Taniela Rawaqa penalties, but what happened next will go down in PNC folklore.

IRB Sevens Player of the Year nominee Alafoti Fa'osiliva replaced George Stowers on the hour mark knowing his side needed two more tries, and within minutes had an immediate impact, scoring both required tries in a three-minute burst.

Firstly, the flanker was on hand to pick the ball up from the base of an offensive scrum on the Fijian line, and his second came immediately after Lolo Lui had converted the first.

From the restart the Fijians were clearly feeling the pressure and an uncharacteristic fumble allowed Census Johnston to capitalise and remarkably the prop kicked ahead for Fa'osiliva, who showed great speed and composure to chase and score the all important bonus point try to send the partisan crowd into raptures.

Any hopes Fiji had of a comeback were dashed though, when they lost Rupeni Nasiga to the sin-bin before David Lemi and Uale Mai combined to secure the 31–9 victory for the hosts, with the latter crossing and Lui adding the conversion.

"We came into this game to win and scoring four tries was a bonus. We knew Fiji was going to be strong so we had to be mentally and physically stronger than them," said head coach Tafua after the final whistle.

"I give credit to the players for their effort and this is a good building ground as we prepare for Rugby World Cup next year.

"The team had been under pressure the whole week and we needed to come out with a super show. The Head of State had told us to improve on our weaknesses and that motivated the players to work harder."

For the first time in the tournament's history, the second and third rounds of matches were streamed live on the IRB website and the 14-day tournament is a fundamental aspect of all four teams' Rugby World Cup 2011 preparations.

Those watching not only witnessed one of the most intense and dramatic finishes in Pacific Nation Cup history but also a preview to next year's RWC with both final round matches.

If this tournament is anything to go by, the passion, desire and quality of rugby from these four nations will make their matches next year must-see spectacles adding a Pacific flavour to the World Cup.

While Fiji will be awaiting a rematch with Samoa on the biggest stage in Pool D alongside current world champions South Africa, Wales and IRB Nations Cup winners Namibia, Tonga will also be chomping at the bit to play Japan in Pool A after they once again lost out by the narrowest margins.

Tonga's 26–23 defeat to Japan in the tournament's penultimate match meant they recorded their third losing bonus point and finished fourth in the tournament standings. The story, however, could have been very different as they lost by three or less points in each of their matches demonstrating the PNC's continuing competitiveness.

In the first round Tonga and eventual winners Samoa were separated by just one point and although they have never beaten the Samoans in the PNC with a number of new players and coach, former All Black Isitolo Maka, the Ikale Tahi came the closest yet, suffering a narrow 24–23 defeat.

Seven days later Tonga held a 31–10 half-time lead and looked to be on course for their fourth victory in five PNC matches against Fiji, but second-half tries from Campese Ma'afu, replacement Kelemedi Bolatagane and captain Dominiko Waqaniburotu brought Samu Domoni's side within striking distance.

With seven minutes remaining Fiji completed a stunning comeback as lock Sekonaia Kalou scored in the corner and Rawaqa converted to secure their second victory of the tournament after a 22–8 victory over Japan in the opening round at Churchill Park in Lautoka, the only match to be played outside of Samoa.

Tonga suffered further heartbreak against Japan in the penultimate match on 26 June. They did, though, end Japan's faint hopes of winning the title after they stopped John Kirwan's side gaining the try-scoring bonus point they needed to stand any chance of adding the Pacific Nations Cup to their HSBC Asian 5 Nations 2010 title.

Having taken the lead in the 67th minute through a fine individual Alipate Fatafehi try and after a Kurt Morath penalty after 76 minutes gave Tonga a 23–19 lead it looked as though they would mark their continuing development with their first victory in their final match.

But after losing captain Aleki Lutui to the sin-bin, Japan's scrum took advantage and were finally awarded a penalty try deep into stoppage time, which James Arlidge converted to secure the win.

Although Arlidge scored 16 points in the match to take his tally to 32, fly half Morath did offer some consolation for Tonga as he ended the tournament as the top point scorer with 39 and Vungakoto Lilo finished as joint top try scorer (three) with Pesamino.

ANZ PACIFIC NATIONS CUP 2010 RESULTS		
12/06/10	**Samoa** 24–23 **Tonga**	Apia Park, **Apia**
12/06/10	**Fiji** 22–8 **Japan**	Churchill Park, **Lautoka**
19/06/10	**Fiji** 41–38 **Tonga**	Apia Park, **Apia**
19/06/10	**Samoa** 23–31 **Japan**	Apia Park, **Apia**
26/06/10	**Japan** 26–23 **Tonga**	Apia Park, **Apia**
26/06/10	**Fiji** 9–31 **Samoa**	Apia Park, **Apia**

FINAL STANDINGS

Team	P	W	D	L	F	A	BP	PTS
Samoa	3	2	0	1	78	63	1	**9**
Fiji	3	2	0	1	72	77	1	**9**
Japan	3	2	0	1	65	68	0	**8**
Tonga	3	0	0	3	84	91	4	**4**

WARRIORS DEFEND THEIR TITLE

By Tom Chick

Bruce Southwick/Zoomfiji/www.oceaniarugby.com

The magnificent Warriors are ecstatic after the final.

The IRB Pacific Rugby Cup 2010 created history in more ways than one this year as the Fiji Warriors became the first team to successfully defend the title, beating the Fiji Barbarians 26–17 in the final at the National Stadium in May.

The all-Fijian contest in Suva meant the tournament witnessed its first-ever single country final with neither of the two Samoan sides –

Upolu Samoa or Savai'i Samoa – represented in the title decider for the first time since the tournament's inception in 2006.

It was the Barbarians' first appearance in a PRC final, a stark contrast to last year when they finished sixth, and ensured that all six sides have now competed in at least one final, demonstrating the ongoing competitiveness of the tournament in its five-year history.

The Warriors had to come from behind to secure their historic victory in a gripping final, and it was left to full-back Taniela Rawaqa, the tournament's leading point scorer with 81, to inspire the comeback in his side's third appearance in a PRC final.

Trailing 17–6 with just 20 minutes to go, it seemed as though the Warriors would fail in their quest to defend the title, but in front of a packed National Stadium, Rawaqa scored the decisive try and added to his personal match tally of 21 points, creating yet another piece of history.

The 21-point haul (one try, four penalties and two conversions) broke the record for the most points scored by an individual in any match in the history of the PRC – the previous best was 19 from Upolu's Josh Keil in 2007 and Savai'i's Ted Sikovi this year – and cemented him as the tournament's all-time leading point scorer with 145.

Replacement Paula Karatu guaranteed the victory in the last minute for the Warriors who had named only one player from the 2009 final in their starting XV, lock Apisalome Ratuniyarawa. The result also reversed an earlier 23–20 defeat to the Barbarians in the first round of matches.

"After having several players drafted into the Flying Fijians, I told the boys they really had to play their hearts out. I told them that this was the stepping stone to the PNC and the Wallabies' tour. They really played well today and I am very proud of them," said Warriors coach Inoke Male after the final whistle.

"Losing to the Barbarians in the first round was a big motivation for us. We were coming back from a good win against the Reds and I think our composure and our control won us the game today. All the boys really played their part and it was a team effort."

The tournament had begun in intriguing fashion, with three local derbies taking place in the opening round of pool matches hosted by Fiji, Samoa and Tonga respectively and included defeats for both of last year's finalists.

The 2006 champions Savai'i shut out their opponents Upolu, who succeeded them as champions and were runners-up in 2009, in the second half to win 23–10 at Apia Park, whilst the Warriors, the first Fijian side to lift the PRC crown in 2009, lost 23–20 to the Barbarians after prop Vesi Rarawa scored a last-minute try to inflict their only defeat of the tournament.

The other opening match saw 2008 champions Tautahi Gold get their campaign off to a solid start against Tau'uta Reds, winning 26–10 at the Teufaiva Stadium thanks to 16 points from wing Tupou Palu.

For the first time the PRC followed a more traditional single-hosting format with the Fiji Rugby Union being awarded the hosting rights for the event that has become a showcase for emerging talent in the Pacific Islands. Fiji hosted rounds two to five as well as the final.

"It's been great, particularly in Fiji which has such a wealth of rugby competitions," the IRB's Regional General Manager for Oceania Will Glenwright admitted on the eve of the final.

"The beauty of changing the format of the tournament and creating a tournament atmosphere and having all of the games in one venue allows the rugby public to develop a better understanding not only of the competition but particularly of the players that are participating in the tournament."

It was Gold who stole the march on the rest of the pack as the only side to maintain a 100% record after the first three rounds. Following their victory over the Reds they went on to beat Savai'i 16–14 before ending the Barbarians' unbeaten record in round three, winning 27–24 in a top of the table clash with Palu adding a further 17 points to his tally.

The win over the Barbarians had taken Gold to the top of the standings with 12 points, two more than the Warriors who leapfrogged the Barbarians on point differential following their 42–20 defeat of Savai'i. However, for the third successive match the 2008 champions failed to achieve a try-scoring bonus point and after losing to the Warriors 21–13 and Upolu 24–20 in rounds four and five, they finished third in the standings with 14 points.

Heading into the final round of pool matches Gold and Savai'i were both still in with a chance of making the final but it was the two Fijian sides that recorded the victories they needed to finish with four wins and 19 points each to gain a final berth – the Warriors doing so in emphatic fashion scoring seven tries against the Reds in the tournament's biggest ever winning margin – 48–0.

The beauty of the Pacific Rugby Cup continued once more this year, providing a pathway for locally based players to put their hands up for national selection, and with Rugby World Cup 2011 on the horizon, there was certainly no shortage of players to emerge and demonstrate they are ready physically and mentally as athletes that can handle the rigours of a big tournament.

IRB PACIFIC RUGBY CUP 2010 RESULTS		
05/05/10	**Upolu Samoa** 10–23 **Savai'i Samoa**	Apia Park, **Apia**
06/05/10	**Tautahi Gold** 26–10 **Tau'uta Reds**	Teufaiva Stadium, **Nuku'alofa**
06/05/10	**Fiji Warriors** 20–23 **Fiji Barbarians**	Lawaqa Park, **Sigatoka**
10/05/10	**Savai'i Samoa** 14–16 **Tautahi Gold**	Churchill Park, **Lautoka**
10/05/10	**Tau'uta Reds** 30–43 **Fiji Barbarians**	Churchill Park, **Lautoka**
10/05/10	**Upolu Samoa** 17–24 **Fiji Warriors**	Churchill Park, **Lautoka**
14/05/10	**Upolu Samoa** 18–19 **Tau'uta Reds**	Churchill Park, **Lautoka**
14/05/10	**Fiji Warriors** 42–20 **Savai'i Samoa**	Churchill Park, **Lautoka**
14/05/10	**Tautahi Gold** 27–24 **Fiji Barbarians**	Churchill Park, **Lautoka**
18/05/10	**Tau'uta Reds** 23–34 **Savai'i Samoa**	Prince Charles Park, **Nadi**
18/05/10	**Fiji Barbarians** 36–25 **Upolu Samoa**	Prince Charles Park, **Nadi**
18/05/10	**Fiji Warriors** 21–13 **Tautahi Gold**	Prince Charles Park, **Nadi**
22/05/10	**Tautahi Gold** 20–24 **Upolu Samoa**	Lawaqa Park, **Sigatoka**
22/05/10	**Fiji Barbarians** 19–14 **Savai'i Samoa**	Lawaqa Park, **Sigatoka**
22/05/10	**Tau'uta Reds** 0–48 **Fiji Warriors**	Lawaqa Park, **Sigatoka**

FINAL STANDINGS

	P	W	D	L	F	A	BP	PTS
Fiji Barbarians	5	4	0	1	145	116	3	**19**
Fiji Warriors	5	4	0	2	155	73	3	**19**
Tautahi Gold	5	3	0	2	102	93	2	**14**
Savai'i Samoa	5	2	0	3	105	110	2	**10**
Upolu Samoa	5	1	0	4	94	122	3	**7**
Tau'uta Reds	5	1	0	4	82	169	1	**5**

FINAL		
29/05/10	**Fiji Barbarians** 17–26 **Fiji Warriors**	National Stadium, **Suva**

JAPAN KEEP THEIR NO 1 SPOT

By Iain Spragg

Getty Images

Japan celebrate lifting another HSBC Asian Five Nations title.

There was far more than pride, or even silverware, at stake in the third annual instalment of the HSBC Asian Five Nations as Japan, Kazakhstan, Hong Kong, Arabian Gulf and South Korea prepared for action, with all five sides acutely aware that the winners of the 2010 tournament would secure automatic qualification for the World Cup in New Zealand in 2011.

Japan began as overwhelming favourites having won the inaugural competition in 2008 and successfully defending their title in 2009, completing both campaigns unbeaten, and the Brave Blossoms did not disappoint as they amassed a phenomenal 326 points in four landslide victories.

Coached by former All Black wing John Kirwan, Japan were simply irresistible throughout the tournament and their crushing 94–5 victory over Hong Kong in the Prince Chichibu Memorial Stadium in Tokyo in

May confirmed they would maintain their proud record of appearing at every World Cup tournament since 1987.

"We have achieved our first goal this year which was to qualify for the World Cup," Kirwan said after his team had dispatched Hong Kong. "The players have worked very hard and that was our best performance in the competition so far. But there is a long way to go. This is a fantastic opportunity for the players whose dream is to play at a World Cup and hopefully we can show the Japanese style of rugby."

The tournament kicked off in late April with the Arabian Gulf, playing their last Asian Five Nations before disbanding to pave the way for their member nations to form their own Test sides, travelling to Kazakhstan and South Korea going to Hong Kong.

Kazakhstan proved too strong for the Gulf in Almaty in a 43–28 triumph but it was Hong Kong who started the competition with a surprise result and a 32–8 victory over the Koreans courtesy of a brace of tries from forward Nigel Clarke, plus one try each by fly-half Keith Robertson and substitute wing Tom McQueen.

"This is an awesome start and just what we wanted," said captain Simon Leung. "It was a great squad effort, but we have to keep our feet on the ground as we still have another three games to go."

The Japanese meanwhile began against South Korea in Kyungsang in early May and the defending champions made an immediate statement of intent with a crushing 71–13 victory over their hosts courtesy of five tries from flying wing Kosuke Endo.

The clash was the only away game of the campaign for Kirwan's side and they returned to Tokyo to prepare for their remaining three games.

The Arabian Gulf, were the first visitors to the Japanese capital and although the final 60–5 scoreline in favour of the home side suggested another rout, the Gulf XV were far from disgraced and grabbed a late consolation try from Sean Hurley

"I couldn't ask much more from the boys," insisted Gulf captain Michael Cox-Hill. "We never gave up and proved that by scoring in the 76th minute. We can take a lot of credit for the way we played."

A week later Japan played host to Kazakhstan in the Prince Chichibu Memorial Stadium and if Kirwan's side had been impressive in their opening two fixtures, they were simply irresistible against Kazakhstan in what proved to be a hugely one-sided encounter.

Shota Horie, Sione Vatuvei, Goshi Tachikawa and Koji Taira all crossed the line inside the first 17 minutes to stun the visitors and wrap up the available bonus point. Kazakhstan did reply midway through the first half through hooker Mikhail Solovyev but it was merely a temporary respite and Japan ran in 11 further tries to complete a 101–7 mauling that took the nation to the verge of World Cup qualification.

It was still mathematically possible for Hong Kong to dethrone the Japanese as champions and finish first with a bonus point victory in the clash between the two sides in the final game of the tournament but Japan knew a draw would be sufficient to ensure they would be playing in New Zealand in 2011.

As it transpired, the home side were never troubled by the visitors in front of a tournament record 10,000-strong crowd in Tokyo and when wing Alisi Tupuailei raced over for the first try of the match, the writing was on the wall for Hong Kong.

Tupuailei went on to complete a hat-trick in the opening 40 minutes, while Endo helped himself to a brace, and Japan stormed to a convincing 94–5 victory which confirmed them as Asian Five Nations champions for a third successive year and rewarded the Brave Blossoms with another opportunity to perform on the world stage.

"It's important we keep growing," said Kirwan after the match. "I want to show the world how much we have improved and I hope we have the courage to play our style of rugby. I have never taken the field to lose a game and won't in New Zealand next year and I am sure the players feel the same."

Defeat was a bitter pill to swallow for Hong Kong but there was worse to follow when the news filtered through that Kazakhstan had triumphed 32–25 over South Korea in Incheon in their final game, snatching second place in the table to claim the right to face Uruguay (which the South Americans won 44–7 in July) in a cross-continental play-off for a place in the World Cup.

"It is really disappointing that our World Cup dream is over but Japan were too good for us and we were blown away," said Hong Kong head coach Dai Rees. "And all credit to Kazakhstan to go to Korea and beat them by four tries to secure the crucial bonus point."

In Division One of the Asian Five Nations, Sri Lanka earned promotion to the top-flight after beating Singapore 23–16 in a thrilling final staged in the Yio Chu Kang Stadium.

The Sri Lankans had beaten Chinese Taipei 37–7 in the semi-final but were taken to the wire by Singapore in the final and had it not been for a dramatic late try, the game could have gone into extra-time. Scrum-half Roshan Weeraratne got the first try of the match for Sri Lanka but the two sides were locked at 16–16 all as the final whistle loomed, only for centre Chamara Vithanage to charge over in the corner for the vital score that settled the issue.

"We fought tremendous odds on and off the field and came through with flying colours mainly due to the tremendous team work," said Sri Lanka captain Pradeep Liyanage. "We promised to bring glory to our motherland and we have done it."

ASIAN FIVE NATIONS 2010 RESULTS

TOP FIVE

Hong Kong 32–8 **South Korea**, **Kazakhstan** 43–28 **Arabian Gulf**, **Arabian Gulf** 16–9 **Hong Kong**, **South Korea** 13–71 **Japan**, **Japan** 60–5 **Arabian Gulf**, **Hong Kong** 19–15 **Kazakhstan**, **Arabian Gulf** 21–19 **South Korea**, **Kazakhstan** 7–101 **Japan**, **Japan** 94–5 **Hong Kong**, **South Korea** 25–32 **Kazakhstan**

DIVISION ONE

Chinese Taipei 7–37 **Sri Lanka**, **Singapore** 22–20 **Malaysia**, **Chinese Taipei** 8–35 **Malaysia**, **Sri Lanka** 23–16 **Singapore**

DIVISION TWO

China 5–94 **India**, **Thailand** 33–53 **Philippines**, **China** 5–56 **Thailand**, **India** 12–34 **Philippines**

DIVISION THREE

Guam 11–44 **Iran**, **Pakistan** 13–11 **Indonesia**, **Guam** 49–12 **Indonesia**, **Iran** 19–6 **Pakistan**

DIVISION FOUR

Uzbekistan 46–0 **Almaty Select XV**, **Jordan** 29–21 **Mongolia**, **Almaty Select XV** 38–21 **Mongolia**, **Uzbekistan** 3–28 **Jordan**

REGIONAL TOURNAMENT: CAMBODIA

Cambodia 9–10 **Brunei**, **Laos** 23–5 **Brunei**, **Cambodia** 3–12 **Laos**

TOP 5 – FINAL STANDINGS

Team	P	W	D	L	F	A	BP	PTS
Japan	4	4	0	0	326	30	4	**24**
Kazakhstan	4	2	0	2	94	173	3	**13**
Hong Kong	4	2	0	2	65	133	2	**12**
Arabian Gulf	4	2	0	2	70	128	0	**10**
South Korea	4	0	0	4	65	156	3	**3**

NAMIBIA EMERGE TRIUMPHANT

By Andrea Wiggins

IRB

The Namibians celebrate their historic win.

Namibia had many reasons to be cheerful heading into the fifth IRB Nations Cup in June, but few would have tipped them for the title despite their impressive Rugby World Cup qualification performances over the previous 12 months.

Returning to the six-team tournament following a three-year absence, Namibia had propped up the table without a win on their previous appearance. In 2010, they were seeking to address that statistic and build on their Africa Cup success the previous year.

Namibia certainly did not have it all their own way in Bucharest and had to come from behind to beat hosts Romania 21–17 in their opening match. In fact it was only an extraordinary try by Llewellyn Winkler at the death that sealed the victory, the right wing side-stepping and dummying his way through a bewildered defence.

Four days later Namibia had to endure a late rally by defending champions Scotland A to triumph 23–20. Scrum-half Eugene Jantjies stood out in an exciting back-line, but it was Namibia's defence in the last ten minutes which proved decisive, repelling wave after wave of Scottish attacks.

These two victories meant that Namibia had the title in their sights as they went into their final match with fellow Rugby World Cup 2011 qualifiers Georgia. However, they weren't the only ones as Italy A had also won their two matches, edging the Argentina Jaguars 22–20 on day one and then Georgia 21–3 with fly-half Luciano Orquera the star of the show against the latter, scoring all of his side's points.

Namibia were first to take to the field on the final day at the stadionul National Arcul de Triumf and their encounter with Georgia was one of tremendous physicality. Georgia were reliant on the rock solid defence that had seen them beat Scotland A on day one, and it was the Lelos who led 13–0 at half-time.

However, the loss of Georgia's inspirational captain Tedo Zibzibadze to a dislocated elbow and then his fellow centre Revaz Gigauri to injury allowed Namibia to grow in confidence, driven on by their captain and star player Jacques Burger.

Burger himself crossed the whitewash first, followed by his impressive and fleet-footed team-mate Chrysander Botha at full-back, who secured the 21–16 victory with a second try to complete a remarkable comeback.

Namibia coach Johan Diergaardt knows that his revitalised team must now use the Nations Cup as a springboard to achieving even better things in 2011. "This is not the end, it's just the beginning as this team has a lot of potential to become a great team. We are thankful for what we have," he insisted.

"At half-time it was a matter of putting all the things together again and telling the boys that we can actually make it. They just had to stop making mistakes, silly mistakes, and start working harder. I do believe they showed a lot of character after the break and I'm feeling great about this team."

Namibia had to endure a few nervous hours to see if the victory was enough to secure them a first ever Nations Cup title, but there was no need for a calculator to determine the champions after Italy A fell at the final hurdle against a resilient new-look Romania, losing a thrilling encounter 27–22.

Romania adapted their style of play and, cheered on by partisan home support, attempted a more attacking approach, throwing off the defensive shackles usually associated with the team who are masters of the driving maul.

Despite dominating the set piece with authority, the Italians were outclassed by a Romanian pack marshalled by captain Sorin Socol, who was later named player of the tournament, and Ovidiu Tonita.

A couple of vintage tries, the first by prop Cezar Popescu and the second by wing Catalin Fercu, along with the accurate and consistent boot of Dan Dumbrava saw Romania to a deserved victory.

The winning margin was enough for Romania to pip Italy A to second spot in the standings on points difference, albeit only just. Italy A had to settle for third place overall, something captain Antonio Pavanello wasn't happy about.

"I'm upset because on the one hand we made unforced errors, which are normal in a match of rugby, but it is not acceptable to give away silly penalties when we should know better," Pavanello said. "On the other hand we did not think properly, making mistake after mistake and allowing them to control the game which we should have won."

His counterpart Socol insisted that "ultimately it was a question of desire, we really wanted this badly", but despite the best ever finish for Romania in a Nations Cup, he too had regrets, albeit not about this match but the opening one that got away against Namibia.

"Although we won two important games, the loss against Namibia, a team we dominated, still hurts," Socol admitted. "In fact, we under-estimated them and they punished us and we deserved it. Namibia made significant progress and we expect them to get some good results at the next World Cup. We hope to play against them again."

In between the Namibia loss and Italy A victory, Romania were convincing 24–8 winners over the Argentina Jaguars, the 2009 runners-up. This victory was the lift that the team and their loyal supporters needed, instilling the belief that under new coaches Steve McDowall and Romeo Gontineac they could go on to achieve bigger and better things.

The IRB Nations Cup – held for a fourth successive year in the Romanian capital – again provided vital experience for the likes of Namibia and Georgia, both nations having confirmed their places at Rugby World Cup 2011 over the preceding eight months.

The tournament also gave more established nations the chance to test new and exciting talent on the international stage, giving many players a chance to stake a claim for a place in their respective country's squads at next year's World Cup in New Zealand.

"I don't know if we were close to our potential or not but we did everything in our power and put all the effort in to progress our game," Argentina Jaguars captain Agustín Guzman said.

"This Nations Cup provided us with a great opportunity to advance our game, experience and playing careers. The most important thing for all of us here is that we came here as a group of players and we are leaving as a team."

The Jaguars finished fifth in the standings, behind Georgia and above Scotland A – the side they beat 33–13 in the other match on the final day. This meant that Scotland A relinquished the title they won under Andy Robinson in 2009 without a victory, having lost 22–21 to Georgia and 23–20 to Namibia.

"You can't criticise the effort of players. The way in which we've come together and trained has been very good," admitted Scotland A coach Sean Lineen. "We scored the first try in every game but couldn't keep up the intensity. I know the players will agree that the area which let us down was individual skills.

"I'm always very positive and what I'll take back from this tournament is the performances shown by players like Fraser McKenzie, Steven Turnbull and Chris Fusaro. Bryan Rennie also put his hand up.

"I'm not sure we respected the tournament enough. This is a tournament where we have two teams in the World Cup. Everyone will learn from this."

RESULTS

11/06/2010	Namibia	21–17	Romania	Bucharest
11/06/2010	Argentina Jaguars	20–22	Italy A	Bucharest
11/06/2010	Scotland A	21–22	Georgia	Bucharest
15/06/2010	Italy A	21–3	Georgia	Bucharest
15/06/2010	Scotland A	20–23	Namibia	Bucharest
15/06/2010	Romania	24–8	Argentina Jaguars	Bucharest
20/06/2010	Georgia	16–21	Namibia	Bucharest
20/06/2010	Argentina Jaguars	33–13	Scotland A	Bucharest
20/06/2010	Italy A	22–27	Romania	Bucharest

FINAL STANDINGS

	P	W	D	L	F	A	BP	PTS
Namibia	3	3	0	0	65	53	0	**12**
Romania	3	2	0	1	68	51	1	**9**
Italy A	3	2	0	1	65	50	1	**9**
Georgia	3	1	0	2	41	63	1	**5**
Argentina Jaguars	3	1	0	2	61	59	1	**5**
Scotland A	3	0	0	3	54	78	2	**2**

MAJOR RUGBY TOURS 2009–10

By Chris Rhys

BLEDISLOE CUP

31 October 2009, Olympic Stadium, Tokyo
Australia 19 (1G 4PG) New Zealand 32 (2G 6PG)

AUSTRALIA: JD O'Connor (Western Force); PJ Hynes (Queensland Reds), RP Cross (Western Force), AP Ashley-Cooper Brumbies), DN Ioane (Queensland Reds); MJ Giteau (Brumbies), SW Genia (Queensland Reds); BA Robinson (NSW Waratahs), ST Moore (Brumbies), BE Alexander (Brumbies), JE Horwill (Queensland Reds), MD Chisholm (Brumbies), RD Elsom (Brumbies)(capt), WL Palu (NSW Waratahs), DW Pocock (Western Force)

SUBSTITUTIONS: T Polata-Nau (NSW Waratahs) & DW Mumm (NSW Waratahs) for Moore & Chisholm (49 mins), GB Smith (Brumbies) for Palu (54 mins)

SCORERS: *Try*: Hynes *Conversion*: Giteau *Penalty goals*: Giteau (4)

NEW ZEALAND: JM Muliaina (Waikato); CS Jane (Wellington), CG Smith (Wellington), MA Nonu (Wellington), SW Sivivatu (Waikato); DW Carter (Canterbury), QJ Cowan (Southland); TD Woodcock (North Harbour), AK Hore (Taranaki), NS Tialata (Wellington), BC Thorn (Canterbury), TJS Donnelly (Otago), AJ Thomson (Otago), R So'oialo (Wellington), RH McCaw (Canterbury)(capt)

SUBSTITUTIONS: IF Afoa (Auckland) for Tialata (46 mins), KJ Read (Canterbury) for So'oialo (53 mins), JJ Eaton (Taranaki) for Donnelly (64 mins), SR Donald (Waikato) for Carter (79 mins)

SCORERS: *Tries*: Sivivatu, C Smith *Conversions*: Carter (2) *Penalty goals*: Carter (6)

REFEREE: SM Lawrence (South Africa)

NEW ZEALAND TO EUROPE 2009

TOUR PARTY

FULL BACKS: JM Muliaina (Waikato), BR Smith (Otago)

THREE QUARTERS: ZR Guildford (Hawke's Bay), CS Jane (Wellington), SW Sivavatu (Waikato), TE Ellison (Wellington), CL McAlister (North Harbour), MA Nonu (Wellington), CG Smith (Wellington)

HALF BACKS: DW Carter (Canterbury), MP Delany (Bay of Plenty), SR Donald (Waikato), QJ Cowan (Southland), AM Ellis (Canterbury), BG Leonard (Waikato)

FORWARDS: AK Hore (Taranaki), CR Flynn (Canterbury), * AP de Malmanche (Waikato), IF Afoa (Auckland), WWV Crockett (Canterbury), OT Franks (Canterbury), NS Tialata (Wellington), TD Woodcock (North Harbour) AF Boric (North Harbour), TJS Donnelly (Otago), JJ Eaton (Taranaki), BC Thorn (Canterbury), RH McCaw (Canterbury), J Kaino (Auckland), LJ Messam (Waikato), AJ Thomson (Otago), TD Latimer (Bay of Plenty), KJ Read (Canterbury), R So'oialo (Wellington)

* Replacement on tour

MANAGER D Shand **COACH** G Henry **ASSISTANT COACHES** S Hansen, W Smith **CAPTAIN** RH McCaw

7 November, Millennium Stadium, Cardiff
Wales 12 (4PG) New Zealand 19 (1G 4PG)

WALES: JW Hook (Ospreys); SL Halfpenny (Cardiff Blues), TGL Shanklin (Cardiff Blues), JH Roberts (Cardiff Blues), SM Williams (Ospreys); SM Jones (Scarlets), GJ Cooper (Cardiff Blues); GD Jenkins (Cardiff Blues), M Rees (Scarlets); P James (Ospreys), A-W Jones (Ospreys), LC Charteris (Newport Gwent Dragons), A Powell (Cardiff Blues), RP Jones (Ospreys)(capt), ME Williams (Cardiff Blues)

SUBSTITUTIONS: M Roberts (Scarlets) for Cooper (54 mins), H Bennett (Ospreys) & DJ Jones (Ospreys) for Rees & James (60 mins), BS Davies (Cardiff Blues) & DAR Jones (Scarlets) for Charteris & Powell (65 mins)

SCORER: *Penalty goals*: SM Jones (4)

NEW ZEALAND: Muliaina; Jane, C Smith, Nonu, Guildford; Carter, Leonard; Crockett, Hore, Tialata, Thorn, Eaton, Kaino, Read, McCaw (capt)

SUBSTITUTIONS: Cowan for Leonard (50 mins), Donnelly for Eaton (54 mins), OT Franks for Crockett (60 mins), Thomson for Read (66 mins)

SCORERS: *Try*: Hore *Conversion*: Carter *Penalty goals*: Carter (4)

REFEREE: C Joubert (South Africa)

14 November, Stadio Guiseppe Meazza (San Siro), Milan
Italy 6 (2PG) New Zealand 20 (5PG 1T)

ITALY: L McLean (Treviso); PK Robertson (Viadana), G-J Canale (ASM Clermont Auvergne), G Garcia (Treviso), Mi Bergamasco (Stade Francais); C Gower (Aviron Bayonnais), T Tebaldi (Gran Parma); S Perugini (Aviron Bayonnais), LL Ghiraldini (Treviso), M-L Castrogiovanni (Leicester Tigers), C-A del Fava (Viadana), Q Geldenhuys (Viadana), A Zanni (Treviso), S Parisse (Stade Francais)(capt), Ma Bergamasco (Stade Francais)

SUBSTITUTIONS: JW Sole (Viadana) for Del Fava (56 mins), I Rouyet (Treviso) for Perugini (58 mins), S Picone (Treviso) for Tebaldi (61 mins), S Favaro (Rugby Parma) for Zanni (66 mins), F Ongaro (Saracens) for Ghiraldini (68 mins)

SCORER: *Penalty goals:* Gower (2)

NEW ZEALAND: Jane; B Smith, Ellison, McAlister, Sivivatu; Delany, Ellis; Crockett, Flynn, Tialata, Donnelly, Boric, Messam, So'oialo (capt), Latimer

SUBSTITUTIONS: Afoa & Cowan for Crockett & Ellis (58 mins), Donald for Delany (63 mins), Muliaina for Jane (68 mins)

SCORERS: *Try*: Flynn *Penalty goals*: McAlister (5)

REFEREE: SJ Dickinson (Australia)

21 November, Twickenham
England 6 (2PG) New Zealand 19 (1G 4PG)

ENGLAND: MJ Cueto (Sale Sharks), MA Banahan (Bath Rugby), DJ Hipkiss (Leicester Tigers), AO Erinle (Biarritz Olympique), UCC Monye (NEC Harlequins); JP Wilkinson (RC Toulon), PK Hodgson (London Irish); TAN Payne (London Wasps), DM Hartley (Northampton Saints), DSC Bell (Bath Rugby), SD Shaw (London Wasps), SW Borthwick (Saracens)(capt), JPR Worsley (London Wasps), JAW Haskell (London Wasps), LW Moody (Leicester Tigers)

SUBSTITUTIONS: TR Croft (Leicester Tigers) for Worsley (2 mins), SG Thompson (CA Brive) for Hartley (48 mins), DG Wilson (Bath Rugby) for Bell (49 mins), SJJ Geraghty (Northampton Saints) for Erinle (62 mins), LP Deacon (Leicester Tigers) for Shaw (65 mins), DS Care (NEC Harlequins) for Hodgson (69 mins), MJM Tait (Sale Sharks) for Banahan (71 mins)

SCORER: *Penalty goals*: Wilkinson (2)

NEW ZEALAND: Muliaina; Guildford, C Smith, Nonu, Sivivatu; Carter, Cowan; Woodcock, Hore, OT Franks, Thorn, Donnelly, Thomson, Read, McCaw (capt)

SUBSTITUTIONS: Afoa & Kaino for Franks & Thomson (57 mins), Boric for Donnelly (60 mins), Ellis for Cowan (70 mins)

SCORERS: *Try*: Cowan Conversion: Carter *Penalty goals*: Carter (4)

REFEREE: JI Kaplan (South Africa)

28 November, Stade Velodrome, Marseille
France 12 (3PG 1DG) New Zealand 39 (4G 2PG 1T)

FRANCE: D Traille (Biarritz Olympique); V Clerc (Stade Toulousain), D Marty (USA Perpignan), Y Jauzion (Stade Toulousain), M Medard (Stade Toulousain): F Trinh-Duc (RC Montpellier-Herault), J Dupuy (Stade Francais); F Barcella (Biarritz Olympique), W Servat (Stade Toulousain), S Marconnet (Stade Francais), S Chabal (Racing Metro 92), R Millo-Chluski (Stade Toulousain), T Dusautoir (Stade Toulousain)(capt), J Bonnaire (ASM Clermont Auvergne), F Ouedraogo (RC Montpellier-Herault)

SUBSTITUTIONS: D Szarzewski (Stade Francais) for Servat (47 mins), N Mas (USA Perpignan) & L Nallet (Metro Racing 92) for Marconnet & Chabal (52 mins), M Parra (ASM Clermont Auvergne) for Dupuy (58 mins), J Puricelli (Aviron Bayonnais) and Y David (Stade Toulousain) for Ouedraogo & Jauzion (63 mins), C Heymans (Stade Toulousain) for Medard (72 mins)

SCORERS: *Penalty goals*: Dupuy (3) *Dropped goal*: Trinh-Duc

NEW ZEALAND: Muliaina; Jane, C Smith, Nonu, Sivivatu; Carter, Cowan; Woodcock, Hore, Tialata, Thorn, Donnelly, Kaino, Read, McCaw (capt)
SUBSTITUTIONS: OT Franks & Boric for Tialata & Thorn (65 mins), McAlister for Nonu (71 mins), Donald, Flynn & Latimer for Carter, Hore & Read (73 mins), Ellis for Cowan (75 mins)
SCORERS: *Tries*: Sivivatu, Muliaina, Kaino, Jane, C Smith *Conversions*: Carter (4) *Penalty goals*: Carter (2)
REFEREE: AC Rolland (Ireland)

5 December, Twickenham
Barbarians 25 (2G 2PG 1T) New Zealand XV 18 (1G 2PG 1T)

Barbarians scorers: *Tries*: BG Habana (3) *Conversions*: MJ Giteau (2) *Penalty goals*: MJ Giteau, M Steyn
New Zealand XV scorers: *Tries*: B Smith, Boric *Conversion*: Donald *Penalty goals*: Donald, Delany
Referee: C Berdos (France)

AUSTRALIA TO EUROPE 2009

TOUR PARTY

FULL BACKS: AP Ashley-Cooper (Brumbies), JD O'Connor (Western Force)
THREE QUARTERS: K Beale (NSW Waratahs), PJ Hynes (Queensland Reds), DN Ioane (Queensland Reds), DA Mitchell (NSW Waratahs), QS Cooper (Queensland Reds), RP Cross (Western Force), RG Horne (NSW Waratahs), LD Turner NSW Waratahs), * T Smith (Brumbies), * L Morahan (Queensland Reds)
HALF BACKS: MJ Giteau (Brumbies), B Barnes (Queensland Reds), L Burgess (NSW Waratahs), WS Genia (Queensland Reds), R Kingi (Queensland Reds), * M Toomua (Brumbies),
FORWARDS: ST Moore (Brumbies), T Polota-Nau (NSW Waratahs), BE Alexander (Brumbies), PJM Cowan (Western Force), MJ Dunning (Western Force), SM Kepu (NSW Waratahs), SL Ma'afu (Brumbies), BA Robinson (NSW Waratahs), MD Chisholm (Brumbies), D Dennis (NSW Waratahs), RD Elsom (Brumbies), JE Horwill (Queensland Reds), DW Mumm (NSW Waratahs), M Chapman (Brumbies), MJ Hodgson (Western Force), DW Pocock (Western Force), GB Smith (Brumbies), RN Brown (Western Force), WL Palu (NSW Waratahs)

* Replacement on tour

MANAGER P Thomson **COACH** RM Deans **ASSISTANT COACHES** JRW Williams, R Graham, P Noriega **CAPTAIN** RD Elsom

3 November, Kingsholm Gloucester
Gloucester Rugby 5 (1T) Australia XV 36 (4G 1PG 1T)

Gloucester Rugby scorer: *Try*: F Burns
Australia XV scorers: *Tries*: Mitchell (2), Cross, T Smith, Cooper *Conversions*: Cooper (4) *Penalty goal*: Cooper

7 November 2009, Twickenham
England 9 (2PG 1DG) Australia 18 (1G 2PG 1T)

ENGLAND: UCC Monye (Harlequins); MJ Cueto (Sale Sharks), DJ Hipkiss (Leicester Tigers), SJJ Geraghty (Northampton Saints), MA Banahan (Bath Rugby); JP Wilkinson (RC Toulon), DS Care (Harlequins); TAN Payne (London Wasps), SG Thompson (CA Brive), DG Wilson (Bath Rugby), LP Deacon (Leicester Tigers), SW Borthwick (Saracens)(capt), TR Croft (Leicester Tigers), JS Crane (Leicester Tigers), LW Moody (Leicester Tigers)
SUBSTITUTIONS: JAW Haskell (Stade Francais) for Crane (52 mins), DM Hartley (Northampton Saints) for Thompson (55 mins), DSC Bell (Bath Rugby) for Wilson (57 mins), PK Hodgson (London Irish) for Care (62 mins), AO Erinle (Biarritz Olympique) for Hipkiss (66 mins), CL Lawes (Northampton Saints) for Deacon (68 mins)
SCORERS: *Penalty goals*: Wilkinson (2) *Dropped goal*: Wilkinson
AUSTRALIA: Ashley-Cooper; Hynes, Ioane, Cooper, Mitchell; Giteau, Genia; Robinson, Moore, Alexander, Horwill, Chisholm, Elsom (capt), Palu, G Smith
SUBSTITUTIONS: Polota-Nau for Moore (59 mins), Cross for Ioane (66 mins), Pocock for Palu (68 mins), Mumm for Chisholm (72 mins), Dunning for Alexander (76 mins)
SCORERS: *Tries*: Genia, Ashley-Cooper *Conversion*: Giteau *Penalty Goals*: Giteau (2)
REFEREE: BJ Lawrence (New Zealand)

15 November, Croke Park, Dublin
Ireland 20 (2G 2PG) Australia 20 (2G 2PG)

IRELAND: RDJ Kearney (Leinster); TJ Bowe (Ospreys), BG O'Driscoll (Leinster)(capt), PW Wallace (Ulster), LM Fitzgerald (Leinster); RJR O'Gara (Munster), TG O'Leary (Munster); CE Healy (Leinster), JP Flannery (Munster), JJ Hayes (Munster), DP O'Callaghan (Munster), PJ O'Connell (Munster), SPH Ferris (Ulster), JPR Heaslip (Leinster), DP Wallace (Munster)

SUBSTITUTIONS: KG Earls (Munster) for Fitzgerald (53 mins), DP Leamy (Munster) for D Wallace (temp 62-64 & 75 mins)

SCORERS: *Tries*: Bowe, O'Driscoll *Conversions*: O'Gara (2) *Penalty goals*: O'Gara (2)

AUSTRALIA: Ashley-Cooper; Hynes, Ioane, Cooper, Mitchell; Giteau, Genia; Robinson, Moore, Alexander, Horwill, Chisholm, Elsom (capt), Palu, Pocock

SUBSTITUTIONS: G Smith for Pocock (temp 20-27 mins), Polota-Nau for Moore (62 mins), O'Connor for Ashley-Cooper (69 mins)

SCORERS: *Tries:* Mitchell, Elsom *Conversions:* Giteau (2) *Penalty goals*: Giteau (2)

REFEREE: JI Kaplan (South Africa)

21 November, Murrayfield
Scotland 9 (2PG 1DG) Australia 8 (1PG 1T)

SCOTLAND: RP Lamont (RC Toulon); SF Lamont (Scarlets), A Grove (Worcester Warriors), GA Morrison (Glasgow Warriors), SCJ Danielli (Ulster); PJ Godman (Edinburgh), CP Cusiter (Glasgow Warriors)(capt); AF Jacobsen (Edinburgh), RW Ford (Edinburgh), MJ Low (Glasgow Warriors), NJ Hines (Leinster), AD Kellock (Glasgow Warriors), AK Strokosch (Gloucester Rugby), JW Beattie (Glasgow Warriors), JA Barclay (Glasgow Warriors)

SUBSTITUTIONS: RGM Lawson (Gloucester Rugby) for Cusiter (20 mins), NJ de Luca (Edinburgh) for Morrison (40 mins), JPR White (ASM Clermont Auvergne) for Strokosch (47 mins), K Traynor (Edinburgh) for Low (56 mins), RJ Vernon (Glasgow Warriors) & CD Paterson (Edinburgh) for Beattie & Danielli (62 mins), DWH Hall (Glasgow Warriors) for Ford (76 mins)

SCORERS: *Penalty goals:* Godman (2) *Dropped goal:* Paterson

AUSTRALIA: Ashley-Cooper; Hynes, Cross, Cooper, Mitchell; Giteau, Genia; Robinson, Moore, Alexander, Horwill, Chisholm, Elsom (capt), Palu, G Smith

SUBSTITUTIONS: Kepu for Robinson (16 mins), Polota-Nau for Moore (45 mins), Mumm for Chisholm (49 mins), Burgess for Genia (62 mins), Brown for Palu (65 mins), O'Connor for Cooper (73 mins)

SCORERS: *Try*: Cross *Penalty goal:* Giteau

REFEREE: R Poite (France)

24 November, City Stadium, Cardiff
Cardiff Blues 3 (1PG) Australia XV 31 (4G 1PG)

Cardiff Blues scorer: *Penalty goal*: B Blair

Australia XV scorers: *Tries:* Beale (2), Cross, Morahan *Conversions:* O'Connor (4) *Penalty goal*: O'Connor

28 November, Millennium Stadium, Cardiff
Wales 12 (4PG) Australia 33 (2G 3PG 2T)

WALES: JW Hook (Ospreys); SL Halfpenny (Cardiff Blues), JH Roberts (Cardiff Blues), J Davies (Scarlets), SM Williams (Ospreys); SM Jones (Scarlets), DJ Peel (Sale Sharks); GD Jenkins (Cardiff Blues)(capt), M Rees (Scarlets), P James (Ospreys), A-W Jones (Ospreys), LC Charteris (Newport Gwent Dragons), DJ Lydiate (Newport Gwent Dragons), A Powell (Cardiff Blues), ME Williams (Cardiff Blues)

SUBSTITUTIONS: T James (Cardiff Blues) for SM Williams (5 mins), M Roberts (Scarlets) for Peel (temp 10-17 & 71 mins), AM Bishop (Ospreys) for Halfpenny (27 mins), H Bennett (Ospreys) for Rees (30 mins), DJ Jones (Ospreys), S Warburton (Cardiff Blues) & J Thomas (Ospreys) for James, Lydiate & Charteris (48 mins)

SCORERS: *Penalty goals*: SM Jones (3), Halfpenny

AUSTRALIA: Ashley-Cooper; Hynes, Ioane, Cooper, Mitchell; Giteau, Genia; Robinson, Moore, Alexander, Horwill, Mumm, Elsom (capt), Palu, Pocock

SUBSTITUTIONS: G Smith for Pocock (40 mins), Polota-Nau for Moore (54 mins), O'Connor for Hynes (60 mins), Dunning, Chisholm & Beale for Alexander, Palu & Mitchell (70 mins), Burgess for Genia (79 mins)

SCORERS: *Tries:* Ioane, Horwill, Pocock, Polota-Nau *Conversions:* Giteau (2) *Penalty goals:* Giteau (3)

REFEREE: W Barnes (England)

TOUR PARTY

FULL BACKS: J Matavesi (Exeter Chiefs), NAS Ligairi (CA Brive)

THREE QUARTERS: V Goneva (Vataru), N Nalaga (ASM Clermont Auvergne), V Delasau (RC Montauban), G Lovobalavu (RC Toulon), S Bai (ASM Clermont Auvergne), J Ratu (Cagimaira), N Roko (Yokogawa), T Nagusa (Ulster)

HALF BACKS: NT Little (Bath Rugby), WS Luveniyali (Airport), MN Rauluni (Saracens), W Vatuvoka (Duavata), K Bola (Kadavu)

FORWARDS: V Veikoso (Mavoci), S Ledua (FTG), VR Sauturaga (Duavata), GC Dewes (Esher) A Yalayalatabua (Navy), DT Manu (Scarlets), V Seuseu (Korovuto), A Tarogi (Le Bugue), RWG Lewaravu (London Welsh), Rawaqa (World Fighting Bull), L Nakarawa (Army), J Domolailai (Lomavatu), A Qera (Gloucester Rugby), J Naikaidawa (Kaite), S Bola (Police), N E Talei (Worcester Warriors), A Boko (Tau), JN Qovu (Senibau), AV Satala (Gloucester Rugby)

MANAGER J Browne **COACH** Glen Ella **ASSISTANT COACHES** S Domoni, M Brewer, I Male **CAPTAIN** S Bai

14 November, Murrayfield
Scotland 23 (2G 3PG) Fiji 10 (1G 1PG)

SCOTLAND: RP Lamont (RC Toulon); SF Lamont (Scarlets), A Grove (Worcester Warriors), GA Morrison (Glasgow Warriors), SCJ Danielli (Ulster); PJ Godman (Edinburgh), CP Cusiter (Glasgow Warriors)(capt); AF Jacobsen (Edinburgh), RW Ford (Edinburgh), MJ Low (Glasgow Warriors), NJ Hines (Leinster), AD Kellock (Glasgow Warriors), AK Strokosch (Gloucester Rugby), JW Beattie (Glasgow Warriors), JA Barclay (Glasgow Warriors)

SUBSTITUTIONS: K Traynor (Edinburgh), MRL Blair (Edinburgh) & CD Paterson (Edinburgh) for Jacobsen, Cusiter & R Lamont (62 mins), JPR White (ASM Clermont Auvergne) for Strokosch (64 mins), DWH Hall (Glasgow Warriors) for Ford (69 mins), NJ de Luca (Edinburgh) & RJ Vernon (Glasgow Warriors) for Blair & Beattie (77 mins)

SCORERS: *Tries:* Beattie, Morrison *Conversions:* Godman (2) *Penalty goals:* Godman (3)

FIJI: Matavesi; Goneva, Lovobalavu, Bai (capt), Nalaga; Little, Rauluni; Yalayalatabua, Veikoso, Manu, Lewaravu, Rawaqa, Domolailai, Boko, Qera

SUBSTITUTIONS: S Bola for Domolailai (23 mins), Dewes for Yalayalatabua (40 mins), Ledua for Veikoso (69 mins), Vatuvoka for Rauluni (71 mins), Ratu for Matavesi (75 mins)

SCORERS: *Try*: Goneva *Conversion*: Little *Penalty goal:* Little

REFEREE: C White (England)

21 November, Royal Dublin Society Showground
Ireland 41 (5G 2PG) Fiji 6 (2PG)

IRELAND: RDJ Kearney (Leinster); SP Horgan (Leinster), BG O'Driscoll (Leinster)(capt), GW D'Arcy (Leinster), KG Earls (Munster); J Sexton (Leinster), EG Reddan (Leinster); TG Court (Ulster), JP Flannery (Munster), JJ Hayes (Munster), LFM Cullen (Leinster), PJ O'Connell (Munster), SPH Ferris (Ulster), JPR Heasley (Leinster), DP Leamy (Munster)

SUBSTITUTIONS: S O'Brien (Leinster) for Leamy (44 mins), TG O'Leary (Munster) for Reddan (54 mins), TD Buckley (Munster) for Hayes (60 mins), AD Trimble (Ulster) & DP O'Callaghan (Munster) for O'Driscoll & O'Connell (67 mins), S Cronin (Connacht) for Flannery (72 mins), PW Wallace (Ulster) for Kearney (74 mins)

SCORERS: *Tries*: Earls (2), O'Driscoll, Kearney, Horgan *Conversions:* Sexton (5) *Penalty goals*: Sexton (2)

FIJI: Ligairi; Goneva, Lovobaluvu, Bai (capt), Roko; Little, Rauluni; Tarogi, Veikoso, Seuseu, Lewaravu, Rawaqa, Satala, Boko, Qera

SUBSTITUTIONS: Nakawara for Rawaqa (40 mins), Nagusa for Ligairi (52 mins), S Bola, Dewes & Ledua for Qera, Tarogi & Veikoso (65 mins), Matavesi for Bai (77 mins)

SCORER: *Penalty goals*: Little (2)

REFEREE: M Jonker (South Africa)

28 November, Stadion Arcul de Triumf, Bucharest
Romania 18 (1G 2PG 1T) Fiji 29 (3G 1PG 1T)

Romania scorers: *Tries:* O Tonita, B Balan *Conversion:* D Dumbrava *Penalty goals:* F Vlaicu (2)

Fiji scorers: *Tries:* Goneva, Naikadawa, Nagusa, Ratu *Conversions:* Matavesi (3) *Penalty goal:* Matavesi

Referee: J Garces (France)

TOUR PARTY

FULL BACKS: H Agulla (CA Brive), L Gonzalez-Amorosino (Leicester Tigers)
THREE QUARTERS: L Borges (RC Albi), M Comuzzi (Pucara), GP Tiesi (Harlequins), M Rodriguez (Atletico de Rosario), BM Urdapilleta (CUBA), F Martin Aramburu (US Dax), HM San Martin (Tala)
HALF BACKS: S Fernandez (Hindu), A Lalanne (London Irish), A Figuerola (CASI), N Vergallo (US Dax)
FORWARDS: ME Ledesma (ASM Clermont Auvergne), A Vernet Basualdo (Stade Toulousain), A Creevy (San Luis), MI Ayerza (Leicester Tigers), R Roncero (Stade Francais), M Scelzo (ASM Clermont Auvergne), JP Orlandi (Racing Metro 92), E Lozada (RC Toulon), PE Albacete (Stade Toulousain), M Carizza (Biarritz Olympique), M Sambucetti (Bristol Rugby), T Leonardi (SIC), A Abadie (Rovigo), AT Campos (RC Montauban), M de Achaval (A Alumni), JM Fernandez Lobbe (RC Toulon)

MANAGER R Jimenez Salice **COACH** S Phelan **ASSISTANT COACHES** F Turnes, M Reggiardo, M Gaitan, F Galthie **CAPTAIN** JM Fernandez Lobbe

14 November, Twickenham
England 16 (1G 2PG 1DG) Argentina 9 (3PG)

ENGLAND: UCC Monye (Harlequins); MJ Cueto (Sale Sharks), DJ Hipkiss (Leicester Tigers), SJJ Geraghty (Northampton Saints), MA Banahan (Bath Rugby); JP Wilkinson (RC Toulon), PK Hodgson (London Irish); TAN Payne (London Wasps), DM Hartley (Northampton Saints), DSC Bell (Bath Rugby), LP Deacon (Leicester Tigers), SW Borthwick (Saracens)(capt), TR Croft (Leicester Tigers), JAW Haskell (Stade Francais), LW Moody (Leicester Tigers)
SUBSTITUTIONS: JPR Worsley (London Wasps) & PPL Doran-Jones (Gloucester Rugby) for Croft & Payne (62 mins), SG Thompson (CA Brive) for Hartley (68 mins), DS Care (Harlequins) & AJ Goode (CA Brive) for Hodgson & Wilkinson (74 mins)
SCORERS: *Try:* Banahan *Conversion*: Wilkinson *Penalty goals:* Wilkinson (2) *Dropped goal:* Wilkinson
ARGENTINA: Agulla; Borges, Tiesi, Rodriguez, Comuzzi; Fernandez, Lalanne; Roncero, Ledesma, Scelzo, Lozada, Albacete, Leonardi, Fernandez-Lobbe (capt), Abadie
SUBSTITUTIONS: Campos for Abadie (33 mins), Carizza for Lozada (54 mins), Ayerza for Scelzo (65 mins), Figuerola for Lalanne (74 mins)
SCORER: *Penalty goals:* Rodriguez (3)
REFEREE: N Owens (Wales)

21 November, Millennium Stadium, Cardiff
Wales 33 (3G 4PG) Argentina 16 (1G 3PG)

WALES: JW Hook (Ospreys); SL Halfpenny (Cardiff Blues), JH Roberts (Cardiff Blues), J Davies (Scarlets), SM Williams (Ospreys); SM Jones (Scarlets), GJ Cooper (Cardiff Blues); GD Jenkins (Cardiff Blues), M Rees (Scarlets), P James (Ospreys), A-W Jones (Ospreys), LC Charteris (Newport Gwent Dragons), A Powell (Cardiff Blues), RP Jones (Ospreys)(capt), ME Williams (Cardiff Blues)
SUBSTITUTIONS: DJ Jones (Ospreys) for James (57 mins), DJ Peel (Sale Sharks) for Cooper (65 mins), H Bennett (Ospreys) & J Thomas (Ospreys) for Rees & Charteris (67 mins), DJ Lydiate (Newport Gwent Dragons), AM Bishop (Ospreys) & T James (Cardiff Blues) for Powell, J Davies & S Williams (72 mins)
SCORERS: *Tries*: SM Williams (2), SM Jones *Conversions*: SM Jones (3) *Penalty goals:* SM Jones (2), Halfpenny (2)
ARGENTINA: Agulla; Borges, Tiesi, Rodriguez, Comuzzi; Fernandez, Figuerola; Roncero, Ledesma, Scelzo, Sambucetti, Albacete, Leonardi, Fernandez-Lobbe (capt), Abadie
SUBSTITUTIONS: Carizza for Sambucetti (62 mins), Ayerza for Scelzo (65 mins), Urdapilleta & Campos for Comuzzi & Abadie (70 mins), San Martin for Tiesi (75 mins), Lalanne for Figuerola (77 mins)
SCORER: *Try*: Rodriguez *Conversion:* Rodriguez *Penalty goals:* Rodriguez (3)
REFEREE: G Clancy (Ireland)

28 November, Murrayfield
Scotland 6 (2PG) Argentina 9 (2PG 1DG)

SCOTLAND: RP Lamont (RC Toulon); SF Lamont (Scarlets), BJ Cairns (Edinburgh), A Grove (Worcester Warriors), TH Evans (Glasgow Warriors); PJ Godman (Edinburgh), CP Cusiter (Glasgow Warriors)(capt); AF Jacobsen (Edinburgh), RW Ford (Edinburgh), MJ Low (Glasgow Warriors), NJ Hines (Leinster), AD Kellock (Glasgow Warriors), AK Strokosch (Gloucester Rugby), JW Beattie (Glasgow Warriors), AR MacDonald (Edinburgh)

SUBSTITUTIONS: CD Paterson (Edinburgh) for R Lamont (48 mins), NJ de Luca (Edinburgh) for Cairns (55 mins), JPR White (ASM Clermont Auvergne) for Hines (59 mins), K Traynor (Edinburgh) & DWH Hall (Glasgow Warriors) for Jacobsen & Ford (64 mins), RJ Vernon (Glasgow Warriors) for Strokosch (71 mins), RGM Lawson (Gloucester Rugby) for Cusiter (73 mins)
SCORER: *Penalty goals:* Godman (2)
ARGENTINA: Agulla; Borges, Tiesi, Rodriguez, Aramburu; Fernandez, Lalanne; Ayerza, Vernet Basualdo, Scelzo, Carizza, Albacete, Campos, Fernandez-Lobbe (capt), Abadie
SUBSTITUTIONS: Creevy for Vernet Basualdo (38 mins), Roncero for Scelzo (53 mins), Leonardi & Figuerola for Abadie & Lalanne (68 mins), San Martin for Aramburu (71 mins)
SCORER: *Penalty goals*: Rodriguez (2) *Dropped goal:* Rodriguez
REFEREE: DA Lewis (Ireland)

SOUTH AFRICA TO EUROPE 2009

TOUR PARTY

FULL BACKS: Z Kirchner (Blue Bulls), E Rose (Lions)
THREE QUARTERS: OM Ndungane (Sharks), JL Nokwe (Cheetahs), J-PR Pietersen (Sharks), BG Habana (Blue Bulls), J Fourie (Lions), AA Jacobs (Sharks), W Olivier (Blue Bulls), M Bosman (Cheetahs), R Viljeon (Griquas), J de Jongh (Western Province), * J de Villiers (Munster)
HALF BACKS: M Steyn (Blue Bulls), F Hougaard (Blue Bulls), R Pienaar (Sharks), PF du Preez (Blue Bulls), H Adams (Blue Bulls)
FORWARDS: BW du Plessis (Sharks), MC Ralepelle (Blue Bulls), JW Smit (Sharks), * JA Strauss (Cheetahs), JN du Plessis (Sharks), T Mtawarira (Sharks), CJ van der Linde (Cheetahs), * WH du Preez (Cheetahs), GG Steenkamp (Blue Bulls), BG Maku (Blue Bulls), HS van der Merwe (Lions), JP Botha (Blue Bulls), V Matfield (Blue Bulls), AJ Hargreaves (Sharks), A Bekker (Western Province), SWP Burger (Western Province), HW Brussow (Cheetahs), DJ Potgieter (Blue Bulls), D Raubenheimer (Griquas), DJ Rossouw (Blue Bulls), AF Johnson (Cheetahs), R Kankowski (Sharks), *JR Deysel (Sharks)

* Replacements on tour

MANAGER A Petersen COACH P de Villiers **ASSISTANT COACHES** D Muir, G Gold, PC Montgomery **CAPTAIN** JW Smit

6 November, Welford Road, Leicester
Leicester Tigers 22 (1G 5PG) South Africa XV 17 (4PG 1T)

Leicester Tigers scorers: *Try*: L Gonzalez-Amorosino *Conversion:* B Youngs *Penalty goals*: B Youngs (5)
South Africa XV scorers: *Try*: Nokwe *Penalty goals:* Pienaar (4)

13 November, Stade Municpial, Toulouse
France 20 (5PG 1T) South Africa 13 (1G 1PG 1DG)

FRANCE: D Traille (Biarritz Olympique); V Clerc (Stade Toulousain), Y David (Stade Toulousain), M Mermoz (USA Perpignan), C Heymans (Stade Toulousain); F Trinh-Duc (RC Montpellier-Herault), J Dupuy (Stade Francais); F Barcella (Biarritz Olympique), W Servat (Stade Toulousain), N Mas (USA Perpignan), L Nallet (Racing Metro 92), R Millo-Chluski (Stade Toulousain), T Dusautoir (Stade Toulousain)(capt), L Picamoles (Stade Toulousain), I Harinordoquy (Biarritz Olympique)
SUBSTITUTIONS: S Marconnet (Stade Francais) & D Marty (USA Perpignan) for Mas & David (49 mins), S Chabal (Racing Metro 92) & D Szarzewski (Stade Francais) for Nallet & Servat (54 mins), J Bonnaire (ASM Clermont Auvergne) for Harinordoquy (55 mins), M Parra (ASM Clermont Auvergne) for Dupuy (66 mins), M Medard (Stade Toulousain) for Heymans (76 mins)
SCORERS: *Try*: Clerc *Penalty goals*: Dupuy (4), Parra
SOUTH AFRICA: Kirchner; Pietersen, Fourie, Jacobs, Habana; M Steyn, F du Preez; Mtawarira, B du Plessis, Smit (capt), JP Botha, Matfield, Burger, Kankowski, Brussow
SUBSTITUTIONS: Bekker for JP Botha (temp 7-17 mins), Rossouw for Burger (47 mins), Van der Linde for Mtawarira (53 mins), Olivier & Strauss for Jacobs & B du Plessis (69 mins)
SCORERS: *Try*: Smit *Conversion*: M Steyn *Penalty goal:* M Steyn *Dropped goal:* M Steyn
REFEREE: W Barnes (England)

17 November, Wembley Stadium
Saracens 24 (1G 3PG 1DG 1T) South Africa XV 23 (1G 2PG 2T)

Saracens scorers: *Tries*: B Barritt, E Joubert *Conversion*: D Hougaard *Penalty goals:* D Hougaard (3) *Dropped goal*: D Hougaard

South Africa XV scorers: *Tries*: Nokwe (2), De Jongh *Conversion:* Pienaar *Penalty goals*: Pienaar (2)

21 November, Stadio Fruili, Udine
Italy 10 (1G 1PG) South Africa 32 (3G 2PG 1T)

ITALY: L McLean (Treviso); M Pratichetti (Viadana), A Sgarbi (Treviso), G Garcia (Treviso), Mi Bergamasco (Stade Francais); C Gower (Aviron Bayonnais), S Picone (Treviso); S Perugini (Aviron Bayonnais), F Ongaro (Saracens), M-L Castrogiovanni (Leicester Tigers), C-A del Fava (Viadana), Q Geldenhuys (Viadana), A Zanni (Treviso), S Parisse (Stade Francais)(capt), S Favaro (Rugby Parma)

SUBSTITUTIONS: I Rouyet (Treviso) for Castrogiovanni (40 mins), LL Ghiraldini (Treviso) for Ongaro (49 mins), T Tebaldi (Gran Parma) for Picone (56 mins), Ma Bergamasco (Stade Francais) for Favaro (60 mins), A Pavanello (Treviso) & JW Sole (Viadana) for Del Fava & Zanni (72 mins)

SCORERS: *Try*: Garcia *Conversion:* Gower *Penalty goal*: Gower

SOUTH AFRICA: Kirchner; Pietersen, Fourie, Jacobs, Habana, M Steyn, F du Preez; W du Preez, Strauss, Smit (capt), JP Botha, Bekker, Rossouw, Kankowski, Brussow

SUBSTITUTIONS: Matfield & Deysel for JP Botha & Kankowski (49 mins), Mtawarira for W du Preez (59 mins), BJ Botha for Strauss (62 mins), Olivier & Pienaar for Jacobs & M Steyn (64 mins), F Hougaard for F du Preez (77 mins)

SCORERS: *Tries*: Habana, Olivier, Fourie, F du Preez *Conversions:* M Steyn (2), Pienaar *Penalty goals:* M Steyn (2)

REFEREE: AC Rolland (Ireland)

28 November, Croke Park, Dublin
Ireland 15 (5PG) South Africa 10 (1G 1DG)

IRELAND: RDJ Kearney (Leinster); TJ Bowe (Ospreys), BG O'Driscoll (Leinster)(capt), PW Wallace (Ulster), KG Earls (Munster); J Sexton (Leinster), TG O'Leary (Munster); CE Healy (Leinster), JP Flannery (Munster), JJ Hayes (Munster), DP O'Callaghan (Munster), PJ O'Connell (Munster), SPH Ferris (Ulster), JPR Heaslip (Leinster), DP Wallace (Munster)

SUBSTITUTIONS: GW D'Arcy (Leinster) for P Wallace (23 mins), S O'Brien (Leinster) for Ferris (40 mins)

SCORER: *Penalty goals*: Sexton (5)

SOUTH AFRICA: Kirchner; Pietersen, Fourie, Olivier, Habana; M Steyn, F du Preez; Mtawarira, Smit (capt), BJ Botha, Bekker, Matfield, Burger, Rossouw, Brussow

SUBSTITUTIONS: Van der Linde for Mtawarira (temp 42-47 mins), BW du Plessis for BJ Botha (47 mins), Potgieter for Bekker (temp 61-68 mins), Pienaar for M Steyn (61 mins), J de Villiers for Olivier (63 mins)

SCORERS: *Try*: Burger *Conversion:* M Steyn *Dropped goal:* M Steyn

REFEREE: N Owens (Wales)

SAMOA TO EUROPE 2009

TOUR PARTY

FULL BACKS: L Lui (Moata'a), T Esau (Afega)

THREE QUARTERS: AT Tuilagi (Sale Sharks), D Lemi (London Wasps), S Tagicakibau (London Irish), IL Mulipola (Tasman), HA Fa'afili (Leeds Carnegie), SJ Mapusua (London Irish), G Williams (ASM Clermont Auvergne), E Fuimaono-Sapolo (Bath Rugby)

HALF BACKS: FP Fili (Wellington), U Mai (Marist), AJ Polu(leuligaga)(Bay of Plenty)

FORWARDS: MM Schwalger (Sale Sharks), A Williams (Marist), JH Va'a (Glasgow Rugby), CAI Johnston (Stade Toulousain), J Fatialofa (Counties Manakau), S Taulafo (Tasman), FHL Levi (Newcastle Falcons), KG Thompson (US Dax), JI Tekori (Castres Olympique), GJ Stowers (London Irish), O Treviranis (Malie), JS Fa'amatuinu (Bath Rugby), M Timoteo (Vaiala), S Semeane (Scopa), H Tuilagi (USA Perpignan)

MANAGER TM Vaea **COACH** FT Tafua **ASSISTANT COACHES** MS Patu, PP Fatialofa, SJ Schuster **CAPTAIN** GJ Stowers

13 November, Millenium Stadium, Cardiff
Wales 17 (4PG 1T) Samoa 13 (1G 2PG)

WALES: JW Hook (Ospreys); SL Halfpenny (Cardiff Blues), TGL Shanklin (Cardiff Blues), JH Roberts (Cardiff Blues), T James (Cardiff Blues); DR Biggar (Ospreys), DJ Peel (Sale Sharks); GD Jenkins (Cardiff Blues), H Bennett (Ospreys), P James (Ospreys), A-W Jones (Ospreys), LC Charteris (Newport Gwent Dragons), A Powell (Cardiff Blues), RP Jones (Ospreys)(capt), S Warburton (Cardiff Blues)

SUBSTITUTIONS: J Davies (Scarlets) for Shanklin (49 mins), C Mitchell (Ospreys) & M Rees (Scarlets) for James & Bennett (63 mins), BS Davies (Cardiff Blues) & J Thomas (Ospreys) for Charteris & Warburton (72 mins)

SCORERS: *Try*: Halfpenny *Penalty goals*: Biggar (3), Halfpenny

SAMOA: Lui; A Tuilagi, G Williams, Mapusua, Lemi; Fili, Polu; Va'a, Schwalger, Johnston, Levi, Tekori, Stowers (capt), H Tuilagi, Treviranis

SUBSTITUTIONS: Fa'afili for A Tuilagi (56 mins), Thompson for Tekori (57 mins), Fa'amatuinu & Mai for Treviranis & Fili (64 mins), Taulafo for Va'a (70 mins)

SCORERS: *Try*: Mapusua *Conversion*: Fili *Penalty goals*: Fili (2)

REFEREE: P Fitzgibbon (Ireland)

21 November, Stade de France, Paris
France 43 (4G 3T) Samoa 5 (1T)

FRANCE: M Medard (Stade Toulousain); B Fall (Aviron Bayonnais), D Marty (USA Perpignan), Y Jauzion (Stade Toulousain), V Clerc (Stade Toulousain); F Trinh-Duc (RC Montpellier-Herault), M Parra (ASM Clermont Auvergne); T Domingo (ASM Clermont Auvergne), D Szarzewski (Stade Francais), S Marconnet (Stade Francais)(capt), S Chabal (Racing Metro 92), P Pape (Stade Francais), T Dusautoir (Stade Francais), J Bonnaire (ASM Clermont Auvergne), A Lapandry (ASM Clermont Auvergne)

SUBSTITUTIONS: G Guirado (USA Perpignan) & J Puricelli (Aviron Bayonnais) for Szarzewski & Dusautoir (47 mins), N Mas (USA Perpignan) for Marconnet (50 mins), R Millo-Chluski (Stade Toulousain) for Chabal (58 mins), J Dupuy (Stade Francais) for Parra (63 mins), Y David (Stade Toulousain) for Marty (66 mins), D Traille (Biarritz Olympique) for Jauzion (72 mins)

SCORERS: *Tries*: Trinh-Duc (2), Szarzewski, Fall, Clerc, Jauzion, Dusautoir *Conversions*: Parra (4)

SAMOA: Lui; Mulipola, Fa'afili, Mapusua, Lemi; Fili, Polu; Taulofo, Schwalger (capt), Johnston, Levi, Thompson, Fa'amatuanu, H Tuilagi, Treviranus

SUBSTITUTIONS: Tekori & Timoteo for Levi & Fa'amatuainu (48 mins), Mai for Polu (51 mins), Fuimaono-Sapolo & Fatialofa for Fa'afili & Johnston (52 mins), A Williams for Schwalger (62 mins), Esau for Fili (67 mins)

SCORER: *Try*: Tekori

REFEREE: D Pearson (England)

28 November, Stadio del Duca, Ascoli Piceno
Italy 24 (1G 3PG 1DG 1T) Samoa 6 (2PG)

ITALY: L McLean (Treviso); PK Robertson (Viadana), G-J Canale (ASM Clermont Auvergne), G Garcia (Treviso), Mi Bergamasco (Stade Francais); C Gower (Aviron Bayonnais), T Tebaldi (Gran Parma); S Perugini (Aviron Bayonnais), LL Ghiraldini (Treviso)(capt), M-L Castrogiovanni (Leicester Tigers), C-A del Fava (Viadana), Q Geldenhuys (Viadana), JW Sole (Viadana), A Zanni (Treviso), Ma Bergamasco (Stade Francais)

SUBSTITUTIONS: S Favaro (Rugby Parma) for Ma Bergamasco (temp 15-23 mins) & Sole (65 mins), A Pavanello (Treviso) for De Fava (60 mins), S Picone (Treviso) for Tebaldi (73 mins), F Ongaro (Saracens) for Ghiraldini (75 mins), I Rouyet (Treviso) for Castrogiovanni (76 mins)

SCORERS: *Tries*: McLean, Penalty try *Conversion*: Mi Bergamasco *Penalty goals*: Mi Bergamasco (2), Gower *Dropped goal*: Tebaldi

SAMOA: Esau; Fa'afili, G Williams, Mapusua, Lemi; Fuimaono-Sapolo, Polu; Johnston, Schwalger, Va'a, Levi, Thompson, Stowers (capt), H Tuilagi, Treviranus

SUBSTITUTIONS: Timoteo for H Tuilagi (9 mins), Taulofo for Johnston (40 mins), Mai for Fuimaono-Sapolo (48 mins), Mulipola & Fa'amatuainu for Esau & Thompson (69 mins), A Williams & Semeane for Schwalger & Treviranus (71 mins)

SCORER: *Penalty goals*: Esau (2)

REFEREE: C Berdos (France)

TONGA TO EUROPE 2009

13 November, Ravenhill, Belfast
Ireland A 48 (2G 3PG 5T) Tonga XV 19 (2G 1T)

Ireland A scorers: *Tries:* DM Cave (2), B Wilkinson, AD Trimble, NAC Best, GW Duffy, IJ Keatley *Conversions*: I Humphreys, IJ Keatley *Penalty goals*: I Humphreys (3)
Tonga XV scorers: *Tries:* VF Lilo, S Hufanga, WM Hafu *Conversions*: K Morath (2)

20 November, Netherdale, Gala
Scotland A 38 (5G 1PG) Tonga XV 7 (1G)

Scotland A scorers: *Tries*: G Laidlaw, J Thompson, BJ Cairns, HFG Southwell, M Robertson *Conversions:* J Thompson (3), C Gregor (2) *Penalty goal*: J Thompson
Tonga XV scorers: *Try*: A Fatafehi *Conversion*: WM Hafu

28 November, Estadio Universitario, Lisbon
Portugal 19 (1G 4PG) Tonga 24 (1G 4PG 1T)

Portugal scorers: *Try*: G Uva *Conversion:* P Cabral *Penalty goals*: P Cabral (4)
Tonga scorers: *Tries*: M Vakaloa, S Valomounga *Conversion*: K Morath *Penalty goals*: P Hola, K Morath (3)

2010 SUMMER TOURS

ENGLAND TO AUSTRALIA AND NEW ZEALAND 2010

TOUR PARTY

FULL BACKS: BJ Foden (Northampton Saints), DA Armitage (London Irish)
THREEQUARTERS: MJ Cueto (Sale Sharks), CJ Ashton (Northampton Saints), MA Banahan (Bath Rugby), UCC Monye (Harlequins), D Strettle (Harlequins), MJ Tindall (Gloucester Rugby), SE Hape (Bath Rugby), MJM Tait (Sale Sharks), OJ Barkley (Bath Rugby), SJJ Geraghty (Northampton Saints), D Waldouck (London Wasps), * BM Barritt (Saracens)
HALF BACKS: TGAL Flood (Leicester Tigers), JP Wilkinson (RC Toulon), CC Hodgson (Sale Sharks), DS Care (Harlequins), BR Youngs (Leicester Tigers), J Simpson (London Wasps), REP Wigglesworth (Sale Sharks)
FORWARDS: SG Thompson (CA Brive), GS Chuter (Leicester Tigers), LA Mears (Bath Rugby), R Webber (London Wasps), TAN Payne (London Wasps), DR Cole (Leicester Tigers), DG Wilson (Bath Rugby), PPL Doran-Jones (Gloucester Rugby), DL Flatman (Bath Rugby), J Golding (Newcastle Falcons), SD Shaw (London Wasps), TP Palmer (Stade Francais), CL Lawes (Northampton Saints), D Attwood (Gloucester Rugby), G Parling (Leicester Tigers), TR Croft (Leicester Tigers), LW Moody (Leicester Tigers), JAW Haskell (Stade Francais), SE Armitage (London Iriish), C Robshaw (Harlequins), JPR Worsley (London Wasps), NJ Easter (Harlequins), H Fourie (Leeds Carnegie), D Ward-Smith (London Wasps), * P Dowson (Northampton Saints)

* Replacement on tour

TEAM MANAGER MO Johnson **ASSISTANT COACHES** M Ford, GC Rowntree, B Smith J Wells **CAPTAIN** LW Moody

8 June, Members Equity Bank Stadium, Perth
Australian Barbarians 28 (2G 3PG 1T) England XV 28 (2G 3PG 1T)

Australian Barbarians scorers: *Tries*: JD O'Connor (3) *Conversions*: JD O'Connor 2 *Penalty goals*: JD O'Connor (2), BS Barnes
England XV scorers: *Tries*: Mears, Ward-Smith, Banahan *Conversions:* Barkley (2) *Penalty goals*: Barkley (3)

12 June, Subiaco Oval, Perth
Australia 27 (3G 2PG) England 17 (2G 1PG)

AUSTRALIA: JD O'Connor (Western Force); DN Ioane (Queensland Reds), RG Horne (NSW Waratahs), BS Barnes (NSW Waratahs), DA Mitchell (NSW Waratahs); QS Cooper (Queensland Reds), L Burgess (NSW Waratahs); BP Daley (Queensland Reds), SM Fainga'a (Queensland Reds), RSL Ma'afu (Brumbies),

DW Mumm (NSW Waratahs), NC Sharpe (Western Force), RD Elsom (Brumbies)(capt), RN Brown (Western Force), DW Pocock (Western Force)
SUBSTITUTIONS: JA Slipper (Queensland Reds) for Daley (65 mins), MD Chisholm (Brumbies) for Mumm (68 mins), KJ Beale (NSW Waratahs) for O'Connor (73 mins), MJ Hodgson (Western Force) & H Edmonds (Brumbies) for Pocock & Fainga'a (78 mins)
SCORERS: *Tries*: Cooper (2), Elsom *Conversions*: O'Connor (3) *Penalty goals*: O'Connor, Cooper
ENGLAND: Foden; Cueto, Tindall, Hape, Ashton; Flood, Care; Payne, Thompson, Cole, Shaw, Palmer, Croft, Easter, Moody (capt)
SUBSTITUTIONS: Youngs for Care (58 mins), Lawes for Shaw (59 mins), Haskell for Moody (65 mins), Wilson for Payne (67 mins), Chuter for Thompson (68 mins), Wilkinson for Tindall (72 mins), Tait for Flood (79 mins)
SCORERS: *Tries:* Penalty tries (2) *Conversions*: Flood (2) *Penalty goal*: Flood
REFEREE: N Owens (Wales)

15 June, Central Coast Stadium, Gosford
Australian Barbarians 9 (3PG) England XV 15 (5PG)

Australian Barbarians scorers: *Penalty goals*: BS Barnes (3)
England XV scorers: *Penalty goals*: Hodgson (2), Barkley (3)

19 June, ANZ Stadium, Sydney
Australia 20 (2G 2PG) England 21 (1G 3PG 1T)

AUSTRALIA: JD O'Connor (Western Force); DN Ioane (Queensland Reds), RG Horne (NSW Waratahs), MJ Giteau (Brumbies), DA Mitchell (NSW Waratahs); QS Cooper (Queensland Reds), SW Genia (Queensland Reds); BP Daley (Queensland Reds), SM Fainga'a (Queensland Reds), RSL Ma'afu (Brumbies), DW Mumm (NSW Waratahs), NC Sharpe (Western Force), RD Elsom (Brumbies)(capt), RN Brown (Western Force), DW Pocock (Western Force)
SUBSTITUTIONS: JA Slipper (Queensland Reds) for Ma'afu (52 mins), MD Chisholm (Brumbies) for Mumm (55 mins), AP Ashley-Cooper (Brumbies) for Ioane (62 mins), H Edmonds (Brumbies) for Fainga'a (71 mins)
SCORERS: *Tries*: Giteau (2) *Conversions*: Giteau (2) *Penalty goals*: Giteau (2)
ENGLAND: Foden; Cueto, Tindall, Hape, Ashton; Flood, Youngs; Payne, Thompson, Cole, Lawes, Palmer, Croft, Easter, Moody (capt)
SUBSTITUTIONS: Wilkinson for Flood (50 mins), Shaw for Lawes (58 mins), Care for Youngs (65 mins), DA Armitage for Tindall (67 mins), Chuter for Thompson (70 mins), Wilson for Cole (temp 4-11, 52-60 mins) & Payne (70 mins)
SCORERS: *Tries:* Youngs, Ashton *Conversion*: Flood *Penalty goals*: Flood (2), Wilkinson
REFEREE: R Poite (France)

23 June, McLean Park, Napier
New Zealand Maori 35 (3G 3PG 1T England XV 28 (2G 3PG 1T)

New Zealand Maori scorers: *Tries*: HE Gear (3), LJ Messam *Conversions:* CL McAlister (3) *Penalty goals*: CL McAlister, W Ripia (2)
England XV scorers: *Tries*: SE Armitage, Ashton, Care *Conversions*: Hodgson (2) *Penalty goals:* Hodgson (3)

SCOTLAND TO ARGENTINA 2010

TOUR PARTY

FULL BACKS: HFG Southwell (Stade Francais), J Thompson (Edinburgh)
THREEQUARTERS: SF Lamont (Scarlets), SCJ Danielli (Ulster), NJ de Luca (Edinburgh), MB Evans (Glasgow), A Grove (Worcester Warriors), GA Morrison (Glasgow)
HALF BACKS: DA Parks (Glasgow), PJ Godman (Edinburgh), MRL Blair (Edinburgh), CP Cusiter (Glasgow), RGM Lawson (Gloucester Rugby)
FORWARDS: RW Ford (Edinburgh), S Lawson (Gloucester Rugby), AG Dickinson (Gloucester Rugby), AF Jacobsen (Edinburgh), MJ Low (Glasgow), G Cross (Edinburgh), RJ Gray (Glasgow), JL Hamilton (Edinburgh), AD Kellock (Glasgow), SJ MacLeod (Edinburgh), JA Barclay (Glasgow), AR MacDonald (Edinburgh), AK Strokosch (Gloucester Rugby), JW Beattie (Glasgow), KDR Brown (Glasgow)

MANAGER G Richardson **COACH** RA Robinson **ASSISTANT COACHES** GPJ Townsend, G Steadman, M Cuttitta, DW Hodge **CAPTAINS** CP Cusiter, AD Kellock

12 June, Estadio Atletico, Tucuman
Argentina 16 (2PG 2T) Scotland 24 (6PG 2DG)

ARGENTINA: M Rodriguez (Stade Francais): L Borges (RC Albi), G-P Tiesi (Stade Francais), S Fernandez (RC Montpellier-Herault), H Agulla (Leicester Tigers); F Contepomi (RC Toulon)(capt), A Lalanne (London Irish); R Roncero (Stade Francais), ME Ledesma (ASM Clermont-Auvergne), M Scelzo (ASM Clermont-Auvergne), M Carizza (Biarritz Olympique), P Albacete (Stade Toulousain), JM Leguizamon (Stade Francais), J-M Fernandez-Lobbe (RC Toulon), G Fessia (Cordoba Athletic)

SUBSITUTIONS: M Ayerza (Leicester Tigers) for Scelzo (44 mins), L Gonzalez-Amorosino (Leicester Tigers) for Borges (47 mins), M Galarza (Universitario La Plata) for Carizza (66 mins), A Creevy (San Luis) for ME Ledesma (68 mins), A Figuerola (CASI) for Lalanne (78 mins)

SCORERS: *Tries*: Tiesi, Leguizamon *Penalty goals*: Contepomi (2)

SCOTLAND: Southwell; MB Evans, De Luca, Morrison, SF Lamont; Parks, RGM Lawson; Jacobsen, Ford, Low, Hamilton, Kellock (capt), Brown, Beattie, Barclay

SUBSTITUTIONS: Strokosch & Blair for Beattie & RGM Lawson (60 mins), S Lawson for Ford (77 mins)

SCORERS: *Penalty goals*: Parks (6) *Dropped goals*: Parks (2)

REFEREE: D Pearson (England)

19 June, Estadio Jose Maria Minella, Mar del Plata
Argentina 9 (3PG) Scotland 13 (1G 2PG)

ARGENTINA: M Rodriguez (Stade Francais): L Gonzalez-Amorosino (Leicester Tigers), G-P Tiesi (Stade Francais), S Fernandez (RC Montpellier-Herault), H Agulla (Leicester Tigers); F Contepomi (RC Toulon)(capt), A Figuerola (CASI); R Roncero (Stade Francais), ME Ledesma (ASM Clermont-Auvergne), M Scelzo (ASM Clermont-Auvergne), M Carizza (Biarritz Olympique), P Albacete (Stade Toulousain), JM Leguizamon (Stade Francais), J-M Fernandez-Lobbe (RC Toulon), G Fessia (Cordoba Athletic)

SUBSITUTIONS: M Ayerza (Leicester Tigers) for Sclezo (temp 37-47 & 73 mins), A Campos (RC Montauban) for Leguizamon (47 mins), R Carballo (RC Begles-Bordeaux) for Contepomi (61 mins), A Creevy (San Luis) for ME Ledesma (63 mins), S Guzman (Tucuman RC) for Carizza (73 mins)

SCORERS: *Penalty goals*: Contepomi (2), Fernandez

SCOTLAND: Southwell; SF Lamont, MB Evans, Morrison, Danielli; Parks, RGM Lawson; Jacobsen, Ford, Low, Hamilton, Kellock (capt), Brown, Beattie, Barclay

SUBSTITUTIONS: MacLeod for Kellock (temp 50-57 & 65 mins), Dickinson & Strokosch for Jacobsen & Beattie (60 mins), S Lawson for Ford (67 mins), Blair for RGM Lawson (68 mins), De Luca for MB Evans (70 mins)

SCORERS: *Try;* Hamilton *Conversion*: Parks *Penalty goals*: Parks (2)

REFEREE: C Berdos (France)

IRELAND TO NEW ZEALAND AND AUSTRALIA 2010

TOUR PARTY

FULL BACKS: RDJ Kearney (Leinster), GEA Murphy (Leicester Tigers), GW Duffy (Connacht)

THREEQUARTERS: TJ Bowe (Ospreys), SP Horgan (Leinster), J Murphy (Leicester Tigers), AD Trimble (Ulster), BG O'Driscoll (Leinster), GM D'Arcy (Leinster), PW Wallace (Ulster)

HALF BACKS: RJR O'Gara (Munster), J Sexton (Leinster), TG O'Leary (Munster), EG Reddan (Leinster), PA Stringer (Munster)

FORWARDS: S Cronin (Connacht), JP Flannery (Munster). J Fogarty (Leinster), D Varley (Munster), TD Buckley (Munster), TG Court (Ulster), JJ Hayes (Munster), MJ Horan (Munster), CE Healy (Leinster), DP O'Callaghan (Munster), MR O'Driscoll (Munster), E O' Donoghue (Ulster), D Tuohy (Ulster), N Ronan (Munster), SM Jennings (Leinster), J Muldoon (Connacht), DP Wallace (Munster), C Henry (Ulster), JPR Heaslip (Leinster), *R Ruddock (Leinster)

* Replacement on tour

MANAGER P McNaughton **COACH** D Kidney **ASSISTANT COACHES** A Gaffney, GP Smal, L Kiss, M Tainton **CAPTAIN** BG O'Driscoll

12 June, Yarrow Stadium, New Plymouth
New Zealand 66 (9G 1PG) Ireland 28 (4G)

NEW ZEALAND: IJA Dagg (Hawke's Bay); CS Jane (Wellington), CG Smith (Wellington), BJ Stanley (Auckland), JT Rokocoko (Auckland); DW Carter (Canterbury), QJ Cowan (Southland); BJ Franks (Tasman), KF Mealamu (Auckland), OT Franks (Canterbury), BC Thorn (Canterbury), AF Boric (North Harbour), J Kaino (Auckland) KJ Read (Canterbury), RH McCaw (Canterbury)(capt)

SUBSTITUTIONS: VVJ Vito (Wellington) for Kaino (37 mins), PAT Weepu (Wellington) for Cowan (40 mins), SL Whitelock (Canterbury) for Thorn (49 mins), NS Tialata (Wellington) for BJ Franks (51 mins), AW Cruden (Manawatu) for Carter (53 mins), AP de Malmanche (Waikato) & ZR Guildford (Hawke's Bay) for Mealamu & Jane (62 mins)

SCORERS: *Tries*: Cowan (2), Smith (2), Whitelock (2), Read, BJ Franks, Tialata *Conversions*: Carter (7), Weepu (2) *Penalty goal*: Carter

IRELAND: Kearney; Bowe, BG O'Driscoll (capt), D'Arcy, Trimble; O'Gara, O'Leary; Healy, Cronin, Buckley, O'Callaghan, MR O'Driscoll, Muldoon, Heaslip, DP Wallace

SUBSTITUTIONS: Jennings for Muldoon (31 mins), Tuohy for MR O'Driscoll (34 mins), Sexton, GEA Murphy & Reddan for O'Gara, Kearney & O'Leary (69 mins), Court & Fogarty for Healy & Cronin (76 mins)

SCORERS: *Tries*: Tuohy, BG O'Driscoll, Bowe, D'Arcy *Conversions*: O'Gara (3), Sexton

SENT OFF: Heaslip (15 mins)

REFEREE: W Barnes (England)

18 June, International Stadium, Rotorua
New Zealand Maori 31 (2G 4PG 1T) Ireland XV 28 (1G 7PG)

New Zealand Maori scorers: *Tries*: HE Gear, D Sweeney, K Lowe *Conversions*: CL McAlister, W Ripia *Penalty goals*: CL McAlister (3), W Ripia

Ireland XV scorers: *Try;* PW Wallace *Conversion*: Sexton *Penalty goals:* Sexton (7)

26 June, Suncorp Stadium, Lang Park, Brisbane
Australia 22 (4PG 2T) Ireland 15 (5PG)

AUSTRALIA: JD O'Connor (Western Force); DA Mitchell (NSW Waratahs), RG Horne (NSW Waratahs), MJ Giteau (Brumbies), AP Ashley-Cooper (Brumbies); QS Cooper (Queensland Reds), L Burgess (NSW Waratahs); BP Daley (Queensland Reds), SM Fainga'a (Queensland Reds), RS Ma'afu (Brumbies), DW Mumm (NSW Waratahs), MD Chisholm (Brumbies), RD Elsom (Brumbies)(capt), RN Brown (Western Force), DW Pocock (Western Force)

SUBSTITUTIONS: KJ Beale (NSW Waratahs) for Horne (40 mins), JA Slipper (Queensland Reds) for Daley (62 mins)

SCORERS: *Tries*: Burgess, Cooper *Penalty goals*: Cooper (2), Giteau (2)

IRELAND: Kearney; Bowe, BG O'Driscoll (capt), PW Wallace, Trimble; Sexton, O'Leary; Healy, Cronin, Buckley, O'Callaghan, MR O'Driscoll, Ronan, Henry, Jennings

SUBSTITUTIONS: Court for Buckley (40 mins), GEA Murphy for Kearney (52 mins), Tuohy for O'Callaghan (temp 52-54 mins) & for MR O'Driscoll (69 mins), Ruddock for Henry (68 mins), Varley for Cronin (69 mins)

SCORER: *Penalty goals:* Sexton (5)

REFEREE: BJ Lawrence (New Zealand)

WALES TO NEW ZEALAND 2010

TOUR PARTY

FULL BACKS: LM Byrne (Ospreys),

THREEQUARTERS: SL Halfpenny (Cardiff Blues), TWJ Prydie (Ospreys), WTM Harries (Newport Gwent Dragons), JH Roberts (Cardiff Blues), AM Bishop (Ospreys), J Davies (Scarlets)

HALF BACKS: SM Jones (Scarlets), DR Biggar (Ospreys), WM Phillips (Ospreys), RS Rees (Cardiff Blues), TD Knoyle (Scarlets)

FORWARDS: M Rees (Scarlets), H Bennett (Ospreys), K Owens (Scarlets), P James (Ospreys), AR Jones (Ospreys), JV Yapp (Cardiff Blues), C Mitchell (Ospreys), A-W Jones (Ospreys), BS Davies (Cardiff Blues), DL Jones (Cardiff Blues), IM Gough (Ospreys), GM Thomas (Newport Gwent Dragons), J Thomas (Ospreys), RJ McCusker (Scarlets), RP Jones (Ospreys)

MANAGER AJ Phillips **COACH** WD Gatland **ASSISTANT COACHES** S Edwards, R Howley, RC McBryde, NR Jenkins **CAPTAIN** RP Jones

19 June, Carisbrook, Dunedin
New Zealand 42 (4G 3PG 1T) Wales 9 (2PG 1DG)

NEW ZEALAND: IJA Dagg (Hawke's Bay); CS Jane (Wellington), CG Smith (Wellington), BJ Stanley (Auckland), JT Rokocoko (Auckland); DW Carter (Canterbury), QJ Cowan (Southland); BJ Franks (Tasman), KF Mealamu (Auckland), OT Franks (Canterbury), BC Thorn (Canterbury), AF Boric (North Harbour), VVJ Vito (Wellington), KJ Read (Canterbury), RH McCaw (Canterbury)(capt)

SUBSTITUTIONS: RD Kahui (Waiktato) for Dagg (40 mins), TD Woodcock (North Harbour) for BJ Franks (45 mins), SL Whitelock (Canterbury) for Boric (56 mins), PAT Weepu (Wellington) for Cowan (59 mins), AJ Thomson (Otago) for Read (69 mins), AW Cruden (Manawatu) for Carter (72 mins), AP de Malmanche (Waikato) for Mealamu (75 mins)

SCORERS: *Tries*: Carter (2), Jane, Kahui, Mealamu *Conversions*: Carter (4) *Penalty goals*: Carter (3)

WALES: Byrne; Halfpenny, Bishop, Roberts, Prydie; SM Jones, Phillips; James, M Rees, AR Jones, BS Davies, A-W Jones, J Thomas, RP Jones (capt), GM Thomas

SUBSTITUTIONS: Yapp & Biggar for AR Jones & SM Jones (56 mins), McCusker for J Thomas (57 mins), J Davies for Roberts (69 mins), Knoyle & Bennett for Bishop & Bennett (73 mins)

SCORERS: *Penalty goals*: Halfpenny, SM Jones *Dropped goal*: SM Jones

REFEREE: G Clancy (Ireland)

26 June, Waikato Stadium, Rugby Park, Hamilton
New Zealand 29 (2G 5PG) Wales 10 (1G 1PG)

NEW ZEALAND: JM Muliaina (Waikato); CS Jane (Wellington), RD Kahui (Waikato), BJ Stanley (Auckland), ZR Guildford (Hawke's Bay); DW Carter (Canterbury), QJ Cowan (Southland); TD Woodcock (North Harbour), KF Mealamu (Auckland), NS Tialata (Wellington), BC Thorn (Canterbury), TJS Donnelly (Otago), J Kaino (Auckland), KJ Read (Canterbury), RH McCaw (Canterbury)(capt)

SUBSTITUTIONS: OT Franks (temp 21–25 mins) (Canterbury) for Woodcock (temp 21-25) & Tialata (54 mins), PAT Weepu (Wellington) & AJ Thomson (Otago) for Cowan & Donnelly (49 mins), RMN Ranger (Northland) for Stanley (54 mins), SL Whitelock (Canterbury) for Read (56 mins), AW Cruden (Manawatu) for Carter (70 mins), AP de Malmanche (Waikato) for Mealamu (71 mins)

SCORERS: *Tries*: Jane, Cruden *Conversions*: Carter, Weepu *Penalty goals*: Carter (5)

WALES: Byrne; Halfpenny, J Davies, Roberts, Prydie; Biggar, Phillips; James, M Rees, AR Jones, BS Davies, A-W Jones, J Thomas, RP Jones (capt), GM Thomas

SUBSTITUTIONS: McCusker for RP Jones (25 mins), DL Jones for BS Davies (56 mins), Mitchell & SM Jones for AR Jones & Biggar (63 mins), Bennett & RS Rees for M Rees & Phillips (66 mins), Harries for Prydie (69 mins)

SCORERS: *Try*: Roberts *Conversion*: SM Jones *Penalty goal*: Halfpenny

REFEREE: JI Kaplan (South Africa)

FRANCE TO SOUTH AFRICA AND ARGENTINA 2010

TOUR PARTY

FULL BACKS: C Poitrenaud (Stade Toulousain), J Porical (USA Perpignan)

THREEQUARTERS: V Clerc (Satde Toulousain), M Andreu (Castres Olympique), A Rougerie (ASM Clermont-Auvergne), J Malzieu (ASM Clermont-Auvergne), M Mermoz (USA Perpignan), D Marty (USA Perpignan), M Bastareaud (Stade Francais), F Fritz (Stade Toulousain), L Mazars (Aviron Bayonnais)

HALF BACKS: F Trinh-Duc (RC Montpellier-Herault), D Skrela (Stade Toulousain), D Yachvili (Biarritz Olympique), M Parra (ASM Clermont-Auvergne)

FORWARDS: D Szarzewski (Stade Francais), G Guirado (USA Perpignan), F Barcella (Biarritz Olympique), T Domingo (ASM Clermont-Auvergne), N Mas (USA Perpignan), J-B Poux (Stade Toulousain), L Ducalcon (Castres Olympique), L Nallet (Racing Metro 92), R Millo-Chluski (Stade Toulousain), P Pape (Stade Francais), J Pierre (ASM Clermont-Auvergne), I Harinordoquy (Biarritz Olympique), L Picamoles (Stade Toulousain), T Dusautoir (Stade Toulousain), J Bonnaire (ASM Clermont-Auvergne), W Lauret (Biarritz Olympique)

MANAGER J Maso **COACH** M Lievremont **ASSISTANT COACHES** E Ntamack, D Retiere, D Ellis, G Quesada **CAPTAIN** T Dusautoir

12 June, Newlands, Cape Town
South Africa 42 (4G 3PG 1T) France 17 (2G 1PG)

SOUTH AFRICA: Z Kirchner (Blue Bulls); GG Aplon (Stormers), J Fourie (Stormers), W Olivier (Blue Bulls), BG Habana (Stormers); M Steyn (Blue Bulls), ER Januarie (Stormers); GG Steenkamp (Blue Bulls), JW Smit (Sharks)(capt), BJ Botha (Ulster); DJ Rossouw (Blue Bulls), V Matfield (Blue Bulls), L-FP Louw (Stormers), PJ Spies (Blue Bulls), SWP Burger (Stormers)
SUBSTITUTIONS: J de Villiers (temp 30-35 mins) (Western Province) for Fourie (temp 30-35) & for Kirchner 60 mins), MC Ralepelle (Blue Bulls) for Smit (40 mins), DJ Potgieter (temp 50-56 mins) (Blue Bulls) for Louw (temp 50-56 & for Burger (60 mins), JN du Plessis (Sharks) for BJ Botha (56 mins), PR van der Merwe (Blue Bulls) & JL de Jongh (Stormers) for Rossouw & Olivier (60 mins), R Pienaar (Sharks) for Steyn (65 mins)
SCORERS: *Tries*: Aplon (2), Spies, Steenkamp, Louw *Conversions*: M Steyn (3), Pienaar *Penalty goals:* M Steyn (3)
FRANCE: Poitrenaud; Rougerie, Marty, Mermoz, Clerc; Trinh-Duc, Parra; Domingo, Szarzewski, Mas, Nallet, Millo-Chluski, Dusautoir (capt), Bonnaire, Lauret
SUBSTITUTIONS: Poux for Domingo (40 mins), Pierre & Picamoles for Millo-Chluski & Lauret (52 mins), Guirado & Andreu for Szarzewski & Marty (63 mins), Yachvili for Parra (66 mins), Skrela for Poitrenaud (71 mins)
SCORERS: *Tries*: Rougerie, Andreu *Conversions*: Parra, Skrela *Penalty goal*: Skrela
REFEREE: BJ Lawrence (New Zealand)

18 June, El Bosque, La Plata Rugby Club
Buenos Aires XV 14 (2G) France XV 37 (3G 2PG 2T)

Buenos Aires XV scorers: *Tries*: M Bustos Buyano, M de Achaval *Conversions:* M Bustos Moyano (2)
France XV scorers: *Tries*: Malzieu (2), Porical, Andreu, Lamboley *Conversions*: Skrela (3) *Penalty goals*: Skrela (2)

26 June, Velez Sarsfield Stadium, Buenos Aires
Argentina 41 (3G 5PG 1T) France 13 (1G 2PG)

ARGENTINA: M Rodriguez (Stade Francais): L Gonzalez-Amorosino (Leicester Tigers), G-P Tiesi (Stade Francais), S Fernandez (RC Montpellier-Herault), R Carballo (RC Begles-Bordeaux); F Contepomi (RC Toulon)(capt), N Vergallo (US Dax); R Roncero (Stade Francais), ME Ledesma (ASM Clermont-Auvergne), M Scelzo (ASM Clermont-Auvergne), M Carizza (Biarritz Olympique), PE Albacete (Stade Toulousain), A Campos (RC Montauban), J-M Fernandez-Lobbe (RC Toulon), G Fessia (Cordoba Athletic)
SUBSITUTIONS: JM Leguizamon (Stade Francais) for Campos (54 mins), J Figallo (RC Montpellier-Herault) for Scelzo (55 mins), M Ayerza (Leicester Tigers) for Roncero (61 mins), A Creevy (San Luis) for ME Ledesma (64 mins), M Galarza (Universitario La Plata) for Carizza (69 mins), H Agulla (Leicester Tigers) for Fernandez (76 mins)
SCORERS: *Tries*: Contepomi (2), Fernandez-Lobbe, Carballo *Conversions*: Contepomi (3) *Penalty goals*: Contepomi (5)
FRANCE: Porical; Clerc, Fritz, Mazars, Malzieu; Trinh-Duc, Parra; Barcella, Szarzewski, Mas, Pape, Nallet, Dusautoir (capt), Picamoles, Bonnaire
SUBSTITUTIONS: Lamboley, Mermoz & Pierre for Picamoles, Mazars & Nallet (50 mins), Yachvili for Parra (61 mins), Guirado for Szarzewski (63 mins), Poux for Mas (71 mins), Poitrenaud for Fritz (74 mins)
SCORERS: *Try*: Malzieu *Conversion*: Parra *Penalty goals*: Porical, Parra
REFEREE: SJ Dickinson (Australia)

ITALY TO SOUTH AFRICA 2010

TOUR PARTY

FULL BACKS: L McLean (Treviso)
THREEQUARTERS: PK Robertson (Viadana), Mirco Bergamasco (Stade Francais), M Pratichetti (Viadana), M Sepe (Viadana), G-J Canale (ASM Clermont-Auvergne), R Bocchino (Rovigo), A Masi (Racing Metro 92)
HALF BACKS: C Gower (Aviron Bayonnais), S Picone (Treviso), T Tebaldi (Gran Parma)
FORWARDS: F Ongaro (Saracens), L Ghiraldini (Treviso), F Sbaraglini (Treviso), S Perugini (Aviron Bayonnais), ML Castrogiovanni (Leicester Tigers), L Cittadini (Treviso), Q Geldenhuys (Viadana), C del Fava (Viadana),

Gallo Images

Gio Aplon was on great form in South Africa's tour match against France, with two tries.

M Bortolami (Gloucester Rugby), V Bernabo (Rugby Roma), P Derbyshire (Padova), M Vosawai (Rugby Parma), S Favaro (Rugby Parma), A Zanni (Treviso), S Parisse (Stade Francais)

MANAGER C Checchinato **COACH** NVH Mallett **ASSISTANT COACHES** C Orlandi, A Troncon **CAPTAIN** S Parisse

19 June, Johann van Riebeeck Stadium, Witbank
South Africa 29 (3G 1PG 1T) Italy 13 (1G 2PG)

SOUTH AFRICA: Z Kirchner (Blue Bulls); GG Aplon (Stormers), J de Villiers (Western Province), AD James (Bath Rugby), BG Habana (Stormers); M Steyn (Blue Bulls), ER Januarie (Stormers); GG Steenkamp (Blue Bulls), MC Ralepelle (Blue Bulls), JN du Plessis (Sharks), JP Botha (Blue Bulls), V Matfield (Blue Bulls)(capt), L-FP Louw (Stormers), PJ Spies (Blue Bulls), DJ Potgieter (Blue Bulls)

SUBSTITUTIONS: AJ Hargreaves (Sharks) for JP Botha (49 mins), CJ van der Linde (Cheetahs) for JN du Plessis (51 mins), JL de Jongh (Stormers) & R Pienaar (Sharks) for Steyn & Januarie (63 mins), BA Basson (Griquas) & R Kankowski (Sharks) for Kirchner & Potgeiter (74 mins), BG Maku (Blue Bulls) for Ralapelle (79 mins)

SCORERS: *Tries*: Habana, Louw, M Steyn, Kirchner *Conversions*: M Steyn (3) *Penalty goal*: M Steyn

ITALY: McLean; Robertson, Pratichetti, Masi, Mi Bergamasco; Gower, Tebaldi; Perugini, Ghiraldini, Castrogiovanni; Bernabo, Geldenhuys, Zanni, Parisse (capt), Favaro

SUBSTITUTIONS: Cittadini for Castrogiovanni (18 mins), Bortolami for Bernabo (49 mins), Ongaro & Canale for Ghiraldini & Masi (57 mins), Derbyshire for Favaro (63 mins), Picone for Tebaldi (67 mins)

SCORERS: *Try:* Parisse *Conversion*: Mi Bergamasco *Penalty goals*: Mi Bergamasco (2)

REFEREE: A Small (England)

26 June, Buffalo City Stadium, East London
South Africa 55 (7G 2PG) Italy 11 (2PG 1T)

SOUTH AFRICA: GG Aplon (Stormers): J de Villiers (Western Province), J Fourie (Stormers), JL de Jongh (Stormers), BG Habana (Stormers); M Steyn (Blue Bulls), ER Januarie (Stormers); GG Steenkamp (Blue Bulls), JW Smit (Sharks)(capt), JN du Plessis (Sharks), JP Botha (Blue Bulls), A Bekker (Stormers), L-FP Louw (Stormers), PJ Spies (Blue Bulls), SWP Burger (Stormers)

SUBSTITUTIONS: BJ Botha (Ulster) & W Olivier (Blue Bulls) for JN du Plessis & De Jongh (51 mins), PR van der Merwe (Blue Bulls) & R Pienaar (Sharks) for JP Botha & Habana (57 mins), DJ Potgeiter (Blue Bulls) & AD James (Bath Rugby) for Burger & M Steyn (60 mins), MC Ralepelle (Blue Bulls) for Smit (62 mins)

SCORERS: *Tries:* M Steyn (2), Spies, JN du Plessis, Habana, Van der Merwe, BJ Botha *Conversions*: M Steyn (5), Pienaar (2) *Penalty goals*: M Steyn (2)

ITALY: McLean; Sepe, Canale, Masi, Mi Bergamasco; Gower, Picone; Perugini, Ongaro, Cittadini; Del Fava, Bortolami, Vosawai, Parisse (capt), Derbyshire

SUBSTITUTIONS: Ghiraldini, Geldenhuys & Tebaldi for Ongaro, Bortolami & Picone (51 mins), Zanni & Sbaraglini for Derbyshire & Cittadini (52 mins), Bocchino for Gower (71 mins)

SCORERS: *Try:* Sepe *Penalty goals*: Mi Bergamasco (2)

REFEREE: A Small (England)

OTHER 2010 INTERNATIONALS

5 June, Canberra Stadium, Canberra
Australia 49 (7G) Fiji 3 (1PG)

AUSTRALIA: KJ Beale (NSW Waratahs); DN Ioane (Queensland Reds), RG Horne (NSW Waratahs), MJ Giteau (Western Force), AP Ashley-Cooper (Brumbies); QS Cooper (Queensland Reds), L Burgess (NSW Waratahs); BE Alexander (Brumbies), H Edmunds (Brumbies), RS Ma'afu (Brumbies), DW Mumm (NSW Waratahs), NC Sharpe (Western Force), RD Elsom (Brumbies)(capt), RN Brown (Western Force), DW Pocock (Western Force)

SUBSTITUTIONS: DA Mitchell (temp 19-31 mins) (NSW Waratahs) for Horne (temp 19-31) & for Ashley-Cooper (54 mins), PJM Cowan (Western Force) for Ma'afu (52 mins), SM Fainga'a (Queensland Reds) for Edmonds (53 mins), MJ Hodgson (Western Force) for Pocock (61 mins)

SCORERS: *Tries*: Beale (2), Ioane (2), Brown, Cooper, Mitchell *Conversions*: Giteau (6), Cooper

FIJI: T Rawaqa (RC Grenoble); S Bobo (Racing Metro 92), R Caucaunibuca (SU Agen), S Radidi (Nadali), T Nagusa (Ulster); WS Luveniyali (Harlequins), E Vucago (Gaunavou); GDC Ma'afu (West Harbour), T Tuapati

(Woodlands), DT Manu (Scarlets)(capt), D Waqaiburotu (Waikato), S Kalou (Kaikorai), A Wise (Vuda), J Qovu (Racing Metro 92), J Naikadawa (Kaite)

SUBSITUTIONS: MSB Volau (temp 7–15 mins) (Police) for Naikadawa (temp 7-15 & 64 mins), R Nasiga (Sigatoka) & R Ratu (RC Aurillac) for Wise & Radidi (54 mins), N Nadolo (NSW Waratahs) for Caucaunibuca (64 mins), V Buatava (Gold Coast) for Luveniyali (67 mins), GC Dewes (Counties Manakau) for Ma'afu (72 mins), V Veikoso (Navoci) for Tuapati (73 mins)

SCORER: *Penalty goal:* Rawaqa

REFEREE: P Fitzgibbon (Ireland)

5 June, Millennium Stadium, Cardiff
Wales 31 (2G 3PG 1DG 1T) South Africa 34 (2G 5PG 1T)

WALES: LM Byrne (Ospreys); SL Halfpenny (Cardiff Blues), JW Hook (Ospreys), JH Roberts (Cardiff Blues), TWJ Prydie (Ospreys); SM Jones (Scarlets), WM Phillips (Ospreys); P James (Ospreys), M Rees (Scarlets), AR Jones (Ospreys), BS Davies (Cardiff Blues), DL Jones (Cardiff Blues), J Thomas (Ospreys), RP Jones (Ospreys)(capt), S Warburton (Cardiff Blues)

SUBSTITUTIONS: A-W Jones (Ospreys) & JV Yapp (Cardiff Blues) for DL Jones & AR Jones (57 mins), RJ McCusker (Scarlets) for Warburton (76 mins)

SCORERS: *Tries*: Hook, Prydie, A-W Jones *Conversions*: SM Jones (2) *Penalty goals*: SM Jones (3) *Dropped goal*: Hook

SOUTH AFRICA: FPL Steyn (Racing Metro 92); GG Aplon (Stormers), J Fourie (Stormers), JL de Jongh (Stormers), OM Ndungane (Sharks); R Pienaar (Sharks), ER Januarie (Stormers); CJ van der Linde (Leinster), JW Smit (Sharks)(capt), BJ Botha (Ulster), DJ Rossouw (Blue Bulls), V Matfield (Blue Bulls), DJ Potgieter (Blue Bulls), JC van Niekerk (RC Toulon), L-FP Louw (Stormers)

SUBSTITUTIONS: BA Basson (Griquas) for Ndungane (33 mins), R Kankowski (Sharks) for Potgeiter (55 mins), JN du Plessis (Sharks) for BJ Botha (57 mins), MC Ralepelle (Blue Bulls) for Van der Linde (73 mins), Z Kirchner (Blue Bulls) & AJ Hargreaves (Sharks) for F Steyn & Rossouw (75 mins)

SCORERS: *Tries*: Ndungane, Potgeiter, De Jongh *Conversions*: Pienaar (2) *Penalty goals*: Pienaar (4), F Steyn

REFREE: DA Lewis (Ireland)

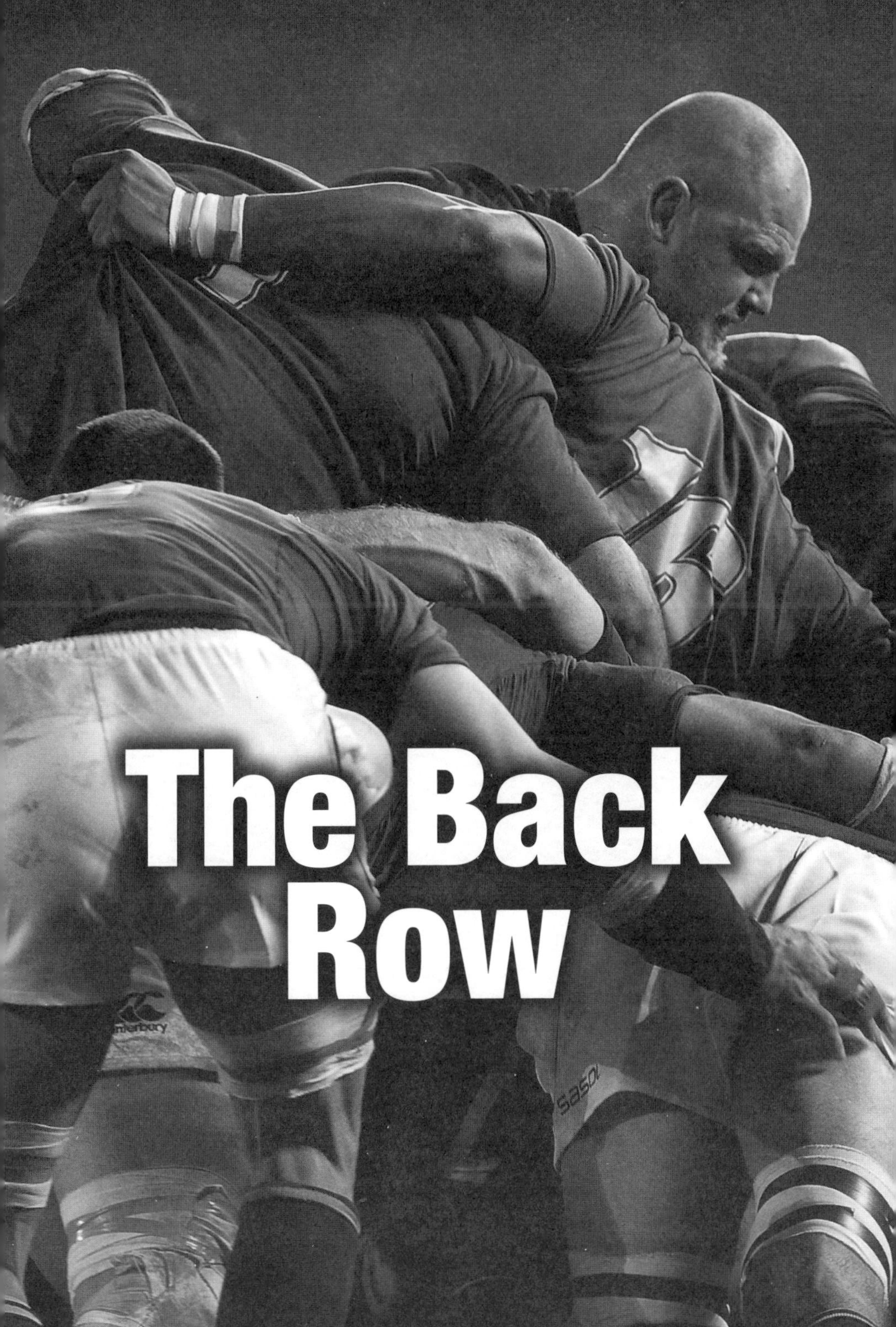

The Back Row

CONSISTENCY THE KEY TO RWC SUCCESS

By Paddy O'Brien,

the IRB Referee Manager.

Stu Forster/Getty Images

In 2007 Alain Rolland achieved the ultimate accolade, refereeing the World Cup final. Who will it be in 2011?

The countdown to Rugby World Cup 2011 is well and truly underway. Over the coming months players from 20 countries will be looking to cement their place in their respective squads to ensure that they have a ticket to participate in rugby's greatest event.

And as the players eye New Zealand 2011 the same can certainly be said for the IRB's international match officials who are also looking to win selection on the RWC referee, assistant referee and television match official panels.

The hard work for the referees started as soon as France 2007 finished, and throughout the cycle advances have been made in the promotion of consistency in key areas, fitness levels and assessment to ensure that our panel of referees are appropriately prepared for the challenges and rigours of a Game that continues to evolve.

Four years ago the IRB Selection Committee adopted a streamlined panel approach for RWC 2007 with 12 referees appointed. The reason was simple – to ensure greater consistency and uniform decision-making across the tournament's 48 matches.

It is a policy that will be followed for RWC 2011 and ten referees, seven assistant referees and four television match officials will be selected for the showcase tournament. The referees will take control of more games than at previous World Cups, meaning they will take to the field for a similar number of matches as the players will during the seven-week tournament.

The streamlined approach further underlines the IRB's commitment to ensuring greater consistency across the board. And as we approach the tournament, I am confident that we are getting the approach right by penalising the clear and obvious and being stricter in the areas relating to space on the field.

Consistency has been the key word in 2010. In May I met with the world's leading coaches in London to discuss all aspects of refereeing practice and global playing trends.

The meeting was extremely constructive and highly productive, the first of its kind between the IRB and the world's top coaches. All found it very beneficial and it was encouraging to see universal support for strict application of the Laws in these five key areas of the Game.

The meeting presented the opportunity to discuss pressing officiating issues and all aspects of referee to coach communication. No new directives have been issued, but it allowed us to clearly outline to all of the coaches the way in which the IRB's referees will approach matches, the commitment to consistency of application across all areas of Law and a commitment to penalise the clear and obvious.

In particular there was a collective determination between the IRB and the coaches to eradicate the number of scrum resets and collapses which are currently prominent at the elite level of the Game. The coaches expressed their full support for referees to employ a zero tolerance to formation offences in this important facet of the Game.

Those coaches present expressed their support for the IRB's commitment to penalising the clear and obvious and reiterated the need for consistency in ensuring strict application of Law in five key areas of the Game:

a) strict refereeing of offside at the breakdown
b) strict refereeing of offside from kicks

Pete Norton/Getty Images

Referees have been instructed to be strict when it comes to offside at the breakdown.

c) strict refereeing of illegal maul formation causing obstruction
d) strict refereeing of players not complying with the slower scrum sequence, front row binding and scrum feeds
e) consistency in the application of the tackle Law

On the whole there was a great improvement throughout the June internationals and the Tri-Nations and I am happy to say that the forum is set to become a regular fixture on the calendar ahead of the annual June and November Tests and will sit alongside three regular annual meetings with the world's top referees and referee managers to promote consistency of performance.

It is not just Law where we are committed to achieving consistency. Physical performance is also a critical area of the modern Game for referees and the guys need to be as fit as the players.

With the ball in play for more time than ever before and players becoming fitter and faster, the world's top referees often cover up to eight kilometres and undertake 400 changes in speed during the average Test match, while heart rates can be up to 70% in the high intensity zone, which is comparable to many athletic disciplines.

We are constantly looking to raise the bar in terms of innovative and effective ways to improve the consistency of the application of Law and the introduction of GPS technology is a core element of a physical conditioning programme that ensures that the official in the middle is in optimum shape for the increasing demands of the Test arena.

The GPS technology devices are housed within a vest worn over the shoulders and record invaluable data on match day and within the training environment that includes heart rate, distance covered, speed of movement, body load (work rate) and field position data. From these areas of improvement, patterns or trends in physical performance can be identified.

After each match the data is downloaded into a web-based performance analysis system (Performance Profiler) and managed by Matt Blair, the IRB's referee conditioning specialist. This data is then made available to the referees and their conditioning coaches and from this training programmes can be adjusted to optimise physical performance and promote consistency across the panel.

The referees meet with Blair as a group once a year and the web-based performance analysis system allows the referees to be supported through the year and at various global locations.

The focus on consistency is not just confined to international rugby. It is important that there is cross-competition buy-in on a global scale and I am happy to report that the Super 14, Heineken Cup and Aviva Premiership amongst others have all met with their clubs to ensure a collaborative approach to achieving consistency.

There is also an exchange policy in operation which allows our top referees to switch between hemispheres and competitions to further promote consistency below international level and to ensure that the referees are able to experience different playing cultures and approaches.

PENALTY KICK
Shoulders parallel with the touchline. Arm angled up, pointing towards non-offending team.

FREE KICK
Shoulders parallel with touchline. Arm bent square at elbow, upper arm pointing towards non-offending team.

TRY AND PENALTY TRY
Referee's back to dead ball line. Arm raised vertically.

ADVANTAGE
Arm outstretched, waist high, towards non-offending team, for a period of approximately five seconds.

SCRUM AWARDED
Shoulders parallel with touchline. Arm horizontal, pointing towards team to throw in the ball.

FORMING A SCRUM
Elbows bent, hands above head, fingers touching.

THROW FORWARD/FORWARD PASS
Hands gesture as if passing an imaginary ball forward.

KNOCK ON
Arm out-stretched with open hand above head, and moves backwards and forwards.

NOT RELEASING BALL IMMEDIATELY IN THE TACKLE

Both hands are close to the chest as if holding an imaginary ball.

TACKLER NOT RELEASING TACKLED PLAYER

Arms brought together as if grasping a player and then opening as if releasing a player.

TACKLER OR TACKLED PLAYER NOT ROLLING AWAY

A circular movement with the finger and arm moving away from the body.

ENTERING TACKLE FROM THE WRONG DIRECTION

Arm held horizontal then sweep of the arm in a semi-circle.

INTENTIONALLY FALLING OVER ON A PLAYER

Curved arm makes gesture to imitate action of falling player. Signal is made in direction in which offending player fell.

DIVING TO GROUND NEAR TACKLE

Straight arm gesture, pointing downwards to imitate diving action.

UNPLAYABLE BALL IN RUCK OR TACKLE

Award of scrum to team moving forward at time of stoppage. Shoulders parallel with the touchline, arm horizontal pointing towards the team to throw in the ball, then pointing the arm and hand towards the other team's goal line whilst moving it backwards and forwards.

UNPLAYABLE BALL IN MAUL

Arm out to award scrummage to side not in possession at maul commencement. Other arm out as if signalling advantage and then swing it across body with hand ending on opposite shoulder..

JOINING A RUCK OR A MAUL IN FRONT OF THE BACK FOOT AND FROM THE SIDE
The hand and arms are held horizontally. Moving sideways.

INTENTIONALLY COLLAPSING RUCK OR MAUL
Both arms at shoulder height as if bound around opponent. Upper body is lowered and twisted as if pulling down opponent who is on top.

PROP PULLING DOWN OPPONENT
Clenched fist and arm bent. Gesture imitates pulling opponent down.

WHEELING SCRUM MORE THAN 90 DEGREES
Rotating index finger above the head.

THROW IN AT SCRUM NOT STRAIGHT
Hands at knee level imitating throw not straight.

FAILURE TO BIND FULLY
One arm out-stretched as if binding. Other hand moves up and down arm to indicate the extent of a full bind.

HANDLING BALL IN RUCK OR SCRUM
Hand at ground level, making sweeping action, as if handling the ball.

THROW IN AT LINEOUT NOT STRAIGHT
Shoulders parallel with touchline. Hand above head indicates the path of the ball, not straight.

CLOSING GAP IN LINEOUT
Both hands at eye level, pointing up, palms inward. Hands meet in squeezing action.

LEANING ON PLAYER IN LINEOUT
Arm horizontal, bent at elbow, palm down. Downward gesture.

PUSHING OPPONENT IN LINEOUT
Both hands at shoulder level, with palms outward, making pushing gesture.

EARLY LIFTING AND LIFTING IN LINEOUT
Both fists clenched in front, at waist level, making lifting gesture.

OBSTRUCTION IN GENERAL PLAY

Arms crossed in front of chest at right angles to each other, like open scissors.

OFFSIDE AT SCRUM, RUCK OR MAUL

Shoulders parallel with touchline. Arm hanging straight down, swings in arc along offside line.

OFFSIDE CHOICE: PENALTY KICK OR SCRUM

One arm is for penalty kick. Other arm points to place where scrum may be taken instead of a kick.

OFFSIDE UNDER 10-METRE LAW OR NOT 10 METRES AT PENALTY AND FREE KICKS

Both hands held open above head.

HIGH TACKLE (FOUL PLAY)
Hand moves horizontally in front of neck.

STAMPING (FOUL PLAY: ILLEGAL USE OF BOOT)
Stamping action or similar gesture to indicate the offence.

PUNCHING (FOUL PLAY)
Clenches fist punches open palm.

DISSENT (DISPUTING REFEREE'S DECISION)
Outstretched arm with hand opening and closing to imitate talking.

AWARD OF DROP-OUT ON 22-METRE LINE
Arm points to centre of 22-metre line.

BALL HELD UP IN IN-GOAL
Space between hands indicates that the ball was not grounded.

BALL IN TOUCH
Flag raised in one hand, the other used to indicate the team to throw in the ball.

FOUL PLAY
Flag held horizontally in front indicating the assistant referee has observed foul play

INTERNATIONAL REFEREES

DISMISSALS IN MAJOR INTERNATIONAL MATCHES

Up to 29 October 2010 in major international matches. These cover all matches for which the eight senior members of the International Board have awarded caps, and also all matches played in Rugby World Cup final stages.

A E Freethy	sent off	C J Brownlie (NZ)	E v NZ	1925
K D Kelleher	sent off	C E Meads (NZ)	S v NZ	1967
R T Burnett	sent off	M A Burton (E)	A v E	1975
W M Cooney	sent off	J Sovau (Fj)	A v Fj	1976
N R Sanson	sent off	G A D Wheel (W)	W v I	1977
N R Sanson	sent off	W P Duggan (I)	W v I	1977
D I H Burnett	sent off	P Ringer (W)	E v W	1980
C Norling	sent off	J–P Garuet (F)	F v I	1984
K V J Fitzgerald	sent off	H D Richards (W)	NZ v W	*1987
F A Howard	sent off	D Codey (A)	A v W	*1987
K V J Fitzgerald	sent off	M Taga (Fj)	Fj v E	1988
O E Doyle	sent off	A Lorieux (F)	Arg v F	1988
B W Stirling	sent off	T Vonolagi (Fj)	E v Fj	1989
B W Stirling	sent off	N Nadruku (Fj)	E v Fj	1989
F A Howard	sent off	K Moseley (W)	W v F	1990
F A Howard	sent off	A Carminati (F)	S v F	1990
F A Howard	sent off	A Stoop (Nm)	Nm v W	1990
A J Spreadbury	sent off	A Benazzi (F)	A v F	1990
C Norling	sent off	P Gallart (F)	A v F	1990
C J Hawke	sent off	F E Mendez (Arg)	E v Arg	1990
E F Morrison	sent off	C Cojocariu (R)	R v F	1991
J M Fleming	sent off	P L Sporleder (Arg)	WS v Arg	*1991
J M Fleming	sent off	M G Keenan (WS)	WS v Arg	*1991
S R Hilditch	sent off	G Lascubé (F)	F v E	1992
S R Hilditch	sent off	V Moscato (F)	F v E	1992
D J Bishop	sent off	O Roumat (Wld)	NZ v Wld	1992
E F Morrison	sent off	J T Small (SA)	A v SA	1993
I Rogers	sent off	M E Cardinal (C)	C v F	1994
I Rogers	sent off	P Sella (F)	C v F	1994
D Mené	sent off	J D Davies (W)	W v E	1995
S Lander	sent off	F Mahoni (Tg)	F v Tg	*1995
D T M McHugh	sent off	J Dalton (SA)	SA v C	*1995
D T M McHugh	sent off	R G A Snow (C)	SA v C	*1995
D T M McHugh	sent off	G L Rees (C)	SA v C	*1995
J Dumé	sent off	G R Jenkins (W)	SA v W	1995
W J Erickson	sent off	V B Cavubati (Fj)	NZ v Fj	1997
W D Bevan	sent off	A G Venter (SA)	NZ v SA	1997

C Giacomel	sent off	R Travaglini (Arg)	F v Arg	1997
W J Erickson	sent off	D J Grewcock (E)	NZ v E	1998
S R Walsh	sent off	J Sitoa (Tg)	A v Tg	1998
R G Davies	sent off	M Giovanelli (It)	S v It	1999
C Thomas	sent off	T Leota (Sm)	Sm v F	1999
C Thomas	sent off	G Leaupepe (Sm)	Sm v F	1999
S Dickinson	sent off	J–J Crenca (F)	NZ v F	1999
E F Morrison	sent off	M Vunibaka (Fj)	Fj v C	*1999
A Cole	sent off	D R Baugh (C)	C v Nm	*1999
W J Erickson	sent off	N Ta'ufo'ou (Tg)	E v Tg	*1999
P Marshall	sent off	B D Venter (SA)	SA v U	*1999
P C Deluca	sent off	W Cristofoletto (It)	F v It	2000
J I Kaplan	sent off	A Troncon (It)	It v I	2001
R Dickson	sent off	G Leger (Tg)	W v Tg	2001
P C Deluca	sent off	N J Hines (S)	US v S	2002
P D O'Brien	sent off	M C Joubert (SA)	SA v A	2002
P D O'Brien	sent off	J J Labuschagne (SA)	E v SA	2002
S R Walsh	sent off	V Ma'asi (Tg)	Tg v I	2003
N Williams	sent off	S D Shaw (E)	NZ v E	2004
S J Dickinson	sent off	P C Montgomery (SA)	W v SA	2005
S M Lawrence	sent off	L W Moody (E)	E v Sm	2005
S M Lawrence	sent off	A Tuilagi (Sm)	E v Sm	2005
S R Walsh	sent off	S Murray (S)	W v S	2006
J I Kaplan	sent off	H T–Pole (Tg)	Sm v Tg	*2007
A C Rolland	sent off	J Nieuwenhuis (Nm)	F v Nm	*2007
N Owens	sent off	N Nalaga (PI)	F v PI	2008
W Barnes	sent off	J P R Heaslip (I)	NZ v I	2010
C Joubert	sent off	D A Mitchell (A)	A v NZ	2010

* Matches in World Cup final stages

OBITUARIES

By Adam Hathaway

ANDY RIPLEY OBE, who died on 17 June 2010, aged 62, was an extravagantly talented all-round sportsman who played 24 times for England, was on the 1974 Lions tour of South Africa, won the BBC Superstars series in 1980, reached the semi-finals of the 400 metres in the AAA Championship in 1978, became a world indoor veteran rowing champion and almost made the Cambridge University Boat Race crew at the age of 50. He then fought a brave and public fight against prostate cancer, a disease that eventually reduced him to a shadow of the rampaging number eight with flowing locks that rugby fans the world over remember so fondly.

Sometimes referred to as the first rock 'n' roll rugby player or memorably 'John Lennon with muscles' by one correspondent, Ripley's refusal to tow the party line endeared him to fans if not to the rugby establishment. As a Lion in 1974 he was forced to attend many ambassadorial functions and at one turned up as if he had just come from the beach, rather than wearing his tour blazer. Manager Alun Thomas told Ripley: "There is another official function on Friday. You will wear the tour blazer, grey trousers and tie". Ripley followed the instructions to the letter, wearing blazer, trousers and tie but nothing else. No shirt, shoes or socks . . . it was typical Ripley.

Ripley was kept out the Test team on that 1974 tour by Welshman Mervyn Davies who described his rival as the 'the best – certainly the most awkward' number eight he had played against. Ripley was dropped by England in 1976, whilst still at his peak, but continued playing for his only club, Rosslyn Park, until he was 41. He was elected club president in 1989, typically turning up at the club on a Triumph motorbike, in jeans and a t-shirt. An accountant by profession, he was also an accomplished linguist and commentated on French television. Ripley was diagnosed with cancer in 2005 but his energy was undiminished and he became an ambassador for the Prostate Cancer Society as well as giving a moving speech at the Rugby Union Writers' Club dinner when he urged everyone in the room to get regular prostate checks. A book followed, *Ripley's World: The Rugby Union Icon's Ultimate Victory over Cancer*, in which he wrote: "Dare we hope? We dare. Can we hope? We can. Should we hope? We must, because to do otherwise is to waste the most precious of gifts, given so freely by God to all of us.

So when we do die, it will be with hope and it will be easy and our hearts will not be broken."

A month before his death Ripley received his OBE from the Prince of Wales at Buckingham Palace.

BILL McLAREN CBE, who died on 19 January 2010, aged 86, was known as the 'Voice of Rugby' and it was impossible to find anyone in the sport – be they player, coach, fan, administrator or colleague – who had a bad word to say about him. Like Peter O'Sullevan in horse racing, Peter Alliss in golf and Richie Benaud in cricket, McLaren's voice is known to those who have no more than a passing interest in their respective sports.

McLaren was a frustrated player, but never showed any bitterness in his commentaries, having been good enough to play for Hawick and have a Scotland trial in 1947 before being struck down with tuberculosis after serving in World War II as a spotter in 20/21 Battery, 5 Medium Regiment. After 19 months in hospital, that denied him any chance of an international cap, McLaren taught PE at local schools and covered rugby for the Hawick Express before getting his break with the BBC. McLaren taught PE until 1987 and coached several players who went on to represent Scotland including Colin Deans, Jim Renwick and Tony Stanger. Typically he did not let his relationship with Stanger affect his commentary when the winger scored the crucial try in Scotland's 1990 Grand Slam win over England at Murrayfield.

In 1953 he covered the Scotland v Wales international for BBC Radio before making the move to television in 1962.

McLaren's attention to detail and his meticulous preparation was appreciated by the players, as were the Hawick balls, sweets that he doled out at training sessions. One former international said he never watched reruns of games he was involved in unless McLaren was commentating.

In 2002 McLaren commentated on his last international, a game between Wales and Scotland in Cardiff that ended with crowd singing 'For He's A Jolly Good Fellow' and a Wales fan displaying a banner proclaiming 'Bill McLaren is Welsh'.

McLaren's services to rugby were recognised in 2002 when the International Rugby Board presented him with the Chairman's Award. He was awarded an MBE in 1979, OBE in 1995 and became a CBE in 2003. Away from rugby he was a keen golfer, playing off ten into his seventies but he and his wife tragically had to deal with the death of their daughter, Janie, from cancer in 2000. McLaren was the subject of an internet campaign calling for him to be knighted with around 8,000 rugby fans signing up.

On hearing of McLaren's death Gerald Davies, the former Wales and

British Lions wing and manager of the Lions tour to South Africa in 2009, summed up the affection with which rugby followers held the commentator. Davies said: "Bill is irreplaceable for several reasons. His command of the English language and obvious love of rugby football and how he transmitted that to everyone across the world was one factor. The completely unbiased commentary on the game was another. He could not possibly harm or insult anybody." The Bill McLaren Foundation has been set up to promote rugby and its values and to encourage youngsters to take up the sport.

RUBEN KRUGER, who died from brain cancer on 27 January 2010, aged 39, was a flanker and a key member of the South Africa side that won the World Cup in 1995, scoring a crucial try in the semi-final against France. That epic season Kruger was named South African Player of the Year.

He made his international debut against Argentina in 1993 and won 36 caps for the Springboks in a distinguished career in which he was dubbed 'The Silent Assassin' by the World Cup-winning coach Kitch Christie. South African Rugby Union president Oregan Hoskins said: "When Ruben was on the field you always knew that the Springboks would not be beaten without a tremendous battle."

Kruger, who came from Vrede in the Free State and played domestic rugby for the Cheetahs and the Bulls, suffered a serious knee injury that looked like finishing his career in 1997 but battled back to be part of the South African squad for Rugby World Cup 1999 before the troublesome joint forced him to quit. In retirement Kruger, the epitome of the rugged Springbok flanker, was a camera salesman, owning a Minolta franchise in Pretoria. Grant Roberts played him in the film of South Africa's World Cup triumph, *Invictus*, directed by Clint Eastwood, which was released in 2009.

ERIC TINDILL, who died on 1 August 2010, aged 99, held the distinction of being the only man to play both rugby and cricket Tests for New Zealand. In November 1999 he became the oldest living Test cricketer, having kept wicket five times for this country between 1937 and 1947, and was also the oldest surviving All Black having won his only cap in the 1936 game against England at Twickenham, known as the 'Obolensky Match' after the Russian prince who scored two spectacular tries. On retirement, Tindill refereed rugby at the highest level, taking charge of two Tests on the Lions tour of New Zealand in 1950 and umpiring New Zealand's cricket Test against England at Lancaster Park in 1959. He was inducted into the New Zealand Sports Hall of Fame in 1995. Tindill also played table tennis for Wellington and wrote a best-selling book with team mate Charlie Oliver – *The Tour of the Third All Blacks* – about the 1935–36 trip.

BARRY BRESNIHAN, who died on 18 July 2010, aged 66, won 25 caps for Ireland, from 1966 to 1971, and was a leading rheumatologist. Bresnihan, a centre, went on two British Lions tours, in 1966 and 1968, played for the Munster side that beat the touring Australians in 1967 and represented University College Dublin, Lansdowne and London Irish at club level. As a Lion he played three of the four Tests in South Africa in 1968 but his medical career overshadowed even these achievements. He qualified as a doctor at UCD before specialising in rheumatology in London, working at Guy's Hospital, the Medical Research Council's rheumatism research unit at Taplow, and the Royal Postgraduate Medical School in Hammersmith. He set up a network of specialised rheumatology clinics in Ireland and produced more than 200 papers on his speciality as well as two books and 13 chapters to specialist rheumatology text books. In 2009, the American College of Rheumatology awarded him the title "Master", an award granted to physicians aged 65 or older who have made outstanding contributions, and UCD created a special Chair of Rheumatology for him.

RON MEAGHER, who died on 24 June 2010, aged 76, played 180 games for Randwick, before turning his attention to rugby administration and refereeing, and was made a life member of the Australian Rugby Union in 1998. Meagher, the son of former Wallaby half-back Wally, was involved in the game for over 60 years but was best known for his role as an official particularly in decisions which determined Wallaby coaching positions during the Bob Dwyer–Alan Jones era. At Randwick, Meagher acted as president (1976–88) and treasurer (1961–64, 1967–72 and 2006–2009) and was made a Life Member in 1979. Amongst his many posts Meagher served on the NSWRU Executive Committee, the NSWRU Board, was NSWRU Rugby Committee Chairman and Sydney Rugby Union Chairman between 1987 and 1995 and was the NSWRU delegate to the ARU between 1991 and 1997. At the Australian Rugby Union he was a member of the ARU Finance Committee, the ARU Tours and Major Matches Committee, the ARU Executive Committee, forerunner to the ARU Board (1991–95), Chairman of the ARU Players Retention Committee (1989–95) and a member of the ARU Referees Selection Committee (1992–95).

CYRIL BURKE, who died on 18 January 2010, aged 84, is considered one of the finest scrum-halves to come out of Australia, occupying a similar status to Nick Farr–Jones and Ken Catchpole. Burke played 26

Tests for the Wallabies from 1946 to 1956, represented New South Wales 36 times and was a life member of the Waratahs and Newcastle Rugby Union. The Cyril Burke Medal, first awarded in 1986, is given to the best player in the First Division. Burke served in Borneo with the RAAF in the Second World War before playing for the Waratahs in their first season, 1946. He made his Test debut in the 14–10 defeat by the All Blacks in Auckland in the same year, one of seven overseas trips he took with the Wallabies including the 1947–48 trip to Britain, France, Canada and the United States making his last international appearance against South Africa in 1956. In between, he played in both 1949 Tests as Australia beat New Zealand 11–6 in Wellington and 16–9 in Auckland to give the Wallabies a first Series victory away from home against New Zealand. On retirement, in 1960, Burke turned to coaching and was involved in the development of notable scrum-halves such as John Hipwell. He was awarded the British Empire Medal in 1974 in recognition of his services to sport.

GWYN ROWLANDS, who died on 29 April 2010, aged 81, is one of a rare group of Welshman, although he was born in England, who have beaten the All Blacks twice in four weeks. In 1953 Rowlands was one of two uncapped players in a Cardiff backline that saw the tourists off 8–3, scoring the second try with a 30-metre dash to the line before he earned his first Welsh cap against the same opponents shortly afterwards when his goal-kicking contributed to a 13–8 triumph at the Arms Park. The Welsh selectors however only capped him four times up to 1956, despite the high regard he was held in by the New Zealanders and supporters of Cardiff, who saw him score 66 tries for the club.

Off the field Rowlands qualified as a doctor and served as a medical officer with the RAF whilst completing his National Service at St Athan and went into general practice with his father in Berkhamsted, later doing stints as captain and president of the local golf club. On retirement he joined the Wellcome Foundation, an organisation that researches human and animal health, and travelled to India and Africa to work with them.

BRIGADIER THOMAS JACKSON OBE, who died on 21 May 2010, aged 88, played 12 times on the wing for Scotland between 1947 and 1949 – making his debut against France at Stade Colombes in Paris on New Year's Day 1947. He scored two tries for his country, one returning to the field although injured against England at Twickenham in 1947 and the other in a 9–8 Scottish win over the French at Murrayfield in 1948. At club level Jackson represented Cheltenham, London Scottish, The Army and Combined Services. Kentish-born Jackson rose to the rank of Brigadier in a distinguished career with the Royal Signals and was awarded an OBE.

MONSIGNOR TOM GAVIN, who died on 25 December 2009, aged 87, was a priest, a teacher and a rugby international who won the Triple Crown with Ireland in 1949. Gavin earned two caps for Ireland as a centre, represented Coventry, Cambridge University and London Irish and was the only serving Catholic priest ever to play Test rugby. Coventry-born to Irish parents, Gavin was ordained in 1946, moving to Cambridge from where he graduated with a first in Classics in 1949. At Ampleforth College for a year he taught the later-to-be Cardinal, Basil Hume, before he went to Cotton College to head the Classics department, before taking over the reins as College Principal from 1967–78. Gavin's first clash with his church came when the Archbishop of Dublin, John Henry McQuaid, asked him to stand down from the Irish rugby team in 1949 as he believed clerics should not play team sports. He got short shrift from Gavin whose apparent disregard for some church bureaucracy is reckoned to have cost him several promotions and any hopes of becoming a bishop. For the last 26 years of his working life Gavin headed up St Thomas More Parish in Coventry, he was a leader in religious education in the West Midlands and co-ordinated a Papal visit in 1992.

JOHNNY MORONEY, who died on 13 December 2009, aged 64, was capped six times on the wing by Ireland although his best position was fly-half, where he starred for Munster, Garryowen and London Irish. In 1969 he was the leading points scorer in England, whilst at London Irish, and won Munster Senior Cup medals with Garryowen in 1969, 1971 and 1974. Tipperary-born Moroney was educated at Rockwell College and joined up with London Irish whilst studying PE at Strawberry Hill in London. Playing in the same era as Mike Gibson and Barry McGann was not the ideal time for an Irish fly-half to force his way into the national team and Moroney duly made his debut in Ireland's 9–6 win over Wales in Dublin in 1968 on the wing. Also as a wing he was part of the Munster side that beat Australia in 1967 and he scored a try, a conversion and three penalties from the same position as France were beaten 17–9 at Lansdowne Road in 1969 before his career was ended with a serious leg injury in 1975. His misfortune paved the way for another Munster fly-half to emerge, Tony Ward.

DUNCAN PATERSON, who died on 21 December 2009, aged 66, won ten caps for Scotland between 1969 and 1972, helping Scotland defeat South Africa on his debut and in his three games against England never lost. Famously, he was a key member of the Scotland XVs who defeated

England in successive weekends in 1971. In the first match, at Twickenham, Paterson's drop-goal and try were instrumental in securing a 16–15 victory – Scotland's first there since 1938. A week later Scotland, with five of Paterson's Gala team mates in the side, won 26–6. Paterson was also a central part of Gala's domination of the seven-a-side circuit in the Borders in the late 1960s and early 1970s and managed the Scotland Sevens team at the inaugural Rugby World Cup Sevens at Murrayfield in 1993. Paterson, who ran his own knitwear and textile business, was elected to the Scottish Rugby Union general committee in 1986 and appointed as Scotland team manager in succession to Bob Munro following the 1990 Grand Slam. He stepped down from the committee in 1998 seeking to put his family first. However, his love of rugby remained and he was a regular spectator at Netherdale.

HARRY SIBSON, who died on 5 January 2010, aged 90, was a Leicester flanker who played 183 times for the club between 1947 and 1954 and continued his involvement with the club after retirement. He variously ran the third team in the 1960s, later was first team secretary and stayed on the committee until the end of the amateur days. Born in Leicester, Sibson, who was partly credited with causing the introduction of a new offside law at the scrum, lived in New Zealand until he was five but returned to England to play for Leicester Schools under-14s before being asked to join Leicester, an invitation team at the time, by A team secretary Doug Norman. He made his first team debut against Birkenhead Park in 1947 and was later a reserve for an England trial. After his service in World War II he worked as a monumental mason.

HAMISH SCOTT, who died on 12 March 2010, aged 86, was a Scottish number eight who once explored the Nepalese Himalayas with Sherpa Tenzing Norgay. Scott won one cap in the Scottish back row in the 13–11 win over England at Murrayfield in 1950 having been educated at Madras College and St Andrews University where he majored in geology, a qualification that explains his link with the sherpa. During World War II he served in the Royal Navy on HMS Scorpion, one of the ships which guarded a secret meeting of Prime Minister Winston Churchill in the North Atlantic. The year before he won his Scotland cap, Scott participated as a scientist in a pioneering expedition to survey an unexplored region of the Himalayas. Among his fellow explorers was Sherpa Tenzing, who four years later became the first man, alongside Sir Edmund Hillary, to conquer Everest. He later lived in Malaya working for the British colonial government as a fish specialist and further overseas posts saw him work in Nigeria and then Canada, where he finally settled with his family in the town of St Andrews, New Brunswick.

ROGER ADDISON, who died on 26 March 2010, aged 65, was a Welsh prop who broke his neck in a game for Pontypool and spent the 44 years up to his death in hospital, having originally being given only three weeks to live. Addison was 21 when he was left paralysed after a scrum collapsed, and would have died there and then but for the quick thinking of his club president, a doctor, who administered on-field treatment. Addison confounded medical thinking with his survival and visitors to his bedside included Elizabeth Taylor and Richard Burton, Tommy Steele and Sean Connery whilst he watched virtually every Welsh international on his bedside television. After his injury Addison, capped at youth level by Wales, was treated at Stoke Mandeville Hospital, then Rookwood Hospital in Cardiff and he died at the University Hospital of Wales in Cardiff. Pontypool RFC sent well wishers to see him every week.

BRIGADIER ROLPH JAMES, who died on 13 June 2010, aged 89, will be remembered for his immense contribution to London Welsh where he was chairman and persuaded Prince Charles, and his then wife, Diana, to attend the club's centenary dinner in 1985. He also sat on the WRU Committee as the Anglo–Welsh representative. When the club was at its lowest, languishing in Division 5 South, James brought in Mike Hamlin and Nigel Scrivens from Gloucester to bolster the side that eventually climbed back up the leagues. Born in Fishguard, he joined the army and made it his career, retiring as a Brigadier and played for Swansea on leave for the army as a hooker in his early days. James was Chairman of the Public School Wanderers and toured with them up until his death and for many years selected Major Stanley XVs when they played Oxford University ahead of the Varsity match. In 1990, James with Terry Cobner, who was a teacher at Oundle School, Peter Taylor and Dafydd Gwynfor Jones established the Welsh Exiles. Over 70 boys have been capped by different Welsh sides from schoolboy to full international over the intervening period. James was also President of the London Pembrokeshire Society and a regular host at the annual Rugby Writers' Dinner in London.

JEFF McLEAN, who died on 6 August 2010, aged 63, was part of a dynasty that has supplied six players to the Australian Test side. A winger he played for Queensland from 1969 to 1974 and 13 times for the Wallabies, between 1971 and 1974, with his final international being against New Zealand in Sydney in 1974, the same match that his younger brother Paul made his debut. McLean played a big role in the rise of Queensland in the 1970s before a badly broken leg ended his career prematurely. Like sibling Paul, he was a noted goal kicker and scored

85 points on Australia's 1972 tour of New Zealand. As well as rugby, McLean was a horse racing fan and one of the driving forces behind the saving of Ipswich Turf Club where he was deputy chairman. The Wallabies wore black armbands in his memory during the 2010 Test match against New Zealand in Christchurch.

ALEX 'ECK' HASTIE, who died on 10 June 2010, aged 74, was a Melrose scrum-half who formed one of Scotland's best half-back partnerships with his long-time club partner David Chisholm. Judges rate the pairing on a par with Roy Laidlaw and John Rutherford and Gary Armstrong and Craig Chalmers in the Scottish roll call of great nine and ten combinations. Hastie won 18 caps for his country, between 1961 and 1968, and Scotland did not lose a match when he and Chisholm were paired together until their 11th appearance in harness. That game was the infamous Test match against the All Blacks, in 1967, when Colin Meads was sent off but New Zealand still won 14–3 but the unfathomable vagaries of selection meant that Hastie and Chisholm never played an entire international season together. Importantly for the Scots however, the pairing never lost a game against England. Hastie was born in Hawick, but attended Melrose Grammar School and played 11 seasons for his local team, making 239 first team appearances. As an amateur rugby player he made his living as a painter and decorator.

JIM GREENWOOD, who died in September 2010, aged 81, was the former Scotland and British Lions back-row forward and pioneer of modern rugby coaching. Known as Mr Rugby in New Zealand, Greenwood arguably made a bigger impression as a coach than he had in a glittering playing career which saw him win 20 caps, captain his country and play in four Tests for the 1955 British Lions on their tour in South Africa. Scotland head coach Andy Robinson was coached by Greenwood when he was a student at Loughborough Colleges. He said: "He was the first top-class coach I worked with and he had a fantastic way of simplifying the game. "His book 'Total Rugby' showed that he was ahead of his time. He was a great inspiration for us as first year students at Loughborough where he lectured us, challenged us and made us think about the game." Born in Fife, James Thomas Greenwood was educated at Dunfermline High School and Edinburgh University and went on to play his club rugby for Dunfermline, Perthshire Accies and a brief spell with Harlequins.

THE DIRECTORY

MEMBER UNIONS OF THE INTERNATIONAL RUGBY BOARD

ANDORRA Federació Andorrana de Rugby
www.far.ad

ARABIAN GULF Arabian Gulf Rugby Football Union
www.agrfu.com

ARGENTINA Union Argentina de Rugby
www.uar.com.ar

AUSTRALIA Australian Rugby Union
www.rugby.com.au

AUSTRIA Osterreichischer Rugby Verband
www.rugby-austria.at

BAHAMAS Bahamas Rugby Football Union
www.rugbybahamas.com

BARBADOS Barbados Rugby Football Union
www.rugbybarbados.com

BELGIUM Fédération Belge de Rugby
www.rugby.be

BERMUDA Bermuda Rugby Union
www.bermudarfu.com

BOSNIA & HERZEGOVINA Ragbi Savez Republike Bosne

BOTSWANA Botswana Rugby Union

BRAZIL Confederação Brazileria de Rugby
www.brasilrugby.com.br

BULGARIA Bulgarian Rugby Federation
www.bfrbg.org

CAMEROON Fédération Camerounaise de Rugby
www.fecarugby.org

CANADA Rugby Canada
www.rugbycanada.ca

CAYMAN Cayman Rugby Union
www.caymanrugby.com

CHILE Federación de Rugby de Chile
www.feruchi.cl

CHINA Chinese Rugby Football Association
www.rugbychina.com

CHINESE TAIPEI Chinese Taipei Rugby Football Union
www.rocrugby.org.tw

COLOMBIA Pro Federacion Colombiana de Rugby
www.rugbycolombia.blogspot.com

COOK ISLANDS Cook Islands Rugby Union

CROATIA Hrvatski Ragbijaški Savez
www.rugby.hr

CZECH REPUBLIC Ceska Rugbyova Unie
www.rugbyunion.cz

DENMARK Dansk Rugby Union
www.rugby.dk

ENGLAND Rugby Football Union
www.rfu.com

FIJI Fiji Rugby Union
www.fijirugby.com

FINLAND Suomen Rugbyliitto
www.rugby.fi

FRANCE Fédération Française de Rugby
www.ffr.fr

GEORGIA Georgian Rugby Union
www.rugby.ge

GERMANY Deutscher Rugby Verband
www.rugby.de

GUAM Guam Rugby Football Union
www.guamrugbyunion.com

GUYANA Guyana Rugby Football Union

HONG KONG Hong Kong Rugby Football Union
www.hkrugby.com

HUNGARY Magyar Rögbi Szövetség
www.rugby.hu

INDIA Indian Rugby Football Union
www.rugbyindia.in

IRELAND Irish Rugby Football Union
www.irishrugby.ie

ISRAEL Israel Rugby Union
www.rugby.org.il

ITALY Federazione Italiana Rugby
www.federugby.it

IVORY COAST Fédération Ivoirienne de Rugby

JAMAICA Jamaica Rugby Football Union
www.jamaicarugby.com

JAPAN Japan Rugby Football Union
www.rugby-japan.jp

KAZAKHSTAN Kazakhstan Rugby Football Federation

KENYA Kenya Rugby Football Union
www.kenyarfu.com

KOREA Korea Rugby Union
www.rugby.or.kr

LATVIA Latvijas Regbija Federācija
www.rugby.lv

LITHUANIA Lietuvos Regbio Federacija
www.litrugby.lt

LUXEMBOURG Fédération Luxembourgeoise de Rugby
www.rugby.lu

MADAGASCAR Fédération Malagasy de Rugby

MALAYSIA Malaysia Rugby Union
www.mru.org.my

MALTA Malta Rugby Football Union
www.maltarugby.com

MAURITIUS Rugby Union Mauritius
www.mauritiusrugby.mu

MEXICO Federación Mexicana de Rugby
www.mexrugby.com

MOLDOVA Federatia de Rugby din Moldovei
www.rugby.md

MONACO Fédération Monégasque de Rugby
www.monaco-rugby.com

MOROCCO Fédération Royale Marocaine de Rugby
www.rugbymaroc.com

NAMIBIA Namibia Rugby Union

NETHERLANDS Nederlands Rugby Bond
www.rugby.nl

NEW ZEALAND New Zealand Rugby Football Union
www.nzru.co.nz

NIGERIA Nigeria Rugby Football Association

NIUE ISLANDS Niue Rugby Football Union

NORWAY Norges Rugby Forbund
www.rugby.no

PAKISTAN Pakistan Rugby Union
www.pakistanrugby.com

PAPUA NEW GUINEA Papua New Guinea Rugby Football Union